VISUAL ENCYCLOPEDIA

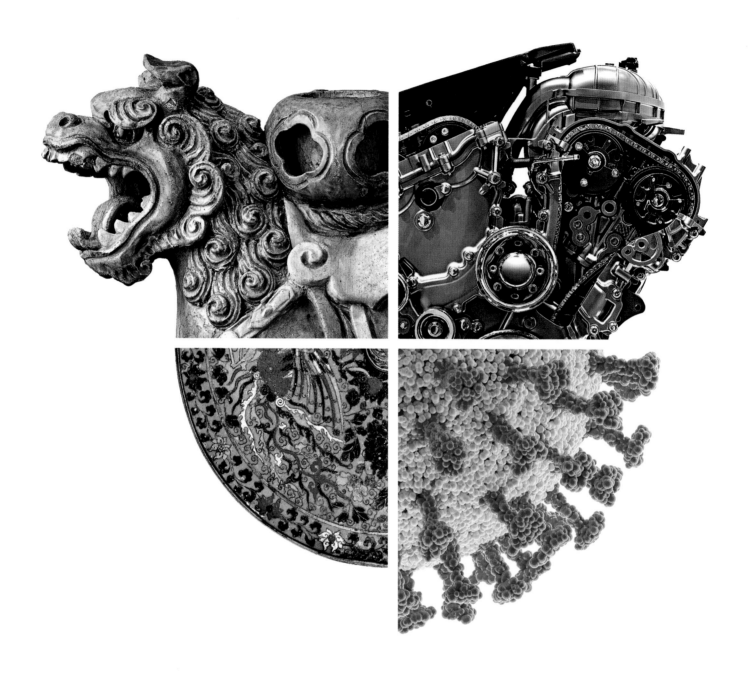

VISUAL ENCYCLOPEDIA

Penguin Random House

First American Edition, 2020
Published in the United States by DK Publishing
1450 Broadway, Suite 801, New York, NY 10018

Copyright © 2020 Dorling Kindersley Limited
DK, a Division of Penguin Random House LLC
20 21 22 23 24 10 9 8 7 6 5 4 3 2
003–310221–Oct/2020

A catalog record for this book
is available from the Library of Congress.
ISBN 978-1-4654-9994-3

DK books are available at special discounts when
purchased in bulk for sales promotions, premiums,
fund-raising, or educational use. For details, contact:
DK Publishing Special Markets,
1450 Broadway, Suite 801, New York, NY 10018
SpecialSales@dk.com

Printed and bound in UAE

For the curious
www.dk.com

Smithsonian

Established in 1846, the Smithsonian is the world's largest
museum and research complex, dedicated to public education,
national service, and scholarship in the arts, sciences, and history.
It includes 19 museums and galleries and the National Zoological
Park. The total number of artifacts, works of art, and specimens
in the Smithsonian's collection is estimated at 156 million.

Smithsonian's National Air and Space Museum
Bob Van der Linden, Margaret Weitekamp, Jim Zimbelman

Smithsonian's National Museum of Natural History
Matthew Miller, Michael Ackerson, Dave Johnson, Darrin
Lunde, Jeremy Jacobs, Carla Dove

Smithsonian's National Museum of American History
Roger Sherman, Jane Rogers, Hal Wallace, Dave Miller

Smithsonian Astrophysical Observatory
Kim Arcand

Smithsonian's National Museum of the American Indian
Ann McMullen

Smithsonian Gardens
Cindy Brown

Smithsonian's Asian Art Museum
Keith Wilson

SMITHSONIAN ENTERPRISES

Product Development Manager
Kealy Gordon

Director, Licensed Publishing
Jill Corcoran

Vice President, Consumer and Education Products
Brigid Ferraro

President, Smithsonian Enterprises
Carol LeBlanc

CONSULTANTS

Alison Ahearn, *Principal Teaching Fellow at Imperial College London, Educational Development Unit, with a special interest in engineering education*

Jamie Ambrose, *author, editor, researcher, and journalist specializing in the natural world, history, and the arts*

Alexandra Black, *author and consultant specializing in cultural and economic history*

Dr. Steve Brusatte, *paleontologist and evolutionary biologist; research explorer at the University of Edinburgh*

Jack Challoner, *former science and math teacher and educator at the London Science Museum; author of more than 40 science and technology books*

Giles Chapman, *motoring author, consultant, and journalist*

Chris Clennett, *horticulturist, botanist, and author of books, scientific papers, and plant profiles*

Dr. Kim Dennis-Bryan, *associate lecturer in life and environmental sciences, Open University*

Chris Hawkes, *sports writer and editor*

Rob Hume, *ornithologist, author, journalist, and former chairman of the British Birds Rarities Committee*

Hilary Lamb, *science and technology writer and consultant; staff reporter for* Engineering and Technology *magazine*

Professor David Macdonald, *Professor of Wildlife Conservation, University of Oxford*

Philip Parker, *author, consultant, and publisher specializing in ancient and medieval political and military systems*

Dr. Kristina Routh, *medical doctor and qualified specialist in Public Health Medicine*

Julius Sen, *Associate Director and Senior Program Advisor, London School of Economics and Political Science*

Marianne Talbot, *Director of Studies in Philosophy, Oxford University's Department for Continuing Education*

Dr. Christopher Thorpe, *Lecturer in sociology, University of Exeter*

DK LONDON

Lead Senior Editor Hugo Wilkinson
Senior Editors Helen Fewster, Rob Houston, Gill Pitts
Project Editor Miezan van Zyl
Editor Hannah Westlake
Assistant Editor Michael Clark
US Editor Karyn Gerhard
US Executive Editor Lori Cates Hand
Production Editor Rob Dunn
Senior Production Controller Meskerem Berhane
Managing Editor Angeles Gavira Guerrero
Associate Publishing Director Liz Wheeler
Publishing Director Jonathan Metcalf

Senior Art Editors Sharon Spencer, Ina Stradins
Project Art Editor Shahid Mahmood
Jacket Design Development Manager Sophia MTT
Senior Jacket Designer Akiko Kato
Managing Art Editor Michael Duffy
Art Director Karen Self
Design Director Phil Ormerod

DK DELHI

Senior Editor Anita Kakar
Editors Sonali Jindal, Aishvarya Misra, Priyanjali Narain, Isha Sharma
Managing Editor Rohan Sinha
Project Picture Researcher Aditya Katyal
Picture Research Manager Taiyaba Khatoon
DTP Designers Syed Mohammad Farhan, Vijay Kandwal
Production Manager Pankaj Sharma

Senior Art Editors Mahua Mandal, Vaibhav Rastogi
Art Editors Rabia Ahmad, Mridushmita Bose, Shipra Jain, Sonakshi Singh
Assistant Art Editors Aarushi Dhawan, George Thomas
Illustrator Anjali Sachar
Managing Art Editor Sudakshina Basu
Senior DTP Designer Shanker Prasad
Pre-production Manager Balwant Singh

Mark Viney, *Professor of Zoology and Head of Department of Evolution, Ecology and Behavior, University of Liverpool*

Karl Warsi, *author and Oxford Publishing Consultant; former mathematics teacher and lecturer at secondary level and further education*

Philip Wilkinson, *author of more than 50 books and consultant specializing in architecture, history, mythology, and the arts*

John Woodward, *author of more than 40 books on animal life and the natural world*

CONTRIBUTORS

Jamie Ambrose, Roxana Baiasu, Dr. Amy-Jane Beer, Alexandra Black, Giles Chapman, Chris Clennett, Kat Day, Clive Gifford, Dr. Sophie Gilbert, Derek Harvey, Jeremy Harwood, Rob Houston, Tom Jackson, Hilary Lamb, Philip Parker, Steve Parker, Gill Pitts, Julius Sen, Giles Sparrow, Dr. Ann Marie Stanley, Dr. Christopher Thorpe, Karl Warsi, Philip Wilkinson

MIX
Paper from
responsible sources
FSC™ C018179

CONTENTS

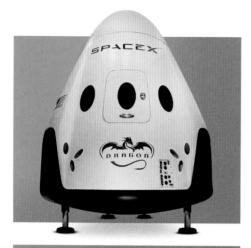

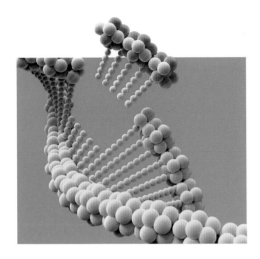
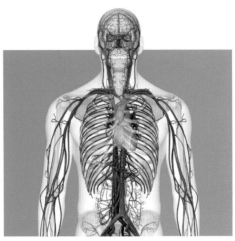
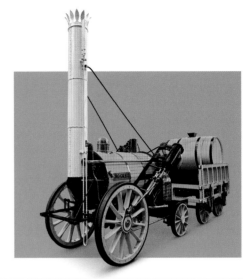

164 SCIENCE AND TECHNOLOGY

292 HISTORY

376 BELIEFS AND SOCIETY

410 ARTS AND LEISURE

Space

The cosmos

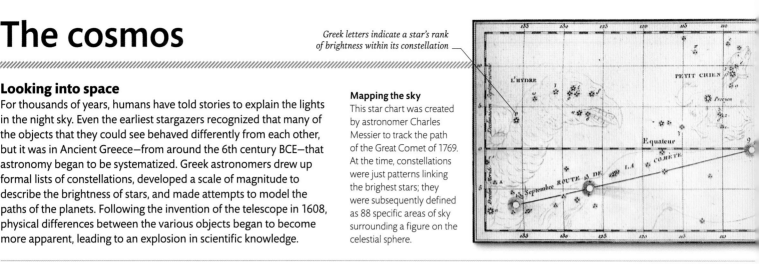

Looking into space

For thousands of years, humans have told stories to explain the lights in the night sky. Even the earliest stargazers recognized that many of the objects that they could see behaved differently from each other, but it was in Ancient Greece—from around the 6th century BCE—that astronomy began to be systematized. Greek astronomers drew up formal lists of constellations, developed a scale of magnitude to describe the brightness of stars, and made attempts to model the paths of the planets. Following the invention of the telescope in 1608, physical differences between the various objects began to become more apparent, leading to an explosion in scientific knowledge.

Mapping the sky

This star chart was created by astronomer Charles Messier to track the path of the Great Comet of 1769. At the time, constellations were just patterns linking the brightest stars; they were subsequently defined as 88 specific areas of sky surrounding a figure on the celestial sphere.

Celestial objects

The universe is full of objects, large and small. Many of the closest bodies in our solar system—asteroids, planets, and moons—are made visible by reflected sunlight. They move against a seemingly fixed background of more distant objects: luminous stars, glowing nebulae, and remote galaxies.

Planets
Planets are spherical bodies that orbit a star on a path mostly clear of other objects.

Dwarf planets
These smaller worlds also circle a star, but may share their orbits with other objects.

Moons
These objects orbit planets. They range from small rocks to complex worlds.

Asteroids
Usually made of rock or metal, asteroids are planetary debris that orbit stars like the sun.

Comets
These icy objects form tails of gas and dust when their orbit brings them close to the sun.

Our solar system

The region of space governed by the sun—and everything contained within it—is known as the solar system. It encompasses eight major planets, at least five dwarf planets, and a wealth of smaller bodies.

How the solar system formed

Our solar system emerged from a collapsing disk of material that was in orbit around the newborn sun some 4.6 billion years ago. Mid-sized bodies called planetesimals gradually formed, and eventually developed into today's planets.

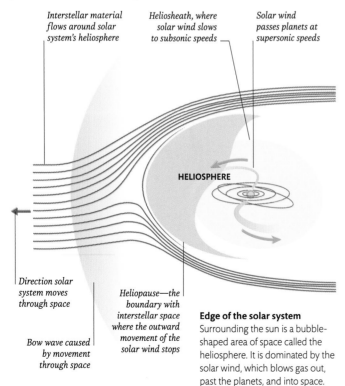

Interstellar material flows around solar system's heliosphere

Heliosheath, where solar wind slows to subsonic speeds

Solar wind passes planets at supersonic speeds

HELIOSPHERE

Direction solar system moves through space

Bow wave caused by movement through space

Heliopause—the boundary with interstellar space where the outward movement of the solar wind stops

Edge of the solar system

Surrounding the sun is a bubble-shaped area of space called the heliosphere. It is dominated by the solar wind, which blows gas out, past the planets, and into space.

❶ Rings formed around the sun
Heat and wind from the sun drove ice and gas away from the inner region, leaving particles of rock and metal.

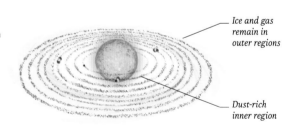

Ice and gas remain in outer regions

Dust-rich inner region

❷ Rocky cores developed
Pebble-sized grains accumulated into planetesimals. Their substantial gravity allowed them to pull in more material.

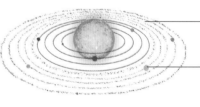

Particles collide and slowly form planetesimals

Planetesimals collide and stick together, forming rocky cores

❸ Giant planets emerged
Away from the sun, rapidly formed cores of rock and ice accumulated gas before it escaped the solar system.

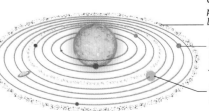

Gas causes pebbles to form large drifts

Drifts collapse suddenly and form large cores

Cores draw in surrounding gas

see also Rocky planets pp.14–15 ▶   Giant planets pp.16–17 ▶   Ancient Greece pp.312–13 ▶   The Enlightenment pp.346–47 ▶

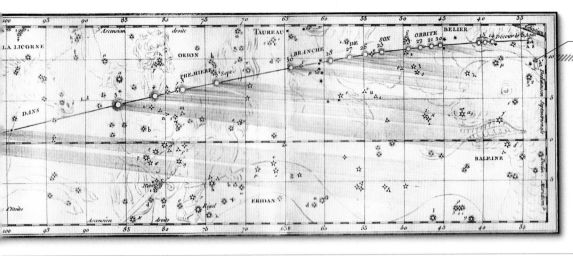

Stars of different magnitudes are depicted at different sizes on a scale of 1–9, in decreasing order of brightness

In perfect conditions, **about 4,000 stars** may be **visible** to the **naked eye** in one moment

Stars
A star is a vast, glowing ball of hot gas that shines due to nuclear reactions in its core.

Asterisms
Asterisms like the sickle are patterns formed in the sky by stars, and the basis of constellations.

Star clusters
Groups of stars that orbit each other may be loose or "open" in structure, or dense, "globular" groups.

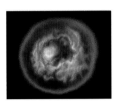

Nebulae (sing. nebula)
Nebulae are interstellar clouds of material that shimmer and glow in the light of nearby stars.

Black holes
These superdense objects are formed by dying stars and in the hearts of galaxies.

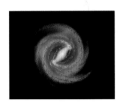

Galaxies
A galaxy is an aggregation of millions of stars with clouds of gas and dust held together by gravity.

Kepler's laws of planetary motion

Three laws, discovered by Johannes Kepler between 1609 and 1619, govern the behavior of planets orbiting the sun, or any object in an elliptical orbit around another. They reflect the changing influence of gravity with distance.

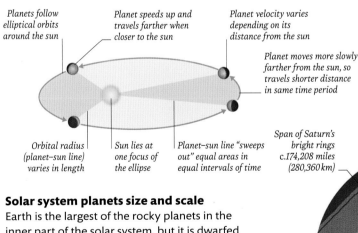

Planets follow elliptical orbits around the sun

Planet speeds up and travels farther when closer to the sun

Planet velocity varies depending on its distance from the sun

Planet moves more slowly farther from the sun, so travels shorter distance in same time period

Orbital radius (planet–sun line) varies in length

Sun lies at one focus of the ellipse

Planet–sun line "sweeps out" equal areas in equal intervals of time

EXOPLANETS

Since the 1990s, astronomers have discovered thousands of "exoplanets"—planets around stars outside our solar system. Hot Jupiters are a class of giant exoplanets that orbit close to their stars; others have highly elongated or tilted orbits. Some exoplanets even orbit one or both stars in a binary (double) star system.

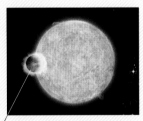

Wasp 18b orbits its star Wasp 18 in less than 23 hours

"HOT JUPITER"

Span of Saturn's bright rings c.174,208 miles (280,360 km)

Diameter of Jupiter c.86,880 miles (139,820 km)

Diameter of sun c.865,000 miles (1.4 million km)

Solar system planets size and scale

Earth is the largest of the rocky planets in the inner part of the solar system, but it is dwarfed in size by the gas giants found in the outer region. These, in turn, are relatively tiny when compared with the vast size of our sun.

Planets in order of size

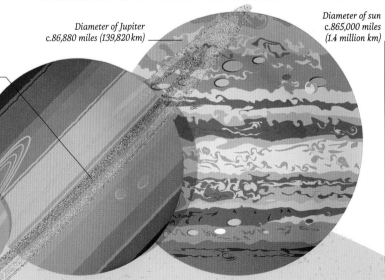

MERCURY **MARS** **VENUS** **EARTH** **NEPTUNE** **URANUS** **SATURN** **JUPITER** **SUN**

Rocky planets

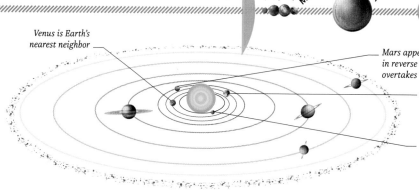

SUN | MERCURY VENUS EARTH MARS | JUPITER | SATURN

The inner planets

The four planets at the center of our solar system—Mercury, Venus, Earth, and Mars—follow orbits that are relatively close to the sun, separated from the much larger outer planets by smaller rocky bodies in the Asteroid Belt. These worlds formed in a warm, ice-free region of the young solar system, so their dominant materials are rocks and metals with high melting points.

Venus is Earth's nearest neighbor

Mars appears to move in reverse when Earth overtakes on the inside

Earth is the only planet in our solar system known to support life

Mercury's tight orbit means it is only seen from Earth for short periods

Mercury

Mercury is the smallest planet, with a heavily cratered surface and practically no atmosphere. Superficially similar to Earth's moon, it bears the scars of huge collisions with rogue asteroids in its distant past, as well as relatively recent widespread volcanic activity.

Tyagaraja Crater

Sobkou Planitia is named after an ancient Egyptian messenger god

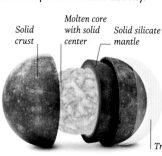

Solid crust

Molten core with solid center

Solid silicate mantle

Inside Mercury
Mercury's core is huge compared to its overall size—perhaps because most of its mantle was blasted away by a huge interplanetary collision early in its history.

Trace atmosphere

Average diameter	3,032 miles (4,879 km)
Mass (Earth = 1)	0.055
Gravity at equator (Earth = 1)	0.38
Mean distance from sun (Earth = 1)	0.39
Axial tilt	0.01°
Rotation period (day)	58.6 Earth days
Orbital period (year)	87.97 Earth days
Minimum temperature	−290°F (−180°C)
Maximum temperature	800°F (430°C)
Moons	0

A single day on Mercury lasts 176 days on Earth

Venus

Venus is only slightly smaller than Earth and orbits just a little closer to the sun, but these slight differences have had radical effects. A runaway greenhouse effect created by carbon dioxide has produced a scorching, superdense atmosphere, while volcanoes have been the biggest influence in shaping the planet's surface.

Maat Mons is Venus's second-highest peak

Greenaway Crater has a rough, radar-bright base

Diana and Dali chasmas form a system of troughs that extend for 4,600 miles (7,400 km)

Average diameter	7,520 miles (12,104 km)
Mass (Earth = 1)	0.82
Gravity at equator (Earth = 1)	0.9
Mean distance from sun (Earth = 1)	0.72
Axial tilt	177.4°
Rotation period (day)	243 Earth days
Orbital period (year)	224.7 Earth days
Average surface temperature	864°F (462°C)
Moons	0

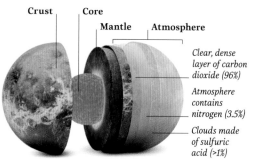

Crust **Core**

Mantle **Atmosphere**

Clear, dense layer of carbon dioxide (96%)

Atmosphere contains nitrogen (3.5%)

Clouds made of sulfuric acid (>1%)

Inside Venus
A lack of water has prevented the crust from splitting into plates. This traps heat in the rocky mantle, which escapes in occasional worldwide volcanic outbursts.

◀ see also The cosmos pp.12–13   Giant planets pp.16–17 ▶   Small worlds pp.18–19 ▶

Earth

Our world is the solar system's largest rocky planet. Although it is structurally similar to its neighbors, Earth's distance from the sun allows water to exist in liquid, solid, and vapor forms, creating a complex fluid environment on top of the rocky crust—and just the right conditions to support life.

Average diameter	7,918 miles (12,742 km)
Axial tilt	23.5°
Rotation period (day)	23 hours 56 minutes
Orbital period (year)	365.26 Earth days
Minimum surface temperature	−128°F(−89°C)
Maximum surface temperature	136°F (58°C)
Moons	1

Pacific Ocean is Earth's largest area of water

Clouds form from water vapor, which may precipitate and fall as rain, sleet, snow, or hail

THE MOON

Formed 4.5 billion years ago by an interplanetary collision, the lunar surface is a mix of bright, cratered highlands and dark, low-lying lava plains caused by volcanic activity.

Copernicus Crater has high central peaks and terraced walls

NEAR SIDE OF THE MOON

Phases of the moon

As the moon orbits Earth, the changing direction affects the amount of sunlight that falls on the near side, and creates a cycle of different phases.

| NEW MOON | WAXING CRESCENT | FIRST QUARTER | WAXING GIBBOUS | FULL MOON | WANING GIBBOUS | LAST QUARTER | WANING CRESCENT |

Spin and orbit

The moon orbits Earth once every 27.3 days. Tidal forces have slowed its spin: it rotates once per orbit, and one hemisphere—the near side—permanently faces Earth.

Apogee—252,000 miles (405,000 km)

Perigee—225,000 miles (362,000 km)

Outer core   Mantle
Inner core   Atmosphere

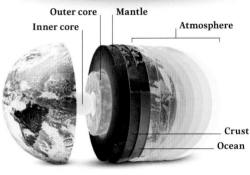

Crust
Ocean

Inside Earth

Churning molten metal in Earth's outer core produces a strong magnetic field around the planet, while heat rising through the mantle drives the forces that shape its crust.

Mars

Mars is the planet that is most similar to Earth. Despite a thin atmosphere and a cold, dry surface that is covered in rusty red dust, Mars has icy polar caps, vast amounts of water ice in its soil, and a landscape marked by ancient riverbeds and huge extinct volcanoes.

MARTIAN MOONS

The two small moons of Mars—Phobos and Deimos—may be asteroids captured by the planet's gravity, or fragments of rock from an ancient collision.

Mars rotates on its axis in 24 hours 37 minutes

Phobos

Deimos

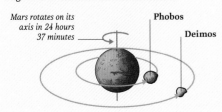

Olympus Mons is the largest volcano on Mars

Valles Marineris is a vast canyon system near the Martian equator

Noachis Terra is a large landmass in the southern highlands

Average diameter	4,212.3 miles (6,779 km)
Mass (Earth = 1)	0.11
Gravity at equator (Earth = 1)	0.38
Mean distance from sun (Earth = 1)	1.52
Axial tilt	25.2°
Rotation period (day)	24.6 hours
Orbital period (year)	687 Earth days
Minimum temperature	−225°F (−143°C)
Maximum temperature	95°F (35°C)
Moons	2

Core   Mantle   Atmosphere
Crust

Inside Mars

The small size of the core means that Mars has lost heat faster than the other planets. Heat from the sun also escapes, due to the thin atmosphere.

see also The Milky Way pp.26-27 ▶ The universe pp.30-33 ▶

Giant planets

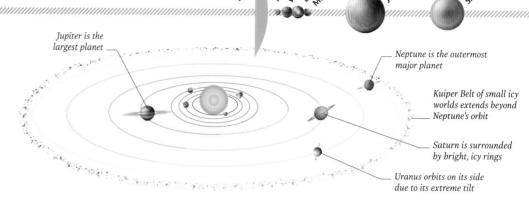

The outer planets

The four giant worlds of the outer solar system—Jupiter, Saturn, Uranus, and Neptune—travel along widely spaced orbits beyond the Asteroid Belt that separates them from the inner planets. Known as "gas giants," these planets formed in a region of the young solar system filled with plentiful amounts of ice and gas, and the structure of each depends on their exact composition.

Jupiter is the largest planet

Neptune is the outermost major planet

Kuiper Belt of small icy worlds extends beyond Neptune's orbit

Saturn is surrounded by bright, icy rings

Uranus orbits on its side due to its extreme tilt

JUPITER'S MOONS

Jupiter has at least 79 satellites—and four of them are among the biggest moons in the solar system. Jupiter's immense gravity heats their interiors, and also powers volcanic activity both on Io, and beneath Europa's icy crust.

 EUROPA **IO** **CALLISTO** **GANYMEDE**

Jupiter

Large enough to consume more than 1,300 Earths, Jupiter is composed primarily of hydrogen—the lightest and simplest element. Clouds in the upper atmosphere are colored by other chemicals, and wrapped into bands running parallel to the equator by Jupiter's rapid spin.

JUPITER

A series of thin dust rings surrounds Jupiter

Equatorial diameter	88,846 miles (142,984 km)
Mass (Earth = 1)	318
Gravity at equator (Earth = 1)	2.4
Mean distance from sun (Earth = 1)	5.20
Axial tilt	3.13°
Rotation period (day)	9.93 hours
Orbital period (year)	11.86 Earth years
Cloud-top temperature	–234°F (–145°C)
Moons	79+

CONVECTION CYCLE

Jupiter's cloud bands consist of high-altitude, light-colored "zones," and darker brownish "belts" lower in the atmosphere. The colors are caused by chemicals condensing at different temperatures and altitudes.

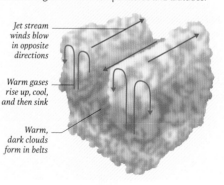

Jet stream winds blow in opposite directions

Warm gases rise up, cool, and then sink

Warm, dark clouds form in belts

Compressed hydrogen molecules form a liquid layer 600 miles (1,000 km) below the surface

Upper atmosphere is dominated by gaseous hydrogen

Layer of liquid metallic hydrogen, formed by the breakdown of molecules deep inside the planet

Jupiter's core—if it exists—is probably quite small

Great red spot is a large oval storm colored by chemicals rising from inside Jupiter

Upper layers also include ammonia, methane, water, and hydrogen sulfide

INSIDE JUPITER

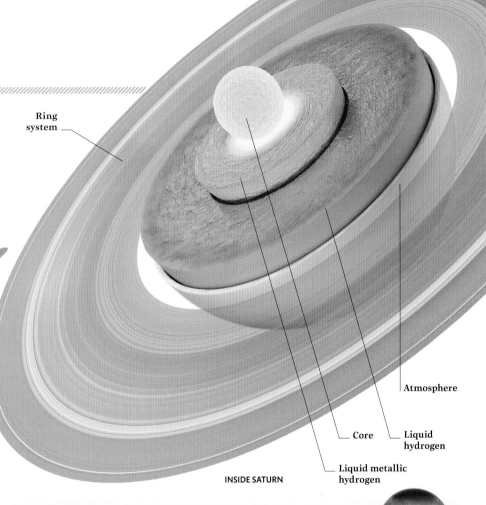

URANUS

NEPTUNE

Saturn

Creamy clouds in Saturn's upper atmosphere conceal stormy conditions beneath. Weaker gravity than Jupiter allows its outer layers to expand, giving the planet a lower average density than water. A ring system consisting of trillions of icy particles, each following its own circular orbit, form narrow ringlets arranged in broad bands around Saturn's equator.

Ring system

Atmosphere

Core

Liquid hydrogen

Liquid metallic hydrogen

INSIDE SATURN

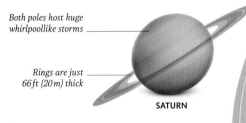

Both poles host huge whirlpoollike storms

Rings are just 66 ft (20 m) thick

SATURN

Saturn's **lightning** has 10,000 times the power of lightning on Earth

Equatorial diameter	74,898 miles (120,536 km)
Mass (Earth = 1)	95.2
Gravity at equator (Earth = 1)	1.02
Mean distance from sun (Earth = 1)	9.58
Axial tilt	26.7°
Rotation period (day)	10.7 hours
Orbital period (year)	29.46 Earth years
Cloud-top temperature	−418°F (−250°C)
Moons	82+

SATURN'S MOONS

Numerous and varied, Saturn's satellites include complex giants like Titan, and smaller Enceladus, which has lakes of liquid water below its surface.

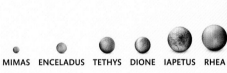   

MIMAS **ENCELADUS** **TETHYS** **DIONE** **IAPETUS** **RHEA** **TITAN**

Uranus

Smaller and denser than both Jupiter and Saturn, Uranus is an "ice giant" with an interior made up of slushy chemicals including water ice, ammonia, and methane. Tilting dramatically on its axis at 98 degrees to its orbit, the planet experiences extreme seasons as it completes its journey around the sun.

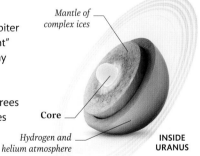

Mantle of complex ices

Core

Hydrogen and helium atmosphere

INSIDE URANUS

Rings formed from dust and rocky material

Equatorial diameter	31,763 miles (51,118 km)
Mass (Earth = 1)	14.5
Gravity at equator (Earth = 1)	0.89
Mean distance from sun (Earth = 1)	19.2
Axial tilt	97.8°
Rotation period (day)	17.2 hours
Orbital period (year)	84.0 Earth years
Cloud-top temperature	−323°F (−197°C)
Moons	27

URANUS

Neptune

The most distant planet from the sun, Neptune is another ice giant. It is similar to Uranus but has more active weather—including some of the strongest winds in the solar system. Neptune's activity is driven by heat from within the planet, produced by chemical changes around the core.

Core

Mantle

Atmosphere

INSIDE NEPTUNE

Wispy clouds of frozen methane

Equatorial diameter	30,775 miles (49,528 km)
Mass (Earth = 1)	17.1
Gravity at equator (Earth = 1)	1.1
Mean distance from sun (Earth = 1)	30.1
Axial tilt	28.3°
Rotation period (day)	16.1 hours
Orbital period (year)	163.7 Earth years
Cloud-top temperature	−330°F (−201°C)
Moons	14

NEPTUNE

see also The Milky Way pp.26–27 ▶ The universe pp.30–33 ▶

Small worlds

Between and beyond the major planets are countless rocky and icy objects that vary in size from boulders to dwarf planets. Most of these asteroids, ice dwarfs, and comets follow roughly circular orbits in areas far away from the major planets' gravity; those with more elliptical orbits risk destruction or exile from the solar system during close encounters with larger worlds.

Belts of bodies

Most objects are in the rocky belt between Mars and Jupiter; the icy Kuiper Belt beyond Neptune; or the remote Oort Cloud (see opposite).

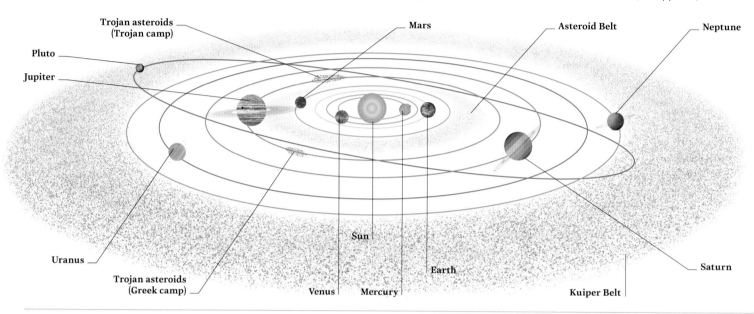

Trojan asteroids (Trojan camp)

Pluto

Jupiter

Uranus

Trojan asteroids (Greek camp)

Mars

Asteroid Belt

Neptune

Sun

Earth

Venus | Mercury

Saturn

Kuiper Belt

Asteroids

Asteroids are small rocky bodies that originally formed across the inner solar system, but were prevented from growing into larger bodies by the gravitational influence of their planetary neighbors. Today, they are mostly confined to a belt between the orbits of Mars and Jupiter, but they frequently collide, so their structure and orbits evolve over time. A number of so-called Trojan asteroids—split into two "camps" inspired by Homer's *Iliad*—circle the sun in gravitational neutral zones aligned with Jupiter's own orbit.

Estimates suggest that the **main asteroid belt** between Mars and Jupiter contains **1.1–1.9 million asteroids**

NEAR-EARTH ASTEROIDS

Collisions and close encounters can push asteroids onto paths that bring them closer to the sun, and—given enough time—eventually destroy or eject them from the solar system. These near-Earth asteroids can be grouped according to their orbit.

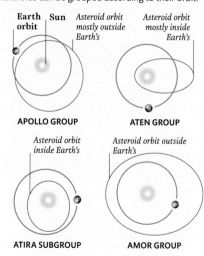

Earth orbit | Sun | Asteroid orbit mostly outside Earth's

Asteroid orbit mostly inside Earth's

APOLLO GROUP

ATEN GROUP

Asteroid orbit inside Earth's

Asteroid orbit outside Earth's

ATIRA SUBGROUP

AMOR GROUP

Types of asteroids

Asteroids vary in size and composition. Some, with dark, carbon-rich surfaces, have changed little since their formation, but others show signs of high metal content or past geological activity. Our knowledge is improved by meteorites that fall to Earth.

Dark, carbon-rich surface

**CARBONACEOUS ASTEROID
C-type**

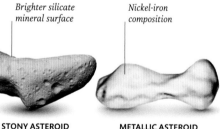

Brighter silicate mineral surface

**STONY ASTEROID
S-type**

Nickel-iron composition

**METALLIC ASTEROID
M-type**

Asteroid evolution

Collisions may play a key role in the formation and compositon of different types of asteroids. A small body is not hot enough for its interior to melt and differentiate. A large one is—but impacts chip off fragments that may then become new asteroids with varied amounts of core and mantle material.

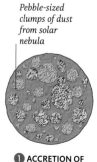

Pebble-sized clumps of dust from solar nebula

❶ ACCRETION OF SMALLER BODIES

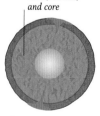

Interior separates into crust, mantle, and core

❷ HEAVIER ELEMENTS SINK TO CENTER

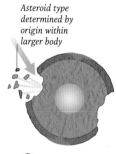

Asteroid type determined by origin within larger body

❸ IMPACTS BREAK OFF FRAGMENTS

The remote object **Sedna** takes around
10,700 years to complete an orbit of the sun

Dwarf planets

These sizeable objects—which circle the sun, and are not moons or satellites—would be considered major planets if it were not for the fact that they share their orbits with large numbers of smaller bodies. Classed officially as dwarf planets, these are objects with gravity that is powerful enough to pull them into a spherical shape—heating their interiors and driving geological activity on their surfaces—but too weak to clear their orbits of smaller objects; this distinguishes them from the rocky planets and gas giants found elsewhere in our solar system.

THE KUIPER BELT

Set in the outer reaches of our solar system, the Kuiper Belt probably contains more than 100,000 objects with a diameter of 62 miles (100 km) or more. Many of these icy worlds formed in the zone beyond the giant planets, but had their orbits altered as Uranus and Neptune moved outward early in their history. Aside from Pluto, the 22 miles (36 km) snowman-shaped Arrokoth is the only Kuiper Belt object to have been studied up close.

The five known dwarfs

Ceres—the largest object in the Asteroid Belt—is a dwarf planet, as are four bodies that orbit beyond Neptune: Pluto, Eris, Makemake, and Haumea. There are probably more to be discovered at the edges of the solar system.

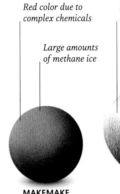

Icy mantle beneath crust

Active, recently formed terrain

Bright, highly reflective surface

Red color due to complex chemicals

Large amounts of methane ice

Huge bulge around equator

Ellipsoid shape caused by rapid speed of rotation

CERES **PLUTO** **ERIS** **MAKEMAKE** **HAUMEA**

Shape formed by two objects that collided and stuck

ARROKOTH

For **75 years**—from 1930 to 2006—**Pluto** was classed as the **9th major planet** in our solar system

---

Comets

Comets are small icy bodies, usually a few miles across. They become visible when they approach the sun from the outer solar system, because they warm up and develop an extensive atmosphere and a tail of escaping ice. Some 1 trillion comets lurk unseen at the edge of the solar system.

Comet origins

Most comets orbit in a spherical shell known as the Oort Cloud. This thick bubble of icy objects extends to about 1 light year from the sun.

Inner cloud extends toward Kuiper Belt

Sun

Comets approach inner solar system from any direction

Outer edges at limit of sun's gravitational grasp

Thick bubble of icy debris

THE OORT CLOUD

Types of comets

Visiting comets are classified according to how often they return to the inner solar system. Their orbits have all been disrupted—initially by encounters in the Oort Cloud, and later by one or more giant planets.

COMET HALLEY

Short period

These comets return to the solar system within 200 years. Multiple episodes of rapid heating remove their ice, which may diminish the display.

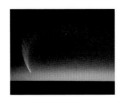

COMET HYAKUTAKE

Long period

The rarer visits of comets that take more than 200 years to make their return are often spectacular events because they retain more ice.

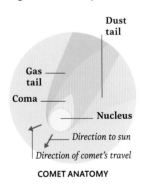

Dust tail

Gas tail

Coma

Nucleus

Direction to sun

Direction of comet's travel

COMET ANATOMY

Comet structure

An active comet consists of a small, solid nucleus, which is surrounded by a planet-sized coma of tenuous gas, and one or more extensive tails.

Comet tails

Formed from escaping dust and ionized vapor, comet tails are caught by the solar wind, so they always point away from the sun.

Gas tail points directly away from sun

Dust tail curves along orbit

Surface warmed by approach to sun

Perihelion passage takes comet near sun

Frozen comet in outer solar system

Tails dwindle as comet retreats

Nucleus refreezes

TYPICAL COMET ORBIT

COMET MCNAUGHT

Single apparition

These comets make just one passage around the sun before they either collide with it, or are flung out of the solar system.

see also The universe pp.30–33 ▶ Missions to the solar system pp.38–39 ▶ **19**

The sun

The sun is our nearest star—a vast ball of mostly hydrogen and helium gas that shines with incandescent light due to nuclear fusion in its core. Cyclical changes alter the sun's appearance from year to year, while electromagnetic radiation (see p.188) and streams of particles from its surface spread out, influencing the entire solar system.

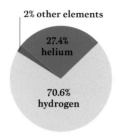

2% other elements

27.4% helium

70.6% hydrogen

Composition by mass
The vast majority of the sun's mass is accounted for by the two lightest elements.

The solar cycle

The sun goes through an 11-year cycle of activity that principally affects dark sunspots on its visible surface, and bright solar flares that erupt from its upper atmosphere. This cycle is driven by changes to the solar magnetic field.

Sunspots

Photographed in January 2014, sunspot AR1944 was one of the largest of the past nine years—Earth is shown to scale.

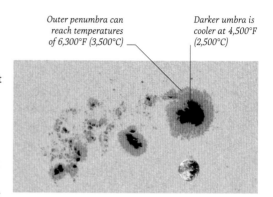

Outer penumbra can reach temperatures of 6,300°F (3,500°C)

Darker umbra is cooler at 4,500°F (2,500°C)

Solar eclipses

Solar eclipses occur when Earth's moon passes in front of the sun. Because the moon's orbit is tilted relative to Earth's, they do not happen at every new moon. The precise alignment required means each eclipse is only visible from a very limited part of Earth's surface.

Total eclipse

During a total eclipse, the moon covers an increasingly large area of the sun before covering it completely at "totality" for up to 7 minutes.

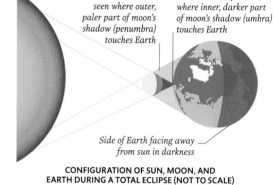

Partial solar eclipse seen where outer, paler part of moon's shadow (penumbra) touches Earth

Total solar eclipse seen where inner, darker part of moon's shadow (umbra) touches Earth

Side of Earth facing away from sun in darkness

CONFIGURATION OF SUN, MOON, AND EARTH DURING A TOTAL ECLIPSE (NOT TO SCALE)

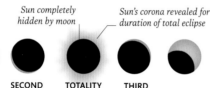

Moon begins to obscure view of sun from Earth

Sun completely hidden by moon

Sun's corona revealed for duration of total eclipse

End of eclipse

FIRST CONTACT **SECOND CONTACT** **TOTALITY** **THIRD CONTACT** **FOURTH CONTACT**

The sun's layers

The sun's structure is divided into layers, where different processes dominate. Energy is produced in the core and makes its way out through the radiative and convective zones. The photosphere is the visible surface—a layer where the sun's gas becomes transparent. Above this lie the thin chromosphere and a vast outer atmosphere or corona.

THE SUN'S SOURCE OF ENERGY

Temperatures and pressures in the sun's core are so high that a process called nuclear fusion is triggered. This involves the forcing-together of lightweight hydrogen nuclei (single particles called protons) in a series of reactions that eventually create nuclei of helium. Along the way, smaller particles (positrons and neutrinos) are released, along with energy in the form of gamma rays.

KEY

- Core
- Radiative Zone
- Convective Zone
- Photosphere
- Chromosphere
- Corona

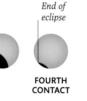

Layers not shown to scale

Features of the sun

By using special filters and cameras that can detect radiations beyond visible light, details on and above the sun's incandescent surface are revealed, which offer clues to the complex structure hidden below the photosphere.

Short-lived jets of gas called spicules, 6,000 miles (10,000 km) tall, scattered across surface

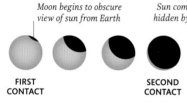

Positron   Neutrino   Gamma ray   Helium-3 nucleus

Hydrogen nucleus (proton)   Energy released   Neutron   Energy released

NUCLEAR FUSION IN THE SUN

Coronal mass ejection

When loops of magnetic field short-circuit high in the sun's outer corona, huge amounts of energy are released, spitting vast clouds of gas into space at speeds of millions of miles per hour.

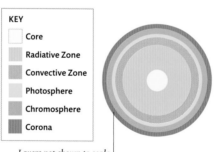

Giant eruptions of gas called prominences suspended above surface by coronal loops may last for days or weeks

Intensely bright regions of sun's mottled surface called faculae, associated with appearance of sunspots

see also Stars pp.22–25 ▶ The universe pp.30–33 ▶ Missions to the solar system pp.38–39 ▶

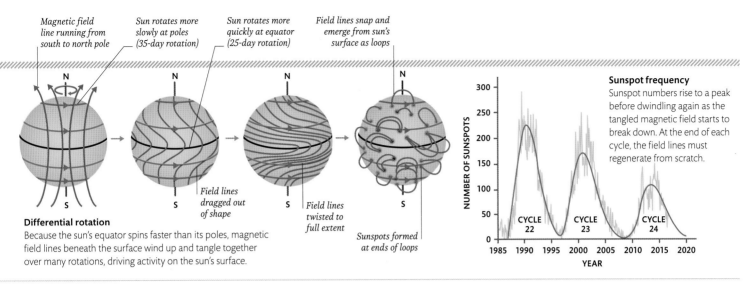

Differential rotation

Because the sun's equator spins faster than its poles, magnetic field lines beneath the surface wind up and tangle together over many rotations, driving activity on the sun's surface.

Magnetic field line running from south to north pole

Sun rotates more slowly at poles (35-day rotation)

Sun rotates more quickly at equator (25-day rotation)

Field lines snap and emerge from sun's surface as loops

Field lines dragged out of shape

Field lines twisted to full extent

Sunspots formed at ends of loops

Sunspot frequency

Sunspot numbers rise to a peak before dwindling again as the tangled magnetic field starts to break down. At the end of each cycle, the field lines must regenerate from scratch.

CYCLE 22

CYCLE 23

CYCLE 24

NUMBER OF SUNSPOTS

YEAR

Solar wind

At its outer edges, the sun's corona merges with the solar wind, a stream of stray particles driven out from the sun by the pressure of radiation behind. As the solar wind streams past Earth, it distorts our planet's magnetic field, before continuing out through the solar system until it eventually slows beyond the orbit of Neptune.

1.3 million Earths would fit inside the sun

Solar wind

Bow shock

Charged particles trapped by magnetic field close to Earth

Earth's magnetic field stretched out on side farthest from sun

EARTH'S MAGNETOSPHERE

Aurora borealis (northern lights)

Particles from the solar wind are drawn down by Earth's magnetosphere above Earth's poles. They energize gas molecules in the upper atmosphere, creating glowing aurorae or northern and southern lights.

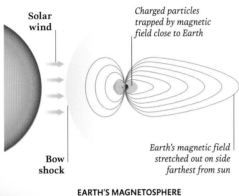

Loops of plasma heated to 1.8 million °F (1 million °C) or higher associated with magnetic field lines

CONVECTIVE ZONE

RADIATIVE ZONE

CORE

Equatorial diameter	865,000 miles (1.4 million km)
Mass (Earth = 1)	333,000
Mean distance from Earth	93 million miles (149.6 million km)
Rotation period (polar)	35 Earth days
Rotation period (equatorial)	25 Earth days
Surface temperature	9,900°F (5,500°C)
Core temperature	27 million °F (15 million °C)

Corona extends outward into space for millions of miles from chromosphere

Irregular layer of atmosphere above photosphere called the chromosphere

Heat and light escape into space at sun's visible surface called the photosphere

Energy carried by convection cells in convective zone generates magnetic field

Energy travels in form of photons of electromagnetic radiation in radiative zone

Nuclear reactions occur in sun's core

Light and matter pp.188–89 ▶   **21**

Types of stars

Stars are huge balls of gas created by the collapse of vast interstellar gas clouds. They shine thanks to energy released by nuclear fusion reactions in their cores. Beyond these two shared characteristics, however, stars vary hugely in properties such as brightness, size, color, and mass, and they range from small, faint dwarfs to enormous, luminous giants.

How stars form
Stars are born when clouds of gas and dust, tens of light years wide, collapse and separate into multiple smaller regions called knots, or Bok globules. Each of these knots produces a single star or a multiple star system.

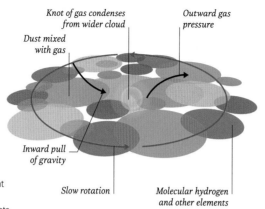

Knot of gas condenses from wider cloud

Outward gas pressure

Dust mixed with gas

Inward pull of gravity

Slow rotation

Molecular hydrogen and other elements

1 MOLECULAR CLOUD

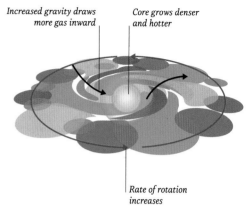

Increased gravity draws more gas inward

Core grows denser and hotter

Rate of rotation increases

2 CORE COLLAPSES

Star classification
A star's spectral class reflects its temperature and color, from blue Class O to red Class M. More complex luminosity classes are broadly divided into dwarfs (stars on or fainter than the expected "main sequence" brightness for their color) and brighter giants.

Hertzsprung-Russell diagram
Plotting stars on a chart comparing color and luminosity reveals that the vast majority lie along the diagonal band called the main sequence.

CLASS		APPARENT COLOR	AVERAGE SURFACE TEMPERATURE	EXAMPLE STAR
O		Blue	Over 54,000°F (30,000°C)	Zeta Puppis, also called Naos (Puppis)
B		Deep bluish white	36,000°F (20,000°C)	Rigel (Orion)
A		Pale bluish white	15,000°F (8,500°C)	Sirius A (Canis Major)
F		White	11,700°F (6,500°C)	Procyon A (Canis Minor)
G		Yellow-white	9,500°F (5,300°C)	The sun
K		Orange	7,150°F (4,000°C)	Aldebaran (Taurus)
M		Red	5,350°F (3,000°C)	Betelgeuse (Orion)

Layers inside stars
Stars with about the same mass as the sun have three internal layers defined by the way in which energy is transported through them to the surface—the core, radiative zone, and convective zone. Low- and high-mass stars, however, have different internal structures.

Inside a high-mass star
Gas around the core absorbs energy and carries it upward by convection. It eventually releases light that passes through a radiative zone to the transparent photosphere.

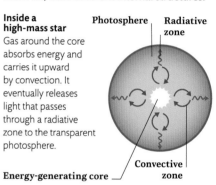

Photosphere

Radiative zone

Energy-generating core

Convective zone

Inside a low-mass star
Energy from the core is absorbed by surrounding gas and carried by convection to the surface, where it is released as light at the photosphere.

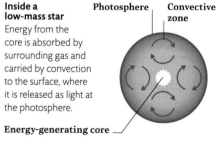

Photosphere

Convective zone

Energy-generating core

Balanced forces
For most of the life of most stars, the forces of gravity and pressure are exactly balanced and the star maintains its size.

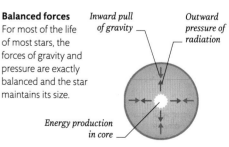

Inward pull of gravity

Outward pressure of radiation

Energy production in core

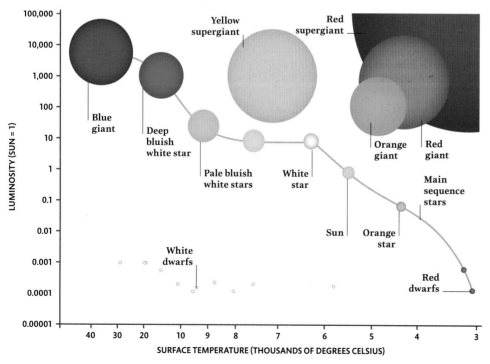

100,000

10,000

Yellow supergiant

Red supergiant

1,000

100

Blue giant

Deep bluish white star

10

LUMINOSITY (SUN = 1)

Pale bluish white stars

White star

Orange giant

Red giant

1

0.1

Main sequence stars

0.01

Sun

Orange star

White dwarfs

0.001

Red dwarfs

0.0001

0.00001

40 30 20 10 9 8 7 6 5 4 3

SURFACE TEMPERATURE (THOUSANDS OF DEGREES CELSIUS)

Astronomers estimate that **about 80 percent of all stars** in our galaxy, the Milky Way, are **faint red dwarfs**; bright stars are in a **small minority**

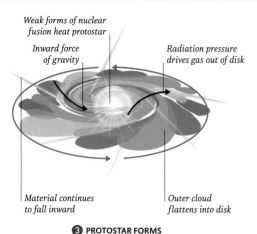

Weak forms of nuclear fusion heat protostar

Inward force of gravity

Radiation pressure drives gas out of disk

Material continues to fall inward

Outer cloud flattens into disk

3 PROTOSTAR FORMS

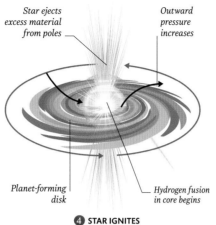

Star ejects excess material from poles

Outward pressure increases

Planet-forming disk

Hydrogen fusion in core begins

4 STAR IGNITES

ANNIE JUMP CANNON

US astronomer Cannon (1863–1941) formulated the most widely used scheme of star classification. By analyzing the light from thousands of stars, she identified patterns that allow their true brightness to be calculated even when their distance is unknown.

Some **700 billion stars** are born in the universe every year

Multiple stars

Star formation frequently leads to systems of two or more stars in orbit around each other. Studying these systems can reveal the relative masses of the stars involved, and also show how stars with different properties evolve at different rates.

The **shortest period** for a **binary star orbit** is **3 hours**; the longest can be hundreds of thousands of years

Barycenter equal distance from stars

Barycenter offset toward more massive star

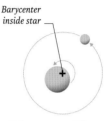

Barycenter inside star

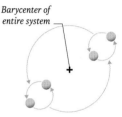

Barycenter of entire system

Equal mass
When two stars in a binary system have equal mass, they will orbit at the same average distance from a common center of gravity, or barycenter.

Unequal mass
If one star weighs more than the other, then the more massive star orbits closer to the barycenter, while the less massive one orbits farther away.

Extreme mass difference
Sometimes the barycenter lies inside the more massive star, which "wobbles" around it, while a much less massive companion star orbits at a distance.

Double binary
In some multiples, two binary pairs orbit each other. Each pair orbits its own shared center of mass, while circling the overall barycenter.

Starbirth nebula

As the first stars born from a nebula begin to shine, their radiation energizes the gas around them, causing it to glow. Fierce stellar winds can hollow out a cavernlike space within the nebula, while pressure from radiation wears dust-rich opaque clouds down to narrow pillars. These surround the locations where star formation is continuing and dense material is best able to resist the erosion.

Mystic Mountain

This spectacular region of the Carina Nebula is shaped by stellar winds and radiation. Embedded in its peak is a newborn star ejecting twin jets of excess matter.

STELLAR RECYCLING

Stars transform lightweight elements into heavier ones throughout their lives, scattering the debris across space as they live and die. As heavy elements enrich the hydrogen-rich nebulae that form new stars, they cause them to burn faster and brighter.

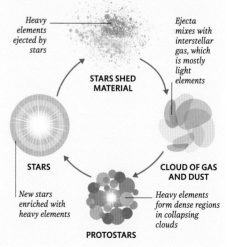

Heavy elements ejected by stars

Ejecta mixes with interstellar gas, which is mostly light elements

STARS SHED MATERIAL

STARS

CLOUD OF GAS AND DUST

New stars enriched with heavy elements

Heavy elements form dense regions in collapsing clouds

PROTOSTARS

see also The lives of stars pp.24–25 ▶ The universe pp.30–33 ▶ The history of the Earth pp.298–99 ▶

The lives of stars

Although many stars vary slightly in brightness over cycles that may take anything from hours to years, their life cycles are so long that astronomers rarely get the chance to observe one type of star turning into another. Instead, the story of stellar evolution has to be pieced together by observing the properties of different types of stars and the numbers of each that we can see in the sky, and linking these to models of the processes that are going on inside these different types. The course of a star's life is determined by its initial mass.

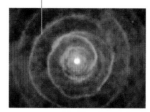

Gas expelled from red giant

LL PEGASI

Different elements glow in different colors

CAT'S EYE NEBULA

Different lives

As a general rule, the greater a star's mass, the brighter it burns but the shorter its lifetime. Stars with more than about eight times the mass of the sun, or more than eight solar masses, also end their lives in a much more spectacular way than lower-mass stars.

Escaping radiation supports star's outer layers

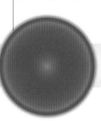

Cool surface, around 5,400°F (3,000°C)

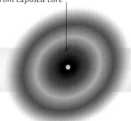

Expelled gas glows in radiation from exposed core

Solar-mass star
Stars with relatively low masses initially burn their internal nuclear fuel—hydrogen—at a slow pace that allows them to shine for billions of years.

Red giant
As the star runs out of hydrogen in its core, it begins to burn helium. This allows it to keep shining, increases its luminosity, and inflates it to an enormous size.

Planetary nebula
Eventually, when all the fuel is used, the red giant becomes unstable and begins to pulsate. Its final act is to eject a series of shells that form a planetary nebula.

Protostars
Stars form in collapsing clouds of gas and dust. As they begin to shine, they go through violent pulsations and eject excess material to achieve stability.

The **lowest-mass stars** may shine feebly for **trillions of years** without exhausting their fuel

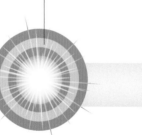

Strong stellar winds blow outer layers into space

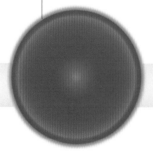

Extended outer atmosphere

Explosion burns through fuel in star's outer layer

High-mass star
Nuclear reactions in heavyweight stars occur at a faster rate than in normal stars, allowing them to shine much more brightly, but for a much shorter time.

Supergiant
Toward the end of their lives, high-mass stars keep shining by developing layers that burn different elements. They swell to huge sizes, and become unstable supergiants.

Supernova
When a supergiant's core runs out of fuel, the surrounding layers collapse and then rebound, creating a supernova explosion that can outshine an entire galaxy.

SUPERGIANTS TO SCALE
Supergiants are the largest stars of all—they may shine with the brightness of a million or more suns, but pressure from this escaping radiation inflates their outer layers to enormous size. The biggest of all the supergiants are the red supergiants. If a red supergiant such as Betelgeuse, for example, replaced the sun at the center of our solar system, it would extend almost to the orbit of Jupiter.

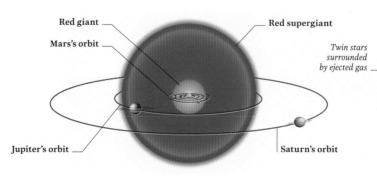

Red giant
Mars's orbit
Red supergiant
Jupiter's orbit
Saturn's orbit

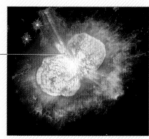

Twin stars surrounded by ejected gas

DYING SUPERGIANT, ETA CARINAE

◀ see also The cosmos pp.12–13   ◀ The sun pp.20–21   ◀ Types of stars pp.22–23

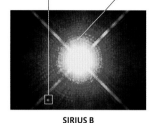

White dwarf Sirius B has same mass as the sun

Sirius, or the Dog Star, has about twice the sun's mass

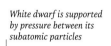

SIRIUS B

Three stages of life
These images capture moments in the death of a sunlike star, as it transforms into an increasingly unstable red giant, sheds its layers to form a planetary nebula, then subsides into a burned-out white dwarf.

White dwarf is supported by pressure between its subatomic particles

The universe is too young for black dwarfs to exist yet

White dwarf
The burned-out core of the star is all that remains at the center of the nebula. With no nuclear reactions to generate energy and support it, it is compressed by gravity to the size of Earth.

Black dwarf
Over many billions of years, the initially incandescent white dwarf slowly cools and changes color. Eventually it will become a cold, dead star known as a black dwarf.

Anything straying too close to black hole is pulled in

Black hole
Supernovae compress the cores of the most massive stars into a single miniscule point with near-infinite density—a black hole.

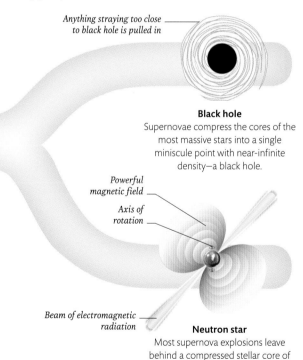

Powerful magnetic field

Axis of rotation

Beam of electromagnetic radiation

Neutron star
Most supernova explosions leave behind a compressed stellar core of incredible density—a city-sized remnant called a neutron star.

A **teaspoon** of **neutron star** material would have a **mass** of 3 billion tons

Cosmic lighthouses
When a supergiant's core is compressed into a neutron star during a supernova explosion, it retains the same "angular momentum" as it previously had, but must spin much more rapidly due to its compression. Its magnetic field is also intensified, channeling its radiation into beams and creating a flashing beacon called a pulsar.

Crab Nebula
The Crab Nebula is the site of a supernova explosion that was seen on Earth in 1054. A fast-spinning pulsar emits regular radio signals from its heart.

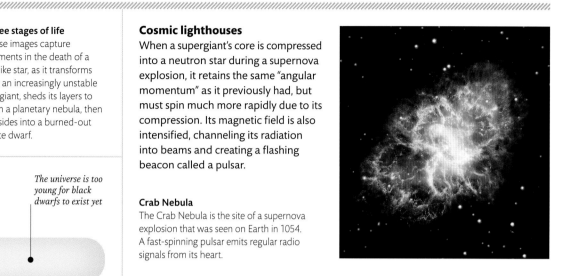

Earth

Radiation beam not aligned with Earth

Radiation beam aligned with Earth

Radiation beam not aligned with Earth

Direction of pulsar's spin **Neutron star**

Smooth, spherical surface

Pulsar off
The pulsar's signal aligns with its magnetic field. If this is tilted to the axis of rotation, its beams sweep around the sky.

Pulsar on
If one or both pulsar beams happen to align with Earth, then we see a brief flash of radiation once in each rotation.

Pulsar off
The beam moves on, but pulsars spin so rapidly that most have a rotation period of a fraction of a second.

The **fastest-spinning** neutron stars rotate more than **700 times per second**

Black holes
If the compressed core of a supernova has more than 1.4 times the sun's mass, then its gravity becomes so great that nothing can halt its collapse. The star's mass becomes compressed to a single point in space called a singularity. A barrier called the event horizon defines a region of space-time (see p.196) around the singularity from which not even light can escape—hence the name black hole.

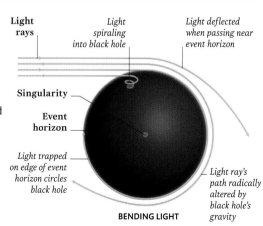

Light rays

Light spiraling into black hole

Light deflected when passing near event horizon

Singularity

Event horizon

Light trapped on edge of event horizon circles black hole

Light ray's path radically altered by black hole's gravity

BENDING LIGHT

see also The universe pp.30–33 ▶   Relativity and grand theories pp.196–97 ▶   The history of the universe pp.294–95 ▶

The Milky Way

Structure of the Milky Way

The Milky Way Galaxy is a vast spiral of stars, gas, and dust—at least 150,000 light years across according to recent estimates, and containing 100–400 billion stars. Its precise structure is hard to determine from our location inside it, but it has several spiral arms (mostly named after the constellations in which they are most prominent) rooted at either end of the central bar. Different types of stars dominate in different regions of the galaxy.

View from Earth
As seen from within, the Milky Way's disk forms a band of light around the sky. It is brightest toward the galactic center in Sagittarius.

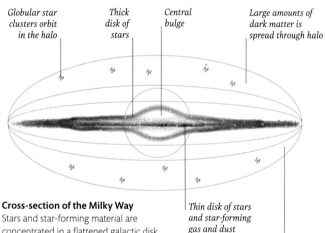

Globular star clusters orbit in the halo

Thick disk of stars

Central bulge

Large amounts of dark matter is spread through halo

Thin disk of stars and star-forming gas and dust

Stray stars orbit in halo region

Cross-section of the Milky Way
Stars and star-forming material are concentrated in a flattened galactic disk around a bulging central hub region packed mainly with red and yellow stars.

90% of the Milky Way's stars and globular clusters lie within **50,000 light years** of the galactic center

HOW SPIRAL ARMS FORM

Spiral arms are not physical structures, but are thought to be areas where orbiting material slows down and jostles together. The spiral region (density wave) is created by a large-scale alignment in the outer, slow-moving regions of elliptical orbits, under the influence of small, nearby galaxies.

Objects follow elliptical orbits around galactic center

PERFECTLY ORDERED ORBITS

Orbits align in many directions

CHAOTIC ORBITS

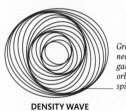

Gravity of nearby galaxies pulls orbits into spiral pattern

DENSITY WAVE

Spiral arms appear bright because the most brilliant and shortest-lived stars never escape the region of their birth

THOUSAND LIGHT YEARS

40　　30　　20　　10

PERSEUS ARM

OUTER ARM

Region that is home to red supergiant V434 Cephei, one of the largest known stars

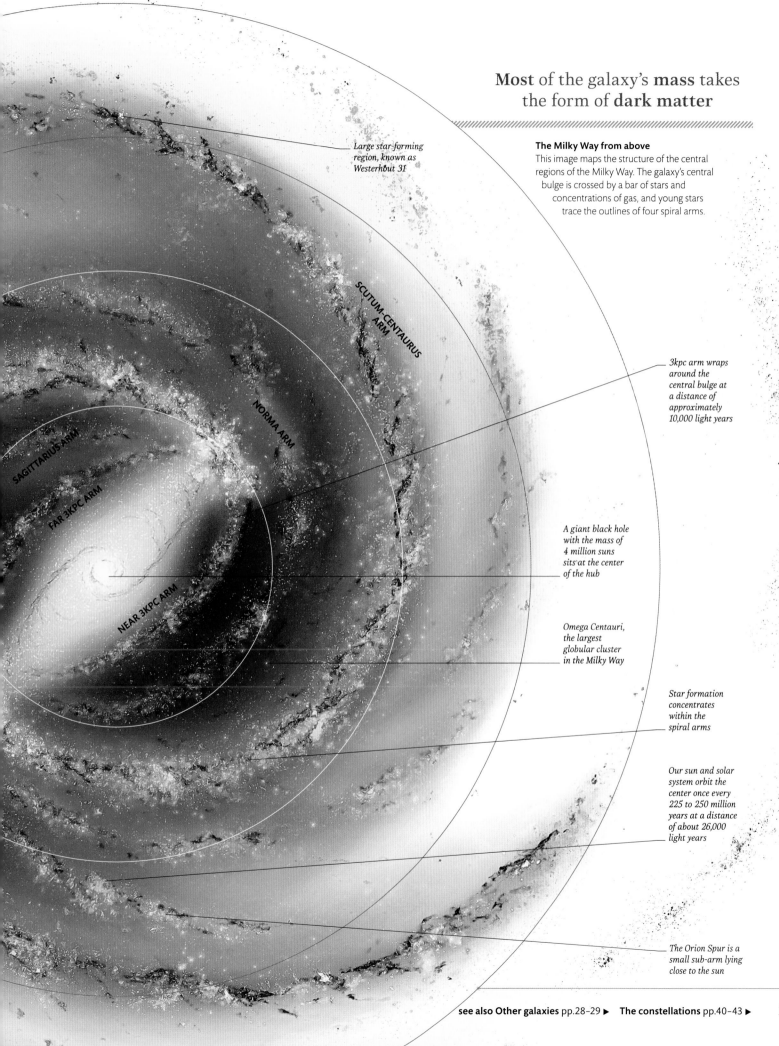

Most of the galaxy's mass takes the form of dark matter

The Milky Way from above
This image maps the structure of the central regions of the Milky Way. The galaxy's central bulge is crossed by a bar of stars and concentrations of gas, and young stars trace the outlines of four spiral arms.

Large star-forming region, known as Westerhout 31

SCUTUM-CENTAURUS ARM

NORMA ARM

SAGITTARIUS ARM

FAR 3KPC ARM

NEAR 3KPC ARM

3kpc arm wraps around the central bulge at a distance of approximately 10,000 light years

A giant black hole with the mass of 4 million suns sits at the center of the hub

Omega Centauri, the largest globular cluster in the Milky Way

Star formation concentrates within the spiral arms

Our sun and solar system orbit the center once every 225 to 250 million years at a distance of about 26,000 light years

The Orion Spur is a small sub-arm lying close to the sun

see also Other galaxies pp.28–29 ▶ The constellations pp.40–43 ▶

Other galaxies

To the limits of our observation, the universe is thought to contain several hundred billion galaxies. They range in shape and size from small, loose clusters of stars, to spirals like our own galaxy, and vast balls formed in collisions. Sometimes their appearance inspires a memorable name, as in the Cigar galaxy, but most are identified by a catalog number, and the constellation in which they are located.

HUBBLE CLASSIFICATION

An influential system of galaxy classification, the "tuning fork" diagram was devised by Edwin Hubble in the 1920s. It includes most major galaxy types, but it is not an evolutionary tree: evidence suggests that galaxies develop via a more complex chain of mergers.

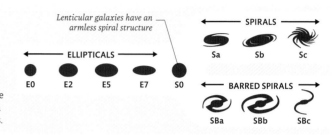

Lenticular galaxies have an armless spiral structure

SPIRALS
ELLIPTICALS

E0 E2 E5 E7 S0

Sa Sb Sc

BARRED SPIRALS

SBa SBb SBc

Spiral galaxies

These galaxies comprise a large ball of stars orbited by a flattened disk of stars, gas, and dust. New stars form in the disk, where gas is compressed, and their brilliant light highlights the spiral structure. The spiral's tightness defines the various galaxy subtypes.

M31 ANDROMEDA GALAXY
Andromeda

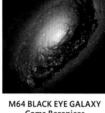

M64 BLACK EYE GALAXY
Coma Berenices

NGC 1448
Horologium

NGC 6753
Pavo

NGC 7793
Sculptor

Barred spiral galaxies

Many galaxies, including our own Milky Way, have spiral arms emerging from the ends of an elongated central bar. As in normal spirals, both the bar and the arms are dense regions where material in the disk slows down and crowds together.

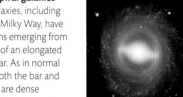

NGC 1015
Cetus

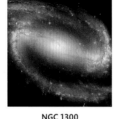

NGC 1300
Eridanus

NGC 1365
Fornax

NGC 2500
Lynx

NGC 6872
Pavo

Lenticular galaxies

These curious galaxies display a spirallike central hub surrounded by an orbiting flattened disk of stars, but no spiral arms. This may represent a "recovery" stage following a major collision or interaction that disrupted the galactic structure.

ESO 381-12
Centaurus

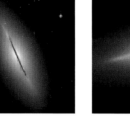

M102 SPINDLE GALAXY
Draco

NGC 4111
Canes Venatici

NGC 2787
Ursa Major

NGC 6861
Telescopium

Elliptical galaxies

These ball-shaped galaxies are classified according to their size and elongation, with the largest E0 "giant ellipticals" being the biggest galaxies of all. Ellipticals are dominated by old red and yellow stars, and show little sign of new star formation.

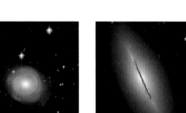

ESO 325-G004
Centaurus

M49
Virgo

M87 VIRGO A
Virgo

NGC 1132
Eridanus

NGC 4623
Virgo

Most galaxies have a **supermassive black hole** at their center, with a mass of **millions or billions of suns**

Irregular galaxies

These gas-rich shapeless clouds are thought by many to be the building blocks of larger galaxies. They are frequently home to regions of intense star formation, and many of the largest examples display the beginnings of a spiral structure.

IC 4710
Pavo

I ZWICKY 18
Ursa Major

M82 CIGAR GALAXY
Ursa Major

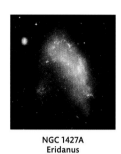

SMALL MAGELLANIC CLOUD
Tucana / Hydra

NGC 1427A
Eridanus

Dwarf galaxies

Often overlooked except in our immediate cosmic neighborhood, dwarf galaxies are small and faint, but may represent the majority of all galaxies. They range from gas-rich irregulars to loose balls of older stars that form dwarf ellipticals and spheroidals.

KISO 5639
Ursa Major

M110
Andromeda

PGC 51017
Boötes

SAGDIG
Sagittarius

UGC 4459
Ursa Major

Active galaxies

Many galaxies display activity that cannot be explained by stars alone, such as clouds of radio emission, or a bright, rapidly variable nucleus. Phenomena like these are generally linked to the consumption of matter by the vast central black hole.

3C 273
Virgo

MESSIER 77
Cetus

NGC 1275 PERSEUS A
Perseus

NGC 5128 CENTAURUS A
Centaurus

NGC 6814
Aquila

Interacting and colliding galaxies

Many objects that do not fit neatly into a standard classification group are, in fact, pairs of galaxies that are either colliding with each other; interacting through gravity during close encounters; or just happen to lie in the same direction in the sky.

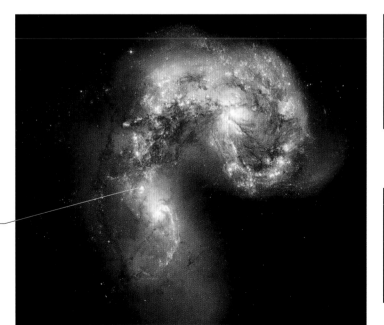

"Antennae" shape created by two colliding spirals whose cores are merging while their arms unwind

**NGC 4038/9
ANTENNAE GALAXIES**
Corvus

ARP 273
Andromeda

AM 0500-620
Dorado

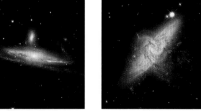

NGC 1531/2
Eridanus

NGC 3314
Hydra

see also The universe pp.30-33 ▶   The constellations pp.40-43 ▶   The history of the universe pp.294-97 ▶   **29**

The universe

The universe is everything there is: an enormous—perhaps infinite—volume of expanding space and all the stars, galaxies, planets, and other material contained within it. Its large-scale structure is composed of vast galaxy clusters in which matter is concentrated in chains and sheets, with the distance to the farthest visible galaxies limited only by how far light has been able to travel since the universe began.

Galaxy clusters and superclusters

About half of all known galaxies are members of distinct clusters. The Milky Way, for example, is one of three major spirals and several dozen smaller galaxies in a cluster called the Local Group. Clusters—which contain anything from a few dozen to several hundred galaxies—are held together by gravity, and merge at the edges to form larger superclusters.

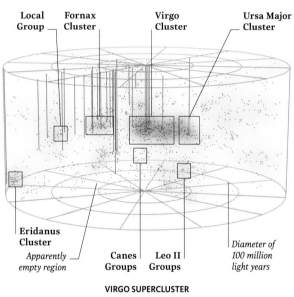

Local Group
Fornax Cluster
Virgo Cluster
Ursa Major Cluster

Eridanus Cluster
Apparently empty region
Canes Groups
Leo II Groups
Diameter of 100 million light years

VIRGO SUPERCLUSTER

Filaments and voids

Surveys show that galaxies in superclusters are concentrated in strands and thin sheets ("filaments") around empty regions ("voids") hundreds of millions of light years across. This may reflect the distribution of matter in the early universe.

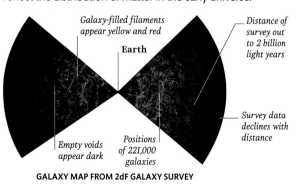

Galaxy-filled filaments appear yellow and red
Earth
Distance of survey out to 2 billion light years
Survey data declines with distance
Empty voids appear dark
Positions of 221,000 galaxies

GALAXY MAP FROM 2dF GALAXY SURVEY

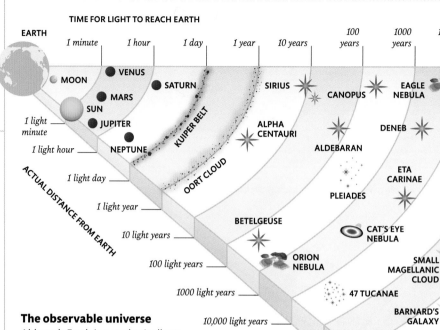

TIME FOR LIGHT TO REACH EARTH

EARTH

1 minute · 1 hour · 1 day · 1 year · 10 years · 100 years · 1000 years · 10...

MOON · VENUS · SATURN · SIRIUS · CANOPUS · EAGLE NEBULA
MARS · SUN · JUPITER · ALPHA CENTAURI · ALDEBARAN · DENEB
NEPTUNE · KUIPER BELT · PLEIADES · ETA CARINAE
OORT CLOUD · BETELGEUSE · CAT'S EYE NEBULA
ORION NEBULA · SMALL MAGELLANIC CLOUD
47 TUCANAE · BARNARD'S GALAXY
VIRGO CLUSTER

ACTUAL DISTANCE FROM EARTH

1 light minute
1 light hour
1 light day
1 light year
10 light years
100 light years
1000 light years
10,000 light years
100,000 light years
1 million light years
10 million light years
100 million light years
1.04 billion light years
16.2 billion light years
46.5 billion light years

The observable universe

Although Earth is not physically at the center of the universe, the limited speed of light means that Earth is at the center of the universe that we can see—because we can see the same distance in every direction. This diagram shows the size of the universe on a logarithmic scale, where each division is ten times larger than the previous one.

> We see **distant cosmic objects** as they looked **millions of billions of years ago**, when their light set out towards Earth

Gravitational lensing

Very large masses in space, such as galaxy clusters, can deflect and magnify rays of light from distant galaxies behind them in an effect called gravitational lensing. This can allow us to see distorted images of objects beyond the range of even the most powerful telescopes.

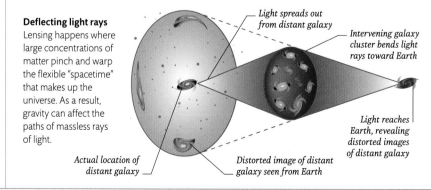

Deflecting light rays
Lensing happens where large concentrations of matter pinch and warp the flexible "spacetime" that makes up the universe. As a result, gravity can affect the paths of massless rays of light.

Light spreads out from distant galaxy
Intervening galaxy cluster bends light rays toward Earth
Light reaches Earth, revealing distorted images of distant galaxy
Actual location of distant galaxy
Distorted image of distant galaxy seen from Earth

Light from the most distant known galaxy, GN-z11, has taken 13.4 billion years to reach Earth

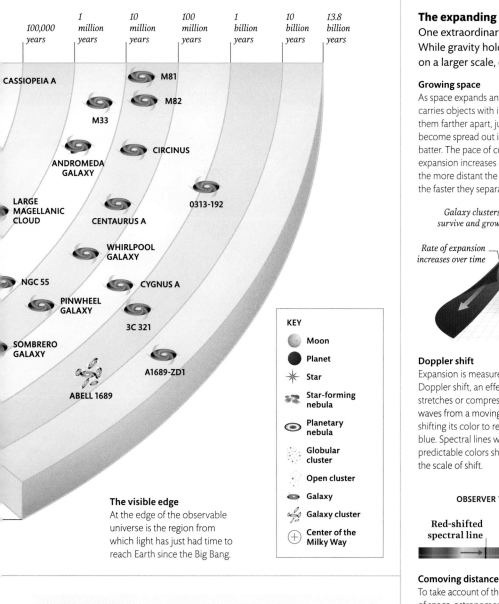

100,000 years	1 million years	10 million years	100 million years	1 billion years	10 billion years	13.8 billion years

CASSIOPEIA A

M81

M82

M33

ANDROMEDA GALAXY

CIRCINUS

LARGE MAGELLANIC CLOUD

0313-192

CENTAURUS A

WHIRLPOOL GALAXY

NGC 55

CYGNUS A

PINWHEEL GALAXY

3C 321

SOMBRERO GALAXY

A1689-ZD1

ABELL 1689

KEY

- ● Moon
- ● Planet
- ✴ Star
- 🌫 Star-forming nebula
- ◎ Planetary nebula
- ⁙ Globular cluster
- ⁙ Open cluster
- 🌀 Galaxy
- ✦ Galaxy cluster
- ⊕ Center of the Milky Way

The visible edge
At the edge of the observable universe is the region from which light has just had time to reach Earth since the Big Bang.

HUBBLE CONSTANT

The Hubble Constant describes the rate at which space expands. It takes its name from Edwin Hubble, who discovered the universe's expanding property in 1929. It measures expansion per unit distance: the more space between two objects, the faster they separate. The Hubble Constant is estimated to be 13.7 miles (22 km) per second per million light years.

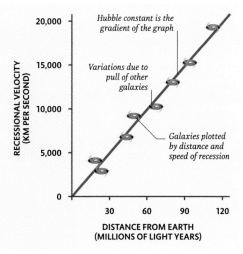

Hubble constant is the gradient of the graph

Variations due to pull of other galaxies

Galaxies plotted by distance and speed of recession

20,000

15,000

RECESSIONAL VELOCITY (KM PER SECOND)

10,000

5,000

0

30   60   90   120

DISTANCE FROM EARTH (MILLIONS OF LIGHT YEARS)

The expanding universe

One extraordinary aspect of the universe is the fact that it is expanding. While gravity holds stars, galaxies, and clusters together at a local level, on a larger scale, everything in the universe is moving farther apart.

Growing space

As space expands and grows, it carries objects with it and moves them farther apart, just as raisins become spread out in rising cake batter. The pace of cosmic expansion increases over time: the more distant the objects, the faster they separate.

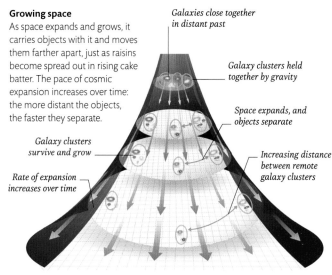

Galaxies close together in distant past

Galaxy clusters held together by gravity

Space expands, and objects separate

Galaxy clusters survive and grow

Increasing distance between remote galaxy clusters

Rate of expansion increases over time

Doppler shift

Expansion is measured using Doppler shift, an effect that stretches or compresses light waves from a moving object, shifting its color to red or blue. Spectral lines with predictable colors show the scale of shift.

Direction of galaxy moving through space

Waves stretched and red-shifted as galaxy recedes from Observer 1

Wavefront of emitted radiation

Galaxy approaching Observer 2

Waves compressed and blue-shifted

OBSERVER 1

OBSERVER 2

Red-shifted spectral line

Blue-shifted spectral line

Comoving distance

To take account of the expansion of space, astronomers chart remote galaxies in terms of "comoving distance"—their present-day separation—rather than the "look-back distance" that the light from a distant galaxy has actually traveled.

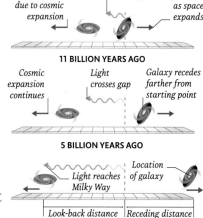

Movement of Milky Way due to cosmic expansion

Light leaves distant galaxy

Galaxy recedes as space expands

11 BILLION YEARS AGO

Cosmic expansion continues

Light crosses gap

Galaxy recedes farther from starting point

5 BILLION YEARS AGO

Light reaches Milky Way

Location of galaxy

Look-back distance | Receding distance

Comoving distance

PRESENT DAY

Comoving distance allows us to see objects 46.5 billion light years from Earth in all directions

see also The universe pp.32–33 ▶ Waves pp.186–87 ▶ The history of the universe pp.294–97 ▶

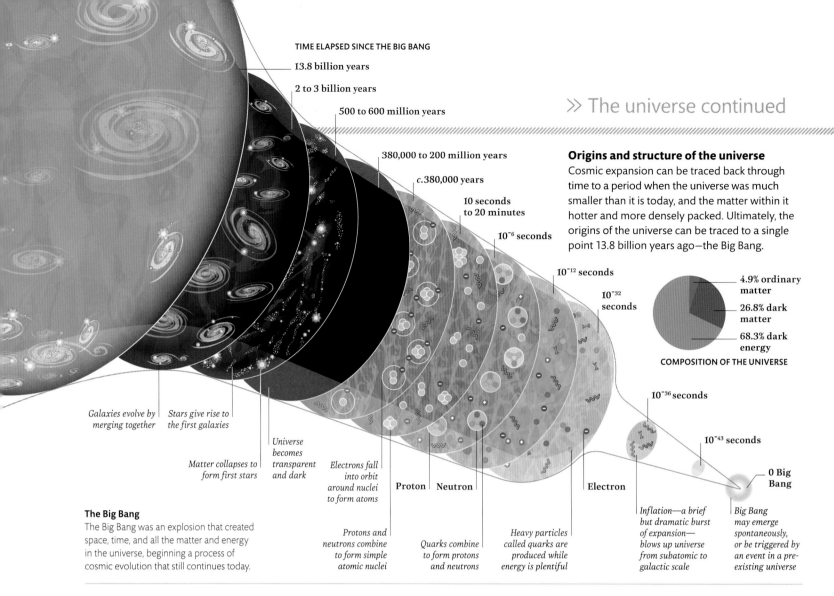

TIME ELAPSED SINCE THE BIG BANG

13.8 billion years

2 to 3 billion years

500 to 600 million years

380,000 to 200 million years

c.380,000 years

10 seconds to 20 minutes

10^{-6} seconds

10^{-12} seconds

10^{-32} seconds

10^{-36} seconds

10^{-43} seconds

0 Big Bang

Origins and structure of the universe

Cosmic expansion can be traced back through time to a period when the universe was much smaller than it is today, and the matter within it hotter and more densely packed. Ultimately, the origins of the universe can be traced to a single point 13.8 billion years ago—the Big Bang.

4.9% ordinary matter

26.8% dark matter

68.3% dark energy

COMPOSITION OF THE UNIVERSE

Galaxies evolve by merging together

Stars give rise to the first galaxies

Matter collapses to form first stars

Universe becomes transparent and dark

Electrons fall into orbit around nuclei to form atoms

Proton | Neutron

Electron

The Big Bang

The Big Bang was an explosion that created space, time, and all the matter and energy in the universe, beginning a process of cosmic evolution that still continues today.

Protons and neutrons combine to form simple atomic nuclei

Quarks combine to form protons and neutrons

Heavy particles called quarks are produced while energy is plentiful

Inflation—a brief but dramatic burst of expansion— blows up universe from subatomic to galactic scale

Big Bang may emerge spontaneously, or be triggered by an event in a pre-existing universe

Dark matter

Ordinary matter—such as stars, gas, and dust that emit light and other radiation—accounts for only one-sixth of the universe's total mass. The remaining "dark" matter is not merely dark, but entirely transparent, and makes itself known only through its influence on visible objects.

NEUTRINO DETECTOR

Most neutrinos pass through matter undetected. Underground detector chambers—which use hundreds of yards of rock to block interference from other particles—sometimes spot their rare interactions with matter.

Light-sensitive tubes detect flashes caused by neutrino interactions

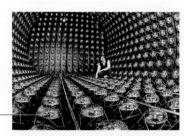

More than **99 percent** of the massive **Dragonfly 44 galaxy** is thought to be **dark matter**

Mapping dark matter

Dark matter is detected through gravitational effects: it does not reflect, absorb, or emit light. Galaxy clusters contain so much matter that they bend light from distant objects by gravitational lensing (see p.30). Astronomers study their lensing effects and build maps of the hidden mass.

Hot gas (ordinary matter) emits x-rays, colored pink

Computer projection (blue) of dark matter concentration

BULLET CLUSTER, COMBINED VISIBLE-LIGHT, X-RAY, AND GRAVITY MAP

Dark matter sources

In 1998, physicists found that neutrinos—particles generated inside stars and supernovas once thought to be massless— actually have significant, but still undefined, mass. Neutrinos probably account for at least some dark matter. The neutrinos from supernovas such as 1987A reach Earth ahead of the light from their explosions and are detected with special apparatus (see box above).

Remnant of supernova 1987A

Superdense **black holes** create warps in space-time from which even **light** cannot escape

Gravity and space-time

Einstein's general theory of relativity—supported by countless experiments—shows that large masses such as stars and galaxies distort both space and the flow of time around them, producing the effects of gravity. The universe is made of four-dimensional "space-time," within which extreme gravity creates distortions known as gravitational wells.

Curved space-time

The sun disrupts space-time, as it acts like a heavy ball on a rubber sheet. Light and objects moving in straight lines curve toward it, in what looks like a gravitational pull.

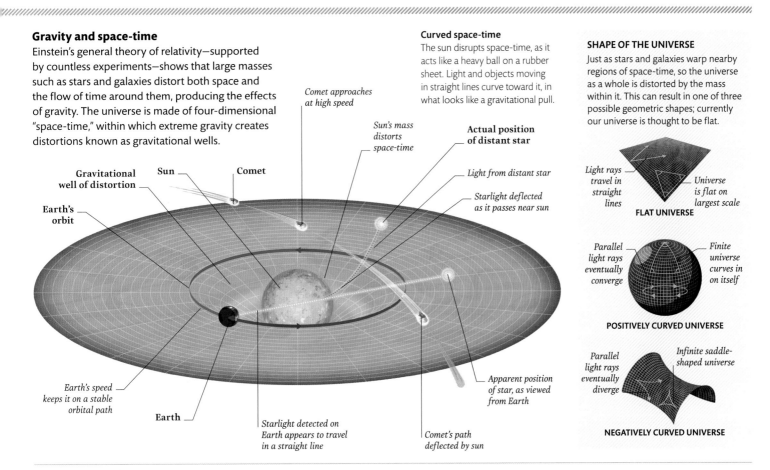

Comet approaches at high speed

Sun's mass distorts space-time

Actual position of distant star

Sun

Comet

Gravitational well of distortion

Light from distant star

Earth's orbit

Starlight deflected as it passes near sun

Earth's speed keeps it on a stable orbital path

Earth

Starlight detected on Earth appears to travel in a straight line

Comet's path deflected by sun

Apparent position of star, as viewed from Earth

SHAPE OF THE UNIVERSE

Just as stars and galaxies warp nearby regions of space-time, so the universe as a whole is distorted by the mass within it. This can result in one of three possible geometric shapes; currently our universe is thought to be flat.

Light rays travel in straight lines

Universe is flat on largest scale

FLAT UNIVERSE

Parallel light rays eventually converge

Finite universe curves in on itself

POSITIVELY CURVED UNIVERSE

Parallel light rays eventually diverge

Infinite saddle-shaped universe

NEGATIVELY CURVED UNIVERSE

Fate of the universe

The balance between cosmic expansion and the inward gravitational pull of all its matter determines whether the universe's growth will eventually stop and reverse, or whether it will continue forever.

Astronomers used to believe that expansion was solely due to the Big Bang and would inevitably slow down. However, in the 1990s they discovered that the rate of expansion is actually accelerating, driven by the mysterious phenomenon that is dark energy.

Future prospects

The fate of the universe is a topic of debate. Competing theories range from the possibility of a total collapse to ideas that it will cool and fade away; tear itself apart; or be replaced by an alternative.

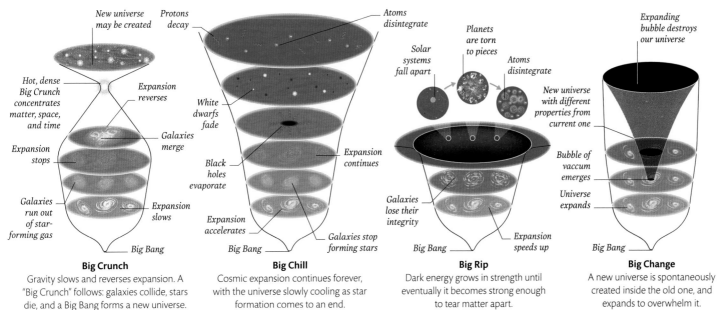

New universe may be created

Protons decay

Atoms disintegrate

Planets are torn to pieces

Solar systems fall apart

Atoms disintegrate

Expanding bubble destroys our universe

Hot, dense Big Crunch concentrates matter, space, and time

Expansion reverses

White dwarfs fade

Galaxies merge

New universe with different properties from current one

Expansion stops

Black holes evaporate

Expansion continues

Bubble of vaccum emerges

Galaxies run out of star-forming gas

Expansion slows

Galaxies lose their integrity

Universe expands

Expansion accelerates

Galaxies stop forming stars

Expansion speeds up

Big Bang

Big Bang

Big Bang

Big Bang

Big Crunch
Gravity slows and reverses expansion. A "Big Crunch" follows: galaxies collide, stars die, and a Big Bang forms a new universe.

Big Chill
Cosmic expansion continues forever, with the universe slowly cooling as star formation comes to an end.

Big Rip
Dark energy grows in strength until eventually it becomes strong enough to tear matter apart.

Big Change
A new universe is spontaneously created inside the old one, and expands to overwhelm it.

see also Relativity and grand theories pp.196–97 ▶   The history of the universe pp.294–97 ▶

Observing the universe

Spiral arms similar to that of the Milky Way

Blue objects are star clusters

Light and other forms of electromagnetic radiation (such as gamma rays and radio waves) are the most important way for us to study and understand other objects in the universe. Telescopes and related instruments that collect distant light and analyze it in various ways are therefore vital tools in learning about the cosmos, including discoveries about the size, age, and formation of the universe.

Distant galaxy
Light from the galaxy NGC 1232 takes 60 million years to reach Earth, giving astronomers a way to look into the past.

Optical telescopes

Invented in the early 17th century, the telescope captures parallel light rays emanating from distant objects and brings them to a focus, creating a magnified image. The greater the area of the collecting lens or mirror (called the objective), the brighter and more detailed the image produced.

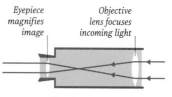

Eyepiece magnifies image *Objective lens focuses incoming light*

Refracting telescope
This design uses a glass objective lens to bend light to a focus before magnifying it with a second eyepiece lens.

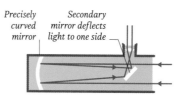

Precisely curved mirror *Secondary mirror deflects light to one side*

Reflecting telescope
This design uses a curved primary mirror to collect and focus the light. A secondary mirror directs the light to an eyepiece.

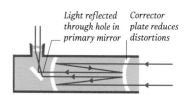

Light reflected through hole in primary mirror *Corrector plate reduces distortions*

Compound telescope
Advanced telescope designs combine a lenslike front "corrector plate" with a mirror to reduce optical distortion.

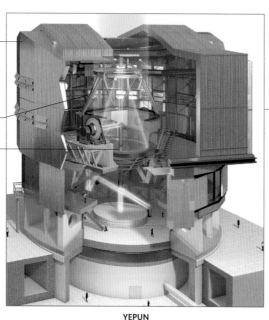

Boxlike observatory structure with a roof that can be closed to protect telescope

Computer-controlled telescope mount

27 ft (8.2 m) primary mirror

The VLT was the first telescope to directly view an exoplanet

YEPUN

Giant telescopes

Modern telescopes have large, thin mirrors, often built from multiple segments. At the European Southern Observatory at Paranal in Chile, a technique called interferometry is used to combine observations from different telescopes in a single super-sharp image.

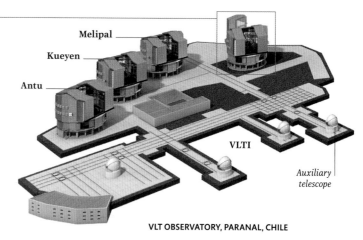

Melipal

Kueyen

Antu

VLTI

Auxiliary telescope

VLT OBSERVATORY, PARANAL, CHILE

COLLECTING AREAS

Advances in manufacturing technology and computer control since the 1990s have seen a huge expansion in the size of mirror-based telescopes. These advances have enhanced the images that can be captured by ground- and space-based telescopes.

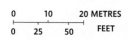

| 0 | 10 | 20 METRES |
| 0 | 25 | 50 FEET |

World's largest refractor, 3 ft (1 m) diameter lens

YERKES OBSERVATORY

Largest functional telescope until 1993, with 16 ft (5 m) mirror

HALE REFLECTOR

First compound mirror, later converted to single lens

MULTI MIRROR TELESCOPE

Largest optical space telescope

HUBBLE SPACE TELESCOPE

Future infrared space telescope

JAMES WEBB SPACE TELESCOPE

Twin telescopes with 2 x 32 ft (10 m) compound mirrors

KECK TELESCOPE

34 ft (10.4 m) mirror with 36 segments

GRAN TELESCOPIO CANARIAS

4 x 27 ft (8.2 m) single mirror telescopes

VERY LARGE TELESCOPE (VLT)

Compound of 7 x 27.5 ft (8.4 m) mirrors

GIANT MAGELLAN TELESCOPE

129 ft (39.3 m) primary made up of 798 segments

EUROPEAN EXTREMELY LARGE TELESCOPE

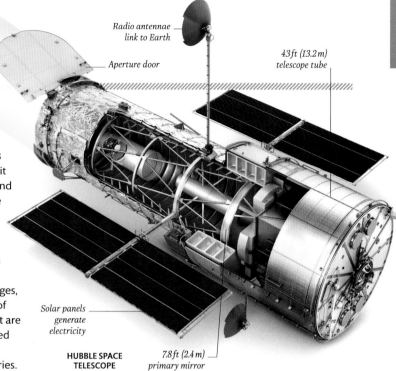

Radio antennae link to Earth

Aperture door

43 ft (13.2 m) telescope tube

Ground-based radio telescopes

The long wavelength of radio waves makes observing with them a challenge. Giant dishes focus waves onto a receiving antenna where they generate weak electric currents. The telescope scans across the sky to build maps of radio emission. Multiple telescopes can combine to improve image sharpness.

Satellite observatories

Telescopes located in orbit around the Earth or beyond can observe the sky more or less continuously, without concern for daylight or bad weather. A location beyond Earth's atmosphere also ensures the sharpest possible images, and allows observations of radiations from space that are either blocked or swamped before they can reach ground-based observatories.

Solar panels generate electricity

HUBBLE SPACE TELESCOPE

7.8 ft (2.4 m) primary mirror

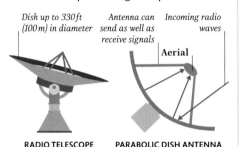

Dish up to 330 ft (100 m) in diameter

Antenna can send as well as receive signals

Incoming radio waves

Aerial

RADIO TELESCOPE   **PARABOLIC DISH ANTENNA**

Different wavelengths

While stars shine mostly in visible light, other astronomical objects at higher or lower temperatures give off invisible radiations with shorter or longer wavelengths. Only a few of these wavelengths reach the ground— the rest are blocked by Earth's atmosphere.

SPECTROSCOPY

A spectroscope deflects light of different wavelengths at different angles so that the composition of colors (called the emission spectrum) within it can be analyzed. The light emitted or absorbed by an object is linked to its atomic and molecular composition.

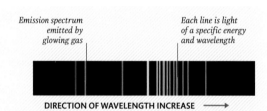

Emission spectrum emitted by glowing gas

Each line is light of a specific energy and wavelength

DIRECTION OF WAVELENGTH INCREASE ⟶

400 MILES (600 KM)

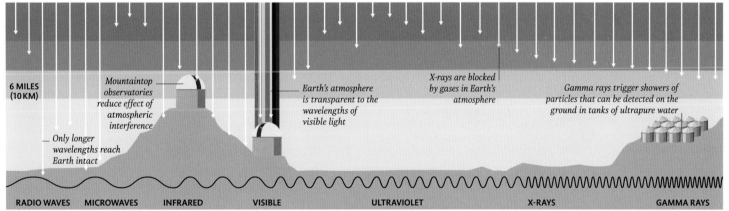

6 MILES (10 KM)

Mountaintop observatories reduce effect of atmospheric interference

Only longer wavelengths reach Earth intact

Earth's atmosphere is transparent to the wavelengths of visible light

X-rays are blocked by gases in Earth's atmosphere

Gamma rays trigger showers of particles that can be detected on the ground in tanks of ultrapure water

RADIO WAVES   MICROWAVES   INFRARED   VISIBLE   ULTRAVIOLET   X-RAYS   GAMMA RAYS

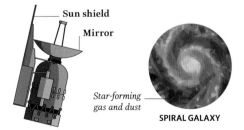

Sun shield

Mirror

Star-forming gas and dust

SPIRAL GALAXY

Infrared telescope

Infrared radiation reveals small, cool stars and interstellar dust. The satellites must be insulated and cooled to avoid the telescope's own warmth swamping weak signals.

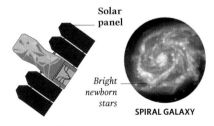

Solar panel

Bright newborn stars

SPIRAL GALAXY

Ultraviolet telescope

Massive stars, far hotter than the sun, shine mostly in the ultraviolet part of the spectrum, but most UV wavelengths are blocked by the atmospheric ozone layer.

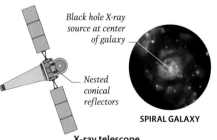

Black hole X-ray source at center of galaxy

Nested conical reflectors

SPIRAL GALAXY

X-ray telescope

X-rays pass straight through reflectors, so observatories, such as Chandra (launched in 1999), focus the rays using curved cones that cause the X-rays to ricochet.

see also Waves pp.186–87 ▶   **Light and matter** pp.188–89 ▶   **The history of the universe** pp.294–97 ▶

Space exploration

In October 1957 the launch of the first artificial satellite ignited a political Space Race between the Soviet Union and United States, culminating in the Apollo Moon landings of 1969–72. Since then, space exploration has focused more on scientific questions, putting satellites and telescopes into orbit, sending astronauts on long-duration missions, and launching increasingly sophisticated robotic space probes to other worlds in our solar system.

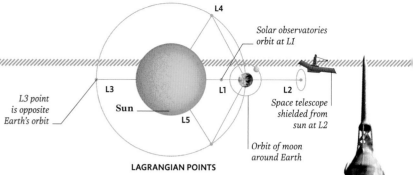

L4

Solar observatories orbit at LI

L3 point is opposite Earth's orbit

L3

Sun

L5

L1

L2

Space telescope shielded from sun at L2

Orbit of moon around Earth

LAGRANGIAN POINTS

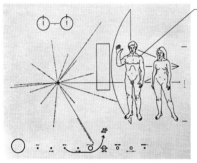

Human figures and information on location of Earth engraved on plaque

PIONEER PLAQUE

Communications antenna

***c.*1770s** Leonhard Euler and Joseph-Louis Lagrange discover points where the gravitational pull of two bodies cancels out, allowing a third to remain in stable orbit. These are later used by many satellites and spacecraft.

March 1972 US space agency NASA launches Pioneer 10, the first space probe to fly past Jupiter. It sends back about 500 images to NASA.

LUNAR ROVER

Wire-mesh wheels

Lightweight aluminum frame

July 1971 The US Apollo 15 mission carries the first Lunar Roving Vehicle to the Moon. This allows astronauts to explore more of the moon's surface.

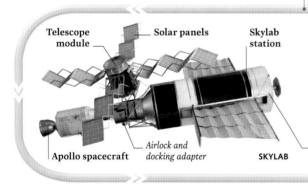

Telescope module

Solar panels

Skylab station

Apollo spacecraft

Airlock and docking adapter

Converted rocket stage

SKYLAB

May 1973 NASA launches Skylab, the first US space station. Over 9 months, three separate crews of astronauts visit Skylab, testing hundreds of experiments in orbit.

November 1973 NASA launches Mariner 10, an unmanned probe that makes flybys of the innermost planet, Mercury, and tests steering techniques used in later missions.

July 1975 A US Apollo spacecraft, launched by a Saturn IB rocket, links up with a Soviet Soyuz capsule in Earth orbit for the Apollo-Soyuz Test Project, a mission that marks a symbolic end to the Space Race.

Two-stage rocket design

SATURN IB

January 2005 ESA entry probe Huygens parachutes into the cloudy atmosphere of Saturn's giant moon Titan and sends back pictures from its surface.

January 2004 NASA's twin Mars Exploration Rovers Spirit and Opportunity touch down on opposite sides of the Red Planet. The robot missions explore the Martian surface for 6 and 14 years respectively.

October 2003 Military pilot Yang Liwei is launched into space aboard the Shenzhou 5 spacecraft, making China the third country to develop its own capacity to launch people into space.

Scaled-down Saturn moon rocket

Total weight of spacecraft is 45,900 lb (20,820 kg)

New engine burns liquid hydrogen

Radio antenna

Navigation and panoramic cameras

Solar panels

Versatile robot arm

Microscopic camera and chemical spectrometer

All-terrain suspension

SPIRIT MARS ROVER

January 2006 NASA's Stardust spacecraft returns a capsule of material from the tail of Comet Wild 2 to Earth after a 7-year mission. Later, scientists studying the material find it contains fragments of interstellar dust similar to that which formed the solar system.

October 2007 Japan's SELENE probe (also known as Kaguya) enters orbit around the moon. Over 20 months, it sends back high-resolution images of the surface and builds a 3D map of the terrain.

Radio antenna

184 lb (83.6 kg) mass

SPUTNIK 1

October 1957 The Soviet Union launches the first artificial satellite, Sputnik 1, into orbit. It sends radio signals to Earth for 3 weeks.

February 1958 Explorer 1, the first US satellite, travels in a higher orbit than Sputnik and discovers 2 dangerous radiation belts created by Earth's magnetic field.

April 1961 Yuri Gagarin, riding aboard the Soviet spacecraft Vostok 1 for less than 2 hours, becomes the first person to journey into space and the first person to orbit Earth.

YURI GAGARIN

March 1965 Soviet cosmonaut Alexei Leonov becomes the first person to walk in space, spending 12 minutes outside of his Voskhod 2 spacecraft.

Concealed pressure suit

Life support connections

Tough but flexible outer layer

APOLLO SPACE SUIT

1971 The Soviet Union launches Salyut 1, the first space station. An early mission to the station, however, ends in tragedy with the death of three cosmonauts.

Salyut crew killed   **SALYUT 1 STAMP**

November 1970 Having lost the race to put people on the moon, the Soviet Union lands Lunokhod 1, the first automated roving robot to investigate the surface.

Radio antenna

Solar panel

Eight separate wheels

LUNOKHOD 1

July 1969 During the US Apollo 11 mission, Neil Armstrong and Buzz Aldrin become the first people to walk on the moon.

Converted 747 carrier aircraft   *Gliderlike Shuttle design*

ENTERPRISE

September 1976 NASA debuts Enterprise, the prototype of its new Space Shuttle, used for reentry tests of the new spacecraft design.

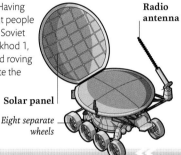

SPACE SHUTTLE COLUMBIA

April 1981 The US launch Columbia, the first in a fleet of reusable shuttles that provide the US space access for the next 30 years.

April 1990 The Hubble Space Telescope (HST) is deployed from the Space Shuttle Discovery. The HST proves to be a vital research tool, and becomes the first large optical telescope in history to reach orbit.

Photovoltaic arrays

US segment of station

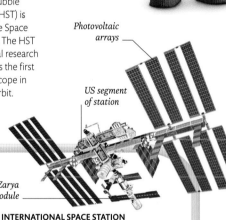

Zarya module

INTERNATIONAL SPACE STATION

February 2001 NASA's NEAR Shoemaker space probe becomes the first mission to touch down on an asteroid, after landing on Eros, a near-Earth asteroid.

Sensor calculates magnetic field of asteroid

Solar panels power spacecraft   **NEAR SHOEMAKER**   *Eight-sided aluminum body*

November 2000 The arrival of the first resident ISS crew and the beginning of Expedition 1 marks the beginning of almost two decades of permanent human presence in space.

November 1998 Construction of the International Space Station (ISS) begins with the launch of the Russian Zarya module, linked 2 weeks later to the Unity module carried aboard the Space Shuttle Endeavour.

Water-rich material scattered by an impact

October 2008 The India Space Research Organization sends its first mission to the moon. The spacecraft maps minerals on the lunar surface for 10 months.

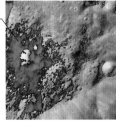

MOON MINERALOGY

September 2011 China launches Tiangong 1, its first space station. Over the next 2 years, it is visited by one uncrewed spacecraft and 2 crewed missions, one of which carries China's first female astronauts.

December 2013 The European Space Agency launches Gaia, a spacecraft built to map the distance to a billion stars via tiny shifts in direction known as parallax.

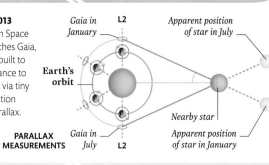

Gaia in January   L2   *Apparent position of star in July*   *Distant stars*

Earth's orbit

Nearby star

PARALLAX MEASUREMENTS   *Gaia in July*   L2   *Apparent position of star in January*

◀ see also Observing the universe pp.34–35   Missions to the solar system pp.38–39 ▶

Missions to the solar system

At present, the solar system is the only part of the universe that we can explore directly, to supplement information gleaned from the light and other types of radiation that come our way from distant stars and galaxies. Human exploration of the solar system has, however, so far gone no further than the moon: to explore other planets and minor bodies of the solar system, we have deployed a variety of robot probes and uncrewed vehicles to deepen our knowledge of our celestial neighborhood.

Moon missions

One of the most significant achievements in human exploration—and arguably the greatest in all of human history so far—was NASA's landing of a dozen astronauts on the moon between 1969 and 1972. Coming just 12 years after the launch of the first artificial satellite, and 8 years after Yuri Gagarin became the first man in space, the huge US effort to reach the moon ahead of their Cold War rivals in the Soviet Union was driven largely by political competition. Nevertheless, the missions returned valuable scientific data, including rock samples that have revealed a wealth of information about the origins and history of the solar system.

Space labs

Since the 1970s, human spaceflight has remained confined to a near-Earth orbit, just a few hundred miles above our planet's surface. To carry out scientific investigations of the space that surrounds Earth, and to learn about—and exploit— the weightless conditions of orbit, larger spacecraft capable of sustaining crews for longer missions were required. While the Soviet Union launched a series of space

stations of increasing complexity, NASA developed a fleet of reusable space shuttles. Since 1998, astronauts from many countries have conducted experiments on the International Space Station (ISS)—a joint enterprise operated by the space agencies of the US, Russia, Europe, Japan, and Canada.

3D cameras mounted on mast

NASA'S CURIOSITY MARS ROVER

Landers and rovers

The first space probes dispatched to the moon aimed merely to hit its surface and send back photographs taken during the final approach, but more sophisticated soft landers soon followed. In the 1970s, similar missions targeted Venus and Mars, with varying degrees of success. The first of the Soviet Union's Venera landers perished during their descent into Venus's hellish atmosphere, but later ones survived for brief periods, and sent back information about the atmosphere and landscape.

NASA's Viking Mars landers proved even more successful when they landed on the Red Planet in 1976. The twin landers collected data until 1980 and 1982— well beyond the mission's expected 90 days. Still further afield in the outer solar system, the European Space Agency's Huygens transmitted images of icy terrain from the surface of Titan—one of Saturn's moons—for several hours in 2005.

Since the late 1990s, several of the landers that have targeted Mars have been equipped with robotic rovers such

◄ Explorer on the moon
Astronaut David Scott during the Apollo 15 mission in 1971. Later Apollo missions used a Lunar Roving Vehicle (background) to widen the range of exploration.

SPACEWALKING FROM THE INTERNATIONAL SPACE STATION

as Curiosity. These are able to cover long distances, allowing them to photograph and analyze more of the planet's surface.

Orbiters

One of the best ways to learn more about other solar system objects is to place spacecraft in orbit around them to enable long-term study. Orbiters present a challenge because the spacecraft must carry engines and fuel to slow down and be captured by the target object's gravity after its high-speed journey across space.

Mariner 9, launched in 1971, revealed the volcanoes, canyons, and ancient riverbeds of Mars for the first time, and later orbiters have mapped the Red Planet in more detail. In the early 1990s, the Magellan mission used radar to reveal the surface of Venus through its clouds. The Galileo (1989–2003) and Cassini (1997–2017) missions to Jupiter and Saturn surveyed not just the giant planets but also their extensive families of moons as well as Saturn's spectacular ring system.

Flyby missions

The flyby approach to space exploration involves launching a spacecraft on a trajectory that will speed past a planet, asteroid, or comet, providing a brief but revealing encounter. Notable early examples include Luna 3, which imaged the far side of the moon in 1959; Mariner 4, which returned close-up views of Mars in 1965; and Mariner 10, which flew past Venus and Mercury in 1974–75.

Pioneer 10 made the first successful Jupiter flyby in 1973, while Pioneer 11 used its encounter with Jupiter to change course and speed, and travel on to Saturn in 1979. Voyager 2 took this technique even further: a series of "slingshot" maneuvers took it past Jupiter, Saturn, Uranus, and Neptune between 1979 and 1989. Flybys are an ideal solution for lightweight, high-speed missions—for instance in 2015, NASA's New Horizons mission flew past Pluto, having taken just under 10 years to reach the edge of the solar system.

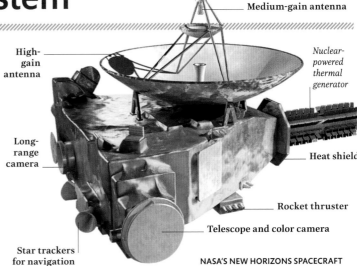

Low-gain antenna
Medium-gain antenna
High-gain antenna
Nuclear-powered thermal generator
Long-range camera
Heat shield
Rocket thruster
Telescope and color camera
Star trackers for navigation

NASA'S NEW HORIZONS SPACECRAFT

> "We have lingered long enough on the shores of the **cosmic ocean**. We are ready at last to set sail for the **stars**."
>
> CARL SAGAN, *Cosmos*, 1980

MISSIONS TO COMETS AND ASTEROIDS

The first comet flybys involved an international flotilla of spacecraft investigating Comet Halley in 1986. In 2000, the NEAR-Shoemaker probe began a yearlong mission to orbit the asteroid Eros. Missions such as Dawn— orbiting asteroids Vesta and Ceres—and Rosetta, which joined a comet on its passage around the sun, have delivered a wealth of discoveries.

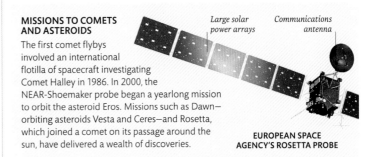

Large solar power arrays
Communications antenna

EUROPEAN SPACE AGENCY'S ROSETTA PROBE

◄ see also Space exploration pp.36–37

The constellations

Mapping the skies

Since ancient times, stargazers have imagined pictures among the stars, and used these to define various constellations of star patterns. Today, the entire sky is divided into 88 constellations with defined boundaries so that every star falls within a particular region. An asterism is the pattern formed by some of the brightest stars in a constellation. The constellations visible in the night sky at a specific time vary depending on the observer's position on Earth, and the sun's location on its annual track through Earth's skies.

The celestial sphere

Astronomers map the sky as the interior of a "celestial sphere" centered on Earth. As Earth spins on its axis, the sky rotates once per day. Earth's annual orbit, meanwhile, means the sun appears against different constellations through the year, along a path called the ecliptic.

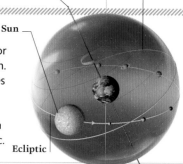

Earth's axis of spin
Celestial equator
Sun
Ecliptic

North polar sky

The stars around the north pole are visible to most northern-hemisphere observers throughout the year. They are said to be circumpolar, neither rising nor setting but simply changing their orientation as they pivot around a central point, the North Celestial Pole.

Long but faint constellation of Draco, the Dragon, wraps around Ursa Minor

Ursa Minor, the Little Bear; the Pole Star marks the tip of its tail

North Celestial Pole—the point in the sky directly above Earth's north pole

Polaris, the pole star, lies within half a degree of the North Celestial Pole

Ursa Major, the Great Bear; its seven brightest stars form the asterism the Plough or Big Dipper within the constellation

Declination (measured in degrees)—celestial equivalent of latitude

Right ascension (measured in hours)—celestial equivalent of longitude

Constellations on map: DRACO, CYGNUS, BOÖTES, URSA MINOR, LACERTA, CEPHEUS, CANES VENATICI, URSA MAJOR, CASSIOPEIA, CAMELOPARDALIS, PERSEUS, LYNX, AURIGA

Of the **88 modern constellations, 48** are from a list created by the Greek-Egyptian astronomer **Ptolemy** in the 2nd century BCE

✴ Brightest stars

Constellation	Star	Magnitude
Ursa Major	Alioth	1.77
Ursa Major	Dubhe	1.79
Ursa Major	Alkaid	1.86
Ursa Minor	Polaris	1.98 avg
Ursa Major	Mizar	2.04

LOCATOR

STAR MAGNITUDES

A star's brightness in Earth's skies is called its magnitude—the lower the magnitude, the brighter the star, and the very brightest stars have negative magnitudes (numbers less than zero). Naked eye magnitudes range from -1.46 (for Sirius, the brightest star in the sky) to about 6.0.

Observing constellations

Earth's size means that we can only ever see half the celestial sphere at a time. For most locations, the area in view changes through the night as Earth rotates, but stars that are too far north or south may never be visible from a particular location.

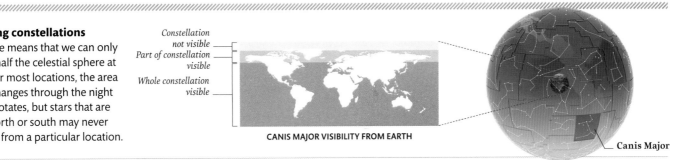

Constellation not visible
Part of constellation visible
Whole constellation visible

CANIS MAJOR VISIBILITY FROM EARTH

Canis Major

South polar sky

The southern circumpolar stars are permanently visible to most southern-hemisphere observers but out of sight from the northern hemisphere. Like the northern circumpolar stars, they change orientation throughout the night and year, but do not rise or set.

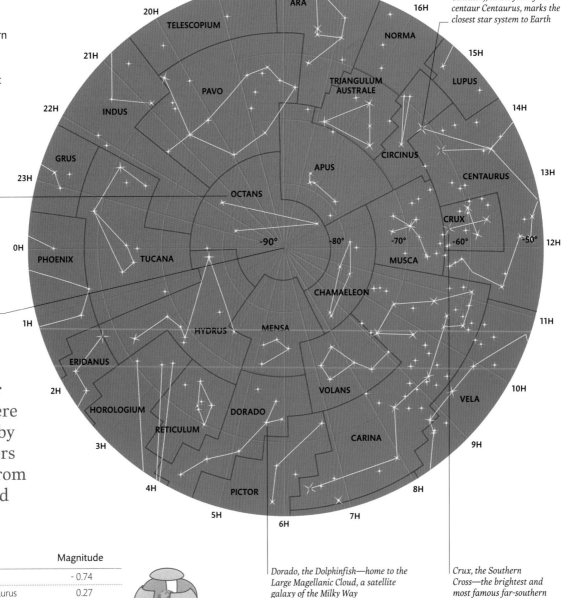

Rigil Kentaurus (Alpha Centauri), at the foot of the centaur Centaurus, marks the closest star system to Earth

Octans, a triangle of stars representing the Octant (a navigational instrument), is home to the South Celestial Pole

There is no bright star (like Polaris in the northern sky) near here

Southern polar constellations were mostly **invented** by European explorers and astronomers from the **1500s** onward

Dorado, the Dolphinfish—home to the Large Magellanic Cloud, a satellite galaxy of the Milky Way

Crux, the Southern Cross—the brightest and most famous far-southern constellation

LOCATOR

☀ Brightest stars

Constellation	Star	Magnitude
Carina	Canopus	- 0.74
Centaurus	Rigil Kentaurus	0.27
Eridanus	Achernar	0.46 avg
Centaurus	Hadar	0.61
Crux	Acrux	0.76

see also Seafaring through history pp.280–81 ▶   **41**

» The constellations continued

Equatorial sky: September, October, November

The sun's movement along the ecliptic means that, circumpolar stars aside, different constellations dominate the night sky at different times of year. Late in the year, the large constellations of Pegasus and Cetus are at their most prominent. For northern-hemisphere observers, these constellations are high in the sky looking south, while in the southern hemisphere, the patterns appear upside down in the sky looking north.

Equatorial sky: June, July, August

Around July, a bright broad swath of the Milky Way—the plane of our galaxy—runs across the sky from north to south, crossing constellations such as Cygnus, Aquila, Scutum, Sagittarius, and Scorpius. These constellations and others nearby are home to many star clusters and star-forming nebulae, while Sagittarius is home to the Milky Way's densest and brightest star clouds, in the direction of the center of the galaxy.

Andromeda (named after a princess in Greek mythology)—home to the nearest major galaxy beyond our own

Serpens, the Snake—the only constellation in the sky split into two parts: Caput (the head) and Cauda (the tail)

Declination (measured in degrees)—celestial equivalent of latitude

First Point of Aries, currently in Pisces, from which right ascension is measured (in hours—celestial equivalent of longitude)

The center of the Milky Way lies about 27,000 light years from Earth in the direction of Sagittarius, the Archer

✳ Brightest stars

Constellation	Star	Magnitude
Piscis Austrinus	Fomalhaut	1.16
Grus	Alnair	1.74
Aries	Hamal	2.00
Cetus	Diphda	2.02
Andromeda	Mirach	2.05 avg

LOCATOR

✳ Brightest stars

Constellation	Star	Magnitude
Lyra	Vega	0.03 avg
Aquila	Altair	0.76
Scorpius	Antares	0.96 avg
Cygnus	Deneb	1.26 avg
Scorpius	Shaula	1.62

LOCATOR

◀ see also The cosmos pp.12–13 ◀ The Milky Way pp.26–27

The constellation **Pegasus** is traditionally represented as being **upside down**—only **southern-hemisphere observers** get to see it **right side up**

Equatorial sky: March, April, May

The constellations that dominate evening skies around April offer some the best view into intergalactic space. Since observers are looking away from the crowded plane of the Milky Way, there is less in the relative foreground to block the view of distant galaxies millions of light years away, and a telescope can reveal dozens of galaxies from the nearest large galaxy cluster in Virgo and neighboring Coma Berenices.

Equatorial sky: December, January, February

Around the turn of the year, another broad swath of the Milky Way, packed with star clusters and nebulae, comes into view. The plane of the galaxy passes through a series of bright constellations including Perseus, Auriga, Orion, and Canis Major. Orion, representing a mythical hunter, faces another bright star pattern in the form of Taurus, the Bull, with his hunting dogs Canis Major and Canis Minor nearby.

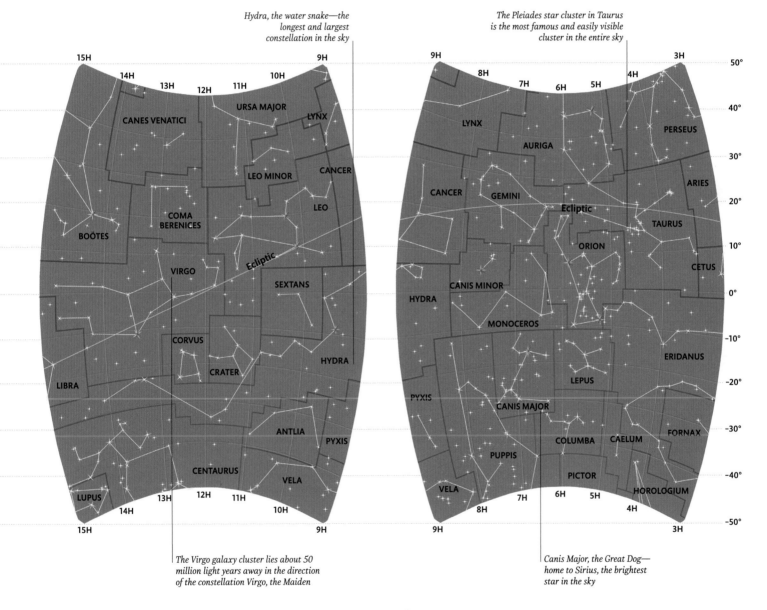

Hydra, the water snake—the longest and largest constellation in the sky

The Pleiades star cluster in Taurus is the most famous and easily visible cluster in the entire sky

The Virgo galaxy cluster lies about 50 million light years away in the direction of the constellation Virgo, the Maiden

Canis Major, the Great Dog—home to Sirius, the brightest star in the sky

Brightest stars

Constellation	Star	Magnitude
Boötes	Arcturus	- 0.05
Virgo	Spica	0.97 avg
Leo	Regulus	1.39
Hyrdra	Alphard	2.00
Leo	Algieba	2.08

LOCATOR

Brightest stars

Constellation	Star	Magnitude
Canis Major	Sirius	-1.46
Auriga	Capella	0.08 avg
Orion	Rigel	0.13 avg
Canis Minor	Procyon	0.34
Orion	Betelgeuse	0.50 avg

LOCATOR

Earth

Inside Earth

Earth's interior is dominated by just a handful of elements. The most important of these are oxygen, silicon, aluminum, iron, calcium, potassium, sodium, and magnesium, though many other elements are present in smaller amounts. Although these raw materials came from the dust and gas that orbited the sun shortly after its formation, 4.5 billion years of chemical and geological processing have transformed them into a complex mix of rocks and minerals. Varying heat, pressure, and chemical composition gives the interior different properties at different depths, creating a broadly three-layered structure with a rocky crust and mantle surrounding a partially molten metallic core. Electric currents generated in churning iron in the outer core power the Earth's magnetism.

Chemical composition of Earth

Over the course of Earth's formation, heavy elements tended to sink toward the center of the planet, while lighter ones rose toward the crust. As a result, the crust and mantle are rich in minerals containing silicon and lightweight metals, while heavier metals dominate the core.

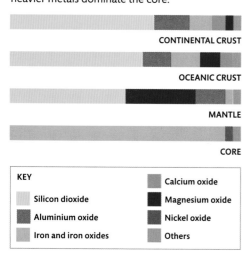

CONTINENTAL CRUST

OCEANIC CRUST

MANTLE

CORE

KEY

- Silicon dioxide
- Aluminium oxide
- Iron and iron oxides
- Calcium oxide
- Magnesium oxide
- Nickel oxide
- Others

SEISMIC WAVES

Geologists study the Earth's internal structure by detecting the paths of seismic waves caused by earthquakes in the crust. As a wave passes through interior layers, each with different properties, the speed of the wave is altered.

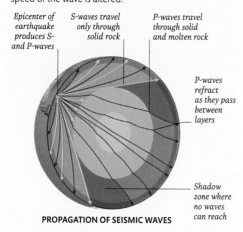

Epicenter of earthquake produces S- and P-waves

S-waves travel only through solid rock

P-waves travel through solid and molten rock

P-waves refract as they pass between layers

Shadow zone where no waves can reach

PROPAGATION OF SEISMIC WAVES

Earth's layers

Chemistry, heat, and gravity have separated the Earth into a number of layers, from the solid inner core to the liquid ocean and the gaseous atmosphere.

Atmosphere extends to about 6,200 miles (10,000 km), but most gas is concentrated in the troposphere— the lowest 6–11 miles (9–17 km)

Earth's water layer has a volume equal to 333 million cubic miles (1.386 billion cubic km)

Crust is broken into tectonic plates that move slowly across a layer of upper mantle rock

Earth's liquid water naturally flows toward low-lying lakes and ocean basins

ATMOSPHERE

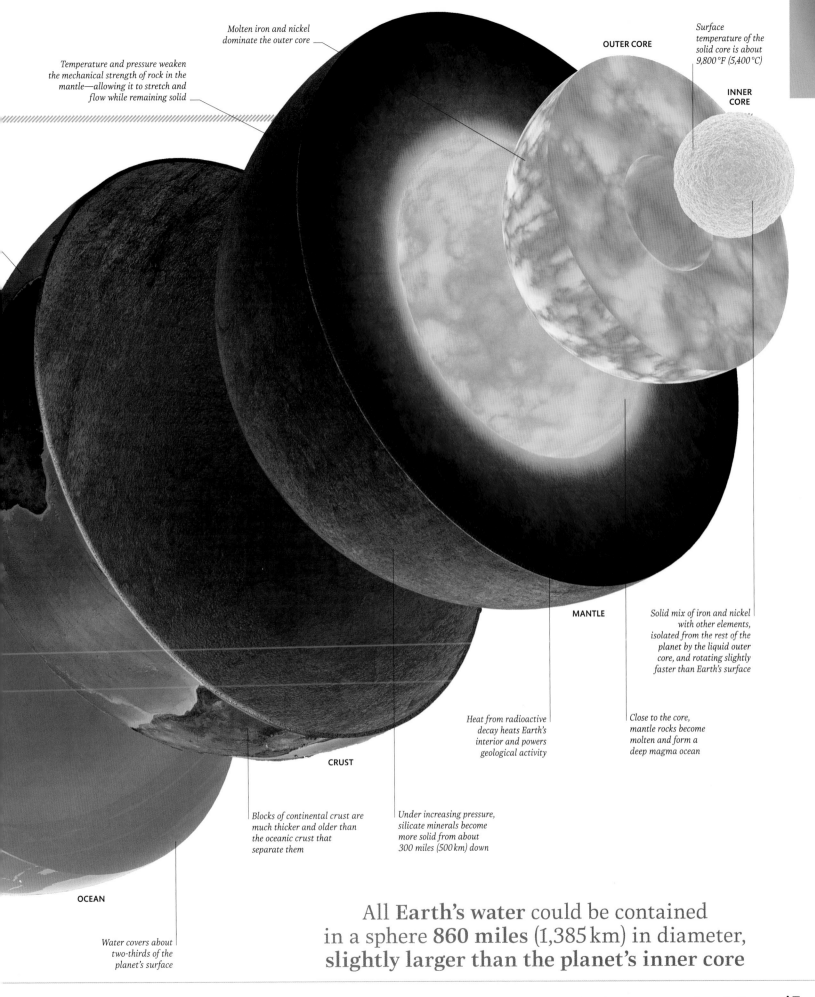

Molten iron and nickel dominate the outer core

Temperature and pressure weaken the mechanical strength of rock in the mantle—allowing it to stretch and flow while remaining solid

OUTER CORE

Surface temperature of the solid core is about 9,800 °F (5,400 °C)

INNER CORE

MANTLE

Solid mix of iron and nickel with other elements, isolated from the rest of the planet by the liquid outer core, and rotating slightly faster than Earth's surface

Heat from radioactive decay heats Earth's interior and powers geological activity

Close to the core, mantle rocks become molten and form a deep magma ocean

CRUST

Blocks of continental crust are much thicker and older than the oceanic crust that separate them

Under increasing pressure, silicate minerals become more solid from about 300 miles (500 km) down

OCEAN

Water covers about two-thirds of the planet's surface

All **Earth's water** could be contained in a sphere **860 miles (1,385 km)** in diameter, slightly larger than the planet's inner core

see also Tectonic plates pp.48–49 ▶ Volcanoes and earthquakes pp.54–55 ▶ Rocks pp.62–63 ▶ **47**

Tectonic plates

Earth is covered in a thin layer of solid rock called the crust. This is not a single, unbroken shell, but consists of sections called tectonic plates. These plates are not fixed, but move around slowly in relation to one another. The term "tectonic" means "to do with building" and the motion of the plates is what constructs large-scale surface features, such as ocean trenches and mountain ranges.

Plates of Earth

Most of Earth's surface is covered by just seven major tectonic plates, although there are several dozen plates in total. The larger ones are labeled below. The others are so-called microplates, which form unstable parts of the crust that are prone to earthquakes. Earthquakes are caused by sudden movements at plate boundaries.

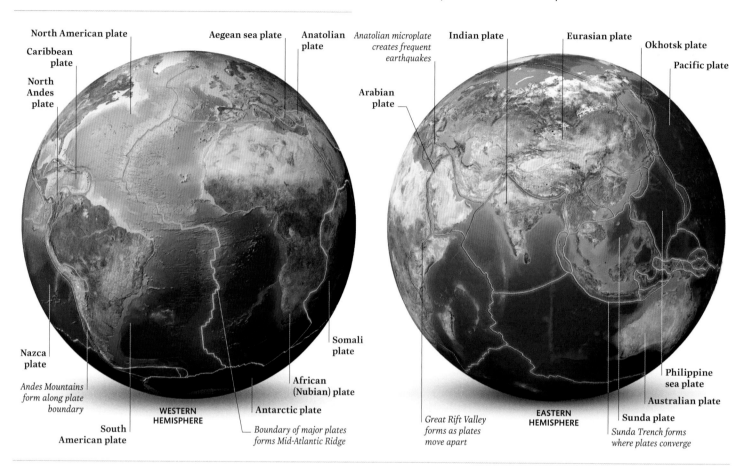

North American plate

Caribbean plate

North Andes plate

Aegean sea plate

Anatolian plate

Anatolian microplate creates frequent earthquakes

Indian plate

Eurasian plate

Okhotsk plate

Pacific plate

Arabian plate

Nazca plate

Andes Mountains form along plate boundary

South American plate

WESTERN HEMISPHERE

African (Nubian) plate

Antarctic plate

Boundary of major plates forms Mid-Atlantic Ridge

Somali plate

Great Rift Valley forms as plates move apart

EASTERN HEMISPHERE

Sunda plate

Sunda Trench forms where plates converge

Philippine sea plate

Australian plate

How plates move

Beneath Earth's solid crust lies a deeper layer called the mantle (see pp.46–47). The heat from the planet's core keeps the rock in the mantle permanently fluid. The tectonic plates float on this fluid material and are moved by currents that flow slowly up, down, and through it.

Convection currents

The motion of the mantle is driven by convection currents (see p.185), which transfer heat from the core to nearer the surface.

Near **Easter Island,** the rift between the **Pacific plate** and **Nazca plate** is spreading by **6 in (15 cm) every year**

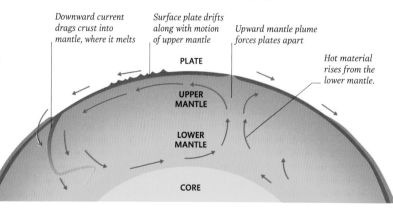

Downward current drags crust into mantle, where it melts

Surface plate drifts along with motion of upper mantle

Upward mantle plume forces plates apart

Hot material rises from the lower mantle.

PLATE

UPPER MANTLE

LOWER MANTLE

CORE

INTERFEROMETRY

Plate movement can be tracked by interferometry. This uses radio waves emitted by a distant galaxy to measure precisely the slowly changing distance between radio telescopes on different plates.

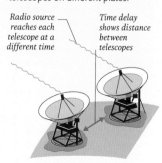

Radio source reaches each telescope at a different time

Time delay shows distance between telescopes

◀ see also Inside Earth pp.46–47 Evolving planet pp.50–51 ▶ Continents pp.52–53 ▶ Volcanoes and earthquakes pp.54–55 ▶

The **mid-ocean ridge** system is the world's **longest mountain range**, at about **40,000 miles** (65,000 km) long

Divergent boundary
Currents in the mantle drag plates apart. This causes a rift in the crust, typically on the ocean floor. Molten rock fills the gap and creates new crust, building a mid-ocean ridge.

Oceanic crust

Rift flanked by mid-ocean ridge

New crust created from solidified magma in bands

Oceanic crust moves away from plate margin

Upper mantle

Magma chamber

Convergent boundary
One plate is pushed under the other, or subducted, melting back into the mantle. The upper plate, if continental crust, is pushed up into a range of fold mountains and often volcanoes.

Continental crust pushed up into fold mountains

Magma forms volcanoes

Continental crust

Subduction causes crust to melt, forming magma

Upper mantle

Oceanic crust

Oceanic crust subducted

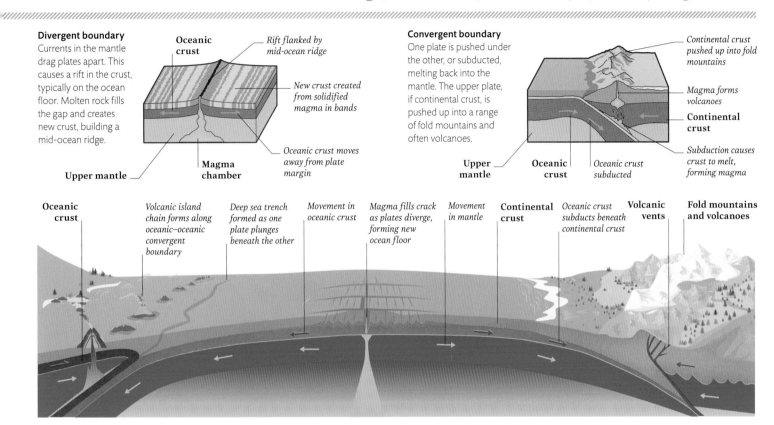

Oceanic crust

Volcanic island chain forms along oceanic–oceanic convergent boundary

Deep sea trench formed as one plate plunges beneath the other

Movement in oceanic crust

Magma fills crack as plates diverge, forming new ocean floor

Movement in mantle

Continental crust

Oceanic crust subducts beneath continental crust

Volcanic vents

Fold mountains and volcanoes

Plate boundaries

Earth's surface is constantly being formed and re-formed by the gradual interaction of tectonic plates. The boundaries between plates are where new crust is created and old crust is destroyed. Additionally these locations are where large-scale surface features, such as mountains and island chains, are being formed (see also pp.56–57), and where destructive events such as earthquakes and volcanic eruptions most often occur (see also pp.54–55).

Transform plate boundary
Plates do not always diverge or converge when they meet. Some move alongside each other, creating a transform boundary. One such is the San Andreas Fault, the boundary of the Pacific and North American plates in California.

Continental drift

Over millions of years, the gradual motion of tectonic plates has altered the shape and position of Earth's continents. This process was first suggested in the 16th century when the first world atlases revealed that the continents could fit together as if parts of an immense jigsaw puzzle, and must have moved apart. The theory was known as continental drift.

Colliding continents
India is known as a subcontinent, and it was a separate landmass before colliding with Asia. The two landmasses are still pushing together, creating the Himalayas.

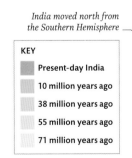

A single supercontinent called Pangaea

Pangaea splits into two

Atlantic separates off the Americas

PANGAEA
270 MILLION YEARS AGO

LAURASIA
GONDWANA
180 MILLION YEARS AGO

NORTH AMERICA
AFRICA
SOUTH AMERICA
66 MILLION YEARS AGO

India moved north from the Southern Hemisphere

EURASIAN PLATE

EQUATOR

INDIA

INDIAN OCEAN

KEY
Present-day India
10 million years ago
38 million years ago
55 million years ago
71 million years ago

ALFRED WEGENER
The movement of continents was proved by this German explorer in 1912. He showed that several rock formations in America and Europe had, in fact, formed in the same place, only to be divided up as continents split apart.

see also Mountain formation pp.56–57 ▶   Rocks pp.62–63 ▶   Oceans pp.64–65 ▶   Thermodynamics pp.184–85 ▶   The history of the Earth pp.298–301 ▶

Evolving planet

Compared to other known rocky planets, Earth has a changeable surface. Since its birth 4½ billion years ago (BYA), its crust has constantly been re-formed by plate tectonics, and its surface and atmosphere transformed by the evolution of life. The changeability is due in part to liquid water. Water is the medium for the chemistry of life, and its presence makes Earth's magma especially fluid, churning with currents that drive tectonic changes at the surface. Traces of Earth's formative times are constantly being discovered in its rocks, revising scientists' estimates of when the earliest events happened.

4.56 BYA The oldest material in the solar system—from which Earth and the other planets will form—is distributed around the young sun in a protoplanetary disk. These materials include rocks, dust, and gas.

4.54 BYA Earth forms from the gradual accretion of particles of dust, metal, and ices, which then coalesce to create a single body with gravity strong enough to pull in other nearby objects.

Planet grows with each collision

FORMATION OF EARTH

Small bodies are planetesimals

Bands of red iron oxide formed as oxygen combined with iron in rocks

BANDED IRONSTONE

2.4–2.1 BYA The Great Oxygenation Event occurs, as oxygen—rarely found in the air before the evolution of photosynthesis—builds up in the air.

Photosynthetic bacteria form filamentous colonies

OSCILLATORIA CYANOBACTERIA

3.5–3.2 BYA Cyanobacteria (blue-green algae) evolve photosynthesis, using light energy to combine carbon dioxide with water to make sugar, giving off oxygen as waste.

3.5 BYA Earth's magnetic field has now formed (new evidence suggests it is 500–700 million years older yet). The field is thought to be created by the spin of Earth's solid inner core within the liquid metal outer core.

Liquid outer core

Geographic north pole

Magnetic north pole

Solid inner core

EARTH'S MAGNETIC FIELD

Magnetic field lines

Magnetic south pole

Geographic south pole

1,300–750 MYA Beginning 1,300 million years ago (MYA), all of Earth's land merges into a supercontinent called Rodinia. Fragments of Rodinia survive in all of today's modern continents.

Sections of today's continents

Ancient landmass

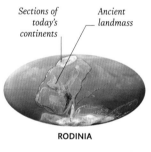

RODINIA

720–635 MYA Earth enters an extreme glacial phase, where almost the entire surface is covered in ice. The cooling is probably caused by photosynthesis removing carbon dioxide from the air.

Thawing created Iapetus Ocean

SNOWBALL EARTH

Ocean ridge forms as plates move away from each other

Tectonic plates are dragged apart, creating new ocean floor

Heat from Earth's molten core causes rocks to rise

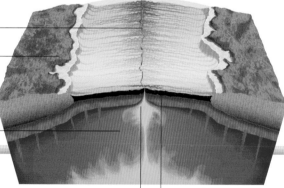

Rising magma fills gap in crust

Oil, made from dead plankton forms under seabed

215–175 MYA The Tethys Ocean appears in a rift that splits Pangaea in two—Laurentia in the north and Gondwana in the south. Today's remnants of the Tethys include the Mediterranean Sea and the Middle East's oil deposits.

FORMATION OF TETHYS OCEAN

252–250 MYA In one of the greatest volcanic events in Earth's history, fissure eruptions create flood basalts known as the Siberian Traps. The volcanic activity could be one cause of the "Great Dying"—Earth's worst-ever mass extinction.

HIMALAYAS

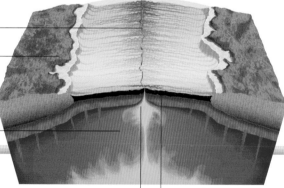

CRYOLOPHOSAURUS

201–66 MYA Earth is warmer than today with no polar ice sheets. Antarctica is drifting south, but still has forests and dinosaurs such as *Cryolophosaurus*.

66 MYA Vast volcanic eruptions that create thick lava fields in India, and the impact of a giant asteroid in Mexico, together result in rapid climate changes that lead to the extinction of the giant dinosaurs.

65 MYA The African and Indian plates collide with Eurasia, leading to a period of mountain building—from the Atlas and Alps in the west to the Himalayas in the east.

55.5 MYA Earth enters its warmest conditions on record during the Paleocene-Eocene Thermal Maximum due to carbon dioxide released from volcanoes.

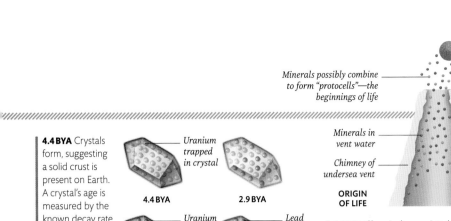

Minerals possibly combine to form "protocells"—the beginnings of life

Protocell released into surrounding seawater

4.4 BYA Crystals form, suggesting a solid crust is present on Earth. A crystal's age is measured by the known decay rate of its radioactive impurities.

Uranium trapped in crystal

4.4 BYA

2.9 BYA

Uranium decays into lead

Lead content reveals age

RADIOMETRIC DATING

1.48 BYA

PRESENT DAY

Minerals in vent water

Chimney of undersea vent

ORIGIN OF LIFE

4.1 BYA Chemicals associated with life, such as fats, proteins, and nucleic acids (RNA and DNA), form, possibly during intense chemical activity in undersea sediments or hydrothermal vents.

GEOLOGICAL TIMESCALE

Geologists divide Earth's history into time periods. The transition from one to the next is defined by a global event that can be verified by fossil evidence. Eons start with significant changes, while epochs are divided by smaller events. For example, the Phanerozoic eon starts with the evolution of multicellular organisms, while the Holocene epoch starts after the end of the last ice age.

	EON	ERA	PERIOD	EPOCH
11,700 years ago	Phanerozoic	Cenozoic	Quaternary	Holocene
2.58 MYA				Pleistocene
5.3			Neogene	Pliocene
23				Miocene
34			Paleogene	Oligocene
56				Eocene
66				Paleocene
145		Mesozoic	Cretaceous	
201			Jurassic	
252			Triassic	
299		Palaeozoic	Permian	
359			Carboniferous	
419			Devonian	
444			Silurian	
485			Ordovician	
541			Cambrian	
2500	Proterozoic			
4000	Archean			
4600	Hadean			

Islands of light rock collide

Continent made of different rocks

Thickened crust

Compressed rock

Oceanic crust

4.1–3.9 BYA In the Late Heavy Bombardment, many asteroids impact Earth and are thought to evaporate most of the oceans and remelt sections of the crust.

Oceanic crust destroyed

BIRTH OF CONTINENTS

4.0–3.6 BYA The first continents begin to form as volcanic islands—formed as lighter crystal material reaches the surface through volcanoes—are pushed together by the first tectonic movements.

First plants are simple and small

ORDOVICIAN

Later plants have stalks

SILURIAN

470–425 MYA Algae and marine animals evolve to live on land by the early Ordovician period. In the Silurian period, land arthropods and taller plants diversify.

Towering trees grew to more than 100 ft (30 m) high

Thick vegetation includes ferns

CARBONIFEROUS PERIOD

Pangaea extends across equator, from one pole to the other

PANGAEA

Outlines of today's continents

280 MYA The foundations of today's continents are merged into the supercontinent Pangaea. The interior is a vast desert because few rainclouds reach this far inland.

359–299 MYA After trees evolved more than 385 MYA, forests spread during the warm, wet Carboniferous period. Their remains form many of today's coal deposits.

Strata (layers) of sedimentary rock provide the geological record

GEOLOGICAL RECORD

45–34 MYA Earth enters a cold phase with a series of ice ages. A permanent ice sheet forms on Antarctica, which had drifted to the South Pole about 100 million years ago.

Ice sheet covers 98 percent of continent

ANTARCTIC ICE SHEET

2.6 MYA The Quaternary ice age begins with ice sheets expanding from both poles. Woolly mammoths live in the nearby grasslands.

Thick coats withstand the harsh cold

WOOLLY MAMMOTH

EARTH'S ANATOMY

see also Prehistoric plants pp.88-89 ▶ The age of dinosaurs pp.90-91 ▶ Prehistoric mammals pp.92-93 ▶ The history of the Earth pp.298-301 ▶

Continents

About one-third of Earth's surface is covered in the extensive areas of dry land called continents. If the planet's rocky crust were smooth and of uniform thickness, Earth would be covered in a single vast, featureless ocean. The continents are regions where the planet's crust is much thicker and more buoyant than in the ocean basins, so most continental crust rises above sea level.

CRATONS

Earth's continents are built around stable regions called shields. The shields correspond to ancient cores called cratons—thick and deeply rooted sections of crust assembled from the remains of primordial mountain ranges. Most are of Archean age, so they have survived 2 billion years of tectonic changes.

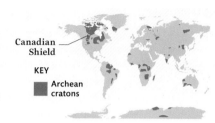

Canadian Shield

KEY

Archean cratons

Types of crust

Continental crust is slightly less dense than the crust forming the ocean floor. When it collides with oceanic crust, it always remains on top and is pushed up into fold mountains. It can therefore become seven times thicker than oceanic crust.

Earth's lithosphere

The crust floats on fluid rocks deep in the mantle. The upper mantle has a different chemical makeup to the crust, but behaves as a solid, and together with the crust, it forms the lithosphere.

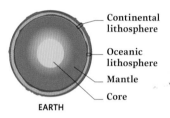

Continental lithosphere

Oceanic lithosphere

Mantle

Core

EARTH

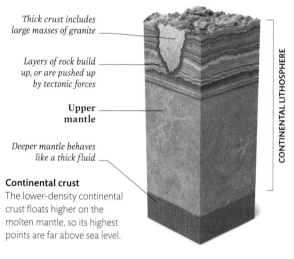

Thick crust includes large masses of granite

Layers of rock build up, or are pushed up by tectonic forces

Upper mantle

Deeper mantle behaves like a thick fluid

CONTINENTAL LITHOSPHERE

Continental crust

The lower-density continental crust floats higher on the molten mantle, so its highest points are far above sea level.

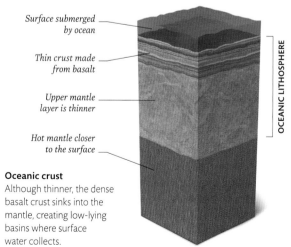

Surface submerged by ocean

Thin crust made from basalt

Upper mantle layer is thinner

Hot mantle closer to the surface

OCEANIC LITHOSPHERE

Oceanic crust

Although thinner, the dense basalt crust sinks into the mantle, creating low-lying basins where surface water collects.

Brooks Range

Rocky Mountains

Great Plains

NORTH AMERICA

Atlas Mountains

①

Canadian Shield is the core of the North American continent and a region without dramatic relief extending from the Arctic to the Great Lakes

Amazon Basin

Planalto da Borborema

SOUTH AMERICA

②

Andes are being created by a fast-moving tectonic plate pressing from the west, creating a chain of fold mountains and fresh volcanoes and earthquakes to this day

Andes

Brazilian Highlands

Earth's seven continents

Earth has four distinct landmasses: the Americas, Afro-Eurasia, Australia, and Antarctica. These are divided into seven continents, for historical and cultural, as well as geographical, reasons. The numbered lines on this map correspond to the cross-section diagrams opposite.

Tierra del Fuego

Marie Byrd Land

Africa is the continent with the **lowest** ratio of coastline to area; **Europe** has the **highest** ratio

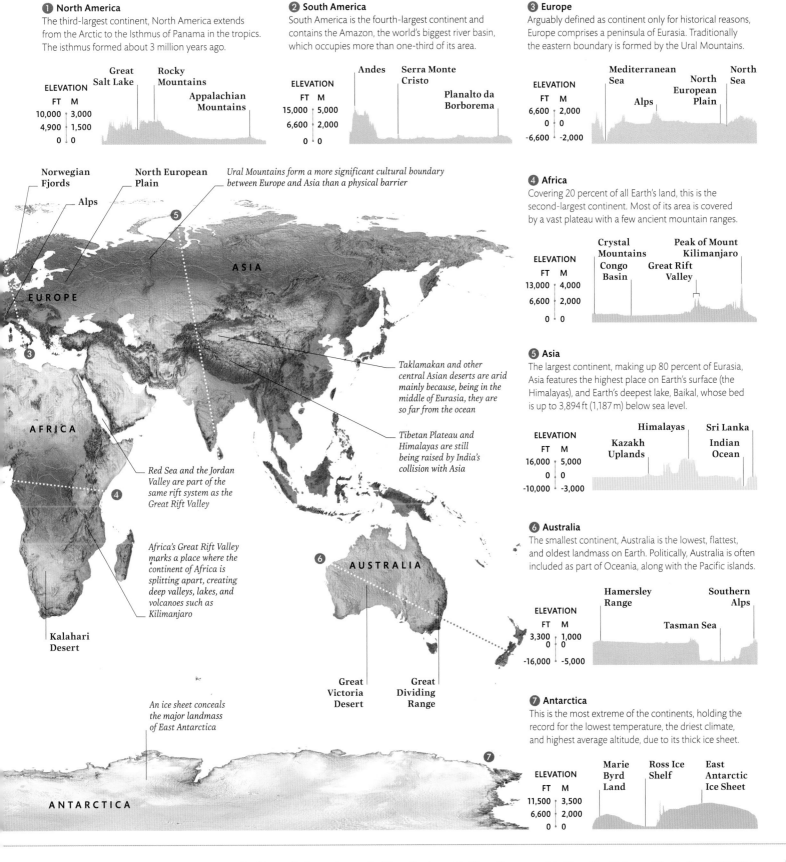

❶ North America
The third-largest continent, North America extends from the Arctic to the Isthmus of Panama in the tropics. The isthmus formed about 3 million years ago.

ELEVATION
FT   M
10,000   3,000
4,900   1,500
0   0

Great Salt Lake | Rocky Mountains | Appalachian Mountains

❷ South America
South America is the fourth-largest continent and contains the Amazon, the world's biggest river basin, which occupies more than one-third of its area.

ELEVATION
FT   M
15,000   5,000
6,600   2,000
0   0

Andes | Serra Monte Cristo | Planalto da Borborema

❸ Europe
Arguably defined as continent only for historical reasons, Europe comprises a peninsula of Eurasia. Traditionally the eastern boundary is formed by the Ural Mountains.

ELEVATION
FT   M
6,600   2,000
0   0
-6,600   -2,000

Mediterranean Sea | North European Plain | North Sea | Alps

❹ Africa
Covering 20 percent of all Earth's land, this is the second-largest continent. Most of its area is covered by a vast plateau with a few ancient mountain ranges.

ELEVATION
FT   M
13,000   4,000
6,600   2,000
0   0

Crystal Mountains | Peak of Mount Kilimanjaro | Congo Basin | Great Rift Valley

❺ Asia
The largest continent, making up 80 percent of Eurasia, Asia features the highest place on Earth's surface (the Himalayas), and Earth's deepest lake, Baikal, whose bed is up to 3,894 ft (1,187 m) below sea level.

ELEVATION
FT   M
16,000   5,000
0   0
-10,000   -3,000

Himalayas | Sri Lanka | Kazakh Uplands | Indian Ocean

❻ Australia
The smallest continent, Australia is the lowest, flattest, and oldest landmass on Earth. Politically, Australia is often included as part of Oceania, along with the Pacific islands.

ELEVATION
FT   M
3,300   1,000
0   0
-16,000   -5,000

Hamersley Range | Southern Alps | Tasman Sea

❼ Antarctica
This is the most extreme of the continents, holding the record for the lowest temperature, the driest climate, and highest average altitude, due to its thick ice sheet.

ELEVATION
FT   M
11,500   3,500
6,600   2,000
0   0

Marie Byrd Land | Ross Ice Shelf | East Antarctic Ice Sheet

Ural Mountains form a more significant cultural boundary between Europe and Asia than a physical barrier

Norwegian Fjords | North European Plain | Alps | ASIA | EUROPE | AFRICA

Taklamakan and other central Asian deserts are arid mainly because, being in the middle of Eurasia, they are so far from the ocean

Tibetan Plateau and Himalayas are still being raised by India's collision with Asia

Red Sea and the Jordan Valley are part of the same rift system as the Great Rift Valley

Africa's Great Rift Valley marks a place where the continent of Africa is splitting apart, creating deep valleys, lakes, and volcanoes such as Kilimanjaro

Kalahari Desert | AUSTRALIA | Great Victoria Desert | Great Dividing Range

An ice sheet conceals the major landmass of East Antarctica

ANTARCTICA

Volcanoes and earthquakes

Volcanoes and earthquakes are the most violent geological events on Earth, releasing large amounts of energy from within our planet. Volcanoes are eruptions of molten rock that release heat from deep inside the Earth, while earthquakes are seismic waves generated as slowly shifting tectonic plates grind past each other, catch, and then abruptly break free with a sudden movement.

Volcano structure

A volcano sits above a pocket of molten rock called a magma chamber. Magma finds its way to the surface through fissures, erupting at the surface as lava, which cools to form layers of rock. The nature of the magma can produce a variety of eruption types, also called styles.

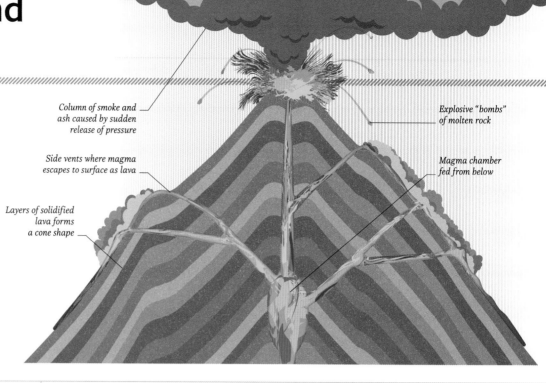

Column of smoke and ash caused by sudden release of pressure

Side vents where magma escapes to surface as lava

Layers of solidified lava forms a cone shape

Explosive "bombs" of molten rock

Magma chamber fed from below

Eruption styles

The strength of an eruption and the properties of erupted material determine its style. A single volcanic event can display several different styles as it runs its course, depending on the pressure from beneath, the chemistry and viscosity of magma, and its gas content.

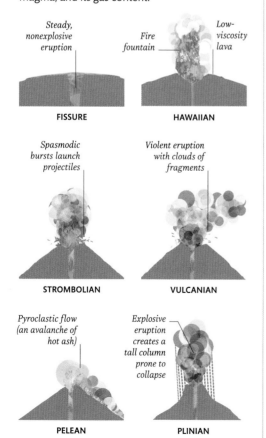

Steady, nonexplosive eruption

FISSURE

Fire fountain

Low-viscosity lava

HAWAIIAN

Spasmodic bursts launch projectiles

STROMBOLIAN

Violent eruption with clouds of fragments

VULCANIAN

Pyroclastic flow (an avalanche of hot ash)

PELEAN

Explosive eruption creates a tall column prone to collapse

PLINIAN

Earthquakes

Although tectonic plates are in constant motion, rocks at the points where they meet have a tendency to lock together, creating strain. When the tension becomes too great, they can break and move suddenly, releasing violent shock waves.

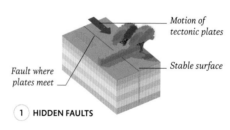

Fault where plates meet

Motion of tectonic plates

Stable surface

(1) **HIDDEN FAULTS**

Fault lines

Earthquakes mostly take place close to major fault lines—tectonic boundaries where two plates have moved in relation to each other.

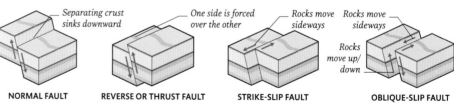

Separating crust sinks downward

NORMAL FAULT

One side is forced over the other

REVERSE OR THRUST FAULT

Rocks move sideways

STRIKE-SLIP FAULT

Rocks move sideways

Rocks move up/down

OBLIQUE-SLIP FAULT

TSUNAMI

Earthquakes on the ocean floor can push up the ocean water above, generating a radiating series of long, low surface waves. As these enter the shallow waters of the continental shelves, they get shorter and steeper, growing in height to become devastating tsunamis.

Effects of earthquake

Tension can build up along a major fault (where tectonic plates move past each other) over a long time. When the stress is released, shock waves spread out from the focus (the point where rocks finally fracture and shift) and are strongest at a point, called the epicenter, on the surface directly above it. As the shock waves spread across Earth's surface, they can shake the ground, altering the landscape.

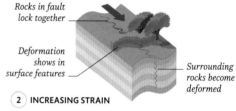

Rocks in fault lock together

Deformation shows in surface features

Surrounding rocks become deformed

(2) **INCREASING STRAIN**

Up to **900,000 earthquakes** go **unnoticed each year**

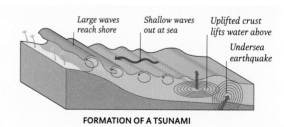

Large waves reach shore

Shallow waves out at sea

Uplifted crust lifts water above

Undersea earthquake

FORMATION OF A TSUNAMI

Mount Yasur, a volcano in Vanuatu, has been continuosly erupting since 1774

How volcanoes form

The formation of a magma chamber is powered by activity at the boundary between Earth's crust and upper mantle, and can take place in a variety of different localities when conditions are right.

Volcano types

A volcano's shape and structure depends on the rate and nature of the its eruptions. Four of the most common shapes are shown here.

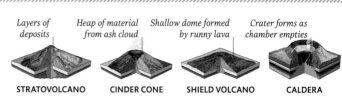

Layers of deposits | *Heap of material from ash cloud* | *Shallow dome formed by runny lava* | *Crater forms as chamber empties*

STRATOVOLCANO   **CINDER CONE**   **SHIELD VOLCANO**   **CALDERA**

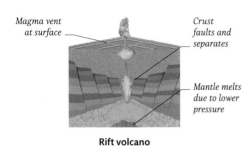

Magma vent at surface — *Crust faults and separates* — *Mantle melts due to lower pressure*

Rift volcano

Where two tectonic plates are separating, new material wells up to fill the gap, forming rift volcanoes. These are found in both continental and oceanic settings.

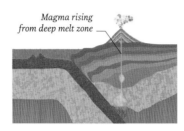

Magma rising from deep melt zone

Subduction zone

Where a submerged oceanic plate is pushed below another plate, the water carried with it can help to melt mantle rocks, creating an arc of volcanic activity.

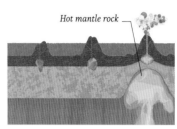

Hot mantle rock

Hotspot volcano

Stationary plumes of heat rising through the mantle can fuel volcanic eruptions. If the crust above a mantle plume is moving, this creates chains of volcanoes.

The strongest earthquake on record happened on May 22, 1960, in Chile. The tsunami it generated reached as far as Japan and Alaska

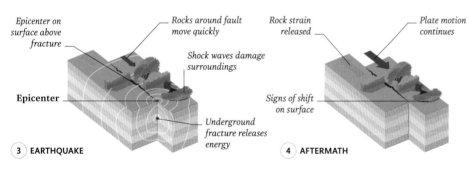

Epicenter on surface above fracture — *Rocks around fault move quickly* — *Shock waves damage surroundings*

Epicenter

Underground fracture releases energy

③ EARTHQUAKE

Rock strain released — *Plate motion continues*

Signs of shift on surface

④ AFTERMATH

Earthquake zones

Earthquakes occur on moving tectonic boundaries around the world, but the most frequent activity is concentrated on the edges of the Pacific and Nazca plates. This area is also known as the Ring of Fire.

KEY

◉ Major earthquakes

— The ring of fire

— Tectonic plate boundaries

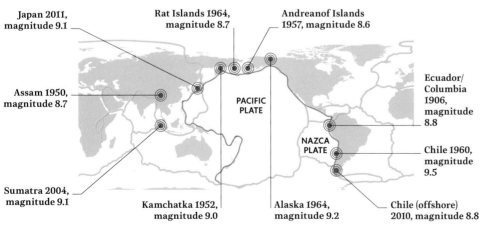

Japan 2011, magnitude 9.1

Rat Islands 1964, magnitude 8.7

Andreanof Islands 1957, magnitude 8.6

Assam 1950, magnitude 8.7

PACIFIC PLATE

Ecuador/ Columbia 1906, magnitude 8.8

NAZCA PLATE

Chile 1960, magnitude 9.5

Sumatra 2004, magnitude 9.1

Kamchatka 1952, magnitude 9.0

Alaska 1964, magnitude 9.2

Chile (offshore) 2010, magnitude 8.8

MEASURING EARTHQUAKES

Earthquake strength is described in terms of "magnitude" on a logarithmic scale. A whole-number increase in magnitude corresponds to 10 times more ground disturbance, and about 32 times more energy released. Most earthquakes are so small that they go largely unnoticed and are only recorded by sensitive instruments called seismometers.

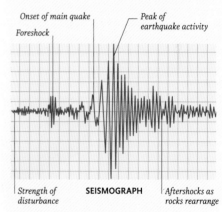

Onset of main quake — *Peak of earthquake activity*

Foreshock

Strength of disturbance   **SEISMOGRAPH**   *Aftershocks as rocks rearrange*

Magnitudes	Level	Effects
1.0–1.9	Micro	Undetectabe
2.0–3.9	Minor	Light shaking
4.0–4.9	Light	Noticeable tremors
5.0–5.9	Moderate	Felt across small area, some damage
6.0–6.9	Strong	Felt across wide area, significant damage
7.0–7.9	Major	Widespread, severe damage
8.0 or more	Great	Severe damage, permanent landscape changes

see also Mountain formation pp.56–57 ▶   Rocks pp.62–63 ▶

Mountain formation

Mountains are the most elevated areas of land on Earth, held aloft against the pull of gravity by the deep roots that build up underneath them and intrude into the denser rocks of Earth's interior. Raising up these huge, heavy rock masses involves the action of powerful forces, which are unleashed when the tectonic plates of Earth's crust collide with each other. As well as folding and transforming preexisting rocks, several types of tectonic collisions also involve volcanic activity that pours new igneous rock onto the Earth's surface, building up new peaks, one layer at a time.

Where mountains form

Earth has two distinct types of crust—thicker continental crust and thinner, but denser, oceanic crust. Collisions between units of crust produce mountains along the boundaries where they meet.

The **ancient seabed** that forms the Himalayan foothills **contains 54-million-year-old** whale fossils

Continent-continent boundary

When two blocks of lightweight continental crust collide, their relative buoyancy means that both resist subduction (being forced downward). The resulting head-on collision produces an extensive crumple zone, where rocks are folded and pushed both upward and downward. These mountains often reinforce a volcanic range, formed by the earlier subduction of oceanic crust as the two landmasses approached each other.

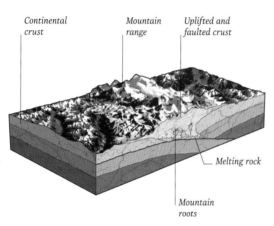

Continental crust
Mountain range
Uplifted and faulted crust
Melting rock
Mountain roots

Alps
Europe's most extensive range, the Alps, formed due to the collision of the Eurasian and the African tectonic plates.

Ocean-continent boundary

When thin oceanic crust and thick continental crust are driven against each other, the denser ocean crust is forced downward at a subduction zone, creating a trench that usually lies offshore. Water in the descending oceanic crust is released into the overlying rock, changing its chemistry and lowering its melting point. This triggers the formation of magma that fuels mountain-building volcanism.

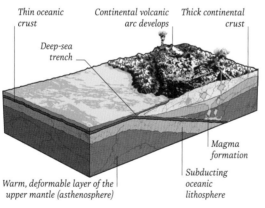

Thin oceanic crust
Continental volcanic arc develops
Thick continental crust
Deep-sea trench
Magma formation
Subducting oceanic lithosphere
Warm, deformable layer of the upper mantle (asthenosphere)

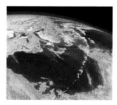

Mount St. Helens
This famous active volcano in the Cascade Range of northwestern North America is powered by the subduction of oceanic crust.

Ocean-ocean boundary

When oceanic plates collide, one plate is inevitably forced beneath the other, creating a deep-sea trench where it descends. The water released as the descending plate melts in the upper mantle causes volcanism in the overlying plate. Lava erupting into the sea along the margin rapidly cools and piles up, eventually emerging at the water's surface as an arc of mountainous volcanic islands.

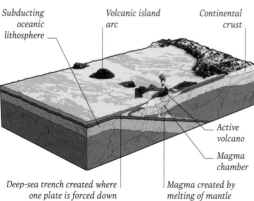

Subducting oceanic lithosphere
Volcanic island arc
Continental crust
Active volcano
Magma chamber
Deep-sea trench created where one plate is forced down
Magma created by melting of mantle

Aleutian island arc
This volcanic chain has formed where the Pacific Ocean plate is forced below a remnant of oceanic crust now welded to North America.

Mountain ranges

The world's great mountain ranges trace past and present episodes of mountain building (orogenesis) along tectonic plate boundaries, and frequently form linear chains called orogenic belts. The Alps and Himalayas, for example, are still sites of ongoing formation, while the Andes and Rockies were mostly created about 60 million years ago. Other ranges, such as the Appalachians, are far more ancient.

KEY			
①	**Alaska Range**	⑨	**Ethiopian Highlands**
②	**Rocky Mountains**	⑩	**Caucasus**
③	**Appalachians**	⑪	**Ural Mountains**
④	**Andes**	⑫	**Tien Shan**
⑤	**Pyrenees**	⑬	**Himalayas**
⑥	**Atlas Mountains**	⑭	**Great Dividing Range**
⑦	**Alps**	⑮	**Trans-Antarctic mountains**
⑧	**Drakensberg**		

Longest ranges

While the system of mid-ocean ridges that runs around the world form a continuous range some 40,400 miles (65,000 km) long, most geologists consider mountain ranges to be chains of peaks above sea level, linked by high ground. According to this definition, the Andes Mountains that run down the western edge of South America form the world's longest range.

Approximate length of range

Andes, South America	4,500 miles (7,200 km)
Rocky Mountains, North America	3,000 miles (4,800 km)
Great Dividing Range, Australia	2,200 miles (3,500 km)
Trans-Antarctic Mountains, Antarctica	2,000 miles (3,200 km)
Himalayas, Asia	1,550 miles (2,500 km)

Driven upward by the collision between Asia and India, the Himalayas are still rising at a rate of $^3/_8$ in (1 cm) per year

How mountains form

Mountains are the result of tectonic events that deform the Earth's crust, usually near tectonic boundaries. During tectonic events, blocks of crust can be disrupted in various ways that leave an impression in the geology of the mountains they create. The nature of this disruption depends on the nature of the tectonic boundary, and the properties of the rocks involved on either side.

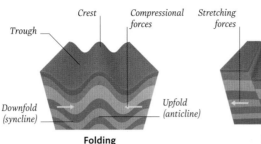

Folding
Pressure and heat can make layers of rocks pliable enough to bend and fold without fracturing, creating ripples on varying scales.

Trough · *Crest* · *Compressional forces* · *Downfold (syncline)* · *Upfold (anticline)*

Rifting
Where continental plates separate or split apart, crust can sink downward along fault lines to form a valley with mountainous edges.

Stretching forces · *Crust collapses* · *Fault lines*

Thrusting
In areas of great compression, fracturing along fault lines (called thrust faults) allows blocks of crust to be pushed upward in stacks.

Movement causes stacking · *Fault lines* · *Compression forces*

Measuring growth

As mountains rise to higher altitudes, they experience different climates. By studying fossil finds, geologists are able to estimate the elevation of a mountain range at the time that the fossil plants grew.

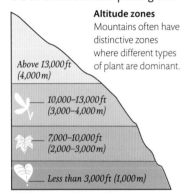

Altitude zones
Mountains often have distinctive zones where different types of plant are dominant.

- *Above 13,000 ft (4,000 m)*
- *10,000–13,000 ft (3,000–4,000 m)*
- *7,000–10,000 ft (2,000–3,000 m)*
- *Less than 3,000 ft (1,000 m)*

World's highest peaks

Earth's hundred tallest mountains are all concentrated in the Himalayas and other nearby ranges. These were formed by the collision of the Indian subcontinent with Asia, caused by the Indian plate moving northward and sliding beneath the Eurasian plate. The highest peak outside of Asia is Argentina's Mount Aconcagua at 22,837 ft (6,961 m).

Approximate height of mountain

Mount Everest, Himalayas	29,035 ft (8,848 m)
K2, Karakoram	28,250 ft (8,611 m)
Kangchenjunga, Himalayas	28,169 ft (8,586 m)
Lhotse, Himalayas	27,940 ft (8,516 m)
Makalu, Himalayas	27,766 ft (8,485 m)

Underwater mountains

In addition to island arcs, a number of other processes build undersea mountains. Where oceanic plates separate from each other, volcanic eruptions pour lava onto the seabed, building chains of mountains on either side of a central rift. "Hot spots" in the mantle can also produce localized volcanoes in the overlying crust.

HIDDEN HEIGHTS

The 29,028 ft (8,848 m) tall Mount Everest is Earth's highest mountain above sea level. However, if measured in terms of the total rise from the base to the peak, Everest is easily beaten by the 33,488 ft (10,207 m) rise of Mauna Kea in Hawaii, a towering extinct volcano formed above a hotspot in Earth's mantle.

Mount Everest 29,028 ft (8,848 m) above sea level · *Mauna Kea 33,488 ft (10,207 m) tall* · *13,803 ft (4,207 m) above sea level* · *19,685 ft (6,000 m) below sea level*

Silfra fissure
As the Mid-Atlantic Ridge crosses Iceland, it forms this 200 ft (60 m) deep tectonic rift.

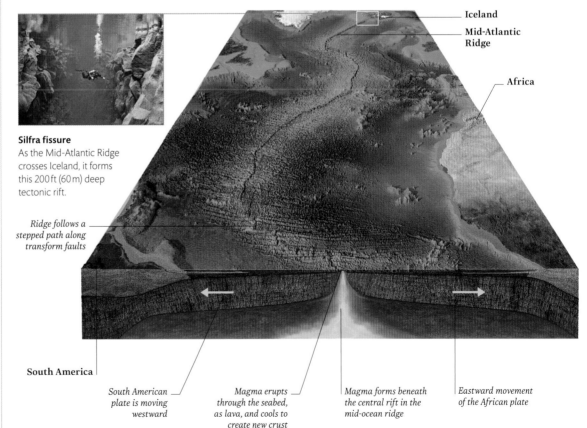

Iceland · *Mid-Atlantic Ridge* · *Africa*

Ridge follows a stepped path along transform faults

South America

South American plate is moving westward · *Magma erupts through the seabed, as lava, and cools to create new crust* · *Magma forms beneath the central rift in the mid-ocean ridge* · *Eastward movement of the African plate*

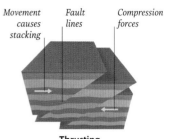

see also Rocks pp.62–63 ▶ **57**

Erosion, weathering, and deposition

Volcanism and plate tectonics are responsible for the formation and uplift of new rocks, but Earth's surface is shaped to an equal extent by processes that wear down, transform, and transport rocks. Erosion encompasses a variety of processes that break down rock and carry it away. Weathering involves the breaking-down of rocks without any immediate transportation.

The **"splash erosion"** from a **single raindrop** can **scatter soil particles** up to 2 ft (0.6 m)

River erosion

The flow of water is one of the most powerful agents of erosion and deposition. Many forms of erosion on land can ultimately be traced back to the action of past and present rivers.

Flow of a river

As a river naturally flows downhill from source to sea, the changing speed of its flow and the shifting balance of erosion and deposition change its shape. Where it flows quickly, the river wears away the terrain, but as the river slows it builds it up.

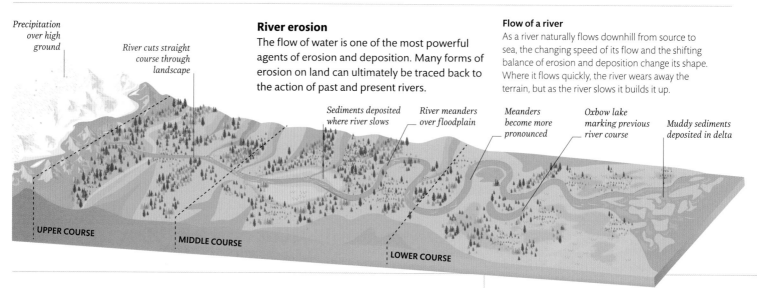

Precipitation over high ground

River cuts straight course through landscape

Sediments deposited where river slows

River meanders over floodplain

Meanders become more pronounced

Oxbow lake marking previous river course

Muddy sediments deposited in delta

UPPER COURSE

MIDDLE COURSE

LOWER COURSE

Wind erosion

The wind can become a powerful force of erosion in situations where loosely bound particles of sediment can be supported for a long time in the air. For example, in very dry climates such as deserts, where there is little moisture or vegetation to hold the soil, wind-blown particles can shape rock into a variety of forms. Through the transportation and deposition of sand, wind also creates dunes.

Particles are repeatedly picked up and dropped

Lower part of rock is eroded

Upper part of rock is unaffected

KEY

→ **Prevailing winds**

Mushroom rocks

When the particles that cause wind erosion are constrained to a certain height, the preferential erosion at low levels can create mushroom-shaped rocks, known as ventifacts.

Coastal erosion

The waves that wash against coastlines can be a powerful erosive force, wearing away rocks and carrying sediments in different ways depending on their strength and the nature of the rocks.

Rocky shores

Waves breaking on a rocky cliff face erode the base more rapidly than the elevated face, ultimately causing the cliff to collapse.

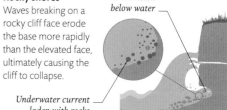

Wave-cut notch below water

Underwater current laden with rocks

Desert pavements

Flat terrain in desert areas often consists of solid areas called pavements. These pavements are made up of layers of interlocking mid-sized pebbles and larger rocks and are formed by wind erosion of finer particles (sand).

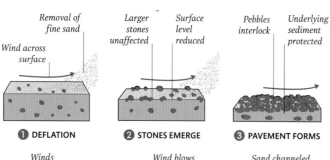

Removal of fine sand

Wind across surface

① DEFLATION

Larger stones unaffected

Surface level reduced

② STONES EMERGE

Pebbles interlock

Underlying sediment protected

③ PAVEMENT FORMS

Sand dunes

Dunes are large deposits of sand created by the saltation (repeated picking up and dropping) of fine sand particles. Their form depends on the prevailing winds. Sand dunes may migrate or become stabilized by vegetation.

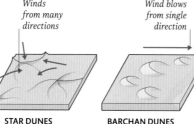

Winds from many directions

STAR DUNES

Wind blows from single direction

BARCHAN DUNES

Sand channeled by wind from two directions

LINEAR DUNES

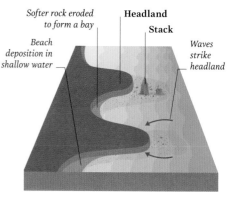

Softer rock eroded to form a bay

Headland

Stack

Waves strike headland

Beach deposition in shallow water

Coast with hard and soft rocks

Harder rocks resist erosion more than soft rocks, forming headlands and isolated stacks separated by bays. The bays may be sheltered from wave energy as waves strike the headlands first.

◀ see also Tectonic plates pp.48–49   ◀ Volcanoes and earthquakes pp.54–55   ◀ Mountain formation pp.56–57

EARTH

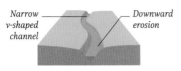

UPPER COURSE

Narrow v-shaped channel

Downward erosion

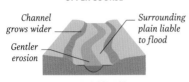

MIDDLE COURSE

Channel grows wider

Gentler erosion

Surrounding plain liable to flood

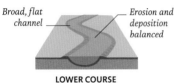

LOWER COURSE

Broad, flat channel

Erosion and deposition balanced

Courses of a river
The profile of a river's course alters as it travels from the elevated uplands around its source, to its eventual outflow at the sea. A typical river has three courses.

CAVE SYSTEMS
In regions of limestone rock, slightly acidic rainwater can dissolve the rock, drain through it, and find a more direct route downhill. As water passes underground, it can hollow out large cave systems which may collapse to form a gorge.

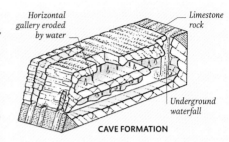

Horizontal gallery eroded by water

Limestone rock

Underground waterfall

CAVE FORMATION

Erosion
Much of water's erosive power comes from its ability to transport sediment grains of varying sizes. Abrasion from these particles wears down the surrounding terrain and particles are carried away.

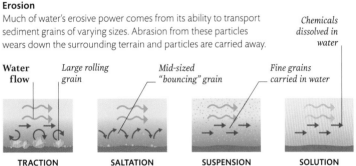

Water flow

Large rolling grain

Mid-sized "bouncing" grain

Fine grains carried in water

Chemicals dissolved in water

TRACTION   **SALTATION**   **SUSPENSION**   **SOLUTION**

Weathering
Weathering processes involve the breaking down of rocks without transportation, usually through physical stress or biological action. Chemical weathering can occur through the interaction of rainwater with atmospheric carbon dioxide to form weak acid.

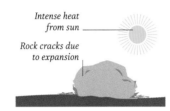

Intense heat from sun

Rock cracks due to expansion

Physical weathering
Repeated cycles of heating and cooling, changes to surrounding pressure, and other physical factors can physically weather rocks.

Glacial erosion
Glaciers are slow-moving masses of ice that act as powerful agents of erosion. Rocks plucked from the ground beneath them become abrasive particles that scour the surrounding landscape, while repeated freezing and thawing at the glacier's edge cause physical weathering of nearby rock.

Icy river
Glaciers are built up from many layers of persistent ice that begin to flow downhill under their own weight, creating a slow but almost unstoppable force.

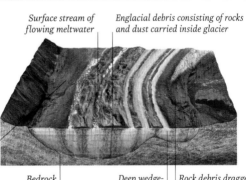

Surface stream of flowing meltwater

Englacial debris consisting of rocks and dust carried inside glacier

Moraines (rock transported on surface)

Bedrock worn smooth

Deep wedge-shaped clefts in the ice surface

Rock debris dragged along and deposited at glacier's sides

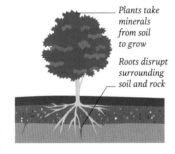

Plants take minerals from soil to grow

Roots disrupt surrounding soil and rock

Biological weathering
Plants and lichens can chemically alter rocks, producing internal stresses that cause them to fragment. Plant roots can also break apart rock.

Deposition
Deposition is the laying-down of transported sediments in a new location at the end of their journey. Sediments settle in different locations depending on their size, shape, and mass, and the speed of the wind or water carrying them, which itself can be influenced by local geography. The accumulation of sediment can, in turn, alter the local geography.

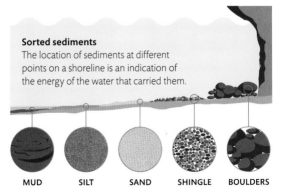

Sorted sediments
The location of sediments at different points on a shoreline is an indication of the energy of the water that carried them.

MUD   **SILT**   **SAND**   **SHINGLE**   **BOULDERS**

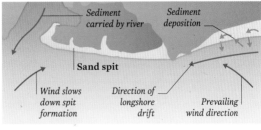

Sediment carried by river

Sediment deposition

Sand spit

Wind slows down spit formation

Direction of longshore drift

Prevailing wind direction

Sediment accumulation
Longshore drift moves sediments along a coast as they are washed in and back out at different angles. Sediments also accumulate in slow-moving or stationary waters.

FORMATION OF OXBOW LAKE
A meandering river erodes the outside bank of its bends but deposits material on the inside bank. Over time this narrows the neck of the meander and the river cuts through.

Deposition on inside banks

① RIVER WITH MEANDER

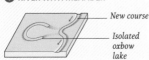

New course

Isolated oxbow lake

② OXBOW LAKE

see also Rocks pp.62–63 ▶   Fresh water and ice pp.68–69 ▶

Minerals

A mineral is a naturally occurring solid, crystalline substance with a repeating molecular structure. Every mineral has a defined chemical composition, from pure elements—such as gold or sulfur—to complex mixtures of metallic and chemical elements. Mineral species are grouped into classes according to the dominant "anion" in their structure.

CRYSTAL SHAPE AND STRUCTURE

The repetitive geometric structure of mineral compounds creates a range of crystal shapes. These can be divided into six systems according to their symmetry.

CUBIC ORTHORHOMBIC HEXAGONAL TETRAGONAL MONOCLINIC TRICLINIC

Mass of quartz rock

Gold deposited from hydrothermal water

Native elements

Elements that exist as pure solids in Earth's crust are known as native elements. Mineralogists also include naturally occurring alloys (metal blends) in this class.

Grapelike (botryoidal) structure

ARSENIC As

Orthorhombic crystals

SULFUR S

Metallic luster

COPPER Cu

Bright, metallic appearance

Rounded surface

GOLD Au

Sulfides

Commonly found in nature, sulfides are often brightly colored and lustrous. They form when metals or semimetals bond with sulfur anions.

Bright red mercury compound

CINNABAR HgS

Elongated, radiating crystals include antimony

STIBNITE Sb$_2$S$_3$

Iridescent copper iron sulfide, also known as "peacock ore"

BORNITE Cu$_5$FeS$_4$

Cubic crystals contain lead

GALENA PbS

Crystals display cubic symmetry

PYRITE FeS$_2$

Halides

Generally soft minerals known as halides form when a metal bonds with a halogen anion such as chlorine, fluorine, bromine, or iodine.

Color caused by elemental impurities

FLUORITE CaF$_2$

Rock salt—a sodium chloride compound

HALITE NaCl

Translucent, glassy appearance

SYLVITE KCl

Deposits of sodium aluminum fluoride

CRYOLITE Na$_3$AlF$_6$

Orthorhombic crystals

CARNALLITE KMgCl$_3$·6H$_2$O

Oxides

Hard minerals known as oxides are created when a metal or semimetal is combined with oxygen, or an oxygen-dominated anionic complex.

Commonly forms in matrix of igneous or metamorphic rock

Semitransparent needlelike crystals

RUTILE TiO$_2$

Steel gray finish

HEMATITE Fe$_2$O$_3$

Dark color caused by iron impurities

CASSITERITE SnO$_2$

Blue coloring indicates iron and titanium

SAPPHIRE (CORUNDUM) Al$_2$O$_3$

Red hue caused by chromium

RUBY (CORUNDUM) Al$_2$O$_3$

Black, metallic finish

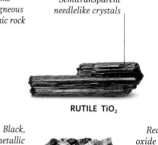

CHROMITE FeCr$_2$O$_4$

Red copper oxide crystals

CUPRITE Cu$_2$O

Red oxide of zinc

ZINCITE ZnO

About **5,500 minerals** are currently known—each with a **unique chemical composition** or structure

Carbonates

Often vividly colored, soft carbonate minerals are formed when a metal bonds to a carbonate substance made up of one carbon and three oxygen atoms (CO_3).

Deep blue copper carbonate crystals

AZURITE
$Cu_3(CO_3)_2(OH)_2$

Large, distinctive crystal formations

CALCITE
$CaCO_3$

Color always a shade of green

MALACHITE
$Cu_2CO_3(OH)_2$

Opaque crystals form marble and dolomite rock

DOLOMITE
$CaMg(CO_3)_2$

Color varies from pink to red

RHODOCHROSITE
$MnCO_3$

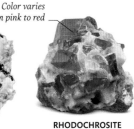

Sulfates

Soft, lightweight sulfate minerals are created when metallic elements bond with sulfate—a combination of sulfur and oxygen atoms (SO_4).

Colorless crystals

ANHYDRITE $CaSO_4$

Prismatic crystals

GYPSUM $CaSO_4 \cdot 2H_2O$

Blue crystals contain strontium

CELESTINE $SrSO_4$

Dense, heavy crystals

BARITE $BaSO_4$

Green to black coloration

BROCHANTITE $Cu_4SO_4(OH)_6$

Phosphates

This large group—defined by the presence of phosphorus and oxygen in a 1:4 ratio (PO_4)—includes many relatively rare mineral compounds.

Blue, glasslike shards

VIVIANITE
$Fe_3(PO_4)_2 \cdot 8H_2O$

Turquoise deposits embedded in iron oxide

TURQUOISE
$CuAl_6(PO_4)_4(OH)_8 \cdot 4H_2O$

Calcium phosphate crystals

APATITE
$Ca_5(PO_4)_3(F,OH,Cl)$

Yellow color fluoresces under ultraviolet light

AUTUNITE
$Ca(UO_2)_2(PO_4)_2 \cdot 10-12H_2O$

Radiating, needlelike crystals

WAVELLITE
$Al_3(PO_4)_2(OH,F)_3 \cdot 5H_2O$

Arsenates

Structurally similar to phosphates, these rare minerals contain an arsenate anion group—AsO_4—based on the toxic metalloid element arsenic.

Botryoidal structure

MIMETITE
$Pb_5(AsO_4)_3Cl$

Vitreous luster

SCORODITE
$FeAsO_4 \cdot 2H_2O$

Dark greenish-blue crystals

CLINOCLASE
$Cu_3(AsO_4)(OH)_3$

Platy green crystals

CHALCOPHYLLITE
$Cu_{18}Al_2(AsO_4)_3(SO_4)_3(OH)_{27} \cdot 33H_2O$

Bright pink "cobalt bloom"

ERYTHRITE
$CO_3(AsO_4)_2 \cdot 8H_2O$

Silicates

Forming some 90 percent of Earth's crust, silicates contain metals mixed with silicon and oxygen, and are the largest and most abundant mineral group.

Elongated crystals

EPIDOTE
$Ca_2Al_2(Fe,Al)(SiO_4)(Si_2O_7)O(OH)$

Pale blue color caused by iron impurities

BERYL
$Be_3Al_2Si_6O_{18}$

Transparent finish

OLIVINE
$(Mg,Fe)_2SiO_4$

Prismatic crystal

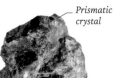

DIOPSIDE $CaMg(Si_2O_6)$

Soapy surface texture

TALC $Mg_3Si_4O_{10}(OH)_2$

Glassy luster

LAZURITE $Na_3Ca(Al_3Si_3O_{12})S$

Purple color caused by radiation and impurities

Vitreous crystals

AMETHYST SiO_2

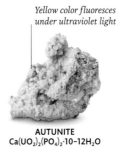

see also Rocks pp.62–63 ▶

Rocks

How rocks form

Rocks are large-scale accumulations of different mineral grains. They form in various ways, as a variety of different chemical and physical processes act on the raw materials erupted onto Earth's surface from pockets of hot magma. The transformation of rocks by forces such as new eruptions, heat, pressure, erosion, and chemical weathering (the reaction of minerals with materials in their surroundings) is an ongoing and endless process.

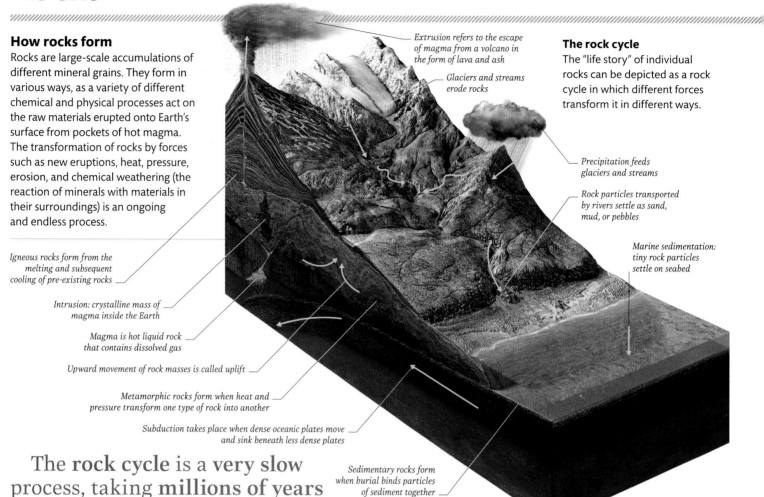

Extrusion refers to the escape of magma from a volcano in the form of lava and ash

Glaciers and streams erode rocks

Igneous rocks form from the melting and subsequent cooling of pre-existing rocks

Intrusion: crystalline mass of magma inside the Earth

Magma is hot liquid rock that contains dissolved gas

Upward movement of rock masses is called uplift

Metamorphic rocks form when heat and pressure transform one type of rock into another

Subduction takes place when dense oceanic plates move and sink beneath less dense plates

Sedimentary rocks form when burial binds particles of sediment together

The rock cycle

The "life story" of individual rocks can be depicted as a rock cycle in which different forces transform it in different ways.

Precipitation feeds glaciers and streams

Rock particles transported by rivers settle as sand, mud, or pebbles

Marine sedimentation: tiny rock particles settle on seabed

The **rock cycle** is a **very slow** process, taking **millions of years**

Igneous rocks

Rocks that have solidified from of magma (a mix of molten rock, minerals, and dissolved gas) are called igneous. Different types of igneous rocks are distinguished by the variations in their mineral content, their chemical composition, and their physical structure.

Volcanic formation

The way in which magma cools and solidifies, either at the Earth's surface (extrusive) or beneath it (intrusive), produces rocks with different mineral properties.

Cinder and ash

Extrusive rock that cools quickly has a glassy to fine-grained matrix

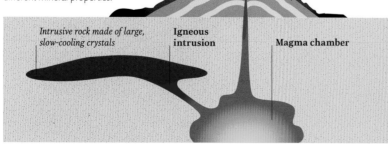

Intrusive rock made of large, slow-cooling crystals

Igneous intrusion

Magma chamber

Devil's tower

This famous rock peak in Wyoming is an igneous intrusion that cooled and solidified underground. It became exposed after surrounding ground and sediment was worn away.

Fine grains **BASALT**

Coarse texture **KIMBERLITE**

Glassy texture **OBSIDIAN**

LAPILLI (PUMICE)

Quartz crystals **RHYOLITE**

Tourmaline crystal **PEGMATITE**

DIORITE

Pink feldspar **GRANITE**

Sedimentary rocks

The actions of wind, water, and changing temperatures erode rocks and carry fragments away. They accumulate as sediment, usually in lakes and on seabeds. Over time, the weight of accumulated material compresses the sediments to create new rock types.

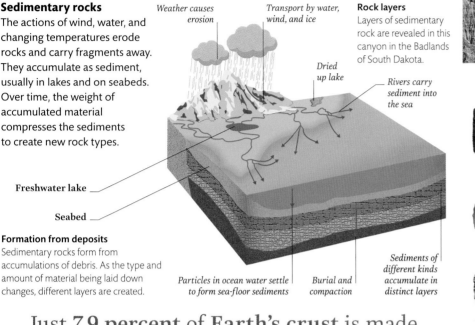

Weather causes erosion

Transport by water, wind, and ice

Dried up lake

Rivers carry sediment into the sea

Freshwater lake

Seabed

Formation from deposits

Sedimentary rocks form from accumulations of debris. As the type and amount of material being laid down changes, different layers are created.

Particles in ocean water settle to form sea-floor sediments

Burial and compaction

Sediments of different kinds accumulate in distinct layers

Rock layers

Layers of sedimentary rock are revealed in this canyon in the Badlands of South Dakota.

Dark color due to carbon

SILTSTONE

Quartz fragment

CONGLOMERATE

Fine-grained texture

SANDSTONE

Rounded grains

LIMESTONE

EVAPORITES

Compact silica

CHERT

BRECCIA

BANDED IRON FORMATION

Red layer rich in hematite

Just **7.9 percent** of **Earth's crust** is made of sedimentary rocks

Metamorphic rocks

When existing rocks experience high temperatures and pressures in the crust, their mineral components and physical structure can be transformed, resulting in metamorphic rocks. One type of metamorphism, called shock metamorphism, occurs when heat and pressure is caused an impact, such as an asteroid strike.

Rock quarry

Slate is a gray rock that splits into countless thin layers. It is formed when sedimentary shale undergoes metamorphosis under high heat and pressure.

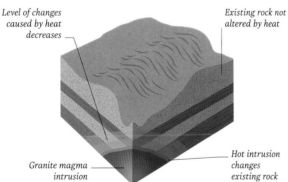

Level of changes caused by heat decreases

Existing rock not altered by heat

Granite magma intrusion

Hot intrusion changes existing rock

Contact metamorphism

On a localized scale, rocks around an underground magma chamber may undergo metamorphosis as their temperatures reach several hundred degrees. Introduction of other chemicals from surrounding rocks (often carried by water) can result in significant chemical changes.

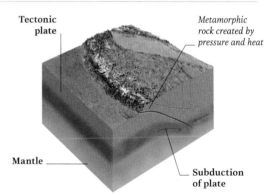

Tectonic plate

Metamorphic rock created by pressure and heat

Mantle

Subduction of plate

Regional metamorphism

Large areas of rock may undergo metamorphosis due to high temperatures combined with vertical pressure deep within Earth's crust, or they may experience horizontal forces as the crust's individual plates are shifted and deformed by plate tectonics (see pp.48–49).

Fine-grained rock

SLATE

GNEISS

Coarse grain

Red garnet

ECLOGITE

JADEITE

SERPENTINITE

Irregular shape as rock is formed by lightning strike

HORNFELS

FULGURITE

Quartzite from sandstone

Marble from limestone

MARBLE

SKARN

QUARTZITE

see also Fresh water and ice pp.68–69 ▶ **63**

Oceans

Earth is a water planet with 71 percent of the surface covered in a saltwater ocean to an average depth of 2.3 miles (3,700 m). The ocean makes up more than 97 percent of all water on Earth's surface.

Oceans of the world

The world's ocean waters are customarily divided into the Pacific, Atlantic, Indian, and Arctic oceans, and sometimes also the Southern Ocean. Nevertheless, all five are interconnected, with water constantly flowing between them.

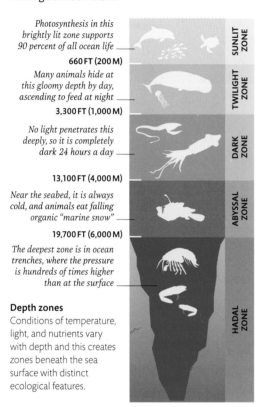

Photosynthesis in this brightly lit zone supports 90 percent of all ocean life

SUNLIT ZONE

660 FT (200 M)

Many animals hide at this gloomy depth by day, ascending to feed at night

TWILIGHT ZONE

3,300 FT (1,000 M)

No light penetrates this deeply, so it is completely dark 24 hours a day

DARK ZONE

13,100 FT (4,000 M)

Near the seabed, it is always cold, and animals eat falling organic "marine snow"

ABYSSAL ZONE

19,700 FT (6,000 M)

The deepest zone is in ocean trenches, where the pressure is hundreds of times higher than at the surface

HADAL ZONE

Depth zones

Conditions of temperature, light, and nutrients vary with depth and this creates zones beneath the sea surface with distinct ecological features.

Hydrothermal vents

There are hot springs even on the ocean floor. Sea water filling cracks in the seabed is warmed by volcanic activity, and returns to the surface as a chemical-rich stream. The dissolved chemicals form a cloudy suspension as the hot stream meets the cold ocean.

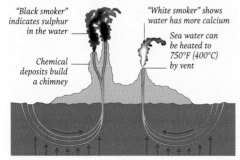

"Black smoker" indicates sulphur in the water

Chemical deposits build a chimney

"White smoker" shows water has more calcium

Sea water can be heated to 750°F (400°C) by vent

Ocean basins

The oceans fill vast basins created by variation in the thickness of Earth's rocky crust. The oceanic crust is about 5 miles (8 km) thick, with the continents being formed of crust commonly 25–30 miles (40–50 km) thick.

The Mid-Atlantic Ridge connects to similar ocean ridges in the Arctic and Indian oceans

ARCTIC OCEAN

The continental shelf between Siberia and Alaska was dry land until 11,000 years ago

The island arc of the Aleutians formed north of an oceanic trench called the Aleutian Trough

The Hawaiian chain formed above a "hotspot"—a deep source of magma that feeds seabed volcanoes, which emerge as islands

Island arcs form where undersea volcanoes, created in the same process that created nearby oceanic trenches, emerge above the surface

ATLANTIC OCEAN

Geographically distinct regions of ocean near the coast are named as seas, for example the Caribbean Sea

PACIFIC OCEAN

Ocean trenches form where the oceanic crust is plunging beneath another tectonic plate, dragging the seabed to enormous depths

The Pacific Ocean comprises 46 percent of Earth's total ocean cover

The Southern Ocean surrounding Antarctica does not have a distinct basin and some geographers do not recognize it

SOUTHERN OCEAN

The boundary between two oceans or seas is often marked by a cape, or promontory of land, such as Cape Horn between the Pacific and Atlantic

The traditional measure of ocean depth is the fathom, which is based on the width of a person's outstretched arms, and now set at **72 in** (183 cm)

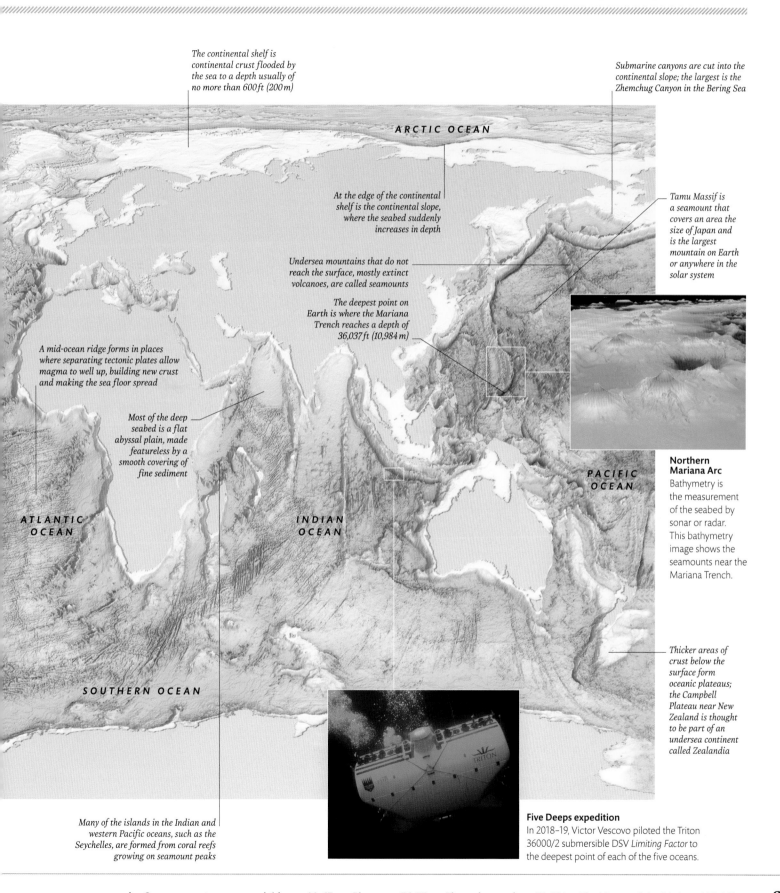

The continental shelf is continental crust flooded by the sea to a depth usually of no more than 600 ft (200 m)

Submarine canyons are cut into the continental slope; the largest is the Zhemchug Canyon in the Bering Sea

ARCTIC OCEAN

At the edge of the continental shelf is the continental slope, where the seabed suddenly increases in depth

Tamu Massif is a seamount that covers an area the size of Japan and is the largest mountain on Earth or anywhere in the solar system

Undersea mountains that do not reach the surface, mostly extinct volcanoes, are called seamounts

The deepest point on Earth is where the Mariana Trench reaches a depth of 36,037 ft (10,984 m)

A mid-ocean ridge forms in places where separating tectonic plates allow magma to well up, building new crust and making the sea floor spread

Most of the deep seabed is a flat abyssal plain, made featureless by a smooth covering of fine sediment

PACIFIC OCEAN

Northern Mariana Arc
Bathymetry is the measurement of the seabed by sonar or radar. This bathymetry image shows the seamounts near the Mariana Trench.

ATLANTIC OCEAN

INDIAN OCEAN

Thicker areas of crust below the surface form oceanic plateaus; the Campbell Plateau near New Zealand is thought to be part of an undersea continent called Zealandia

SOUTHERN OCEAN

Five Deeps expedition
In 2018–19, Victor Vescovo piloted the Triton 36000/2 submersible DSV *Limiting Factor* to the deepest point of each of the five oceans.

Many of the islands in the Indian and western Pacific oceans, such as the Seychelles, are formed from coral reefs growing on seamount peaks

Ocean currents, waves, and tides

Ocean water is in constant motion. At the surface, the water rises and falls due to waves created by the wind. Meanwhile along the coast, the water surges up and down the shoreline according to a regular pattern due to the tide—a longer-period rise and fall of the ocean caused by the moon's pull of gravity. On the largest scale, the oceans are set in motion by currents flowing at a variety of depths, which are slowly but continuously mixing the water and profoundly affecting the pattern of Earth's climates.

PLANKTON BLOOM

Currents

An ocean current is a stream of water that moves continuously in a consistent direction at a few miles an hour. The routes of ocean currents are defined by a complex interaction of depth, temperature, salinity, the shape of the coast, and Earth's rotation.

Surface currents

Currents that move surface water, many of which are named, greatly affect climate. Cold currents along tropical coasts bring extreme dry weather, while warmer water causes rain. Surface currents are linked to deepwater currents (see opposite).

KEY
→ Warm ocean current
→ Cold ocean current

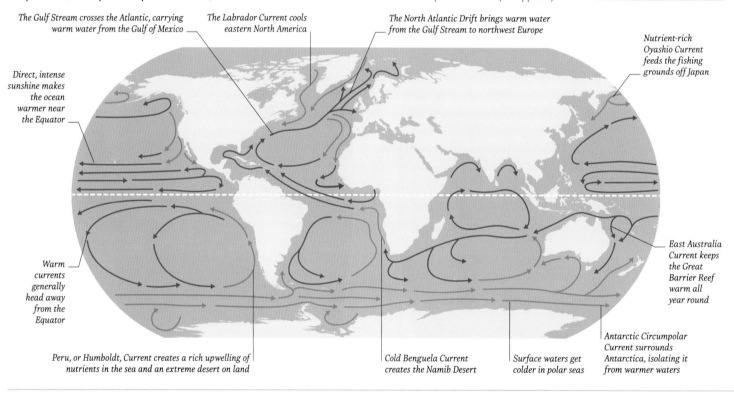

The Gulf Stream crosses the Atlantic, carrying warm water from the Gulf of Mexico

The Labrador Current cools eastern North America

The North Atlantic Drift brings warm water from the Gulf Stream to northwest Europe

Nutrient-rich Oyashio Current feeds the fishing grounds off Japan

Direct, intense sunshine makes the ocean warmer near the Equator

Warm currents generally head away from the Equator

East Australia Current keeps the Great Barrier Reef warm all year round

Peru, or Humboldt, Current creates a rich upwelling of nutrients in the sea and an extreme desert on land

Cold Benguela Current creates the Namib Desert

Surface waters get colder in polar seas

Antarctic Circumpolar Current surrounds Antarctica, isolating it from warmer waters

Waves

Ocean waves are caused by the friction between the water surface and the wind blowing over it. Waves form in a zone of clear water called a fetch. Larger waves form when the fetch is longer (it can be hundreds of miles), and when the wind speed is higher and it blows for longer. Wind waves above a height of 50 ft (15 m) are rare. Tsunamis (see p.54), caused by sudden disturbance of the water, can be higher.

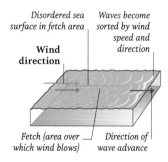

Disordered sea surface in fetch area
Waves become sorted by wind speed and direction
Wind direction
Fetch (area over which wind blows)
Direction of wave advance

❶ Building waves
The wind blowing over a fetch creates a region of ripples, which combine into a unified wave with a consistent direction.

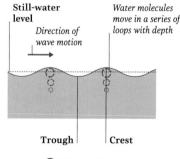

Still-water level
Direction of wave motion
Water molecules move in a series of loops with depth
Trough   **Crest**

❷ Water motion
Water molecules do not move forward. The water moves in looping tube shapes, which creates the rise and fall called swell.

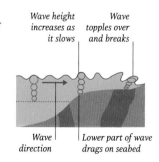

Wave height increases as it slows
Wave topples over and breaks
Wave direction
Lower part of wave drags on seabed

❸ Waves break on shore
As the wave enters shallow water, the bottom of the wave drags, but the upper part continues unabated and breaks.

The **largest recorded tsunami** was caused by a landslide on the coast of **Alaska in 1958**; it surged up an **opposing mountainside to a height of 1,700 ft** (520 m)

PLANKTON

Any marine organisms that cannot swim strongly against ocean currents are classed as plankton. They range from microscopic bacteria to giant jellyfish and can be divided into plantlike "phytoplankton" and the animal and animallike "zooplankton" that eat them.

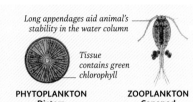

Long appendages aid animal's stability in the water column

Tissue contains green chlorophyll

PHYTOPLANKTON
Diatom

ZOOPLANKTON
Copepod

Gyres

The rotation of Earth deflects winds and wind-driven ocean currents from their routes, especially those that flow north and south. This phenomenon, called the Coriolis Effect, creates oceanic-scale circles of currents called gyres.

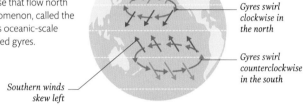

Northern winds skew right

Gyres swirl clockwise in the north

Gyres swirl counterclockwise in the south

Southern winds skew left

Ocean conveyor

Ocean currents are linked by a large-scale circulation called the ocean conveyor. Surface currents are joined to deep currents by vertical water movement called upwelling and downwelling. The conveyor is driven by the differences in water density caused by varying saltiness and temperature.

A diffuse upwelling occurs in the North Pacific

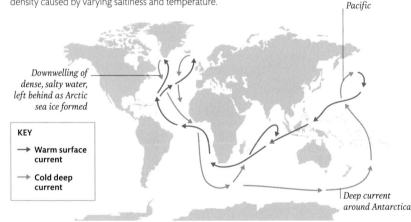

Downwelling of dense, salty water, left behind as Arctic sea ice formed

Deep current around Antarctica

KEY

→ Warm surface current

→ Cold deep current

Frozen seas

Salty seawater freezes at 28.4°F (−2°C) to form sea ice. Water reduces in density as it freezes (seawater more so because it leaves the salt behind in the water), and so the ice floats on the surface. About one-eighth of the world's oceans freeze over at some point each year, but the extent of sea ice varies considerably between summer and winter, especially in the Antarctic, where the area shrinks by almost 85 percent. The icebergs in cold oceans are not sea ice, but calved from glaciers.

KEY

⬚ Extent of summer sea ice

▨ Extent of winter sea ice

→ Routes of icebergs

ARCTIC OCEAN

SOUTHERN OCEAN

Drift ice
Sea ice can be made up of ice floes that drift with the ocean currents (drift ice) or fast ice connected to the shore.

Multi-year ice
After one winter, sea ice is 3–7 ft (1–2 m) thick, but thicker pressure ridges develop (above), which can stay frozen for many years.

Tides

The gravitational pull of the moon and sun creates a bulge in the ocean's surface, which sweeps around the globe as Earth turns. Barely 2 ft (60 cm) in open water, the bulge surges up the shore when it hits land, making a high tide.

Spring and neap tides

Spring tides with especially high and low waters occur when the pull of the moon and sun align. When they work at odds, their gravity creates milder neap tides.

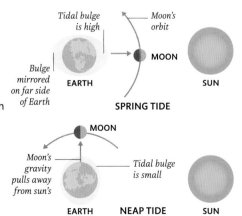

Tidal bulge is high

Moon's orbit

MOON

Bulge mirrored on far side of Earth

EARTH

SUN

SPRING TIDE

MOON

Moon's gravity pulls away from sun's

Tidal bulge is small

EARTH

NEAP TIDE

SUN

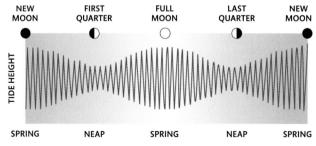

NEW MOON	FIRST QUARTER	FULL MOON	LAST QUARTER	NEW MOON

TIDE HEIGHT

SPRING   NEAP   SPRING   NEAP   SPRING

Tidal pattern
The pattern of spring and neap tides follows the phases of the moon. The phases are an indication of the relative positions of the moon and sun. During a New and Full moon, the sun and moon are aligned and there are corresponding spring tides.

see also Waves pp.186–87 ▶   States of matter pp.198–99 ▶   Types of living things pp.216–17 ▶

Fresh water and ice

Most of the water on Earth is salt water, which contains a variety of dissolved minerals. A small amount of the planet's water is fresh, meaning that the concentration of salt is below 500 parts per million molecules of water. Fresh water is found frozen in icecaps and glaciers, beneath Earth's surface, and in lakes, streams, and rivers.

The water cycle

Earth's water is in a constant state of motion as it moves between land, the oceans, and the atmosphere. In this chain of processes, known as the water cycle, the sun heats up water in rivers, lakes, and seas, evaporating it into vapor. This vapor condenses and forms clouds, which eventually release rain or snow. This precipitation redistributes the water across the Earth's surface, restarting the process.

> Apart from ice delivered in **asteroid and comet impacts**, the volume of Earth's water and ice remains unchanged since the planet's birth

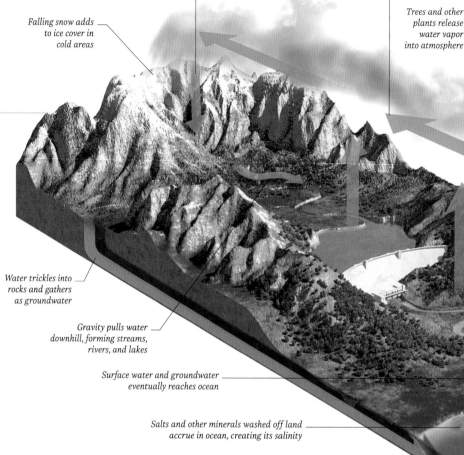

Buildup of water droplets in the air leads to rain

Winds blow clouds from warm ocean over colder land

Falling snow adds to ice cover in cold areas

Trees and other plants release water vapor into atmosphere

Water trickles into rocks and gathers as groundwater

Gravity pulls water downhill, forming streams, rivers, and lakes

Surface water and groundwater eventually reaches ocean

Salts and other minerals washed off land accrue in ocean, creating its salinity

Lakes

Lakes form in any basin surrounded by higher land as water flows down into the basin, usually through a number of inflow channels. Unlike rivers, lakes usually do not have a consistent current, although some have currents caused by inflow channels, or by wind.

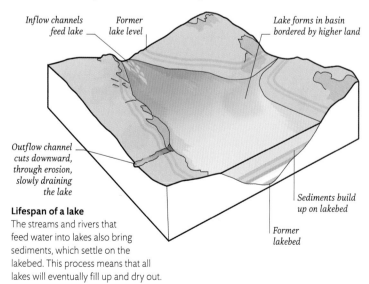

Inflow channels feed lake

Former lake level

Lake forms in basin bordered by higher land

Outflow channel cuts downward, through erosion, slowly draining the lake

Sediments build up on lakebed

Former lakebed

Lifespan of a lake

The streams and rivers that feed water into lakes also bring sediments, which settle on the lakebed. This process means that all lakes will eventually fill up and dry out.

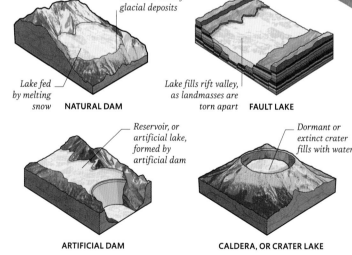

Basin formed by a natural dam of glacial deposits

Lake fed by melting snow **NATURAL DAM**

Lake fills rift valley, as landmasses are torn apart **FAULT LAKE**

Reservoir, or artificial lake, formed by artificial dam

Dormant or extinct crater fills with water

ARTIFICIAL DAM

CALDERA, OR CRATER LAKE

Types of lakes

Lake basins form in many ways—these are just four examples. They can be dammed by humans or by landslides or glaciers. The largest and deepest lakes, such as Baikal in Russia, are fault lakes, formed by movements in Earth's tectonic plates. The world's highest lakes, however, tend to be crater lakes, which form when water gathers in a volcanic crater, which can be active or inactive.

As temperature falls, larger droplets form in cloud

At high altitude, water vapor cools and condenses into clouds of tiny droplets

Solar heating makes water evaporate into water vapor that rises into air

97.5 percent is saline sea water

2.5 percent is fresh water

0.3 percent is in rivers and lakes

68.9 percent is in polar ice caps and glaciers

Earth's water distribution

The vast majority of Earth's water is salt water, which makes up the oceans. Most fresh water is locked away as ice or in groundwater. Only a tiny fraction of fresh water is flowing through the world's river systems.

30.8 percent is in groundwater held in porous rocks

EARTH'S WATER

Lambert Glacier, the world's largest, covers over 386,000 sq miles (1 million sq km)

IRRIGATION

As well as flowing downhill, water also flows down into Earth's crust through layers of porous rock. Boreholes called artesian wells are used to access aquifers—subterranean reservoirs that act as a source of irrigation water. These wells use the natural pressure created by the flow of groundwater, which pushes water up to the surface.

Rain soaks into the ground

Groundwater flows through rock layer

Artesian well used to raise water to surface

ARTESIAN WELL

Desalination

In coastal deserts where fresh water is scarce, the salt can be removed from nearby sea water using energy in an industrial process called desalination. The most efficient way to do this is by reverse osmosis, where the water is forced through membranes at high pressure.

Membranes block passage of dissolved minerals

Water cleaned by filtering it through sand beds

Sea water enters plant

Solid debris is removed

Saline waste returned to ocean

Desalinated water tapped off

DESALINATION PROCESS

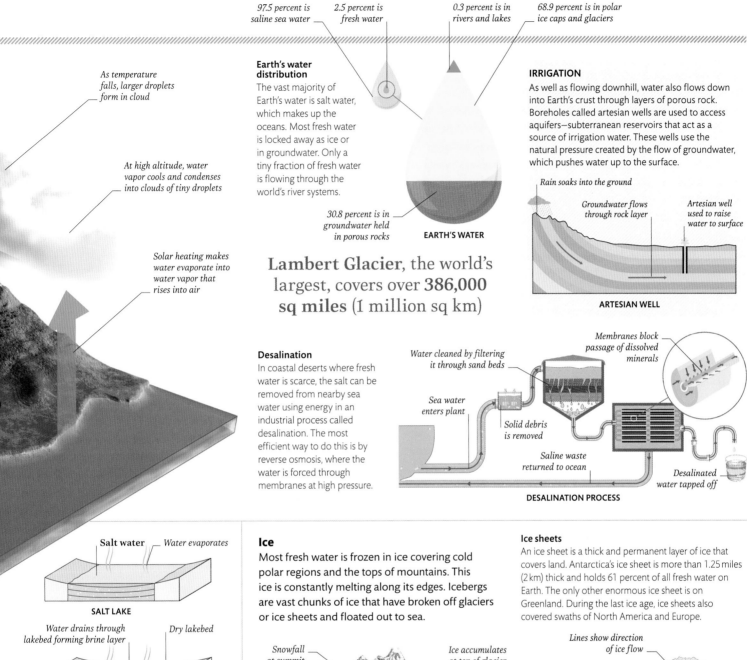

Salt water — Water evaporates

SALT LAKE

Water drains through lakebed forming brine layer — Dry lakebed

SALT PAN

Layers of salt build up

SALT CRUST

Salt lakes

Salt lakes form when there is no outflow, because evaporation exceeds inflow. Evaporation leaves behind any dissolved minerals, which build up in the remaining water. When there is very little inflow, the lake can dry to form a salt pan.

Ice

Most fresh water is frozen in ice covering cold polar regions and the tops of mountains. This ice is constantly melting along its edges. Icebergs are vast chunks of ice that have broken off glaciers or ice sheets and floated out to sea.

Snowfall at summit

Ice accumulates at top of glacier

Ice begins to melt on lower section

Gravity pulls snow and ice downhill

Glaciers

A glacier is a slowly moving river of ice, which flows downhill. It can do so because the great pressure at its base melts its lower surface, and the water lubricates its movement.

Ice sheets

An ice sheet is a thick and permanent layer of ice that covers land. Antarctica's ice sheet is more than 1.25 miles (2 km) thick and holds 61 percent of all fresh water on Earth. The only other enormous ice sheet is on Greenland. During the last ice age, ice sheets also covered swaths of North America and Europe.

Lines show direction of ice flow

Ice shelves extend from land over sea

Ice erodes deep valley

ANTARCTIC ICE SHEET

Snout of glacier releases water and sediments

In cold periods glacier extends downhill

see also Weather pp.74-75 ▶

Earth's atmosphere

Planet Earth is surrounded by an envelope of gases called the atmosphere. The gases extend several thousand miles into space. The atmosphere becomes increasingly thin with altitude, and three-quarters of its gas content lies within 6.8 miles (11 km) of ground level. This lowest, densest layer of the atmosphere is the medium for the entire world's weather, so it has a profound effect on conditions on the planet's surface.

Composition

The atmosphere contains a mixture of gases, known as air. The air's composition is in a dynamic equilibrium with natural processes, mostly biological in nature, constantly adding and removing different gases. Earth is the only planet in the solar system to have significant amounts of oxygen in its air.

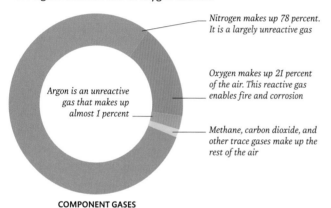

Nitrogen makes up 78 percent. It is a largely unreactive gas

Oxygen makes up 21 percent of the air. This reactive gas enables fire and corrosion

Argon is an unreactive gas that makes up almost 1 percent

Methane, carbon dioxide, and other trace gases make up the rest of the air

COMPONENT GASES

Atmospheric pressure

The pressure of the atmosphere is the force applied by the air on another object. This can be visualized as the weight of all the air above the object pushing down. At sea level, the atmosphere applies a weight of about 15 lb per sq in (1 kg per sq cm) of Earth's surface. However, the exact value varies from place to place and in time.

Pressure systems

Cold air is denser and heavier than warm air, and tends to sink. The atmospheric pressure beneath a cold air mass is therefore higher than it is under a warm air mass. Air forced out of a high-pressure zone blows toward low-pressure zones as wind.

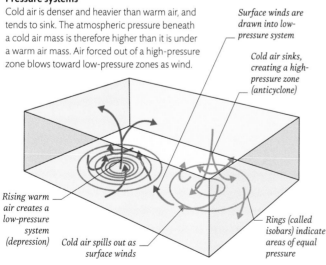

Surface winds are drawn into low-pressure system

Cold air sinks, creating a high-pressure zone (anticyclone)

Rising warm air creates a low-pressure system (depression)

Cold air spills out as surface winds

Rings (called isobars) indicate areas of equal pressure

Trapping heat

The air is largely transparent to sunlight coming from space and it shines right through. (Blue light is scattered widely, which makes the sky appear blue.) By contrast, heat radiating from Earth's surface is trapped by greenhouse gases in the atmosphere. This elevates the planet's average temperature.

Greenhouse effect

The warming process is called the greenhouse effect because the gases work like the glass of a greenhouse, letting light in but preventing some heat from escaping.

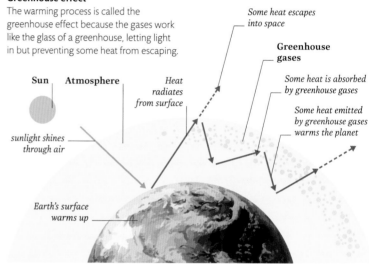

Some heat escapes into space

Greenhouse gases

Some heat is absorbed by greenhouse gases

Some heat emitted by greenhouse gases warms the planet

Sun   **Atmosphere**   *Heat radiates from surface*

sunlight shines through air

Earth's surface warms up

Lights in the atmosphere

There are phenomena that cause light disturbances in the atmosphere, the best-known of which are the auroras. An aurora is a pattern of glowing particles that forms high in the atmosphere, most commonly in the polar regions. In the far north, this is called the aurora borealis or northern lights (see p.21); in the far south, the aurora australis.

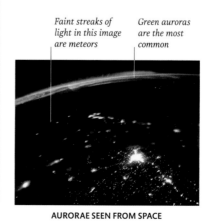

Faint streaks of light in this image are meteors

Green auroras are the most common

AURORAE SEEN FROM SPACE

WATER IN THE ATMOSPHERE

Water enters the air as vapor when liquid on Earth's surface evaporates. The amount of water vapor in the air is measured as humidity, and in warm tropical regions the atmosphere tends to be more humid. As air cools, the vapor condenses into droplets, forming clouds and rain.

HOW AURORAS WORK

The Earth's magnetic field forms a protective boundary and also pulls the solar wind toward the poles. High-energy particles from the sun collide with gases present in the atmosphere to create glowing colors. Colors vary due to altitude and the type of atom that is struck.

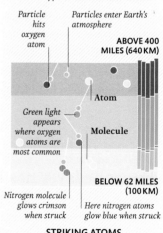

Particle hits oxygen atom

Particles enter Earth's atmosphere

ABOVE 400 MILES (640 KM)

Atom

Green light appears where oxygen atoms are most common

Molecule

Nitrogen molecule glows crimson when struck

Here nitrogen atoms glow blue when struck

BELOW 62 MILES (100 KM)

STRIKING ATOMS

The gas in **Earth's atmosphere weighs 5,500 trillion tons** (5,000 trillion tonnes), which is **less than a millionth** of the **planet's total mass**

Shielding the Earth

The atmosphere has a diffuse layer of ozone at an altitude of between 9 and 22 miles (15 and 35 km). Ozone is an unstable form of oxygen, where molecules are made of three atoms of oxygen, not two. High-energy ultraviolet radiation from the sun is absorbed by the ozone. In this way the ozone layer filters out dangerous rays from sunlight.

Ozone depletion

Ozone is both created and destroyed naturally by UV, but artificial gases called CFCs, used in refrigerators and aerosols, also destroy it and create a hole on the ozone layer. In the 1980s, these chemicals were banned.

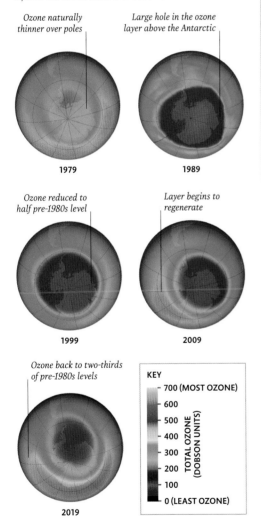

Ozone naturally thinner over poles

1979

Large hole in the ozone layer above the Antarctic

1989

Ozone reduced to half pre-1980s level

1999

Layer begins to regenerate

2009

Ozone back to two-thirds of pre-1980s levels

2019

KEY

700 (MOST OZONE)
600
500
400
300
200
100
0 (LEAST OZONE)

TOTAL OZONE (DOBSON UNITS)

The **ozone layer** has **10 ozone molecules** for every million air molecules, **30 times more** than in normal air

Layers of the atmosphere

While the pressure of the atmosphere decreases with altitude in a relatively uniform fashion, air temperature does not. The way temperature fluctuates with altitude creates distinct boundaries between five atmospheric layers.

Boundaries

In the atmosphere's lowest layer, the troposphere, temperature drops with altitude. However, it then rises in the stratosphere. Next, the mesosphere forms the coldest part of the atmosphere at –120°F (–85°C), and above that the upper two layers reach very high temperatures, although the layers also become very diffuse.

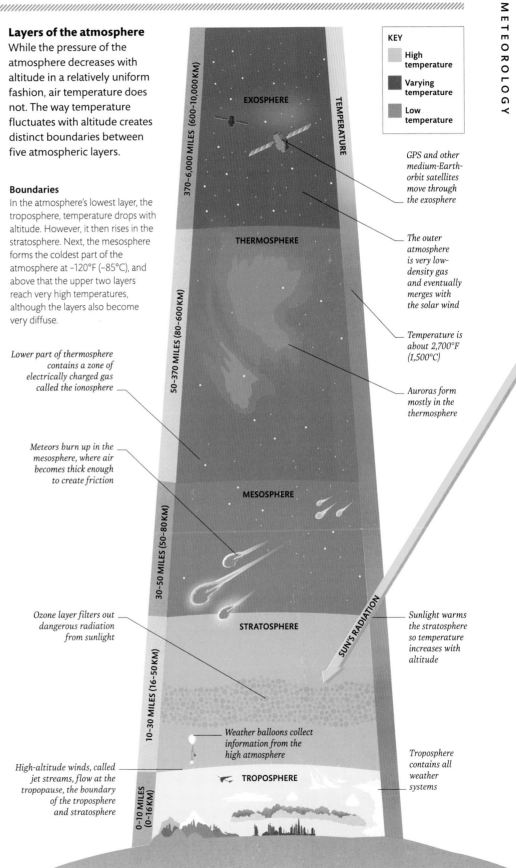

KEY

High temperature

Varying temperature

Low temperature

370–6,000 MILES (600–10,000 KM)

EXOSPHERE

TEMPERATURE

GPS and other medium-Earth-orbit satellites move through the exosphere

THERMOSPHERE

50–370 MILES (80–600 KM)

The outer atmosphere is very low-density gas and eventually merges with the solar wind

Temperature is about 2,700°F (1,500°C)

Lower part of thermosphere contains a zone of electrically charged gas called the ionosphere

Auroras form mostly in the thermosphere

Meteors burn up in the mesosphere, where air becomes thick enough to create friction

MESOSPHERE

30–50 MILES (50–80 KM)

Ozone layer filters out dangerous radiation from sunlight

STRATOSPHERE

SUN'S RADIATION

Sunlight warms the stratosphere so temperature increases with altitude

10–30 MILES (16–50 KM)

Weather balloons collect information from the high atmosphere

Troposphere contains all weather systems

High-altitude winds, called jet streams, flow at the tropopause, the boundary of the troposphere and stratosphere

TROPOSPHERE

0–10 MILES (0–16 KM)

see also Atmospheric circulation pp.72–73 ▶ Weather pp.74–75 ▶ Biomes pp.76–77 ▶ **71**

Atmospheric circulation

The atmosphere is always in motion, with the flow of air masses creating winds. The movement of air masses is driven by solar heating, which warms the Earth's surface. The distribution of heat is uneven and it is much warmer at the Equator than it is at the poles. Circulation cells form as warm, lighter air rises and cooler, denser air sinks, moving the air and creating the winds that then distribute heat around the globe.

Large-scale circulation

On a global scale, air circulates in 3D zones called cells, each circling the planet at a particular latitude. Rising warm air near the Equator flows north and south and a similar circulation occurs in the polar cells. Air in the cells that form between the tropical and polar cells flows in the opposite direction.

Dry air sinks into subtropical zone creating calm, drought conditions

Equatorial convergence zone, or doldrums, known for gloomy weather

POLAR DESERTS

The air circulating in polar cells is much colder than in other cells, which means it is much drier. Precipitation is rare, and mostly falls as snow rather than rain, so Earth's polar regions are classified as deserts. Almost all fresh water takes the form of ice.

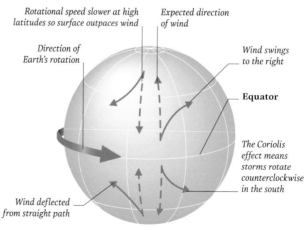

DISKO BAY, GREENLAND

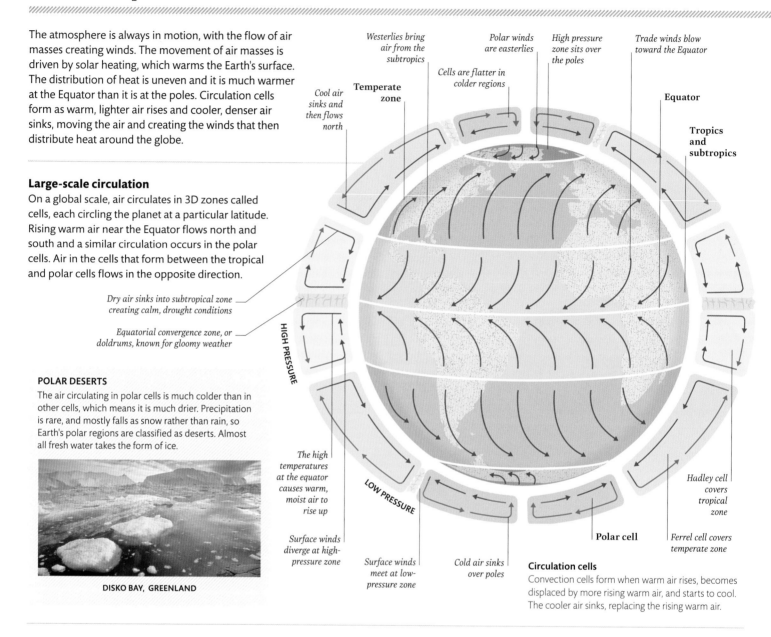

Cool air sinks and then flows north

Westerlies bring air from the subtropics

Polar winds are easterlies

High pressure zone sits over the poles

Trade winds blow toward the Equator

Temperate zone

Cells are flatter in colder regions

Equator

Tropics and subtropics

HIGH PRESSURE

LOW PRESSURE

The high temperatures at the equator causes warm, moist air to rise up

Surface winds diverge at high-pressure zone

Surface winds meet at low-pressure zone

Cold air sinks over poles

Hadley cell covers tropical zone

Polar cell

Ferrel cell covers temperate zone

Circulation cells

Convection cells form when warm air rises, becomes displaced by more rising warm air, and starts to cool. The cooler air sinks, replacing the rising warm air.

Coriolis effect

Earth's surface winds do not simply flow directly north or south but veer off course, creating the diagonal westerly and easterly winds. This is due to the Coriolis Effect created by the west-to-east rotation of the planet, which deflects winds clockwise in the northern hemisphere and counterclockwise in the southern hemisphere. The effect is strongest at the poles.

Rotational speeds

Points on the equator are moving eastward more rapidly than points at high latitudes. Wind blowing toward high latitudes outpaces the surface's eastward motion, so it changes course if plotted on a map.

Rotational speed slower at high latitudes so surface outpaces wind

Direction of Earth's rotation

Expected direction of wind

Wind swings to the right

Equator

The Coriolis effect means storms rotate counterclockwise in the south

Wind deflected from straight path

GASPARD-GUSTAVE DE CORIOLIS

The Coriolis effect is named after the French mathematician and engineer Gaspard-Gustave de Coriolis (1792–1843), who explained the phenomenon in 1835. The effect was first noticed in Italy in 1651, by scientists who saw that cannonballs fired at long range were deflected from their target.

◄ see also Ocean currents, waves, and tides pp.66–67   ◄ Fresh water and ice pp.68–69   ◄ Earth's atmosphere pp.70–71

Prevailing winds create ocean currents, which are used by non-sailing commercial ships to hasten their journey

Prevailing winds

The large-scale circulation created by cells produces zones of winds around the world. Each region of Earth's surface has a prevailing wind, which blows in a predictable direction. Cooler winds blow toward the Equator, while warmer ones head toward the poles. The higher pressure zones in the subtropics are called the "Horse latitudes," known for their calm and frequently windless conditions.

Surface winds

The planet's surface is split into zones of prevailing winds. The dominant winds are named primarily for the direction from which they blow.

Jet streams

High-altitude winds bands of fast-moving air, called jet streams, form where two circulation cells meet. The main jets circle the poles and the subtropical zone. The jets follow wavelike paths and then have a big influence on the weather; creating high- and low-pressure zones. Unusually large waves are associated with extreme weather conditions, such as droughts and floods.

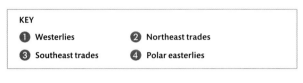

KEY
1. Westerlies
2. Northeast trades
3. Southeast trades
4. Polar easterlies

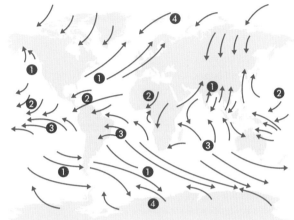

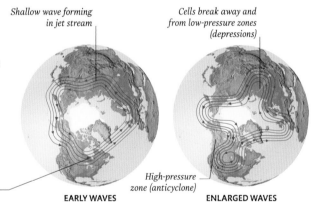

Shallow wave forming in jet stream

Cells break away and from low-pressure zones (depressions)

Jet stream shifting south brings wet weather

High-pressure zone (anticyclone)

EARLY WAVES

ENLARGED WAVES

BEAUFORT SCALE

In 1805, Sir Francis Beaufort, an Irish naval officer, developed a wind force scale based on sea conditions. The scale has since been adapted for use on land.

BEAUFORT NO.	WIND SPEED MPH (KPH)	DESCRIPTION
0	0-1 (0-2)	Calm; smoke rises vertically, air feels still
1	1-3 (2-6)	Light air; smoke drifts
2	4-7 (7-11)	Slight breeze; wind detectable on face, some leaf movement
3	8-12 (12-19)	Gentle breeze; leaves and twigs move
4	13-18 (20-29)	Moderate breeze; loose paper blows around
5	19-24 (30-39)	Fresh breeze; small trees sway
6	25-31 (40-50)	Strong breeze; difficult to use an umbrella
7	32-38 (51-61)	High wind; whole trees bend
8	39-46 (62-74)	Gale; twigs break off trees, walking into wind is difficult
9	47-54 (75-87)	Severe gale; roof tiles blow away
10	55-63 (88-101)	Whole gale; trees break and are uprooted
11	64-74 (102-119)	Storm; damage is extensive, cars overturn
12	75+ (120+)	Hurricane; widespread devastation

The wind speeds of the main jet streams have been measured at up to 250 mph (400 kph)

Seasonal variation

Atmospheric conditions vary considerably between seasons due to a change in the amount of solar heating. This is the result of Earth's tilting axis, which means that the sun is high overhead in the summer, giving long days, but low in the sky in winter, giving short days.

Solstices and equinoxes

An equinox is a day in spring or fall when the length of the day and night are the same. The summer solstice has the longest day and winter solstice has the longest night.

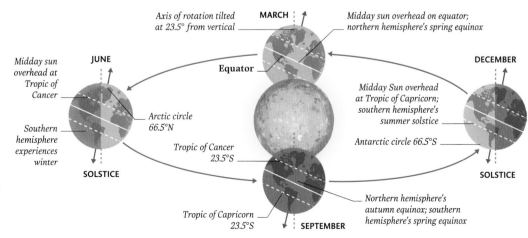

Axis of rotation tilted at 23.5° from vertical

MARCH

Midday sun overhead on equator; northern hemisphere's spring equinox

JUNE

Equator

DECEMBER

Midday sun overhead at Tropic of Cancer

Arctic circle 66.5°N

Southern hemisphere experiences winter

SOLSTICE

Tropic of Cancer 23.5°S

Midday Sun overhead at Tropic of Capricorn; southern hemisphere's summer solstice

Antarctic circle 66.5°S

SOLSTICE

Tropic of Capricorn 23.5°S

SEPTEMBER

Northern hemisphere's autumn equinox; southern hemisphere's spring equinox

see also Weather pp.74-75 ▶ Biomes pp.76-77 ▶

Weather

The science of weather is called meteorology, from the Greek for "things high in the air." In fact, nearly all weather occurs within the troposphere, the bottom layer of atmosphere that extends to an altitude of about 7.5 miles (10 km). The weather is the state of the atmosphere at one location at a particular time, and includes factors such as temperature, humidity, and air pressure. These interact to create the prevailing conditions, such as rain.

Air masses

The atmosphere is divided into a series of vast air masses. Each is associated with a particular region, but they grow and shrink as the seasons change. The boundaries between air masses are zones that experience changeable weather.

Coldest air masses are near the poles

Air masses over continents tend to be drier than maritime air

Continental polar air is cold and dry

Air is warmer near to the equator

Masses over tropical waters are warm and moist

Masses over ocean tend to be moist

SOURCE REGIONS OF AIR MASSES

Weather fronts

Changes in the weather occur when masses of air with differing characteristics, such as temperature and humidity, collide. The boundary between the air masses is called the weather front, and the particular conditions along the front dictate what weather system will develop.

Warm fronts

This system forms when warm, humid air pushes into colder, dry air. The warm air rises slowly over the colder mass, forming a region of light and persistent rain.

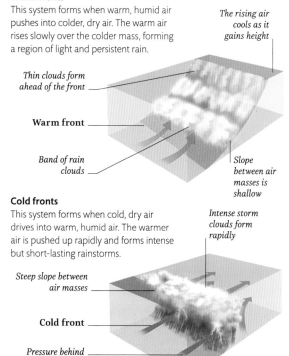

The rising air cools as it gains height

Thin clouds form ahead of the front

Warm front

Band of rain clouds

Slope between air masses is shallow

Cold fronts

This system forms when cold, dry air drives into warm, humid air. The warmer air is pushed up rapidly and forms intense but short-lasting rainstorms.

Intense storm clouds form rapidly

Steep slope between air masses

Cold front

Pressure behind front increases

Occluded fronts

This type of front forms when a warm front meets a cold front and they merge. The boundary between air masses is lifted off the ground, and a mix of unsettled weather occurs.

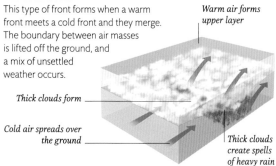

Warm air forms upper layer

Thick clouds form

Cold air spreads over the ground

Thick clouds create spells of heavy rain

Cloud types

Clouds are made from water droplets and ice crystals suspended in the air. There are three basic types of clouds, which may merge in some cases. Cumulus clouds are fluffy, cirrus clouds are wispy, and stratus clouds are layered. The term nimbus is added to indicate a raincloud, while the prefix "alto-" refers to mid-level formations.

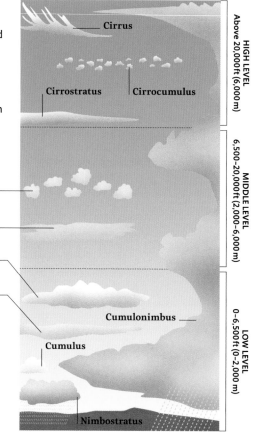

Cirrus

Cirrostratus

Cirrocumulus

HIGH LEVEL
Above 20,000ft (6,000 m)

Altocumulus clouds indicate a thunderstorm is forming

Altostratus clouds create overcast skies

Stratocumulus are the most common clouds

Stratus clouds are flat and can be low enough to the ground to form fog

MIDDLE LEVEL
6,500–20,000ft (2,000–6,000 m)

Cumulonimbus

Cumulus

Nimbostratus

LOW LEVEL
0–6,500ft (0–2,000 m)

122,000 cubic miles (505,000 cubic km) of rain and other precipitation falls on Earth every year

Precipitation and its types

Any form of water falling from the sky is called precipitation. It starts with tiny droplets forming clouds, but when the size of the droplets becomes too big to stay suspended in the air, they fall due to gravity.

Rain
The most common form of precipitation occurs as water vapor condenses as the air cools.

Snow
Fluffy flakes grow as tiny ice crystals and stick together when blown through very cold but moist air.

Sleet
When snowflakes begin to melt as they fall, the result is a mixture of rain and ice, called sleet.

Hail
Raindrops blown upward freeze into a hailstone. Repeating this process makes the stones larger.

Fog and mist
When a cloud of suspended water droplets touches the ground, it creates mist and fog.

Weather systems

Predicting dangerous weather such as tornadoes and hurricanes can reduce deaths and damage. In order to forecast the weather, meteorologists need to understand how each type of weather system forms and functions. All weather systems are the interaction of air of different temperatures, humidities, and pressures.

Tornadoes

Also known as a whirlwind, a tornado is a funnel of wind that forms when thunderclouds touch the ground. At their edges they have the fastest winds measured on Earth, with the largest tornadoes spiraling at 300 mph (480 kph). In the center of the tornado is a low-pressure area.

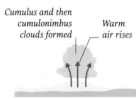

❶ Stage 1
A tornado forms from a large thunderstorm called a supercell. A supercell is created over land by warm air rising rapidly.

Cumulus and then cumulonimbus clouds formed

Warm air rises

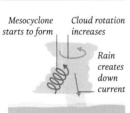

❷ Stage 2
High in the thunder cloud a region begins to rotate slowly. This leads to the formation of a structure called a mesocyclone.

Mesocyclone starts to form

Cloud rotation increases

Rain creates down current

❸ Stage 3
The mesocyclone moves below the base of the cloud and contacts the ground and starts to suck air up into the storm.

Spiraling wind column touches ground

Downward currents eventually stop updraft

Monsoons

A monsoon is a wind that changes direction halfway through the year. This reversal brings about seasonal weather changes. When it blows inland from the ocean, the wind brings moisture, creating a "monsoon season" of heavy rains. When the direction reverses, the air becomes dry. Monsoons typically occur in tropical areas.

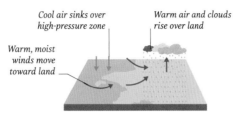

Cool air sinks over high-pressure zone

Warm air and clouds rise over land

Warm, moist winds move toward land

Monsoon season
In summer, warm air rises more rapidly over land, drawing moist air in from the ocean. This humid air then rises and drops its water as rain.

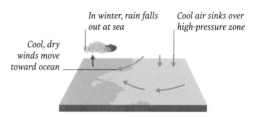

In winter, rain falls out at sea

Cool air sinks over high-pressure zone

Cool, dry winds move toward ocean

Dry season
In winter, the ocean is warmer than the land, so the circulation of air is reversed. Cold air sinks over land and moves out to sea as a dry wind.

Tropical storms

The largest storm systems form over equatorial oceans where surface water temperatures exceed 78°F (26°C). The warm air rising from the ocean builds vast circulating storms.

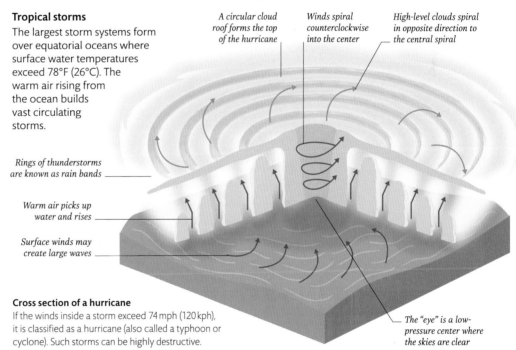

A circular cloud roof forms the top of the hurricane

Winds spiral counterclockwise into the center

High-level clouds spiral in opposite direction to the central spiral

Rings of thunderstorms are known as rain bands

Warm air picks up water and rises

Surface winds may create large waves

The "eye" is a low-pressure center where the skies are clear

Cross section of a hurricane
If the winds inside a storm exceed 74 mph (120 kph), it is classified as a hurricane (also called a typhoon or cyclone). Such storms can be highly destructive.

Climate

While weather is a description of the state of the atmosphere at a certain time, climate is an understanding of the kinds of weather a region is likely to experience from one year to the next. Weather changes frequently but a region's climate changes only slowly over decades. The globe is divided into broad climate zones closely mapped to latitude.

There are 1.4 billion flashes of lightning and claps of thunder every year

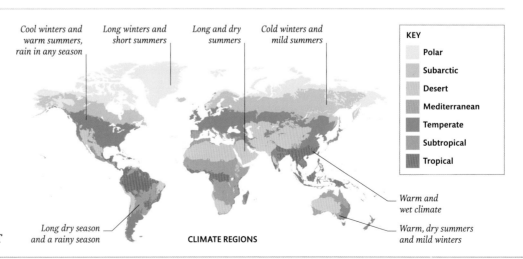

Cool winters and warm summers, rain in any season

Long winters and short summers

Long and dry summers

Cold winters and mild summers

KEY
- Polar
- Subarctic
- Desert
- Mediterranean
- Temperate
- Subtropical
- Tropical

Warm and wet climate

Long dry season and a rainy season

CLIMATE REGIONS

Warm, dry summers and mild winters

see also Biomes pp.76–77 ▶

Biomes

A biome is a characteristic community of wildlife that is closely associated with a particular climate. The land surface of Earth can be divided into biomes, closely allied with the globe's varying climate zones. A biome does not fill a continuous region but is fragmented across continents. The separated sections of a biome share the same broad environmental conditions that lead to a broad type of vegetation, be it shrubland or broadleaf forest, although the particular animals and plants that survive there may vary a lot between continents.

Biomes of the world

This map divides Earth's surface into 16 biomes, mostly on land. Biomes differ in climatic conditions, such as rainfall and temperature range, plus any seasonal variation. Polar and boreal areas are cold for most of the year. Temperate regions have a range of mild conditions, while the tropics are hot all year. The biome concept can be extended to marine habitats, such as coral reef and mangrove.

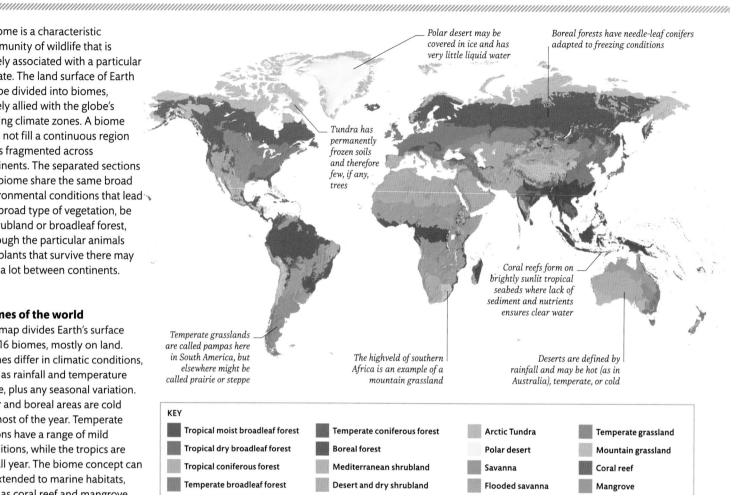

Polar desert may be covered in ice and has very little liquid water

Boreal forests have needle-leaf conifers adapted to freezing conditions

Tundra has permanently frozen soils and therefore few, if any, trees

Coral reefs form on brightly sunlit tropical seabeds where lack of sediment and nutrients ensures clear water

Temperate grasslands are called pampas here in South America, but elsewhere might be called prairie or steppe

The highveld of southern Africa is an example of a mountain grassland

Deserts are defined by rainfall and may be hot (as in Australia), temperate, or cold

KEY

■ Tropical moist broadleaf forest	■ Temperate coniferous forest	■ Arctic Tundra	■ Temperate grassland
■ Tropical dry broadleaf forest	■ Boreal forest	■ Polar desert	■ Mountain grassland
■ Tropical coniferous forest	■ Mediterranean shrubland	■ Savanna	■ Coral reef
■ Temperate broadleaf forest	■ Desert and dry shrubland	■ Flooded savanna	■ Mangrove

Buttress roots support trees in the thin soil

Trees form a thick canopy 100 ft (30 m) above the forest floor

Slow-growing savanna trees have deep roots that collect water

Wide-open grasslands are suited to large, fast-running animals

Some desert trees have deep tap roots that search for buried water stores

Rain sinks rapidly into the dry sandy soils

Succulent desert plants retain water

Leaves turn brown as trees remove their valuable green chlorophyll

Fallen leaves create a deep and fertile soil

Tropical broadleaf forest
Evergreen tropical forest (rainforest) grows in regions that are warm and wet all year round. The soil is shallow and nutrients are cycled through it quickly. A seasonally dry variant, monsoon forest, is deciduous.

Savanna
Also called tropical grassland, this biome exists where there is not enough rainfall for dense stands of trees to survive, but more rainfall than in a desert. Fast-growing grass sprouts whenever rain does fall.

Desert
A desert forms wherever the annual rainfall drops below 10 in (250 mm), while land that gets less than 24 in (600 m) will be a semidesert. With limited water, desert plants and animals are sparse.

Temperate broadleaf forest
These woodlands grow in latitudes where there is a short, cold winter. To prevent frost damage, most temperate trees are deciduous, dropping their leaves in fall and growing new ones in spring.

Coral reefs contain one-quarter of marine species but cover one percent of the ocean's area

Vertical zones

Climate changes with altitude, so biome communities form in zones on mountainsides. High altitudes are always colder because the air is thinner, so it holds less heat. In addition, with fewer obstructions, the high-altitude wind speeds are greater, which has a drying effect.

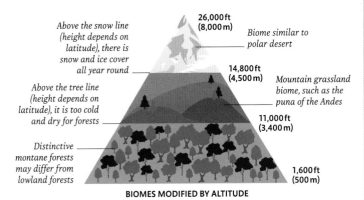

Above the snow line (height depends on latitude), there is snow and ice cover all year round

26,000 ft (8,000 m)

Biome similar to polar desert

14,800 ft (4,500 m)

Mountain grassland biome, such as the puna of the Andes

Above the tree line (height depends on latitude), it is too cold and dry for forests

11,000 ft (3,400 m)

Distinctive montane forests may differ from lowland forests

1,600 ft (500 m)

BIOMES MODIFIED BY ALTITUDE

LATITUDE ZONES

Earth's cycle of seasons has different impacts on the biomes at different latitudes. The tropical zone has warm weather all year with little seasonal variation. The temperate region has a short, cold winter, while the polar region has long, dark winters with little sunshine.

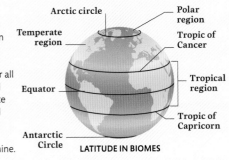

Arctic circle

Polar region

Temperate region

Tropic of Cancer

Equator

Tropical region

Antarctic Circle

Tropic of Capricorn

LATITUDE IN BIOMES

Microhabitats

Within a biome there can be many microhabitats, where the conditions are different. The life-forms that live in each microhabitat tackle different challenges. In the emergent trees of a tropical forest, organisms must cope with far drier, windier, and sunnier conditions than on the forest floor.

Emergent trees grow above the canopy and access more sunlight

The canopy is formed when crowns of tall trees form a dense layer

The understory has smaller shrubs and trees that grow in the gloom

On the ground, saplings wait for a gap in the canopy

TROPICAL FOREST MICROHABITATS

Forest layers

A rainforest is a highly complex ecosystem with at least four identifiable microhabitats, which form layers, or stories, in the habitat.

KEY

Emergent trees | Understory
Canopy | Ground layer

Ecological succession

A biome represents a climax community, which takes maximum advantage of a habitat and its climate. If new land opens up, due to a landslide, volcanic eruption, or human activity, the community develops from bare earth by a process called succession. Many factors can stop succession reaching the climax, such as waterlogged soil leading to wetland instead of forest.

The highest tree lines are at around 16,000 ft (4,900 m) in the Andes and in southern Tibet

Succession in a temperate forest

It can take hundreds of years for a forest to develop. It takes several stages, each paving the way for the next. At each stage, the habitat is occupied by transient communities, which are replaced in an increasingly predictable way toward the climax.

Tall trees form a broken canopy, with smaller plants growing in clearings

Mature forest has trees more than 50 years old

A young forest emerges after about 25 years

These thick-stemmed plants survive for several years

Bare earth could result from tree fall creating a clearing

Specialty pioneers—herbs, grasses, and fast-growing ferns—sprout

Shrubs crowd out the pioneers

◄ see also Atmospheric circulation pp.72–73   ◄ Weather pp.74–75   The web of life pp.80–81 ►

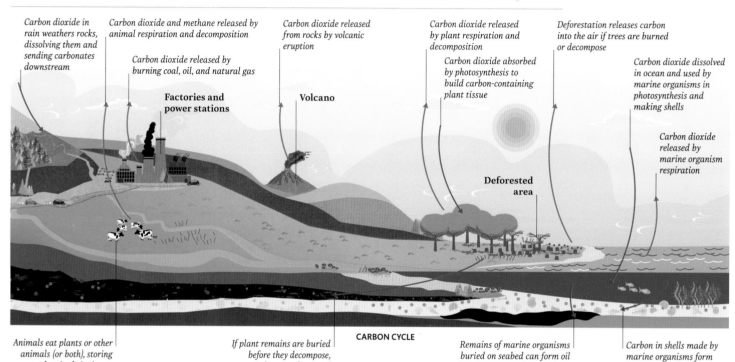

The carbon cycle

Carbon is an essential ingredient in all types of life. Every living thing takes in carbon in various forms from the environment and gives it out again. Together with physical processes this creates the carbon cycle. The carbon cycle is naturally balanced, but human activities are upsetting that balance.

Carbon in the environment

Compounds of carbon are found in the air, water, soils, and rocks. The fastest components of the cycle are plants taking carbon dioxide (CO_2) from the air and water by photosynthesis and all kinds of life breathing out carbon dioxide, or releasing it when rotting.

KEY

→ Carbon released into air as CO_2 and methane

→ CO_2 absorbed into organisms, ocean, and rock

Carbon dioxide in rain weathers rocks, dissolving them and sending carbonates downstream

Carbon dioxide and methane released by animal respiration and decomposition

Carbon dioxide released by burning coal, oil, and natural gas

Factories and power stations

Carbon dioxide released from rocks by volcanic eruption

Volcano

Carbon dioxide released by plant respiration and decomposition

Carbon dioxide absorbed by photosynthesis to build carbon-containing plant tissue

Deforestation releases carbon into the air if trees are burned or decompose

Carbon dioxide dissolved in ocean and used by marine organisms in photosynthesis and making shells

Carbon dioxide released by marine organism respiration

Deforested area

Animals eat plants or other animals (or both), storing carbon in their tissues

If plant remains are buried before they decompose, they may form coal

CARBON CYCLE

Remains of marine organisms buried on seabed can form oil and natural gas

Carbon in shells made by marine organisms form limestone and chalk

Long-term natural sinks

Carbon compounds are not always cycled quickly through the environment. There are several routes out of the short-term cycle to sinks, where the carbon accrues for long periods. The sinks contain 30 times as much carbon as the air, soil, and oceans.

Limestone and chalk

The shells of many ocean organisms are made from calcium carbonate, which settles on the seabed to form carbonate-containing rocks.

Shell is made with carbon extracted from sea water

COCCOLITHOPHORE

How coal forms

Coal is the remains of vegetation that becomes buried before it rots significantly. It is squeezed over millions of years by the weight of sediments above it, making it transform into a carbon-rich rock.

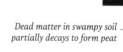

Prehistoric plants topple and die

Pressure of sediment layers squeezes out water and air

Rock is now coal, a combustible rock rich in carbon

Dead matter in swampy soil partially decays to form peat

Pressure of sediment layers builds

Deposits lose water and gas, concentrating their carbon levels

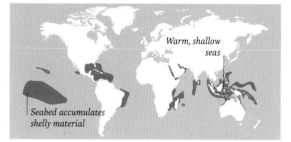

Warm, shallow seas

Seabed accumulates shelly material

TODAY'S LIMESTONE- AND CHALK-FORMING REGIONS

HOW DIAMOND IS MADE

Diamonds are hard crystals of pure carbon. They form under enormous pressures and high temperatures. While asteroid impacts can create these conditions, mostly diamonds form in the mantle beneath mountain-building regions.

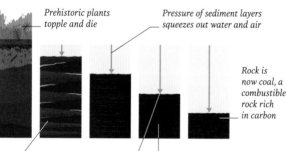
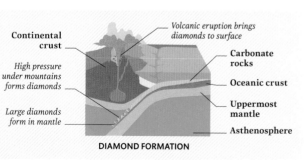

Continental crust

High pressure under mountains forms diamonds

Large diamonds form in mantle

Volcanic eruption brings diamonds to surface

Carbonate rocks

Oceanic crust

Uppermost mantle

Asthenosphere

DIAMOND FORMATION

Carbon is the 15th most abundant element on Earth

Disturbing the cycle

Human activity is disrupting the carbon cycle, chiefly by adding more CO_2 to the air than is removed (see p.82). Most of this additional CO_2 is released by burning fossil fuels, where carbon has been stored for millions of years. CO_2 is a greenhouse gas (see p.70) so excess leads to a rise in the average temperature of Earth's atmosphere and changing climates (see p.83).

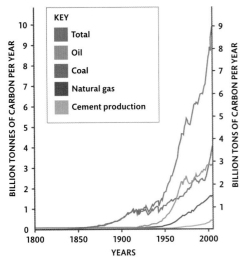

KEY
- Total
- Oil
- Coal
- Natural gas
- Cement production

BILLION TONNES OF CARBON PER YEAR / BILLION TONS OF CARBON PER YEAR — YEARS (1800, 1850, 1900, 1950, 2000)

Adding carbon to the atmosphere
Most carbon dioxide of human origin in the atmosphere has been added since 1950, by burning fossil fuels and producing cement, which involves roasting carbonate minerals.

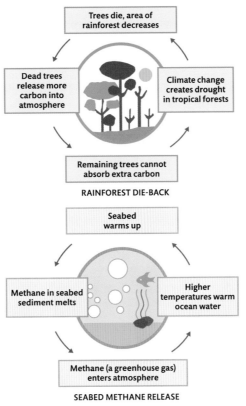

Trees die, area of rainforest decreases

Dead trees release more carbon into atmosphere

Climate change creates drought in tropical forests

Remaining trees cannot absorb extra carbon

RAINFOREST DIE-BACK

Seabed warms up

Methane in seabed sediment melts

Higher temperatures warm ocean water

Methane (a greenhouse gas) enters atmosphere

SEABED METHANE RELEASE

Vicious circles
The increase in Earth's temperature is creating feedback loops in the carbon cycle. Some, such as increased rates of photosynthesis by plants and plankton, offset artificial

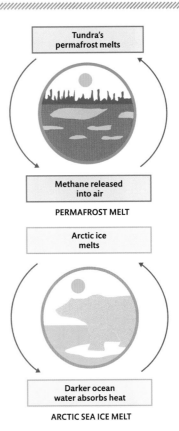

Tundra's permafrost melts

Methane released into air

PERMAFROST MELT

Arctic ice melts

Darker ocean water absorbs heat

ARCTIC SEA ICE MELT

climate change and have a regulating effect. In contrast, positive feedback loops (above) are vicious circles. They result in a further increase in atmospheric carbon—and a further increase in temperature.

Carbon capture

To reduce the buildup of atmospheric CO_2 and slow global warming, it is not enough to reduce or even halt emissions. Experts are therefore developing methods of actively removing CO_2 from the air and sequestering it, which means isolating it in an inert form that will not return to the atmosphere.

New and replanted forests
If forests are replaced or replanted, the growing trees capture carbon from the atmosphere as they grow and store it in biomass.

Carbon dioxide is absorbed

Soil storage
Biochar is charcoal made by heating plant waste, preventing it from decomposing. Adding it to soil makes the soil an effective long-term carbon store.

Ocean fertilization
Adding vast quantities of iron-rich chemicals will boost the growth of algae in the oceans. Their remains will add to natural carbon sinks.

Bioenergy and carbon capture
Plant matter absorbs carbon as it grows. If it is burned in power stations with carbon-capture technology, no CO_2 is released.

Carbon captured and sequestered

Enhanced weathering
Minerals that react with dissolved CO_2 in rain water could be crushed and spread on land, accelerating this natural process, which carries carbon to the seabed.

Direct air capture (DAC)
New technologies could take carbon dioxide gas from the air. No system has yet proven to be effective on an industrial scale.

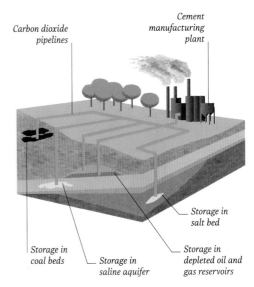

Carbon dioxide pipelines

Cement manufacturing plant

Storage in salt bed

Storage in coal beds

Storage in saline aquifer

Storage in depleted oil and gas reservoirs

Captured carbon storage
Instead of releasing the carbon dioxide produced by power plants and cement factories, it can be captured, liquidized, and sequestered in artificial carbon sinks, such as abandoned mines and oil fields.

see also Organic chemistry pp.208–209 ▶ Environmental chemistry pp.212–13 ▶ Respiration and metabolism pp.222–23 ▶ Energy pp.262–63 ▶

The web of life

No species survives independently of other organisms in its habitat. Together, all living things are interconnected, creating an intricate web of life. The most obvious connections between them are food chains, where one species eats another, and so on. Additionally, there are various types of partnerships where unrelated species help each other survive.

Top predators are very rare; a **snow leopard** may range over **77 sq miles** (200 sq km)

Interactions between species

Every organism has to secure the resources and living space it needs to survive and reproduce. To do so, it must compete with others of its own species, but it may also have to compete with similar species in its habitat and avoid or resist getting eaten by predators or consumers. Some organisms have strong pairwise bonds with other species and live in intimate associations called symbiosis. A symbiosis, which means "living together," can benefit both partners, or may be neutral or harmful to one of them.

KEY
→ Benefits from relationship
→ Harmed by relationship

Types of interactions

Interactions can be classified according to the relative harm and benefit to each participant. Symbiosis, the close interaction between two species, includes both cooperative relationships (mutualism) and parasitic ones.

COMPETITION

VULTURE — Vultures and hyenas are both scavengers and compete with each other for the same kinds of food. — **HYENA**

PREDATION

TIGER — Predator and prey are in an evolutionary arms race. Tigers try to kill goats, which try to evade capture. — **GOAT**

PARASITISM

TICK — A tick takes food from its host, a hedgehog, which is weakened but not killed by the relationship. — **HEDGEHOG**

MUTUALISM

FLOWERING PLANT — Both species benefit. A flower provides food for a bee, which transfers pollen between blooms. — **BEE**

PREDATOR–PREY CYCLE

In certain conditions, populations of a predator species and its prey follow a cycle. As the prey population grows, so do numbers of predators, but more predators result in a drop in prey abundance. The predator population crashes, which allows the prey to recover, and the cycle repeats.

KEY
— Hare population — Lynx population

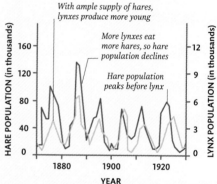

With ample supply of hares, lynxes produce more young

More lynxes eat more hares, so hare population declines

Hare population peaks before lynx

Niches

Every species is adapted by its anatomy and behavior to exploit its habitat uniquely, so in theory, no two species share the same feeding niche. For example, waders' bills vary in length and shape according to diet.

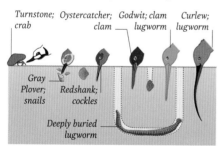

Turnstone; crab *Oystercatcher; clam* *Godwit; clam lugworm* *Curlew; lugworm*

Gray Plover; snails *Redshank; cockles*

Deeply buried lugworm

RESOURCE PARTITIONING IN WADING BIRDS

GAIA HYPOTHESIS

Presented in the 1970s by British chemist James Lovelock and American biologist Lynn Margulis, this idea shows how all of the biological and physical activities on Earth interact to create a self-regulating biosphere that maintains the stable conditions needed for life.

Ecological levels

The natural world can be understood and investigated at several levels or scales. The smallest scale is an individual organism of a particular species, and the largest is the entire biosphere—all of the parts of the Earth that support life. In between there are collections of organisms of various complexity.

Ecological scale

Each ecological level reveals different phenomena about how living things interact, survive, and evolve—and how they may be made extinct by environmental damage.

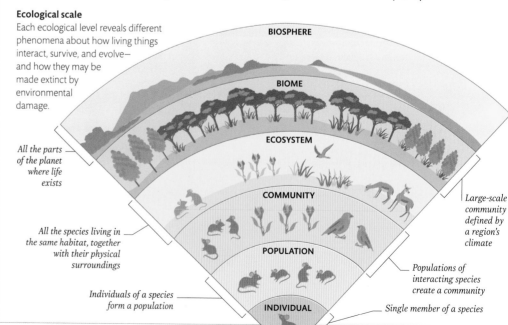

BIOSPHERE
BIOME
ECOSYSTEM
COMMUNITY
POPULATION
INDIVIDUAL

All the parts of the planet where life exists

All the species living in the same habitat, together with their physical surroundings

Individuals of a species form a population

Large-scale community defined by a region's climate

Populations of interacting species create a community

Single member of a species

The White-tailed Eagle occupies the same ecological niche in Eurasia as the Bald Eagle does in North America

Food web

In every community, one population of organisms feeds on another, creating a web of connections between species. Photosynthetic species, such as plants and algae, do not eat food. They are autotrophs, or primary producers, and form the starting point of a food web. Animals are consumers of food, or heterotrophs.

Trophic levels

Members of a food web are positioned by what they eat and what eats them. Primary producers are at one end, and top predators with no natural enemies are at the other.

PRIMARY PRODUCERS	PRIMARY CONSUMERS	SECONDARY CONSUMERS	HUNTERS	TOP PREDATORS

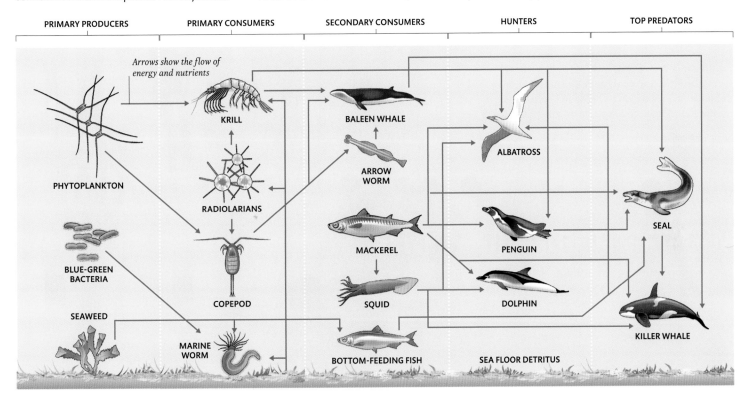

Arrows show the flow of energy and nutrients

KRILL · BALEEN WHALE · ALBATROSS · PHYTOPLANKTON · ARROW WORM · RADIOLARIANS · SEAL · BLUE-GREEN BACTERIA · MACKEREL · PENGUIN · COPEPOD · SQUID · DOLPHIN · SEAWEED · MARINE WORM · BOTTOM-FEEDING FISH · SEA FLOOR DETRITUS · KILLER WHALE

Chemoautotrophs

The food web around a hydrothermal vent, or black smoker, on the dark seabed is not based on a photosynthetic organism. Instead, it starts with chemoautotrophs that extract energy from chemicals in the water.

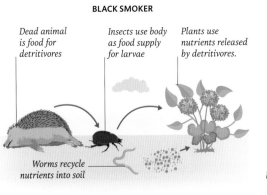

Mineral deposits create a chimney

Dark "smoky" water contains chemicals used by bacteria

Tube worms house chemoautotrophic bacteria

Shrimps consume bacteria

Crabs are secondary consumers

BLACK SMOKER

Detritivores

All food webs include detritivores, or "waste eaters"—animals that ingest and digest dead organisms and animal waste internally. Fungi and bacteria are decomposers, which means they break down and absorb nutrients from organic matter through external chemical and biological processes.

Dead animal is food for detritivores

Insects use body as food supply for larvae

Plants use nutrients released by detritivores.

Worms recycle nutrients into soil

RECYCLING NUTRIENTS

Energy pyramid

Ecologists picture the distribution of energy and biomass (living material) in a food web using an energy pyramid. Only a small proportion—about 10 percent—of the energy passes from one trophic level to the next. This is why there are always fewer predators than prey.

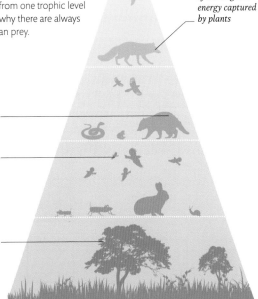

Top predators can access only a tiny fraction of the original energy captured by plants

Secondary consumers include omnivores (which eat both plants and animals)

Primary consumers, or herbivores, make up the majority of animal biomass

Energy enters the pyramid as it is captured by primary producers, almost exclusively from sunlight

see also The story of life pp.86–87 ▶   Types of living things pp.216–17 ▶   Evolution pp.228–29 ▶

Environmental impact

Human activities have an impact on ecosystems. More often than not, those artificial changes damage the abilities of wildlife communities to coexist in ways that have evolved gradually over many generations. Some species benefit from human activities, swell in numbers, and become pests, but many more species become endangered by human impact.

Since 1970, human activities have reduced wild animal populations on average by 60 percent

Pollution

Pollution is the result of something added to the environment in excessive amounts so that it has a harmful effect on an ecosystem. The most familiar pollutants are chemicals added to soil, water, and air, but sound, light, and heat can also be pollution.

Polluted water courses

Toxic chemicals kill wildlife if added to rivers, but any biologically active chemicals, such as medicines and farm fertilizers, can also cause pollution. The excess nutrients in fertilizers do not benefit natural flora, but boost algal growth at the expense of other species.

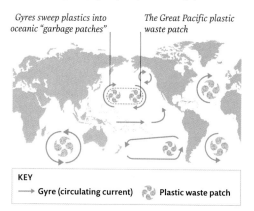

- Carbon dioxide, 80% of greenhouse gas emissions
- Methane, 10%
- Nitrous oxide, 7%
- Tetrafluoroethane
- Carbon tetrafluoride — F gases, 3%
- Trichlorofluoromethane

GREENHOUSE GASES

Atmospheric pollution

Some gases added to the air cause acid rain and smog. Others add to the Greenhouse Effect. Some artificial greenhouse gases (F gases) are potent in tiny quantities.

Gyres sweep plastics into oceanic "garbage patches"

The Great Pacific plastic waste patch

KEY

→ Gyre (circulating current) ⬰ Plastic waste patch

Plastic in the sea

Over 9 billion tons (8 million tonnes) of plastic is dumped in the ocean every year. It does not rot. Fragments enter the food chain and accumulate in seafloor sediments.

Chemical fertilizers added to fields to help crops grow

Fertilizers washed into rivers

Farm animal waste enters rivers

Streams and springs deliver nutrients and oxygen to lake

Human waste enters water

Clean water supports diverse wildlife

Nutrients boost algal growth

Algal bloom blocks out light, then dies and decays, which consumes oxygen

Water becomes "eutrophic" (full of nutrients), but deoxygenated

EUTROPHICATED WATER SYSTEM

CLEAN WATER SYSTEM

Habitat damage

Human activity can destroy natural habitats, replacing them with urban development or farmland. Habitats can also be damaged by being fragmented and degraded. This is most evident in complex habitats such as rainforests, where there are many specific species that cannot adapt even to small changes.

Humans have cut down 46 percent of all forest habitats on Earth

Forests burned to make space for crops

Destruction
Rainforest is cleared by people to make way for fields and animal pastures. Natural vegetation and animal habitats are lost.

Road presents barrier

Small patch of habitat may not sustain species with large ranges

Fragmentation
Access roads divide up the remaining forests. The fragmented habitat is not as diverse as a single patch with the same area.

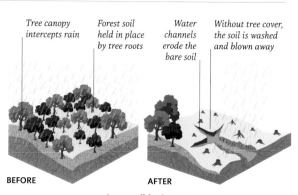

Tree canopy intercepts rain

Forest soil held in place by tree roots

Water channels erode the bare soil

Without tree cover, the soil is washed and blown away

BEFORE

AFTER

Irreversible damage
Converting tropical rainforest to farmland is an unsustainable change. The forest soil is thin, and nutrients are cycled through it very fast by the trees. After a few years of farming, the land becomes infertile. But even if abandoned, the land may not return to forest for centuries, due to irreversible soil erosion.

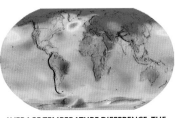

Between 1880–2020, average **sea level rose about 9 in** (24 cm) due to **glacier melt** and **thermal expansion**

Climate change

Climate change is not only global warming, but also the associated changes in weather patterns, observed and predicted. It is being driven by the addition of carbon dioxide and other greenhouse gases to the atmosphere (see p.79). This enhances the Greenhouse Effect (see p.70), which traps Earth's heat. During the 20th century, Earth's average temperature rose about 1.4°F (0.8°C), and it is predicted to continue rising.

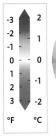

AVERAGE TEMPERATURE DIFFERENCE: THE PERIOD 2015–19 COMPARED TO 1951–80

Extreme weather

The frequency of climate-related disasters, such as storms, floods, and wildfires, increased in 1980–2015, while the rate of other natural disasters was unchanged. The suspected cause is global warming—a greater amount of heat energy in the atmosphere drives more energetic storms and sends the weather into more violent patterns.

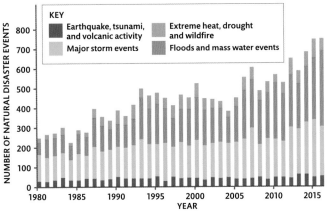

KEY
- Earthquake, tsunami, and volcanic activity
- Major storm events
- Extreme heat, drought and wildfire
- Floods and mass water events

NUMBER OF NATURAL DISASTER EVENTS — YEAR (1980–2015)

Uneven heating

Global warming is not even—northern areas are warming more quickly. The average temperature increase is small, but the temperature range is also increasing in these regions, resulting in much higher maximum temperatures.

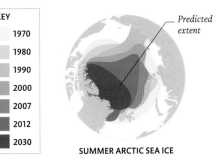

KEY
- 1970
- 1980
- 1990
- 2000
- 2007
- 2012
- 2030

Predicted extent

SUMMER ARCTIC SEA ICE

Coral bleaching

When coral is stressed by higher ocean temperature and acidity, it bleaches. The acidity is caused by more dissolved carbon dioxide. If bleaching is repeated and persistent, the coral dies.

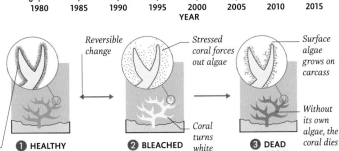

Algae live inside healthy coral, providing nutrients

1 HEALTHY CORAL

Reversible change

Coral turns white

2 BLEACHED CORAL

Stressed coral forces out algae

Surface algae grows on carcass

Without its own algae, the coral dies

3 DEAD CORAL

Arctic sea ice

The area of sea ice covering the Arctic Ocean grows in winter and shrinks in summer. The extent of summer ice cover has reduced since 1970, as Arctic temperatures rise. The ocean could be ice-free in summer by 2100.

Feeding the world

About one-third of Earth's land surface is used to grow food. As the human population rises, so does demand. Farmers increase production by increasing the area of farmland or using chemical fertilizer and pesticides to boost yields, and both these strategies damage the natural world.

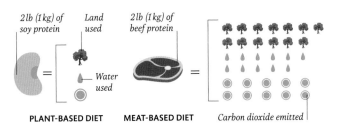

2 lb (1 kg) of soy protein — *Land used* — *2 lb (1 kg) of beef protein*

Water used

PLANT-BASED DIET **MEAT-BASED DIET** *Carbon dioxide emitted*

Impact of eating meat

Plant foods can be produced much more efficiently. Beef production requires 13 times more land, 11 times more water, and emits 10 times more CO₂ than producing soybeans.

HUMAN POPULATION

Natural populations are limited by factors in an ecosystem, such as the availability of food, space, and threats of disease and predators. Human civilization has been able to mitigate these limitations with medicine and technology, and as a result, the global population of the species has been able to grow exponentially. However, the population is predicted to plateau in the middle of this century.

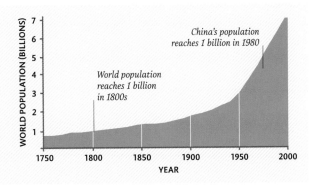

China's population reaches 1 billion in 1980

World population reaches 1 billion in 1800s

WORLD POPULATION (BILLIONS) — YEAR (1750–2000)

Biodiversity

It is thought that there are about 9 million species of organisms on Earth—and potentially many more. Much of this diversity is contributed by species that live only in small and isolated ecosystems. About one-quarter of all species that have been assessed are at risk of extinction.

Endangered organisms

Animals at risk of extinction, such as these two, are conserved by protecting their habitat, banning hunting, and helping them breed.

Population less than 250

Critically endangered

KAKAPO
(Strigops habroptila)

SUMATRAN ORANGUTAN
(Pongo abelii)

Extinction

The extinction rate has seen a ten times increase due to human activities. At least 900 plant and animal species have been made extinct by people.

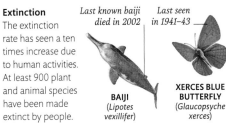

Last known baiji died in 2002

Last seen in 1941–43

BAIJI
(Lipotes vexillifer)

XERCES BLUE BUTTERFLY
(Glaucopsyche xerces)

◀ see also Biomes pp.76–77   ◀ The carbon cycle pp.78–79   ◀ The web of life pp.80–81   Environmental chemistry pp.212–13 ▶

Life

The story of life

Life is more than 4 billion years old, first emerging when Earth was only one-tenth of its present age. As the hot new planet cooled and oceans formed, the first life emerged—probably deep under water in stable environments near the young ocean floor. Within a few million years, the first living cells had evolved into microbes—and for billions of years after that,

the world belonged only to them. Bigger, more complex life-forms—multicellular life—evolved only in the last billion years of Earth's history. These are the organisms that evolved into the familiar plants and animals of recent times. It was then that life could emerge from the microscopic and would fill the oceans and land with greenery and fast-moving creatures.

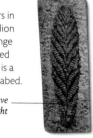

Before tectonic mountain building, high land is formed by crater rims

Crust still mainly hot and unstable

EARTH AROUND 4.4–4.2 BYA

Early seas may have filled craters

4.4–4.2 BYA
The first permanent oceans form over 4 BYA (billion years ago), providing the first habitat for life.

Backward-facing spine, one of two pairs

Short, broad antenna, one of two pairs of antennae

Twenty-six segments, each with a pair of legs and gill branches

635–541 MYA A wave of experimental evolution occurs in the ocean from 600 MYA (million years ago) and produces a range of early animals, together called the Ediacaran Fauna. *Charnia* is a plantlike example from the seabed.

541–485 MYA
The "Cambrian Explosion" of animal life occurs, with rapid evolution of animals into many different body forms, including early arthropods, such as *Marrella*.

Fronds may have captured sunlight

CHARNIA FOSSIL

MARRELLA

Branched, feathery gill

Long, thin antenna

Stiff but flexible body

Chevron-shaped blocks of muscle

HAIKOUICHTHYS

530 MYA The oldest known vertebrate—a fish called *Haikouichthys*—leaves fossilized remains. It swims using a stiff but flexible rod called a notochord that would later evolve into a backbone.

419–359 MYA
A flowering of several major types of fishes gives this period the name "The Age of Fishes." Vertebrate jaws first evolve, as shown by the giant predator, *Dunkleosteus*.

DUNKLEOSTEUS

Large eyes aided nocturnal lifestyle

Low crouch helped animal to leap out of danger

Long tail, typical of sauropods

Broad ribcage

Neck made up of long vertebrae

MEGAZOSTRODON

225–201 MYA Mammals evolve from their reptilian ancestors. One of the earliest mammals is *Megazostrodon*, from the start of the Jurassic, 201 MYA.

Upright gait

SAUROPOD DINOSAUR
Barapasaurus

252–66 MYA
During the "Age of Reptiles," dinosaurs dominate on land, pterosaurs in the air, and ichthyosaurs, plesiosaurs, pliosaurs, and others dominate the ocean.

Long tail supported by bone, unlike modern birds

Mouth full of teeth, like non-avian dinosaurs

160–150 MYA The earliest known birds emerge, notably *Archaeopteryx* (150 MYA), but also related animals such as *Aurornis* (160 MYA). These animals evolved gradually from birdlike dinosaurs.

66 MYA A mass extinction kills nonflying dinosaurs, pterosaurs, and large sea reptiles. The blame probably lies with an asteroid, which leaves traces of a crater now buried in Mexico.

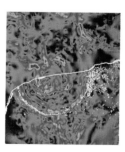

CHICXULUB CRATER, MEXICO

ARCHAEOPTERYX

Flight feathers are asymmetrical, like those of modern birds

 ◄ see also Inside Earth pp.46–47   ◄ Evolving planet pp.50–51   ◄ The web of life pp.80–81

Fossil trackways are signs that unidentified arthropods invaded land 530 million years ago

4.2–3.5 BYA Life arises from nonliving matter. Self-assembling molecules build the first cells, which reproduce simply by splitting into two.

RNA (ancestor of DNA)

PARENT CELL SPLITTING

Each daughter cell contains its parent's RNA

Cell membrane

DAUGHTER CELLS

DNA occurs in closed loops

BACTERIA

Flagellum

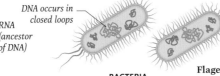

2.9–2.6 BYA The simplest organisms alive today—bacteria—invade land. Soils rich in organic matter date back 2.9 million years, while the first fossil soil-surface bacteria are 2.6 million years old.

2.2–1.5 BYA Complex cells, with DNA wrapped up in a nucleus, first evolve, probably by bacteria combining with other simple cells. Life is more complex, but it is still single-celled.

Diatom is a single-celled marine alga

Many marine microbes have spines that prevent sinking

COMPLEX CELLS

Diatoms range in shape from cigars to rugby balls

1.6–1.05 BYA The earliest fossils of multicellular life appear. One of these, from 1.05 billion years ago, belongs to a red seaweed, *Bangiomorpha*. It is named after the very similar modern seaweed, *Bangia*.

Individual cells

Cells connected in filaments

BANGIA

2.4–2.1 BYA Some microbes invent photosynthesis and gradually fill the air with oxygen—previously absent from the atmosphere. Many microbes go extinct, but new ones emerge.

Oxygen released into air

Mushroom-shaped colonies of microbes

Iron-rich rocks react with oxygen and form red bands

DURING OXYGENATION

Old microbes go extinct

Sky turns blue

New, oxygen-loving microbes thrive

Evidence is buried

AFTER OXYGENATION

385–359 MYA Fossilized trees are first preserved as fossils and provide evidence of the first forests. Early trees include *Archaeopteris*, which had dense wood similar to that of some modern conifers.

Modern coniferlike outline

ARCHAEOPTERIS

375 MYA The first land vertebrates—tetrapods—evolve from lobe-finned fishes, which had fins on short bony supports. The first tetrapods had various numbers of digits (toes), but eventually, the standard number became five.

Humerus
Radius
Ulna
Fin ray

LOBE-FINNED FISH

Limb bones evolved from fin stalk bones

Digits evolved from fin rays

EARLY TETRAPOD

Five digits

LATER TETRAPOD

Compound eye with many facets

Wingspan reached 27 in (69 cm)

Wing made of a substance called chitin

---

252 MYA The greatest mass extinction ever, called the Great Dying, kills off 90 percent of plant species, 70 percent of terrestrial animals, and 96 percent of marine species, including the last trilobites. Rare survivors on land include the dicynodont reptiles.

Kidney-shaped eye

TRILOBITE
Ditomopyge

Spines projected from head

Barrel-shaped body digested plant food

Tough, horny beak

DICYNODONT
Lystrosaurus

359–299 MYA The Carboniferous is a period of warm, wet climate globally. Swampy forests decay to form coal, while insects such as *Meganeura* (a griffinfly, related to dragonflies) grow enormous, possibly connected with high levels of oxygen in the atmosphere.

Abdomen of 10 segments, like modern dragonflies

MEGANEURA

Giant beak may have cracked nuts and seeds

Body same size as the carnivorous terror birds, at 6 ft 6 in (2 m) tall

FLIGHTLESS BIRD
Gastornis

65–30 MYA New animals evolve, replacing those lost in the mass extinction. The first large land predators are giant "terror birds." Mammals diversify into hoofed types and many others.

Even-toed hoofed feet

HOOFED MAMMAL
Mesoreodon

2.6 MYA Earth enters the most recent of many ice ages, known as the Pleistocene Ice Age. It lasts until 10,000 years ago. Thickly furred mammals live in tundra habitats beside the ice.

Shaggy outer hairs over dense undercoat

Front horn 3 ft (1 m) long

WOOLLY RHINOCEROS

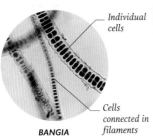

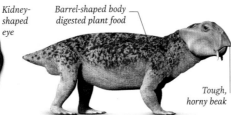

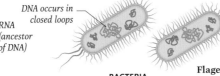

see also The plant kingdom pp.96–97 ▶ The animal kingdom pp.106–107 ▶ Types of living things pp.216–17 ▶

Prehistoric plants

The invasion of land

Plants evolved from freshwater algae when they began to invade land. At least 470 MYA (million years ago), algae developed drought-resistant spores, probably as a way of dispersing to other ponds or rivers or for waiting out dry spells. To become land plants, however, they needed further adaptations, including a cuticle (a waterproof covering) with stomata (openings) that allowed intake of carbon dioxide.

Pioneer

Aglaophyton evolved around 410 MYA and was similar to the first land plants. It might have had a cuticle and stomata but, like today's mosses, it did not have stiffened vascular (water transport) tissues.

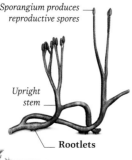

Sporangium produces reproductive spores

Upright stem

Rootlets

Water uptake and support

Land plants needed fast uptake of water to replace water lost through stomata, and they developed vascular tissue—water transport vessels. The vessels needed to resist collapse, so they were stiffened with lignin (the stiff substance in wood).

ANNULAR **SPIRAL** **LADDER-LIKE** **BORDERED**

Supporting vessels

The vessels that evolved for water transport became thickened in different patterns. Their stiffness gave plants support, allowing them to grow upward.

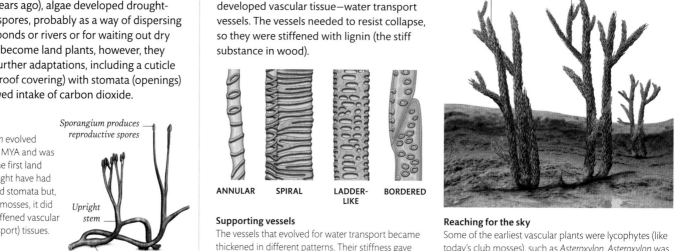

Covering of small, scalelike "leaves"

Main shoot has side branches at intervals

Reaching for the sky

Some of the earliest vascular plants were lycophytes (like today's club mosses), such as *Asteroxylon*. *Asteroxylon* was one of the tallest plants 410 MYA, at 20 in (50 cm) high.

HOW FOSSILS FORM

Fossils can reveal fine details of the biological structure of long-extinct life forms. They form if dead plants or animals are buried before their bodies decompose, in which case their tissues can be turned to stone over millions of years. Plants growing in swamps, mangroves, or river floodplains are frequently buried during floods or storm tides.

1 Living tree
Trees in river floodplains, swamps, or mangroves live in habitats often inundated by water.

2 Recently dead tree
As a dead tree falls, it may be buried, before it rots, by mud or sand brought by flood water.

3 Fossilized tree
Mineral-rich water seeps through the buried tree's porous tissues, depositing rock-forming minerals.

4 Exposed fossil
The tree, now turned to rock, may be exposed if the overlying rock is worn away by erosion.

Trees

Plants with strong support tissue included ancestors of today's ferns, club mosses, and horsetails. Some examples of all these types grew to be several feet tall, becoming the first trees. Plants also diversified into many groups now long extinct. One group, the progymnosperms, included the first plants to develop dense wood and true leaves.

The trees that formed the first coal forests were not conifers, but giant club mosses

Fernlike fronds reached a height of 26 ft (8 m)

Scars left by shed fronds

Frondlike branches, some bearing capsules containing spores

Trunk formed from dense wood

Up to 65 ft (20 m) tall

Growth form resembles modern horsetails

Crown up to 130 ft (40 m) high

Bark bore distinctive pattern of diamond-shaped scars

Eospermatopteris
One of the earliest trees was *Eospermatopteris*, a fernlike plant living around 400 MYA.

Archaeopteris
The progymnosperm *Archaeopteris* formed the first forests on a global scale, 385 MYA.

Calamites
Giant treelike horsetails called *Calamites* grew in the Carboniferous period, 350 MYA.

Lepidodendron
Dominating the swampy coal forests of the Carboniferous was the giant club moss, *Lepidodendron*.

The **colonization of land** by plants has happened **only once** in Earth's history

Seed plants

Seeds were a quantum leap in the evolution of plants. Their appearance around 360 MYA occurred together with the evolution of pollen—both adaptations broke plants' reliance on water bodies and freed them to colonize the entire land.

NON-SEED PLANTS

Before pollen, all plants reproduced by releasing spores, like ferns and mosses do today. Spores grow into gametophytes, which release sperm into water or moist soil. If a sperm fertilizes the egg of another gametophyte, a new fern grows.

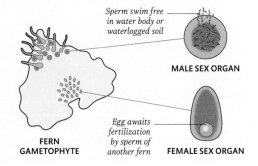

Sperm swim free in water body or waterlogged soil

MALE SEX ORGAN

FERN GAMETOPHYTE

Egg awaits fertilization by sperm of another fern

FEMALE SEX ORGAN

Pollen organ of the Carboniferous seed plant Potoniea

Fossil seeds from the early seed plant Medullosa (300 MYA)

Pollen
Pollen lands on an adult plant and fertilizes its ovules (eggs) directly or by sperm swimming in the plant's tissues. Some seed plants produced pollen in special organs.

Seeds
Seeds are water-resistant capsules containing an embryonic plant, which can remain dormant, developing only when it reaches a suitable environment.

Types of early seed plants

The first seed plants were called seed ferns, because of the shape of their leaves, but they are unrelated to today's ferns. Lacking true cones or flowers, they grew their seeds in packages of ovules on their leaves.

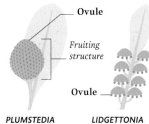

Ovule

Fruiting structure

Ovule

Cupule containing an ovule

PLUMSTEDIA   LIDGETTONIA   DENKANIA

Conifers and relatives

Seed plants developed seed cones, which gave seeds protection. Conifers (cone-bearing plants) appeared around 320 MYA. As dry conditions prevailed in the Permian period (299–252 MYA), conifers took over and diversified, along with other new groups, together called the gymnosperms.

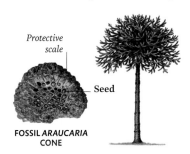

Protective scale

Seed

FOSSIL *ARAUCARIA* CONE

Petallike bract

Central receptacle

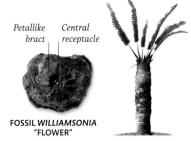

FOSSIL *WILLIAMSONIA* "FLOWER"

Monkey puzzle
Araucaria, which still lives today as the familiar monkey puzzle tree, was a widespread conifer in the Jurassic period (201–145 MYA).

Bennettitaleans
One group of gymnosperms called the bennettitaleans developed structures much like flowers. *Williamsonia* is an example from the Jurassic.

Flowers

True flowers evolved around 120 MYA, in the latter half of the age of the dinosaurs (see pp.90–91). Angiosperms (flowering plants) had broad, veined leaves and flowers, which produced pollen, seeds, or both. The seeds developed inside a fruit. Angiosperms diversified alongside the later dinosaurs, but branched out further after the dinosaurs' extinction, and formed the first closed-canopy forests by 56 MYA.

Showy flower
In this magnolialike plant from 100 MYA, the flowers are large and conspicuous— evidence that angiosperms were already attracting insects for pollination.

Tightly packed follicles containing seeds

Petallike perianth

Broad leaf

ARCHAEANTHUS

Prominent midrib

Grass and grasslands

Grasses first evolved around 55 MYA (in the Paleogene period), but it was not until the climate became cooler and drier 15–9 MYA (in the Neogene period) that grasslands became an extensive habitat. Grasses' secrets of success included their wind-pollinated flowers and their growth from the base, which allowed them to continue to grow and spread into a ground-covering mat despite being cropped at their tips by grazing animals.

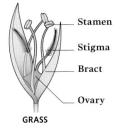

Stamen

Stigma

Bract

Ovary

GRASS FLOWER

Tropical grassland, 1 MYA
The spread of grasslands created a new habitat. Grass formed the base of new food chains featuring grazers both large (hoofed mammals) and small (termites).

Wildebeests are typical large, fast-running mammals of grasslands

Grazed grasses form ground cover

Trees dot grassland habitats in the tropics

Termite nest

see also Flowering plants pp.100–103 ▶   Reproduction pp.226–27 ▶

The age of dinosaurs

Ruling reptiles

The Mesozoic Era (252–66 MYA, million years ago), was dominated by large reptiles. Dinosaurs represent just one of many groups. Reptiles in the sea were not closely related to dinosaurs and included turtles, plesiosaurs, crocodilians, and even giant lizards. The winged reptiles were relatives of dinosaurs called pterosaurs. On land, dinosaurs were joined by numerous other reptiles, including the ancestors of today's lizards and crocodiles.

Bristlelike feathers may have been present

Forward-facing eyes typical of a predator

Nostrils led to highly developed olfactory (smell) organs

Serrated teeth, common to most theropod dinosaurs

Animal walked on the tips of three toes

Hallux, or dew claw

TYRANNOSAURUS

Evolution of the dinosaur

Early in the Mesozoic, many types of large reptiles emerged. Among these were the archosaurs, a group that includes today's crocodiles. Some archosaurs evolved in a different direction, developing not only an upright gait, but also bipedalism (walking on two legs). Dinosaurs evolved from such a group of advanced, bipedal archosaurs.

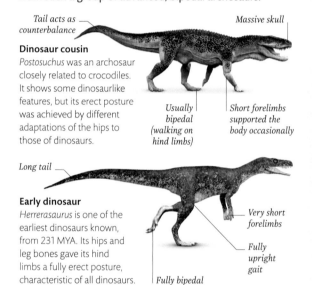

Tail acts as counterbalance

Massive skull

Dinosaur cousin

Postosuchus was an archosaur closely related to crocodiles. It shows some dinosaurlike features, but its erect posture was achieved by different adaptations of the hips to those of dinosaurs.

Usually bipedal (walking on hind limbs)

Short forelimbs supported the body occasionally

Long tail

Early dinosaur

Herrerasaurus is one of the earliest dinosaurs known, from 231 MYA. Its hips and leg bones gave its hind limbs a fully erect posture, characteristic of all dinosaurs.

Very short forelimbs

Fully upright gait

Fully bipedal

UPRIGHT STANCE

As archosaurs evolved, some began to stand upright, and, unlike the sprawling legs of lizards and crocodiles, their legs supported the body high above the ground, allowing agile and efficient running.

Sprawling leg

LIZARD STANCE

Intermediate gait

CROCODILIAN STANCE

Upright leg

DINOSAUR STANCE

Sea reptiles

Monstrous reptilian predators populated the Mesozoic seas. Except for turtles and crocodilians, they all went extinct along with the dinosaurs. The largest grew to giant size—*Mosasaurus* could reach lengths greater than 43 ft (13 m).

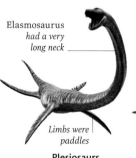

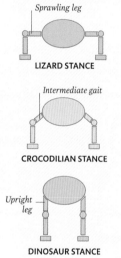

Ophthalmosaurus had very large eyes

Ichthyosaurs

These streamlined, dolphin-shaped hunters swam with a sharklike tail and gave birth to young in water.

Liopleurodon had crocodilelike teeth

Tail of Mosasaurus probably ended in a sharklike fluke

Elasmosaurus had a very long neck

Limbs were paddles

Mosasaurs

Giant marine lizards called mosasaurs evolved from small lizards that lived on land.

Plesiosaurs

These carnivorous reptiles swam with four flippers. Many had long necks and small heads.

Pliosaurs

These predators were a type of plesiosaur, but had short necks and huge heads with powerful jaws.

Pterosaurs

The first vertebrates to evolve powered flight, these reptiles appeared around 228 MYA. Early pterosaurs had short necks and long tails. Later species, the pterodactyloids, had greater agility in the air due to their short tail and long-necked body.

Short neck

Long tail

RHAMPHORHYNCHUS

Wing held taut by a single finger

Flight surface made of skin

Long neck

QUETZALCOATLUS

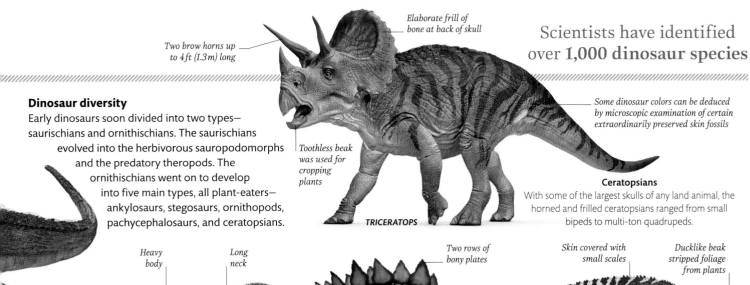

Two brow horns up
to 4 ft (1.3 m) long

Elaborate frill of
bone at back of skull

Scientists have identified
over **1,000 dinosaur species**

Dinosaur diversity

Early dinosaurs soon divided into two types—
saurischians and ornithischians. The saurischians
evolved into the herbivorous sauropodomorphs
and the predatory theropods. The
ornithischians went on to develop
into five main types, all plant-eaters—
ankylosaurs, stegosaurs, ornithopods,
pachycephalosaurs, and ceratopsians.

Toothless beak
was used for
cropping
plants

Some dinosaur colors can be deduced
by microscopic examination of certain
extraordinarily preserved skin fossils

TRICERATOPS

Ceratopsians
With some of the largest skulls of any land animal, the
horned and frilled ceratopsians ranged from small
bipeds to multi-ton quadrupeds.

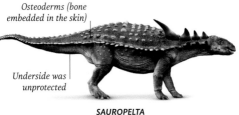

Heavy
body

Long
neck

Long tail

DIPLODOCUS

Sauropodomorphs
Early species (prosauropods) were bipedal, but most later
members of this group (sauropods) walked on four legs
and had a long neck and tail. Some became gigantic.

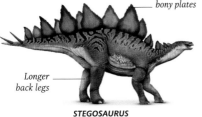

Two rows of
bony plates

Longer
back legs

STEGOSAURUS

Stegosaurs
With plates and spikes running down their backs and tail,
and occasionally protruding from their shoulders, these
large herbivores were well defended.

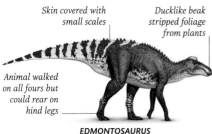

Skin covered with
small scales

Ducklike beak
stripped foliage
from plants

Animal walked
on all fours but
could rear on
hind legs

EDMONTOSAURUS

Ornithopods
Some of these hugely successful and varied herbivores
had showy crests for display and hundreds of plant-
crushing teeth. Smaller species walked on two legs.

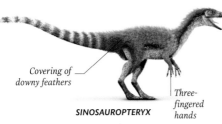

Osteoderms (bone
embedded in the skin)

Underside was
unprotected

SAUROPELTA

Ankylosaurs
Various bony plates and spikes armed the wide bodies
of these herbivorous dinosaurs. Many species also
wielded a bony club at the end of the tail.

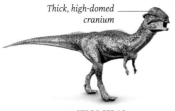

Covering of
downy feathers

Three-
fingered
hands

SINOSAUROPTERYX

Theropods
Theropods were bipedal, like the first dinosaurs. They
ranged from small, birdlike animals to *Tyrannosaurus rex*.
Nearly all were predators, but some ate plants.

Thick, high-domed
cranium

STEGOCERAS

Pachycephalosaurs
These bipedal plant-eaters had heads made for combat,
with flattened or dome-shaped skulls up to 10 in (25 cm)
thick, which protected the brain from heavy blows.

Evolution of birds

Biologists regard birds as flying
dinosaurs that evolved from
nonflying theropods more than
150 MYA. Close relatives of birds,
such as *Velociraptor*, had swiveling
wrist joints like those of birds.
Anchiornis, like *Archaeopteryx* (see
p.86), could fly weakly. *Liaoxiornis*
had more powerful flight muscles.

EVOLUTION OF FEATHERS

Feathers began as filamentous
or tufty structures that may have
insulated dinosaurs. Later, some
feathers developed a stiff shaft,
or rachis. Some such feathers had
barbs and barbules knitted into a
flat surface, but only those with
a shorter leading edge had the
right aerodynamics for flight.

Tuft of
barbs

Rachis

Rachis

Short
leading
edge

Unbranched
filament

Barb

Barb

Long
trailing
edge

Barbules

Probably
covered in
insulating
feathers

COMPSOGNATHUS

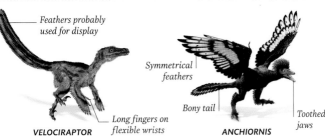

Feathers probably
used for display

Symmetrical
feathers

Bony tail

Long fingers on
flexible wrists

VELOCIRAPTOR

Toothed
jaws

ANCHIORNIS

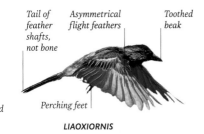

Tail of
feather
shafts,
not bone

Asymmetrical
flight feathers

Toothed
beak

Perching feet

LIAOXIORNIS

see also Reptiles pp.126–33 ▶ Birds pp.134–39 ▶ Classification pp.158–63 ▶

Prehistoric mammals

How mammals evolved

Mammals evolved from a group of mammallike reptiles called cynodonts, 230–205 million years ago (MYA), in the Triassic period. Today, mammals are defined by their furry, glandular skin, especially mammary glands, but there is no direct fossil record of these. There is an extensive record, however, of changes in the skull and teeth.

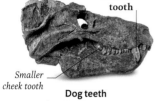

Canine tooth

Smaller cheek tooth

Dog teeth
Cynognathus, like other cynodonts, had stabbing canines (cynodont means "dog tooth"). While reptiles have uniform teeth, mammals have teeth of contrasting kinds.

Distinct waist in front of hips, like mammals

Legs held beneath body, unlike reptiles

Furry reptile
Cynodonts probably acquired fur and warm-bloodedness gradually. This cynodont, *Thrinaxodon*, is pictured as hairy, although we cannot be sure it was.

Mammalian external ear flap may have been present

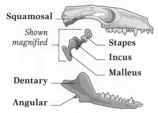

Mammal-shaped
By the late Triassic, very mammallike animals had evolved. To some experts, *Morganucodon* is a mammal. To others, it is a mammaliaform, or "mammal-shaped."

> **Mammals** had already lived for **140–160 million years** when the dinosaurs went extinct

JAW BONES TO EAR BONES
Reptiles and other vertebrates have a single ear ossicle (a tiny bone called the stapes) that transfers sound to the inner ear. Mammals evolved a better arrangement. Extra ossicles evolved from the quadrate and articular bones, which, having lost their role in the jaw hinge, linked in a chain with the stapes, forming a highly sensitive ear.

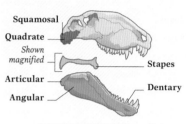

Squamosal
Quadrate
Shown magnified
Stapes
Articular
Dentary
Angular

ANCESTRAL REPTILE (*Dimetrodon*)

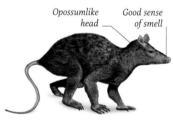

Squamosal
Shown magnified
Stapes
Incus
Malleus
Dentary
Angular

MAMMALLIKE REPTILE (Cynodont)

Mesozoic mammals

In the Mesozoic (the age of the dinosaurs—the Triassic, Jurassic, and Cretaceous periods) many mammals had only some modern mammal features. They were probably all furry, but nearly all still laid eggs. They were mainly tiny, probably nocturnal, and many were adept burrowers or climbers. Most were members of families that are now long extinct.

Slim snout

Stout chin

Still not quite a mammal
Sinoconodon, like many Mesozoic animals, had mixed features—it had mammal ear bones, but its teeth were replaced throughout life, like a reptile's.

Rodent-like gnawing incisors

Clawed toes

The beginning of gnawing
Nemegtbaatar was a multituberculate— a widespread type of mammal in the Cretaceous period. It foreshadowed rodents, with its gnawing teeth.

Walked on the soles of its feet   *Pointed teeth in front*

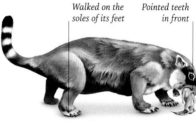

Dinosaur hunter
Most mammals that lived alongside dinosaurs were tiny. *Repenomamus*, however, was a badger-sized predator that could take baby dinosaurs.

Mouse-sized mammal   *Badger-sized mammal*

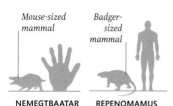

NEMEGTBAATAR   REPENOMAMUS

Tiny dinosaur neighbors
Repenomamus was much larger than average Mesozoic mammals. Most, such as *Nemegtbaatar*, were squirrel-sized or smaller.

Marsupials and placentals

Survivors of the Mesozoic included two live-bearing groups—eutherians and metatherians. Metatherians gave rise to marsupials, while some eutherians evolved into placentals.

Opossumlike head   *Good sense of smell*

Marsupials
Marsupials dispensed with eggs and gave birth directly to live young. *Alphadon* lived at least 70 MYA, but the marsupial fossil record could stretch back 125 million years.

Long, slender limbs   *Long, narrow snout*

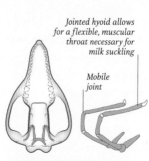

Placental mammals
Zalambdalestes was a eutherian. Eutherians gave rise in the Cretaceous to the placentals—mammals that nourish their unborn young with a placenta.

EVIDENCE OF SUCKLING
Modern mammals have a jointed bone in the throat called the hyoid that allows the flexibility needed to suckle. Most cynodonts had a rigid, reptilian hyoid, but mammaliaforms (the most mammallike cynodonts) had hyoids like those of mammals, suggesting they produced milk.

View of upper skull from below, showing position of hyoid bone

Rigid hyoid typical of reptiles, which swallow without chewing

CYNODONT (*Thrinaxodon*)

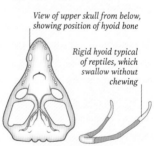

Jointed hyoid allows for a flexible, muscular throat necessary for milk suckling

Mobile joint

MAMMALIAFORM (*Microdocodon*)

After the dinosaurs

With the disappearance of most large land animals 66 million years ago, for the survivors, there were many empty niches to fill. Mammals, both marsupials and placentals, diversified, and hoofed mammals thrived. "Terror birds" (see p.87) were the first large land predators to replace carnivorous dinosaurs, in addition to predatory mammals called creodonts.

A thin, flexible tail would have brushed away biting insects

Hornlike knobs are not horn, but bony outgrowths of the skull

Upper canine elongated into a tusk, probably used in display

Feet supported by wedges of soft tissue behind the toes

EARLY HOOFED MAMMAL
Uintatherium

Rapid evolution

Within 10 million years of the death of the dinosaurs, the ancestors of most major living groups of mammals, such as primates, whales, bats, and rodents, had evolved.

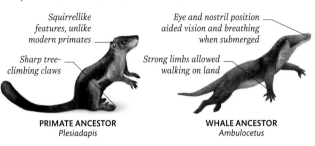

Squirrellike features, unlike modern primates

Sharp tree-climbing claws

PRIMATE ANCESTOR
Plesiadapis

Eye and nostril position aided vision and breathing when submerged

Strong limbs allowed walking on land

WHALE ANCESTOR
Ambulocetus

Long fingers support wing

Claws on first two digits

EARLY BAT
Icaronycteris

Patagium (flight membrane)

EARLY RODENT
Eomys

OUR LOST MEGAFAUNA

As recently as 20,000 years ago, Earth was much richer in large mammals, or "megafauna." Many, including the giant armadillos and ground sloths, of the Americas, went extinct at the same time as they first encountered humans. Others may have succumbed to climate change as the Ice Age ended.

Animal walked on the sides of its feet

Mouth contained sharp slicing teeth

Giant claws used to pull vegetation towards mouth

GIANT GROUND SLOTH
Megatherium

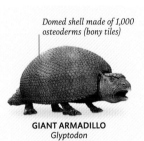

Domed shell made of 1,000 osteoderms (bony tiles)

GIANT ARMADILLO
Glyptodon

Thick fur coat

WOOLLY MAMMOTH
Mammuthus primigenius

Modern mammals

Between 40 and 10 MYA, mammals became more similar to today's. Whales lost their hind limbs and became entirely marine, horses lost all but their middle toes, and the first cats and apes appeared.

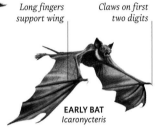

Long arms good for swinging in trees

EARLY APE
Dryopithecus

Forelimbs have become flippers

Tail ended in a fluke

EARLY WHALE
Basilosaurus

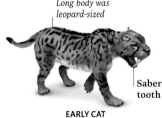

Long body was leopard-sized

Saber tooth

EARLY CAT
Eusmilus

Middle, hoofed toes carried all the weight

Three-toed feet

EARLY HORSE
Merychippus

Mammalian milestones

Mammals evolved, step by step, over millions of years. Some milestones are only hinted at by the fossil record. Milk glands, for instance, are unlikely to fossilize, but the developmental pattern of fossil *Morganucodon* juveniles suggests that they were milk-fed.

225 MYA *Adelobasileus evolves. Once known as the earliest mammal due to its mammallike inner ear, it could be ancestral to all mammals*

210 MYA *The mammallike Morganucodon has toothless young, which then develop "milk teeth" replaced by adult teeth*

165 MYA *Microdocodon fossil shows the earliest jointed hyoid bone, which is evidence of suckling*

160 MYA *Juramaia evolved. It is the oldest known eutherian and is on the evolutionary line that led to placental mammals*

125 MYA *Sinodelphys appears. Scientists describe it as the earliest known marsupial on its discovery, but others argue it is a eutherian*

66–63 MYA *The earliest undisputed placental mammals, such as the early carnivore Ravenictis, appear*

Human evolution

Fewer than 10 million years ago, the ancestors of humans, called hominins, split from those of chimpanzees. Their initial difference was that they walked increasingly upright on two feet, but some species gained additional distinctive features, including a larger brain and the ability to craft and use complex stone tools. More than 20 species of hominin lived and died, but one species, *Homo sapiens*, prevailed.

Human species

Sahelanthropus, living in Africa about 7 million years ago (MYA), shows signs of habitually walking upright, and some experts regard it as the earliest hominin. There followed a diversity of upright apes. Powerful jaws and large back teeth, ideal for eating tough, fibrous foods, appeared in some species. Large brains relative to body size and smaller jaws and teeth appeared in others. Below is a selection of ten species, including our own.

One species, the **Denisovans**, known from a **few bones and their DNA**, still lacks a scientific name

Heavy brow ridge · *Nose is wide and flat, unlike human noses*

Sahelanthropus
This animal may have walked on two legs, possibly linking it more closely to hominins than to other apes.

Wide cheekbone extends far beyond eye socket · *Cranium housed brain barely bigger than chimp's*

Australopithecus afarensis
Australopithecus species were similar in size to a chimpanzee, but bipedal and with a slightly larger brain.

Distance between eyes is small · *Round cranium*

Australopithecus africanus
This southern African species had a larger jaw and cheek teeth than *Australopithecus afarensis*, and longer arms.

Eyes set more widely apart · *Nose more pronounced*

Homo habilis
The first known member of the genus *Homo* to evolve, this species is called "handyman" due to its use of stone tools.

Slightly larger braincase than those of Australopithecus · *Nostrils point down, as in modern humans*

Homo ergaster
Like all earlier hominins, *Homo ergaster*, whose name means "workman" due to its crafting skills, lived only in Africa.

Walking upright

Many of the anatomical differences between humans and apes are connected with the unique bipedal (two-legged) locomotion and upright stance of humans. It has led to evolutionary modifications all over the skeleton.

Cone-shaped ribcage maximizes shoulder flexibility for climbing · *Leg bones much shorter than humans'* · *Gorillas and chimpanzees are knuckle walkers*

Spinal cord enters through base of skull · *Barrel-shaped ribcage allows arms to swing freely when walking* · *Arched foot acts as a springy shock absorber*

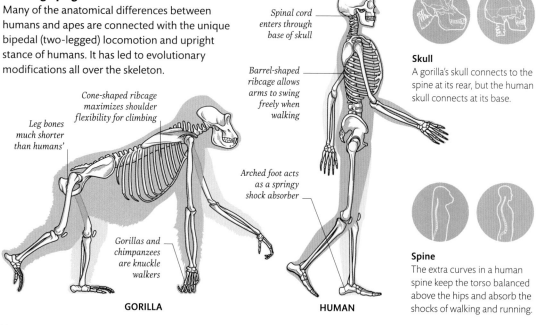

GORILLA · **HUMAN**

Skull
A gorilla's skull connects to the spine at its rear, but the human skull connects at its base.

Spine
The extra curves in a human spine keep the torso balanced above the hips and absorb the shocks of walking and running.

Foot
The human big toe has no grasping function. It is aligned with the others, contributing to a supportive platform.

Pelvis
The broad, flat human pelvis brings the base of the spine near the hip joint, providing stability when upright.

TOOLMAKING TECHNOLOGIES
Archaeologists identify phases of increasing sophistication in hominin toolmaking. The earliest known is called the Lomekwian culture. These tools were made by unknown hominins around 3.3 MYA. Although crude, they were superior to any chimpanzee tools.

Cutting edge could be made by a single blow

Oldowan chopper
Associated with *Homo habilis* 2.5 MYA, Oldowan tools were simple cores and flakes produced by a "hammerstone."

Blade sharpened by blows on both sides
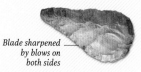

Acheulean handaxe
Acheulean tools, associated with *Homo ergaster* or *Homo erectus*, are more finely crafted and sharper.

The largest **hominin brains** have **tripled in size**, from *Australopithecus* 4 million years ago to *Homo sapiens* today

EVOLUTION TIMELINE

The hominin family tree is constantly being revised as more fossils are discovered. This chart gives an overview of the last 5 million years, according to current knowledge. Each bar indicates the time range for a species, and its color indicates the genus the species belongs to.

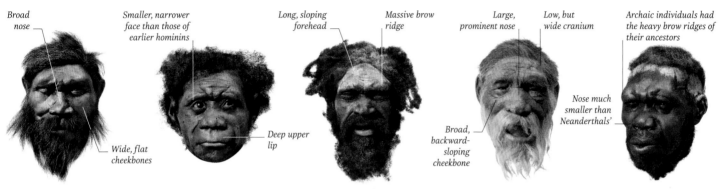

KEY

■ *Ardipithecus*   ▥ *Australopithecus*   ▥ *Homo*

Australopithecus sediba   *Homo sapiens*
Australopithecus garhi   *Homo neanderthalensis*
Homo naledi
Homo heidelbergensis
Australopithecus africanus   *Homo antecessor*
Australopithecus bahrelghazali   *Homo erectus*
Australopithecus afarensis   *Homo ergaster*   *Homo luzonensis*
Australopithecus anamensis   *Homo georgicus*   *Homo floresiensis*
Ardipithecus   *Homo habilis*
ramidus

| 5 MYA | 4 MYA | 3 MYA | 2 MYA | 1 MYA |

Broad nose — Smaller, narrower face than those of earlier hominins — Long, sloping forehead — Massive brow ridge — Large, prominent nose — Low, but wide cranium — Archaic individuals had the heavy brow ridges of their ancestors

Wide, flat cheekbones — Deep upper lip — Broad, backward-sloping cheekbone — Nose much smaller than Neanderthals'

Homo erectus
This species possibly led the first expansion of hominins outside Africa, reaching as far as China and Indonesia.

Homo floresiensis
This diminuitive species probably descended from *Homo erectus* and was isolated on the Indonesian island of Flores.

Homo heidelbergensis
This widespread hominin is probably the ancestor of modern humans in Africa, and Neanderthals in Europe.

Homo neanderthalensis
Living in western Asia and Europe, Neanderthals coexisted with, and interbred with, *Homo sapiens* and the mysterious Denisovans.

Homo sapiens
The oldest *Homo sapiens* fossils have "archaic" features, like earlier species, such as the lack of a protruding chin.

Humans colonize the world

Hominins started life in Africa, but from 2.1 MYA onward, they dispersed beyond Africa in waves. Half a million years ago, there were probably several species of *Homo* living in different parts of the world. However, from 200,000 years ago (YA), *Homo sapiens* began emerging from Africa. In places, it coexisted and interbred with earlier species, but eventually, it replaced them.

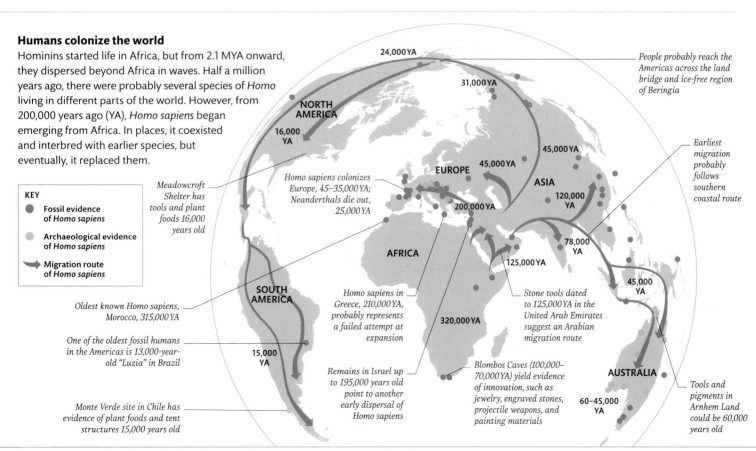

KEY

● Fossil evidence of *Homo sapiens*

○ Archaeological evidence of *Homo sapiens*

➜ Migration route of *Homo sapiens*

24,000 YA

31,000 YA

NORTH AMERICA

16,000 YA

EUROPE

ASIA

45,000 YA

45,000 YA

120,000 YA

200,000 YA

78,000 YA

AFRICA

125,000 YA

45,000 YA

SOUTH AMERICA

320,000 YA

15,000 YA

AUSTRALIA

60–45,000 YA

People probably reach the Americas across the land bridge and ice-free region of Beringia

Earliest migration probably follows southern coastal route

Meadowcroft Shelter has tools and plant foods 16,000 years old

Homo sapiens colonizes Europe, 45–35,000 YA; Neanderthals die out, 25,000 YA

Oldest known Homo sapiens, Morocco, 315,000 YA

One of the oldest fossil humans in the Americas is 13,000-year-old "Luzia" in Brazil

Monte Verde site in Chile has evidence of plant foods and tent structures 15,000 years old

Homo sapiens in Greece, 210,000 YA, probably represents a failed attempt at expansion

Remains in Israel up to 195,000 years old point to another early dispersal of *Homo sapiens*

Blombos Caves (100,000–70,000 YA) yield evidence of innovation, such as jewelry, engraved stones, projectile weapons, and painting materials

Stone tools dated to 125,000 YA in the United Arab Emirates suggest an Arabian migration route

Tools and pigments in Arnhem Land could be 60,000 years old

see also The human body pp.230–31 ▶   The skeletal system pp.232–33 ▶   Prehistory to 3000 BCE pp.302–303 ▶

The plant kingdom

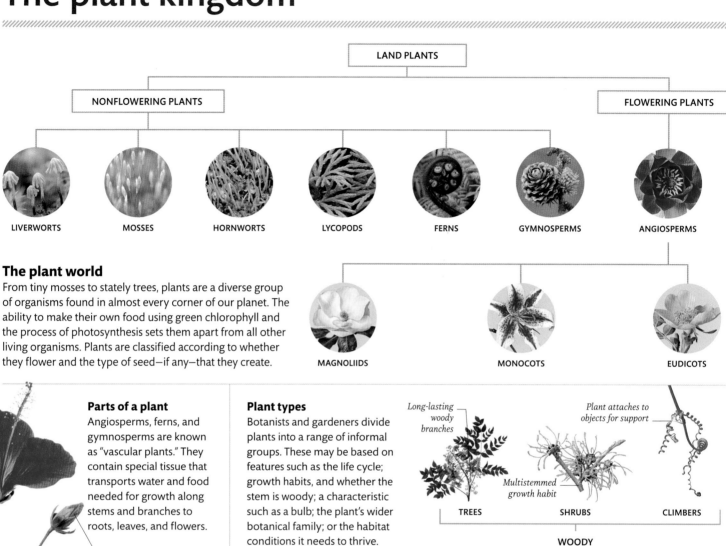

LAND PLANTS

NONFLOWERING PLANTS

FLOWERING PLANTS

LIVERWORTS · MOSSES · HORNWORTS · LYCOPODS · FERNS · GYMNOSPERMS · ANGIOSPERMS

MAGNOLIIDS · MONOCOTS · EUDICOTS

The plant world

From tiny mosses to stately trees, plants are a diverse group of organisms found in almost every corner of our planet. The ability to make their own food using green chlorophyll and the process of photosynthesis sets them apart from all other living organisms. Plants are classified according to whether they flower and the type of seed—if any—that they create.

Parts of a plant

Angiosperms, ferns, and gymnosperms are known as "vascular plants." They contain special tissue that transports water and food needed for growth along stems and branches to roots, leaves, and flowers.

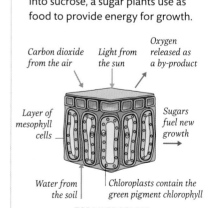

Flowers hold the reproductive organs, and are often brightly colored

Leaf captures sunlight to make energy for growth, and releases excess water via transpiration

Petiole, or leaf stalk, may be long, short, or absent altogether

Branch places leaves away from the stem, which allows them to capture more sunlight

Stem supports the plant, and carries nutrients up from the roots

Roots anchor the plant to the ground, and draw water and nutrients from the soil

Plant types

Botanists and gardeners divide plants into a range of informal groups. These may be based on features such as the life cycle; growth habits, and whether the stem is woody; a characteristic such as a bulb; the plant's wider botanical family; or the habitat conditions it needs to thrive.

Long-lasting woody branches

Plant attaches to objects for support

Multistemmed growth habit

TREES · SHRUBS · CLIMBERS

WOODY

Plant leaves

Leaves come in all shapes and sizes. Their variety reveals how plants balance the dual functions of photosynthesis and transpiration in different habitats: a big leaf may trap more light, but will lose more water through evaporation.

Needles shrug off snow

Tiny scales minimize water loss

SCALES

NEEDLES

Leaves are shed each year

DECIDUOUS BROAD-LEAVES

Plant always has some green leaves

Fleshy leaves store water

SUCCULENT LEAVES

EVERGREEN BROAD-LEAVES

Photosynthesis

Inside leaves, mesophyll cells with light-absorbing chloroplasts make glucose by combining light, carbon dioxide, and water. This is turned into sucrose, a sugar plants use as food to provide energy for growth.

Carbon dioxide from the air

Light from the sun

Oxygen released as a by-product

Layer of mesophyll cells

Sugars fuel new growth

Water from the soil

Chloroplasts contain the green pigment chlorophyll

TOP LAYER OF LEAF

◀ see also Prehistoric plants pp.88–89   Nonflowering plants pp.98–99 ▶   Flowering plants pp.100–103 ▶

Scientists have identified about 391,000 species of vascular plants

How plants grow

All seed-producing plants follow the same growth pattern. A seed begins to germinate when it is exposed to conditions that break its dormancy, triggering the release of hormones that regulate every aspect of growth.

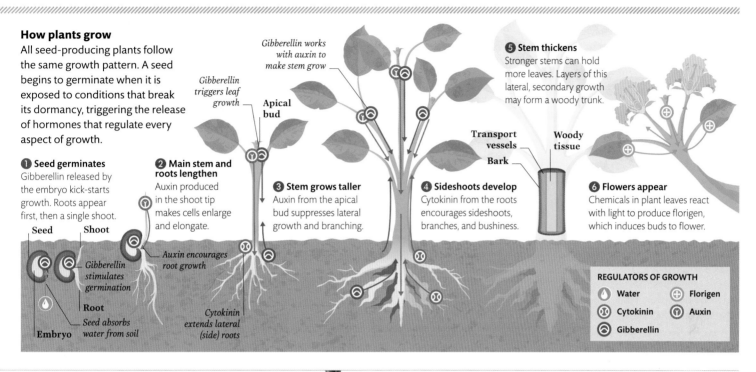

Gibberellin works with auxin to make stem grow

Gibberellin triggers leaf growth

Apical bud

5 Stem thickens
Stronger stems can hold more leaves. Layers of this lateral, secondary growth may form a woody trunk.

Transport vessels

Woody tissue

Bark

1 Seed germinates
Gibberellin released by the embryo kick-starts growth. Roots appear first, then a single shoot.

Seed **Shoot**

Gibberellin stimulates germination

Root

Seed absorbs water from soil

Embryo

Auxin encourages root growth

2 Main stem and roots lengthen
Auxin produced in the shoot tip makes cells enlarge and elongate.

Cytokinin extends lateral (side) roots

3 Stem grows taller
Auxin from the apical bud suppresses lateral growth and branching.

4 Sideshoots develop
Cytokinin from the roots encourages sideshoots, branches, and bushiness.

6 Flowers appear
Chemicals in plant leaves react with light to produce florigen, which induces buds to flower.

REGULATORS OF GROWTH
- Water
- Cytokinin
- Gibberellin
- Florigen
- Auxin

Entire life cycle completed in 1 year

ANNUAL

Flowers appear in the 2nd year of 2-year life cycle

BIENNIAL

Top growth dies back and regrows for several years

PERENNIAL

Bulb stores food

BULBOUS

Flowers held on spikes of bracts

GRASS

Segmented stems

BAMBOO

Spines help to conserve water

CACTUS

Leaves absorb water from the air

AIR PLANT

HERBACEOUS

Parts of a flower

Flowers have male and/or female parts. The sepals and petals that surround them can offer protection as well as attracting pollinators.

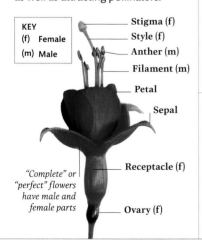

KEY
(f) Female
(m) Male

- Stigma (f)
- Style (f)
- Anther (m)
- Filament (m)
- Petal
- Sepal
- Receptacle (f)
- Ovary (f)

"Complete" or "perfect" flowers have male and female parts

Pollination and fertilization

Pollination occurs when the male sperm cells (pollen) produced by the anthers are transferred to the female stigma. Pollen is carried from one flower to another by insects, birds, animals, or wind. Plants with multiple flowers can "self-pollinate" if pollen from one bloom is transferred to another.

Fertilization
Pollen grains produce a long tube which passes the male sperm cells into a flower's ovary, where they fuse with female ovules.

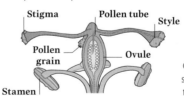

Stigma
Pollen tube
Style
Pollen grain
Ovule
Stamen

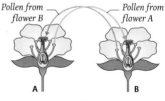

Pollen from flower B
Pollen from flower A

A **B**

Cross-pollination
Cross-pollination—when pollen is from a separate plant of the same species—helps to maintain the species' genetic diversity.

Seeds and fruit

Gymnosperm and angiosperm seeds are either "naked" (unprotected), or enclosed in fruits that develop from flower ovaries. Fruits have different roles: some encourage distribution, while others protect seeds until the conditions for germination are met.

Seeds held on upper sides of scales

SEED CONE

Wings formed by flower carpel

DRY FRUIT

Each fruitlet (drupe) holds a single seed

FLESHY FRUIT

Hard-walled fruit encloses seed

NUT

see also Classification pp.158–59 ▶ Types of living things pp.216–17 ▶

Nonflowering plants

Once primitive plants emerged from water onto dry land, some 500 million years ago, they needed new biology to survive. Initially, tiny green plants were forced to live in damp places. Over time, new forms evolved with adaptations to reduce their reliance on water. These were able to grow and reproduce in more hostile environments. Examples of most of these evolutionary plant stages are still alive.

Liverworts

Most liverworts are flat green plants. They have no system to conduct water or nutrients, so these can only move from cell to cell. To reproduce, the male sperm swims in surface water to the female cell, as in mosses (see below).

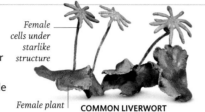

Female cells under starlike structure

Female plant

COMMON LIVERWORT
(Marchantia polymorpha)

Hornworts

These relatives of liverworts form a rosette-shaped plant. Male and female organs grow within the flat plant. The spore-bearing stage grows as a long hornlike structure, which splits open from the top to release spores.

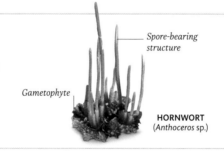

Spore-bearing structure

Gametophyte

HORNWORT
(Anthoceros sp.)

Lycopods

Lycopods and club mosses form larger plants than mosses or liverworts, as they have vascular cells to move water and nutrients. The green plant is the spore-bearing stage. Ancient, treelike lycopods formed most coal deposits.

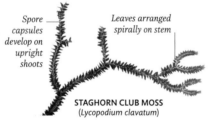

Spore capsules develop on upright shoots

Leaves arranged spirally on stem

STAGHORN CLUB MOSS
(Lycopodium clavatum)

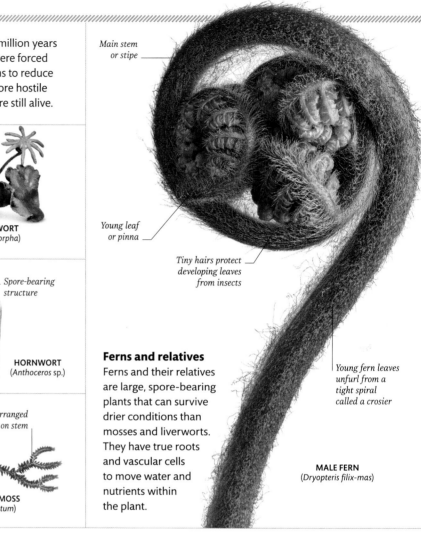

Main stem or stipe

Young leaf or pinna

Tiny hairs protect developing leaves from insects

Young fern leaves unfurl from a tight spiral called a crosier

MALE FERN
(Dryopteris filix-mas)

Ferns and relatives

Ferns and their relatives are large, spore-bearing plants that can survive drier conditions than mosses and liverworts. They have true roots and vascular cells to move water and nutrients within the plant.

Mosses

Most mosses are small, clump-forming plants without true roots. Their spores are shed into the wind from capsules on tall stems, but they still rely on surface water for their male sperm to reach a female shoot. The green, leaflike part of the moss is called the gametophyte. It produces food using solar energy, but mosses do not contain veins to transport water and nutrients. Instead, these are directly absorbed into the cells.

> Mosses have **grown** in **damp places** as early as **300 million years ago**

Life cycle of moss

This complex life cycle is called alternation of generation. Spores grow into separate male or female plants. Male cells swim to the female cells, then a new spore-bearing capsule develops.

Spore-bearing structure

CAPILLARY THREAD MOSS
(Bryum capillare)

Gametophyte

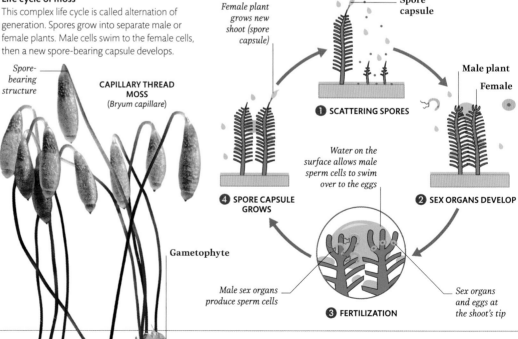

Female plant grows new shoot (spore capsule)

Spore capsule

❶ **SCATTERING SPORES**

Male plant

Female

Water on the surface allows male sperm cells to swim over to the eggs

❹ **SPORE CAPSULE GROWS**

❷ **SEX ORGANS DEVELOP**

Male sex organs produce sperm cells

❸ **FERTILIZATION**

Sex organs and eggs at the shoot's tip

 ◄ see also Prehistoric plants pp.88–89

There are **more than 10,500** known **species** of fern **alive today**

Whorls of green shoots on sterile stem

HORSETAIL
(*Equisetum* sp.)

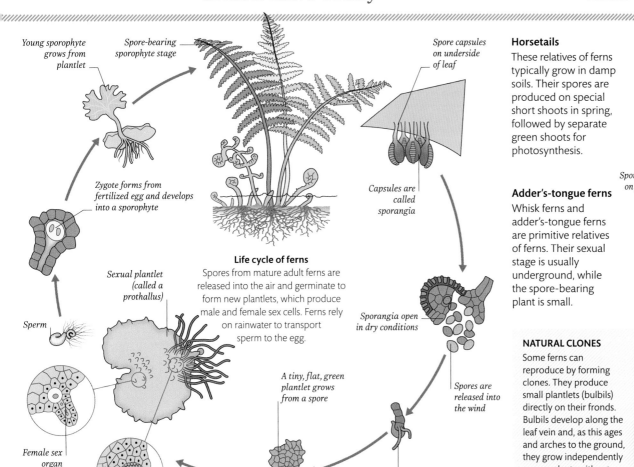

Young sporophyte grows from plantlet

Spore-bearing sporophyte stage

Spore capsules on underside of leaf

Zygote forms from fertilized egg and develops into a sporophyte

Capsules are called sporangia

Life cycle of ferns
Spores from mature adult ferns are released into the air and germinate to form new plantlets, which produce male and female sex cells. Ferns rely on rainwater to transport sperm to the egg.

Sexual plantlet (called a prothallus)

Sperm

Female sex organ

Male sex organ

A tiny, flat, green plantlet grows from a spore

Sporangia open in dry conditions

Spores are released into the wind

Spores germinate on damp soil

Horsetails
These relatives of ferns typically grow in damp soils. Their spores are produced on special short shoots in spring, followed by separate green shoots for photosynthesis.

Adder's-tongue ferns
Whisk ferns and adder's-tongue ferns are primitive relatives of ferns. Their sexual stage is usually underground, while the spore-bearing plant is small.

Sporangia on fertile blade

Barren blade

ADDER'S-TONGUE FERN
(*Ophioglossum* sp.)

NATURAL CLONES
Some ferns can reproduce by forming clones. They produce small plantlets (bulbils) directly on their fronds. Bulbils develop along the leaf vein and, as this ages and arches to the ground, they grow independently as new plants without any sexual stage.

Tiny green crosier develops

First leaves are undefined

DIPLAZIUM PROLIFERUM
(*Diplazium proliferum*)

Gymnosperms
These flowerless plants have woody stems, tough leaves, and seeds. They can grow in much harsher environments than other nonflowering plants because most gymnosperms do not need surface water at any stage to reproduce.

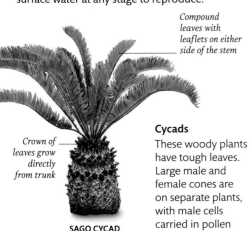

Compound leaves with leaflets on either side of the stem

Crown of leaves grow directly from trunk

SAGO CYCAD
(*Cycas revoluta*)

Cycads
These woody plants have tough leaves. Large male and female cones are on separate plants, with male cells carried in pollen to reach females.

Ginkgo
Separate trees produce male pollen cones or female ovules. The ovules develop into an unpleasant smelling, fruitlike structure after male pollen reaches them.

MAIDENHAIR TREE
(*Ginkgo biloba*)

Conifers
Conifers dominate cold-climate woodland. Their narrow leaves resist cold and drought. Seeds are formed in cones that may take three years to mature.

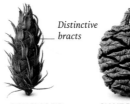

Distinctive bracts

DOUGLAS FIR
(*Pseudotsuga menziesii*)

Dense, woody cone

GIANT REDWOOD
(*Sequoiadendron giganteum*)

ATLAS CEDAR
(*Cedrus atlantica*)

Gnetophytes
Unlike other gymnosperms, the plants in this group have advanced water-conducting vessels (like those found in the flowering plants).

Two evergreen leaves

WELWITSCHIA
(*Welwitschia mirabilis*)

Seeds between cone scales

COULTER PINE
(*Pinus coulteri*)

Seed within fruitlike aril

YELLOW-BERRIED YEW
(*Taxus baccata* 'Lutea')

◀ see also The plant kingdom pp.96–97   Flowering plants pp.100–103 ▶   **99**

Flowering plants

Flowers evolved to use insects as pollinators, although some flowering plants rely on wind pollination. There are three main groups of flowering plants: magnoliids, monocotyledons, and eudicotyledons. The most advanced have developed complex flowers and specialized methods of growth to ensure their survival and seed production for future generations.

Seeds
A seed contains an embryo and its food stores in endosperm or cotyledons. A protective coat ensures the embryo survives until conditions allow it to grow.

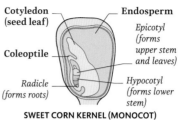

Cotyledon (seed leaf) — Endosperm
Epicotyl (forms upper stem and leaves)
Coleoptile
Radicle (forms roots) — Hypocotyl (forms lower stem)

SWEET CORN KERNEL (MONOCOT)

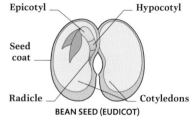

Epicotyl — Hypocotyl
Seed coat
Radicle — Cotyledons

BEAN SEED (EUDICOT)

Roots
Roots anchor the plant. They absorb water and nutrients from soil to allow growth. Some roots, such as carrots, also store nutrients for later use.

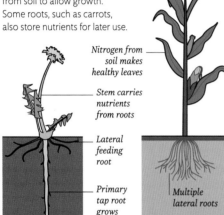

Nitrogen from soil makes healthy leaves
Stem carries nutrients from roots
Lateral feeding root
Primary tap root grows down vertically

DANDELION (EUDICOT)

Multiple lateral roots

CORN (MONOCOT)

Leaves
Leaves are the energy factories for the plant. As their veins do not branch, monocot leaves are usually narrow, but eudicotyledon leaves are often broad.

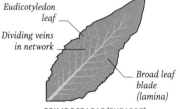

Monocotyledon leaf
Parallel veins
Narrow leaf blade (lamina)

PALM GRASS (MONOCOT)

Eudicotyledon leaf
Dividing veins in network
Broad leaf blade (lamina)

PRIMROSE LEAF (EUDICOT)

Flowers
Flowers contain the plant's reproductive parts. The stamens are male and carry the pollen, while the ovary, style, and stigma are female. The flower's appearance is linked to its method of pollination.

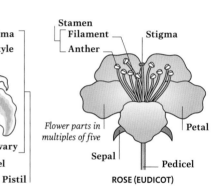

Stamen
Anther
Filament
Stigma
Style
Flower parts in multiples of three
Tepal (petallike structure)
Ovary
Pedicel

LILY (MONOCOT) — Pistil

Stamen
Filament
Anther
Stigma
Flower parts in multiples of five
Sepal
Petal
Pedicel

ROSE (EUDICOT)

Magnoliids
These are among the most primitive of flowering plants. Their flowers are often simple, may lack petals, and do not produce nectar. Many magnoliids are trees or shrubs and are sources of essential oils and spices, such as cinnamon, nutmeg, and black pepper.

Single large seed within fleshy fruit
Tepals attract beetles
Leathery evergreen leaves

AVOCADO (Persea americana)

Stigmas and ovaries in conelike structure
Multiple large tepals

SOUTHERN MAGNOLIA (Magnolia grandiflora)

ANCIENT ANGIOSPERMS
Early in the evolution of flowering plants, the group known as ancient angiosperms diverged from the rest of the angiosperms. This group has flowers with multiple petals and other flower parts. While some are shrubs, many are aquatic plants where their flowers are thrust out of the water for pollinators to reach. These ancient angiosperms include star anise and water lilies.

WATER LILY (Nymphaea sp.)

 ◀ see also The plant kingdom pp.96–97

Flowering plants first started appearing with the dinosaurs 125 million years ago

Monocotyledons

This group of flowering plants are distinguished by their seeds having only a single seed leaf (cotyledon). They include many economically important plants, such as wheat, barley, rice, corn, and millet, as well as grasses, palms, irises, lilies, and orchids.

Protective spathe

Male flowers above females on spadix

Arum

These plants have flowers on a spadix. Tiny separate male and female flowers grow in a dense spike, often enclosed by a protective bract called a spathe.

PSEUDODRACONTIUM
(*Pseudodracontium lacourii*)

Silks (styles) catch pollen

Grasses and grains

These plants have flowers without petals, as they are wind pollinated. Their leaves grow from the base, not the tip, allowing them to survive grazing by animals.

Husk protects ovaries

CORN
(*Zea mays*)

Strong woody stems

Lateral shoots appear at nodes

Bamboo

Bamboos are large, woody grasses. The largest grows to 82 ft (25 m) tall, and they can grow 3 ft (90 cm) in 24 hours. Many bamboos die after producing seeds.

BAMBOO
(*Phyllostachys* sp.)

Arched stem (rachis)

Flowers protected by glumes (bracts)

SPANGLE GRASS
(*Chasmanthium latifolium*)

Palms

These are the only treelike monocots. They often have only one tall, but thin, stem, which cannot thicken or branch like those of real trees.

Divided (pinnate) leaf

COCONUT
(*Cocos nucifera*)

Leaflets separated by rachis

Young developing fruit

Old leaf bases protect the stem

Lilies

These are mostly herbaceous plants, and only a few develop woody stems. Many have bulbs, allowing them to survive cold or drought. Their three sepals and three petals are indistinguishable, and termed tepals.

Flower spike

Flowers open in sequence

Colorful tepals

STARGAZER LILY
(*Lilium orientalis* 'Stargazer')

Flowerhead stem (peduncle)

TORCH LILY
(*Kniphofia uvaria*)

Orchids

There are more species of orchid than any other plant. They are the most advanced monocots. Many orchids have very specialized systems of pollination, leading to bizarre appearances.

Some orchids may live for more than 100 years

Petal

Large, colorful sepal attracts pollinators

Highly modified petal

Lip or slipper

Flower stem (pedicel)

VENUS SLIPPER ORCHID
(*Paphiopedilum* sp.)

Colorful, upright sepal

Narrow, unbranched trunk

Flower mimics insects to attract pollinators

Scars where the leaves grew remain visible

WOODCOCK ORCHID
(*Ophrys scolopax*)

see also Nonflowering plants pp.98–99 ◄ Flowering plants continued pp.102–103 ► Classification pp.158–59 ►

>> Flowering plants continued

Eudicots

Most trees, ornamental flowers, fruit, and vegetables are eudicots. Unlike other angiosperms, eudicot pollen grains have three or more pores, from which the pollen tube grows. They are highly varied and complex organisms and only a selection of eudicot orders are represented here.

Proteas

The Proteales are some of the least advanced (or basal) eudicots. Most are from the Southern Hemisphere and have complex flowers pollinated by birds or small mammals.

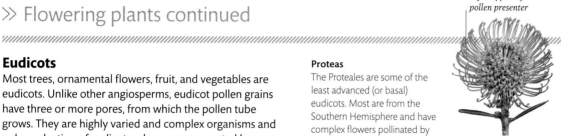

Style tipped by pollen presenter

Tiny flowers make up the inflorescence

RED PINCUSHION PROTEA
(*Leucospermum cordifolium*)

KING PROTEA FLOWER
(*Protea cynaroides*)

Cacti and relatives

This varied group contains all cacti and many succulent plants, which have developed water storage systems to survive prolonged drought. The Caryophyllales also includes climbers and annuals, such as quinoa.

Flower buds protected by spines and hairs

Large head holding tiny flowers

Colorful bracts surround white flowers

Brightly colored flowers clustered together

OWL-EYE CACTUS
(*Mammillaria perbella*)

COCKSCOMB
(*Celosia cristata*)

BOUGAINVILLEA
(*Bougainvillea glabra*)

AIRPLANE PLANT
(*Crassula perfoliata* var. minor)

Oaks, birches, and beeches

This botanical group (Fagales) is distinguished by usually having separate male and female flowers, the males growing in long, dense catkins. They are generally wind pollinated, flowering before the leaves grow in spring.

Large tree with spreading habit

Two nuts within spiny cupule

Male flowers grow in hanging catkins

Large deciduous leaves

LARGE ENGLISH OAK
(*Quercus robur*)

SWEET CHESTNUT
(*Castanea sativa*)

CHINESE RED-BARKED BIRCH
(*Betula albosinensis*)

STRANDZHA OAK
(*Quercus hartwissiana*)

Cabbages

Although cabbages and broccoli are distinguished by four-petaled flowers, other members of the Brassicales are more varied. Many plants in this group are edible and contain glucosinolate, or mustard oil.

Densely packed leaves

Bright petals attract long-tongued pollinators

Scented flowers attract pollinators

Black seeds within the berry

WILD CABBAGE
(*Brassica oleracea*)

COMMON NASTURTIUM
(*Tropaeolum majus*)

HOARY STOCK
(*Matthiola incana*)

PAPAYA TREE
(*Carica papaya*)

Heathers

Heathers are usually long-lived woody plants. Tea plants are also members of this order (Ericales). Their other relatives, however, include herbs like primrose and, bizarrely, the carnivorous American pitcher plants.

Small flowers held above the leaves

Flowers grow in small clusters

Leaves trap and digest flies

Strawberrylike fruit takes a year to develop

COMMON HEATHER
(*Calluna vulgaris*)

STRAWBERRY TREE
(*Arbutus unedo*)

ALBRECHT'S AZALEA
(*Rhododendron albrechtii*)

PITCHER PLANT
(*Sarracenia* sp.)

Parsley and carrots

Carrots and most of their relatives are distinguished by their small flowers being borne in large flat inflorescences called umbels. This group, the Apiales, also includes ivy and ginseng.

Small flowers in a flat umbel

Tiny flowers packed into conical head

Small flowers above bracts

Flower head curls inward after flowering

WILD CARROT
(*Daucus carota* 'Dara')

SEA HOLLY
(*Eryngium maritimum*)

GREAT MASTERWORT
(*Astrantia major* 'Rubra')

QUEEN ANNE'S LACE
(*Daucus carota*)

Over 50 percent of plant species are eudicots

Buttercups

The Ranunculales are a relatively primitive group among the eudicots with large, symmetrical, open flowers pollinated by bees. Most are herbs, although there are some woody species.

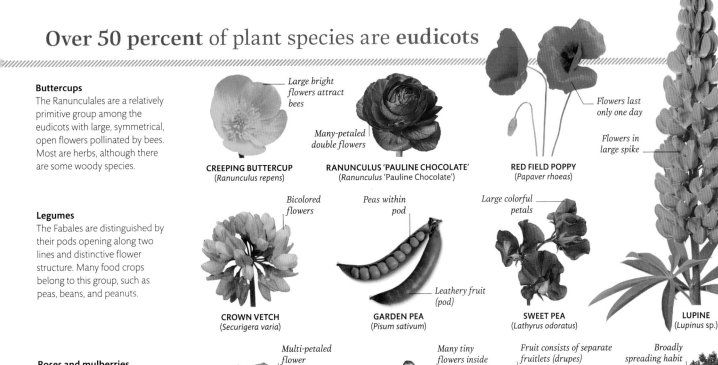

Large bright flowers attract bees

Many-petaled double flowers

Flowers last only one day

Flowers in large spike

CREEPING BUTTERCUP
(*Ranunculus repens*)

RANUNCULUS 'PAULINE CHOCOLATE'
(*Ranunculus 'Pauline Chocolate'*)

RED FIELD POPPY
(*Papaver rhoeas*)

Legumes

The Fabales are distinguished by their pods opening along two lines and distinctive flower structure. Many food crops belong to this group, such as peas, beans, and peanuts.

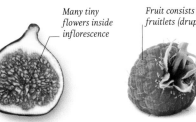
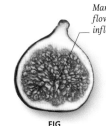

Bicolored flowers

Peas within pod

Large colorful petals

Leathery fruit (pod)

CROWN VETCH
(*Securigera varia*)

GARDEN PEA
(*Pisum sativum*)

SWEET PEA
(*Lathyrus odoratus*)

LUPINE
(*Lupinus sp.*)

Roses and mulberries

Rosales contains a wide variety of plants, from strawberries and roses to figs, mulberries, and hemp. This group includes many edible fruits and are mostly pollinated by insects.

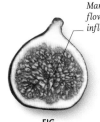

Multi-petaled flower

Many tiny flowers inside inflorescence

Fruit consists of separate fruitlets (drupes)

Broadly spreading habit

ROSE 'FRAGRANT CLOUD'
(*Rosa 'Fragrant Cloud'*)

FIG
(*Ficus carica*)

RASPBERRY
(*Rubus idaeus*)

APPLE TREE
(*Malus domestica*)

Maples

Mostly trees and shrubs, the Sapindales often have tiny flowers that are pollinated by bees and flies, like maples and lychee, but also includes citrus (oranges, lemons, and relatives).

Pendulous flowers

Two winged seeds derived from flower with two carpels

Red fruit within enlarged calyx

Fiery autumn color

CORREA 'MARIAN'S MARVEL'
(*Correa 'Marian's Marvel'*)

AMUR MAPLE
(*Acer tataricum subsp. ginnala*)

WINTER CHERRY
(*Withania somnifera*)

NORWAY MAPLE
(*Acer platanoides*)

Foxgloves

Most of this group (Lamiales) have tubular flowers with a flat lip, ideally suited to bee pollination. The flowers of the plants in this group all have only a single line of symmetry.

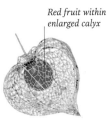

Tubular flowers in spike

Leaf hairs retain moisture

Bracts attract pollinators

Disk florets

COMMON FOXGLOVE
(*Digitalis purpurea*)

LAVENDER
(*Lavandula sp.*)

PURPLE SAGE
(*Salvia officinalis 'Purpurascens'*)

Daisies

The Asterales are the most advanced of the eudicots. Their flowers are complex, each head appearing as a single bloom, but actually consisting of numerous tiny flowers (florets), each with petals, stamens, and carpels.

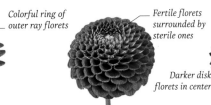

Colorful ring of outer ray florets

Fertile florets surrounded by sterile ones

Spiny bracts

Darker disk florets in center

CAPE DAISY
(*Osteospermum 'Stardust'*)

DAHLIA 'IVANETTI'
(*Dahlia 'Ivanetti'*)

CORNFLOWER
(*Centaurea cyanus*)

CARDOON
(*Cynara cardunculus*)

see also Classification pp.158–59 ▶

Fungi

What are fungi?

Once grouped with plants, fungi are classified in their own kingdom. They can be simple, single-celled organisms such as yeasts, flat molds that form visible colonies, or more sophisticated multicellular forms such as mushrooms. Fungi are widespread and found in most habitats on Earth.

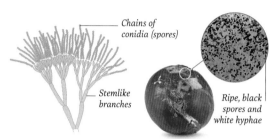

Chains of conidia (spores)

Stemlike branches

Ripe, black spores and white hyphae

Penicillium
Some species of the *Penicillium* genus of fungi produce the medicinal antibiotic penicillin; others are used to make cheese.

Mold
Like all fungi, molds obtain their nutrition from dead and decaying organic matter, or from living plants or animals.

LICHEN

A lichen is actually two to three living things—a fungus and an alga and/or a cyanobacterium—that function as a single entity for mutual benefit. Fungi cannot photosynthesize or fix nitrogen (see p.212), but algae and cyanobacteria can, offering the fungi extra nutrients in return for its protective structure, which includes pigments that absorb harmful UV light.

Dishlike lobes may be green-gray or yellow-orange

Pale, foliate lobes may be very flat or bumpy

LOBED LICHEN   **FOLIOSE LICHEN**

Mushrooms and toadstools

Both mushrooms and toadstools are the fruiting bodies of fungi, and for many people, they are the most familiar manifestation of what a fungus is. Although there is no scientific distinction between the two terms, "toadstool" is often used to refer to poisonous mushroom species.

Mushroom anatomy

With its familiar stem and cap, a mushroom is the visible fruiting, or spore-producing, part of what is actually a vast fungus. Apart from when it reproduces, the fungus remains hidden underground, where it absorbs water and nutrients through a network of thin, threadlike, branching structures called hyphae. The entire network is known as a mycelium, which remains dormant until conditions, such as ground temperature and sufficient rainfall, are favorable for it to reproduce.

Mushrooms are nearly 90 percent water

HYPHAE

Hyphae are the basis of any fungus. They have tubular cells with rigid walls that are usually made of chitin, a glucose derivative. In some hyphae, cells are separated by porous "cross-walls" called septa. As well as absorbing nutrients, hypha cells contain genetic material.

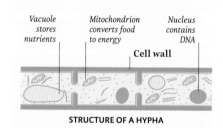

Vacuole stores nutrients

Mitochondrion converts food to energy

Nucleus contains DNA

Cell wall

STRUCTURE OF A HYPHA

Life cycle of a mushroom

One mushroom may release a billion spores (reproductive cells) a day, but only a few will germinate. In the presence of enough moisture and food, spores send out fine, threadlike hyphae underground, which spread, forming a mycelium. Hyphae from two spore mating-types fuse, as the mycelium grows. Environmental conditions trigger it to send fruiting bodies above ground, which mature into mushrooms that release spores.

Beneficial relationship

Mycorrhizal fungal hyphae penetrate plant roots, which helps the plant to absorb water and mineral nutrients from the soil. In return, the fungus has access to carbohydrates produced by the plant.

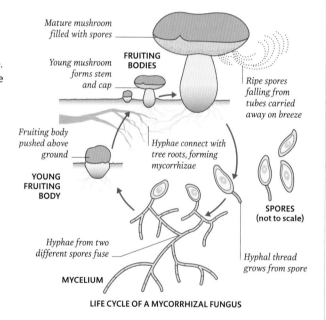

Mature mushroom filled with spores

Young mushroom forms stem and cap

FRUITING BODIES

Ripe spores falling from tubes carried away on breeze

Fruiting body pushed above ground

YOUNG FRUITING BODY

Hyphae connect with tree roots, forming mycorrhizae

SPORES (not to scale)

Hyphae from two different spores fuse

Hyphal thread grows from spore

MYCELIUM

LIFE CYCLE OF A MYCORRHIZAL FUNGUS

Fruiting bodies

Although stem-and-cap mushrooms are by far the most familiar fungi, fruiting bodies come in a wide variety of shapes. They occur either singly or in clusters, and range from sponge-like morels or shelflike bracket fungi to puffballs, cups, stars—even tentaclelike appendages.

Spherical shape

Smooth, ear- or cuplike shape

Bird's-nest fungi resemble egg-filled nests

Grooves (asci) release spores

Concentric "rings" show years of growth

BALL   **CUP**   **NEST**   **LOBED**   **BRACKET**

Entire forests are connected by mycorrhizal fungi in a network nicknamed the wood wide web

Caps

Many fungi produce fruiting bodies with caps on a raised stem. Cap shapes range from the classic dome to those with pleats or honeycomb-like folds that resemble tiny sponges. Although they help to identify many fungi, cap shape can change as the fruiting body matures.

Tapers to a central point

CONICAL

Cap resembles half a sphere

CONVEX

Honeycomblike shape

FOLDED

Outer margin rolled downward

FUNNEL-SHAPED

Raised, central "boss"

UMBONATE

Flattened or domed scarlet cap

Hole where wart has broken off

Warts wash off as mushroom ages

Raised white wart

FLY AGARIC
(Amanita muscaria)

Raised warts are remnants of original white membrane

Stalk

Ring (annulus)

Bulb (volva)

CROSS-SECTION

Stems

Fungi stems offer identification clues to some species. They can be long or short, thick or thin, and some may have rings, bulbs, or other structures.

Long, slender stem roots directly in soil

ROOTING

Clublike base

CLAVATE

Ring (annulus)

STEM AND RING

Stem girth decreases toward base

TAPERED TO BASE

Gills and pores

Most, but not all, stemmed fungi have true gills, or lamellae, beneath their caps. Spores line the gills' surface, ready for dispersal. Gill thickness and spacing, and how they attach to the stem help identify different species.

Stem free from cap and gills

Tightly packed, parallel gills

CROWDED

Widely spaced gills attach to stem

BROADLY SPACED

Gills attach to stem

Extent of gills varies

UNEQUAL LENGTH

Gills run length of cap to stem

EQUAL LENGTH

Very wide, branching, gill-like pores

BRANCHING

Small holes beneath cap

PORES

Crustlike growth

SKIN

Branching outgrowths resemble coral

CORAL

Stomach-shaped sac contains spores

STAR

Funnel-shaped cap

Gills on underside

TRUMPET

Stem tapers toward top

PHALLIC

Yellow head releases spores

Narrow, stem

CLUB

Pestle-shaped fruiting body

PEAR

see also Environmental chemistry p.212 ▶ Types of living things p.216 ▶ The history of medicine pp.250–51 ▶ Modern medicine pp.252–53 ▶

The animal kingdom

About 1.5 million species of animals have been described by science, with perhaps millions more to be discovered. They form a biological kingdom of multicellular organisms, distinct from plants, fungi, protozoa, chromists, bacteria, and archaea. Animals vary enormously in size, form, and lifestyle, and are found in some of the most hostile places on Earth.

Animal characteristics

Animals are heterotrophic, meaning they obtain the energy to live by consuming organic material, including the tissues of other organisms. All but one animal breathes oxygen, most are mobile at some point in their life history, and most reproduce by producing eggs and sperm, though many can also reproduce asexually.

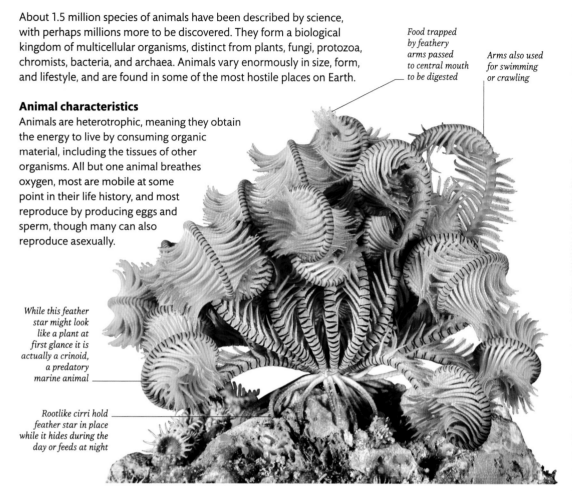

Food trapped by feathery arms passed to central mouth to be digested

Arms also used for swimming or crawling

While this feather star might look like a plant at first glance it is actually a crinoid, a predatory marine animal

Rootlike cirri hold feather star in place while it hides during the day or feeds at night

ANIMAL CLASSIFICATION

Animals are classified hierarchically according to the extent of shared characteristics.

▼ **KINGDOM** An overall division containing organisms that work in fundamentally similar ways, such as the kingdom Animalia

▼ **PHYLUM** A major subdivision of a kingdom, containing one or more classes, such as the phylum Chordata

▼ **CLASS** A major subdivision of a phylum, containing one or more orders, such as the class Mammalia (see p.140)

▼ **ORDER** A major subdivision of a class, containing one or more families, such as the order Carnivora (see p.152)

▼ **FAMILY** A subdivision of an order, containing one or more genera, such as the family Canidae, the dog family (see p.152)

▼ **GENUS** A subdivision of a family, containing one or more species, such as the genus *Canis*

▼ **SPECIES** A group of similar individuals that are able to interbreed in the wild, such as *Canis lupus*, the Gray Wolf (see p.152)

▼ **SUBSPECIES** A group of individuals that is significantly different from other groups of the same species, such as *Canis lupus familiaris*, the domestic dog (see p.153)

▼ **BREED** A group of domesticated animals that have been bred by humans to have a specific appearance and characteristics, such as the Labrador Retriever

Animals range in size from the **huge Blue Whale** to **fairyflies** that are **invisible** to the naked eye

MICROORGANISMS

As single-celled organisms, microorganisms belong in separate kingdoms, but many share animallike characteristics such as heterotrophy. Others are plantlike and make their own food through photosynthesis; others can do both.

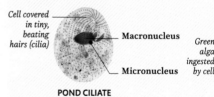

Cell covered in tiny, beating hairs (cilia) — **Macronucleus**

Micronucleus

POND CILIATE
(*Colpoda cucullus*)

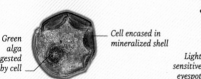

Green alga ingested by cell

Cell encased in mineralized shell

ARCELLA BATHYSTOMA

Spiny shell made of sand and algae cell walls

CENTROPYXIS ACULEATA

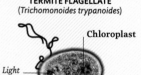

Chloroplast

Light sensitive eyespot

GREEN EUGLENA
(*Euglena viridis*)

Single posterior flagellum runs along body

4 anterior flagella

TERMITE FLAGELLATE
(*Trichomonoides trypanoides*)

Radial spines fuse into central body

STAR RADIOLARIAN
(*Astrolithium* sp.)

Filamentous pseudopods used to catch food

Siliceous surface scales

SCALY CERCOZOA
(*Euglypha* sp.)

Alveolates
The alveolates exhibit a flexible layer of flattened sacs that support the cell membrane. They include ciliates and dinoflagellates.

Amoebas
The loose term "amoeba" refers to a variety of naked and armored single-celled organisms capable of extending tentaclelike pseudopods.

Flagellates
Flagellates are single-celled organisms bearing whiplike structures (flagella), used to propel the cell through water or create a feeding current.

Rhizarians
Radiolarians build glassy shells out of silica and foraminiferans have shells of calcite, sand, or organic material. Some cercozoa have a shell.

Invertebrates

What is an invertebrate?

The invertebrates are a loose and diverse collection of more than 30 animal phyla, including the great majority of animal species on Earth, grouped together simply because they lack the spinal column or notochord seen in vertebrates.

ANIMAL SPECIES

Invertebrates comprise the majority of known animal taxa, with more than 1.4 million described species, compared to about 67,000 vertebrates.

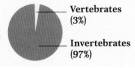

- Vertebrates (3%)
- Invertebrates (97%)

Sponges

The sedentary sponges have no specialized organs and no circulatory, digestive, or nervous systems. Water is drawn through the body via interconnected pores and channels on currents created by the beating of tiny flagella. Particles of food trapped in these narrow spaces are engulfed by cells that line the channels.

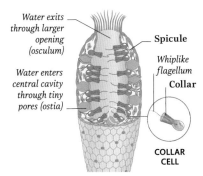

- Water exits through larger opening (osculum)
- Water enters central cavity through tiny pores (ostia)
- Spicule
- Whiplike flagellum
- Collar
- COLLAR CELL

SIMPLE SPONGE BODY SYSTEM

Worms

"Worm" is a term used to describe animals of several unrelated phyla with soft, tubular bodies. They occupy a wide range of marine, freshwater, and terrestrial habitats and many are parasitic.

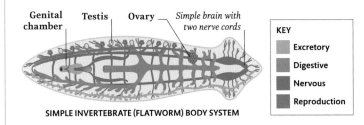

- Genital chamber
- Testis
- Ovary
- Simple brain with two nerve cords

SIMPLE INVERTEBRATE (FLATWORM) BODY SYSTEM

KEY
- Excretory
- Digestive
- Nervous
- Reproduction

- Spicules surround opening
- Tube-shaped body

SYCON SPONGE
(*Sycon* sp.)

Calcareous sponges

About 650 species of this exclusively marine group live in relatively shallow waters. The gelatinous body filling is supported by a skeleton of three-pointed spicules made of calcium carbonate.

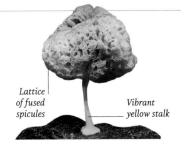

- Lattice of fused spicules
- Vibrant yellow stalk

BOLOSOMA GLASS SPONGE
(*Bolosoma* sp.)

Glass sponges

The skeletal elements of glass sponges comprise four- or six-pointed spicules made of silicon, fused to form a robust latticework. They are found worldwide, generally in deeper water than calcareous sponges.

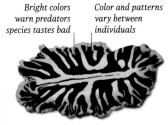

- Bright colors warn predators species tastes bad
- Color and patterns vary between individuals

DIVIDED FLATWORM
(*Pseudoceros dimidiatus*)

Flatworms

Flatworms (including flukes and tapeworms) have simple bodies, lacking organs for respiration or circulation, and a simple nervous system. Food is digested in a simple pouch with a single opening.

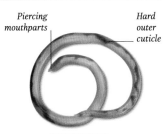

- Piercing mouthparts
- Hard outer cuticle

"PORK WORM"
(*Trichinella spiralis*)

Roundworms

Roundworms, also known as nematodes, are the most widespread and abundant form of animal life on Earth. They range from a few microns to over 3 ft (100 cm) in length. A third of known species are parasitic.

- Very large opening (osculum)
- Deeply ridged body can grow up to 6 ft (2 m) tall
- Large group of more than 30 tubes

BARREL SPONGE
(*Xestospongia testudinaria*)

Demosponges

This diverse group of more than 7,000 species includes crusts, mounds, and tubular forms. Most demosponges are marine, but about 150 species live in brackish or fresh water.

STOVEPIPE SPONGE
(*Aplysina archeri*)

Segmented worms

The bodies of annelids are divided into repeating segments. Annelids include the marine ragworms and tubeworms, the terrestrial earthworms, and leeches.

- Head
- Tail

COMMON EARTHWORM
(*Lumbricus terrestris*)

- Whorls of tentacles extended from tube for filter feeding and respiration

CHRISTMAS TREE TUBE WORM
(*Spirobranchus giganteus*)

Cnidarians

These simple aquatic animals may live as solitary or colonial forms. They have a radially symmetrical body plan and an armory of stinging cells (cnidocytes) used to capture prey and in self-defense. Individuals of many species alternate between swimming medusa and sedentary polyp life stages.

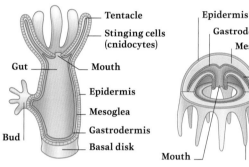

Tentacle
Stinging cells (cnidocytes)
Gut
Mouth
Epidermis
Mesoglea
Gastrodermis
Bud
Basal disk

Epidermis
Gastrodermis
Mesoglea
Gut
Mouth
Tentacle

Polyp
Sedentary polyps live attached to the seabed or other substrate. A circlet of tentacles directs prey to the central, upward-facing mouth.

Medusa
The bell-shaped medusa is a free-swimming form with a fringe of tentacles used to trap prey. The mouth is in the center of the underside.

Anemones and corals

The exclusively marine class Anthozoa includes the anemones and the soft and hard corals. Colonies of the latter secrete the stony matrix that forms the basis of coral reefs, and thus support huge biodiversity. Anthozoans disperse as planktonic larvae, which settle and metamorphose into sessile polyps. Most can reproduce both sexually and by budding.

Sticky foot (basal disk) anchors anemone to reef

Polyp can grow up to 3ft (1m) in diameter

MAGNIFICENT SEA ANEMONE
(*Heteractis magnifica*)

Polyps protrude from fingerlike mass

DEAD-MAN'S FINGERS
(*Alcyonium glomeratum*)

Tough, flexible stem with many polyp-bearing branches

COMMON SEA FAN
(*Gorgonia ventalina*)

Lateral polyps on side branches

ORANGE SEA PEN
(*Ptilosarcus gurneyi*)

Grooved, spherical shape of this hard coral colony

LOBED BRAIN CORAL
(*Lobophyllia* sp.)

Mollusks

Most members of this huge group of more than 110,000 marine, freshwater, and terrestrial species carry a protective external shell or shells made of calcium carbonate and protein. However, in slugs and cephalopods the shell is either reduced, absent, or internal.

Siphon
Adductor muscle
Mantle
Shell
Hinge ligament
Foot
Gills
Digestive system

Bivalve
The shell has two parts (valves) joined by a flexible hinge. Adductor muscles open and close the shell.

Digestive system
Tentacle
Radula
Jaw
Eye
Funnel
Gills
Shell
Mantle cavity

Cephalopod
Only nautiloids retain an external shell. That of squid, cuttlefish, and octopuses is internalized or absent.

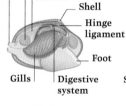

Digestive system
Mantle
Gill
Radula
Coiled shell
Foot
Sensory tentacles

Gastropod
All modern gastropods evolved from a common ancestor with a single shell and a muscular foot.

Cephalopods

These tentacled, agile, color-changing mollusks include the Colossal Squid, the largest invertebrate at up to 43 ft (13 m) long. Cephalopods are predators of other marine animals.

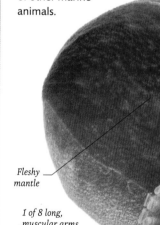

Fleshy mantle

1 of 8 long, muscular arms

Bivalves

Exclusively aquatic, bivalves are filter feeders with a planktonic larval stage. Most species are sedentary as adults and live attached to a substrate by gluey threads, but scallops can swim using their valves and mantle.

GIANT CLAM
(*Tridacna gigas*)

Siphon draws in water

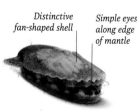

Distinctive fan-shaped shell

Simple eyes along edge of mantle

QUEEN SCALLOP
(*Aequipecten opercularis*)

Ribbed shell

COMMON EDIBLE COCKLE
(*Cerastoderma edule*)

Growth rings

WEST AFRICAN TELLIN
(*Peronaea madagascariensis*)

Asymmetrical shell

COMMON MUSSEL
(*Mytilus edulis*)

Translucent bell of up to
12 in (30 cm) diameter

Jellyfish

True jellyfish (Scyphozoa) have a central mouth that opens into four stomach (gastric) pouches. The "jelly" is a clear substance called mesoglea, which lies between the two layers of cells: the outer epidermis and inner gastrodermis.

HOW JELLYFISH SWIM

A medusa swims using muscle fibers, called coronal muscle, that encircle the bell-shaped body. Like other cnidarians, jellyfish have no brain, but simple sense organs allow them to respond to light and gravity, and many species rise to feed in surface waters at night, and sink deeper by day.

Jellyfish propelled
forward

Coronal muscle
relaxes and bell
opens out

Water
enters bell

Coronal muscle
contracts

Water forced
out of bell

POWER STROKE　　**RECOVERY STROKE**

BLUE JELLYFISH
(*Cyanea lamarckii*)

Regularly spaced reflective
crystalline spots

**WHITE-SPOTTED
JELLYFISH**
(*Phyllorhiza punctata*)

**UPSIDE-DOWN
JELLYFISH**
(*Cassiopea andromeda*)

MOON JELLYFISH
(*Aurelia aurita*)

Hydrozoans

Many species of this diverse group have a polyp and a medusa stage. Most are colonial, comprising tens to thousands of polyps. The Portuguese Man-of-War is a colony of four different types of polyps that create the impression of a more complex single animal.

Offspring budding
from parent polyp

COMMON HYDRA
(*Hydra vulgaris*)

Tip of
branching
colony

FIRE CORAL
(*Millepora* sp.)

Polyp at tip of
branching stem

**PINK-HEARTED
HYDROID**
(*Tubularia* sp.)

Gas-filled float
(pneumatophore)

Stinging tentacles
trail for 33 ft (10 m)
or more below surface

**PORTUGUESE
MAN-OF-WAR**
(*Physalia physalis*)

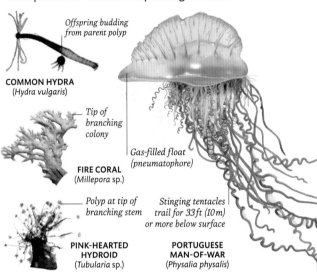

External,
chambered,
bouyant shell

8 arms and 2 tentacles
attached to head

Bright warning
coloration

CHAMBERED NAUTILUS
(*Nautilus pompilius*)

COMMON CUTTLEFISH
(*Sepia officinalis*)

BLUE-RINGED OCTOPUS
(*Hapalochlaena lunulata*)

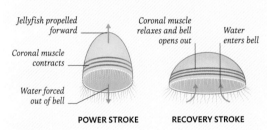

A **Common Octopus** has about **500 million**
neurons in its body—most of them in its **arms**

Prominent
sophisticated eye

Cuplike suckers
have taste and
touch sensors

COMMON OCTOPUS
(*Octopus vulgaris*)

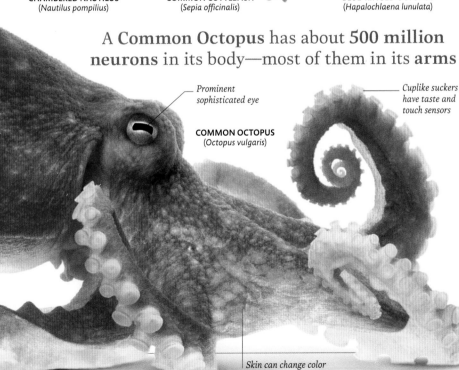

Skin can change color
or texture

Gastropods

By far the largest class of mollusks, gastropods include the familiar slugs and snails seen in gardens. Some gastropods are graceful swimmers, others are slow-moving herbivores, while cone snails fire darts containing paralyzing neurotoxins at their prey.

Glossy
shell

Flare-lipped
shell

Eye at tip of first pair
of tentacles

TIGER COWRIE
(*Cypraea tigris*)

QUEEN CONCH
(*Lobatus gigas*)

ROMAN SNAIL
(*Helix pomatia*)

Two pairs of
sensory tentacles

Respiratory
opening

APPLE SNAIL
(*Ampullariidae*)

COMMON GARDEN SLUG
(*Arion distinctus*)

Tentacle
(rhinophore)
sensitive to touch
and chemicals

Exposed gills
for respiration

Mantle

ANNA'S SEA SLUG
(*Chromodoris annae*)

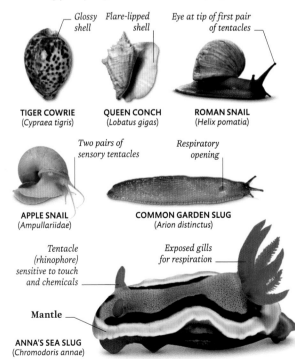

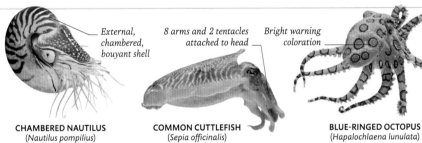

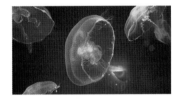

see also Invertebrates classification p.159 ▶　Reproduction pp.226–27 ▶　**109**

» Invertebrates continued

Echinoderms

The adult bodies of these marine animals typically exhibit five-way symmetry. Most have moveable spines and all have a skeleton (test) of calcium carbonate plates. Echinoderms lack a brain and use hydraulic tube feet connected by a water vascular system to move, feed, and respire.

Sea urchins

Sea urchins have robust, spiny, spherical or discoid adult bodies, supported by a rigid test with tiny perforations through which the tube feet extend. They feed using a five-toothed apparatus, the Aristotle's lantern.

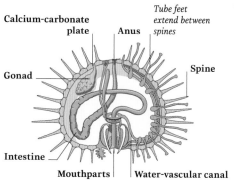

Calcium-carbonate plate — Anus — *Tube feet extend between spines*
Gonad — Spine
Intestine — Mouthparts — Water-vascular canal

SEA URCHIN BODY SECTION

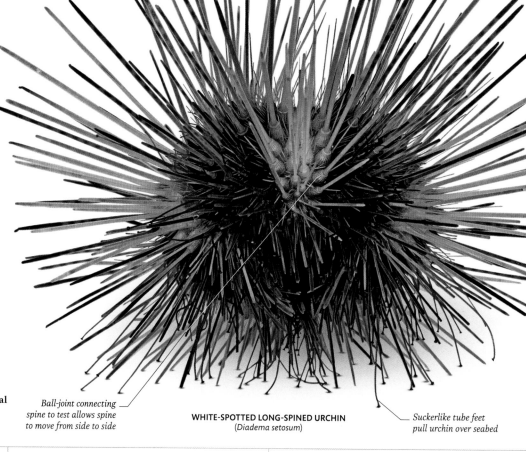

Hard-tipped hollow spine releases mild venom if broken

Ball-joint connecting spine to test allows spine to move from side to side

WHITE-SPOTTED LONG-SPINED URCHIN
(*Diadema setosum*)

Suckerlike tube feet pull urchin over seabed

Brittle starfish

These seabed dwellers typically resemble skinny, hyperactive starfish, with mobile arms allowing them to crawl, climb, and even swim in open water. Like starfish they can regenerate their arms if they are broken off.

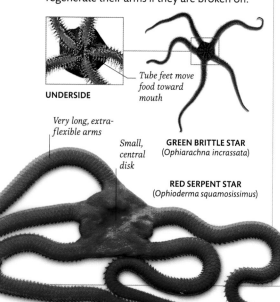

UNDERSIDE

Tube feet move food toward mouth

Very long, extra-flexible arms

Small, central disk

GREEN BRITTLE STAR
(*Ophiarachna incrassata*)

RED SERPENT STAR
(*Ophioderma squamosissimus*)

Starfish

Starfish occur from tidal zones to ocean floors. Most have five arms but many species have more. The mouth and tube feet are located in grooves on the underside. Most are carnivorous and can open bivalve shells with their tube feet.

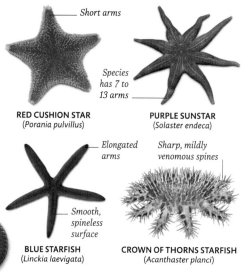

Short arms

RED CUSHION STAR
(*Porania pulvillus*)

Species has 7 to 13 arms

PURPLE SUNSTAR
(*Solaster endeca*)

Elongated arms

Sharp, mildly venomous spines

Smooth, spineless surface

BLUE STARFISH
(*Linckia laevigata*)

CROWN OF THORNS STARFISH
(*Acanthaster planci*)

Sea cucumbers

Elongation gives sea cucumbers a front and back end, but the five-way symmetry is still usually apparent in the arrangement of feeding tentacles and the rows of tube feet that run along the body in most species.

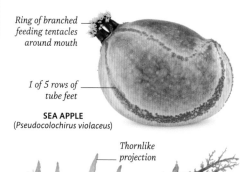

Ring of branched feeding tentacles around mouth

1 of 5 rows of tube feet

SEA APPLE
(*Pseudocolochirus violaceus*)

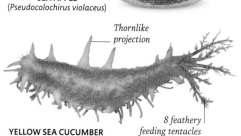

Thornlike projection

YELLOW SEA CUCUMBER
(*Colochirus robustus*)

8 feathery feeding tentacles extended into current

◀ see also The animal kingdom p.106

ANIMALS

Flexible test enables urchin to enter crevices

FIRE URCHIN
(Asthenosoma varium)

Mouth at front end

Distinctive "heart" shape

HEART URCHIN
(Echinocardium cordatum)

Blunt, solid spines

Spherical test up to 6in (15cm) in diameter

SLATE PENCIL URCHIN
(Heterocentrotus mamillatus)

Arthropods

The phylum Arthropoda contains about 80 percent of known animal species. Arthropods have bilateral symmetry, an external skeleton, and a segmented body with multifunctional paired appendages. They are adapted to live in every type of habitat.

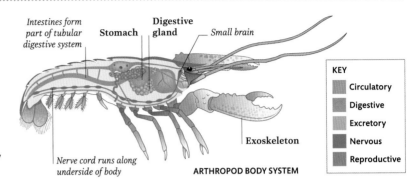

Intestines form part of tubular digestive system
Stomach
Digestive gland
Small brain

Nerve cord runs along underside of body

Exoskeleton

ARTHROPOD BODY SYSTEM

KEY
- Circulatory
- Digestive
- Excretory
- Nervous
- Reproductive

Insects

Nine out of 10 arthropods are insects. They have six legs and a body in three sections: head, thorax, and abdomen. They are the only invertebrate group capable of powered flight.

Insect exoskeleton

A lightweight, rigid exoskeleton provides insects with immense strength for their size. Adults breathe air through openings in it.

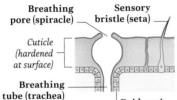

Breathing pore (spiracle)
Sensory bristle (seta)
Cuticle (hardened at surface)
Breathing tube (trachea)
Epidermis

Thorax
Simple eyes (ocelli) on top of head
Forewings partly cover hindwings at rest
Abdomen
Breathing pore (spiracle)
Head
Movable, segmented feelers (antennae) detect airborne scents
Compound eye
Cutting and chewing mouthparts (mandibles)
Claw
Pollen basket on rear legs of some bee species
Fourth leg segment (tibia)
Third leg segment (femur)
Fifth leg segment (metatarsus)
Foot (tarsus)

HONEY BEE
(Apis mellifera)

Crinoids

Crinoids orient themselves mouth upward and their five arms have many branches. They take two forms: the stalked sea lilies and unstalked feather stars.

Arms spread to feed

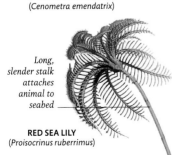

PRETTY FEATHER STAR
(Cenometra emendatrix)

Long, slender stalk attaches animal to seabed

RED SEA LILY
(Proisocrinus ruberrimus)

METAMORPHOSIS

Most insects undergo a process of developmental change from a larval to adult form. Complete metamorphosis involves a single transformation in which the larva's body is liquified and remodeled as the adult inside a pupa or chrysalis.

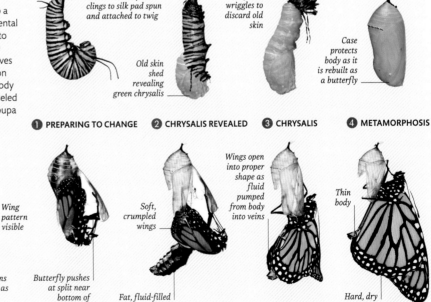

Monarch caterpillar clings to silk pad spun and attached to twig
Old skin shed revealing green chrysalis
Chrysalis wriggles to discard old skin
Case protects body as it is rebuilt as a butterfly

1 PREPARING TO CHANGE **2** CHRYSALIS REVEALED **3** CHRYSALIS **4** METAMORPHOSIS

Wing pattern visible
Chrysalis darkens after 9–10 days as butterfly's body turns black
Butterfly pushes at split near bottom of chrysalis
Soft, crumpled wings
Fat, fluid-filled body
Wings open into proper shape as fluid pumped from body into veins
Thin body
Hard, dry wings

5 READY TO EMERGE **6** CHRYSALIS SPLITS **7** OUT OF SHAPE **8** WINGS EXPAND **9** READY TO FLY

Dragonflies are the fastest flying insects, reaching top speeds of 35 mph (56 km/h)

Insect orders

Insects account for more species than any other class of animals. More than 1 million species have been identified, but scientists think many millions more have yet to be discovered. Species are grouped into orders based on distinctive features they have in common. They range from simple, wingless insects, such as silverfish and parasitic lice and fleas, to social bees, wasps, and ants, which are the most advanced insects in the world.

LITTLE AND LARGE

The award of world's largest flying insect depends on whether body length or wingspan is measured, but the horn of a male Hercules Beetle makes its body longer than a human hand. By contrast, the world's smallest flying insect, the fairyfly (a type of wasp), is so tiny it would fit inside a period. Males are even smaller than females but lack wings.

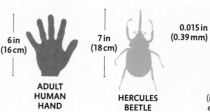

6 in (16 cm)
ADULT HUMAN HAND

7 in (18 cm)
HERCULES BEETLE
(Dynastes hercules)
Beetles

0.015 in (0.39 mm)
FAIRYFLY
(Dicopomorpha echmepterygis)
Bees, wasps, ants, and sawflies

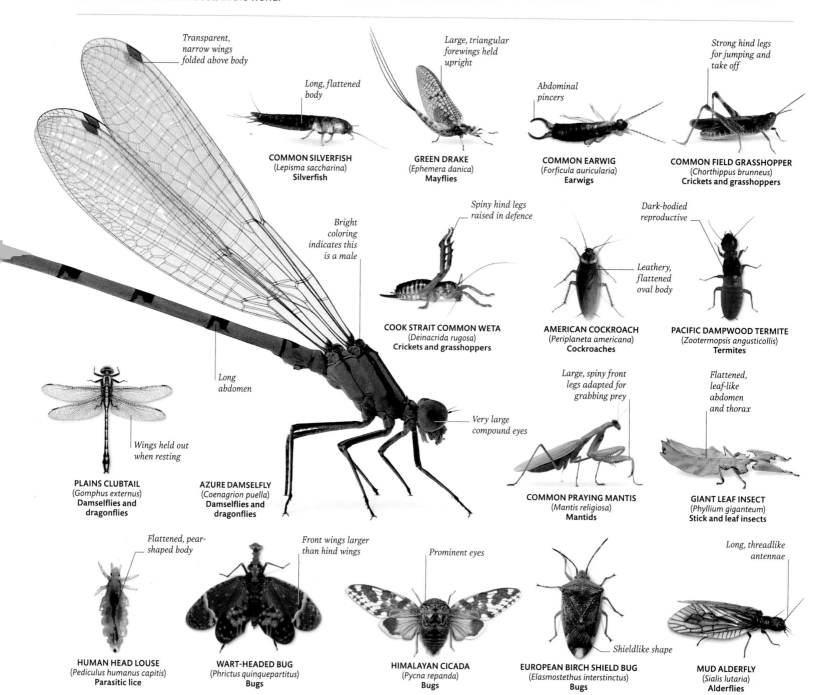

Transparent, narrow wings folded above body

Long, flattened body

COMMON SILVERFISH
(Lepisma saccharina)
Silverfish

Large, triangular forewings held upright

GREEN DRAKE
(Ephemera danica)
Mayflies

Abdominal pincers

COMMON EARWIG
(Forficula auricularia)
Earwigs

Strong hind legs for jumping and take off

COMMON FIELD GRASSHOPPER
(Chorthippus brunneus)
Crickets and grasshoppers

Bright coloring indicates this is a male

Spiny hind legs raised in defence

COOK STRAIT COMMON WETA
(Deinacrida rugosa)
Crickets and grasshoppers

Leathery, flattened oval body

AMERICAN COCKROACH
(Periplaneta americana)
Cockroaches

Dark-bodied reproductive

PACIFIC DAMPWOOD TERMITE
(Zootermopsis angusticollis)
Termites

Long abdomen

Very large compound eyes

Wings held out when resting

PLAINS CLUBTAIL
(Gomphus externus)
Damselflies and dragonflies

AZURE DAMSELFLY
(Coenagrion puella)
Damselflies and dragonflies

Large, spiny front legs adapted for grabbing prey

COMMON PRAYING MANTIS
(Mantis religiosa)
Mantids

Flattened, leaf-like abdomen and thorax

GIANT LEAF INSECT
(Phyllium giganteum)
Stick and leaf insects

Flattened, pear-shaped body

HUMAN HEAD LOUSE
(Pediculus humanus capitis)
Parasitic lice

Front wings larger than hind wings

WART-HEADED BUG
(Phrictus quinquepartitus)
Bugs

Prominent eyes

HIMALAYAN CICADA
(Pycna repanda)
Bugs

Shieldlike shape

EUROPEAN BIRCH SHIELD BUG
(Elasmostethus interstinctus)
Bugs

Long, threadlike antennae

MUD ALDERFLY
(Sialis lutaria)
Alderflies

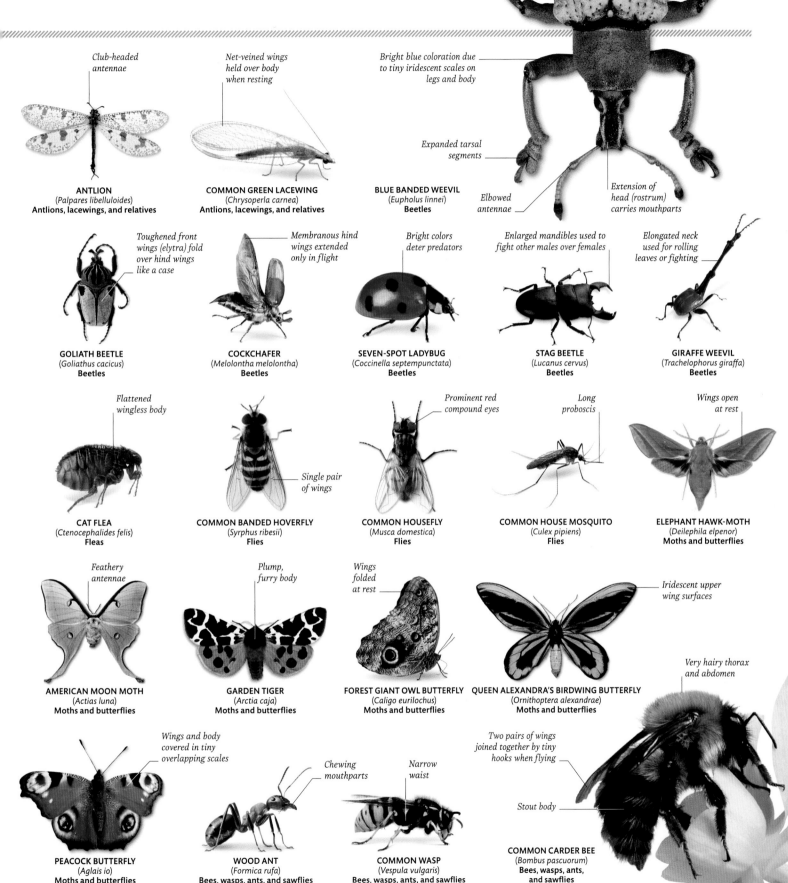

Club-headed antennae

ANTLION
(*Palpares libelluloides*)
Antlions, lacewings, and relatives

Net-veined wings held over body when resting

COMMON GREEN LACEWING
(*Chrysoperla carnea*)
Antlions, lacewings, and relatives

Bright blue coloration due to tiny iridescent scales on legs and body

Expanded tarsal segments

Elbowed antennae

Extension of head (rostrum) carries mouthparts

BLUE BANDED WEEVIL
(*Eupholus linnei*)
Beetles

Toughened front wings (elytra) fold over hind wings like a case

GOLIATH BEETLE
(*Goliathus cacicus*)
Beetles

Membranous hind wings extended only in flight

COCKCHAFER
(*Melolontha melolontha*)
Beetles

Bright colors deter predators

SEVEN-SPOT LADYBUG
(*Coccinella septempunctata*)
Beetles

Enlarged mandibles used to fight other males over females

STAG BEETLE
(*Lucanus cervus*)
Beetles

Elongated neck used for rolling leaves or fighting

GIRAFFE WEEVIL
(*Trachelophorus giraffa*)
Beetles

Flattened wingless body

CAT FLEA
(*Ctenocephalides felis*)
Fleas

Single pair of wings

COMMON BANDED HOVERFLY
(*Syrphus ribesii*)
Flies

Prominent red compound eyes

COMMON HOUSEFLY
(*Musca domestica*)
Flies

Long proboscis

COMMON HOUSE MOSQUITO
(*Culex pipiens*)
Flies

Wings open at rest

ELEPHANT HAWK-MOTH
(*Deilephila elpenor*)
Moths and butterflies

Feathery antennae

AMERICAN MOON MOTH
(*Actias luna*)
Moths and butterflies

Plump, furry body

GARDEN TIGER
(*Arctia caja*)
Moths and butterflies

Wings folded at rest

FOREST GIANT OWL BUTTERFLY
(*Caligo eurilochus*)
Moths and butterflies

Iridescent upper wing surfaces

QUEEN ALEXANDRA'S BIRDWING BUTTERFLY
(*Ornithoptera alexandrae*)
Moths and butterflies

Very hairy thorax and abdomen

Wings and body covered in tiny overlapping scales

PEACOCK BUTTERFLY
(*Aglais io*)
Moths and butterflies

Chewing mouthparts

WOOD ANT
(*Formica rufa*)
Bees, wasps, ants, and sawflies

Narrow waist

COMMON WASP
(*Vespula vulgaris*)
Bees, wasps, ants, and sawflies

Two pairs of wings joined together by tiny hooks when flying

Stout body

COMMON CARDER BEE
(*Bombus pascuorum*)
Bees, wasps, ants, and sawflies

see also Invertebrates classification p.159 ▶

» Invertebrates continued

Crustaceans

This diverse group of arthropods, named for the "crust" of exoskeleton that serves as both support and armor, ranges from microscopic plankton to spider crabs with a leg span of 13 ft (4 m). Most species are aquatic.

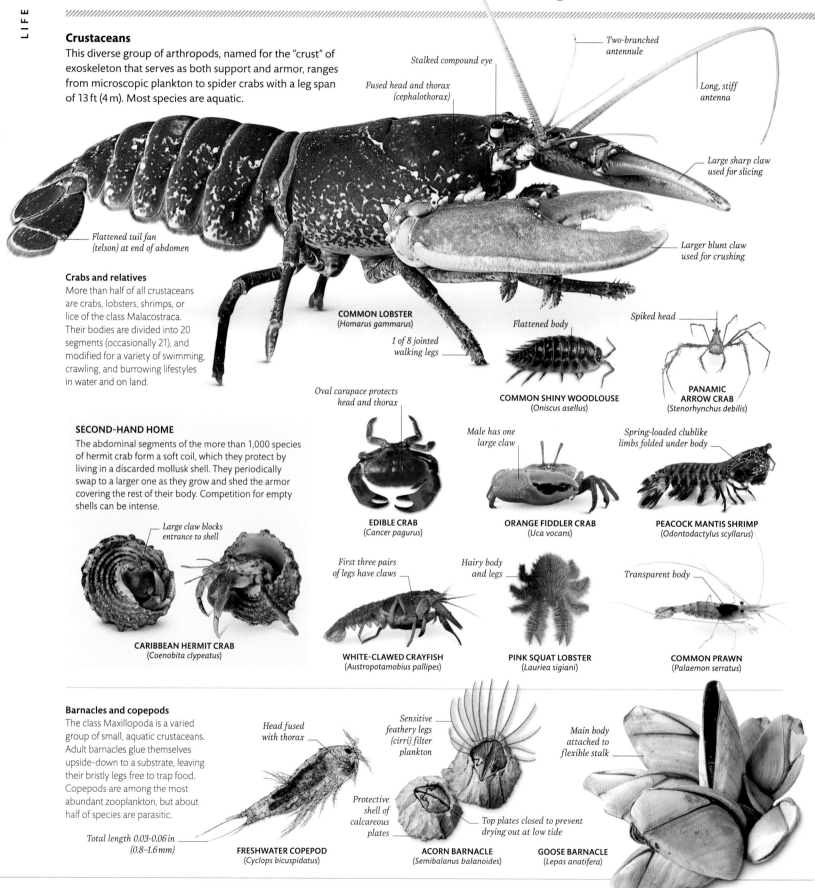

Two-branched antennule

Stalked compound eye

Fused head and thorax (cephalothorax)

Long, stiff antenna

Large sharp claw used for slicing

Flattened tail fan (telson) at end of abdomen

Larger blunt claw used for crushing

COMMON LOBSTER
(Homarus gammarus)

1 of 8 jointed walking legs

Flattened body

Spiked head

Crabs and relatives

More than half of all crustaceans are crabs, lobsters, shrimps, or lice of the class Malacostraca. Their bodies are divided into 20 segments (occasionally 21), and modified for a variety of swimming, crawling, and burrowing lifestyles in water and on land.

COMMON SHINY WOODLOUSE
(Oniscus asellus)

PANAMIC ARROW CRAB
(Stenorhynchus debilis)

Oval carapace protects head and thorax

Male has one large claw

Spring-loaded clublike limbs folded under body

SECOND-HAND HOME

The abdominal segments of the more than 1,000 species of hermit crab form a soft coil, which they protect by living in a discarded mollusk shell. They periodically swap to a larger one as they grow and shed the armor covering the rest of their body. Competition for empty shells can be intense.

Large claw blocks entrance to shell

EDIBLE CRAB
(Cancer pagurus)

ORANGE FIDDLER CRAB
(Uca vocans)

PEACOCK MANTIS SHRIMP
(Odontodactylus scyllarus)

First three pairs of legs have claws

Hairy body and legs

Transparent body

CARIBBEAN HERMIT CRAB
(Coenobita clypeatus)

WHITE-CLAWED CRAYFISH
(Austropotamobius pallipes)

PINK SQUAT LOBSTER
(Lauriea sigiani)

COMMON PRAWN
(Palaemon serratus)

Barnacles and copepods

The class Maxillopoda is a varied group of small, aquatic crustaceans. Adult barnacles glue themselves upside-down to a substrate, leaving their bristly legs free to trap food. Copepods are among the most abundant zooplankton, but about half of species are parasitic.

Head fused with thorax

Sensitive feathery legs (cirri) filter plankton

Main body attached to flexible stalk

Total length 0.03–0.06 in (0.8–1.6 mm)

Protective shell of calcareous plates

Top plates closed to prevent drying out at low tide

FRESHWATER COPEPOD
(Cyclops bicuspidatus)

ACORN BARNACLE
(Semibalanus balanoides)

GOOSE BARNACLE
(Lepas anatifera)

Arachnids

All arachnids have two main body segments, the cephalothorax and abdomen, and four pairs of legs. Additional appendages, known as chelicerae and pedipalps, serve a variety of sensory, feeding, reproductive, and defensive functions. Arachnids include the familiar spiders, scorpions, and harvestmen, and mites and ticks.

Spider silk is a stretchy protein with a tensile strength greater than steel

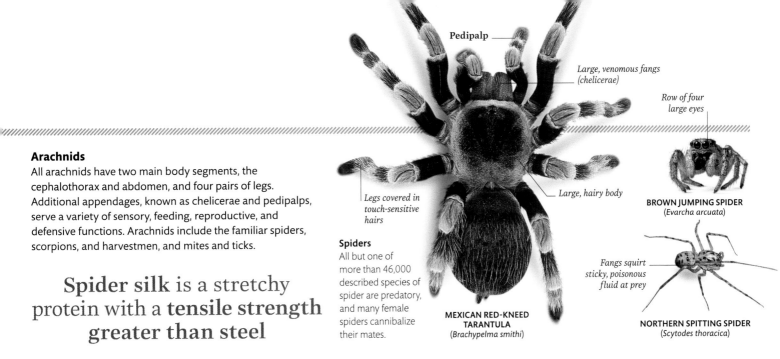

Pedipalp

Large, venomous fangs (chelicerae)

Legs covered in touch-sensitive hairs

Large, hairy body

MEXICAN RED-KNEED TARANTULA
(Brachypelma smithi)

Row of four large eyes

BROWN JUMPING SPIDER
(Evarcha arcuata)

Fangs squirt sticky, poisonous fluid at prey

NORTHERN SPITTING SPIDER
(Scytodes thoracica)

Spiders
All but one of more than 46,000 described species of spider are predatory, and many female spiders cannibalize their mates.

MAKING A SILK TRAP

Spiders use modified appendages to spin silk as it is extruded from abdominal glands. The familiar orb web species produce silk covered in sticky droplets that help snare passing insects.

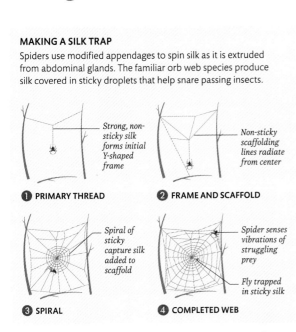

Strong, non-sticky silk forms initial Y-shaped frame

① PRIMARY THREAD

Non-sticky scaffolding lines radiate from center

② FRAME AND SCAFFOLD

Spiral of sticky capture silk added to scaffold

③ SPIRAL

Spider senses vibrations of struggling prey

Fly trapped in sticky silk

④ COMPLETED WEB

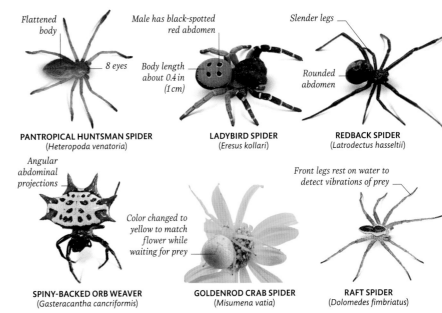

Flattened body

8 eyes

PANTROPICAL HUNTSMAN SPIDER
(Heteropoda venatoria)

Male has black-spotted red abdomen

Body length about 0.4 in (1 cm)

LADYBIRD SPIDER
(Eresus kollari)

Slender legs

Rounded abdomen

REDBACK SPIDER
(Latrodectus hasseltii)

Angular abdominal projections

SPINY-BACKED ORB WEAVER
(Gasteracantha cancriformis)

Color changed to yellow to match flower while waiting for prey

GOLDENROD CRAB SPIDER
(Misumena vatia)

Front legs rest on water to detect vibrations of prey

RAFT SPIDER
(Dolomedes fimbriatus)

Scorpions and relatives

The pedipalps of scorpions are modified into pincers. The long, upcurved tail has a venomous sting at the tip, used in hunting and defense. Whip scorpions have a whip-like, stingless tail and pseudoscorpions have a bulbous rear end.

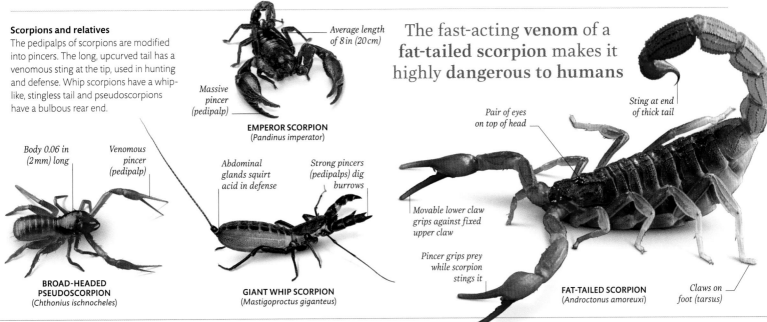

Average length of 8 in (20 cm)

Massive pincer (pedipalp)

EMPEROR SCORPION
(Pandinus imperator)

The fast-acting venom of a fat-tailed scorpion makes it highly dangerous to humans

Pair of eyes on top of head

Sting at end of thick tail

Body 0.06 in (2 mm) long

Venomous pincer (pedipalp)

BROAD-HEADED PSEUDOSCORPION
(Chthonius ischnocheles)

Abdominal glands squirt acid in defense

Strong pincers (pedipalps) dig burrows

GIANT WHIP SCORPION
(Mastigoproctus giganteus)

Movable lower claw grips against fixed upper claw

Pincer grips prey while scorpion stings it

FAT-TAILED SCORPION
(Androctonus amoreuxi)

Claws on foot (tarsus)

see also Invertebrates classification p.159 ▶   **115**

Fishes

What is a fish?

The earliest vertebrates resembled fishes, but the term "fish" refers to a diverse group of more than 33,000 aquatic animals descended from several different ancestors. All have a brain surrounded by a braincase (cranium) and most are vertebrates, divided into bony (having skeletons made of bone), cartilaginous (having skeletons made of cartilage), or primitive jawless types. The majority live exclusively in water, have scales, are cold-blooded, and use gills to breathe.

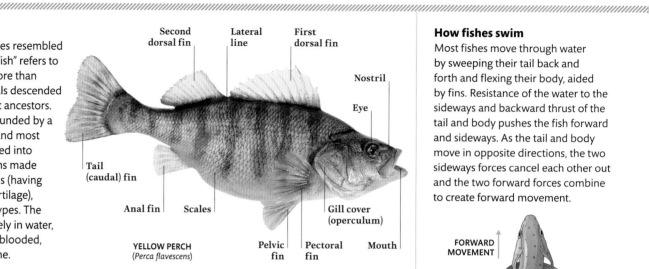

Second dorsal fin · Lateral line · First dorsal fin · Nostril · Eye · Gill cover (operculum) · Mouth · Pectoral fin · Pelvic fin · Scales · Anal fin · Tail (caudal) fin

YELLOW PERCH
(*Perca flavescens*)

How fishes breathe

Most fishes obtain oxygen through their gills. Water is taken in through the mouth and forced over the gills. Blood-rich gill filaments absorb oxygen, passing it into the bloodstream to circulate around the body. At the same time carbon dioxide in the blood is removed and released into the water.

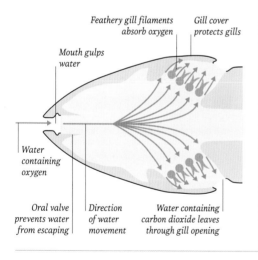

Feathery gill filaments absorb oxygen · Gill cover protects gills · Mouth gulps water · Water containing oxygen · Oral valve prevents water from escaping · Direction of water movement · Water containing carbon dioxide leaves through gill opening

Detecting movement

A fish uses sense organs called lateral lines to help it navigate. Running along both sides of its body and over its head, these channels contain neuromasts, which convert subtle changes in water pressure into electrical pulses, alerting the fish to avoid collisions or elude predators.

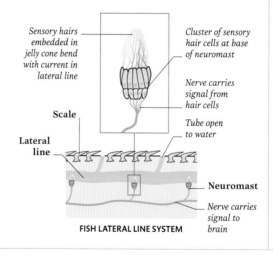

Sensory hairs embedded in jelly cone bend with current in lateral line · Cluster of sensory hair cells at base of neuromast · Nerve carries signal from hair cells · Tube open to water · Scale · Lateral line · Neuromast · Nerve carries signal to brain

FISH LATERAL LINE SYSTEM

How fishes swim

Most fishes move through water by sweeping their tail back and forth and flexing their body, aided by fins. Resistance of the water to the sideways and backward thrust of the tail and body pushes the fish forward and sideways. As the tail and body move in opposite directions, the two sideways forces cancel each other out and the two forward forces combine to create forward movement.

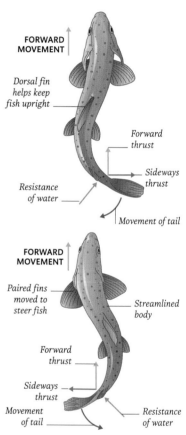

FORWARD MOVEMENT · Dorsal fin helps keep fish upright · Forward thrust · Sideways thrust · Resistance of water · Movement of tail

FORWARD MOVEMENT · Paired fins moved to steer fish · Streamlined body · Forward thrust · Sideways thrust · Movement of tail · Resistance of water

Jawless fishes

Lampreys and hagfishes both lack biting jaws, paired fins, scales, and a stomach. While hagfishes have a simple, soft braincase, they lack vertebrae, so they are not true vertebrates.

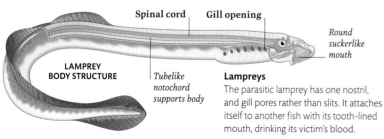

Spinal cord · Gill opening · Round suckerlike mouth · **LAMPREY BODY STRUCTURE** · Tubelike notochord supports body

Lampreys
The parasitic lamprey has one nostril, and gill pores rather than slits. It attaches itself to another fish with its tooth-lined mouth, drinking its victim's blood.

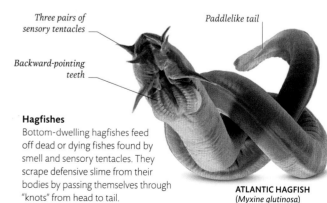

Three pairs of sensory tentacles · Paddlelike tail · Backward-pointing teeth

Hagfishes
Bottom-dwelling hagfishes feed off dead or dying fishes found by smell and sensory tentacles. They scrape defensive slime from their bodies by passing themselves through "knots" from head to tail.

ATLANTIC HAGFISH
(*Myxine glutinosa*)

Cartilaginous fishes

Unlike bony fishes, fishes such as sharks and rays have skeletons made of cartilage. Their exposed gills are not protected by a cover as in bony fishes, and some bottom-dwelling species also breathe through spiracles—respiratory openings on the top of the head behind the eyes—as well as gills. Cartilaginous fishes have small, hard placoid scales, or denticles (tiny, toothlike scales with backward-facing barbs), unequal tail lobes, and reproduce by internal fertilization.

Teeth

The teeth of a cartilaginous fish reflect its diet. The flat teeth of rays are used to crush mollusk shells, while sharks need sharp pointed teeth and teeth with serrations to bite into and tear flesh.

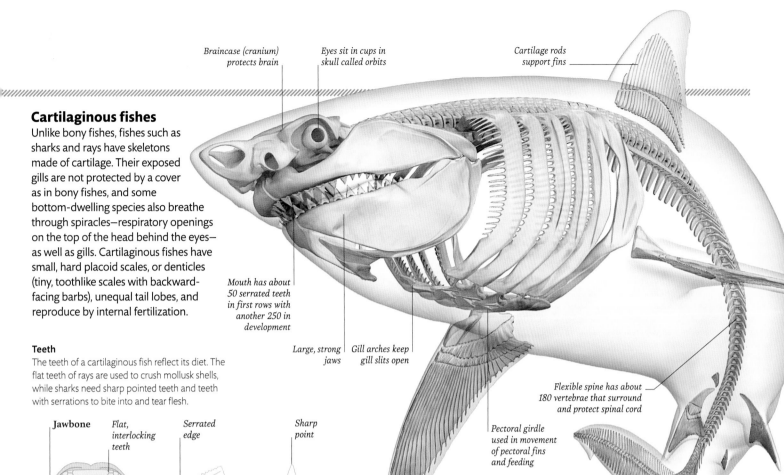

Braincase (cranium) protects brain

Eyes sit in cups in skull called orbits

Cartilage rods support fins

Mouth has about 50 serrated teeth in first rows with another 250 in development

Large, strong jaws

Gill arches keep gill slits open

Flexible spine has about 180 vertebrae that surround and protect spinal cord

Pectoral girdle used in movement of pectoral fins and feeding

SHARK SKELETON

Jawbone

Flat, interlocking teeth

Serrated edge

Sharp point

GRINDING **CUTTING** **GRIPPING**

A White Shark can grow up to **20,000 teeth** in its lifetime

Reproduction

Unlike most bony fishes, which fertilize eggs outside the body, cartilaginous fishes usually either bear live young or lay fertilized eggs that are surrounded by egg cases. These protect and feed the developing embryos until they hatch.

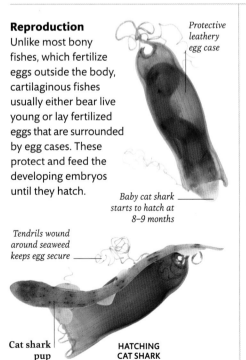

Protective leathery egg case

Baby cat shark starts to hatch at 8–9 months

Tendrils wound around seaweed keeps egg secure

Cat shark pup

HATCHING CAT SHARK

Sensing electric fields

Electroreception—sensing changes in electric fields—is highly developed in sharks and rays. Pores called ampullae of Lorenzini, concentrated on a shark's head, react to minute electric charges produced by muscle movements, alerting a shark whenever a prey species moves.

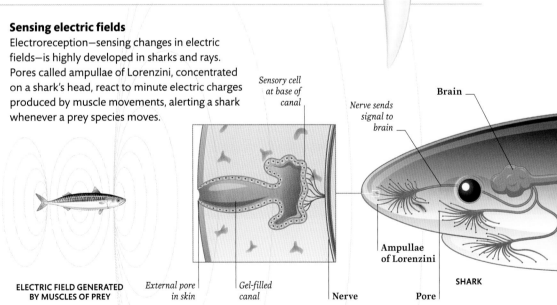

Sensory cell at base of canal

Nerve sends signal to brain

Brain

ELECTRIC FIELD GENERATED BY MUSCLES OF PREY

External pore in skin

Gel-filled canal

Nerve

Ampullae of Lorenzini

Pore

SHARK

Sharks can **detect a change** in an electrical signal as small as **1 billionth** of a volt

see also Classification p.158 ▶ Fishes classification p.160 ▶ Types of living things p.217 ▶

» Fishes continued

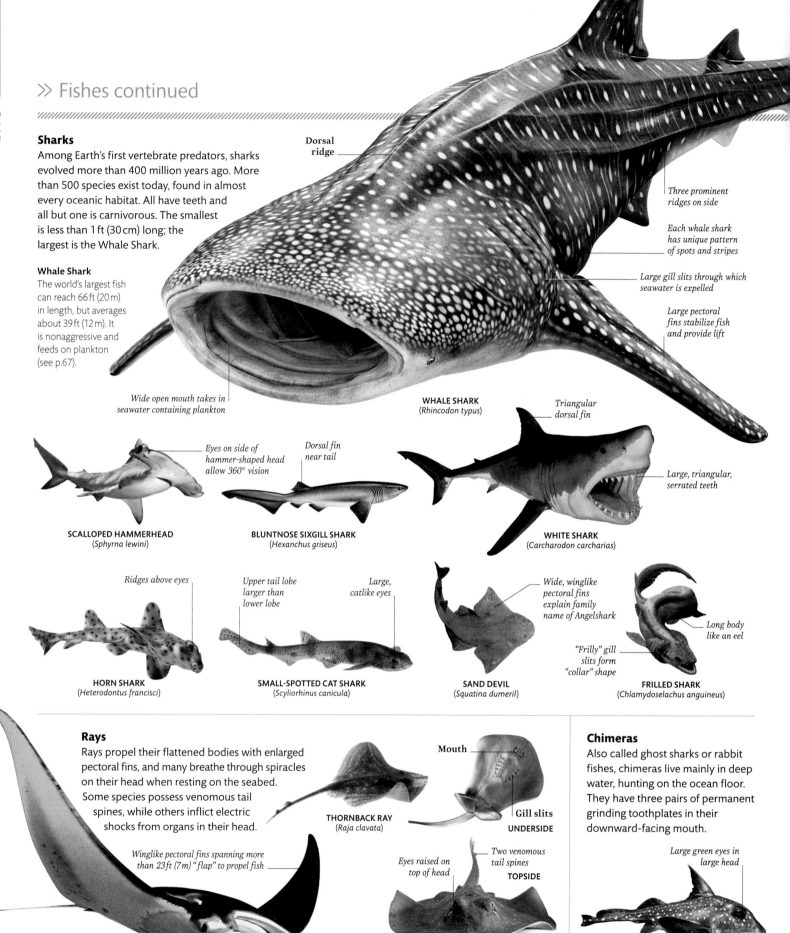

Sharks

Among Earth's first vertebrate predators, sharks evolved more than 400 million years ago. More than 500 species exist today, found in almost every oceanic habitat. All have teeth and all but one is carnivorous. The smallest is less than 1 ft (30 cm) long; the largest is the Whale Shark.

Whale Shark

The world's largest fish can reach 66 ft (20 m) in length, but averages about 39 ft (12 m). It is nonaggressive and feeds on plankton (see p.67).

Dorsal ridge

Three prominent ridges on side

Each whale shark has unique pattern of spots and stripes

Large gill slits through which seawater is expelled

Large pectoral fins stabilize fish and provide lift

Wide open mouth takes in seawater containing plankton

WHALE SHARK
(*Rhincodon typus*)

Triangular dorsal fin

Eyes on side of hammer-shaped head allow 360° vision

Dorsal fin near tail

Large, triangular, serrated teeth

SCALLOPED HAMMERHEAD
(*Sphyrna lewini*)

BLUNTNOSE SIXGILL SHARK
(*Hexanchus griseus*)

WHITE SHARK
(*Carcharodon carcharias*)

Ridges above eyes

Upper tail lobe larger than lower lobe

Large, catlike eyes

Wide, winglike pectoral fins explain family name of Angelshark

"Frilly" gill slits form "collar" shape

Long body like an eel

HORN SHARK
(*Heterodontus francisci*)

SMALL-SPOTTED CAT SHARK
(*Scyliorhinus canicula*)

SAND DEVIL
(*Squatina dumeril*)

FRILLED SHARK
(*Chlamydoselachus anguineus*)

Rays

Rays propel their flattened bodies with enlarged pectoral fins, and many breathe through spiracles on their head when resting on the seabed. Some species possess venomous tail spines, while others inflict electric shocks from organs in their head.

Winglike pectoral fins spanning more than 23 ft (7 m) "flap" to propel fish

Mouth

THORNBACK RAY
(*Raja clavata*)

Gill slits
UNDERSIDE

Eyes raised on top of head

Two venomous tail spines
TOPSIDE

GIANT MANTA RAY
(*Manta birostris*)

BLUE-SPOTTED RIBBONTAIL RAY
(*Taeniura lymma*)

Chimeras

Also called ghost sharks or rabbit fishes, chimeras live mainly in deep water, hunting on the ocean floor. They have three pairs of permanent grinding toothplates in their downward-facing mouth.

Large green eyes in large head

SPOTTED RATFISH
(*Hydrolagus colliei*)

Bony fishes

Of the three groups of fishes, bony fishes evolved most recently and are considered the most advanced. With more than 32,000 species, they represent the largest class of vertebrates on Earth, and make up about 96 percent of all fish species. Found in almost every aquatic habitat, from deep oceans to high-altitude lakes, most bony fishes have scales, two nostrils, a swim bladder, and one pair of gill openings.

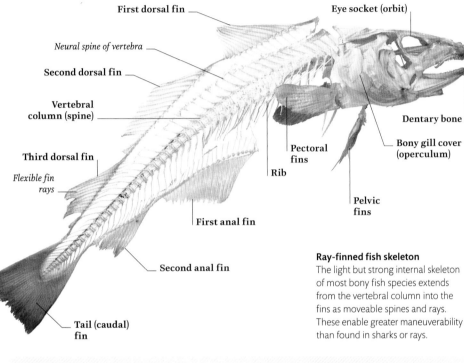

- First dorsal fin
- Neural spine of vertebra
- Second dorsal fin
- Vertebral column (spine)
- Third dorsal fin
- Flexible fin rays
- First anal fin
- Second anal fin
- Tail (caudal) fin
- Eye socket (orbit)
- Dentary bone
- Bony gill cover (operculum)
- Pectoral fins
- Rib
- Pelvic fins

Ray-finned fish skeleton
The light but strong internal skeleton of most bony fish species extends from the vertebral column into the fins as moveable spines and rays. These enable greater maneuverability than found in sharks or rays.

Buoyancy

Most bony fishes have an internal, expandable, usually gas-filled buoyancy organ called a swim bladder. By adjusting the amount of gas (mostly oxygen) the bladder contains, the fishes can maintain a certain depth, rise, or sink. Cartilaginous fishes lack a swim bladder, but do have a large oil-filled liver, which is less dense than water and so increases their bouyancy. Some bottom-dwelling fishes have no swim bladder.

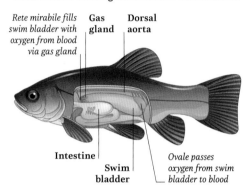

- Rete mirabile fills swim bladder with oxygen from blood via gas gland
- Gas gland
- Dorsal aorta
- Intestine
- Swim bladder
- Ovale passes oxygen from swim bladder to blood

Deep-sea fishes have a higher concentration of **oxygen** in their swim bladders

FROM FINS TO LIMBS

Most fishes use fins for swimming, but in some species, they have other locomotive functions. In flyingfishes, elongated pectoral fins serve as gliding wings, but in mudskippers, they have shortened into structures for moving over land. Several bottom-dwelling fish species, such as frogfishes and some scorpionfishes, also use specially adapted fins to crawl or "walk" along the seabed. The frogfish's pectoral fins have a flexible joint that allows it to bend, giving the fish better control when walking.

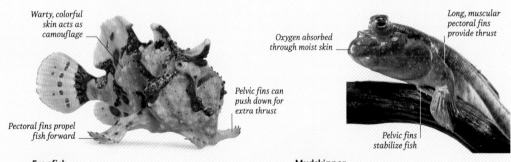

- Warty, colorful skin acts as camouflage
- Pectoral fins propel fish forward
- Pelvic fins can push down for extra thrust
- Oxygen absorbed through moist skin
- Long, muscular pectoral fins provide thrust
- Pelvic fins stabilize fish

Frogfish
Using its modified lower fins, a frogfish "walks" slowly along the seabed, pausing to attract prey by waggling a movable stalk between its eyes.

Mudskipper
Mudskippers live most of their lives on land, and see better in air than underwater. Adapted fins and evolved "shoulder" joints allow them to climb and crawl.

Fleshy-finned fishes

Fleshy- or lobe-finned fishes like coelacanths and lungfishes are believed to share an ancestor with land vertebrates. They differ from other bony fishes by having lost or greatly reduced fin rays, and their highly mobile fins are covered in fleshy muscle. Coelacanths live in deep marine waters, whereas lungfishes live in lakes, rivers, and swamps, and can breathe air with their primitive lungs.

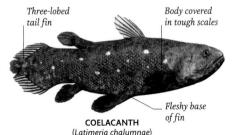

- Three-lobed tail fin
- Body covered in tough scales
- Fleshy base of fin

COELACANTH
(*Latimeria chalumnae*)

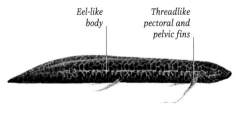

- Eel-like body
- Threadlike pectoral and pelvic fins

MARBLED LUNGFISH
(*Protopterus aethiopicus*)

see also Classification p.158 ▶   Fishes classification p.160 ▶   **119**

» Fishes continued

Ray-finned fishes

The fins of these bony fishes are supported by a fan of stiff, flexible rods, called rays, covered with skin. By far the largest group of fishes, with some 32,000 species, ray-finned fishes are divided into more than 10 superorders, the most important of which are shown here. However, the classification of the fishes in this group is constantly changing as scientists discover new species and find out more about the relationships between them.

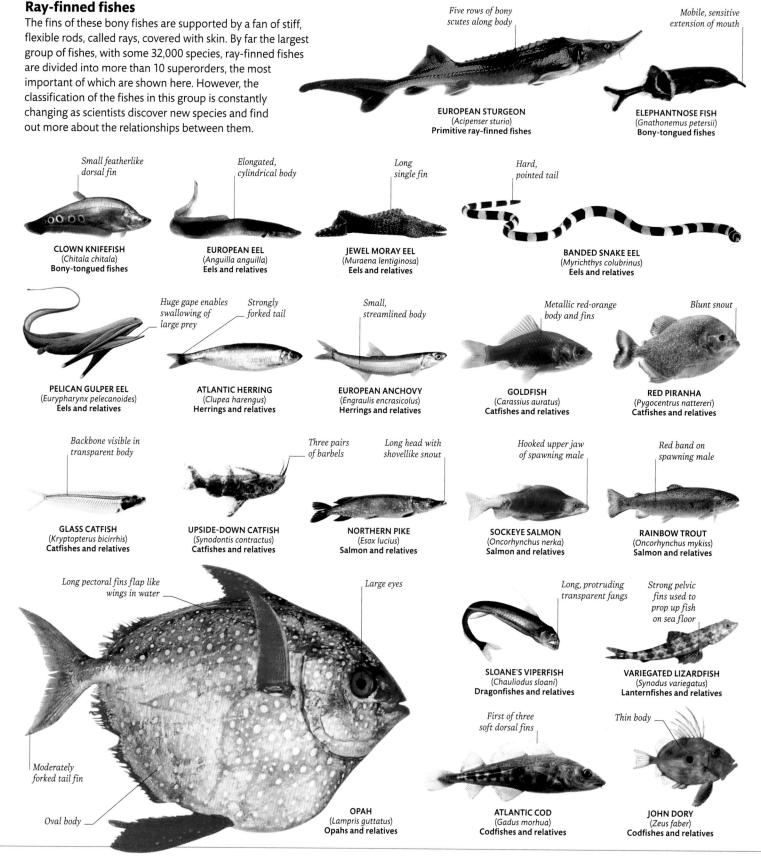

Five rows of bony scutes along body

EUROPEAN STURGEON
(*Acipenser sturio*)
Primitive ray-finned fishes

Mobile, sensitive extension of mouth

ELEPHANTNOSE FISH
(*Gnathonemus petersii*)
Bony-tongued fishes

Small featherlike dorsal fin

CLOWN KNIFEFISH
(*Chitala chitala*)
Bony-tongued fishes

Elongated, cylindrical body

EUROPEAN EEL
(*Anguilla anguilla*)
Eels and relatives

Long single fin

JEWEL MORAY EEL
(*Muraena lentiginosa*)
Eels and relatives

Hard, pointed tail

BANDED SNAKE EEL
(*Myrichthys colubrinus*)
Eels and relatives

Huge gape enables swallowing of large prey

PELICAN GULPER EEL
(*Eurypharynx pelecanoides*)
Eels and relatives

Strongly forked tail

ATLANTIC HERRING
(*Clupea harengus*)
Herrings and relatives

Small, streamlined body

EUROPEAN ANCHOVY
(*Engraulis encrasicolus*)
Herrings and relatives

Metallic red-orange body and fins

GOLDFISH
(*Carassius auratus*)
Catfishes and relatives

Blunt snout

RED PIRANHA
(*Pygocentrus nattereri*)
Catfishes and relatives

Backbone visible in transparent body

GLASS CATFISH
(*Kryptopterus bicirrhis*)
Catfishes and relatives

Three pairs of barbels

UPSIDE-DOWN CATFISH
(*Synodontis contractus*)
Catfishes and relatives

Long head with shovellike snout

NORTHERN PIKE
(*Esox lucius*)
Salmon and relatives

Hooked upper jaw of spawning male

SOCKEYE SALMON
(*Oncorhynchus nerka*)
Salmon and relatives

Red band on spawning male

RAINBOW TROUT
(*Oncorhynchus mykiss*)
Salmon and relatives

Long pectoral fins flap like wings in water

Large eyes

Moderately forked tail fin

Oval body

OPAH
(*Lampris guttatus*)
Opahs and relatives

Long, protruding transparent fangs

SLOANE'S VIPERFISH
(*Chauliodus sloani*)
Dragonfishes and relatives

Strong pelvic fins used to prop up fish on sea floor

VARIEGATED LIZARDFISH
(*Synodus variegatus*)
Lanternfishes and relatives

First of three soft dorsal fins

ATLANTIC COD
(*Gadus morhua*)
Codfishes and relatives

Thin body

JOHN DORY
(*Zeus faber*)
Codfishes and relatives

Weighing up to **5,000 lb** (2,300 kg), the **Ocean Sunfish** is the **world's largest bony fish**

Spiny-rayed fishes

Containing almost half of all species of fishes, this is by far the largest superorder of ray-finned fishes, encompassing 32 orders. As well as flexible fin rays, spiny-rayed fishes have harder, sharp, bony spines in the front part of their dorsal, anal, and pelvic fins. In some fishes, these spines have been adapted as weapons of defense or attack. For example, the spines of scorpionfishes, such as the Red Lionfish, are venomous.

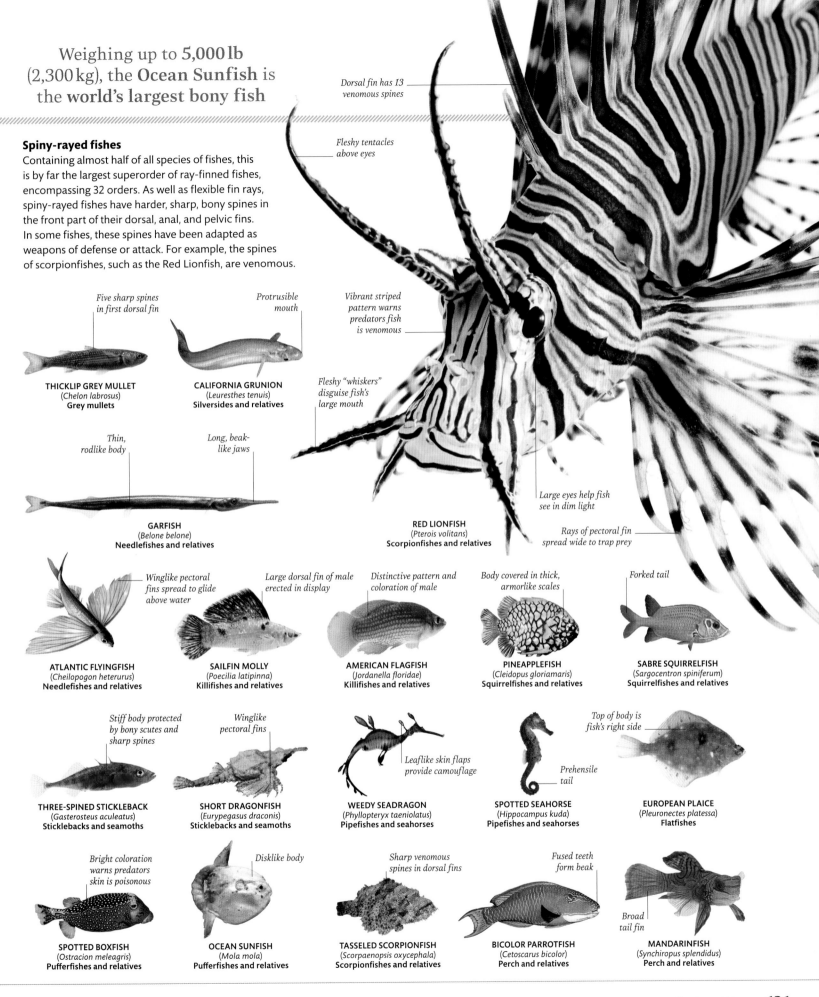

Dorsal fin has 13 venomous spines

Fleshy tentacles above eyes

Five sharp spines in first dorsal fin

Protrusible mouth

Vibrant striped pattern warns predators fish is venomous

THICKLIP GREY MULLET
(*Chelon labrosus*)
Grey mullets

CALIFORNIA GRUNION
(*Leuresthes tenuis*)
Silversides and relatives

Fleshy "whiskers" disguise fish's large mouth

Thin, rodlike body

Long, beak-like jaws

GARFISH
(*Belone belone*)
Needlefishes and relatives

RED LIONFISH
(*Pterois volitans*)
Scorpionfishes and relatives

Large eyes help fish see in dim light

Rays of pectoral fin spread wide to trap prey

Winglike pectoral fins spread to glide above water

Large dorsal fin of male erected in display

Distinctive pattern and coloration of male

Body covered in thick, armorlike scales

Forked tail

ATLANTIC FLYINGFISH
(*Cheilopogon heterurus*)
Needlefishes and relatives

SAILFIN MOLLY
(*Poecilia latipinna*)
Killifishes and relatives

AMERICAN FLAGFISH
(*Jordanella floridae*)
Killifishes and relatives

PINEAPPLEFISH
(*Cleidopus gloriamaris*)
Squirrelfishes and relatives

SABRE SQUIRRELFISH
(*Sargocentron spiniferum*)
Squirrelfishes and relatives

Stiff body protected by bony scutes and sharp spines

Winglike pectoral fins

Leaflike skin flaps provide camouflage

Prehensile tail

Top of body is fish's right side

THREE-SPINED STICKLEBACK
(*Gasterosteus aculeatus*)
Sticklebacks and seamoths

SHORT DRAGONFISH
(*Eurypegasus draconis*)
Sticklebacks and seamoths

WEEDY SEADRAGON
(*Phyllopteryx taeniolatus*)
Pipefishes and seahorses

SPOTTED SEAHORSE
(*Hippocampus kuda*)
Pipefishes and seahorses

EUROPEAN PLAICE
(*Pleuronectes platessa*)
Flatfishes

Bright coloration warns predators skin is poisonous

Disklike body

Sharp venomous spines in dorsal fins

Fused teeth form beak

Broad tail fin

SPOTTED BOXFISH
(*Ostracion meleagris*)
Pufferfishes and relatives

OCEAN SUNFISH
(*Mola mola*)
Pufferfishes and relatives

TASSELED SCORPIONFISH
(*Scorpaenopsis oxycephala*)
Scorpionfishes and relatives

BICOLOR PARROTFISH
(*Cetoscarus bicolor*)
Perch and relatives

MANDARINFISH
(*Synchiropus splendidus*)
Perch and relatives

see also Classification p.158 ▶   Fishes classification p.160 ▶

Amphibians

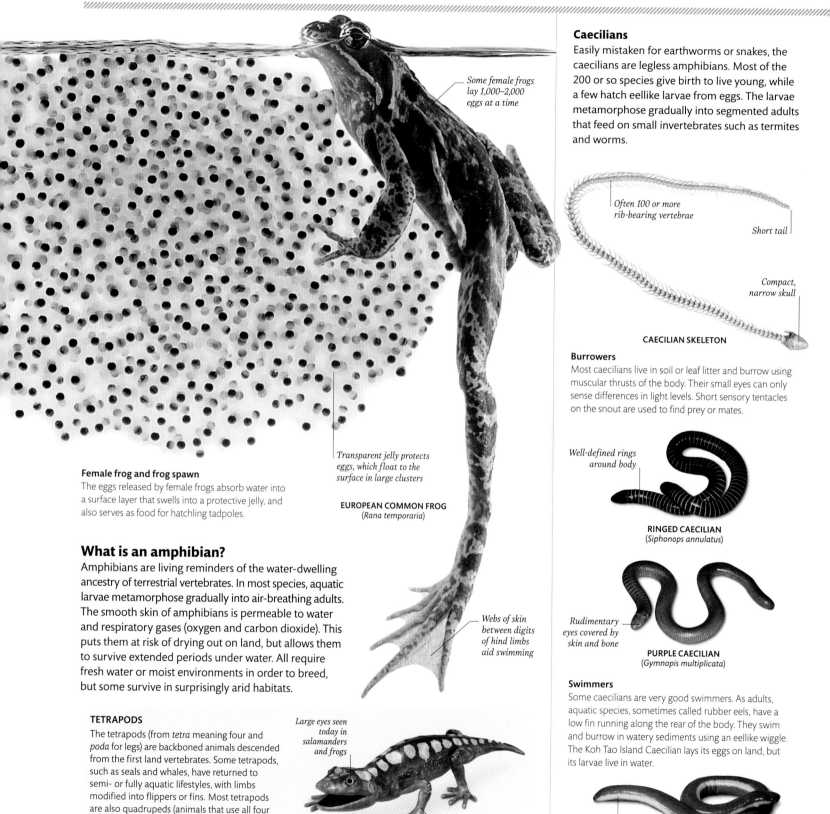

Some female frogs lay 1,000–2,000 eggs at a time

Transparent jelly protects eggs, which float to the surface in large clusters

EUROPEAN COMMON FROG
(Rana temporaria)

Webs of skin between digits of hind limbs aid swimming

Female frog and frog spawn
The eggs released by female frogs absorb water into a surface layer that swells into a protective jelly, and also serves as food for hatchling tadpoles.

What is an amphibian?
Amphibians are living reminders of the water-dwelling ancestry of terrestrial vertebrates. In most species, aquatic larvae metamorphose gradually into air-breathing adults. The smooth skin of amphibians is permeable to water and respiratory gases (oxygen and carbon dioxide). This puts them at risk of drying out on land, but allows them to survive extended periods under water. All require fresh water or moist environments in order to breed, but some survive in surprisingly arid habitats.

TETRAPODS
The tetrapods (from *tetra* meaning four and *poda* for legs) are backboned animals descended from the first land vertebrates. Some tetrapods, such as seals and whales, have returned to semi- or fully aquatic lifestyles, with limbs modified into flippers or fins. Most tetrapods are also quadrupeds (animals that use all four limbs to move on land) but exceptions include caecilians, snakes, birds, and humans.

Large eyes seen today in salamanders and frogs

AMPHIBAMUS— EARLY TETRAPOD

Forelimbs and hind limbs were same size

Caecilians
Easily mistaken for earthworms or snakes, the caecilians are legless amphibians. Most of the 200 or so species give birth to live young, while a few hatch eellike larvae from eggs. The larvae metamorphose gradually into segmented adults that feed on small invertebrates such as termites and worms.

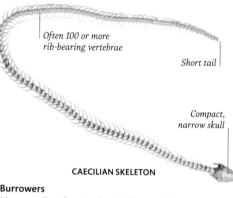

Often 100 or more rib-bearing vertebrae

Short tail

Compact, narrow skull

CAECILIAN SKELETON

Burrowers
Most caecilians live in soil or leaf litter and burrow using muscular thrusts of the body. Their small eyes can only sense differences in light levels. Short sensory tentacles on the snout are used to find prey or mates.

Well-defined rings around body

RINGED CAECILIAN
(Siphonops annulatus)

Rudimentary eyes covered by skin and bone

PURPLE CAECILIAN
(Gymnopis multiplicata)

Swimmers
Some caecilians are very good swimmers. As adults, aquatic species, sometimes called rubber eels, have a low fin running along the rear of the body. They swim and burrow in watery sediments using an eellike wiggle. The Koh Tao Island Caecilian lays its eggs on land, but its larvae live in water.

Yellow band runs length of body

KOH TAO ISLAND CAECILIAN
(Ichthyophis kohtaoensis)

Large, flattened skull

Five digits on hind limbs

Short ribs

Four digits on front limbs

Long backbone

Short limbs of similar length

Long tail

Newts and salamanders

Like the earliest terrestrial vertebrates, most newts and salamanders have a long, slender body, a long tail, and four limbs spreading to the sides of the body. Their smooth, moist, delicate skin requires them to live in water or in cool, damp places.

Salamander skeleton

The limbs of a salamander exhibit the five-digit (pentadactyl) structure from which all tetrapod feet derive, although the front limbs have since lost a digit.

Chinese Giant Salamanders are the world's **largest amphibians** and the **longest lived, at 50 years** or more

Newts and European salamanders

Newts are semiaquatic salamanders, with a life cycle including a tadpolelike larva, a land-dwelling juvenile called an "eft," then the adult form.

Crest on male

GREAT CRESTED NEWT
(*Triturus cristatus*)

Row of poison glands

EMPEROR NEWT
(*Tylototriton shanjing*)

Finlike tail aids swimming

ALPINE NEWT
(*Ichthyosaura alpestris*)

Bright yellow markings warn predators salamander is toxic

FIRE SALAMANDER
(*Salamandra salamandra*)

COMPLEX LIFE CYCLES

Amphibious newt larvae transition to life on land via a juvenile "eft" stage, whereas aquatic salamander larvae develop in water. Land-living salamander larvae hatch from eggs laid on land and the juveniles mature there.

Adult

Eft

Larva

Eggs laid one at a time

Courting adults

AMPHIBIOUS

Mole salamanders

The mole salamanders of North America mostly live in burrows by day and forage at night. However, the unusual and critically endangered axolotl retains its gilled, fully aquatic larval form into adulthood.

Blood-rich, feathery external gills

Rounded snout

AXOLOTL
(*Ambystoma mexicanum*)

TIGER SALAMANDER
(*Ambystoma tigrinum*)

Adult

Larva

Lots of small eggs laid

AQUATIC

Lungless salamanders

With more than 400 species, this is by far the largest family of salamanders. They never develop lungs, breathing solely through their moist skin. They feed mostly on small invertebrates, and possess an additional scent organ located in a vertical slit between their nostrils and mouth.

Sticky skin secretions protect salamander from predators

MISSISSIPPI SLIMY SALAMANDER
(*Plethodon mississippi*)

Prominent eyes

ENSATINA SALAMANDER
(*Ensatina eschscholtzii*)

Webbed feet

CUKRA CLIMBING SALAMANDER
(*Bolitoglossa striatula*)

Relatively few large eggs laid

Adult

Juvenile

Larva developing inside egg

TERRESTRIAL

Giant salamanders

Adults of the aquatic Chinese Giant Salamander can grow to 6 ft (1.8 m) in length and weigh 104 lb (47 kg). The American Hellbender (also known as snot otter) ranges from 1–2 ft (30 to 60 cm) in length.

Splayed limbs

CHINESE GIANT SALAMANDER
(*Andrias davidianus*)

Flattened head for burrowing

HELLBENDER
(*Cryptobranchus alleganiensis*)

see also Frogs and toads pp.124–25 ▶   Amphibians classification p.160 ▶   Types of living things p.217 ▶   **123**

LIFE

Frogs and toads

Strictly speaking, all 7,000-plus species of the order Anura are frogs, with toads as a subgroup with warty skin. Most frogs and toads begin life as aquatic larvae (tadpoles) and develop via gradual metamorphosis to four-legged, air-breathing adults. Frogs are active predators, and their skin is colored for camouflage or to warn that they secrete defensive toxins.

Long, muscular legs

Smooth, moist skin

Short body

Large, protruding eyes

Nostrils on top of snout

Ear drum (tympanum) clearly visible

Vocal sac

Short front limbs

PICKEREL FROG
(Lithobates palustris)

Large eye sockets

Broad, flat skull

Short, stiff backbone to cope with stress of leaping and landing

Elongated pelvis articulates with long, powerful legs

Shorter digits on front limbs

Long toes

The Pickerel Frog's **toxic skin** makes it the only **poisonous frog native to the US**

Frog skeleton

Adult frogs have no tail. The legs fold under the body, and are used for crawling, hopping, and swimming. The flat skull features large eye sockets, a wide gape, and tiny teeth.

Communication

Frogs deploy a range of audible, tactile, and visual signals to share information about their status. They use a variety of displays to warn potential predators, intimidate rivals, and attract potential mates.

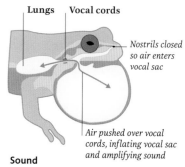

Lungs   Vocal cords

Nostrils closed so air enters vocal sac

Air pushed over vocal cords, inflating vocal sac and amplifying sound

Sound

Most frog species have a unique croak, chirp, or whistle. Their calls travel through air and water and can exceed 100 decibels, or as loud as a motorcycle.

Female strokes chosen male to indicate she is ready to lay eggs

Touch

Touch can be an important aspect of frog courtship, triggering calls and other behavior. This recently discovered form of communication may be widespread.

Hand waved to declare territory to rival male

Posturing

Visual signaling is useful in species living in noisy environments such as by fast-flowing water. Signals include arm-waving, leg-stretching, bobbing, and swaying.

Preparing to move to land

The transition from gilled, fishlike larva to air-breathing, four-legged adult requires a complex metamorphosis, which takes place gradually over several weeks or months. Gills are absorbed as lungs develop. The tail shrinks and is replaced as the means of locomotion by legs, while feeding behavior becomes increasingly predatory.

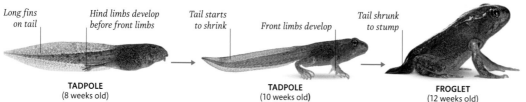

Long fins on tail

Hind limbs develop before front limbs

Tail starts to shrink

TADPOLE
(8 weeks old)

Front limbs develop

Tail shrunk to stump

TADPOLE
(10 weeks old)

FROGLET
(12 weeks old)

FEET AND HANDS

The hands and feet of frogs and toads are adapted to suit their lifestyles. Webs of skin between digits increase swimming efficiency, broad pads aid grip on smooth surfaces like leaves, and species that crawl or burrow develop horny protuberances on their hind feet.

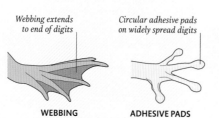

Webbing extends to end of digits

Circular adhesive pads on widely spread digits

Large tubercle used for digging

WEBBING

ADHESIVE PADS

TUBERCLES

The **Golden Poison Frog** is the **most poisonous animal** in the world—its skin has enough poison to **kill 10 people**

"Horn" above eye

Frogs

Frogs are generally distinguished by their smooth, moist, permeable skin. This remarkable skin is also their biggest weakness, as it makes them vulnerable to the fungal disease chytridiomycosis. The greatest diversity of frogs is found in tropical rainforests.

South American horned frogs

The wide mouth and voracious appetite of this family earns them the nickname "Pac-Man frogs". Some individuals even try to engulf prey almost as large as themselves.

ORNATE HORNED FROG
(*Ceratophrys ornata*)

Poison-dart frogs

The gaudy colors of these tiny South American species warn of highly toxic skin secretions. Darts or arrows tipped in frog poison help native hunters to paralyze large prey quickly.

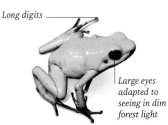

Long digits

Large eyes adapted to seeing in dim forest light

GOLDEN POISON FROG
(*Phyllobates terribilis*)

Characteristic dark patch behind eyes

Rounded snout

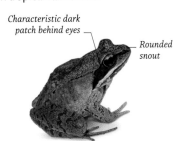

WOOD FROG
(*Lithobates sylvaticus*)

Warts and ridges on the skin

Very wide mouth

AFRICAN BULLFROG
(*Pyxicephalus adspersus*)

Sticky skin secretion protects frog against predator

TOMATO FROG
(*Dyscophus antongilii*)

Bright coloration warns predators frog is toxic

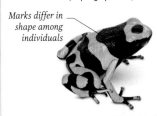

STRAWBERRY POISON-DART FROG
(*Oophaga pumilio*)

True frogs

Members of the archetypal frog family are present on six continents. They have long, powerful legs, and range in size from 1/3–13 in (8 mm to 33 cm).

Bullfrogs

"Bullfrogs" are species from several different families characterized by large size. An African bullfrog can live for 30 years and males may weigh 4 1/3 lb (2 kg).

Narrow-mouthed frogs

These small, mostly ground-dwelling frogs have plump bodies, short snouts, and stout hind legs. They hunt small prey, including ants and termites.

Marks differ in shape among individuals

YELLOW-BANDED POISON-DART FROG
(*Dendrobates leucomelas*)

Webbed feet on extended limbs enable frog to glide between far-apart trees

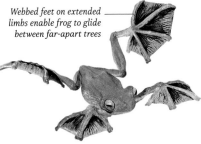

WALLACE'S FLYING FROG
(*Rhacophorus nigropalmatus*)

Digits have adhesive pads for gripping

RED-EYED TREE FROG
(*Agalychnis callidryas*)

Heart visible through skin

LA PALMA GLASS FROG
(*Hyalinobatrachium valerioi*)

Coloration varies among individuals

DYEING POISON FROG
(*Dendrobates tinctorius*)

Flying frogs

Several species of Afro-Asian tree frogs have extensive webs of skin between elongated digits, which act as parachutes, extending leaps into long glides.

Tree frogs

These arboreal frogs spawn in puddles of trapped rainwater or onto leaves overhanging water so that hatching tadpoles can drop right in.

Glass frogs

Named for the transparent skin on the belly, the arboreal glass frogs lay eggs on leaves and the males guard them from predators until they hatch.

Toads

Toads are not biologically distinct from frogs, but the term is often applied to slow-moving land-dwellers with thicker, warty skin. The skin is less permeable than that of other frogs, allowing some toads to occupy arid habitats, including deserts, where they may only breed after it rains. The "warts" are associated with glands secreting foul-tasting compounds as a deterrent to predators.

Large parotid glands secrete powerful toxin

CANE TOAD
(*Rhinella marina*)

Vertical pupils

Eggs attached to male's rear

MIDWIFE TOAD
(*Alytes obstetricans*)

Stout body

COUCH'S SPADEFOOT
(*Scaphiopus couchii*)

True toads

Most members of the large and diverse family Bufonidae are typically toadlike, with shortened front limbs and hind legs used for walking or hopping.

Midwife toads

Male midwife toads carry strands of fertilized eggs on their back and wrapped around their hind legs to protect them from predators.

American spadefoot toads

Horny growths on the feet aid rapid burrowing in this small group of closely related species. Living mostly underground allows them to survive arid conditions.

see also Amphibians classification p.160 ▶

Reptiles

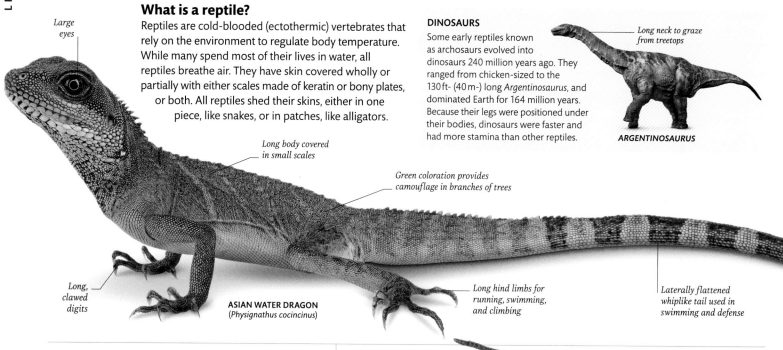

What is a reptile?

Reptiles are cold-blooded (ectothermic) vertebrates that rely on the environment to regulate body temperature. While many spend most of their lives in water, all reptiles breathe air. They have skin covered wholly or partially with either scales made of keratin or bony plates, or both. All reptiles shed their skins, either in one piece, like snakes, or in patches, like alligators.

*Large
eyes*

*Long body covered
in small scales*

*Green coloration provides
camouflage in branches of trees*

*Long,
clawed
digits*

ASIAN WATER DRAGON
(*Physignathus cocincinus*)

*Long hind limbs for
running, swimming,
and climbing*

*Laterally flattened
whiplike tail used in
swimming and defense*

DINOSAURS

Some early reptiles known as archosaurs evolved into dinosaurs 240 million years ago. They ranged from chicken-sized to the 130 ft- (40 m-) long *Argentinosaurus*, and dominated Earth for 164 million years. Because their legs were positioned under their bodies, dinosaurs were faster and had more stamina than other reptiles.

*Long neck to graze
from treetops*

ARGENTINOSAURUS

Egg with a shell

Although some snakes and lizards give birth to live young (viviparous), most reptiles lay eggs after internal fertilization, depositing them in nests in the soil or sand. Temperature is crucial to the embryo's development, and in some species determines the gender of the hatchlings.

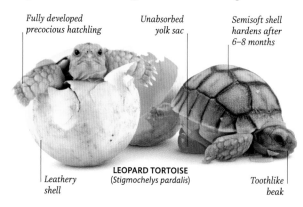

*Fully developed
precocious hatchling*

*Unabsorbed
yolk sac*

*Semisoft shell
hardens after
6–8 months*

*Leathery
shell*

LEOPARD TORTOISE
(*Stigmochelys pardalis*)

*Toothlike
beak*

Heat regulation

Small reptiles are only active for short periods because slight temperature changes affect their metabolic rate. In warm surroundings, body temperatures rise, but activity levels drop rapidly as conditions cool. Overnight, the metabolism of some species slows almost to the point of torpor.

KEY

— Air temperature

— Lizard's body temperature

▨ Sheltering to avoid cold

▨ Basking

▨ Normal activity

▨ Sheltering to avoid heat

[Graph: TEMPERATURE °C (0, 15, 30, 45) and TEMPERATURE °F (32, 50, 70, 90, 110) vs TIME OF DAY (06:00, 09:00, 12:00, 15:00, 18:00, 20:00)]

Inside a reptile egg

Unlike hard-shelled birds' eggs, most reptile eggs are encased in a more flexible, leathery shell. A cushionlike fluid-filled sac (amnion) surrounds and protects the embryo, while the yolk provides food for it as it develops.

*Shell permeable to
respiratory gasses*

Embryo   **Amnion**

Air cell

*Allantois
passes oxygen
to embryo*

**CROSS SECTION
OF AN ALLIGATOR EGG**

Yolk sac

LIVING FOSSIL

New Zealand's Tuatara is the sole survivor of an ancient group of reptiles. Unlike lizards, tuataras have no visible earhole and a light-sensitive "third eye" on the top of their heads is believed to help them sense seasons or the time of day. They live in burrows.

*Soft, jagged
crest*

*Head covered
in small scales*

TUATARA
(*Sphenodon punctatus*)

Stout limbs

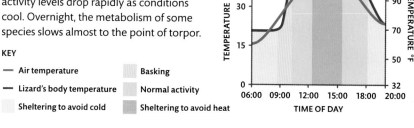

*Opening behind eye socket
(orbit) found in all reptiles
except turtles and tortoises*

Bony arch

**TUATARA
SKULL**

Teeth

SERRATED JAWS

A tuatara's teeth are actually serrated extensions of its jawbones. One row in its lower jaw slots in between two in its upper jaw—a formidable arrangement suited to tearing apart hard-shelled beetles, their main prey.

LIFE

Turtles and tortoises

Turtles and tortoises are some of the most primitive reptiles, found all over the world apart from the Arctic and Antarctic. Their bodies are encased in hard, protective shells comprised of bone plates covered either with horny scutes made of keratin, or with tough, rubbery skin. Apart from clambering ashore to lay eggs or bask, turtles spend most of their lives in water, while tortoises spend theirs on land.

LOGGERHEAD TURTLE
(*Caretta caretta*)

Paddlelike flippers

Freshwater turtles

Found in wetlands, streams, and rivers, most freshwater turtles have hard shells, retreating into them when threatened. Some remain underwater all winter, obtaining oxygen from the water.

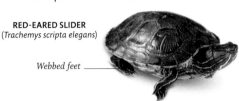

RED-EARED SLIDER
(*Trachemys scripta elegans*)

Webbed feet

Eyes and nostrils on top of head

ORNATE BOX TURTLE
(*Terrapene ornata*)

Short neck draws head straight into shell

EUROPEAN POND TURTLE
(*Emys orbicularis*)

Row of spines on carapace

FALSE MAP TURTLE
(*Graptemys pseudogeographica*)

Streamlined body

GREEN TURTLE
(*Chelonia mydas*)

Leathery carapace

LEATHERBACK TURTLE
(*Dermochelys coriacea*)

Hooked upper and lower beak delivers powerful bite

ALLIGATOR SNAPPING TURTLE
(*Macrochelys temminckii*)

Long neck bends sideways so head rests under edge of shell

COMMON SNAKE-NECKED TURTLE
(*Chelodina longicollis*)

Extended snout used as snorkel

SPINY SOFTSHELL
(*Apalone spinifera*)

Sea turtles

All seven species of sea turtle come ashore to lay their eggs in nests dug out of sand on tropical and subtropical beaches, then return to the ocean. Some species eat seagrass, whiles others hunt jellyfish, sponges, or crabs.

Tortoises

Tortoises are in the same order as turtles but belong to a different family. They are strictly land-dwellers, found in habitats as diverse as deserts and tropical forests. Most are herbivores, and range from 3 in (8 cm) to 6 ft (2 m) long.

Some **tortoises** can live for more than **200 years**

Saddle-backed shell lets tortoise browse shrubs

GALAPAGOS TORTOISE
(*Chelonoidis nigra*)

Growth rings in scutes

DESERT TORTOISE
(*Gopherus agassizii*)

Domed scutes

INDIAN STAR TORTOISE
(*Geochelone elegans*)

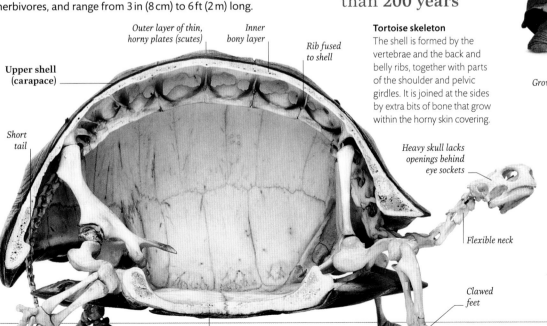

Outer layer of thin, horny plates (scutes)

Inner bony layer

Rib fused to shell

Upper shell (carapace)

Short tail

Lower shell (plastron)

Tortoise skeleton

The shell is formed by the vertebrae and the back and belly ribs, together with parts of the shoulder and pelvic girdles. It is joined at the sides by extra bits of bone that grow within the horny skin covering.

Heavy skull lacks openings behind eye sockets

Flexible neck

Clawed feet

see also Types of living things p.217 ▶ **127**

LIFE

Dark brown and tan markings camouflage python when resting among dead leaves

Smooth, scaly skin

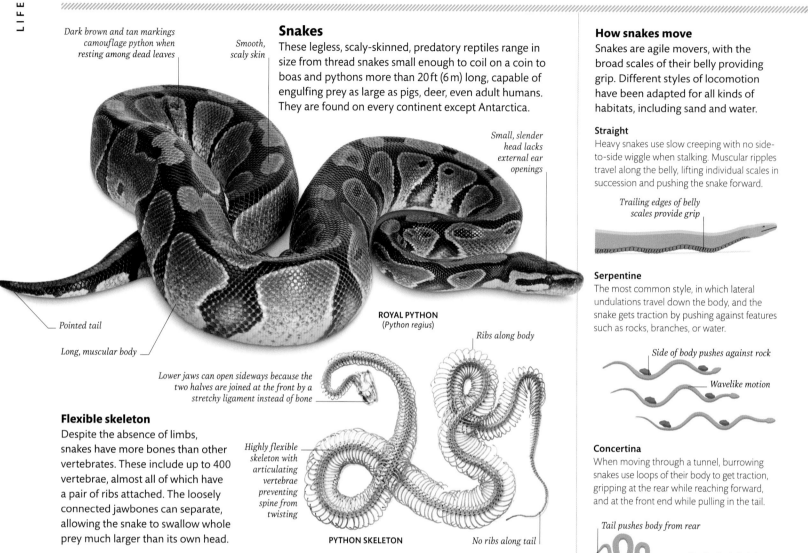

Small, slender head lacks external ear openings

Snakes

These legless, scaly-skinned, predatory reptiles range in size from thread snakes small enough to coil on a coin to boas and pythons more than 20 ft (6 m) long, capable of engulfing prey as large as pigs, deer, even adult humans. They are found on every continent except Antarctica.

ROYAL PYTHON
(*Python regius*)

Pointed tail

Long, muscular body

Lower jaws can open sideways because the two halves are joined at the front by a stretchy ligament instead of bone

Ribs along body

Flexible skeleton

Despite the absence of limbs, snakes have more bones than other vertebrates. These include up to 400 vertebrae, almost all of which have a pair of ribs attached. The loosely connected jawbones can separate, allowing the snake to swallow whole prey much larger than its own head.

Highly flexible skeleton with articulating vertebrae preventing spine from twisting

PYTHON SKELETON

No ribs along tail

Large, lidless eyes with vertical pupils

Nostrils supplement scent collected by flicking tongue

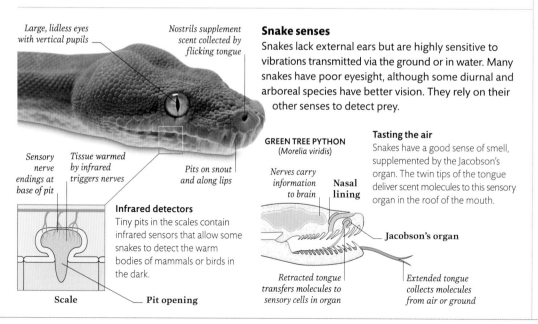

Snake senses

Snakes lack external ears but are highly sensitive to vibrations transmitted via the ground or in water. Many snakes have poor eyesight, although some diurnal and arboreal species have better vision. They rely on their other senses to detect prey.

Sensory nerve endings at base of pit

Tissue warmed by infrared triggers nerves

Pits on snout and along lips

Infrared detectors

Tiny pits in the scales contain infrared sensors that allow some snakes to detect the warm bodies of mammals or birds in the dark.

Scale

Pit opening

GREEN TREE PYTHON
(*Morelia viridis*)

Tasting the air

Snakes have a good sense of smell, supplemented by the Jacobson's organ. The twin tips of the tongue deliver scent molecules to this sensory organ in the roof of the mouth.

Nerves carry information to brain

Nasal lining

Jacobson's organ

Retracted tongue transfers molecules to sensory cells in organ

Extended tongue collects molecules from air or ground

How snakes move

Snakes are agile movers, with the broad scales of their belly providing grip. Different styles of locomotion have been adapted for all kinds of habitats, including sand and water.

Straight

Heavy snakes use slow creeping with no side-to-side wiggle when stalking. Muscular ripples travel along the belly, lifting individual scales in succession and pushing the snake forward.

Trailing edges of belly scales provide grip

Serpentine

The most common style, in which lateral undulations travel down the body, and the snake gets traction by pushing against features such as rocks, branches, or water.

Side of body pushes against rock

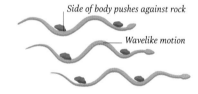

Wavelike motion

Concertina

When moving through a tunnel, burrowing snakes use loops of their body to get traction, gripping at the rear while reaching forward, and at the front end while pulling in the tail.

Tail pushes body from rear

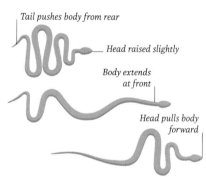

Head raised slightly

Body extends at front

Head pulls body forward

Sidewinding

Sidewinding is used on loose surfaces such as a sandy slope. The snake propels itself with muscular waves that lift sections of its body and push it forward.

Head and front of body raised

Direction of travel

Sections of body pushing against ground

Raised section of body

Snakes have no eyelids so they **cannot blink**—they **sleep** with their **eyes open**

Boas

These powerful, sometimes very large snakes kill by constriction, tightening their coils with every exhalation of their prey. Once dead, the prey is swallowed head first. All but one species of boa give birth to live young.

COMMON BOA
(*Boa constrictor*)

Forked tongue

Transparent scale covers eye

ROSY BOA
(*Lichanura trivirgata*)

GREEN ANACONDA
(*Eunectes murinus*)

Powerful coils used for support and to kill prey

EMERALD TREE BOA
(*Corallus caninus*)

Weighing up to
550 lb (250 kg),
the **Green Anaconda**
is the **world's heaviest snake**

Pythons

Pythons grab prey with their mouth but kill by constriction. They differ from the superficially similar boas in that the females lay eggs, which they coil around to protect them from predators during the 2–3 months of incubation.

GREEN TREE PYTHON
(*Morelia viridis*)

Bright green coloration helps hide snake in trees

Long, muscular body

Arrowhead marking on head

BURMESE PYTHON
(*Python bivittatus*)

RETICULATED PYTHON
(*Python reticulatus*)

Longest snake
At up to 30 ft (9 m), the Reticulated Python is the world's longest snake. Reports of individuals being as much as 39 ft (12 m) long are based on stretched skins.

6 FT (2 M)

30 FT (9 M)

Colubrid snakes

This varied family comprises 70 percent of all snake species. Colubrids either actively hunt small prey or wait in ambush. A third of species have a venomous bite, the rest kill by constriction. Most lay eggs.

Characteristic yellow collar

GRASS SNAKE
(*Natrix natrix*)

Solid fangs at rear of mouth deliver venom to bite wound by capillary action

REAR-FANGED SNAKE

Distinctive colors and pattern of captive-bred snake

EASTERN CORN SNAKE
(*Pantherophis guttatus*)

Coloration mimics that of some venomous snakes

SINALOAN MILKSNAKE
(*Lampropeltis polyzona*)

Vipers

Vipers inject relatively slow-acting venom into the vital organs of their prey via long, hollow, hinged fangs at the front of the mouth, which fold away when not in use. Most vipers give birth to live young. Heat detection is more advanced in the pit vipers than other snakes.

Loud warning
The rattle is a horny section at the end of the tail made up of loosely connected segments that are added to each time the snake sheds its skin. When the snake vibrates its tail, the segments knock against each other.

Small "birth button" scale

Two lobes of segment hidden inside older segments

Visible external lobe of single dry segment

Newest segment has live tissue

RATTLE

Short tail

Thick body

Cobras and relatives

The cobras and their relatives, including mambas and sea snakes, are all venomous. Many of them produce a potent neurotoxic venom that is deadly to humans.

Fixed, hollow fang injects venom

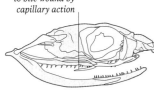

FRONT-FANGED SNAKE

Bright coloration warns predators snake is venomous

CENTRAL AMERICAN CORAL SNAKE
(*Micrurus nigrocinctus*)

Spread hood acts as warning

MONOCLED COBRA
(*Naja kaouthia*)

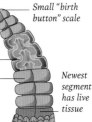

Rattle raised and vibrated as warning

WESTERN DIAMONDBACK RATTLESNAKE
(*Crotalus atrox*)

Heat-sensing pits between eyes and nostrils

Large, triangular head

GABOON VIPER
(*Bitis gabonica*)

MALAYAN PIT VIPER
(*Calloselasma rhodostoma*)

see also Reptiles classification p.160 ▶ **129**

Lizards

Lizards are the largest and most successful group of reptiles. They are adapted to a wide range of habitats, from forests and deserts to wetlands and even the sea. Most have four legs, although some are limbless. Some species give birth to live young, but most reproduce by laying eggs.

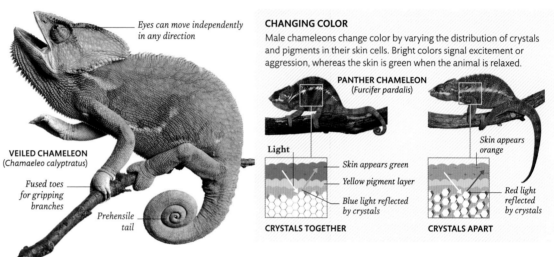

Four limbs attached to side of body

Long neck

Opening in skull behind eye socket (orbit)

Pelvic girdle

Long, whiplike tail

Ribs attached to spine

Five digits on all limbs ending in sharp claws

MONITOR LIZARD SKELETON

Chameleons

Chameleons are color-changing reptiles from Africa and Eurasia. They use their highly elastic, projectile tongue, up to twice the length of their body, to capture prey including insects and other small animals.

Eyes can move independently in any direction

CHANGING COLOR

Male chameleons change color by varying the distribution of crystals and pigments in their skin cells. Bright colors signal excitement or aggression, whereas the skin is green when the animal is relaxed.

PANTHER CHAMELEON
(*Furcifer pardalis*)

Light

Skin appears orange

Skin appears green

Yellow pigment layer

Blue light reflected by crystals

Red light reflected by crystals

CRYSTALS TOGETHER

CRYSTALS APART

Body shape and coloration resembles dead leaf

BEARDED PYGMY CHAMELEON
(*Rieppeleon brevicaudatus*)

VEILED CHAMELEON
(*Chamaeleo calyptratus*)

Fused toes for gripping branches

Prehensile tail

Iguanas and relatives

Despite their large size and fearsome appearance, adult iguanas are plant eaters. True iguanas live in the Americas and on islands in the Caribbean and Pacific Ocean. Their smaller cousins, the anoles and helmeted lizards, are mostly slim, agile tree dwellers from the New World.

Skin color changes according to mood or temperature

Long, slender tail

GREEN ANOLE
(*Anolis carolinensis*)

Sharp claws and pads on toes aid climbing

Male flicks its large pink throat fan (dewlap) as signal to females or rival males

Long tail used as whip in defense

GREEN IGUANA
(*Iguana iguana*)

Prominent helmetlike crest

Marine Iguanas sneeze to expel salt filtered from their blood by glands near their nose

High dorsal crest and tail crest aid swimming

Bright colors to attract females derived from pigments in seaweed growing around southern Galápagos Islands

Flattened, oar-shaped tail powers swimming

Long toes and claws for clinging to rocks

GREEN BASILISK
(*Basiliscus plumifrons*)

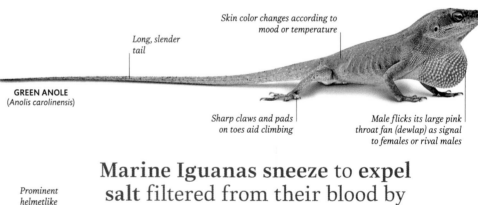

Sticky feet can support the weight of an
11 oz (300 g) gecko hanging **upside down**

Geckos

Most geckos have soft, thin skin covered in usually
tiny, granular scales. They are mostly arboreal and
can cling to smooth surfaces, and even hang upside
down from ceilings, thanks to specially adapted feet.
Many geckos can shed their tail if it is seized by a
predator (and then regrow it), and in some species
the tail is head-shaped, to confuse the aggressor.

*Long-clawed
toes*

RING-TAILED GECKO
(*Cyrtodactylus louisiadensis*)

*Bright
coloration*

MADAGASCAR DAY GECKO
(*Phelsuma madagascariensis*)

*Large eyes enable this nocturnal
gecko to see well in the dark*

*Distinctive
orange spots*

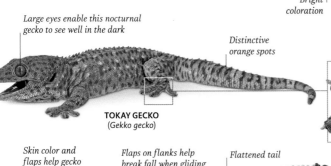

TOKAY GECKO
(*Gekko gecko*)

Sticky feet
The toe pads are covered
in millions of tightly
packed, microscopic
hairs that generate strong
adhesive forces.

*Skin color and
flaps help gecko
blend against tree
bark when it lands*

*Flaps on flanks help
break fall when gliding*

Flattened tail

KUHL'S FLYING GECKO
(*Ptychozoon kuhli*)

Webbed feet
The webbed toes and skin
flaps of the "flying" geckos
help them turn leaps into
moderately well-controlled
glides when threatened.

Skinks and relatives

This large family of thick-necked
lizards with bony head scales are
mostly burrow dwellers, but many
are agile climbers and others swim
well. Some lay eggs, some give
birth to live young, and at least one
species can do both.

Short legs

EASTERN BLUE-TONGUED SKINK
(*Tiliqua scincoides*)

*Long tail
and body*

FIRE SKINK
(*Lepidothyris fernandi*)

*Pointed snout aids
swimming through sand*

SANDFISH SKINK
(*Scincus scincus*)

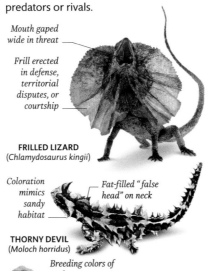

*High dorsal
crest in
older males*

*Sharp teeth in blunt
snout used to scrape
seaweed from
underwater rocks*

MARINE IGUANA
(*Amblyrhynchus cristatus*)

Short legs

Agama lizards

Many agama lizards have spectacular-
looking adornments such as tail spikes,
spines, or colorful frills, which function
as weapons or to intimidate potential
predators or rivals.

*Mouth gaped
wide in threat*

*Frill erected
in defense,
territorial
disputes, or
courtship*

FRILLED LIZARD
(*Chlamydosaurus kingii*)

*Coloration
mimics
sandy
habitat*

*Fat-filled "false
head" on neck*

THORNY DEVIL
(*Moloch horridus*)

*Breeding colors of
male*

RAINBOW LIZARD
(*Agama agama*)

Wall and girdled lizards

Wall lizards are mostly slim, agile predators,
while girdled lizards are named for the
rings of spiny scales on their tail.

OCELLATED LIZARD
(*Timon lepidus*)

VIVIPAROUS LIZARD
(*Zootoca vivipara*)

*Mouth holds spiny tail
to form protective ring*

ARMADILLO GIRDLED LIZARD
(*Ouroborus cataphractus*)

see also Reptiles pp.132–33 ▶   Reptiles classification p.160 ▶   **131**

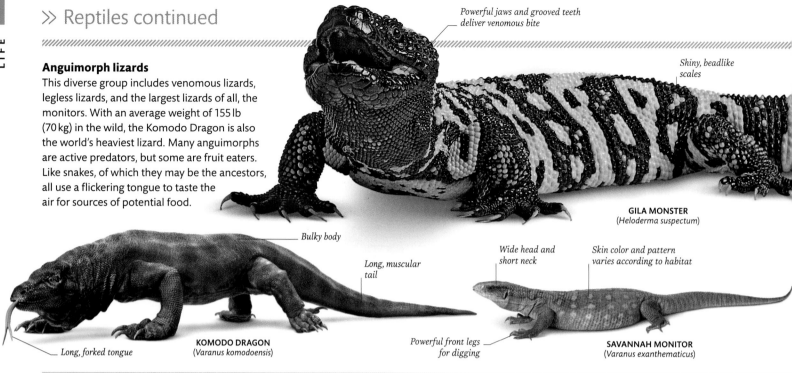

Powerful jaws and grooved teeth deliver venomous bite

Shiny, beadlike scales

Anguimorph lizards

This diverse group includes venomous lizards, legless lizards, and the largest lizards of all, the monitors. With an average weight of 155 lb (70 kg) in the wild, the Komodo Dragon is also the world's heaviest lizard. Many anguimorphs are active predators, but some are fruit eaters. Like snakes, of which they may be the ancestors, all use a flickering tongue to taste the air for sources of potential food.

Bulky body

Long, muscular tail

GILA MONSTER
(*Heloderma suspectum*)

Wide head and short neck

Skin color and pattern varies according to habitat

Long, forked tongue

KOMODO DRAGON
(*Varanus komodoensis*)

Powerful front legs for digging

SAVANNAH MONITOR
(*Varanus exanthematicus*)

Crocodiles and alligators

This 250-million-year-old group has scarcely changed in the 66 million years since dinosaurs roamed the Earth. All crocodilians, which comprise crocodiles, alligators, caimans, and gharials, breed on land, where despite short legs and an usually sprawling stance they can sprint short distances. They hunt a variety of prey in water, and propulsion is generated by a tail powerful enough to launch their entire body into the air.

MATERNAL CARE

Baby crocodilians hatch from eggs buried in sand, mud, or a mound of vegetation, and call to their mother guarding the nest. The hatchlings are vulnerable to predation, so the mother escorts or, more usually, carries them in her mouth to the relative safety of water. She may move them repeatedly if she senses danger, and stays with them for several months.

Crocodiles

These tropical reptiles are formidable semiaquatic predators. The Saltwater and the Nile Crocodiles have the strongest recorded bite force of any animal, although the muscles responsible for opening the jaws are surprisingly weak.

Dark spots on throat and flanks

Large, bony scales of crocodilians shed singly or in pieces

Keeled scales on tail

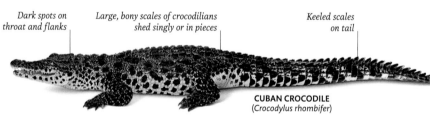

CUBAN CROCODILE
(*Crocodylus rhombifer*)

Open mouth prevents overheating when basking

Eyes and nose of crocodilians set high on head so they can see and breathe while body is partly submerged

Dorsal scales reinforced by underlying bony plates

Short hind limbs have four toes, forelimbs have five

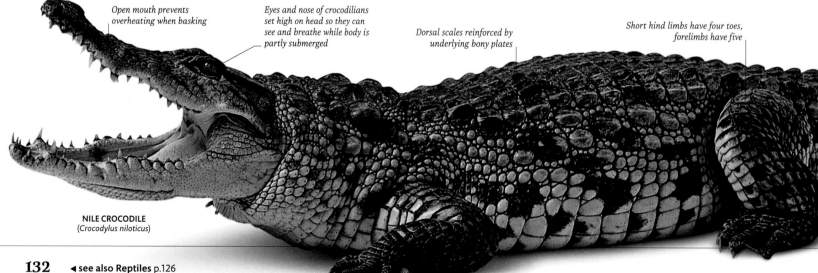

NILE CROCODILE
(*Crocodylus niloticus*)

Weighing up to **2,200 lb** (1 tonne), the Saltwater Crocodile is the **largest living reptile**

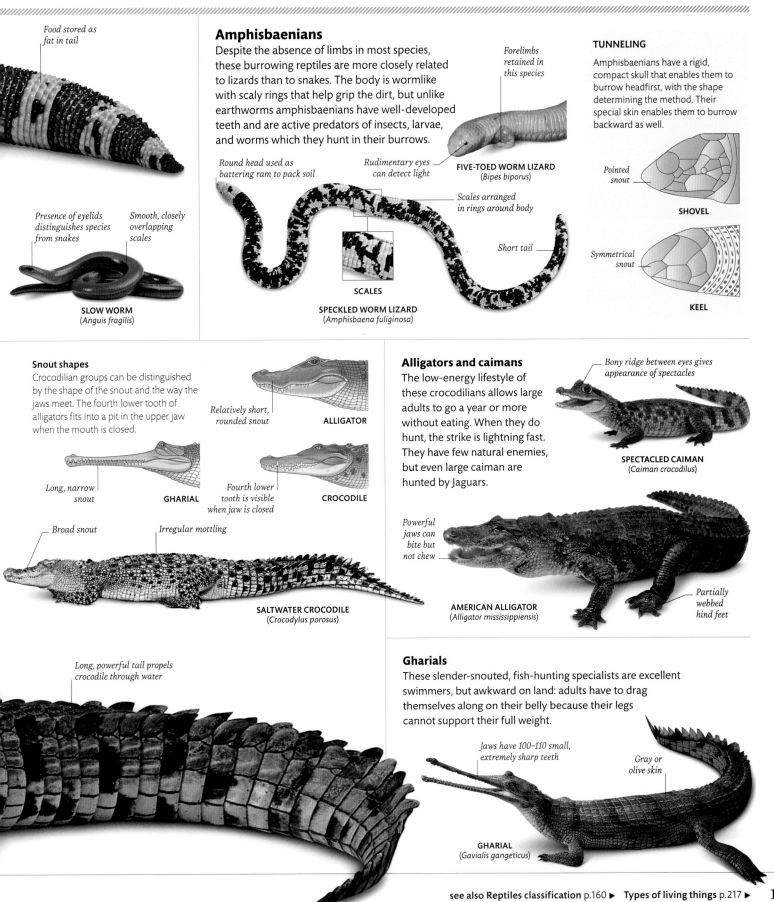

Food stored as fat in tail

Amphisbaenians

Despite the absence of limbs in most species, these burrowing reptiles are more closely related to lizards than to snakes. The body is wormlike with scaly rings that help grip the dirt, but unlike earthworms amphisbaenians have well-developed teeth and are active predators of insects, larvae, and worms which they hunt in their burrows.

Forelimbs retained in this species

TUNNELING

Amphisbaenians have a rigid, compact skull that enables them to burrow headfirst, with the shape determining the method. Their special skin enables them to burrow backward as well.

Round head used as battering ram to pack soil

Rudimentary eyes can detect light

FIVE-TOED WORM LIZARD
(*Bipes biporus*)

Pointed snout

SHOVEL

Presence of eyelids distinguishes species from snakes

Smooth, closely overlapping scales

Scales arranged in rings around body

Short tail

Symmetrical snout

KEEL

SCALES

SLOW WORM
(*Anguis fragilis*)

SPECKLED WORM LIZARD
(*Amphisbaena fuliginosa*)

Snout shapes

Crocodilian groups can be distinguished by the shape of the snout and the way the jaws meet. The fourth lower tooth of alligators fits into a pit in the upper jaw when the mouth is closed.

Relatively short, rounded snout

ALLIGATOR

Long, narrow snout

GHARIAL

Fourth lower tooth is visible when jaw is closed

CROCODILE

Alligators and caimans

The low-energy lifestyle of these crocodilians allows large adults to go a year or more without eating. When they do hunt, the strike is lightning fast. They have few natural enemies, but even large caiman are hunted by Jaguars.

Bony ridge between eyes gives appearance of spectacles

SPECTACLED CAIMAN
(*Caiman crocodilus*)

Broad snout

Irregular mottling

Powerful jaws can bite but not chew

SALTWATER CROCODILE
(*Crocodylus porosus*)

AMERICAN ALLIGATOR
(*Alligator mississippiensis*)

Partially webbed hind feet

Long, powerful tail propels crocodile through water

Gharials

These slender-snouted, fish-hunting specialists are excellent swimmers, but awkward on land: adults have to drag themselves along on their belly because their legs cannot support their full weight.

Jaws have 100–110 small, extremely sharp teeth

Gray or olive skin

GHARIAL
(*Gavialis gangeticus*)

see also Reptiles classification p.160 ▶ Types of living things p.217 ▶

Birds

What is a bird?

Birds are the only vertebrates with feathers. These egg-laying animals with hornlike, toothless bills are most closely related to reptiles, yet are warm-blooded (endothermic) and have four-chambered hearts, like mammals. Hollow bones and aerodynamic wings allow most of the more than 10,000 bird species to fly, and all are bipedal—using two hind limbs to hop, walk, run, paddle, perch, or capture prey. They are found on every continent and many remote islands.

THE FIRST BIRDS

Birds evolved from carnivorous dinosaurs about 150 million years ago. When the most famous Jurassic bird fossil, *Archaeopteryx*, was discovered in the 1860s, its wings, flight, and tail feathers revealed it was capable of rudimentary flight, but like small feathered dinosaurs (theropods) of the time, it had teeth and a long, bony tail. It was about the size of a crow (see skeleton below).

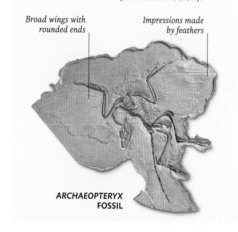

Broad wings with rounded ends

Impressions made by feathers

ARCHAEOPTERYX FOSSIL

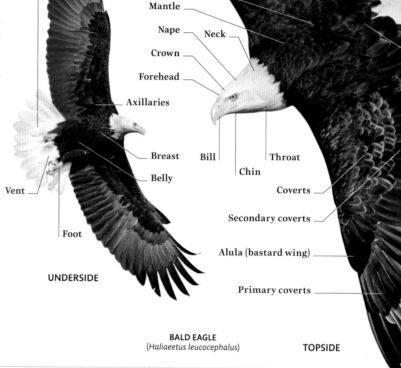

Long flight feathers (primaries)

Secondaries

Upper tail coverts

Tail feathers

Under tail coverts

Scapulars

Mantle

Nape

Neck

Crown

Forehead

Axillaries

Rump

Breast

Bill

Throat

Chin

Belly

Coverts

Vent

Secondary coverts

Foot

Alula (bastard wing)

Primary coverts

UNDERSIDE

BALD EAGLE
(*Haliaeetus leucocephalus*)

TOPSIDE

Skeleton

Bird skeletons are made up of thin-walled but strong, dense bones filled with air cavities (pneumatization). They have fewer bones than reptiles or mammals, and many of them are reduced in size and even fused together, such as in the wrist and digital bones of the wing. Unlike other vertebrates, many bird species can move both upper and lower mandibles (jawbones).

The **skeleton** of most flying birds **weighs less** than their **feathers**

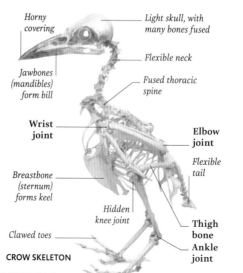

Horny covering

Light skull, with many bones fused

Jawbones (mandibles) form bill

Flexible neck

Fused thoracic spine

Wrist joint

Elbow joint

Flexible tail

Breastbone (sternum) forms keel

Hidden knee joint

Thigh bone

Clawed toes

Ankle joint

CROW SKELETON

Spongy bone in head end distributes forces

Strengthening transverse bone strut

Bone shaft

Air-filled space

Hollow bone

Not all of a bird's bones contain marrow, the substance that produces blood cells. Instead, many have air cavities and internal bony supports called trabeculae, which function like struts inside an airplane wing to prevent the bones from collapsing under pressure during flight.

In 2007, a Bar-tailed Godwit flew 7,200 miles (11,570 km) nonstop in eight days

Flight

To fly, a bird uses powerful muscles to move its wings in a repetetive motion. Air flows over a wing's curved upper surface faster than it moves underneath, causing a difference in pressure above and below the wing. This lifts the bird, while wingbeats create thrust to propel the animal upward and forward.

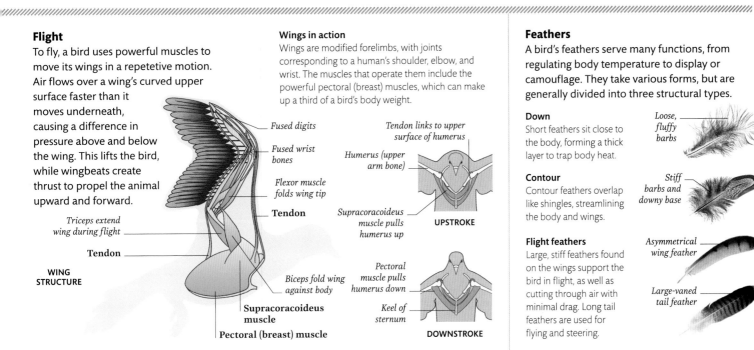

Triceps extend wing during flight

Tendon

WING STRUCTURE

Fused digits

Fused wrist bones

Flexor muscle folds wing tip

Tendon

Biceps fold wing against body

Supracoracoideus muscle

Pectoral (breast) muscle

Wings in action

Wings are modified forelimbs, with joints corresponding to a human's shoulder, elbow, and wrist. The muscles that operate them include the powerful pectoral (breast) muscles, which can make up a third of a bird's body weight.

Tendon links to upper surface of humerus

Humerus (upper arm bone)

Supracoracoideus muscle pulls humerus up

UPSTROKE

Pectoral muscle pulls humerus down

Keel of sternum

DOWNSTROKE

Feathers

A bird's feathers serve many functions, from regulating body temperature to display or camouflage. They take various forms, but are generally divided into three structural types.

Down
Short feathers sit close to the body, forming a thick layer to trap body heat.

Contour
Contour feathers overlap like shingles, streamlining the body and wings.

Flight feathers
Large, stiff feathers found on the wings support the bird in flight, as well as cutting through air with minimal drag. Long tail feathers are used for flying and steering.

Loose, fluffy barbs

Stiff barbs and downy base

Asymmetrical wing feather

Large-vaned tail feather

FLIGHT FEATHER STRUCTURE
Flight feathers have one wide and one narrow vane, or section, divided by a central shaft (rachis). Each vane contains barbs that branch into interlocking barbules, creating a smooth, aerodynamic surface.

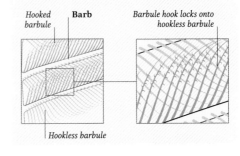

Hooked barbule   **Barb**   *Barbule hook locks onto hookless barbule*

Hookless barbule

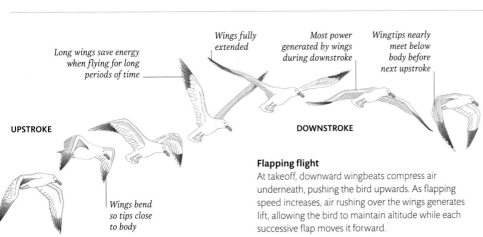

Long wings save energy when flying for long periods of time

Wings fully extended

Most power generated by wings during downstroke

Wingtips nearly meet below body before next upstroke

UPSTROKE

DOWNSTROKE

Wings bend so tips close to body

Flapping flight
At takeoff, downward wingbeats compress air underneath, pushing the bird upwards. As flapping speed increases, air rushing over the wings generates lift, allowing the bird to maintain altitude while each successive flap moves it forward.

Types of feet

A bird's foot shape and structure depend on how it moves, its environment, and its dietary habits. Predatory species have clawlike talons for grasping prey, while passerine (perching) birds' toes are arranged so that three face forward and one backward, allowing them to grasp twigs and reeds as well as balancing them when they hop. Waterfowl and some other birds that swim have flexible skin (webbing) connecting their toes.

The Ostrich can run at speeds of up to 45 mph (70 km/h)

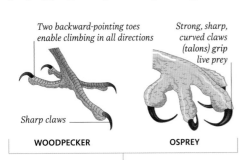

Two backward-pointing toes enable climbing in all directions

Strong, sharp, curved claws (talons) grip live prey

Sharp claws

WOODPECKER   **OSPREY**

GRIPPING AND HOLDING

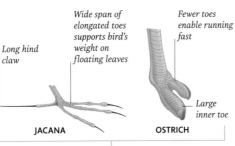

Wide span of elongated toes supports bird's weight on floating leaves

Fewer toes enable running fast

Long hind claw

Large inner toe

JACANA   **OSTRICH**

WALKING AND RUNNING

Wide lobes on toes open when foot kicks backward

Webbing provides extra thrust when swimming

COOT   **DUCK**

SWIMMING

see also Birds classification p.161 ▶   Types of living things p.217 ▶

>> Birds continued

Respiration

Compared to other vertebrates, birds have relatively small lungs for their body size, but their anatomy compensates for this with nine additional air sacs positioned at different points throughout their body. These sacs continuously feed fresh air directly to a bird's lungs, which means birds can take in oxygen while both inhaling and exhaling.

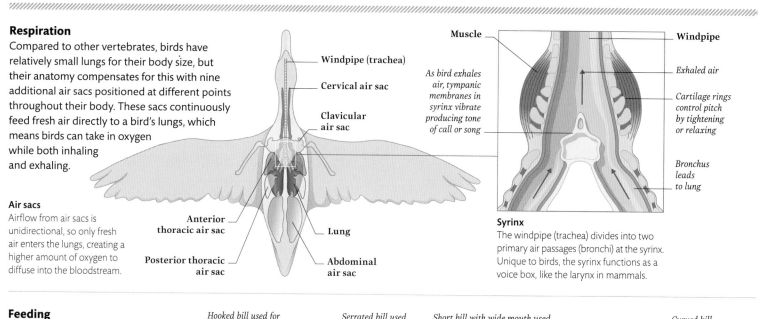

Windpipe (trachea)

Cervical air sac

Clavicular air sac

Anterior thoracic air sac

Lung

Posterior thoracic air sac

Abdominal air sac

Muscle

Windpipe

As bird exhales air, tympanic membranes in syrinx vibrate producing tone of call or song

Exhaled air

Cartilage rings control pitch by tightening or relaxing

Bronchus leads to lung

Air sacs
Airflow from air sacs is unidirectional, so only fresh air enters the lungs, creating a higher amount of oxygen to diffuse into the bloodstream.

Syrinx
The windpipe (trachea) divides into two primary air passages (bronchi) at the syrinx. Unique to birds, the syrinx functions as a voice box, like the larynx in mammals.

Feeding

A variety of bill shapes reflects how birds have evolved in response to habitat and food sources. Although many species eat both live prey and seasonal vegetation, most specialize in a particular food item, such as fishes, insects, or nectar.

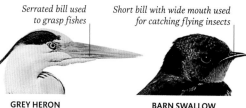

Hooked bill used for tearing meat

Serrated bill used to grasp fishes

Short bill with wide mouth used for catching flying insects

Curved bill used to sweep for shrimp

GOLDEN EAGLE
(*Aquila chrysaetos*)

GREY HERON
(*Ardea cinerea*)

BARN SWALLOW
(*Hirundo rustica*)

PIED AVOCET
(*Recurvirostra avosetta*)

Nest types

The need for a safe place to lay eggs is common to all birds, but nests vary enormously, ranging from simple scrapes to highly sophisticated constructions or precarious cliffside dwellings. Some species, like the oystercatcher, rely solely on the camouflaged shells to protect their eggs.

Woven nest
Male weaver birds construct their elaborate, hollow nests with a down-facing entrance by weaving grass and leaves together on the end of a branch.

Nest hangs from thin branch, out of reach of most predators

Strong feet make it easier to hang upside down

Bill used to cut and weave grass

Entrance will be at bottom of nest

SOUTHERN MASKED WEAVER
(*Ploceus velatus*)

Most small birds make open nests with a soft, warm lining

CUP NEST

Swallows build nests with soft, sticky mud and grass

ADHERENT NEST

Woodpeckers chisel holes in tree trunks with their strong, sharp bill

CAVITY NEST

Storks build huge nests on tall trees or buildings

PLATFORM NEST

Grebes make nests of weeds anchored in place

FLOATING NEST

Some shorebirds lay their eggs directly on the ground

NO NEST

Sight

Birds see the world in two main ways. Species with eyes on either side of the head rely on monocular vision, focusing each eye on different objects simultaneously to help them avoid predators. The forward-facing eyes of predatory species use binocular vision, using both eyes to focus on prey.

Eagles can **see prey** as **small** as a rabbit **2 miles (3 km) away**

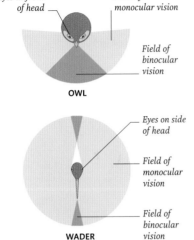

Eyes at front of head

Field of monocular vision

Field of binocular vision

OWL

Eyes on side of head

Field of monocular vision

Field of binocular vision

WADER

Migration

Many birds stay in just one area, while others migrate, changing locations in search of food or nesting grounds. Some travel only short distances, such as from higher to lower elevations, while others fly thousands of miles twice a year.

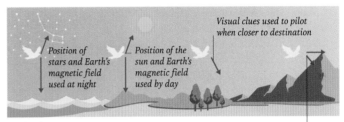

Position of stars and Earth's magnetic field used at night

Position of the sun and Earth's magnetic field used by day

Visual clues used to pilot when closer to destination

Navigation

Magnetic fields, celestial objects like the stars and the sun, and mountain ranges and other landmarks are thought to help birds follow migratory paths.

Visual clues and distinctive smells used to find home

Long bill useful in probing mud for worms

LONG-BILLED CURLEW
(*Numenius americanus*)

Bristle-lined bill sieves microorganisms

LESSER FLAMINGO
(*Phoeniconaias minor*)

Fine bill used to extract seeds

GOLDFINCH
(*Carduelis carduelis*)

Powerful bill used to crack nuts

MACAW
(*Ara ararauna*)

Pointed bill used for picking berries

BLACKBIRD
(*Turdus merula*)

Long, pointed bill used to reach nectar inside flowers

SPARKLING VIOLETEAR
(*Colibri coruscans*)

Hatching

Chicks may take hours or days to break out of an egg. Most chicks have an egg tooth, which they use first to punch a tiny hole in the shell, then to make cracks in a circle, until the shell breaks apart. Most hatchlings are blind and lack feathers so must be cared for by their parents, but in waterfowl and gamebirds, the hatchlings have down and can feed themselves within hours.

More than **one trillion hen's eggs** are consumed in the world **every year**

DOMESTICATION

Animals bred purposefully by humans develop characteristics unlike those of their wild relatives. The most well-known domesticated bird is the chicken, which has been kept by people for up to 10,000 years. It is believed a genetic mutation allows chickens to breed and lay eggs all year, not just seasonally. DNA analysis shows that one of their wild ancestors is the Red Junglefowl (*Gallus gallus*), native to Southeast Asia.

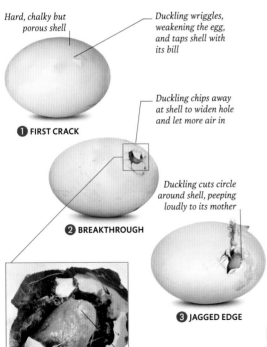

Hard, chalky but porous shell

Duckling wriggles, weakening the egg, and taps shell with its bill

1 FIRST CRACK

Duckling chips away at shell to widen hole and let more air in

Duckling cuts circle around shell, peeping loudly to its mother

2 BREAKTHROUGH

Egg tooth (hard, sharp bump on bill) used to strike shell

3 JAGGED EDGE

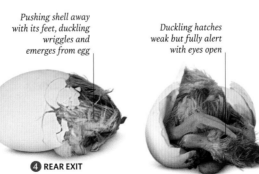

Pushing shell away with its feet, duckling wriggles and emerges from egg

4 REAR EXIT

Duckling hatches weak but fully alert with eyes open

5 HATCHED

Legs and feet not yet strong enough to support weight

Stumpy wings lack flight feathers

Damp down feathers

6 DRYING OUT

see also Birds classification p.161 ▶ **137**

›› Birds continued

Bird orders

Advances in DNA analysis and species comparison have revolutionized the way modern birds are classified, particularly in terms of orders. Taxonomic sources vary, but the system used in this book divides the class Aves into 40 orders—shown here—according to genetic makeup as well as physical similarities. Some of these orders contain only a few species—the Hoatzin is the sole member of its order, for example—but the Passeriformes order of perching birds (passerines) includes more than 6,000.

FLIGHTLESS BIRDS

At different points in evolution, many birds lost the ability to fly, developing dense bones, smaller wings, and larger bodies. Some, such as land-dwelling kiwis and ostriches, are known as ratites and have flattened breastbones. Ratites lack a "keel:" the bony ridge that anchors flying muscles. Penguins retained a keel, but evolved paddlelike wings to "fly" underwater.

Stiff, flipperlike wings adapted for swimming

EMPEROR PENGUIN
(*Aptenodytes forsteri*)
Penguins

Plump body

RED-WINGED TINAMOU
(*Rhynchotus rufescens*)
Tinamous

Two-toed feet

COMMON OSTRICH
(*Struthio camelus*)
Ostriches

Three-toed feet

GREATER RHEA
(*Rhea americana*)
Rheas

Loose, hairlike plumage

SOUTHERN CASSOWARY
(*Casuarius casuarius*)
Cassowaries and emus

Nostrils at tip of bill

NORTH ISLAND BROWN KIWI
(*Apteryx mantelli*)
Kiwis

Broad, flattened bill

MALLARD
(*Anas platyrhynchos*)
Waterfowl

Bright plumage on males

INDIAN PEAFOWL
(*Pavo cristatus*)
Game birds

Streamlined body

RED-THROATED DIVER
(*Gavia stellata*)
Divers

Thick coat of short, stiff, overlapping feathers

KING PENGUIN
(*Aptenodytes patagonicus*)
Penguins

Tubular nostrils

SOUTHERN ROYAL ALBATROSS
(*Diomedea epomophora*)
Albatrosses and petrels

Small head on thin neck

GREAT CRESTED GREBE
(*Podiceps cristatus*)
Grebes

Angled bill

CHILEAN FLAMINGO
(*Phoenicopterus chilensis*)
Flamingos

Long tail streamers

WHITE-TAILED TROPIC BIRD
(*Phaethon lepturus*)
Tropic birds

Daggerlike bill

WHITE STORK
(*Ciconia ciconia*)
Storks

Elongated toes

SCARLET IBIS
(*Eudocimus ruber*)
Herons and relatives

All four toes connected by webs

BLUE-FOOTED BOOBY
(*Sula nebouxii*)
Gannets, cormorants, and relatives

Powerful hooked bill

BALD EAGLE
(*Haliaeetus leucocephalus*)
Hawks, eagles, and relatives

Male inflates neck feathers in display

LITTLE BUSTARD
(*Tetrax tetrax*)
Bustards

Short, rounded wings

WHITE-BREASTED MESITE
(*Mesitornis variegatus*)
Mesites

Raised crest of feathers at base of bill

RED-LEGGED SERIEMA
(*Cariama cristata*)
Seriemas

 ◄ see also The story of life pp.86–87 ◄ Birds pp.134–37

There are **more species** of **perching birds** than in all of the other **orders** combined

Crest of stiff golden feathers

Pearl-gray feathers on long, thick neck

Long, slender bill

SUNBITTERN
(*Eurypyga helias*)
Kagu and Sunbittern

Large, colorful bill

ATLANTIC PUFFIN
(*Fratercula arctica*)
Waders, gulls, and auks

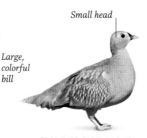

Small head

CROWNED SANDGROUSE
(*Pterocles coronatus*)
Sandgrouse

Plump, full-breasted body

ROCK DOVE
(*Columba livia*)
Pigeons

Broad wings aid balance

HOATZIN
(*Opisthocomus hoazin*)
Hoatzin

Red color of wings due to turacin pigment

RED-CRESTED TURACO
(*Tauraco erythrolophus*)
Turacos

Long tail

GREATER ROADRUNNER
(*Geococcyx californianus*)
Cuckoos

Large, forward-facing eyes

BARN OWL
(*Tyto alba*)
Owls

Tiny bill, but large mouth fringed with bristles

EUROPEAN NIGHTJAR
(*Caprimulgus europaeus*)
Nightjars and frogmouths

Highly flexible wings

SPARKLING VIOLETEAR
(*Colibri coruscans*)
Hummingbirds and swifts

Reversible outer toe

BLUE-NAPED MOUSEBIRD
(*Urocolius macrourus*)
Mousebirds

Bare skin around eyes

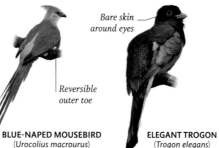

ELEGANT TROGON
(*Trogon elegans*)
Trogons

Zygodactyl feet (two toes facing forward, two toes facing back)

CUCKOO ROLLER
(*Leptosomus discolor*)
Cuckoo Roller

Large head and bill

LILAC-BREASTED ROLLER
(*Coracias caudatus*)
Kingfishers and relatives

Fan-shaped crest

EURASIAN HOOPOE
(*Upupa epops*)
Hoopoes and hornbills

Huge, colorful bill

TOCO TOUCAN
(*Ramphastos toco*)
Woodpeckers and toucans

Small "tooth" on bill

PEREGRINE FALCON
(*Falco peregrinus*)
Falcons and caracaras

Flexible hooked bill

SCARLET MACAW
(*Ara macao*)
Parrots

Feet—unique to perching birds—can wrap around small stems

BLUE TIT
(*Cyanistes caeruleus*)
Passerines

Long legs for wading through grasses and marshland

Well-developed hind toes aid perching in trees

GRAY CROWNED CRANE
(*Balearica regulorum*)
Rails, cranes, and relatives

see also Birds classification p.161 ▶   Types of living things p.217 ▶

Mammals

What is a mammal?

Mammals are a highly diverse group, with different species living on and under the ground, in trees or in oceans, but they all share several characteristics that set them apart from other animals. They have hair, a lower jaw hinged directly to the skull, and three middle-ear bones, while female mammals feed their young with milk-producing mammary glands. All mammals are also warm-blooded (endothermic)—a trait they share with birds.

Body mostly covered in fur

SUCKLING YOUNG

Milk producers

Female mammals possess mammary glands—modified sweat glands activated by hormones released during birth. Initially, the mammaries produce colostrum, containing antibodies and proteins, followed by fat-rich milk usually exuded through nipples or teats.

Kittens suckle milk directly from mother's teats

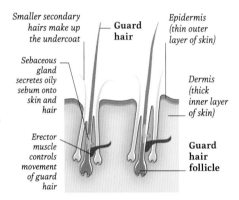

Smaller secondary hairs make up the undercoat

Guard hair

Epidermis (thin outer layer of skin)

Sebaceous gland secretes oily sebum onto skin and hair

Dermis (thick inner layer of skin)

Erector muscle controls movement of guard hair

Guard hair follicle

Hair

Mammal hair consists of threadlike strands of a protein called keratin that cover most or part of their bodies. It has three forms: a soft, insulating undercoat; stiff, protective guard hairs; and sensitive whiskers.

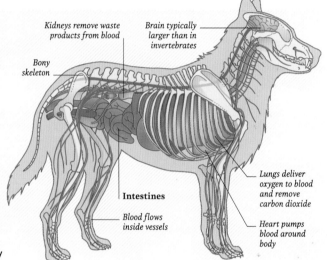

VERTEBRATE BODY SYSTEMS

Like all vertebrates, the mammalian body operates via interdependent systems, from protective skin to the skeletal framework that supports muscles activated by brain signals via the nervous system. Neither the brain nor the heart muscle, which controls circulation, can function without most other systems. Apart from reproduction, all systems interact to keep one individual alive.

Kidneys remove waste products from blood

Brain typically larger than in invertebrates

Bony skeleton

Intestines

Blood flows inside vessels

Lungs deliver oxygen to blood and remove carbon dioxide

Heart pumps blood around body

KEY

■ Reproductive	■ Digestive
■ Circulatory	■ Excretory
■ Nervous	■ Respiratory

Monotremes

Found only in Australia and New Guinea, monotremes lay eggs rather than giving birth to live young. Only five species exist—the duck-billed platypus and four echidna, or spiny anteater, species. All have highly modified, beaklike snouts, and adult monotremes are toothless.

Spines longer than fur

Long, tubular snout probes for food

Waterproof fur

Flattened bill

Flattened tail acts as rudder

Fully webbed front feet

SHORT-BEAKED ECHIDNA
(*Tachyglossus aculeatus*)

DUCK-BILLED PLATYPUS
(*Ornithorhynchus anatinus*)

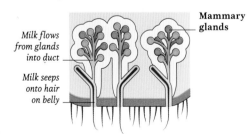

Milk flows from glands into duct

Mammary glands

Milk seeps onto hair on belly

Monotreme mammary glands

Monotremes lack nipple or teats. Instead, females exude milk directly onto their skin via a series of ducts that form two flat, fur-covered milk patches from which their young can feed.

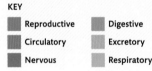

Baby echidnas, known as **puggles**, are about $\frac{1}{2}$ in (12 mm) long when they **hatch**, and weigh just $\frac{2}{100}$ oz (0.57 g)

SUPER-SENSITIVE BILL

A platypus closes its eyes, ears, and nose to dive underwater, but specialized receptor cells in its bill enable it to hunt bottom-dwelling crustaceans, insect larvae, and worms. About 40,000 electroreceptors detect electrical signals given off by muscular contractions of prey animals, while about 60,000 mechanoreceptors track pressure and motion changes in the water.

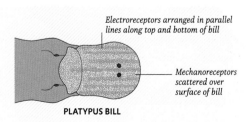

Electroreceptors arranged in parallel lines along top and bottom of bill

Mechanoreceptors scattered over surface of bill

PLATYPUS BILL

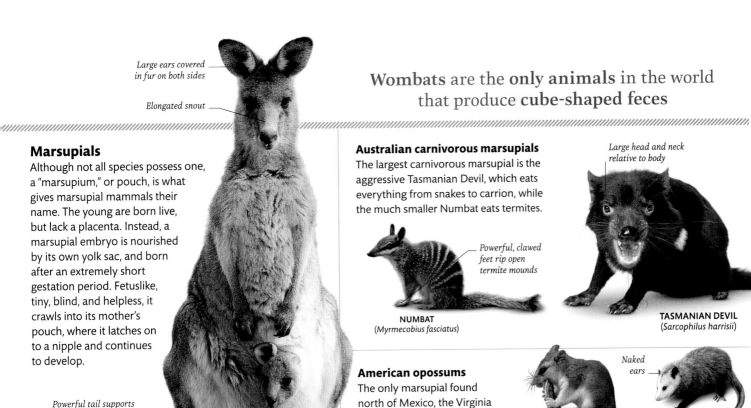

Large ears covered
in fur on both sides

Elongated snout

Wombats are the **only animals** in the world that produce **cube-shaped feces**

Marsupials

Although not all species possess one, a "marsupium," or pouch, is what gives marsupial mammals their name. The young are born live, but lack a placenta. Instead, a marsupial embryo is nourished by its own yolk sac, and born after an extremely short gestation period. Fetuslike, tiny, blind, and helpless, it crawls into its mother's pouch, where it latches on to a nipple and continues to develop.

Powerful tail supports
bipedal stance and balances
body when hopping

Joey stays in mother's
forward-facing pouch
for up to 11 months

EASTERN GRAY KANGAROO
(Macropus giganteus)

Australian carnivorous marsupials

The largest carnivorous marsupial is the aggressive Tasmanian Devil, which eats everything from snakes to carrion, while the much smaller Numbat eats termites.

Large head and neck
relative to body

Powerful, clawed
feet rip open
termite mounds

NUMBAT
(Myrmecobius fasciatus)

TASMANIAN DEVIL
(Sarcophilus harrisii)

American opossums

The only marsupial found north of Mexico, the Virginia Opossum is one of 103 species of opossum living in the Americas. Like most opossums, it is a semiarboreal omnivore that eats eggs, small mammals, insects, and fruit. Many species have a prehensile tail that grasps branches when they are climbing.

Naked
ears

PATAGONIAN OPOSSUM
(Lestodelphys halli)

VIRGINIA OPOSSUM
(Didelphis virginiana)

Long, prehensile tail

COMMON MOUSE OPOSSUM
(Marmosa murina)

WOOLLY MOUSE OPOSSUM
(Marmosa demerae)

Kangaroo joeys are born about **28 days** after conception

DOUBLE UTERUS
Female marsupials have two vaginas connected to two uteruses, with a central vagina forming a birth canal. In kangaroos, one embryo develops in one uterus while another remains dormant.

Uterus with 1-month-
old undeveloped
infant, ready for birth

Fallopian tube

Ovary

Second
uterus

First
vagina

Second vagina used
for insemination

Third vagina
(birth canal)

Kangaroos and relatives

Kangaroos and wallabies are part of the macropod family, noted for their powerful hind legs. Despite differences in appearance, koalas, wombats, gliders, and possums are close relatives of macropods, as all belong to the order Diprotodontia.

Joey carried
on back after
leaving mother's
downward-
facing pouch

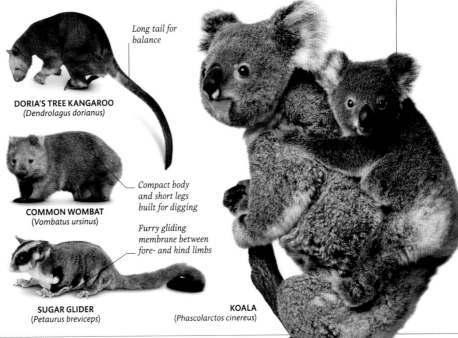

Long tail for
balance

DORIA'S TREE KANGAROO
(Dendrolagus dorianus)

Compact body
and short legs
built for digging

COMMON WOMBAT
(Vombatus ursinus)

Furry gliding
membrane between
fore- and hind limbs

Marsupial moles

Just two species of marsupial mole exist, both found only in Australia. Unlike true moles, they don't create permanent tunnels as they dig, but "swim" through light, sandy soil in search of prey.

Large claws on front feet for
digging and holding prey

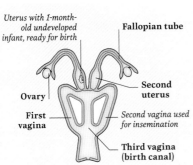

SOUTHERN MARSUPIAL MOLE
(Notoryctes typhlops)

SUGAR GLIDER
(Petaurus breviceps)

KOALA
(Phascolarctos cinereus)

see also Mammals classification pp.162–63 ▶ Types of living things p.217 ▶

» Mammals continued

PLACENTAL UTERUS

A complex organ comprising layers of tissue, a placenta is formed by the uterus once a fetus is implanted. It connects the mother's body with the fetus via an umbilical cord, supplying oxygen and nutrients from the mother, as well as removing carbon dioxide and waste material from the fetus.

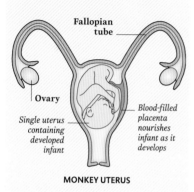

Fallopian tube

Ovary

Single uterus containing developed infant

Blood-filled placenta nourishes infant as it develops

MONKEY UTERUS

Placental mammals

Apart from monotremes and marsupials, all mammals are placental mammals, or eutherians. From tiny shrews to enormous blue whales, all of these animals give birth to live young that gestate, or develop, for much longer periods inside the womb compared to non-eutherians. Such longer gestation periods provide greater amounts of nourishment to eutherian fetuses.

Single young carried, fed, and groomed by mother for 3–4 years

CHIMPANZEE MOTHER AND INFANT

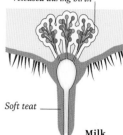

Mammary glands produce milk in response to hormones released during birth

Soft teat

Milk

Placental mammary glands

Mammary glands—specialized, modified sweat glands that clump together to form milk-secreting organs—are associated with teats or nipples in female eutherians.

> The Common Tenrec has **litters of up to 32 babies,** although females have a **maximum of 29 teats**

Tenrec and golden moles

Golden moles are all burrowers, while tenrecs are adapted to a range of habitats. These tiny insectivores are endemic to Africa and Madagascar, respectively.

Rolls into spiky ball if threatened

LESSER HEDGEHOG TENREC
(*Echinops telfairi*)

Coarse fur scattered with spines

LOWLAND STREAKED TENREC
(*Hemicentetes semispinosus*)

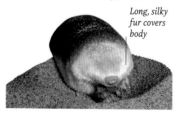

Long, silky fur covers body

GRANT'S DESERT GOLDEN MOLE
(*Eremitalpa granti*)

Sengis

Sengis, or elephant shrews, are native to Africa. Mainly insectivorous, they also hunt spiders and earthworms, which they detect with their long, flexible nose. They have long, powerful back legs and can run swiftly.

Long tail and legs

ROUND-EARED SENGI
(*Macroscelides proboscideus*)

Large ears and eyes

FOUR-TOED SENGI
(*Petrodromus tetradactylus*)

Aardvark

While it resembles an anteater, the Aardvark is more closely related to elephants and is indigenous to Africa. It emerges from its burrow at night to sniff out ants and termites, which it captures with its long, sticky tongue.

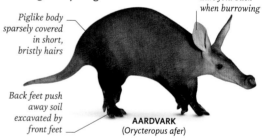

Piglike body sparsely covered in short, bristly hairs

Ears fold back when burrowing

Back feet push away soil excavated by front feet

AARDVARK
(*Orycteropus afer*)

Dugong and manatees

Aquatic dugongs and manatees are the only herbivorous marine mammals on Earth, feeding largely on seagrass. Dugongs are found mainly in shallow coastal waters of the Indian and western Pacific oceans, while manatees inhabit slow-moving rivers, bays, and coastal areas in the east of the Americas, the Amazon Basin, and West Africa.

Thick-skinned, streamlined body

Fluked, flattened tail

DUGONG
(*Dugong dugon*)

Thick, sensory bristles

Paddle-shaped tail

Nostrils closed underwater

Paddlelike front limb

WEST INDIAN MANATEE
(*Trichechus manatus*)

African Savanna Elephant's trunk ends in two opposing, fingerlike tips

Elephants

Weighing up to 7$\frac{1}{2}$ tons (6.8 tonnes), elephants are Earth's largest land animals. These highly intelligent, social mammals are often called natural landscapers, as they carve paths through dense undergrowth, clear trees and shrubs, and replant forests as they defecate seeds. The African Savanna and Forest elephants are indigenous to sub-Saharan Africa, while the smaller Asian Elephant is native to India and Southeast Asia.

An **African elephant's** trunk contains **40,000** muscle bundles

Long, thick, forward-curving ivory tusks (upper incisors) weigh over 220 lb (100 kg) in largest males

Large, veined ears radiate excess heat

Tough, loose, wrinkled skin

Eyelashes up to 5 in (12.7 cm) long

AFRICAN SAVANNA ELEPHANT
(*Loxodonta africana*)

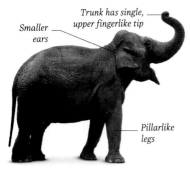

Trunk has single, upper fingerlike tip

Smaller ears

Pillarlike legs

ASIAN ELEPHANT
(*Elephas maximus*)

LIGHTENED SKULL

The average adult elephant skull weighs 115 lb (52 kg), which is still relatively light for such a massive animal. Tiny air pockets pervade the skull, making the bone less dense, but still providing enough mass to support the bulky neck muscles needed for movement.

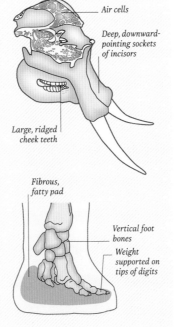

Air cells

Deep, downward-pointing sockets of incisors

Large, ridged cheek teeth

CUSHIONED FEET

An elephant is a digitigrade, meaning its feet are structured so that it walks on its toes. These are supported by thick pads of fatty tissue on the soles of the feet, which act as shock absorbers, and also provide stability over uneven terrain.

Fibrous, fatty pad

Vertical foot bones

Weight supported on tips of digits

Hyraxes

Native to Africa and southwest Asia, hyraxes, or dassies, are herbivores, yet have a pair of continuously growing, tusklike upper incisors used for defense. The first and third digits of their hind feet are hoofed, indicating hyraxes are related to primitive hoofed mammals.

Plump body

SOUTHERN TREE HYRAX
(*Dendrohyrax arboreus*)

Opposable toe on hind foot

Moist feet act like suction cups on hard surfaces

ROCK HYRAX
(*Procavia capensis*)

see also Mammals classification pp.162–63 ▶

Sloths **descend** to the forest floor
about **once a week** to defecate

Armadillos

Related to sloths and anteaters, armadillos are found only in the Americas, mostly near the equator. Their diet includes insects, plants, and eggs, and all 21 species are protected from predators by segmented, keratin-coated, bony plates (osteoderms).

Six to eight armored bands

SIX-BANDED ARMADILLO
(*Euphractus sexcinctus*)

Tail lacks protective osteoderms

NORTHERN NAKED-TAILED ARMADILLO
(*Cabassous centralis*)

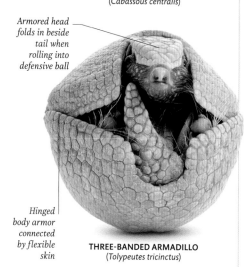

Armored head folds in beside tail when rolling into defensive ball

Hinged body armor connected by flexible skin

THREE-BANDED ARMADILLO
(*Tolypeutes tricinctus*)

Sloths and anteaters

Sloths, anteaters, and armadillos have extra lumbar vertebrae joints that strengthen their back and hips. This frees the forelimbs to dig for insects or forage for leaves, saving energy for these animals, which have low metabolisms.

Two hook-clawed toes on front feet (three on hind feet)

Forelegs longer than hind legs

SOUTHERN TWO-TOED SLOTH
(*Choloepus didactylus*)

Hair grows away from belly

SLOTH FORELIMB ANATOMY

Sloth limbs evolved to suspend their body from branches, and the reduced number of digits end in elongated, hooklike claws. The pulling muscles are much stronger in the forelimbs, while the hind limbs have larger extension muscles.

Humerus   Radius   Phalanges

Carpals

Ulna   Metacarpals

Three toes on all feet

BROWN-THROATED SLOTH
(*Bradypus variegatus*)

Long, tubular snout

GIANT ANTEATER
(*Myrmecophaga tridactyla*)

Prehensile tail

COLLARED ANTEATER
(*Tamandua tetradactyla*)

Rabbits, hares, and pikas

These vegetarian animals are known as lagomorphs. Widely hunted by carnivores and birds of prey, their large eyes and ears help detect danger, while long back legs allow many to outrun predators.

Short, thick fur

AMERICAN PIKA
(*Ochotona princeps*)

Ears furred on both surfaces

Eyes on either side of head

Huge ears radiate excess body heat

Long hind legs

Brown fur turns white in winter

EUROPEAN RABBIT
(*Oryctolagus cuniculus*)

BLACK-TAILED JACKRABBIT
(*Lepus californicus*)

EUROPEAN HARE
(*Lepus europaeus*)

MOUNTAIN HARE
(*Lepus timidus*)

Colugos

Native to Southeast Asia, the nocturnal colugos glide up to 230 ft (70 m) between trees using a fur-covered membrane (patagium).

SUNDA COLUGO
(*Galeopterus variegatus*)

Tree shrews

Also found in Southeast Asia, tree shrews eat insects and fruit. Some species also lap nectar from giant pitcher plants, leaving droppings inside the plant's tube.

Snout lacks whiskers

COMMON TREE SHREW
(*Tupaia glis*)

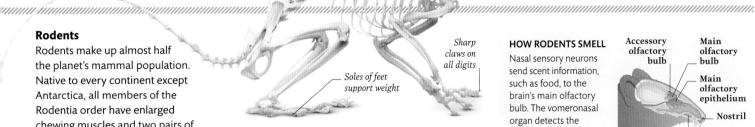
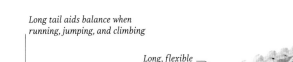

Long tail aids balance when running, jumping, and climbing

Long, flexible spine aids jumping

Skull and jaws adapted for gnawing

Wide gap separates gnawing teeth (incisors) from chewing teeth (molars)

Long, curved, continuously growing incisors

Sharp claws on all digits

Soles of feet support weight

Rodents

Rodents make up almost half the planet's mammal population. Native to every continent except Antarctica, all members of the Rodentia order have enlarged chewing muscles and two pairs of continuously growing, enlarged upper and lower incisors. Most have acute senses of smell and hearing, and long, touch-sensitive whiskers (vibrissae).

Squirrel skeleton
Tree-dwelling squirrels have clawed toes, heavy jawbones, and the long tail common to many land-based rodents. Squirrels jump and climb, however, so require longer hind limbs.

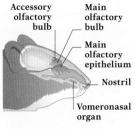

HOW RODENTS SMELL
Nasal sensory neurons send scent information, such as food, to the brain's main olfactory bulb. The vomeronasal organ detects the pheromones of other animals and connects with the accessory olfactory bulb.

Accessory olfactory bulb

Main olfactory bulb

Main olfactory epithelium

Nostril

Vomeronasal organ

MOUSE OLFACTORY SYSTEM

Squirrellike rodents
These burrowing ground-dwellers or nesting tree-dwellers are found in habitats as diverse as tropical rainforests and Arctic tundra. Most eat plants, seeds, and nuts.

Forepaws grasp food

Bushy tail

Tail almost as long as body

EURASIAN RED SQUIRREL
(*Sciurus vulgaris*)

EASTERN CHIPMUNK
(*Tamias striatus*)

Small ears close to head

Large, black eyes

BLACK-TAILED PRAIRIE DOG
(*Cynomys ludovicianus*)

AFRICAN DORMOUSE
(*Graphiurus sp.*)

Mouselike rodents
Often found in urban habitats, mice and their relatives are among the smallest rodents. They are also the most successful, due to their high birth rate and adaptability.

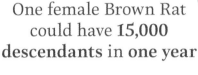

Large cheek pouches store food when foraging

MALAGASY GIANT RAT
(*Hypogeomys antimena*)

GOLDEN HAMSTER
(*Mesocricetus auratus*)

Prehensile tail wraps around stalks

Tail used for balance when hopping at speed

Naked tail

Forepaws free to grasp another stalk

LESSER EGYPTIAN JERBOA
(*Jaculus jaculus*)

BROWN RAT
(*Rattus norvegicus*)

HARVEST MOUSE
(*Micromys minutus*)

> One female Brown Rat could have **15,000** descendants in one year

---

Cavylike rodents
Cavies such as guinea pigs, maras, and pig-sized capybaras, the largest living rodent, are found only in South America. Like Old and New World porcupines, they differ from other rodents in having small tails, larger, heavier bodies, and shorter limbs.

Barb-tipped quills

Ears, eyes, and nose set high on head

Thick, soft fur for warmth

Large head with blunt snout

CAPE PORCUPINE
(*Hystrix africaeaustralis*)

CAPYBARA
(*Hydrochoerus hydrochaeris*)

CHILEAN CHINCHILLA
(*Chinchilla lanigera*)

LONG-HAIRED GUINEA PIG
(*Cavia porcellus*)

Springhares
Large hind limbs make these African rodents excellent jumpers, while sharp-clawed forelimbs allow them to dig burrows. Springhares are herbivores, feeding mainly on stems, roots, and fruit.

Large, upright ears

Tail used as support when sitting

SOUTH AFRICAN SPRINGHARE
(*Pedetes capensis*)

Beaverlike rodents
Beavers are large rodents, weighing up to 66 lb (30 kg). They build large dams in wetlands and streams, altering landscapes. They are grouped with kangaroo rats and gophers due to similarities in jaw and teeth formation.

Long whiskers aid spatial awareness in dark

Bulky body

Flat, scaly tail slaps water as alarm signal

Large hind legs and feet for hopping

ORD'S KANGAROO RAT
(*Dipodomys ordii*)

AMERICAN BEAVER
(*Castor canadensis*)

See also Mammals classification pp.162–63 ▶ **145**

Tarsiers cannot move their huge eyes—instead they can rotate their heads almost 180 degrees

Primates

The third most diverse mammal group after rodents and bats, the Primates order contains 480 species, split into prosimians, monkeys, and apes (which includes humans). All primates have relatively large brains and five digits on hands and feet, and most have flat nails on the fingers and toes.

As well as improving hygiene, grooming is relaxing

Social grooming

Most primates live in social groups and bonds between members are reinforced by grooming sessions, as shown by these macaques.

MONKEY ARM ANATOMY

Most prosimians and monkeys are quadrupedal, so they have the same basic arm and hand structure as humans, but with elongated, more robust arm bones for weight-bearing locomotion.

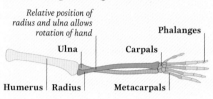

Relative position of radius and ulna allows rotation of hand

Humerus | Radius | Ulna | Carpals | Metacarpals | Phalanges

Prosimians

Meaning "pre-monkey," prosimian refers to the most primitive primates. Most are arboreal and have a more highly developed sense of smell than other primates. A long claw on the second toe is used for grooming.

Lemurs

More than 100 lemur species live in Madagascar. Diurnal species live in family groups, while nocturnal ones are solitary. Smaller lemurs feed on insects and fruit, while most larger species are herbivorous.

Slender, catlike body

Narrow face

RING-TAILED LEMUR
(*Lemur catta*)

Tail used to signal to other members of troop

Long tail aids balance

Large, moveable ears

Large eyes

BROWN GREATER GALAGO
(*Otolemur crassicaudatus*)

MAHOLI BUSHBABY
(*Galago moholi*)

Galagos

Also known as bushbabies, galagos are small, tree-dwelling primates native to sub-Saharan Africa. Because of their arboreal lifestyle, their feet have elongated bones with thick, roughened pads on the soles for grasping branches. All galagos are nocturnal, and feed mainly on fruit, insects, tree gum, and nectar.

Mouse lemurs are the smallest primates in the world

Forward-facing eyes for judging distance

LAC ALAOTRA BAMBOO LEMUR
(*Hapalemur alaotrensis*)

Thick, woolly fur

Male has reddish-brown cheeks

Long, bushy tail

MONGOOSE LEMUR
(*Eulemur mongoz*)

Fat stored in tail and hind legs

RUFOUS MOUSE LEMUR
(*Microcebus rufus*)

Lorises and pottos

These small primates move slowly amid forest branches, clinging tightly with hands and feet. Native to Asia and Africa, lorises and pottos use their mildly poisonous saliva licked onto their fur for defense.

Pincerlike grip

PYGMY SLOW LORIS
(*Nycticebus pygmaeus*)

Arms raised for balance

Large, furry ears

Muscular legs used to gallop across open ground

COQUEREL'S SIFAKA
(*Propithecus coquereli*)

Very short tail, just 2in (5cm) long

INDRI
(*Indri indri*)

Coarse fur with white guard hairs

AYE-AYE
(*Daubentonia madagascariensis*)

Tarsiers

Native to Southeast Asia, tarsiers are nocturnal, insect-eating tree-dwellers. Long legs and elongated ankles allow them to leap up to 10ft (3m) at a time, while their long, slender fingers have disklike pads at the tips for grip.

Eye weighs slightly more than brain

PHILIPPINE TARSIER
(*Tarsius syrichta*)

◄ see also Prehistoric mammals pp.92–93   ◄ Human evolution pp.94–95

Monkeys

Divided into two geographically distinct subgroups, more than 300 species make this the largest group of primates. Although both monkeys and apes are inquisitive animals with large brains, monkeys have smaller bodies and narrower chests, and most have long tails.

Naked gripping pad on underside of tail

Adult male has long, full beard but both sexes roar

Thick, soft, close-curled fur

Strong prehensile (grasping) tail used as fifth limb can support body weight

GRAY WOOLLY MONKEY
(*Lagothrix cana*)

New World monkeys

New World monkeys have flat noses with side-facing nostrils. Found in Mexico and Central and South America, they range from 3 oz (85 g) Pygmy Marmosets to 33 lb (14.5 kg) howlers. Most lack opposable thumbs, many have prehensile tails.

Red howler monkey **calls** can reach **90 decibels**—loud enough to **damage hearing**

Flattened nails protect sensitive fingertips

RED HOWLER MONKEY
(*Alouatta seniculus*)

Distinctive white mask around eyes

Owllike face gives alternate name of Owl Monkey

Nonprehensile tail used only for balance

Large pads on fingers and toes

NORTHERN NIGHT MONKEY
(*Aotus trivirgatus*)

COMMON SQUIRREL MONKEY
(*Saimiri sciureus*)

Distinctive cap of dark fur

Relatively short limbs

BLACK-CAPPED CAPUCHIN
(*Sapajus apella*)

No bare skin on prehensile tail

Adult males and females have white moustaches

Clawed fingers and toes

EMPEROR TAMARIN
(*Saguinus imperator*)

Old World monkeys

Native to Asia, the Middle East, Africa, and Gibraltar, Old World monkeys have narrow noses, slender septums, and downward-facing nostrils. Generally larger than New World monkeys, they have hairless, padded buttocks, and many have opposable thumbs.

Hard sitting pad on buttock

Distinctive white band across forehead

VERVET MONKEY
(*Chlorocebus pygerythrus*)

Large cheek pouches store food

MONA MONKEY
(*Cercopithecus mona*)

No hair on face

One of two pectoral mammary glands

RHESUS MACAQUE
(*Macaca mulatta*)

Short tail indicates this is a ground-dwelling monkey

Cranium contains large brain compared to body size

Long, doglike snout

MANDRILL
(*Mandrillus sphinx*)

Bare rump and face

HAMADRYAS BABOON
(*Papio hamadryas*)

No cheek pouches

Hands have rudimentary thumbs

Unspecialized teeth indicates omnivorous diet

Arms as long as legs for walking on all fours

Long fingers

MACAQUE SKELETON

Large, thick cape of adult male

Dextrous hands pick grasses when sitting

GELADA
(*Theropithecus gelada*)

Pointed tuft of hair

Tail longer than body

TUFTED GREY LANGUR
(*Semnopithecus priam*)

Legs longer than arms for leaping

GUEREZA
(*Colobus guereza*)

see also Apes p.148 ▶ Mammals classification pp.162–63 ▶

Apes

The group of highly intelligent primates known as apes are the closest relatives to humans. Apes differ from other primates in several ways, including having larger, more complex brains and no visible, external tail.

Great apes

Native to African and Southeast Asian tropical forests, great apes are the largest of the apes, the largest being the Mountain Gorilla, which can grow to 6 ft (1.82 m) tall and weigh up to 485 lb (220 kg). At night, they sleep in nests made from leaves or branches in trees or on the ground.

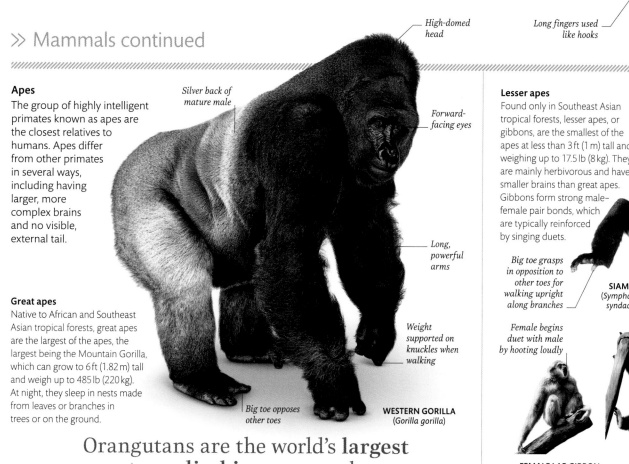

High-domed head

Silver back of mature male

Forward-facing eyes

Long, powerful arms

Weight supported on knuckles when walking

Big toe opposes other toes

WESTERN GORILLA
(Gorilla gorilla)

Orangutans are the world's largest tree-climbing mammals

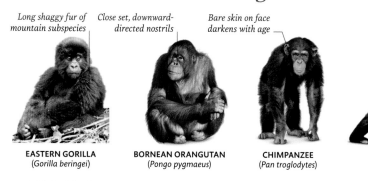

Long shaggy fur of mountain subspecies

EASTERN GORILLA
(Gorilla beringei)

Close set, downward-directed nostrils

BORNEAN ORANGUTAN
(Pongo pygmaeus)

Bare skin on face darkens with age

CHIMPANZEE
(Pan troglodytes)

Center parting in hair on head

BONOBO
(Pan paniscus)

DEXTROUS HANDS

Four fingers and an opposable thumb give great apes both power and precision hand grips. Opposability allows the thumb to move independently, enabling apes to manipulate small objects, such as twigs, as well as grasping larger ones, such as branches, for support.

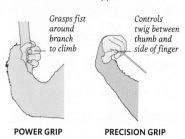

Grasps fist around branch to climb

Controls twig between thumb and side of finger

POWER GRIP

PRECISION GRIP

Great apes and humans

Humans and the great apes evolved from a common ancestor that lived 8–6 million years ago, which makes genetic differences among great ape species very small. Humans' closest relatives are the Chimpanzee and the Bonobo, with whom they share 98.8 percent of their noncoding (junk) DNA.

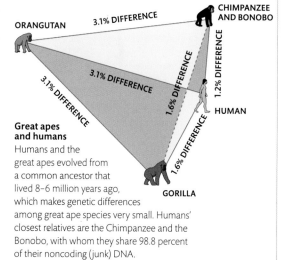

ORANGUTAN

3.1% DIFFERENCE

CHIMPANZEE AND BONOBO

3.1% DIFFERENCE

3.1% DIFFERENCE

1.6% DIFFERENCE

1.2% DIFFERENCE

HUMAN

1.6% DIFFERENCE

GORILLA

Lesser apes

Found only in Southeast Asian tropical forests, lesser apes, or gibbons, are the smallest of the apes at less than 3 ft (1 m) tall and weighing up to 17.5 lb (8 kg). They are mainly herbivorous and have smaller brains than great apes. Gibbons form strong male–female pair bonds, which are typically reinforced by singing duets.

Long fingers used like hooks

Arms up to 2.5 times length of body

Big toe grasps in opposition to other toes for walking upright along branches

SIAMANG
(Symphalangus syndactylus)

Female begins duet with male by hooting loudly

Most gibbons are dimorphic, with males being much darker

FEMALE LAR GIBBON
(Hylobates lar)

MALE LAR GIBBON
(Hylobates lar)

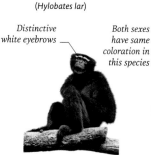

Distinctive white eyebrows

Both sexes have same coloration in this species

HOOLOCK GIBBON
(Bunopithecus hoolock)

SILVERY GIBBON
(Hylobates moloch)

BRACHIATION

Gibbons are mainly arboreal, moving through the trees using a hand-over-hand swing known as brachiation. Extra-long forelimbs and highly flexible shoulder, elbow, and wrist joints allow them to move efficiently with minimal effort.

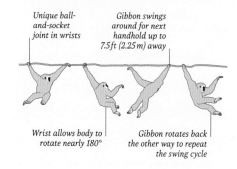

Unique ball-and-socket joint in wrists

Gibbon swings around for next handhold up to 7.5 ft (2.25 m) away

HUMAN

Wrist allows body to rotate nearly 180°

Gibbon rotates back the other way to repeat the swing cycle

Bats

The only mammals capable of true flight, bats are found in almost every habitat on Earth except the poles and extreme deserts. Many bats are voracious insectivores, eating their own weight in insects each night, but more than 300 species of plants depend upon bats as pollinators.

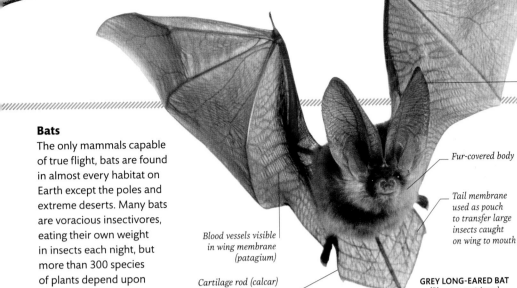

Large, mobile ears

Fur-covered body

Tail membrane used as pouch to transfer large insects caught on wing to mouth

Blood vessels visible in wing membrane (patagium)

Cartilage rod (calcar) holds tail membrane taut

GREY LONG-EARED BAT
(*Plecotus austriacus*)

BAT WING ANATOMY

Bat wing bones are the same as in human forearms and hands, just greatly modified. The elongated fingers support the patagium, the skin membrane stretched between the arm and body.

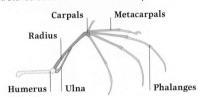

Carpals *Metacarpals*
Radius
Humerus *Ulna* *Phalanges*

Echolocation

Some bats have excellent eyesight and all have a good sense of smell, but all microchiroptera rely on echolocation to hunt and navigate at night. Pulses of sound ("chirps") emitted via the mouth or nose hit objects and create echoes that bounce back to the bat's ears, providing information about size, shape, and location.

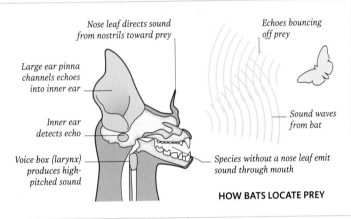

Nose leaf directs sound from nostrils toward prey

Echoes bouncing off prey

Large ear pinna channels echoes into inner ear

Inner ear detects echo

Voice box (larynx) produces high-pitched sound

Species without a nose leaf emit sound through mouth

Sound waves from bat

HOW BATS LOCATE PREY

Hibernation

Bats that live in areas with cold winters either migrate to warmer places or hibernate. They hang upside down in caves or buildings or squeeze into crevices. Their body temperature lowers and their metabolic rate and breathing slow as they deep-sleep through the cold months.

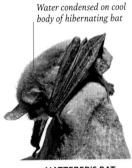

Water condensed on cool body of hibernating bat

NATTERER'S BAT
(*Myotis nattereri*)

Megachiroptera

Also called Old World fruit bats, these tropical and subtropical bats include flying foxes and feed mainly on flowers and fruit. Generally larger than the microchiroptera, they have big eyes that see well at night, small ears, and a clawed index finger. Their long-muzzled faces lack the necessary features for echolocation.

Hooklike claws on feet

Foxlike face

Leathery wings enclose body when resting

FRANQUET'S EPAULETTED BAT
(*Epomops franqueti*)

Rearward-facing knees

LARGE FLYING FOX
(*Pteropus vampyrus*)

Clawed thumb used for climbing

LYLE'S FLYING FOX
(*Pteropus lylei*)

INDIAN FLYING FOX
(*Pteropus giganteus*)

Microchiroptera

The majority of bat species are "microbats," found worldwide from the tropics to temperate zones. Most hunt insects, but some of the larger species feed on small vertebrates and all three species of vampire bats eat only blood.

Weighing just $\frac{1}{20}$ oz (1.5 g), the **Bumblebee Bat** is the **world's smallest mammal**

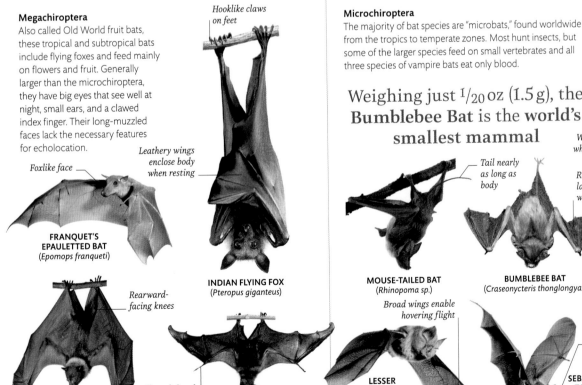

Tail nearly as long as body

MOUSE-TAILED BAT
(*Rhinopoma sp.*)

Relatively large, dark wings

BUMBLEBEE BAT
(*Craseonycteris thonglongyai*)

Wings folded when roosting

Feet clenched when relaxed

COMMON NOCTULE
(*Nyctalus noctula*)

Broad wings enable hovering flight

LESSER HORSESHOE BAT
(*Rhinolophus hipposideros*)

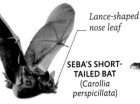

Lance-shaped nose leaf

SEBA'S SHORT-TAILED BAT
(*Carollia perspicillata*)

COMMON VAMPIRE BAT
(*Desmodus rotundus*)

see also Mammals classification pp.162–63 ▶ **149**

An adult pangolin's scales account for about 20 percent of its total body weight

Hedgehogs and moonrats

Although they look dissimilar, hedgehogs and moonrats belong to the same ancient family. Hedgehogs are native to Eurasia and Africa, while moonrats, or gymnures, live in Southeast Asia. Both have diets ranging from invertebrates to fruit, and they are good swimmers and climbers.

Large ears disperse heat

LONG-EARED HEDGEHOG
(Hemiechinus auritus)

Long, scaly tail

MOONRAT
(Echinosorex gymnura)

Prickly defense

Hedgehogs are covered in hollow spines. Temporary ones emerge about an hour after they are born, followed by permanent spines usually 1–2 days later. Curled up, a hedgehog is protected from most predators—unlike furry moonrats, which emit a noxious smell when threatened.

All vulnerable parts protected

CURLED IN A TIGHT BALL

Head and front legs emerge once danger passed

EMERGING FROM BALL

Spines (modified hairs) 1 in (2–3 cm) long

EUROPEAN HEDGEHOG
(Erinaceus europaeus)

Pangolins

Highly endangered, pangolins use their extraordinarily long tongues—up to 16 in (40 cm)—to feed on termites and ants. They lack teeth and a muscular stomach "chews" their food. Their bodies are almost completely protected by tough, overlapping scales, and all eight African and Asian species will roll into a ball when threatened.

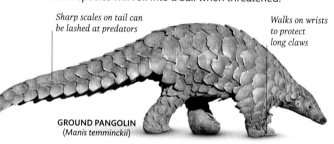

Sharp scales on tail can be lashed at predators

Walks on wrists to protect long claws

GROUND PANGOLIN
(Manis temminckii)

SCALE FORMATION

Like human hair, pangolin scales are made of keratin, but in pangolins the keratin fuses to form overlapping, continuously growing, armorlike plates.

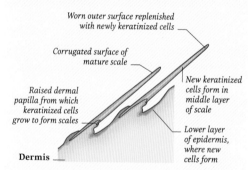

Worn outer surface replenished with newly keratinized cells

Corrugated surface of mature scale

Raised dermal papilla from which keratinized cells grow to form scales

New keratinized cells form in middle layer of scale

Lower layer of epidermis, where new cells form

Dermis

Shrews and moles

Moles have enlarged forefeet for burrowing, while the desmans developed semiwebbed forefeet to hunt underwater. Solenodons and shrews hunt insects and other prey, some species using venomous saliva.

Paler fur may darken with age

HISPANIOLAN SOLENODON
(Solenodon paradoxus)

Long, naked tail

Sharp claws

Stiff hairs on feet and tail aid swimming

Elongated, mobile snout for detecting food

EURASIAN WATER SHREW
(Neomys fodiens)

Ears hidden by short fur

Small eyes

NORTH AMERICAN LEAST SHREW
(Cryptotis parva)

Long snout used like a snorkel or to probe for food

PYRENEAN DESMAN
(Galemys Pyrenaicus)

Forefeet push soil sideways and back

EUROPEAN MOLE
(Talpa europaea)

Cetaceans

Most modern cetaceans are marine mammals thought to have evolved from land-based mammals about 50 million years ago. Adaptations include flippers instead of forelimbs, a fluked tail instead of hind limbs, and nostrils on top of their head to breathe air. A few cetaceans live in fresh water.

Two horizontal flukes on tail

Cuvier's Beaked Whale can dive to depths of almost 2 miles (3 km) and stay underwater for up to 2 hours 18 minutes

DOLPHIN FLIPPER ANATOMY

Flippers help cetaceans turn underwater and prevent their bodies from rolling, but they contain the same bones as terrestrial mammal forelimbs, although greatly modified. The number of carpal (wrist) bones varies between species. Some cetaceans also use flippers for social touching.

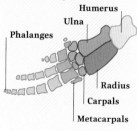

Humerus

Ulna

Phalanges

Radius

Carpals

Metacarpals

LIFE

Dorsal fin helps stability

Hairless, streamlined body

Blowhole

Jaws extended to form beak

Flippers used for steering

LONG-BEAKED COMMON DOLPHIN
(*Delphinus capensis*)

Baleen whales

Baleen whales use their comblike baleen plates, made of keratin, to trap plankton and krill inside their mouth as they force water out. They have two blowholes. At up to 107 ft (32.6 m) long, the Blue Whale is Earth's largest animal.

Mottled skin encrusted with barnacles and other growths

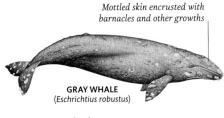

GRAY WHALE
(*Eschrichtius robustus*)

Fatty pad at base of dorsal fin

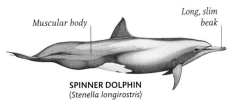  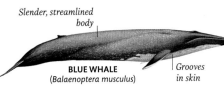

Flippers up to one-third of body length

HUMPBACK WHALE
(*Megaptera novaeangliae*)

Slender, streamlined body

BLUE WHALE
(*Balaenoptera musculus*)

Grooves in skin

Toothed whales

Toothed whales have simple, pointed teeth, either in one or both jaws, and a single blowhole. They range in size from the critically endangered 5 ft- (1.5 m-) long Vaquita to the 63 ft- (19.2 m-) long Sperm Whale.

Muscular body

Long, slim beak

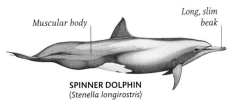

SPINNER DOLPHIN
(*Stenella longirostris*)

Small, rounded head

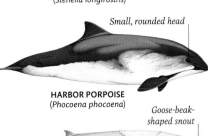

HARBOR PORPOISE
(*Phocoena phocoena*)

Goose-beak-shaped snout

CUVIER'S BEAKED WHALE
(*Ziphius cavirostris*)

Massive blunt head makes up one-third of whale's length

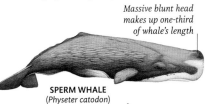

SPERM WHALE
(*Physeter catodon*)

Dorsal fin up to 6 ft (1.8 m) tall in males

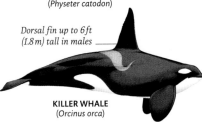

KILLER WHALE
(*Orcinus orca*)

Continuously growing upper incisor forms long spiral tusk

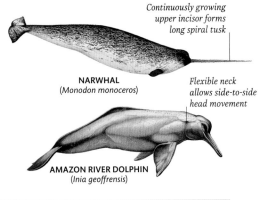

NARWHAL
(*Monodon monoceros*)

Flexible neck allows side-to-side head movement

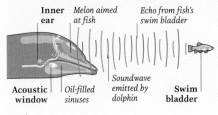

AMAZON RIVER DOLPHIN
(*Inia geoffrensis*)

Jaws and teeth

Wide mouths and a flexible lower jaw allow baleen whales to take in vast amounts of water, sieving lots of food at once. Toothed whales have narrower mouths, with strong jaws to catch and grip individual prey.

Conical teeth in lower jaw fit into sockets in upper jaw

SPERM WHALE

Simple, conical teeth on upper and lower jaws

Jaws open vertically

DOLPHIN

Large upper jaw holds hundreds of baleen plates

Unfused at front, lower jawbones turn outward to take in water

Lower jaw joint flexes laterally and vertically

BALEEN WHALE

ECHOLOCATION

High-frequency sonar clicks produced by toothed whales are focused by a fat-filled organ (the melon) in their heads. The whale uses soundwaves reflected off objects such as prey to pinpoint its target.

Inner ear *Melon aimed at fish* *Echo from fish's swim bladder*

Acoustic window *Oil-filled sinuses* *Soundwave emitted by dolphin* **Swim bladder**

BENGAL TIGER
(Panthera tigris tigris)

Carnivores

Meat-eating mammals of the Carnivora order must either kill other animals or scavenge carcasses to survive. On land, carnivores range from the tiny Least Weasel, which can weigh as little as 1 oz (25 g), to the Polar Bear, can weigh up to 1,430 lb (650 kg).

Skeleton

Carnivores must outthink, outrun, overpower, or outmaneuver prey. Adaptations such as shorter forelimbs and powerful, longer hind limbs aid stability and speed when hunting.

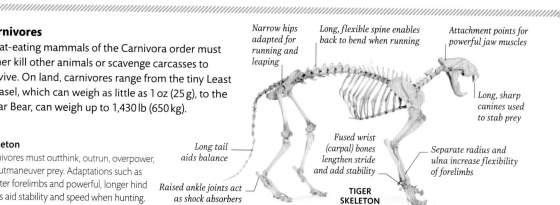

Narrow hips adapted for running and leaping

Long, flexible spine enables back to bend when running

Attachment points for powerful jaw muscles

Long, sharp canines used to stab prey

Long tail aids balance

Fused wrist (carpal) bones lengthen stride and add stability

Separate radius and ulna increase flexibility of forelimbs

Raised ankle joints act as shock absorbers

TIGER SKELETON

Sea lions, seals, and walrus

Pinnipeds—flipper-footed marine mammals—are also carnivores. Fishes, cephalopods, and crustaceans are their usual prey, but the leopard seal also hunts other pinnipeds.

Walruses use their **tusks as ice picks** to haul themselves onto ice floes or land

Small external ears

CALIFORNIA SEA LION
(Zalophus californianus)

Rear flippers turn forward when on land

ANTARCTIC FUR SEAL
(Arctocephalus gazella)

Rear flippers provide no support on land

GRAY SEAL
(Halichoerus grypus)

Fleshy, inflatable nose (trunk) of male

SOUTHERN ELEPHANT SEAL
(Mirounga leonina)

Oversized canine teeth (tusks) grow to 3 ft (1 m) in mature males

WALRUS
(Odobenus rosmarus)

Dogs and relatives

Hypercarnivores like wolves have a diet consisting of at least 70 percent meat. Most canid species, however, are mesocarnivores: consuming 30–70 percent meat, but also foraging for plant matter such as berries and roots, or fungi.

Each digit has a hard pad

GRAY WOLF
(Canis lupus)

WOLF SKULL AND TEETH

Predatory carnivores have large carnassials—modified bladelike upper premolars and lower molars that shear against each other.

Upper carnassial tooth

Lower carnassial tooth

Wild canids

Members of the Canidae family use scent, hearing, and eyesight to track prey. Foxes and coyotes tend to hunt singly or in pairs, while wolves and wild dogs hunt in packs.

Long, pointed muzzle

Short, blunt, nonretractable claws provide traction when running

Toes support weight when walking or running

COYOTE
(Canis latrans)

White winter coat twice as thick as summer coat

ARCTIC FOX
(Alopex lagopus)

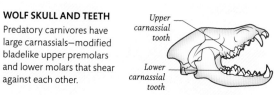

Long, bushy tail (brush)

RED FOX
(Vulpes vulpes)

Black mask

Short-haired fur on legs

RACCOON DOG
(Nyctereutes procyonoides)

Large, erect ears

Long, slender legs

MANED WOLF
(Chrysocyon brachyurus)

BLACK-BACKED JACKAL
(Canis mesomelas)

Coat pattern reflects scientific name of "painted wolf"

Five digits on forefeet (four on hind feet)

AFRICAN WILD DOG
(Lycaon pictus)

Prominent shoulder hump

Upright stance used to identify a threat or food source

Bamboo makes up 99 percent of a panda's diet

Rounded face

Large snout

AMERICAN BLACK BEAR
(*Ursus americanus*)

GIANT PANDA
(*Ailuropoda melanoleuca*)

Dense coat usually dark brown, but may be black or blonde

Long, rough fur

Small ears to minimize heat loss

BROWN BEAR
(*Ursus arctos*)

Soles of large, strong paws support weight when walking or standing

Bears

Earth's largest land carnivores, all but one of the eight bear species are hypocarnivores, depending on meat for less than 30 percent of their diet. The exception is the polar bear, a hypercarnivore, which feeds mainly on seals.

Long, nonretractable claws used for digging and climbing

SLOTH BEAR
(*Melursus ursinus*)

POLAR BEAR
(*Ursus maritimus*)

Domestic dogs

Gray wolves and dogs diverged from an extinct wolf species around 15,000 to 40,000 years ago. Dogs were domesticated at least 14,000 years ago.

Chaser, a **Border collie**, was trained to recognize the names of **1,022 objects**

Broad head and chest

High-set, drop ears

Large muzzle packed with odor-detecting sensors

Weatherproof double coat protects muscular, athletic body

Long, narrow head

SCHNAUZER
Utility

BORDER COLLIE
Pastoral

SMOOTH-HAIRED DACHSHUND
Scent hound

SALUKI
Sight hound

LABRADOR RETRIEVER
Gundog

Short, strong legs and paws used for digging

Long, curly tail carried over back

Powerful, muscular thighs

BREED SIZES

Despite the long history of domestication, most modern dog breeds were developed within the last few centuries, usually to perform tasks, such as herding or vermin hunting, or as small companion dogs. Today, sizes range from teacup-sized Chihuahuas to giant Irish Wolfhounds.

5 in
(13 cm)

CHIHUAHUA

32 in
(81 cm)

IRISH WOLFHOUND

JACK RUSSELL TERRIER
Terrier

BICHON FRISE
Toy

SIBERIAN HUSKY
Working

Cats

From domestic cats to leopards and tigers, all 37 species of the Felidae family are highly specialized hunters. In the wild, they are entirely dependent on prey they hunt, and their diet consists almost exclusively of meat.

Wild felines

Except for Antarctica and Australia, cats are native to almost every part of the world. Their varied coats often hint at their habitat, from buff-colored lions of African savannas to jaguars that hunt in dappled rainforest shade.

ACUTE HEARING

Like most mammals, cats' ears are made up of an inner, middle, and outer ear, but the mobile, triangular outer pinna channels sound deep into the middle ear, allowing cats to detect a remarkably wide range of sounds and pinpoint their source.

MAMMALIAN EAR STRUCTURE

Ear canal

Ear bones (ossicles) vibrate and send sound to fluid in inner ear

Auditory nerve carries signal to brain

Pinna funnels sound waves into ear canal

Cochlea converts sound waves into electrical signal

Eardrum (tympanum) vibrated by sound waves entering ear

Middle ear

Thick, dark mane signals fitness of adult male

LION
(*Panthera leo*)

Individual's unique pattern of rosettes provides camouflage

JAGUAR
(*Panthera onca*)

Long, thickly furred tail can be wrapped around body for extra warmth

Short limbs aid climbing

SNOW LEOPARD
(*Panthera uncia*)

Tail acts as counterbalance when turning at speed

Long, muscular legs enable stride length of 23 ft (7 m)

Light, slender body built for sprinting at 70 mph (115 kph)

CHEETAH
(*Acinonyx jubatus*)

Muscular shoulders and forelimbs used to haul prey into trees

LEOPARD
(*Panthera pardus*)

Large forelimbs and very large paws for holding down prey

PUMA
(*Puma concolor*)

Distinctive ear tufts and facial ruff

Short, bobbed tail

CANADIAN LYNX
(*Lynx canadensis*)

Short, dense fur

OCELOT
(*Leopardus pardalis*)

Very large ears pinpoint location of prey

SERVAL
(*Leptailurus serval*)

Domestic cats

More than 100 breeds of domestic cats exist today, the result of selective breeding for body and coat type and character.

Tabby coat pattern found in many breeds

BRITISH SHORTHAIR

Dark extremities

SIAMESE CAT

WILD ANCESTOR

All domestic cats are believed to descend from a North African/Southwest Asian wildcat. The process is thought to have begun about 12,000 years ago when humans began to cultivate grain crops. Grains attracted rodents, which attracted cats, and the human and feline species began to interact.

AFRICAN WILDCAT
(*Felis silvestris lybica*)

Short muzzle

PERSIAN CAT

Thick, shaggy, waterproof coat

MAINE COON

Short-haired, blue coat

BLUE KORAT

Dark patches around eyes protect against glare of desert sun

Meerkats can **spot aerial predators** more than **985 ft** (300 m) away

Mongooses

More than 30 species of mongoose live in Africa, Asia, and Europe. Although small, they are formidable predators, hunting rodents, lizards, and even venomous snakes and scorpions.

Coarse, grizzled fur

Upright stance when on lookout

BANDED MONGOOSE
(*Mungos mungo*)

MEERKAT
(*Suricata suricatta*)

Civets and relatives

Although they resemble cats, civets have longer bodies, long tails, short legs, and a longer muzzle. They eat small animals, eggs, and fruit.

Long, slender body

Tapered muzzle

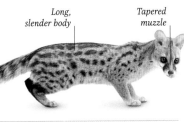

COMMON GENET
(*Genetta genetta*)

Hyenas and Aardwolf

Although strikingly similar, the Aardwolf eats mainly termites, while hyenas are meat-eaters with powerful, bone-crushing jaws. Both are more closely related to cats and civets than wolves.

Back slopes downward from shoulder to tail

Neck and back mane

AARDWOLF
(*Proteles cristata*)

STRIPED HYENA
(*Hyaena hyaena*)

Weasels and relatives

Nearly 60 species belong to the Mustelidae, or weasel, family. Usually long-bodied, with short legs, they have anal glands that produce a musky odor. Most are terrestrial, but minks and otters range from semi- to fully aquatic.

Small, flattened head aids entering mouse burrows

Slender neck and body

Bushy tail

Long, coarse hair on back and flanks

EUROPEAN PINE MARTEN
(*Martes martes*)

EURASIAN BADGER
(*Meles meles*)

Partly webbed feet enables hunting in water and on land

LEAST WEASEL
(*Mustela nivalis*)

AMERICAN MINK
(*Neovison vison*)

Stocky, bearlike build

Stiff whiskers detect prey movements in water

EURASIAN OTTER
(*Lutra lutra*)

Strong jaws

WOLVERINE
(*Gulo gulo*)

WHISKERS

Whiskers, or vibrissae, are specialized sensory hairs that transmit information from the environment to the brain. Movement by touch, water, or air activates the whisker (vibrissal) nerve in the center of each shaft.

Superficial whisker nerve

Whisker

Epidermis

Most superficial whisker nerve endings encircle whisker

Deep whisker nerve endings run alongside whisker's root

Whisker capsule

Dermis

Deep whisker nerve

Whisker grows from base of follicle

Raccoons and relatives

These small- to medium-sized mammals are native to forests of the Americas. All are omnivores, eating fruit, nuts, and plants as well as rodents, eggs, insects, frogs, and crayfish.

Distinctive black face mask

Strongly prehensile tail

NORTHERN RACCOON
(*Procyon lotor*)

KINKAJOU
(*Potos flavus*)

Skunks

The skunks of the Americas and the Asian stink badgers all have anal scent glands that spray a noxious fluid when these animals are threatened.

Black-and-white warning coloration

STRIPED SKUNK
(*Mephitis mephitis*)

Red Panda

The Red Panda is the only living member of the Ailuridae family. It lives in montane forests of China and the Himalayas, and feeds mainly on bamboo, as well as fruit, fungi, and animal protein.

Soft, dense fur

RED PANDA
(*Ailurus fulgens*)

see also Mammals classification pp.162–63 ▶ **155**

Odd-toed hoofed mammals

Hoofed mammals are the dominant terrestrial herbivores. Many species have been domesticated. In odd-toed hoofed mammals, the weight is borne by the central (third) toe, and the toes are protected by tough, keratinized hoofs.

RHINOCEROS LEG ANATOMY

Rhinos have relatively slim legs given their bulk, but the shortened, strong bones can support a body weight of up to $2\frac{1}{2}$ tons (2.3 tonnes) between the four legs. Fatty pads in the feet may spread some of the load borne by the toes.

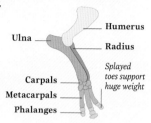

Humerus
Ulna
Radius
Carpals
Metacarpals
Phalanges
Splayed toes support huge weight

Rhinoceroses

Rhinoceroses include some of the world's largest land animals. Wild rhinos are endangered due to poaching for their keratinized horns; depending on the species, they have either one or two. Two species are native to Africa and three to Asia.

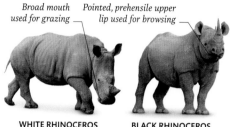

Broad mouth used for grazing *Pointed, prehensile upper lip used for browsing*

WHITE RHINOCEROS
(*Ceratotherium simum*)

BLACK RHINOCEROS
(*Diceros bicornis*)

Tapirs

Tapirs live in forested areas and spend daylight hours foraging for fruit and vegetation. They flee into water if threatened, or to keep cool, as they are excellent swimmers.

Hard-skinned, piglike body *Short, extensible trunk can be used as snorkel*

MALAYAN TAPIR
(*Tapirus indicus*)

Horses and relatives

Equids, or members of the horse family, have one toe on each foot in the form of a single hoof. They are built for speed and have great stamina. Equids are mainly grazers, although some species eat bark, leaves, and other plant material, and most live in herds controlled by a single male.

Upright mane

PRZEWALSKI'S HORSE
(*Equus caballus przewalskii*)

Long, coarse coat

DONKEY
(*Equus asinus asinus*)

Distinctive striped pattern

GRANT'S ZEBRA
(*Equus quagga boehmi*)

> The horse and the donkey were **domesticated** around **5,500** years ago

HORSE LEG ANATOMY

A horse's long, slender legs are adapted to quick, efficient movement, allowing it to run at speeds of up to 43 mph (70 kph) or more for short periods when threatened—or in a race.

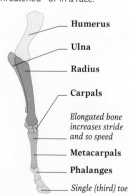

Humerus
Ulna
Radius
Carpals
Elongated bone increases stride and so speed
Metacarpals
Phalanges
Single (third) toe

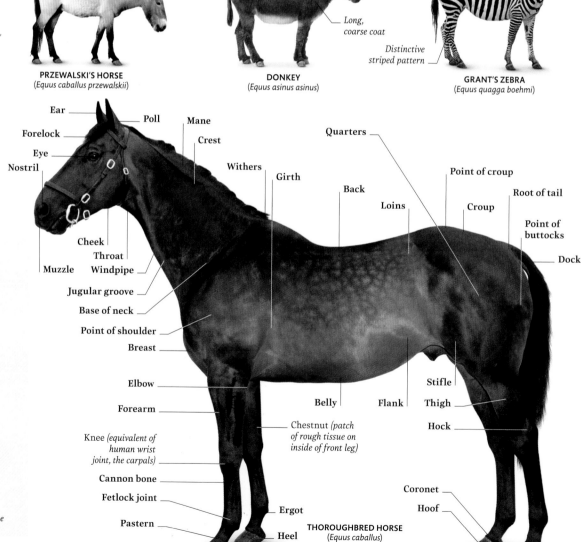

Ear
Poll
Mane
Forelock
Crest
Eye
Quarters
Nostril
Withers
Girth
Point of croup
Back
Root of tail
Loins
Croup
Point of buttocks
Cheek
Dock
Throat
Muzzle Windpipe
Jugular groove
Base of neck
Point of shoulder
Breast
Elbow
Stifle
Belly Flank Thigh
Forearm
Hock
Chestnut (*patch of rough tissue on inside of front leg*)
Knee (*equivalent of human wrist joint, the carpals*)
Cannon bone
Coronet
Fetlock joint
Hoof
Ergot
Pastern
THOROUGHBRED HORSE
Heel
(*Equus caballus*)

The **black** color of a giraffe's **tongue** protects it from being **burned by the sun** when the giraffe is feeding

Even-toed hoofed mammals

Most animals in this group have two or four toes on each foot, each encased in a keratinized hoof. Apart from pigs and hippopotamuses, all are ruminants—cud-chewing herbivores with multi-chambered stomachs.

Pigs

Although most wild pigs are forest-dwellers, warthogs live on the African savannas. All pigs have an excellent sense of smell and a strong snout that ends in a cartilaginous nasal disk, used to root for plant and animal food.

Tuft on long, pointed ear

RED RIVER HOG
(*Potamochoerus porcus*)

WILD BOAR
(*Sus scrofa*)

Strong snout used like bulldozer when foraging

Short, skin-covered ossicones (horns)

Thin, mobile lips aid browsing

Neck up to almost 8 ft (2.4 m) long

Camels and relatives

All camelids have broad padded feet—an adaptation to walking on sand or snow—with two large toes protected by nails instead of hoofs. Wild Bactrian Camels have two humps in which fat is stored, the domesticated Dromedary has one.

Long, slender leg

DROMEDARY
(*Camelus dromedarius*)

Split upper lip

GUANACO
(*Lama guanicoe*)

Giraffes and Okapi

The tallest living animals at up to 18 ft (5.5 m), giraffes, and their much smaller relative, the Okapi, are indigenous to Africa. Giraffes inhabit savannas, while Okapis live in thick tropical rainforest. A giraffe's foot is about 1 ft (30 cm) in diameter, which prevents it from sinking in loose sand.

RETICULATED GIRAFFE
(*Giraffa camelopardalis reticulata*)

Deer

Most deer have branched, solid bone antlers that are shed then regrown from the skull every year. Apart from Reindeer, females usually lack horns or have small stubs. Species that do not have antlers usually have tusklike canines.

Palmate antler

Antler with multiple points

MOOSE
(*Alces americanus*)

RED DEER
(*Cervus elaphus*)

Hippopotamuses

Weighing up to 5 tons (4.5 tonnes), hippos spend most daylight hours in water, which helps to support their mass as well as keeping their skin moist. Their mouth has an average gape of 4 ft (1.2 m)—the largest of any land animal.

Skin almost hairless

Eyes, ears, and nostrils at top of head

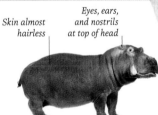

HIPPOPOTAMUS
(*Hippopotamus amphibius*)

AMERICAN BISON
(*Bison bison*)

Shaggy coat and beard

Cattle and relatives

Cattle and other bovids have unbranched, bony horns surrounded by keratin. They are present in both sexes in most species and are never shed. Bovids range from graceful, slender-limbed antelope to hefty bison and the Gaur.

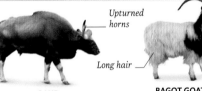

Upturned horns

GAUR
(*Bos gaurus*)

Long hair

BAGOT GOAT
(*Capra hircus*)

Horns of males may weigh as much as skeleton

BIGHORN SHEEP
(*Ovis canadensis*)

Long, spiral horns of males

GREATER KUDU
(*Tragelaphus strepsiceros*)

CATTLE LEG ANATOMY

All cattle and their relatives have divided (cloven) hoofs, with the often extremely heavy weight of the animal supported by the two central toes on each foot. As with all hoofed mammals, each leg is embedded in the body wall as far as the elbow or knee joint.

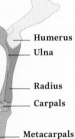

— Humerus
— Ulna
— Radius
— Carpals
— Metacarpals
— Phalanges

Classification

Principles of classification

For centuries, scientists have grouped species of organisms into a series of taxa (singular, taxon). Each taxon in the series is more inclusive, larger, and has a higher "rank." Species are grouped with other similar species into genera (singular, genus), genera grouped into families, and so on, in a hierarchy ending in the highest-ranked taxon, the kingdom (see pp.106, 216). Since the mid-19th century, scientists have been investigating the evolutionary history of organisms by analyzing shared features to establish how closely they are related.

Cladistics

The classification of life is more natural (less artificial) if it reflects evolutionary history. Cladistics is a set of rules that help us do this. Every taxon in cladistics must be a "clade." A clade is a group that includes all the descendants of a particular ancestor, which share one or more unique features first found in that ancestor. Applying cladistics means reorganizing groups, and in some places abandoning the neat hierarchy and ranks of traditional classification.

Cladistic classification of vertebrates

Cladistics splits fishes into clades, the last of which, the fleshy-finned fishes, includes their many thousands of descendants—all land vertebrates, or tetrapods (reptiles, amphibians, mammals, and birds).

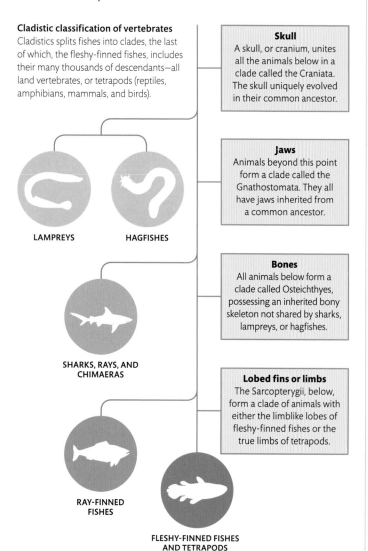

LAMPREYS

HAGFISHES

SHARKS, RAYS, AND CHIMAERAS

RAY-FINNED FISHES

FLESHY-FINNED FISHES AND TETRAPODS

Skull
A skull, or cranium, unites all the animals below in a clade called the Craniata. The skull uniquely evolved in their common ancestor.

Jaws
Animals beyond this point form a clade called the Gnathostomata. They all have jaws inherited from a common ancestor.

Bones
All animals below form a clade called Osteichthyes, possessing an inherited bony skeleton not shared by sharks, lampreys, or hagfishes.

Lobed fins or limbs
The Sarcopterygii, below, form a clade of animals with either the limblike lobes of fleshy-finned fishes or the true limbs of tetrapods.

The kingdoms of life

As knowledge grows, experts are dividing life into varying numbers of kingdoms, or even higher-level taxa called domains. In this book, we use a seven-kingdom system. Bacteria and archaea are simple and single-celled. Protozoa and chromists are also mainly single-celled, but more complex.

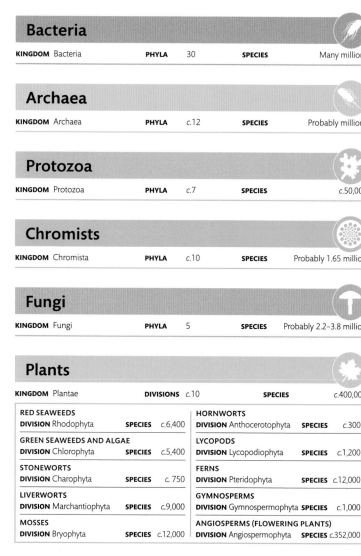

Bacteria

KINGDOM	Bacteria	PHYLA	30	SPECIES	Many millions

Archaea

KINGDOM	Archaea	PHYLA	c.12	SPECIES	Probably millions

Protozoa

KINGDOM	Protozoa	PHYLA	c.7	SPECIES	c.50,000

Chromists

KINGDOM	Chromista	PHYLA	c.10	SPECIES	Probably 1.65 million

Fungi

KINGDOM	Fungi	PHYLA	5	SPECIES	Probably 2.2–3.8 million

Plants

KINGDOM	Plantae	DIVISIONS	c.10	SPECIES	c.400,000

RED SEAWEEDS			HORNWORTS		
DIVISION Rhodophyta	SPECIES	c.6,400	DIVISION Anthocerotophyta	SPECIES	c.300
GREEN SEAWEEDS AND ALGAE			LYCOPODS		
DIVISION Chlorophyta	SPECIES	c.5,400	DIVISION Lycopodiophyta	SPECIES	c.1,200
STONEWORTS			FERNS		
DIVISION Charophyta	SPECIES	c.750	DIVISION Pteridophyta	SPECIES	c.12,000
LIVERWORTS			GYMNOSPERMS		
DIVISION Marchantiophyta	SPECIES	c.9,000	DIVISION Gymnospermophyta	SPECIES	c.1,000
MOSSES			ANGIOSPERMS (FLOWERING PLANTS)		
DIVISION Bryophyta	SPECIES	c.12,000	DIVISION Angiospermophyta	SPECIES	c.352,000

Animals

KINGDOM	Animalia	PHYLA	More than 30	SPECIES	c.1.3 million

Animal groups and names

The following pages summarize the classification scheme used in the animal kingdom section (see pp.106–157). It represents current thinking and is a compromise between cladistics and traditional classification. As in cladistics, groups are "nested" to show how they are related; informal, "traditional" groups with no distinct biological identity, such as the jawless fishes on p.160, are bounded by dotted lines. Some of the species totals, particularly for the invertebrates, are based on estimates and can be subject to rapid change. More than 1 million species of insects have been described, but scientists think there may be many more millions of species living on Earth.

Invertebrates

Invertebrates form a diverse collection of more than 30 phyla, which vary enormously in size. They can be grouped, informally, because they all lack the spinal column found in vertebrates. They comprise the vast majority—97 percent—of known animal species. Only the major invertebrate phyla are included in the animal kingdom section of this book (see pp.106–115). Almost all of the minor phyla listed below contain marine species or animals that live in damp habitats.

MINOR PHYLA

COMB JELLIES
PHYLUM Ctenophora   SPECIES   c.200

PEANUT WORMS
PHYLUM Sipuncula   SPECIES   c.150

BRYOZOANS
PHYLUM Bryozoa   SPECIES   c.6,000

ROTIFERS
PHYLUM Rotifera   SPECIES   c.2,000

RIBBON WORMS
PHYLUM Nemertea   SPECIES   c.1,400

BRACHIOPODS
PHYLUM Brachiopoda   SPECIES   c.400

HORSESHOE WORMS
PHYLUM Phoronida   SPECIES   c.20

ARROW WORMS
PHYLUM Chaetognatha   SPECIES   c.150

WATER BEARS
PHYLUM Tardigrade   SPECIES   c.1,000

VELVET WORMS
PHYLUM Onychophora   SPECIES   c.180

SPOONWORMS
PHYLUM Echiura   SPECIES   c.200

HEMICHORDATES
PHYLUM Hemichordata   SPECIES   c.130

10 OTHER MINOR INVERTEBRATE PHYLA

SPONGES
PHYLUM Porifera   CLASSES 3   ORDERS 24   FAMILIES 127   SPECIES c.10,000

CNIDARIANS
PHYLUM Cnidaria   CLASSES 6   ORDERS 24   FAMILIES 300   SPECIES c.11,000

FLATWORMS
PHYLUM Platyhelminthes   CLASSES 6   ORDERS 41   FAMILIES 424   SPECIES c.30,000

SEGMENTED WORMS
PHYLUM Annelida   CLASSES 4   ORDERS 17   FAMILIES 130   SPECIES c.18,000

ROUNDWORMS
PHYLUM Nematoda   CLASSES 2   ORDERS 17   FAMILIES 160   SPECIES c.26,000

MOLLUSKS
PHYLUM Mollusca   CLASSES 7   ORDERS 53   FAMILIES 609   SPECIES c.110,000

ECHINODERMS
PHYLUM Echinodermata   CLASSES 5   ORDERS 38   FAMILIES 173   SPECIES c.7,000

INVERTEBRATE CHORDATES
Chordates are animals with a backbone or notochord (the evolutionary precursor of a backbone), and they all belong to the phylum Chordata. The phylum is split into three subphyla—one being the vertebrates (see p.160). The other two are invertebrates, because they have only a notochord, no backbone. The fishlike lancelets have a notochord throughout life, but most tunicates (which include sea squirts) have one only in their tadpolelike larvae.

TUNICATES
SUBPHYLUM Urochordata   CLASSES 3   ORDERS 7   FAMILIES 36   SPECIES c.2,900

LANCELETS
SUBPHYLUM Cephalochordata   CLASSES 1   ORDERS 1   FAMILIES 1   SPECIES 30

ARTHROPODS
PHYLUM Arthropoda

MANDIBULATES
SUBPHYLUM Mandibulata   CLASSES 16   ORDERS 109   FAMILIES c.2,230   SPECIES c.1.2 million

HEXAPODS
SUPERCLASS Hexapoda   CLASSES 4   ORDERS 32   FAMILIES c.1,047   SPECIES c.1.1 million

SPRINGTAILS
CLASS Collembola   ORDERS 1   FAMILIES 32   SPECIES c.8,100

PROTURANS
CLASS Protura   ORDERS 1   FAMILIES 7   SPECIES c.760

DIPLURANS
CLASS Diplura   ORDERS 1   FAMILIES 8   SPECIES c.975

INSECTS
CLASS Insecta   ORDERS 29   FAMILIES c.1,000   SPECIES c.1.1 million

BRISTLETAILS
ORDER Archaeognatha   SPECIES c.470

SILVERFISH
ORDER Thysanura   SPECIES c.570

MAYFLIES
ORDER Ephemeroptera   SPECIES c.3,000

DAMSELFLIES AND DRAGONFLIES
ORDER Odonata   SPECIES c.5,600

CRICKETS AND GRASSHOPPERS
ORDER Orthoptera   SPECIES c.10,500

STONEFLIES
ORDER Plecoptera   SPECIES c.3,000

ROCK CRAWLERS
ORDER Grylloblattodea   SPECIES 30

EARWIGS
ORDER Dermaptera   SPECIES c.1,900

STICK AND LEAF INSECTS
ORDER Phasmatodea   SPECIES c.2,500

MANTIDS
ORDER Mantodea   SPECIES c.2,300

COCKROACHES
ORDER Blattodea   SPECIES c.4,600

TERMITES
ORDER Isoptera   SPECIES c.3,000

WEB-SPINNERS
ORDER Embioptera   SPECIES c.400

ANGEL INSECTS
ORDER Zoraptera   SPECIES c.43

BARKLICE AND BOOKLICE
ORDER Psocoptera   SPECIES c.5,600

PARASITIC LICE
ORDER Phthiraptera   SPECIES c.5,200

BUGS
ORDER Hemiptera   SPECIES c.88,000

THRIPS
ORDER Thysanoptera   SPECIES c.7,400

DOBSONFLIES AND ALDERFLIES
ORDER Megaloptera   SPECIES c.300

SNAKEFLIES
ORDER Raphidioptera   SPECIES c.200

ANTLIONS, LACEWINGS, AND RELATIVES
ORDER Neuroptera   SPECIES c.11,000

BEETLES
ORDER Coleoptera   SPECIES c.370,000

STREPSIPTERANS
ORDER Strepsiptera   SPECIES c.580

SCORPIONFLIES
ORDER Mecoptera   SPECIES c.550

FLEAS
ORDER Siphonaptera   SPECIES c.2,500

FLIES
ORDER Diptera   SPECIES c.150,000

CADDISFLIES
ORDER Trichoptera   SPECIES c.10,000

MOTHS AND BUTTERFLIES
ORDER Lepidoptera   SPECIES c.165,000

BEES, WASPS, ANTS, AND SAWFLIES
ORDER Hymenoptera   SPECIES c.198,000

MYRIAPODS
SUPERCLASS Myriapoda   CLASSES 2   ORDERS 21   FAMILIES 171   SPECIES c.13,150

CRUSTACEANS
SUPERCLASS Crustacea   CLASSES 7   ORDERS 56   FAMILIES c.1,000   SPECIES c.70,000

CHELICERATES
SUBPHYLUM Chelicerata   CLASSES 3   ORDERS 14   FAMILIES 675   SPECIES c.104,350

SEA SPIDERS
CLASS Pycnogonida   ORDERS 1   FAMILIES 13   SPECIES c.1,330

HORSESHOE CRABS
CLASS Merostomata   ORDERS 1   FAMILIES 1   SPECIES 4

ARACHNIDS
CLASS Arachnida   ORDERS 12   FAMILIES 661   SPECIES c.103,000

see also Types of living things pp.216–17 ▶   Bacteria and viruses pp.218–19 ▶   **159**

Vertebrates

FISHES

FOUR CLASSES

The term "fish" refers to a diverse group of aquatic vertebrates descended from several different ancestors. In this book, the more than 30,000 species of fishes alive today are classified in the four classes listed below.

JAWLESS FISHES

HAGFISHES						
CLASS Myxini	**ORDERS**	1	**FAMILIES**	1	**SPECIES**	78

LAMPREYS						
CLASS Cephalaspidomorphi	**ORDERS**	1	**FAMILIES**	1	**SPECIES**	c.43

CARTILAGINOUS FISHES

CLASS Chondrichthyes	**ORDERS** 14	**FAMILIES** 54	**SPECIES** c.1,200

SHARKS AND RAYS						
SUBCLASS Euselachii						
SHARKS	**ORDERS**	9	**FAMILIES**	34	**SPECIES**	c.510
RAYS	**ORDERS**	4	**FAMILIES**	17	**SPECIES**	c.650

CHIMAERAS						
SUBCLASS Holocephali	**ORDERS**	1	**FAMILIES**	3	**SPECIES**	48

BONY FISHES

CLASS Osteichthyes	**ORDERS** 67	**FAMILIES** 481	**SPECIES** c.31,000

FLESHY-FINNED FISHES						
SUBCLASS Sarcopterygii	**ORDERS**	2	**FAMILIES**	4	**SPECIES**	48

RAY-FINNED FISHES
SUBCLASS Actinopterygii

PRIMITIVE RAY-FINNED FISHES	**ORDERS**	4	**FAMILIES**	5	**SPECIES**	49
BONY-TONGUED FISHES **ORDER** Osteoglossiformes	**ORDERS**	1	**FAMILIES**	5	**SPECIES**	244
TARPONS AND EELS **SUPERORDER** Elopomorpha	**ORDERS**	4	**FAMILIES**	24	**SPECIES**	c.1,000
HERRINGS AND RELATIVES **SUPERORDER** Clupeomorpha	**ORDERS**	1	**FAMILIES**	5	**SPECIES**	405
SLICKHEADS AND TUBESHOULDERS **SUPERORDER** Alepocephali	**ORDERS**	1	**FAMILIES**	3	**SPECIES**	137
CATFISHES AND RELATIVES **SUPERORDER** Ostariophysi	**ORDERS**	5	**FAMILIES**	85	**SPECIES**	c.10,500
SALMON AND RELATIVES **SUPERORDER** Protacanthopterygii	**ORDERS**	2	**FAMILIES**	14	**SPECIES**	355
SMELTS AND DRAGONFISHES **SUPERORDER** Osmeromorpha	**ORDERS**	4	**FAMILIES**	14	**SPECIES**	c.600
LANTERNFISHES AND RELATIVES **SUPERORDER** Scolepomorpha	**ORDERS**	2	**FAMILIES**	19	**SPECIES**	c.520
SUPERORDER Cyclosquamata	**ORDERS**	1	**FAMILIES**	1	**SPECIES**	c.13
OPAHS AND OARFISHES **SUPERORDER** Lamprimorpha	**ORDERS**	1	**FAMILIES**	6	**SPECIES**	c.22
CODFISHES AND RELATIVES **SUPERORDER** Paracanthopterygii	**ORDERS**	5	**FAMILIES**	24	**SPECIES**	c.667
SPINY-RAYED FISHES **SUPERORDER** Acanthopterygii	**ORDERS**	32	**FAMILIES**	284	**SPECIES**	c.14,800

AMPHIBIANS

CLASS Amphibia

While new species of frogs are being discovered every year, their thin, moist skin makes them particularly susceptible to the chytridiomycosis fungal disease, and about 90 species have become extinct in the wild over the past 50 years.

NEWTS AND SALAMANDERS				
ORDER Caudata	**FAMILIES**	9	**SPECIES**	707

CAECILIANS				
ORDER Gymnophiona	**FAMILIES**	10	**SPECIES**	205

FROGS AND TOADS				
ORDER Anura	**FAMILIES**	56	**SPECIES**	c.6,700

REPTILES

CLASS Reptilia

Squamates—snakes, lizards, and amphisbaenians—are by far the most successful reptiles, accounting for more than 95 percent of species alive today. The Tuatara is the last survivor of an ancient group of reptiles.

TORTOISES AND TURTLES				
ORDER Chelonia	**FAMILIES**	14	**SPECIES**	346

TUATARAS				
ORDER Rhyncocephalia	**FAMILIES**	1	**SPECIES**	1

SQUAMATES				
ORDER Squamata	**FAMILIES**	52	**SPECIES**	10,000

SNAKES				
SUBORDER Serpentes	**FAMILIES**	19	**SPECIES**	c.4,500

BLIND AND THREAD SNAKES				
SUPERFAMILY Scolecophidia	**FAMILIES**	5	**SPECIES**	441

BOAS, PYTHONS, AND RELATIVES				
SUPERFAMILY Henophoidea	**FAMILIES**	12	**SPECIES**	218

COLUBRIDS AND RELATIVES				
SUPERFAMILY Caenophidia	**FAMILIES**	3	**SPECIES**	4,000
COLUBRIDS	**FAMILY** Colubridae		**SPECIES**	3,300
VIPERS	**FAMILY** Viperidae		**SPECIES**	337
ELAPIDS	**FAMILY** Elapidae		**SPECIES**	361

LIZARDS				
SUBORDER Lacertilia	**FAMILIES**	37	**SPECIES**	c.6,300

IGUANAS AND RELATIVES				
SUPERFAMILY Iguanoidea	**FAMILIES**	14	**SPECIES**	1,840

GECKOS AND SNAKE LIZARDS				
SUPERFAMILY Gekkonidae	**FAMILIES**	7	**SPECIES**	c.1,700

SKINKS AND RELATIVES				
SUPERFAMILY Scincomorphoidea	**FAMILIES**	8	**SPECIES**	2,477

ANGUIMORPH LIZARDS				
SUPERFAMILY Anguimorpha	**FAMILIES**	9	**SPECIES**	250

AMPHISBAENIANS				
SUBORDER Amphisbaenia	**FAMILIES**	6	**SPECIES**	196

CROCODILES AND ALLIGATORS				
ORDER Crocodilia	**FAMILIES**	3	**SPECIES**	25

With almost 1,900, **Colombia has more species of birds** than any other country

BIRDS

CLASS Aves

In the classification scheme used in this book, birds are separated into 40 orders according to their genetic make-up as well as physical similarities. Passerines, or perching birds, are the largest order with over 130 families.

TINAMOUS
ORDER Tinamiformes   **FAMILIES** 1   **SPECIES** 47

OSTRICH
ORDER Struthioniformes   **FAMILIES** 1   **SPECIES** 2

RHEAS
ORDER Rheiformes   **FAMILIES** 1   **SPECIES** 2

CASSOWARIES AND EMUS
ORDER Casuariiformes   **FAMILIES** 2   **SPECIES** 4

KIWIS
ORDER Apterygiformes   **FAMILIES** 1   **SPECIES** 5

WATERFOWL
ORDER Anseriformes   **FAMILIES** 3   **SPECIES** 177

GAMEBIRDS
ORDER Galliformes   **FAMILIES** 5   **SPECIES** 299

DIVERS
ORDER Gaviiformes   **FAMILIES** 1   **SPECIES** 6

PENGUINS
ORDER Sphenisciformes   **FAMILIES** 1   **SPECIES** 18

ALBATROSSES AND PETRELS
ORDER Procellariiformes   **FAMILIES** 4   **SPECIES** 147

GREBES
ORDER Podicipediformes   **FAMILIES** 1   **SPECIES** 23

FLAMINGOS
ORDER Phoenicopteriformes   **FAMILIES** 1   **SPECIES** 6

TROPICBIRDS
ORDER Phaethontiformes   **FAMILIES** 1   **SPECIES** 3

STORKS
ORDER Ciconiiformes   **FAMILIES** 1   **SPECIES** 19

HERONS AND RELATIVES
ORDER Pelecaniformes   **FAMILIES** 5   **SPECIES** 118

GANNETS, CORMORANTS, AND RELATIVES
ORDER Suliformes   **FAMILIES** 4   **SPECIES** 60

HAWKS, EAGLES, AND RELATIVES
ORDER Accipitriformes   **FAMILIES** 4   **SPECIES** 265

BUSTARDS
ORDER Otidiformes   **FAMILIES** 1   **SPECIES** 26

MESITES
ORDER Mesitornithiformes   **FAMILIES** 1   **SPECIES** 3

SERIEMAS
ORDER Cariamiformes   **FAMILIES** 1   **SPECIES** 2

KAGU AND SUNBITTERN
ORDER Eurypygiformes   **FAMILIES** 2   **SPECIES** 2

RAILS, CRANES, AND RELATIVES
ORDER Gruiformes   **FAMILIES** 6   **SPECIES** 189

WADERS, GULLS, AND AUKS
ORDER Charadriiformes   **FAMILIES** 19   **SPECIES** 384

SANDGROUSE
ORDER Pteroclidiformes   **FAMILIES** 1   **SPECIES** 16

PIGEONS
ORDER Columbiformes   **FAMILIES** 1   **SPECIES** 342

HOATZIN
ORDER Opisthocomiformes   **FAMILIES** 1   **SPECIES** 1

TURACOS
ORDER Musophagiformes   **FAMILIES** 1   **SPECIES** 23

CUCKOOS
ORDER Cuculiformes   **FAMILIES** 1   **SPECIES** 149

OWLS
ORDER Strigiformes   **FAMILIES** 4   **SPECIES** 242

NIGHTJARS AND FROGMOUTHS
ORDER Caprimulgiformes   **FAMILIES** 4   **SPECIES** 123

HUMMINGBIRDS AND SWIFTS
ORDER Apodiformes   **FAMILIES** 4   **SPECIES** 470

MOUSEBIRDS
ORDER Coliiformes   **FAMILIES** 1   **SPECIES** 6

TROGONS
ORDER Trogoniformes   **FAMILIES** 1   **SPECIES** 43

CUCKOO ROLLER
ORDER Leptosomiformes   **FAMILIES** 1   **SPECIES** 1

KINGFISHERS AND RELATIVES
ORDER Coraciiformes   **FAMILIES** 6   **SPECIES** 160

HOOPOES AND HORNBILLS
ORDER Bucerotiformes   **FAMILIES** 4   **SPECIES** 74

WOODPECKERS AND TOUCANS
ORDER Piciformes   **FAMILIES** 9   **SPECIES** 447

FALCONS AND CARACARAS
ORDER Falconiformes   **FAMILIES** 1   **SPECIES** 66

PARROTS
ORDER Psittaciformes   **FAMILIES** 4   **SPECIES** 397

PASSERINES
ORDER Passeriformes   **FAMILIES** 131   **SPECIES** 6,430

◀ see also Birds pp.134–39   **161**

>> Vertebrates continued

MAMMALS

CLASS Mammalia

Classification schemes differ but in this book, mammals are separated into 29 orders, with marsupials (mammals with a pouch) split into seven orders within the infraclass Marsupialia, and monkeys and apes are divided into two groups.

EGG-LAYING MAMMALS
ORDER Monotremata **FAMILIES** 2 **SPECIES** 5

MARSUPIALS
INFRACLASS Marsupialia **FAMILIES** 19 **SPECIES** 363

AMERICAN OPOSSUMS
ORDER Didelphimorphia **FAMILIES** 1 **SPECIES** 103

AUSTRALASIAN CARNIVOROUS MARSUPIALS
ORDER Dasyuromorphia **FAMILIES** 2 **SPECIES** 75

BANDICOOTS
ORDER Peramelemorphia **FAMILIES** 3 **SPECIES** 19

MARSUPIAL MOLES
ORDER Notoryctemorphia **FAMILIES** 1 **SPECIES** 2

KANGAROOS AND RELATIVES
ORDER Diprotodontia **FAMILIES** 11 **SPECIES** 156

SHREW OPOSSUMS
ORDER Paucituberculata **FAMILIES** 1 **SPECIES** 6

MONITO DEL MONTE
ORDER Microbiotheria **FAMILIES** 1 **SPECIES** 1

SENGIS
ORDER Macroscelidea **FAMILIES** 1 **SPECIES** 15

TENRECS AND GOLDEN MOLES
ORDER Afrosoricida **FAMILIES** 2 **SPECIES** 51

AARDVARK
ORDER Tubulidentata **FAMILIES** 1 **SPECIES** 1

DUGONG AND MANATEES
ORDER Sirenia **FAMILIES** 2 **SPECIES** 4

ELEPHANTS
ORDER Proboscidea **FAMILIES** 1 **SPECIES** 3

HYRAXES
ORDER Hyracoidea **FAMILIES** 1 **SPECIES** 5

ARMADILLOS
ORDER Cingulata **FAMILIES** 1 **SPECIES** 21

SLOTHS AND ANTEATERS
ORDER Pilosa **FAMILIES** 4 **SPECIES** 10

RABBITS, HARES, AND PIKAS
ORDER Lagomorpha **FAMILIES** 2 **SPECIES** 92

RODENTS
ORDER Rodentia **FAMILIES** 34 **SPECIES** 2,478

SQUIRRELLIKE RODENTS
SUBORDER Sciuromorpha **FAMILIES** 3 **SPECIES** 332

BEAVERLIKE RODENTS
SUBORDER Castorimorpha **FAMILIES** 3 **SPECIES** 109

MOUSELIKE RODENTS
SUBORDER Myomorpha **FAMILIES** 7 **SPECIES** 1,737

CAVYLIKE RODENTS
SUBORDER Hystricomorpha **FAMILIES** 18 **SPECIES** 301

SPRINGHARES AND RELATIVES
SUBORDER Anomaluromorpha **FAMILIES** 2 **SPECIES** 9

COLUGOS
ORDER Dermoptera **FAMILIES** 1 **SPECIES** 2

TREE SHREWS
ORDER Scandentia **FAMILIES** 2 **SPECIES** 20

PRIMATES
ORDER Primates **FAMILIES** 12 **SPECIES** 480

PROSIMIANS
SUBORDER Strepsirrhini **FAMILIES** 4 **SPECIES** 139

MONKEYS AND APES
SUBORDER Haplorhini

MONKEYS
FAMILIES 6 **SPECIES** 315

APES
FAMILIES 2 **SPECIES** 26

BATS
ORDER Chiroptera **FAMILIES** 18 **SPECIES** 1,330

HEDGEHOGS AND RELATIVES
ORDER Erinaceomorpha **FAMILIES** 1 **SPECIES** 24

SHREWS AND RELATIVES
ORDER Soricomorpha **FAMILIES** 4 **SPECIES** 428

PANGOLINS
ORDER Pholidota **FAMILIES** 1 **SPECIES** 8

Wild mammals are rare compared to other animals—in terms of biomass, arthropods outweigh them globally **143 times** over

CARNIVORES

ORDER Carnivora	**FAMILIES**	16	**SPECIES**	279
DOGS AND RELATIVES	**FAMILY**	Canidae	**SPECIES**	35
BEARS	**FAMILY**	Ursidae	**SPECIES**	8
SEA LIONS AND FUR SEALS	**FAMILY**	Otariidae	**SPECIES**	34
WALRUS	**FAMILY**	Odobenidae	**SPECIES**	1
EARLESS SEALS	**FAMILY**	Phocidae	**SPECIES**	18
SKUNKS	**FAMILY**	Mephitidae	**SPECIES**	12
RACCOONS AND RELATIVES	**FAMILY**	Procyonidae	**SPECIES**	13
RED PANDA	**FAMILY**	Ailuridae	**SPECIES**	1
MUSTELIDS	**FAMILY**	Mustelidae	**SPECIES**	57
MALAGASY CARNIVORES	**FAMILY**	Eupleridae	**SPECIES**	8
AFRICAN PALM CIVET	**FAMILY**	Nandiniidae	**SPECIES**	1
MONGOOSES	**FAMILY**	Herpestidae	**SPECIES**	34
CIVETS AND RELATIVES	**FAMILY**	Viverridae	**SPECIES**	34
LINSANGS	**FAMILY**	Prionodontidae	**SPECIES**	2
CATS	**FAMILY**	Felidae	**SPECIES**	37
HYENAS AND AARDWOLF	**FAMILY**	Hyaenidae	**SPECIES**	4

ODD-TOED HOOFED MAMMALS

ORDER Perissodactyla	**FAMILIES**	3	**SPECIES**	17
HORSES AND RELATIVES	**FAMILY**	Equidae	**SPECIES**	7
RHINOCEROSES	**FAMILY**	Rhinocerotidae	**SPECIES**	5
TAPIRS	**FAMILY**	Tapiridae	**SPECIES**	5

EVEN-TOED HOOFED MAMMALS

ORDER Artiodactyla	**FAMILIES**	10	**SPECIES**	376
PIGS	**FAMILY**	Suidae	**SPECIES**	17
PECCARIES	**FAMILY**	Tayassuidae	**SPECIES**	3
HIPPOPOTAMUSES	**FAMILY**	Hippopotamidae	**SPECIES**	2
CAMELS AND RELATIVES	**FAMILY**	Camelidae	**SPECIES**	7
DEER	**FAMILY**	Cervidae	**SPECIES**	53
CHEVROTAINS	**FAMILY**	Tragulidae	**SPECIES**	10
MUSK DEER	**FAMILY**	Moschidae	**SPECIES**	7
PRONGHORN	**FAMILY**	Antilocapridae	**SPECIES**	1
GIRAFFE AND OKAPI	**FAMILY**	Giraffidae	**SPECIES**	5
CATTLE AND RELATIVES	**FAMILY**	Bovidae	**SPECIES**	279

CETACEANS

ORDER Cetacea	**FAMILIES**	4	**SPECIES**	89

BALEEN WHALES **SUBORDER** Mysticeti	**FAMILIES**	4	**SPECIES**	14

TOOTHED WHALES **SUBORDER** Odontoceti	**FAMILIES**	10	**SPECIES**	75

Bats (21.8%) · Primates (7.9%) · Shrews and relatives (7%) · Even-toed hoofed mammals (6.2%) · Marsupials (5.9%) · Carnivores (4.6%) · Rabbits, hares, and pikas (1.5%) · Cetaceans (1.5%) · All other mammal groups (3%) · Rodents (40.6%)

The **world's largest rodent** is the **Capybara** at up to 143 lb (65 kg), while the **smallest** is the **Balochistan Pygmy Jerboa** at 0.14 oz (4 g)

Mammal species by group
Of the more than 6,000 species of mammals alive today, rodents make up the largest group with just under 2,500 species, and comprise almost half of the world's mammal population. Like the second-largest group, bats, they are native to every continent except Antarctica.

Science and Technology

Numbers

The need to count

Counting is a skill that most likely dates back to prehistory. Although there is strong evidence that mammals and some other animals engage in a form of counting without numbers, the need for humans to count numerically developed as the hunter-gatherer lifestyle succumbed to settled cultures involving land, livestock, and trade.

Whole numbers
This is the simplest type of number, comprising all the complete (whole) numbers, including zero.

Negative numbers
If zero is the whole number before 1, negative numbers are numbers less than zero.

Fractions
A fraction describes the numbers "in between," as a proportion involving two whole numbers.

Decimal
The decimal, or base 10, system is used as a global standard to express numbers.

Numerals

Many ancient civilizations independently developed their own system of symbols to express numbers. The universally recognized Hindu-Arabic system evolved through ancient Indian and medieval Arab cultures.

Systems of the ancient world
The Hindu–Arabic system is considered the easiest to use for calculations, but Roman numerals, for example, endure today on clocks and watches.

MODERN HINDU-ARABIC	1	2	3	4	5	6	7	8	9	10
MAYAN	•	••	•••	••••	—	⎯•⎯	••	•••	••••	⹀
CHINESE	一	二	三	四	五	六	七	八	九	十
ANCIENT ROMAN	I	II	III	IV	V	VI	VII	VIII	IX	X
ANCIENT EGYPTIAN	|	||	|||	||||	|||||	||||||	|||||||	||||||||	|||||||||	∩
BABYLONIAN	𒀸	𒐀	𒐁	𒐂	𒐃	𒐄	𒐅	𒐆	𒐇	⟨

Types of numbers

Numbers can be categorized in a variety of number sets. Natural numbers are a subset of whole numbers. The whole numbers, fractions, and decimals form part of a wider set of numbers, called rational numbers, which in turn fall within an even wider set called real numbers. Real numbers are included in a set called complex numbers, which also includes imaginary numbers. As science and technology has become more advanced, each of these sets has found practical use.

Natural numbers

The set of natural numbers is whole counting numbers. These numbers stretch to infinity in the positive direction, but do not include zero or any negative numbers.

> Mathematically, **zero is considered** to be an **even number**

First number
The number 1 is the first in the counting sequence, and the basic unit in our number system.

Even prime
The number 2 is unique in being the only even prime number.

Triangular number
A triangular numer is the sum of consecutive whole numbers, e.g. 1+2=3.

Composite number
This is the first composite number, being a non-prime positive integer.

Prime number
Five is a prime number, as it has no factors other than 1 and itself.

Perfect number
A number is perfect if its proper divisors add up to the number itself, e.g. 6=1+2+3

Not the sum of squares
Seven is the first integer that is not the sum of the squares of three integers.

Fibonacci number
In the Fibonacci sequence (see p.171), each number is obtained by adding the previous two.

Highest decimal
This is the highest value single digit in our decimal system, and it is also a square number.

Base number
Ten is the basis of our decimal system, which is also known as base 10.

Integers

This set of numbers comprises all of the natural numbers, together with the number zero and the negative whole numbers.

A natural number

-2

Rational numbers

The set of rational numbers comprises all numbers that can be expressed as a fraction a/b, where a and b are integers.

3/2 = 1.5   *2 and 3 are integers*

1/3 = 0.33333...   *Repeating pattern*

Real numbers

This set comprises both rational and irrational numbers—numbers that cannot be expressed as a ratio of two integers, such as √2 and π.

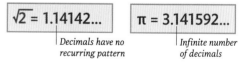

$\sqrt{2} = 1.14142...$ *Decimals have no recurring pattern*

$\pi = 3.141592...$ *Infinite number of decimals*

Complex numbers

The set of complex numbers comprises both real and imaginary numbers, where the latter are square roots of negative numbers.

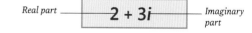

Real part   2 + 3*i*   *Imaginary part*

Squares

The power of a number represents the number of times that the number is multiplied by itself. Roots can be thought of as the inverse of powers.

Squared number

Geometrically, a squared number represents the area of a square.

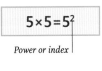

Five rows, with five units in each row

Square of a number

The small 2 indicates "5 to the power of 2" or "5 squared," which means it is multiplied by itself once.

$$5 \times 5 = 5^2$$

Power or index

Square root of a number

A square root is the number that is multiplied by itself to give the number under the root sign.

Positive square root

$$\sqrt{25} = 5$$

Cubes

Multiplying a number by itself twice gives its cube. The power of a cube number is 3. A cube root is a number that, multiplied by itself twice, equals a given number.

Cube number

A cube number can be represented as a cube, with all sides the same number of units.

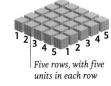

Number of units

Cube of a number

Multiplying a number by itself twice is described as "cubing" the number.

$$5 \times 5 \times 5 = 5^3$$

Power or index

Cube root of a number

The cube root is the number that, when cubed, equals the number under the cube root sign.

Cube root symbol *Cube root*

$$\sqrt[3]{125} = 5$$

Powers and standard form

Standard form is used to express very large and very small numbers concisely. These numbers are written in the form $a \times 10^n$ where a is a number between 1 and 10, and n is an integer.

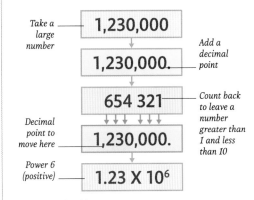

Take a large number
1,230,000

Add a decimal point
1,230,000.

Count back to leave a number greater than 1 and less than 10
654 321

Decimal point to move here
1,230,000.

Power 6 (positive)
1.23 X 10⁶
$$1.23 \times 10^6$$

Using standard form

Large numbers are written in standard form with a positive power, while small numbers have a negative power.

Prime numbers

A prime number is a whole number that is only divisible by 1 and itself. This may not appear significant in itself, but every single integer can be generated by multiplying prime numbers together. Another aspect of primes is that they show no obvious regular pattern.

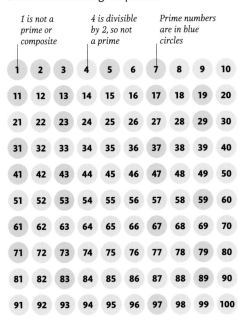

1 is not a prime or composite
4 is divisible by 2, so not a prime
Prime numbers are in blue circles

Sieve of Eratosthenes

This method to find smaller primes is called the Sieve of Eratosthenes, named after a Greek mathematician. Use the flowchart (right) to calculate the primes.

Populating the sieve

This flowchart is used to calculate whether a whole number between 1 and 100 is prime by checking if it is divisible by any of the primes 2, 3, 5, and 7.

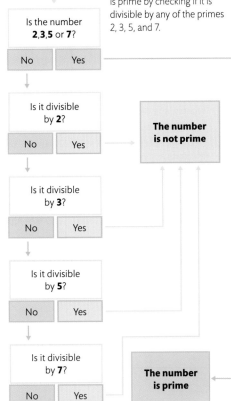

Pick a number from **1** to **100**

Is the number **2**,**3**,**5** or **7**?
No / Yes

Is it divisible by **2**?
No / Yes

Is it divisible by **3**?
No / Yes

Is it divisible by **5**?
No / Yes

Is it divisible by **7**?
No / Yes

The number is not prime

The number is prime

The **largest** known prime number has 24,862,068 digits

PRIME NUMBERS IN CYBERSECURITY

An algorithm, known as RSA, enables electronic messages, such as emails, to be encrypted using prime numbers. This system works on the principle that very large numbers are a product of two primes and finding those prime factors is extremely difficult.

MARIN MERSENNE

Marin Mersenne (1588–1648) was a French mathematician best known for his work on devising a formula for generating primes. He found that the formula $2^n - 1$ works for certain values of n. These types of primes are known as Mersenne Primes.

see also Computer technology pp.274–75 ▶

Calculations

The concept of numbers emerged over millennia and a natural extension of this idea was to take two or more numbers and combine them. Basic calculations may have been motivated by the need to total up a number of different goods for barter (addition) or to compare two quantities of goods (subtraction), but mathematicians devised increasingly complex problems and rules for performing calculations.

SCIENCE AND TECHNOLOGY

Numbers and operations

Calculations typically involve taking one or more numbers, and operating on them in some way. The most common operations are addition, subtraction, multiplication, and division. The operation is typically positioned between two numbers, such as 12 x 7.

$$17 - (4 + 6) \div 2 + 36 = 48$$

Adding, subtracting, multiplication, and division

These are the four basic operations, and they are intrinsically related. Subtraction, multiplication, and division can all be thought to emerge from the idea of addition. The early development of arithmetic was devoted largely to developing effective methods of calculation using these operations, including mechanical aids such as an abacus.

Multiplication

One way of looking at multiplication is that it is repeated addition. So 5 x 3 is a shorter way of saying 3 + 3 + 3 + 3 + 3. It can also be expressed as 5 + 5 + 5.

Addition

The most basic of the operations, addition is just the summation of two or more quantities. So, 1 plus 3 equals 4.

Subtraction

Subtraction is the inverse of addition. You can look at the above calculation in a different way, so 4 minus 3 equals 1.

Division

Division means sharing or grouping something equally, but it can also be seen as repeated subtraction.

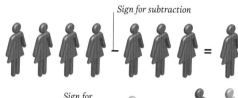
Sign for addition

Sign for subtraction

Sign for division

Sign for multiplication

JOHN NAPIER

John Napier (1550–1617) grew up in a wealthy Scottish family. Although he was clearly talented at mathematics, he devoted much of his time to his estates and to the advancement of Protestant theology. He is now most well-known for the invention of logarithms, created to enable calculation with large numbers. Napier also popularized the use of the decimal point.

Order of operations

Combining more than one operation can lead to more than one answer, depending on the sequence in which the calculations are made. For example, 2 + 3 x 4 could be viewed as 5 x 4, with an answer of 20. However, due to the agreed order of priority with operations, the correct answer is 14. The order of operations is often shortened with the acronym PEMDAS (or BEDMAS), which stands for Parentheses (Brackets), Exponents, Multiplication, Division, Addition, and Subtraction.

$$4 \times (2 + 3) = 20$$

❶ Parentheses

When calculations are enclosed in parentheses, this is an instruction to do this first. Here, the 2 plus 3 should be done first, and then the result is multiplied by 4.

$$5 + 2 \times 3^2 = 23$$

❷ Exponents

Exponents, or powers, come next. The power 2, or "squared," is an example of this, instructing you to multiply the number by itself. So $3^2 = 3 \times 3$.

$$8 \div 2 \times 3 = 12$$

❸ Multiplication

Multiplication has the same order of priority as division. When they both appear together, as in this example, the convention is to work from left to right.

$$6 + 4 \div 2 = 8$$

❹ Division

Division and multiplication come next in the order of operations. In the example above, you solve 4 divided by 2 first, and then add the result to 6.

$$9 \div 3 + 12 = 15$$

❺ Addition

Finally addition, with subtraction, takes last place in the order of operations. In the example above, solve 9 divided by 3 first, and then add 12.

$$10 - 3 + 4 = 11$$

❻ Subtraction

Subtraction has the same order of priority as addition. If the two operations appear together, as in the example here, work from left to right.

FOUR FOUR'S CHALLENGE

Using four 4s, write calculations with the answers 0 to 20. You can use the operations +, -, x, and ÷, with brackets and square roots. There are other solutions to the examples below.

$$4 + 4 - 4 - 4 = 0$$

$$44 \div 44 = 1$$

$$\frac{4}{4} + \frac{4}{4} = 2$$

$$(4 + 4 + 4) \div 4 = 3$$

$$\sqrt{4} + \sqrt{4} + 4 - 4 = 4$$

$$\sqrt{4} + 4 - \frac{4}{4} = 5$$

French mathematician **Blaise Pascal designed** a **mechanical calculator** in **1642**

Percentage calculations

Percentages are fractions out of 100. So, 35% is the same as $^{35}/_{100}$. They allow you to figure out proportions, such as when a quantity is increasing or decreasing. Percentages are particularly useful in the context of money and presenting large amounts of information.

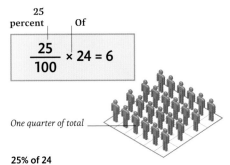

25 percent — Of

$$\frac{25}{100} \times 24 = 6$$

One quarter of total ⎯

25% of 24

You can simplify a calculation by working in smaller fractions. Remember 25 out of 100 is 1 out of 4. So, 25% is one quarter, and ¼ of 24 is 24 ÷ 4.

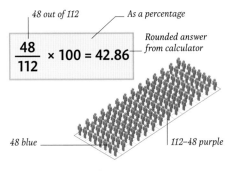

48 out of 112 — As a percentage

$$\frac{48}{112} \times 100 = 42.86$$

Rounded answer from calculator

48 blue ⎯ 112–48 purple

48 as a percentage of 112

To determine a figure as a percentage (proportion) of the total means dividing that figure by the total. "Out of" is an instruction to divide, in this case 48 ÷ 112.

Calculating interest

Banks pay interest on the money that savers invest with them (capital), and charge interest on money that is borrowed from them. Interest is given as a percentage, and there are two types: simple and compound. Interest can be added to the principal a number of times per year. This is called the compounding frequency. For example, when the interest is added every month, the compound frequency is 12. The effective interest rate (EIR), also called annual equivalent rate (AER), is calculated by taking into account the number of compounding periods in order to compare products with different compounding frequencies.

Simple interest

With simple interest, the interest is applied to the initial loan or investment, called the principal, over a number of years.

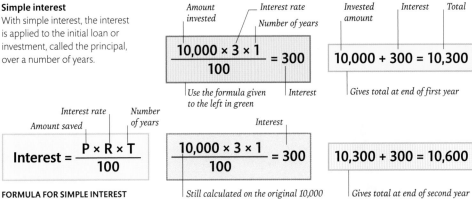

Amount invested — Interest rate — Number of years

$$\frac{10,000 \times 3 \times 1}{100} = 300$$

Use the formula given to the left in green | Interest

Invested amount — Interest — Total

$$10,000 + 300 = 10,300$$

Gives total at end of first year

Amount saved — Interest rate — Number of years

$$\text{Interest} = \frac{P \times R \times T}{100}$$

FORMULA FOR SIMPLE INTEREST

Interest

$$\frac{10,000 \times 3 \times 1}{100} = 300$$

Still calculated on the original 10,000

$$10,300 + 300 = 10,600$$

Gives total at end of second year

Compound interest

Much more commonly used by banks and businesses, compound interest is calculated on the capital amount at any particular time.

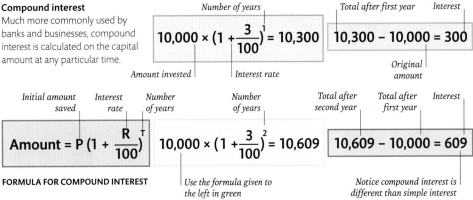

Number of years

$$10,000 \times \left(1 + \frac{3}{100}\right)^1 = 10,300$$

Amount invested | Interest rate

Total after first year — Interest

$$10,300 - 10,000 = 300$$

Original amount

Initial amount saved — Interest rate — Number of years

$$\text{Amount} = P\left(1 + \frac{R}{100}\right)^T$$

FORMULA FOR COMPOUND INTEREST

Number of years

$$10,000 \times \left(1 + \frac{3}{100}\right)^2 = 10,609$$

Use the formula given to the left in green

Total after second year — Total after first year — Interest

$$10,609 - 10,000 = 609$$

Notice compound interest is different than simple interest

Rounding and estimation

You use estimation whenever you figure out roughly how long it will take to complete a task or how tall something is. Estimation is used in practical situations when an exact answer is not needed. Rounding, or rounding off, is a process of replacing one number with another to make a number easier to use.

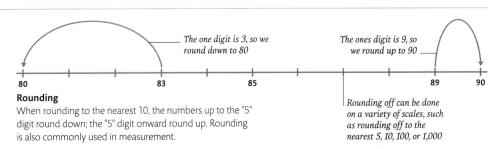

The one digit is 3, so we round down to 80

The ones digit is 9, so we round up to 90

80   83   85   89   90

Rounding

When rounding to the nearest 10, the numbers up to the "5" digit round down; the "5" digit onward round up. Rounding is also commonly used in measurement.

Rounding off can be done on a variety of scales, such as rounding off to the nearest 5, 10, 100, or 1,000

All **measurements of length** involve **some rounding**, however accurate the ruler or tape measure

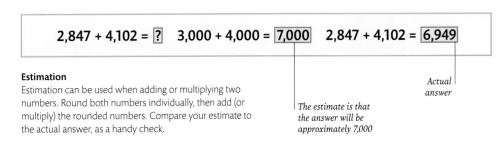

$$2,847 + 4,102 = \boxed{?} \quad 3,000 + 4,000 = \boxed{7,000} \quad 2,847 + 4,102 = \boxed{6,949}$$

Estimation

Estimation can be used when adding or multiplying two numbers. Round both numbers individually, then add (or multiply) the rounded numbers. Compare your estimate to the actual answer, as a handy check.

The estimate is that the answer will be approximately 7,000

Actual answer

see also Algebra pp.170–71 ▶ Statistics and probability pp.176–77 ▶

Algebra

As techniques for dealing with numbers and arithmetic evolved, so too did the notion that there were rules worked in all situations. For example, it is possible to add numbers in any order and always get the same result. The idea of generalized arithmetic led to the branch of math known as algebra, in which letters and symbols represent numbers and the relationship between them. All of our electronic devices rely on algebraic formulas.

Elements of algebra

Everyone learns at least one language from an early age as a means of everyday communication. Algebra is like a language; it allows people to communicate mathematically in a universally understood way, and contains its own elements ("words") and rules ("grammar").

Term
A term can be a letter, a number, or a combination of both.

Operation
Addition, subtraction, multiplication, and division are operations.

Variable
This is an unknown number or quantity you are trying to find.

Equals
This means the sides of an equation are balanced.

Constant
Any term with a value that is always the same is called a constant.

Expressions
An expression is a collection of terms (numbers, letters, or a combination of both) separated by symbols (such as + or – signs for addition or subtraction).

Equations
An equation is a pair of expressions or terms separated by an equal sign. The sides of the equation must be equal.

MUHAMMAD IBN MUSA AL-KHWARIZMI
By the 9th century, the Islamic world had become a great center of mathematical learning. One of its finest scholars was al-Khwarizmi (*c.*780–850 CE). His work at the House of Wisdom in Baghdad laid the foundations of the algebra that we use today. Among his achievements was a treatise on Hindu numerals, which led to the "Arabic numerals" used around the world today.

Uses of algebra
Algebra's main purpose is often regarded as "finding x," or determining the value of an unknown number or quantity. This is certainly important, but it has other essential purposes, such as in describing the world around us using a mathematical model. This involves reducing the phenomenon being studied, such as the angles in a triangle, to a simplified mathematical version that is true in all situations.

Using algebra to solve equations
Solving an equation means finding the value of an unknown quantity. Medieval Arab scholars, such as al-Khwarizmi, formalized the rules for solving them. As equations came to be used to describe ever more complex phenomena, their methods of solution became more complex, too.

> Some **equations** can only be solved with the help of a **computer**

INEQUALITIES
An inequality shows that one quantity is not the same as another. Inequality symbols (such as < meaning "less than") show that the numbers on each side of the symbol are different in size. Inequalities are used commonly in business, computer programming, and engineering.

$x > y$ — *Greater than*

$x \geq y$ — *Greater than or equal to*

$x \neq y$ — *Not equal to*

$x < y$ — *Less than*

$x \leq y$ — *Less than or equal to*

Proving results
Algebra not only enables us to articulate rules precisely, but it can also prove that those rules are true. One of the most famous examples in modern times is the proof of Fermat's Last Theorem by the British mathematician Andrew Wiles, which draws together different fields of mathematics, such as number theory and algebra.

Linear equations
These are the simplest type of equations. In the example here, the solution is x = 4 ($3 \times 4 = 12$; $12 - 2 = 10$).

$3x - 2 = 10$ — *Solve using inverse operations*

Quadratic equations
These contain a squared term, as well as a linear expression, like the example to the right. These equations typically have two solutions.

$3x^2 + 2x - 8 = 0$ — *The solutions are $x = \frac{1}{3}$ and $x = -2$*

Simultaneous equations
These are pairs of equations that contain the same unknown variables, x and y. They are solved together using elimination, substitution, or with a graph.

$4x + 5y = 17$ — *The y terms can be eliminated*

$3x - 5y = 4$ — *The solutions are $x = 3$ and $y = 1$*

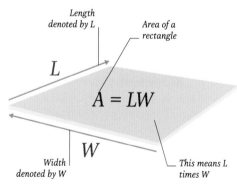

Length denoted by L

Area of a rectangle

$$A = LW$$

Width denoted by W

This means L times W

A RECTANGULAR FLOOR

Formulas
Formulas are mathematical rules that link variables, and can be used to describe real-world phenomena, such as the speed of sound or the interest paid on a loan. In the diagram above, the formula $A = LW$ is used to find the area of a rectangular floor.

Algebra and number sequences

There are many patterns hidden within number sequences and shapes, and algebra allows us to describe these patterns by using rules. These rules also enable us to predict how the patterns will evolve, which has many practical uses. An example of real-life application is population growth, where algebra can be used to predict future population size.

Arithmetic sequence

In an arithmetic sequence, the difference between successive numbers (or "terms") is the same. In other words, you add (or subtract) the same amount each time.

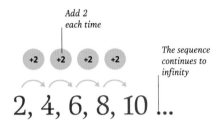

Add 2 each time

The sequence continues to infinity

+2 +2 +2 +2

2, 4, 6, 8, 10 ...

Geometric sequence

In a geometric sequence, the ratio (but not the difference) between successive terms is constant. For example, each term in the sequence might be twice the size of the one before it.

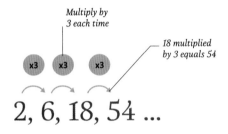

Multiply by 3 each time

18 multiplied by 3 equals 54

x3 x3 x3

2, 6, 18, 54 ...

Square numbers

A square number is formed when a term is multiplied by itself. It can be represented using a square pattern, with the length of a side representing the number that is multiplied by itself.

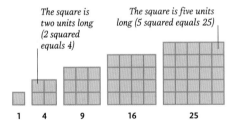

The square is two units long (2 squared equals 4)

The square is five units long (5 squared equals 25)

1   4   9   16   25

Fibonacci sequence

Found commonly in nature, the Fibonacci sequence works by adding the two previous terms to get the next term. The sequence can be found in the shapes of seashells, ferns, and sunflowers.

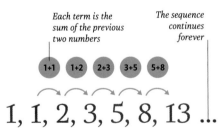

Each term is the sum of the previous two numbers

The sequence continues forever

1+1 1+2 2+3 3+5 5+8

1, 1, 2, 3, 5, 8, 13 ...

Golden spiral

If you represent the Fibonacci numbers as squares (the lengths of which correspond to the sequence), and then draw a curve through opposite corners, you get a spiral that approximates to shapes found in nature, such as in this nautilus shell.

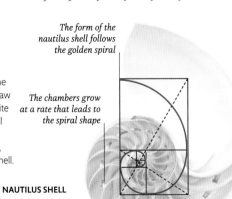

The form of the nautilus shell follows the golden spiral

The chambers grow at a rate that leads to the spiral shape

NAUTILUS SHELL

Graphical algebra

French philosopher and mathematician René Descartes (1596–1650) developed a way of representing algebra through geometry (and vice versa) in the form of a graph. It is often easier to understand a picture than an equation: a graph allows you to see the underlying shape of the equation, and allows you to solve it approximately.

Linear

Used to represent linear sequences and linear equations, these graphs have a uniform slope or gradient. They are often used to represent proportional relationships.

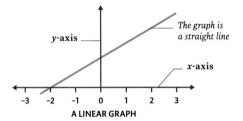

y-axis

The graph is a straight line

x-axis

-3 -2 -1 0 1 2 3

A LINEAR GRAPH

Quadratic

Used to represent quadratic equations, these graphs have a "parabolic" shape with a single vertex (a maximum or minimum point). They can be used to model the path of an object thrown in the air.

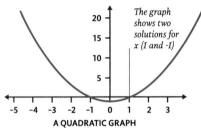

The graph shows two solutions for x (1 and -1)

20
15
10
5

-5 -4 -3 -2 -1 0 1 2 3

A QUADRATIC GRAPH

Cubic

Related to cubic equations, containing an x^3 term, these typically have a maximum point and a minimum point along the curve. Cubic equations generally have three solutions, which can be read off the graph.

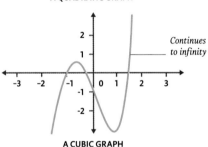

Continues to infinity

2
1

-3 -2 -1 0 1 2 3

-1
-2

A CUBIC GRAPH

Exponential

The rate at which exponential graphs change at any point is related to the value at that point. In the graph to the right, the larger a value is, the faster it grows.

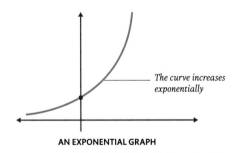

The curve increases exponentially

AN EXPONENTIAL GRAPH

CALCULUS

This powerful branch of math resulted from the attempts to solve two different problems. One was the need to model and predict rates of change, and the other was to calculate the areas of curved shapes. From the first came differential calculus, and from the second came integral calculus. Algebra shows that these are mutually inverse processes.

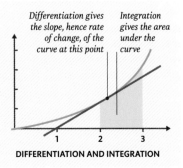

Differentiation gives the slope, hence rate of change, of the curve at this point

Integration gives the area under the curve

1   2   3

DIFFERENTIATION AND INTEGRATION

Geometry

Similar to arithmetic being based on numbers, the branch of math known as geometry is based on shapes and their properties—such as lines, angles, symmetry, and area. The term derives from the ancient Greek for "Earth measurement." Early humans saw myriad shapes in the world around them, many of which were irregular. However, geometry evolved as a system that could make sense of this world by modeling it using abstract shapes. The most common of these shapes and their properties are dealt with here.

Basic 2D and 3D shapes

Our world is three-dimensional (3D), yet some of the most familiar shapes only have two dimensions—meaning that they exist on a flat surface or plane. The triangle is the simplest closed 2D shape with straight edges and this highly stable shape is commonly used in architecture.

Three edges — TRIANGLE
Four equal edges and 90° angles — SQUARE
A single edge — CIRCLE
Uniform cross-section — PRISM
Tapers to a point — PYRAMID
All square faces — CUBE

Quadrilaterals

Shapes with many sides, such as triangles, quadrilaterals, pentagons and so on are collectively known as polygons. Quadrilaterals, or four-sided shapes, come in a number of different types, and are often used in design.

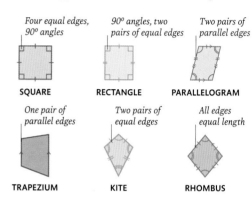

Four equal edges, 90° angles — SQUARE
90° angles, two pairs of equal edges — RECTANGLE
Two pairs of parallel edges — PARALLELOGRAM
One pair of parallel edges — TRAPEZIUM
Two pairs of equal edges — KITE
All edges equal length — RHOMBUS

Circles

The circle is defined as a shape whose single curved edge (circumference) is the same distance from a fixed point (center) all along its length. In the real world, perfect circles are rare or virtually nonexistent.

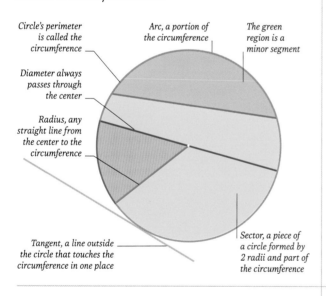

Circle's perimeter is called the circumference
Arc, a portion of the circumference
The green region is a minor segment
Diameter always passes through the center
Radius, any straight line from the center to the circumference
Tangent, a line outside the circle that touches the circumference in one place
Sector, a piece of a circle formed by 2 radii and part of the circumference

Angles

Angle is a measure of the change in direction, or turn, between two lines that intersect at a point. Angles are commonly measured in degrees (°), and there are 360° in a complete turn. There are four main types of angles, each named according to their size.

An acute angle is less than 90° — 55° ACUTE ANGLE
A right angle is 90° — 90° RIGHT ANGLE
An obtuse angle is between 90° and 180° — 120° OBTUSE ANGLE
A reflex angle is greater than 180° — 210° REFLEX ANGLE

Sum of angles

Knowing that there are 360 degrees in a circle allows us to solve geometrical problems. It also follows that there are 180 degrees on a straight line.

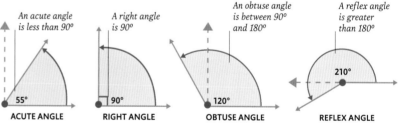

a+b+c+d=180°. So b= 40°
a=20° b c=90° d=30°
ON A STRAIGHT LINE

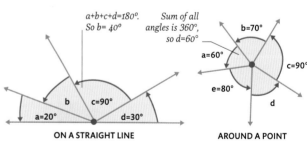

Sum of all angles is 360°, so d=60°
a=60° b=70° c=90° e=80° d
AROUND A POINT

Spheres, cones, and cylinders

Some 3D shapes are seen commonly in the real world. The cylinder and sphere are used frequently in engineering, while the cone is the shape made by light emanating from a source, such as a flashlight.

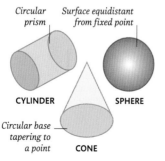

Circular prism — CYLINDER
Surface equidistant from fixed point — SPHERE
Circular base tapering to a point — CONE

Coordinate geometry

Plotting geometric shapes on a graph (known as a Cartesian grid) allows mathematicians to define a shape's position and makes it possible to calculate the results of movements, such as rotations and translations (see opposite).

Coordinates

In a 2D Cartesian coordinate system, points are described by two coordinates: their horizontal distance and their vertical distance from a fixed point.

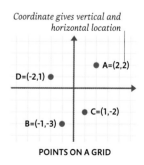

Coordinate gives vertical and horizontal location
A=(2,2)
D=(-2,1)
C=(1,-2)
B=(-1,-3)
POINTS ON A GRID

Any two points can be connected by one, and only one, straight line

Reflective symmetry

Shapes can be described by their properties, and among the most basic of these is symmetry. Most plants and animals possess reflective, or line, symmetry. We commonly think of "the left-hand side matching the right-hand side."

Lines of symmetry

The isosceles triangle shown here has one line of symmetry, whereas the square has four.

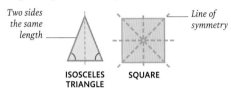

Two sides the same length

Line of symmetry

ISOSCELES TRIANGLE   SQUARE

Planes of symmetry

3D shapes have planes of reflective symmetry rather than lines, such as the shapes shown here.

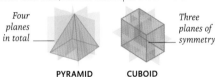

Four planes in total

Three planes of symmetry

PYRAMID   CUBOID

Rotational symmetry

A shape is said to have rotational symmetry when it can be moved around a center point and still fit into its original outline. The number of ways a shape can fit into its original outline when it is rotated is called its "order" of rotational symmetry.

Points of symmetry

Two-dimensional shapes have rotational symmetry around a point. An equilateral triangle—its sides are of equal length—has rotational symmetry of order 3. A square has order 4 rotational symmetry.

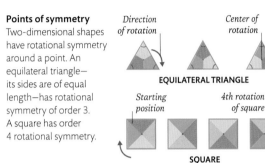

Direction of rotation   *Center of rotation*

EQUILATERAL TRIANGLE

Starting position   *4th rotation of square*

SQUARE

Axes of symmetry

Unlike 2D shapes that rotate around a point, 3D shapes will rotate around an axis, or a number of axes in the case of some shapes.

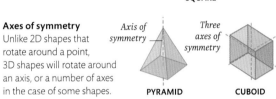

Axis of symmetry   *Three axes of symmetry*

PYRAMID   CUBOID

Tessellations

Tessellation referes to the degree to which shapes tessellate, or fit together exactly. The pattern of regular hexagons shown can be extended infinitely in all directions.

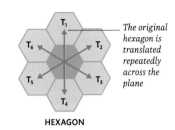

The original hexagon is translated repeatedly across the plane

HEXAGON

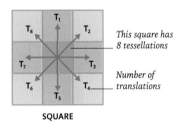

This square has 8 tessellations

Number of translations

SQUARE

Rotation, reflection, translation, and enlargement

Shapes can be transformed, and this idea is commonly used in graphic design. The four principal types of 2D transformation are reflection, rotation, translation, and enlargement. The transformation is performed on a starting object, resulting in an image.

Reflection

A reflection is defined simply by its mirror line, known as the axis of reflection.

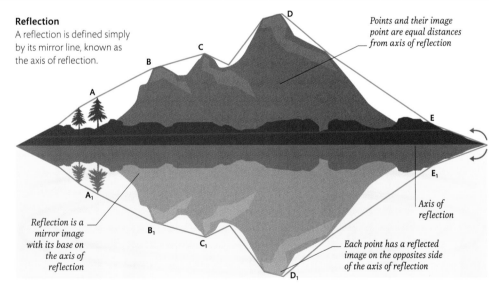

Points and their image point are equal distances from axis of reflection

Reflection is a mirror image with its base on the axis of reflection

Axis of reflection

Each point has a reflected image on the opposites side of the axis of reflection

Rotation

To rotate a shape, you need three things: the angle of turn, the direction (clockwise or counterclockwise), and the center of rotation.

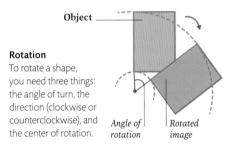

Object

Angle of rotation   *Rotated image*

Translation

Translation is the act of shifting an object within the plane. The shape can be moved horizontally and vertically, but retains its orientation. In the image, all points of the object are moved the same distance from their original positions.

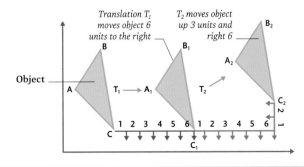

Translation T_1 moves object 6 units to the right   *T_2 moves object up 3 units and right 6*

Object

Enlargement

An enlargement is a transformation that produces an image of an object that is the same shape but a different size.

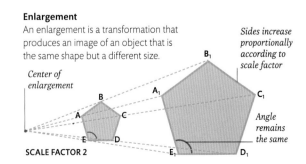

Center of enlargement

Sides increase proportionally according to scale factor

Angle remains the same

SCALE FACTOR 2

see also Measurement and construction pp.174-75 ▶ **173**

Measurement and construction

When people first began to make objects, the concept of measurement became important. In order to make measurements, standard units were created for quantities such as length, mass, and capacity. Through measurements and constructions (accurate drawings), the rules of geometry can be applied to many aspects of everyday life. Architects and engineers use it to design and create safe structures, and navigation systems require geometry to plot routes.

Calculating π

All circles have the same proportions. One of the great challenges in ancient times was in determining the ratio of a circle's circumference to its diameter. This proportion is known by the Greek letter π (*pi*), and its value is 3.141592 ... The digits of this number are thought to continue infinitely.

The circumference is the distance around the edge (perimeter) of the circle

The circumference can be calculated as π × diameter

π has been calculated to over 31 trillion digits

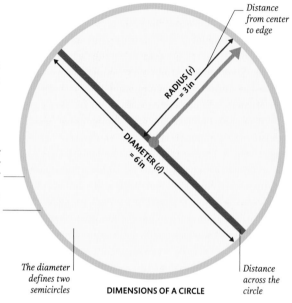

Distance from center to edge

RADIUS (*r*) = 3 in

DIAMETER (*d*) = 6 in

The diameter defines two semicircles

DIMENSIONS OF A CIRCLE

Distance across the circle

Tools in geometry

Many geometry instruments derive from tools that originated centuries ago. Those shown here focus on the measuring and constructing (drawing) of shapes.

Compass
Primarily used for constructing circles or arcs of circles. A pencil moves in a fixed distance from a central point.

Ruler
A ruler is used to measure and draw straight lines. They often have different scales, such as millimeters and inches.

Set square
Ideal for drawing common angles, they typically come in two shapes: 90°, 45°, and 45°; or 90°, 60°, and 30°.

Calculator
Used for performing calculations on the measurements or to apply trigonometry formulas.

Protractor
This tool is used for measuring and drawing angles. Protractors are typically marked from 0° to 180°.

Constructions

Constructions are created using a straight edge and compasses, and are used for accurate technical drawing. The diagram shows a perpendicular bisector, which is a straight line that cuts another straight line in half.

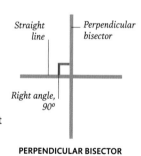

Straight line

Perpendicular bisector

Right angle, 90°

PERPENDICULAR BISECTOR

Much of geometry comes from the Greek philosopher Euclid

Scale drawings

Architects and engineers use scale drawings to create accurate plans for large and small objects. By using a set scale factor (ratio) to convert actual measurements, drawings can be scaled down for large objects, such as bridges, or scaled up to design small items, such as components for electronic products.

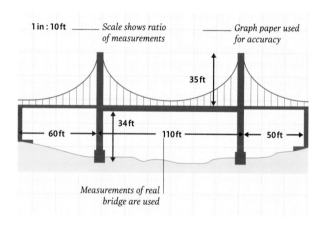

1 in : 10 ft — Scale shows ratio of measurements

Graph paper used for accuracy

35 ft

60 ft   34 ft   110 ft   50 ft

Measurements of real bridge are used

Loci

The locus (plural loci) describes the path of a point (or between two points) where the path adheres to a given rule. For example, the path that is always the same distance from a straight line segment.

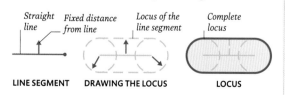

Straight line

Fixed distance from line

Locus of the line segment

Complete locus

LINE SEGMENT   **DRAWING THE LOCUS**   **LOCUS**

Bearings

Using angles in degrees, bearings show direction accurately. They are measured clockwise from North. Bearings are used to guide ships and aircraft over great distances and to plot routes that include changes in direction.

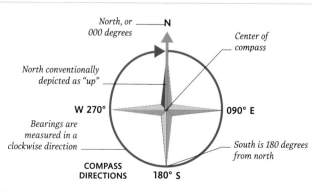

North, or 000 degrees — N

Center of compass

North conventionally depicted as "up"

W 270°

090° E

Bearings are measured in a clockwise direction

South is 180 degrees from north

COMPASS DIRECTIONS   180° S

> "I have often admired the **mystical way of Pythagoras,** and the **secret magic of numbers.**"
>
> SIR THOMAS BROWNE, *Religio Medici*, 1634

Perimeter and area of plane shapes

Measuring a 2D shape focuses on two things: its perimeter (the length around the edges) and its area (size of its surface). For many 2D shapes, if some of their dimensions are known it is possible to calculate the perimeter and area.

Calculating perimeter

To find the perimeter of a shape, you can either use a simple formula, or just add up the total length of its sides.

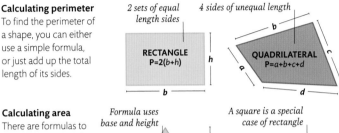

2 sets of equal length sides

RECTANGLE
$P=2(b+h)$

4 sides of unequal length

QUADRILATERAL
$P=a+b+c+d$

Calculating area

There are formulas to calculate the area of standard shapes, if you know their dimensions. Area is measured in square units, for example cm².

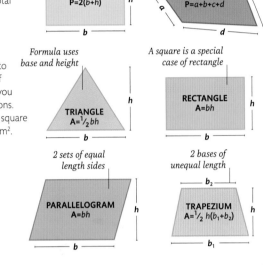

Formula uses base and height

TRIANGLE
$A=\frac{1}{2}bh$

A square is a special case of rectangle

RECTANGLE
$A=bh$

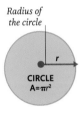

Radius of the circle

CIRCLE
$A=\pi r^2$

2 sets of equal length sides

PARALLELOGRAM
$A=bh$

2 bases of unequal length

TRAPEZIUM
$A=\frac{1}{2}h(b_1+b_2)$

Volume and surface area

Our world is 3D, and the objects within it possess both volume (V) and surface area (SA). Volume is a measure of the amount of space that an object occupies; surface area is the total area of its surfaces. Volume is measured in cubed units, and surface area is measured in squared units.

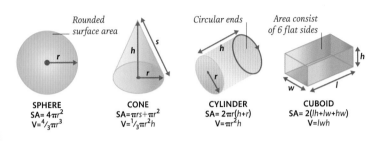

Rounded surface area

SPHERE
$SA=4\pi r^2$
$V=\frac{4}{3}\pi r^3$

CONE
$SA=\pi rs+\pi r^2$
$V=\frac{1}{3}\pi r^2 h$

Circular ends

CYLINDER
$SA=2\pi r(h+r)$
$V=\pi r^2 h$

Area consist of 6 flat sides

CUBOID
$SA=2(lh+lw+hw)$
$V=lwh$

Mass and density

All objects possess mass (M), which we experience as a weight force under gravity. The amount of mass that fits into a given volume (V) of a particular substance is called its density (D). Knowing two of the measurements, it is possible to figure out the third.

$M=DV$
$D=M/V$
$V=M/D$

M — Mass

D   V — Volume

Trigonometry

Trigonometry uses the relationships between the length of the sides and the angles of a triangle to calculate unknown sides or angles. Its uses in the modern world include electronic engineering and satellite navigation.

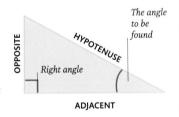

The angle to be found

HYPOTENUSE

OPPOSITE

Right angle

ADJACENT

The sine formula

For a right-angled triangle, sine (sin) is the ratio of the opposite side and the hypotenuse.

$$\sin A = \frac{\text{opposite}}{\text{hypotenuse}}$$

The cosine formula

For a right-angled triangle, cosine (cos) is the ratio of the adjacent side and the hypotenuse.

$$\cos A = \frac{\text{adjacent}}{\text{hypotenuse}}$$

The tangent formula

For a right-angled triangle, tangent (tan) is the ratio of the opposite and the adjacent sides.

$$\tan A = \frac{\text{opposite}}{\text{adjacent}}$$

Pythagorean theorem

This famous theorem describes the relationship between the sides of a right-angled triangle. The sum of the squares of the two shorter sides equals the square of the longer side. This allows you to calculate unknown lengths. There is more than one proof of the theorem.

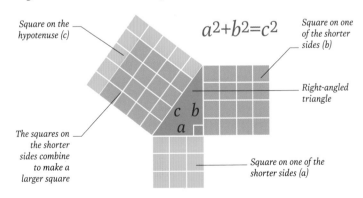

Square on the hypotenuse (c)

$a^2+b^2=c^2$

Square on one of the shorter sides (b)

Right-angled triangle

The squares on the shorter sides combine to make a larger square

Square on one of the shorter sides (a)

c b
a

PYTHAGORAS

Pythagoras was a Greek philosopher who lived in the 6th century BCE. He is most famous for his theorem relating to triangles, but he also established a community in Southern Italy, which made advances in the understanding of numbers and how they related to real life. Their principal belief was that everything in the universe could be explained by mathematical rules.

see also Symbols, charts, and measurements pp.180-81 ▶   **Structures and construction** pp.266-67 ▶   **175**

Statistics and probability

Mathematics is often linked with certainty. However, we live in a world in which data has become an important commodity, and being able to process it requires statistics.

In addition, in the last hundred years scientists have built a new "quantum" model of the universe based on uncertainty, which requires a deep understanding of probability.

Data

In the modern world, data is increasing at a very rapid pace. Statistics is about making sense of that data, and it often starts with a question, a statement, or hypothesis that can be analyzed using a range of techniques.

> **"Facts are stubborn things, but statistics are pliable."**
>
> Attributed to MARK TWAIN

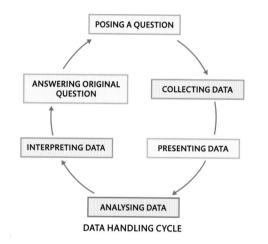

POSING A QUESTION

ANSWERING ORIGINAL QUESTION

COLLECTING DATA

INTERPRETING DATA

PRESENTING DATA

ANALYSING DATA

DATA HANDLING CYCLE

Analyzing data: average values

Data analysis often begins by determining typical or average values, and looking at how they are affected by deviant values in the range or spread.

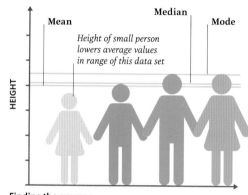

Mean | Median | Mode

Height of small person lowers average values in range of this data set

HEIGHT

Finding the average
Averages are calculated in three ways. The mode is the most frequent value; median is the middle value; and mean is the sum of all values, divided by their number.

Presenting data

Once raw data has been collected from a survey, experiment, or by electronic data harvesting, it needs to be represented in diagrams to allow the distribution, or shape, to be assessed. The diagrams used depend on the type of data. Data can have continuous numerical values, such as length, or discrete numerical values, such as number of legs, or a qualitative attribute, such as color. Across whole data sets, however, qualitative data can be counted as frequency of occurrence in a certain category (categorical data) and analyzed numerically, like discrete and continuous numerical data.

CATEGORY	FREQUENCY
GREEN	4
ORANGE	8
YELLOW	6
BLUE	4
MAUVE	5

Table of data
A table is an easy way to organize data. If it is categorical, frequency measures how often a value occurs in a category.

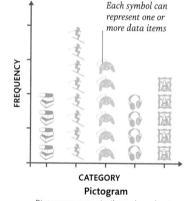

Height of bar indicates frequency

FREQUENCY

X VALUE, OR CATEGORY
Bar chart
A bar chart can show data with discrete *x* values or categories. The number of times each value occurs is the frequency.

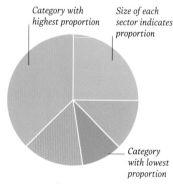

Each symbol can represent one or more data items

FREQUENCY

CATEGORY
Pictogram
Pictograms are similar to bar charts, but show frequencies with pictures and work better with categorical data.

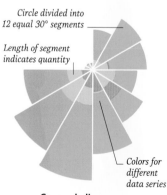

Circle divided into 12 equal 30° segments

Length of segment indicates quantity

Colors for different data series

Coxcomb diagram
Coxcomb diagrams are like radial bar charts, useful for data with cyclical *x* values, such as months of the year.

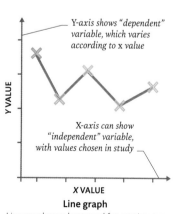

Y-axis shows "dependent" variable, which varies according to x value

Y VALUE

X-axis can show "independent" variable, with values chosen in study

X VALUE
Line graph
Line graphs are best used for continuous quantitative data that can assume any value in a range—like trends over time.

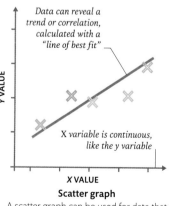

Data can reveal a trend or correlation, calculated with a "line of best fit"

Y VALUE

X variable is continuous, like the y variable

X VALUE
Scatter graph
A scatter graph can be used for data that is continuous in *x* and *y* variables. It can show if there is a link between *x* and *y*.

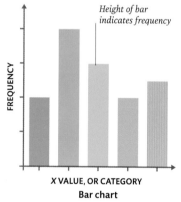

Category with highest proportion

Size of each sector indicates proportion

Category with lowest proportion

Pie chart
Pie charts show data that are proportions of a whole, showing the fraction of data falling into each category.

"We do not know **anything** for **certain**, but **everything probably**."

CHRISTIAAN HUYGENS, *Oeuvres Completes*, 1673

Probability

Probability is the study of uncertainty, and it provides us with a way of working out how likely something is to occur. It is commonly used in fields as diverse as medicine and insurance.

0 IMPOSSIBLE

Identical snowflakes
The likelihood of this event happening is close to zero—almost impossible.

UNLIKELY

A hole in one
Depending on the golfer's ability, hitting a hole in one is a fairly rare event.

0.5 EVEN CHANCE

Heads or tails
If the coin is unbiased, the probability of either result is equally likely.

LIKELY

Being right-handed
The probability that a person is right-handed is reasonably high.

1 CERTAIN

Earth turning
The probability of Earth continuing to turn tomorrow is close to 1—almost certain.

Scale of probability
Probability is expressed as a fraction, a decimal, or occasionally as a percentage. You can think of it on a scale from 0 (impossible) to 1 (certain).

Theoretical probability

Theoretical probability is based on assumptions that may or may not be true. In rolling a dice, the main assumption might be that each "outcome"—the number it lands on—is equally likely.

Possible outcomes for rolling a single dice once
There are 6 possible outcomes to a single roll of the dice: 1, 2, 3, 4, 5, or 6. Each number is equally likely to occur, which means the probability for any one number is $\frac{1}{6}$.

Outcome of rolling a 2

Combined probabilities

Quite often, we want to determine the likelihood of two completely unrelated, or "independent," events happening at the same time. Alternatively,

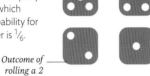

Front of coin

HEADS

Back of same coin

TAILS

$\frac{1}{2}$ *1 in 2 chance*

Tossing a coin
Tossing a fair coin gives 2 possible outcomes, "Heads" or "Tails," each with a probability of $\frac{1}{2}$.

Rolling a 4

$\frac{1}{6}$ *1 in 6 chance*

Rolling a dice
Rolling an unbiased dice gives 6 possible outcomes, each with a probability of $\frac{1}{6}$.

Experimental probability

Experimental probability, as the name suggests, is based on experiment. For example, by rolling a dice a large number of times you can determine the actual likelihood of getting each outcome.

Outcome of a probability experiment
In reality, you are unlikely to obtain 1, 2, 3, 4, 5, and 6 in just 6 rolls of the dice—but in 1,000 attempts, the amount of times each number comes up will be about the same.

Outcome of rolling three 6s, followed by three 5s

we might want to figure out what the chances are of either one event or the other event happening. You can use simple arithmetic to calculate these combined probabilities.

Multiply to calculate probability of getting tails and a 4

$\frac{1}{2}$

x

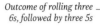

$\frac{1}{6}$

=

$\frac{1}{12}$ *$\frac{1}{2} \times \frac{1}{6}$*

Both events
The probability of a combined outcome of Tails and a 4 can be calculated through multiplication.

Dependent events

Many combined events are not independent of each other. For example, a disease may affect a known proportion of the population. The outcome of a diagnostic test—positive or negative—depends on whether the individual has the disease. The reliability of the test can be estimated with probability, using the test results and the known disease prevalence.

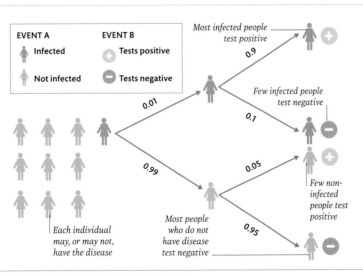

EVENT A	EVENT B
Infected	Tests positive
Not infected	Tests negative

Most infected people test positive — 0.9

0.01

Few infected people test negative — 0.1

0.99

0.05

Few non-infected people test positive

Most people who do not have disease test negative — 0.95

Each individual may, or may not, have the disease

BAYES' THEOREM

Bayes' Theorem allows you to work out "conditional" probabilities as described to the left. In the example of the diagnostic test, you can figure out, for instance, the likelihood of getting a positive result (Event B), given that you have already contracted the disease (Event A). Bayes' Theorem is given by this formula:

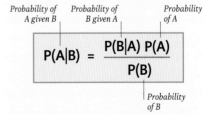

Probability of A given B *Probability of B given A* *Probability of A*

$$P(A|B) = \frac{P(B|A)\ P(A)}{P(B)}$$

Probability of B

see also Modern mathematics pp.178–79 ▶ Quantum mechanics pp.192–93 ▶

Modern mathematics

The turn of the 20th century marked a pivotal time for the development of mathematics. Central to this was the German mathematician David Hilbert (1862–1943), whose 19th-century work included the development of a modern axiomatic approach to geometry. The 23 unsolved major problems in mathematics that Hilbert listed in 1900 would help to shape mathematics research in the 20th century and beyond, into directions such as set theory and logic, as well as chaos theory.

Topology

Topology has its roots in the 18th-century work of Swiss mathematician Leonhard Euler on polyhedra (many-sided shapes). It is the study of shapes without measurements and is concerned with the unchangeable properties of a shape, with no regard to its lengths, proportions, or angles.

"Outside"
"Inside"
Twist

Möbius strip
A Möbius strip is a geometric shape that has only a single surface. It can be created by taking a length of paper, twisting it, and joining the ends.

6 faces
8 vertices
12 edges

Euler's formula
For any polyhedron, such as a cube, the number of corners (vertices, V), edges (E), and faces (F) are related by Euler's formula: $V + F - E = 2$.

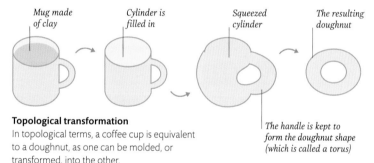

Mug made of clay
Cylinder is filled in
Squeezed cylinder
The resulting doughnut

Topological transformation
In topological terms, a coffee cup is equivalent to a doughnut, as one can be molded, or transformed, into the other.

The handle is kept to form the doughnut shape (which is called a torus)

> "**Topology** is the science of **fundamental pattern** and **structural relationships** of event constellations." BUCKMINSTER FULLER, 1963

MATHEMATICS IN SPACEFLIGHT
Before electronic computers, the complex calculations needed for developing spaceflight had to be performed by mathematicians. Mathematician and engineer Mary Jackson (1921–2005) helped to pioneer the use of computers to calculate trajectories, launch windows, and safe return routes for spacecraft as part of NASA's Mercury program.

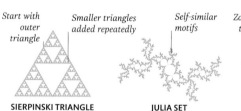

MARY JACKSON AT NASA'S LANGLEY RESEARCH CENTER

Chaos theory

Chaos theory was popularized through the so-called "butterfly effect," based on the idea that the flapping of a butterfly's wings in one place can result in a tornado in another part of the world. Many dynamical phenomena, such as orbiting planets, are predictable. However, as soon as you introduce any greater complexity, a high degree of unpredictability results. Chaos theory seeks to find patterns in this unpredictability.

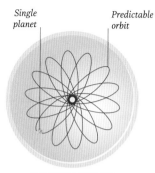

Single planet
Predictable orbit

PREDICTABLE ORBITS

Geodesic path
The "geodesic path" (orbit) that a hypothetical planet follows becomes highly unpredictable when other bodies have an influence on its gravitational field.

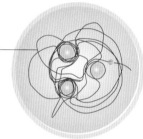

Path of planet becomes unpredictable

SCRAMBLED ORBITS

Interacting variables
American mathematician Edward Lorenz worked on climate modeling and devised a graphic representation of how three climate variables might interact. Although a minuscule change in one could result in huge differences in the others, the overall resulting system, or "Lorenz attractor," is stable and has a well-defined shape.

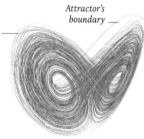

Individual paths never repeat
Attractor's boundary

LORENZ ATTRACTOR

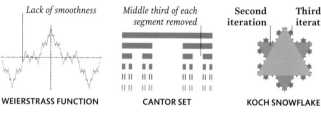

Lack of smoothness

Middle third of each segment removed

Second iteration
Third iteration

WEIERSTRASS FUNCTION
CANTOR SET
KOCH SNOWFLAKE

Start with outer triangle
Smaller triangles added repeatedly
Self-similar motifs
Zoom in on the detail

SIERPINSKI TRIANGLE
JULIA SET
MANDELBROT SET

Fractals
In the late 19th century, mathematicians became intrigued by the properties of shapes that possess "self-similarity," such that when you zoom in, you find a smaller replica of the shape. The most famous of the "fractal" shapes is the Mandelbrot set.

> "In the mind's eye, a **fractal** is a way of seeing infinity." JAMES GLEICK, 2011

> "A geometry able to **include mountains and clouds** now exists."
>
> BENOÎT MANDELBROT, *A Lecture on Fractals*, 1990

Graph theory

Many problems in the real world can be interpreted mathematically by "modeling" them as networks; for example, the most efficient way to distribute goods from a warehouse. Graph theory establishes rules and algorithms (sequences of rules) relating the points (nodes) in a network with their connecting edges (arcs). It has application in fields such as computer science and biology.

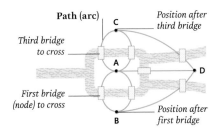

Path (arc)
Position after third bridge
Third bridge to cross
Position after first bridge
First bridge (node) to cross

Bridges of Konigsberg
In this problem, it is impossible to find a path (arc) that crosses over each bridge (node) only once and returns to the starting point (A).

Social mathematics

Social mathematics is concerned with the concept of connectedness, and finding ways in which to quantify or represent it. Related to graph theory, social mathematics has gained increasing importance in the modern era of social media, but it has applications in fields as diverse as psychology, sociology, and mathematical epidemiology.

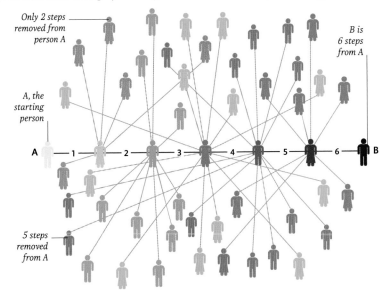

Only 2 steps removed from person A

B is 6 steps from A

A, the starting person

A — 1 — 2 — 3 — 4 — 5 — 6 — B

5 steps removed from A

Six degrees of separation
Connectedness is made popular in the idea that, on average, each person in the world is only six steps (degrees) removed by acquaintance from any other person.

Six degrees of separation is also sometimes called the six handshakes rule

Four-color theorem

Any political map of the world is usually colored in such a way that no two adjacent countries have the same color. This raises the question, "What is the minimum number of colors you need to color a map?" The four-color theorem, proved by computer in 2005, states that no more than four colors are needed to ensure that no two adjacent regions have the same color.

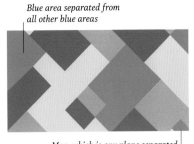

Blue area separated from all other blue areas

Map, which is any plane separated into contiguous (touching) regions

Set theory and logic

Set theory was devised as mathematicians searched for a new axiomatic approach to numbers. It is based on applying Boolean algebra (where values are either true or false) to sets of numbers or elements and examining their properties.

Logic gates

Logic gates provide the means by which computer binary code (composed of zeros and ones) can be manipulated. The different types of logic gate are categorized by Boolean commands, such as AND, OR, NOT, or a combination of them.

NOT gate
A NOT gate has a single input A. The output is the opposite of the input, so it inverts the signal.

Single input, either 0 or 1

INPUT	OUTPUT
1	0
0	1

AND gate
An AND gate has two inputs: A and B, but the output can only be 1 when both A and B are 1.

Two inputs

INPUT		OUTPUT
A	B	A AND B
0	0	0
0	1	0
1	0	0
1	1	1

OR gate
An OR gate also has two inputs: A and B. The output of an OR gate is 1 if either A or B (or both) are 1.

INPUT		OUTPUT
A	B	A AND B
0	0	0
0	1	1
1	0	1
1	1	1

NAND gate
A NAND gate is an AND gate (resulting in 0, 0, 0, 1) followed by a NOT gate. Its output is 1 unless both its inputs are 1.

Signifies the NOT gate

INPUT		OUTPUT
A	B	A AND B
0	0	1
0	1	1
1	0	1
1	1	0

NOR gate
A NOR gate is an OR gate followed by a NOT gate. Its output is 1 only when both its inputs are 0.

INPUT		OUTPUT
A	B	A AND B
0	0	1
0	1	0
1	0	0
1	1	0

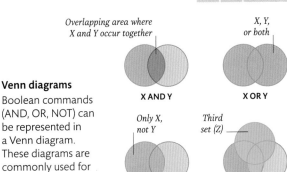

Overlapping area where X and Y occur together

X, Y, or both

Venn diagrams

Boolean commands (AND, OR, NOT) can be represented in a Venn diagram. These diagrams are commonly used for two or three sets, as shown here.

X AND Y

X OR Y

Only X, not Y

Third set (Z)

X NOT Y

(X AND Y) OR Z

see also **The spread and control of disease** pp.254–55 ▶

Symbols, charts, and measurements

Mathematics is a huge subject, including the study of numbers, quantities, patterns, and shapes, as well as relationships between entities and the operations that can be performed on them. Though much of mathematics may seem complex, many commonly used symbols, calculations, measurements, and conversions have practical uses in day-to-day life. Some of this information is summarized here.

Squares, cubes, and roots

Square numbers are $1 \times 1 = 1$, $2 \times 2 = 4$, and so on. Conversely, the square root of 9 is 3, because $3 \times 3 = 9$. These facts can be abbreviated: $3^2 = 9$ and $\sqrt{9} = 3$. In a similar way, 4 cubed, or 4^3, equals $4 \times 4 \times 4$, or 64. And conversely, $\sqrt[3]{64} = 4$.

NO.	SQUARE	CUBE	SQUARE ROOT	CUBE ROOT
1	1	1	1.000	1.000
2	4	8	1.414	1.260
3	9	27	1.732	1.442
4	16	64	2.000	1.587
5	25	125	2.236	1.710
6	36	216	2.449	1.817
7	49	343	2.646	1.913
8	64	512	2.828	2.000
9	81	729	3.000	2.080
10	100	1,000	3.162	2.154

Prime numbers

A prime number is an integer (whole number) that has only two factors: 1 and the number itself. So, for example, 17 is a prime number because only 1 and 17 will go into it without leaving a remainder. Using this definition, 1 is not a prime number. Here are the first 100 prime numbers.

2	3	5	7	11	13	17	19	23	29
31	37	41	43	47	53	59	61	67	71
73	79	83	89	97	101	103	107	109	113
127	131	137	139	149	151	157	163	167	173
179	181	191	193	197	199	211	223	227	229
233	239	241	251	257	263	269	271	277	281
283	293	307	311	313	317	331	337	347	349
353	359	367	373	379	383	389	397	401	409
419	421	431	433	439	443	449	457	461	463
467	479	487	491	499	503	509	521	523	541

> "If **numbers** aren't **beautiful,** I don't know what is."
>
> PAUL ERDŐS, Attributed

Multiplication table

Mental arithmetic can be useful in many aspects of everyday life. One set of calculations that can be learned is multiplication tables, or times tables, which help establish essential numeracy skills. The table below gives the multiples of the numbers 1 to 12. This may be helpful when scaling up recipes or calculating the material required for a DIY project.

	1	2	3	4	5	6	7	8	9	10	11	12
1	1	2	3	4	5	6	7	8	9	10	11	12
2	2	4	6	8	10	12	14	16	18	20	22	24
3	3	6	9	12	15	18	21	24	27	30	33	36
4	4	8	12	16	20	24	28	32	36	40	44	48
5	5	10	15	20	25	30	35	40	45	50	55	60
6	6	12	18→	24	30	36	42	48	54	60	66	72
7	7	14	21	28	35	42	49	56	63	70	77	84
8	8	16	24	32	40	48	56	64	72	80	88	96
9	9	18	27	36	45	54	63	72	81	90	99	108
10	10	20	30	40	50	60	70	80	90	100	110	120
11	11	22	33	44	55	66	77	88	99	110	121	132
12	12	24	36	48	60	72	84	96	108	120	132	144

Mathematical signs and symbols

Mathematics is like a language, and it has its own set of universally accepted notations. There are some variations, for example multiplication can be expressed by × or by • . Different branches of mathematics have specialized notations, but here are the most common symbols.

SYMBOL	DEFINITION
+	Plus; positive
−	Minus; negative
±	Plus or minus; positive or negative; degree of accuracy
∓	Minus or plus; negative or positive
×	Multiplied by (6 × 4)
·	Multiplied by (6 · 4); scalar product of two vectors (A·B)
÷	Divided by (6 ÷ 4)
/	Divided by; ratio of ($^6/_4$)
—	Divided by; ratio of ($\frac{6}{4}$)
=	Equals
≠	Not equal to
≡	Identical with; congruent to
≢	Not identical with
≙	Corresponds to
:	Ratio of (6:4)
::	Proportionately equal (1:2: :2:4)
≈, ≐, ≏	Approximately equal to; equivalent to; similar to
≅	Congruent to; identical with
>	Greater than
≫	Much greater than
≯	Not greater than

SYMBOL	DEFINITION
<	Less than
≪	Much less than
≮	Not less than
≥ ≧ ≳	Equal to or greater than
≤ ≦ ≲	Equal to or less than
∝	Directly proportional to
( )	Parentheses, can mean multiply
—	Vinculum: division w(a-b); chord of circle or length of line (AB);
$\overrightarrow{AB}$	Vector
$\overline{AB}$	Line segment
$\overleftrightarrow{AB}$	Line
∞	Infinity
n^4	Power, index
$\sqrt[2]{}, \sqrt[3]{}$	Square root, cube root, etc.
%	Percent
°	Degrees (°C); degree of arc, e.g. 90°
∠, $\angle^s$	Angle(s)
π	(pi) = 3.141592 ...
⊥	Perpendicular
∟	Right angle
∥	Parallel
⌐m	Measured by

SCIENCE AND TECHNOLOGY

Between 1889 and 1960, a **meter** was **defined as the distance** between two lines marked on the **prototype alloy bar** made of platinum and iridium

Units of measurement

Throughout history, people have attempted to create standard units of measurement in order to be able to quantify or compare lengths, masses, and temperatures. The internationally recognized system, called *Système Internationale d'Unités* or SI, developed from the French metric system. Measurement based on the British imperial system are also still in use.

TEMPERATURE

	FAHRENHEIT	CELSIUS	KELVIN
Boiling point of water	212°	100°	373°
Freezing point of water	32°	0°	273°
Absolute zero	-459°	-273°	0°

LIQUID VOLUME

METRIC

1,000 milliliters (ml)	=	1 liter (l)
100 liters (l)	=	1 hectoliter (hl)
10 hectoliters (hl)	=	1 kiloliter (kl)
1,000 liters (l)	=	1 kiloliter (kl)

IMPERIAL

8 fluid ounces (fl oz)	=	1 cup
20 fluid ounces (fl oz)	=	1 pint (pt)
4 gills (gi)	=	1 pint (pt)
2 pints (pt)	=	1 quart (qt)
4 quarts (qt)	=	1 gallon (gal)

LENGTH

METRIC

10 millimeters (mm)	=	1 centimeter (cm)
100 centimeters (cm)	=	1 meter (m)
1,000 millimeters (mm)	=	1 meter (m)
1,000 meters (m)	=	1 kilometer (km)

IMPERIAL

12 inches (in)	=	1 foot (ft)
3 feet (ft)	=	1 yard (yd)
1,760 yards (yd)	=	1 mile
5,280 feet (ft)	=	1 mile
8 furlongs	=	1 mile

MASS

METRIC

1,000 milligrams (mg)	=	1 gram (g)
1,000 grams (g)	=	1 kilogram (kg)
1,000 kilograms (kg)	=	1 tonne (t)

IMPERIAL

16 ounces (oz)	=	1 pound (lb)
14 pounds (lb)	=	1 stone
112 pounds (lb)	=	1 hundredweight
20 hundredweight	=	1 ton

TIME

METRIC AND IMPERIAL

60 seconds	=	1 minute
60 minutes	=	1 hour
24 hours	=	1 day
7 days	=	1 week
52 weeks	=	1 year

AREA

METRIC

100 square millimeters (mm²)	=	1 square centimeter (cm²)
10,000 square centimeters (cm²)	=	1 square meter (m²)
10,000 square meters (m²)	=	1 hectare (ha)
100 hectares (ha)	=	1 square kilometer (km²)
1 square kilometer (km²)	=	1,000,000 square meters (m²)

IMPERIAL

144 square inches (sq in)	=	1 square foot (sq ft)
9 square feet (sq ft)	=	1 square yard (sq yd)
1,296 square inches (sq in)	=	1 square yard (sq yd)
43,560 square feet (sq ft)	=	1 acre
640 acres	=	1 square mile (sq mile)

Conversion tables

Metric measurements are the most commonly used around the world, but it can still be handy to convert readily between metric and imperial. Knowing the ratios between common measures makes it easy to convert between the two systems when necessary.

AREA

METRIC		IMPERIAL	IMPERIAL		METRIC
1 square centimeter (cm²)	=	0.155 square inch (sq in)	1 square inch (sq in)	=	6.4516 square centimeters (cm²)
1 square meter (m²)	=	10.764 square feet (sq ft)	1 square foot (sq ft)	=	0.0929 square meter (m²)
1 square meter (m²)	=	1.196 square yard (sq yd)	1 square yard (sq yd)	=	0.8361 square meter (m²)
1 hectare (ha)	=	2.4711 acres	1 acre	=	0.4047 hectare (ha)
1 square kilometer (km²)	=	0.3861 square miles	1 square mile	=	2.59 square kilometers (km²)

LENGTH

METRIC	IMPERIAL
1 millimeter (mm) =	0.03937 inch (in)
1 centimeter (cm) =	0.3937 inch (in)
1 meter (m) =	1.0936 yards (yd)
1 kilometer (km) =	0.6214 mile

IMPERIAL	METRIC
1 inch (in) =	2.54 centimeters (cm)
1 foot (ft) =	0.3048 meter (m)
1 yard (yd) =	0.9144 meter (m)
1 mile =	1.6093 kilometers (km)
1 nautical mile =	1.853 kilometers (km)

MASS

METRIC		IMPERIAL
1 milligram (mg)	=	0.0154 grain
1 gram (g)	=	0.0353 ounce (oz)
1 kilogram (kg)	=	2.2046 pounds (lb)
1 tonne/metric ton (t)	=	0.9842 imperial ton

IMPERIAL		METRIC
1 ounce (oz)	=	28.35 grams (g)
1 pound (lb)	=	0.4536 kilogram (kg)
1 stone	=	6.3503 kilogram (kg)
1 hundredweight (cwt)	=	50.802 kilogram (kg)
1 imperial ton	=	1.016 tonnes/metric tons

VOLUME

METRIC		IMPERIAL
1 cubic centimeter (cm³)	=	0.061 cubic inch (in³)
1 cubic decimeter (dm³)	=	0.0353 cubic foot (ft³)
1 cubic meter (m³)	=	1.308 cubic yard (yd³)
1 liter (l)/1 dm³	=	1.76 pints (pt)

IMPERIAL		METRIC
1 cubic inch (in³)	=	16.387 cubic centimeters (cm³)
1 cubic foot (ft³)	=	0.0283 cubic meters (m³)
1 fluid ounce (fl oz)	=	28.413 milliliters (ml)
1 pint (pt)/20 fl oz	=	0.5683 liter (l)
1 gallon/8 pt	=	4.5461 liters (l)

◀ see also Geometry pp.172–73   ◀ Measurement and construction pp.174–75   **181**

Classical mechanics

Classical mechanics is a branch of physics that describes the motion of physical objects. It can be applied to all motion, from athletics to space exploration, and is based on the principle that using energy to apply forces to objects causes their motion (or shape) to change. It was established centuries ago by Isaac Newton and remains accurate for predicting the motion of familiar objects or for determining their movements in the past.

Types of energy

Changing the motion of an object by applying a force (an example of doing "work") requires energy to be transferred to that object. Energy is stored in many different forms and is transferred between them to enact change.

 Chemical energy
Chemical processes can release the stores of energy binding atoms to each other.

 Elastic potential
Stretched, squashed, or twisted objects may have the potential to return to their original shape.

 Radiant energy
Visible light is an energy that travels as fluctuations in magnetic and electrical fields.

 Thermal energy
The motion (or vibration) of atoms within an object is called thermal energy.

 Gravitational potential
Objects lifted up against gravity have the potential to accelerate as they fall.

 Electrical potential
A battery has the potential to move charges around a circuit, generating a current.

Nuclear energy
Atomic nuclei contain huge amounts of energy, which can be released.

 Electrical energy
Energy carried by a flow of charges (electric current) can be used to power devices.

Acoustic energy
The energy carried in a sound wave squeezes and stretches the air (or other medium).

 Kinetic energy
This is the energy that all moving objects have associated with their motion.

Conservation of energy

Energy cannot be created or destroyed, but it is constantly being transferred between different forms. A process as simple as pushing a load of bricks up a slope involves the transfer of energy between many forms.

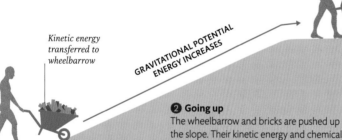

Kinetic energy transferred to wheelbarrow

Chemical potential energy stored in body has decreased

Gravitational potential energy begins to change to kinetic energy

GRAVITATIONAL POTENTIAL ENERGY INCREASES

❷ Going up
The wheelbarrow and bricks are pushed up the slope. Their kinetic energy and chemical energy stored in the body are transferred into gravitational potential energy.

❶ On the move
A person uses chemical energy stored in the body to do work on the brick-filled wheelbarrow. The wheelbarrow begins to move and gains kinetic energy.

❸ Release of potential
When the bricks are tipped out of the wheelbarrow, their gravitational potential energy is transferred into kinetic energy as they fall to the ground.

As bricks fall, their kinetic energy increases and their gravitational potential energy decreases

When bricks stop falling, their kinetic energy is converted into heat and acoustic energy

Doing work

Applying forces to change the motion of objects is called doing "work." For example, striking a tennis ball applies a force to the ball, sending it hurtling into a new direction.

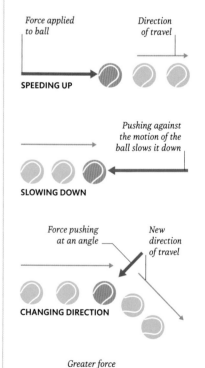

Force applied to ball — *Direction of travel*
SPEEDING UP

Pushing against the motion of the ball slows it down
SLOWING DOWN

Force pushing at an angle — *New direction of travel*
CHANGING DIRECTION

Greater force changes the shape more
CHANGING SHAPE
Forces are equal

INERTIA

An object's motion does not change unless it experiences a net external force; for example, a skater continues to glide along the ice until friction and air resistance slows them to a standstill. This resistance to change in motion is known as inertia. Gravity and resistive forces on Earth, such as friction, partially conceal the effects of inertia, making it appear that moving objects tend to slow down.

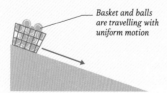

Basket and balls are travelling with uniform motion

Equal motion
The basket and balls keep moving at the same speed in the same direction unless a force is applied.

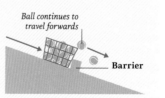

Ball continues to travel forwards

Barrier

Inertial shift
A barrier exerts a force on the basket, halting its movement, but the balls continue moving.

see also Thermodynamics pp.184–85 ▶   Electricity and magnetism pp.190–91 ▶   Quantum mechanics pp.192–93 ▶

Newton's laws of motion

Newton's three laws of motion describe how forces acting on a massive object influence its motion. They form the core of classical mechanics, and can be used as the starting point for predicting and explaining a range of phenomena in physics, such as the launch of a rocket into space. For a rocket to launch, it needs force to change its stationary state of motion. The rocket's acceleration depends on the mass and the thrust provided by combustion. The acceleration is diminished somewhat by the force of air resistance, or drag, acting against it.

> "If I have **seen further**, it is by **standing** upon the **shoulders of giants.**"
>
> ISAAC NEWTON, In a letter to Robert Hooke, 1675

ISAAC NEWTON

Sir Isaac Newton (1642–1727) was an English polymath recognized as one of the most influential scientists in history. In addition to devising laws of mechanics and gravitation, Newton also made significant contributions in optics, astronomy, fluid dynamics, and mathematics, developing calculus independently of his contemporary, Gottfried Leibniz. He was closely associated with the University of Cambridge and the Royal Society.

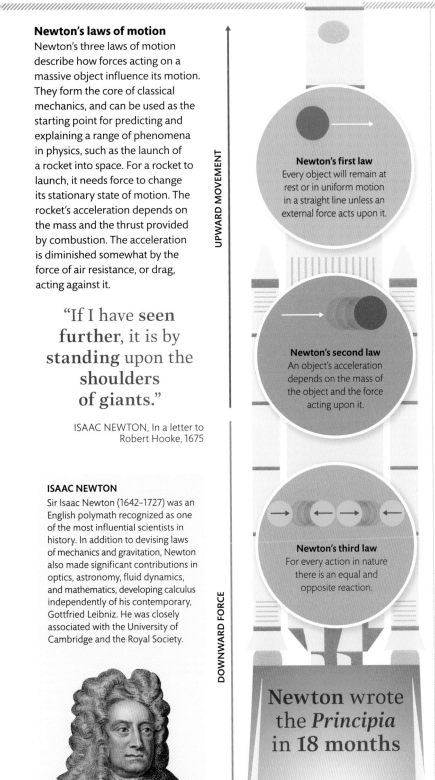

UPWARD MOVEMENT

DOWNWARD FORCE

Newton's first law
Every object will remain at rest or in uniform motion in a straight line unless an external force acts upon it.

Newton's second law
An object's acceleration depends on the mass of the object and the force acting upon it.

Newton's third law
For every action in nature there is an equal and opposite reaction.

Newton wrote the *Principia* in 18 months

Newton's law of gravitation

Isaac Newton's law of universal gravitation, which he laid out in his *Principia*, states that every massive object exerts an attractive force on every other massive object. The strength of this force depends on the masses of the objects and the distance separating them.

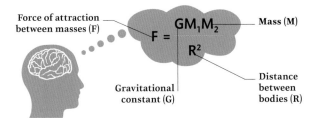

Force of attraction between masses (F)

$$F = \frac{GM_1M_2}{R^2}$$

Mass (M)

Gravitational constant (G)

Distance between bodies (R)

Gravity and mass
The gravitational force (F) between two objects is directly proportional to their masses (M); for instance, doubling one object's mass doubles the force between the objects.

Gravity and distance
Gravitational attraction is inversely proportional to the square of the distance (D) between the objects—e.g., doubling their separation decreases the attraction by a factor of four.

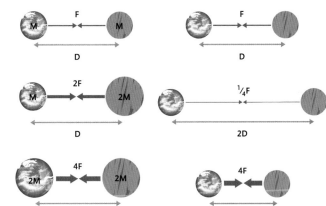

Mass and weight

The weight of an object is the gravitational force exerted on it. On Earth, weight is experienced as a force pulling toward the ground. The mass of an object is a measurement of the amount of material it contains. Although massive objects experience more weight, all objects fall to the ground at the same rate.

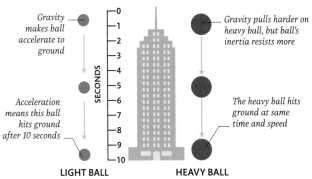

Gravity makes ball accelerate to ground

Acceleration means this ball hits ground after 10 seconds

SECONDS

Gravity pulls harder on heavy ball, but ball's inertia resists more

The heavy ball hits ground at same time and speed

LIGHT BALL

HEAVY BALL

see also Energy pp.262–63 ▶ **183**

Thermodynamics

The physics of heat, temperature, and certain properties of matter is called thermodynamics. It deals with how energy, in the form of heat, is transferred between different forms of matter and from one place to another. At the core of thermodynamics is a set of four laws that describe entropy and how heat behaves in an enclosed system.

Thermodynamics was born out of **efforts to improve** the efficiency of **early steam engines**

Kinetic theory of gases
Kinetic theory describes gases as a collection of many pointlike particles in random motion, continually colliding with each other and the walls of their container. The model may be a simplification, but it is effective for understanding observable properties such as temperature, pressure, and volume. Heating a gas adds kinetic energy to its particles, causing them to move more rapidly and undergo more frequent and energetic collisions. This causes the gas to expand in volume or—if trapped inside a container—to exert more pressure as its particles collide more frequently with the walls of the container.

Pressure and temperature
The kinetic theory of gases is used to explain why gas, even when inside a pressurized container, expands as it rises towards the surface of water.

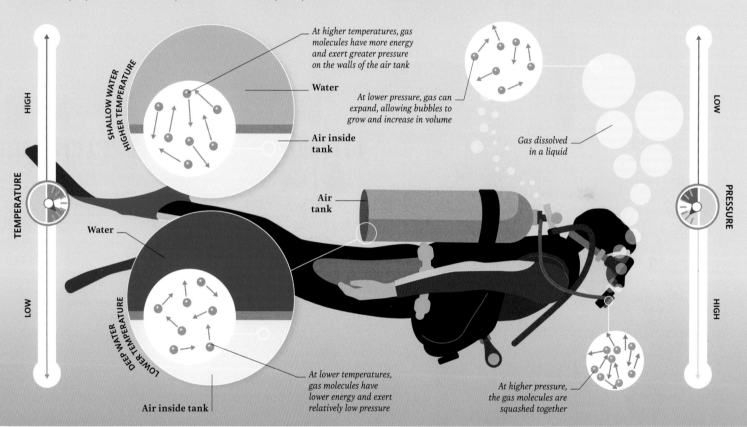

TEMPERATURE — HIGH / LOW

SHALLOW WATER HIGHER TEMPERATURE

At higher temperatures, gas molecules have more energy and exert greater pressure on the walls of the air tank

Water

At lower pressure, gas can expand, allowing bubbles to grow and increase in volume

Air inside tank

Gas dissolved in a liquid

Water

Air tank

DEEP WATER LOWER TEMPERATURE

At lower temperatures, gas molecules have lower energy and exert relatively low pressure

Air inside tank

At higher pressure, the gas molecules are squashed together

PRESSURE — LOW / HIGH

The laws of thermodynamics
The four laws of thermodynamics describe behaviour of thermal energy in a system. Crucially, they state that energy cannot be created or destroyed, and that heat naturally moves in one "direction" (from hot to cold). These principles are among the most important rules in science. The four laws are not numbered conventionally because the first law conceptionally was the last to be formulated.

Zeroth Law
Two systems each in thermal equilibrium with a third are in thermal equilibrium with each other.

Law 1
Energy can change forms but cannot be created or destroyed.

Law 2
Entropy (disorder or randomness) in an isolated system increases over time.

Law 3
There is a minimum temperature, but in reality, it is not possible to reach absolute zero.

Fate of the universe
Entropy, a measure of the disorder in any closed system, always increases over time. A consequence is that the universe will eventually reach a state of maximum entropy, where no more "work" can be done.

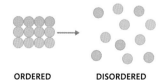

ORDERED → DISORDERED

Water can exist as **solid ice, liquid water, and gaseous vapor** at +32.01°F

Energy vs. temperature

Thermal energy, also called heat, is the total internal energy in a particular sample of a substance and depends on its mass, the type of particle, and the speed of the particles. Temperature, however, refers to the average energy of its particles. Glowing specks from sparklers have high temperatures, but not much heat due to their size.

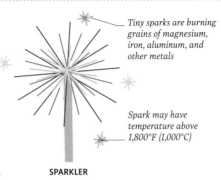

Tiny sparks are burning grains of magnesium, iron, aluminum, and other metals

Spark may have temperature above 1,800°F (1,000°C)

SPARKLER

Measuring temperature

Kelvin (K), Celsius (°C), and Fahrenheit (°F) are temperature scales. Certain natural phenomena occur at defined temperatures on these scales; for example, water boils at 212°F (100°C). Physicists mostly use the Kelvin scale, which begins at the minimum possible temperature: "absolute zero."

KEY	
°C Celsius	K Kelvin
°F Fahrenheit	

Temperature scales

Using the temperatures at which certain natural phenomena occur as fixed points allowed scientists to create temperature scales.

WILLIAM THOMSON

William Thomson (1828–1907), also known as Lord Kelvin, figured out that if an object lost all of its heat energy until its particles could not move, its temperature would be –460°F (–273°C), known as absolute zero.

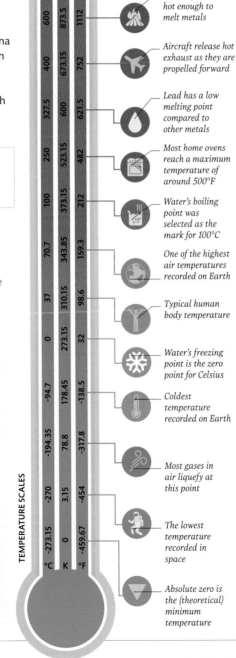

TEMPERATURE SCALES

°C	K	°F
600	873.5	1112
400	673.15	752
327.5	600	621.5
250	523.15	482
100	373.15	212
70.7	343.85	159.3
37	310.15	98.6
0	273.15	32
–94.7	178.45	–138.5
–194.35	78.8	–317.8
–270	3.15	–454
–273.15	0	–459.67

A wood fire is hot enough to melt metals

Aircraft release hot exhaust as they are propelled forward

Lead has a low melting point compared to other metals

Most home ovens reach a maximum temperature of around 500°F

Water's boiling point was selected as the mark for 100°C

One of the highest air temperatures recorded on Earth

Typical human body temperature

Water's freezing point is the zero point for Celsius

Coldest temperature recorded on Earth

Most gases in air liquefy at this point

The lowest temperature recorded in space

Absolute zero is the (theoretical) minimum temperature

Transfer of heat

Heat is transferred between objects via three processes: convection, conduction, and radiation. The way heat is transferred depends on the objects' properties; for instance, solids are good at conducting heat due to their close-packed atomic structure.

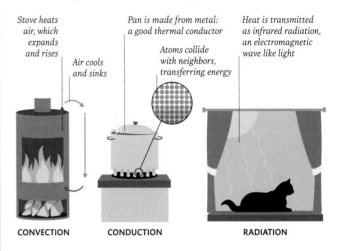

Stove heats air, which expands and rises

Air cools and sinks

Pan is made from metal: a good thermal conductor

Atoms collide with neighbors, transferring energy

Heat is transmitted as infrared radiation, an electromagnetic wave like light

CONVECTION **CONDUCTION** **RADIATION**

Thermal equilibrium

Heat always travels spontaneously from hot to cold objects. This process of heat transfer continues until the objects reach the same temperature and can be said to be in a state of thermal equilibrium.

Thermal energy spreads out until it is evenly distributed

Thermal equilibrium is reached

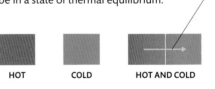

HOT **COLD** **HOT AND COLD** **WARM**

Phase transitions and latent heat

Matter exists in different states, including solids, liquids, and gases. Adding energy to matter causes its particles to move more energetically and eventually break the bonds between them, changing state. During these phase transitions, the energy works as latent heat, which does not raise the temperature of the matter.

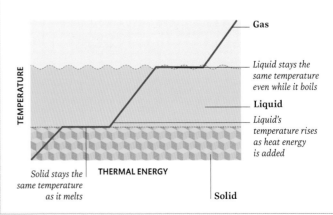

TEMPERATURE

Gas

Liquid stays the same temperature even while it boils

Liquid

Liquid's temperature rises as heat energy is added

THERMAL ENERGY

Solid stays the same temperature as it melts

Solid

see also Electricity and magnetism pp.190–91 ▶   Nuclear and particle physics pp.194–95 ▶

Waves

SCIENCE AND TECHNOLOGY

Waves are regular, repeated oscillations (fluctuations) around a fixed midpoint. They take many different forms—for example, they can stand still or transfer energy as they travel through a substance or a vacuum—but waves can all be described with a common set of behaviors. Light, sound, and mechanical waves (such as ripples on water) are among the most familiar waves found in nature.

Nature of waves

Waves can transfer energy from one location to another through oscillations. These motions arise in various forms, with their properties depending on the substance that they travel through. Sound waves, for instance, are oscillations in pressure traveling through a substance.

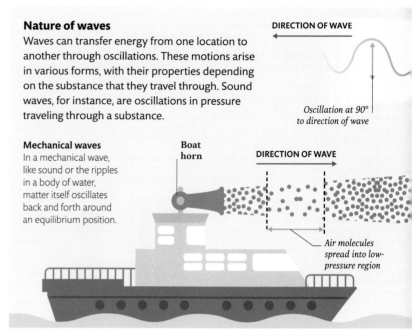

DIRECTION OF WAVE

Oscillation at 90° to direction of wave

Mechanical waves

In a mechanical wave, like sound or the ripples in a body of water, matter itself oscillates back and forth around an equilibrium position.

Boat horn

DIRECTION OF WAVE

Air molecules spread into low-pressure region

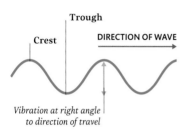

Crest

Trough

DIRECTION OF WAVE

Vibration at right angle to direction of travel

Transverse wave

The oscillations of a transverse wave are perpendicular to its direction of travel. Electromagnetic waves, such as light, are examples of transverse waves.

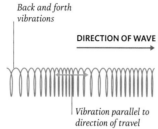

Back and forth vibrations

DIRECTION OF WAVE

Vibration parallel to direction of travel

Longitudinal wave

The oscillations of a longitudinal wave are in the same direction as the wave's direction of travel. Sound is an example of a longitudinal wave.

Properties of waves

Waves can be described quantitatively by measuring a set of properties common to all waves. A wave's frequency is the number of complete oscillations per second, while wavelength is the distance covered by one oscillation. The wave's size or "height"—called its amplitude—indicates its power.

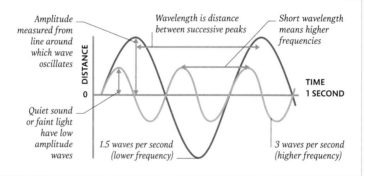

Amplitude measured from line around which wave oscillates

Wavelength is distance between successive peaks

Short wavelength means higher frequencies

DISTANCE

0

TIME 1 SECOND

Quiet sound or faint light have low amplitude waves

1.5 waves per second (lower frequency)

3 waves per second (higher frequency)

Diffraction

When waves pass through a gap, they bend and spread out. This is called diffraction. Diffraction only occurs if the gap is small compared to the size of the wavelength; if it is too large, the bending is barely perceptible.

When a short wave travels through a wide gap, very little diffraction occurs

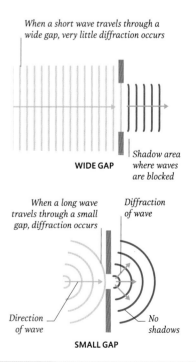

WIDE GAP

Shadow area where waves are blocked

When a long wave travels through a small gap, diffraction occurs

Diffraction of wave

Direction of wave

SMALL GAP

No shadows

Reflection

When waves hit an obstacle or boundary, they are reflected from that boundary at the same angle (called the angle of reflection) that they approached it at (the angle of incidence). The shape of a reflected wave depends on the shape of the incident wave and the shape of the boundary encountered.

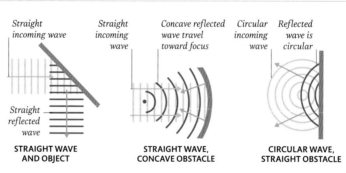

Straight incoming wave

Straight reflected wave

STRAIGHT WAVE AND OBJECT

Straight incoming wave

Concave reflected wave travel toward focus

STRAIGHT WAVE, CONCAVE OBSTACLE

Circular incoming wave

Reflected wave is circular

CIRCULAR WAVE, STRAIGHT OBSTACLE

Refraction

Waves travel at different speeds as they pass through different substances. Light, for example, is slower in water than in air. When waves cross boundaries between substances, their speed and angle changes; this is known as refraction.

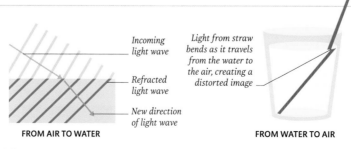

Incoming light wave

Refracted light wave

New direction of light wave

FROM AIR TO WATER

Light from straw bends as it travels from the water to the air, creating a distorted image

FROM WATER TO AIR

Waves do not transfer matter, they transfer energy

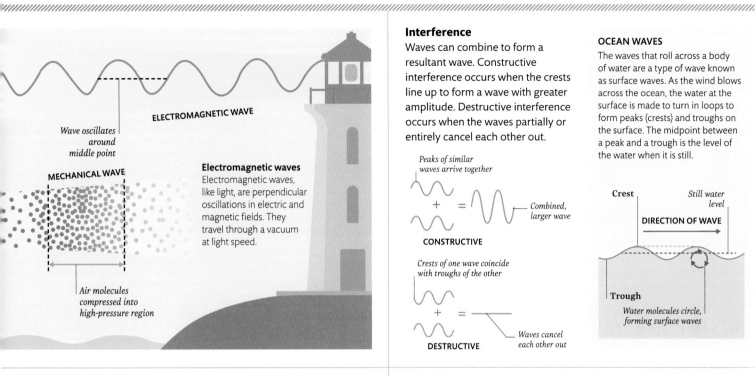

ELECTROMAGNETIC WAVE

Wave oscillates around middle point

MECHANICAL WAVE

Electromagnetic waves
Electromagnetic waves, like light, are perpendicular oscillations in electric and magnetic fields. They travel through a vacuum at light speed.

Air molecules compressed into high-pressure region

Interference
Waves can combine to form a resultant wave. Constructive interference occurs when the crests line up to form a wave with greater amplitude. Destructive interference occurs when the waves partially or entirely cancel each other out.

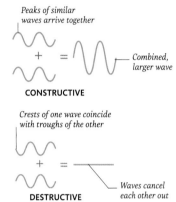

Peaks of similar waves arrive together

+ = — *Combined, larger wave*

CONSTRUCTIVE

Crests of one wave coincide with troughs of the other

+ =

DESTRUCTIVE

Waves cancel each other out

OCEAN WAVES
The waves that roll across a body of water are a type of wave known as surface waves. As the wind blows across the ocean, the water at the surface is made to turn in loops to form peaks (crests) and troughs on the surface. The midpoint between a peak and a trough is the level of the water when it is still.

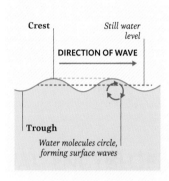

Crest

Still water level

DIRECTION OF WAVE

Trough

Water molecules circle, forming surface waves

Doppler effect
Even fast waves, such as sound waves, are affected by the movement of their source. As a vehicle with a siren approaches, the sound waves are squashed together, raising their frequency. As the vehicle passes and moves away, the waves are stretched out. This is known as the Doppler effect.

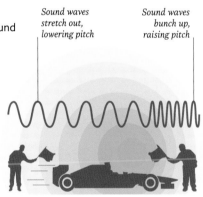

Sound waves stretch out, lowering pitch

Sound waves bunch up, raising pitch

How waves transfer energy
Waves can transfer energy as they propagate, but not matter. Mechanical waves disturb matter locally as they pass, although matter does not move with the water. This is what causes floating objects to bob as a wave passes.

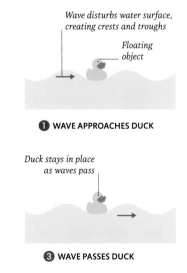

Wave disturbs water surface, creating crests and troughs

Floating object

❶ WAVE APPROACHES DUCK

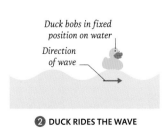

Duck bobs in fixed position on water

Direction of wave

❷ DUCK RIDES THE WAVE

Duck stays in place as waves pass

❸ WAVE PASSES DUCK

Equilibrium
Oscillations occur not just in waves but in many natural phenomena. For example, a pendulum swings around its equilibrium position (hanging straight down) with a type of oscillation called simple harmonic motion. This means that the further the pendulum travels from equilibrium, the stronger the restoring force pulling it back to equilibrium.

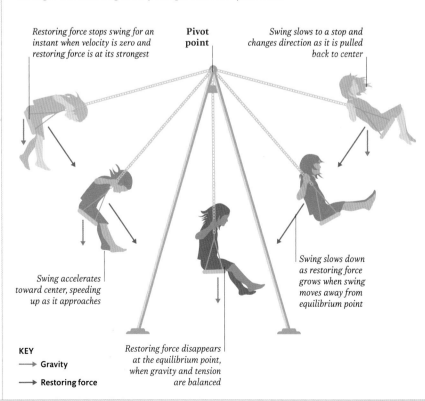

Restoring force stops swing for an instant when velocity is zero and restoring force is at its strongest

Pivot point

Swing slows to a stop and changes direction as it is pulled back to center

Swing accelerates toward center, speeding up as it approaches

Swing slows down as restoring force grows when swing moves away from equilibrium point

KEY

→ Gravity

→ Restoring force

Restoring force disappears at the equilibrium point, when gravity and tension are balanced

see also Electricity and magnetism pp.190–91 ▶   Nuclear and particle physics pp.194–95 ▶   Relativity and grand theories pp.196–97 ▶

Light and matter

The physics of light and its interactions with matter is known as optics. The visible light with which we perceive the world is a wave found in the middle of the electromagnetic spectrum. Each type of electromagnetic wave has distinct properties, depending on its wavelengths. They all interact with matter, but in various ways, depending on their energy (wavelength). Many interactions between light and matter can be understood by thinking of light as a wave. However, other phenomena required physicists in the early 20th century to challenge this convention and also describe light as a particle, known as a photon.

Spectrum of light
The electromagnetic spectrum is the range of synchronized vibrations of electric and magnetic fields. It ranges from long wavelength, low energy waves to short wavelength, high energy waves.

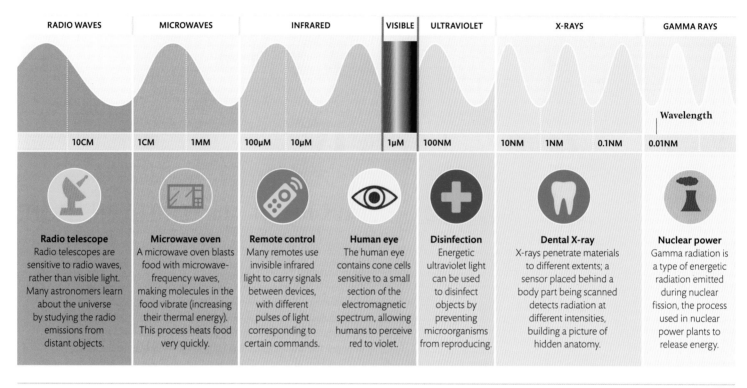

| RADIO WAVES | MICROWAVES | INFRARED | VISIBLE | ULTRAVIOLET | X-RAYS | GAMMA RAYS |

Wavelength

| 10CM | 1CM | 1MM | 100μM | 10μM | 1μM | 100NM | 10NM | 1NM | 0.1NM | 0.01NM |

Radio telescope
Radio telescopes are sensitive to radio waves, rather than visible light. Many astronomers learn about the universe by studying the radio emissions from distant objects.

Microwave oven
A microwave oven blasts food with microwave-frequency waves, making molecules in the food vibrate (increasing their thermal energy). This process heats food very quickly.

Remote control
Many remotes use invisible infrared light to carry signals between devices, with different pulses of light corresponding to certain commands.

Human eye
The human eye contains cone cells sensitive to a small section of the electromagnetic spectrum, allowing humans to perceive red to violet.

Disinfection
Energetic ultraviolet light can be used to disinfect objects by preventing microorganisms from reproducing.

Dental X-ray
X-rays penetrate materials to different extents; a sensor placed behind a body part being scanned detects radiation at different intensities, building a picture of hidden anatomy.

Nuclear power
Gamma radiation is a type of energetic radiation emitted during nuclear fission, the process used in nuclear power plants to release energy.

Light as waves and particles
Light has properties of waves and particles. A simple way to show the wavelike behavior of light is called the double-slit experiment. Although the wave model of light was dominant in science for many years, physicists struggled to explain electromagnetic emission related to temperature using this model. Their observations could only be explained if light can also be characterized as small, discrete packages of energy (known as photons).

Light travels at almost **186,000 miles/s** **(300,000 km/s)** in a **vacuum**

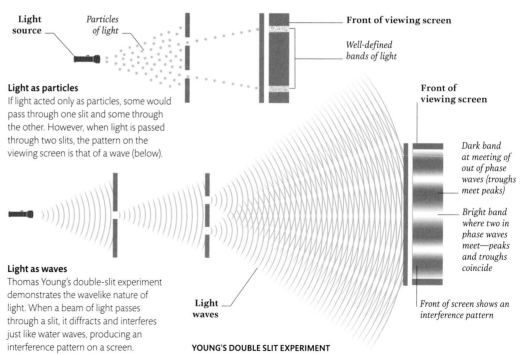

Light source / Particles of light / Front of viewing screen / Well-defined bands of light

Light as particles
If light acted only as particles, some would pass through one slit and some through the other. However, when light is passed through two slits, the pattern on the viewing screen is that of a wave (below).

Front of viewing screen

Dark band at meeting of out of phase waves (troughs meet peaks)

Bright band where two in phase waves meet—peaks and troughs coincide

Light as waves
Thomas Young's double-slit experiment demonstrates the wavelike nature of light. When a beam of light passes through a slit, it diffracts and interferes just like water waves, producing an interference pattern on a screen.

Light waves

Front of screen shows an interference pattern

YOUNG'S DOUBLE SLIT EXPERIMENT

The **momentum of light particles** from the sun can **propel spacecraft** with solar sails

Light and matter

The way we see the properties of a material depends on how it interacts with light; for instance, a clear material allows a lot of light through, while an opaque object lets through almost none. The color of an object depends on which wavelengths of light are reflected and which are absorbed.

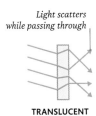

Light passes through clearly

TRANSPARENT

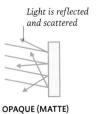

Light scatters while passing through

TRANSLUCENT

Light is reflected and scattered

OPAQUE (MATTE)

Light reflected in single beam

OPAQUE (SHINY)

Refraction

Light changes speed as it passes from one substance into another, often causing it to bend. As white (mixed) light travels through a prism, it splits into separate colors due to each wavelength being bent by a slightly different angle.

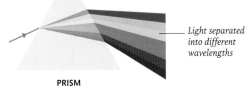

Light separated into different wavelengths

PRISM

Mirrors

Most objects have tiny irregularities on the surface, causing light to be reflected from them at all angles (scattering). However, mirrors have an extremely smooth surface, allowing light beams to be reflected at their original alignment and generating clear, virtual images.

Light hits object and is reflected onto mirror

Mirror image

A mirror creates a "virtual image," which appears to be reversed and also to be "behind" the mirror.

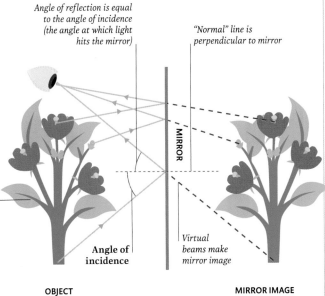

Angle of reflection is equal to the angle of incidence (the angle at which light hits the mirror)

"Normal" line is perpendicular to mirror

MIRROR

Angle of incidence

Virtual beams make mirror image

OBJECT

MIRROR IMAGE

Lenses

A lens is a transparent object that manipulates light through refraction. It has two curved surfaces, so light enters and leaves it at different angles, and is refracted by different amounts. The two main types are convex (bends light inward) and concave (spreads light out).

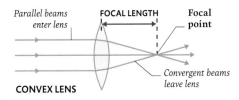

Parallel beams enter lens

FOCAL LENGTH

Focal point

CONVEX LENS

Convergent beams leave lens

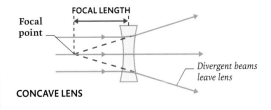

FOCAL LENGTH

Focal point

Divergent beams leave lens

CONCAVE LENS

How atoms emit light

Atoms absorb and emit energy in the form of light when electrons move between their energy shells. When an electron absorbs a photon it moves to a higher energy shell, and when the electron drops to a lower energy shell, it releases the energy difference in the form of a photon.

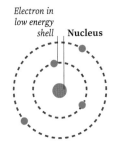

Electron in low energy shell **Nucleus**

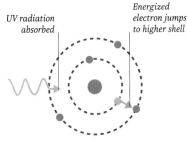

UV radiation absorbed

Energized electron jumps to higher shell

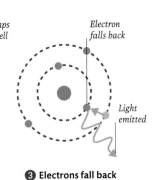

Electron falls back

Light emitted

❶ Stable atom
Electrons fill up the energy levels (shells) that surround the atomic nucleus.

❷ Electron jumps up
An electron absorbs a photon and it becomes excited, jumping to a higher energy level.

❸ Electrons fall back
The electron quickly falls back to a lower energy level, releasing excess energy as light.

How fluorescence works

Fluorescence is one of several ways in which light is emitted. Fluorescent objects absorb photons and subsequently release them, normally at a longer wavelength (lower energy) than the absorbed light. For instance, an object may absorb ultraviolet light and emit visible light.

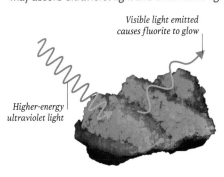

Visible light emitted causes fluorite to glow

Higher-energy ultraviolet light

FLUORITE

see also Quantum mechanics pp.192–93 ▶

Electricity and magnetism

Electromagnetism is the physics of charged objects and their interactions, which occur through electric and magnetic fields. Electricity and magnetism were once thought to be separate forces, but James Clerk Maxwell (1831–79) unified them, describing them as aspects of the same force. The electromagnetic force is, after gravitation, the most familiar of the four fundamental forces; it runs electrical devices and gives rise to electromagnetic waves, such as light.

Static electricity

Atoms contain a positively charged nucleus surrounded by negatively charged electrons, which can flow freely to other objects. An object with a surplus of electrons becomes negatively charged, attracting positively charged objects, which have a deficit of electrons.

KEY

⚫ Electron   ⊕ Positive Charge

Surplus of electrons

❸ Shock
As the electrons jump to the conductive metal handle, the person experiences a small electric shock and sometimes there is a visible spark.

Whole body gains a small negative charge

Neutral door handle

Electrons leap to door handle, producing a small shock

Negative charge of body

❷ Discharge
As the hand approaches the door handle, some electrons are transferred to the handle, leaving the body electrically neutral.

Electrons move to the body

Neutral carpet

❶ Charge from friction
As the foot rubs against the fibers in the carpet, electrons are transported from the ground to the body, making the body slightly negatively charged.

Making a current

An electric current is a flow of electrical charge, such as through the wires in a circuit. Charged particles are pulled toward an opposite charge and in a current, such as one produced by a battery, the difference in electrical charge between two electrodes keeps the current flowing. Materials that are good at carrying a current are called conductors. Materials that block electric currents are called insulators.

KEY
— Wire
→ Direction of electrons

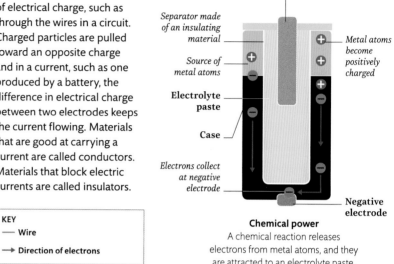

Positive electrode

Separator made of an insulating material

Source of metal atoms

Electrolyte paste

Case

Electrons collect at negative electrode

Metal atoms become positively charged

Negative electrode

Chemical power
A chemical reaction releases electrons from metal atoms, and they are attracted to an electrolyte paste.

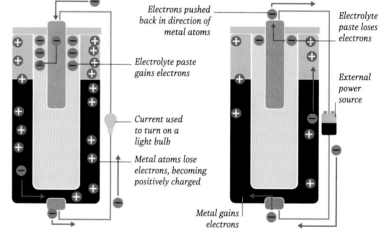

Electrons pushed back in direction of metal atoms

Electrolyte paste gains electrons

Current used to turn on a light bulb

Metal atoms lose electrons, becoming positively charged

Electrolyte paste loses electrons

External power source

Metal gains electrons

Discharging
The electrodes are separated, forcing electrons to travel to the positive electrode via a connecting wire.

Recharging
Some batteries can be recharged by forcing electrons to flow back toward the negative electrode.

Magnetic fields and forces

A magnet has two poles—north and south—and is surrounded by a field that exerts attractive and repulsive forces on other magnetic materials. A magnetic field stretches out in all directions, but quickly weakens with distance. The behavior of particles inside materials gives rise to different types of magnets.

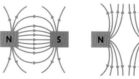

OPPOSITES ATTRACT   **LIKE POLES REPEL**

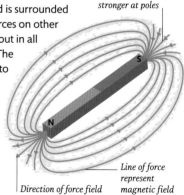

Magnetic field stronger at poles

Line of force represent magnetic field

Direction of force field

Electromagnetism

Electricity and magnetism are aspects of one phenomenon, called electromagnetism. It describes the relationship between electric and magnetic fields, such as the direction of a magnetic field in relation to an electric one.

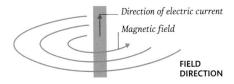

Direction of electric current

Magnetic field

FIELD DIRECTION

Induction

A changing magnetic field can interact with a circuit to generate a current, with strength and direction varying with the magnetic field. This is known as electromagnetic induction.

Inducing current

Electrical generators induce an electric current by rapidly moving a wire through a magnetic field.

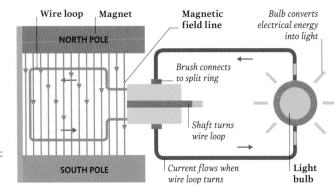

Wire loop   Magnet

Magnetic field line

Bulb converts electrical energy into light

NORTH POLE

Brush connects to split ring

Shaft turns wire loop

SOUTH POLE

Current flows when wire loop turns

Light bulb

Electromagnets

An electromagnet is a magnet created when an electric current is passed through a tightly wound coil of wire (called a solenoid). An electromagnet's field can be controlled by varying the strength of the current running through the magnet.

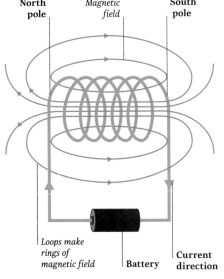

North pole   Magnetic field   South pole

Loops make rings of magnetic field   Battery   Current direction

Electrical motors

Induction is at the core of many electrical devices. A motor is like a generator run in reverse. In a motor, a coil (called an armature) inside a magnetic field rotates as a current flows through it.

Fleming's left hand rule

The "left-hand rule" is a method for working out the direction of motion in an electric motor using three fingers.

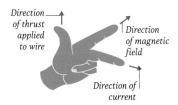

Direction of thrust applied to wire

Direction of magnetic field

Direction of current

Inside a power drill

A drill is an example of a device that uses a motor to generate rotational movement from an electric current.

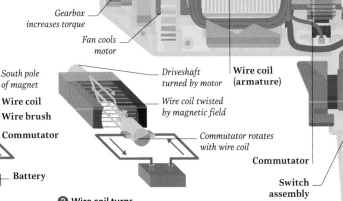

Gearbox increases torque

Fan cools motor

Driveshaft turned by motor

Wire coil (armature)

Wire coil twisted by magnetic field

Commutator rotates with wire coil

Commutator

Switch assembly

Power supply

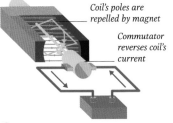

South pole of magnet

Wire coil

Wire brush

Commutator

Magnetic field line

Battery

❶ Current flows into coil
A battery provides an electric current to flow through wire brushes and a wire coil positioned in a magnetic field.

❷ Wire coil turns
Wire coil is repelled by the magnet's like poles, creating the torque (rotational force) that turns the drive shaft.

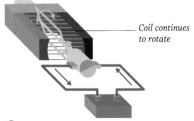

Coil's poles are repelled by magnet

Commutator reverses coil's current

Coil continues to rotate

❸ Reversing current
A component called a commutator reverses the electric current's direction every time the coil flips over.

❹ Poles repel
The coil's poles change with every turn, repelled and then attracted by the magnet, keeping it rotating in the same direction.

Electromagnetic waves

Electromagnetic waves, such as visible light, are changes (oscillations) in electric and magnetic fields, perfectly in sync but at right angles to each other.

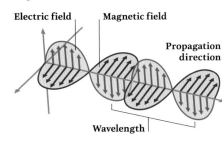

Electric field   Magnetic field

Propagation direction

Wavelength

see also Quantum mechanics pp.192–93 ▶   Nuclear and particle physics pp.194–95 ▶

Quantum mechanics

What is a quantum?

A "quantum" simply refers to the smallest possible amount of some physical quantity, such as energy, time, or angular momentum. For example, the smallest amount of electromagnetic energy (like visible light) is a photon. Quantization is at the core of quantum mechanics—the field of physics concerned with how nature behaves at the atomic and subatomic scales.

Uncertainty principle

On the quantum scale, there is a limit to the precision with which some pairs of physical properties can be measured. This is because the act of measuring a particle can disturb it, rendering other measurements less precise. One of these pairs is position and velocity—the more precisely a particle's position is known, the more uncertain its velocity is.

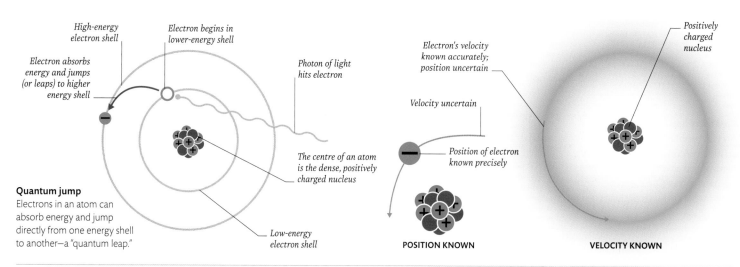

High-energy electron shell

Electron begins in lower-energy shell

Electron absorbs energy and jumps (or leaps) to higher energy shell

Photon of light hits electron

The centre of an atom is the dense, positively charged nucleus

Quantum jump
Electrons in an atom can absorb energy and jump directly from one energy shell to another—a "quantum leap."

Low-energy electron shell

Positively charged nucleus

Electron's velocity known accurately; position uncertain

Velocity uncertain

Position of electron known precisely

POSITION KNOWN

VELOCITY KNOWN

Quantum tunneling

On the quantum scale, objects can tunnel through energy barriers by momentarily "borrowing" energy from their surroundings. This is known as quantum tunneling, and it is fundamental to how nuclear fusion and some electronics work.

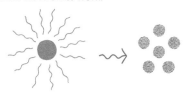

WAVES

PARTICLES

"**Particles** have **wavelike** properties."

ERWIN SCHRÖDINGER,
Austrian-Irish physicist, 1887–1961

Classical picture

Objects require a minimum amount of energy to surmount a barrier in classical mechanics. For example, an electron needs a certain amount of energy to penetrate a negatively-charged electric field. If it lacks this energy, the electron will be deflected by the barrier.

Quantum picture

In quantum mechanics, the uncertainty principle means that no position is absolutely certain or impossible for a subatomic particle, such as an electron. This means that there is the small possibility for a particle to exist on the opposite side of a barrier such as an electric field.

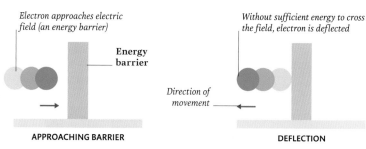

Electron approaches electric field (an energy barrier)

Energy barrier

Without sufficient energy to cross the field, electron is deflected

Direction of movement

APPROACHING BARRIER

DEFLECTION

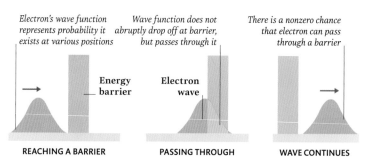

Electron's wave function represents probability it exists at various positions

Wave function does not abruptly drop off at barrier, but passes through it

There is a nonzero chance that electron can pass through a barrier

Energy barrier

Electron wave

REACHING A BARRIER

PASSING THROUGH

WAVE CONTINUES

Timeline

Quantum mechanics was born in the early 20th century, after physicists found that some phenomena could not be explained with classical physics. The quantum revolution marked a departure from the predictable "clockwork" models of the universe.

1900 Max Planck suggests that light could be quantized

1913 Niels Bohr presents atomic model with discrete electron energy levels

1926 Erwin Schrödinger publishes a vital equation describing quantum systems

1850

1930

1905 Albert Einstein explains the photoelectric effect using the concept of photons

1924 Louis de Broglie proposes that matter has wavelike properties

1927 Werner Heisenberg formulates the uncertainty principle describing quantum states

Quantum mechanics has **applications** in electronics, computing, and **medical imaging**

Schrödinger's equation

Schrödinger's equation predicts how the state of a quantum mechanical system (its wave function) develops over time, given an initial set of conditions. For instance, the equation can be used to calculate the probability of finding a particle at a certain point. Physicists have used the equation to build models of phenomena such as alpha decay (an element losing two protons and two neutrons to become another element).

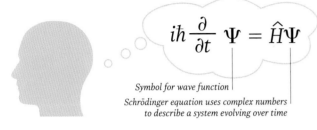

$$i\hbar \frac{\partial}{\partial t}\Psi = \hat{H}\Psi$$

Symbol for wave function

Schrödinger equation uses complex numbers to describe a system evolving over time

Quantum superposition

A superposition is a combination of multiple quantum states. Particles exist in a superposition until they are observed and adopt a definite state, causing its superposition to collapse.

UNDECIDED STATE

Many-worlds interpretation

Another interpretation of quantum mechanics proposes that—during quantum events—the universe splits into all of the alternate timelines for each possible outcome.

PARALLEL WORLDS

Schrödinger's cat

Quantum superposition can have bizarre implications. For example, a radioactive atom could be in a superposition of "not-decayed" and "decayed." In Schrödinger's thought experiment, decay prompts the release of poison, killing a captive cat. The only way to know if the cat is alive or dead is to look inside the box. As long as the system is unobserved, the cat is both dead and alive.

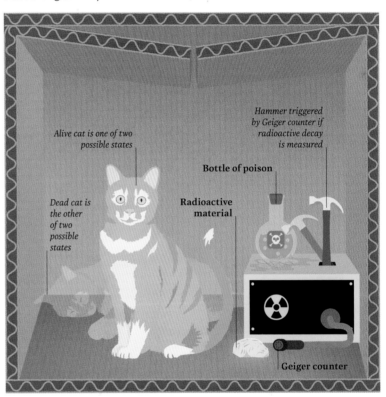

Alive cat is one of two possible states

Dead cat is the other of two possible states

Radioactive material

Hammer triggered by Geiger counter if radioactive decay is measured

Bottle of poison

Geiger counter

SCHRÖDINGER'S CAT THOUGHT EXPERIMENT

Quantum entanglement

Quantum entanglement occurs when pairs of particles become linked (entangled). When this happens, the state of one particle cannot be described independently of the other. This means that manipulating one particle instantly alters the other, even when the two particles are separated by vast distances.

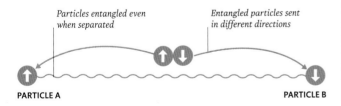

Particles entangled even when separated

Entangled particles sent in different directions

PARTICLE A   **PARTICLE B**

The **uncertainty principle** allows for **"virtual particles"** to **pop in and out of existence**

Quantum computers

A quantum computer uses quantum phenomena, such as superposition, to complete calculations. Although still in the early stages of development, they could become vastly more powerful than classical computers.

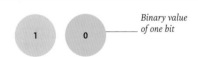

Binary value of one bit

Traditional bit
A bit—the basic unit of data in classical computing—can take on one of two values at a time: either a 0 or a 1.

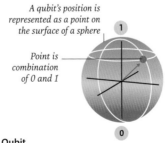

A qubit's position is represented as a point on the surface of a sphere

Point is combination of 0 and 1

Qubit
A qubit (quantum bit) is not limited to just two states—it can represent 0, 1, or a superposition of the two. This increases the amount of information it can carry.

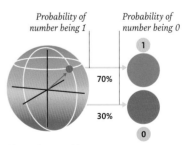

Probability of number being 1

Probability of number being 0

70%

30%

Measuring a cubit
A quantum computer measures the state of each qubit (the chance of it being 0 and the chance of it being 1) to produce a classical output: a 0 or a 1.

Nuclear and particle physics

For millennia, scientists and philosophers have sought to understand what the fundamental building blocks of matter are and how they work. Although atoms (meaning "indivisible") were long believed to be the smallest possible objects, 20th-century physics revealed a dazzling variety of particles hidden within the atom.

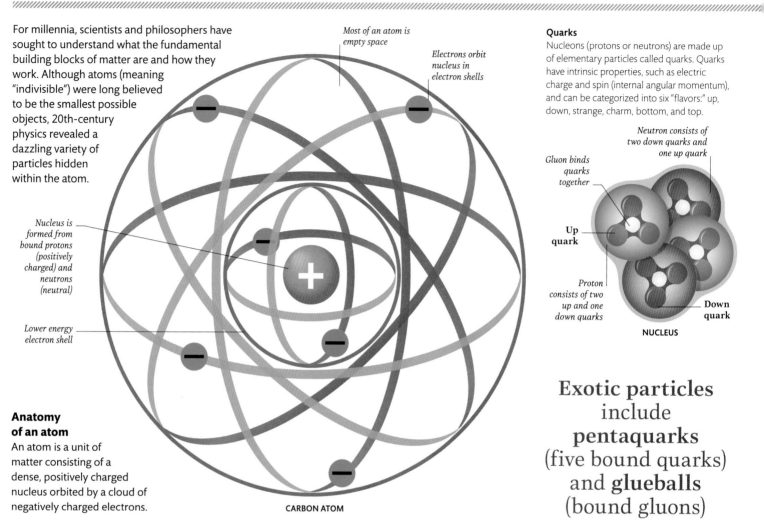

Most of an atom is empty space

Electrons orbit nucleus in electron shells

Nucleus is formed from bound protons (positively charged) and neutrons (neutral)

Lower energy electron shell

CARBON ATOM

Anatomy of an atom

An atom is a unit of matter consisting of a dense, positively charged nucleus orbited by a cloud of negatively charged electrons.

Quarks

Nucleons (protons or neutrons) are made up of elementary particles called quarks. Quarks have intrinsic properties, such as electric charge and spin (internal angular momentum), and can be categorized into six "flavors:" up, down, strange, charm, bottom, and top.

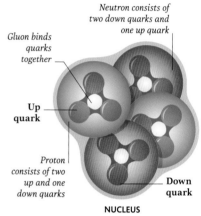

Neutron consists of two down quarks and one up quark

Gluon binds quarks together

Up quark

Proton consists of two up and one down quarks

Down quark

NUCLEUS

Exotic particles include pentaquarks (five bound quarks) and glueballs (bound gluons)

The subatomic world

Below the atomic scale there is a "particle zoo" of subatomic particles with all sorts of properties. Many natural phenomena can be attributed to the interactions between these particles.

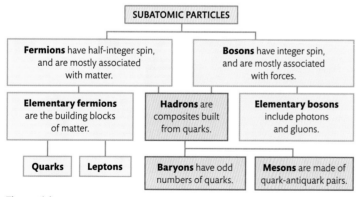

SUBATOMIC PARTICLES

Fermions have half-integer spin, and are mostly associated with matter.

Bosons have integer spin, and are mostly associated with forces.

Elementary fermions are the building blocks of matter.

Hadrons are composites built from quarks.

Elementary bosons include photons and gluons.

Quarks **Leptons**

Baryons have odd numbers of quarks.

Mesons are made of quark-antiquark pairs.

The particle zoo

Subatomic particles can be broadly separated into fermions and bosons, which obey different sets of rules. Some subatomic particles are elementary and others are composite particles.

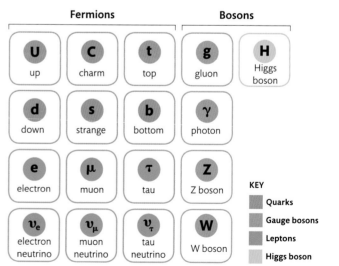

Fermions			Bosons	
U up	**C** charm	**t** top	**g** gluon	**H** Higgs boson
d down	**s** strange	**b** bottom	**γ** photon	
e electron	**μ** muon	**τ** tau	**Z** Z boson	
ν_e electron neutrino	**ν_μ** muon neutrino	**ν_τ** tau neutrino	**W** W boson	

KEY

- Quarks
- Gauge bosons
- Leptons
- Higgs boson

Standard model

The standard model is a framework classifying known elementary particles. All particles are divided according to their properties into fermions (the building blocks of matter) and bosons (force-carrying particles).

Gravity is the **weakest** of the four fundamental forces

Fundamental forces

All interactions in nature can be reduced to four fundamental types: the strong, weak, electromagnetic, and gravitational forces. Most of the fundamental interactions are carried by known "force carrier" particles.

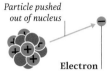

Strong force
- Strong force
- Neutron
- Proton

The strong force binds quarks (and nucleons) together. It is carried by gluons.

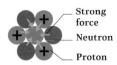

Particle pushed out of nucleus

Electron

Weak force
The weak force causes some types of radioactive decay. It is carried by W and Z bosons.

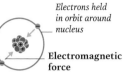

Electrons held in orbit around nucleus

Electromagnetic force

Electromagnetic force
This force is responsible for interactions between charged particles. It is carried by photons.

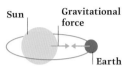

Sun / Gravitational force

Earth

Gravity
Gravity causes attraction between massive objects. It has no known force carrier.

The Higgs boson model

Particles gain mass by interacting with the Higgs field, an invisible energy field. Some particles interact strongly with it, causing them to slow down—like wading through quicksand—and gain a lot of mass. Others only interact weakly and gain less mass, and some, like photons, do not interact at all. The existence of the Higgs boson—the force carrier for the interaction—was confirmed by physicists in 2012.

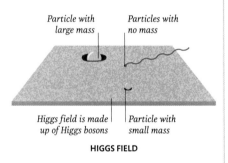

Particle with large mass

Particles with no mass

Higgs field is made up of Higgs bosons

Particle with small mass

HIGGS FIELD

Particle accelerators

Particle accelerators use electric fields to accelerate beams of charged particles to high energies and smash them apart. Particle accelerators allow physicists to create extreme conditions (including the moments after the Big Bang), and discover new phenomena and particles among the remains of collisions.

Large Hadron Collider
The Large Hadron Collider particle accelerator is the world's largest machine. Physicists use it for a huge range of experiments, including the successful search for the Higgs Boson.

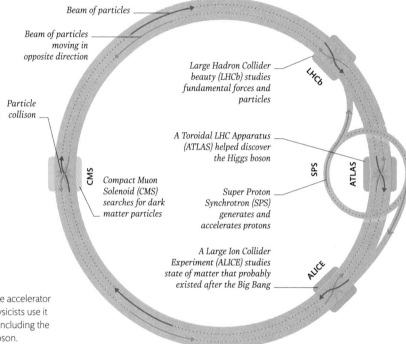

Beam of particles

Beam of particles moving in opposite direction

Particle collison

Large Hadron Collider beauty (LHCb) studies fundamental forces and particles

A Toroidal LHC Apparatus (ATLAS) helped discover the Higgs boson

Compact Muon Solenoid (CMS) searches for dark matter particles

Super Proton Synchrotron (SPS) generates and accelerates protons

A Large Ion Collider Experiment (ALICE) studies state of matter that probably existed after the Big Bang

LHCb

SPS ATLAS

ALICE

CMS

Radioactivity

Some atomic nuclei are radioactive—prone to break apart (decay) over time. These unstable nuclei have a different number of neutrons compared to stable nuclei of the same element. There are three main ways through which a nucleus emits radiation: alpha, beta, and gamma decay.

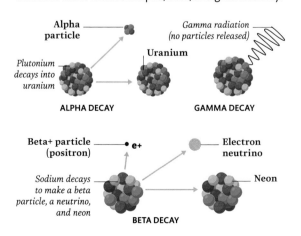

Alpha particle

Gamma radiation (no particles released)

Uranium

Plutonium decays into uranium

ALPHA DECAY

GAMMA DECAY

Beta+ particle (positron)

e+

Electron neutrino

Neon

Sodium decays to make a beta particle, a neutrino, and neon

BETA DECAY

Nuclear fission and fusion

Nuclear fission is the splitting of a heavy nucleus and nuclear fusion is the joining together of lighter nuclei; both processes release huge quantities of energy. Nuclear power stations harness nuclear fission (using Uranium-238) for power generation, although scientists hope to eventually be able to use nuclear fusion as a clean and sustainable energy source.

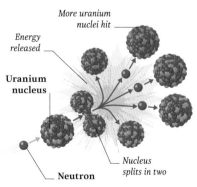

More uranium nuclei hit

Energy released

Uranium nucleus

Nucleus splits in two

Neutron

Fission of uranium
A neutron strikes the target nucleus, breaking it into two smaller nuclei and a handful of high-speed neutrons which strike other nuclei.

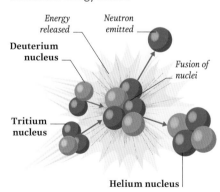

Energy released

Neutron emitted

Deuterium nucleus

Fusion of nuclei

Tritium nucleus

Helium nucleus

Formation of helium
Helium is produced through the fusion of two hydrogen nuclei (deuterium and tritium). This process sustains stars through most of their lifetimes.

Relativity and grand theories

In the 20th century, physicist Albert Einstein proposed his theories of special and general relativity, transforming our understanding of the universe. Relativity describes space and time as malleable and deeply entwined and predicts phenomena such as black holes and gravitational waves. Perhaps physics' greatest challenge is uniting relativity with its other great pillar—quantum mechanics—into a single "theory of everything."

Mass–energy equivalence

The famous equation E=mc² describes the interchangeable relationship between mass and energy. One of the consequences of this equivalence is that objects accelerated to near light speed gain mass.

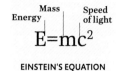

$$E=mc^2$$

EINSTEIN'S EQUATION

Special relativity

Special relativity addresses, among other things, contradictions in observations of the speed of light, which is constant regardless of your frame of reference. The theory explains this by saying objects moving faster through space move more slowly through time.

> "The distinction between **past**, **present**, and **future** only has the meaning of an **illusion**."
>
> ALBERT EINSTEIN, In a private letter

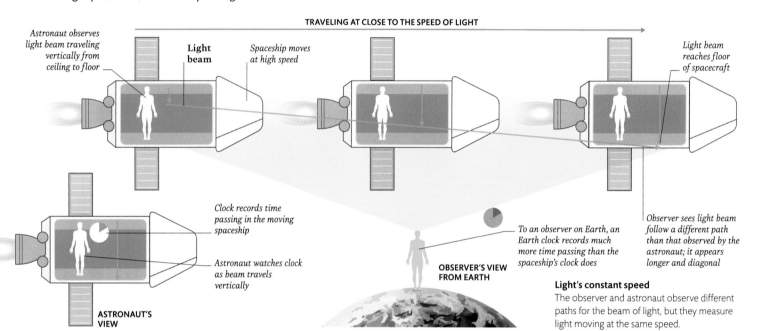

TRAVELING AT CLOSE TO THE SPEED OF LIGHT

Astronaut observes light beam traveling vertically from ceiling to floor

Light beam

Spaceship moves at high speed

Light beam reaches floor of spacecraft

Clock records time passing in the moving spaceship

Astronaut watches clock as beam travels vertically

ASTRONAUT'S VIEW

OBSERVER'S VIEW FROM EARTH

To an observer on Earth, an Earth clock records much more time passing than the spaceship's clock does

Observer sees light beam follow a different path than that observed by the astronaut; it appears longer and diagonal

Light's constant speed

The observer and astronaut observe different paths for the beam of light, but they measure light moving at the same speed.

General relativity

Einstein's theory of general relativity remodeled gravity to be compatible with special relativity, which closely links space and time. General relativity conceptualizes space-time as a continuum warped by massive objects, causing gravitational effects.

Gravity bends light

Warped space-time does not only affect objects such as stars, but also bends the path of light. Evidence for general relativity was obtained in 1919 when the apparent position of a star changed when the sun moved between the star and Earth.

Sun's gravity warps space-time

Star

Path of light from star

WARPING LIGHT

Star's apparent location

Space-time

Space and time can be combined into a four-dimensional concept in which objects move in three dimensions in space and one in time. This can be represented by stacking successive snapshots of space.

Equivalence principle

An important principle of general relativity is that the forcelike effects of acceleration and gravity are equivalent. They would be indistinguishable to someone inside an elevator, whether it is accelerating upward or in a gravitational field. Using this principle, Einstein realized that gravity affects light in the same way as acceleration, and that it does this by warping space-time.

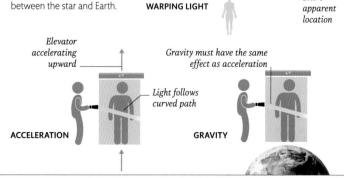

Elevator accelerating upward

Gravity must have the same effect as acceleration

Light follows curved path

ACCELERATION

GRAVITY

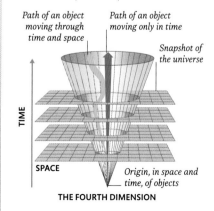

Path of an object moving through time and space

Path of an object moving only in time

Snapshot of the universe

TIME

SPACE

Origin, in space and time, of objects

THE FOURTH DIMENSION

There is a **black hole** at the core of the Milky Way
millions of times more massive than the **sun**

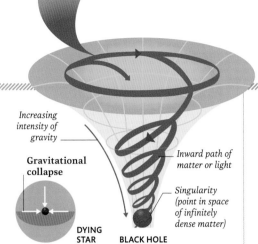

Increasing intensity of gravity

Gravitational collapse

Inward path of matter or light

Singularity (point in space of infinitely dense matter)

DYING STAR

BLACK HOLE

Black holes

Under general relativity, space-time can be distorted into a bottomless well by the remains of a collapsed giant star, forming an infinitely dense object—a black hole. Within a certain distance (the event horizon), nothing can escape its gravity.

Gravitational waves

Gravitational waves are ripples in space-time caused by extreme astronomical phenomena such as black hole collisions. Einstein predicted them in 1916 and physicists detected them a century later.

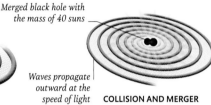

STRETCHING

SQUEEZING

DIRECTION OF WAVE

How waves are generated

As two black holes orbit each other, they lose orbital energy through gravitational waves. As they fall toward each other, they emit more intense gravitational waves.

How wave travels through space

The waves cause the distance between objects to fluctuate with the frequency of the wave. This can be detected only with very sensitive instruments.

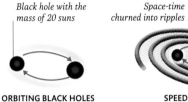

Black hole with the mass of 20 suns

ORBITING BLACK HOLES

Space-time churned into ripples

SPEED INCREASES

Merged black hole with the mass of 40 suns

Waves propagate outward at the speed of light

COLLISION AND MERGER

Theories of everything

Physicists suspect that the four fundamental forces of the universe were once a single force that split in the first fraction of a second after the Big Bang. They do not yet understand how this happened. If physicists could describe gravity in the same theoretical framework as the three nongravitational forces, which are understood in terms of quantum mechanics, they would find a holy grail of physics—a theory of everything.

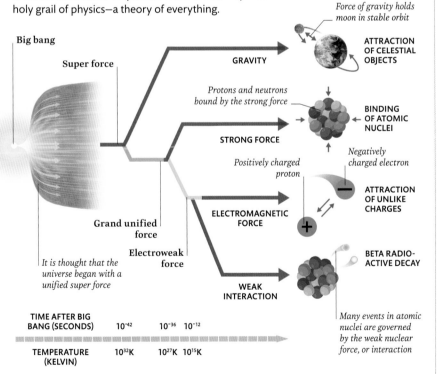

Big bang

Super force

It is thought that the universe began with a unified super force

Grand unified force

Electroweak force

Force of gravity holds moon in stable orbit

GRAVITY

ATTRACTION OF CELESTIAL OBJECTS

Protons and neutrons bound by the strong force

STRONG FORCE

BINDING OF ATOMIC NUCLEI

Positively charged proton

Negatively charged electron

ELECTROMAGNETIC FORCE

ATTRACTION OF UNLIKE CHARGES

WEAK INTERACTION

BETA RADIO-ACTIVE DECAY

Many events in atomic nuclei are governed by the weak nuclear force, or interaction

TIME AFTER BIG BANG (SECONDS)	10^{-42}	10^{-36}	10^{-12}
TEMPERATURE (KELVIN)	10^{32}K	10^{27}K	10^{15}K

Relativity teaches us the **connection** between the **different descriptions** of one and the same **reality**

ALBERT EINSTEIN

Albert Einstein (1879–1955) was a German-born physicist and one of history's greatest scientists. His achievements include contributions to quantum and statistical mechanics, in addition to his theories of relativity. He moved to Switzerland to study as a young man and later settled in the US. He was awarded the 1921 Nobel Prize in Physics.

String theory

String theory models particles as one-dimensional "strings," which vibrate at different frequencies like the strings of an instrument. It is a candidate theory of everything, although it has been criticized for its lack of falsifiability—it seems impossible to disprove.

Filaments of energy

The strings in string theory are filaments of nearly the shortest length possible. They can be open or closed (a ring), and their properties are determined by their multidimensional vibrations.

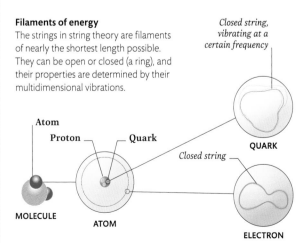

Closed string, vibrating at a certain frequency

Atom

Proton

Quark

QUARK

Closed string

MOLECULE

ATOM

ELECTRON

States of matter

A substance can exist in three different states: solid, liquid, or gas. For example, water can be ice, liquid water, or steam, and transforming water from one to the other does not alter its chemical formula. Water is a liquid at room temperature, but other elements and compounds may be solid or gaseous at room temperature.

Adding salt to ice slightly lowers the **melting point** of water

Molecules exert pressure on the surfaces they hit

A gas can form into a solid by the process of deposition

DEPOSITION

SUBLIMATION

Molecules move in any direction

Gas
In a gas, the molecules are not connected to their neighbors and are free to move. As a result, a gas spreads out to fill any container and can be any shape or volume.

Molecules break free from one another and become gases

EVAPORATION

CONDENSATION

Strong bonds create a high melting point

Solids can sublimate into a gas, bypassing the liquid state

Gas molecules cluster together to form droplets of liquid

A liquid takes the shape of its container

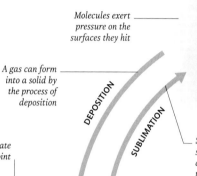

Changing states of matter
Materials change state as they gain or lose energy. Solid is the low-energy state; warming it makes it melt into a liquid, which in turn boils into a gas. Melting and boiling points are specific to each substance.

Molecules cling together

Bonds make the solid rigid

Shape of solid is fixed

Liquid
About one in ten of the molecules in a liquid have broken free of the bonds that connected it to its neighbors. As a result of this, a liquid can flow into any shape. However, its volume remains fixed.

Solid
In a solid, each molecule is securely bonded to its neighbors. This creates a structure that has a fixed shape and volume. Adding heat to a solid will make the bonds vibrate more until they begin to break.

Heating a solid breaks bonds, making a liquid

Cooling liquid closes broken bonds

FREEZING

MELTING

Exotic states of matter
Substances can take on exotic states of matter but in changing into them, both their chemical and physical natures are altered. Heating gas can create plasma; cooling substances to very low temperatures creates strange condensates where all of the atoms merge into a single entity.

This glow is plasma made by electrifying gases

PLASMA BALL

Gas at room temperature
When cool, the gas atoms are not charged. They exert only small forces on each other and do not conduct electricity.

Atom

Electrons orbit nucleus

Atoms are electrically neutral

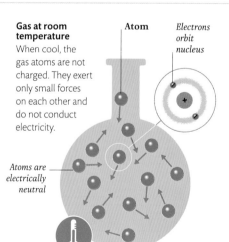

Charged plasma
At high temperatures, the extreme energy breaks atoms into positively charged ions and negatively charged electrons, forming a conductive plasma.

Atom

Electron is not bound to nucleus

Electrons and ions are free to move

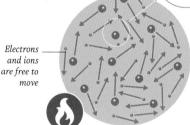

◀ **see also Light and matter** pp.188–89   ◀ **Nuclear and particle physics** pp.194–95

Gas laws

The temperature, volume, and pressure of a gas are all related to each other. If one measure changes and a second stays constant, the third will always change in proportion to the first. These relationships are described by the three gas laws, each named after its discoverer.

HEAT AND GAS

At the atomic level, heat (measured as temperature) is the motion of atoms. As materials get hotter, their atoms move faster. In a gas, hotter molecules move faster, spread out in all directions, and hit surfaces more often.

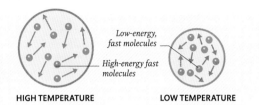

Low-energy, fast molecules

High-energy fast molecules

HIGH TEMPERATURE   **LOW TEMPERATURE**

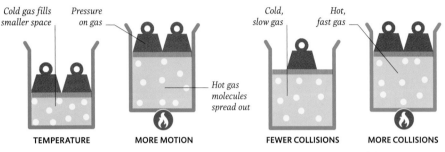

Pressure pushing on gas   *Dispersed molecules*   *Double the pressure*   *Compressed molecules*

DIFFUSION   **PRESSURE**

Cold gas fills smaller space   *Pressure on gas*

Hot gas molecules spread out

TEMPERATURE   **MORE MOTION**

Cold, slow gas   *Hot, fast gas*

FEWER COLLISIONS   **MORE COLLISIONS**

Boyle's law

This law says that gas pressure is inversely proportional to volume. Doubling the pressure will halve the volume, if the temperature stays constant.

Charles's law

This law states that heating a gas will increase the volume. Heat makes molecules move faster and if the pressure is to stay constant they need more space.

Gay-Lussac's law

If the volume is kept constant, then the pressure of a gas is proportional to the temperature. When the temperature of a gas increases, so does the pressure.

Crystalline and amorphous solids

The atoms in a solid are all linked together to form a rigid structure. When that structure follows a repeating pattern, the solid is classified as a crystal. Noncrystalline or amorphous solids have no repeating atomic structure.

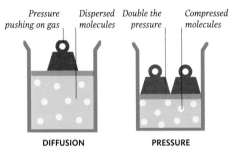

Regular pattern of atoms and molecules

Crystal lattice pattern

SALT

SUGAR

SAND

Crystalline solids

Examples of crystalline solids include individual grains of salt, sugar, and sand, which are all made from units that repeat as a crystal lattice.

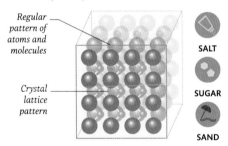

Irregular pattern of atoms and molecules

Random tangle of bonds

GLASS

RUBBER

BUTTER

Amorphous solids

Unlike crystalline solids, amorphous solids lack long-range order. Although rubber can be stretched or compressed, it will not take the shape of its container or flow.

Viscosity of liquids

The ability of a liquid to flow is described as its viscosity. A highly viscous liquid flows slowly in a single stream. A liquid with low viscosity flows quickly and splashes and drips easily. Viscosity depends on properties like the size of molecules and the bond strength between molecules.

Water has low viscosity

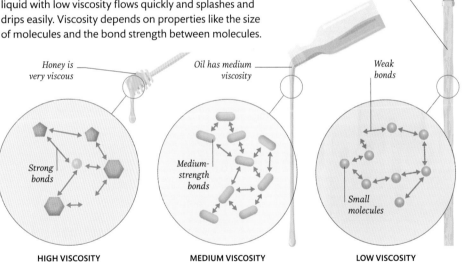

Honey is very viscous

Oil has medium viscosity

Weak bonds

Strong bonds

Medium-strength bonds

Small molecules

HIGH VISCOSITY   **MEDIUM VISCOSITY**   **LOW VISCOSITY**

Tar pitch, a highly viscous liquid, takes **several years** to **form a single drop** in room temperature

NON-NEWTONIAN FLUIDS

Non-Newtonian fluids are strange fluids that have a variable viscosity that depends on how much force is applied to them. Examples include toothpaste, suspensions of corn starch in water, quicksand, and even blood plasma.

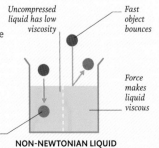

Uncompressed liquid has low viscosity   *Fast object bounces*

Slow object sinks   *Force makes liquid viscous*

NON-NEWTONIAN LIQUID

see also The periodic table pp.200–201 ▶   Mixtures, compounds, solvents, and solutions pp.204–205 ▶   Organic chemistry pp.208–209 ▶   **199**

The periodic table

The periodic table is a chart that shows all of the chemical elements together, and it uses a system that allows chemists to predict the likely properties of each substance at a glance from its position in the table. An element's physical and chemical properties are dependent on the unique structure of its atoms. The table arranges the elements in order of atomic number, which increases in line with the structural complexity of each element's atoms. The table is the result of many contributions over the past 230 years, although its chief architect is the Russian chemist Dmitri Mendeleev, who published his version in 1869.

KEY

- Hydrogen—a reactive gas

REACTIVE METALS

- Alkali metals—soft, very reactive metals
- Alkaline earth metals—moderately reactive metals

TRANSITION ELEMENTS

- Transition metals—a varied group of metals, many with valuable properties

MAINLY NON-METALS

- Metalloids—elements with properties between those of metals and nonmetals
- Other metals—mostly relatively soft metals with low melting points
- Carbon and other nonmetals
- Halogens—very reactive nonmetals
- Noble gases—colorless, very unreactive gases

RARE EARTH METALS

- Also called lanthanoids (57–71) and actinoids (89–103), these are reactive metals—some are rare or synthetic

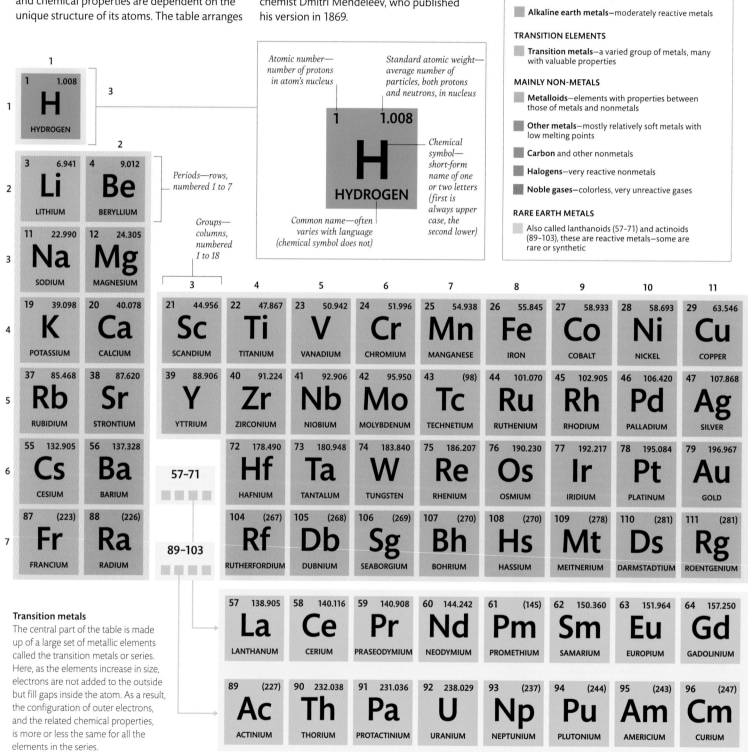

Atomic number—number of protons in atom's nucleus

Standard atomic weight—average number of particles, both protons and neutrons, in nucleus

Chemical symbol—short-form name of one or two letters (first is always upper case, the second lower)

Common name—often varies with language (chemical symbol does not)

Periods—rows, numbered 1 to 7

Groups—columns, numbered 1 to 18

Transition metals

The central part of the table is made up of a large set of metallic elements called the transition metals or series. Here, as the elements increase in size, electrons are not added to the outside but fill gaps inside the atom. As a result, the configuration of outer electrons, and the related chemical properties, is more or less the same for all the elements in the series.

Periods and groups

The elements are ordered by increasing atomic number—that is, increasing number of protons in the nucleus—and as they grow, the number of electrons also goes up. Electrons sit in shells, which have a fixed amount of space. When one shell is filled, a new one starts. A row, or period, represents the elements with the same number of electron shells in their atoms. Period 1 contains just two elements because the innermost electron shell holds just two electrons. A new shell starts to fill in period 2, and holds eight electrons, while period 7 has 32 elements. Once in their rows, the elements also form columns, or groups, containing elements that have the same number of outer electrons. These electrons are involved in making chemical bonds, and so members of a group all react in similar ways.

DMITRI MENDELEEV

Russian chemist Mendeleev (1834–1907) developed the periodic table in 1869 with no knowledge of atomic structure. Instead, he ordered elements according to valence or combining power.

An extended version of this table recognizes **synthetic elements** with **atomic numbers** up to **118**

					18
					2 4.003 **He** HELIUM
13	14	15	16	17	
5 10.810 **B** BORON	6 12.011 **C** CARBON	7 14.007 **N** NITROGEN	8 15.999 **O** OXYGEN	9 18.998 **F** FLUORINE	10 20.180 **Ne** NEON
13 226.982 **Al** ALUMINUM	14 28.085 **Si** SILICON	15 30.974 **P** PHOSPHORUS	16 32.060 **S** SULFUR	17 35.450 **Cl** CHLORINE	18 39.948 **Ar** ARGON

12						
30 65.380 **Zn** ZINC	31 69.723 **Ga** GALLIUM	32 72.630 **Ge** GERMANIUM	33 74.922 **As** ARSENIC	34 78.971 **Se** SELENIUM	35 79.904 **Br** BROMINE	36 83.798 **Kr** KRYPTON
48 112.414 **Cd** CADMIUM	49 114.818 **In** INDIUM	50 118.710 **Sn** TIN	51 121.760 **Sb** ANTIMONY	52 127.600 **Te** TELLURIUM	53 126.904 **I** IODINE	54 131.293 **XE** XENON
80 200.592 **Hg** MERCURY	81 204.380 **Tl** THALLIUM	82 207.200 **Pb** LEAD	83 208.980 **Bi** BISMUTH	84 (209) **Po** POLONIUM	85 (210) **At** ASTATINE	86 (222) **Rn** RADON
112 (285) **Cn** COPERNICIUM	113 (286) **Nh** NIHONIUM	114 (289) **Fl** FLEROVIUM	115 (289) **Mc** MOSCOVIUM	116 (293) **Lv** LIVERMORIUM	117 (294) **Ts** TENNESSINE	118 (294) **Og** OGANESSON

65 158.925 **Tb** TERBIUM	66 162.500 **Dy** DYSPROSIUM	67 164.930 **Ho** HOLMIUM	68 167.259 **Er** ERBIUM	69 168.934 **Tm** THULIUM	70 173.055 **Yb** YTTERBIUM	71 174.967 **Lu** LUTETIUM
97 (247) **Bk** BERKELIUM	98 (251) **Cf** CALIFORNIUM	99 (252) **Es** EINSTEINIUM	100 (257) **Fm** FERMIUM	101 (258) **Md** MENDELEVIUM	102 (259) **No** NOBELIUM	103 (262) **Lr** LAWRENCIUM

ALLOTROPES OF CARBON

When pure, the atoms of an element may link together in more than one way, creating alternative forms called allotropes. Carbon has four main allotropes, shown below. These are all pure carbon, but their differing internal structures gives them varied and useful properties.

Diamond

Each atom forms a bond with four of its neighbors, thus creating a repeating tetrahedral structure. The crystal lattice is very rigid and equally strong in all directions, making diamond the hardest substance known.

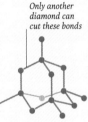

Only another diamond can cut these bonds

Graphite

The atoms are arranged in weakly linked sheets of hexagons that slide over one another. Each atom has just three bonds; the fourth electron wanders through the sheet, which enables graphite to conduct electricity.

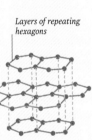

Layers of repeating hexagons

Graphene

Made up of a single sheet of graphite, graphene is incredibly thin but very strong and resistant to tearing, and can be rolled into fibers. Chemical engineers are developing graphene for use in electronics and nanotechnology.

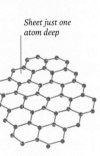

Sheet just one atom deep

Fullerenes

Also known as a buckyball, the basic fullerene contains 60 carbon atoms organized like the surface of a soccer ball. Larger forms with 72, 76, 84, and even 100 atoms are possible but less stable.

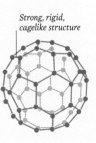

Strong, rigid, cagelike structure

see also Molecules, ions, and bonds pp.202–203 ▶

Molecules, ions, and bonds

A molecule is two or more atoms connected by at least one shared pair of electrons, which is known as a covalent bond. The atoms may be the same, as is the case for chlorine (Cl_2) or oxygen (O_2), or different, as in water (H_2O) or ethanol (CH_3CH_2OH). Atoms can also lose and gain electrons to form ions and ionic bonds. Substances formed this way, for example table salt (NaCl), are not molecules—they are called ionic compounds.

Electron shells

Electrons exist in "shells" around the nucleus of an atom. Other than in noble gas atoms, the electron shell farthest from the nucleus is only partially filled, and the electrons in these shells may be shared to form covalent bonds, or gained or lost to form ions.

KEY

⊖ Electron

Magnesium's electron shells
The first two electron shells in a magnesium atom are full. The outermost shell is unfilled, containing only two electrons.

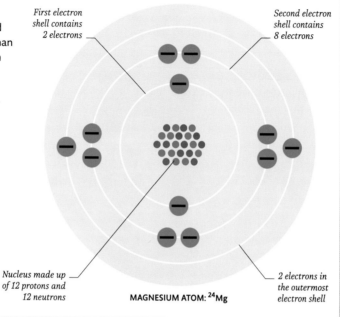

First electron shell contains 2 electrons

Second electron shell contains 8 electrons

Nucleus made up of 12 protons and 12 neutrons

2 electrons in the outermost electron shell

MAGNESIUM ATOM: ^{24}Mg

Covalent bonds

A covalent bond is a shared pair of electrons between atoms. By sharing, each effectively acquires a full outer shell.

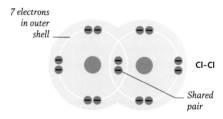

7 electrons in outer shell

Cl–Cl

Shared pair

Single bond
Each chlorine atom has seven electrons in its outer shell. The shared pair means both have a share in eight (a full outer shell).

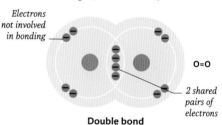

Electrons not involved in bonding

O=O

2 shared pairs of electrons

Double bond
Each oxygen atom has six electrons in its outer shell. Four electrons (two pairs) are shared to form a double bond.

What is an ion?

Ions have positive or negative charges. They form when atoms gain or lose electrons. Because the number of (negative) electrons is no longer equal to the number of (positive) protons, the charges are unbalanced. When there are more electrons, the result is a negative ion. When there are fewer electrons than protons, a positively charged ion is formed.

Sodium ion
A neutral sodium atom has 11 electrons in total, but only one electron in its outermost electron shell. This outermost electron is easily lost, turning it into a positively charged sodium ion, written as Na⁺.

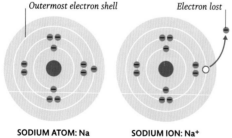

Outermost electron shell

Electron lost

SODIUM ATOM: Na

SODIUM ION: Na⁺

Chloride ion
A neutral chlorine atom has seven electrons in its outermost electron shell. This shell has the capacity to hold eight electrons, so chlorine readily gains an electron to form a negatively charged ion (Cl⁻).

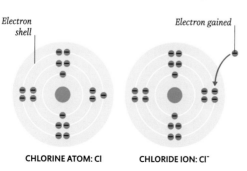

Electron shell

Electron gained

CHLORINE ATOM: Cl

CHLORIDE ION: Cl⁻

Ionic bonding

Ionic bonds form because of the interaction between positive and negative ions. Often metal ions (positive) and non-metal ions (negative) are involved. Positive and negative ions are attracted to each other, forming a lattice of ionic bonds. It takes a lot of energy to disrupt all of these attractions, so ionic compounds often have high melting points.

❶ Electron transfer
The ionic compound sodium chloride (NaCl) forms when sodium atoms lose their outermost electron to form sodium ions (Na+), and chlorine atoms gain those electrons to form chloride ions (Cl-).

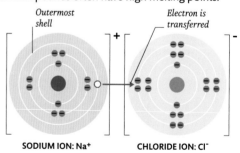

Outermost shell

Electron is transferred

SODIUM ION: Na⁺

CHLORIDE ION: Cl⁻

❷ Ionic bond formed
An ionic bond is an electrostatic attraction between positive and negative ions. Ionic bonds do not exist alone—an ionic compound is a repeating, 3D lattice of positive and negative ions. The formula is the smallest repeating unit.

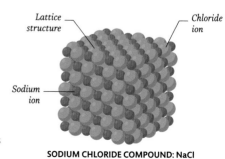

Lattice structure

Chloride ion

Sodium ion

SODIUM CHLORIDE COMPOUND: NaCl

Iron is Earth's **most abundant element** by mass, at more than **30 percent**, but **aluminum** is the most **plentiful metal** in the crust at **8 percent**

Metallic bonding

The atoms of metallic elements lose their electrons easily. Inside solid metal, the electrons become "delocalized," belonging to all the atoms at once. The resulting metal ions are held in place within a "sea" of these delocalized electrons. This metallic bonding gives rise to the properties of metals.

Properties of metals

Metals are good conductors of heat and electricity and are shiny, ductile, malleable, and sonorous (ring when hit). Many have high melting and boiling points.

Alloys

An alloy is a mixture of elements, at least one of which is a metal. Through experimentation or design, scientists have created many alloys, with useful properties, such as extreme hardness or high melting points.

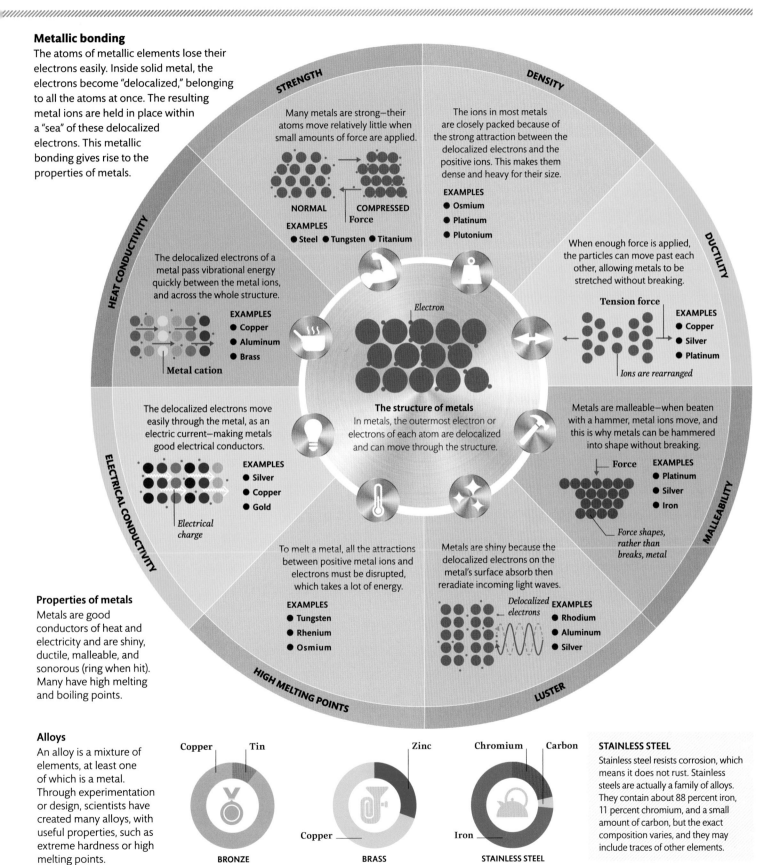

STRENGTH

Many metals are strong—their atoms move relatively little when small amounts of force are applied.

NORMAL   COMPRESSED
Force
EXAMPLES
● Steel ● Tungsten ● Titanium

DENSITY

The ions in most metals are closely packed because of the strong attraction between the delocalized electrons and the positive ions. This makes them dense and heavy for their size.

EXAMPLES
● Osmium
● Platinum
● Plutonium

HEAT CONDUCTIVITY

The delocalized electrons of a metal pass vibrational energy quickly between the metal ions, and across the whole structure.

EXAMPLES
● Copper
● Aluminum
● Brass

Metal cation

DUCTILITY

When enough force is applied, the particles can move past each other, allowing metals to be stretched without breaking.

Tension force

EXAMPLES
● Copper
● Silver
● Platinum

Ions are rearranged

Electron

The structure of metals
In metals, the outermost electron or electrons of each atom are delocalized and can move through the structure.

ELECTRICAL CONDUCTIVITY

The delocalized electrons move easily through the metal, as an electric current—making metals good electrical conductors.

EXAMPLES
● Silver
● Copper
● Gold

Electrical charge

MALLEABILITY

Metals are malleable—when beaten with a hammer, metal ions move, and this is why metals can be hammered into shape without breaking.

Force

EXAMPLES
● Platinum
● Silver
● Iron

Force shapes, rather than breaks, metal

HIGH MELTING POINTS

To melt a metal, all the attractions between positive metal ions and electrons must be disrupted, which takes a lot of energy.

EXAMPLES
● Tungsten
● Rhenium
● Osmium

LUSTER

Metals are shiny because the delocalized electrons on the metal's surface absorb then reradiate incoming light waves.

Delocalized electrons

EXAMPLES
● Rhodium
● Aluminum
● Silver

Alloys

Copper   Tin

BRONZE

Zinc

Copper

BRASS

Chromium   Carbon

Iron

STAINLESS STEEL

STAINLESS STEEL
Stainless steel resists corrosion, which means it does not rust. Stainless steels are actually a family of alloys. They contain about 88 percent iron, 11 percent chromium, and a small amount of carbon, but the exact composition varies, and they may include traces of other elements.

see also Mixtures, compounds, solvents, and solutions pp.204–205 ▶ Chemical reactions pp.206–207 ▶ **203**

Mixtures, compounds, solvents, and solutions

The substances all around us are rarely made of one single element. Different atoms bond to form compounds, and different compounds (and sometimes elements) can be combined to form mixtures. Many of the most familiar "liquid" substances are actually solutions, where one substance is dissolved in another. Tap water, for example, typically contains sodium, calcium, and chloride ions dissolved in water.

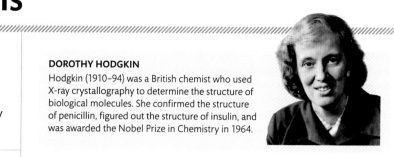

DOROTHY HODGKIN
Hodgkin (1910–94) was a British chemist who used X-ray crystallography to determine the structure of biological molecules. She confirmed the structure of penicillin, figured out the structure of insulin, and was awarded the Nobel Prize in Chemistry in 1964.

Mixtures

A mixture contains substances that are not chemically bonded to each other. For example, if iron and sulfur are combined at room temperature, the sulfur does not become chemically bonded to the iron. The particles are randomly arranged, and the substances can be easily separated with a magnet.

IRON FILINGS   **SULFUR**   **MIXTURE**

IRON AND SULFUR MIXTURE

Elements in a mixture
Sulfur forms molecules containing eight atoms (S_8). These atoms are covalently bonded to each other (they share a pair of electrons), but in a mixture of iron and sulfur there are no bonds between the sulfur and the iron.

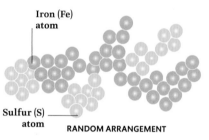

Iron (Fe) atom

Sulfur (S) atom

RANDOM ARRANGEMENT

EVERYDAY MIXTURES
The Earth's atmosphere is a mixture of nitrogen, oxygen, argon, carbon dioxide, and other gases. It also contains varying amounts of water, depending on weather conditions. Clouds, a type of colloid (see below), form when tiny drops of liquid water are dispersed in the air.

Compounds

A compound contains two or more elements chemically combined. For example, if a mixture of iron and sulfur is heated, a chemical reaction occurs and iron (II) sulfide, a compound, forms with chemical bonds between iron and sulfur. It takes a lot of energy to split this compound into pure iron and pure sulfur.

IRON FILINGS   **SULFUR**   **HEAT**   **COMPOUND**

IRON AND SULFUR COMPOUND

Elements in a compound
Iron (II) sulfide is a chemical compound containing iron ions (Fe^{2+}) and sulfide ions (S^{2-}). The differently charged ions (see p.202) are attracted electrostatically and they form a repeating pattern with a consistent formula (FeS).

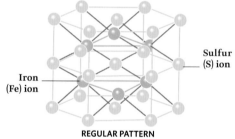

Sulfur (S) ion

Iron (Fe) ion

REGULAR PATTERN

When **eggs are overcooked,** the surface of the **yolk** turns **greenish** due to the formation of **iron (II) sulfide**

Types of mixtures

In a mixture, the substances might be loosely mixed, as in mud, or intimately associated, as in a solution. A colloid is an intermediate state between these two. One way to identify types of mixtures is to shine a beam of bright light at them. The light will pass straight through a solution if the solute is completely dissolved in the solvent. However, in colloids and suspensions, light is scattered by particles suspended in the liquid.

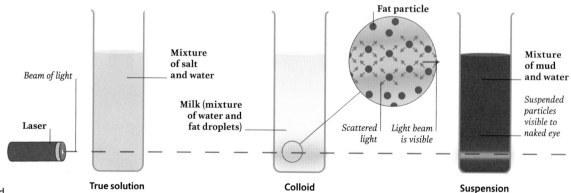

Fat particle

Beam of light

Laser

Mixture of salt and water

Milk (mixture of water and fat droplets)

Scattered light

Light beam is visible

Mixture of mud and water

Suspended particles visible to naked eye

True solution
If the solute (in this case, salt) is completely dissolved in the solvent (in this case, water) the solution is transparent, meaning light passes through.

Colloid
Colloids, such as milk, have tiny particles dispersed in a fluid, but not dissolved. The suspended particles will reflect light shone through the mixture.

Suspension
Larger particles suspended in liquid tend to separate out over time, and the mixture is more likely to be completely opaque, meaning no light passes through.

◄ **see also States of matter** pp.198–99   ◄ **The periodic table** pp.200–201   ◄ **Molecules, ions, and bonds** pp.202–203

During "dry" cleaning, garments are soaked in a nonpolar solvent, which **dissolves** oily (nonpolar) stains

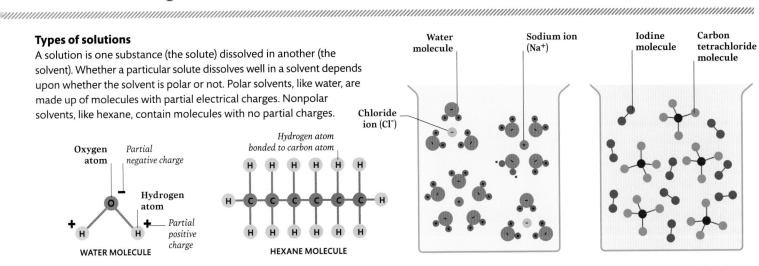

Types of solutions

A solution is one substance (the solute) dissolved in another (the solvent). Whether a particular solute dissolves well in a solvent depends upon whether the solvent is polar or not. Polar solvents, like water, are made up of molecules with partial electrical charges. Nonpolar solvents, like hexane, contain molecules with no partial charges.

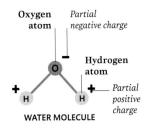

Oxygen atom *Partial negative charge*
Hydrogen atom
Partial positive charge
WATER MOLECULE

Polar solvent
Water is polar: oxygen attracts bonding electrons more than hydrogen, so oxygen has a partial negative charge, and the hydrogens have partial positive charges.

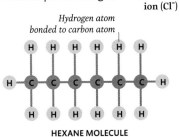

Hydrogen atom bonded to carbon atom
HEXANE MOLECULE

Nonpolar solvent
Hexane is nonpolar: the atoms have similar electronegativities (tendency to attract bonding electrons), so overall there are no partial charges.

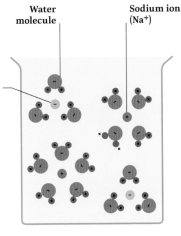

Water molecule **Sodium ion (Na$^+$)** **Iodine molecule** **Carbon tetrachloride molecule**

Chloride ion (Cl$^-$)

Ionic solute in polar solvent
An ionic solute, such as salt (NaCl), dissolves well in a polar solvent. The ions are attracted to the partial charges on the water molecules.

Nonpolar solute in nonpolar solvent
Nonpolar molecules will not dissolve in a polar solvent like water, because there are no electric charges for the water to attract—but they will dissolve well in a nonpolar solvent.

Solubility

Solid, liquid, and gaseous substances (solutes) can dissolve in other substances (solvents). This property is called solubility. How soluble a solute is in a solvent depends on various conditions, such as temperature and pressure. Generally, solids are more soluble in warmer liquids, while gases are more soluble in cooler liquids. The maximum amount of solute that will dissolve in a given amount of solvent at a specific pressure and temperature is called its saturation point.

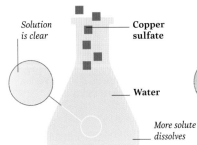

Solution is clear **Copper sulfate**
Water
More solute dissolves

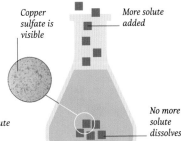

Copper sulfate is visible *More solute added*
No more solute dissolves

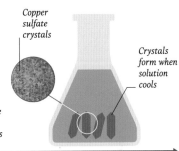

Copper sulfate crystals
Crystals form when solution cools

INCREASING CONCENTRATION

Unsaturated solution
When a small amount of solute, in this case solid copper sulfate, is added to water, it dissolves easily and completely, which means the solution is unsaturated.

Saturated solution
If more copper sulfate is added, eventually it stops dissolving and solid particles remain visible. This is called a saturated solution.

Supersaturated solution
If the solution is heated, even more solute will dissolve—this is called supersaturation. As the solution cools, crystals form as the solute solidifies out of the solution.

Transition metals

Transition metals are a large group of elements found in the middle of the periodic table. They have variable oxidation states, which means they can form ions with different positive charges. They also form ionic compounds that dissolve in water, with different ions producing different colors. They have a range of properties and uses, and some are good catalysts (see p.206). Vanadium is a particularly interesting transition metal because it has a wide range of oxidation states and colors.

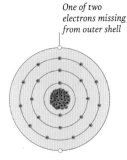

One of two electrons missing from outer shell

Vanadium 2+
The color of the solution depends on how many electrons the atom has lost. Solutions containing vanadium 2+ ions are violet in color.

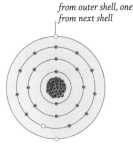

Two electrons missing from outer shell, one from next shell

Vanadium 3+
The different colors are caused by the ways light interacts with the varying number of electrons. In this case, the solution is green.

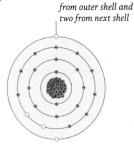

Two electrons missing from outer shell and two from next shell

Vanadium 4+
Solutions containing vanadium 4+ ions are blue. Vanadium oxides are sometimes used to give glass a blue or green tint.

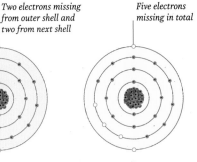

Five electrons missing in total

Vanadium 5+
Vanadium pentoxide is used as a catalyst in manufacturing sulfuric acid and in making ceramics. Solutions containing vanadium 5+ ions are yellow.

see also Chemical reactions pp.206–207 ▶ Chemical techniques pp.210–11 ▶

Chemical reactions

A chemical reaction is a process by which two or more chemical substances change to form new kinds of substances. The substances present before and after a reaction can be elements or compounds, and in every chemical reaction, bonds between atoms are broken or made. The number of atoms, and so the total mass of substance, remains the same.

Cesium is so reactive it explodes on contact with water

Reactants and products

The starting materials of a chemical reaction are called the reactants. The reaction transforms them into a new substance called the product. The reaction does not create or destroy atoms.

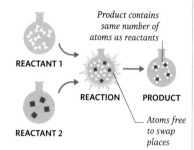

Product contains same number of atoms as reactants

REACTANT 1

REACTION   PRODUCT

REACTANT 2

Atoms free to swap places

Energetics of chemical reactions

Chemical reactions need an input of energy to start, which is called the activation energy and is normally applied as heat. The making of bonds between the reactants also releases energy, in the form of heat.

Exothermic reaction
Mixing the reactants to create a product releases more energy than is absorbed during this type of reaction.

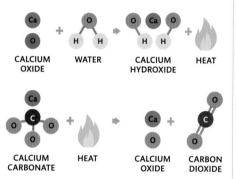

CALCIUM OXIDE   WATER   CALCIUM HYDROXIDE   HEAT

Endothermic reaction
Breaking up the reactant requires more energy to be absorbed than is released during this type of reaction.

CALCIUM CARBONATE   HEAT   CALCIUM OXIDE   CARBON DIOXIDE

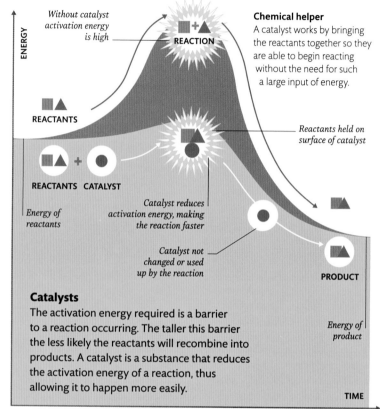

Without catalyst activation energy is high

ENERGY

REACTION

REACTANTS

REACTANTS   CATALYST

Energy of reactants

Catalyst reduces activation energy, making the reaction faster

Catalyst not changed or used up by the reaction

Chemical helper
A catalyst works by bringing the reactants together so they are able to begin reacting without the need for such a large input of energy.

Reactants held on surface of catalyst

PRODUCT

Energy of product

TIME

Catalysts

The activation energy required is a barrier to a reaction occurring. The taller this barrier the less likely the reactants will recombine into products. A catalyst is a substance that reduces the activation energy of a reaction, thus allowing it to happen more easily.

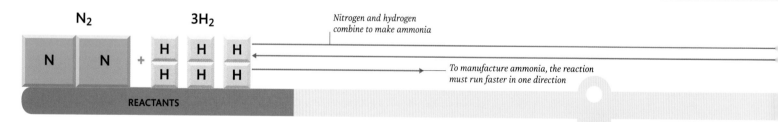

N_2 $3H_2$

N   N   +   H H H / H H H

Nitrogen and hydrogen combine to make ammonia

To manufacture ammonia, the reaction must run faster in one direction

REACTANTS

Dynamic equilibrium

In principle, all chemical reactions are reversible: products can react to remake the reactants, since all the atoms are still present. Many simple reactions do proceed easily in either direction. There is a point called equilibrium, however, at which a reaction is proceeding at equal speed in both directions. That equilibrium is dynamic: it can change, depending upon conditions such as temperature, pressure, and the concentration of the reactants and products.

Equilibrium can only be achieved in a closed system—a canned fizzy drink is in equilibrium until the can is opened

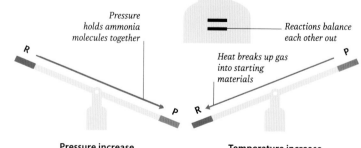

Pressure holds ammonia molecules together

Reactions balance each other out

Heat breaks up gas into starting materials

R   P

P   R

Pressure increase
An increase in pressure tips the balance toward more ammonia being manufactured.

Temperature increase
Adding more heat energy reduces the amount of ammonia as the extra energy enables more decomposition.

An **enzyme** is a **powerful biological catalyst** that **accelerates a specific chemical reaction** by a **factor** of as much as a **million or more**

Types of reactions

Chemists organize reactions into different types depending on what kinds of changes are occurring. Chemical reactions can be used to create, or synthesize, new compounds, or reduce a compound into pure elements.

Synthesis
In this reaction, two or more reactants combine to make a single product. These reactions often have a low activation energy.

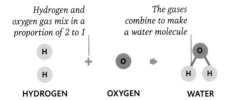

Hydrogen and oxygen gas mix in a proportion of 2 to 1

The gases combine to make a water molecule

HYDROGEN OXYGEN WATER

Decomposition
In this reaction, a single reactant breaks apart into two or more products. Often heat is required for the reaction to work.

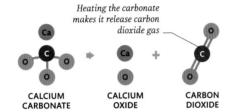

Heating the carbonate makes it release carbon dioxide gas

CALCIUM CARBONATE CALCIUM OXIDE CARBON DIOXIDE

Displacement
Some elements are more reactive than others, and will push weaker atoms out of compounds and take their place in a displacement reaction.

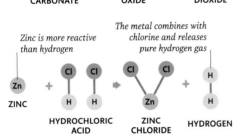

Zinc is more reactive than hydrogen

The metal combines with chlorine and releases pure hydrogen gas

ZINC HYDROCHLORIC ACID ZINC CHLORIDE HYDROGEN

Unlike hydrogen, the **noble gases are unreactive** and do not form compounds easily

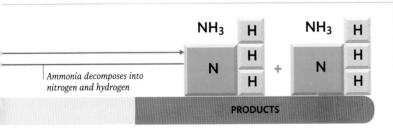

NH₃ NH₃

Ammonia decomposes into nitrogen and hydrogen

PRODUCTS

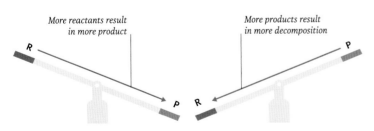

More reactants result in more product

More products result in more decomposition

Reactants concentration increase
Adding more reactants so they outweigh the product makes the reaction go in the forward direction.

Product concentration increase
Allowing the products to outweigh the reactants means the reverse reaction will dominate.

Acids and alkalis

An acid is a compound that releases hydrogen ions (H+) when dissolved in water. The ions are highly reactive. The opposite of an acid is an alkali (also called a base), which releases an equally reactive hydroxide ion (OH⁻) when dissolved in water.

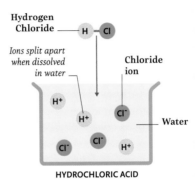

Hydrogen Chloride

Ions split apart when dissolved in water

Chloride ion

Water

HYDROCHLORIC ACID

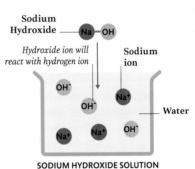

Sodium Hydroxide

Hydroxide ion will react with hydrogen ion

Sodium ion

Water

SODIUM HYDROXIDE SOLUTION

ACID (HCL) ALKALI (NaOH) SALT (NACL) WATER (H₂O)

Neutralization
When an acid and alkali react, their reactive ions combine to make neutral water molecules. The other ions form an unreactive compound called a salt—in this case, sodium chloride, or common salt.

pH SCALE

The strength of an acid or alkali is given by its pH value. This is related to the number of hydrogen ions present in a solution. Pure water, neither acid nor alkali, has a pH of 7.

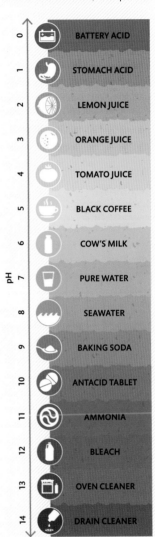

pH	
0	BATTERY ACID
1	STOMACH ACID
2	LEMON JUICE
3	ORANGE JUICE
4	TOMATO JUICE
5	BLACK COFFEE
6	COW'S MILK
7	PURE WATER
8	SEAWATER
9	BAKING SODA
10	ANTACID TABLET
11	AMMONIA
12	BLEACH
13	OVEN CLEANER
14	DRAIN CLEANER

Electrolysis

Water conducts electricity because a few of the molecules split into positively charged hydrogen ions (H+) and negatively charged hydroxide ions (OH⁻). When an electric current is passed through water, these ions respectively gain and lose electrons and turn into hydrogen and oxygen gas.

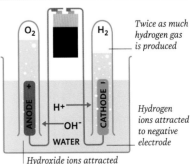

Twice as much hydrogen gas is produced

O₂ H₂

ANODE + CATHODE –

H+ OH⁻

WATER

Hydrogen ions attracted to negative electrode

Hydroxide ions attracted to positive electrode

see also Chemical techniques pp.210–11 ▶ **207**

Organic chemistry

Organic chemistry is the study of carbon-based compounds. Carbon can form the long molecular chains that are the basis of life, such as proteins and starches. The simplest organic compounds are called hydrocarbons—containing only hydrogen and carbon. They are familiar as the key component of fuels, such as gasoline, and can also be used to make plastics. Alcohols and carboxylic acids are organic molecules that also contain oxygen. Fullerenes, graphene, and carbon nanotubes are relatively recently discovered materials that contain only carbon atoms. Of these materials, graphene and carbon nanotubes have high tensile strength and are good conductors of electricity.

Hydrocarbons

Hydrocarbons are covalently bonded molecules made up of hydrogen and carbon atoms. They release a lot of energy when reacting with oxygen (during combustion) and so are often used as fuels. An example is methane (CH_4), also known as natural gas.

Single bond
The simplest hydrocarbon is methane (CH_4). Four single covalent bonds join the central carbon atom to four hydrogen atoms.

Molecular chain
Hydrocarbons can form long chains of carbon atoms. In a long-chain molecule, each carbon atom forms four bonds, while hydrogen atoms each form one.

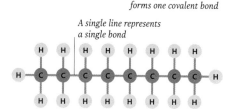

Each carbon atom forms four covalent bonds

Each hydrogen atom forms one covalent bond

Displayed formula
A chemical formula can be shown as a displayed formula. All the bonds are shown as straight lines, and atoms are identified by their atomic symbols.

A single line represents a single bond

Isomers

Isomers are compounds that have the same formula (the same number and type of atoms), but which are arranged differently. Isomers have different chemical and physical properties. Chemists use systematic names to make the exact structures of different isomers clear.

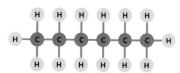

Hexane (C_6H_{14})
The compound with the formula C_6H_{14} can be arranged in several different ways. The straight chain is called hexane.

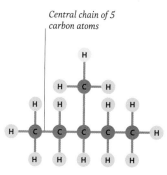

Central chain of 5 carbon atoms

3-methylpentane (C_6H_{14})
In this isomer, a CH_3 group is joined to the central carbon in a chain of five. This is still C_6H_{14}, but is named 3-methylpentane.

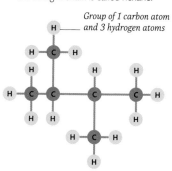

Group of 1 carbon atom and 3 hydrogen atoms

2,3-Dimethylbutane (C_6H_{14})
Here, the longest chain contains four carbons, with two CH_3 groups branching off. This is also C_6H_{14}, but is named 2,3-dimethylbutane.

Alkanes, alkenes, and alkynes

Carbon atoms can form double and triple bonds. A hydrocarbon chain with only single bonds is called an alkane. Alkenes contain at least one double, C=C, bond. Alkynes contain at least one triple, C≡C, bond. Multiple bonds are less stable, so molecules with double or triple bonds are more reactive than molecules with single bonds.

REACTIVITY INCREASING

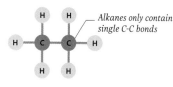

Alkanes only contain single C-C bonds

Ethane (C_2H_6)
Alkane names end in "ane." Alkanes have the general formula C_nH_{2n+2}—that is, twice as many hydrogens as carbons, plus two.

Alkenes contain at least one C=C bond

Ethene (C_2H_4)
Alkene names end in "ene." Alkenes have the general formula C_nH_{2n}—that is, twice as many hydrogens as carbons.

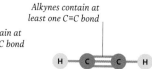

Alkynes contain at least one C≡C bond

Ethyne (C_2H_2)
Alkyne names end in "yne." Alkynes have the general formula C_nH_{2n-2}—that is, twice as many hydrogens as carbons, minus two.

POLYMERIZATION AND MANUFACTURING PLASTICS

Crude oil is a mixture of hydrocarbons that is separated into its constituent parts, called fractions. Some of the parts are used as fuels, while others are used to make plastics, medicines, and other chemicals. Hydrocarbons with long molecules are broken down (cracked) to form smaller molecules.

❶ Crude oil
Most hydrocarbons come from crude oil. Crude oil is a mixture of hydrocarbons of different lengths, which must be separated into fractions, which have their own distinct compositions and boiling points.

An oil platform is used to extract crude oil

CRUDE OIL EXTRACTED

❷ Distillation
The crude oil is heated and the fractions separate by boiling point. High boiling point fractions are collected at the bottom.

Crude oil enters furnace

Furnace

CRUDE OIL HEATED

Fractional distillation column

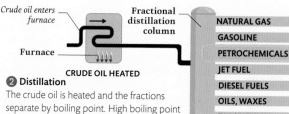

NATURAL GAS
GASOLINE
PETROCHEMICALS
JET FUEL
DIESEL FUELS
OILS, WAXES
TAR/ BITUMEN

Carboxylic acids

Carboxylic acids are carbon-based molecules which contain a C=O connected to an O-H (usually written as COOH). They are weak acids that partially ionize in water to release H+ ions.

Carboxylic acids contain a COOH group of atoms

Methanoic acid
The smallest carboxylic acid is methanoic acid, also known as formic acid. Many species of ants produce formic acid.

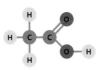

Ethanoic acid
Ethanoic acid (CH₃COOH), also called acetic acid, is the chemical that gives vinegar its distinctive smell and taste.

Alcohols

Alcohols are organic molecules that contain an O-H group attached to a carbon atom. They make good fuels—releasing a lot of energy when burned and producing less soot than is released when burning hydrocarbons. A number of alcohols are also good solvents (chemicals that can dissolve other substances). The best-known alcohol is ethanol.

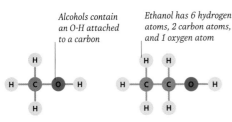

Alcohols contain an O-H attached to a carbon

Ethanol has 6 hydrogen atoms, 2 carbon atoms, and 1 oxygen atom

Methanol
The smallest alcohol is methanol (CH₃OH), which is also known as wood alcohol. It is used as a precursor to produce other chemicals.

Ethanol
Ethanol (C₂H₅OH) is the type of alcohol found in alcoholic beverages. It is also commonly used as a disinfectant and also as a preservative.

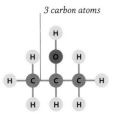

3 carbon atoms

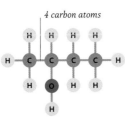

4 carbon atoms

Propan-2-ol
Propan-2-ol (C₃H₇OH) is also known as isopropyl alcohol. It is commonly used in antiseptics and household detergents.

Butan-2-ol
Butan-2-ol (C₄H₉OH), also called sec-butanol, is an alcohol mainly used in the production of the industrial solvent butanone.

Monomers and polymers

Polymer molecules are long chains, which are made by joining together lots of smaller molecules, called monomers. The most common kind of polymer is the addition polymer. Addition polymers are made from alkenes, and one of the most common is polyethylene (polythene), which is made from ethene (C₂H₄) molecules.

C=C (double) bond

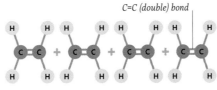

Monomers
Ethene is made up of monomers. During polymerization, one bond in each C=C bond breaks, and monomers join in a chain containing C-C bonds.

C-C (single) bond

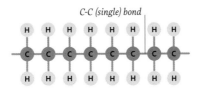

Polymer
Polyethylene is made by joining, or adding, lots of ethene molecules. Polymer molecules are very large, and are sometimes called "macromolecules."

PROTEIN   **STARCH**   **CELLULOSE**   **DNA**

Natural polymers
Naturally occurring polymers are all condensation polymers, which release a small molecule (usually water) when the monomers join into a chain.

FULLERENES AND GRAPHENE

Allotropes are different forms of the same element (see p.201) but each with different structures and properties. Buckminsterfullerene (C₆₀) is a carbon allotrope in which the atoms are arranged in a sphere. In another form known as graphene, the carbon atoms form a layer of hexagons. Fullerenes and graphene layers can be used to produce tubes, called carbon nanotubes, which are about 10,000 times thinner than human hair.

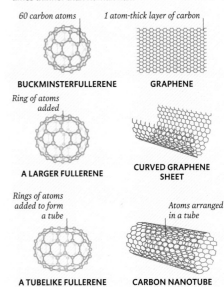

60 carbon atoms   *1 atom-thick layer of carbon*

BUCKMINSTERFULLERENE   **GRAPHENE**

Ring of atoms added

A LARGER FULLERENE   **CURVED GRAPHENE SHEET**

Rings of atoms added to form a tube   *Atoms arranged in a tube*

A TUBELIKE FULLERENE   **CARBON NANOTUBE**

The carbon-based polymer **polyethylene** is the **most common type of plastic** in the world

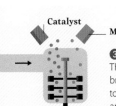

Catalyst

Monomer

3 Polymerization
The C=C bond in alkenes can break, allowing lots of molecules to join, forming long chains, which are described as a polymer, or plastic. A catalyst is used to speed up and control the reaction.

POLYMERIZATION REACTION

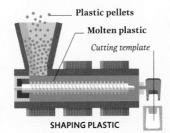

Plastic pellets

Molten plastic

Cutting template

SHAPING PLASTIC

4 Shaping plastics
Plastics can be made into lots of different shapes. Plastic pellets are melted, compressed, and then shaped. This can be done by injecting it into a mold or making it into sheets, which are cut into shapes.

Plastic bag

5 End product
Different plastics have different properties. Thermoplastics melt at relatively low temperatures, while thermoset plastics, once molded, do not melt—only burn. The plastic used to make plastic bags is water resistant and lightweight.

see also Environmental chemistry pp.212–13 ▶   What is "alive?" pp.214–15 ▶

Chemical techniques

Separating substances, and then working out what they are, is an essential part of chemistry. Chemists use lots of different techniques to separate mixtures, to identify specific compounds and elements, and also to work out the exact amounts of the substances that are present in a mixture or compound.

Filtration

Filtration is a way of separating a liquid from an undissolved solid. It uses a filter, such as filter paper—special paper that is strong when wet, and allows liquid to pass through while blocking particles of solid. One example is sand and sea water. The sand is insoluble and can be filtered out; the dissolved salt will need to be removed another way.

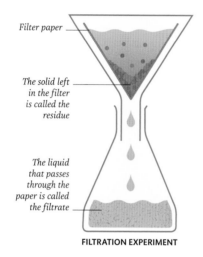

Filter paper

The solid left in the filter is called the residue

The liquid that passes through the paper is called the filtrate

FILTRATION EXPERIMENT

The first **water treatment** facility **used filtration** to produce **clean drinking water**

Chromatography

The first part of the word chromatography comes from the Greek for "color," because it was originally developed to separate plant pigments. Chromatography involves a stationary phase (such as paper) and a mobile phase (such as water). A mixture dissolves in the mobile phase and is separated as it moves across the stationary phase. A similar technique can be used for gases.

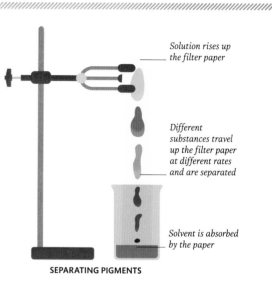

Solution rises up the filter paper

Different substances travel up the filter paper at different rates and are separated

Solvent is absorbed by the paper

SEPARATING PIGMENTS

GAS CHROMATOGRAPHY

In gas chromatography, or GC, the mobile phase is a gas, while the stationary phase is a microscopic coating on a solid support, which is packed into a thin glass or metallic tube (called a column). GC can tell us the number of different compounds in a mixture and how much of each there is. It is often paired with mass spectrometry (MS) and GC-MS is used in forensics and drug testing.

SAMPLE VIALS ON GAS CHROMATOGRAPH

pH indicators

Litmus is one of the oldest pH indicators— substances that change color in the presence of acids or alkalis. Litmus changes from red (acid) to blue (alkali). Paper impregnated with litmus can be used to test solutions and gases quickly.

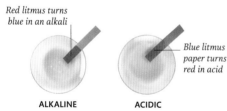

Red litmus turns blue in an alkali

Blue litmus paper turns red in acid

ALKALINE   **ACIDIC**

JUSTUS VON LIEBIG

Justus von Liebig was one of the first chemists to focus on empirical research (based on observation and measurement). He developed an apparatus for determining the amount of hydrogen, carbon, and oxygen in organic substances, and was a pioneer of practical chemistry education.

Titration

To determine concentration, a technique called titration is used. A known volume of one solution is combined with another with a known concentration. The volume needed for them to react completely is measured, and the unknown concentration is calculated.

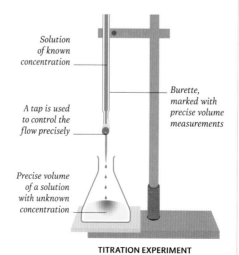

Solution of known concentration

A tap is used to control the flow precisely

Precise volume of a solution with unknown concentration

Burette, marked with precise volume measurements

TITRATION EXPERIMENT

Precipitation

Sometimes a solution contains a mixture of different ions, one of which forms an insoluble precipitate (solid) when another substance is added. For example, when lead ions are mixed with a solution containing iodide ions, bright yellow lead iodide forms.

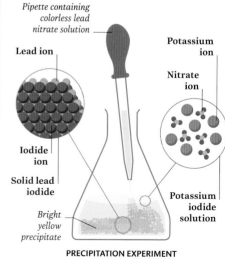

Pipette containing colorless lead nitrate solution

Lead ion

Potassium ion

Nitrate ion

Iodide ion

Solid lead iodide

Bright yellow precipitate

Potassium iodide solution

PRECIPITATION EXPERIMENT

Mass spectrometry

This method is used to determine what compounds are present in a mixture. A mass spectrometer bombards a sample with electrons. These knock some electrons off the molecules, producing ions. The ions are accelerated toward a detector; a magnetic field causing them to follow a curved path. Since ions with small masses curve more than those with large mass, the ions are separated out by mass.

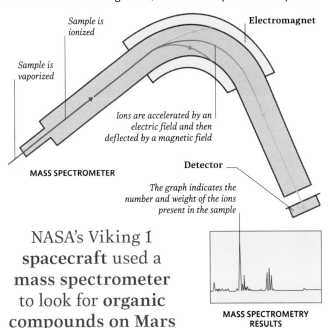

Sample is ionized

Sample is vaporized

Electromagnet

Ions are accelerated by an electric field and then deflected by a magnetic field

MASS SPECTROMETER

Detector

The graph indicates the number and weight of the ions present in the sample

NASA's Viking 1 spacecraft used a mass spectrometer to look for organic compounds on Mars

MASS SPECTROMETRY RESULTS

Distillation

One way to separate liquids that have different boiling points is called distillation. When the mixture is gently heated, the substance with the lowest boiling point is the first to vaporize. The resultant gas moves upward and into a "condenser." There it moves past cold surfaces, where it condenses back into a liquid, separate from the original mixture.

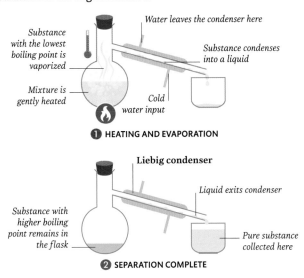

Substance with the lowest boiling point is vaporized

Water leaves the condenser here

Substance condenses into a liquid

Mixture is gently heated

Cold water input

❶ HEATING AND EVAPORATION

Liebig condenser

Liquid exits condenser

Substance with higher boiling point remains in the flask

Pure substance collected here

❷ SEPARATION COMPLETE

Centrifuging

A centrifuge works by spinning a sample of mixed substances at high speed around a fixed axis. This applies a strong, outward (centrifugal) force on the mixture. Dense substances and large particles move outward, and less dense substances move in the opposite direction. Centrifuges are used to quickly separate insoluble substances that would naturally separate slowly.

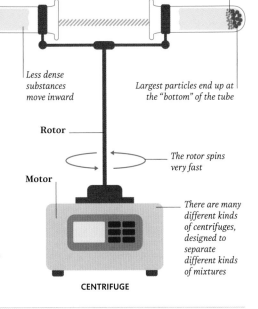

More dense substances move outward

Less dense substances move inward

Largest particles end up at the "bottom" of the tube

Rotor

The rotor spins very fast

Motor

There are many different kinds of centrifuges, designed to separate different kinds of mixtures

CENTRIFUGE

Evaporation

This technique is used to separate a soluble solid from a solvent. Heat is used to remove most of the solvent but, usually, some is left to evaporate naturally to avoid decomposition of the solid residue.

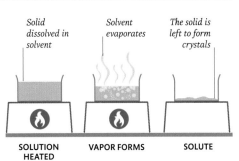

Solid dissolved in solvent

Solvent evaporates

The solid is left to form crystals

SOLUTION HEATED

VAPOR FORMS

SOLUTE

Flame tests

Flame tests are used to identify metals in compounds by heating them. Electrons in the hot atoms are excited and emit light in the visible spectrum, characteristic to particular elements. For example, barium salts produce a green flame.

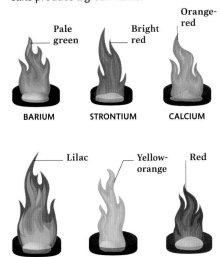

Pale green

Bright red

Orange-red

BARIUM

STRONTIUM

CALCIUM

Lilac

Yellow-orange

Red

POTASSIUM

SODIUM

LITHIUM

BUNSEN BURNER

The Bunsen burner was designed by German chemist Robert Bunsen to produce a very hot, sootless, and non-luminous flame, specifically to make it easier to see the colors produced by metals in different compounds. The burner mixes air with the gas before it burns and this design is still used in laboratories.

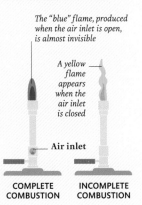

The "blue" flame, produced when the air inlet is open, is almost invisible

A yellow flame appears when the air inlet is closed

Air inlet

COMPLETE COMBUSTION

INCOMPLETE COMBUSTION

◀ see also Chemical reactions pp.206–207   Environmental chemistry pp.212–13 ▶   Diagnosis pp.258–59 ▶

Environmental chemistry

Environmental chemistry is the study of chemical processes that occur on Earth, both those that occur naturally and those caused by human activities. It includes the study of the chemistry in the air and water, and on land. Environmental chemistry is often linked to "green chemistry," which specifically aims to reduce pollution from chemical processes.

Heavy metals

Heavy metals include arsenic, mercury, and lead, and can build up as a result of activities such as mining and waste disposal. They are toxic, causing poisoning at high levels. Regular low-level exposure leads to health problems over time.

Wastewater
Wastewater is water that has been contaminated by human use. It includes sewage as well as water from the mining industry and manufacturing processes, and runoff from urban areas.

Air pollutants

In addition to water vapor, our atmosphere contains about 78 percent nitrogen (N_2), 21 percent oxygen (O_2), nearly 1 percent argon (Ar), 0.04 percent carbon dioxide (CO_2), and traces of other gases. Industries produce other substances.

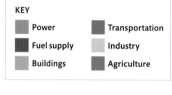

KEY

- Power
- Fuel supply
- Buildings
- Transportation
- Industry
- Agriculture

80 percent of all pollution in the oceans comes from sources on land

PRIMARY POLLUTANTS

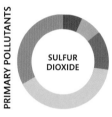

SULFUR DIOXIDE

NITROGEN OXIDES

PARTICULATE MATTER

CARBON MONOXIDE

VOLATILE ORGANIC COMPOUNDS

AMMONIA

This gas forms when certain fossil fuels are burned. It is also produced by volcanic activity. Sulfur dioxide causes respiratory problems and acid rain.

Nitrogen oxides form when fuels are burned at high temperatures. These emissions cause respiratory problems, as well as smog and acid rain.

Microscopic particles of solid or liquid suspended in the air, formed during various processes, have been linked to cancers and other health problems.

Carbon monoxide is an odorless gas that forms when fossil fuels are burned in a limited oxygen supply. It is deadly if inhaled in large quantities.

There are many types of VOCs and they are linked to numerous health problems. An example is formaldehyde, which evaporates from some types of paint.

The biggest source of ammonia is agriculture, where it is used to make fertilizers. It can cause breathing problems and affect soil chemistry.

Oxygen cycle

The oxygen cycle explains the chemical changes that atmospheric oxygen undergoes. It links photosynthesis—carried out by green plants, algae, and some bacteria—with respiration: the process by which all living things release energy from glucose.

Night and day
Plants use sunlight to create food through photosynthesis. Oxygen is a by-product created during the day, when plants are exposed to sunlight.

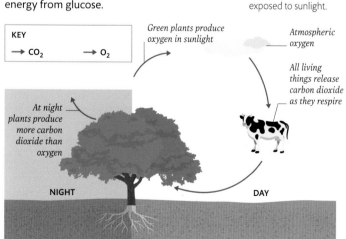

KEY
→ CO_2 → O_2

Green plants produce oxygen in sunlight

Atmospheric oxygen

All living things release carbon dioxide as they respire

At night plants produce more carbon dioxide than oxygen

NIGHT

DAY

Nitrogen cycle

The nitrogen cycle explains the chemical changes atmospheric nitrogen undergoes, before being released into the atmosphere as nitrogen again. Nitrogen is a key component of nucleic acids (such as DNA) and proteins and is therefore needed by all living things for growth.

Nitrogen fixation
Nitrogen gas (N_2) is inert. Fixation is the process of forming ammonia (NH_3) or other compounds, such as nitrates (NO_3^-), from nitrogen.

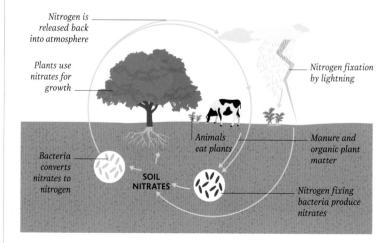

Nitrogen is released back into atmosphere

Plants use nitrates for growth

Nitrogen fixation by lightning

Animals eat plants

Manure and organic plant matter

Bacteria converts nitrates to nitrogen

SOIL NITRATES

Nitrogen fixing bacteria produce nitrates

A **lightning strike** has a **distinct smell** because it **produces ozone** (O_3)

Pesticides and herbicides

Pesticides and herbicides control animal and plant pests. Production of food crops on a large scale would be impossible without them, but they can have environmental consequences, such as harming pollinating insects or aquatic plants. They may also harm humans if not carefully controlled.

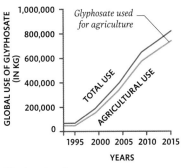

Glyphosate sales

Globally, the use of pesticides has decreased since the 1970s, but the use of some weed killers, such glyphosate, has increased.

BIOMAGNIFICATION

Organisms are linked in the environment: if a larger creature eats a lot of smaller organisms contaminated with a toxin, it can absorb large amounts of the chemical over time. This increases up the food chain in a process called biomagnification.

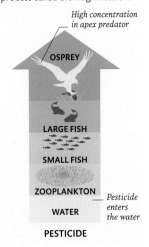

High concentration in apex predator

OSPREY

LARGE FISH

SMALL FISH

ZOOPLANKTON

WATER — *Pesticide enters the water*

PESTICIDE

Acidification of the oceans

Oceans absorb carbon dioxide directly from the atmosphere. As atmospheric CO_2 levels have increased due to the burning of fossil fuels, the oceans have in turn absorbed more CO_2, lowering pH, and causing harm to organisms, such as corals and mollusks.

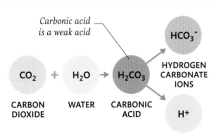

Carbonic acid is a weak acid

CO_2 CARBON DIOXIDE + H_2O WATER → H_2CO_3 CARBONIC ACID

HCO_3^- HYDROGEN CARBONATE IONS

H^+ HYDROGEN ION

Chemistry of acidification

When carbon dioxide dissolves in water it forms carbonic acid, which in turn releases hydrogen ions (H^+), lowering the pH of the solution.

Plastic pollution

It can take years for plastic debris to break down. Microscopic particles, formed from larger pieces of litter, can enter the food chain and cause harm, either because they contain toxins or simply because they build up.

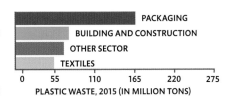

PACKAGING

BUILDING AND CONSTRUCTION

OTHER SECTOR

TEXTILES

PLASTIC WASTE, 2015 (IN MILLION TONS)

Excess plastic waste

Millions of tons of plastic waste are produced each year. Plastic waste includes synthetic materials created by the textile industry.

Acid rain

Rainwater is naturally slightly acidic (~ pH 5.5), but when atmospheric moisture mixes with emissions of sulfur dioxide (SO_2) or nitrogen oxides (NO_X) it becomes more so, harming life and causing erosion.

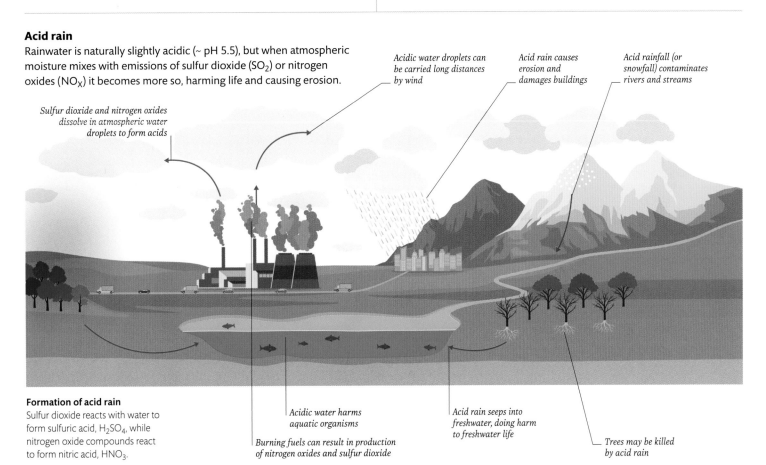

Sulfur dioxide and nitrogen oxides dissolve in atmospheric water droplets to form acids

Acidic water droplets can be carried long distances by wind

Acid rain causes erosion and damages buildings

Acid rainfall (or snowfall) contaminates rivers and streams

Formation of acid rain

Sulfur dioxide reacts with water to form sulfuric acid, H_2SO_4, while nitrogen oxide compounds react to form nitric acid, HNO_3.

Acidic water harms aquatic organisms

Burning fuels can result in production of nitrogen oxides and sulfur dioxide

Acid rain seeps into freshwater, doing harm to freshwater life

Trees may be killed by acid rain

◂ **see also** Chemical reactions pp.206–207   ◂ Organic chemistry pp.208–209   Respiration and metabolism pp.222–23 ▸   **213**

What is "alive?"

The word "biology" means "the study of life," but defining exactly what life is has proved impossible—even for biologists. For millennia, theologians, philosophers, and scientists from disciplines as diverse as chemistry, biology, physics, and robotics have proposed more than a hundred different definitions of what constitutes life, but none have been universally accepted. And the more science progresses, the less agreement there is. Right now, the only way to distinguish living from nonliving things is by studying the basic functions that all living organisms have in common.

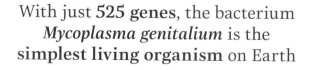

With just **525 genes**, the bacterium *Mycoplasma genitalium* is the simplest living organism on Earth

The seven characteristics of life
Despite the huge variety of life on Earth, all of the many millions of species share a combination of traits. The list is not foolproof—computer programs and crystals, for example, grow and replicate—but if all seven characteristics are exhibited by something it is deemed to be alive.

Nutrition
To sustain life, organisms must take in or produce food for energy and nutrients, as these support and sustain all other functions, such as growth, movement, and respiration.

Reproduction
Reproduction is when one living thing creates another either asexually, such as by simple cell division, or sexually, by the fusion of genetic material from two individuals.

Movement
All living things move to a greater or lesser degree, and while plants may not walk, their roots push through the earth and leaves and flowers may turn toward the sun.

Growth
An increase in an organism's size is made possible when enough energy is available to fuel the production of new cells, or for their cells to grow in size. This allows organisms to grow as big as a whale.

Living organism
The single-celled organism Green Euglena both consumes food, as animals must do, and photosynthesizes, as plants do.

Excretion
Living organisms must eliminate waste products, otherwise a buildup could produce life-threatening toxins. Even single-celled bacteria excrete waste in liquid, gas, or solid form.

Sensitivity
The ability of an organism to sense and respond to changes in its environment, such as chemical, light, or temperature, is critical to its survival. Each stimulus triggers a specific set of coordinated responses.

Respiration
To survive, living things need a steady supply of energy, derived by breaking down food in chemical reactions. Complex, multicellular organisms accomplish this by using oxygen to break down sugars.

Carbon makes up about **20 percent** of the **weight** of a **human body,** whereas **plants are 45 percent carbon**

NOT ALIVE

Some nonliving things may appear alive, because they seem to have one or more of the seven signs of life. However, if they do not possess the full set of characteristics—and unless they can die—they are not alive.

Internal combustion engine
Man-made engines take in fuel and emit waste products, but they cannot be considered living because they lack sensitivity and neither reproduce nor grow.

Crystals
Crystals show some signs of life, as they grow in response to chemical changes, and some even move in response to light. However, they cannot reproduce.

Computer
Computers are programmed to respond to their environment and store information, and some can replicate programs, but none does so independently.

Viruses
Viruses fall between alive and not alive. While they respond to their environment by adaptation, and replicate within living organisms, they do not feed, respire, or grow.

Ingredients for life

Most living things on Earth are constructed from the same essential elements: hydrogen, oxygen, nitrogen, and carbon, as well as phosphorus and sulfur. When these atoms combine, they not only create the water, ammonia, and methane necessary to form a rudimentary atmosphere and oceans, but these simple molecules can bond to produce amino acids, laying the foundations for complex proteins, or simple sugars.

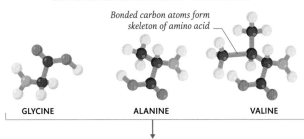

SIMPLE INGREDIENTS

Oxygen Hydrogen WATER
Carbon Nitrogen AMMONIA
METHANE

SIMPLE ORGANIC MOLECULES—AMINO ACIDS

Bonded carbon atoms form skeleton of amino acid

GLYCINE ALANINE VALINE

COMPLEX ORGANIC MOLECULES—LINKED AMINO ACIDS

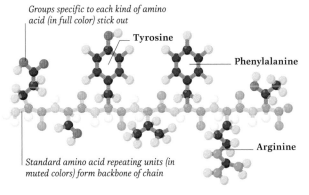

Groups specific to each kind of amino acid (in full color) stick out

Tyrosine

Phenylalanine

Arginine

Standard amino acid repeating units (in muted colors) form backbone of chain

Creating compartments

Chains of life-giving, carbon-based molecules are not the same as living cells, which require a membrane to concentrate and protect their contents. These cell membranes are provided by phospholipids: oily molecules that aggregate to form membranes in water—where life began.

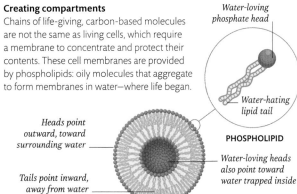

Water-loving phosphate head

Water-hating lipid tail

PHOSPHOLIPID

Heads point outward, toward surrounding water

Water-loving heads also point toward water trapped inside

Tails point inward, away from water

MEMBRANE FORMING A SPHERE

Conditions for life

In 1952, Stanley Miller and Harold Urey at the University of Chicago tested the hypothesis that complex organic molecules can form from simple, inorganic materials. By energizing their inorganic mixture with a spark to simulate lightning, they recreated the conditions of the young Earth and formed simple amino acids— the building blocks of life.

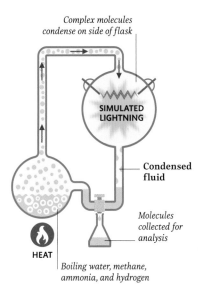

Complex molecules condense on side of flask

SIMULATED LIGHTNING

Condensed fluid

Molecules collected for analysis

HEAT

Boiling water, methane, ammonia, and hydrogen

THE MILLER-UREY EXPERIMENT

CAN ANYTHING LIVE FOREVER?

Most living organisms have limited lifespans—apart from the "immortal jellyfish," *Turritopsis dohrnii*. Jellyfish begin as polyps attached to the seabed. Polyps release free-swimming medusae, which mature, spawn to create larvae that become polyps, then die. *Turritopsis*, however, can regress from a medusa to a ball of tissue that becomes a polyp, thus rebooting itself.

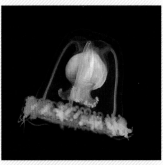

IMMORTAL JELLYFISH MEDUSA

Types of living things

Living organisms are found from icy poles and scorching deserts to thermal vents far beneath the ocean surface. Scientists study the anatomy and DNA of these living things to discover how they are related. With this information, they classify the organisms in a system of ever-smaller groups, beginning with kingdoms, in order to understand the sheer diversity—and often surprising forms—life on Earth can take.

All organisms, whether living or extinct, are thought to be genetically related

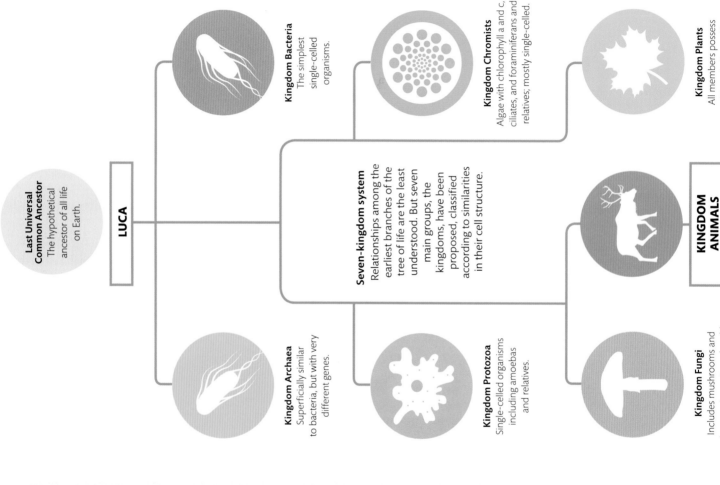

Last Universal Common Ancestor The hypothetical ancestor of all life on Earth.

LUCA

Kingdom Bacteria The simplest single-celled organisms.

Kingdom Chromists Algae with chlorophyll a and c, ciliates, and foraminiferans and relatives; mostly single-celled.

Kingdom Plants All members possess chlorophyll a and b.

Seven-kingdom system Relationships among the earliest branches of the tree of life are the least understood. But seven main groups, the kingdoms, have been proposed, classified according to similarities in their cell structure.

KINGDOM ANIMALS

Kingdom Archaea Superficially similar to bacteria, but with very different genes.

Kingdom Protozoa Single-celled organisms including amoebas and relatives.

Kingdom Fungi Includes mushrooms and microscopic yeasts and molds.

HIERARCHY OF PLANT TAXA

Classification specialists called taxonomists traditionally arrange living things into groups called taxa, which are ranked from kingdom, the highest level, to species, the smallest group. The plant kingdom is split first into divisions, which compare basic form and structure. The criteria for each rank then become increasingly specific, such as physiology and the detailed structure of flowers and fruits. Evidence from the fossil record and DNA analysis is used to place each plant into the correct taxon.

▼ **Division** Separates plants according to key features, for example, angiosperms and gymnosperms

▼ **Class** Divides plants according to fundamental differences, such as monocots and eudicots

▼ **Order** A major subdivsion of a class, containing one or more families, such as the order Rosales

▼ **Family** A group of several genera that share a set of underlying natural characteristics, such as the family Rosaceae (the rose family)

▼ **Genus (genera)** A group of species that share a range of distinctive characteristics, such as the genus Rosa

▼ **Species** A group of individuals that interbreed naturally to produce offspring with similar characteristics, such as the species Rosa gallica

▼ **Variety** A group of individuals that differ slightly in botanical structure from other individuals of the same species, such as the variety Rosa gallica var. officinalis

▼ **Cultivar** A selected, or artificially bred, distinct variant of a species or variety, such as the cultivar Rosa gallica var. officinalis "Versicolor"

Tree of life

Scientists classify organisms according to their phylogeny—their evolutionary relationships to other life forms. A phylogenetic tree, also known as a "tree of life," depicts these connections. To create such a diagram, scientists look for features that organisms have in common, but only those that are due to their shared ancestry are used. That way, the scientists group not only similar organisms, but those that are closely related.

"The **affinities** of all the **beings of the same class** have sometimes been **represented** by a **great tree.** I believe this simile largely **speaks the truth.**" CHARLES DARWIN, *On the Origin of Species,* 1859

Invertebrates

Invertebrates as an unnatural group

All animals that lack a backbone are called invertebrates. However, although they have a common ancestor, they have no feature in common, and some are simple, others complex. Also, since backboned animals (fishes and their ancestors) evolved from one group of invertebrates, excluding these descendants makes this group incomplete, and not a clade.

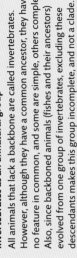

Sponges

Cnidarians, including anemones and jellyfishes

Arthropods, mollusks, and most kinds of worms

Starfishes and relatives

Fishes

Fishes as an unnatural group

Like invertebrates, fishes do not form a clade. All fishes do share a common ancestor, but four-limbed animals (tetrapods), which evolved from fleshy-finned bony fishes, are not classed as "fishes." Unlike invertebrates, however, fishes are much more similar in complexity and have many traits in common, so they form a type of group called a "grade."

Jawless fishes (lampreys and hagfishes)

Sharks, rays, and chimeras

Ray-finned bony fishes

Fleshy-finned bony fishes

Natural and unnatural groups

Modern classification avoids two kinds of unnatural groups—groups of unrelated organisms, and incomplete groups. If birds were grouped with insects, for instance, because both have wings, this would be unnatural, because they evolved their wings separately and are unrelated. An incomplete group is avoided by including all known descendants of a common ancestor. Such a complete group is called a clade. Many familiar groups such as fishes and invertebrates are not, in fact, clades.

Tetrapods

Tetrapods as a natural group

Tetrapods form a clade because the group includes all of the descendants of the first animal to evolve four limbs. Some tetrapods, such as whales and snakes, have lost limbs, but they are included because they are related. Classifying all living things into clades makes it difficult to stick to traditional ranked taxa, because groups become nested within groups instead of being ranked alongside each other.

Birds

Crocodilians

Archosaurs

Archosaurs means "ruling reptiles," and this clade features many extinct reptiles including dinosaurs—the ancestors of birds. Crocodiles and alligators are the closest living relatives of birds.

Lizards and snakes

Modern reptiles and birds

All living reptiles and birds belong to this clade. Some extinct reptiles, including the ancestors of mammals, are excluded.

Turtles

Amniotes

Amniotes includes all animals whose eggs have a waterproof membrane, or amnion. The first amniote was the ancestor of all reptiles, mammals, and birds.

Amphibians

Mammals

Bacteria and viruses

Bacteria and viruses are two very different entities. Viruses cannot survive independently of a host cell and are therefore not usually considered to be "alive," whereas bacterial cells are found living in many different environments. Some viruses, called bacteriophages, infect bacterial cells.

Types of bacteria

Bacterial species have evolved to live in many different habitats. Their cells can be spherical (cocci), rod-shaped (bacilli), or curved or spiral-shaped (spirochetes).

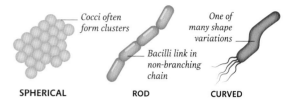

Cocci often form clusters

One of many shape variations

Bacilli link in non-branching chain

SPHERICAL **ROD** **CURVED**

Bacteria

Bacteria are small, single-celled microorganisms, with a single loop of chromosomal DNA (see pp.224–25). Some bacteria have additional small loops of DNA called plasmids, which contain extra genes that confer advantages such as antibiotic resistance. Bacteria have been found all over the Earth, from icy Arctic snow to hot hydrothermal vents deep on the ocean floor, and there are more bacterial cells living in your body than your own human cells. Bacteria living in the soil or on dead plant matter help to release nutrients back into the environment, and bacteria also make the essential vitamin B12, which is needed by all life forms to make DNA and proteins.

Bacterial cell structure

Bacteria are prokaryotes, meaning that the inside of the cell is one big compartment, unlike animal or plant cells (eukaryotes). They have a range of features that help them survive.

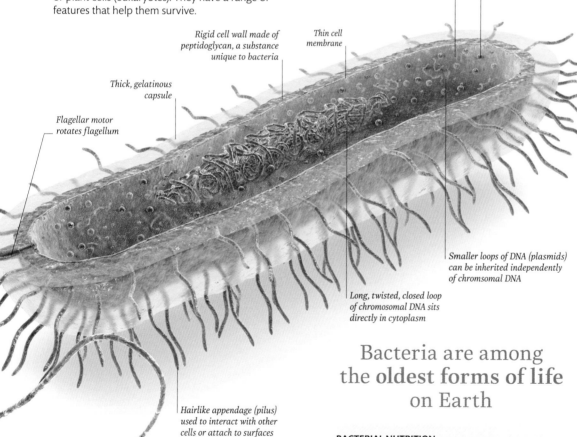

Fluid cytoplasm containing proteins, metabolites, and other cell structures fills cell

Molecular machines called ribosomes make proteins for cell

Rigid cell wall made of peptidoglycan, a substance unique to bacteria

Thin cell membrane

Thick, gelatinous capsule

Flagellar motor rotates flagellum

Smaller loops of DNA (plasmids) can be inherited independently of chromsomal DNA

Long, twisted, closed loop of chromosomal DNA sits directly in cytoplasm

Hairlike appendage (pilus) used to interact with other cells or attach to surfaces

Long, whiplike tail (flagellum) drives bacterium through fluid

Bacteria are among the **oldest forms of life** on Earth

BACTERIAL NUTRITION

Like other organisms, bacteria need nutrients to survive and grow. Many bacteria are autotrophs, which means they are able to use either light (photosynthesis) or chemical energy (chemosynthesis) to change carbon dioxide into sugar. Some bacteria partner with, or infect, other organisms to access nutrients.

How a bacterium replicates

Bacteria most commonly reproduce by binary fission, a form of asexual reproduction during which a cell copies its DNA and divides in half to make two new identical "daughter" cells. Division can happen as quickly as every 20 minutes.

DNA contains genetic information

❶ Parent cell

If the conditions are suitable, and the cell has enough energy, it will activate the machinery required for cell division.

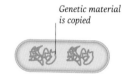

Genetic material is copied

❷ DNA replicates

First, the cell must make another complete, identical copy of its DNA, in a process called DNA replication.

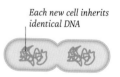

Each new cell inherits identical DNA

❸ Cell begins to divide

The two identical copies of DNA are segregated at each end of the cell as the cell begins to divide.

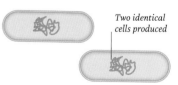

Two identical cells produced

❹ Daughter cells

As cell division completes, two new cells are created that are genetically identical copies (clones) of the original parent cell.

The **smallpox virus killed 300–500 million people**
in the 12,000 years it existed until it was declared **eradicated in 1980**

Types of viruses

Different viruses have varying shapes and sizes, and can use either DNA or RNA (a chemical related to DNA) to encode their genetic information.

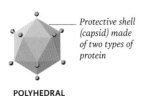

Protective shell (capsid) made of two types of protein

POLYHEDRAL

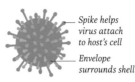

Spike helps virus attach to host's cell

Envelope surrounds shell

ENVELOPED

Protein subunit of capsid (capsomere)

HELICAL

Head (capsid)

Sheath

Tail fibers

COMPLEX

How a virus replicates

Viruses are essentially just fragments of genetic code that protect themselves with an outer coat. Features of their coat also help them to invade a host cell. Since they do not have their own cell, viruses cannot make their own proteins and instead must hijack the host cell's machinery to both replicate their genetic material and make new coat proteins. All viruses are, therefore, parasites.

❶ Virus attaches
Viral coat proteins have evolved to attach to specific features on the host cell. The virus's ability to recognize a specific feature ensures that it is infecting a host cell that is suitable for its own replication.

❷ Virus penetrates cell
Viruses enter cells either by membrane fusion or by forming a pore, or hole, in the membrane. If a virus is enveloped by the host cell's membrane on entry, it breaks down the membrane "bubble" once it is inside the cell.

❸ Virus coat breaks apart
Once the virus is inside the host cell, it must release its genetic material into the cell. This process of shedding its coat is called "uncoating."

❹ Viral genes replicate
To make new virus particles, the genetic code of the virus must both replicate itself and use itself to instruct the host to make new viral proteins. These include proteins for its coat and proteins that can alter the host cell.

❺ Virus sabotages host's protein-making machinery
Some viruses block the host's protein synthesis so that the machinery spends more time making viral proteins instead. Some viruses even change the behavior of the host, to increase their chance of infecting the next host.

❻ New viruses assembled
Once the host's ribosomes have made new viral coat proteins, and the viral genetic code has been replicated, new virus particles are assembled, helped by the host cell's machinery.

❼ New virus particles released
The new viral particles are released from the cell's surface, each one ready to infect a new host cell. This release may rupture and kill the original cell.

ROSALIND FRANKLIN

The British scientist Rosalind Franklin (1920–58), well-known for her role in solving the structure of DNA, also used X-ray diffraction to solve the structure of the tobacco mosaic virus, the first virus to be discovered. This pioneered work on the structure of other human viruses such as the polio virus.

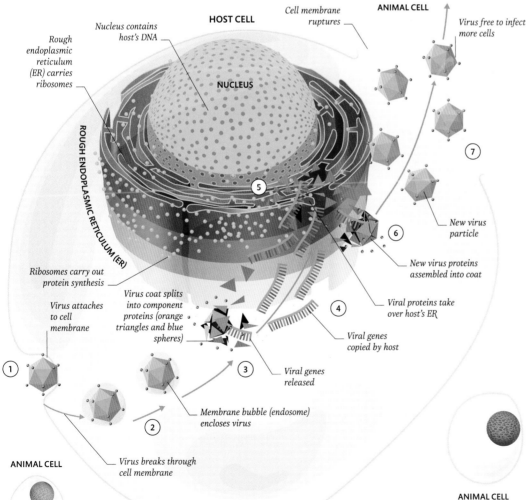

HOST CELL

Cell membrane ruptures

ANIMAL CELL

Virus free to infect more cells

Nucleus contains host's DNA

Rough endoplasmic reticulum (ER) carries ribosomes

NUCLEUS

ROUGH ENDOPLASMIC RETICULUM (ER)

Ribosomes carry out protein synthesis

Virus attaches to cell membrane

Virus coat splits into component proteins (orange triangles and blue spheres)

Membrane bubble (endosome) encloses virus

Viral genes released

Viral genes copied by host

Viral proteins take over host's ER

New virus proteins assembled into coat

New virus particle

ANIMAL CELL

Virus breaks through cell membrane

ANIMAL CELL

see also How cells work pp.220–21 ▶ How genes work pp.224–25 ▶ Modern medicine pp.252–53 ▶   **219**

How cells work

Cells are the basic units of life. Organisms may consist of just a single cell or be made up of many specialized cells working together. Each cell has its own copy of DNA (see p.224), which it uses to make the protein machinery it needs to survive. There are two main categories of cells: prokaryotic (see Bacteria, p.218, for example) and eukaryotic. Eukaryotic cells have membrane-bound compartments called organelles, which perform different functions in the cell. Examples include the nucleus, which stores the DNA, and mitochondria, which are the sites of respiration. Animal and plant cells are eukaryotic.

There are up to
500,000 chloroplasts
in a square
millimeter of leaf

Plant cell structure and function

Plants cells have evolved many specialized features. They have a cell wall, which keeps the cells rigid, helping to both keep their shape and to prevent them from bursting as they absorb water. Plant cells also have organelles called chloroplasts. These are the sites of photosynthesis, where energy from sunlight is turned into chemical energy that can be stored. Chloroplasts contain a pigment called chlorophyll that reflects green light, which is why plants appear green.

1 Receiving instructions
The nucleus contains the plant's DNA, which encodes instructions for making every single protein that the plant needs to live. Temporary copies of the instructions are made using a molecule called messenger RNA (mRNA) and transported out of the nucleus.

2 Manufacture
The mRNA contains the instructions to make a protein, and it must therefore be "translated." It is carried to ribosomes, which are able to translate the genetic code and build the protein. Ribosomes are concentrated on the rough endoplasmic reticulum, (ER) giving it its rough appearance.

3 Packaging
Once the protein has been made, it travels through the cytoplasm in a small bubble of membrane called a vesicle to the Golgi body. Here the proteins are sorted and may be modified by the addition of other molecules that help their function, such as sugars or fats.

4 Shipping
Once the protein is ready, it is sent from the Golgi body to where it is needed inside, or sometimes outside, the cell. The protein is packaged inside vesicles that are molecularly tagged for where they are going—like a zip code. Vesicles carrying proteins for outside the cell fuse with the cell membrane to release them.

Nucleus stores DNA, which acts as a library of instructions for making proteins

Nucleolus, where ribosomes are made

Rough endoplasmic reticulum (ER), where proteins are built and assembled

Smooth endoplasmic reticulum (ER) makes and transports fats and steroid hormones

Ribosomes make protein

Vacuole stores water and nutrients, and provides internal pressure to help plant keep its shape

Cell wall made of the complex carbohdryate cellulose, which provides support and structure

Chloroplasts carry out photosynthesis

Mitochondrion provides energy for the cell

Cytoplasm—fluid inside cell membrane

Vesicles carry products around the cell

Cell membrane forms a controlled barrier

Golgi body processes and modifies proteins and other molecules before sending them around the cell

Vesicles can release proteins and other substances out of the cell

Lysosome contains enzymes that digest waste products

NUCLEUS · mRNA · NUCLEOLUS · ROUGH ER · RIBOSOMES · SMOOTH ER · VACUOLE · CELL WALL · MITOCHONDRION · VESICLE · GOLGI BODY · CHLOROPLAST · LYSOSOME · CELL MEMBRANE

Types of plant cells

Plants have many different specialized cells that carry out specific functions. For example, root hair cells absorb water and minerals from the soil. Xylem cells carry water from the roots to the leaves, while phloem tissue transports glucose and other nutrients. Mesophyll cells, found in leaves, have chloroplasts that carry out photosynthesis.

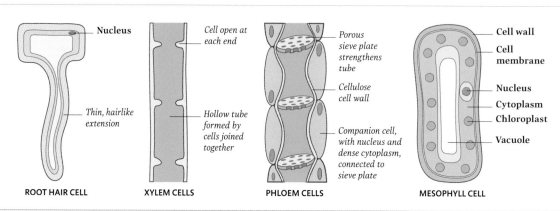

Nucleus

Thin, hairlike extension

ROOT HAIR CELL

Cell open at each end

Hollow tube formed by cells joined together

XYLEM CELLS

Porous sieve plate strengthens tube

Cellulose cell wall

Companion cell, with nucleus and dense cytoplasm, connected to sieve plate

PHLOEM CELLS

Cell wall

Cell membrane

Nucleus

Cytoplasm

Chloroplast

Vacuole

MESOPHYLL CELL

The **smallest** human cell is the **male sperm cell** at 0.05 mm long, while the **widest** is the **female egg cell** at 0.1 mm across

Animal cell structure and function

Animal cells are different from plant cells in that they do not have a cell wall, so their shape is much more flexible, and they do not have chloroplasts to make sugar. Because of this, animals have evolved a support system to keep the shape of their bodies stable—either an internal hydrostatic or bony skeleton, or an external shell or body case—and they must eat sugar made from plants or other organisms to survive. However, like plant cells, animal cells have a nucleus, mitochondria, endoplasmic reticulum, and Golgi bodies that all carry out the same functions as in plants.

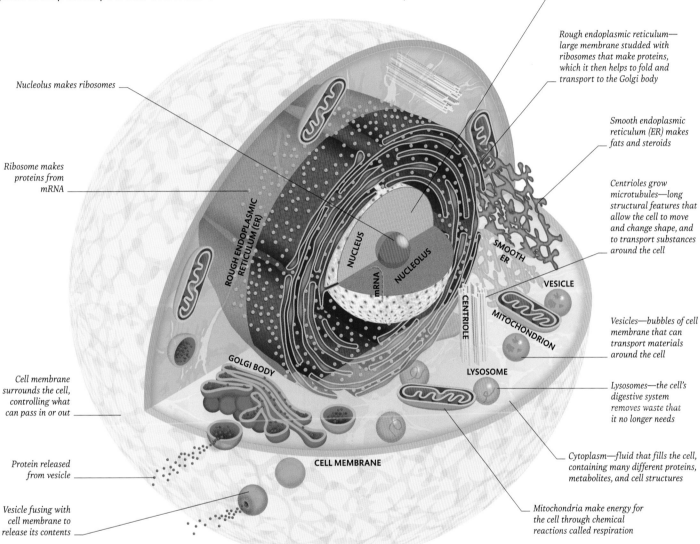

Nucleolus makes ribosomes

Ribosome makes proteins from mRNA

ROUGH ENDOPLASMIC RETICULUM (ER)

NUCLEUS

mRNA

NUCLEOLUS

Cell membrane surrounds the cell, controlling what can pass in or out

GOLGI BODY

Protein released from vesicle

CELL MEMBRANE

Vesicle fusing with cell membrane to release its contents

CENTRIOLE

SMOOTH ER

MITOCHONDRION

VESICLE

LYSOSOME

Nucleus stores and protects the DNA, and is surrounded by a membrane that only allows certain substances in or out

Rough endoplasmic reticulum— large membrane studded with ribosomes that make proteins, which it then helps to fold and transport to the Golgi body

Smooth endoplasmic reticulum (ER) makes fats and steroids

Centrioles grow microtubules—long structural features that allow the cell to move and change shape, and to transport substances around the cell

Vesicles—bubbles of cell membrane that can transport materials around the cell

Lysosomes—the cell's digestive system removes waste that it no longer needs

Cytoplasm—fluid that fills the cell, containing many different proteins, metabolites, and cell structures

Mitochondria make energy for the cell through chemical reactions called respiration

Types of animal cells

As in plants, animal cells are specialized to carry out different functions. An extreme example is a nerve cell, which relays information and in some animals can reach several yards long. Other examples include muscle cells, which contain lots of mitochondria for energy, and red blood cells that carry oxygen around the body.

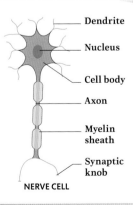

Dendrite

Nucleus

Cell body

Axon

Myelin sheath

Synaptic knob

NERVE CELL

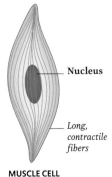

Nucleus

Long, contractile fibers

MUSCLE CELL

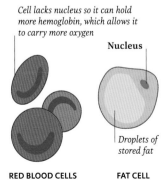

Cell lacks nucleus so it can hold more hemoglobin, which allows it to carry more oxygen

Nucleus

RED BLOOD CELLS

Droplets of stored fat

FAT CELL

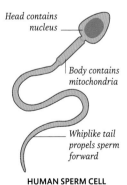

Head contains nucleus

Body contains mitochondria

Whiplike tail propels sperm forward

HUMAN SPERM CELL

see also Respiration and metabolism pp.222-23 ▶ How genes work pp.224-25 ▶ **221**

Respiration and metabolism

Respiration and metabolism are the chemical reactions that take place inside a cell to give it the energy and the molecules that it needs to survive. Respiration is the series of reactions that release energy from sugar—glucose—to make molecules called adenosine triphosphate (ATP), which can be used by the cell to drive its machinery. The entire array of chemical processes in the cell, from respiration to building proteins to the removal of toxic waste products, is called metabolism.

HANS KREBS

While working at the University of Sheffield, German-born British scientist Hans Krebs (1900–81) investigated the mechanism by which cells break down glucose using oxygen to release energy. He discovered the chemical reaction sequence that happens in mitochondria, which is now known as the Krebs cycle.

Energy and fuel

Most life on Earth is sustained by organisms that use energy from sunlight to produce sugar, in a process called photosynthesis. If an organism cannot photosynthesize, it must ingest other organisms that can, such as plants, or organisms that have themselves eaten plants. This sugar acts as fuel to make energy.

Respiration in an animal

In animal cells, most of the chemical reactions of respiration take place inside the mitochondria, which use oxygen to release energy in a process called aerobic respiration. If there is no oxygen available, the cell can still use anaerobic respiration, but this is much less efficient.

❶ Delivering the fuel
In larger animals, nutrients, including the sugar glucose, are absorbed from food in the digestive system and are transported around the body in the blood. Oxygen is absorbed from the skin, lungs, or gills, where it binds to the protein hemoglobin in red blood cells.

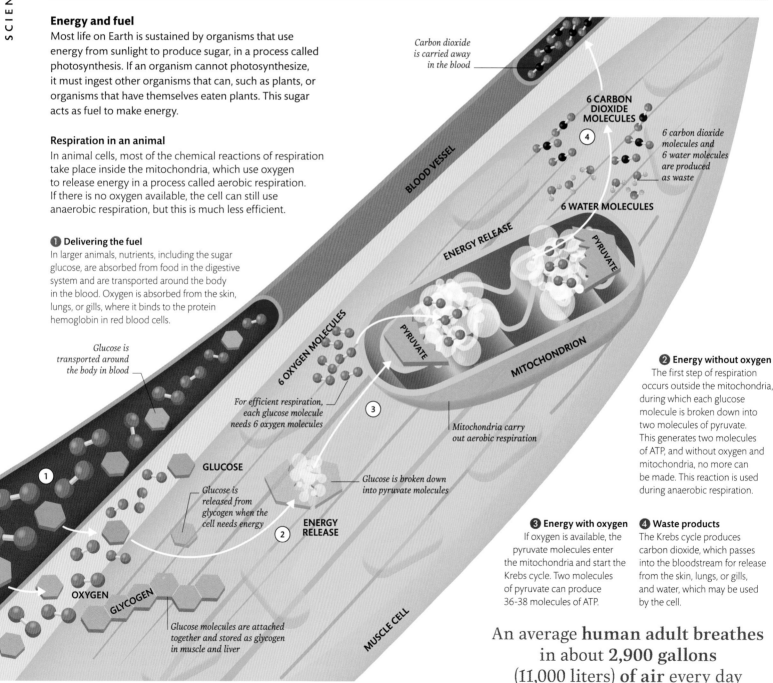

Carbon dioxide is carried away in the blood

6 CARBON DIOXIDE MOLECULES

6 carbon dioxide molecules and 6 water molecules are produced as waste

6 WATER MOLECULES

BLOOD VESSEL

ENERGY RELEASE

PYRUVATE

6 OXYGEN MOLECULES

PYRUVATE

MITOCHONDRION

For efficient respiration, each glucose molecule needs 6 oxygen molecules

Mitochondria carry out aerobic respiration

Glucose is transported around the body in blood

GLUCOSE

Glucose is released from glycogen when the cell needs energy

Glucose is broken down into pyruvate molecules

ENERGY RELEASE

OXYGEN

GLYCOGEN

Glucose molecules are attached together and stored as glycogen in muscle and liver

MUSCLE CELL

❷ Energy without oxygen
The first step of respiration occurs outside the mitochondria, during which each glucose molecule is broken down into two molecules of pyruvate. This generates two molecules of ATP, and without oxygen and mitochondria, no more can be made. This reaction is used during anaerobic respiration.

❸ Energy with oxygen
If oxygen is available, the pyruvate molecules enter the mitochondria and start the Krebs cycle. Two molecules of pyruvate can produce 36-38 molecules of ATP.

❹ Waste products
The Krebs cycle produces carbon dioxide, which passes into the bloodstream for release from the skin, lungs, or gills, and water, which may be used by the cell.

An average **human adult breathes** in about **2,900 gallons** (11,000 liters) **of air** every day

Aerobic respiration and photosynthesis

Aerobic respiration uses oxygen and sugar to release energy; by consuming energy from the sun, plants can reverse this reaction during photosynthesis. The process of turning carbon dioxide into sugar is called "carbon fixation."

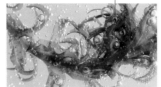

Bubbles of oxygen released when photosynthesizing

CANADIAN PONDWEED

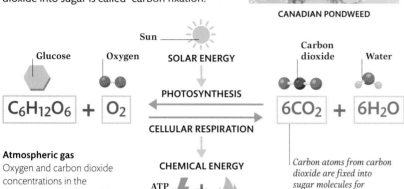

Sun

Glucose   Oxygen   **SOLAR ENERGY**   Carbon dioxide   Water

$C_6H_{12}O_6$ + O_2 **PHOTOSYNTHESIS** $6CO_2$ + $6H_2O$

CELLULAR RESPIRATION

CHEMICAL ENERGY

ATP + Heat

Atmospheric gas
Oxygen and carbon dioxide concentrations in the atmosphere are balanced by respiration and photosynthesis.

Carbon atoms from carbon dioxide are fixed into sugar molecules for storage by the plant

Anaerobic respiration

If oxygen runs out, cells keep themselves alive by switching to anaerobic respiration. Although this does not require oxygen, it is very inefficient and generates toxic waste products such as lactic acid, which causes cramps.

Intense exercise
During intense exercise, oxygen cannot reach the muscles fast enough, which causes them to switch to anaerobic respiration. When at rest, the waste product lactic acid is broken down into carbon dioxide and water.

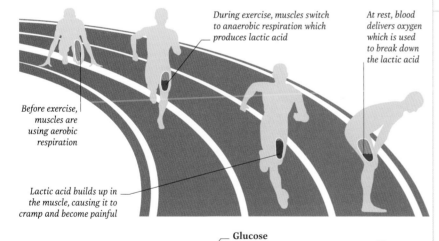

During exercise, muscles switch to anaerobic respiration which produces lactic acid

At rest, blood delivers oxygen which is used to break down the lactic acid

Before exercise, muscles are using aerobic respiration

Lactic acid builds up in the muscle, causing it to cramp and become painful

Anaerobic respiration in animals
Anaerobic respiration is the breakdown of one glucose molecule into two pyruvate molecules that are converted into lactic acid.

Glucose   Lactic Acid

$C_6H_{12}O_6$ ⟶ $2C_3H_6O_3$

Anaerobic respiration in plants and yeast
Anaerobic respiration in plants and yeast produces the waste product ethanol, which is toxic and eventually kills the organism.

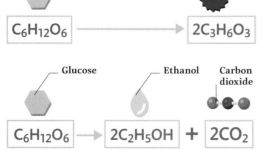

Glucose   Ethanol   Carbon dioxide

$C_6H_{12}O_6$ ⟶ $2C_2H_5OH$ + $2CO_2$

---

*Most of the **energy a person expends** is through their **resting metabolism***

What is metabolism?

Metabolism is every chemical reaction that takes place inside a cell or an organism. This includes the processes of digestion, muscle contraction, heat production, protein building, DNA replication, and waste clearance. Lots of these processes are chains of chemical reactions, driven by enzymes.

Enzymes
Enzymes are proteins that act as biological catalysts that speed up biochemical reactions. Catalysts also reduce the energy needed for chemical reactions, and make reactions more efficient.

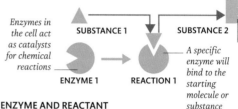

Enzymes in the cell act as catalysts for chemical reactions

SUBSTANCE 1   **SUBSTANCE 2**

A specific enzyme will bind to the starting molecule or substance

The enzyme converts the starting substance into a second, intermediate molecule

ENZYME 1   **REACTION 1**

ENZYME AND REACTANT

Enzyme 2 converts the intermediate molecule into the final product

Second molecule may move to a different part of the cell or stay where it was made

SUBSTANCE 2   **FINAL PRODUCT**

A second enzyme binds to the intermediate molecule

ENZYME 2   **REACTION 2**

FINAL PRODUCT CREATED

How is energy used?

Energy from respiration in the form of ATP is used by enzymes to drive the chemical reactions in the cell that keep the organism alive. Additional energy is needed to grow or move.

Plant
Plants need energy from respiration to both maintain and make new cells, allowing them to grow, and for reproduction.

During the day, plants create and store energy from sunlight

Cold-blooded snake
Cold-blooded animals warm themselves directly from the sun by basking on rocks. However, they still need energy to move.

Most animals spend a large amount of energy on movement

Warm-blooded adult mouse
Warm-blooded animals use their own energy to keep warm so that they don't need to rely on the sun.

Warm-blooded animals must consume a lot of fuel to control their body heat

KEY

■ Reproduction   ■ Growth
■ Metabolism   ■ Movement   ■ Generating body heat

---

see also The muscular system pp.234–37 ▶ Respiratory and cardiovascular systems pp.240–41 ▶ **223**

How genes work

What are genes?

Genes are short sequences of DNA that usually encode instructions to make a protein. Any changes to a gene result in changes to the protein, and can change how it works. Variation in gene sequences mean that despite having the same set of genes, individuals can look different to each other. New changes to the gene sequence are called mutations. Although most mutations stop the protein functioning and can cause genetic diseases, a few may be beneficial.

How genes build proteins

The DNA code is made of four different chemical units called bases, denoted by letters: adenine (A), thymine (T), cytosine (C) and guanine (G). These are read as 3-letter "words" called codons. Each codon corresponds to a specific amino acid—amino acids are the building blocks of proteins. The order of the bases determines the order of the amino acids in the protein.

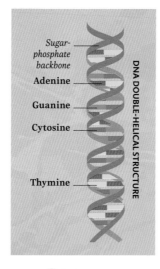

DNA DOUBLE-HELICAL STRUCTURE

Sugar-phosphate backbone
Adenine
Guanine
Cytosine
Thymine

❶ DNA structure
The four bases form the "rungs" of the DNA ladder by pairing specifically: A is always with T, and C with G.

Unzipped DNA

Base sequence now exposed and can act as a template

❷ DNA unzips
In order for a gene to be read, the two strands of DNA must be unzipped in a specific place to expose the bases along one strand.

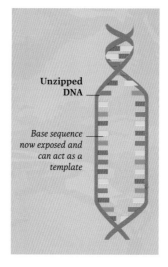

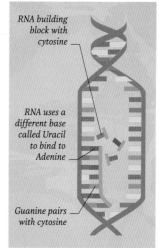

RNA building block with cytosine

RNA uses a different base called Uracil to bind to Adenine

Guanine pairs with cytosine

❸ Transcription
RNA bases pair with the exposed DNA bases to form a temporary copy of the gene, in a process called transcription.

Genes and genomes

Humans have over 25,000 genes arranged over 3 billion base pairs of DNA. The DNA is made up of 46 individual strands, called chromosomes. The entire sequence of DNA is called the genome. Each species has a different-sized genome.

Controlling genes

A main function of the stretches of DNA between genes is to act as a switch, turning genes on and off so that they only make proteins when they are needed.

If all the **DNA in a human body** was stretched out and joined end to end it would be about **50 billion miles (80 billion km) long**

Bases on one side of helix always pair with the complementary base on other side of helix

Adenine (red) always pairs with thymine (yellow)

Cytosine (blue) always pairs with guanine (green)

DNA helix tightly coiled many times over

Outer edges of ladder made of alternating sugar and phosphate units

DNA

Packaging DNA

Nearly every cell contains an entire copy of the genome. In humans, this is 6½ ft (2 m) of DNA per cell. To fit inside the nucleus, the DNA is tightly wound into coils, and during cell division it is wound even tighter into supercoils.

Chromosomes form X-shape during cell division

HUMAN CELL

CHROMOSOME

THE DNA DOUBLE HELIX

In 1953, the respectively American and British scientists James Watson and Francis Crick published what is now the most famous biological structure of all time: the DNA double helix. Their structure of DNA was based on work by Rosalind Franklin (see p.219). Watson and Crick realized that if the two strands of the DNA helix were separated, each could be used as a template to build the other side of the helix, allowing DNA to be copied.

Model made of metal plates and wires

JAMES WATSON

Sex chromosomes

A pair of sex chromosomes helps to determine the sex of the individual. In humans, these are called X and Y. Females usually have two Xs, whereas males usually have an X and a Y.

X (long) and Y (short) chromosomes of male

Nucleus contains 23 pairs of chromosomes

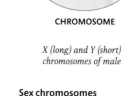

The animal with the **smallest** number of chromosomes is the **Jack Jumper ant,** with only one pair, while the **Atlas Blue butterfly** has the **largest** number of chromosomes with 452 (226 pairs)

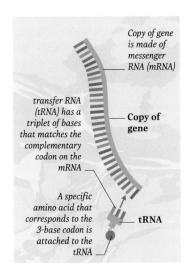

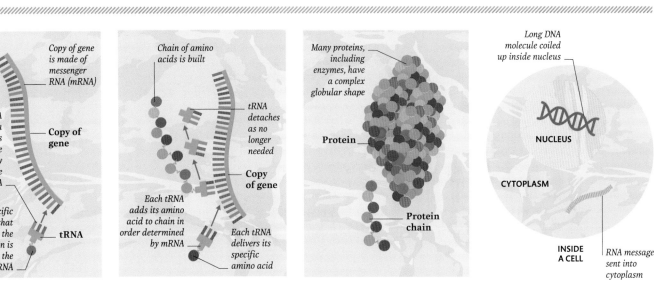

transfer RNA (tRNA) has a triplet of bases that matches the complementary codon on the mRNA

Copy of gene is made of messenger RNA (mRNA)

Copy of gene

A specific amino acid that corresponds to the 3-base codon is attached to the tRNA

tRNA

Chain of amino acids is built

tRNA detaches as no longer needed

Copy of gene

Each tRNA adds its amino acid to chain in order determined by mRNA

Each tRNA delivers its specific amino acid

Many proteins, including enzymes, have a complex globular shape

Protein

Protein chain

Long DNA molecule coiled up inside nucleus

NUCLEUS

CYTOPLASM

INSIDE A CELL

RNA message sent into cytoplasm

④ RNA leaves the nucleus
The finished messenger RNA (mRNA) strand travels from the nucleus to the cytoplasm, where transfer RNA (tRNA) molecules are matched to each codon.

⑤ Translation into amino acid chain
Each tRNA molecule is attached to a specific amino acid, which join together to form a protein chain. In this way, the base sequence is translated into amino acids.

⑥ Amino acids fold into protein
Once the protein chain is made, it folds up into a 3D structure. The exact shape is determined by the order of the amino acids in the chain.

Where it all happens
DNA is packaged inside the nucleus for protection. RNA transmits the code to the protein-making machinery in the cytoplasm.

How we inherit genes

Genes are passed from parents to their offspring, forming the units of inheritance. The rules of inheritance were discovered by a monk named Gregor Mendel in the 19th century. By studying sweet peas, he realized that an individual must inherit one copy of every gene from each parent, but he did not know which molecule was responsible for this inheritance.

Mendelian inheritance

Different versions of each gene are called alleles. When an individual inherits a different allele from each parent, one allele is often dominant (always expressed) and the other is recessive. To show a recessive trait, an individual must inherit a recessive allele from both parents.

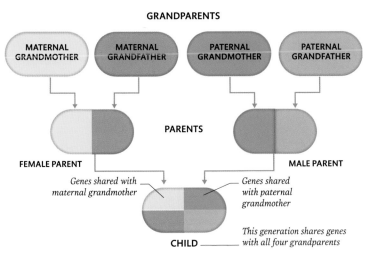

GRANDPARENTS

MATERNAL GRANDMOTHER | **MATERNAL GRANDFATHER** | **PATERNAL GRANDMOTHER** | **PATERNAL GRANDFATHER**

PARENTS

FEMALE PARENT

MALE PARENT

Genes shared with maternal grandmother

Genes shared with paternal grandmother

This generation shares genes with all four grandparents

CHILD

Dominant allele for detached earlobes

Recessive allele for attached earlobes

MALE PARENT

FEMALE PARENT

DOUBLE DOMINANT | **DOMINANT-RECESSIVE** | **DOMINANT-RECESSIVE** | **DOUBLE RECESSIVE**

Both copies of gene recessive

DETACHED EARLOBES

ATTACHED EARLOBE

Genes in families
Averaged across the genome—and across the population of individuals—a grandchild shares about half of its genes with each parent and one-quarter of its genes with each grandparent.

> **New mutations** in humans happen at a rate of **1 in 10 million base pairs** per generation

Polygenic traits
Many characteristics, such as human height, are not controlled by a single gene or allele of that gene. Instead, many genes contribute, and many different heights result from the different combinations.

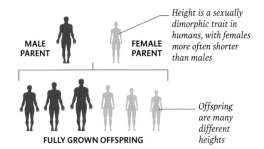

MALE PARENT

FEMALE PARENT

Height is a sexually dimorphic trait in humans, with females more often shorter than males

Offspring are many different heights

FULLY GROWN OFFSPRING

see also Reproduction pp.226–27 ▶ Evolution pp.228–29 ▶ Medical advances pp.260–61 ▶

Reproduction

One of the defining characteristics of living things is their ability to reproduce. Strategies for reproduction have been evolving since the beginning of life, so it is not surprising that many different methods now exist. However, most of these strategies fall into one of two categories: asexual reproduction, where the genetic material of only one individual is used to make a new organism, or sexual reproduction, in which two individuals contribute DNA to create a new organism. Asexual reproduction produces new individuals quickly, whereas sexual reproduction introduces genetic variety, making the species more robust.

Asexual reproduction

Asexual reproduction is the process of making a new individual using just one parent's genetic material, which means the offspring have the same DNA as the parent. Because asexual reproduction produces organisms that have the same DNA, there is very little genetic variation in the population, so if the environment changes, or a new predator appears, every individual is equally vulnerable to the new threat.

Making copies

Asexual reproduction results in the production of clones, which contain exactly the same DNA as each other. Single-celled organisms such as amoebas reproduce in this way.

Parental DNA is copied and each cell inherits a copy

Each offspring contains identical DNA

PARENT   **DIVISION**   **OFFSPRING**

Sexual reproduction

During sexual reproduction, two individuals contribute DNA to make offspring. This means that the offspring inherit a random mixture of traits from both parents, which maintains genetic variation and increases a species' chances of surviving change. To reproduce sexually, parents must produce specialized cells called gametes in a process called meiosis. Gametes contain half of the parent's DNA, so that when two gametes combine, the new individual contains a full set of DNA.

There are approximately **6 million differences** in the **DNA sequence** of **any two humans** on Earth

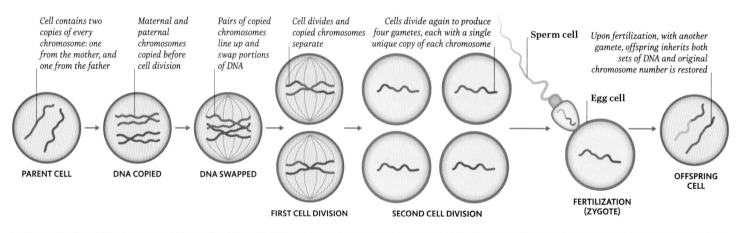

Cell contains two copies of every chromosome: one from the mother, and one from the father

Maternal and paternal chromosomes copied before cell division

Pairs of copied chromosomes line up and swap portions of DNA

Cell divides and copied chromosomes separate

Cells divide again to produce four gametes, each with a single unique copy of each chromosome

Sperm cell

Upon fertilization, with another gamete, offspring inherits both sets of DNA and original chromosome number is restored

Egg cell

PARENT CELL   **DNA COPIED**   **DNA SWAPPED**   **FIRST CELL DIVISION**   **SECOND CELL DIVISION**   **FERTILIZATION (ZYGOTE)**   **OFFSPRING CELL**

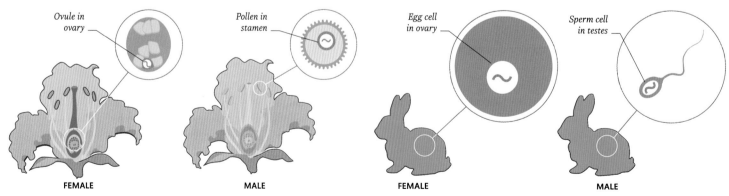

Ovule in ovary   *Pollen in stamen*   *Egg cell in ovary*   *Sperm cell in testes*

FEMALE   **MALE**   **FEMALE**   **MALE**

Sex in flowering plants
The sexual organ of flowering plants is the flower. At the base of the flower is the ovary, which contains the ovules, the female gametes, while the stamens surrounding the ovary produce pollen, the male gametes.

Sex in animals
In animals, the female gamete is the egg cell and male gametes are sperm cells. Sperm cells have a long, whiplike tail, which they use to swim toward the much larger egg, with their many mitochondria providing the energy.

In optimal conditions, a **bacteria cell** can **divide every 20 minutes**, which means one bacterium will have **69 billion descendants after 12 hours**

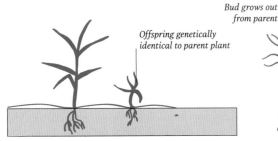

Offspring genetically identical to parent plant

PLANT PRODUCING RUNNERS

Vegetative reproduction
Some plants, such as strawberries, raspberries, and spider plants, can reproduce asexually. They do this by extending runners (stolons) that grow over or just under the ground before producing their own roots and leaves.

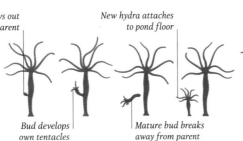

Bud grows out from parent

New hydra attaches to pond floor

Bud develops own tentacles

Mature bud breaks away from parent

HOW A HYDRA BUDS

Budding
Hydra are small aquatic animals. They can reproduce sexually, but when food is plentiful they reproduce asexually by budding. In this process, a bud forms from the parent before detaching to become independent.

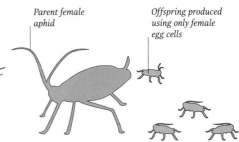

Parent female aphid

Offspring produced using only female egg cells

APHID ASEXUAL REPRODUCTION

Parthenogenesis
Parthenogenesis is the development of a female egg into an adult without fertilization. Some plants, some invertebrates, including nematodes and aphids, and even some fishes, amphibians, and reptiles are able to reproduce this way.

Mating behavior
Choosing the right mate can be crucial for successful reproduction and many animals have evolved complex behaviors that allow them to display their reproductive fitness to a potential partner or partners.

Male songbirds, like this Eurasian Wren, sing to attract a mate

Colorful male Peacock Spiders woo females by dancing

SINGING

DANCING

Courtship and competition
Many animals perform complex courtship rituals to woo potential mates. Their success at courtship determines if they will reproduce. Male animals often perform to attract females, with displays of skill ranging from singing or dancing to complex diving routines. Male or females of some species win access to mates through combat.

Fallow Deer stags fight for the right to mate

Grebe pairs bond through elaborate courtship displays

FIGHTING

BONDING

Reproductive flexibility
Sexual reproduction between two individuals is the best way to maintain a healthy gene pool. However, some animals have evolved reproductive strategies to produce offspring when males are not present. These include the Komodo Dragon, where lone females have reproduced by parthenogenesis in captivity.

KOMODO DRAGON

Reproductive strategies
Reproduction is energy-consuming. Energy must be invested to rear vulnerable young, and energy is required from the body to produce offspring in the first place. By balancing these two energy requirements, organisms have the best chance of producing young that will pass on their genes, and different strategies have evolved in animals to achieve this.

FISH

FISH SPAWN

Many offspring
Fishes lay hundreds—sometimes millions—of eggs at a time. Most of these eggs will not survive, but the vast number laid ensures that a few will grow up to become adult fish.

A **male Emperor Penguin** will lose nearly half his **body weight** incubating a **single egg** over an Antarctic winter

CONDOR

CONDOR EGG

Few offspring
Condors lay just one egg every two years, allowing both parents to raise their dependent chick until the next egg is laid, thus increasing its chance of survival.

OSKAR HERTWIG
Oskar Hertwig (1849–1922) was a German embryologist and anatomist who discovered how a sperm cell fertilizes an egg. At the time, scientists did not know whether sperm cells just touched the egg or whether the sperm entered it. By studying fertilization in transparent sea urchin eggs, Hertwig observed that sperm did enter the egg, and that once this occurred, other sperm cells were blocked from entering.

see also Evolution pp.228–29 ▶ Reproductive and endocrine systems pp.246–47 ▶ The human life cycle pp.248–49 ▶

Evolution

Evolution is one of the most important theories in biology. It is the process by which organisms change over time, and it helps to explain how new species arise. Evolution is driven by natural selection, whereby individuals with favorable heritable characteristics are more likely to survive and pass them to their offspring. As a result, these characteristics spread through the population, better adapting it to the environment of the time.

Natural selection

In any population, random mutations arise in the genome, giving rise to genetic variation. Some of these mutations will be advantageous, giving the organism a trait that improves its ability to survive. These organisms then pass this trait on to the next generation. This process is called natural selection, and drives evolution.

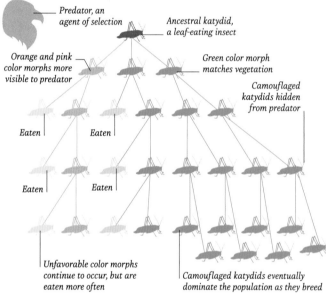

Predator, an agent of selection

Ancestral katydid, a leaf-eating insect

Orange and pink color morphs more visible to predator

Green color morph matches vegetation

Camouflaged katydids hidden from predator

Eaten | Eaten

Eaten | Eaten

Unfavorable color morphs continue to occur, but are eaten more often

Camouflaged katydids eventually dominate the population as they breed

Survival of the fittest
Natural selection works because of the different selective pressures acting on populations. Organisms with features that confer some sort of advantage, such as camouflage, are more likely to survive and reproduce than those without them. This is more popularly known as "the survival of the fittest"—a phrase inspired by Darwin's work.

CHARLES DARWIN
Charles Darwin (1809–82) was a British naturalist who traveled to South America on the *HMS Beagle*, captained by Robert FitzRoy. He brought back to England many samples of the different species that he encountered during the voyage. The ship reached the Galápagos Islands in September 1835, and Darwin's observations of the islands' birds laid the foundation for his revolutionary theory of evolution, which he published in 1859 in his book *On the Origin of Species*.

Speciation

Speciation is the evolution of two or more separate species from one ancestral species. This can occur due to geographical separation of different populations of the ancestral species, after which each population takes a separate evolutionary route, or because members of the original species start to specialize in different ways, such as eating different foods.

Geographic isolation
Individuals from a single population may get separated and end up on either side of an obstruction, such as a mountain range. The two subpopulations continue to evolve independently, eventually resulting in two separate species.

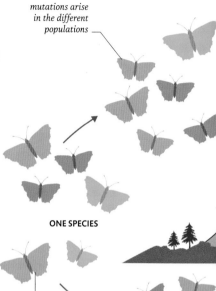

Random mutations arise in the different populations

ONE SPECIES

Original population separated into two populations

The **majority of species** that have evolved are **now extinct,** but their **genes survive** in living descendants

Adaptive radiation

Adaptive radiation is the process whereby a species evolves in many different directions at the same time. This can happen if new food sources become available, or the environment changes, thereby opening up new habitats.

Galápagos finches
Darwin observed that finches living on the Galápagos Islands displayed different characteristics. Finches that fed on large, hard seeds and nuts had large, deep bills, while finches that ate insects had smaller, sharper bills. He realized that each finch population had evolved in a different direction, leading to many new species.

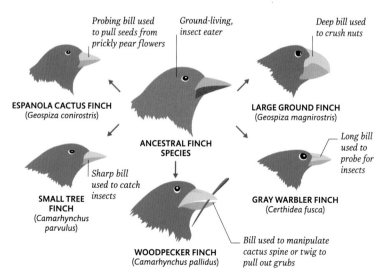

Probing bill used to pull seeds from prickly pear flowers

Ground-living, insect eater

Deep bill used to crush nuts

ESPANOLA CACTUS FINCH
(*Geospiza conirostris*)

LARGE GROUND FINCH
(*Geospiza magnirostris*)

ANCESTRAL FINCH SPECIES

Long bill used to probe for insects

Sharp bill used to catch insects

SMALL TREE FINCH
(*Camarhynchus parvulus*)

GRAY WARBLER FINCH
(*Certhidea fusca*)

WOODPECKER FINCH
(*Camarhynchus pallidus*)

Bill used to manipulate cactus spine or twig to pull out grubs

Most **stickleback fishes** live in **salt water**, but new **freshwater species** have evolved from ancestors that were **trapped in lakes** during the **last ice age**

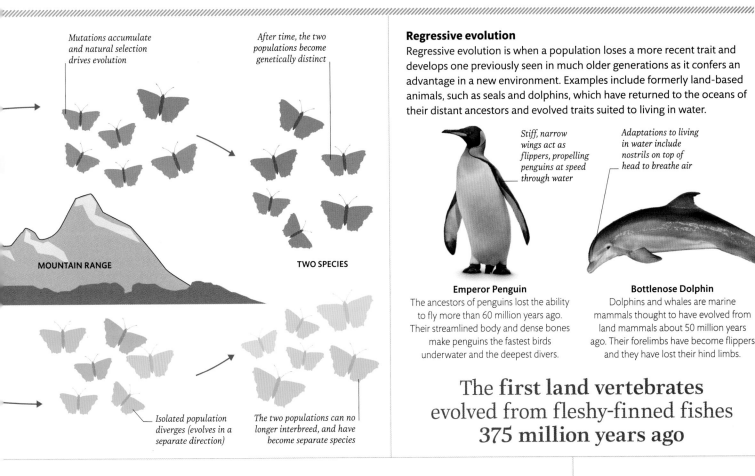

Mutations accumulate and natural selection drives evolution

After time, the two populations become genetically distinct

MOUNTAIN RANGE

TWO SPECIES

Isolated population diverges (evolves in a separate direction)

The two populations can no longer interbreed, and have become separate species

Regressive evolution

Regressive evolution is when a population loses a more recent trait and develops one previously seen in much older generations as it confers an advantage in a new environment. Examples include formerly land-based animals, such as seals and dolphins, which have returned to the oceans of their distant ancestors and evolved traits suited to living in water.

Stiff, narrow wings act as flippers, propelling penguins at speed through water

Adaptations to living in water include nostrils on top of head to breathe air

Emperor Penguin
The ancestors of penguins lost the ability to fly more than 60 million years ago. Their streamlined body and dense bones make penguins the fastest birds underwater and the deepest divers.

Bottlenose Dolphin
Dolphins and whales are marine mammals thought to have evolved from land mammals about 50 million years ago. Their forelimbs have become flippers and they have lost their hind limbs.

The **first land vertebrates** evolved from fleshy-finned fishes **375 million years ago**

Divergent evolution

Over vast periods of time, repeated speciation leads to new descendant species becoming markedly different from their common ancestor—this is known as divergent evolution. For example, all organisms that live on land have diverged from their water-living ancestors. And all species of mammals alive today diverged from an ancestral shrewlike mammal that lived around 210 million years ago.

Shared ancestry

Although a horse's leg looks very different to a bat's wing, the shared sequence of the bones in their limbs reveals all mammals have evolved from a common ancestor.

Ulna

Radius   Carpals

Metacarpals

Phalanges

DOLPHIN FLIPPER   **BAT WING**   **MONKEY ARM**   **HORSE LEG**

Coevolution

Coevolution occurs in organisms that have a close association and develop reciprocal adaptations. This can happen if one organism provides a necessary function for a second organism, which in turn provides the first organism with resources such as food or shelter. For example, bees, hummingbirds, and some bats pollinate flowers when feeding on nectar.

Convergent evolution

Convergent evolution occurs when different organisms independently evolve a similar trait or appearance as a result of living in the same environment. For example, bats, birds, and butterflies all have wings and can fly, but they are not closely related and, unlike the mammal limbs shown above, their wings are not the result of shared ancestry but of convergence.

Similar body forms

Ichthyosaurs were carnivorous marine reptiles that lived 250–90 million years ago. They evolved features seen today in predatory fishes such as sharks.

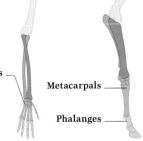

Streamlined body built for speed

Strong tail propels shark through water

Dorsal fin prevents rolling

Paired flippers

Dorsal fin

Distinct tail

ICHTHYOSAUR

Paired fins moved for steering

SHARK

Body coated in pollen from other agave plants

Bat uses long tongue to reach nectar at base of agave flowers

As bat feeds, it pollinates plant

LESSER LONG-NOSED BAT
Leptonycteris yerbabuenae

◀ see also How genes work pp.224–25   ◀ Reproduction pp.226–27   **229**

The human body

The human body's components exist in a hierarchical structure of increasing complexity, in which each "level" contributes to a greater whole. Chemicals are combined into cells; cells are joined together to form tissues; and tissues develop with others to form organs, which in turn work together to carry out the body's essential processes.

DNA and chromosomes
Genes—the instructions to make and maintain a body—are stored in a chemical form called DNA (deoxyribonucleic acid). Each gene has the code to build a body substance—a protein. The DNA is stored as enormously long and tightly coiled molecules called chromosomes.

The human genome
In each body cell, DNA exists as 46 chromosomes in 23 pairs, together making up the human genome. One of each pair is from the mother and the other from the father. Under the microscope, the pattern of bands indicates groups of genes.

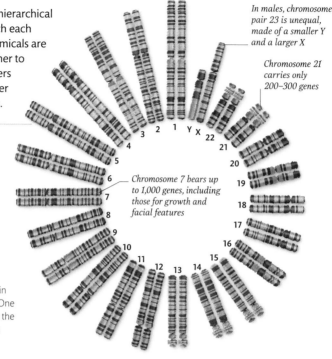

In males, chromosome pair 23 is unequal, made of a smaller Y and a larger X

Chromosome 21 carries only 200–300 genes

Chromosome 7 bears up to 1,000 genes, including those for growth and facial features

ANDREAS VESALIUS
In 1543, Flemish anatomist Vesalius (1514-1564) published a major landmark in life sciences called *On the Fabric of the Human Body*. It marked a break from ancient, unquestioned, and constantly repeated teachings and heralded a new era of firsthand observation and experimentation.

Organization of the body
The body can be viewed as a hierarchy of organization. The basic units are about 30–40 trillion microscopic cells. Cells of a similar kind make up a particular type of tissue, and several kinds of tissues form each of the main working units, known as organs.

From cells to body systems
As cells form tissues, which make organs, so a set of organs work together to fulfill one major body function, such as digestion. This is termed a body system. Overall health and body efficiency depends on body systems working together.

A series of organs that work together to break down food is called the digestive system

Cell varieties and tissue types
There are more than 100 different kinds of cells, each with its own shape and structure adapted to its task. These are variations of only four basic cell and tissue types: epithelial, connective, muscular, and nervous.

Skin is **one-sixth of the body weight** of an average adult

Nerve
Nerve cells have long, thin extensions that carry tiny electrical pulses known as nerve signals.

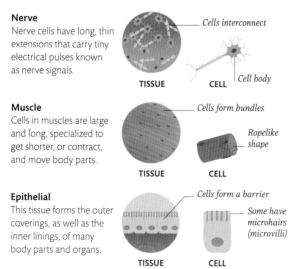

Cells interconnect

TISSUE   **CELL**   *Cell body*

Muscle
Cells in muscles are large and long, specialized to get shorter, or contract, and move body parts.

Cells form bundles

Ropelike shape

TISSUE   **CELL**

Epithelial
This tissue forms the outer coverings, as well as the inner linings, of many body parts and organs.

Cells form a barrier

Some have microhairs (microvilli)

TISSUE   **CELL**

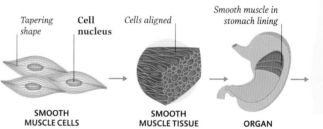

Tapering shape   **Cell nucleus**   *Cells aligned*   *Smooth muscle in stomach lining*

SMOOTH MUSCLE CELLS   **SMOOTH MUSCLE TISSUE**   **ORGAN**   **SYSTEM**

STEM CELLS
As life starts, the fertilized egg divides repeatedly to form dozens of similar cells known as stem cells. Each has the potential to become any cell type in the body. As development continues, these groups of cells lose this general ability and become differentiated into specialized cell types.

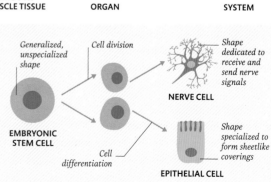

Generalized, unspecialized shape   *Cell division*   *Shape dedicated to receive and send nerve signals*

EMBRYONIC STEM CELL   **NERVE CELL**

Cell differentiation

Shape specialized to form sheetlike coverings

EPITHELIAL CELL

Skin and hair

The largest organ, the skin of an adult on average covers about 17–19 sq ft (1.6–1.8 sq m). It detects touch and protects inner parts from physical damage and drying out. Its surface layer of dead, flakelike cells is rapidly replaced from beneath as the cells rub off. Skin also produces vitamin D under the influence of sunlight. Head and body hairs help retain heat; they are dead except at the root.

Ultraviolet protection

The sun's ultraviolet rays can harm body tissues. Naturally dark skin shields the parts below from damage. The color is due to the pigment melanin, produced by cells called melanocytes. Light skin can gradually adapt by making more melanin than usual.

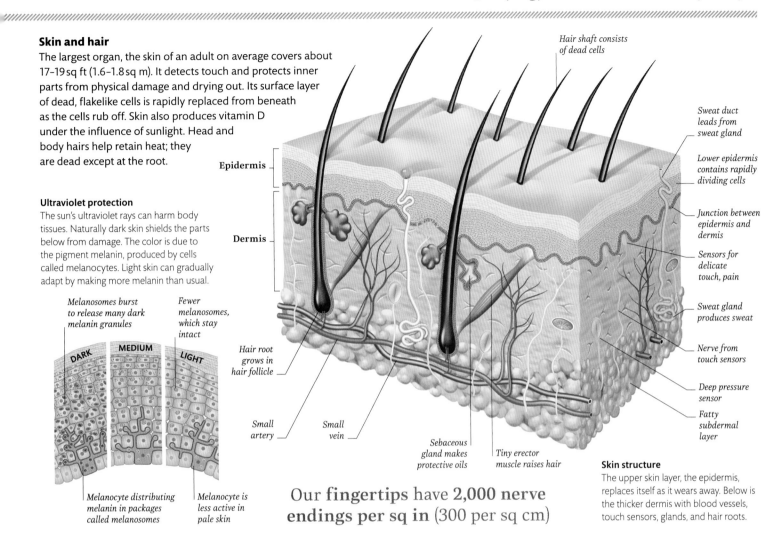

Hair shaft consists of dead cells

Epidermis

Dermis

Sweat duct leads from sweat gland

Lower epidermis contains rapidly dividing cells

Junction between epidermis and dermis

Sensors for delicate touch, pain

Sweat gland produces sweat

Nerve from touch sensors

Deep pressure sensor

Fatty subdermal layer

Hair root grows in hair follicle

Small artery

Small vein

Sebaceous gland makes protective oils

Tiny erector muscle raises hair

Melanosomes burst to release many dark melanin granules

Fewer melanosomes, which stay intact

DARK **MEDIUM** **LIGHT**

Melanocyte distributing melanin in packages called melanosomes

Melanocyte is less active in pale skin

Our **fingertips** have **2,000 nerve endings per sq in** (300 per sq cm)

Skin structure

The upper skin layer, the epidermis, replaces itself as it wears away. Below is the thicker dermis with blood vessels, touch sensors, glands, and hair roots.

Thermoregulation

Skin helps maintain constant body temperature. When the body is too hot, the skin's blood vessels widen, bringing more warm blood near the surface where it loses heat to the exterior. Heat is also lost through sweat, which evaporates from the skin surface, and hairs lie flatter to trap less insulating air. If the body is too cold, these processes are reversed.

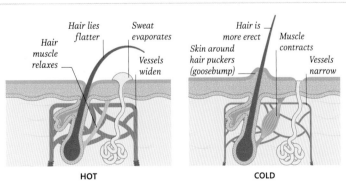

Hair lies flatter *Sweat evaporates* *Hair muscle relaxes* *Vessels widen*

HOT

Hair is more erect *Muscle contracts* *Skin around hair puckers (goosebump)* *Vessels narrow*

COLD

NAILS

Nails are made of keratin—the same tough, durable substance that forms hairs and is also in upper epidermal skin cells. A nail grows from its root under the skin and slides along the nail bed to the end of the finger or toe. Nails are constantly self-repairing.

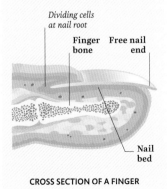

Dividing cells at nail root

Finger bone **Free nail end**

Nail bed

CROSS SECTION OF A FINGER

Skin healing

Skin damage is quickly sealed as blood vessels narrow and the blood thickens into a gellike mass, the clot. Gradually this hardens to keep out infecting germs, while cells around it multiply and spread into the damaged area.

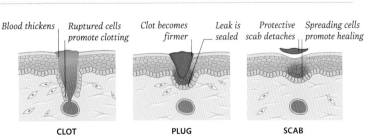

Blood thickens *Ruptured cells promote clotting* *Clot becomes firmer* *Leak is sealed* *Protective scab detaches* *Spreading cells promote healing*

CLOT **PLUG** **SCAB**

The skeletal system

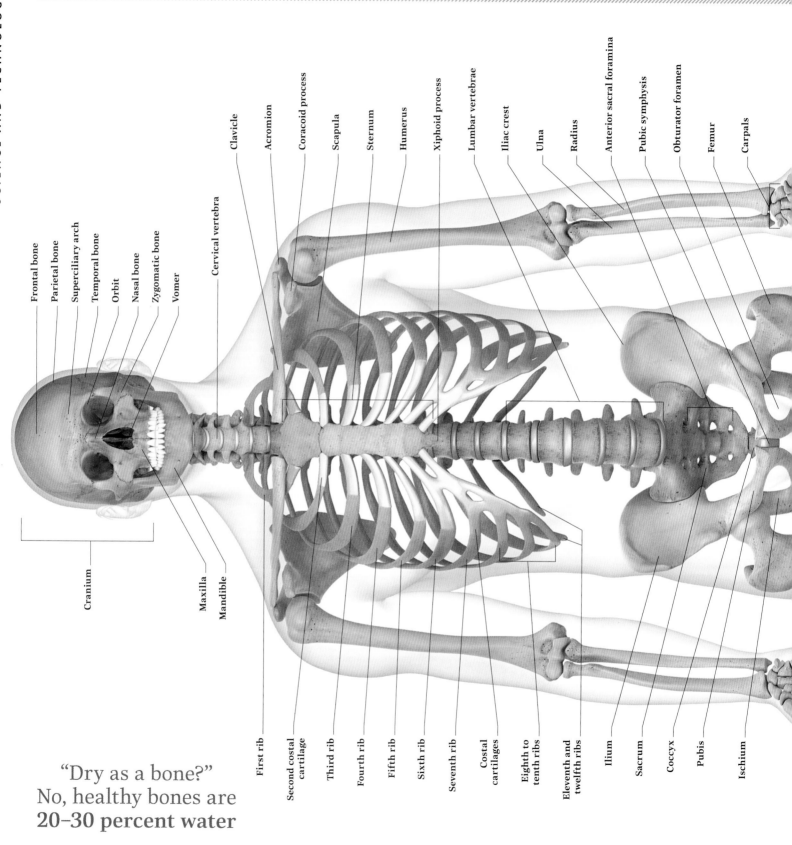

Frontal bone
Parietal bone
Superciliary arch
Temporal bone
Orbit
Nasal bone
Zygomatic bone
Vomer
Cervical vertebra
Clavicle
Acromion
Coracoid process
Scapula
Sternum
Humerus
Xiphoid process
Lumbar vertebrae
Iliac crest
Ulna
Radius
Anterior sacral foramina
Pubic symphysis
Obturator foramen
Femur
Carpals

Cranium
Maxilla
Mandible

First rib
Second costal cartilage
Third rib
Fourth rib
Fifth rib
Sixth rib
Seventh rib
Costal cartilages
Eighth to tenth ribs
Eleventh and twelfth ribs
Ilium
Sacrum
Coccyx
Pubis
Ischium

"Dry as a bone?"
No, healthy bones are
20–30 percent water

The skeleton forms **one-seventh** of total **body weight**

The skeleton's 206 bones form a strong yet moveable inner framework that supports the softer body parts. Bones also protect—the cranium (upper skull), for instance, surrounds the brain. More than half of the body's bones—106—are in the wrists, hands, ankles, and feet. Another 28 are in the head. The skeleton's central axis, including the skull, vertebral column (spine), and ribs, is termed the axial skeleton. The hips, legs, shoulders, and arms form the appendicular skeleton. Each bone has an anatomical name, and so does each of its parts, hollows, holes, and lumps (processes). Many bones or their parts also have common names, such as the cheekbone, which is the maxillary process of the zygomatic bone.

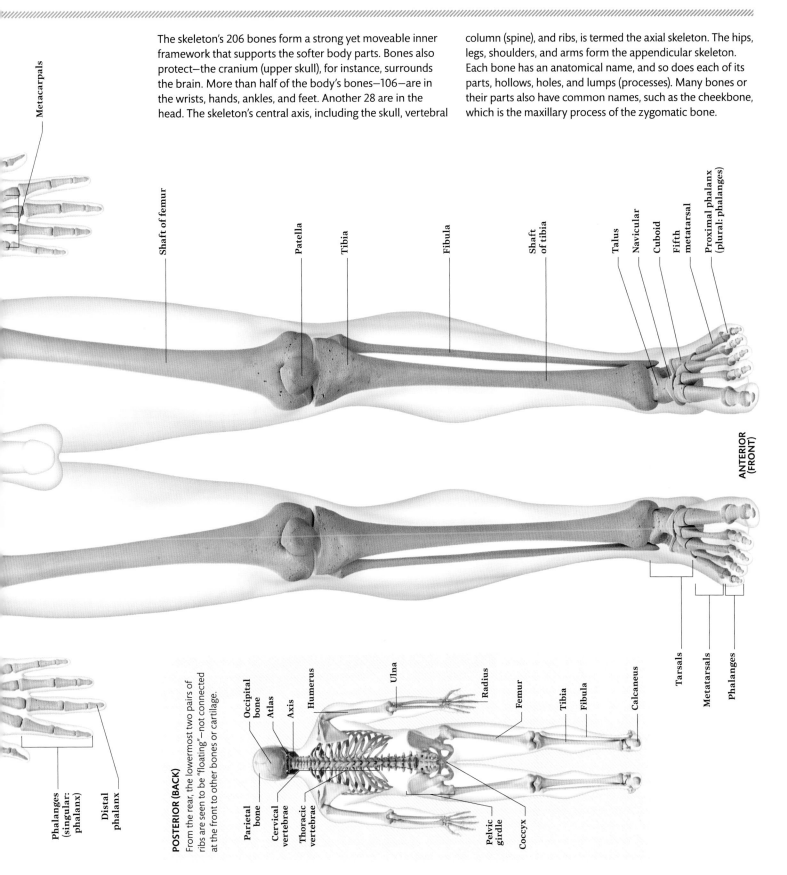

Metacarpals

Shaft of femur

Patella

Tibia

Fibula

Shaft of tibia

Talus

Navicular

Cuboid

Fifth metatarsal

Proximal phalanx (plural: phalanges)

ANTERIOR (FRONT)

Tarsals

Metatarsals

Phalanges

Phalanges (singular: phalanx)

Distal phalanx

POSTERIOR (BACK)
From the rear, the lowermost two pairs of ribs are seen to be "floating"—not connected at the front to other bones or cartilage.

Occipital bone

Atlas

Axis

Humerus

Ulna

Radius

Femur

Tibia

Fibula

Calcaneus

Parietal bone

Cervical vertebrae

Thoracic vertebrae

Pelvic girdle

Coccyx

see also The muscular system pp.234–37 ▶ **233**

The muscular system

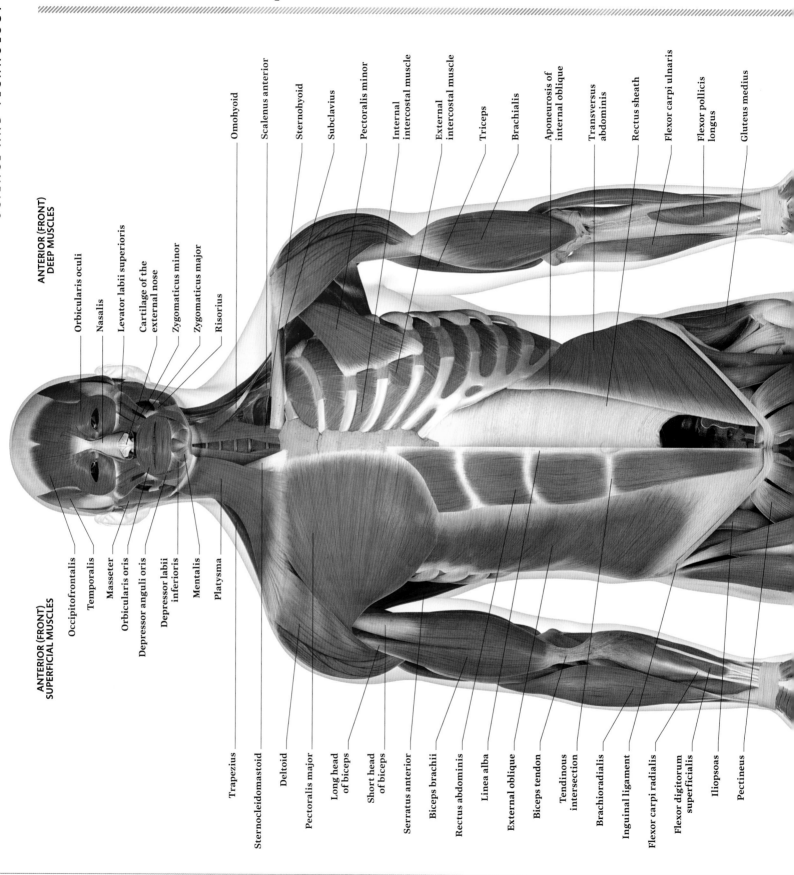

ANTERIOR (FRONT) DEEP MUSCLES

Orbicularis oculi
Nasalis
Levator labii superioris
Cartilage of the external nose
Zygomaticus minor
Zygomaticus major
Risorius

Omohyoid
Scalenus anterior
Sternohyoid
Subclavius
Pectoralis minor
Internal intercostal muscle
External intercostal muscle
Triceps
Brachialis
Aponeurosis of internal oblique
Transversus abdominis
Rectus sheath
Flexor carpi ulnaris
Flexor pollicis longus
Gluteus medius

ANTERIOR (FRONT) SUPERFICIAL MUSCLES

Occipitofrontalis
Temporalis
Masseter
Orbicularis oris
Depressor anguli oris
Depressor labii inferioris
Mentalis
Platysma

Trapezius
Sternocleidomastoid
Deltoid
Pectoralis major
Long head of biceps
Short head of biceps
Serratus anterior
Biceps brachii
Rectus abdominis
Linea alba
External oblique
Biceps tendon
Tendinous intersection
Brachioradialis
Inguinal ligament
Flexor carpi radialis
Flexor digitorum superficialis
Iliopsoas
Pectineus

Our **tiniest muscle**, the ear's **stapedius**,
is less than $1/10$ in (2 mm) long

Anterior muscles

Skeletal muscles are those connected to bones or to each other, to move body parts. There are typically more than 650 named muscles comprising two-fifths of the total body weight. The exact muscle number varies. For example, some people lack the platysma—a broad, sheetlike muscle in the neck. Muscles tend to be arranged in layers. Outer, or superficial, muscles are just under the skin, with intermediate layers beneath, and deep muscles adjacent to bones. Muscles exert force only by shortening and pulling. They cannot push actively. Therefore they are arranged in groups, some pulling a bone one way and others moving it in opposing directions.

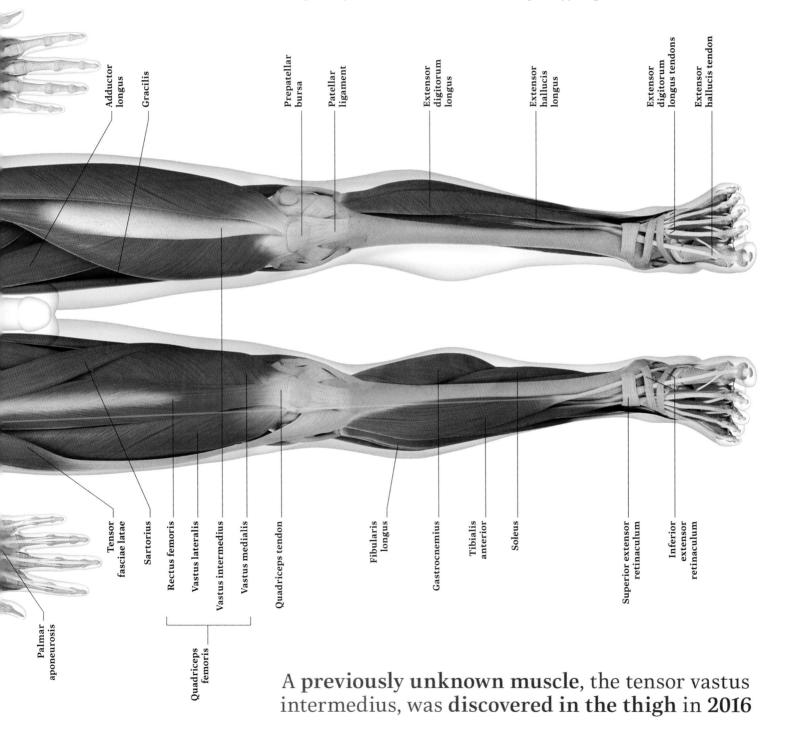

Adductor longus
Gracilis
Prepatellar bursa
Patellar ligament
Extensor digitorum longus
Extensor hallucis longus
Extensor digitorum longus tendons
Extensor hallucis tendon

Palmar aponeurosis
Tensor fasciae latae
Sartorius
Rectus femoris
Vastus lateralis
Vastus intermedius
Vastus medialis
Quadriceps tendon
Fibularis longus
Gastrocnemius
Tibialis anterior
Soleus
Superior extensor retinaculum
Inferior extensor retinaculum

Quadriceps femoris

A **previously unknown muscle**, the tensor vastus intermedius, was **discovered in the thigh** in 2016

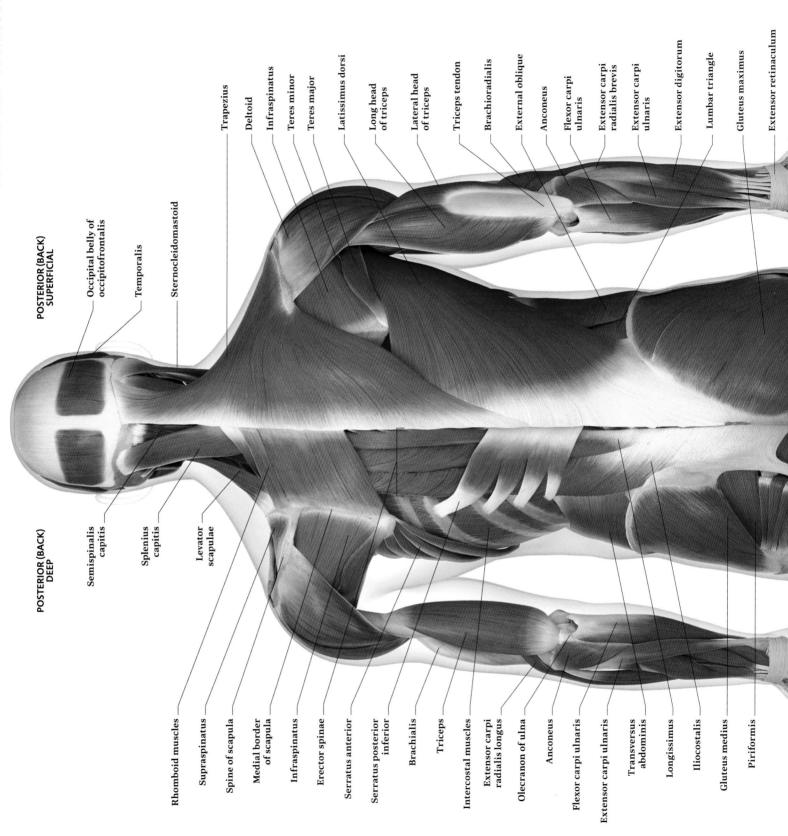

POSTERIOR (BACK)
SUPERFICIAL

Occipital belly of occipitofrontalis

Temporalis

Sternocleidomastoid

Trapezius

Deltoid

Infraspinatus

Teres minor

Teres major

Latissimus dorsi

Long head of triceps

Lateral head of triceps

Triceps tendon

Brachioradialis

External oblique

Anconeus

Flexor carpi ulnaris

Extensor carpi radialis brevis

Extensor carpi ulnaris

Extensor digitorum

Lumbar triangle

Gluteus maximus

Extensor retinaculum

POSTERIOR (BACK)
DEEP

Semispinalis capitis

Splenius capitis

Levator scapulae

Rhomboid muscles

Supraspinatus

Spine of scapula

Medial border of scapula

Infraspinatus

Erector spinae

Serratus anterior

Serratus posterior inferior

Brachialis

Triceps

Intercostal muscles

Extensor carpi radialis longus

Olecranon of ulna

Anconeus

Flexor carpi ulnaris

Extensor carpi ulnaris

Transversus abdominis

Longissimus

Iliocostalis

Gluteus medius

Piriformis

Posterior muscles

A rear—posterior, or dorsal—view shows the body's largest muscle, the gluteus maximus in the buttock. It attaches into the pelvis (hip bone) above and the femur (thigh bone) below. Tensing it keeps the back and thigh in line when standing upright, while contraction pulls the thigh rearward to walk, run, and jump. Also visible is the body's largest, thickest tendon, the calcaneal, or Achilles tendon. It links the gastrocnemius and other calf muscles into the calcaneus (heel bone) below and is more prominent when standing on tiptoe. Several longer, much slimmer tendons pass from muscles in the forearm and under a fibrous strap in the wrist, the extensor retinaculum, to straighten the fingers.

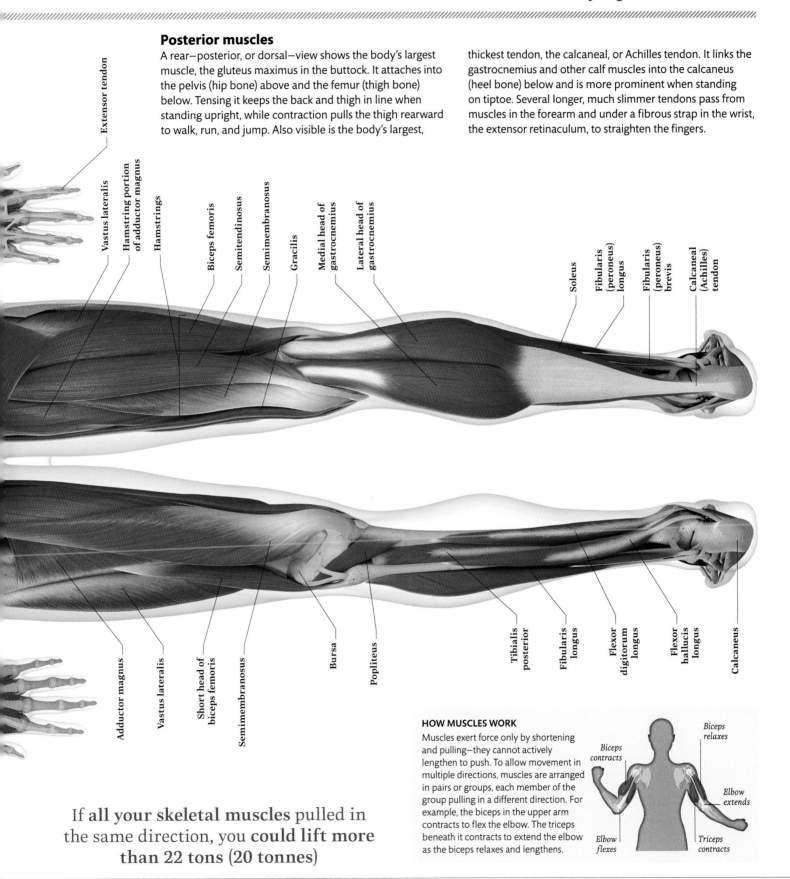

Extensor tendon

Vastus lateralis

Hamstring portion of adductor magnus

Hamstrings

Biceps femoris

Semitendinosus

Semimembranosus

Gracilis

Medial head of gastrocnemius

Lateral head of gastrocnemius

Soleus

Fibularis (peroneus) longus

Fibularis (peroneus) brevis

Calcaneal (Achilles) tendon

Adductor magnus

Vastus lateralis

Short head of biceps femoris

Semimembranosus

Bursa

Popliteus

Tibialis posterior

Fibularis longus

Flexor digitorum longus

Flexor hallucis longus

Calcaneus

HOW MUSCLES WORK

Muscles exert force only by shortening and pulling—they cannot actively lengthen to push. To allow movement in multiple directions, muscles are arranged in pairs or groups, each member of the group pulling in a different direction. For example, the biceps in the upper arm contracts to flex the elbow. The triceps beneath it contracts to extend the elbow as the biceps relaxes and lengthens.

Biceps contracts

Elbow flexes

Biceps relaxes

Elbow extends

Triceps contracts

If **all your skeletal muscles** pulled in the same direction, you **could lift more than 22 tons (20 tonnes)**

see also Medical advances pp.260–61 ▶   **237**

The nervous system

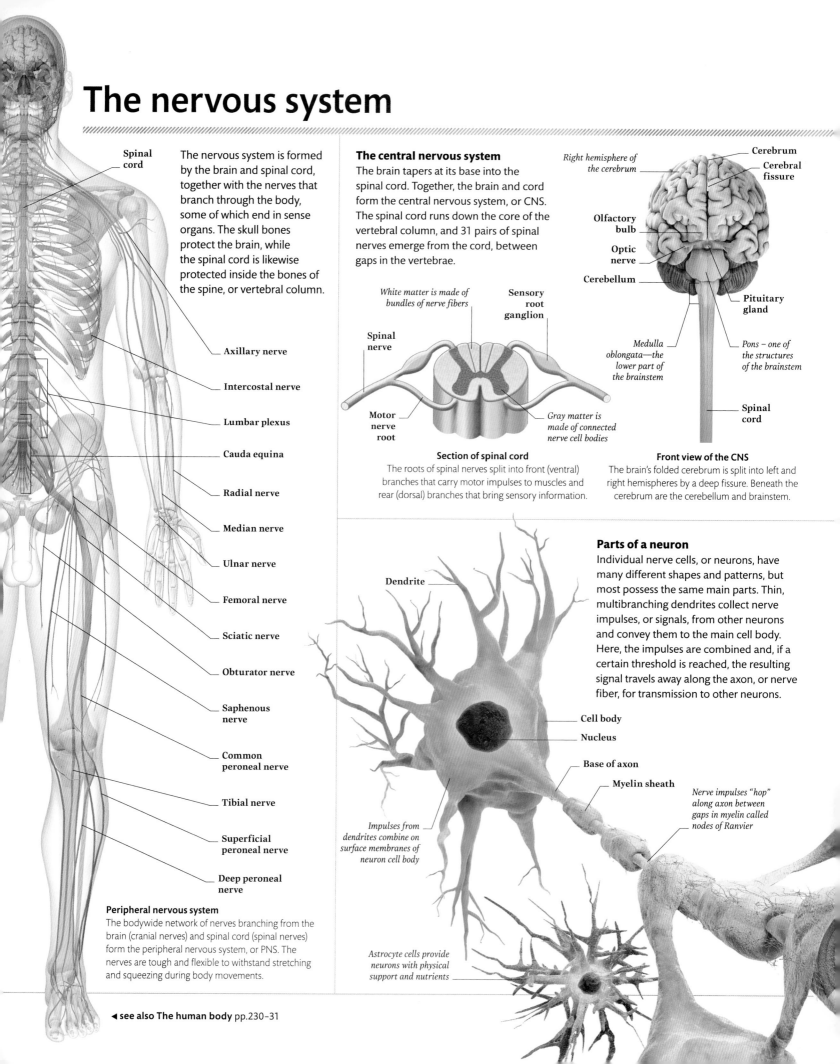

Spinal cord

The nervous system is formed by the brain and spinal cord, together with the nerves that branch through the body, some of which end in sense organs. The skull bones protect the brain, while the spinal cord is likewise protected inside the bones of the spine, or vertebral column.

Axillary nerve

Intercostal nerve

Lumbar plexus

Cauda equina

Radial nerve

Median nerve

Ulnar nerve

Femoral nerve

Sciatic nerve

Obturator nerve

Saphenous nerve

Common peroneal nerve

Tibial nerve

Superficial peroneal nerve

Deep peroneal nerve

Peripheral nervous system

The bodywide network of nerves branching from the brain (cranial nerves) and spinal cord (spinal nerves) form the peripheral nervous system, or PNS. The nerves are tough and flexible to withstand stretching and squeezing during body movements.

◀ see also The human body pp.230–31

The central nervous system

The brain tapers at its base into the spinal cord. Together, the brain and cord form the central nervous system, or CNS. The spinal cord runs down the core of the vertebral column, and 31 pairs of spinal nerves emerge from the cord, between gaps in the vertebrae.

White matter is made of bundles of nerve fibers

Sensory root ganglion

Spinal nerve

Motor nerve root

Gray matter is made of connected nerve cell bodies

Section of spinal cord
The roots of spinal nerves split into front (ventral) branches that carry motor impulses to muscles and rear (dorsal) branches that bring sensory information.

Right hemisphere of the cerebrum

Cerebrum

Cerebral fissure

Olfactory bulb

Optic nerve

Cerebellum

Pituitary gland

Medulla oblongata—the lower part of the brainstem

Pons – one of the structures of the brainstem

Spinal cord

Front view of the CNS
The brain's folded cerebrum is split into left and right hemispheres by a deep fissure. Beneath the cerebrum are the cerebellum and brainstem.

Parts of a neuron

Individual nerve cells, or neurons, have many different shapes and patterns, but most possess the same main parts. Thin, multibranching dendrites collect nerve impulses, or signals, from other neurons and convey them to the main cell body. Here, the impulses are combined and, if a certain threshold is reached, the resulting signal travels away along the axon, or nerve fiber, for transmission to other neurons.

Dendrite

Cell body

Nucleus

Base of axon

Myelin sheath

Nerve impulses "hop" along axon between gaps in myelin called nodes of Ranvier

Impulses from dendrites combine on surface membranes of neuron cell body

Astrocyte cells provide neurons with physical support and nutrients

Each **neuron** in the cortex may connect to more than **10,000** others

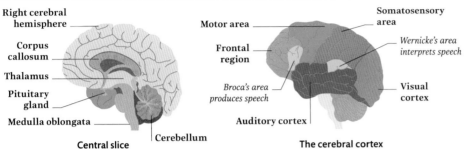

Central slice
A vertical slice viewed from the side shows that the brain's hemispheres are linked by a strap of nerve fibers, the corpus callosum.

Right cerebral hemisphere
Corpus callosum
Thalamus
Pituitary gland
Medulla oblongata
Cerebellum

Motor area
Frontal region
Broca's area produces speech
Auditory cortex
Somatosensory area
Wernicke's area interprets speech
Visual cortex

The cerebral cortex
The cortex is the outer 2–3 mm layer of the cerebrum. All cortical areas work together, but some have specific functions, including processing images and words.

The brain is **2 percent of the body** by weight but consumes **20 percent of its energy**

Processing touch information
The somatosensory area of the cortex receives information from skin all over the body. The most sensitive regions, such as the hand, lips, and tongue have the largest sections of cortex.

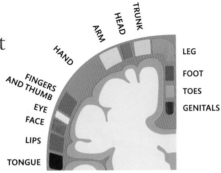

TRUNK
HEAD
ARM
HAND
FINGERS AND THUMB
EYE
FACE
LIPS
TONGUE
LEG
FOOT
TOES
GENITALS

The senses
The main senses are sight, hearing, smell, taste, and touch, but senses also include internal information, such as the position of body parts and the directional pull of gravity.

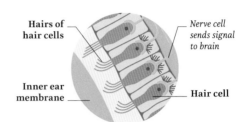

Hairs of hair cells
Inner ear membrane
Nerve cell sends signal to brain
Hair cell

Ears
In the inner ear, sounds cause vibrations, which shake a membrane in which micro-hairs are embedded. This triggers the hair cells to produce nerve impulses.

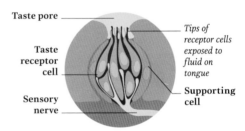

Taste pore
Taste receptor cell
Sensory nerve
Tips of receptor cells exposed to fluid on tongue
Supporting cell

Tongue
Up to 10,000 microscopic taste buds on the tongue's upper surface detect a mixture of five main flavors: sweet, salty, sour, bitter, and savory (umami).

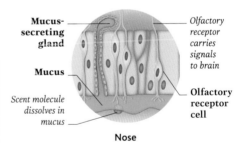

Mucus-secreting gland
Mucus
Scent molecule dissolves in mucus
Olfactory receptor carries signals to brain
Olfactory receptor cell

Nose
Like the tongue, the nose responds to specific chemical substances. They are detected by 50 million olfactory receptor cells in two patches in the roof of the nasal cavity.

PASSING THE SIGNAL TO THE NEXT NERVE CELL

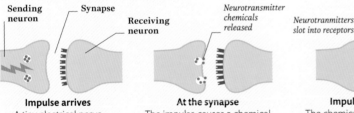

Sending neuron
Synapse
Receiving neuron
Neurotransmitter chemicals released
Neurotransmitters slot into receptors
Signal triggered in receiving neuron

Impulse arrives
A tiny electrical nerve impulse from the preceding nerve cell's axon reaches a junction, or synapse.

At the synapse
The impulse causes a chemical called a neurotransmitter to be released, and this passes across a microscopic gap, the synaptic cleft.

Impulse continues
The chemicals trigger receptors in the receiving nerve cell, altering its membrane and stimulating the next electrical impulse.

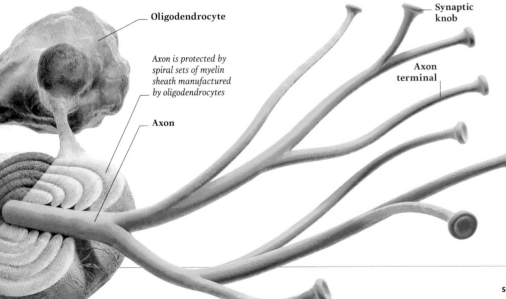

Oligodendrocyte
Axon is protected by spiral sets of myelin sheath manufactured by oligodendrocytes
Axon
Synaptic knob
Axon terminal

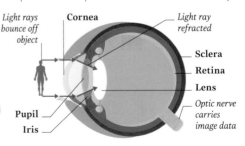

Light rays bounce off object
Cornea
Light ray refracted
Sclera
Retina
Lens
Optic nerve carries image data
Pupil
Iris

Eyes
Light rays are refracted (bent) by the domed cornea, pass through the gap, or pupil, in the iris, and are focused by the adjustable lens onto the light-sensitive retina.

Respiratory and cardiovascular systems

Respiration and blood circulation are the most vital and immediate body systems. If one stops for even a few minutes, life ceases. Respiration, or breathing, obtains essential oxygen from air and also removes carbon dioxide from the body, which is deadly if allowed to accumulate. The cardiovascular system of heart, blood vessels, and blood distributes oxygen, nutrients, and hundreds of other substances around the body, as well as collecting carbon dioxide and other wastes.

Respiratory system

The upper respiratory airways are the nose, pharynx (throat), and larynx. They lead to the trachea, or windpipe, which branches into two air passages called bronchi, each leading to a lung. The bronchi in turn branch into narrower bronchioles within each lung.

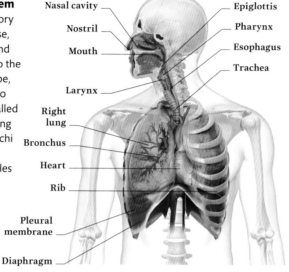

Nasal cavity
Nostril
Mouth
Larynx
Right lung
Bronchus
Heart
Rib
Pleural membrane
Diaphragm

Epiglottis
Pharynx
Esophagus
Trachea

Inhaling and exhaling

To inhale, the dome-shaped diaphragm muscle beneath the lungs contracts and flattens, while the intercostal muscles between the ribs contract to expand the chest. Both movements stretch the spongy lungs larger to draw in air. As these muscles relax, the lungs shrink and exhale.

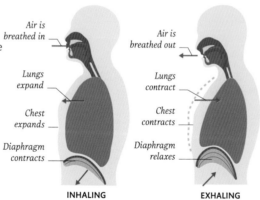

Air is breathed in
Lungs expand
Chest expands
Diaphragm contracts

INHALING

Air is breathed out
Lungs contract
Chest contracts
Diaphragm relaxes

EXHALING

From air to blood

Deep in the lungs, bronchioles branch repeatedly and end in microscopic air spaces called alveoli, each surrounded by a network of tiny capillary blood vessels. Oxygen moves, or diffuses, from the alveolar air, where it is more concentrated, into the low-oxygen blood. Carbon dioxide is more concentrated in the blood, so it diffuses in the other direction.

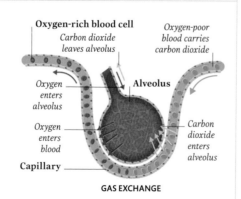

Oxygen-rich blood cell
Carbon dioxide leaves alveolus
Oxygen-poor blood carries carbon dioxide
Oxygen enters alveolus
Alveolus
Oxygen enters blood
Carbon dioxide enters alveolus
Capillary

GAS EXCHANGE

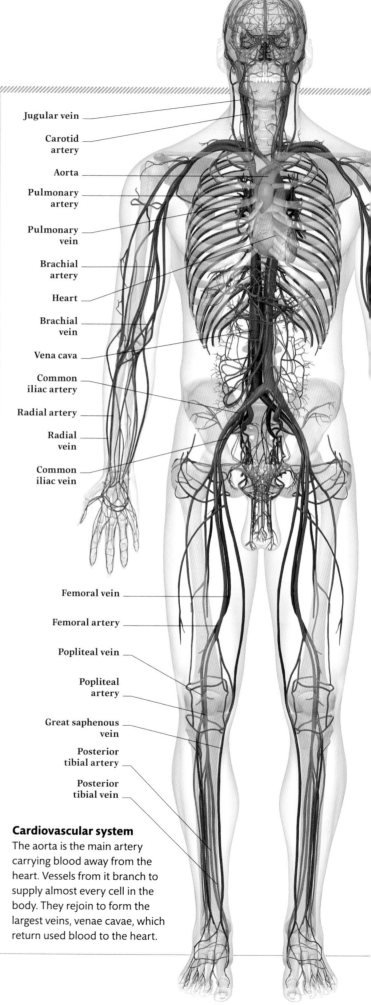

Jugular vein
Carotid artery
Aorta
Pulmonary artery
Pulmonary vein
Brachial artery
Heart
Brachial vein
Vena cava
Common iliac artery
Radial artery
Radial vein
Common iliac vein

Femoral vein
Femoral artery
Popliteal vein
Popliteal artery
Great saphenous vein
Posterior tibial artery
Posterior tibial vein

Cardiovascular system

The aorta is the main artery carrying blood away from the heart. Vessels from it branch to supply almost every cell in the body. They rejoin to form the largest veins, venae cavae, which return used blood to the heart.

A person's **blood vessels joined** end to end would
go **around the world almost three times**

How the heart beats
The heart walls consist of thick, strong cardiac muscles.
Every second or so they undergo a coordinated cycle of
contraction and relaxation known as the heart beat. The
muscles' electrical activity can be detected and displayed
as an undulating line, the electrocardiogram (ECG).

Atria contract
Tiny electrical signals
from the heart's natural
pacemaker, the sinoatrial
node, trigger its two small
upper chambers, or atria,
to contract. Blood flows
through valves to the lower
ventricle chambers. The
ECG makes a "P" wave.

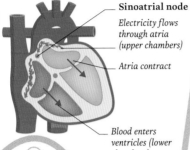

Sinoatrial node
*Electricity flows
through atria
(upper chambers)*

Atria contract

*Blood enters
ventricles (lower
chambers)*

Signals relayed
The ventricles have thicker,
stronger muscles. The
electrical signals are relayed
by the atrioventricular
node along specialized
conducting fibers in the
walls of the ventricles
to their bases.

*Atria relax
and veins
refill them
with blood*

Atrioventricular node
*Electricity travels
down wall between
ventricles*

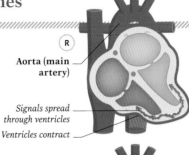

**Aorta (main
artery)**

*Signals spread
through ventricles*

Ventricles contract

Ventricles contract
As signals pass from the ventricular
bases up through their muscular walls,
they stimulate contractions that squeeze
blood upward through valves into the
main arteries from the heart. The ECG
forms a peak identified as "R."

*Blood pumped
to body*

*Muscles'
electrical state
recovers*

Muscles finish contraction
On the ECG, the complete contracting
actions of the thick ventricular walls are
known as the QRS complex. The down-
peaking S wave signifies these muscle
actions are finished and recovering.

*Atria full
of blood*

Heart recharges
Electrical activity returns to neutral
and cardiac muscles recover and relax.
However, the heart does not actively
enlarge to suck in more blood. Rather,
the pressure within the main veins
pushes blood into the atria for the
next beating cycle.

How blood travels
Arteries conveying blood from
the heart have strong walls and
can change diameter to control
flow to each body part. Each artery
divides many times into narrower
arterioles and finally capillaries, 10
times thinner than hairs, where gas
exchange occurs. Capillaries unite
via venules into main veins, whose
one-way valves ensure blood
flows back to the heart.

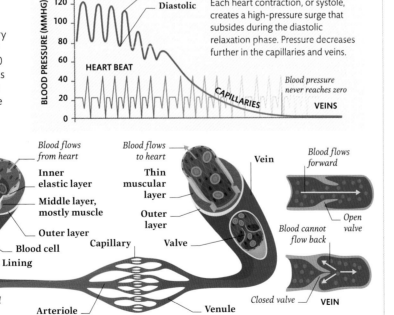

ARTERIES **Systolic**

Diastolic

HEART BEAT

CAPILLARIES

VEINS

*Blood pressure
never reaches zero*

BLOOD PRESSURE (MMHG): 0, 20, 40, 60, 80, 100, 120

BLOOD PRESSURE
Each heart contraction, or systole,
creates a high-pressure surge that
subsides during the diastolic
relaxation phase. Pressure decreases
further in the capillaries and veins.

Blood flow

Artery

*Blood flows
from heart*

**Inner
elastic layer**

**Middle layer,
mostly muscle**

Outer layer

Blood cell

Lining

*Artery wall
contracts*

ARTERY

*Vessel narrows and
limits blood flow*

Capillary

Arteriole

*Blood flows
to heart*

**Thin
muscular
layer**

**Outer
layer**

Valve

Venule

Vein

*Blood flows
forward*

*Open
valve*

*Blood cannot
flow back*

Closed valve

VEIN

Double circulation
The heart is the crossover point
of a double circulation. Low-oxygen
blood flows from the heart's right
side to the lungs for more oxygen
(pulmonary circulation). It returns
to the left side and is pumped
around the body to cells and
tissues (systemic circulation) before
returning to the right side.

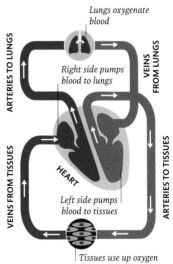

*Lungs oxygenate
blood*

ARTERIES TO LUNGS

VEINS FROM LUNGS

*Right side pumps
blood to lungs*

VEINS FROM TISSUES

ARTERIES TO TISSUES

HEART

*Left side pumps
blood to tissues*

Tissues use up oxygen

At any moment, **80 percent of blood** is in **veins,** 10 in
arteries, 5 in **capillaries,** and 5 percent **in the heart**

see also Lymphatic and immune systems pp.242–43 ▶ **Digestive and urinary systems** pp.244–45 ▶ **The human life cycle** pp.248–49 ▶

Lymphatic and immune systems

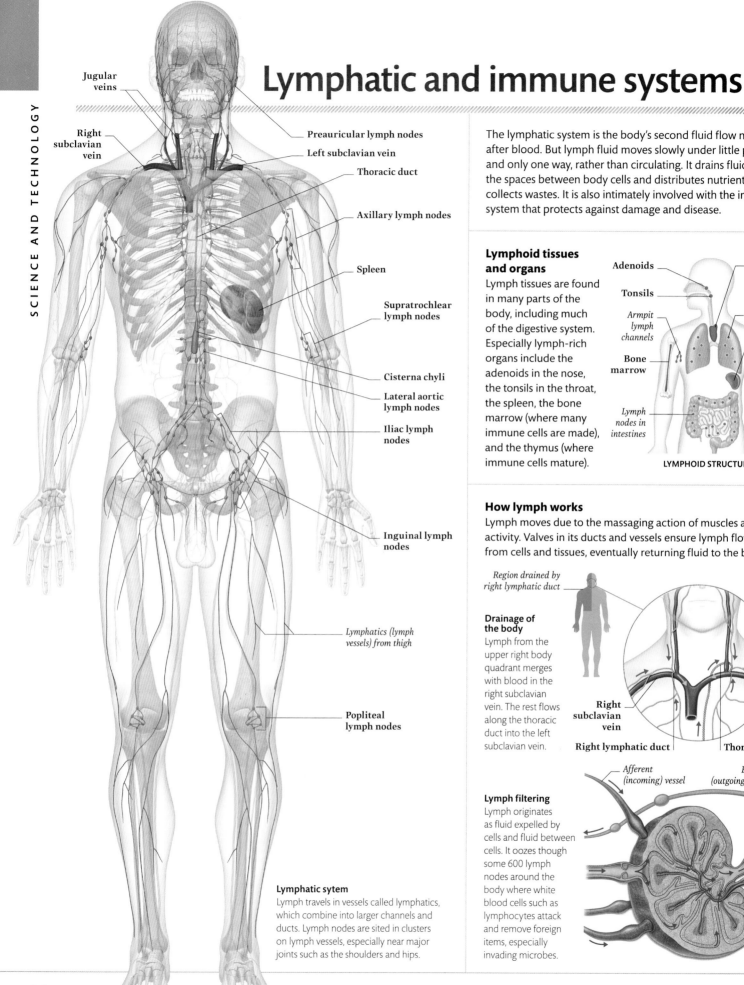

Jugular veins

Right subclavian vein

Preauricular lymph nodes

Left subclavian vein

Thoracic duct

Axillary lymph nodes

Spleen

Supratrochlear lymph nodes

Cisterna chyli

Lateral aortic lymph nodes

Iliac lymph nodes

Inguinal lymph nodes

Lymphatics (lymph vessels) from thigh

Popliteal lymph nodes

Lymphatic sytem
Lymph travels in vessels called lymphatics, which combine into larger channels and ducts. Lymph nodes are sited in clusters on lymph vessels, especially near major joints such as the shoulders and hips.

The lymphatic system is the body's second fluid flow network, after blood. But lymph fluid moves slowly under little pressure, and only one way, rather than circulating. It drains fluid from the spaces between body cells and distributes nutrients and collects wastes. It is also intimately involved with the immune system that protects against damage and disease.

Lymphoid tissues and organs

Lymph tissues are found in many parts of the body, including much of the digestive system. Especially lymph-rich organs include the adenoids in the nose, the tonsils in the throat, the spleen, the bone marrow (where many immune cells are made), and the thymus (where immune cells mature).

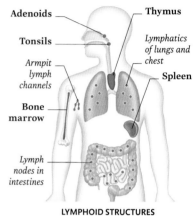

Adenoids

Tonsils

Armpit lymph channels

Bone marrow

Lymph nodes in intestines

Thymus

Lymphatics of lungs and chest

Spleen

LYMPHOID STRUCTURES

How lymph works

Lymph moves due to the massaging action of muscles and body activity. Valves in its ducts and vessels ensure lymph flows one way, from cells and tissues, eventually returning fluid to the blood.

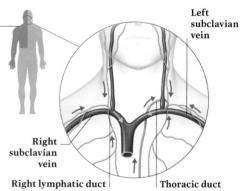

Region drained by right lymphatic duct

Drainage of the body
Lymph from the upper right body quadrant merges with blood in the right subclavian vein. The rest flows along the thoracic duct into the left subclavian vein.

Left subclavian vein

Right subclavian vein

Right lymphatic duct

Thoracic duct

Lymph filtering
Lymph originates as fluid expelled by cells and fluid between cells. It oozes though some 600 lymph nodes around the body where white blood cells such as lymphocytes attack and remove foreign items, especially invading microbes.

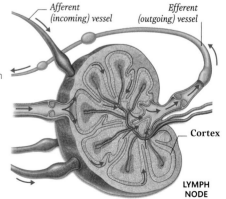

Afferent (incoming) vessel

Efferent (outgoing) vessel

Cortex

LYMPH NODE

◄ see also Bacteria and viruses pp.218–19   ◄ How cells work pp.220–21   ◄ The human body pp.230–31

Some **macrophages** can consume more than **200 bacteria** before they destroy themselves by "overeating"

Immune system

The immune system is a network of organs, tissues, and cells spread throughout the body. Its main task is to recognize and neutralize threats to health, such as invading microbes.

Immune cells

Many immune cells are types of white blood cells. They include phagocytes that engulf particles such as bacteria.

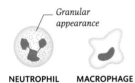

Granular appearance

NEUTROPHIL (*phagocyte*)　　**MACROPHAGE** (*phagocyte*)

High surface area　　*Large nucleus*

NATURAL KILLER CELL　　**DENDRITIC CELL**　　**B LYMPHOCYTE**

Inflammatory response

As well as repelling invaders, the immune system also helps to recognize and repair damage. Many white cells are involved. At an injury site, mast cells release histamine that makes local blood vessels widen to bring in many defenders. The area becomes red, hot, swollen, and perhaps painful—the four signs of inflammation.

First line defenses

At a breach in the skin, the local reaction makes blood capillary walls wide and porous. White cells squeeze through gaps into the battle zone.

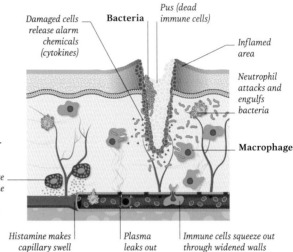

Damaged cells release alarm chemicals (cytokines)　　**Bacteria**　　*Pus (dead immune cells)*

Inflamed area

Neutrophil attacks and engulfs bacteria

Macrophage

Mast cells release histamine

Histamine makes capillary swell　　*Plasma leaks out*　　*Immune cells squeeze out through widened walls*

Adaptive immune responses

The general reaction to almost any kind of damage or invasion is called the innate immune response. A further stage is the adaptive immune response, which is a more specific reaction—for example, targeted to a particular kind of infecting bacterium.

Recognizing self and non-self

Every body cell is coated in marker proteins, or antigens, that are unique to each individual. The antigens are a signal to the immune cells, so that they are recognized and tolerated.

Antigens coat body cell　　*Antigen of a different shape*

BODY CELL　　**FOREIGN CELL**

Antibody-based immune response

The immune system recognizes "non-self" antigens on invaders. White cells known as B lymphocytes (or B cells) make antibodies that join to the antigens to neutralize and destroy them.

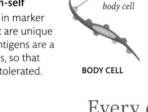

Macrophage swallows invader　　*Macrophage presents invader's antigens*

B cell binds with antigen　　*Specific memory B cells proliferate for later use*

MEMORY B CELL

Macrophage engulfs damaged invader

Antibodies produced and released　　*Antibodies deactivate invader*

Antigen　　**B CELL**　　**PLASMA B CELL**　　**ANTIBODIES**

❶ Presenting antigens
Macrophages begin the process by swallowing invaders and displaying the invader's antigens to other immune cells.

❷ Antibody production
A B cell binds to the foreign antigen and clones itself to make memory B cells and antibody-producing plasma B cells.

❸ Antibody release
The antibodies enter the bloodstream and stick to invaders, marking them for attack by other immune cells.

Every drop of blood contains 375,000 immune cells

IMMUNIZATION

After combating a particular invader, such as a virus, the immune system can mount another attack very rapidly, using memory cells. In immunization, a disabled virus, or parts of it, are put into the body as a vaccine. This does not cause illness, but the antigens provoke an immune response that can quickly be activated in future encounters.

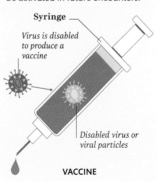

Syringe

Virus is disabled to produce a vaccine

Disabled virus or viral particles

VACCINE

Cell-based immune response

Like the antibody-based system, the cell-based immune response generates memory cells, which mount a faster attack the second time around.

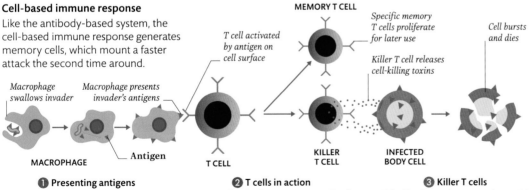

MEMORY T CELL

T cell activated by antigen on cell surface　　*Specific memory T cells proliferate for later use*　　*Cell bursts and dies*

Killer T cell releases cell-killing toxins

Macrophage swallows invader　　*Macrophage presents invader's antigens*

MACROPHAGE　　**Antigen**　　**T CELL**　　**KILLER T CELL**　　**INFECTED BODY CELL**

❶ Presenting antigens
Again, immune cells, such as macrophages or dendritic cells, swallow invaders and display the foreign antigens.

❷ T cells in action
Triggered by the foreign antigen, a T cell (or T lymphocyte) clones itself to produce memory T cells and killer T cells.

❸ Killer T cells
Killer T cells attack unwanted material directly. Specific memory T cells are stored for the next attack.

◀ see also **Respiratory and cardiovascular systems** pp.240–41　　**Modern medicine** pp.252–53 ▶　　**The spread and control of disease** pp.254–55 ▶

Digestive and urinary systems

The abdomen contains two body systems concerned with input and output. Digestion breaks down food, taking its energy and nutrients into the blood to distribute to the body. Excretion removes unwanted substances collected by the blood from cells and tissues. The main product of excretion is urine, and the system is known as the urinary system.

The **liver** is the **body's largest** internal organ and has more than **500** functions

The teeth

Digestion begins with the lips, mouth, tongue, and teeth. Each tooth has a root in the jawbone and a crown covered by the body's hardest substance, enamel, for biting and chewing. Under this is less hard, shock-absorbing dentine. At the center is the pulp with nerves and blood vessels.

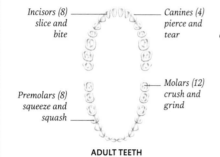

Incisors (8) slice and bite

Canines (4) pierce and tear

Premolars (8) squeeze and squash

Molars (12) crush and grind

ADULT TEETH

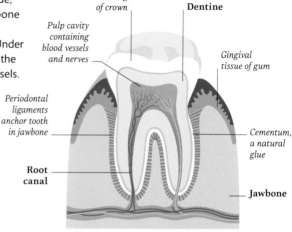

Enamel covering of crown

Dentine

Pulp cavity containing blood vessels and nerves

Gingival tissue of gum

Periodontal ligaments anchor tooth in jawbone

Cementum, a natural glue

Root canal

Jawbone

CROSS SECTION OF A MOLAR TOOTH

The digestive system

Initial digestion in the mouth is mainly physical mashing and crushing. However, chemical digestion also occurs as enzymes in the watery, lubricating saliva attack starchy carbohydrates. The stomach uses physical squeezing but also adds powerful acids and enzymes. Intestinal digestion is mainly chemical.

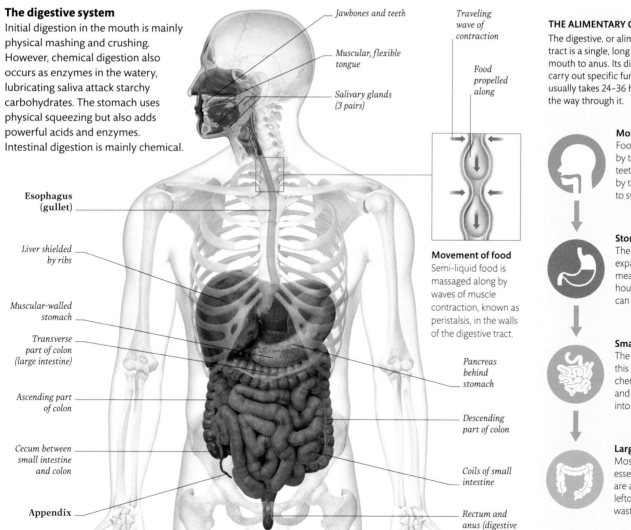

Jawbones and teeth

Muscular, flexible tongue

Salivary glands (3 pairs)

Esophagus (gullet)

Liver shielded by ribs

Muscular-walled stomach

Transverse part of colon (large intestine)

Ascending part of colon

Cecum between small intestine and colon

Appendix

Traveling wave of contraction

Food propelled along

Movement of food
Semi-liquid food is massaged along by waves of muscle contraction, known as peristalsis, in the walls of the digestive tract.

Pancreas behind stomach

Descending part of colon

Coils of small intestine

Rectum and anus (digestive outlet)

THE ALIMENTARY CANAL

The digestive, or alimentary, canal or tract is a single, long passageway from mouth to anus. Its different regions carry out specific functions, and food usually takes 24–36 hours to pass all the way through it.

Mouth and throat
Food is captured by the lips, chewed by teeth, and molded by the tongue, ready to swallow.

Stomach
The baglike stomach expands to hold a meal for several hours so digestion can proceed.

Small intestine
The longest part, this region continues chemical digestion and absorbs products into the blood.

Large intestine
Most of the water and essential body salts are absorbed, and the leftovers formed into waste feces.

The two kidneys are **less than 1 percent** of body weight yet receive **more than one-fifth** of the heart's **total blood output**

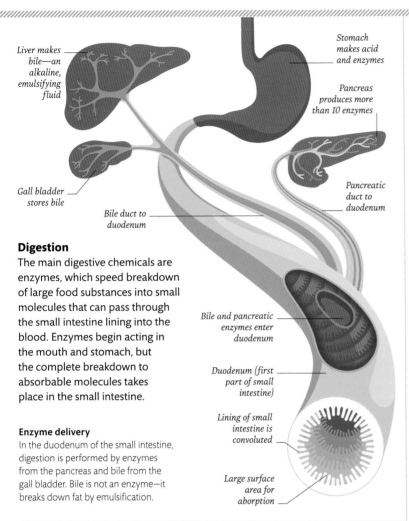

Liver makes bile—an alkaline, emulsifying fluid

Stomach makes acid and enzymes

Pancreas produces more than 10 enzymes

Gall bladder stores bile

Pancreatic duct to duodenum

Bile duct to duodenum

Digestion

The main digestive chemicals are enzymes, which speed breakdown of large food substances into small molecules that can pass through the small intestine lining into the blood. Enzymes begin acting in the mouth and stomach, but the complete breakdown to absorbable molecules takes place in the small intestine.

Bile and pancreatic enzymes enter duodenum

Duodenum (first part of small intestine)

Lining of small intestine is convoluted

Large surface area for absorption

Enzyme delivery

In the duodenum of the small intestine, digestion is performed by enzymes from the pancreas and bile from the gall bladder. Bile is not an enzyme—it breaks down fat by emulsification.

The urinary system

The two kidneys are the core of the urinary system. They sit in the upper rear abdomen and filter urea and dozens of other waste substances from blood to a form a liquid, urine. The kidneys also adjust overall water balance, either retaining water and making urine concentrated, or removing excess water, making urine more dilute.

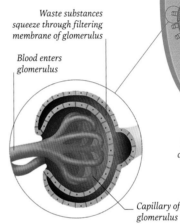

Cortex containing glomeruli

Renal artery brings waste-laden blood

Waste substances squeeze through filtering membrane of glomerulus

Blood enters glomerulus

Renal vein carries filtered blood

Medulla of kidney

Ureter carries urine to bladder

Capillary of glomerulus

Filter close-up

Water and wastes are removed from blood flowing through a knot of capillaries, the glomerulus.

Kidney function

The outer layer, or cortex, contains a million microfilters (glomeruli). Urine collects in the central area.

Nutrition

A healthy body needs to receive balanced amounts of five main nutrient groups—carbohydrates, proteins, fats, vitamins, and minerals. Vitamins and minerals are essential, but are needed only in small quantities compared to carbohydrates, proteins, and fats.

Carbohydrates
Sugars and starches are the main energy providers, broken apart in cells to fuel life processes.

Vitamins
About 13 vitamins are necessary for body processes, from skin renewal to digestion.

Proteins
These are split into amino acid subunits, and rebuilt as the body's structural molecules in all tissues.

Minerals
Mostly simple chemical substances, minerals include calcium for teeth and bones.

Fats
Certain fats are needed in limited amounts for healthy nerves and other tissues, and for energy.

Water
Most of the body's metabolism takes place in watery fluids inside and between cells.

Male and female tracts

Urine flows from the kidneys down tubes called ureters to be stored in a stretchy muscle bag, the bladder. In females, the urethra tube emptying urine from the bladder opens into the genital area. In males, the urethra is five times longer and opens at the end of the male genitalia.

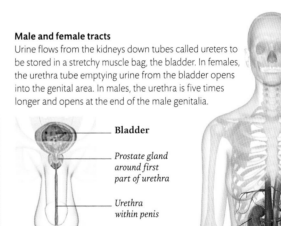

Bladder

Prostate gland around first part of urethra

Urethra within penis

MALE

Right kidney

Right ureter from right kidney

Bladder

Urethra

FEMALE

Reproductive and endocrine systems

There are many close links between the reproductive system, for producing offspring, and the endocrine or hormonal system, which controls and coordinates many processes such as digestion, excretion, blood formation, heart rate and blood pressure, the sleep-wake cycle, and overall growth and sexual maturation. These are also the only two systems with major differences between female and male.

Reproductive systems

The reproductive systems of male and female bodies differ greatly, due to their contrasting roles in their joint function. The female system includes the mammary glands in the breasts that produce milk for the newborn infant, as well as the ovaries and uterus, where the young develops before birth.

Female system

The main parts of the female system are the ovaries, which produce and ripen ova, or egg cells, the fallopian, or uterine, tubes where an egg may be fertilized by a male sperm, the uterus where the embryo grows, and the vagina, or birth canal.

How the male system works

Sperm are produced by rapid division of cells called spermatogonia in the long, thin seminiferous tubules packed within each testis. They mature, developing tails, and are stored in a 20 ft- (6 m-) long coiled tube called the epididymis, next to the testis.

> **Sperm** are produced in the two testes at the rate of more than **1,500** every second

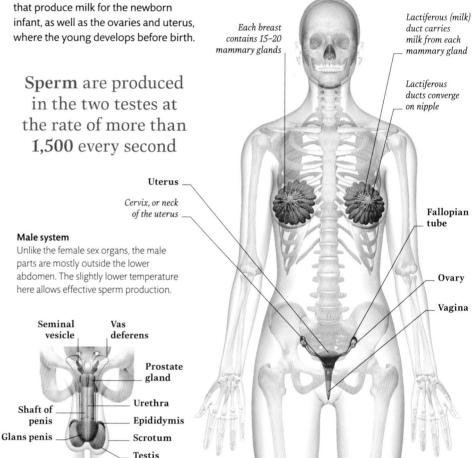

Each breast contains 15–20 mammary glands

Lactiferous (milk) duct carries milk from each mammary gland

Lactiferous ducts converge on nipple

Uterus

Cervix, or neck of the uterus

Fallopian tube

Ovary

Vagina

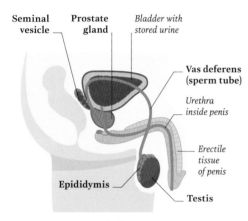

Seminal vesicle   **Prostate gland**   *Bladder with stored urine*

Vas deferens (sperm tube)

Urethra inside penis

Erectile tissue of penis

Epididymis

Testis

Path of sperm

At sperm release (ejaculation), sperm pass along the vas deferens. The prostate and seminal vesicles add nutritional fluids to form semen, which exits along the urethra.

Male system

Unlike the female sex organs, the male parts are mostly outside the lower abdomen. The slightly lower temperature here allows effective sperm production.

Seminal vesicle   **Vas deferens**

Prostate gland

Shaft of penis

Glans penis

Urethra

Epididymis

Scrotum

Testis

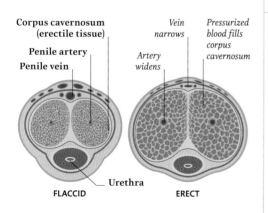

Corpus cavernosum (erectile tissue)

Penile artery

Penile vein

Vein narrows

Artery widens

Pressurized blood fills corpus cavernosum

Urethra

FLACCID   ERECT

Structure of the penis

To make the penis rigid and erect for sexual intercourse, its arteries widen to bring more blood, but the veins narrow. Blood under pressure engorges the spongy corpus cavernosum tissues.

How the female system works

Every month, the reproductive system of a woman prepares for the possibility of pregnancy. Each of the two ovaries holds many thousands of dormant eggs, one of which begins maturing inside a follicle, while the uterus lining, or endometrium, grows thick, ready to nourish the egg.

Ovulation

Egg cells grow, ripen, and are ovulated, or released from the ovary, during the hormone-controlled menstrual cycle (see opposite).

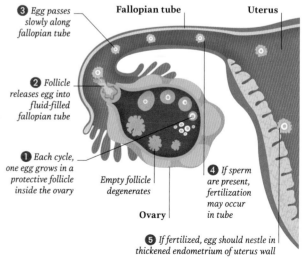

❸ *Egg passes slowly along fallopian tube*

Fallopian tube   **Uterus**

❷ *Follicle releases egg into fluid-filled fallopian tube*

❶ *Each cycle, one egg grows in a protective follicle inside the ovary*

Empty follicle degenerates

❹ *If sperm are present, fertilization may occur in tube*

Ovary

❺ *If fertilized, egg should nestle in thickened endometrium of uterus wall*

A female baby is born with **all her egg cells**, totaling between **500,000 and 1 million**, already waiting in her **ovaries**

Endocrine system

Hormones are produced in endocrine glands or tissues. They circulate in blood and affect certain parts known as their target organs or tissues. Some hormones have effects throughout the body. Insulin from the pancreas gland controls how all body cells use glucose as an energy source. Other hormones are very specific. Aldosterone from the adrenal gland controls kidney function to regulate the body's water balance.

Main endocrine glands

Most glands are multifunctional. The many thyroid hormones include those that regulate the speed of the body's metabolism. The adrenal gland also secretes many hormones, including adrenaline.

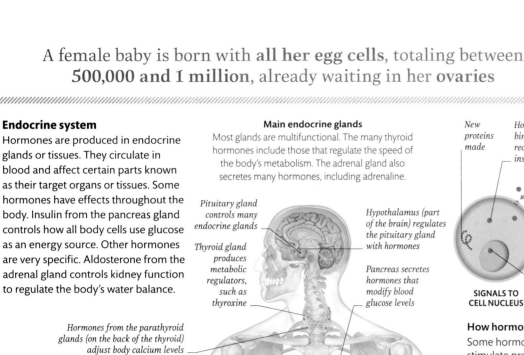

Pituitary gland controls many endocrine glands

Thyroid gland produces metabolic regulators, such as thyroxine

Hypothalamus (part of the brain) regulates the pituitary gland with hormones

Pancreas secretes hormones that modify blood glucose levels

Hormones from the parathyroid glands (on the back of the thyroid) adjust body calcium levels

Adrenal gland on top of the kidney makes hormones that adjust blood volume and pressure

Testosterone from the testes in males affects sexual development and sperm production

Additional female endocrine glands

The two ovaries produce hormones such as the main female hormone estrogen, which controls sexual development and the reproductive, or menstrual, cycle.

Ovary

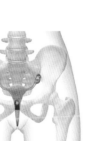

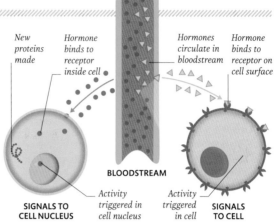

New proteins made

Hormone binds to receptor inside cell

Hormones circulate in bloodstream

Hormone binds to receptor on cell surface

BLOODSTREAM

Activity triggered in cell nucleus

SIGNALS TO CELL NUCLEUS

Activity triggered in cell

SIGNALS TO CELL

How hormones work

Some hormones pass straight into the cell nucleus to stimulate production of the target substance. In others, the hormone triggers a membrane receptor.

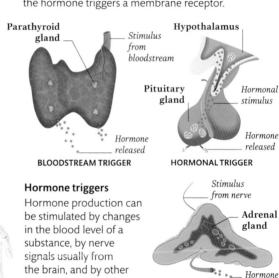

Parathyroid gland

Stimulus from bloodstream

Hypothalamus

Pituitary gland

Hormonal stimulus

Hormone released

BLOODSTREAM TRIGGER

Hormone released

HORMONAL TRIGGER

Hormone triggers

Hormone production can be stimulated by changes in the blood level of a substance, by nerve signals usually from the brain, and by other hormones or hormone-releasing factors.

Stimulus from nerve

Adrenal gland

Hormone released

NERVOUS TRIGGER

Hormonal cycle

Estrogen stimulates growth of the endometrium, and its peak triggers further hormones, which cause ovulation on or around day 14. Progesterone further stimulates endometrial growth, but if no fertilized egg implants, its level falls, reducing blood supply to the endometrium and causing it to shed its outer layer.

KEY

Estrogen	Luteinizing hormone
Progesterone	Follicle-stimulating hormone (FSH)

MENSTRUAL CYCLE

The menstrual cycle lasts about 28 days but can be significantly irregular. Day 1 is the start of the period, as the blood-filled endometrium (uterus lining) breaks down and is lost through the vagina.

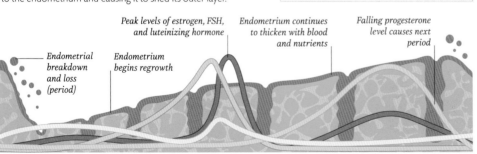

Peak levels of estrogen, FSH, and luteinizing hormone

Endometrium continues to thicken with blood and nutrients

Falling progesterone level causes next period

Endometrial breakdown and loss (period)

Endometrium begins regrowth

MENSTRUATION **LINING GROWS** **HORMONE SURGE** **FURTHER GROWTH**

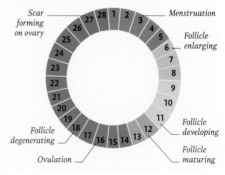

Scar forming on ovary

Menstruation

Follicle enlarging

Follicle degenerating

Follicle developing

Ovulation

Follicle maturing

◄ see also Evolution pp.228–29   ◄ The human body pp.230–31   The human life cycle pp.248–49 ►   **247**

The human life cycle

The development of a human begins with the union of its male parent's and female parent's DNA within an egg cell, and continues when that cell implants in the lining of its female parent's uterus. Development usually progresses through childhood to maturity, but human lifespan is inevitably limited.

Fertilization

The human body begins life as a female egg cell about 0.1 mm across, which is joined, or fertilized, by a much smaller male sperm only 0.05 mm long. The fertilized egg divides into two cells, then four, and so on. These cells continue to multiply and specialize as they form different tissues and organs.

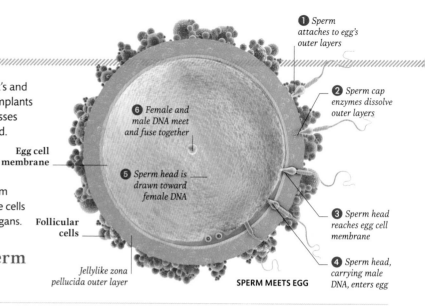

① Sperm attaches to egg's outer layers

② Sperm cap enzymes dissolve outer layers

⑥ Female and male DNA meet and fuse together

Egg cell membrane

⑤ Sperm head is drawn toward female DNA

③ Sperm head reaches egg cell membrane

④ Sperm head, carrying male DNA, enters egg

Follicular cells

Jellylike zona pellucida outer layer

SPERM MEETS EGG

Healthy semen contains **1.4–10 billion sperm** per fl oz (40–300 million per ml)

Gestation

Pregnancy lasts about 9 months from fertilization. The embryo's first organs to form are the heart, which is beating by 3 weeks, and the brain and spinal cord. By 8 weeks, all main organs are present. The embryo is then known as a fetus.

Head and face formed

Wall of uterus (womb)

10 WEEKS

Placenta in uterine wall

Arms and legs taking shape

14 WEEKS

Hands very active, touching face and body

Limb movement can be felt by mother

24 WEEKS

Fetus positioned head-down for birth

Umbilical cord links fetus to placenta

40 WEEKS

Birth

Birth can take less than 1 hour or more than 1 day, but is generally shorter for a mother's second and subsequent children. The main birth hormone is oxytocin, made in the hypothalamus (in the brain, see p.247) and released into the blood by the pituitary gland. It stimulates powerful contractions of the muscles in the uterus wall. Stronger and more frequent contractions widen the cervix and move the baby along the birth canal.

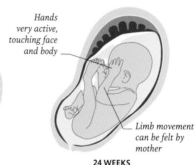

Layers of smooth muscle

Waves of uterine contraction

Gap in pelvis

Cervix thins

Head presses on cervix

① Contractions
Muscles in the uterus wall periodically shorten to press the baby's head against the cervix, which becomes thinner.

Head is baby's widest part

Cervical opening widens

Vaginal canal

② Dilation of the cervix
The contractions of labor become longer, stronger, and closer together. The opening in the cervix gradually widens, or dilates.

Baby may twist around

Head usually emerges first

③ Delivery of the baby
The cervix dilates further, and contractions push the baby's head through. The rest of the body usually follows quickly.

PLACENTA

The fetus receives oxygen, fluids, nutrients, and energy from the mother through a disk-shaped organ called the placenta, which is grown jointly by mother and fetus. Inside the placenta, fetal blood vessels are surrounded by pools of maternal blood. Substances can pass, or diffuse, through the membranes separating the two.

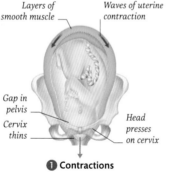

Capillaries of mother

Pools of maternal blood

Oxygen passes from maternal to fetal blood

Capillaries of fetus

High-oxygen blood in umbilical vein to fetus

Low-oxygen blood in umbilical arteries from fetus

Umbilical cord

TWINS

There are two processes that can result in two babies who develop together and are born usually minutes apart. In monozygotic twins, one fertilized egg divides in two, then each of these two cells continues to develop into a baby. In dizygotic twins, two egg cells are released at once, and each is fertilized by its own sperm.

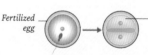

Fertilized egg

After one division, each cell develops into a baby, so twins have the same genetic material

MONOZYGOTIC (IDENTICAL)

Two fertilized eggs

Each egg develops into a baby, so the twins' similarities are the same as for any siblings

DIZYGOTIC (FRATERNAL)

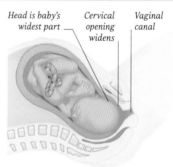
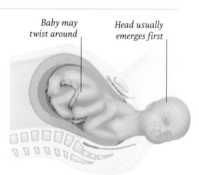

A **newborn's brain** is about one-quarter of its **adult size**

New baby

In the first seconds and minutes, the newborn body undergoes major changes. Breathing starts as the lungs inflate and begin to absorb oxygen. The pulmonary blood vessels supplying them widen, while the umbilical vessels to the placenta narrow and degenerate. The digestive system prepares for the first feeds of breast milk.

BABY TEETH

The full set of 20 baby, or deciduous, teeth, which appear from front to back, is complete by 24–26 months. They begin to fall out, again from front to back, from about 6 years.

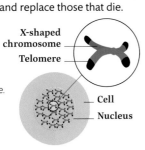

Lateral incisor   First molar

UPPER TEETH

LOWER TEETH

Canine, or cuspid   Second molar

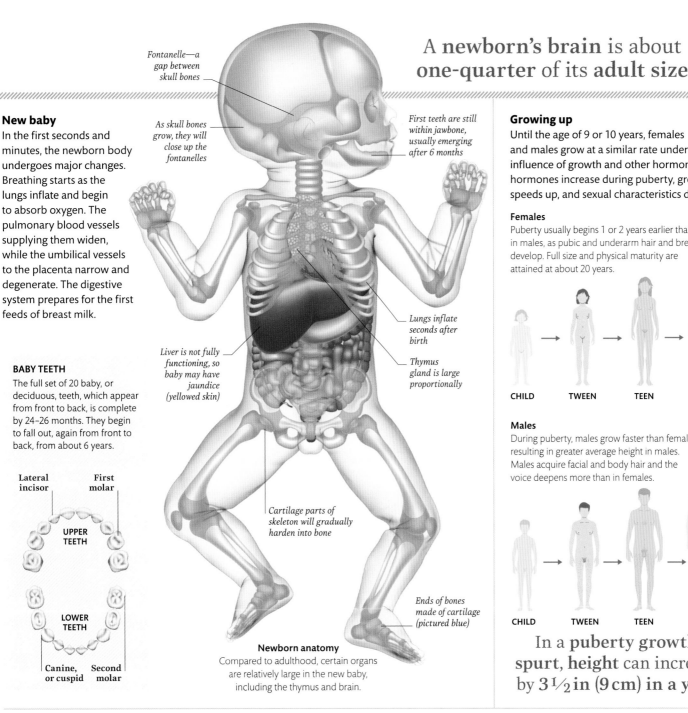

Fontanelle—a gap between skull bones

As skull bones grow, they will close up the fontanelles

First teeth are still within jawbone, usually emerging after 6 months

Lungs inflate seconds after birth

Thymus gland is large proportionally

Liver is not fully functioning, so baby may have jaundice (yellowed skin)

Cartilage parts of skeleton will gradually harden into bone

Ends of bones made of cartilage (pictured blue)

Newborn anatomy
Compared to adulthood, certain organs are relatively large in the new baby, including the thymus and brain.

Growing up

Until the age of 9 or 10 years, females and males grow at a similar rate under the influence of growth and other hormones. Sex hormones increase during puberty, growth speeds up, and sexual characteristics develop.

Females

Puberty usually begins 1 or 2 years earlier than in males, as pubic and underarm hair and breasts develop. Full size and physical maturity are attained at about 20 years.

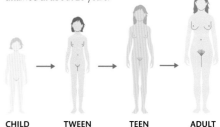

CHILD   TWEEN   TEEN   ADULT

Males

During puberty, males grow faster than females, resulting in greater average height in males. Males acquire facial and body hair and the voice deepens more than in females.

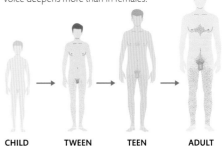

CHILD   TWEEN   TEEN   ADULT

In a **puberty growth spurt, height** can increase by 3½ in (9 cm) in a year

Aging

How fast a body ages depends on factors including genes, diet, activity and lifestyle, disease history, and environmental conditions. It seems that body cells can divide only so many times, to maintain and replace those that die.

Telomeres

At the end of each chromosome arm is a protective tip of DNA called a telomere. It acts as a point of attachment for the molecular machinery of cell division.

X-shaped chromosome
Telomere

Cell
Nucleus

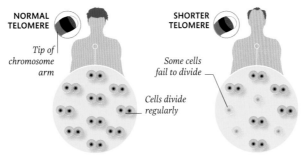

NORMAL TELOMERE

Tip of chromosome arm

Cells divide regularly

❶ Normal cell renewal
Molecules attach to telomeres to control the copying of DNA during cell division. At the end of the process, the last bit of telomere is not copied.

SHORTER TELOMERE

Some cells fail to divide

❷ Telomeres depleted
With continuing cell division, each telomere becomes shorter. Gradually, molecule attachment becomes more difficult.

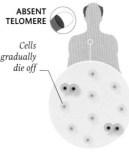

ABSENT TELOMERE

Cells gradually die off

❸ Telomeres lost
Eventually telomeres become so short, the replication molecules can no longer attach. The cell dies without being able to replace itself.

◀ see also The human body pp.230–31   ◀ Reproductive and endocrine systems pp.246–47   Diagnosis pp.256–59 ▶   **249**

The history of medicine

The origins of medicine stretch back millennia. The earliest practitioners may well have been people who wanted to help the injured or ill and realized they could develop the skills to do so. For much of its history, medical practice was entwined with faiths and religions. However, in 15th-century Europe, during the Renaissance period, new approaches to medicine based on the principles of reason and involving observation, experimentation, and record-keeping became common. The scientific method was developed during the 19th century, and the 20th and 21st centuries saw an increase in the use of technology.

Circular incisions made using a drill

c.5,000 BCE People practice trepanning—chipping or drilling holes into a patient's skull—to treat anything from skull fractures to mental disorders.

SKULL TREPANNING

Jenner vaccinated his 11-month-old son against smallpox in an attempt to prove it was safe

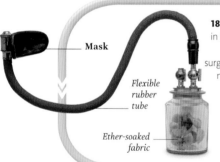

1796 British surgeon Edward Jenner infects a young boy with cowpox and then smallpox in order to test the protective potential of one virus against another. In doing so, he popularizes vaccination and establishes the principles of immunization.

EDWARD JENNER PERFORMING SMALLPOX VACCINATION

1628 After years of research, British physician William Harvey publishes *De motu cordis*—the first full account of the circulatory system.

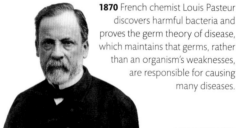

Depiction of nervous system, complete with brain, spinal cord, and nerves

600–1500 CE A golden age in Islamic medicine ensues as eminent physicians, including Ibn Sina (known as Avicenna in the West), delve into the details of how the body's various systems—such as the nervous and circulatory systems—work.

AVICENNA'S *CANON OF MEDICINE*, 1025

Mask

Flexible rubber tube

Ether-soaked fabric

1840s Developments in the field of inhaled anesthetics allow surgeons to administer nitrous oxide, ether, or chloroform to numb pain.

LETHEON ETHER INHALER

1870 French chemist Louis Pasteur discovers harmful bacteria and proves the germ theory of disease, which maintains that germs, rather than an organism's weaknesses, are responsible for causing many diseases.

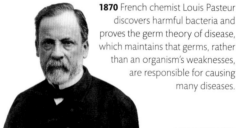

LOUIS PASTEUR

1895 German physicist Wilhelm Roentgen's discovery of X-rays leads to the first images of the body's insides for medical purposes.

Metal ring blocks X-rays

FIRST X-RAY

1970s British engineer Godfrey Hounsfield combines X-ray images taken from different angles to create a three-dimensional (3D) picture known as a computerized tomography (CT) scan.

GODFREY HOUNSFIELD

1953 American biologist James Watson and British physicist Francis Crick discover the helical coil structure of DNA (deoxyribonucleic acid), stimulating numerous advances across the biological and medical sciences.

Double helix backbone

Cross-rungs of nucleobases that carry genetic code

DOUBLE-HELIX DNA STRUCTURE

1950s The invention of miniaturized electronic components such as transistors allows for heart pacemakers initially to be worn externally, on the body, and eventually fully implanted within the chest area.

Wires connect to heart

IMPLANTABLE CARDIAC PACEMAKER, 1958 SERIES

1980s The World Health Organization (WHO) declares the eradication of smallpox—two decades after the eradication by immunization plan was initiated in 1959.

1983 French virologists Françoise Barré-Sinoussi and Luc Montaigner discover a retrovirus that would later become known as the Human Immunodeficiency Virus (HIV).

FRANCOISE BARRE-SINOUSSI

Image guidance screen

Surgeon controls robot from operating console

Robot arms with surgical instruments

1998 Robotics and almost instant electronic communications contribute to the first robot-assisted surgery and telesurgery by remote control.

Table-side assistance, should it be required

ROBOTIC SURGERY

Written on palm leaf, the Sushruta-Samhita is among the founding texts of Ayurveda

TREATISE ON AYURVEDIC MEDICINE

3000 BCE Ayurveda emphasizes balancing the body's life forces, *doshas*, and constitution, *prakriti*. It has a long oral history and Indian physician Sushruta writes a seminal work on Ayurvedic medicine and surgery *c.*800 BCE.

Statue of Imhotep holding a papyrus across his knees

c.2650 BCE Egyptian King Djoser's chief attendant, Imhotep is also a gifted healer and a high priest. He establishes several medico-religious practices that persist for 3,000 years.

STATUE OF IMHOTEP

Points marked indicating where to insert needles in order to treat an illness

c.2200 BCE Chinese medicine evolves to include making some diagnoses on the basis of pulse readings, and using herbs and acupuncture to balance the flow of life energy, or *chi*.

ACUPUNCTURE CHART

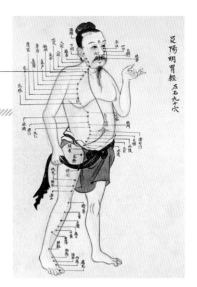

---

27 BCE–410 CE In ancient Rome, surgery advances as doctors are increasingly called on to treat soldiers wounded in wars, and arena gladiators who suffer terrible injuries in the name of entertainment.

Shears for cutting through tissue

SURGICAL INSTRUMENTS

Associated with liver and summer

HOT **DRY**

YELLOW BILE (FIRE)

BLOOD (AIR) **BLACK BILE (EARTH)**

Associated with heart and spring

Associated with spleen and autumn

WET **PHLEGM (WATER)** **COLD**

Associated with brain and winter

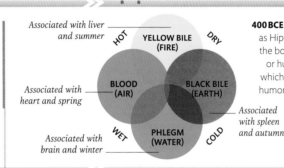

400 BCE Greek physicians, such as Hippocrates, maintain that the body contains four fluids, or humors, an imbalance in which leads to illnesses. Each humor is also associated with an element, an organ, and a season.

THE FOUR HUMORS

1901 In Austria, immunologist Karl Landsteiner categorizes blood into three groups—A, B, and O—allowing for safer blood transfusions.

Electrical circuit and battery housed in clear artifical resin

Funnel to collect blood

Syringe to draw blood

Tube to inject blood

BLOOD TRANSFUSION

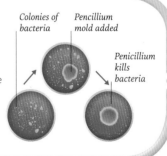

1922 In order to treat people dying from diabetes, Canadian doctor Frederick Banting and American scientist Charles Best administer a pancreas extract containing the hormone insulin.

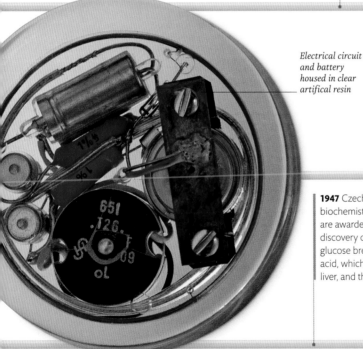

1947 Czech-American biochemists Gerty and Carl Cori are awarded a Nobel Prize for the discovery of the cycle by which glucose breaks down into lactic acid, which is recycled by the liver, and then stored as glycogen.

1928 In Scotland, scientist Alexander Fleming finds that the penicillium mold releases a bacteria-killing substance, penicillin. This leads to the creation of the first modern antibiotic.

Colonies of bacteria

Pencillium mold added

Penicillium kills bacteria

HOW PENICILLIUM DESTROYS BACTERIA

2000 The first draft of the Human Genome Project—an initiative to identify and sequence every gene in a typical human genome—is achieved, paving the way to treat hundreds of medical conditions, inherited and otherwise.

Pairs of human chromosomes

Chromosomes contain genetic instructions

HUMAN GENOME

2019–20 A coronavirus disease (called COVID-19) emerges in Wuhan, China, and quickly spreads. This leads to a global pandemic with large numbers of cases and fatalities.

Coronavirus named for its crownlike spikes

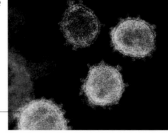

NOVEL CORONAVIRUS

see also Modern medicine pp.252-53 ▶ The spread and control of disease pp.254-55 ▶

Modern medicine

General medicine can be divided into dozens of specialized fields, and is often a specialty in its own right. Causes of ill health include infections, accidents and deliberate injury, deficiencies such as inadequate diet, lack of hygiene, poor environment, substance abuse, physiological conditions like diabetes, cancers, malfunction of major systems such as brain and nerves or heart and blood, inherited problems, and degenerative diseases ranging from arthritic joints to dementias.

Infectious diseases

Infections and related diseases are caused by pathogens—harmful viruses or microorganisms such as bacteria, fungi, and parasites—entering the body, or attaching to its surface, and then multiplying. Contagious infections (see p.254) are those spread by direct or close contact between individuals, via bodily products like blood and sputum, or contaminated objects or surfaces.

Bacteria
A typical bacterium is about 100 times smaller in volume than a human body cell. There are a huge variety of shapes, many with long whiplike extensions called flagella. Harmful bacterial infections may be treated with antibiotics.

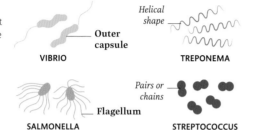

Helical shape

Outer capsule

VIBRIO

TREPONEMA

Flagellum

Pairs or chains

SALMONELLA

STREPTOCOCCUS

Viruses
Much tinier than even bacteria, viruses cannot reproduce independently. They invade host cells to make copies of themselves, destroying the hosts cells in the process. The best protection against a virus is vaccination.

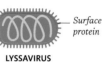
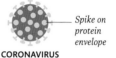

Surface protein

DNA

LYSSAVIRUS

ADENOVIRUS

Spike on protein envelope

Capsid (protein shell)

CORONAVIRUS

HERPESVIRUS

Protists and parasitic animals
Protists (single-celled organisms) often spread via contaminated water. Parasitic animals include worms, flukes, and insect larvae. Tapeworms can be over 66 ft (20 m) long.

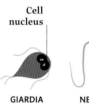
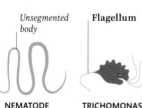

Cell nucleus

Unsegmented body

Flagellum

GIARDIA

NEMATODE

TRICHOMONAS

Fungi
Related to mushrooms, parasitic fungi spread in the form of tiny, tough spores. They dissolve surrounding tissues, from skin to lung, and absorb the nutrients.

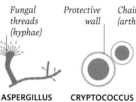
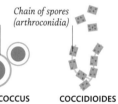

Fungal threads (hyphae)

Protective wall

Chain of spores (arthroconidia)

ASPERGILLUS

CRYPTOCOCCUS

COCCIDIOIDES

Accidents and trauma
Specialist departments deal with urgent treatment of wounds, bone fractures, and other damage, usually accidental, but also in some cases due to the use of weapons. These departments also treat the initial stages of medical emergencies such as heart attacks, severe asthma, and substance abuse.

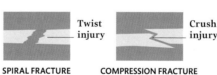

Bone breaks skin

Skin unbroken

Crack or split

OPEN FRACTURE

CLOSED FRACTURE

GREENSTICK FRACTURE

Several pieces

Twist injury

Crush injury

COMMINUTED FRACTURE

SPIRAL FRACTURE

COMPRESSION FRACTURE

Mental health
Mental health problems affect the mind at various levels, from awareness of self and others, and disturbed routine behavior and social interactions, to severe anxiety and depressive states, and potentially life-endangering responses under physical and emotional stress. Many parts of the brain may be involved.

Types of medicine
Modern medicine is divided up into many specialties. Some are based on body parts or systems, such as cardiology. Others deal with life stages, including obstetrics, pediatrics, and geriatrics (related to conditions of aging). Various specialties often work together.

> **Doctors** in ancient Rome **specialized** in particular **fields** of medicine

 Anesthesia
Suppressing sensation, such as pain perception (local) and consciousness (general).

 Cardiology
Concerned with disorders of the heart and major circulatory vessels.

 Dentistry
Specializing in the teeth, gums, and mouth, including tongue and oral hygiene.

 Dermatology
Treatment of problems of the skin, hair, and nails, including cosmetic disorders.

 Emergency medicine
Diagnosis and treatment of acute (sudden) and possibly life-threatening conditions.

 General medicine
Generalized medical care, especially conditions involving multiple systems.

 Medical genetics
Study and diagnosis of genetic material (DNA) and inherited disorders.

 Neurology
Concerning the brain and nervous system, including nerve–muscle conditions.

 Obstetrics and gynecology
Female reproductive and associated organs, fertility, pregnancy, and childbirth.

 Oncology
Diagnosis, study, and treatment of tumors, especially cancerous ones.

 Ophthalmology
Problems of the eyes and associated parts such as tear glands and eyelids.

 Orthopedics
Dealing with problems of bones, joints, muscles, tendons, and allied parts.

The **fastest A-fibers** carry pain signals at more than **330 ft (100 m)** per second, the **slowest C-fibers** at less than **3.3 ft (1 m)** per second

How drugs work

Drugs are chemicals that can cure or slow down disease, relieve symptoms, or ease pain. Some drugs, especially painkillers (analgesics), interfere with the ways in which nerve signals are generated or travel along fibers and through junctions (synapses) to the brain.

Types of drugs

Most cells have specialized receptor areas and various body chemicals bind to these to control processes within the cell. Drugs called agonists bind to specific cell receptors; antagonists block the receptors.

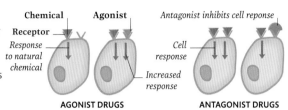

Chemical · Agonist · *Antagonist inhibits cell reponse*

Receptor · *Response to natural chemical* · *Cell response* · *Increased response*

AGONIST DRUGS · **ANTAGONIST DRUGS**

Feeling pain

Sensations of pain usually come from damaged tissues where cells break apart and leak chemicals. These stimulate sensory nerve endings, which produce nerve signals bound for the brain.

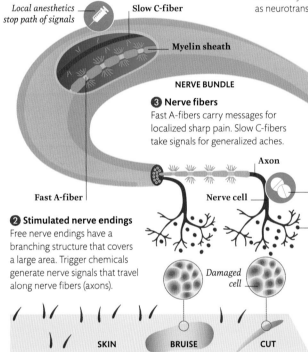

Local anesthetics stop path of signals

Slow C-fiber

Myelin sheath

NERVE BUNDLE

Fast A-fiber

3 Nerve fibers
Fast A-fibers carry messages for localized sharp pain. Slow C-fibers take signals for generalized aches.

Axon

Nerve cell

2 Stimulated nerve endings
Free nerve endings have a branching structure that covers a large area. Trigger chemicals generate nerve signals that travel along nerve fibers (axons).

Damaged cell

SKIN · BRUISE · CUT

4 Nerve junction
At the spinal cord, peripheral nerve fibers have junctions with cord fibers. Signals pass across the junction gap as neurotransmitters.

Some painkillers may block chemical signals here

Chemical message for pain

SYNAPSE

Some painkillers block production of prostaglandins at the site of the injury

Prostaglandin molecule released by cell

1 Trigger chemicals
Prostaglandin chemicals leaking from broken cells activate not only nerve messages representing pain, but also inflammation as blood and fluid flow to the area increases.

5 Reaching the brain
Spinal cord fibers link to nerve cells in the thalamus, which sends them to appropriate brain areas, especially the touch centers.

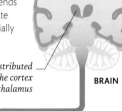

Pain signals are distributed to various areas of the cortex by the thalamus

BRAIN

Nerve traveling up to brain

SPINAL CORD

Body nerve connecting to spinal cord

SURGICAL PROCEDURES

Surgical procedures are used to remove, repair, or replace damaged tissue in the body. It may also involve implanting artificial devices, such as a pacemaker. Operations may range from highly invasive to minimally invasive keyhole surgery and advances in technology have increased the safety and effectiveness of surgical procedures, increased success rates, and shortened recovery times.

Pediatrics
Care of infants, children, and adolescents, often including changes during puberty.

Pathology
Broadly, the study of disease; in particular, the effects of disease on cells, tissues, and fluids.

Pharmaceutical medicine
Developing, assessing, monitoring, and regulating medicines for the benefit of patients.

Physiotherapy
Physical therapies including exercise for treatment and rehabilitation.

Podiatry
Treating disorders of the toes and toenails, foot, ankle, calf, and lower extremities.

Psychiatry
Dealing with mental disorders, including cognitive, perceptual, and emotional.

Radiology
Use of X-rays, ultrasound, and nuclear magnetic resonance for diagnosis and treatment.

Surgery
Operations using instruments to cut into the body to treat injuries or disorders.

TRADITIONAL MEDICAL SYSTEMS

Many regions have developed methods of diagnosis and treatment over millennia. They include Ayurveda in Southern Asia, and herbalism and divination in Africa. In China, the Theory of the Five Elements emphasizes interactions between the body and universe.

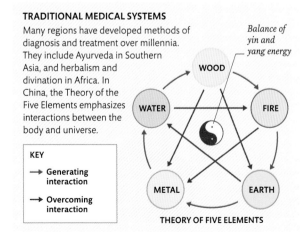

Balance of yin and yang energy

WOOD

WATER · **FIRE**

METAL · **EARTH**

KEY
→ Generating interaction
→ Overcoming interaction

THEORY OF FIVE ELEMENTS

see also The spread and control of disease pp.254–55 ▶ **Diagnosis** pp.256–59 ▶ **The fight against disease** pp.364–65 ▶

The spread and control of disease

Throughout history, infectious diseases—those that can spread from person to person among a population—have had devastating effects. The study of what causes them, and how and why they spread, and how they can be controlled or limited, is called epidemiology.

Requirements

Infectious diseases require certain elements to spread. The pathogens must be present, they must have favorable conditions to thrive, and the hosts must not be immune or otherwise resistant.

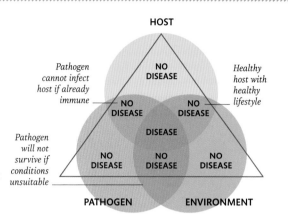

HOST

Pathogen cannot infect host if already immune

Healthy host with healthy lifestyle

NO DISEASE

NO DISEASE

NO DISEASE

DISEASE

Pathogen will not survive if conditions unsuitable

NO DISEASE

NO DISEASE

NO DISEASE

PATHOGEN

ENVIRONMENT

IS IT CATCHING?

- **Infection** A disease caused by invasive organisms living and reproducing in or on the body.
- **Pathogen** Organism that causes disease.
- **Vector** Organism that transmits pathogens from person to person.
- **Transmissible or Communicable** Able to spread from person to person.
- **Contagious** Spread only by close contact.
- **Outbreak** A sudden, localized increase in the occurrence of an infectious disease.
- **Epidemic/Pandemic** Affecting many thousands/ millions across a wide region/continents.

Studying outbreaks

Epidemiologists examine patterns of disease spread. They study where a disease spreads, for instance within a particular city zone. And they study who is infected, for example people of a certain age group or doing specific jobs.

BROAD STREET

REGENT STREET

GOLDEN SQUARE

BREWER STREET

London's 1854 cholera outbreak

John Snow mapped deaths from cholera in London. He realized they centered on a communal water pump in Broad Street. Disabling the pump drastically reduced the outbreak (see p.365).

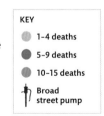

KEY

- 1–4 deaths
- 5–9 deaths
- 10–15 deaths
- Broad street pump

JOHN SNOW

The analysis of the 1854 cholera outbreak by English physician Snow (1813–58) helped to found the medical science of epidemiology. It also spurred advances in sewage disposal, hygiene, and other aspects of public health.

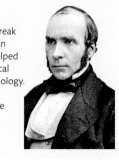

Diseases and society

Patterns of infections and other diseases differ around the world, often according to culture and tradition, and the patterns have also changed through time. According to the World Health Organization, the most important environmental factor for disease reduction is a supply of clean water for drinking, cooking, and washing.

Diseases of poverty

Major historical causes of ill health include poor hygiene. Education, increased public awareness, and government policy help to lessen the effects.

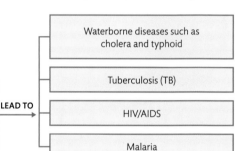

| Malnutrition due to poor diet |
| Lack of fresh water and poor sanitation |
| Lack of access to healthcare and health advice |

LEAD TO

| Waterborne diseases such as cholera and typhoid |
| Tuberculosis (TB) |
| HIV/AIDS |
| Malaria |

| Increased use of cars |
| Decreased exercise |
| Increased sedentary employment |
| Easy access to large amounts of low-cost processed foods |
| Greater access to low-cost alcohol and tobacco |
| Lower consumption of fresh and seasonal food |

LEAD TO

Diseases of affluence

Wealth and advanced economies have brought risks of different diseases to the fore, especially those linked to obesity and aging.

| Type 2 diabetes |
| Heart disease |
| Some types of cancer |
| Alcohol- and drug-related issues |
| Obesity |

How diseases spread

Communicable diseases have several person-to-person routes. One of the most contagious is measles. The virus is spread by airborne droplets from coughs and sneezes, by direct contact, and by contaminated objects.

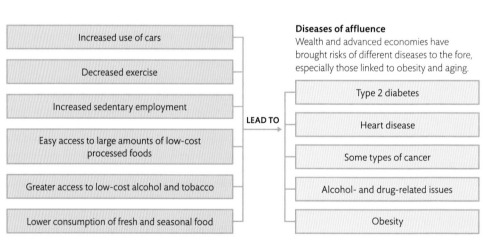

INSECT OR OTHER VECTOR

DIRECT CONTACT

AIR

INDIRECT CONTACT

INFECTED PERSON

FOOD

HEALTHY PERSON

Ebola virus disease has an average fatality rate of 50 percent, but this has been as high as **90 percent** in some outbreaks

Types of vaccines

A vaccine contains deactivated pathogens, parts of them, or toxic products from them that are harmless, but which still activate the body's immune system to defend itself and repel the disease, as happens during a natural infection.

Disease-causing pathogen
Different pathogens are treated in different ways to produce effective vaccines with few side effects. For example, in the vaccine for bubonic plague, the pathogen is inactivated.

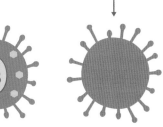

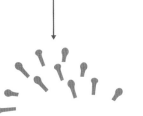

Pieces of pathogen
Fragments that initiate the immune response, rather than whole pathogens. Used for human papillomavirus (HPV), hepatitis B.

Pathogen genetic material
Injected, this causes body cells to produce pathogen substances that trigger the immune system. Used for Japanese encephalitis.

Inactivated pathogen
Heat, radiation, or chemicals kill the pathogen, but it still instigates an immune reaction. Used for influenza, cholera.

Closely related organism
The vaccine contains a pathogen that causes a similar disease in another species, but no or few human symptoms. Used for tuberculosis (TB).

Disarmed pathogen
The pathogen is alive, but the parts that make it harmful are removed or disabled. Used for measles, mumps, rubella (MMR).

Neutralized toxins
Harmful substances produced by the pathogen are incapacitated by radiation, heat, or chemicals. Used for tetanus, diphtheria.

Preventing or containing infectious diseases

For many infections, immunization using vaccines is the most effective way to prevent their spread. The ready-and-waiting defense systems of immunized people attack the pathogen so rapidly that it does not have time to multiply and then be passed to others.

Zero immunization

The disease spreads unchecked through a population, although there may be some individuals who already have some form of natural immunization. Smallpox killed 300–500 million people before it was eradicated by a vaccination campaign.

Minority immunization

The disease maintains its transmission through the population because those individuals who are infected continue to pass it on. However, the infected are fewer in number than if there had been no vaccinations.

Majority immunization

Above about 80 percent vaccination in the population may bring herd immunity, where those who are protected do not spread the pathogen, so the unvaccinated do not encounter it. Without new hosts to infect, the pathogen may die out.

Immunization

No vaccine is 100 percent effective, and some have side effects, which are usually minor but may be more severe for some individuals. However, overall the drawbacks of vaccination outweigh the risks of not being immunized.

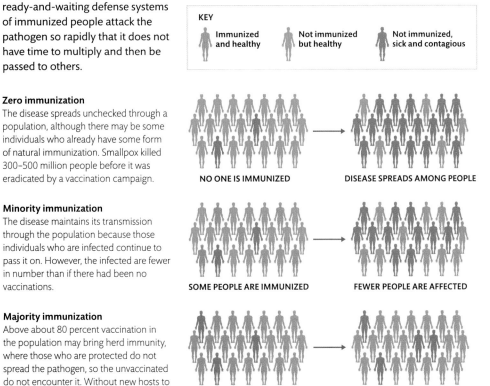

KEY

Immunized and healthy
Not immunized but healthy
Not immunized, sick and contagious

NO ONE IS IMMUNIZED → **DISEASE SPREADS AMONG PEOPLE**

SOME PEOPLE ARE IMMUNIZED → **FEWER PEOPLE ARE AFFECTED**

MOST PEOPLE GET IMMUNIZED → **SPREAD OF DISEASE IS CONTAINED**

Conquering smallpox

Following a massive 20-year worldwide campaign using a series of highly effective vaccines with few side-effects, smallpox was finally declared eradicated in 1980.

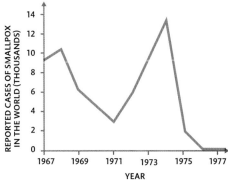

Screening for disease

Checking for early signs of potentially serious illnesses is especially important for non-transmissible conditions such as cancers and heart disease.

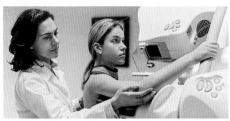

MAMMOGRAPHY SCREENING FOR BREAST CANCER

Diagnosis

Before an illness can be truly treated and cured, its root cause should be identified. This is the act of diagnosis, sometimes referred to as an exercise in scientific logic combined with a medical art form. The physician amalgamates and evaluates evidence from a potentially huge array of sources, from initial observations of the patient during the physical, clinical, or medical, examination, to the most complex of scanned images and sample analysis.

Physical examination

A medical examination has several components. One is the history, including the patient's own account and medical records. Another is the physical exam, from observing the patient's manner, to studying parts such as eyes, tongue, and skin. Also featured may be basic tests, such as blood pressure and listening to the heart.

Blood pressure

The pressure exerted by blood as it surges through vessels, measured by a sphygmomanometer, is a valuable pointer to numerous conditions. The cuff inflates enough to stop arterial flow, then releases to measure the highest pressure. The lowest pressure is taken with the cuff deflated.

Eye check
The ophthalmoscope shines a light into the eyeball for a magnified view of the retina and other parts. This can reveal signs of disorders.

Ear check
Gently realigning the ear flap straightens the ear canal and allows the doctor to use an otoscope to see an enlarged view of the eardrum.

BODY WEIGHT

Several calculations relate weight, height, chest, waist and hip size, and other body dimensions. For example BMI (Body Mass Index), is weight (lbs) divided by height (in) squared times 703. These figures give a general idea of overall health and degree of obesity.

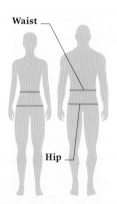
Waist
Hip

GENDER	FEMALE	MALE
HEALTHY	<0.8	<0.9
MODERATE RISK	0.8–0.89	0.9–0.99
HIGH RISK	≥0.9	≥1.0

WAIST/HIP RATIO

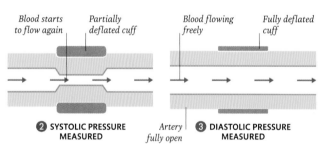

Blood flow stopped | **Compressed artery wall** **Artery**

Inflated cuff

① THE CUFF IS INFLATED

Blood starts to flow again | *Partially deflated cuff*

② SYSTOLIC PRESSURE MEASURED

Blood flowing freely | *Fully deflated cuff*

Artery fully open | **③ DIASTOLIC PRESSURE MEASURED**

Blood pressure reading

The upper number is systolic pressure—the highest exerted when the heart contracts. Below is the lower, or diastolic, pressure. The number for diastolic is lower because it is the arterial pressure when the heart relaxes.

$$\frac{120}{80}$$

Systolic pressure
Diastolic pressure

Rigid endoscope

This design is available in diameters ranging from 1 mm to more than $^1/_{25}$–$^2/_5$ in (10mm). Different types are used to visualize inside the nose (rhinoscopy), bladder (cystoscopy), and abdomen (laparoscopy).

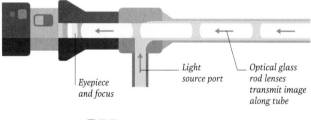

Eyepiece and focus
Light source port
Optical glass rod lenses transmit image along tube

Flexible endoscope

This type of device can be bent and curled to steer through the body, along parts such as the digestive tract or large blood vessels.

Internal examination

Endoscopes provide an internal view, take biopsy samples of tissues and fluids, and execute minor procedures such as sealing blood vessels. They are named according to the parts they access, such as a bronchoscope, which can examine the lungs.

CAPSULE ENDOSCOPY

The size of a large pill, the capsule endoscope houses a tiny camera and electronics for wireless communication. Usually swallowed, it takes pictures of the gut interior and sends them wirelessly.

Ring of LEDs provide light for camera

CAPSULE ENDOSCOPE

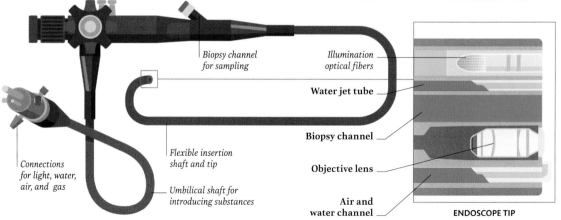
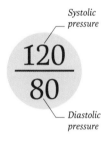

Connections for light, water, air, and gas

Flexible insertion shaft and tip

Umbilical shaft for introducing substances

Biopsy channel for sampling

Illumination optical fibers

Water jet tube

Biopsy channel

Objective lens

Air and water channel

ENDOSCOPE TIP

The **electromagnet** in an **MRI scanner** generates a magnetic field 40,000 times as strong as Earth's

Scans and imaging

Since the first X-ray pictures for medical purposes in 1895, noninvasive diagnostic imaging has developed into a huge field. In the 1970s, computers began assembling series of X-ray images into 3D images viewable from any angle. There are now more than 20 techniques for looking inside the body, using sound waves, magnetism, X-rays and other electromagnetic waves, chemicals that block X-rays, and substances that emit other forms of radiation. In a related medical specialty, similar machines are used for treatment, as in precisely targeted radiotherapy to shrink and remove tumors.

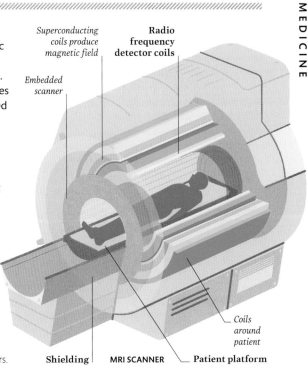

Superconducting coils produce magnetic field — **Radio frequency detector coils**

Embedded scanner

Coils around patient

Shielding | **MRI SCANNER** | **Patient platform**

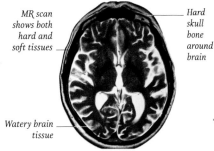

Lung tissues appear dark — *Clavicle (collar bone)*

Heart behind sternum (breast bone) — *Air passages faintly visible, due to cartilage*

Standard X-rays

X-ray images show harder tissues, which do not allow X-rays to pass, as pale shapes—chiefly bone, cartilage, and teeth. Injecting substances that absorb X-rays, known as radiopaque, outlines softer parts where they collect.

MR scan shows both hard and soft tissues — *Hard skull bone around brain*

Watery brain tissue

Magnetic resonance imaging, MRI

A powerful magnetic field around the body makes its hydrogen atoms align. When the magnetism ceases, the atoms return to normal, giving off tiny pulses of radio waves that are recorded by detectors.

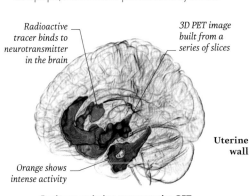

Radioactive tracer binds to neurotransmitter in the brain — *3D PET image built from a series of slices*

Orange shows intense activity

Positron emission tomography, PET

A dye substance containing radioactive tracer is injected, swallowed, or inhaled. Depending on the specific tracer, it is absorbed by certain tissues with higher chemical activity, and these show up brighter in the image.

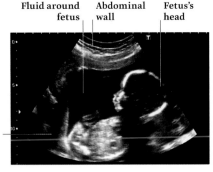

Fluid around fetus | **Abdominal wall** | **Fetus's head**

Uterine wall

Ultrasound, US

Very high-pitched sound waves are reflected by tissues in different ways. A receiver detects the echoes, which are assembled into real-time changing images. This technique uses no X-ray-like radiation and is common in pregnancy.

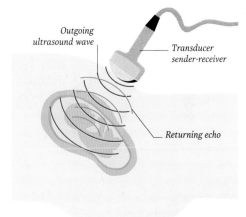

Outgoing ultrasound wave — *Transducer sender-receiver*

Returning echo

ULTRASOUND IMAGING OF FETUS

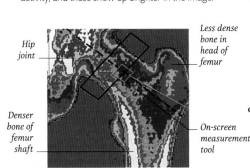

Less dense bone in head of femur

Hip joint

Denser bone of femur shaft — *On-screen measurement tool*

Dual-energy X-ray absorptiometry, DEXA

Also known as a bone density scan, DEXA uses low-dose X-rays to analyze the density or strength of bones. It is used, for instance, to monitor bone thinning in certain conditions or during some forms of treatment.

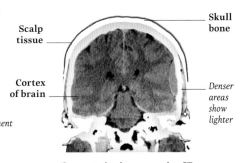

Scalp tissue — **Skull bone**

Cortex of brain — *Denser areas show lighter*

Computerized tomography, CT

CT scanning employs X-rays from a source that rotates around the body along with detectors on the opposite sides. As in all radiation techniques, the amount of X-rays is adjusted to minimize harmful side effects.

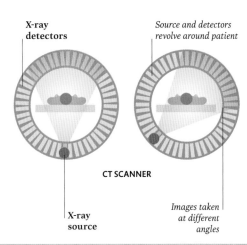

X-ray detectors — *Source and detectors revolve around patient*

CT SCANNER

X-ray source — *Images taken at different angles*

◄ see also The skeletal system pp.232–33   ◄ Respiratory and cardiovascular systems pp.240–41   ◄ The history of medicine pp.250–51

>> Diagnosis continued

Electrical diagnostics

The body is naturally alive with tiny electrical signals. The brain, nerves, heart, and muscles are especially busy. Their impulses can be detected by electrodes on the skin, or in more complex and precise situations, by inserting sensors into organs and tissues. Their display on screens or paper traces reveal the health of their sources.

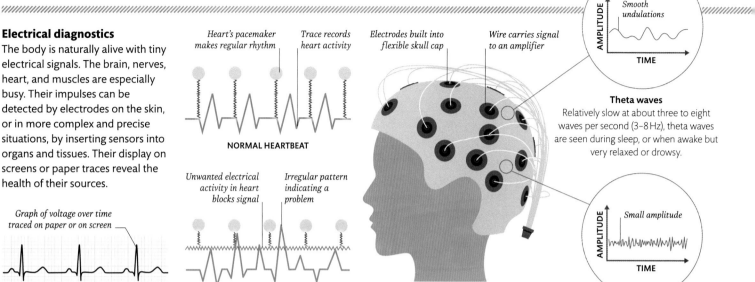

Heart's pacemaker makes regular rhythm

Trace records heart activity

NORMAL HEARTBEAT

Unwanted electrical activity in heart blocks signal

Irregular pattern indicating a problem

IRREGULAR HEARTBEAT

Electrodes built into flexible skull cap

Wire carries signal to an amplifier

ELECTROENCEPHALOGRAPH, EEG

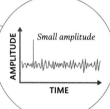

Smooth undulations

AMPLITUDE / TIME

Theta waves
Relatively slow at about three to eight waves per second (3–8 Hz), theta waves are seen during sleep, or when awake but very relaxed or drowsy.

Graph of voltage over time traced on paper or on screen

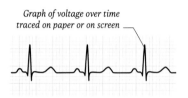

AMPLITUDE / TIME

Small amplitude

Electrocardiogram, ECG
Electrodes attached to the chest and limbs pick up the heart's electrical activity as the signals ripple outward through the tissues to the skin.

Reading the ECG
The ECG trace shows the heart rate (beats per minute) and the way electrical signals stimulate the muscular walls to contract, forcing out blood.

EEG cap
A skull cap ensures that eletrodes are placed correctly over the head for an EEG to show the brain's electrical activity, which occurs in coordinated waves.

Gamma waves
From 30 to more than 100 per second, gamma waves indicate the person's brain is busy with conscious attention and memory formation.

Sample taking and testing

Small amounts, or samples, of almost any body substance may be extracted and examined to gauge state of health. Fluids, such as sputum and urine, and fecal matter are obtained relatively easily. Blood is one of the most commonly taken samples. Biopsy involves taking cells or tissues, for example, from the skin, or from the gut wall or lung lining during endoscopy (see p.256).

Types of tests
Some chemical tests are on-the-spot, such as glucose in blood for diabetes. Others are based in the laboratory. Genetic tests investigate DNA for faulty genes.

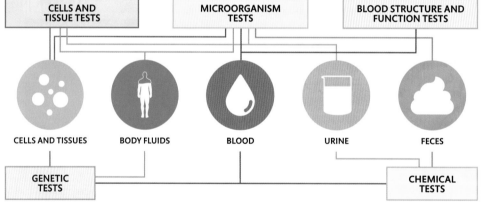

CELLS AND TISSUE TESTS	MICROORGANISM TESTS	BLOOD STRUCTURE AND FUNCTION TESTS

CELLS AND TISSUES　　BODY FLUIDS　　BLOOD　　URINE　　FECES

GENETIC TESTS　　　　　CHEMICAL TESTS

Plunger withdrawn slowly

Sample carefully labeled

Common tests require 2.5–3 ml

May contain substances to prevent clotting

Absorbent paper containing reactant chemicals

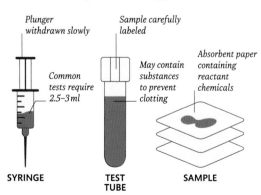

SYRINGE　　**TEST TUBE**　　**SAMPLE**

Blood samples
Blood is usually withdrawn into a syringe using a needle into an arm vein. Larger quantities are stored in bags or beakers. Drops of blood come from skin pricks.

Fatty tissue around glands

Tissue of mammary glands

Blood vessels are avoided

Breast lump

Fine needle draws up cells and fluid

Biopsies
Fine-needle aspiration extracts a biopsy sample from soft, pliable tissue near the body surface, like the breast, using a very narrow needle and syringe.

AUTOPSY

Since medieval times, surgeons have conducted autopsies, or postmortems, to ascertain the cause of death. This can be linked to the patient's symptoms and condition in life, to improve future treatments.

16TH-CENTURY AUTOPSY

Electroencephalograms (EEGs) can be used to assess **brain activity** in **coma patients**

In vitro tests

Meaning "in glass," in vitro tests take place in containers and equipment rather than in the body ("in vivo") and number in the thousands. Most commonly analyzed are blood and urine. Usually, blood is first separated into its main constituents of cells and plasma.

Blood may be tested for more than **100 different substances**

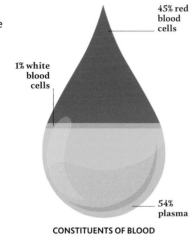

45% red blood cells

1% white blood cells

54% plasma

CONSTITUENTS OF BLOOD

Uric acid

Bicarbonate ions

CREATININE

POTASSIUM IONS

SODIUM IONS

CHLORIDE IONS

UREA

Double-concave saucerlike shape   *Red color due to hemoglobin*

Red blood cells
These blood cells contain hemoglobin, which picks up oxygen in the lungs and releases it near the body's cells.

Neutrophil

White blood cells
The main types of white cells (see p.243) help to defend the body from infection and remove harmful substances.

Antibody   **Nutrient**

Plasma
Plasma carries hundreds of telltale substances including nutrients, hormones, antibodies, and blood-clotting chemicals.

Substances in urine
The acidity of urine or the presence of blood or sugar can help diagnose a huge range of conditions, including diabetes.

COMPONENT	TESTS FOR
Red blood cells	Numbers, shape, and size affected by genetic and other disorders
White blood cells	Cells affected by infection and blood cancers such as leukemia
Hemoglobin	Low levels may indicate anemia, or severe blood loss
Plasma	Tests may indicate inflammation or certain autoimmune conditions

Blood glucose

Testing the concentration of glucose (sugar) in the blood can help to diagnose and monitor diabetes. Diabetes is a disorder of blood glucose regulation. Glucose is the major energy source for all body cells. Its blood level is controlled by two pancreatic hormones (see p.247), insulin and glucagon. Insulin triggers cells to use glucose, so blood glucose falls. Glucagon triggers the release of stored glucose.

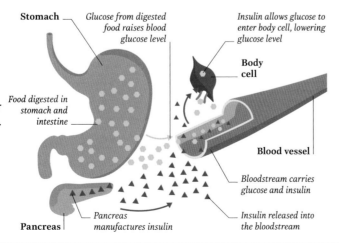

Stomach   *Glucose from digested food raises blood glucose level*

Insulin allows glucose to enter body cell, lowering glucose level

Body cell

Food digested in stomach and intestine

Blood vessel

Bloodstream carries glucose and insulin

Pancreas   *Pancreas manufactures insulin*

Insulin released into the bloodstream

Pathology

Pathology is broadly the causes and effects of disease. However, it usually refers to activities in the "path lab"—laboratory tests of fluids, cells, tissues, and microbes, especially for diagnosis and to monitor treatment. Much of this work involves microscopes and tissue-coloring substances called stains.

Cytopathology
This is the study of disease at the level of cells. Microscopic examination can identify foreign cells, or cells abnormal in number, shape, or arrangement, typical of disease, especially many cancers.

Clival chordoma (a type of cancer)

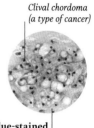

Blue-stained sample

Histopathology
Examining whole tissues and groups of tissues is called histopathology. Tissues are scrutinized under a microscope to look for abnormalities of cells and the structures around them.

Slice of stained bone tissue

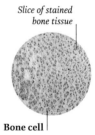

Bone cell

Until the 1960s, **pregnancy tests** involved injecting urine into an **African clawed frog** to see if it **ovulated**

FORENSIC PATHOLOGY

This speciality of pathology focuses on studying corpses and body products, such as blood stains, hair, and saliva. Tests include extracting DNA and proteins that can be probed in molecular detail. Aims are to determine cause of death and provide evidence for legal cases.

INTERPRETING DNA GEL

MEDICINE

◀ see also Lymphatic and immune systems pp.242–43   ◀ Digestive and urinary systems pp.244–45   ◀ Modern medicine pp.252–53

Medical advances

Almost every year, great strides are made in medical diagnosis, treatment, and care. Some of these advances transfer from other areas or research, such as computer science, robotics, microscopy, nanotechnology, and genetic studies. Other advances are generated from within medicine itself, such as innovative microsurgical techniques, and new vaccines and novel drugs to combat newly discovered and age-old diseases and disorders. However, all progress in medicine should be slow and careful because false hopes can cause pain and suffering, and ultimately, lives are at stake.

Three-dimensional printing

Computerized 3D printing is being applied to medicine in several ways. Frameworks printed from bio-friendly substances act as scaffolding for cells to colonize and make components such as bones, cartilage, and muscle. Actual cells can be arranged by the printer into multi-tissue parts, such as ears.

Printed human tissue
Research into test-printing small "organoids" has yielded a mini human heart, complete with blood vessels, muscular walled chambers, and valves.

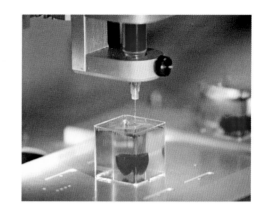

Genetic manipulation

The complete human genome of genetic instructions, in the form of DNA, was determined in 2003. Major applications include identifying faulty gene sequences that cause problems, such as inherited conditions and some forms of cancer, and repairing or replacing them by targeted genetic manipulation.

Gene editing
Molecules can be custom-made to attach to a defective length of DNA. Enzymes and other chemicals then snip out the problem sequence and replace it with a corrected version so that the cell can function normally.

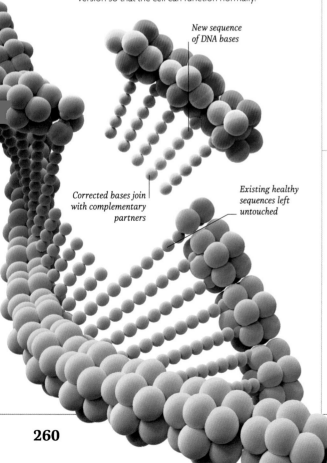

New sequence of DNA bases

Corrected bases join with complementary partners

Existing healthy sequences left untouched

Hi-tech aids

Even the body's most complex and mysterious part, the brain, is gradually yielding its secrets as to how it works. At the same time, electronic devices are becoming tinier, more complex, and more intricate. This is enabling microtechnology to aid and even enhance brain function.

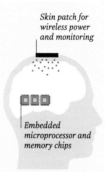

MEMORY CHIPS
Microprocessors and memory chips can be implanted into different areas of the brain to expand retention and recall abilities. An area of particular interest is the hippocampus, which is active in changing short-term experiences into long-term memories.

Skin patch for wireless power and monitoring

Embedded microprocessor and memory chips

HIPPOCAMPAL IMPLANTS

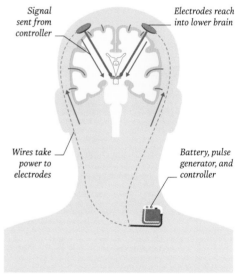

Signal sent from controller

Electrodes reach into lower brain

Wires take power to electrodes

Battery, pulse generator, and controller

Deep brain stimulation
In this treatment, electrodes are placed into parts of the lower brain, commonly in areas that help control movement. Controlled electrical pulses sent to the electrodes alter the patterns of surrounding nerve signals.

Stem cell therapy

Stem cells are those that have not yet specialized (differentiated) into nerve, blood, or other specific cell types. They have the potential to become any kind of cell. Stem cell therapy uses undifferentiated cells produced from transforming adult cells, such as the hematopoietic cells found in bone marrow. These are introduced into body parts to specialize and form new tissues.

Stem cells could help **restore** some **movement** after a **spinal cord injury**

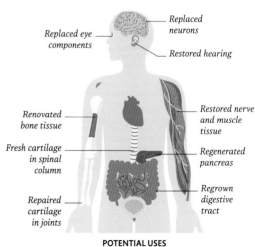

Replaced eye components

Replaced neurons

Restored hearing

Renovated bone tissue

Restored nerve and muscle tissue

Fresh cartilage in spinal column

Regenerated pancreas

Repaired cartilage in joints

Regrown digestive tract

POTENTIAL USES

There are **immunotherapy treatments available** for about **20 types of cancer**

Personalized medicine

It is well known that people may vary in their responses to the same medication. Analyzing certain sequences in a person's genome may show if a particular drug is likely to be more or less effective, so drug therapies can be tailored to the individual.

Immunotherapy

Immunotherapy boosts the body's own defenses to fight cancer. In one type of immunotherapy, a custom-made vaccine is produced, which prepares T cells to attack specific cancer cells. T cells may not recognize the threat, because the cancer cells are produced by the body.

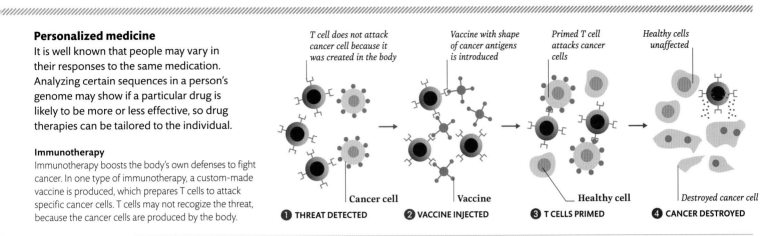

T cell does not attack cancer cell because it was created in the body

Vaccine with shape of cancer antigens is introduced

Primed T cell attacks cancer cells

Healthy cells unaffected

Cancer cell

Vaccine

Healthy cell

Destroyed cancer cell

❶ THREAT DETECTED **❷ VACCINE INJECTED** **❸ T CELLS PRIMED** **❹ CANCER DESTROYED**

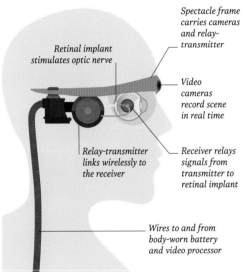

Retinal implant stimulates optic nerve

Spectacle frame carries cameras and relay-transmitter

Video cameras record scene in real time

Relay-transmitter links wirelessly to the receiver

Receiver relays signals from transmitter to retinal implant

Wires to and from body-worn battery and video processor

Sensory implants

Electronic versions of the eye and ear progress yearly. In one system, a camera captures the scene as electrical signals that travel to an external relay, which transmits them wirelessly to a retinal implant.

Prosthetic body parts were used in Egypt about 3,000 years ago

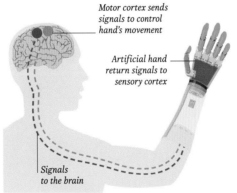

Motor cortex sends signals to control hand's movement

Artificial hand return signals to sensory cortex

Signals to the brain

Prosthetic hand

The latest prostheses have two-way function. The brain sends signals to control their movements and the prosthesis has sensory receptors to feel touch and pressure, and transmit signals back to the brain.

NANOMEDICINE

Nano- is the next tiniest level from micro-, smaller than cells and at the scale of molecules and even atoms. Therapeutic nanomachines could travel around the body, programmed to destroy germs, cancerous cells, or toxic substances. Nanoelectronic robots might help ailing cells or damaged cells and nanoparticles may slow-release their drug contents directly into target tissues.

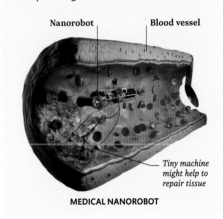

Nanorobot **Blood vessel**

Tiny machine might help to repair tissue

MEDICAL NANOROBOT

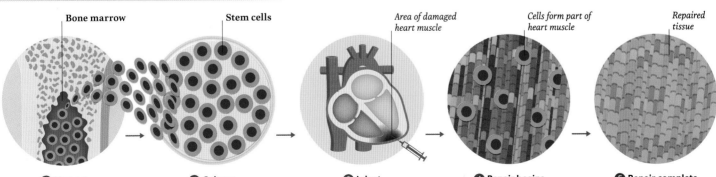

Bone marrow **Stem cells** *Area of damaged heart muscle* *Cells form part of heart muscle* *Repaired tissue*

❶ Harvest
Certain types of stem cells are removed from adult bone marrow. These hematopoietic stem cells naturally make different kinds of blood cells.

❷ Culture
The cells are put into specialized nutrient solutions with substances that enhance their potential to "despecialize" to become other cell types.

❸ Inject
The stem cells are placed into a damaged heart wall—a suitable environment to encourage them to differentiate into heart muscle cells.

❹ Repair begins
The stem cells continue to multiply, but some undergo changes to produce specialist heart muscle cells known as cardiac myocytes.

❺ Repair complete
The muscular heart wall, which may have been damaged by a heart attack (myocardial infarction), gradually undergoes restoration.

Energy

Energy makes things happen. It cannot be created or destroyed, but it is constantly converted between its many different forms. Electrical energy is valuable to humanity because it can be easily stored, transported, and converted into other types of useful energy, so a lot of effort is put into generating electricity. Energy is measured in joules (J). The rate at which it is converted between forms is known as power, which is measured in watts (W).

How a power station works

Power stations are facilities for generating electrical power from energy sources, such as oil or nuclear fuel. Most power stations contain generators, which convert kinetic (motion) energy into electrical energy. This electrical energy is then transferred to buildings through a network known as a power grid.

Coal began forming hundreds of millions of years ago from **decaying living matter**

Coal-fired power station

In a coal-fired power station, burning coal releases its chemical energy, heating and boiling water. The steam turns a turbine, which drives an electricity generator.

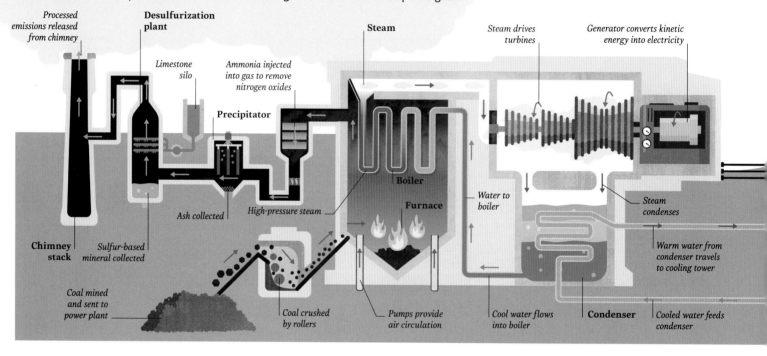

Processed emissions released from chimney

Desulfurization plant

Limestone silo

Ammonia injected into gas to remove nitrogen oxides

Precipitator

Steam

Steam drives turbines

Generator converts kinetic energy into electricity

Boiler

Water to boiler

Steam condenses

Chimney stack

Sulfur-based mineral collected

Ash collected

High-pressure steam

Furnace

Warm water from condenser travels to cooling tower

Coal mined and sent to power plant

Coal crushed by rollers

Pumps provide air circulation

Cool water flows into boiler

Condenser

Cooled water feeds condenser

Water power

The movement of water can be used to generate electricity. This involves capturing the kinetic energy of naturally ebbing water (tidal power), or of falling water (hydropower). These are clean, renewable sources of electricity, although they have some impact on their local environments.

Hydroelectric power

Hydroelectric power captures the energy of falling or fast-flowing water. Often water is collected in a reservoir and released when demand is high, turning turbines and driving generators.

Reservoir

Water flows through penstock

Powerhouse

Transformer

Electricity transported via cables supported by pylons

Movement converted into electricity

Water intake

Electricity pylons

Large objects filtered out

Flow drives turbine

Generator

Water outlet

Geothermal power

The natural thermal energy generated and stored in the Earth can be harnessed by tapping into underground wells of hot water, or pumping water through hot regions of the ground.

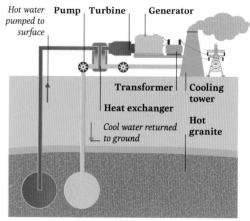

Hot water pumped to surface

Pump **Turbine** **Generator**

Transformer

Heat exchanger

Cool water returned to ground

Cooling tower

Hot granite

GEOTHERMAL POWER PLANT

CLEANING EMISSIONS

Gas produced in the furnace is processed to remove the majority of harmful pollutants before release. However, pollutants such as sulfur dioxide are still emitted by coal-fired plants.

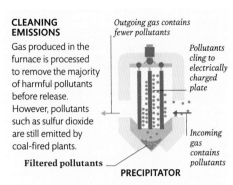

Outgoing gas contains fewer pollutants

Pollutants cling to electrically charged plate

Incoming gas contains pollutants

Filtered pollutants

PRECIPITATOR

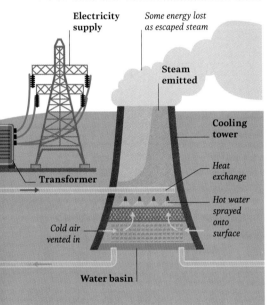

Electricity supply

Some energy lost as escaped steam

Steam emitted

Cooling tower

Transformer

Heat exchange

Hot water sprayed onto surface

Cold air vented in

Water basin

Nuclear power

Nuclear power plants generate electricity using the nuclear energy released when atomic nuclei are split apart (fission). These reactions are controlled to ensure a steady release of energy. In the future, electricity may also be generated from the fusion of nuclei.

The **first nuclear reactor** was **built** in 1942 under a football stadium in Chicago, Illinois

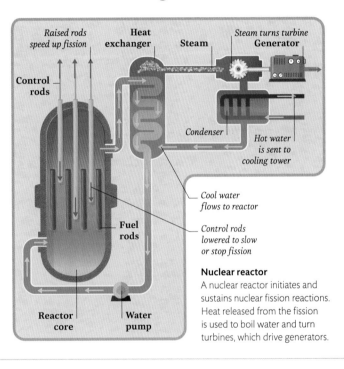

Raised rods speed up fission

Heat exchanger

Steam

Steam turns turbine **Generator**

Control rods

Condenser

Hot water is sent to cooling tower

Cool water flows to reactor

Control rods lowered to slow or stop fission

Fuel rods

Reactor core

Water pump

Nuclear reactor

A nuclear reactor initiates and sustains nuclear fission reactions. Heat released from the fission is used to boil water and turn turbines, which drive generators.

Radioactive waste disposal

Some waste produced by nuclear power stations is radioactive, and must be processed and stored carefully to stop radiation from leaking.

Fuel rods left to cool

❶ FUEL BUNDLE

Copper container

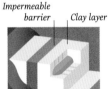

❷ DISPOSED CANISTER

Impermeable barrier *Clay layer*

❸ SEALED WITH CLAY

Waste could be buried for long-term storage

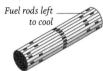

❹ BURIAL SITE

Wind energy

Wind turbines use the kinetic energy of the wind to drive generators and produce electricity. Wind is a clean and renewable source of energy, though it only allows electricity to be generated while the wind is blowing, so it is not suitable for every environment.

WIND

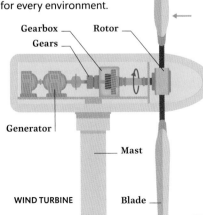

Gearbox **Rotor**

Gears

Generator

Mast

WIND TURBINE **Blade**

Solar energy

The sun can be used directly to generate electricity, such as by boiling water to turn turbines, or using solar panels composed of cells, that generate a direct current from incident sunlight, known as photovoltaic cells. Solar power is a rapidly growing method of generating clean and renewable energy.

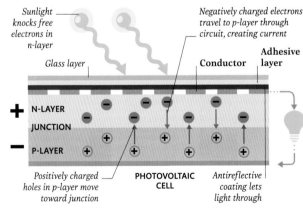

Sunlight knocks free electrons in n-layer

Negatively charged electrons travel to p-layer through circuit, creating current

Glass layer

Conductor

Adhesive layer

+ **N-LAYER**

JUNCTION

− **P-LAYER**

Positively charged holes in p-layer move toward junction

PHOTOVOLTAIC CELL

Antireflective coating lets light through

BIOENERGY

Burning biomass, such as wood and sewage, releases chemical energy. This energy is renewable, although it emits carbon dioxide and requires land to produce matter to burn.

INDUSTRIAL RESIDUE **ANIMAL WASTE** **SEWAGE** **AGRICULTURAL** **FORESTRY**

◄ see also Weather pp.74–75 ◄ The carbon cycle pp.78–79 The car pp.286–87 ►

Materials

All objects are made of materials—substances or combinations of substances. Materials have different properties, making them suitable for a diverse range of applications. Some occur naturally and others, such as steel or nylon, are processed or synthesized for certain purposes. The creation of materials with novel properties is essential for the advancement of technology.

Concrete

Concrete is an artificial material that has been used for thousands of years to build structures. It is strong and durable like stone, but also cheap and easy to produce. Wet concrete can be poured into molds of almost any shape and will harden in that shape when set.

Making concrete

Concrete is composed of a binder and filler. The binder is a pastelike fluid made of water and cement. The filler is aggregate; gravel or grainy sand.

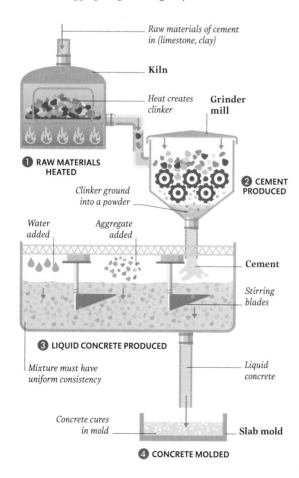

Raw materials of cement in (limestone, clay)

Kiln

Heat creates clinker

Grinder mill

① **RAW MATERIALS HEATED**

Clinker ground into a powder

② **CEMENT PRODUCED**

Water added

Aggregate added

Cement

Stirring blades

③ **LIQUID CONCRETE PRODUCED**

Mixture must have uniform consistency

Liquid concrete

Concrete cures in mold

Slab mold

④ **CONCRETE MOLDED**

Concrete was a **popular** material in the **Roman Empire;** it was used in the **Colosseum** and **Pantheon**

Metals

Metals comprise a family of materials that includes certain elements and combinations of elements. Metals are used extensively in the modern world in everything from jewelry to electronics. Due to their properties (see p.203) they conduct heat and electricity well, and tend to be strong yet malleable.

Steelmaking process

Steel is an alloy that contains iron, a small amount of carbon, and occasionally traces of other elements. It can be produced by melting iron ore (rock containing iron) in a blast furnace, or scrap steel in an electric arc furnace.

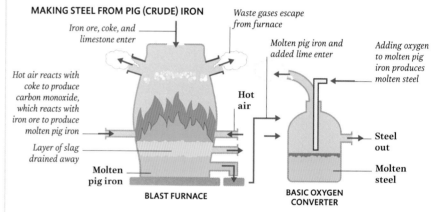

MAKING STEEL FROM PIG (CRUDE) IRON

Iron ore, coke, and limestone enter

Waste gases escape from furnace

Hot air reacts with coke to produce carbon monoxide, which reacts with iron ore to produce molten pig iron

Molten pig iron and added lime enter

Adding oxygen to molten pig iron produces molten steel

Hot air

Layer of slag drained away

Molten pig iron

Steel out

Molten steel

BLAST FURNACE

BASIC OXYGEN CONVERTER

ALLOYS

An alloy is a combination of metals (or metals and other elements) that retain metallic properties. Combining metals allows for the creation of materials with properties different from the pure metal. For example, steel (an alloy of iron and carbon) is harder and stronger than pure iron, and rose gold (an alloy of gold and copper) has a pink tone which makes it popular for use in jewelry. A few alloys can occur naturally, such as electrum (an alloy of silver and gold), but most are created by humans.

Shaping metals

The atoms in metals form crystalline structures. The structures break down when heated, causing the metal to become soft and easier to shape. In some cases they can also be shaped without heat.

The **first** human-made **alloy** was **bronze**

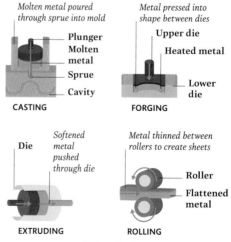

Molten metal poured through sprue into mold

Plunger
Molten metal
Sprue
Cavity

CASTING

Metal pressed into shape between dies

Upper die
Heated metal
Lower die

FORGING

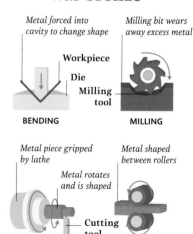

Metal forced into cavity to change shape

Workpiece
Die

BENDING

Milling bit wears away excess metal

Milling tool

MILLING

Die

Softened metal pushed through die

EXTRUDING

Metal thinned between rollers to create sheets

Roller
Flattened metal

ROLLING

Metal piece gripped by lathe

Metal rotates and is shaped

Cutting tool

TURNING

Metal shaped between rollers

ROLLING

Hot methods

Heated, softened metal can be reworked into a new shape. As it cools, the atoms recrystallize and become hard again.

Cold methods

Metals can be formed into new shapes without heat; these cold methods use mechanical stresses to rework the metal.

Glass

Glass is a solid material that is often transparent and brittle. It is made by cooling molten substances (such as silica sand) so quickly that the atoms are trapped in a disordered, amorphous structure.

Sand can be fused into glass naturally when **lightning strikes** it

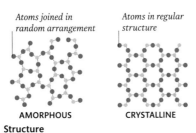

Atoms joined in random arrangement

Atoms in regular structure

AMORPHOUS **CRYSTALLINE**

Structure
Glass is amorphous—this means that its atoms are not arranged into a regular structure, like that of crystalline solids.

PROPERTIES OF GLASS
Glass is widely used in buildings and ornaments. It is usually transparent or translucent, thanks to its amorphous structure. Its water and corrosion resistance make it an ideal barrier and container. However, it is brittle, so must be toughened for use in vehicles and phone screens.

 BRITTLE
 TRANSPARENT
 WATER-RESISTANT
 CORROSION-RESISTANT

Plastics

Plastics are synthetic materials made from polymers—long chains of repeating molecules. They are extremely versatile, allowing for a range of properties, and are cheap and easy to produce.

Thermoplastics
The bonds between polymers break during heating and join again during cooling.

 Weak attractive force

Thermosetting plastics
When heated, cross-linking bonds form, causing it to harden permanently.

 Strong cross-link bond

Making polyethylene
Polyethylene is made by linking ethylene into polymer chains. Different processes produce low-density polyethylene (used for plastic bags and wraps), or high-density polyethylene (used for bottles and pipes).

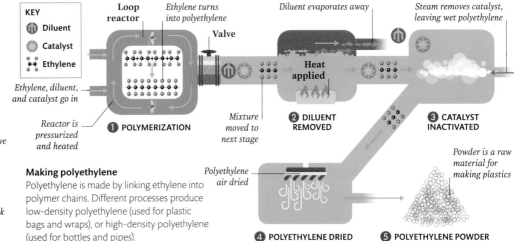

KEY
- Diluent
- Catalyst
- Ethylene

Loop reactor

Ethylene turns into polyethylene

Valve

Ethylene, diluent, and catalyst go in

Reactor is pressurized and heated

1 POLYMERIZATION

Mixture moved to next stage

Diluent evaporates away

Heat applied

2 DILUENT REMOVED

Steam removes catalyst, leaving wet polyethylene

3 CATALYST INACTIVATED

Polyethylene air dried

Powder is a raw material for making plastics

4 POLYETHYLENE DRIED **5 POLYETHYLENE POWDER**

Composites

A composite material is made from materials that combine to give the composite distinct properties from its constituents. Composites occur naturally and are also designed by humans to have useful properties, such as carbon fiber.

Natural composites
Most materials in the natural world are composites, including wood and rock. Human bodies also contain many composite materials, such as our nails and bones. Bones are made mainly from brittle hydroxyapatite with soft, flexible collagen, which gives them the properties they need to support our bodies.

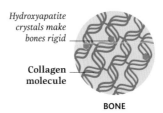

Hydroxyapatite crystals make bones rigid

Collagen molecule

BONE

Lignin molecule

Cellulose mixed with other materials

WOOD

Making carbon fiber polymer
Carbon fiber polymer is extraordinarily light and strong. It is produced through complex processes involving many steps and a variety of substances.

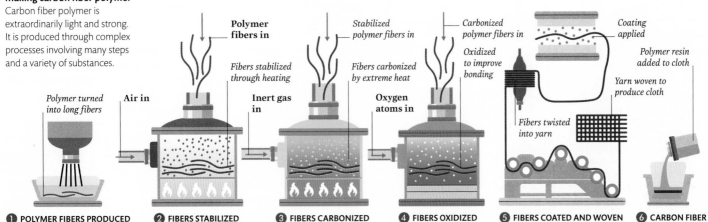

Polymer turned into long fibers

Air in

Polymer fibers in

Fibers stabilized through heating

Inert gas in

Stabilized polymer fibers in

Fibers carbonized by extreme heat

Oxygen atoms in

Carbonized polymer fibers in

Oxidized to improve bonding

Coating applied

Polymer resin added to cloth

Yarn woven to produce cloth

Fibers twisted into yarn

1 POLYMER FIBERS PRODUCED **2 FIBERS STABILIZED** **3 FIBERS CARBONIZED** **4 FIBERS OXIDIZED** **5 FIBERS COATED AND WOVEN** **6 CARBON FIBER**

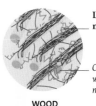

Structures and construction

Our lives are lived in and around the built environment: the human-made world filled with structures such as houses, bridges, roads, and sewers. These structures are designed by engineers to fulfill their functions safely, and are constructed from different parts and materials using heavy machinery such as cranes and diggers.

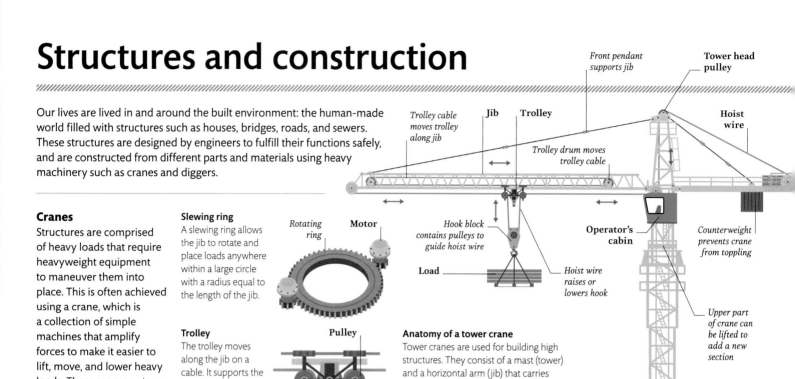

Front pendant supports jib

Tower head pulley

Trolley cable moves trolley along jib

Jib   **Trolley**

Hoist wire

Trolley drum moves trolley cable

Hook block contains pulleys to guide hoist wire

Operator's cabin

Counterweight prevents crane from toppling

Load

Hoist wire raises or lowers hook

Upper part of crane can be lifted to add a new section

Tower contains steps for operator to climb

Cranes

Structures are comprised of heavy loads that require heavyweight equipment to maneuver them into place. This is often achieved using a crane, which is a collection of simple machines that amplify forces to make it easier to lift, move, and lower heavy loads. There are many types of cranes designed for various purposes.

Slewing ring

A slewing ring allows the jib to rotate and place loads anywhere within a large circle with a radius equal to the length of the jib.

Rotating ring   **Motor**

Trolley

The trolley moves along the jib on a cable. It supports the hook block, which is raised and lowered by the hoist wire.

Pulley

Hoist wire

Anatomy of a tower crane

Tower cranes are used for building high structures. They consist of a mast (tower) and a horizontal arm (jib) that carries a pulley on a moving trolley. The rear jib carries a concrete counterweight, winding gear, and motors.

Earth movers

A crucial process in construction is digging, moving, and depositing earth in order to make space to lay the foundations of a building. Earth-moving machines such as diggers, bulldozers, and front-end loaders use levers and hydraulics to manipulate a large volume of earth.

LEVERS

A lever is a machine used to amplify force or movement in different directions. Levers can be divided into three classes distinguished by where the effort force (also known as input) and output force (load) are located relative to the fulcrum.

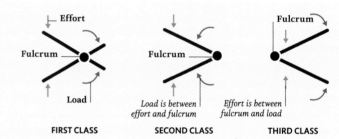

Effort

Fulcrum

Load

FIRST CLASS

Fulcrum

Load is between effort and fulcrum

SECOND CLASS

Fulcrum

Effort is between fulcrum and load

THIRD CLASS

Excavator

Excavators are designed to shovel huge amounts of material. At the heart of an excavator is an engine that drives the tracks and pump (which in turn powers its hydraulic systems).

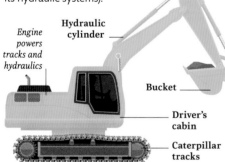

Engine powers tracks and hydraulics

Hydraulic cylinder

Bucket

Driver's cabin

Caterpillar tracks

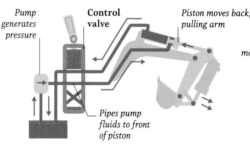

Pump generates pressure

Control valve

Piston moves back, pulling arm

Pipes pump fluids to front of piston

❶ Moving the arm forward

The pump generates hydraulic pressure, applying force to the fluid contained within a closed pipe system. This force pushes the piston rod backward, causing the dipper arm to be pulled forward.

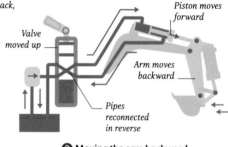

Piston moves forward

Valve moved up

Arm moves backward

Pipes reconnected in reverse

❷ Moving the arm backward

A valve controlled by the operator reverses the flow of hydraulic fluid in the pipes, exerting pressure on the other side of the piston. This pushes the piston back in the opposite direction, pulling the arm backward.

Hydraulics

Liquids cannot be compressed, so a force that is applied to a liquid is instead transferred through it. When a force is applied to one end of a liquid inside a closed cylinder, it passes through to the other end. The force can be amplified greatly by changing the relative widths of the piston rod and the cylinder.

❶ Multiplying a force

The force applied by a piston in a narrow cylinder can be multiplied by a wider cylinder and piston at the other end, even though liquid pressure remains the same.

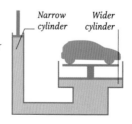

Narrow cylinder   *Wider cylinder*

❷ Double the force, half the distance

A large piston with twice the area of the narrow piston doubles the force exerted. However, the force operates over only half the distance.

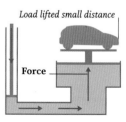

Load lifted small distance

Force

Bridges

A bridge is a structure spanning an obstacle that would be time-consuming, dangerous, or impossible to cross otherwise. Whether a bridge crosses a stream or connects two countries, it is crucial that it can withstand and transfer the forces of tension and compression from the bridge's weight and load.

Main cable structure
Main cables are made of many strands of high-tensile steel twisted together. They are also wrapped with steel wire.

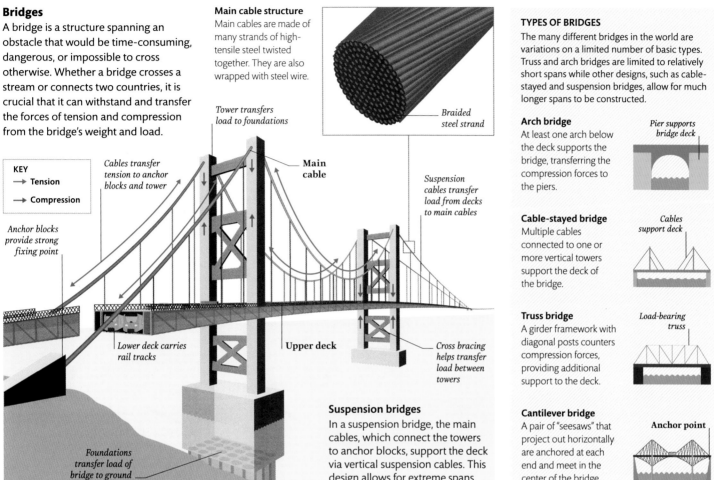

Braided steel strand

Tower transfers load to foundations

Main cable

Cables transfer tension to anchor blocks and tower

Suspension cables transfer load from decks to main cables

KEY
→ Tension
→ Compression

Anchor blocks provide strong fixing point

Lower deck carries rail tracks

Upper deck

Cross bracing helps transfer load between towers

Foundations transfer load of bridge to ground

Suspension bridges
In a suspension bridge, the main cables, which connect the towers to anchor blocks, support the deck via vertical suspension cables. This design allows for extreme spans.

TYPES OF BRIDGES

The many different bridges in the world are variations on a limited number of basic types. Truss and arch bridges are limited to relatively short spans while other designs, such as cable-stayed and suspension bridges, allow for much longer spans to be constructed.

Arch bridge
At least one arch below the deck supports the bridge, transferring the compression forces to the piers.

Pier supports bridge deck

Cable-stayed bridge
Multiple cables connected to one or more vertical towers support the deck of the bridge.

Cables support deck

Truss bridge
A girder framework with diagonal posts counters compression forces, providing additional support to the deck.

Load-bearing truss

Cantilever bridge
A pair of "seesaws" that project out horizontally are anchored at each end and meet in the center of the bridge.

Anchor point

Modern buildings

From small stone cottages to towering skyscrapers with hundreds of apartments, perhaps the most important artificial structures are those which humans inhabit. Modern living structures should be safe, secure, offer shade and shelter from extreme weather, and provide access to vital utilities such as water and electricity.

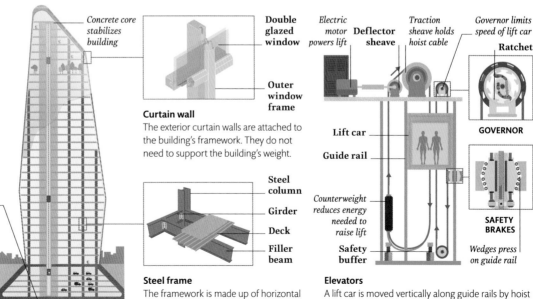

Concrete core stabilizes building

Piles below foundation support building

Skyscrapers

High-rise buildings offer a large amount of space while occupying a relatively small amount of land, making them a popular structure in densely populated cities. Advances in technology have allowed for higher skyscrapers to be built.

Double glazed window

Outer window frame

Curtain wall
The exterior curtain walls are attached to the building's framework. They do not need to support the building's weight.

Steel column

Girder

Deck

Filler beam

Steel frame
The framework is made up of horizontal girders and a vertical steel column, with extra support from filler beams.

Electric motor powers lift

Deflector sheave

Traction sheave holds hoist cable

Governor limits speed of lift car

Ratchet

Lift car

Guide rail

GOVERNOR

Counterweight reduces energy needed to raise lift

Safety buffer

SAFETY BRAKES

Wedges press on guide rail

Elevators
A lift car is moved vertically along guide rails by hoist cables that pass over a pulley powered by a motor. At the other end of the hoist cables is a counterweight.

see also Elements of architecture pp.454–55 ▶ Details of architecture pp.458–59 ▶

Home technology

Homes are filled with technology, from comparatively simple mechanical systems to complex computers. This includes machines of all types for heating, cooling, cleaning, and managing the home. Many of these devices rely on utilities such as electricity, water, and an Internet connection, with infrastructure in every modern home (such as plumbing and fiber-optic cables) required to support them.

Refrigerators

A refrigerator cools its interior by pumping out energy through the movement of a coolant around a closed system of pipes. The coolant is compressed and expanded, changing between liquid and gas, and drawing out heat from the interior of the fridge in the process.

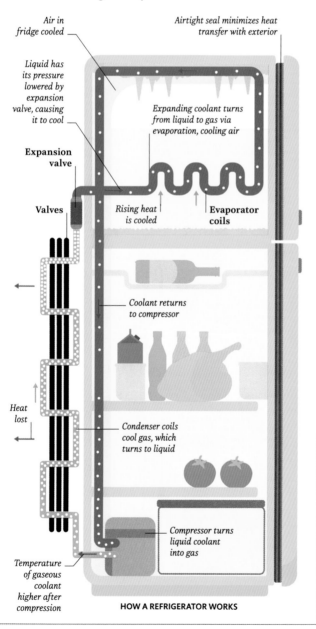

Air in fridge cooled

Airtight seal minimizes heat transfer with exterior

Liquid has its pressure lowered by expansion valve, causing it to cool

Expanding coolant turns from liquid to gas via evaporation, cooling air

Expansion valve

Valves

Rising heat is cooled

Evaporator coils

Coolant returns to compressor

Heat lost

Condenser coils cool gas, which turns to liquid

Compressor turns liquid coolant into gas

Temperature of gaseous coolant higher after compression

HOW A REFRIGERATOR WORKS

Microwave ovens

Microwave ovens use microwaves—a form of electromagnetic wave—to heat food. Microwaves penetrate food, exciting water and fat molecules to emit energy. Food can be cooked much faster than in a conventional oven.

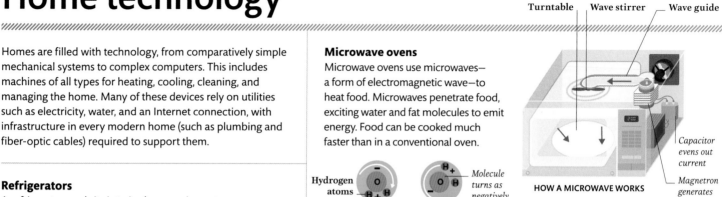

Turntable   Wave stirrer   Wave guide

Capacitor evens out current

Magnetron generates microwaves

HOW A MICROWAVE WORKS

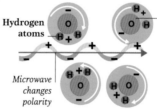

Hydrogen atoms

Molecule turns as negatively charged oxygen attracted to positive charge

Microwave changes polarity

Generating heat
Water molecules align with the electric field of the microwave. The field switches polarity rapidly, causing the molecules to flip and release heat built up by friction.

Kettles

When a kettle is turned on, an electric current runs through the heating element, which heats up and transfers thermal energy to the water. When a thermostat detects that the boiling temperature has been reached, it interrupts the current flow. Bimetallic thermostats use metals that bend when heated; when the desired temperature has been reached, the metals bend away, breaking the electrical circuit.

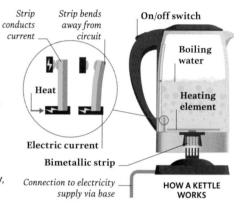

Strip conducts current

Strip bends away from circuit

On/off switch

Boiling water

Heat

Heating element

Electric current

Bimetallic strip

Connection to electricity supply via base

HOW A KETTLE WORKS

Washing machines

A washing machine contains an outer drum, held in place by springs and shock-absorbing dampers, containing an inner drum. The inner drum is spun by an electric motor to turn clothing, water, and detergent.

HOW DETERGENTS WORK
The molecules in laundry detergent are hydrophilic (attracted to water molecules) at one end, and attracted to oil at the other. This allows them to pull oily stains out of fabric, to be rinsed away.

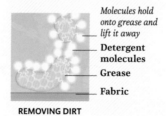

Molecules hold onto grease and lift it away

Detergent molecules

Grease

Fabric

REMOVING DIRT

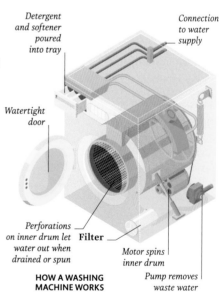

Detergent and softener poured into tray

Connection to water supply

Watertight door

Perforations on inner drum let water out when drained or spun

Filter

Motor spins inner drum

HOW A WASHING MACHINE WORKS

Pump removes waste water

Some **washing machines spin** as fast as **1,800 revolutions** per minute

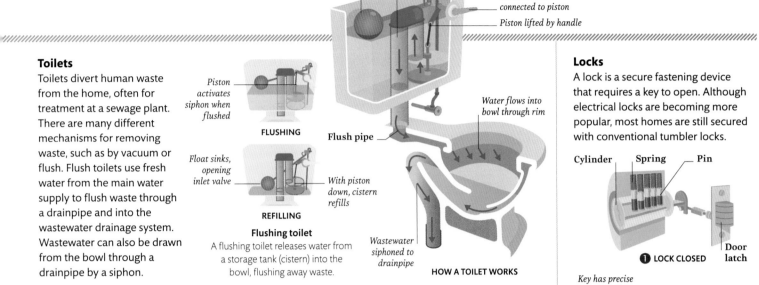

Float rises and falls with water level in cistern

Siphon empties cistern water into bowl

Inlet valve

Flush handle connected to piston

Piston lifted by handle

Water flows into bowl through rim

FLUSHING

Piston activates siphon when flushed

Flush pipe

Float sinks, opening inlet valve

With piston down, cistern refills

REFILLING

Flushing toilet
A flushing toilet releases water from a storage tank (cistern) into the bowl, flushing away waste.

Wastewater siphoned to drainpipe

HOW A TOILET WORKS

Toilets

Toilets divert human waste from the home, often for treatment at a sewage plant. There are many different mechanisms for removing waste, such as by vacuum or flush. Flush toilets use fresh water from the main water supply to flush waste through a drainpipe and into the wastewater drainage system. Wastewater can also be drawn from the bowl through a drainpipe by a siphon.

Locks

A lock is a secure fastening device that requires a key to open. Although electrical locks are becoming more popular, most homes are still secured with conventional tumbler locks.

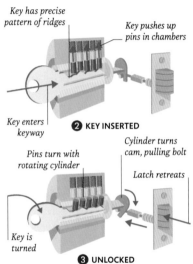

Cylinder   **Spring**   **Pin**

Door latch

❶ LOCK CLOSED

Key has precise pattern of ridges

Key pushes up pins in chambers

Key enters keyway

❷ KEY INSERTED

Cylinder turns cam, pulling bolt

Pins turn with rotating cylinder

Latch retreats

Key is turned

❸ UNLOCKED

Tumbler locks
A tumbler lock unfastens when the cylinder inside rotates. A series of chambers containing pins of various lengths prevents it from turning unless the correct key is inserted.

Thermostat

Thermostats control the temperature in homes or other buildings. When the interior temperature drops below a certain point set by the user, the thermostat completes a circuit, which sends a signal instructing the boiler to fire and generate more heat. Thermostats are also used in air conditioning systems to maintain a room's temperature below a certain point, and in incubators to keep the temperature within a narrow range.

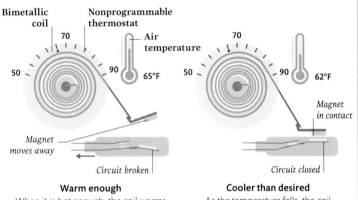

Bimetallic coil   **Nonprogrammable thermostat**

Air temperature

70   50   90   65°F

Magnet moves away

Circuit broken

Warm enough
When it is hot enough, the coil warms and straightens, pulling the magnet away from its contact and breaking the circuit. This stops the boiler.

70   50   90   62°F

Magnet in contact

Circuit closed

Cooler than desired
As the temperature falls, the coil bends and the magnet moves toward the contact. This closes the circuit and signals that the boiler should start.

Underfloor domestic heating was discovered in a Neolithic site in present-day North Korea

Digital assistants

Small, sound-activated computers known as smart speakers use voice recognition to turn spoken commands into instructions. Their functions include simple Internet searches, music playback, and commands for connected "smart" devices around the home, including door entry systems, thermostats, or refrigerators.

How a smart speaker works
Smart speakers capture audio and transfer it to cloud servers via an Internet connection to process and return a response.

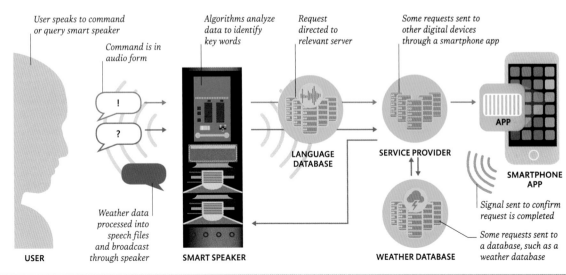

User speaks to command or query smart speaker

Command is in audio form

Algorithms analyze data to identify key words

Request directed to relevant server

Some requests sent to other digital devices through a smartphone app

! ?

USER

Weather data processed into speech files and broadcast through speaker

SMART SPEAKER

LANGUAGE DATABASE

SERVICE PROVIDER

APP

SMARTPHONE APP

Signal sent to confirm request is completed

Some requests sent to a database, such as a weather database

WEATHER DATABASE

see also Computer technology pp.274–75 ▶   Modern globalization and economic growth pp.370–71 ▶   The early 21st century pp.374–75 ▶   **269**

Sound, light, and vision technology

Technological advances made over the centuries—from lenses to computers—allow us to capture, store, manipulate, and produce sound and light for applications ranging from surgery to live entertainment.

Today, anybody with a smartphone can record and replay audio-visual information. It is coded and stored as a sequence of binary digits from which the original sound and images can be reconstructed.

Electric lighting

Fluorescent, incandescent, and LED (light-emitting diode) lighting all use an electric current to emit light. In fluorescent lamps, the inside of the tube is covered in a luminescent substance (phosphors).

Binoculars

Binoculars produce magnified images of faraway objects, making them easier to see. They consist of a pair of frame-mounted telescopes containing prisms that flip the inverted image and bend light back on itself, allowing for a long focal length (see p.493) despite the limited size of binoculars.

The difference in vision between user's eyes is corrected by a rotating focusing ring

Cross section of a binocular

Light entering binoculars passes through a series of lenses and glass prisms that focus, magnify, and flip the image before reaching the eye.

Eye — Bridge

Antireflective coating applied to lenses (and all glass in binoculars)

Image magnified by eyepiece lenses

Prisms flip reflect light internally

Eyepieces and lenses moved in and out by focusing mechanism

Incoming light focused by objective lens

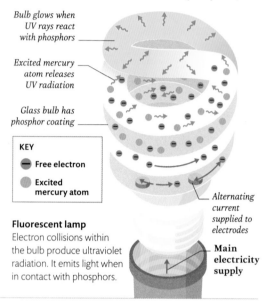

Bulb glows when UV rays react with phosphors

Excited mercury atom releases UV radiation

Glass bulb has phosphor coating

KEY
- − **Free electron**
- **Excited mercury atom**

Fluorescent lamp

Electron collisions within the bulb produce ultraviolet radiation. It emits light when in contact with phosphors.

Alternating current supplied to electrodes

Main electricity supply

Speakers

A speaker is a device that converts an audio signal (an electrical signal representing sound data) to sound. An electric current carrying the signal is applied to a coil of wire on an electromagnet. Electromagnetic induction (see p.191) forces the coil to move, vibrating a diaphragm. This pushes on air in front of the speaker, producing sound waves that match the pattern in the audio signal.

Printers

A printer is a device that allows a document stored on a computer to be represented as a physical object, usually with ink markings on paper. The most common printers are inkjet and laser printers.

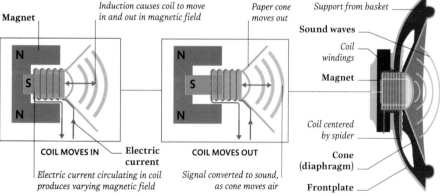

Magnet

Induction causes coil to move in and out in magnetic field

COIL MOVES IN — **Electric current**

Electric current circulating in coil produces varying magnetic field

Paper cone moves out

COIL MOVES OUT

Signal converted to sound, as cone moves air

Support from basket

Sound waves

Coil windings

Magnet

Coil centered by spider

Cone (diaphragm)

Frontplate

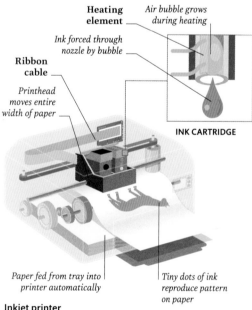

Heating element *Air bubble grows during heating*

Ink forced through nozzle by bubble

Ribbon cable

Printhead moves entire width of paper

INK CARTRIDGE

Paper fed from tray into printer automatically

Tiny dots of ink reproduce pattern on paper

Inkjet printer

Inkjet printers form markings of tiny ink droplets, using computer binary code as a guide. The ink cartridges combine yellow, magenta, cyan, and black pigments, then spray ink on the paper as it moves beneath them.

DIGITAL SOUND

Sound can be stored as a sequence of binary digits. Sound waves are translated by a microphone into electrical signals represented in binary form. These binary digits are then used to reconstruct the original audio signal and play it through a speaker.

Voltage is assigned binary numbers

Hard drive stores digital information

Binary numbers recreate the audio signal

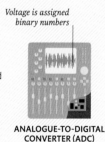

ANALOGUE-TO-DIGITAL CONVERTER (ADC)

STORAGE DEVICE

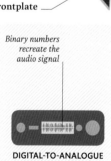

DIGITAL-TO-ANALOGUE CONVERTER (DAC)

Projectors

A projector projects a rapid series of bright images, or frames, onto a surface, The images are either stored digitally or on a physical reel of film.

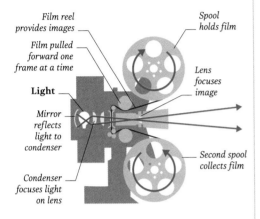

Film reel provides images
Spool holds film
Film pulled forward one frame at a time
Lens focuses image
Light
Mirror reflects light to condenser
Second spool collects film
Condenser focuses light on lens

Film projector

A film projector contains a rotating shutter, which allows light to pass briefly through each still image (frame) of the film reel before moving to the next frame on the film.

Digital cameras

Digital cameras capture and store photographs digitally, rather than on film. Light enters the camera through a lens that focuses an image inside the camera. A sensor measures the color and brightness of every bit of that image and a processor converts those details into a string of binary digits. Digital cameras are often miniaturized and incorporated into other devices, such as smartphones and tablets.

DSLR (digital single-lens reflex) camera

A DSLR camera contains a mirror that directs light from the main lens toward an eyepiece lens. The mirror flips up when the shutter button is released, allowing light to hit the sensor.

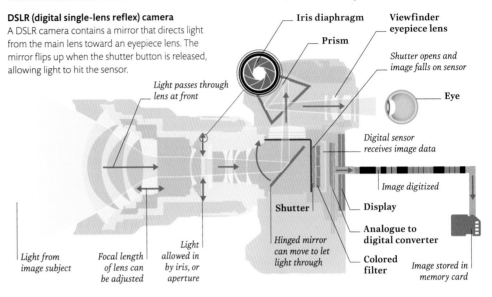

Iris diaphragm
Prism
Viewfinder eyepiece lens
Shutter opens and image falls on sensor
Light passes through lens at front
Eye
Digital sensor receives image data
Image digitized
Light from image subject
Focal length of lens can be adjusted
Light allowed in by iris, or aperture
Shutter
Hinged mirror can move to let light through
Display
Analogue to digital converter
Colored filter
Image stored in memory card

Lasers

A laser ("light amplification by stimulated emission of radiation") produces an intense beam of light. It is different from other light because its beam is collimated (spreads minimally) and coherent (the light waves are all in step and of the same frequency).

LASER PRINTER

A laser passes over a rotating drum, causing some areas to become negatively charged. Positively charged toner clings to the roller in these areas, and is subsequently bonded to the paper.

Laser falls on drum, producing image as negative charge
Mirror reflects laser onto drum
Toner fused to paper with heated rollers
Toner attracted to negative charge
LASER PRINTING

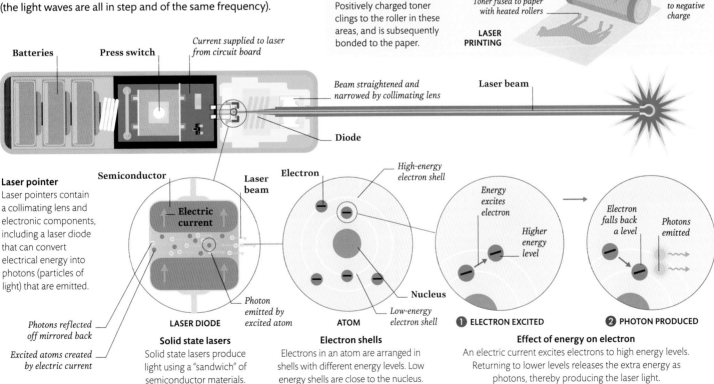

Batteries
Press switch
Current supplied to laser from circuit board
Beam straightened and narrowed by collimating lens
Laser beam
Diode

Laser pointer

Laser pointers contain a collimating lens and electronic components, including a laser diode that can convert electrical energy into photons (particles of light) that are emitted.

Photons reflected off mirrored back
Excited atoms created by electric current

Semiconductor
Electric current
Laser beam
Electron
High-energy electron shell
Energy excites electron
Higher energy level
Electron falls back a level
Photons emitted
Photon emitted by excited atom
Nucleus
Low-energy electron shell
① ELECTRON EXCITED
② PHOTON PRODUCED
LASER DIODE
ATOM

Solid state lasers

Solid state lasers produce light using a "sandwich" of semiconductor materials.

Electron shells

Electrons in an atom are arranged in shells with different energy levels. Low energy shells are close to the nucleus.

Effect of energy on electron

An electric current excites electrons to high energy levels. Returning to lower levels releases the extra energy as photons, thereby producing the laser light.

see also **Communications technology** pp.272–73 ▶   **Computer technology** pp.274–75 ▶   **Photography** pp.492–95 ▶   **271**

Communications technology

Many activities in the modern world, such as phone calls or television broadcasts, depend on being able to send and receive information very quickly. Something as straightforward as sending a text message may use multiple layers of communications infrastructure, such as a mobile messaging applications, fiber-optic cables in which data races as pulses of light, and transmitters and receivers to relay information encoded in radio waves.

Television broadcasting

Television broadcasting allows anybody with a television set to watch video content transmitted by broadcasters. Real-life scenes are captured with video cameras and microphones as electrical signals that are modulated and then transmitted to homes via ground-based antennas, satellites, or cables.

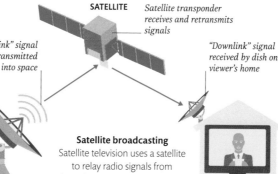

SATELLITE

Satellite transponder receives and retransmits signals

"Uplink" signal transmitted into space

"Downlink" signal received by dish on viewer's home

SATELLITE DISH

Electrical signals sent to satellite dish

Satellite broadcasting
Satellite television uses a satellite to relay radio signals from broadcaster to home. It can be accessed even in remote areas.

SATELLITE TELEVISION

Signals sent to ground-based tower

TELEVISION STATION

TRANSMISSION TOWER

Tower transmits signals in form of radio waves

Antenna on viewer's home receives radio signals

Terrestrial broadcasting
Terrestrial television transmits radio signals from a station to homes. A tower transmits the signals as radio waves.

TERRESTRIAL TELEVISION

Radio signals

Radio waves are used in telecommunications, broadcasting, and navigation to share data without connecting cables. The data is then encoded into radio waves by modifying wave features. The signals are sent and received by antennas, then decoded to extract the data.

❶ Radio broadcast
A presenter in a studio speaks into a microphone, which transforms the sounds of the voice into an electric current.

❷ Studio transmitter link (STL)
An STL receives the audio signal from the studio and relays it to a transmission antenna via microwave links or fiber-optic cables.

❸ Transmission signal
The current in the antenna causes electrons to vibrate, generating varying electric and magnetic fields and radiating electromagnetic waves.

❹ Radio broadcast received
An antenna turns waves back into current, causing a speaker cone to vibrate and emit sound waves, reconstructing the presenter's voice.

The World Wide Web

The World Wide Web is a vast and growing network of information accessed via the Internet. It is made up of billions of interlinked web pages formatted in a common language, hosted on millions of servers, and each identified by a unique address. It is navigated and downloaded through a program called a browser.

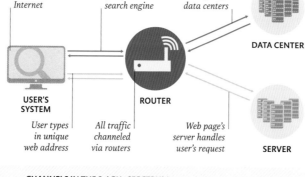

User's computer is part of the Internet

User makes query with search engine

Queries processed by huge data centers

DATA CENTER

USER'S SYSTEM

ROUTER

SERVER

User types in unique web address

All traffic channeled via routers

Web page's server handles user's request

Wi-Fi signals
Wi-Fi utilizes radio waves within set frequency ranges to allow nearby Wi-Fi enabled devices to exchange data wirelessly. Multiple devices share the specific channels the data is transmitted through. Overlapping channels, such as in the 2.4 GHz spectrum, can cause interference. The 5 GHz spectrum has no overlap, making it the most efficient.

CHANNELS IN THE 2.4 GHz SPECTRUM

Lowest frequency in spectrum is 2.412 GHz

Only three of 14 channels do not overlap with others

No overlap on the 11th channel in the spectrum

Overlapping channels cause interference

2.462 GHz

Telecommunications network

Telecommunications networks enable the exchange of information. They are made of connected nodes that direct signals through wires, cables, satellites, and other infrastructure to reach their destination.

Mobile phone communication
Making a mobile phone call begins with the transmission of radio signals from a phone with information about the call destination.

MOBILE PHONE

BASE STATION

Landline communication
Outgoing landline calls transmit electrical signals via handsets that are physically wired to the local telephone exchange with cables.

Call placed on handset wired to overhead cables

Aboveground cables are easier to maintain

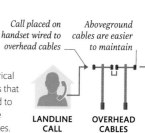

LANDLINE CALL

OVERHEAD CABLES

GPS is just **one** of several **satellite navigation systems**

Satellite navigation

Location information from satellite navigation systems is provided by networks of satellites. A receiver calculates its own position by measuring how long radio signals take to travel from satellites.

Satellites repeatedly transmit radio signals to Earth with precise location and time data

Radio signals travel at the speed of light between satellites and receivers

SATELLITE 3

SATELLITE 2

SATELLITE 1

Command center calculates satellite positions and sends them navigation instructions

SATELLITE 4

Receiver calculates its distance from satellites based on signal travel time, and finds its position via trilateration

Ground stations collect satellite data to relay to command center

KEY
→ Exchange of data   → Time taken

GPS RECEIVER

GROUND STATION   **COMMAND CENTER**   **GROUND STATION**

GPS satellites

Satellite navigation systems use satellites that orbit Earth twice a day. GPS satellites orbit in six planes containing four satellites each, to ensure at least four are detectable anywhere on Earth at all times.

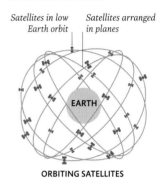

Satellites in low Earth orbit   *Satellites arranged in planes*

EARTH

ORBITING SATELLITES

Trilateration

A receiver finds it own position by calculating the distance to multiple satellites. Results sent from each satellite give a large sphere, but the receiver's position falls within the small intersection of the possible locations and is narrowed down with each additional satellite.

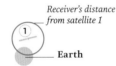

Receiver's distance from satellite 1

— Earth

Satellite 1
Calculating the distance from one satellite places receiver within the area intersected by a massive sphere.

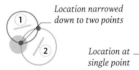

Location narrowed down to two points

Location at single point

Satellite 2
The distance from two satellites restricts the possible position to between one of two points where the spheres intersect.

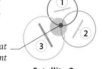

Precise position confirmed

Satellite 3
Finding the distance from a third satellite narrows the receiver's position down to one possible point.

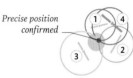

Satellite 4
A fourth satellite corrects inaccuracies caused by the receiver's clock and satellites' clocks not being synchronized.

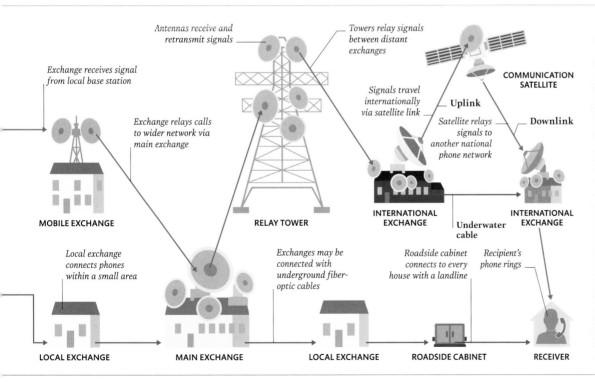

Antennas receive and retransmit signals

Towers relay signals between distant exchanges

Exchange receives signal from local base station

Exchange relays calls to wider network via main exchange

Signals travel internationally via satellite link

COMMUNICATION SATELLITE

— **Uplink**

Satellite relays signals to another national phone network

— **Downlink**

MOBILE EXCHANGE

Local exchange connects phones within a small area

RELAY TOWER

Exchanges may be connected with underground fiber-optic cables

INTERNATIONAL EXCHANGE   **Underwater cable**   **INTERNATIONAL EXCHANGE**

Roadside cabinet connects to every house with a landline

Recipient's phone rings

LOCAL EXCHANGE   **MAIN EXCHANGE**   **LOCAL EXCHANGE**   **ROADSIDE CABINET**   **RECEIVER**

DIAL-UP INTERNET

Millions of people today still use the telephone network to access the Internet. The user's computer sends information down a telephone line to the Internet via their Internet service provider (ISP). This process requires a modem to encode and decode the audio signals that are sent through the telephone line.

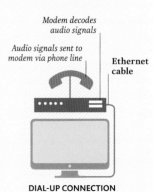

Modem decodes audio signals

Audio signals sent to modem via phone line

Ethernet cable

DIAL-UP CONNECTION

see also Computer technology pp.274–75 ▶   **273**

Computer technology

Computers are machines that execute sequences of commands (programs) automatically. Modern computers, such as laptops and smartphones, can be made to follow countless different programs, allowing them to handle a range of tasks only limited by hardware and computing power. Computers are crucial for running many aspects of the world.

Laptop computers

The brain of a laptop is its central processing unit (CPU), which carries out commands in programs. The rest of its hardware is designed for input, output, and the storage of data.

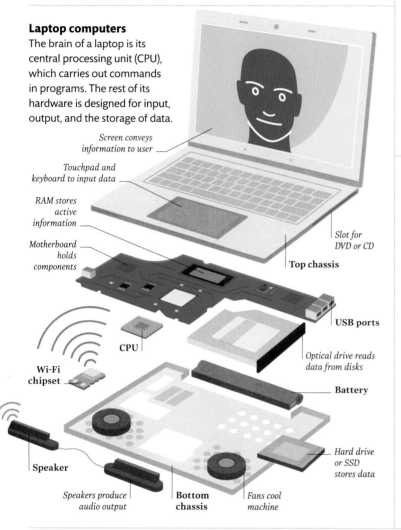

Screen conveys information to user

Touchpad and keyboard to input data

RAM stores active information

Motherboard holds components

CPU

Wi-Fi chipset

Speaker

Speakers produce audio output

Bottom chassis

Fans cool machine

Top chassis

Slot for DVD or CD

USB ports

Optical drive reads data from disks

Battery

Hard drive or SSD stores data

Storage

Computers store and manipulate data. Data required by programs are stored in RAM (random access memory) for instant access, while inactive data (such as documents and photos) are stored on a drive which retains information even when the computer is off.

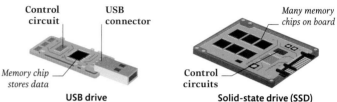

Control circuit **USB connector**

Memory chip stores data

USB drive
A USB drive is an example of removable storage. It allows a limited amount of data to be transferred.

Many memory chips on board

Control circuits

Solid-state drive (SSD)
Data stored on an SSD can be accessed and rewritten much faster compared to a regular hard drive.

Mobile touch technology

Mobile devices are portable computers. Most mobile devices can connect to other devices and the Internet. Some are designed for a narrow range of tasks, such as e-readers, while others, such as smartphones, are much more versatile.

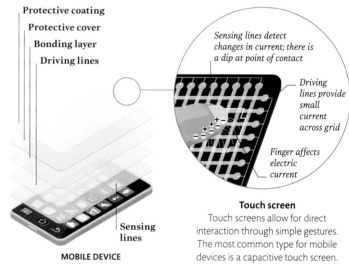

Protective coating
Protective cover
Bonding layer
Driving lines

Sensing lines detect changes in current; there is a dip at point of contact

Driving lines provide small current across grid

Finger affects electric current

Sensing lines

MOBILE DEVICE

Touch screen
Touch screens allow for direct interaction through simple gestures. The most common type for mobile devices is a capacitive touch screen.

How computers work

At the core of a computer is its CPU, which runs programs. It communicates with the rest of the computer, taking inputs (such as from the keyboard and mouse), manipulating memory, and generating outputs (such as via the screen or speakers).

The motherboard
The CPU and other components are arranged on a printed circuit board known as the motherboard.

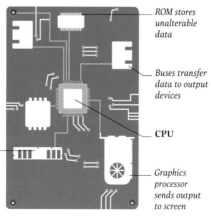

ROM stores unalterable data

Buses transfer data to output devices

CPU

RAM stores active data

Graphics processor sends output to screen

Inside the CPU

A control unit directs the CPU's operations, while an arithmetic logic unit (ALU) performs the operations. The results of the operations are temporarily held in registers.

ALU performs an operation on the data

Control unit reads and directs data to register

| CONTROL UNIT | REGISTER | ALU |

Register stores result of an operation

Data accessed from RAM

RAM

ALU sends results to the register

Result may be sent to RAM

The **World Wide Web** was invented in 1989 for scientists to **share information** with each other

Software

Software is a collection of commands and resources that tell a computer what to do. Unlike hardware they are intangible, existing only as electric signals. Software is written in various machine languages: sequences of binary units (0s and 1s) representing instructions.

Algorithms

An algorithm is a sequence of steps, each one a precise instruction that tells a computer how to perform a specific task. Computer programs are collections of algorithms.

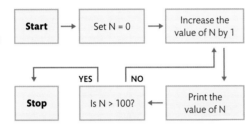

Start → Set N = 0 → Increase the value of N by 1

YES | NO

Stop | Is N > 100? | Print the value of N

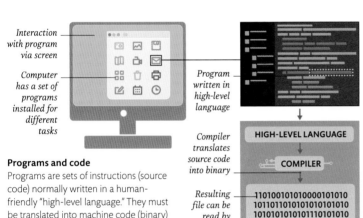

Interaction with program via screen

Computer has a set of programs installed for different tasks

Program written in high-level language

HIGH-LEVEL LANGUAGE

COMPILER

Compiler translates source code into binary

Resulting file can be read by machine

11010010101000010101010
10110111010101010101010
10101010101011101010

Programs and code

Programs are sets of instructions (source code) normally written in a human-friendly "high-level language." They must be translated into machine code (binary) for a computer to execute them.

The Internet

The Internet is the global network of computers that exchange data according to a shared set of rules (the Internet protocol suite). The Internet is at the core of modern communications, supporting applications such as the World Wide Web and email.

Exchanging data

Layers of software arrange for data to be divided into "packets" and sent through the Internet infrastructure to their destination.

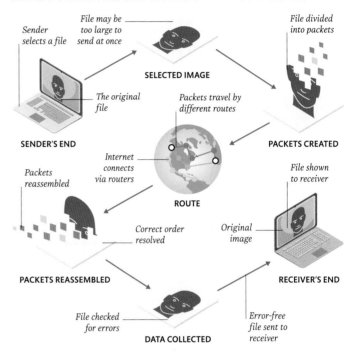

Sender selects a file

File may be too large to send at once

SELECTED IMAGE

File divided into packets

The original file

Packets travel by different routes

SENDER'S END

PACKETS CREATED

Internet connects via routers

File shown to receiver

Packets reassembled

ROUTE

Correct order resolved

Original image

PACKETS REASSEMBLED

RECEIVER'S END

File checked for errors

Error-free file sent to receiver

DATA COLLECTED

Artificial intelligence (AI)

AI is intelligence demonstrated by machines. This can range from the ability to perform limited tasks such as predictive text, to more "general" intelligence such as driving a car. A lot of AI research is focused on machine learning—in which computers learn to perform tasks without being programmed to do so by a human.

Artificial neural networks

Machine learning can be achieved with artificial neural networks. Like biological neurons, artificial neurons produce outputs, based on information received. These are processed through multiple hidden layers of neurons, which "learn" as they process more information.

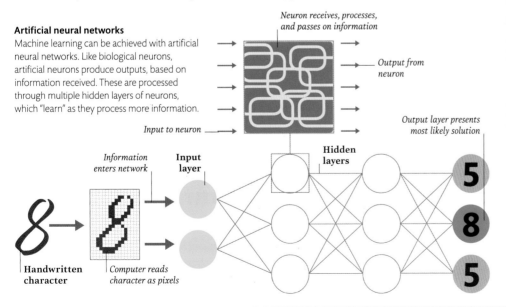

Neuron receives, processes, and passes on information

Output from neuron

Input to neuron

Information enters network

Input layer

Hidden layers

Output layer presents most likely solution

Handwritten character

Computer reads character as pixels

APPLICATIONS OF AI

AI has an extremely wide range of applications, including transportation, medicine, and finance. Although computers cannot rival humans in general intelligence, they can be taught to perform narrow tasks with great speed and precision.

Suggestions for music
AI can be used to identify music preferences, and suggest songs based on these preferences.

Helping doctors diagnose illnesses
An AI tool trained on health records could suggest likely diagnoses based on a patient's symptoms.

Self-driving cars
Autonomous cars use real-time information from a range of sensors to operate safely on roads.

Image recognition
Computers can be taught to recognize objects in digital images, based on patterns of pixels.

see also Transportation in the 21st century pp.290–91 ▶ Modern globalization and economic growth pp.370–71 ▶ The early 21st century pp.374–75 ▶ **275**

3D printing and robotics

New machines are constantly being invented in order to make tasks easier. 3D printers allow almost any shape to be printed from a digital design, rather than created through manufacturing. Robots are machines that perform tasks with minimal human guidance, such as assembling devices in a factory.

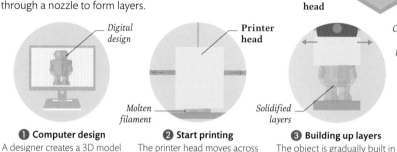
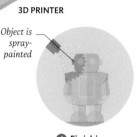

Printer head moves left and right

Solid filament is heated

Molten filament extruded

Data from computer

Vertical head

Spool of filament

Base plate moves back and forth

3D PRINTER

3D printing

While conventional printers create flat images from ink, 3D printers build structures layer by layer, guided by a digital design. This allows for the cheap and efficient production of items of almost any shape imaginable, although creating more detailed objects takes longer.

It is **possible** to 3D print objects from **concrete, chocolate,** and **living cells**

Process of 3D printing

A 3D printer creates structures from a filament (often plastic). This filament is heated and softened, then extruded through a nozzle to form layers.

Digital design

Molten filament

Printer head

Solidified layers

Object is spray-painted

❶ Computer design
A designer creates a 3D model of the desired structure on a computer.

❷ Start printing
The printer head moves across the plate, melting and extruding filament.

❸ Building up layers
The object is gradually built in multiple layers from the bottom up.

❹ Finishing
The grainy, plain 3D-printed objects may be smoothed and painted.

How robots work

A robot is a machine that can execute computer-guided actions. They come in various different shapes and sizes and are used in healthcare, manufacturing, and many other industries. Most robots are capable of movement in and around their surroundings, moving their parts with actuators.

END EFFECTORS

The "hand" of a robotic arm is known as the end effector. Various tools can be attached, allowing the robot to carry out different tasks, such as drilling, gripping, welding, or manipulating objects.

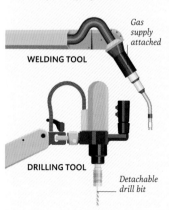

Gas supply attached

WELDING TOOL

DRILLING TOOL

Detachable drill bit

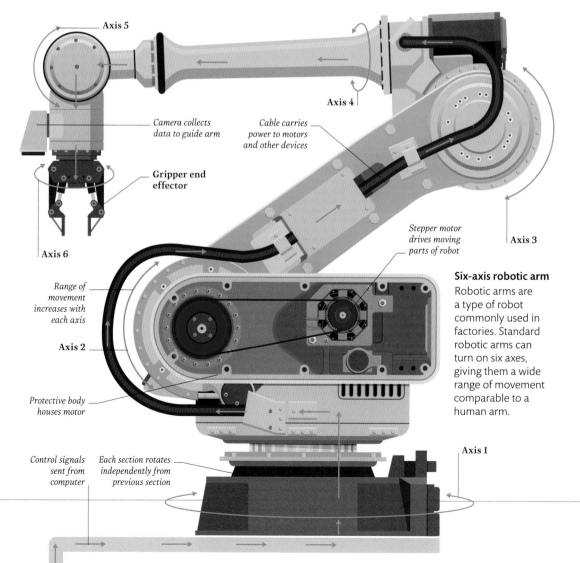

Axis 5

Camera collects data to guide arm

Cable carries power to motors and other devices

Axis 4

Gripper end effector

Axis 6

Range of movement increases with each axis

Stepper motor drives moving parts of robot

Axis 3

Axis 2

Protective body houses motor

Control signals sent from computer

Each section rotates independently from previous section

Axis 1

Six-axis robotic arm

Robotic arms are a type of robot commonly used in factories. Standard robotic arms can turn on six axes, giving them a wide range of movement comparable to a human arm.

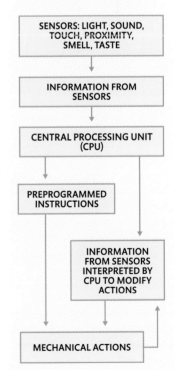
The word **"robot"** was **introduced** in the **1920** Czech play *R.U.R*, referring to **forced labor**

Uses of 3D printers

Although 3D printing is not widely used for mass manufacturing, it is used to produce custom-made items for industries such as healthcare, catering, and sports.

Pills
3D printing can be used to create pills that contain a precise combination of substances, and dissolve very quickly.

Sports shoes
Some athletes wear custom 3D-printed shoes. These allow for a perfect fit, and are designed to be lightweight.

Prosthetics
Missing bone can be replaced with synthetic prostheses or 3D-printed titanium to replicate the original shape.

Musical instruments
Musical instruments such as guitars and flutes can be fully or partially 3D printed. They sound slightly different.

Stepper motors

Stepper motors are composed of a rotor, which is a magnet, surrounded by a ring of electromagnets (stator). Activating different sets of electromagnets brings the poles in and out of alignment, turning the rotor step by step.

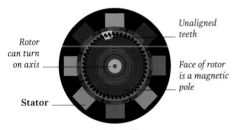

Rotor can turn on axis

Unaligned teeth

Face of rotor is a magnetic pole

Stator

Motor off
A magnetic rotor sits inside the stator, which is made of a ring of paired, static electromagnets. There are teeth on both the rotor and stator.

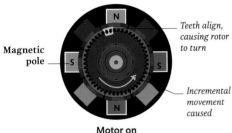

Magnetic pole

Teeth align, causing rotor to turn

Incremental movement caused

Motor on
Activating the electromagnet pairs in turn sets the teeth with opposing poles into alignment, while matching poles are pushed out of alignment, forcing the rotor to turn.

Autonomy and AI

Some robots carry out decisions and actions autonomously, based on the data they collect from their sensors. Both autonomous and semiautonomous robots use AI, learning to perform tasks without being explicitly programmed to do so.

Semiautonomous robot
Semiautonomous robots follow commands from a remote operator, and they have an internal computer to help them execute tasks.

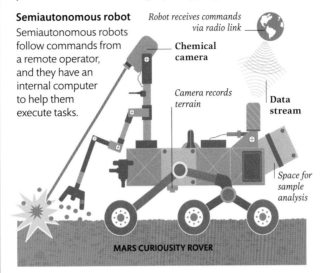

Robot receives commands via radio link

Chemical camera

Camera records terrain

Data stream

Space for sample analysis

MARS CURIOUSITY ROVER

Autonomous robot
Robots perform well in controlled settings like factories, but struggle with the complexity of the real world. Fully autonomous robots require powerful computers, well-trained AI, and sophisticated sensors to make decisions.

Sensors analyze environment

Hydraulic limbs

Robot can use tools and manipulate objects of various size

Strain on joints measured by force-torque sensors

Lower limbs gather data about the terrain

HUMANOID ROBOT

Sensory data
Autonomous robots collect data about their environment with cameras, radar, and other sensors. They make decisions based on this data; for instance, autonomous cars are trained to stop when they detect a pedestrian.

Gyroscope helps robot balance

Infrared sensors detect objects

Optical camera "eyes"

DATA INPUT

TYPES OF ROBOTS

Robots are designed for all sorts of tasks, from assembling cars to assisting in surgery. However, each robot can only perform a limited number of tasks, based on its design and programming.

AUTONOMOUS	SEMI-AUTONOMOUS
SELF-DRIVING CAR	RESCUE ROBOT
VACUUM CLEANER	MISSILE
FACTORY ROBOT	SURGICAL ROBOT

ELEMENTS OF ROBOT ACTION

A robot's CPU (the "brain") chooses actions guided by the sensory data it collects, and executes the actions with preprogrammed instructions. As they carry out actions, they collect more informative data.

> **SENSORS: LIGHT, SOUND, TOUCH, PROXIMITY, SMELL, TASTE**
>
> ↓
>
> **INFORMATION FROM SENSORS**
>
> ↓
>
> **CENTRAL PROCESSING UNIT (CPU)**
>
> ↓
>
> **PREPROGRAMMED INSTRUCTIONS**
>
> ↓
>
> **INFORMATION FROM SENSORS INTERPRETED BY CPU TO MODIFY ACTIONS**
>
> ↓
>
> **MECHANICAL ACTIONS**

The origins of modern transportation

Walking, riding horses and other animals, and paddling simple boats were the only transportation options available to prehistoric peoples. As a result, they traveled rarely and mostly over short distances. As transportation developed on land, sea, and air, so people, goods, and raw materials were able to travel faster and farther. Innovations in transportation technology have sparked mass migrations of people and global trade, as well as enabling the exploration of Earth and space.

From trails to roads

Pounded earth, logs, and stone were all used to reinforce well-worn trails, turning them into robust roads. The ancient Romans advanced road construction using concrete, multiple layers of materials, and a curved camber to drain away rainwater. About 250,000 miles (400,000 km) of Roman roads were built, some of which still remain. Asphalt, first used to surface streets by the Babylonians around 625 BCE, was reintroduced in the 1820s and now covers most highways.

Exploring the seas

The first voyagers took to water using simple rafts and dug-out canoes fashioned from tree trunks, and sails harnessing the power of the wind were first deployed more than 5,000 years ago. From the 15th century onward, a golden age of exploration saw European sailing ships discovering lands and establishing trade routes with Africa, Asia, and the Americas. In the 19th century, steam and diesel engines enabled more reliable long-distance shipping.

Wooden wheel fitted with iron rim

1869 MICHAUX VELOCIPEDE FROM FRANCE

The invention of the bicycle

In 1817, German civil servant Karl von Drais mounted two wooden wheels on a frame with handlebars and a saddle. His *Laufmaschine* (running machine) lacked pedals; the rider paddled their feet on the ground to gain speed instead. Pedals were later fitted directly to the front wheel of velocipedes in the 1860s. In Britain in 1885, John Kemp Starley invented the forerunner of the modern bicycle, the safety bicycle, with pedals driving a chain that turned the rear wheel.

HENRY FORD AND THE MODEL T

US automotive pioneer Henry Ford popularized the moving assembly line where car bodies were carried along conveyor belts and their parts fitted. This sped up production, lowering costs and making Ford's Model T far more affordable. Over 15 million Model T cars were produced between 1908 and 1927.

MODEL T FORDS AT FORD'S MICHIGAN FACTORY

Trains and railroads

Steam engines, first used to pump water out of mines, were adapted to power wheeled locomotives that ran along iron rails in the early 19th century. Steam locomotives hauled passengers and freight for the first time in the 1820s and 1830s, reducing journey times. Tens of thousands of miles of railroad networks sprang up all around the world and the first underground city railroad opened in London in 1863. Called the Metropolitan Railway, it consisted of wooden, gas-lit carriages pulled by steam locomotives. Six years later the first Transcontinental Railroad crossing the entire US was completed. Diesel and electric-powered locomotives superseded steam in the 20th century with high-speed electric trains, running at more than 168 mph (270 km/h), creating rapid links between major cities.

Motor vehicles arrive

Steam-powered carriages were the first motorized vehicles on roads, but proved slow, heavy, and unreliable. In 1876,

19,000 built. Iconic, affordable cars such as the Model T Ford (1908), the Volkswagen Beetle (1938), and the BMC Mini (1959) were produced in the millions. Safety innovations followed, including the triple point seat belt (1959), airbags (1970s), and crumple zones (1950s) which channel crash forces safely away from the driver and passengers. In the early 21st century, growing environmental concerns about the use of fossil fuels led to increasing numbers of electric vehicles.

Taking to the skies

People had long dreamed of flight before the French Montgolfier brothers built and flew the first manned and untethered hot air balloon in 1783. Gliding experiments by pioneers including German aviator Otto Lilienthal were seized upon by two American brothers, Orville and Wilbur Wright. After years of experimentation, they flew the first heavier-than-air powered aircraft in 1903.

The Wright brothers sparked an aviation boom which led to the arrival of passenger, airmail, and cargo planes

The **longest flight** on the Wright Flyer's **launch** day was **59 seconds** long

German engineer Nikolaus Otto perfected a type of engine suitable for propelling wheeled vehicles on land. In his four stroke internal combustion engine, gasoline and air were mixed, compressed, and burned inside a cylinder to produce expanding gases that drove a piston (see p.286). In 1885 a similar engine was used by Karl Benz to produce the first motorcar, the Benz Patent Motorwagen, a three-wheeler with a top speed of up to 10 mph (16 km/h).

Car manufacture quickly advanced in Europe and the US, where Ransom Olds' Oldsmobile Curved Dash became the first mass-produced car in 1901 with

in the three decades that followed. All were flown using propellers driven by internal combustion engines until the development of faster, more powerful, jet engines in the 1930s by Frank Whittle in the UK and Hans von Ohain in Germany. Jet-engined airliners enabled inexpensive, rapid travel between continents within hours, where journeys had previously taken days or weeks by ship or propeller aircraft making multiple stops. The world's largest airliner, the Airbus A380, entered service in 2007. Boasting a maximum capacity of 853 passengers, more than 190 million people had flown on A380s by 2019.

Timeline

Transportation relied on human, animal, or natural power such as wind for thousands of years. From the 18th century onward, development of engines using wood, coal, or oil-products as fuel provided the power to propel vehicles faster and farther than ever before.

4000 BCE

*c.***3500 BCE** *The wheel is invented in the Tigris-Euphrates valley, western Asia*

3000–1500 BCE *Using early catamaran ships, Austronesian settlers colonize the Indo-Pacific region*

1492 *Italian explorer Christopher Columbus reaches the Americas by sea*

*c.***300 BCE** *The first Roman roads are built, connecting towns and military bases*

*c.***800 CE** *The Vikings begin using clinker-built longships for exploration and raiding*

*c.***1500s** *The oldest known inclined elevator railway operates in Austria*

L'ARMENIE SOVIETIQUE

◀ A new era of mobility
A stylized 1930s poster from the Soviet Union depicts the freedom that traveling on a fast steam train or car could provide.

Into space
Escaping Earth's gravity to travel into space requires huge power. Rocket engines mix and burn fuel and their own supply of oxygen or oxidizer (an oxygen-creating substance) so they can function outside Earth's oxygen-rich lower atmosphere. In the 1950s, rocket-powered long-range missiles were converted into the first launch vehicles, carrying artificial satellites and other machines into space, beginning with the Soviet Union's Sputnik satellite in 1957. Twelve years later, the largest and most powerful launch vehicle ever built, the 363 ft (110.6 m) tall Saturn V, carried the Apollo 11 mission to land humans on the moon for the first time.

Eagle represents code name of Apollo 11 lunar module

REPLICA APOLLO 11 MISSION PATCH

At liftoff, the **Saturn V** consumed over **14 tons** (13 tonnes) of **fuel and oxygen** per second

1804 *British inventor Richard Trevithick builds the first full-scale steam locomotive*

1886 *German engineer Karl Benz builds the first production motor-car, the Benz Patent-Motorwagen*

1905 *US inventors, the Wright brothers, build the Wright Flyer III, the first heavier-than-air aircraft that can maneuver on three axes*

1997 *Japanese carmaker Toyota introduces the Prius—the first mass-produced hybrid electric car*

2000

1816 *Scottish engineer John Loudon McAdam designs the first modern roads*

1817 *German inventor Karl Drais builds the "running machine," an early form of the bicycle*

1903 *The first Tour de France cycle race takes place*

1952 *The de Havilland Comet becomes the first jet airliner to enter service*

1961 *Soviet cosmonaut Yuri Gagarin becomes the first person to travel in space*

see also The car pp.286–87 ▶ Aviation through history pp.288–89 ▶ Transportation in the 21st century pp.290–91 ▶ **279**

Seafaring through history

Seafaring has come a long way since the dugout canoes of ancient times, and has enabled trade, exploration, and even the building of empires. With the advent of sails more than 5,000 years ago, people began harnessing wind energy to power their seagoing craft over longer distances. Sails dominated seafaring for millennia until the arrival of steam power in the 18th and 19th centuries. Steam was, in turn, superseded by diesel engine-powered sea travel.

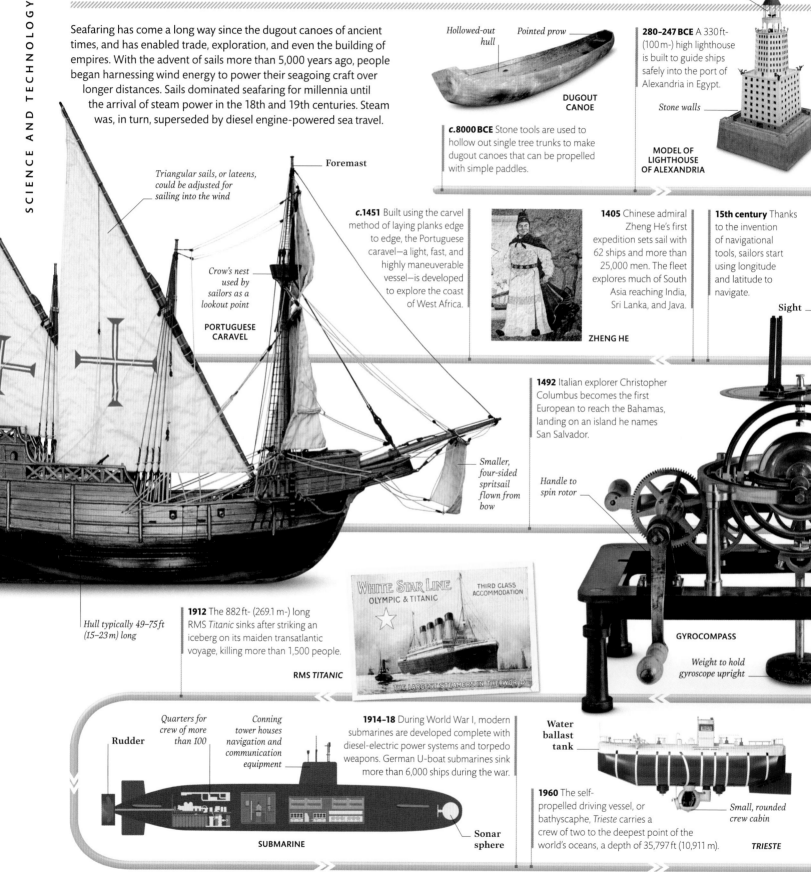

Hollowed-out hull

Pointed prow

DUGOUT CANOE

c.8000 BCE Stone tools are used to hollow out single tree trunks to make dugout canoes that can be propelled with simple paddles.

Ships guided by furnace-lit fire at night and sun-reflecting mirror during day

280–247 BCE A 330 ft- (100 m-) high lighthouse is built to guide ships safely into the port of Alexandria in Egypt.

Stone walls

MODEL OF LIGHTHOUSE OF ALEXANDRIA

Triangular sails, or lateens, could be adjusted for sailing into the wind

Foremast

c.1451 Built using the carvel method of laying planks edge to edge, the Portuguese caravel—a light, fast, and highly maneuverable vessel—is developed to explore the coast of West Africa.

1405 Chinese admiral Zheng He's first expedition sets sail with 62 ships and more than 25,000 men. The fleet explores much of South Asia reaching India, Sri Lanka, and Java.

15th century Thanks to the invention of navigational tools, sailors start using longitude and latitude to navigate.

Sight

Crow's nest used by sailors as a lookout point

PORTUGUESE CARAVEL

ZHENG HE

1492 Italian explorer Christopher Columbus becomes the first European to reach the Bahamas, landing on an island he names San Salvador.

Handle to spin rotor

Smaller, four-sided spritsail flown from bow

Hull typically 49–75 ft (15–23 m) long

1912 The 882 ft- (269.1 m-) long RMS *Titanic* sinks after striking an iceberg on its maiden transatlantic voyage, killing more than 1,500 people.

RMS *TITANIC*

WHITE STAR LINE OLYMPIC & TITANIC

THIRD CLASS ACCOMMODATION

THE LARGEST STEAMERS IN THE WORLD

GYROCOMPASS

Weight to hold gyroscope upright

Quarters for crew of more than 100

Conning tower houses navigation and communication equipment

Rudder

1914–18 During World War I, modern submarines are developed complete with diesel-electric power systems and torpedo weapons. German U-boat submarines sink more than 6,000 ships during the war.

Water ballast tank

1960 The self-propelled driving vessel, or bathyscaphe, *Trieste* carries a crew of two to the deepest point of the world's oceans, a depth of 35,797 ft (10,911 m).

Small, rounded crew cabin

SUBMARINE

Sonar sphere

TRIESTE

Fixed outer disk, or
mater, with degree and
hour scale marked

Brass plate depicts
celestial sphere
with star positions

Shorter third, or mizzen,
sail at stern for stability
rather than propulsion

**Main
sail**

Foresail

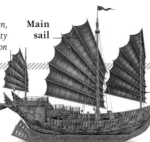

CHINESE JUNK

220–150 BCE Greek
mathematician Apollonius
of Perga develops the
astrolabe, which enables
sailors to navigate by
determining their ship's
latitude—how far north or
south of the equator they
are—based on the positions
of the sun and stars in the sky.

Star pointer

ASTROLABE

***c.*87 BCE** The ancient
Greek Antikythera
mechanism—an early
mechanical computer—
may have been used to
predict the position of
the stars in the sky as
a navigational aid.

***c.*220 CE** Foreign ships reaching China
inspire the development of the junk. With
hulls of softwood, these vessels have
multiple, fan-shaped sails stiffened by
battens—strips of bamboo or wood.

***c.*1280** Sailing in
large canoes across
stretches of the
southern Pacific,
eastern Polynesian
people reach
and settle in
New Zealand.

**Double hull
for stability**

POLYNESIAN CANOE

11th century In China,
the compass pointing to
magnetic north is first
used for navigation. It
reduces explorers'
dependence on
celestial navigation.
They appear in Europe
in the 12th century.

**Degree
scale**

**North
marker**

EARLY MARINERS' COMPASS

***c.*1000** Icelandic
explorer Leif Erikson
becomes the first
European to reach
North America when
he sails to Vinland,
believed to be the
coast of Newfoundland,
Canada.

9th century Vikings cross the
Atlantic ocean on longships—long,
narrow, and shallow
vessels with square sails—
raiding and colonizing
faraway lands.

*Hull built using
clinker method of
overlapping planks*

VIKING LONGSHIP

*Plate mounted on
gyroscope frame*

*Gyroscope
rotor*

***c.*1514** The cross-staff, developed
centuries earlier, is improved
for use in navigation at sea. It
measures the angle between
the horizon and the sun or a
star to determine latitude.

*Sliding crosspiece to
line up with horizon
at one end and star
on the other*

Star

Scale

**Sea's
surface**

Navigator

Horizon

CROSS-STAFF FOR MARITIME NAVIGATION

1519–22 Portuguese
explorer Ferdinand
Magellan embarks
westward from Spain
on an around-the-
world voyage. Only 18
of the more than 260
crew survive this trip.

**FERDINAND
MAGELLAN**

1729 English
physician and
inventor John Allen
receives the first
patent for a boat
powered by a
steam engine.

***c.*1908** The
gyrocompass uses a
fast-spinning disk
instead of
magnetized needles
to find true north,
unaffected by iron
and steel, to enable
more accurate
navigation.

1906 Norwegian
explorer Roald
Amundsen makes
the first successful
navigation of
the Northwest
Passage—a route
through the Arctic
to the Pacific.

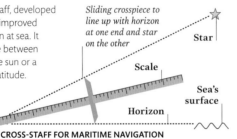

**FRANKLIN
EXPEDITION**

1848 All hands lost on English naval officer
John Franklin's expedition to find a route
through Arctic waters to the Pacific Ocean.

18th century Using
sextants as a
navigational tool
becomes popular. The
device uses mirrors to
enable the precise
calculation of angles
to find a ship's latitude
with greater accuracy.

*Mirror
reflects light
from star
or sun*

Eyepiece

*Scale
depicts
angle*

Movable arm

SEXTANT

***c.*1980s** The first mega-cruise ships
are launched. At 1,184 ft (361 m)
long and with a capacity of
6,680 passengers, *Symphony
of the Seas* is the world's
largest cruise ship.

*Passenger
cabin
balconies*

Lifeboats

**Crew
quarters**

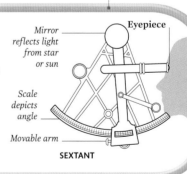

Bow

**A CRUISE
SHIP**

1994 Global Positioning System
(GPS) becomes fully operational.
Signals sent to and from a
network of 27 satellites provides
pinpoint accuracy of navigation
at sea and on land.

*Satellite orbits at altitude
of 12,427 miles (20,000 km)*

Earth

GPS SATELLITE CONSTELLATION

see also The ship pp.282–83 ▶   **Trade and exploration** pp.340–41 ▶

Sailing ships

Exploration and trade

Boats with sails traveled on rivers and close to coasts for thousands of years, but from the 14th century onward, large wooden ships could be made stable enough and fitted with deep holds, and multiple masts and sails, to begin voyaging farther from shore. Sailing from China, admiral and diplomat Zheng He explored Asia and Africa, while a number of ships from Portugal, Italy, and Spain voyaged to islands and continents never before seen by Europeans in an era of widespread exploration.

Crossing the ocean
In 1492, the Italian explorer Christopher Columbus sailed the *Santa Maria*—a nao, or carrack ship—from Spain across the Atlantic Ocean to islands in the Caribbean. The ship ran aground in December 1492.

Types of sails

Sails were once made from beaten, flattened plant fibers before robust fabric such as cotton canvas was used. Over the centuries, varying shapes and designs were developed, each with different attributes, which allowed ships to explore and navigate the world.

Square sail

The earliest sails were rectangular or square, and were suspended from a horizontal yard. They were efficient at sailing downwind at speed.

Yard is square to the mast

Spritsail

Hoisted below a bowsprit—the long spar that extends in front of the ship's bow—spritsails were employed on most carracks.

Spritsail yard arm at an angle to bowsprit

Lateen sail

These irregular sails, developed during the Roman era, gave ships the ability to tack into the wind in a zig-zagging pattern.

Rear edge is called a leach

Angled yard supports top of sail

Bermuda sail

A triangular sail with only its luff or front edge attached to the mast; it is still used as the mainsail on some yachts.

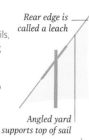

Bottom edge of sail called a foot

Mizzen yard

Ship's pennant

Flag of the expedition's Spanish sponsors

Mizzen backstay

Ropes, called stays, help to stabilize masts

Main topsail yard from where topsail is flown

Line called a topsail topping lift

Main topmast stay

Observation point known as the crow's nest

Main yard, where mainsail is tied up

Main stay

Mizzenmast

Mainsail is largest sail hoisted by the ship

Falconet swiveling gun

Main mast

Ratlines acted as rope ladders to reach the mast top

Aftcastle deck above captain's cabin gave views over the ship

Long boat for rowing ashore

Captain's cabin

Quarterdeck contained tiller and navigation instruments

Quarterdeck

Rudder connected to tiller deflects water flow to steer the ship

Hold stored spare sails, rigging, and supplies, and stone ballast to keep ship stable

Chinese explorer Zheng He is estimated to have sailed
124,240 miles (200,000 km) on his seven voyages of discovery

Modern sails

Modern sails are mostly made from strong, flexible artificial materials including nylon, Dacron, and Kevlar. Large sails are often constructed out of panels, stitched or glued together, and sometimes stiffened and supported by horizontal spars called battens. When flown, sails form an airfoil and act in a similar way to an aircraft's wings, generating lift through changes in air pressure as the air flows over both sides of the sail. Sailors can adjust their sail type and position to maximize the amount of lift produced. By doing this, a sailboat can tack (moving forward in a zig-zag pattern) into an oncoming wind.

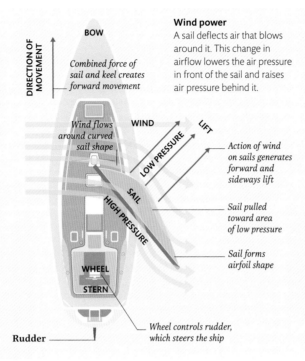

DIRECTION OF MOVEMENT

BOW

Combined force of sail and keel creates forward movement

Wind flows around curved sail shape

WIND

LIFT

LOW PRESSURE

SAIL

HIGH PRESSURE

WHEEL

STERN

Rudder

Wheel controls rudder, which steers the ship

Wind power

A sail deflects air that blows around it. This change in airflow lowers the air pressure in front of the sail and raises air pressure behind it.

Action of wind on sails generates forward and sideways lift

Sail pulled toward area of low pressure

Sail forms airfoil shape

Hydrodynamic keels

The development of the keel, a large flat blade or panel attached to the bottom of a vessel's hull, transformed sailing. The keel generates its own lift as it travels through water. It enabled vessels to not just sail mostly downwind but to still move forward when encountering wind from the front and side which produces a strong sideways force known as heeling.

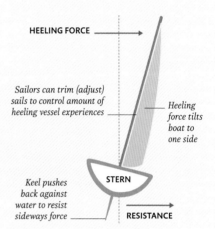

HEELING FORCE

Sailors can trim (adjust) sails to control amount of heeling vessel experiences

Heeling force tilts boat to one side

STERN

Keel pushes back against water to resist sideways force

RESISTANCE

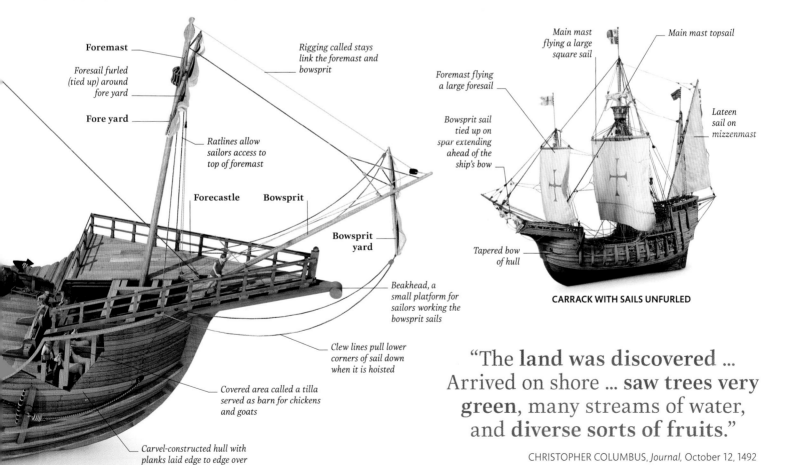

Foremast

Foresail furled (tied up) around fore yard

Fore yard

Rigging called stays link the foremast and bowsprit

Ratlines allow sailors access to top of foremast

Forecastle   Bowsprit

Bowsprit yard

Beakhead, a small platform for sailors working the bowsprit sails

Clew lines pull lower corners of sail down when it is hoisted

Covered area called a tilla served as barn for chickens and goats

Carvel-constructed hull with planks laid edge to edge over a strong frame of wooden ribs

Main mast flying a large square sail

Main mast topsail

Foremast flying a large foresail

Lateen sail on mizzenmast

Bowsprit sail tied up on spar extending ahead of the ship's bow

Tapered bow of hull

CARRACK WITH SAILS UNFURLED

"The land was discovered ... Arrived on shore ... saw trees very green, many streams of water, and diverse sorts of fruits."

CHRISTOPHER COLUMBUS, *Journal*, October 12, 1492

see also Ancient China pp.308–309 ▶   Trade and exploration pp.340–41 ▶   The Middle Ages in the Americas pp.342–43 ▶

Trains and railroads

Trains and railroads developed from steam-powered haulage locomotives used at mines and metal foundries. From the 1820s, railroads sprang up first in Britain, and then Europe and elsewhere. In the US, railroad networks underwent phenomenal expansion in the 19th century—from 2,800 miles (4,506 km) of lines in 1840 to 163,500 miles (263,000 km) 50 years later.

Steam locomotives, pulling multiple passenger carriages or freight cars, slashed travel times between cities and countries all over the world. In the 20th century, diesel- and electric-powered locomotives, neither of which had to stop for coal and water supplies, gained popularity. Today, high-speed electric trains can travel at speeds much greater than those achieved previously.

Waste gases exit locomotive through tall smokestack chimney

STEPHENSON'S ROCKET

1830 The *Stephenson's Rocket* locomotive runs on the world's first intercity railroad line, between Liverpool and Manchester, UK.

Trains are used to carry around **40 percent** of the **world's freight cargo**

1896 Snowdon Mountain Railroad trains are fitted with cogs that move along toothed rails to travel up a steep gradient in Wales, UK.

SNOWDON RAILROAD

1879 The first electric locomotive, invented by German engineer Werner von Siemens, is demonstrated on a 984 ft- (300 m-) long circular track at the Berlin Industrial Exposition.

WERNER VON SIEMENS

1900s Color-coded electric lights are added to railroad semaphore signals, which use raised and lowered arms to instruct train drivers to stop or proceed.

Both arms in horizontal position indicates "danger: stop"

SEMAPHORE SIGNAL

Veranda at rear of train allows crew access to roof

1913 As rail networks boom across North America, short rail cars called cabooses hitched to a train's rear are widely used as an office and quarters for the train's crew.

H&B.T. 16

CABOOSE NO. 16

1961 Built to test high-speed coaches, Germany's No. 18.201 has a top speed of $113\frac{1}{3}$ mph (182.4 km/h). Still maintained and operational, the locomotive last ran in 2005.

Smokebox door features distinctive conical shape

18 201

NO. 18.201

1955 The half pantograph is invented, enabling high-speed trains to receive electricity from an overhead line.

Contact wire of power line

Pantograph collects power from cable

Roof of railroad car

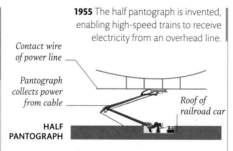

HALF PANTOGRAPH

1964 The world's first high-speed electric rail service, the Shinkansen or bullet train, reduces journey times between the Japanese cities of Tokyo and Osaka by more than half.

SHINKANSEN

ELECTRIC LOCOMOTIVE

Transformer reduces voltage

1960s Thousands of miles of railroad lines are electrified. Electric locomotives are quieter and less polluting than steam and diesel.

Electric motor turns wheel

Japan's **L0 maglev** is the world's **fastest train,** reaching up to **375 mph** (603 km/h)

1860s American industrialist Cornelius Vanderbilt builds a number of new railroads, including the Hudson River and New York Central Railroads.

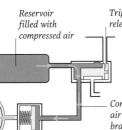

CORNELIUS VANDERBILT

1863 The Class B No. 147, or *Thatcher Perkins*, operates on the Baltimore and Ohio (B&O) railroad's steepest gradient lines. This wood-burning engine is used to move Union troops during the Civil War and stays in service for 29 years.

Chimney fitted with spark arrester

Warning bell operated from driver's cab

Headlight illuminated tracks ahead

1869 American engineer George Westinghouse invents the triple-valve air brake to provide powerful and effective braking.

Reservoir filled with compressed air

Triple slide valve releases air

"Cowcatcher" pushes aside stray animals

Brake stops wheel

Compressed air flows to brake cylinder

AIR BRAKE APPLICATION

B&O CLASS B NO. 147 THATCHER PERKINS

1920s As train travel for leisure and vacations increases in popularity across the US, Europe, and the UK, train companies create colorful advertising posters to encourage passengers.

TRAIN ADVERTISEMENT

Copper-topped chimney releases gases from coal-burning furnace

1930 Named after British kings, the powerful King Class locomotives haul heavy express trains, mostly on lines between London and the west of England.

KING EDWARD II

1931 The Reading Multiple Unit (MU) electric railroad cars begin service in Philadelphia. Each car is 72 ft 11½ in (22.2 m) long, and has a capacity of 86 passengers.

READING MU NO. 800

1938 The A4 *Mallard* reaches a speed of 126 mph (203 km/h), a world record for a steam train. It remained in service in the UK until 1963, clocking a total of 1.5 million miles (2.4 million km).

Body houses 18 ft- (5.5 m-) long, high-pressure boiler

Streamlined wedge shape reduces air resistance

MALLARD

1933 The Class SVT 877, or *Fliegender Hamburger*, enters service. Germany's first fast diesel train, its top speed of 99 mph (160 km/h) remained unmatched on the Hamburg–Berlin line until 1997.

FLIEGENDER HAMBURGER

1982 The luxurious *Palace on Wheels* begins operating in India. Carrying a maximum of 104 passengers in its 23 cars, the train features two dining cars, a spa, and a lounge.

PALACE ON WHEELS' DINING CAR

Floor of maglev train

Guide magnets on train maintain gap

Guideway's electromagnetic coils and train's support magnets repulse, levitating the train

2004 China's Shanghai Maglev (magnetic levitation) train, using magnets to suspend itself above its track, enters service with a record top speed of 268 mph (431 km/h).

MAGLEV TRAIN

see also Transportation in the 21st century pp.290–91 ▶

The car

The development of the gas-powered internal combustion engine was a breakthough in personal transportation. At first, cars were the unreliable playthings of the rich. Soon, mass production dramatically lowered prices, and this, alongside improvements in roads and infrastructure, meant that cars dominated transportation throughout the 20th century. Racing and sports car development led to innovations such as better braking and safer tires, as well as ever-higher top speeds. Safety improvements and the effects of fossil fuels such as gas and diesel became key issues by the 1970s. In the 21st century, scientists turned to alternative fuels, while artificial intelligence (AI) is automating the driving process itself.

SAFETY

Laminated glass—the first safety-orientated innovation—was introduced in the 1920s. Deformable crumple zones were developed in the 1950s, but it is features such as seatbelts, antilock brakes, and airbags that have made the greatest contributions to occupant safety.

AIRBAG DEPLOYED IN A CRASH TEST

Inside the car

The primary role of every car is to carry seated passengers. It needs a power unit to create propulsion, a braking system for stopping, a gearing mechanism to cope with different gradients, a suspension system to cushion the impact of road surfaces, and steering so the driver can change direction accurately. Together these elements are known as the drivetrain.

Considerable engineering expertise is used to combine these facets and, in a modern car, the driver is now isolated from many mechanical functions. Electrical systems were introduced in the 1920s, initially to automate the starting process, but this extended to lighting and heating. Later developments include powered windows, air conditioning, in-car entertainment, and even digital communication.

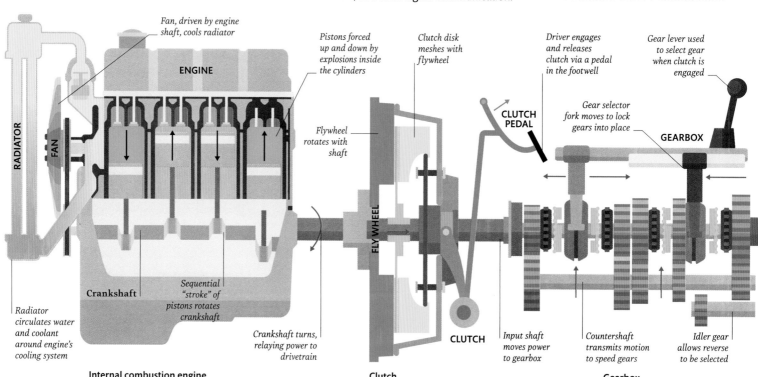

Fan, driven by engine shaft, cools radiator

ENGINE

Pistons forced up and down by explosions inside the cylinders

Clutch disk meshes with flywheel

Driver engages and releases clutch via a pedal in the footwell

Gear lever used to select gear when clutch is engaged

RADIATOR

FAN

Flywheel rotates with shaft

CLUTCH PEDAL

Gear selector fork moves to lock gears into place

GEARBOX

FLYWHEEL

Crankshaft

Sequential "stroke" of pistons rotates crankshaft

Radiator circulates water and coolant around engine's cooling system

Crankshaft turns, relaying power to drivetrain

CLUTCH

Input shaft moves power to gearbox

Countershaft transmits motion to speed gears

Idler gear allows reverse to be selected

Internal combustion engine
The engine captures the energy produced by the ignition of a mixture of fuel and air. Small explosions force pistons up and down, which turns a central shaft.

Clutch
The clutch disconnects the engine's power output from the drivetrain when changing gear. It may be automatic or manual.

Gearbox
The gearbox allows a driver to match the engine speed to the level required by road conditions. Today, cars have at least five different "ratios" of gears to select from.

Timeline

Many hundreds of companies have been involved in automotive manufacturing, but today only a dozen organizations dominate the global car industry. In 2009, China overtook the US to become the world's biggest car market.

1885 *Karl Benz's three-wheeled Patent Motor-Wagen is the first "car" with an internal combustion engine*

1908 *Henry Ford launches the Model T; after the price is reduced, 15 million cars are produced*

1850

1902 *The Oldsmobile Curved Dash becomes the first mass-produced car built on a production line*

1934 *Pioneering Citroën Traction Avant is introduced with front-wheel drive and a unitary body construction*

> "You can **have** it in **any color** you want, as long as it is **black**."
>

Differentials

When a car turns a corner, the outside wheels must rotate faster than the inside ones. Differential gears allow each wheel to turn at a different speed, distributing equal amounts of torque. With rear-wheel drive, the differential is part of the rear axle; with front-wheel drive, it is built into each drive unit.

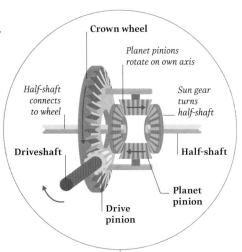

Crown wheel

Planet pinions rotate on own axis

Half-shaft connects to wheel

Sun gear turns half-shaft

Driveshaft

Half-shaft

Planet pinion

Drive pinion

Rubber tire grips road surface

Output shaft carries drive power to wheels

DRIVESHAFT

Wheel turns to push car forward or backward

Italy built the **world's first road** for fast, **intercity** car driving in 1924 between **Milan** and **Varese**

Car design

Some early cars featured seats set above the power unit; the introduction of front-mounted engines reduced height and improved stability. Steel welding techniques followed and, by the late 1930s, the closed sedan (saloon) body style was common and designers began to incorporate aerodynamics. With the onset of front-wheel drive in the 1960s, cars became more spacious and versatile.

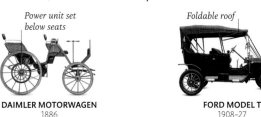

Power unit set below seats

DAIMLER MOTORWAGEN
1886

Foldable roof

FORD MODEL T
1908–27

Low-slung chassis boosts roadholding

ASTON MARTIN MK II
1934

Streamlined body reflects art-deco design

LINCOLN ZEPHYR
1936

Air-cooled engine housed in trunk

VOLKSWAGEN BEETLE
1938

Wheels cushioned by hydropneumatic suspension

CITROËN DS
1955

Huge tail-fins echo 1950s jet age

CADILLAC SERIES 62
1959

Fuel-injected engine boosts road and track performance

BMW 3.0 CSL
1972

Ground-hugging wedge shape typical of high-performance supercars

LAMBORGHINI COUNTACH
1988

Hybrid gas / electric powertrain—a Prius first

TOYOTA PRIUS MKII
2004

1959 *British Motor Corporation's (BMC) Mini with a transverse engine profoundly alters global car design*

1987 *Ferrari F40 becomes the first production road car that can top 200 mph (322 km/h)*

2005 *BMW runs successful real-world trials of hydrogen fuel-cell-powered cars*

2020

1964 *The sporty Ford Mustang is launched; a million cars are sold in the first two years*

2012 *Tesla's luxury electric Model S is unveiled; this has a major impact on the established car industry*

Aviation through history

Humankind has always dreamed of flight. Numerous early attempts with winged gliders ended in death and disaster, until experiments in the 18th and 19th centuries brought about greater understanding of the principles of flight. Balloons and airships were lifted using hot air or lighter-than-air gases, and gliders were followed by powered aircraft. The 20th century saw a boom in aviation with the development of military aircraft, helicopters, jet engines, air freight, and giant passenger airliners.

Wooden pulley system for flapping wings

MODEL OF DA VINCI'S FLYING MACHINE

Wing made of wooden ribs covered in fabric

c.16th century Italian scientist and artist Leonardo da Vinci creates designs of flying machines modeled on the movements of bats and birds.

MANFRED VON RICHTHOFEN

1914–18 Military aviation develops during World War I, introducing ace pilots such as Germany's Manfred von Richthofen.

POSTER ADVERTISEMENT FOR THE FLYING MEET

1909 The first international flying meet is held at Reims, France. It does much to promote the idea of aircraft as a practical form of transportation.

1907 French aviator Henri Farman piloting a Voisin biplane makes the first flight of a minute or more in Europe. More than 60 Voisin biplanes are built as a result of this newly earned fame.

Rudder turns to steer aircraft left and right

1903 Brothers Orville and Wilbur Wright build and fly the world's first heavier-than-air aircraft in North Carolina, USA. Rising 10ft (3m) above ground, this controlled and powered flight lasts 12 seconds.

1929 The heaviest-ever flying boat, the Dornier Do X, is introduced. It requires 12 engines to lift its 108,027 lb (49,000 kg) loaded weight.

Metal hull with three decks

DORNIER DO X

1932 American Amelia Earhart becomes the first female aviator to make a solo transatlantic flight, traveling from Newfoundland, Canada, to Northern Ireland in a Lockheed Vega 5B.

AMELIA EARHART

1937 The giant German passenger airship LZ 129 *Hindenburg* catches fire while docked at a US naval base. It is destroyed and 36 lives are lost.

HINDENBURG DISASTER

1974 The F-16 Fighting Falcon makes its first flight. More than 4,600 of these versatile supersonic fighters enter service in more than 20 countries.

Shock wave spreads out

THE SOUND BARRIER

Aircraft travels faster than sound, creating sonic boom

1969 The Anglo-French supersonic airliner, the Concorde, takes to the skies flying at almost twice the speed of sound. It stays in service from 1976 to 2003.

Lightweight aluminium alloy airframe

HARRIER GR 3

Wingspan of 32ft 6in (9.9m)

F-16 FIGHTING FALCON

Ruddervators combine functions of rudders and elevators

1967 The Harrier—the first operational aircraft capable of vectoring thrust from its engines to take off and land vertically—takes flight. It is developed by British corporation Hawker Siddeley.

Faceted panels provide F-117 with most of its stealth

1983 The Lockheed F-117 enters service in the US. It is the first military aircraft designed with stealth technology to avoid detection by enemy radar.

1986 The two-seater Rutan Model 76 Voyager takes off from Mojave, California, becoming the first aircraft to fly around the world without landing or refueling.

LOCKHEED F-117 NIGHTHAWK

VOYAGER STAMP

◀ see also The origins of modern transportation pp.278–79

German aviator **Otto Lilienthal** made over **2,000 glider flights** between 1890 and 1896

MONTGOLFIER BALLOON

Balloon envelope made of taffeta

1783 The first manned flight of a hot air balloon—designed and built by French papermakers the Montgolfier brothers—reaches 3,000 ft (910 m) above Paris and stays aloft 25 minutes.

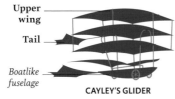

Upper wing

Tail

Boatlike fuselage

CAYLEY'S GLIDER

1849 British inventor George Cayley builds a glider with multiple wings to generate lift. It makes a short flight carrying a small boy.

1891 Ferdinand von Zeppelin resigns from the German army to devote himself to designing rigid airships, the first of which, the LZ1, flies in 1900.

FERDINAND VON ZEPPELIN

1896 American scientist Samuel P. Langley flies a large model aircraft to distances of up to 4,800 ft (1,460 m) using a catapult to launch the plane.

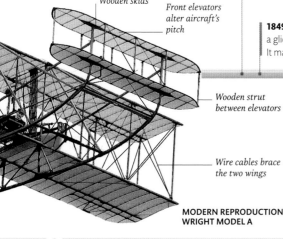

Wooden skids

Front elevators alter aircraft's pitch

Wooden strut between elevators

Wire cables brace the two wings

MODERN REPRODUCTION WRIGHT MODEL A

c.1900s German Martin Kutta and Russian Nikolai Joukowski develop a theorem that helps calculate the lift an airfoil shape such as a wing generates when moving through air.

KUTTA-JOUKOWSKI THEOREM

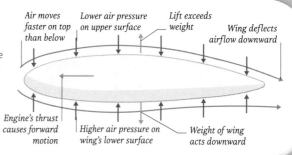

Air moves faster on top than below

Lower air pressure on upper surface

Lift exceeds weight

Wing deflects airflow downward

Engine's thrust causes forward motion

Higher air pressure on wing's lower surface

Weight of wing acts downward

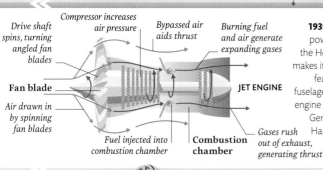

Compressor increases air pressure

Drive shaft spins, turning angled fan blades

Bypassed air aids thrust

Burning fuel and air generate expanding gases

Fan blade

JET ENGINE

Air drawn in by spinning fan blades

Fuel injected into combustion chamber

Combustion chamber

Gases rush out of exhaust, generating thrust

1939 The first jet-powered aircraft, the Heinkel He 178, makes its first flight. It features a metal fuselage and turbojet engine developed by German designer Hans von Ohain.

Shoulder harness strap

TYPE T5 PARACHUTE

1939–45 World War II sees the first large-scale use of parachutes to save aircrew from damaged aircraft and to land airborne troops on the ground.

1942 The Messerschmitt Me 262 debuts its jet-powered capabilities. Twin jet engines give this German plane a top speed of 560mph (900 kph).

1952 The Boeing B-52 Stratofortress makes its debut. This large, long-range strategic bomber can carry up to 70,000 lb (31,500 kg) of weapons.

*c.1950s** The United States introduces advances to flight suit technology. Pressure suits and anti-g suits allow pilots to fly safely at very high altitudes.

AIR PRESSURE SUIT

1949 The de Havilland Comet 1 prototype makes its maiden flight. The world's first jet airliner, it can fly faster and higher than propeller-driven planes.

1945 The first mass-produced helicopter, the Sikorsky R-4 enters service. This US-built helicopter seats two.

Spinning rotor blades generate force of lift

Rotor head tilts to fly forward

TYPICAL HELICOPTER DYNAMICS

Tail fin allows stability in forward flight

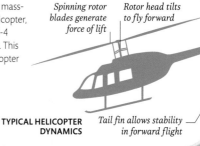

2005 The world's largest jet airliner, the Airbus A380, first flies. This double-decker seats up to 853 passengers within its 239½ ft- (72.7 m-) long fuselage.

Winglet reduces turbulence

Wingspan of 262 ft (79.8 m)

AIRBUS A380

2015 The Solar Impulse 2 sets a world record by flying for 117 hours on solar power, from Nagoya, Japan, to Hawaii.

More than 17,000 solar cells cover the aircraft's surface

Rudder controls side-to-side movement

SOLAR IMPULSE 2

see also Transportation in the 21st century pp.290-91 ▶ **289**

Transportation in the 21st century

Much of the world's population has become increasingly mobile during the first two decades of the 21st century. The demand for fast, safe, and affordable transportation options across land, sea, and air has grown enormously, as has global trade and the freight of goods and raw materials. With an ever-increasing global population and mounting concerns over environmental issues, the future of transportation presents many challenges.

Maglev trains
Magnetic levitation (maglev) systems made their commercial debut in 1984 with a low-speed shuttle ferrying passengers from Birmingham airport, UK, to a nearby train station. Only a handful of maglev lines have been constructed since, but the future promises many more. Maglev replaces traditional wheels and rails with powerful electromagnets that raise a train above its guideway, then push and pull it along its route. With no contact friction, maglev promises less noise, vibration, and wear and tear as well as greater fuel efficiency. Speeds eclipsing conventional high-speed rail are also possible—in 2015, a Japanese L0 maglev achieved a world train speed record of 375 mph (603 kph).

MAGLEV TRAIN

Electric vehicles
Electric vehicles (EVs) have a long history: the first EV was built in the 1830s by Scottish inventor Robert Anderson. Only in the 21st century, however, did they become a practical alternative to internal combustion engine vehicles, which burn fossil fuels and lead to localised pollution. Promising quieter and cleaner road transportation, EVs can travel increasingly further between recharges, thanks to improvements in rechargeable batteries and electric motor design. By 2019, there were 15 times more electric vehicles on the world's roads than there were in 2013, with over 40 per cent of all EVs found in China. They can cut global warming if they use renewable energy.

Hybrid cars
Hybrid cars, using both electric and gasoline engines, have become increasingly popular in the 21st century, following the introduction of the Toyota Prius in 1997. Hybrid electric vehicles (HEVs) use the small gas-fueled motor both to recharge batteries and to drive; the battery is also charged via regenerative braking—the car converts kinetic energy into electrical energy that is stored in the battery. Plug-in hybrid electric vehicles (PHEVs) are plugged into electrical outlets to recharge. In addition to lower harmful emissions, hybrids offer greater fuel economy than regular vehicles—as much as 50 miles per gallon (2.5 liters per 100 km).

Driverless cars
Robotics research in the 2000s led to the adoption of intelligent driving aids, such as parking collision avoidance sensors and adaptive cruise control. In self-driving (autonomous) vehicles, a human driver is replaced with a computer controller, receiving data from a sophisticated package of sensors. These sensors include radar, which detects the speed and distance of objects nearby, and Light Detection and Ranging (LiDAR), whose pulses of laser light build a detailed 3-D picture of the vehicle's surroundings.

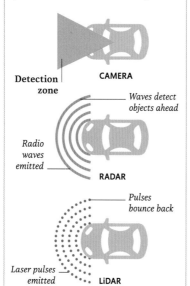

Detection zone

CAMERA

Waves detect objects ahead

Radio waves emitted

RADAR

Pulses bounce back

Laser pulses emitted

LiDAR

Air travel in the 21st century
In 2018, aircraft carried more than 4.2 billion passengers. New, more energy-efficient aircraft, pilotless cargo-carrying drones, and greater automation at airports all aid the demand for air transportation, which doubled between 2000 and 2020. Although many airports are at capacity, larger aircraft are not predicted: the end of production of the 853-passenger capacity Airbus A380 was announced in 2019, and smaller, twin-engine jet airliners appear to be the way forward. At the start of 2020, the world's longest nonstop scheduled service was Singapore Airlines' Newark–Singapore route, covering a distance of 9,534 miles (15,344 km).

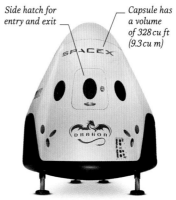

Side hatch for entry and exit

Capsule has a volume of 328 cu ft (9.3 cu m)

SpaceX DRAGON MANNED SPACECRAFT

Space tourism
In the modern world, not everyone who goes into space needs to be a trained astronaut. In 2001, US businessman Dennis Tito became the world's first space tourist. He paid more than $20 million for a stay of 7 days and 22 hours on board the International Space Station, ferried to and from the space station by a Soyuz TM spacecraft. Since then, various companies have begun development of their own private spacecraft, expected to be capable of carrying passengers on short, suborbital trips into space or into low Earth orbit. These include Boeing's Starliner project, Virgin Galactic, and American entrepreneur Elon Musk's SpaceX.

Hyperloop
A rapid ground transportation technology under development in the 21st century, hyperloop pods carrying passengers are

▶ Modern high-speed train
A CRH380 high-speed train pulls into Beijing station in China. The Beijing–Shanghai high-speed rail line carries 160 million passengers per year at speeds of up to 217 mph (350 kph).

designed to float on air skis—cushions of air—much like an air hockey puck, or by using magnetic levitation. According to the concept, the pods travel inside a long tube, from which most of the air is sucked out by a fan. This air is then blown behind or underneath the hyperloop to help propel it. With far less air resistance to encounter, the pods move efficiently, using less energy than regular rail travel, and are potentially capable of moving as fast as 746 mph (1,200 kph). Proposed hyperloop projects in the US, Spain, and India aim to reduce travel times between cities by three-quarters or more.

Transportation and the environment
The 21st century has seen an increased awareness of the harmful impacts that burning fossil fuels has on the environment, particularly the major threats posed by air pollution and climate change. Improvements in engine efficiency and the streamlining of vehicles to reduce air resistance have improved fuel economy, but motor vehicles and aircraft remain major contributors of carbon dioxide (CO_2), nitrous oxides, and other harmful emissions into the atmosphere. For emissions targets to be met, significant changes need to occur, with solutions focusing on cleaner fuels, renewable energy, and improved public transportation, including cycle facilities.

URBAN BICYCLE RENTAL

In 2019, transportation accounted for **a quarter of all** CO_2 **emissions worldwide**

History

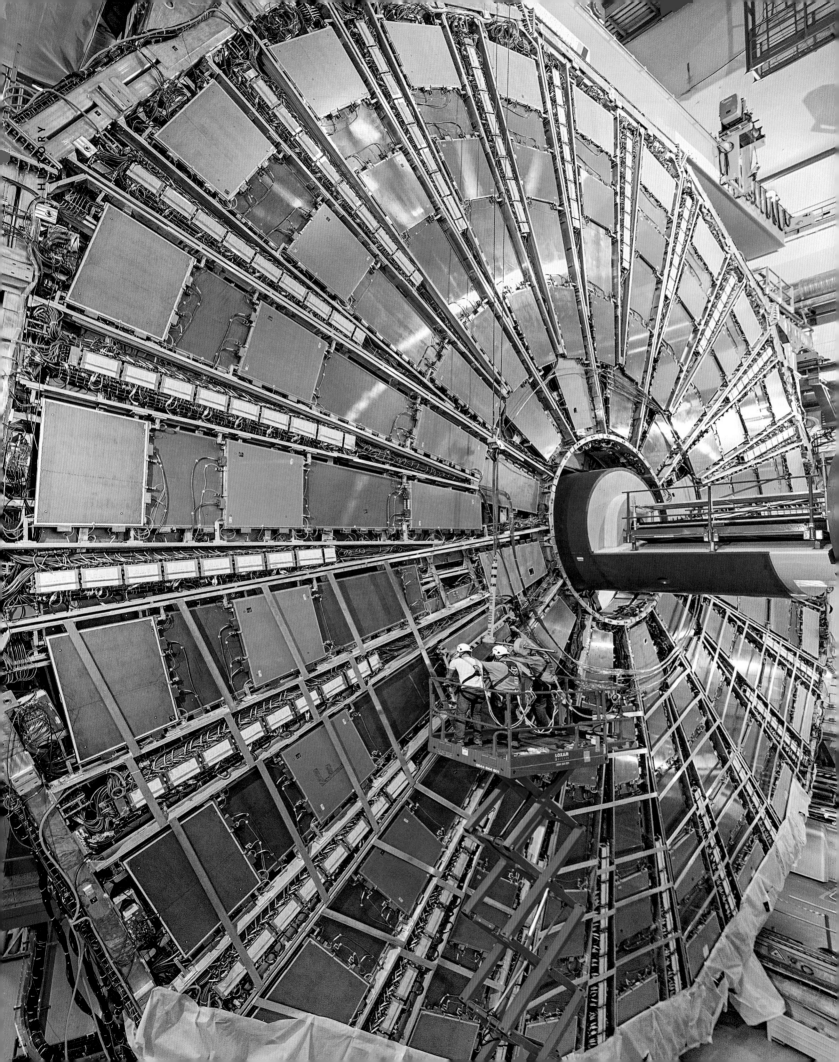

The history of the universe

Our universe was born in a vast, explosive expansion some 13.8 billion years ago—an event known as the Big Bang. This vast outpouring of energy was accompanied by the creation of four dimensions—three of space and one of time itself, so that it is meaningless to ask what came "before" the Big Bang. The first few minutes of creation saw energy coalesce into vast quantities of densely packed matter—the raw ingredients of all the material in the universe today.

How do we know?

The concept of the Big Bang traces its origins to the simple observation that the universe is expanding, and therefore must once have been smaller. The idea of cosmic expansion first emerged in the 1920s after Edwin Hubble discovered that nearly all galaxies are moving away from us.

In 1931, Belgian priest and cosmologist Georges Lemaître traced today's expanding universe back to a state that was compact, dense, and hotter than any temperatures known today. He called this the "primeval atom" (the name "Big Bang" was coined later, initially to belittle the idea).

In 1948, physicists showed how the expanding primeval atom could have transformed energy into atoms of the simplest elements in the exact proportions measured from the early universe. Then in 1964, astronomers detected the afterglow of radiation from the Big Bang itself. Today, we continue to build on this theory through observations of the distant universe and particle accelerator experiments that recreate the energy conditions of 13.8 billion years ago.

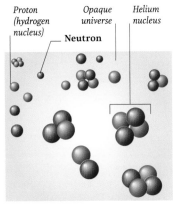

PROTONS AND NEUTRONS FORMING THE FIRST ATOMIC NUCLEI

Proton (hydrogen nucleus) Opaque universe Helium nucleus **Neutron**

◀ **Giant particle accelerator**
The Large Hadron Collider at CERN near Geneva, Switzerland, conducts experiments that probe particle physics at temperatures approaching those of the Big Bang, helping us to build our picture of the origins of the universe.

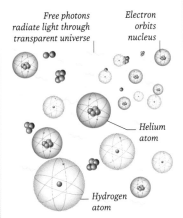

Free photons radiate light through transparent universe Electron orbits nucleus

Helium atom

Hydrogen atom

FORMATION OF THE FIRST ATOMS

In the beginning

The Big Bang began with an instantaneous outburst of energy whose conditions were just right to trigger expansion rather than collapse. Energy poured into the infant universe in the first 10^{-43} seconds (or the first 10 million trillion trillion trillionth of a second). This period is known as the Planck Epoch, whose conditions were so extreme that the laws of physics as we know them did not apply.

At the end of the Planck Epoch, physical laws, such as electromagnetism, began to establish themselves as the universe rapidly expanded and cooled from near-infinite temperatures. Around 10^{-32} seconds into cosmic history, a dramatic event called Inflation blew up the scale of space by a factor of 10^{28} (or by 10 billion billion billion times) in a tiny fraction of a second, transforming submicroscopic fluctuations in the density of matter into the seeds that would one day become vast clusters of galaxies.

The birth of matter

The newborn universe was so hot that mass and energy were interchangeable according to Einstein's famous equation $E = mc^2$ (see p.196). Particles of matter—heavyweight quarks and lighter leptons (which include electrons)—were able to wink in and out of existence, usually created in pairs with an oppositely charged "antiparticle." In the first microsecond, temperatures had already fallen so far that

quarks could no longer be produced, though production of the most stable leptons (electrons and electron neutrinos) continued for about 10 seconds.

Protons and neutrons

The quarks now began to bind in trios, creating the protons and neutrons (as well as their antiparticles) now found within the nuclei of atoms. The vast majority of particles and antiparticles destroyed each other in bursts of energy where they met, but a small proportion of matter particles survived, with protons outnumbering neutrons by seven to one. In 2–20 minutes after the Big Bang, falling temperatures allowed protons and neutrons to bind, creating nuclei of the simplest elements, such as helium and lithium.

Toward the first atoms

As the creation of matter came to an end, the vast majority of energy in the universe was in the form of high-energy gamma-ray photons. However, density was so great that these rays could travel only tiny distances before colliding with, or being diverted by, particles of matter. This heated the particles and scattered the photons in new directions, with slightly less energy. The abundant radiation was so intense, it exerted a pressure that prevented gravity from clumping matter together. The universe remained effectively opaque—an expanding fireball of incandescent fog.

As photon scattering slowly reduced the energy in radiation, the cosmic energy balance changed. Gamma rays faded

into lower-energy X-rays, then ultraviolet radiation. After about 47,000 years, most radiation energy had been absorbed by matter. Meanwhile, the universe inexorably cooled as it expanded.

In about 380,000 years, temperatures finally fell low enough (about 3,000°C, or 5,400°F) for nuclei and electrons to combine into atoms. This produced a

In less than **an hour**, all the **atomic nuclei in the universe** were made

sudden drop in the number of free particles. The fog finally cleared and photons, now in the form of visible light, could race from the edges of the fireball at light speed, creating the oldest visible radiation in the universe. It still arrives at Earth from all directions and we call it the Cosmic Microwave Background (CMB). Mapping its variation across the sky can still reveal details of the early universe.

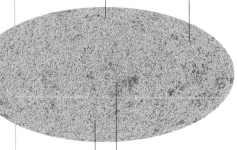

Red areas are 0.0004°F (0.0002°C) warmer than average Blue areas are 0.0004°F (0.0002°C) cooler than average

Warmer red areas are where matter is dense Cooler blue areas are where matter is less dense

WHOLE-SKY IMAGE OF CMB VARIATION

DISCOVERING THE CMB

The Cosmic Microwave Background (CMB) is a faint afterglow from the moment that photons were first free to radiate through space. It is diminished to weaker microwaves by its 13.8-billion-year journey. It was predicted in 1948, but the telltale radiation was only discovered by chance in 1964. Arno Penzias and Robert Wilson had built a giant microwave antenna for satellite communication experiments, but found it was plagued by a persistent faint signal from all over the sky.

PENZIAS AND WILSON'S ANTENNA

◀ see also The cosmos pp.12–13   ◀ The universe pp.30–33   ◀ Observing the universe pp.34–35   **295**

>> The history of the universe continued

The Big Bang generated all the matter and energy in the universe and saw the establishment of fundamental forces that govern how it works. The period that followed, however, was also vital to establishing the universe we know today. Matter clumped into the first stars and galaxies, and lightweight elements began converting into the heavier ones that enable complex chemistry and the formation of rocky planets such as Earth.

From darkness to light

The event known as decoupling, when light was freed from matter 380,000 years after the Big Bang (see p.295) marked a major shift in cosmic history. The universe suddenly became transparent, but as radiation from the early fireball faded, it also became completely dark.

During this cosmic dark age, other forces were at work. No longer driven apart by radiation pressure, matter particles could at last coalesce under the influence of gravity. In fact, this process had begun earlier; the mysterious dark matter (see pp.32–33), which comprises 85 percent of all matter, is unaffected by radiation and therefore began to coalesce well before decoupling, concentrating around any slightly denser regions.

About 150–300 million years after the Big Bang, some knots of matter became so dense and hot that they ignited to create the first generation of stars. These were very different to the stars we know today. Composed of raw materials formed in the Big Bang, they were made almost entirely of pure hydrogen and helium, and they could grow to be hundreds of times more massive than our sun. Nevertheless, they quickly burned through their hydrogen in just a few million years, lighting up the early universe and producing heavier elements, such as carbon and oxygen, in their cores—in the same way as present-day massive stars.

Seeding the universe

The first stars died in supernova explosions that may have been very different from those seen today (see p.25). Theoretical models predict that a sudden wave of nuclear fusion spread through the entire star, flinging out vast quantities of heavy elements and leaving no remnant where the star had been. Fierce radiation from

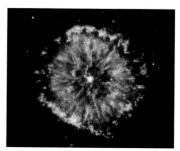

MATTER SHED FROM A DYING STAR

these supernovas probably began energizing the giant clouds of hydrogen that filled the early universe, splitting their molecules and stripping their electrons in an event called reionization. Interstellar space today is a tenuous plasma created by this reionization, and nearly all radiation can pass through it.

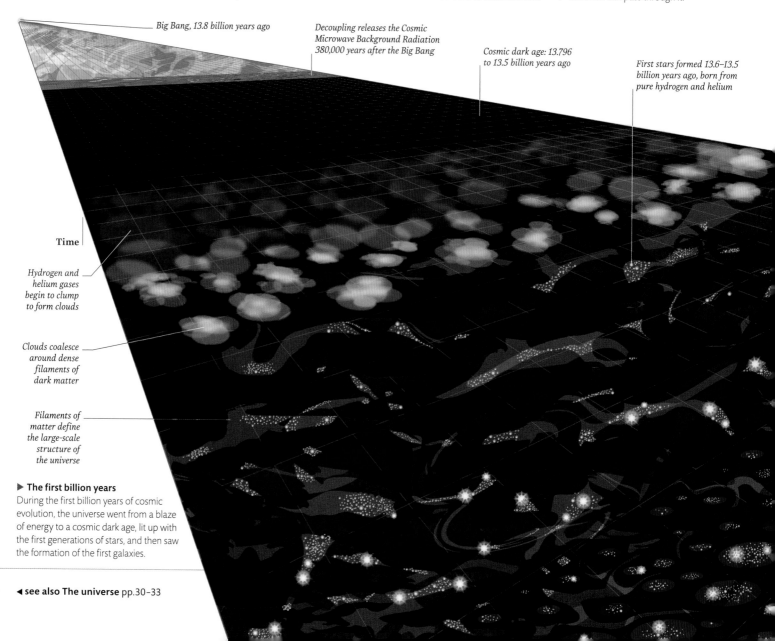

Big Bang, 13.8 billion years ago

Decoupling releases the Cosmic Microwave Background Radiation 380,000 years after the Big Bang

Cosmic dark age: 13.796 to 13.5 billion years ago

First stars formed 13.6–13.5 billion years ago, born from pure hydrogen and helium

Time

Hydrogen and helium gases begin to clump to form clouds

Clouds coalesce around dense filaments of dark matter

Filaments of matter define the large-scale structure of the universe

▶ The first billion years

During the first billion years of cosmic evolution, the universe went from a blaze of energy to a cosmic dark age, lit up with the first generations of stars, and then saw the formation of the first galaxies.

Early **galaxies called quasars** burn **so bright** that they are visible across **13 billion light years** of space

The life and death of the first generation of stars began a process that is ongoing today, enriching the cosmos with heavy elements. As the second generation of stars formed, the presence of these elements caused them to burn faster and more brightly, but also meant that they could no longer grow so massive. As this second generation of giants exhausted their fuel a few million years later, they exploded much like today's supernovas, generating smaller amounts of heavy elements and leaving behind their collapsed cores—tiny, dense neutron stars and infinitely dense black holes.

The first galaxies

The first galaxies coalesced in the same regions of concentrated matter as the first stars, though probably a little later. According to current theories, the earliest were small and shapeless, mixing raw hydrogen gas from intergalactic space with heavier elements forged in the first generations of stars. Collisions and near misses between these galaxies created ripples that triggered new waves of star formations. The galaxies also harbored increasing numbers of black holes left behind by second-generation and later stars. As these collided and merged, eventually most galaxies developed giant black holes in their centers. These acted as gravitational anchors, drawing galaxies together if they happened to collide, and ensuring the growth of larger and more complex systems. At the centers of these coalescing galaxies, the giant black holes also merged and gorged on their surroundings. The superheated disks of infalling matter around them shone as brilliant beacons of radiation called quasars.

STAR BIRTH

Toward the Earth

As galaxies grew, large-scale mergers became less frequent and central black holes became quiet and dark. Large surviving galaxies including our own infant Milky Way developed spiral arms, as clouds of gas and dust orbiting in disks around the center of the galaxy found themselves pushed together in spiral "traffic jams." Here, gravity steered this congestion into new generations of stars. The largest of these lived and died in just a few million years, again scattering heavy elements into the interstellar medium (the matter between stars) as they turned supernova.

Our own sun began to form from the interstellar medium, concentrated by gravity into a spinning disk of gas and dust, about 4.6 billion years ago. Since many generations of stars and supernovas had passed, its raw materials contained the elements needed to create solid matter and rocky planets. As our sedate, long-lived star emerged from its birthplace to join the general population of the galactic disk, it carried with it a newborn solar system.

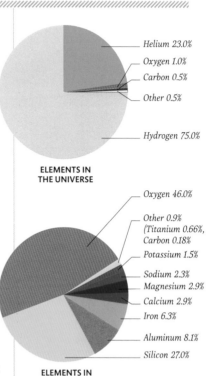

Helium 23.0%
Oxygen 1.0%
Carbon 0.5%
Other 0.5%
Hydrogen 75.0%

ELEMENTS IN THE UNIVERSE

Oxygen 46.0%
Other 0.9% (Titanium 0.66%, Carbon 0.18%)
Potassium 1.5%
Sodium 2.3%
Magnesium 2.9%
Calcium 2.9%
Iron 6.3%
Aluminum 8.1%
Silicon 27.0%

ELEMENTS IN EARTH'S CRUST

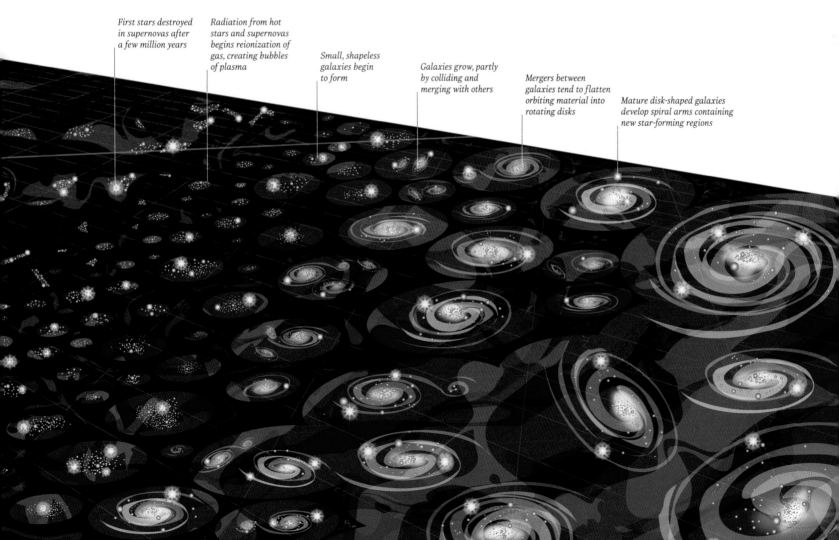

First stars destroyed in supernovas after a few million years

Radiation from hot stars and supernovas begins reionization of gas, creating bubbles of plasma

Small, shapeless galaxies begin to form

Galaxies grow, partly by colliding and merging with others

Mergers between galaxies tend to flatten orbiting material into rotating disks

Mature disk-shaped galaxies develop spiral arms containing new star-forming regions

The history of the Earth

Our planet's story began with a cloud of interstellar gas and dust, which eventually became a complex world that has a temperate climate ideal for supporting life. Along the way, interactions between geology, atmosphere, oceans, and life have seen Earth pass through several distinct phases. The direct evidence from the earliest times has been largely wiped out by 4.5 billion years of continuous change, but scientists have built a picture of what happened from material preserved in meteorites, the surfaces of other, less active, worlds, and computer models.

Asteroid-sized bodies formed by accretion

Planetesimal formed by pebble accretion remains cool at first

Drift of coalescing pebbles

❶ Accretion
Over millions of years, dust particles probably joined to form pebble-sized bodies by accretion—first by weak static electric forces, then increasingly by gravity.

❷ First planetesimals
Spherical moon-sized to Mars-sized bodies, called planetesimals, formed by gradual growth, or perhaps suddenly, when loose aggregations of pebbles collapsed.

The birth of the solar system

Our solar system was born from an interstellar nebula—the same cloud of gas and dust that gave birth to the sun (and many other stars), in a process that began about 4.6 billion years ago. The events may have been triggered by shockwaves from a nearby supernova that enriched the nebula with radioactive elements.

The process began when clumps of gas within the nebula began to collapse under their gravity, forming opaque clouds called Bok globules (see pp.22–23). As our globule collapsed, and mass concentrated near its center, it rotated faster (just as a pirouetting skater increases their spin by drawing in their arms). Collisions between clumps of gas and dust particles in different orbits gradually flattened the cloud into a broad, rotating disk of material that spiraled toward the center.

Eventually, conditions at the center of the nebula were so hot and dense that nuclear fusion reactions were possible and the sun was born. The outward pressure of radiation and the solar wind reduced the amount of material falling into the sun, leaving a broad doughnut of matter where our solar system is today. The heat close to the young sun ensured that easily melted, volatile materials such as ice evaporated into gas and were driven into the outer solar system, leaving only high-melting-point dust behind.

Coming together

Within the protoplanetary disk circling the newborn sun, planets came together through a process known as accretion. In Earth's part of the solar system, grains of dust gradually clumped together, probably attracted to each other through weak static electric forces. As the clumps grew, they began to exert gravitational influence over their surroundings, pulling in more and more material, until they formed a swarm of roughly moon-to-Mars-sized worlds, or planetesimals,

The **oldest** remnants of Earth's crust are **4.4-billion-year-old chemicals** trapped inside **crystals of zircon**

which collided with each other and grew into the planets. According to a current theory, one of the last collisions, thought to have taken place 4.5–4.4 billion years ago, was between the proto-Earth and a Mars-sized world, sometimes called Theia. The collision destroyed Theia and blasted its material, along with

a substantial chunk of our own planet's mantle, into space. Much of the material fell onto Earth or escaped into space. However, a substantial cloud remained in orbit and coalesced, in a matter of decades, to form the moon.

After the collision with Theia, impacts trailed off sharply as stray debris in the inner solar system was "soaked up" by the planets. Another spike, known as the Late Heavy Bombardment, occurred about 3.9 billion years ago when shifts in the orbits of the giant planets sent ice-rich material toward the inner solar system.

Separation into layers

Each collision that contributed to the creation of the planets heated up the materials involved, so the early Earth is assumed to have been extremely hot. Even before its formation was complete, this internal heat triggered a process called differentiation, which sorted the elements into spherical layers through the effects of gravity. Residual heat, along with that released by radioactive materials from the solar nebula, allowed

◀ Hell on Earth
The time between Earth's birth and about 4 billion years ago is known as the Hadean era, after Hades, the Greek god of the Underworld. The moon was nearer than today and lava covered Earth's surface.

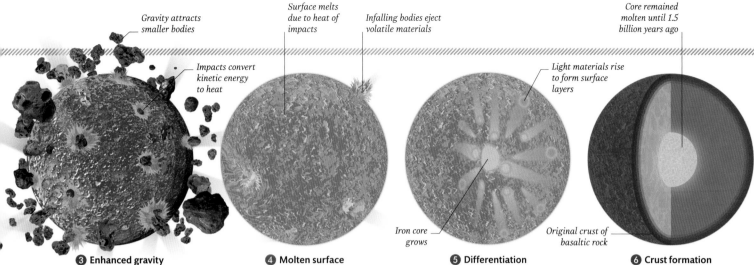

Gravity attracts smaller bodies

Surface melts due to heat of impacts

Infalling bodies eject volatile materials

Core remained molten until 1.5 billion years ago

Impacts convert kinetic energy to heat

Light materials rise to form surface layers

Iron core grows

Original crust of basaltic rock

❸ Enhanced gravity

The intense gravity of larger planetesimals drew in other objects. Ultimately the few dozen planetesimals collided and merged to form planets, including Earth.

❹ Molten surface

The heat generated by collisions and released by radioactive elements raised the temperature of early Earth, giving it a molten surface and a mobile interior.

❺ Differentiation

The fluid state of Earth's interior allowed the planet's materials to separate into layers: dense, metallic elements sank, and lightweight elements rose.

❻ Crust formation

As Earth cooled an initial crust formed, capping the underlying mantle. Heat continued to escape the interior at such a rate that volcanoes were widespread.

Earth's interior to melt and separate; heavy elements sank toward the center and lighter ones formed overlying layers.

Over time, the interior developed into layers similar to those seen today. The distribution of different elements was driven partly by their relative density and partly by the tendency to react chemically with others. The formation of an iron core also took with it most of Earth's so-called siderophile, or "iron-loving" elements

and the Earth was so hot that the planet formed in a very arid state, and water for the oceans must have arrived after it cooled. Now it is thought that oceans may have been present at least 4.4 billion years ago. One explanation for such early oceans is that impacts of ice-rich bodies, late in Earth's formation, ejected water vapor into the atmosphere. Another is that water was trapped under pressure within Earth's minerals even when temperatures were at

The first continents

Earth's original crust was a solid, single-piece shell, pockmarked by volcanic vents that let out heat. But about 4 billion years ago, the crust broke into plates that began to move, starting the cycle of crust activity known as plate tectonics (see pp.48–49). The Late Heavy Bombardment may have begun this process when it pulverized Earth's surface. As the plates moved, some plates were forced below their neighbors,

The increasingly elevated terrain was prone to erosion by wind and water, which not only produced the first sedimentary rocks, but also began to transform Earth's atmosphere. As part of a new chemical weathering process, carbon dioxide slowly reacted with silicate rocks, eventually converting them to carbonates. The balance of silicate and carbonate rocks in the crust continues to regulate carbon dioxide levels over millions of years.

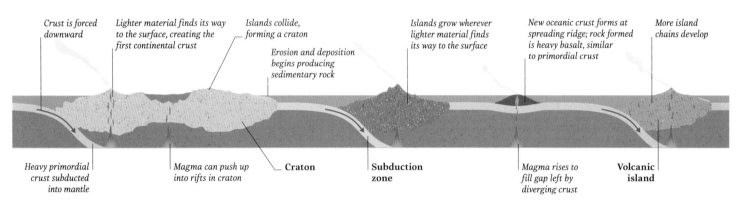

Crust is forced downward

Lighter material finds its way to the surface, creating the first continental crust

Islands collide, forming a craton

Erosion and deposition begins producing sedimentary rock

Islands grow wherever lighter material finds its way to the surface

New oceanic crust forms at spreading ridge; rock formed is heavy basalt, similar to primordial crust

More island chains develop

Heavy primordial crust subducted into mantle

Magma can push up into rifts in craton

Craton

Subduction zone

Magma rises to fill gap left by diverging crust

Volcanic island

(gold, platinum, cobalt, and nickel). Those that react readily with oxygen or other lightweight elements (lithophiles and chalcophiles respectively) tended toward the surface, forming a thick mantle topped by a solid but unstable crust of the lightest elements. This initial crust was thin and fairly featureless.

Early atmosphere and oceans

Overlying the rocks of early Earth were layers of water and gas—the oceans and atmosphere. The source of Earth's water is still debated. It was thought that the inner regions of the solar nebula were so dry

their peak, and only escaped through volcanoes, which relieved the pressure. It is likely that both processes, as well as water from comets, contributed. It also seems clear that cataclysmic events during Earth's early history resulted in at least one complete evaporation of the oceans followed by later recondensation.

Earth's atmosphere was also in a state of change. Initially, it was composed of lightweight hydrogen and helium, but as the solar wind swept these away, volcanic eruptions transformed it into a hot, dense mix of gases, rich in carbon dioxide, that created a powerful greenhouse effect.

or subducted. Subduction produced heat that melted overlying rocks, giving rise to volcanoes that brought lighter rocks to the surface. The buoyancy of this new crust allowed it to pile up to greater heights, forming volcanic islands. As the plates jostled, these resisted subduction. Heavy primordial crust was always subducted in preference, so continental crust continued to build. As the islands piled into one another, they formed larger landmasses called cratons—the ancient cores of today's continents. Earth was still giving off heat much faster than it does today, speeding the continent-building process.

▲ Formation of continents

The cores of the continents formed in the early stages of plate tectonics through repeated collision and merging of island chains made of relatively lightweight rocks.

Rocks from the early days of plate tectonics, **3.8 billion years ago,** can still be found in **Greenland**

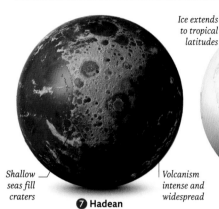

Ice extends to tropical latitudes

Hot, arid interior

Tropical coasts

Colliding plates along Pacific Coast of North America produce Rocky Mountains

Shallow seas fill craters

Volcanism intense and widespread

❼ Hadean
About 4 billion years ago, Earth's early crust of basaltic rock was still pockmarked with impact craters resulting from the Late Heavy Bombardment.

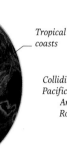

❽ Snowball Earth
About 800 million years ago, with the continents concentrated around the tropics, factors conspired to cool Earth, triggering an almost global glaciation.

❾ Pangea
The most recent supercontinent, known as Pangea, coalesced about 300 million years ago. Isolated from coastal rainfall, large areas of land turned to desert.

South America moves north

❿ Warm period
About 55 million years ago, a global warm period saw ice caps melt and higher seas flood many low-lying areas of land. The continents were gradually drifting toward their present-day distribution.

About **55.5 million years** ago, Earth's average temperature **increased by 14.4°F (8°C)** as volcanoes released **carbon dioxide** into the atmosphere

Life takes hold

The beginnings of plate tectonics about 4 billion years ago marked the end of the early Hadean era, and the start of the Archean era, which lasted 1.5 billion years. Most of the evidence for Earth's history in this period has been destroyed or buried by subsequent plate tectonics, but a few rare finds reveal what was going on inside Earth—and on its surface. New continental crust continued to form, adding to existing landmasses at a greater rate than it was

Antiquity of Earth
Investigation of complex rock formations, as seen in this 1787 sketch showing rock layers at Jedburgh, Scotland, inspired early geologists. The Scottish geologist James Hutton wrote of a world with "no vestige of a beginning, no prospect of an end."

eroded, and gradually built up Earth's land surface. By the end of the Archean, the area of dry land reached 80 percent of today's extent. Earth's magnetic field, already in place at least 3.5 billion years ago, gained in strength, increasing its ability to deflect the radiation of the powerful solar wind. This is just as well, since the Archean was also the era when life became widespread. The earliest fossil evidence of life dates to about 3.5 billion years ago (though there are older chemical traces possibly made by life). These fossils were cyanobacteria— colonial bacteria that harvest energy from sunlight and build complex biochemicals from carbon dioxide.

New atmosphere and new life
The Proterozoic era began 2.5 billion years ago. Rocks surviving from this era reveal how the planet was changing. The early Proterozoic seems to have been a time of active tectonics with continents splitting and reuniting—at certain times nearly all of Earth's land was united into a single supercontinent, while at others it was widely spread out. But it was changes to Earth's atmosphere and to its life that would have a permanent impact.

A billion years of photosynthesis by cyanobacteria had reduced carbon dioxide levels in the atmosphere, resulting in a cooler planet; the first evidence of ice ages comes from early in this era. Meanwhile, oxygen made as a waste product of photosynthesis by this early

life produced new minerals in Earth's crust, due to the reactive nature of oxygen. Over hundreds of millions of years, oxygen built up in these mineral "sinks" through reactions with iron and other chemicals in Earth's oceans.

About 2.4 billion years ago, the mineral sinks were full, so oxygen began to build up in the oceans and atmosphere. This turned out to be an apocalypse for most life, which, unaccustomed to life in oxygen, was poisoned by its own waste. Organisms that survived this so-called "Great Oxygenation Event" had evolved to become consumers of oxygen. The need to live in an oxygenated environment may have even triggered the changes that led to more complex life (see pp.220–21).

Cycles of life
About 775 million years ago, toward the end of the Proterozoic, there is evidence for the beginning of a series of prolonged ice ages that extended over most of the planet—a time known as Snowball Earth. As Earth emerged from the last of these, there was a blossoming of new types of multicellular life, including early animals. This marks the start of the Phanerozoic Eon (or Eon of Visible Life)—a time that began around 541 million years ago and extends to the present. Throughout this eon, geology, climate, and life have been bound together. The diversity of living species has waxed and waned through a series of mass extinction events, linked to

Eurasian ice sheet during height of the glaciation

Much of present-day Europe covered by shallow seas

Laurentian (North American) ice sheet, at maximum extent

Ocean pack ice

Isthmus of Panama cuts off Atlantic circulation from the Pacific

⓫ Ice age
Some 2.6 million years ago, the Americas joined and transformed ocean circulation, tipping Earth into an ice age. Maximum glaciation occurred 20,000 years ago.

Sahara region of North Africa is flooded

dramatic changes in climate. The causes of the extinctions are complex and varied. Some probably had physical triggers, such as widespread volcanism, impacts from space, or changes to the global heat balance linked to land distribution and ocean currents. Others seem to have been prompted by life itself. They range from the gradual removal of atmospheric greenhouse gases as plants first spread onto land, to the sudden release of these same gases by human activity in the recent past. The links between Earth's atmosphere, rocks, oceans, and living inhabitants will dictate our planet's future just as it has shaped its past.

CHARLES LYELL
Scottish geologist Lyell (1797–1875) proposed the principle known as uniformitarianism, which says that Earth was shaped by the same forces that are acting on it today, at a similar rate. This slow formation of rock layers made it clear that Earth was much older than the few thousand years previously believed.

◀ see also The carbon cycle pp.78–79   ◀ Environmental impact pp.82–83   ◀ The story of life pp.86–87   ◀ Types of living things pp.216–17

Prehistory to 3000 BCE

Starting with the ancient human ancestors and the first true humans in Africa, prehistory ended with the advent of writing millions of years later. During the Stone Age—divided into the Paleolithic (old), Mesolithic (middle), and Neolithic (new) periods—humans went from being hunter-gatherers to being farmers. It was followed by the Bronze Age, when humans discovered how to work metals. By the Iron Age, people across Europe, Asia, and parts of Africa began making tools and weapons from iron and steel.

3.3–1.76 MYA The earliest stone tools are made by hominins—humanlike primates. Around 1.76 MYA, Paleolithic peoples start making stone hand axes and other large cutting tools.

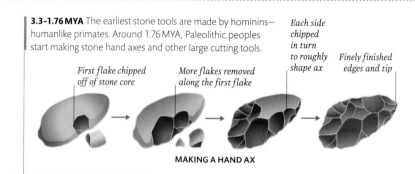

First flake chipped off of stone core

More flakes removed along the first flake

Each side chipped in turn to roughly shape ax

Finely finished edges and tip

MAKING A HAND AX

Impressed decoration resembles rope

c.13,000 BCE The earliest pottery was produced by hunter-gatherers in China. By 13,000 BCE, the first Japanese people, or Jomons, produce open-fired vessels.

ADVANCED JOMON POTTERY

c.14,000 BCE Dogs are the first animals to be domesticated by humans. A dog's skeleton was found buried with the remains of a woman at Eynan, Israel.

Skeleton of a 28-week-old puppy

CAST OF WOMAN BURIED WITH DOG

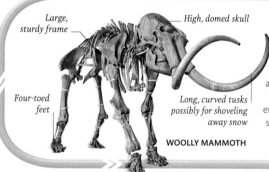

Large, sturdy frame

High, domed skull

Four-toed feet

Long, curved tusks possibly for shoveling away snow

WOOLLY MAMMOTH

c.9700 BCE The Ice Age ends as a result of dramatic global warming, which may have been triggered by shifting ocean currents and increased carbon dioxide in the atmosphere. As their environment changes, animals such as the woolly mammoth begin to go extinct.

c.10,500–9,500 BCE Farming originates in the Fertile Crescent—an area ranging from Egypt through present-day Turkey to parts of modern-day Iraq. A wild predecessor of modern wheat is among the many crops grown here.

Slim head with small grains

Tight husks

Seed head intact until threshing

Larger, fatter head

WILD WHEAT

WILD EINKORN WHEAT

DOMESTICATED EMMER WHEAT

MODERN BREAD WHEAT

Spouted jar made of copper alloy

c.4000 BCE The world's first cities, such as Uruk, are built in Mesopotamia (mostly present-day Iraq and Kuwait). These cities flourish and enter into trade with each other.

JAR FROM URUK

c.4000 BCE Wet rice cultivation begins in China in the valleys of the lower and middle Yangtze and upper Huang-ho rivers. The rice is grown in muddy paddy fields.

Circular bank and ditch encircle stone pillars

Holes for wooden posts

↑
N

c.4500 BCE Neolithic communities in Europe construct monuments for tombs and sites where religious rites are celebrated. Stonehenge in the UK is thought to be one such ceremonial and burial site.

Three-stone arch, or trilithon

STONEHENGE

Ring of 30 large, upright stones

OX

SUN

FISH

CUNEIFORM

c.3300–2900 BCE The Sumerians of Mesopotamia, in present-day Iraq, develop cuneiform—the earliest-known form of writing. This writing is soon adopted by other civilizations in the region.

c.3200 BCE Chariots, the first form of wheeled transportation, are used widely in warfare. The Standard of Ur (2600 BCE) bears some of the earliest depictions of such wheeled transportation.

Sumerian war chariot with solid wheels drawn by wild asses

STANDARD OF UR

c.210,000 YA Having spread through much of Africa, the first *Homo sapiens*, following their hominin ancestors, migrate to Europe via the Middle East and reach central and eastern Asia.

H. sapiens begin migrating out of Africa

Humans start the slow, challenging sea crossing to Australia

HUMAN MIGRATION

58,000–38,000 BCE Seafarers cross from Indonesia into northern Australia when sea levels are relatively low. Humans then spread throughout the continent.

c.44,000 BCE Stone Age peoples create vivid cave paintings. One of the oldest yet discovered depicts a pig and buffalo hunt and appears on the back wall of a cave in Sulawesi, Indonesia.

Depiction of anoa, a smaller relative of water buffalo

SULAWESI CAVE PAINTING

c.26,000–19,000 BCE In Europe, the early Paleolithic people produce small statues of women, collectively called Venus figurines. They are carved from soft stone, bone, and ivory, or shaped from clay, which is then fired.

Complex hair or hat arrangement

VENUS FIGURINE

c.28,000–14,000 BCE In the last Ice Age, reduced sea levels expose a land bridge that allows humans and animals to cross from Asia into North America. Once the ice recedes, thousands of years later, people move further south.

c.38,000 BCE The last Neanderthals disappear from Europe. They may have struggled with climate change and then found it impossible to compete for resources with early *H. sapiens*.

c.43,000 BCE Evidence for the presence of European early modern humans (EEMH) in western Europe was discovered in the Cro-Magnon cave in France, in 1868.

Rounded skull

High, almost vertical forehead

EEMH CRANIUM

Few facial features, if any

c.9000 BCE Massive stone pillars arranged in circles are erected in Gobekli Tepe, Turkey. These are thought to be the first temple in human history.

Large T-shaped pillars set in stone walls

NEOLITHIC SHRINE

c.8000 BCE In Palestine, Jericho becomes the first place to be protected by a specially constructed defensive stone wall. Its towers are even older.

Staircase leading up to tower

Defensive wall

FIRST WALLED SETTLEMENT

Fertile region along River Nile

Memphis

LOWER EGYPT

UPPER EGYPT

ANCIENT EGYPT

c.5000 BCE Llamas are domesticated from camellike guanacos in the Peruvian Andes in South America. They are used as pack animals, most notably by the Incas.

c.5000 BCE Knowledge of working copper to make tools, weapons, and ornaments arrives in Egypt via Mesopotamia.

Cutting edge

Socket to fit wooden handle

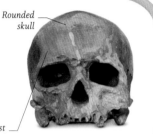

COPPER ADZE

Emphasis on hips and breasts possibly to depict fertility

c.3100 BCE The ruler of Upper Egypt, possibly called Menes or Narmer, invades Lower Egypt, and unifies the two kingdoms with Memphis as the capital.

Ceremonial sun disk with two bulls and a stag

c.3000 BCE In western Asia, people combine tin with copper to produce bronze—an even stronger metal, ideal for creating everything from weaponry to ornamentation—thus ushering in the Bronze Age.

BRONZE ARTIFACT, TURKEY

The first civilizations

As the climate warmed after the last Ice Age, and populations increased, prehistoric peoples across the world independently abandoned hunter-gathering in favor of agriculture, and their settlements grew into villages, towns, and cities. The first cities were founded in Mesopotamia's fertile river-plains in c. 4000 BCE; others—notably Memphis and Thebes in Egypt, and Harappa and Mohenjo Daro in the Indus Valley—followed.

Trade

Although the practice of exchanging goods is often associated with urban life, archaeological evidence suggests that a thriving trade in weapons and tools made of obsidian—a hard, black, volcanic glass—significantly predates the first settlements and cities. Obsidian artifacts found in Kenya's Olorgesailie basin—where the material does not occur locally—date to around 396,000 years ago, so must have been transported, and traded, by people from distant parts where the

Settling down

No one knows for certain why Stone Age peoples began to work the land in about 10,000 BCE. It may have been convenient to transplant wild crops closer to what became their new homes, or it could be that they simply recognized the potential of germinating seeds as a source of food. What we do know is that the peoples in each area developed specific crops to suit the local climate. In Mesoamerica, corn was being raised around 7000 BCE. Wheat had been domesticated in Mesopotamia

Carved lapis lazuli bead

Biconical carnelian bead

MESOPOTAMIAN BEAD BELT

material was more easily available. The obsidian used for tools and weapons discovered at Franchthi on the Greek mainland is thought to have been mined on the island of Minos and then traded across the Aegean more than 15,000 years ago. Carnelian and lapis lazuli jewelry were also traded widely, notably between the Indus Valley and Mesopotamia, and amber artifacts from Sicily were being traded in Spain by around 4000 BCE.

some 2,000 years earlier, while in China and southern Asia, rice cultivation started between 8000 BCE and 7000 BCE.

In some parts of the world, animals were domesticated before crops. Africa may have had domesticated cattle as early as 8500 BCE, but cereals, such as millet and sorghum, were not domesticated until about 4500 BCE and 3500 BCE. In Europe, pigs, sheep, and goats were also domesticated around 8500 BCE; the first evidence of domesticated horses dates to 3,500 years later.

Creating a surplus

Farming revolutionized prehistoric life. Raising crops and herding livestock demanded that people stayed put for long enough to reap the benefits. It provided a reasonably reliable source of nourishment that could satisfy immediate needs—and when crop yields were good, the surplus could be stockpiled for when times became harder. In Mesopotamia, the development of granaries meant that any surplus could be safely stored.

Traditionally, the changes farming brought about were thought to be sudden and dramatic. The modern view, however, is that the process was slower and more gradual than previously believed.

Earthenware decorated with pigments

Loop handle

NEOLITHIC CHINESE POT C. 2350 BCE

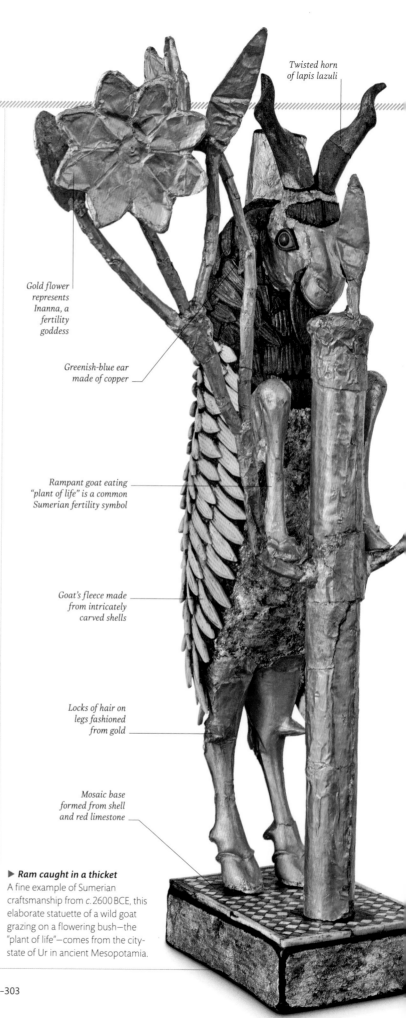

Twisted horn of lapis lazuli

Gold flower represents Inanna, a fertility goddess

Greenish-blue ear made of copper

Rampant goat eating "plant of life" is a common Sumerian fertility symbol

Goat's fleece made from intricately carved shells

Locks of hair on legs fashioned from gold

Mosaic base formed from shell and red limestone

▶ **Ram caught in a thicket**
A fine example of Sumerian craftsmanship from c. 2600 BCE, this elaborate statuette of a wild goat grazing on a flowering bush—the "plant of life"—comes from the city-state of Ur in ancient Mesopotamia.

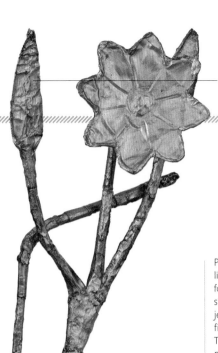

Leaf or bud always seen with flowers on "plant of life"

Gold leaf covers branches and tree trunk

"When **tillage** begins, **other arts** follow. **The farmers**, therefore, are the **founders of civilization**"

DANIEL WEBSTER, *On the Agriculture of England*, 1840

Pottery was a feature of the new settled lifestyle, and the same clay that was used for building houses was fashioned into storage vessels. Other craftspeople made jewelry and artworks, including striking figurines carved from stone and bone. They learned to weave, and produced material that was both useful and artistic.

Weaponry was also influenced by advances in technology. Warriors used copper for daggers, axes, and arrowheads that had initially been made of stone mounted on wooden handles and shafts.

The first towns

At the western end of Mesopotamia's Fertile Crescent—the land along the Tigris, Euphrates, and Nile rivers where the first farming settlements emerged at the dawn of the Neolithic Age—Çatalhöyük, in central Turkey, is thought to be one of the world's oldest towns. It was settled *c.*9,500 years ago; at its peak, it had as many as 8,000 inhabitants who grew wheat, barley, lentils, peas, and other legumes, and herded sheep and goats.

Houses in Çatalhöyük were built back-to-back with no doors or windows. They were accessed through an opening in the roof by a ladder which led to a single main room containing a hearth, oven, and sleeping platforms. Two ancillary rooms were used for storage and domestic work.

Elsewhere in Mesopotamia, Egypt, the Indus Valley, and China, towns like Çatalhöyük continued to grow, and

developed into cities. Urbanizaton on this scale was, until recently, thought to be a feature of the Old World. However, the Norte Chico civilization of Peru achieved a similar scale and compexity in cities like Caral. Set on an Andean plateau in the Supe Valley, the city was once a thriving metropolis with six stone pyramids, amphitheaters, ornate plazas, and houses. It was founded around 2600 BCE—about the same time as the Egyptian pyramids.

Ancient religions

It is difficult to pinpoint where religion began. It seems every culture developed its own belief in supernatural entities to explain natural phenomena—night, day, and the seasons—or to help individuals make sense of themselves. Most early religions were polytheistic, worshipping many gods, but some were henotheistic, with one god who took many forms.

In Mesopotamia, the first records of religious practice date from *c.*3500 BCE. Its powerful deities included Marduk, who defeated Tiamat and the forces of chaos to create the world, and Inanna, goddess of love, sex, and war. Ahura Mazda was the supreme god of ancient Indo-Iranians, supported by others, including Anahita, goddess of fertility, health, healing, water, and wisdom. The ancient Egyptians had multiple gods, but also regarded their pharaohs as deities. In Mesoamerica, the Maya worshipped more than 250 deities, each with their own sphere of influence.

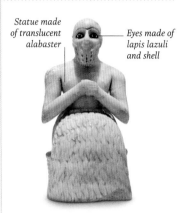

Statue made of translucent alabaster

Eyes made of lapis lazuli and shell

STATUE OF EBIH-IL, SUPERINTENDENT OF MARI, MESOPOTAMIA, C. 2400 BCE

Across the world, temples were filled with decorative objects and statues. Examples from Mari, in modern Syria, include votive statues of the worshippers themselves, a practice that allowed significant members of society, such as Ebih-Il (above), to be ever-present before their god.

City-states

Of all the factors that contributed to the evolution of human civilization, a source of water was one of the most important. This was certainly true of Mesopotamia, where Uruk, in Sumer, is considered to be the world's first city-state. At its height in *c.*2800 BCE, it had between 40,000 and 80,000 inhabitants who sheltered behind 6 miles (10 km) of defensive walls.

By *c.*1500 BCE city-states had flourished in the fertile basin of China's Yellow River and the Indus Valley in modern India and Pakistan. In the latter, the Harappans prospered from 3300 BCE to 1900 BCE, when their culture suddenly collapsed, either due to Aryan invaders moving south, or perhaps because tectonic shifts affected the rivers on which they relied.

Specialization

With the advent of agriculture, more food became available, and the size of populations grew. Settlements were set up, and these then expanded to become the first villages and towns. Specialized workers within them took advantage of the development of more advanced tools, especially towards the end of the Neolithic era (*c.*10,000–2500 BCE), when people started to use tools made from copper rather than stone. These Neolithic specialists included home-builders, who baked clay into bricks to create more substantial houses. Some also built defensive walls to protect themselves and their fellow citizens from outside attack.

INVENTION OF WRITING

As society grew more complex, record-keeping became a priority. Sumerian pictographs dating from *c.*3400 BCE represent the earliest-known form of writing, which was later simplified into wedge-shaped marks called cuneiform. The ancient Egyptians developed hieroglyphs, a pictorial form in which individual symbols represented ideas, sounds, and syllables. Written scripts also emerged in China, Mesoamerica, and possibly the Indus Valley. The earliest-known Chinese script was inscribed on oracle bones by fortune tellers in about 1200 BCE.

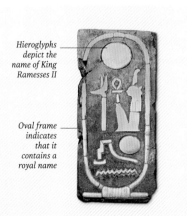

Hieroglyphs depict the name of King Ramesses II

Oval frame indicates that it contains a royal name

EGYPTIAN TILE WITH HIEROGLYPHS

SACRED CITY OF CARAL-SUPE, PERU

see also The ancient world pp.306–307 ▶   World religions pp.378–81 ▶   The history of writing pp.462–63 ▶

The ancient world
(3000 BCE–600 CE)

Complex states became established in North Africa and the Middle East in the early 4th millennium BCE, and later in China and the Americas. It is the period from which we have the first substantial written records, allowing historians to reconstruct the narrative of the rise of the empires of pharaonic Egypt, the Persian Achaemenids, and the Romans. As well as architectural splendors such as the pyramids and the temples of Teotihuacan in Mexico, this was a period of great religious ferment, giving rise to Confucianism, Buddhism, Judaism, classical Hinduism, and Christianity.

c.2580 BCE The huge Great Pyramid at Giza in Egypt is created to house the body of the pharaoh Khufu. Built of massive hand-cut limestone blocks, it originally stands 481 ft (147 m) high.

King's Chamber · Grand Gallery · Air shaft · Air shaft · Queen's Chamber · Entrance · Subterranean chamber

GREAT PYRAMID

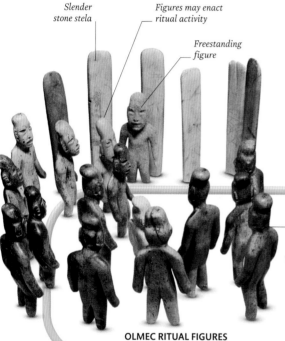

Slender stone stela
Figures may enact ritual activity
Freestanding figure
Figure made of jade

OLMEC RITUAL FIGURES

1274 BCE Armies led by Egyptian pharaoh Ramesses II and Hittite ruler King Muwatalli II clash in the Battle of Kadesh, a Syrian city and important center of trade. Both sides claim victory.

Ramesses's "victory" inscribed on temple walls

RELIEF OF WAR PRISONERS FROM KADESH

1500–1200 BCE The Vedas—religious, spiritual, and secular literature—are written in archaic Sanskrit, forming one of the earliest literary records of the people of northwest India.

1200 BCE The Olmec establish the city of San Lorenzo in southeast Mexico. The first great Mesoamerican culture, they excel at stone-carving and are famed for producing 9 ft- (3 m-) high basalt heads.

Shallow mortar for grinding plant matter

900 BCE The Chavín civilization flourishes in Peru, and culminates in a massive stone-block complex called Chavín de Huántar.

CHAVÍN JAGUAR STONE MORTAR

GREEK TERACOTTA POT

Eastern border
Western border

ROMAN EMPIRE IN WESTERN EUROPE, 14 CE

☐ Roman empire

27 BCE Following the assassination of Julius Caesar, Octavius, known as Augustus, becomes the first Roman emperor. By his death in 14 CE, the Roman Empire stretches from the English Channel to Egypt.

221 BCE After centuries of war between feudal states, the militaristic Qin state, in modern Shaanxi province, seizes all neighboring states. This creates a unified Chinese empire ruled by Shi Huang Di.

Ornamental "torana" ("gateway")

322 BCE Chandragupta Maurya overthrows the Nanda dynasty's Kingdom of Magadha in eastern India and founds the pan-Indian Maurya Empire, which eventually rules most of the subcontinent.

SANCHI STUPA, BUDDHIST SHRINE

220 CE The powerful and innovative Han Dynasty— which opened the Silk Road for trade between East and West— collapses, plunging China into disunity.

Central mountain connects to heaven

HAN ARTEFACT

300–600 CE Centered in modern northern Ethiopia, the Kingdom of Aksum reaches its apogee. Its kings derive huge wealth from controlling the trade in gold and ivory, becoming the first rulers in sub-Saharan Africa to mint coins.

KING EZRA'S STELA

378 CE Western pagan Gothic tribes rebel, defeating a Roman army, and killing Emperor Valens at the Battle of Adrianople. The Roman Empire begins to crumble.

Emperor Valens

ROMAN GOLD COIN

Square tablet

Raised projection

Raised images of animals, humans, and plant motifs

Undeciphered text

Carved from soft stone

INDUS SEALS

Stone is fired for durability

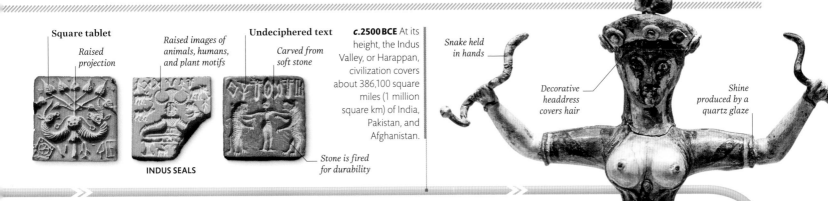

Small cat sits atop headdress

Snake held in hands

Decorative headdress covers hair

Shine produced by a quartz glaze

c.2500 BCE At its height, the Indus Valley, or Harappan, civilization covers about 386,100 square miles (1 million square km) of India, Pakistan, and Afghanistan.

Tight waistband with vertical stripes

c.1650 BCE The Shang dynasty is founded in northeast China. It is the first Chinese dynasty to leave written records and a highly developed calendar, as well as sophisticated bronze work.

Inscriptions

SHANG BRONZE GU (VESSEL)

Shamash, Babylonian god of justice

c.1775 BCE Hammurabi, king of Babylon, orders the Code of Hammurabi carved into a large black stone stela. It contains 282 laws on trade, fines, and more.

LAW CODE STELA

c.2000 BCE Wealthy Minoan rulers on the island of Crete build luxurious palaces, some housing hundreds of people, filled with decorative objects and complete with water and sewer systems.

SNAKE "GODDESS"

c.800 BCE Following a dark age, the Greek population sees a large increase. Preceding the Classical period, this Archaic age witnesses the founding of poleis, Greek city-states defined by their centrality in administrative and religious spheres.

Geometric patterns

509 BCE After centuries of rule by monarchs, Romans founded the Roman Republic by instituting government by elected magistrates.

Letters mean "Roman Senate and People"

EMBLEM OF ROMAN REPUBLIC

SPQR

334 BCE Macedon's Alexander III, known as "the Great," invades Persia in a campaign that sees him conquer most of their known world.

ALEXANDER THE GREAT

c.450 BCE Based in Switzerland, the Iron Age Celtic culture known as La Tène reaches its peak, characterized by advanced metalwork.

ANCIENT OSTRACON

508 BCE Cleisthenes, leader of the Greek city of Athens, introduces a system of political reforms called demokratia or "rule by the people," creating the first democracy.

Ceremonial clothing

Layered floor-length skirt

c. 5th century CE Buddhism is established in China, brought from India by traders. Chinese monks such as Faxian (in 399) travel to India in search of Buddhist texts and others spread the religion further afield.

Decoration carved into stone

BUDDHA RELIEF, CHINA, c.420–589

476 CE German warrior Odoacer overthrows Roman emperor Augustulus to become king of Italy, signaling the end of the Western Roman Empire. Odoacer is later ousted by Gothic ruler Theodoric.

Woodcut of Odoacer

ODOACER AND THEODORIC

531 CE The reign of Khosrow I, Sassanian Persia's greatest king, begins. He reforms the taxation system, reduces the power of provincial aristocrats, and engages in a series of successful military campaigns. The empire's borders expand to the east.

Ancient China

By about 4500 BCE, Neolithic cultures along the banks of China's Yangtze and Yellow Rivers, thriving on the surplus produced from millet and rice-growing, had begun to develop into states. A series of imperial dynasties vied for control until 221 BCE, when the whole country was united under the Qin. This marked the beginning of a long period of prosperity in which China projected its power into neighboring areas of central and Southeast Asia.

The beginning of China

From about 4500 BCE, a series of complex Neolithic cultures emerged in China. The Hongshan of the northeast were skilled workers in jade, making turtles and dragons, while the Yangshao of the Yellow River valley may have had a shamanistic religious system, and built a small town protected by a moat at Banpo. Around 3000 BCE, they were succeeded by the Longshan, who used the potter's wheel to make delicate black ceramics. Then, around 1900 BCE, they developed into the Erlitou culture, China's first Bronze Age civilization, whose rich graves indicate a more hierarchical society possibly associated with the Xia, widely regarded as China's first ruling dynasty.

Geometrical patterns painted in red and dark brown **Handle**

NEOLITHIC MAJIAYAO JAR

Shang dynasty

Numerous small states had appeared by 2000 BCE—a period known as *wan guo* ("ten thousand states"). Around 1650 BCE, the Shang established a capital at Zhengzhou in Henan, becoming China's first historically attested dynasty. The capital had huge defensive earthwork walls. "Oracle bones" were discovered within—animal bones used for divination and inscribed with the earliest form of Chinese writing. The Shang also made high-quality bronze objects used in religious rituals. Royal graves found at Anyang were lavish: that of Queen Fu Hao contained 468 bronze items, 755 jade objects, and several ivory cups.

Elaborately decorated hilt   *Broad blade*

RITUAL SHANG DAGGER-AXE

Zhou China

According to Chinese tradition, the last Shang king was a cruel, leisure-loving man who neglected the government, sparking a revolt in the subordinate kingdom of Zhou in the west. Around 1046 BCE, its ruler, Wu, took the Shang capital and began his own Zhou dynasty, with its capital at Fenghao, near modern Xian. The Zhou adopted many Shang practices but also introduced *fengjian*—a new system designed to control their extended domain—in which large areas were ruled semiautonomously by relatives of the king. The system broke down in 771 BCE after rebels allied with invading northern barbarians, forcing the Zhou to retreat to a smaller area around Luoyang.

The Warring States period

During the Spring and Autumn period (771–481 BCE), a growing number of states broke away from Zhou rule, and warfare between them was frequent. However, the period was culturally rich in political theorists and philosophers such as Confucius and Laozi, the founders of Confucianism and Daoism respectively.

As the Warring States period (481–221 BCE) began, the states gradually consolidated until about 300 BCE, by which time only seven remained. The westernmost, Qin, then initiated reforms that bolstered its armies, before launching a campaign of conquest against the other six states.

First Emperor and Terracotta Army

Within 25 years of his accession to the throne of Qin in 246 BCE, Prince Zheng had conquered all of the other warring states to become Qin Shi Huangdi, first emperor of a unified China. He enforced a policy of rigid centralization, transplanting the families of defeated states to live in the royal capital Xianyang and burning their dynastic records. He abolished feudal fiefs, imposed uniform weights and a script, and built the first version of the Great Wall of China to act as a defense against barbarians. The latter part of his reign was marred by his compulsive search for elixirs of immortality, and when he died he was buried with 8,000 life-size terracotta warriors intended to serve him in the afterlife.

The Han and the Silk Road

In 202 BCE, Liu Bang, one of a series of rebels against Qin Shi Huangdi's unpopular son, Qin Er Shi, emerged victorious and declared himself Gaozu, first emperor of the Han. From his capital at Changan, trading caravans could now travel deep into central Asia across a network of routes that became known as the Silk Road. They carried Chinese goods as far west as the Roman Empire, with gold, silver, and prized commodities such as central Asian horses traveling in the opposite direction. The Silk Road helped establish Chinese power in a series of oasis towns along its length, and also allowed new ideas, such as Buddhism, to cross into China.

Han technology

The long Han dynasty (202 BCE–220 CE) saw many advances in technology, such as an improved moldboard plough for tilling, a chain pump powered by waterwheels to assist irrigation, and an early version of the compass, which used a magnetized metal ladle. In the 1st century BCE, a type of wheelbarrow was devised for carrying loads small distances, while the invention of paper in 105 CE made record-keeping cheaper. The Han scholar Zhang Heng even demonstrated a seismometer in 132 in which balls dropping from the mouths of metal dragons indicated the direction of the earth tremor.

> "He is **merciless** ... should he succeed in **conquering the empire**, we shall **all** become his **captives**."
>
> WEI LIAO, On the Emperor Qin Shi Huangdi, *c.*220 BCE

◀ **Emperor Wu-ti**
In this illustrated history of Chinese emperors, painted on silk, Emperor Wu-ti (141–87 BCE) exits his palace.

Han expansion in central and Southeast Asia

The Han state was stronger than its predecessors and soon began to expand China's borders. Under Wu-ti (141–87 BCE), the empire reached the height of its power. He fought wars against the Xiongnu on the northern border, which enabled him to conquer the Hexi Corridor in 121 BCE and then push into the Tarim Basin, establishing control over a large part of central Asia, which the Chinese referred to as the Western Regions. Wu-ti also conquered northern Vietnam in 111 BCE, occupied part of Korea in 128 BCE, and expanded the state's control over southern China.

Arm acts as funnel, trapping smoke in body

Kneeling servant girl

HAN OIL LAMP

The decline of the Han

In 9 CE, the Han were briefly deposed by a usurping official. Despite their restoration in 25 CE, they failed to recover their former prestige. Their new eastern capital at Luoyang became increasingly vulnerable to palace intrigues and the domination of the court by eunuch-ministers. A series of child-emperors were helpless to enact reforms, corrupt ministers siphoned revenue, and a series of droughts and floods heightened rural unrest. In 184–186 a revolt by the Yellow Turbans, a religious sect, shattered the eunuchs' power. After the last Han emperor was deposed in 220, China once again broke apart into a group of warring kingdoms.

see also China: the Tang, Song, and Ming dynasties pp.322–23 ▶   Trade and exploration pp.340–41 ▶   Great philosophers p.386 ▶

Ancient Egypt

Egypt was the ancient world's most enduring civilization, lasting for 3,000 years. During this time, 32 dynasties of pharaohs ruled a kingdom centered on the Nile river, and constructed temples, palaces, and lavish tombs (including pyramids) on which they left hieroglyphic inscriptions recording their achievements and praising their vast array of gods. They created a period of prosperity and cultural continuity that ended only with Egypt's conquest by the Roman empire in 30 BCE.

The land and the Nile
Egypt was referred to as the "gift of the Nile" as the river's annual flooding deposited fertile silt along its banks, vastly enhancing the land's agricultural potential, and encouraging the early development of irrigation techniques. All of Egypt's main population centers clustered in a thin ribbon around the river. This *kemet*, or "black land," stood in stark contrast to the *deshret*, or "red land," of the Western and Eastern Desert, where only a few oases and mines gave incentive to venture.

The unification of Egypt
Politically, early Egypt was divided into two kingdoms: Upper Egypt, in the south, and Lower Egypt, in the north. Around 3100 BCE, the ruler of Upper Egypt conquered the north and united the country, symbolically joining the *deshret*, or "red crown," of Lower Egypt to his own *hedjet*, or "white crown." While his exact identity remains uncertain, he was named in later histories as Menes, but may be the Narmer depicted on a contemporary siltstone palette, or Aha, the founder of the First Dynasty.

The Old Kingdom
During the Egyptian Old Kingdom, from 2686 to 2181 BCE, a centralized state emerged, based around the capital at Memphis. The pharaohs divided the land into regions called *nomes*, each with its own *nomarch* (governor), and began to build large stone monuments. They also projected Egyptian power abroad, with military expeditions to Canaan in the east and Nubia in the south.

The age of the pyramids
Early pharaohs were buried in mud-brick rectangular tombs, but around 2650 BCE Pharaoh Djoser created a step pyramid when he instructed his chief minister Imhotep to have several layers of these bricks placed on top of each other. During the 4th Dynasty (2613–2494 BCE), true pyramids of stone appeared. The largest of these was Khufu's Great Pyramid, or the Great Pyramid of Giza, which required over 2 million blocks of stone and the employment of thousands of laborers.

The Middle Kingdom
The Old Kingdom ended with a period of famine and the dissolution of Egypt into regional kingdoms. Around 2050 BCE Mentuhotep II, the ruler of Thebes in the south, reunified Egypt, initiating the Middle Kingdom era, which lasted until 1640 BCE. Strong central rule was restored and Egypt sent trading expeditions to the land of Punt, south of Nubia. The power of the *nomarchs* was severely curtailed, impeding the emergence of independent regions, which had destabilized the Old Kingdom, and Middle Kingdom pharaohs resumed the building of pyramid tombs at el-Lisht and Dahshur. Under the 12th Dynasty (1991–1786 BCE), Egypt's armies fought in Syria, Palestine, and Nubia, but the Middle Kingdom had lost its vigor, and when the Hyksos (invaders from West Asia) settled in the Nile Delta around 1725 BCE, Egypt once again split up into competing states.

> "I am the dirt beneath the sandals of the king ... **My lord is the Sun** who comes forth over all lands day by day."
>
> KING OF TYRE, Letter to Amenhotep IV, *c.*1417 BCE

Religion and beliefs about the dead
The Egyptian pantheon included many gods, chief among them Horus, the sky god, the sun deity, Re, his consort, Isis, and Osiris, lord of the dead. Many of these gods were often depicted with animal heads, such as the king of the gods, Amon (a ram), and the god of the underworld, Anubis (a jackal).

The Egyptians mummified noble corpses and carried out complex rituals to ensure the survival of the soul after death. Tomb walls were covered with spells to help the dead safely journey to the underworld and to undergo ordeals such as the weighing of their sins against a feather.

The New Kingdom
Egypt reached its greatest level of power and prosperity in the New Kingdom era (1567–1085 BCE). In 1330 BCE Tutankhamun (1334–1325 BCE) began to restore the shrines of Amon, reversing damage inflicted during his father's rule. Later, the longest-reigning ruler, Rameses II (1290–1223 BCE), built a huge temple at Abu Simbel in Egypt's far south.

— **Ceremonial beard**

TUTANKHAMUN'S DEATH MASK

Egypt's empire in the Near East
While Egypt had intervened in the Near East during the Middle Kingdom, its armies campaigned further afield in the New Kingdom. Tuthmosis III (1504–1450 BCE) sent almost 20 expeditions to Syria and Palestine, reaching as far as the Euphrates and forcing the Mitanni people to accept Egyptian overlordship. After Rameses II suffered a defeat at the hands of the Hittites at Qadesh in 1274 BCE, Egypt's power in the area waned.

Human features housed spirit of deceased

Highly decorated wooden exterior

22ND DYNASTY SARCOPHAGUS

SCIENCE, MATHS, AND MEDICINE
Egyptians invented the first ox-drawn plow around 4000 BCE and also the *shaduf*, a water-transfer device to aid irrigation. Mathematicians could solve quadratic equations, while doctors, although unaware of the functioning of internal organs, still carried out basic surgery.

EYE DOCTOR AT WORK

Temples and the Valley of the Kings
There were sanctuaries to local deities in most Egyptian towns. Among the largest is the Great Hypostyle Hall in the temple of Amun-Re at Karnak (*c*.1250 BCE). On the opposite bank of the Nile, New Kingdom pharaohs were buried in opulent tombs in the Valley of the Kings.

Late-period Egypt
After the New Kingdom's collapse, Egypt experienced a period of fragmentation, including rule by Libyan and Nubian dynasties. The restoration of native Egyptian rule under Psamtik I in 664 BCE marked ancient Egypt's final period of flourishing. Even so, it suffered more than a century of Persian rule (525–404 BCE), and then Ptolemy, one of Alexander the Great's former generals, established a final, Macedonian, dynasty in 323 BCE.

The Ptolemies
During the Ptolemaic era (323–30 BCE), most pharaohs married their siblings to maintain a purely Macedonian lineage. The victory of Ptolemy III (246–221 BCE) in 241 BCE against the Seleucids, a Hellenistic dynasty, solidified Egypt's power, but infighting among its leaders and a gradual increase in Roman influence saw Egypt falter, before losing independence entirely with the Roman conquest of 30 BCE.

◀ Tomb fresco
Pharaoh Ramesses I (left) stands with Ptah, a god believed to grant the deceased the ability to eat and drink in the afterlife.

see also Mythology pp.388–89 ▶ **311**

Ancient Greece

The Greek island of Crete was home to Europe's earliest developed civilization about 4,000 years ago. Greece's small mainland city-states eventually developed a vibrant culture as well, colonizing the Mediterranean and giving rise to advances in science, philosophy, and democracy. However, feuding sapped their power and, despite fighting off challenges from Persia, they eventually succumbed to Alexander the Great's Macedon.

The Minoans

Minoan culture developed around 2000 BCE in Cretan cities, which became rich trading throughout the eastern Mediterranean. Its rulers, based around elaborate palaces such as Knossos and Phaistos, were both political and religious leaders. The Minoans created sophisticated administrations, with records kept in Linear A, an as yet-undeciphered script. They were not warlike, and around 1450 BCE an earthquake and invasions by the Mycenaeans led to their decline.

Mycenaeans

Around 1600 BCE Mycenaean palace-culture arose in the Peloponnese in southern Greece. The Mycenaeans built fortress strongholds, such as Mycenae, Pylos, and Tiryns, with monumental stone walls, buried their rulers in shaft-graves packed with lavish grave goods, and left extensive archives in Linear B script. Their decorated pottery and colorful painted frescoes were influenced by the Minoan culture. Most Mycenaean palatial centers suffered catastrophic destruction around 1200 BCE, possibly at the hands of raiders.

Emergence of the city-states

After the fall of Mycenaean civilization, Greece entered a dark age from which no written records survive. Gradually, smaller centers expanded to become *poleis* (city-states), with control over a hinterland of villages. Most were originally monarchies, but around 650 BCE tyrants took power in many city-states. Fighting between the city-states' hoplites, or citizen-soldiers, was frequent, and by about 600 BCE Thebes, Corinth, Sparta, and Athens became dominant.

Greek colonization

Starting in the late 9th century BCE, the Greek city-states had sent colonists throughout the Mediterranean and western Asia Minor. They founded new settlements tied to their original home city by bonds of kinship. Among the first was Syracuse, founded in eastern Sicily around 733 BCE. The colonization in southern Italy was so dense that the area became known as *Magna Graecia* ("Greater Greece"), which became a conduit for Greek influence on emerging Roman culture.

Greek religion and temples

The Greek pantheon encompassed many gods, headed by Zeus and his wife Hera, who were believed to live on Mount Olympus with other immortals such as Athena, goddess of wisdom and patron goddess of Athens. Temples dedicated to the gods proliferated in most Greek cities. Oracles, such as that of the god Apollo at Delphi attracted many visitors seeking counsel, and an annual cycle of festivals and ceremonies honored the gods, such as the Panathenaea in Athens.

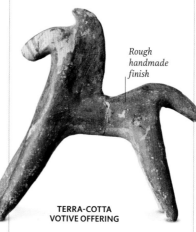

Rough handmade finish

TERRA-COTTA VOTIVE OFFERING

Greek philosophy

The Greeks might have been the first civilization to think about the nature of the world beyond considering it the plaything of the gods. From the 6th to the 3rd century BCE philosophers studied geometry, ethics, and speculated about the prime material of the universe, with Thales of Miletus (624–546 BCE) believing it was water. Successors, such as Socrates (469–399 BCE), Plato (427–347 BCE), and Aristotle (384–322 BCE) brought a new rigor to philosophy and remain influential to this day.

▶ Greek "red figure" cup

The decoration on this ancient Greek cup, dating from about 490 BCE, depicts a diner reclining at a banquet, entertained by a musician playing pipes.

Greco-Persian Wars

In 499 BCE, Athens aided the Greek cities of western Asia Minor in their revolt against Persian rule. In revenge, Persian ruler Darius (550–487 BCE) invaded in 490 BCE. Against the odds, the Athenians defeated him at Marathon. Ten years later Xerxes (519–465 BCE), Darius' son, mounted an even larger invasion. Some Greek city-states defected, but steadfast Spartan resistance at Thermopylae and an Athenian naval victory at Salamis turned the tide.

Peloponnesian war

Rivalry between Athens and Sparta grew as Sparta sought to export its model of a military elite, while Athens promoted democracy. In 432 BCE war broke out between the two powers when the city of Potidaea, an Athenian ally, sought to defect to Sparta. In 415 BCE, Athens was repelled from Syracuse, a Spartan ally. Besieged Athens eventually surrendered to Spartan rule in 404 BCE.

Hellenistic world

Alexander the Great inherited the Greek states from his conquering father, Philip (382–336 BCE), and went on to conquer the Persian Empire and beyond. After his death, Alexander's empire broke up into successor states, such as the Ptolemies in Egypt. He had ordered the foundation of Greek colonies in his empire and these cities became centers through which Greek culture, known as Hellenism, spread further east, reaching what is now modern India and Afghanistan.

> ## "Like frogs around a pond we have settled upon the shores of this sea."
>
> SOCRATES, In Plato's *Phaedo*

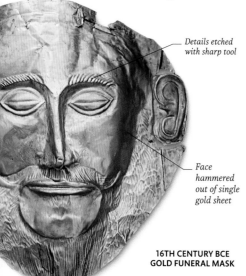

Details etched with sharp tool

Face hammered out of single gold sheet

16TH CENTURY BCE GOLD FUNERAL MASK

Athenian democracy

The city-state of Athens developed an early form of democracy in which the citizenry (which excluded women, slaves, and foreigners) had a greater say than they did under tyranny. In 508 BCE Cleisthenes (570–507 BCE), a magistrate, devised a new constitution under which 140 *demes* (voting districts) annually chose members to a 500-strong council. Any man who qualified for Athenian citizenship could also attend a meeting of the *ekklesia* (the principal assembly of Athens), which gathered to vote on important matters, including military strategy and the choice of military leaders. Members could also vote to exile politicians by a special vote known as an ostracism.

ALEXANDER THE GREAT

In 336 BCE, Alexander (356–323 BCE) became king of Macedon, a Greek kingdom, succeeding his father, Philip, who had already conquered most of Greece. In 334 BCE Alexander invaded the Persian Achaemenid empire, defeating its ruler Darius III (381–330 BCE) in several battles, despite being hugely outnumbered. By 331 BCE he was the master of Persia, but continued to press on even further, into India. Only the threat of mutiny from homesick soldiers, and his death from fever in 323 BCE, put an end to Alexander's military campaigns.

Ancient Rome

From its beginnings as an obscure hilltop town in central Italy in the mid-8th century BCE, Rome steadily expanded and conquered until it controlled first Italy, then southern and most of western Europe, North Africa, and large parts of the Near East. Roman-style towns with temples and amphitheatres sprang up throughout the empire, defended by an incredibly effective army. The imperial system remained dominant until barbarian invaders in the 4th and 5th centuries CE caused its collapse.

The origins of Rome

Later Roman tradition related that the city had been founded in 753 BCE by Romulus, the son of the war-god Mars. In reality, the first settlement, which dated from the early 8th century BCE, formed on the boundary of influence between local Latin tribes and the sophisticated Etruscan states to the north. It was ruled by a series of seven kings, some of them of Etruscan origin. The second king, Numa Pompilius, was said to have established many Roman religious traditions, and the later king Servius Tullius gave Rome its first defensive wall in the mid-6th century BCE. Although the kings expanded Rome's territory in central Italy, the last, Tarquinius Superbus, was a cruel tyrant and in 510 BCE was expelled from Roman territory in a successful aristocratic uprising.

Romulus and Remus suckle from a she-wolf

CAPITOLINE WOLF STATUE

50,000: the approximate **capacity** of the **Colosseum** in Rome, the **largest amphitheater** in the empire

The Republic

After the monarchy's fall, Rome became a Republic governed by a Senate and two annually elected consuls, whose main duty was to lead the army. The infant Republic was troubled by a struggle between rich landowners, the patricians, and the more numerous, landless, plebeians until the creation of the Tribunes of the Plebs in 494 BCE to protect their interests.

The conquest of Italy

Beginning with victories against the alliance of local towns—the Latin League—in 499 BCE, Roman armies steadily gained territory. Three wars with the Samnites in central Italy between 343 and 290 BCE resulted in the annexation of central Italy, and having defeated Greeks in the south and Etruscans to the north, by 264 BCE the Romans ruled the entire Italian peninsula.

Hannibal and the Punic Wars

Rome faced its greatest military challenge during the three Punic Wars against the Carthaginians, a maritime people with an empire in North Africa and Sicily. During the second Punic War (218–201 BCE) the Carthaginian general Hannibal invaded Italy and inflicted several devastating defeats against the Romans before withdrawing. Only with the destruction of Carthage in 146 BCE did the threat end.

Julius Caesar

By the late Republic, power in Rome had devolved to military strongmen. In 49 BCE civil war broke out between Pompey, a popular general, and Julius Caesar, who had won glory conquering Gaul (France). Caesar won a decisive victory and was made dictator for life in 44 BCE, but was then assassinated by traditionalists who feared he wanted to make himself king.

The Roman army

A formidable force, the army under the early Empire consisted of about 28 legions, each with 5,000 men supported by noncitizen troops, including specialist units of cavalry and archers. The disciplined legionaries were devastating against less well-trained opponents.

Sloping neck guard for extra protection

REPLICA LEGIONARY HELMET

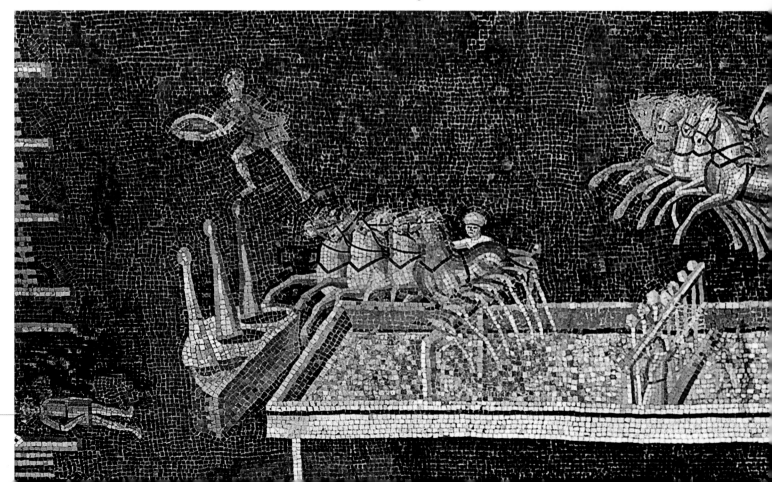

> "I had **extinguished the flames** of civil war ... **For this service** on my part **I was given the title of Augustus** by decree of the Senate."
>
> *Res Gestae Divi Augusti (The Will of Emperor Augustus)*, 14 CE

The dawn of the Imperial system

After Julius Caesar's death in 44 BCE, his supporters first defeated his assassins and then fought among themselves. In 31 BCE Caesar's heir, Octavian (r.27 BCE–14 CE), defeated Mark Antony, his former ally, in a naval battle at Actium. Four years later he had the Senate grant him extraordinary powers. Taking the title Augustus, he became Rome's first emperor, making conquests along the Danube and in Germany, before bequeathing the empire to Tiberius (r.14–37 CE) in 14 CE.

The Empire at its height

The pace of expansion was slower after Augustus. Trajan (r.98–117 CE), the first non-Italian emperor, expanded the Empire to its greatest extent, seizing Dacia (modern Romania) and much of Mesopotamia in western Asia. After his death, his adoptive son Hadrian (r.117–138 CE) concentrated on stabilizing the empire's borders, ordering the building of Hadrian's Wall across the northern frontier in Britain.

Military anarchy

Successive emperors struggled to make the government of the vast empire more manageable, and after the murder of Alexander Severus in 235 CE, the system broke down. A half-century of short-lived rulers, mainly soldiers, destabilized the empire and Gaul and Britain broke away, followed by most of the east under Zenobia, queen of Palmyra, Syria, in the 260s. Aurelian (214–275) reunited the empire by 273, but it was severely weakened.

Diocletian and the reorganization

In 284 CE, the army raised an officer, Diocletian, to be emperor. Rather than trying to rule alone, he chose a former colleague, Maximian, to share the imperial throne with him. Diocletian ruled the Eastern Empire, and Maximian the Western. In 293, each of them picked another junior emperor (or "Caesar") to assist him. This Tetrarchy (system of four emperors), worked at first, but collapsed after Diocletian abdicated in 305.

Constantine and Christianity

Declared emperor in the Western Empire by his army in 306 CE, six years later Constantine defeated his rival to the position, Maxentius (son of Maximan), outside Rome. He was the first emperor to legalize Christianity, and he outlawed religious persecution. Further victories meant that by 324 he was undisputed emperor, allowing him to reform the administration, separating military and civil positions, and call the Council of Nicaea, a council of bishops, in 325, resulting in the first uniform Christian doctrine.

THE DONATION OF CONSTANTINE

Barbarian invasion

Pressure on the imperial frontiers grew from the 3rd century CE, as federations of Germanic barbarians beyond the borders grew in strength. Incursions into the empire became more frequent and in 378 the Visigoths broke through and destroyed a large Roman army at Adrianople. In 406, a large barbarian army crossed the Rhine and rampaged through Gaul, occupying much of Spain and crossing into North Africa.

Collapse and survival

As barbarians seized more Roman provinces the empire could no longer raise the tax revenue to pay its army. Rome itself was sacked in 410 and 455 CE, and the emperors became puppets of their Germanic army chiefs. Finally in 476 one of the chiefs, Odoacer, deposed the last western Roman emperor Romulus Augustulus. A separate line of emperors survived in the eastern part of the empire until 1453. Its capital was Constantinople, formerly called Byzantium.

▼ Imperial games

This late-2nd century CE Roman mosaic shows a chariot race in progress. Horse races were a favorite pastime.

Ancient Americas

By 1000 BCE, a series of advanced cultures had emerged from the corn-growing villages of the Americas, based around large ceremonial centers. The Olmecs of Mexico and Chavín of Peru constructed cities with elaborate temples and palaces at their heart, while in North America less dense settlements formed part of wide-ranging trading networks. In Central America, writing systems documented a series of struggles between Maya city-states that may have contributed to their collapse around 900 CE.

No eye holes indicates mask was not for wearing

Cleft head characteristic of Olmec carvings

OLMEC MASK

Olmecs

Date	1500 BCE–400 BCE
Location	Mexico

The Olmecs established Central America's first civilization, building cities such as La Venta and San Lorenzo with drainage systems, pools for religious rituals and bathing, plazas, and temples. They carved colossal stone heads from boulders of basalt, weighing up to 55 tons (50 tonnes), which may represent powerful Olmec rulers. Their art depicts jaguars and human-animal hybrid creatures, and they may have developed a writing system as early as 900 BCE, which would be the earliest in the Western Hemisphere.

Maya

Date	750 BCE–1697 CE
Location	Mexico, Guatemala, Honduras, Belize

The Maya people lived in a series of city-states linked by trading networks, which flourished from around 750 BCE, each with central plazas and great stone-built temples, pyramids, buildings for astronomical observations, and courts for a ritual ball-game. The reason for the collapse of the Maya cities is still unknown, but today about 8 million descendants still reside in their original homeland of Mesoamerica.

Chavín culture

Date	500 BCE–300 BCE
Location	Peru

Among the earliest advanced cultures of South America, the corn-growing Chavín built a massive temple complex at Chavín de Huantar, centered on the Lanzón, a 16 ft- (5 m) high thin granite shaft, called a stela. The Lanzón depicts a hybrid human-jaguar deity, an image frequently found in Chavín art, and likely predates the construction around it. The temple complex oversaw the convergence and dissemination of ideological, cultural, and religious ideas. Their gods included a smiling deity, an alligator god, and a divine figure bearing two staffs.

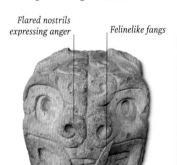

Flared nostrils expressing anger

Felinelike fangs

SMILING GOD

Adena culture

Date	1000 BCE–100 CE
Location	Central Ohio Valley

The Adena, Native American hunters and cultivators of pumpkin, squash, and tobacco, lived in settlements along the Ohio River. They built huge earthwork mounds, which they used for burials and as ceremonial platforms. They painted the bodies of their dead with ocher and other bright pigments, and interred them in log-lined tombs with grave goods including fine flint blades, clay pipes, copper bracelets, marine shells, and stone tablets engraved with animal designs. The mounds may also have functioned as territorial markers.

Face of lightning deity Cociyo

Forked snake tongue

CLAY URN DEPICTING ZAPOTEC GOD

Zapotecs

Date	500 BCE–900 CE
Location	Oaxaca Valley, Mexico

From their hilltop stronghold of Monte Albán, the Zapotecs overlooked and united most of Mexico's Oaxaca Valley. Zapotec rulers expanded their territory through military conquest and colonization, integrating defeated settlements into the Zapotec empire. They used the wealth from their conquests to build pyramids and ritual ball-game courts, and one of their temples depicts captive rival chieftains in grotesque poses, known as the *danzantes* ("dancers") friezes. Glyphs carved into these stone friezes at Monte Albán reveal a sophisticated writing system and calendar. Zapotec religion was polytheistic, with many of their deities linked to agriculture and fertility, and they also worshipped gods from other Mesoamerican cultures. For unknown reasons, by 900 CE Monte Albán was deserted, and remained so for centuries.

Cacao was first cultivated in **Central America. A thick drink made from cocoa beans** was consumed by the **ruling elite** as far back as 1900 BCE

◀ **Zapotec tomb mural**
Archaeologists discovered 170 tombs in Monte Albán in southern Mexico, each one filled with carvings and artifacts, and decorated with vivid paintings.

Nazca

Date	100 BCE–800 CE
Location	Southern Peru

Village-dwelling farmers, hunters, and metalworkers with a large ceremonial center at Cahuachi, the Nazca produced beautiful polychrome ceramics depicting humanized mythical beings. They also created geoglyphs, enormous drawings etched into the desert, showing a range of animals and abstract shapes. These highly elaborate shapes, with examples including a hummingbird sucking nectar, can only be seen in full from the air. The civilization vanished suddenly around 800 CE.

Ceremonial tumi knife to sever head

Half-human half-jaguar "Decapitator" deity

NAZCA POT

Hopewell

Date	100 BCE–500 CE
Location	Midwest of the US

Centered in the Ohio valley, the Hopewell culture farmed corn and squash, hunted for wild game, and produced high-quality metalwork of beaten copper. They built elaborate burial mounds, such as the 1,246 ft- (380 m-) long Great Serpent Mound in southern Ohio, in which they buried their elite in log-lined tombs, with grave goods including fine squat pottery decorated with bird motifs. Exotic raw materials, which the Hopewell used to make intricate works of art, came to the Hopewell's territory through long-distance trade networks that stretched as far as the Rocky Mountains, the Carolinas, and the Gulf of Mexico.

Nomads and tribes

In ancient times, central Asia was home to an unstable series of kingdoms, tribal federations, and nomadic groups. Over time, as these broke up, waves of peoples were pushed to migrate, often displacing settled peoples, such as the Celts and the Goths of Europe. Nomadic life bred skilled warriors, especially horse-borne archers, allowing groups such as the Huns and the Mongols to carve out huge empires spanning multiple continents.

Hallstatt and La Tène cultures
Developing out of the late Bronze-Age Urnfield culture of central Europe around 1250 BCE, the Hallstatt people were most likely ancestors of the Celts. They had a strong warrior tradition, a tribal structure, and a love of horses. By 500 BCE they had developed into the Iron Age La Tène, who lived in small, self-sufficient settlements in France, and spread into eastern Europe. La Tène culture was characterized by swirling, spiral patterns in their jewelry and metalwork.

Two joined pieces of sheet-bronze

HALLSTATT HELMET

Celts in the British Isles
It remains unclear whether large numbers of Celts migrated to Britain or whether the native British simply adopted Celtic culture. Nonetheless, by about 800 BCE Hallstatt culture, and shortly after 500 BCE, La Tène culture had reached Britain (and soon after, Ireland). Celtic tribal kingdoms flourished for hundreds of years. In England, Wales, and southern Scotland the Celts ruled until the Roman conquest in 43 CE; in Ireland they survived into the 12th century.

Scabbard decorated with bronze strips

CELTIC DAGGER IN SHEATH

Pazyryk burials
In the high valleys of the Altai mountains in Siberia around the 6th–2nd centuries BCE, the Pazyryk people buried their dead in huge mounds or *kurgans*, together with beautifully preserved textiles, including depictions of horsemen—archaeological evidence suggests the Pazyryk people were nomadic horse-riding herders. The buried men bore tattoos depicting mythological creatures.

The Scythians
The Scythians were fearsome warriors who lived in southern Russia and Ukraine from the 9th century BCE. Fighting on horseback with bows, arrows, and axes, they raided as far as Babylon and Assyria, and at home grew rich on trade with the Greek cities around the Black Sea. This allowed them to produce beautiful golden objects including discs in the form of birds of prey. Around 300 CE, they finally succumbed to waves of attacks from Germanic tribes moving westward.

The Hephthalites and Saka
An ethnically Iranian people, the Saka ruled a series of kingdoms on the steppes from around the 6th century BCE before attacking northern India around 88 BCE. There, they set up kingdoms that lasted about two centuries. The Hephthalites (or White Huns) dominated central Asia from the mid-6th to the mid-7th century CE and exerted great pressure on the Sassanian Persian Empire from the east, weakening it severely.

The Xiongnu
From the 3rd century BCE, the Xiongnu were nomadic cattle breeders who carved out an empire on the Mongolian steppes. Their light cavalry, armed with composite bows, harassed the borders of the Han Chinese Empire, who sent princesses to marry Xiongnu leaders in 200 BCE in a bid to stop the raids. The Xiongnu controlled a key sector of the Silk Road trade route between China and the West until their replacement by the Xianbei, another nomadic federation, around 90 CE.

The age of the Huns
The Huns erupted from central Asia in the 370s CE, attacking the Roman Empire, the Persian Empire, and the Gupta Empire (in northern India). Later, in the 430s, the various Hun tribes united under Attila and fought the Roman Empire in nearly two decades of highly destructive warfare, until 453, when Attila died, and the Hun Empire soon fell apart.

The Goths divide
In the late 4th century CE the Goths—a Germanic people settled around the Black Sea—launched a series of attacks against the Roman Empire. They went on to divide into two groups, the Ostrogoths and Visigoths, and established kingdoms in Italy, southwest France, and Spain.

OSTROGOTHIC COIN

The birth of Hungary
The Magyar were nomadic horse warriors who migrated from central Asia, reaching the southern Russian steppes by the early 9th century CE. In the 860s they began raids into central Europe, which eventually spanned from Constantinople in the east to Bremen in the west. In the 890s, led by Árpád, the Magyars conquered land along the Danube, subjugating the area's Slav and Hun inhabitants. There, they became Christian, and established the kingdom of Hungary about a century later.

The Mongol Empire
In 1206, Genghis Khan (1162–1227) united the disparate nomadic Mongol tribes into a powerful federation with a disciplined military structure. He and his successors led the Mongol mounted archers to conquer vast swaths of central Asia, Russia, Iran, and China. At its peak, the Mongol Empire was the largest contiguous empire in human history. By 1294, however, the empire had fragmented into a series of smaller khanates that dwindled in power and eventually became obsolete.

▶ **Hunting scene**
This Pazyryk saddle, made from leather, felt, fur, hair, and gold, depicts griffins attacking mountain goats.

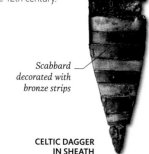

Helmet adorned with feather

Luxurious golden robe

STATUE OF ÁRPÁD

At its peak in 1279, the Mongol Empire reached over **9 million sq miles** (23 million sq km) in size

The Middle Ages and beyond (600-1750)

After the fall of the Roman Empire, western Europe entered a long period of disunity before centralized states gradually began to reemerge. In China, by contrast, a reunified state prospered under the Tang, Song, and Ming dynasties, while an Islamic empire held sway for three centuries over much of the Middle East and North Africa. Toward the end of the period, Europe's military technology advanced and its explorers began reaching other parts of the globe, ultimately leading to European dominance.

618 CE The Tang dynasty is established in China. Its first two emperors, Gaozu and Taizong, unite the country and usher in an era of prosperity. The Tang maintain control until their collapse in 907.

622 CE In Western Arabia, Prophet Muhammad flees Mecca for Medina upon facing hostility. The year of this *Hijra*, or migration, marks the start of the Islamic calendar.

EMPEROR TAIZONG

Pivotal win for longbow-weilding English over fragmented French opposition

1337 The Hundred Years' War breaks out over Edward III of England's claim to the French throne. By its end in 1453, England has lost almost all its French territory.

BATTLE OF CRECY, 1346

Shrine to god of rain
Shrine to god of war
Successive rulers built over existing temples

1325 After migrating, the Aztecs build the city of Tenochtitlán on an island in Lake Texcoco, which becomes the center of their empire in Mexico.

MODEL OF AZTEC TEMPLE

1347 The bubonic plague spreads rapidly through Europe, killing one-third of the population and causing social and economic changes.

EUROPE
ASIA
AFRICA

KEY ▨ Affected areas → Plague progress

1368 Former Buddhist monk Hongwu drives out the Mongols and establishes the Ming dynasty in China, restoring strong government and economic prosperity.

MING MIRROR (BACK)

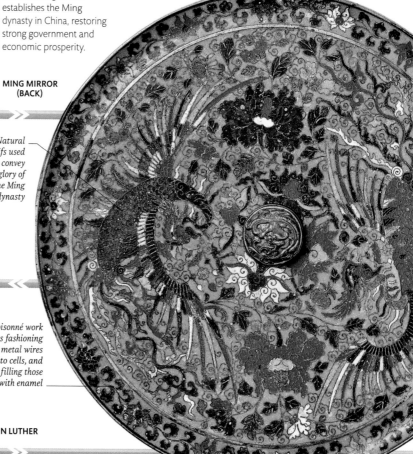

Natural motifs used to convey glory of the Ming dynasty

1508-12 Italian artist Michelangelo paints frescoes on the ceiling of the Sistine Chapel in Rome, creating one of the artistic masterpieces of the Renaissance.

SECTION OF SISTINE CHAPEL CEILING

1517 German monk Martin Luther publishes *95 Theses*, condemning corrupt practices in the Catholic Church. This sparks the Reformation—a movement to remedy the transgressions of churches—and helps establish Protestant churches, dividing Europe on religious grounds.

Cloisonné work involves fashioning fine metal wires into cells, and filling those with enamel

MARTIN LUTHER

 see also China: the Tang, Song, and Ming dynasties pp.322-23 ▶ Japan: from Nara to Tokugawa pp.324-25 ▶

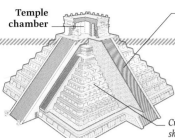

Temple chamber

365 steps represent 365 days in Mayan solar year

Cross-section shows smaller, earlier temple under present one

KUKULKAN TEMPLE, CHICHÉN ITZÁ

*c.***600s CE** Mayan cities such as Tikal and Chichén Itzá are enlarged and become regional centers. Chichén Itzá remains a major city until the 13th century.

793 CE Scandinavian Vikings attack the island monastery of Lindisfarne in England—the first of more than two centuries of raids on northern Europe.

Minaret built by Qutb-ud-din Aibak as symbol of victory

800 CE Pope Leo III crowns Carolingian Frankish king Charlemagne Emperor of Rome, giving rise to the Holy Roman Empire.

Bronze finish

STATUETTE OF CAROLINGIAN NOBLEMAN

988 CE Vladimir, the Grand Prince of Kiev, forges an alliance with the Byzantine Empire and adopts Greek Orthodox Christianity, introducing the religion to Russia.

1235 Sundiata Keita establishes the Mali empire, which dominates large parts of West Africa for more than 300 years.

MALI FIGURINE OF SOLDIER ON HORSEBACK

1215 Led by Genghis Khan, the Mongols capture Zhongdu (modern Beijing), capital of the Jurchen Jin dynasty, to become the dominant power in northern China.

1206 Qutb-ud-din Aibak founds the Muslim-ruled Delhi Sultanate. Despite initial instability, by the 14th century, its rule extended into southern India.

QUTB MINAR, DELHI

1099 The first of many European military expeditions, or crusades, to recover Christian pilgrimage sites from the Muslims captures the holy city of Jerusalem.

1066 Duke William of Normandy conquers England after defeating its Anglo-Saxon King Harold at Hastings. He divides much of its land between his Norman followers.

Sheet iron construction

NORMAN HELMET

1438 The Inca ruler Pachacuti expands his empire over the central and southern Andes and coastal Peru. The site of Machu Picchu is built for him in *c.*1450.

MACHU PICCHU

*c.***1440** German printer Johannes Gutenberg establishes Europe's first printing press using movable type, in Mainz. This allows books to be mass-produced.

Wooden frame

PRINTING PRESS

1453 Ottoman Turkish sultan Mehmed II captures Constantinople after a seven-week siege, putting an end to the Byzantine Empire. He makes the city his capital.

Nose guard

Columbus's flagship the Santa María

1492–93 Genoese navigator Christopher Columbus sets out across the Atlantic to find a sea route to East Asia, but instead makes landfall in the Americas.

ILLUSTRATION OF COLUMBUS'S FLEET

1480 Grand Prince Ivan III of Moscow defeats the ruler of the Mongol Great Horde, ending Mongol domination of Russia. Moscow's rise to dominance in the region begins.

GRAND PRINCE IVAN III

1467 The Onin Wars break out in Japan between competing *daimyo* (feudal lords), starting a century of civil war and disunity in the country.

1521 Spanish conqueror Hernán Cortés captures the city of Tenochtitlán with his soldiers and local allies, ending the Aztec empire and establishing Spanish rule in Mexico.

1526 Central Asian prince Babur defeats the Delhi sultan at Panipat, founding the Mughal Empire. By 1700, the Mughals control most of the Indian subcontinent.

BATTLE OF PANIPAT

1600 Japanese shogun (ruler of the military) Tokugawa Ieyasu's victory at Sekigahara puts an end to the Warring States period and brings Japanese reunification.

TOKUGAWA IEYASU

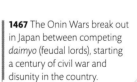

see also **Rulers of India** pp.326–27 ▶ **Faith and feudalism** pp.330–31 ▶ **Early Russia** pp.336–37 ▶

China: the Tang, Song, and Ming dynasties

In the millennium between 600 and 1600 CE, China was ruled by three great dynasties—the Tang, Song, and Ming. Each of them provided cultural and bureaucratic continuity with the past, enabling long periods of political and economic stability. Each of them in turn, however, fell victim to factionalism, corruption, and pressure from nomadic groups beyond the frontier, leading to fresh periods of instability before the establishment of a new strong dynasty.

The reunification of China

After the collapse of the Han dynasty in 221 CE, China underwent centuries of disunity and was divided into as many as 20 separate states. The Northern Zhou unified in 577 CE. Later in 588, the first ruler of the Sui dynasty, Wendi, invaded the south, toppled its main state the Chen, and finally brought China back under the rule of a single emperor. Wendi's ambitious public works and expensive foreign campaigns resulted in growing popular opposition to the taxes needed to fund them, and in 617 the Sui were overthrown by Li Yuan, a former general, who, as Emperor Gaozu, established the Tang dynasty.

Tray catches wax drips

"Sancai" (three color) glaze of green, amber, and cream

TANG DYNASTY CANDLE HOLDER

The Tang in central Asia

Gaozu, the first Tang emperor, and his successors, such as Taizong (626–649 CE), inaugurated a golden age for China with a reunited empire, wealth through the newly open Silk Road, and efficient bureaucracy bringing peace and prosperity. The Tang launched campaigns to regain territory lost since the time of the Han, conquering a string of towns along the Silk Road in central Asia, such as Khotan. Pressure from nomadic tribes, however, meant large garrisons were needed to defend them, putting severe strain on the Tang finances.

An Lushan Rebellion and the decline of the Tang

By the middle years of the Tang, their borders were under pressure. A defeat by an Arab Muslim army at the Talas River in 751 CE and the rising power of frontier generals led one of them, An Lushan, to rebel in 755, beginning a decade of civil war in which northern China was devastated and the eastern capital, Luoyang, sacked. Although An Lushan was defeated, the Tang never fully recovered. Many areas on the frontier were lost and the emperors became puppets of military commanders and eunuch bureaucrats. Finally, in 907 the last Tang emperor, Aidi, was deposed.

Imperial capitals

The founding emperors of new dynasties often established new cities (although commonly near the site of existing imperial centers). The Sui refounded Chang'an (modern Xian), previously the capital under the Han, endowing it with lavish new buildings. Further to the east, Luoyang had been the capital under the later Han in the 1st and 2nd centuries CE, and was restored briefly by Wu Zetian, China's only female empress regnant, at the end of the 7th century. Kaifeng, even farther to the east, became the capital of the Song in 960, until they lost northern China to nomads in 1126 and set up a new capital in the south at Hangzhou.

> ## "The **State is destroyed,** the mountains and rivers remain."
>
> DU FU, Tang dynasty poet,
> *The View in Spring*, 712–770 CE

The Song economy

After another period of disunity after the collapse of the Tang, China was reunited in 960 CE by Taizu, first emperor of the Song dynasty. A series of long-lived emperors restored civilian rule and brought stability and economic prosperity to China. The population more than doubled, to about 100 million by 1100, and trade along China's system of canals flourished. As the cash economy grew the demand for money increased and, in 1120, the Song created the world's first government-issued paper money. Chinese industry also reached new levels of technical sophistication, with government workshops for silk production and large-scale production of ceramics, paper, and iron.

PORTRAIT OF KUBLAI KHAN

Nomadic invasions and the collapse of the Song

The Song government became increasingly faction-ridden and weighed down by bureaucratic regulations. An attempt in 1068 by Emperor Shenzong's chief minister Wang Anshi to institute reforms and collect tax more efficiently failed in the face of opposition by traditionalists, and ended up weakening the dynasty. Unable to defend the crucial northern border, in 1126 the Song succumbed to an invasion by Jurchen nomads (who took the name Jin when they ruled), who captured both the capital Kaifeng and the emperor Huizong. Song rule in northern China collapsed, but loyalists regrouped in the south, where they ruled as the Southern Song dynasty until 1279.

Mongol China

In 1234, the Mongol ruler Ögedei Khan, son of Genghis (see p.318), conquered northern China. Genghis's grandson Kublai transferred the Mongol capital to Beijing and in 1275 sent his armies south of the Yangtze river where, after four years, they conquered the Southern Song. Ruling as the Yuan dynasty, Kublai and his successors kept apart from the Chinese, retaining their own customs and employing Chinese bureaucrats to administer the government. Even so, the need to reward Mongol and Jin followers led to inefficiency and corruption, and by the 1350s the Yuan were weakened, facing a series of revolts by Chinese rebels.

Hongwu and the rise of the Ming

Zhu Yuanzhang, a peasant who had risen to head the Red Turbans, one of many anti-Yuan rebel groups, captured Beijing and deposed the last Yuan emperor in 1368. Declaring himself Hongwu, the first emperor of the Ming dynasty, he reformed the army, devolved responsibility for taxation to local communities, and strengthened the bureaucracy. The Ming emperors restored Chinese influence in Southeast Asia, and between 1405 and 1433 sent a series of expeditions under the eunuch Zheng He (see p.341) across the Indian Ocean and to East Africa.

Decline of the Ming

Although the Ming rebuilt the Great Wall (see p.308), they still faced raids by Mongol tribes north of the frontier. The capture of Emperor Yingzong after a campaign against them in 1449, and his subsequent eight-year captivity, seriously undermined the dynasty. Later Ming emperors such as Wanli (1572–1620) neglected the government and spent so lavishly in palace entertainment that the treasury became almost bankrupt. Poor harvests in the 1620s led to rural uprisings, one of whose leaders, Li Zicheng, took Beijing in 1644, ending the Ming dynasty.

Candle holder

Green glaze applied to stoneware surface

MING DYNASTY LION FIGURE

▶ Ming lacquered panel

This panel from the 1430s, intricately designed with a pattern of a dragon, phoenix, and flowers, demonstrates the sophisticated technical prowess of craftsmen during the middle Ming period.

Hard lacquer on surface applied with a brush over a base of wood or cloth

Dragon, a symbol of good fortune that was also used by Chinese emperors to represent imperial power

Winged phoenix—in Chinese folklore, a mythical bird and an omen of the harmonious ascension of a new emperor

Smaller phoenix used as decorative motif

see also **Japan: from Nara to Tokugawa** pp.324–25 ▶ **Trade and exploration** pp.340–41 ▶

Japan: from Nara to Tokugawa

Japan developed into a centralized state early in its history, but its emperors came to be dominated by a series of shoguns, or military rulers, backed by their samurai retainers. Periodic civil wars between rival factions caused the country to break down into a series of domains ruled by rival warlords until it was reunified in the late 17th century. After briefly encouraging international trade, Japan relapsed into an isolation in which technological advances stalled, but social and political stability flourished.

The spread of Buddhism
Buddhism arrived in Japan in the mid-6th century CE from the Baekje kingdom of Korea. It was taken up by the powerful Soga clan, and officially recognized by the Empress Suiko (592–628) in 594. By the mid-7th century, there were dozens of Buddhist temples in Japan. For centuries, Buddhism was a threat to the dominant Shinto religion at the court. It also conflicted with the ideals of a Confucian bureaucratic state, which had originated in Tang dynasty China and were written into law in 701.

Amida Buddha (of the Pure Land sect)

Golden lacquer finish exterior

JAPANESE BUDDHA STATUE

The Nara period
A centralized Japanese state known as *Wa*, or *Yamato*, had emerged by the 5th century CE. In 710, Empress Genmei (707–15) moved its capital to Nara, a new city based on the Chinese Tang capital of Chang'an. Chinese influence permeated religion, government, and the arts, and Chinese characters were adapted to write the Japanese language. The Nara emperors, notably Kanmu (781–806) expanded their territory significantly in wars fought with the Emishi people of the north.

The Heian period and the Fujiwara ascendancy
In 794 CE, the court moved to Heian (Kyoto) to escape the growing power of Buddhist institutions. In 801, Emperor Kanmu bestowed the title *sei tai-shogun* ("barbarian-crushing general") on Sakanoue no Tamuramaro, who had conquered the Emishi. Abbreviated to "shogun," the title was adopted by later military leaders. In 858, the shogun Fujiwara Yoshifusa became regent for the child emperor Seiwa, beginning a line of Fujiwara shoguns that ruled for more than 300 years. After 1086, imperial power was further diminished by the practice of "cloistered emperors," who would abdicate in favor of a child successor, leaving real power to the shogun.

Clan rivalries and the Genpei War
As the emperor's authority waned and conflict between rival clans increased, a new class emerged—the samurai, military retainers to the clan leaders bound by a code of honor. As the Fujiwara lost influence, a struggle broke out between the Taira and Minamoto families, who had backed alternate claimants to the throne. This erupted into the Genpei War (1180–85) from which the Minamoto emerged as shoguns after naval victory at Dan-no-ura.

Kamakura shogunate
After the Genpei War, Minamoto Yoritomo set up court at Kamakura, where the shoguns established a new capital. From there, they repelled Mongol invasions in 1274 and 1281 (the latter destroyed by a storm—the *kamikaze*, or "divine wind"). In 1333, the last Kamakura shogun was usurped after Emperor Go-Daigo tried to seize power. Under the Ashikaga shogunate (1338–1573), power devolved to regional warlords, or *daimyo*.

Japanese literary culture
In the early 8th century CE, in the Nara period, Japanese literature emerged with a series of historical chronicles and collections of poetry. The Heian was the classical age of Japanese literature—a refined court culture producing elegant poetry and rich prose such as *The Tale of Genji* (c.1010), written by the female courtier Murasaki Shikibu. As the imperial court declined in power, folk tales and war stories such as *The Tale of the Heike* (c.1240) became more common, although poetry, such as the *Shin kokinshū* (c.1205) by Fujiwara Sadaie, remained popular.

WOODBLOCK PRINTS

> "If you **wish for peace, prepare for war.**"
>
> Attributed to
> ODA NOBUNAGA

The age of disunity
In 1467, a succession dispute over the shogunate erupted into the Onin War, which lasted 11 years and shattered central authority. Fighting between the *daimyo* and their samurai armies then became endemic in a 100-year period known as the Sengoku ("Age of disunity"). The later Ashikaga shoguns were mere puppets of the more powerful *daimyo*, whose domains became virtual mini-kingdoms, and most were deposed and died in exile. Samurai armies roamed the countryside, and castles were built throughout Japan as *daimyo* strongholds.

The unification of Japan
In 1560, Oda Nobunaga, a minor *daimyo*, began to expand from his small domain in central Japan. In 1568, he captured Kyoto. Steadily gaining power, he was lord of most of Japan by the time of his assassination in 1582. Nobunaga's general Toyotomi Hideyoshi took up his mantle and completed the unification of Japan in 1590. After he died in 1598, a new power struggle broke out between the *daimyo*, from which Tokugawa Ieyasu emerged victorious after the Battle of Sekigahara in 1600.

Tokugawa Reforms and culture
Establishing a new court at Edo (Tokyo) in 1603, Tokugawa Ieyasu ordered the former *daimyo* to build palaces there and reside at the court annually, in a bid to keep them under his authority. To ensure social stability, he established a hierarchy of four social classes (samurai, artisans, merchants, and farmers), and severely restricted social mobility between the classes. External trade was encouraged, and Portuguese and Dutch traders arrived in Japan, bringing Christianity with them.

Latticework around central compartment

Base designed to mount wooden pole

EDO PERIOD LAMP

Japan's period of isolation
From the 1630s, the Tokugawa shoguns, fearful of the extent of foreign influence on Japan, issued a series of decrees expelling Christian missionaries and imposing restriction on Japanese converts. From 1633, Japanese subjects were banned from trading abroad. By 1639, the only foreign trade permitted was with the Dutch on a small island near Nagasaki. Japan would remain isolated from the outside world for more than 200 years, until the arrival of an American naval expedition in 1853.

◀ Battle of Nagashino (1575)
In this 1857 illustration by Utagawa Yoshikazu, Takeda Katsuyori's forces clash with those of Oda Nobunaga and Tokugawa Ieyasu outside the besieged Nagashino fort.

Fine metal blade

Hilt made of stingray skin

SAMURAI SHORT SWORD

see also Trade and exploration pp.340–41 ▶   World religions pp.378–81 ▶   What is philosophy? pp.382–83 ▶   **325**

Rulers of India

Centuries of political division in India followed the collapse of the Gupta Empire in the 6th century CE. Many smaller states developed, including the Delhi Sultanate, but none emerged as the dominant power until the appearance of the Mughal Empire in the 16th century. Based around Delhi, its combination of military might, religious tolerance, and a patronage of the arts held together a potentially unstable coalition of Muslim and Hindu potentates and produced one of the great epochs in Indian history.

Rulers of medieval India

Date	606–1015
Location	North India

After the fall of the Gupta Empire (c.250–543 CE), India was briefly reunited under the emperor Harsha in the 7th century, but fragmented into smaller kingdoms. Dynasties such as the Cholas later achieved supremacy in the south in the 9th century, but failed to extend their power northward. Instead, Islam gradually established itself in the north after a series of invasions led by Mahmud of Ghazni between 1001 and 1025.

Circle of flames

Shiva as dancer on lotus pedestal

CHOLA STATUE OF LORD SHIVA

The Delhi Sultanate

Date	1206–1526
Location	Delhi and north India

In 1193, another Muslim invader from central Asia, Muhammad of Ghor, captured Delhi and conquered the Rajput Hindu principalities. After his death, his deputy Qutb-ud-Din declared himself sultan and established the Delhi Sultanate. At first it was unstable, with five of the first 11 sultans assassinated and disputes often emerging between its Turkic and Afghan factions. In the early 14th century, the sultanate stabilized, conquered part of the south and, under the rule of sultan Muhammad bin Tughluq in the 1320s, moved the capital to Daulatabad. Invasion in 1398 by Timur, a descendent of the Mongol Genghis Khan, weakened the Delhi Sultanate and by the time the Lodi dynasty came to power in 1451 its territory was much reduced.

Babur and the foundation of the Mughal Empire

Date	1526–55
Location	North India

In 1526, a descendant of Timur named Babur, who had failed to establish an empire in central Asia, invaded northern India. Using artillery Babur defeated Ibrahim, the last Delhi sultan, at Panipat, and then seized the Lodi dynasty capital of Agra. His victory over the Rajput chieftain Mewar Singh the following year persuaded his followers to remain in India, but the Mughal Empire he then established almost collapsed when his son Humayun was expelled from Delhi in 1540 by Sher Shah Suri, an Afghan chieftain.

The reign of Akbar

Date	1556–1605
Location	North and central India

Humayun died soon after his restoration in 1555, and the near half-century rule of his son Akbar that followed saw the apogee of the Mughal Empire, which grew vastly to Kashmir in the north and Bengal in the east. A vigorous ruler, he took part in many campaigns, and strengthened the empire's administration, establishing a centralized system staffed by warrior-aristocrats, the *mansabdars*, who derived their position from loyalty rather than heredity. He was liberal in religion, taking a Hindu Rajput princess as his wife and removing the *jizya*, the poll tax on non-Muslims. In 1571, he moved the capital to a newly constructed city at Fatehpur Sikri, west of Agra, from where he presided over a glittering court and promoted Din-I-Ilahi, a religion combining elements of all the existing faiths of India.

Vijayanagara

Date	1336–1565
Location	South India

The initial failure of the Mughals to conquer southern India was due in part to the founding in 1336 of Vijayanagara ("the city of Victory"), a vast fortified city which became a regional bulwark of Hinduism under the Sangama dynasty. To secure the power of the Sangama, a 10-day reconsecration festival (the *mahanavami*) was held each year, while a system of *najaka*, or local military commanders, was created to collect taxes. Efforts to expand north by the Sangama were thwarted by the Bahmani sultans of the Deccan. In the 16th century, the Sangamas were replaced by the Tuluvas and then the Aravidis, who in 1565 were defeated by local Muslim rulers, after which Vijayanagara was destroyed and the empire fell apart.

The reign of Shah Jahan

Date	1628–58
Location	North and central India

Akbar's death in 1605 was followed by a civil war from which his son Jahangir emerged victorious. After Jahangir died in 1627, a vicious conflict between his four sons was won by Khurram, who took the name Shah Jahan as Mughal emperor. He built a new capital at Delhi (including the Red Fort), renaming it Shahjahanabad, while his most abiding legacy was the Taj Mahal, at Agra, a mausoleum for his wife Mumtaz Mahal, who died in childbirth in 1631. Elsewhere, Shah Jahan's forces made major advances to the south, annexing Ahmednagar and subjugating Golconda and Bijapur, but he was deposed by his sons when he fell gravely ill in 1657 and spent the last nine years of his life as a prisoner in his own palace.

Aurangzeb and the decline of the Mughal Empire

Date	1658–1707
Location	India

A civil war between the sons of Shah Jahan was won by the emperor Aurangzeb. He aggressively secured rebellious provinces in Bengal and on the Afghan border, and expanded almost to the southern tip of India, while challenged by the rise of the Maratha kingdom and a revolt by his own son. Aurangzeb's restoration of legal restrictions on non-Muslims and the overstretching of resources strained the empire, and after his death in 1707, caused it to fall apart. By the early 19th century it was reduced to a small enclave around Delhi.

Mughal art and culture

Date	1526–1707
Location	India

The Mughal emperors were great patrons of the arts. Akbar fostered architectural excellence with large-scale building projects such as Fatehpur Sikri, while also establishing a royal workshop in which artists illustrated manuscripts with exquisite miniature paintings. Akbar's son, Jahangir, continued to promote Mughal art, cultivating artists such as Abu al-Hasan, known as "the Wonder of the Age." Under the later Mughals, however, art became more formalized and rigid as the empire itself contracted.

Positions of stars marked on globe

Band shows zodiac

Longitude markings

MUGHAL CELESTIAL GLOBE

▶ **Akbar arrests Shah Abu'l-Maali**
In this page from the *Akbarnama*, Akbar's official chronicle, his forces capture the man who had murdered his stepmother in order to gain control over Kabul.

AKBAR THE GREAT
The military prowess of the Mughal Emperor Akbar (r.1556–1605) led to him being known as "the Great". His reforms of the army, including a more effective use of horses, along with his support of new technologies and personal leadership in battle, were fundamental in creating a fighting machine that was unrivalled in the Indian subcontinent. He also encouraged religious debate and nurtured the arts and culture at his court.

Curved blade can pierce chain mail in battle

Elaborate elephant adorns handle

Sharp spikes screwed into metal globe

MUGHAL MACE   **WAR PICK**

The rise of the Marathas

Date	c.1650–1818
Location	Central west India

The Maratha kingdom appeared in the 1640s when aristocrat Shivaji Bhonsle began to carve out an independent territory on the west coast of central India. Although at first contained by the Mughals under Aurangzeb, Shivaji rebelled again in 1670, proclaiming himself king in 1674. Based in a string of mountaintop forts, the Marathas proved almost impossible for the Mughals to subdue, and even after an extensive campaign by Aurangzeb in the 1680s, their confederacy reemerged in the early 18th century under Shivaji's grandson Shahu. Thereafter their *peshwas*, or ministers, dominated much of central west India until a final defeat by the British East India Company in 1818 during the Third Anglo-Maratha War.

> "If **on earth** there is a **garden of bliss**, it is this, it is this, **it is this.**"

SAADULLAH KHAN,
Verse inscribed on the Diwan-i-Khas (Hall of Private Audiences) in the Red Fort, Delhi, c.1648

see also Colonial empires pp.356–57 ▶

The rebuilding of Europe

The dissolution of the western Roman Empire in the late 5th century CE left much of its former territory in the hands of Germanic successor kingdoms. The rulers of these kingdoms began a long process of rebuilding, aided in places by the survival of elements of Roman administration. Despite the devastation caused by raiders in the 9th and 10th centuries, they survived and formed the nucleus of many modern European countries.

Merovingian Gaul and Visigothic Spain

The Franks were a Germanic barbarian group which pressed westward into Roman Gaul in the 5th century CE. Clovis united them into a single kingdom, overcoming the remnants of the Roman Empire, and converting to Catholicism in about 496. His descendants, the Merovingians, created a hybrid Frankish-Roman culture, preserving much of Roman learning and issuing written law codes in the Roman style. The Merovingian tradition of dividing the realm among several heirs led to frequent civil wars and so enfeebled the dynasty that in 768, Pepin the Short, their mayor of the palace (a senior official), overthrew the last of them and declared himself king. The Visigoths, another Germanic group, initially settled in southwest Gaul, but were pushed out into Spain after a defeat by the Franks in 507. From their capital at Toledo, they united the entire Iberian Peninsula under their rule, until an invasion by a Berber-Arab Muslim army in 711 destroyed a Visigothic kingdom already weakened by civil war.

The Anglo-Saxon kingdoms

In the aftermath of the collapse of the Roman Empire in 411 CE, a series of Germanic invaders (Jutes, Angles, and Saxons), collectively known as the Anglo-Saxons, invaded Britain. By around the year 500 they had founded a series of small kingdoms in the east. From there they pushed westward, until by the late 6th century they occupied most of England. The principal Anglo-Saxon states were Wessex in the south and west, Mercia in the Midlands, and Northumbria in the north. They engaged in a series of wars of supremacy, which ended after the others were destroyed by Viking armies in the 9th century and Alfred the Great of Wessex defeated the invaders, allowing his kingdom to become the kernel from which a united England emerged in the 10th century.

Ostrogoths, Lombards, and Byzantines

The Ostrogoths entered Italy from the Balkans in 488 CE, at the invitation of Zeno, the eastern Roman emperor, who wanted revenge against Odoacer, who overthrew the last western Roman emperor. Their king, Theodoric, established a stable kingdom, employing many Romans in his administration. However, in 533 the Byzantine (eastern Roman) emperor Justinian launched a war of reconquest which dragged on until 554. Although the Byzantines recaptured most of Italy, the peninsula was devastated, and in 568 the Lombards, another Germanic group, invaded and established a series of duchies, which eventually coalesced into a kingdom that survived until its conquest by the Franks in 774.

The Carolingians and the Holy Roman Empire

Pepin the Short's son, Charlemagne (d.814), strengthened the new Carolingian dynasty, expanding its borders to encompass parts of Spain, Saxony, and Italy. He oversaw a cultural flourishing, later termed the Carolingian Renaissance, and promoted the reform of the Frankish church and his kingdom's administrative systems. In 800 CE, Charlemagne had himself crowned Emperor of the Romans,

Made from gold and enamel

Christian cross-shape in middle

ANGLO-SAXON PENDANT

symbolically reviving the Roman empire in the west. His successors, though, failed to maintain unity and in 840 the kingdom was divided between his three grandsons, sapping its strength. The rulers of the eastern portion, the ancestor of modern Germany, inherited and revived the imperial title, beginning with Otto I in 962.

The spread of Christianity

Christianity, which had flourished in western and southern Europe under the

> "Beware **discord**, beware **civil wars**, which are **wiping you and your people out.**"
>
> GREGORY OF TOURS, *History of the Franks, Book V,* 594 CE

▲ **Bayeux tapestry**
The almost 230 ft- (70 m-) long tapestry provides a visual narration of William of Normandy's conquest of England in 1066.

late Roman Empire, survived its fall, but the rulers of the new Germanic kingdoms which replaced it were largely pagan. By the early 6th century CE they had begun to convert to Christianity. Some, as in Visigothic Spain, initially to Arianism, a heretical form of the religion. Before long, missionaries departed from this Christian core to evangelize regions where it had withered away or never been established. In 597, St. Augustine, dispatched by Pope Leo II, arrived in England to begin a process of conversion which was largely complete within half a century. In the 8th century, Christianity reached Frisia (in the Netherlands) and then radiated out northward and eastward. Denmark and Poland were converted in the 960s and the last main pagan outposts in Europe, in Sweden and Lithuania, became Christian between the 11th and 14th centuries.

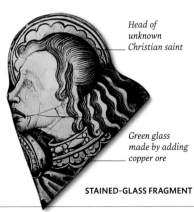

Head of unknown Christian saint

Green glass made by adding copper ore

STAINED-GLASS FRAGMENT

The Bulgarian Empire
In the 7th century CE, Slav invaders overwhelmed much of the Byzantine-controlled Balkans. One group, the Bulgars, established a kingdom on the lower Danube in the 680s, which under Khan Krum in the early 9th century doubled its territory to become a serious threat to the Byzantines. Bulgaria reached the height of its power in the 9th and 10th centuries, its conversion to Christianity in 864 cementing its position as the chief cultural center of the southern Slavs. Khan Simeon won a string of victories against the Byzantines, taking the title of emperor and even besieging Constantinople in 922. Yet the Byzantines recovered, and a crushing defeat at Kleidion in 1014 put an end to the Bulgarian empire, which then experienced a revival in the 12th and 13th century as Byzantine power in the Balkans once more collapsed.

The Vikings
In the late 8th century CE, seaborne raiders emerged from Scandinavia to begin a two-century period in which they terrorized the coastlines of northwestern Europe, their mobility aided by longships whose speed and shallow draft allowed them to assault a wide range of targets. Propelled by overpopulation, political instability, and lack of opportunity at home, the Vikings first attacked England and Ireland, then France, and even as far afield as Constantinople. In northern England, eastern Ireland,

48,000 lb (22,000 kg) of silver was paid by King Aethelred II in 1012 to the Vikings to **stop them from raiding England**

Scotland, Normandy, and Sicily they established states of their own, which survived into the 10th and 11th centuries. Further afield, the Vikings explored new lands in the north Atlantic, settling in Iceland around the year 870, Greenland around 980, and reaching North America around 1000.

The Normans
The Normans (or "north men") were originally Vikings who settled in northern France after their chief, Rollo, made a treaty with the French King Charles the Bald to protect the region from other raiders. By the 11th century their lands encompassed all of Normandy, and Duke William, a descendent of Rollo, succeeded in adding England after his defeat of the Anglo-Saxon king Harold at Hastings in 1066. From the 1030s, Norman mercenaries also became involved in factional disputes between southern Italian states, and under Robert Guiscard and his brother Roger they carved out Norman states there and in Sicily, which lasted until the end of the 12th century.

ILLUMINATED 12TH CENTURY MANUSCRIPT

see also Faith and feudalism pp.330–31 ▶ Early Russia pp.336–37 ▶ The Renaissance pp.338–39 ▶

Faith and feudalism

By the 11th century, the nucleus of the modern states of Europe had appeared, but the continent was beset by warfare as monarchs struggled to expand their realms. As towns grew, merchants became rich on trade, but the conservative system of feudalism, which tied peasants to their land, impeded economic progress. Although secular rulers exerted their authority in this era, the Christian church remained the dominant power.

The medieval church: papacy and reform
The early medieval Papacy had struggled to impose its authority on bishops outside Italy. Pope Gregory VII (r.1073–85) undertook a process of reform, insisting on the supremacy of the Papacy within the Church. In 1074 he forbade priests to marry. He also ruled that only the Pope (and not secular rulers) had the power to invest bishops in their office.

The investiture controversy
In 1075 a dispute broke out between Gregory VII and German Emperor Henry IV, who claimed the right to invest bishops. Emperor Henry IV tried to have Gregory deposed, leading the Pope in turn to excommunicate him. His authority damaged, the Emperor was forced to perform a humiliating penance in 1077.

The new monastic orders
By the 11th century, monastic life was in decay as abbeys became repositories more of wealth than of prayer. A desire for spiritual renewal led to the founding of new religious orders, such as the Carthusians (1084) and the Cistercians (1098). These new monastic orders emphasized the importance of physical work and prayer, and were followed by orders of friars such as the Franciscans (1212), who practiced absolute poverty and preached directly to ordinary people.

The Holy Roman Empire
In 800 CE, the Frankish ruler Charlemagne had crowned himself emperor in a symbolic revival of the Roman empire in the West. From 962, the title was held by dynasties such as the Ottonians and Salians based in Germany. Ruling a hierarchy of princes and dukes, by the 11th century the power of the Emperor (Holy Roman Emperor from 1157) depended on the personality of its incumbent.

The Crusades
Following an appeal from Byzantine emperor Alexius I, in 1095 Pope Urban II preached a crusade, an armed pilgrimage to free the holy city Jerusalem from Muslim rule. The army of this crusade (the first of nine between 1095 and 1271) captured the city in 1099 and established a series of Christian states, which survived until 1291.

Trading cities: Venice and Genoa
Well-placed to exploit trade in the Mediterranean, the Italian city-states of Genoa and Venice grew in wealth from the 12th century. After the capture of the Byzantine capital Constantinople in 1214 by a Venetian-led army, the two cities monopolized trade in the former empire. Venice's defeat of Genoa in 1381 allowed it to become the supreme trading power in the Mediterranean until the 16th century.

The Reconquista
The Arab invasion of Visigothic Spain in 711 CE had left a small area in the north controlled by Christians. This gradually expanded in a process known as the Reconquista, which accelerated in the 11th century as the Muslim emirate of Cordoba weakened. A victory at Las Navas de Tolosa in 1212 left only the Kingdom of Granada in Muslim hands until 1492.

The Hundred Years' War
The war broke out in 1337 after the English king Edward III invaded France to assert a claim to the French throne inherited from his grandfather. An early victory at Crécy (1346) enabled him to conquer much of northern France, but the French pushed back. Henry V renewed the war, defeating the French at Agincourt (1415) and occupying the country north of the Loire, but a French recovery, inspired by the leadeship of a young peasant woman, Joan of Arc, left the English in control of only Calais when the war ended in 1453.

Flight groove

MEDIEVAL CROSSBOW

Feudalism and the medieval economy
In the early medieval period (c.500–1000 CE), a system of land tenure known as feudalism arose by which nobles held their land from the king in return for providing their retainers to serve in royal armies. Peasants in turn gave labor service in exchange for land, and were normally not allowed to leave it.

The Black Death and its aftermath
In 1348 a devastating epidemic struck Europe, spread by fleas carried on black rats. Known as the Black Death or bubonic plague, it was characterized by buboes, swellings on the neck and groin. Appearing in Italy in 1347, it spread rapidly, killing between a third and half of Europe's population. It left a labor shortage in its wake that increased the bargaining power of the peasantry and helped weaken feudalism.

Poland-Lithuania
After Mongols had destroyed the Kievan Rus capital of Kiev in 1240, the Grand Duchy of Lithuania emerged as the

ST. BENEDICT, MONASTIC FOUNDER

> "The condition of the people was **pitiable** to behold. They **sickened by the thousands** daily, and **died unattended** ..."
>
> GIOVANNI BOCCACCIO,
> *The Decameron*, 1353

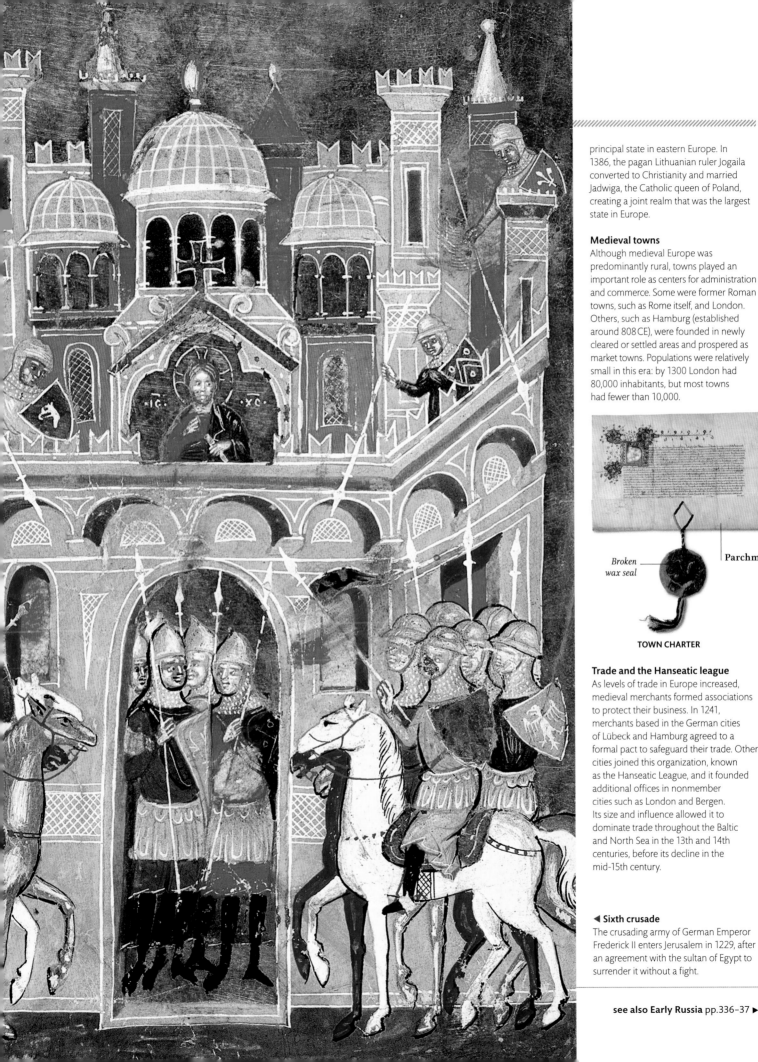

principal state in eastern Europe. In 1386, the pagan Lithuanian ruler Jogaila converted to Christianity and married Jadwiga, the Catholic queen of Poland, creating a joint realm that was the largest state in Europe.

Medieval towns

Although medieval Europe was predominantly rural, towns played an important role as centers for administration and commerce. Some were former Roman towns, such as Rome itself, and London. Others, such as Hamburg (established around 808 CE), were founded in newly cleared or settled areas and prospered as market towns. Populations were relatively small in this era: by 1300 London had 80,000 inhabitants, but most towns had fewer than 10,000.

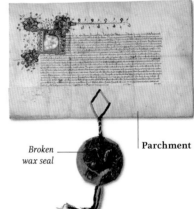

Broken wax seal · Parchment

TOWN CHARTER

Trade and the Hanseatic league

As levels of trade in Europe increased, medieval merchants formed associations to protect their business. In 1241, merchants based in the German cities of Lübeck and Hamburg agreed to a formal pact to safeguard their trade. Other cities joined this organization, known as the Hanseatic League, and it founded additional offices in nonmember cities such as London and Bergen. Its size and influence allowed it to dominate trade throughout the Baltic and North Sea in the 13th and 14th centuries, before its decline in the mid-15th century.

◀ Sixth crusade

The crusading army of German Emperor Frederick II enters Jerusalem in 1229, after an agreement with the sultan of Egypt to surrender it without a fight.

The Islamic world

Beginning in central Arabia, the Islamic empire expanded rapidly in the 7th century CE until its reach extended from Spain to Afghanistan. Within this enormous realm, centered on the caliphal capital of Baghdad, a rich culture flourished, with advances in architecture, astronomy, and medicine. By the 10th century, the empire had begun to fragment, but the emergence of large Islamic states in Turkey, Iran, and India in the 16th century partially restored its unity.

The birth of Islam

In the 6th century CE, Arabia was divided between believers in pagan gods and Christian and Jewish communities. In about 610, the prophet Muhammad, born into a wealthy merchant clan in the caravan city of Mecca, had a religious revelation. He began to preach a new religion, Islam, which taught submission to a single god. Facing opposition from traditionalists, he fled to nearby Medina in 622, and from here his believers conquered almost the entire Arabian Peninsula by his death in 632.

The Arab conquests and the Umayyads

Muhammad's successors (or caliphs) easily overcame the Byzantine and Persian empires, which had been weakened by decades of warfare. In 637 CE, Caliph Umar's forces captured the holy city of Jerusalem, and defeated the Sassanian Persians in 642. Muslim armies pushed deep into north Africa and central Asia, but they were hindered by civil wars between rival claimants to the caliphate. In 661, the Umayyad dynasty emerged victorious, and reestablished a united caliphate with its capital at Damascus.

The Abbasid caliphate

The Umayyads were plagued by divisions between the mainstream Sunni, who acknowledged the Ummayads' rule, and the Shia, who believed the descendants of Muhammad's cousin Ali to be the rightful rulers. In 750 CE, a Shia uprising overthrew the last Umayyad and installed a new dynasty, the Abbasids. Their second caliph, al-Mansur, built a new capital at Baghdad in 762, heralding a time of great prosperity, but ruling such a vast empire proved impossible, and many areas began to break away in the 9th and 10th centuries.

Star pointer indicates position of specific stars

Rotating bar

ISLAMIC ASTROLABE

Baghdad and Islamic Science

The early Abbasid caliphs were great patrons of science. Al-Mansur (774–75 CE) founded the Bayt al-Hikmah ("House of Wisdom") in his new capital to further the translation of Greek and Persian scientific works into Arabic. Scholars such as the astronomer al-Biruni (973–1052) and the physician Ibn Sina (980–1037) expanded the frontiers of knowledge, and their works were studied for centuries.

The Fatimids and the Ayyubids

As the Abbasid empire fell apart, new dynasties arose in its former territory. In 969 CE, the Shia Fatimids conquered Egypt where they founded Cairo, a new capital. Declaring themselves caliphs in opposition to the Abbasids, they fought lengthy wars with their rivals, capturing Yemen, Syria, and, in 1058, even Baghdad. However, they became over-dependent on Turkish mercenaries, and in 1169 the last Fatimid was ousted and replaced by the Ayyubids under Saladin, an Iraqi Kurd.

> "In **Baghdad I am the Shah,** in Byzantine realms **I am the Caesar,** and in Egypt **the Sultan."**
>
> SULEYMAN THE MAGNIFICENT,
> Inscription on the citadel of Bender, Moldova, 1558

The Seljuk empire spreads

In 1038 Tughril Beg, the ruler of the Seljuq Turks based at Nishapur in northeastern Iran, declared himself sultan. The Seljuqs expanded steadily, taking Baghdad in 1060. In 1071, they obliterated a Byzantine army at Manzikert and captured much of Asia Minor. Later, a revolt in 1086 led the Seljuq sultanate to split and wane in power.

The rise of the Ottomans

The Ottomans began as a small Turkish emirate on the borders of the Byzantine empire in western Anatolia. In 1324, the Ottoman sultan Orhan captured the key city of Bursa, making it his capital. From there, the Ottomans took most of the other Byzantine cities in Asia Minor, and, in 1354, crossed over into Europe.

The conquest of Constantinople

A Mongol invasion in 1402 nearly destroyed the Ottoman empire, but it recovered, and regained lost lands in Asia Minor and the Balkans. In 1453, Sultan Mehmed II laid siege to Constantinople, the last major possession of the Byzantine empire—and its capital. The defenders resisted for two months, but finally the Ottomans captured the city, which Mehmed made his new capital.

The Golden Age of Süleyman I

From 1520–66, under Süleyman the Magnificent, the Ottoman empire grew to its largest extent. His father Selim I had conquered Egypt in 1517, and he gained Rhodes and most of Hungary, which he annexed in 1529. He then besieged but failed to capture Vienna, the Austrian Hapsburg capital. Known as Kanun ("the lawgiver"), he codified the Ottoman laws, subsidized educational institutions, and supported the arts—he himself was a poet.

MEHMED II

Mehmed (1432–81) ruled twice. During his first reign, after his father Murad II was deposed, he defeated the last major Christian crusade at Varna in 1444. Mehmed became sultan again in 1451, and his capture of Constantinople in 1453 earned him both the nickname "the Conqueror" and a prestige that allowed him to pursue further conquests. His armies advanced as far as Belgrade, which they besieged in 1456. Mehmed captured the remaining Byzantine possessions in Greece in 1460-61, conquered Albania in 1478-79, and even briefly occupied Otranto, in southern Italy, in 1480.

▶ **Ottoman court, 16th-century**
In this illuminated manuscript, Süleyman the Magnificent is attended by the courtiers of his palace as he legislates.

Shah Ismail I and the Safavid empire

By the 14th century, the Safavids, an order of Sufi mystics, had established themselves at Ardabil in the northeast of Persia. As civil war broke out in the late 15th century, the Safavids expanded. Shah Ismail I took Tabriz in 1501, made it his capital, and resisted Ottoman attacks from 1514–17, establishing a stable frontier in the west.

The height of Safavid power

In 1598, Shah Abbas moved the Safavid capital to the Persian city of Isfahan, which he adorned with lavish mosques, religious schools, markets, and a grand public square. During his reign, he reestablished central authority, fortified the government, and recovered territory lost to the Uzbeks and Ottomans. After his death in 1629 the empire slowly declined, until its collapse in 1722.

Brass cover

SAFAVID CERAMIC JAR

The story of gunpowder

A chemical compound that started as a medical curiosity in China, gunpowder went on to change the way wars were waged, heralding a new era of projectile weapons. Gunpowder weaponry spread from China to the Islamic world and Europe, with artillery and handguns seeing use in conflicts across the world. Firing mechanisms were refined so that medieval single-shot hand cannons were succeeded in the 20th century by machine-guns with firing rates of 6,000 rounds per minute. In the same period, range increased from a few dozen metres to the 3.5 km (2 miles) of modern rifles.

GUNPOWDER

9th century CE Chinese alchemist Chao Nai-An stumbles upon an early form of gunpowder in his quest to create an immortality elixir.

960–1279 The Chinese develop *pao-chang*—bamboo crackers using gunpowder—and then add fuses and colored smoke to these to create fireworks.

FIREWORKS

Wheel cover

Trigger causes a serrated wheel to spin, igniting a spark against iron pyrite

WHEEL LOCK

c.1530 The wheel lock is invented, with a wheel-based ignition mechanism ideal for shorter-barreled cavalry weapons.

Powder flask

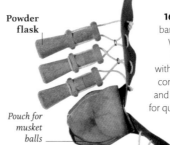

Pouch for musket balls

16th century The bandolier appears. Worn across the body, it is a belt with compartments containing powder and shot and allows for quicker reloading.

BANDOLIER

16th century Paper cartridges preloaded with shot and a measure of gunpowder appear in Europe. They have to be bitten open before being loaded into the gun.

Shot held at one end

PAPER CARTRIDGES

Hindu goddess

16th century Portuguese traders introduce matchlocks to Japan in the 1550s. Matchlocks also reach India via the Ottoman empire, aiding the Mughal rise to power.

INDIAN MATCHLOCK POWDER FLASK

17th century Barrels of gunpowder are used as blasting agents in mines in Italy, and to widen mountain roads. Its use soon spreads across Europe.

Sulphur 10%
Saltpeter 75%

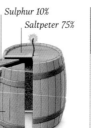

Charcoal 15%

COMPOSITION OF GUNPOWDER

1620s In flintlocks, a flint strikes a metal plate to ignite the charge. These are easier to manufacture than wheel locks and flintlock pistols can be operated with one hand.

Striking steel

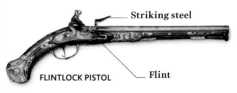

FLINTLOCK PISTOL

Flint

1884 American inventor Hiram Maxim's improved machine gun uses the recoil action to load, fire, and eject cartridges while the trigger is held.

HIRAM MAXIM

1880s French pharmacist Paul Vieille uses guncotton—cotton treated with saltpeter—to develop a new, smokeless form of gunpowder.

SMOKELESS POWDER

1862 American inventor Richard Gatling's gun is used in the American Civil War for the first time. It has multiple barrels rotating around a central axis, is operated by a crank, and can fire 600 rounds per minute.

Folding trail seat

GATLING GUN

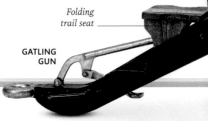

Hammer drives firing pin into cartridge

Barrel

Trigger releases hammer

Bullets

SEMIAUTOMATIC PISTOL

1891 Gunsmiths in Austria-Hungary and Germany adapt the Maxim-gun's recoil loading action to handguns to produce pistols with high rates of fire.

1919 Using a friction blowback mechanism in which the energy of the spent cartridge reloads the next one, American designer John Thompson develops the first American submachine gun, with firing rates up to 700 rpm.

Cocking handle

Cooling fin

THOMPSON GUN AND MAGAZINE

 ◀ see also Chemical reactions pp.206–207   ◀ China: the Tang, Song, and Ming dynasties pp.322–23

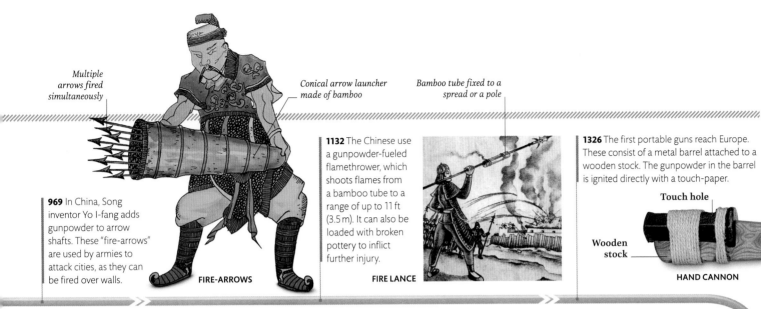

Multiple arrows fired simultaneously

Conical arrow launcher made of bamboo

Bamboo tube fixed to a spread or a pole

969 In China, Song inventor Yo I-fang adds gunpowder to arrow shafts. These "fire-arrows" are used by armies to attack cities, as they can be fired over walls.

FIRE-ARROWS

1132 The Chinese use a gunpowder-fueled flamethrower, which shoots flames from a bamboo tube to a range of up to 11 ft (3.5 m). It can also be loaded with broken pottery to inflict further injury.

FIRE LANCE

1326 The first portable guns reach Europe. These consist of a metal barrel attached to a wooden stock. The gunpowder in the barrel is ignited directly with a touch-paper.

Touch hole

Wooden stock

HAND CANNON

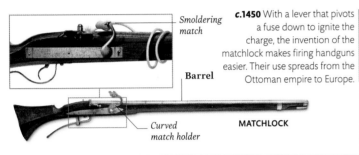

Smoldering match

Barrel

Curved match holder

MATCHLOCK

c.1450 With a lever that pivots a fuse down to ignite the charge, the invention of the matchlock makes firing handguns easier. Their use spreads from the Ottoman empire to Europe.

c.1431 Stronger cannon tubes make it possible for cast-iron shots to be used instead of stone ones. First employed by the Duke of Burgundy, Philip the Good, in the Hundred Years' War, these reduce city walls to rubble.

Vent **Powder charge** **Shot** **Rammer**

NAVAL CANNON

c.1431 European navies mount heavy cannons with muzzle-loaded balls that inflict devastating damage on the wooden ships of the time.

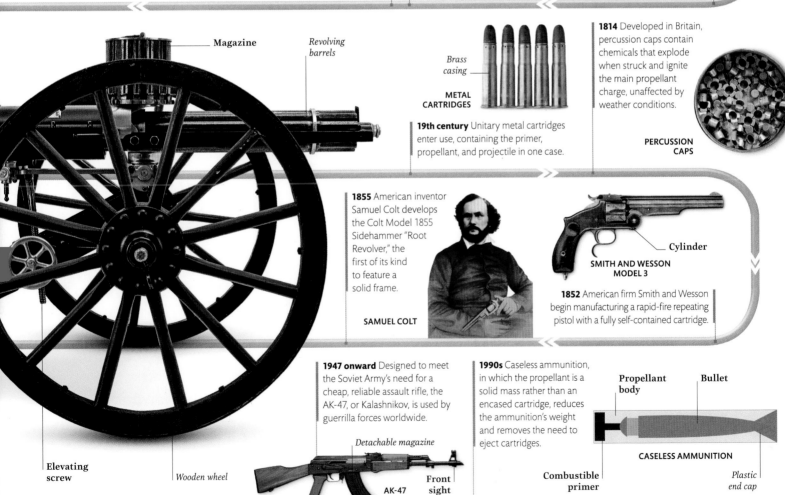

Magazine

Revolving barrels

Brass casing

METAL CARTRIDGES

19th century Unitary metal cartridges enter use, containing the primer, propellant, and projectile in one case.

1814 Developed in Britain, percussion caps contain chemicals that explode when struck and ignite the main propellant charge, unaffected by weather conditions.

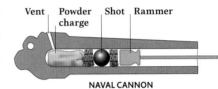

PERCUSSION CAPS

1855 American inventor Samuel Colt develops the Colt Model 1855 Sidehammer "Root Revolver," the first of its kind to feature a solid frame.

SAMUEL COLT

Cylinder

SMITH AND WESSON MODEL 3

1852 American firm Smith and Wesson begin manufacturing a rapid-fire repeating pistol with a fully self-contained cartridge.

Elevating screw

Wooden wheel

1947 onward Designed to meet the Soviet Army's need for a cheap, reliable assault rifle, the AK-47, or Kalashnikov, is used by guerrilla forces worldwide.

Detachable magazine

AK-47

Front sight

1990s Caseless ammunition, in which the propellant is a solid mass rather than an encased cartridge, reduces the ammunition's weight and removes the need to eject cartridges.

Propellant body

Bullet

CASELESS AMMUNITION

Combustible primer

Plastic end cap

see also The Industrial Revolution pp.354–55 ▶ The age of global conflicts pp.360–63 ▶

Early Russia

For centuries, nomadic tribes migrated through the area that would become Russia as they ventured westward, until states began to develop there in the 9th century CE under the influence of Viking invaders. Kievan Rus, the most powerful of these, dominated the area culturally and politically, until it divided into smaller principalities and was destroyed by Mongol invaders in the 13th century. From its ruins came the principality of Muscovy, which in turn gave rise to the modern state of Russia.

Peoples of Russia

Russia's ethnic history is complex because of its geographical position, lying on the route taken by nomadic peoples as they crossed the steppes from central Asia. In the south, Scythians, who ruled from the 8th century BCE, were followed by Sarmatians, Goths, Huns, Avars, Khazars, and Turkic groups such as the Pechenegs. To the north Finno-Ugric tribes vied with Slavs, whose original homeland may have been in the middle Dnieper basin. From the 8th century CE, Vikings from Sweden began to migrate southward from the Baltic coast, founding trading settlements that formed the nucleus of the future medieval states of Russia.

Foundation of Kievan Rus

At first the Vikings simply sought to trade from bases such as Staraya Ladoga (near modern St. Petersburg). According to tradition, in 862 CE the people of Novgorod invited a group of Vikings led by the chieftain Rurik to defend them. Twenty years later Rurik's son Oleg captured the city of Kiev to the south. This became the center of a Viking-ruled realm known as Rus. Under Oleg's progeny, Kievan Rus became a powerful principality, spanning much of the terrain of modern Ukraine and western Russia.

Russia and Byzantium

Constantinople, known to the Vikings as Miklagard ("The Great City"), was the capital of the Eastern Roman Empire, or Byzantium. It was both an attractive destination for traders and a target for raiders. In 860 CE and 907, the Vikings attacked the city, leading to a treaty in 911 setting the terms under which Vikings could trade in the city. Each year they came with a fleet and wintered in the mouth of the Dnieper. Further attacks in 940 and 944 led to restrictions on Viking traders, but the conversion of the Rus to Christianity in the late 10th century finally brought peace.

Conversion to Christianity

Both the Vikings and the Slavs amongst whom they settled were pagan and worshipped a pantheon of gods. However, neighboring Poland became Christian with the conversion of its ruler in 960 CE. Once Christianity began spreading into the Vikings' Scandinavian heartlands, Vladimir, the Grand Prince of Kiev, found himself increasingly isolated. In 988 he was baptized into the Greek Orthodox Christianity of Byzantium, beginning the Christian era in Russian history.

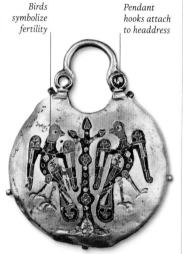

Birds symbolize fertility

Pendant hooks attach to headdress

12TH-CENTURY PENDANT

Yaroslav the Wise

Vladimir's son, Yaroslav (980–1054), fought a 20-year civil war with his brothers before securing power over all of Kievan Rus in the 1030s. Under him, Kiev reached the height of its power. Three of his daughters became queens in western Europe (of France, Norway, and Hungary) and he lavished Kiev with new defenses and promulgated the first written Russian law code. He encouraged the spread of Christianity by building a grand new church of St. Sophia to rival its namesake in Constantinople, and appointed Ilarion as the first non-Greek metropolitan bishop of Kiev. His military ventures, however, were less successful, as nomadic groups such as the Pechenegs began to press from the south, and an expedition against Byzantium in 1043 ended in defeat.

Novgorod and the Russian principalities

After the death of Yaroslav in 1054, Kievan Rus broke up into about a dozen principalities, including Kiev itself. Vladimir Monomakh briefly reunited these states between 1113 and 1125, but the pressure of Polovtsian raiders in the south cut off Kiev from trade with Constantinople and forced it into decline. As Russia fractured once more, the northern state of Novgorod became prominent. Ruled by an assembly of citizens, its princes were

elected rather than hereditary, and they vied for supremacy with the neighboring principality of Vladimir-Suzdal, which attracted migrants as Kiev collapsed into anarchy. There, in about 1147, Moscow, Russia's future capital, was founded.

Mongol invasions

The Mongol armies of Genghis Khan first attacked southern Russia in 1223, heavily defeating a combined army of several principalities. The Mongols—known in Russia as Tatars—attacked again in 1237, sacking Ryazan, Moscow, and Vladimir-Suzdal. Three years later they devastated southern Russia, including Kiev. Russia became the westernmost outpost of the Mongol empire, ruled by the khans of the Golden Horde. The Mongols left many local rulers in place, but these leaders were forced to gather enormous tributes for their Mongol overlords and to provide recruits for the Mongol army. Russian resentment at these demands increased under the Mongol occupation, which lasted until the 15th century and was known as the "Tatar Yoke."

The rise of Moscow

Moscow (or Muscovy) was originally a minor settlement in Vladimir-Suzdal. Comparatively sheltered from the full rigors of the Tatar Yoke, the princes of Moscow prospered, and in the early

14th century, Prince Daniel expanded his lands to the south, northeast, and west, until he had more than doubled the principality's territory. Moscow's lands expanded further under Dmitry Donskoy and Vasily I in the late 14th and early 15th centuries. It eclipsed the power of states such as Vladimir-Suzdal and Tver and became the seat of the Metropolitan Bishop of the Russian Church.

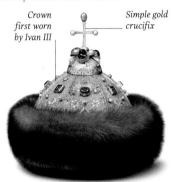

Crown first worn by Ivan III

Simple gold crucifix

GOLDEN CAP

Establishment of the Tsardom

Ivan III became Grand Prince of Moscow in 1462 and ruled for more than 40 years. He defeated the Mongol Ahmed Khan in 1480 and then withheld Moscow's tribute, before turning his attention to expanding Muscovy's territory, destroying the power of Novgorod and deporting thousands of

> "Our land is great and rich but there is **no order** in it. Come to **rule us** and **reign over us.**"
>
> SAINT NESTOR THE CHRONICLER, Relating Novgorod's 9th-century appeal to the Varangians, *Russian Primary Chronicle*, 1113

its inhabitants whom he replaced with Muscovites. He introduced a law code and made land grants to the nobility dependent on military service rather than lineage. His power almost unchallenged, Ivan awarded himself the titles "Tsar" and "autocrat," the former in imitation of Roman emperors.

Worn and stained paper

THE CODE OF LAW OF TSAR IVAN IV

Ivan the Terrible

Becoming ruler as a small boy, Ivan IV's (1530–84) childhood was dominated by the boyars, military nobility whose feuding nearly tore Moscow apart. As an adult, Ivan sent Moscow's armies east, where they captured the khanate of Astrakhan, and west to the Baltic where they took most of Livonia. He was formally crowned Tsar in 1547, before establishing a permanent military force called the *Streltsy*. Later in his reign, his rule became much harsher, employing the *oprichnina*, a private militia, which sacked Novgorod

in 1570, murdering swaths of Ivan's opponents, including boyars. This cruelty and the treatment of the peasantry, who were now forbidden to leave their land, earned Ivan the nickname "the Terrible."

▼ **Warrior procession**

In this 1550s icon (religious work of art), Alexander Nevsky (prince of Novgorod) and Saint George lead a host of heavenly warriors into battle.

The Renaissance

From the 14th century, European thinkers began to break free of the constraints of medieval tradition, looking to Classical antecedents for inspiration. This movement, known as the Renaissance, began in Italy, before spreading to northern and western Europe, creating an international network of scholars. Creativity in the arts flourished, and pioneers, aided by the advent of the printing press, made advances in fields as diverse as medicine, astronomy, and cartography.

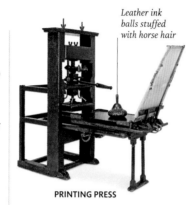

Crossed keys are symbol of papacy

Coat of arms has six balls

Latin inscription at base

MEDICI CREST

in which a number of city-states vied for power. Merchants from these states formed a wide range of ruling houses with money to lavish on artists whose works enhanced their reputations. The Medici rulers of Florence, who made their fortune in banking, were patrons to many artists including Michelangelo, Raphael (1483–1520), and Botticelli (1445–1510).

Medieval universities and scholasticism

During the Middle Ages, institutions dedicated to higher learning had begun to spring up. Known as *studia generalia*, or universities, the first appeared in Bologna, Italy, in 1088, and then spread to France, Germany, Britain, and across Europe. Their curriculum was conservative, focusing on *trivium* (logic, rhetoric, and grammar) and *quadrivium* (arithmetic, astronomy, geography, and music) with advanced studies in theology, church law, and medicine. Scholasticism—the major school of critical thinking that flourished—aimed to reconcile contradictions in Classical sources such as Aristotle, whose works on logic became known in the 12th century. While scholars such as St. Thomas Aquinas (1224–74) produced enormously influential works, such as his *Summa Theologica*, the rigidity of scholasticism could result in a lack of openness to new ideas.

Leather ink balls stuffed with horse hair

PRINTING PRESS

The invention of printing

Printing using movable type was introduced into Europe by Johannes Gutenberg (c.1400–68), a printer from Mainz, in 1455. His printing press allowed for the production of large print-runs of books, as opposed to the slow process of copying text by hand. Most early books were printed in Latin, but from the 16th century works in local languages began to

Art and patrons

From the 14th century, artists in Italy developed a new style that was distinct from the formulaic works of the Middle Ages. Beginning with Giotto di Bondone (1267–1337), artists began to experiment with perspective, a technique that had been lost since Roman times. Painters such as Piero della Francesca (1412–92) and Leonardo da Vinci (1452–1519), sculptors such as Donatello (1386–1466) and Michelangelo (1475–1564), and architects such as Leon Battista Alberti (1404–72) created works that embodied the spirit of the Renaissance. These artists were also helped by the competitive nature of northern Italian politics,

Bruneschelli and architecture

Filippo Brunelleschi (1377–1446), a trained Florentine goldsmith, initially worked as a sculptor, but found his greatest fame as an architect. In 1418, he was commissioned to complete the city's cathedral, which had

> ## "We, by our **arts**, may be called the **grandsons of God**."
>
> LEONARDO DA VINCI, *Notebooks (Vol. 1)*, c.1478–1519

The rise of humanism

From the 14th century an increasing number of ancient Greek and Roman manuscripts were rediscovered, mainly in Italy, by scholars such as the poet Petrarch (1304–74) who compiled a comprehensive version of the works of Roman historian Livy. Humanism, a new intellectual movement, presented knowledge as human, not divine, and emphasized the benefits of recovering and reinterpreting ancient works, many of which had been lost, misunderstood, or embellished during the Middle Ages. Humanists such as the papal secretary Poggio Bracciolini continued this movement in the 15th century, and it spread across Europe, where scholars such as Desiderius Erasmus (1466–1536) produced new versions of the Old Testament in Greek and Latin, and polemical works of theology.

appear in print as well, and in huge numbers. In Venice alone, from 1450–1500, some two and a half million books were printed. This vast increase in the dissemination of knowledge allowed for rapid progress in the sciences.

FLORENCE CATHEDRAL

remained without a dome since the mid-14th century. Brunelleschi used a herringbone pattern of brickwork to spread the weight of the dome, and built a secondary interior dome to strengthen it. While Renaissance architects designed a wide range of churches and civic buildings, Brunelleschi's Dome remains the greatest architectural feat of this era, and at 377 ft (115 m) in height it is the largest brick dome ever constructed.

Renaissance astronomy

In 1543, Polish astronomer Nicolaus Copernicus published *On the Revolutions of the Heavenly Spheres*, which argued that instead of the sun orbiting the Earth—the prevalent theory since the 1st century CE—the opposite was true. This heliocentric theory helped to explain anomalies such as the retrograde motion of planets. In 1597 German astronomer Johannes Kepler, refining the Copernican model, calculated that the orbits of the planets around the sun were elliptical, not spherical. In 1609, Italian polymath Galileo Galilei, using the recently invented telescope, discovered craters on the moon

and four satellites of Jupiter. While the Catholic Church convicted Galileo of heresy in 1633 for his defense of the heliocentric model, by then the model itself had become widely accepted.

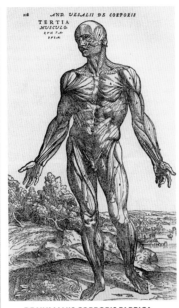

DE HUMANIS CORPORIS FABRICA

Vesalius and medicine

Medical science had remained profoundly conservative into the 16th century, influenced by the theory of humors (see p.251) put forward by Greco-Roman doctor Galen (*c.*130–216 CE). Some practical advances were made when Italian universities began carrying out public dissection in the 14th century, allowing students to observe internal organs first hand. In 1543, the anatomist Andreas Vesalius published *De humanis corporis fabrica* ("On the Fabric of the Human Body"), which

was accompanied by detailed illustrations of bones, muscles, arteries, and organs, forming an important tool for surgeons and physicians in understanding the human body. This enabled English doctor William Harvey (1578–1657) to devise an accurate theory of the circulation of blood around the body via the heart, further promoting observational methods and distancing medicine from the theoretical notions of the ancient world.

Renaissance and the Reformation

The advent of humanist ideas and the spread of printing had loosened the Catholic Church's monopoly on religious ideas, already weakened by 14th-century schisms that had produced rival popes in Rome and Avignon. Studies of Classical philosophers such as Aristotle and Plato allowed for novel and varied ways of thinking, and new translations of the Bible made Biblical teachings accessible to the general populace. This trend was accentuated when translations began to appear in local languages, with a French New Testament appearing in 1523, and one in English in 1525. This environment enabled the ideas of religious reformers such as Martin Luther (1483–1546) to spark the Reformation, a European-wide movement for religious reform. Although the Catholic Church reacted by stifling dissent, it also used the Renaissance to promote its own reforms, including the creation of new religious orders, such as the Jesuits (founded in 1540), to counter the spread of Protestantism.

Mapmaking and discovery

In the late 14th century, the rediscovery of Ptolemy's 2nd-century CE work *Geography*, which divided the world up into a grid of latitudes and longitudes, sparked a new interest in mapping the globe. Exploring Africa, Portugese mariners reached the Cape of Good Hope at the continent's southern tip in 1488, before Christopher Columbus discovered the Americas in 1492. New techniques were needed to map these areas, and in 1533 the Dutch cartographer Gemma Frisius (1508–55) described the technique of triangulation as a means to identify the distance between any two points. In 1569, his assistant Gerardus Mercator (1512–94) produced a world map using a projection which represented the curved surface of the Earth in a flat, two dimensional format. Showing compass courses as straight lines, this method simplified the process of navigation, and allowed for greater accuracy than ever before.

MICHELANGELO

Born to Florentine ex-nobility, Michelangelo (1475–1564) was apprenticed to the painter Domenico Ghirlandaio at 14 before studying at the Medici humanist academy. He carved two of his masterpieces, *Pietà* (1499) and *David* (1501), before the age of 30. His Sistine Chapel ceiling (1508–12) is often cited as one of the greatest works of art ever made. He died in Rome at the age of 88, and was buried in Florence.

> ## "As though seated on a royal throne, **the sun** governs the family of planets **revolving around it.**"
>
> NICOLAUS COPERNICUS, *On the Revolutions of Heavenly Spheres*, 1543

> There are approximately **300** figures depicted in the **frescoes** on the ceiling of the **Sistine Chapel**, in Rome. Commissioned by **Pope Julius II** in 1508, the ceiling took **four years** to complete

see also The Reformation pp.344–45 ▶ The history of painting pp.442–43 ▶

Trade and exploration

Since early times, trade and exploration went hand in hand. The first long-distance trade route between ancient Mesopotamia and the Indus Valley was established by around 3000 BCE. Later, China prospered by trading jade, spices, and silk along land routes developed to link east and west. Their closure by Ottoman Turkey in the 15th century denied these luxuries to the west and drove Europeans to seek other routes to the east, sparking a whole new era of global maritime exploration.

Polynesian exploration of the Pacific
Originally from Southeast Asia, the ancestors of the Polynesians were a seafaring people who began spreading southward and eastward across the Pacific Ocean from around 3000 BCE. By about 1 CE, they had reached the islands of Tonga and Samoa, venturing on from there as far as Hawaii to the north, Easter Island to the east, and New Zealand to the far southwest. Their boats, which comprised two outrigger canoes either side of a main hull, could carry up to 24 people along with plants to cultivate and chickens and pigs to rear on the islands they discovered.

FERDINAN. MAGALA.

Outrigger canoe to side

Central hull beside canoes

POLYNESIAN VOYAGER

The Silk Road

Established by the Han dynasty in China in about 130 BCE, the Silk Road was a network of land trade routes linking various parts of the ancient world. The trade along it was two-way. A variety of imports, including precious metals, animal furs, glassware, and wool blankets and carpets, were shipped from west to east, while tea, porcelain, jade, spices, and, above all, silk were among the luxuries traveling in the other direction. Silk was particularly sought-after in ancient Rome, even after several Roman emperors, including Augustus, attempted to ban its wearing for being immoral.

Viking expansion in the Atlantic

The Vikings of Scandinavia began their explorations in the North Atlantic in about 800 CE, when they settled the Faroe Islands. From there, their ships ranged westward, sighting Iceland in the 830s. Erik the Red discovered Greenland in 986; his second son, Leif Erikson, reached the North American coast shortly after 1000. There, he discovered Baffin Island, which he named Helluland; a forested region with white sand beaches he called Markland; and finally to the southwest an area he named Vinland after the wild grapes he found growing there. Artifacts discovered in 1961 at the northern tip of Newfoundland confirmed the Viking presence in North America.

Chinese exploration

Between 1405 CE and 1433, China enjoyed a golden age of maritime expansion thanks largely to Zheng He, the Head Eunuch of Yongle, the third Ming Emperor. On the first of seven voyages, Zheng visited Vietnam, Java, Sumatra, and Malacca before rounding the southern tip of India to reach Cochin and Calicut.

◀ Magellan's global voyage

This 16th-century colored, copper engraving by Theodore de Bry provides a fantastical depiction of Ferdinand Magellan's journey aboard the *Victoria*, the only ship of an original fleet of five to actually complete this circumnavigation.

Later, he voyaged to the Persian Gulf and the coast of East Africa, but with his death, Xuande, Yongle's successor, abruptly stopped any more exploration on the grounds of its exorbitant cost.

The Portuguese and West Africa

Sponsored by Prince Henry the Navigator, Portuguese sailors in their small, highly maneuverable caravels began to explore the West African coast in the first half of the 15th century. Later, they reached Cape Verde in 1456, Bartolomeu Dias sailed round the Cape of Good Hope in 1488, and Vasco da Gama circumnavigated Africa and crossed the Indian Ocean to reach India in 1497. There, the Portuguese made Goa their major trading center, while in West Africa, they traded for gold, ivory, pepper, and slaves with Ghana, Mali, Benin, and other tribal kingdoms.

Columbus and the New World

Having convinced the rulers of Spain to finance the voyage, Genoese sea captain Christopher Columbus set sail from Palos de la Frontera in August 1492 confident that, by sailing west across the Atlantic Ocean, he could find a new route to China and the east, in particular the Spice Islands (the Moluccas) of the Indies. He and his three ships, *Santa María*, *Pinta*, and *Niña*, made their first landfall on October 12 on an island in the Bahamas he christened San Salvador; three later voyages in 1493, 1498, and 1502 took him further into the Caribbean, where he established a colony on Hispaniola, and to the South American coastline. Yet, despite the physical evidence, he refused to accept that he had discovered a new continent. Instead, he clung to the belief that he had reached the Indies and that somewhere a sea passage must exist that would lead him to his original goal.

The spice trade and the Indies

Following the Ottoman closure of the overland trade routes that for centuries had brought spices from the east to Europe, the Portuguese led the drive to establish a new direct sea route to the spice regions of the Indies. In 1501, Pedro Álvares Cabral became the first man to bring spices from India to Europe via the Cape of Good Hope, while Francisco Serrão reached the Spice Islands 11 years later. Throughout these years, the Portuguese remained the dominant force in the European exploration of the east. Their control of the spice trade, however, lasted only until 1602, after which traders of what would become known as the Dutch East India Company ousted them, thereafter monopolizing the trade in spices such as nutmeg, mace, cloves, and pepper for the next two centuries.

> ## "It was **so wonderful** that I do not know **how to describe ...**"
>
> BERNAL DIAZ, Spanish conquistador, On first sight of Tenochtitlán,
> *The Conquest of New Spain*, 1565

Exploration of North America

Though the Spanish were the first Europeans to found a permanent settlement in North America, in 1565 at St. Augustine, Spanish Florida, it was the French and English who led the way in the further exploration of the continent. In Canada, French navigator Jacques Cartier explored the St. Lawrence river between 1534 and 1542, the French later founding their first settlement there in 1605 at Port-Royal, Nova Scotia. They also claimed a vast area of territory along the Mississippi river, which they named Louisiana. Jamestown, the first successful English settlement, was founded in 1607 in what would later become the colony of Virginia. Futher English settlement along the Atlantic coast quickly followed with 13 separate colonies established by the end of the 17th century.

Circumnavigating the globe

In 1519, Portuguese navigator Ferdinand Magellan, sailing in the service of Spain, set out to sail around the world. Although the expedition was successful, his Spanish subordinate Juan Sebastián Elcano completing the voyage in 1522, Magellan was killed the year before in a conflict with Filipino natives over their conversion to Christianity. However, as he had previously traveled to the Philippines from the west he became credited as the first mariner to complete a circumnavigation. Later, Sir Francis Drake became the second person to sail aound the globe. His voyage aboard the *Golden Hind* between 1577 and 1580 was extremely profitable. Drake brought back vast amounts of gold and silver seized from the Spanish off the coast of Peru, as well as cloves from the Spice Islands.

"Hispaniarum Rex" inscription

Royal coat of arms

SPANISH COINS FROM 1770

Spanish America and the silver trade

Mexico came under Spanish control when Hernán Cortés crushed the Aztecs in 1519–21, while Peru's Inca rulers were conquered by Francisco Pizarro between 1531 and 1535. The wealth the Spanish extracted from these South and Central American empires fueled their economy. Silver was discovered in 1545 at Potosi in the Andes, where 160,000 Peruvians and slaves from Africa labored, and at Zacatecas in Mexico a year later. It was shipped back to Spain annually in vast treasure fleets and much was used to mint the *peso*, or Spanish dollar, the world's first globally accepted currency.

MARCO POLO

In the late 13th century, the Venetian merchant and explorer Marco Polo (*c.*1254–1324) traveled along the Silk Road to China, where he spent 17 years serving Kublai Khan, the country's Mongol overlord. On his return home, he compiled an account of his journeys, *The Travels of Marco Polo*. Although a bestseller that today is an invaluable insight into life in East Asia at the time, few of its early readers believed his tales of adventure.

The Middle Ages in the Americas

The Teotihuacan culture, which flourished between 1 and 750 CE, was one of the most influential in Mesoamerica, the area extending from central Mexico down through to northern Costa Rica. Further south in the Andes Mountains, various cultures thrived along the coast. Centuries later, two powerful empires, the Aztec and the Inca, emerged in Mexico and Peru. In North America, nomadic societies settled, built cliff dwellings and fortified settlements, and established wide-ranging trade networks.

Teotihuacan

Between the 1st and 7th centuries CE, Teotihuacan became one of the largest and most powerful cultural centers in ancient Mesoamerica. The city, located in the Valley of Mexico, reached its peak of importance around 500–550 CE, when its population numbered as many as 200,000. Its remarkable ruins, most notably the Pyramid of the Sun and Pyramid of the Moon, are a surviving testament to its importance. Its people produced pottery and textiles, and created colorful reliefs.

Tiwanaku

The site of Tiwanaku (in modern Bolivia) stands almost 13,000 ft (4,000 m) above sea level. Little is known about its early history, but it became an important pre-Columbian religious center. At the height of its power, its influence extended through the southern Andes and into modern Peru, Chile, and Argentina. Though Tiwanaku was abandoned sometime after 1000 CE, probably due to climate change impacting the agriculture on which it depended, it retained its religious significance. The Inca believed it to be the birthplace of humankind.

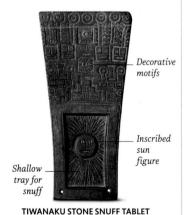

Decorative motifs

Inscribed sun figure

Shallow tray for snuff

TIWANAKU STONE SNUFF TABLET

◀ **Codex Borbonicus**
A page from a Codex, written and illustrated by Aztec priests, shortly before or after the Spanish conquest. It details the cycles of two calendars.

The Toltecs

The original Toltecs were likely migrants who moved into central Mexico from the northwestern desert. The civilization they established there flourished between the 10th and mid-12th centuries CE. They were ferocious warriors, who frequently went to war to spread the cult of Quetzalcoatl, the greatest of their gods. Tula, the capital, became renowned for its sumptuous buildings; its craftsmen were skilled potters and metalworkers. Why the Toltec civilization suddenly collapsed remains unknown; it may have been precipitated by drought or invading peoples from the north.

Opening in handle

Stirrup-shaped spout connects to head and back of female figure

Shapes made by molds
EARLY CHIMU VESSEL

The Chimú

Chimú civilization flourished along the northern coast of Peru between 1100 and 1470 CE, when it was conquered by the expanding Inca Empire. Its people were skilled farmers, who devised elaborate irrigation systems to water their lands, dramatically increasing their agricultural productivity. Chan Chan, in the state of Chimor, was their capital. At the peak of Chimú power it had a population of up to 40,000. Many Chimú were gifted craftspeople, producing fine metalwork, striking monochromatic pottery, and colorful textiles.

Mississippian cultures and Cahokia

Thought to begin around 1000 CE, the Mississippian culture spread through much of the North American Midwest and Southeast. Owing its prosperity to its efficiency in cultivating corn, beans, and squash, it was a socially complex society, whose chiefs ruled from fortified urban centers with large temples. Cahokia, near modern-day St. Louis, was the largest of them. It flourished from around 1050 to 1350, when it was abandoned, possibly due to soil depletion or political unrest.

Peoples of the North American Southwest

Corn farming encouraged the nomadic peoples of the Southwest to settle, living in shallow pit-dwellings grouped near mountain streams or along ridges. Between 400 CE and c.1200, they built cliff dwellings in the faces of rocky crags, or along canyons and mesa walls. The Puebloans, as they became known, devised complex irrigation systems to raise crops even in the hot sun. Their descendants became skilled potters and basket-makers; some mined turquoise, which they traded with the Toltecs.

THE COLUMBIAN EXCHANGE

The Columbian exchange, named after Christopher Columbus, refers to the widespread transfer of plants, precious metals, animals, culture, technology, human populations, and diseases between the Old World, the Americas, and West Africa. Contact and trade in the 15th and 16th centuries saw the interchange of many of these things, some beneficial, and some detrimental.

The Aztecs

Around 1325, the Aztecs (also known as the Mexica) founded the city of Tenochtitlán in Mexico, on marshy land in Lake Texcoco. Just a century later, its ruler Izcoatl expanded Aztec power by forming an alliance with two other powerful city-states, Texcoco and Tlacopán. Rapid expansion continued under four successive Aztec rulers, who established control over most of northern Mexico. Tenochtitlán grew to become one of the largest cities in pre-Columbian America with a population of at least 200,000. Continued Aztec dominance

The **Pyramid of the Sun** is the **third largest pyramid** in the world

The Incas

Starting in their homeland in Peru's Cuzco Valley, from 1438 the Incas carved out a vast and wealthy South American empire. By 1500 it stretched from modern-day Ecuador to Chile, far to the south. Their leader, the Sapa Inca, ruled over as many as 12 million people from Cuzco, the empire's capital, which lay at the heart of a 40,000-km (25,000-mile) road network connecting it with other major Inca cities. An efficient tax and administrative system served to consolidate the Sapa Inca's power over what was the largest pre-Columbian empire.

Realistic design

Hammered gold

INCA LLAMA FIGURINE

in the region, however, depended on the ability to keep its vassals in check. Conquered peoples were required to send regular shipments of tribute to the city, which were closely recorded. Aztec warriors engaged in warfare in order to capture prisoners of war, as the religion of Tenochtitlán required regular human sacrifices to appease the gods.

The Spanish in the Americas

When Hernán Cortés landed in Mexico in 1519 he very quickly allied himself with Aztec vassal city-states that were discontented with Moctezuma II, the Aztec emperor. Cortés met no resistance when he entered Tenochtitlán and took Moctezuma prisoner. When the city fell in August 1521, the Aztec Empire fell with it.
   The Inca Empire in Peru was already disintegrating when Francisco Pizarro arrived in 1531. He captured Atahualpa, the reigning Sapa Inca, in a bloody ambush fought at Cajamarca and put him to death. The city of Cuzco fell without further struggle and all Inca resistance was finally crushed in 1572.

see also Colonial empires pp.356–57 ▶ **343**

The Reformation

In 1517, decades of discontent with both the Catholic Church and the popes that governed it came to a head with the publication of German theologian Martin Luther's *Ninety-five Theses* condemning many Church practices, particularly the sale of indulgences—the remission of sins in exchange for money. The splits that followed led to the birth of a new Protestant faith, which quickly spread across northern Europe. Years of bitter religious conflict between Catholics and Protestants followed.

Lollards and Hussites

Long before Luther, in the late 14th century English theologian John Wycliffe and his followers, known as the Lollards, became the first group to question papal authority. They took their name from the medieval Dutch word lollaert ("mumble"), probably a reference to the importance they placed on reading the Bible's scriptures. They disliked the corruption they saw as endemic in the Church, as well as some of its religious teachings. The movement was tolerated at first, but under Henry IV and Henry V they suffered persecution, and after their failed uprising in 1414 they were forced underground. Nevertheless, their example influenced others across Europe, notably the Czech theologian Jan Hus. He and his followers, the Hussites, were similarly persecuted for their radical views; Hus himself was burned at the stake for heresy in 1415.

Catholic pressures and disunity

The Catholic Church had been weakened by the Papal Schism, which stemmed from the decision of Pope Clement VII in 1378 to move the papacy from Rome to Avignon, in France, where it had earlier sat for much of the century. It saw two popes, one in Rome and one in Avignon, joined in 1409 by a third in Pisa, each claim the supreme authority of the Church. The rift was only healed in 1417, when Martin V was elected as sole Pope by the Council of Constance. In response to criticism of the Church, some of its leading intellectuals advocated its reform. They included Spain's Cardinal Francisco Jiménes de Cisneros, the Archbishop of Toledo, and, most notably, the Dutch humanist Desiderius Erasmus.

The theses of Martin Luther

Although the story that Martin Luther nailed his *Ninety-five Theses* to the door of the castle church in Wittenberg is likely a myth, there is no doubting the impact of their publication. The text asserted that the Bible alone was the ultimate religious authority and that salvation could be achieved only through faith, not by deeds. Luther also attacked the corrupt finances of the Church, whose sale of indulgences had been supported by papal decree or "bull."

SATIRICAL ANTI-LUTHERAN ENGRAVING

Growth of reformed churches

Luther's message of reform attracted followers across a sympathetic Europe. In 1525, Albrecht, Duke of Prussia, declared himself Lutheran, becoming the first European ruler to establish Protestantism as an official state religion. His actions were soon followed by other leaders, most notably the princes of Saxony, Hesse, and Schleswig-Holstein. In Scandinavia, Sweden's King Gustav Vasa renounced Catholicism in 1536, while Denmark and Norway became Protestant by 1537.

Calvinism

In the 1540s, the French theologian John Calvin established Geneva, in Switzerland, as a base from where his pastors could be sent out to teach the precepts of his new brand of Protestantism. In Scotland, they created Presbyterianism, and in England and the Netherlands they helped inspire the Puritan movement; by 1562, two million people in France were Calvinists. Calvin was more radical in his thinking than Luther and, particularly in the work *Institutes of the Christian Religion*, preached God's sole sovereignty and the notion of predestination, in which God preselects those destined to find salvation.

Bible translations and literacy

Protestants agreed that people had a right to read the Bible in their own languages. Although John Wycliffe had produced an English Bible in 1382 and Jan Hus a Czech version in 1406, it was not until the invention of the printing press later in the 15th century that wider access to new translations became practical. The first such work was by William Tyndale, whose English New Testament (1526) was smuggled from Germany into England. Tyndale was executed in 1536, but by that time Martin Luther's German-language Bible had already become a standard reference work.

> "I **detest dissension** ... it goes against the **teachings of Christ** and against a **secret inclination** of nature."
>
> DESIDERIUS ERASMUS, Dutch philosopher and scholar, Letter to Marcus Laurinus, 1523

Wars in Germany and France

From the outset, Holy Roman Emperor Charles V had sought to suppress Lutheranism, but the resistance of the Protestant princes from 1530 led to decades of war. In Germany, a peace was eventually agreed at Augsburg in 1555 that allowed Protestants to worship freely, but only in already Protestant states. In France, Catholics and Protestants, known as Huguenots, fought a series of bitter religious wars starting in 1562. The conflicts ended in 1598, when Henri IV, a former Huguenot who had reconverted to Catholicism, granted the Huguenots religious toleration.

Quill

Stained glass shows venerated opponent of Protestant Reformation

SIR THOMAS MORE

The Reformation in Britain

Protestant ideas made little headway in England until Henry VIII, enraged by the Pope's refusal to annul his marriage, broke with Rome in 1534 and established the Church of England with himself as its head. Chancellor Thomas More criticized Henry, and was beheaded. Under Henry's successor, Edward VI, protestant reform increased, but his changes were reversed by Mary, his Catholic half-sister; Elizabeth I later restored the Protestant status quo. In Scotland, Catholic and Calvinist rivalries threatened civil war after Mary, Queen of Scots, ascended the throne, but her flight to England ensured a Protestant victory.

> **"We thought** that the clergy ... had been **our subjects wholly ... but they be but half our subjects ... "**
>
> KING HENRY VIII,
> Attacking the English clergy's allegiance to the pope, 1532

The Counter-Reformation

In 1545, the Council of Trent, which met until 1563, began what became known as the Counter-Reformation, demonstrating that Catholicism had recognized its failings and was prepared to change. During this period, the Council upheld papal supremacy, clarified Church dogma, and tackled abuses such as the sale of indulgences. A list of forbidden books was established, the Roman Inquisition was revived—having been founded in 1542 to punish heresy—and the Society of Jesus was tasked with reconverting people back to Catholicism from Protestantism.

The Thirty Years' War

Triggered by a Protestant rebellion in Bohemia in 1618 against the Catholic Ferdinand II, the Thirty Years' War spread across the Holy Roman Empire and lasted until 1648 when the Treaty of Westphalia gave all Protestants the right to worship freely. Spain and the Catholic League fought on the imperial side, while Denmark, Sweden, and France supported the Protestants. Millions of people died in the conflict.

Quillon crossguard for grip and protection

Cutting edges on each side

Thrusting and stabbing point

REFORMATION WARS-ERA DAGGER

◀ **The "weight" of the Bible**
In this allegory of the Reformation, scales assess the relative merits of each side, with the Protestant Bible easily outweighing the earthly riches of the Catholic Church.

see also The Enlightenment pp.346–47 ▶ World religions pp.378–81 ▶ **345**

The Enlightenment

Also known as the Age of Reason, the Enlightenment was a period of intellectual and philosphical thought that began in the mid-17th century, when a scientific revolution sparked off new investigative methods and ways of thinking. Social and political philosophers applied the same methods to further their own studies of the nature of humanity. The result was an explosion of scientific activity and philosophical thought that challenged many long-accepted preconceptions, dogmas, and beliefs.

René Descartes and philosophy

Widely regarded as the father of modern Western philosophy, French philosopher René Descartes (1596-1650) was the founder of "rationalism"—a way of understanding the world using reason as a means of attaining knowledge. He proposed that deduction was the only way to achieve this, epitomized in the phrase he coined, *"Cogito ergo sum"* (I think, therefore I am) and argued that the teachings of philosophers such as Aristotle were flawed because they were irrational.

Galileo and the new astronomy

Italian astronomer Galileo Galilei (1564-1642) helped revolutionize understanding of the universe using a telescope of his own design. His observations confirmed the belief first proposed by 16th-century Polish astronomer Nicolaus Copernicus that the planets orbited the sun. This led to Galileo's conviction for heresy by the Roman Catholic Inquisition and he spent his last years under house arrest. Other influential astronomers include Johannes Kepler (1571-1630), who devised the Laws of Planetary Motion, and Giovanni Cassini (1625-1712), who measured how long it took Jupiter and Mars to rotate.

Rousseau, Locke, and Enlightenment philosophy

Two political philosophers, the British John Locke (1632-1704) and Swiss-born Jean-Jacques Rousseau (1712-78), were key contributors to Enlightenment thinking. Locke argued for a social contract to help people protect their rights and a representative form of government—but stipulated that only adult male property owners should vote. Rousseau thought people were naturally good, but society corrupted them—to live peacefully they had to put individual wishes after what he called the collective or general will.

Newton and gravity

British mathematician Sir Isaac Newton (1642-1727) laid the foundation of modern physics in his book *Principia Mathematica*, first published in 1687. The book, which took him two years to write,

encapsulated more than 20 years of thinking and experimentation. In it Newton outlined his theory of calculus, his three Laws of Motion and, most significantly, his Theory of Universal Gravitation. His observations on gravity went unchallenged until the early 1900s, when German-born physicist Albert Einstein put forward an alternative proposal in his General Theory of Relativity.

Eye piece on side of main tube

Globe-shaped stand

NEWTON'S REFLECTOR TELESCOPE

Robert Boyle and chemistry

When British scientist Robert Boyle (1627-91), with his assistant Robert Hooke (1635-1703), devised his air pump, he laid the groundwork for a new approach to scientific investigation—that practical experimentation was the only way to verify a theory. He established that air was needed for sound transmission, to keep a flame burning, and for life itself. He formulated Boyle's Law: the pressure exerted by a mass of gas is inversely proportionate to the volume it occupies.

ADAM SMITH

A leading figure in the Scottish Enlightenment, Adam Smith (1723-90), known as the father of economics and capitalism, came to prominence after becoming a professor at Glasgow University in 1751. His first book, *The Theory of Moral Sentiments*, was published in 1759, but *The Wealth of Nations* cemented his reputation.

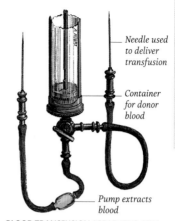

Needle used to deliver transfusion

Container for donor blood

Pump extracts blood

BLOOD TRANSFUSION APPARATUS, 1876

Medical advances

This period saw great advances in medical knowledge. In 1628, British physician William Harvey (1578-1657) showed that the heart pumped blood through the body. In 1676, Dutch investigator Antonie van Leeuwenhoek (1632-1723) discovered blood cells and observed living bacteria using his new microscope. In the late 18th century, Scottish brothers John and William Hunter (1728-93 and 1718-83) made advances in anatomy, and Edward Jenner (1749-1823) pioneered vaccination.

Scientific societies

The 17th and 18th centuries saw the introduction of scientific societies. In 1603, Galileo was a prominent member of Rome's new *Accademia dei Lincei*. In France, Louis XIV founded the *Academie Royale des Sciences* in 1666. London's Royal Society was set up in 1660, and Charles II became its patron in 1662. Similar groups were founded across Europe and North America; the American Philosophical Society opened in Philadelphia in 1743.

Adam Smith and *The Wealth of Nations*

In his book *The Wealth of Nations*, first published in 1776, Scottish thinker and economist Adam Smith argued that all human beings possessed the natural tendency to put their own needs and

interests first. Economic progress, he stated, relied on the pursuit of enlightened self-interest, what he called the "division of labor," and freedom of trade. He also argued that governments should interfere as little as possible in the running of the economy, allowing what he termed the "invisible hand" of the market to regulate it. His views had an enormous impact on the rising middle classes throughout Europe and in the newly independent US.

"**My country** is the **world**, and **my religion** is to **do good**."

THOMAS PAINE, *The Rights of Man*, 1792

Diderot and the *Encyclopédie*

The French philosopher Denis Diderot (1713–84), his coauthor and editor the mathematician Jean Le Rond d'Alembert (1717–83), and more than 140 other contributors, sought to document all existing branches of human knowledge in one extensive work, *Encyclopédie*. Diderot began publication by volume in 1751, and by the time the work was finished, it consisted of 17 volumes of text, 11 of illustrations, and six supplementary volumes. Although the text was completed by 1765, it was not until 1772 that all the accompanying plates were ready for publication. The work was enormously influential, as well as controversial. Diderot and his fellow encyclopedists came under sustained attack from religious and government elements because of the liberal views they expressed.

Absolutism

Certain influential 18th-century thinkers, such as the French writer Voltaire (1694–1778) and Rousseau, believed that social, economic, and educational reforms could only be achieved by a new type of monarch— the so-called enlightened despot. The Prussian emperor, Frederick the Great, sought Voltaire's advice on how to be such a ruler. In Russia, Peter the Great tried to modernize his country, and in Austria, Empress Maria Theresa, and later her son Joseph II, became prominent reformers.

▼ *An experiment on a bird in the air pump*, **Jospeph Wright, 1768**
This British study shows a dove being observed as it is deprived of air in an experiment.

African kingdoms

Just as in Europe, Asia, and South America, empires flourished in Africa throughout the Middle Ages and beyond, and some even rivaled the might of ancient Rome or Persia. Three of these in the west of the continent—Ghana, Mali, and Songhai—evolved into powerful trading hubs, controlling the flow of gold, salt, and other merchandise between north and sub-Saharan Africa. Their wealth also transformed them into centers of culture and learning.

The Ghana Empire

An established presence in West Africa from the 6th to the 13th centuries, the Ghana Empire controlled the regional trade in gold, ivory, ostrich feathers, hides, and slaves into North Africa. Unlike modern Ghana, this empire encompassed present-day Mali and Mauritania in the western Sudan savanna, and was policed by a formidable army, which included cavalry. Its capital, Koumbi Saleh, one of the largest African cities of its time, became the wealthiest city in West Africa. It was home to about 20,000 people and to the Ghana kings, who reputedly stockpiled gold nuggets.

Arabic script   *Handpainted decorations*

QUR'AN, TIMBUKTU MANUSCRIPTS

Timbuktu and the spread of Islam

After the Muslim Arabs conquered North Africa in the 7th century, merchants, scholars, and missionaries brought Islam into West Africa. It was initially peaceful, as African rulers either tolerated Islam or converted to it, but it met with resistance in the East in Christian kingdoms such as Nubia and Axum, and was imposed by force. Islam helped spread the art of writing in Africa, which flourished in cities such as Timbuktu. By the 14th century, Timbuktu had several mosques and universities, and was a center for Muslim scholars.

The Kanem Empire

Kanem controlled the region surrounding Lake Chad from the 9th to the 14th centuries; its heart, however, lay on the lake's eastern shores. Although its ruler converted to Islam in the late 11th century, the religion was not widely embraced until the 13th century. Kanem's location at the end of a Saharan caravan route made it a natural hub that facilitated trade between the merchants of North and central Africa and those of central Africa and the Nile Valley. Its wealth funded an efficient cavalry and allowed for its expansion northward into the Sahara.

The Songhai Empire

Dating from at least the 9th century, Songhai overcame territory losses to the Mali empire in the 14th century to become West Africa's most powerful empire between c.1460 and c.1591. Its success reached a zenith under Sunni Ali (1464–92), known as "Sunni the Merciless." Using shrewd battle strategy, the king repulsed attackers and secured the empire's territories by around 1468. Besides an armored cavalry, Songhai possessed one of North Africa's few navies, which Sunni Ali used to seize part of the failing Mali Empire.

Ethiopia (Zagwe and Solomonid)

By the end of the 9th century, the Agau people of the Ethiopian highlands had overthrown the Aksumite rulers who once dominated the Red Sea coast. They established the Christian Zagwe dynasty, which ruled Ethiopia in the 12th and 13th centuries. The Zagwe are best known for building 11 churches out of solid rock in the capital city of Roha. In the late 13th century, the Zagwe were replaced by the powerful Solomonid dynasty, which claimed descendance from King Solomon. The Solomonids remained in power until 1974, when Haile Selassie I was deposed.

Figures show exaggerated facial features

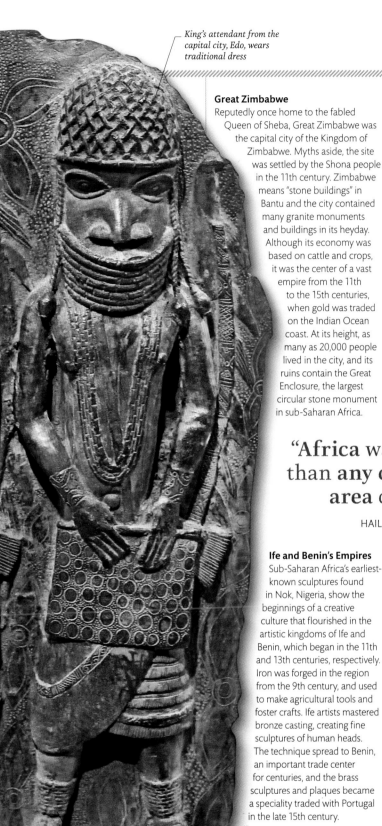

King's attendant from the capital city, Edo, wears traditional dress

Great Zimbabwe

Reputedly once home to the fabled Queen of Sheba, Great Zimbabwe was the capital city of the Kingdom of Zimbabwe. Myths aside, the site was settled by the Shona people in the 11th century. Zimbabwe means "stone buildings" in Bantu and the city contained many granite monuments and buildings in its heyday. Although its economy was based on cattle and crops, it was the center of a vast empire from the 11th to the 15th centuries, when gold was traded on the Indian Ocean coast. At its height, as many as 20,000 people lived in the city, and its ruins contain the Great Enclosure, the largest circular stone monument in sub-Saharan Africa.

The Mali Empire

Founded by Sundiata Keita (r.1230–55), the Mali Empire spanned four centuries. At its height under Mansa ("King") Musa I (r.1312–37) it was the largest empire Africa had ever seen, stretching from the Atlantic to the intellectual trading hub of Timbuktu, and into the Sahara. Mali's wealth was fueled by natural resources such as gold and salt, as well as by its control and taxation of regional trade routes. When Musa, a devout Muslim, embarked on his Hajj pilgrimage to Mecca in 1324, he took with him large quantities of gold and tens of thousands of soldiers and slaves.

The Jolof Empire

The Jolof, or Wolof, Empire rose to power in the mid-14th century. It was situated between West Africa's Senegal and Gambia rivers, in what had once been an agricultural part of the Mali Empire. It grew rich from dealing in, among other commodities, gold, ivory, hides, textiles, gum, and slaves—transactions that were

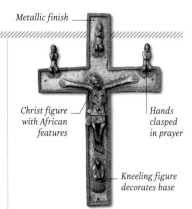

Metallic finish

Christ figure with African features

Hands clasped in prayer

Kneeling figure decorates base

16TH–17TH CENTURY KONGOLESE CRUCIFIX

The Kingdom of Kongo

Located south of the Congo River on the central African west coast, the Kingdom of Kongo was formed in the late 14th century by an alliance of various local principalities. It became a trading empire, with the slave trade creating a large proportion of its wealth. At its height it had a population of more than 2 million. Although ruled by a single monarch, who in the 16th century adopted Catholicism, Kongo's government included a council of elders, governors, and local officials, as well as an army of up to 20,000 slaves.

European settlement and slave trade

Wealthy African empires attracted trade with Europeans merchants. By the 16th century, interest shifted from luxury items to slaves; an estimated 12.5 million were shipped across the Atlantic. The impact was devastating. Warfare increased, slave-raiding was common, and only those supplied with European firearms could resist. Farms were destroyed, resulting in famines, and European diseases such as syphilis and smallpox were introduced.

> ## "Africa was born no later ... than any other geographical area on this globe."
>
> HAILE SELASSIE, Emperor of Ethiopia, 1930–74

Ife and Benin's Empires

Sub-Saharan Africa's earliest-known sculptures found in Nok, Nigeria, show the beginnings of a creative culture that flourished in the artistic kingdoms of Ife and Benin, which began in the 11th and 13th centuries, respectively. Iron was forged in the region from the 9th century, and used to make agricultural tools and foster crafts. Ife artists mastered bronze casting, creating fine sculptures of human heads. The technique spread to Benin, an important trade center for centuries, and the brass sculptures and plaques became a speciality traded with Portugal in the late 15th century.

often conducted with European merchants from France and Portugal. Until 1600, slaves comprised a third of Jolof's "merchandise," but this declined as slaves from this empire were replaced by those captured in other parts of Africa.

Anklets

◄ Benin bronzes
Highly decorated plaques, made using the lost-wax casting technique decorated the palace of the oba, or king, of Benin. Many depict the king and his attendants.

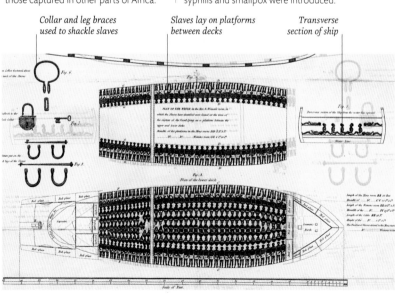

Collar and leg braces used to shackle slaves

Slaves lay on platforms between decks

Transverse section of ship

PLAN OF A TRADE SHIP SHOWING HOW AFRICAN SLAVES WERE TRANSPORTED, 1823

see also Colonial empires pp.356–57 ▶ The struggle for independence pp.368–69 ▶

The modern world (1750 onward)

The last three centuries have ushered in unprecedented change, as revolutions reshaped boundaries, empires fell, new nations were born, and colonialism and slavery became a thing of the past. Rapid industrialization and burgeoning capitalist economies sparked many disputes, some of which escalated into civil—and, later, global— conflicts as agrarian and industrial, then capitalist and communist societies collided. Religious and ethnic divisions erupted into violence in other parts of the globe. Economies rose, fell, and rose again, and while science created a frightening weapon that ended a world war, the struggle for land, power, and resources continues.

Motto reads "Glory and fatherland"

1754 The Seven Years' War breaks out in Europe. New alliances form, fuelling hostilities in existing conflicts such as the French and Indian War (1754–63) in North America.

PRUSSIAN WAR BANNER

Imperial eagle

October 1929 The New York Stock Exchange crashes as panic selling causes stock prices to plummet. Banks fail in the early 1930s and the Great Depression begins.

1922 Benito Mussolini's march on Rome elevates him to prime minister of Italy, bringing Fascism to the world stage.

Benito Mussolini

BENITO MUSSOLINI'S MARCH ON ROME

March 15, 1917 In Russia, centuries of Romanov rule come to an end when Tsar Nicholas II abdicates after demonstrators in Petrograd demand socialist reforms.

Slogan reads: "15 years of struggle for the General Party Line 1917–1932"

RUSSIAN PROPAGANDA POSTER

90/105 mm main gun

Main gun sight

Turret holds one of three crew

1930s Overfarming and drought lead to soil depletion in the US. Dust storms ravage agrarian states as farmers are forced to migrate in search of work.

MIGRANT WORKER, US, 1936

AMX-13 TANK, AS USED IN THE SIX-DAY WAR

June 1967 In the Six-Day War, Arab states Egypt, Syria, and Jordan fight Israel, which wins control of the Sinai Peninsula, the Gaza Strip, East Jerusalem, and the Golan Heights.

East and West Germans sit atop the Berlin Wall, celebrating the end of the Cold War

American soldiers help South Vietnamese forces at the Battle of Khe Sanh

US SOLDIERS IN VIETNAM

March 8, 1965 Two US Marine battalions arrive at Da Nang, as America enters the war between Communist North and independent South Vietnam.

1979 The Shah of Iran Mohammad Reza Shah Pahlavi flees the country after an Islamic uprising led by the religious leader Ruhollah Khomeini forces him from power.

96.3 mile- (155 km-) long wall of concrete and barbed wire

MOHAMMAD REZA SHAH PAHLAVI

November 9, 1989 In Germany, East Berlin's Communist Party announces free movement between East and West Berlin. Destruction of the 28-year-old Berlin Wall begins.

FALL OF BERLIN WALL

Signatories include US founding father Benjamin Franklin, who also helped draft the declaration

In October 1789, Parisian women march to Versailles protesting the rising price of bread

July 4, 1776 Fifteen months after the first skirmish between British and American troops, the Continental Congress signs a Declaration severing American colonies' ties with Britain.

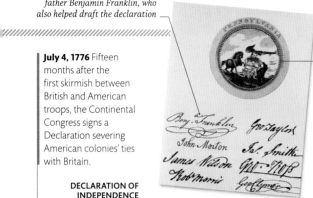

State of Pennsylvania's seal

DECLARATION OF INDEPENDENCE

July 4, 1789 In France, a mob of Parisians storm the Bastille—a state-run armory, prison, and symbol of French King Louis XVI's oppressive rule. The French Revolution begins.

SCENE FROM THE FRENCH REVOLUTION

June 28, 1914 Serbian nationalist Gavrilo Princip assassinates Austrian Archduke Franz Ferdinand and his wife in Bosnia, sparking World War I.

FRANZ FERDINAND

US CIVIL WAR CARTOON

April 1865 The four-year-long US civil war draws to a close with the Confederate South surrendering to the Union.

NAPOLEON'S EMPIRE, 1812

KEY

■ French Empire
□ French client states
■ Independent allies
□ Opposing Napoleon

1815 Led by the Duke of Wellington, Arthur Wellesley, British and allied forces defeat Napoleon at the Battle of Waterloo, ending 23 years of war.

1807 The Abolition of the Slave Trade Act makes slave trade illegal throughout British colonies.

Medal depicts slave breaking free of shackles

MEDAL COMMEMORATING THE ABOLITION ACT

NAZI INSIGNIA

Swastika symbol

September 1, 1939 German forces, under the command of *Führer* Adolf Hitler, attack Poland by land and air. World War II begins.

August 1945 US bombers drop atomic bombs on the Japanese cities of Hiroshima and Nagasaki, killing an estimated 120,000 people. Japan surrenders unconditionally on August 15, ending World War II.

Fast explosive   *Slow explosive*

Plutonium core   *Tamper/ Pusher*

Neutron initiator

CROSS-SECTION OF ATOM BOMB

August 15, 1947 The Indian Independence Bill ends 200 years of British rule in India and Pakistan, recognizing them as independent nations.

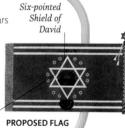

STATESMEN JAWAHARLAL NEHRU (LEFT) AND MUHAMMAD ALI JINNAH

1960 Seventeen African territories gain independence from European rule. Ghanaian President Kwame Nkrumah proclaims "a new era" at the United Nations Assembly.

Nose-mounted jet intake

Swept-back tail design

MIG-15

June 25, 1950 Communist forces from Soviet-backed North Korea invade US-supported South Korea, sparking three years of bloodshed as the Korean War begins.

October 1, 1949 Communist leader Mao Zedong serves as the chairman of People's Republic of China, with Zhou Enlai as premier.

May 14, 1948 The first Jewish state in 2,000 years is created in Tel Aviv, as David Ben-Gurion proclaims the state of Israel and becomes its first prime minister.

Six-pointed Shield of David

Twelve stars possibly representing 12 tribes of Israel

PROPOSED FLAG DESIGN, 1918

January 16, 1991 President George H.W. Bush announces the beginning of Operation Desert Storm to remove Iraqi forces that had invaded Kuwait. The first Gulf War begins.

Leaflet encouraging Iraqi forces to surrender

GULF WAR LEAFLET, 1991–92

September 11, 2001 The twin towers of New York's World Trade Center are destroyed as two passenger planes hijacked by Islamic extremists are flown into them.

2008 Financial firms, such as the investment bank Lehman Brothers, collapse, leading to the worst global financial crisis since the Great Depression.

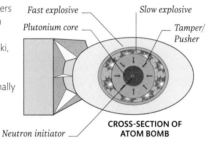

GLOBAL WARMING

2000s With higher temperatures being recorded the world over, the issue of global warming comes into sharper focus.

2011 Following the immolation of Tunisian street trader Mohamed Bouazizi in December 2010, a series of pro-democracy protests result in regime changes in Arab countries including Tunisia, Egypt, and Libya.

see also Political revolutions pp.352–53 ▶ Modern civil wars pp.358–59 ▶ The struggle for independence pp.368–69 ▶

enté par le Sr cholat lun des Vainqueur de la Bastille.   Siege de la B

Political revolutions

In the late 18th century, revolutions in North America and France fueled demands for social and political freedoms that were to transform the world. The 19th century saw nationalist movements flower in Europe, which then spread to different parts of the globe. Attempts to bring about the sovereignty of the people went hand in hand with this, although they did not necessarily bring democracy in their wake, as events in Russia and China were to show.

Red enamel coating

Hammer and plow

RED ARMY CAP BADGE, 1919

The American Revolution
Tension between Britain and its North American colonists, fueled by British efforts to impose new taxes, snapped in 1775, when armed conflict broke out. The 13 colonies declared independence in 1776, and seven more years of war ensued, with the Patriots fighting British troops and Loyalists. After France joined them in 1778, the tide turned in favor of the Patriots. The British defeat at Yorktown in 1781 proved decisive, and Britain conceded American independence in 1783.

Painted canvas with "Liberty" embroidered in cartouche

Insignia of company

1776 KNAPSACK OF 4TH MARYLAND INDEPENDENT COMPANY

The French Revolution of 1789–99
The revolution reached its first climax in 1789, with the National Assembly abolishing feudalism and adopting the Declaration of the Rights of Man. In 1791, it moved to a constitutional monarchy. From 1792, more extreme factions seized power, proclaimed a republic, and executed King Louis XVI. The Committee of Public Safety took dictatorial powers and executed 20,000 counterrevolutionaries. A more moderate regime took hold until 1799, when Napoleon (see p.361) seized power.

◀ **The Bastille falls**
The Paris mob attacked the Bastille fortress on July 14, 1789, seeing it as a symbol of royal oppression.

Parliamentary democracy: Britain and France
Though the Glorious Revolution of 1688 had established constitutional monarchy in Britain, the country was far from a full parliamentary democracy—in 1800, only 10 percent of the adult male population had the vote. Reform acts in 1832, 1867, and 1884 broadened the franchise, but full adult suffrage was not achieved until 1928. At least Britain had a parliament, however. In France, the Estates-General, which did not even meet from 1614 to 1789, had no legislative power. Its three estates, representing the clergy, nobility, and the common people, could only advise the king.

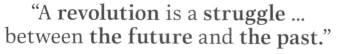

> "A **revolution** is a **struggle** ... between **the future** and **the past**."
>
> FIDEL CASTRO, Cuban revolutionary leader, 1959

Italian unification
After the end of the Napoleonic Wars of 1799–1815, Italy was redivided into a patchwork of small, independent states, and the country was largely controlled by Spanish Bourbons and Austrian Hapsburgs (see pp.344–45). However, the desire for national unity could not be assuaged. From 1815, Giuseppe Mazzini and Giuseppe Garibaldi led the cause, though their initial efforts failed. Having masterminded an alliance with Napoleon III's France, Piedmont-Sardinia's prime minister, the Count of Cavour, tricked Austria into war in 1859, as a result of which Sardinia gained Lombardy. Central Italy voted to join Sardinia, Garibaldi liberated Sicily and Naples, and, in 1861, a united Italy was proclaimed. Austria was forced to turn Venice over to the new kingdom in 1866; Rome followed in 1871.

The 1848 uprisings
In 1848, many parts of Europe were about to erupt as popular discontent with the established order grew. Revolutions broke out first in Sicily and France, where King Louis Philippe I was overthrown. Revolts flared up in the rest of Italy and the Austrian empire, while, in Germany, nationalist assemblies in Berlin and Frankfurt called for the country to be united under Prussian rule. The apparent success was short-lived. With the exception of France, where Louis Napoleon (later Napoleon III) emerged to take power, the status quo eventually was restored everywhere else.

German unification
In the early 1850s, Germany was still a loose confederation of individual states dominated by Austria, but in the 1860s the state of Prussia took the lead in pressing for German unification. The Prussian chief minister, Otto von Bismarck, engineered a war with Austria in 1866. Prussia's victory, achieved in just seven weeks, led to the formation of the North German Confederation. Another war four years later, this time with France, led to the South German states allying themselves with the North in 1870. The French were defeated and the German empire was proclaimed in 1871, with Bismarck as its first chancellor.

The Russian Revolution
There was not one but two revolutions in Russia in 1917, when the war-weary Russians rose up to topple Tsar Nicholas II, ending 304 years of despotic Romanov rule. The first, in February, forced the tsar's abdication and led to the installation of a well-meaning, but weak, democratic government. In the second, in October, the Bolsheviks, led by Lenin, who had returned to Russia after years of exile, seized power. They went on to defeat their opponents in a bitter civil war and set up the Soviet Union in 1922, a one-party Communist federation. This survived World War II and became a global super-power, but collapsed in 1991, when the fall of Communism led to its dissolution.

The Chinese Revolution
The Communist Party of China (CPC) was founded in Shanghai in 1921. In 1927, its nationalist rivals, the Kuomintang (KMT), forced the CPC back into the south. In 1934, Mao Zedong led the CPC north to Shaanxi in the Long March, taking a year to make the 3,700 mile (6,000 km) trek. After World War II, a bitter civil war ended in 1949 with Mao's proclamation of the People's Republic of China.

The Cuban Revolution
Revolt against Fulgencio Batista's regime began in 1953, when Fidel Castro led an abortive raid on an army barracks. By 1958, guerrilla war engulfed the island; in 1959, Batista fled and Castro took power. His aim to break the US stranglehold on the Cuban economy led him to ally with the USSR. The Soviets' attempt to set up missile bases in Cuba in 1961 brought the world to the brink of nuclear war.

The Iranian Revolution
In 1978, opposition to the autocratic rule of Shah Mohammad Reza Pahlavi led to riots calling for Shia religious leader Ayatollah Khomeini's return. In 1979, the shah fled the country. Khomeini returned and established the Islamic Republic, which he ran on strict religious and social lines. Its anti-Western sentiments and support for radical Shia groups abroad led to ongoing tensions with the US.

CHE GUEVARA
An Argentine-born revolutionary, Che Guevara (1928–67) sprang to prominence during the revolution in Cuba that propelled Fidel Castro to power. After serving as a minister in Castro's new government, he left the island in 1965 to fulfill his ambition of fermenting revolutions in other parts of the developing world, first in the Congo and then in Bolivia, where he was captured and executed.

see also The age of global conflicts pp.360–63 ▶   Self-determination and civil rights pp.366–67 ▶   What is politics? pp.392–93 ▶

The Industrial Revolution

Starting in Britain in the late 18th century, the Industrial Revolution gradually spread across Europe and into the US. It was characterized by technological innovation and growth in industry, with the invention of new machines such as the steam engine, spinning jenny, and power loom leading to industrialization on a massive scale. The consequent economic growth, also spurred by a population boom, transformed the lives of people throughout the world.

Origins of the revolution

The Industrial Revolution began in Britain, driven by a number of factors. Advances in agriculture fueled a population boom of potential workers. The island's wealth of mineral resources, particularly iron ore and coal, facilitated iron and steel production and powered steam engines. Technological developments pioneered by a generation of inventive geniuses, such as James Watt, the inventor of an improved steam engine, and Richard Arkwright, who devised a spinning frame that improved textile production, also led to an increase in industry. Britain's geographical location and command of the sea made it easy to boost its export trade.

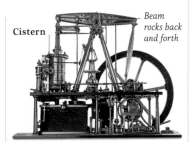

Cistern

Beam rocks back and forth

WATT STEAM ENGINE

James Watt and steam power

Though Scottish mathematical instrument-maker James Watt is generally regarded as the father of the steam engine, he did not actually invent it.

Realizing that existing steam engines were extremely inefficient (the repeated cooling and reheating of their cylinders wasted vast amounts of useful steam), he devised a separate condensing cylinder to solve the problem. Although Watt devised the condensing chamber in 1765, he did not patent it until 1769. In 1774, he began working in partnership with Birmingham foundry-owner Matthew Boulton. The engines the two men manufactured went on to revolutionize the mining, iron-making, textile, and manufacturing industries in Britain and internationally.

The iron and steel industries

Abraham Darby I revolutionized iron-making in 1709 by pioneering the use of coke, rather than the traditional charcoal, as a fuel. In the 1780s, Henry Cort devised a faster way to make wrought iron, and over the next 20 years, iron production increased by 400 percent. Steel, however, remained expensive until Henry Bessemer invented the "Bessemer converter" in 1856. As a result, steel could be made quickly and cheaply for the first time.

Textiles

Textile manufacturing was one of the industries that benefited the most from the Industrial Revolution. In Britain, many inventions, such as the spinning jenny, a multispindle spinning frame, turned a cottage industry into an industrial one. In the US, the cotton gin made it quicker and easier to remove unwanted seeds from cotton. Cotton imports from North America and India provided the raw materials for the creation of a new mass-market in cotton textiles, manufactured by the mills that sprang up to feed it.

COTTON MILL

> "It was a town of **machines and tall chimneys** out of which interminable **serpents of smoke** trailed themselves for ever ..."
>
> CHARLES DICKENS, Description of Coketown, *Hard Times*, 1854

Canals and railroads

Better transportation links were an essential prerequisite for the Industrial Revolution's spread. Canals allowed the quick and efficient transport of heavy goods. By 1850, however, canals were battling for survival with railroads (see pp.284–85). By the end of the century, Britain was crisscrossed with railroad lines. British engineering expertise lay behind the building of railroads in Europe, Asia, and South America. In the US, a railroad-building boom peaked following the Civil War (see p.359).

The spread of the industrialization

Though Britain's industrial growth led contemporaries to christen it the "workshop of the world," its dominance lasted for only about 50 years before other countries caught up. In Europe, Belgium led the way, followed later by Germany and France. In the US, the Industrial Revolution started in the northeast, when Samuel Slater, an enterprising British immigrant, established the first US cotton mill. Following the Civil War (1861–65), widespread industrialization progressed at breakneck speed.

Urbanization

As the Industrial Revolution progressed, towns and cities grew apace, fueled by a major population shift away from the countryside farms and villages. In preindustrial Britain, over 80 percent of the population lived in rural areas; by 1850, over 50 percent lived in cities and towns. As industrialization spread elsewhere in Europe and North America, they, too, became urbanized. In the second half of the 19th century, Chicago became the world's fastest-growing city; between 1860 and 1900 its population grew from just 112,000 to 1,698,000.

Factories and model settlements

Factories had one main purpose: to maximize productivity and profit. They were often cluttered, dirty, poorly lit, and unsafe. The men, women, and children who worked in them labored for 12 to 16 hours a day, six days a week. Few employers tried to change things until the early 1800s, when manufacturer and social reformer Robert Owen pioneered better conditions at New Lanark Mill, Scotland. In the US, George Pullman had success with the town he founded for his employees.

The new working class and unions

During the Industrial Revolution, workers had few, if any, rights, and the government did little to protect them. In Britain, for instance, the Combination Acts made strikes illegal and banned the formation of trade unions. Though the Acts were repealed in 1824, it was only from the 1850s onward that trade unions started to win hard-fought concessions. The story was similar in the US, where the ever-expanding population had workers competing for limited jobs. This meant that employers could dictate how much or how little they would pay.

The Second Industrial Revolution

Between 1870 and 1914, rapid advances in steelmaking and the advent of electricity spurred industrial production to new heights of ingenuity. Technological and manufacturing innovations, most notably the development of machine tools, made it possible to mass produce all types of goods. Communication was transformed with the invention of the telegraph and telephone. Transportation, too, was revolutionized by the invention of the internal combustion engine (see pp.286-87). By the end of the 19th century, Germany's industrial output outstripped that of Britain, while the US emerged as a leading industrial power.

SOCIAL CONDITIONS AND PHILANTHROPY

Inspired by the poor social conditions caused by industrialization, modern philanthropy took shape between about 1885 and 1914, as some wealthy people looked for socially beneficial ways of utilizing their surplus wealth. Donations often went to hospitals, the poor, or educational institutions.

CHILD WORKER IN TEXTILE FACTORY

◀ **Sheffield, England, 1800s**
The smokestacks of steel factories in this British industrial city are shown pumping out smoke in this contemporary handcolored woodcut.

Colonial empires

Colonialism is the practice of acquiring political control of overseas territories, generally for economic exploitation, and often involving the violent subjugation of the territory's population. It emerged as a distinct phenomenon in the 16th century led by various European powers who by 1900 had colonized much of the world, including virtually all of Africa. Stifling local political development, these measures removed the autonomy of entire regions and caused irreparable damage to entire societies.

The roots of modern colonialism

Voyages conducted by European explorers in the 16th century saw once-separate empires and nations come into contact with each other for the first time. These explorers were initially sent out by their sovereigns to find routes to the source of valuable spices such as pepper and cloves.

The economic gains to be made through trade and exploitation of these lands gradually attracted more European adventurers who began to settle, displacing local people, and often by force. These patterns emerged in a time when political competition in Europe had created a system of strong centralized states with military and technological advantages over the societies they took over, which were often hampered by political division, civil war, or disease.

The rise of empires

In the Americas, the Portuguese empire occupied modern Brazil from the early 16th century, while Spanish conquest destroyed the indigenous Aztec and Inca empires by 1533 and established control as far north as California. In North America, Britain and France founded settler colonies, beginning with Jamestown, established by Britain in 1607.

European outposts had been formed in West Africa in the 16th century as embarkation points for the shipment of enslaved Africans to the Americas. In the 17th century, the slave trade accelerated rapidly, as forced labour fueled the growth of new colonial territories. Two centuries later the "Scramble for Africa" (1881–1914) saw the pace of colonization quicken again as almost the entire continent became occupied by European powers.

TIPU SULTAN

Resistance

Indigenous peoples have strongly resisted European colonization. In North America, native Americans fought wars from the early 17th century against the settlers' occupation of their lands, while in 1775 colonists in the 13 British-controlled colonies revolted and established an independent United States in 1783. In India, local rulers such as Tipu Sultan, Sultan of Mysore, waged wars against the encroaching British, but ultimately failed (and in 1799 Mysore was conquered).

In Australia, aboriginal peoples saw entire communities eradicated as they fought and lost skirmishes against British colonizers, while the Maori in New Zealand fought wars between 1845 and 1872 that enabled them to retain at least some of their lands and way of life. In some cases, resistance took on a religious aspect, as in Sudan in the 1880s, where the Mahdi led an Islamic uprising to expel the British, while in India the British managed to anger both Muslim and Hindu soldiers serving in their army, which led to the Sepoy Uprising in 1857 that came close to overthrowing British rule in the area.

SAMUEL MAHARERO

In January 1904, Maharero (d.1923), a chief of the Herero, in South West Africa (now Namibia), led an uprising against German occupiers. Losses were huge. About 75 percent of all Herero died and Maharero was forced into exile in British-ruled Bechuanaland, where he died in 1923. In Namibia he is widely regarded as a national hero.

From 1872–1921, **under British rule,** life expectancy in India fell by **20 percent**

Colonizer portrayed as bringing order to natives

1923 NEWSPAPER ILLUSTRATION

The effects of colonization

Colonization led to the removal of local rulers and the loss of independence for many peoples. Colonized peoples were rarely accorded the same rights as citizens of the invading country. The slave trade, over three centuries, saw 12.5 million Africans shipped across the Atlantic to work on plantations in the Americas. Colonies were exploited for the economic gain of the colonizers, with no benefit accruing to indigenous peoples, with silver mined in Bolivia and diamonds in South Africa profiting the European powers.

Colonies were seen as producers of mineral or agricultural wealth and were not, after the Industrial Revolution, urged to develop their own industries, which might have rivaled those of the colonial power. Even those countries that retained their independence, such as China, had their ability to act freely severely curtailed: the British fought two wars against China in the 1840s and 1850s for the right to export opium there, and afterward occupied ports in which they traded free from Chinese jurisdiction.

◀ **Opium warehouse**
Workers pack opium in Patna, northeast India. Much of the drug's production was destined for shipment to China.

Colonization today

Although most colonies once ruled by European powers have now won their independence, a few territories regarded as too small to be viable as independent nations remain under colonial control, such as St. Helena (ruled by Britain). Others are the subject of international conflicts, such as the Falklands, the dispute over which broke out into war between Britain and Argentina in 1982. Some former colonies, such as French Guiana, remain fully absorbed into the political structure of the European power.

In independent former colonies, however, the impact of colonization remains. The economies of many became overspecialized, such as Caribbean countries dependent on banana or sugar production. After independence many suffered from a lack of education and healthcare facilities, a lack of other basic infrastructure, and a lack of access to the financial resources needed to build these.

Their borders, determined by the colonial powers, often did not match the distribution of ethnic groups, leading to damaging civil wars, while postcolonial European support for dictatorial regimes impeded the growth of civil societies in many countries. The legacy of colonialism is one of poverty halting the growth of a modern economy in growing populations with increasingly limited resources.

FALKLANDS WAR

> "The worst thing that **colonialism** did was to **cloud our view** of our past."
>
> BARACK OBAMA,
> *Dreams from My Father: A Story of Race and Inheritance, 1995*

see also Global conflicts pp.360–63 ▶   Self determination and civil rights pp.366–67 ▶   The struggle for independence pp.368–69 ▶

Modern civil wars

Civil wars have taken place throughout history, and the modernizing world saw such conflicts continue, driven by political movements, independence struggles, ethnic tensions, and more. By the late 20th century they were almost endemic: since 1945, it is estimated that as many as 25 million people perished fighting civil wars, while millions more have been displaced and impoverished. Some key conflicts from the modern era are detailed here.

Civil war in the US

The US Civil War grew from decades of tension between the northern and southern states over the enslavement of Black people and states' rights. The election of the antislavery Abraham Lincoln as president in 1860 led to the secession of the southern states to form the Confederacy, and war with the rest of the United States, or the Union, broke out in 1861. The war raged for four years, during which time over 700,000 lives were lost. A pivotal Union victory at the Battle of Gettysburg in July 1863 ended Confederate incursions into the Union's territory; eventually the weakened Confederate forces surrendered in April 1865.

The Mexican Civil War

The complex and bloody Mexican Civil War began in 1910 when dictator Porfirio Díaz was overthrown by liberal politician Francisco Madero. Madero was ousted by an army coup in early 1913, but General Victoriano Huerta, the coup's leader, failed to reimpose dictatorial rule. A guerrilla uprising broke out led by Emiliano Zapata and Francisco (Pancho) Villa, who fought for the rights of landless peasants and Mexico's *mestizo* (mixed-race) majority. Wealthy landowner Venustiano Carranza became president in 1917, but was reluctant to redistribute land to poor Mexicans. Stability was only restored in 1920 when Álvaro Obregón became president.

The Russian Civil War

After the October 1917 revolution (see p.353), the Bolsheviks' hold on power was by no means secure, and civil war with the right-wing White Russians broke out in June 1918. The White forces were initially supported by Britain, France, Italy, the US, and Japan, but this ended in 1919. The war lasted until late 1920, by which time the Communists had secured victory, achieved in part through their control of

the country's industrial heartland and most of the railway network They also possessed charismatic leadership, primarily that of Vladimir Lenin and Leon Trotsky, who convinced Russians that their success would lead to better living standards rather than a return to the repressive ways of the Tsarist regime.

Commanders   Soviet troops

PRO-BOLSHEVIK POSTER

The Chinese Civil War

Mao Zedong's Communists and the Nationalist Party, led by Chiang Kai-shek, battled for control of China in 1927–49. At first the Communists—who aimed to abolished the power of landowners and redistribute land to the collective control of the peasantry—were forced to retreat to the south of the country and then, in the Long March (see p.353), to the remote north, where they established a base. War with Japan in 1937 led to an uneasy truce, and after World War II ended in 1945, civil war broke out again. By 1949, Mao's forces were victorious and more than a million of Chiang Kai-shek's supporters fled from the mainland to Taiwan, around 60 miles (100 km) off the coast.

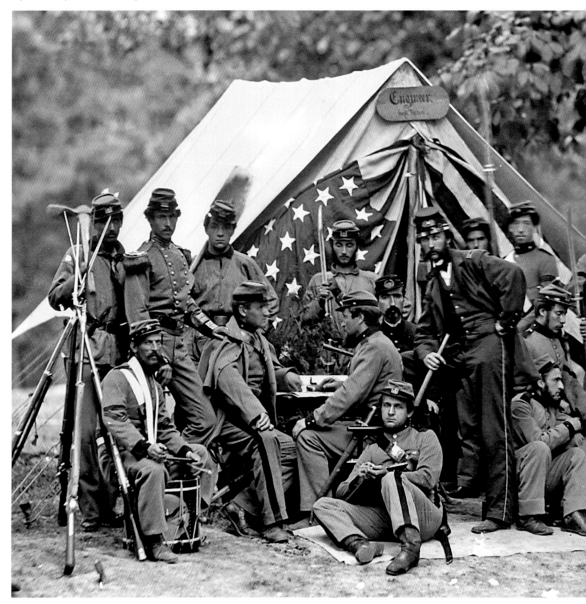

▶ **US Civil War troops, 1860s**
Engineers of the New York state militia rest in camp before going into action against opposing Confederate forces.

The Spanish Civil War

Starting in July 1936, generals Emilio Mola and Francisco Franco launched a Nationalist uprising aimed at overthrowing Spain's democratically elected Republican government. This triggered the Spanish Civil War, the bloodiest conflict western Europe had seen since the end of World War I. The uprising started in Spanish Morocco and quickly spread to southwestern Spain. The city of Madrid, however, held out against the Nationalists.

The turning point came in late 1938, when, having won the battles of Teruel and the Ebro, Franco's forces marched on Barcelona. The city's capture in January 1939 was followed by the occupation of the whole of Catalonia. When Madrid finally surrendered to the Nationalists on March 27, the war was effectively over. Franco's victory was partly achieved thanks to tacit military aid from Fascist Italy and Nazi Germany.

Nigeria and Biafra

In May 1967 the southeastern state of Biafra declared independence from the rest of Nigeria, following the massacre of thousands of the region's Igbo people by Nigerian soldiers. A civil war broke out in July when Nigerian forces attacked. Although the Biafrans held their ground at first, Nigerian forces gradually made inroads into their territory, capturing the oil fields that Biafras relied on for economic survival.

BIAFRAN TROOPS IN 1968

With no money to pay for imported food, famine ensued; it is estimated that between half a million and three million Biafrans died. The war ended in January 1970 when the Biafran government surrendered, after the loss of its last stronghold.

African backing. While the FNLA grew weaker, UNITA became more powerful. By 1992, it had gained control of about two-thirds of the country. Repeated attempts to reach a compromise eventually resulted in a peace agreement in 2002.

> "There are occasions when it **pays better** to fight and be beaten than **not to fight** at all."
>
> GEORGE ORWELL, *Homage to Catalonia*, 1938

Yugoslav civil wars

A federation of six republics, Yugoslavia erupted in civil war in 1991 after Croatia and Slovenia declared independence. Serbia sent troops to both territories; the Slovenes triumphed relatively quickly, but it took until 1995 for the Croats to win back control of their country. Bosnia declared independence in 1992, but Bosnian Serbs resisted and drove over a million Muslims and Croats from their homes. Conflict continued in the region until 2001.

The Angolan Civil War

After Angola gained independence from Portugal in 1975, tensions between three of its competing political groups led to a protracted civil war that lasted until 2002. The Cuban- and Soviet-backed People's Movement for the Liberation of Angola (MPLA) fought the National Liberation Front of Angola (FNLA) and the National Union for the Total Independence of Angola (UNITA), both of which had South

The Algerian Civil War

Having been ruled by the secular National Liberation Front (FLN) since independence from France in 1962, Algerians voted in large numbers for the Islamic Salvation Front (FIS) in the election of 1992. Rather than accept the result, the FLN organized a military crackdown against the FIS. The FIS took to the mountains and launched a guerilla campaign. Various factions emerged, some of which massacred civilians. The rebels were defeated in 2002.

The Yemeni Civil War

Mass protests led to the fall of President Ali Abdullah Saleh in 2012, but the new government struggled to maintain control of the country. In 2014, fighting intensified between the Sunni-dominated government, backed by Saudi Arabia and other Sunni Arab nations, and the Houthi, champions of Yemen's Shia Muslim minority, backed by Shia-ruled Iran. The fighting led to a humanitarian crisis.

CONFLICTS IN AFGHANISTAN

Following the Soviet withdrawal from Afghanistan in 1988, rebels seized control of much of the country. The rebels took Kabul in 1992, overthrowing the secular government. Rival factions, often divided by ethnic group, fought for dominance, until the Islamist Taliban militia took power in 1996. After the terror attacks on the US in 2001 (see p.374), US troops invaded, aiming to remove the Taliban from power.

"Stinger" rocket launcher

AFGHAN SOLDIER

The age of global conflicts

The French and Indian War (known as the Seven Years' War (1756–63) in Europe) was the first conflict to be fought on a truly global scale, in which France, Spain, Austria, Russia, and their allies battled Britain and Prussia at home and in colonial territories. This heralded a new era of large-scale wars in which major alliances battled for territory and dominance. The Napoleonic Wars (1803–15) were fought across Europe, as was the Franco-Prussian War (1870–71), which ended with the emergence of a reunified Germany as a world power. A newly industrialized Japan also entered the world stage with its unexpected defeat of Russia in the 1904–1905 Russo-Japanese War.

The Seven Years' War in Europe
This conflict arose in 1756 from Austria's move to reclaim the province of Silesia from Prussia. Europe's powers formed two alliances: France, Austria, Saxony, Sweden, and Russia on one side and Prussia, Hanover, and Britain on another. While Prussia battled on the continent, Britain renewed its attacks on France's colonies in North America and targeted France's possessions in India and the Caribbean. Peace was restored in 1763.

▼ **Japan's naval triumph**
This highly stylized painting shows Admiral Togo's decimation of the Russian fleet at the battle of Tsushima in May 1905.

Timeline
Warfare on a global scale is a relatively recent consequence of both technological developments in transportation and weapons, and intensified campaigns of colonial expansion. These conflicts paved the way for World War I and II in the 20th century.

1750

September 13, 1759 *In the French and Indian War, the Battle of Quebec lasts one hour*

February 10, 1763 *The Treaty of Paris peace document ends the French and Indian War*

August 26, 1789 *Declaration of the Rights of Man and of the Citizen is published*

May 17, 1756 *The Seven Years' War breaks out in Europe*

February 15, 1763 *The Treaty of Hubertusburg ends the Seven Years' War*

July 14, 1789 *The Storming of the Bastille occurs*

September 22, 1792 *The First Republic of France is established*

During **Napoleon's Egypt campaign**, a French soldier discovered ancient Egyptian artifact the **Rosetta Stone**

The French and Indian War

In North America, conflict between Britain, France, and their colonists and respective Native American allies had been raging since 1754. A string of British defeats was followed by a stalemate until 1759, when Britain conquered French Canada. In 1763, France ceded its North American lands.

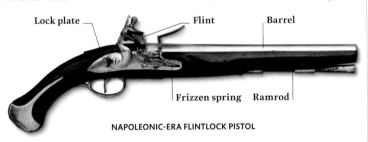

Lock plate   Flint   Barrel

Frizzen spring   Ramrod

NAPOLEONIC-ERA FLINTLOCK PISTOL

The French Revolutionary Wars

As a result of the French Revolution (see p.353), France went to war as Austria and Prussia intervened to restore the monarchy in 1792. Facing defeat, the French government ordered mass conscription. The new revolutionary armies threw back the invaders and took the offensive in Italy. French commander Napoleon's successes there forced the Austrians to make peace.

The Napoleonic Wars

Napoleon's military success made him a natural choice to lead France when Austria, Russia, Britain, and the Ottoman Empire formed a new coalition by 1799.

THE CONGRESS OF VIENNA AND EUROPEAN ALLIANCES

Convened in Vienna in 1814, the Congress aimed to restore order after the Napoleonic Wars; under its terms, France lost territory to Russia, Prussia, and Austria. Subsequently, the latter three nations headed the Holy Alliance, whose aim was to preserve the status quo. The system worked; in 1848, for example, Russia helped Austria suppress a revolution in Hungary.

Having siezed power in 1799, he forced the Austrians and Russians out of the war. Britain, too, came to a short-lived peace. When fighting resumed in 1803 with the British declaring war, Napoleon continued to win victory after victory, making peace with Russia and turning Austria and Prussia into reluctant allies. By 1809, he was the master of continental Europe.

Napoleon at bay

Having abandoned plans to invade Britain, Napoleon turned to a trade blockade to force British capitulation. However, it turned the Russians against him again. His 1812 invasion of Russia ended in a catastrophic retreat and Russia and other countries formed the Fourth Coalition against him. They were again financed by the British, who had already beaten the French at sea and began securing victories on land in the later years of the Peninsular War (1807–14) in Portugal and Spain.

The Hundred Days' War and the defeat of Napoleon

In April 1814, Napoleon was forced to abdicate by the victorious Allied powers, who exiled him to the Mediterranean island of Elba. Escaping captivity the following February, he returned to France, where he toppled the restored Bourbon monarchy within a month. The Allies declared him an outlaw and resolved to put an end to his rule once and for all. Following his defeat at Waterloo in June 1815, Napoleon abdicated again. This time, he was exiled to remote St. Helena in the South Atlantic. He died there in 1821, possibly from poor living conditions, cancer, or poisoning.

The Franco-Prussian War

The 1870–71 conflict between Prussia and its allies in the North German Confederation and France was the final link in the forging of a new unified Germany. It was the result of a diplomatic intrigue engineered by the Prussian chief minister Otto von Bismarck, which provoked Napoleon III into declaring war. This prompted the southern German states to ally with the Confederation, and they swiftly achieved victory. The new German Empire was proclaimed at Versailles in 1871, just days before peace negotiations with the French started.

The Spanish-American War of 1898

Provoked by the unexplained sinking of the US battleship *Maine* in Havana Harbor, Cuba, the Spanish-American War was short-lived. Fighting began in the Philippines in May 1898, followed by US landings in Cuba in June. In the Treaty of Paris (1898), which ended the war that December, Spain renounced all claims to Cuba, ceded Guam and Puerto Rico to the US, and sold the Philippine islands to the US for $20 million. It was the end of the Spanish Empire in the Indies.

US AFRICAN-AMERICAN REGIMENT

Oversized pickelhaube, *a German helmet*

Cavalry sword

CARTOON OF KAISER WILHELM I

The Russo-Japanese War

Tensions between Russia and Japan over disputed territories in Manchuria and Korea led to war in February 1904, when the Japanese launched a surprise attack on Port Arthur. On land, the Japanese took Port Arthur and beat the Russians at the Yalu River and Mukden; at sea, they scored a decisive victory at Tsushima. In the peace that followed and the resulting Treaty of Portsmouth (1905), Russia agreed to evacuate Manchuria and ceded Port Arthur and Korea to Japan.

Guerrilla warfare

Irregular armed forces, known as guerrillas, have featured throughout the history of warfare. They played a notable role in the Seven Years' War, as Croatian, Hungarian, and Serbian irregulars harassed Frederick the Great's Prussians in Bohemia and Moravia; during the Napoleonic Wars, French invaders suffered greatly at the hands of Spanish guerillas in the Peninsular War, and from attacks by bands of peasants and Cossacks during the long retreat from the ruins of Moscow.

> "Nothing except a **battle lost** can be half as **melancholy** as a **battle won**."
>
> DUKE OF WELLINGTON, British commander, Letter after Waterloo, 1815

May 18, 1804 *Napoleon Bonaparte crowns himself Emperor of the French*

July 19, 1870 *The Franco-Prussian War breaks out*

May 10, 1871 *The Treaty of Frankfurt ends the Franco-Prussian War*

December 10, 1898 *The Spanish-American War ends with a treaty*

1910

June 18, 1815 *The Battle of Waterloo marks the defeat of Napoleon, who is exiled*

January 18, 1871 *The German Empire is founded under Wilhelm I*

April 20, 1898 *The Spanish-American War breaks out in Cuba*

February 8, 1904 *The battle of Port Arthur begins*

May 27–28, 1905 *The battle of Tsushima takes place*

see also The struggle for independence pp.368–69 ▶ **361**

World War I was expected to last a few months, but the conflict raged for four years in the stalemate of trench warfare. New weapons such as machine guns and gas took their toll, and millions of lives were lost. World War II was even more destructive and far-reaching, and it ended with the US and the USSR as dominant world powers. They remained locked in ideological conflict for decades until the collapse of Communism in Europe and the USSR left the US as an unchallenged military superpower.

The outbreak of World War I

As the 20th century began, Europe split into new alliances. France and Russia formed a secret Dual Alliance to counterbalance the Triple Alliance between Germany, Austria-Hungary, and Italy. In 1904, Britain signed the Entente Cordiale with France, and Russia allied with Britain three years later. With the assassination of Archduke Franz Ferdinand of Austria by a Serbian nationalist in 1914, Vienna declared war on Serbia. Germany backed Austria-Hungary, Russia supported the Serbs, and France backed Russia. German violation of Belgian neutrality led Britain to declare war on Germany on August 4, 1914. Italy joined the Entente (or Allied) powers in 1915.

The Battle of the Somme

Within months, forces were dug into trenches in Belgium and France; action also took place in Prussia, the Balkans, Italy, Egypt, and more. Fought between July 1 and November 18, 1916, the Battle of the Somme was one of the most bitterly contested of World War I. Allied commanders wanted a "big push" to break the stalemate, but instead it turned into a battle of attrition at tremendous cost on both sides. The British, who bore the brunt of the fighting, advanced a total of 7 miles (11 km); on the first day of the battle, 19,240 were killed. A campaign at Passchendaele in 1917 saw similar losses.

The final offensives and the peace

The US joined the Allies in 1917. In March 1918, Germany launched a series of large-scale offensives, aiming to take advantage of their numerical superiority before US troops could be fully deployed. Despite

1914 Star

British War Medal awarded to World War I forces

British Victory Medal

THREE WORLD WAR I MEDALS

sweeping gains, the German effort ground to a halt. Allied counteroffensives at the Second Battle of the Marne on July 18 and at Amiens on August 8 drove back the exhausted Germans. Defeat coincided with revolution at home and, on November 11, delegates from the new German government signed an armistice.

The outbreak of World War II

German Nazi Party leader Adolf Hitler was determined to make Germany the dominant European power. He reintroduced conscription, created the Luftwaffe (air force), and built up a massive fighting force. The Third Reich embarked on a campaign of short, fast, and powerful attacks, known as *blitzkrieg* (lightning war) to achieve this ambition. This tactic proved effective in Germany's invasion of Poland in 1939, triggering the start of the World War II in Europe. From 1940, Denmark, Norway, the Low Countries, France, Greece, and Yugoslavia were subjected to *blitzkrieg*.

The Battle of Britain

The USSR, France, and Britain allied against Germany. After Germany conquered France in June 1940, Britain rejected Hitler's peace proposals, and German high command began planning to invade. German air assaults began in July with attacks on coastal targets and shipping. From August 13 onward, the attack moved inland, concentrating on Britain's Royal Air Force (RAF) airfields and communications centers before Hermann Goering, the Luftwaffe's commander, switched to targeting London in September. The RAF buckled under the strain, but did not break. By September 17, Goering's deadline, it was clear that air superiority was not going to be achieved and the invasion was abandoned.

HEINKEL HE111 GERMAN MEDIUM BOMBER

Operation Barbarossa

Hitler's invasion of the USSR on June 22, 1941, took the Soviets by surprise. By mid-July the Germans had advanced over 400 miles (640 km) and were 200 miles (320 km) from Moscow, but weeks were wasted while Hitler and his generals disputed which direction to take next. By the time the advance resumed, the weather had broken and it was too late. On December 5, the Soviet counteroffensive forced the Germans into a retreat, driving them back 150 miles (240 km). Germany's advance was stalled until the following spring.

The Normandy landings

The US had joined the war after Japan's attack on its Pacific fleet at Pearl Harbor in December 1941. On June 6, 1944, Allied forces launched a massive naval, air, and land assault on Nazi-occupied France. This marked the start of the final struggle to liberate northwest Europe from Nazi rule. Though the Germans had been expecting the invasion, the choice of landing sites was a surprise. By the end of the day, the Allies had established a firm foothold along the coast, though it took almost three months to break out from their beachheads and begin a drive into the French heartlands.

THE FIRST TANKS

Devised to cross barbed wire and trenches, tanks were a British invention. They made their debut during the 1916 Somme offensive, but did not make their mark until 460 Mark IV tanks broke through the German lines at Cambrai the following fall. Although initially crude and unreliable, they became widely used in modern land warfare.

Brushwood fascine was detached to help the tank cross trenches

MARK IV TANK

One of two 6-pounder guns

The defeat of Germany

In December 1944, with the Allies closing in on Germany, Hitler launched a counter-offensive in the Ardennes in France. Bad weather had grounded Allied air forces. However, the advance turned into a full-scale German retreat as the weather improved. The Allies crossed the Rhine in March 1945, the Eastern Front collapsed in the face of a massive Soviet offensive in early 1945, and Berlin fell to the Soviets on May 2. Germany formally surrendered on May 8.

War in the Pacific

At the same time as its assault on the US Pacific fleet at Pearl Harbor in December 1941, Japan had launched attacks in Southeast Asia. Hong Kong, Malaya, and Singapore fell, followed by the Dutch East Indies, the Philippines, and Burma. A US naval victory at Midway in June 1942 ended Japanese expansion. The capture of Iwo Jima and Okinawa in 1945 gave the US air bases from which to launch bombings, culminating in the atomic bombing of Hiroshima and Nagasaki on August 6 and 9. Japan surrendered on September 2, ending the war.

The Cold War: Korea and Vietnam

The first armed conflict between the post-World War II capitalist West and Communist East occurred in Southeast Asia. In June 1950, Communist North Korea invaded the US- and UN-backed South. UN forces were pushed south when Communist Chinese troops intervened. The war ended in a stalemate in July 1953.

The Vietnam War was a lengthy guerrilla struggle between the Communist North and US-backed South. US and South Vietnamese forces struggled against the well-organized Communist Viet Cong and the US withdrew in 1973. The South fell to Communist forces in 1975.

Wars in the Middle East

Post-World War II, the Middle East has seen a number of conflicts, some with the open or covert involvement of foreign powers. After its founding in 1948, Israel battled for survival and went to war with its Arab neighbors in 1948, 1956, 1967, and 1973. Three major wars have been fought in the Persian Gulf, the longest between Iraq and Iran in 1980–88. In 1990, Iraqi dictator Saddam Hussein invaded Kuwait for its oil, leading to the 1991 Gulf War, in which a US-led coalition drove the Iraqis back. A second Gulf War in 2003 overthrew Hussein. In 2011, a civil war broke out in Syria between the government and rebels.

▲ First Gulf War

US and Saudi Arabian aircraft patrol the skies over Kuwait as coalition ground forces advance on the capital. The pillars of smoke rise from oil fields deliberately set on fire by the retreating Iraqi forces.

> "Your **name** is unknown. Your **deed** is immortal."
>
> Inscription on Tomb of the Unknown Soldier, Alexander Gardens, Moscow

July 27, 1953 *The Korean Armistice is signed, ending the conflict*

September 22, 1980 *Iraq invades Iran, triggering conflict*

August 20, 1988 *Peace negotiations end the Iran-Iraq War*

September 11, 2001 *Terrorists launch four attacks against the US*

December 18, 2011 *US forces withdraw from Iraq*

2015

March 8, 1965 *US troops land in South Vietnam*

April 30, 1975 *The fall of Saigon marks the end of the Vietnam War*

August 2, 1990 *The Persian Gulf War breaks out*

February 28, 1991 *A ceasefire is declared, ending the Persian Gulf War*

March 20, 2003 *The Second Gulf War breaks out*

see also The struggle for independence pp.368–69 ▶ The early 21st century pp.374–75 ▶

The fight against disease

Until the 19th century, physicians had few means to combat infectious diseases other than keeping the patient comfortable and isolated from others. Then, a series of advances in understanding how germs transmit disease, in vaccinations to provide immunity, and finally in antibiotics to combat them, removed the threat of infections that had killed many millions. Advances in medical procedures, in particular anesthesia and antiseptics, also helped save the lives of many patients.

Malthus and Malthusianism

The English economist Thomas Malthus theorized in his *An Essay on the Principle of Population* (1798) that the food supply increased only in an arithmetical progression (by a steady amount each time period), while population grew in a geometric progression (doubling every so many years), so that food shortages were inevitable. Malthusians suggested that war, famine, and disease combined to keep food and populations levels in balance, and that the only way to prevent food shortages was through measures such as birth control.

The cholera pandemics

Cholera is an intestinal disease that causes death from severe diarrhea and vomiting. It spread from India around the world in a series of pandemics from 1817, causing hundreds of thousands of deaths. In 1854, the English doctor John Snow recognized it as a waterborne disease after finding a cluster of cases around a London water pump. The discovery of the cholera bacterium by the German epidemiologist Robert Koch in 1883 helped reinforce measures such as the building of modern sewers to retard the disease, but cholera pandemics have continued, the seventh and most recent beginning in 1961.

◄ **Louis Pasteur**
The "father of microbiology" examines the spinal cord of a rabbit that had been infected with rabies. He developed a vaccine against the virus in 1885.

Pasteur and germ theory

Before the mid-19th century, the most common theories of how diseases spread were that they were caused by tiny animals, or "germs," which appeared spontaneously, or by miasma, noxious vapors in the air that penetrated the lungs. In 1861, the French scientist Louis Pasteur observed that if germs were excluded from a nutrient gel, then mold did not grow even though it was in contact with the air, thus disproving the miasma theory. He concluded that diseases were spread by the germs themselves, and his germ theory eventually became established. In 1876, Robert Koch discovered the germ (a bacterium) responsible for anthrax—the first time a specific microorganism was linked to a disease. Five years later, Pasteur publicly demonstrated in France a vaccine he had developed for anthrax. Koch continued his own research and identified the bacteria responsible for tuberculosis (in 1882) and cholera.

LONDON SEWAGE SYSTEM, 1859

Antiseptics and sanitation

Physicians since Hippocrates in the 4th century BCE had understood that wounds deteriorated if not kept clean. In 1865, the British surgeon Joseph Lister discovered that carbolic acid applied to a compound fracture prevented germs from infecting it. Four years later he developed this into an antiseptic spray, which reduced deaths in surgery and enabled more complex operations. In the 1870s, the Scottish surgeon William Macewen introduced the steam sterilization of surgical instruments.

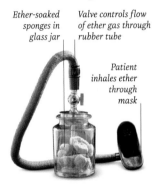

Ether-soaked sponges in glass jar

Valve controls flow of ether gas through rubber tube

Patient inhales ether through mask

EARLY (1847–48) INHALER FOR ETHER ANESTHESIA

Anesthesia

Early surgeons had little to offer patients in the way of pain relief. In 1846, the American dentist William Morton used an ether-impregnated handkerchief to reduce the pain during a tooth extraction. Morton refined the process to deliver the ether through a mask and it was soon being used in more complex surgery, such as amputations. In the 1850s, ether was replaced by chloroform, a faster-acting anesthetic gas.

Public healthcare

The growth in urban populations during the Industrial Revolution highlighted the need for centrally directed public healthcare programs. In the UK, social reformer Edwin Chadwick set in motion the mandatory notification of infectious diseases in 1889. In the US, physician Sara Josephine Baker began a healthcare campaign in 1907 to instruct poorer families on basic hygiene. Her work cut child mortality rates in New York by half.

Penicillin and antibiotics

Even after Pasteur and Koch's discovery of the role of bacteria in spreading infectious diseases, doctors had few ways to treat them. In 1928, the Scottish physician Alexander Fleming accidentally left a culture of bacteria exposed for several weeks and found that a mold that had grown on the plates had retarded the bacteria's growth. He named the mold penicillin—the first antibiotic. In the 1940s, Howard Florey and Ernst Chain at Oxford University devised a process for its mass production, and antibiotics became a routine part of treating diseases that had previously been incurable.

Vaccines

In 1796, the English physician Edward Jenner discovered that injecting patients with infected cowpox material gave them immunity to smallpox (caused by the variola virus). Years later, Pasteur developed vaccines against fowl cholera (1879), anthrax (1881), and rabies (1885). The introduction of a vaccine against polio in 1955 in the US helped control a virus that had paralyzed tens of thousands of children each year, and a series of international vaccination programs has now eradicated it in all but a handful of countries. Smallpox was declared completely eradicated in 1980.

"Vaccinate your children against polio"

ITALIAN POLIO VACCINE POSTER, 1962

MODERN NURSING

British reformer Florence Nightingale's experiences in the poorly run military hospitals during the Crimean war of 1854–56 convinced her that a formal nursing profession was needed. In 1860, she established a nursing school at St. Thomas's Hospital in London, which provided medically trained nurses. In the US, similar reforms were pioneered by an American nurse, Clara Barton, who in 1864 was appointed superintendent of nurses for the Union Army during the Civil War.

FIVE THOUSAND BY JUNE

GRADUATE NURSES YOUR COUNTRY NEEDS YOU

WORLD WAR 1 RECRUITMENT POSTER

> "It may seem a strange principle to enunciate as the **very first requirement** in a **hospital** that it should **do the sick no harm**."
>
> FLORENCE NIGHTINGALE,
> *Notes on Hospitals*, 1863

◄ **see also** Bacteria and viruses pp.218–19   ◄ The spread and control of disease pp.254–55   ◄ Medical advances pp.260–61   Modern health pp.372–73 ►

Self-determination and civil rights

Self-determination, the right of a people to determine their own destiny, was recognized by Article 1 of the United Nations Charter in 1945, which stated: "All peoples have the right to self-determination ... [to] freely determine their political status and freely pursue their economic, social, and cultural development." In contrast, civil rights ensure that individuals are treated equally under law, regardless of race, sex, religion, or other personal traits. The struggle for civil rights is ongoing.

Latin American wars of independence

Between 1791 and 1826, all French, Spanish, and Portuguese colonies in Latin America, apart from Puerto Rico and Cuba, became independent nations after three centuries of imperial rule. Haiti threw off French control in 1804, followed by a wave of conflicts that resulted in Spanish colonies from Argentina to Mexico becoming republics. By 1826, Brazil, too, had won its independence from Portugal.

Greece's war of independence

The War of Greek Independence (1821–32), began officially on March 25, 1821, when revolutionaries on the Peloponnese peninsula and several surrounding islands instigated sporadic revolts against Turkish forces of the ruling Ottoman Empire. By January 1822, Greek independence was declared, but fighting, interventions, and negotiation continued until the Treaty of Constantinopole was signed in 1832.

The Irish Question

This phrase was used to describe how to deal with Irish nationalism after Ireland became part of the UK in 1801. Following the Anglo-Irish War of 1919–21, six mainly Protestant counties of the northeast became Northern Ireland, under UK control, in 1922, while the remaining 26 Catholic counties seceded, eventually becoming the Republic of Ireland in 1937.

Green and orange taken from Irish flag

Year on back of medal

MEDAL COMMEMORATING THE 1916 UPRISING OF IRISH REPUBLICANS

New states after World War I

The aftermath of World War I redefined European national boundaries as land controlled by the former Russia, Austria-Hungary, and Germany became Austria, Hungary, Czechoslovakia, and Yugoslavia; Poland regained its independence; and Finland, Estonia, Latvia, Lithuania and Greater Romania were created. The former Ottoman Empire retained only Turkey.

Women's suffrage in Europe and the US

Voting in national elections used to be a male privilege, often dependent on owning property. During the 1800s, British and American women lobbied strenuously—via peaceful protests, hunger strikes, and even violence—for the right to vote, finally receiving it in 1918 in Britain for most women over age 30, and 1920 in the US.

Ta moko *(facial tattoo)*

Tewhatewha *(hand weapon)* with a paua *(abalone) eye* marks Nene's status

MAORI CHIEF TAMATI WAKA NENE

"We must **learn to live together** as brothers or perish together as fools." MARTIN LUTHER KING, JR., 1964

The civil rights movement in the US

Despite the freedom received after the US Civil War, oppression continued for many former African slaves. A mass protest movement of marches, boycotts, and acts of civil disobedience began in the 1950s in the South, finally resulting in the passage of desegregation laws during 1964–68 to prevent racial discrimination in areas such as education and housing.

Indigenous rights in North America, Australia, and New Zealand

The battles for the basic human rights of native, or indigenous, peoples that were taken away by colonialists led to the US, New Zealand, and Canada recognizing native rights to some land and resources in the late 18th to mid-19th centuries. The fight for Australia's Aboriginal population's constitutional recognition continues.

Dictators and civil rights: Uganda

Having seized power, dictators quickly remove human rights such as the freedom of speech and religion. Idi Amin rose through the ranks of Uganda's military before overthrowing prime minister Milton Obote in 1971 and declaring himself president. During his eight-year rule, Amin ordered the executions of some 300,000 people.

The Arab Spring

In winter 2010 and spring 2011, uprisings swept through Muslim countries in Africa and the Middle East, including Morocco, Syria, Tunisia, Libya, Egypt, and Bahrain, in reaction to oppression and human rights violations by autocratic governments. Although not all were successful, regimes changed in Tunisia, Libya, and Egypt. The catalyst for what became known as the Arab Spring was Mohamed Bouazizi, a Tunisian street vendor who set himself on fire to protest harassment by local police.

▼ Women's Freedom League

Members of the newly formed Women's Freedom League demonstrate against the UK's "Man-Made Laws" on the streets of London in 1907.

MARTIN LUTHER KING, JR

After earning his doctorate in theology in Boston, King (1929–68) returned to his native South to work in the civil rights movement. A Nobel Peace Prize-winner renowned for his eloquent speeches and nonviolent protests, he was assassinated in 1968.

The struggle for independence

At the beginning of the 20th century, a small number of mostly northern European countries ruled over most of Africa and Asia. During the first half of the century, organizations were set up in these colonies that would, in time, turn into mass movements demanding full independence. Some of these movements relied on peaceful means, while others turned to violent struggle. By 1980, almost 80 independent nations had been created.

American pioneers
The first successful uprisings against the colonial powers were in the Americas, where the 13 colonies broke free of British control in 1776 to form the United States. The ideas sparked by the French Revolution of 1789 helped to inspire the Haitian Revolution in 1791, and Spanish and Portuguese control of South America was overthrown between 1809 and 1833. By the early 20th century, organizations calling for home rule or independence were also being established in colonies throughout Asia and Africa.

India and Pakistan
Inspired by the charismatic example of Mahatma Gandhi, the Indian National Congress launched a nationwide, nonviolent civil disobedience campaign against British rule in 1915. The Hindu-dominated Indian National Congress demanded a single independent India, while the All-India Muslim League called for a separate, Muslim-controlled state—Pakistan. India and Pakistan won independence in 1947. More than 10 million Hindus, Sikhs, and Muslims fled across the new borders, with at least a million dying in the violence.

◀ Algerian freedom
Jubilant crowds in the streets of Algiers finally celebrated winning independence from France in July 1962.

MAHATMA GANDHI
Known as the Mahatma (Great Soul) by his followers, Gandhi (1869–1948) was the Indian National Congress's most inspiring leader. The peaceful movements he launched made him an international figure. During World War II, his call for Britain to "Quit India" eventually led to the negotiations that brought about independence. However, his attempts to reconcile all faiths failed and he was assassinated in 1948.

Israel and Palestine
The UK struggled to reconcile conflicting pledges it made to both Arabs and Jews—it had offered support to Arab nationalists during World War I, and expressed support for the establishment of a Jewish homeland in Palestine in 1917. In 1936, the Arabs in Palestine rose in a three-year revolt, opposing British rule and the arrival of Jewish settlers fleeing persecution in Europe. After World War II, many more Jews moved to Palestine, and Jewish fighters launched a guerrilla war against the British. In 1948, the state of Israel was created, and about 250,000 Palestinians were forced to leave their homeland.

Kenyan independence
In Kenya, discontent with British rule led to an uprising in 1952, when a group called the Mau Mau began attacking farmsteads owned by white settlers, as well as fellow Kenyans loyal to Britain. A drastic suppression by Britain saw more than 10,000 Mau Mau killed and about 20,000 imprisoned. The uprising, and the way it was dealt with, boosted the call for independence, which was won in 1963.

War in Algeria
Opposition to French rule over Algeria exploded after World War II, when Arab Algerians demanded the same rights as French Algerians. The Front de Libération Nationale (FLN) launched an uprising in 1954, and a bloody war for independence followed. French forces launched harsh reprisals against the rebels, and thousands died on both sides of the conflict. French president Charles de Gaulle negotiated independence with the FLN in 1962, and a million French settlers fled Algeria.

Victorious Viet Minh leader Ho Chí Minh

VIET MINH PROPAGANDA

Struggles in Southeast Asia
In French Indochina, opposition to colonial rule grew in the early 20th century, leading up to a failed army mutiny in 1930. Following this, Vietnamese nationalists, led by Ho Chí Minh, increasingly looked to communism for inspiration. Following the defeat of Japan in 1945, France failed to reassert control over Indochina, and fought the nationalists for control of Vietnam for eight years before its defeat at Dien Bien Phu in 1954 (see p.363).

French West Africa
In contrast to elsewhere, France's colonies in West Africa made a relatively smooth transition to independence. In part, this was due to careful negotiations between African political leaders and France's governing elites. In 1958, they won internal self-government; two years later, full independence followed.

The year of independent nations
By 1960, what British Prime Minister Harold MacMillan called a "wind of change" swept through Africa. Seventeen sub-Saharan African nations, including 14 former French colonies, secured independence from their onetime European masters.

South Africa and apartheid
In 1948, the government of South Africa, led by the National Party, introduced a policy of apartheid that violently enforced racial segregation, and imposed white-minority rule. Opposition groups, including the African National Congress (ANC), organized resistance to this, with little success. The ANC and Pan Africanist Congress (PAC) were banned in 1960 and their leaders imprisoned. The ANC continued to operate as an underground organization, launching guerilla attacks on targets associated with the apartheid regime. By the late 1980s, international sanctions and continuing protests had weakened the regime. In 1990 the ANC was unbanned, and in 1994 the ANC won the first free elections, and Nelson Mandela became president.

> "... the idea that the **British Empire** could ever end was **inconceivable.**"
>
> DORIS LESSING, British-Zimbabwean author, Speaking about her pre-war colonial childhood, 2003

COLD WAR FEARS
Although the US initially sympathized with anti-colonialism, it feared that new nations might become Communist. This led it to support South Vietnam against a Communist takeover by the North (see p.363). The US developed the "domino" theory to justify interventions, and saw Cuba as a gateway through which Communism might spread across Latin America and the Caribbean (see p.353).

◀ see also Political revolutions pp.352–53   ◀ Colonial empires pp.356–57   ◀ The age of global conflicts pp.360–63

Modern globalization and economic growth

Globalization had its earliest roots in the Silk Road around the 1st century BCE. In the 20th century, however, two world wars and a depression caused international trading links to break down and millions to lose their lives, halting economic expansion. Despite these tragedies, war also led to the creation of new technologies, which, once adapted to the civilian arena, combined with sophisticated new communications networks and allowed trade to flourish, paving the way for today's global economy.

The postwar recovery

By World War II's end in 1945, trade accounted for just five percent of the world gross domestic product (GDP). It was the lowest figure for more than a century. However, having escaped the destruction endured by Europe, the US, with its vast natural resources, quickly emerged as the new economic superpower. Cars and aircraft that had shipped weapons during wartime began to ship goods instead, and global trade flourished—initially controlled by the US and Europe in the West, and the Soviet Union in the East.

Multinational companies

The International Monetary Fund (IMF), created in 1945, implemented a system of exchange rates to allow transactions between member countries. Fostering international stability via economic growth was also central to capitalist US policy. By the mid-1950s, US corporations had built factories abroad, and multinational companies have proliferated ever since, creating new markets, bypassing trade restrictions, and accessing cheaper labor.

Gas stations in the US had to use signs to turn away customers

Sorry... NO GAS

SIGN FROM THE FUEL CRISIS

The oil shock

Industrial economies run on oil, and any sudden change in its supply can destabilize developed countries. In 1973, in retaliation for Western support of Israel during the Arab-Israeli conflicts (see p.363), Arab members of the Organization of the Petroleum Exporting Companies (OPEC) quadrupled the price of oil, prohibited its sale to the US, Japan, and western Europe, and triggered a global recession that continued throughout the 1970s. The Iranian Revolution of 1979 also resulted in a loss of oil output, and prices rose again.

The Asian Tigers

In Asia during the 1950s and 1960s, Hong Kong, Singapore, South Korea, and Taiwan all maintained consistently high economic growth levels by investing in rapid industrialization and the development of a massive export trade. Known as the "Asian Tigers," they each have specialized strengths, with Hong Kong and Singapore acting as vital world financial centers, while South Korea and Taiwan are global leaders in the manufacture and export of automotive and electronic components, alongside information technology. The Asian Tigers have remained stable throughout financial and credit crises and now rank among the IMF's 39 most advanced economies lists.

The global financial crisis

Between 2007 and 2009, panic in the form of a financial crisis swept financial markets worldwide. This was due partly to excessive risk-taking in what had been a booming US economy, when banks lent customers mortgages for amounts close to or even above houses' value. To fund the loans, US banks and investment companies also overborrowed, often from other foreign banks and investors.

When US house prices fell in 2006, thousands of borrowers defaulted on loans, banks incurred heavy losses, and financial markets and investors around the world panicked as US financial firms, such as Lehman Brothers, failed.

The "BRICs"

BRIC is an acronym coined by US investment bank Goldman Sachs for Brazil, Russia, India, and China. These are four rapidly developing countries the firm predicted will become the world's main suppliers of raw materials, services, and manufactured goods by 2050. In 2010, South Africa became the fifth such emerging economy, and the term was changed to BRICS. The predicted rise of the BRICS is mainly due to their low labor and production costs compared to Western economies. In 1990, the original BRIC countries accounted for 11 percent of global GDP; by 2014, that figure was almost 30 percent.

New global industries

Artificial intelligence (AI) as a field of study was founded in 1956, but progress to create machines that could even rudimentarily mimic human intelligence was slow. It stalled several times until the late 1990s, when IBM's Deep Blue computer beat chess champion Garry Kasparov. Today, machine learning is an intrinsic part of many online services, fueling the rise of robotics in fields such as medical research and the automotive and space industries. Genetic manipulation, including gene splicing, exploded when coupled with computerized processing systems and inventions such as the electron microscope.

ASSEMBLY ROBOT

The information technology (IT) revolution

IT began to develop in earnest on May 22, 1973, when Bob Metcalfe at Xerox's Research Center in California wrote a memo outlining how an "Ethernet" could connect computers to share data. Computer-related activities were confined mainly to interactions between a single person and a computer until 1989, when Tim Berners-Lee invented the World Wide Web while working at CERN (the European Organization for Nuclear Research), in Switzerland. The rise of local and global connectivity networks, and the invention of personal smartphones in the 1990s, ushered in "data mining" for profit, as well as countless other applications in industry. Today, IT has moved from being a simple processing tool to an intrinsic part of most businesses, powering everything from global stock exchanges to banking.

> "The ultimate **goal of the Web** is to **support and improve** our weblike existence in the world."
>
> TIM BERNERS-LEE, *Weaving the Web*, 1999

Rustbelts and regional decline

At the same time as digital and information technologies were coming into their own, traditional industries began to decline, particularly in certain areas of the US. The territory stretching roughly from New York to the Midwest had been dominated by coal and steel production and manufacturing. As these industries declined sharply during the 1970s, factories closed and were left to decay, earning the region the name "Rust Belt." The term has since extended to any former industrial region that has experienced a downturn due to rising labor costs and the capital-intensive nature of manufacturing; the automotive industry is a case in point.

Globalization and international trade

The info-tech revolution and rise of computers use made it easier to conduct trade between countries around the world, fostering opportunities for growth beyond a business's home country. Not only was international trade good for growth and expansion of various companies, it also stimulated enormous expansion in related sectors, particularly transportation and the information and communications technology industry itself. As trade became increasingly international, it also had the side-effect of making nations interdependent on each other, due to ever-increasing interconnectedness. Global trading became the standard for businesses wishing to operate over a certain size.

The shifting economic balance

In the decades following World War II, the United States, Japan, Germany, the UK, France, and Italy emerged as advanced economies. Together they formed a political forum known as the G6, becoming the G7 in 1976 with Canada's inclusion, then the G8 between 1996 and 2014 with Russia's brief inclusion. In the year 2000, China's economy amounted to barely a tenth of that of the US. By 2010, however, this picture had altered considerably: China's economy was half that of the US, Japan had stalled, and the BRICS nations were rising rapidly. The BRICS' collective economic power may soon surpass that of the G7 nations.

◀ Port of Singapore

Shipping containers are carried by cargo ships to ports all around the world. Global shipping on such a scale could not be coordinated without the Internet.

Modern health

The 20th and 21st centuries saw enormous strides in medicine. Healthcare systems improved as doctors began to understand more about nutrition and scientists developed advanced therapies and antibiotics. Yet enormous challenges remained—populations grew beyond the capacity of countries to provide healthy environments, and new diseases associated with changing lifestyles emerged. The world struggled with the threat of pandemic diseases to which humans had little or no resistance.

Nutritional advances

In the premodern era, there was very little understanding of the role that nutrition plays in human health. In 1747, James Lind discovered that feeding sailors a diet rich in citrus fruit staved off scurvy, and gradually scientists discovered the role of vitamins in achieving this. Vitamin B_1 was synthesized in 1926 and Vitamin C isolated in 1928. Vitamin D_2 was described in 1936, and Vitamin A in 1947. Today, nutritionists know that a balance between these vitamins is necessary to maintain a healthy body, allowing medical practitioners to effectively treat many diseases through appropriate nutrition.

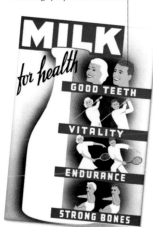

Images of healthy living encourage people to drink milk

US HEALTH POSTER, 1948

Healthcare systems

Complex healthcare systems emerged in the 19th century, with the modern nursing profession developing from the school founded by Florence Nightingale in 1860, after her experiences during the Crimean War (see pp.364–65). There was very little

◀ **Student nurses**
A student nurse holds a newborn at the National Training School for Midwives in London, UK, in 1948. That year, the UK's National Health Service (NHS) was founded, offering free healthcare to all.

central funding for healthcare, however, and hospitals depended on charitable foundations or patient fees. In 1948, the UK established the National Health Service (NHS), a universal free healthcare system paid for by taxation. The US and other countries favored funding hospitals through a private insurance-backed system or, as in Singapore, a government-run one.

The Green Revolution

The increase in the world's population to 2.5 billion in 1950 strained the ability of developing countries to produce enough food. In the 1940s, researchers in Mexico developed new disease-resistant, higher-yield wheat varieties. The technology of this "Green Revolution" spread to India, where a new strain of rice, IR8, massively increased yields. Yet the Green Revolution has been criticized for its large-scale use of fertilizers, dependence on only a few strains of crops (making them vulnerable to disease), and failure to repeat its successes in Africa.

The AIDS crisis

In 1981, doctors in Los Angeles detected a disease that attacked patients' immune systems. It was labeled Acquired Immune Deficiency Syndrome (AIDS) the following year. In 1983, researchers discovered it was caused by Human Immunodeficiency Virus, or HIV. The disease, spread by bodily fluids, especially during sexual contact, swept across the world. It is now treatable by antiretroviral drugs, but no cure has been found. About 70 million people have been infected, and 35 million have died.

Biotech and GM

Biotechnology, the modification of natural organisms for industrial purposes, has its roots in the breeding programs of the past. In the 1970s, the development of recombinant DNA techniques, where strands of DNA from different organisms are spliced together, allowed the development of genetically modified (or GM) foodstuffs, with the first crops planted in the US in 1987. Although GM techniques increased yields, resistance to them grew because of fears they had not been assessed for long-term health implications.

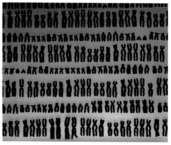

HUMAN CHROMOSOMES

The human genome

The discovery in 1953 of the structure of deoxyribonucleic acid (DNA), which contains the genetic instructions that determine the form of living beings, set off a search to sequence the genome (the complete genetic code) of organisms. By 1995, scientists had managed this for bacteria, and in 2000 for that of a fruit fly. In 1990, the Human Genome Project was established to coordinate an international effort to sequence the human genome, and in 2001, it published its first draft, opening the way for genetic therapies to treat many diseases caused by genetic faults.

Population and land use

The population of the world increased more than five-fold, from 1.5 billion in 1900 to around 7.8 billion in 2020, with cities in developing countries such as Lagos in Nigeria approaching 20 million inhabitants. The strain on nations with limited infrastructure became severe, leading to the overexploitation of marginal land. Shanty towns around established cities, such as the favelas of Brazil, have limited access to clean water or medical facilities, risking creating a new medical underclass deprived of the public healthcare advances of the last century.

Aging and wealth-related illness

As life expectancies increased, industrialized countries found themselves with aging populations (there were 962 million people over the age of 60 in 2017). Death rates from diseases that strike later in life rose, and healthcare systems had to cope with increasing numbers of dementia patients. More sedentary lifestyles and changes in diet led to a rise in diabetes, a disorder of the pancreas, with over 450 million sufferers by 2018.

MODERN PANDEMICS

The modern era saw the emergence of new diseases, often transmitted by close contact with populations of diseased animals, and the threat of their uncontrolled spread as a global pandemic. Ebola, which causes severe hemorrhaging and death in about half of cases, killed 11,000 people in an outbreak in West Africa in 2013–16, and SARS, a respiratory infection that emerged in southern China in 2002, spread to 26 countries, killing 774 people. In late 2019, a new virus, COVID-19, was identified in Wuhan in China. Despite efforts to contain it, the virus spread rapidly worldwide, causing hundreds of thousands of deaths and a severe economic recession.

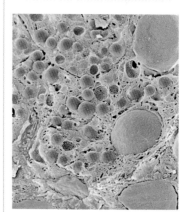

PANCREAS TISSUE

New technologies

As technology advanced, new opportunities opened up in medicine. Computers allowed more efficient monitoring of healthcare systems, and in 1971 the first computerized tomography (CT) scanner, which uses multiple X-ray beams to build a 3D image of a body, was used to detect a brain tumor. Laparoscopic (keyhole) surgery, in which surgeons make a small incision and use a camera and instruments inserted on a thin rod to conduct surgery, reduced the impact on patients. By 2020, artificial intelligence (AI) was being used to interpret the results of CT and magnetic resonance imaging (MRI) scans, helping doctors to achieve an effective diagnosis.

> "Of all the **forms of inequality**, injustice in **healthcare** is the most **shocking**."
>
> MARTIN LUTHER KING, JR.,
> In a speech to healthcare workers, March 1966

◀ **see also Modern medicine** pp.252–53   ◀ **The spread and control of disease** pp.254–55   ◀ **Medical advances** pp.260–61   ◀ **The fight against disease** pp.364–65

The early 21st century

The collapse of the Communist bloc in the early 1990s offered the hope of a new era of peace and economic prosperity. However, war and instability in the Middle East and Africa, a global financial crisis, resurgences in nationalism, rising population, and climate change and environmental degradation challenged this optimism and created an era of deepening political uncertainty. Even liberating new technologies such as the Internet affected society in unforeseen ways.

The War on Terror

On September 11, 2001, attacks by the Islamist group al-Qaeda killed almost 3,000 people in the US, most of whom died in the World Trade Center in New York. In response, President George W. Bush declared a "war on terror" and later that year launched air strikes against the Taliban regime in Afghanistan, which was hosting al-Qaeda cells. The war expanded to Iraq, Somalia, Libya, the Philippines, and Mali, but the results were mixed and the involvement often protracted. Other such Islamist groups, including ISIS, later grew amid the instability of these wars.

Twin Towers logo

BADGE FOUND AT WORLD TRADE CENTER

The Arab Spring and its aftermath

In January 2011, demonstrations sparked by the suicide of a street vendor in protest against corruption led to the fall of the Tunisian President Ben Ali. Soon, crowds in other Arab nations protested against their governments. Egypt's Hosni Mubarak resigned in February, and Libya's Muammar al-Gaddafi was overthrown and killed in October. Hopes of a democratic future were largely disappointed as Egypt's old guard regained power in 2014, and Libya, Yemen, and Syria became engulfed in civil wars.

Russia, Ukraine, and Syria

Russian President Vladimir Putin had wanted to restore his country's global status, diminished after the Soviet Union's collapse in 1990. When the pro-Russian government of Ukraine was toppled in 2014, he sent Russian forces to occupy and then annex Crimea, which had a Russian ethnic majority. The following year, Putin sent Russian forces to help President Bashar al-Assad recapture ground lost during Syria's civil war.

Globalization and populism

The international financial crisis of 2007–2008, which sent countries into recession and undermined faith in money markets, helped fuel a feeling in advanced nations that many had been left behind by the globalization of business. Populist parties, such as Front National in France, used this discontent to attract voters, while also blaming migrant groups for many of their economic problems.

North Korea's nuclear capability

From 1948, North Korea's regime kept the country in isolation and practiced *juche*, or self-reliance, and by 2006 it had advanced sufficiently on its own to begin testing nuclear weapons. Various diplomatic initiatives followed, including a 2018 summit between US President Donald Trump and the North Korean leader Kim Jong-un, but all failed to convince the country to abandon its nuclear ambitions.

▶ **National pride**

In a choreographed display, North Korean schoolchildren use boards to create the image of a soldier during the 2008 Arirang Mass Games.

Iranian and Saudi rivalry

The clerical regime that had gained power in Iran after the 1979 revolution sought to spread its influence throughout the entire Middle East, creating a "Shia crescent" that extended across countries with large Shia Muslim populations such as Iraq, Syria, and Lebanon. This clashed with the similar ambitions of predominantly Sunni Muslim Saudi Arabia to achieve regional control. Relations deteriorated further after Iran and Saudi Arabia funded rival groups during the Syrian Civil War from 2011. Saudi Arabia also accused Iran of backing Houthi militia in the civil war in Yemen and of destabilising its own eastern provinces, which have a sizeable Shia minority population.

> "We are ... **the last generation** that can **take steps** to avoid the worst impacts of **climate change.**"
>
> BAN KI-MOON, Secretary-General of the United Nations,
> Speaking in Leuven, Belgium, May 28, 2015

The European Union and "Brexit"

With the accession of Croatia to the European Union (EU) as its 28th member in 2013, the future and strength of the organization seemed assured. However, uncertainties over whether the EU should further integrate in areas such as defense, the rise of populist parties espousing nationalist policies, and the arrival of large numbers of refugees fleeing Middle East conflicts caused a major crisis. In Britain, where governments had been skeptical of deeper integration, a referendum in 2016 saw a vote to leave the EU. Lengthy negotiations resulted in Britain's exit (known as "Brexit") in 2020, but the nature of the EU's relationship with its former member remained uncertain.

Radical South America

Following the election of Hugo Chávez in Venezuela in 1999, many countries in South America chose governments that rejected the conservative policies and free-market economics of the recent past. Charismatic leaders, such as Chávez, Luiz Inácio Lula da Silva ("Lula") in Brazil, and Evo Morales in Bolivia, introduced left-wing policies and opposed the influence of the United States on the region. Their policies dominated the continent for nearly two decades.

Artificial Intelligence

In the global economy of the 21st century, increasing amounts of work once performed by people can now be mechanized or carried out by complex algorithms. The development of Artificial Intelligence (AI) systems has potential uses in areas such as medical examinations, legal advice, and accountancy, placing the advanced world's labor needs in a state of uncertainty.

AUTONOMOUS CAMERA DRONE

The rise of Africa

Between 2000 and 2020, living standards improved in many African countries, with Ethiopia recorded as one of the world's fastest-growing economies in 2019. Populations grew, with sub-Saharan Africa expected to account for over half of global population growth by 2050. South Africa established itself as a modern democracy, but other countries, such as Zimbabwe and the Democratic Republic of Congo, suffered from misgovernment or civil war.

CLIMATE CHANGE AWARENESS

Climate change became a major political issue in the 21st century, with 9 of the 10 warmest years on record occurring since 2005. Activists such as Sweden's Greta Thunberg (below) protested to stop irreversible environmental damage.

STRIKE FOR CLIMATE ACTION

Beliefs and Society

World religions

Belief in a spiritual realm that governs human existence is common to most parts of the world, and is expressed as religion. While each of the world's most-followed religions has a unique identity, some have common elements, such as a belief in reincarnation. And Judaism, Christianity, and Islam are known as Abrahamic religions, as all three acknowledge the prophet Abraham as a spiritual founder. These shared aspects are a result of religions evolving in geographical proximity, and of holy texts, which helped to spread ideas after the invention of writing around 3200 BCE.

OM SYMBOL

Hinduism

Date	2300–1500 BCE
Location	Indus Valley (near modern-day Pakistan)

Hinduism is the third largest religion after Christanity and Islam. The main beliefs are that the supreme god Brahman is present everywhere and in everything (including animals), and that life is a cycle of birth, death, and rebirth. Brahman takes three main forms: Brahma, the creator; Vishnu, who keeps the balance of good and evil; and Shiva, who destroys the universe in order to recreate it. The primary sacred texts are the Vedas (1500 BCE), which are written in Sanskrit.

FARAVAHAR

Zoroastrianism

Date	6th century BCE–637 CE
Location	Persia (modern-day Iran)

Considered one of the world's oldest continuously practiced religions, Zoroastrianism is centered on the worship of one god, Ahura Mazda, and is named after the prophet Zarathustra, or Zoroaster. It was the state religion of Persia until the 7th century when Muslim invaders converted or persecuted Zoroastrians. Many fled to Gujarat, India, where they became known as Parsis. Zoroastrianism is passed down through the male family line and does not permit conversion to the religion.

STAR OF DAVID

Judaism

Date	c.19th century BCE
Location	Mesopotamia (modern-day Iraq)

The religion of the Jewish people, Judaism is one of the oldest monotheist religions, meaning worship of one god. Beliefs and early history are recorded in the Tanakh, the Hebrew Bible, which has the same books as the Christian Old Testament. These scriptures explain that God, Yahweh, made a covenant with Abraham, stating he would become the leader of a new nation, Israel, in return for obedience to God.

AHIMSA HAND

Jainism

Date	6th–5th century BCE
Location	India

The word Jain comes from the Sanskrit *jina*, meaning the path of victory, which entails living a life of ethical and spiritual purity in order to escape karma and liberate the soul. Unlike many other religions there are no gods, spiritual beings, or priests in Jainism. The writings of Mahavira form the basis of Jain beliefs, the most important of which is to live without violence. This includes not harming animals, so all Jains are vegetarian.

WHEEL OF LAW

Buddhism

Date	6th–4th century BCE
Location	Nepal

The teachings of Siddhartha Gautama underpin Buddhism and its three universal truths: nothing is lost in the universe; everything changes; and every action has an equal reaction (the concept of karma). Buddhists strive to adhere to five precepts: to refrain from killing (including animals), stealing, sexual misconduct, lying, and being intoxicated. As with Hinduism, from which Buddhism emerged, meditation is practiced to reach spiritual enlightenment.

WATER SYMBOL

Confucianism

Date	6th–5th century BCE
Location	China

Founded by the scholar Confucius as a system of ethics and social philosophy, Confucianism views life as a melding of heaven, nature, and humanity. It is not concerned with how the world was created, nor concepts of a personal god; instead, it emphasizes the importance of family history and relationships, the need for a hierarchical society, and the role of education in enriching the individual, society, and politics. It is not an organized religion, but spread from China to other parts of Asia through Chinese literature.

Yoga has its roots in Hinduism

◀ **Leshan Giant Buddha**
Carved out of a sandstone cliff in 713–803 near Leshan, Sichuan Province, China, this 233 ft (71 m) tall statue depicts Maitreya, a future Buddha.

see also Great philosophers pp.386–87 ▶   **379**

YIN YANG

Daoism

Date	6th century BCE
Location	Eastern China

A philosophical teaching and a way of life, Taoism is based on the principle of living with the flow of the natural world. This entails living unselfishly, simply, and spontaneously, embracing time, change, gain, and loss. The goal of following this *tao* (the Chinese word for path) is to ultimately be free of human constructs and society, and live at one with nature. Taoism is influenced by the sage Laozi, who is also venerated by Confucianists.

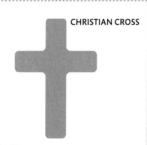

CHRISTIAN CROSS

Christianity

Date	1st century
Location	Palestine

The world's most-followed religion, Christianity is named after Jesus Christ, who is worshipped as the son of God and the Messiah, or savior. Jesus offered believers forgiveness from bad thoughts and deeds, and a place in heaven after death, in return for confession through prayer. According to Christianity's holy text, the Bible, Jesus was crucified and rose from the dead three days later. He joined God in heaven, and his spirit guides believers.

TORII

Shinto

Date	6th century
Location	Japan

Considered Japan's indigenous religion, Shinto is based on belief in spiritual beings called *kami*, who intervene in daily life to help humans in return for devotion and ritual worship. Shinto rituals take place at shrines, especially at New Year but also for important occasions such as to pray for exam success, or to seek blessing for a wedding. *Kami* are perceived as part of the human world, and religious arts such as poetry and painting are important aspects.

THE STAR AND CRESCENT

Islam

Date	7th century
Location	Mecca (present-day Saudi Arabia)

Followers of Islam are called Muslims, and they believe in one God, Allah, who passed his teachings to the prophet Muhammad through the angel Gabriel. These revelations are written in the Qur'an, which sets out five tenets: Shahada, the profession of faith; Salat, a prayer ritual five times daily; Sawm, fasting during Ramadan; Zakat, a tax paid to help the poor; and Hajj, a pilgrimage to Mecca.

THE KHANDA

Sikhism

Date	15th century
Location	Punjab

Based on the teachings of 10 gurus, starting with founder Guru Nanak, Sikhism rejects the caste system of Hinduism, proclaims one God, and stresses the importance of equality, community service, hard work, and doing good deeds in order to escape reincarnation. The Sikh holy book, Guru Granth Sahib, contains the words of the 10 gurus as well as Sikh, Hindu, and Muslim saints. Sikhs do not cut their hair out of respect for God's creation.

NINE-POINTED STAR

Baha'i

Date	19th century
Location	Iran

Founded by Baha'u'llah, the son of an Iranian government minister, Baha'i grew out of the Babi movement calling for social change and women's rights. Baha'u'llah was imprisoned for supporting Babi, then exiled to Baghdad where he claimed he was the manifestation of God and established the Baha'i faith. He preached world peace, advocating racial and gender equality, and education for all. His writings form the basis of Baha'i.

THE DIVINE EYE

Cao Dai

Date	1926
Location	Vietnam

Incorporating insights from other religions such as Buddhism and Daoism, Cao Dai was founded by Ngô Văn Chiêu, a spiritualist who claimed to have received instruction from a godlike entity named Cao Dai to establish a new religion. Caodaiists worship one god, creator of the universe, but also revere a goddess figure, the mother of all things in the universe. Prayer ceremonies are held in temples three times daily.

More than **eight out of ten** people in the world identify with a **religious group**

▼ Sultan Ahmed Mosque
Also known as the Blue Mosque after the tiles that decorate its interior, this Muslim place of worship was built in 1609–16 in Istanbul (present-day Turkey).

What is philosophy?

The practice of philosophy seeks to make sense of the world and our place in it. Ancient Greek philosophers gave the name to this discipline, which means "love of wisdom." It asks big questions about everything there is, such as: Who are we? What is the fundamental nature of reality? What is it to have a mind and consciousness? What gives everything meaning? What can we know? Can we have knowledge of God? What is the meaning of life and of us being here? How to live one's life? How can we understand values such as goodness or beauty?

What do philosophers do?

Philosophers seek to answer fundamental questions about humans and the world by employing philosophical methods to address them. They use argumentation to support their views, and they develop them through logical thinking and analysis of concepts and experience. Philosophers undertake critical thinking to develop and defend their positions, and to support, criticize, or refute other views. Their views are often presented in writing (such as in books and articles), but may also be expressed during talks in public forums of discussion or in debates with other philosophers at conferences or public events. Recent developments and uses of philosophy outside academia or school include the teaching of philosophy for professionals, philosophical counseling, and festivals of philosophy.

Philosophy and science

In the ancient world, philosophy and science were not separate—for a long time science was called "natural philosophy." With the development of modern science, some philosophers view philosophy and science as different disciplines with distinct methods and issues of inquiry. Others think they still have much in common, and that they complement each other.

Philosophy of religion

The philosophy of religion is the philosophical study of the concepts involved in the main religious traditions (see pp.378–81). In particular, it is concerned with concepts of God and of the divine attributes of God. The philosophy of religion also includes the debates over the existence of God and those concerned with arguments about the creation of the universe, the problem of evil, the nature of ultimate reality, religious experience, and miracles.

Metaphysics and ontology

There are different definitions of ontology and metaphysics, though ontology is considered a part of metaphysics. According to a traditional account, ontology is the study of what there is (what exists) or of being in general. Metaphysics is the study of particular domains of being (the nature of what exists), such as the mind (consciousness), bodies, freedom, or God. Metaphysical debates are concerned with fundamental concepts such as being, existence, essence, identity, possibility, object, property, relation, fact, freedom, the world, and the relevant methods with which to approach these issues.

Epistemology

Epistemology is the theory of knowledge. A traditional view may be that in order to have knowledge, we need to form a belief or opinion, have some justification for holding that belief, and the belief must be true. But is that an adequate explanation of knowledge? And what is justification? What is truth? These are questions that competing theories of knowledge address and debate.

Philosophy of mind

Philosophy of mind investigates the very idea of the mind—the nature and structure of the human mind, and its relation to the brain and body and with the rest of the physical world. Central issues include the "mind–body problem"—if mind and body are distinct, how do they interact?—and the issue of our lived, subjective experience: how, if at all, can our subjective experience of, for example, color or taste be explained in terms of physical processes in the brain?.

> "For it is **owing to their wonder** that men both now begin and at **first** began to philosophize."
>
> ARISTOTLE, *Metaphysics*, 4th century BCE

Aesthetics

Aesthetics is the philosophical study of the nature of beauty, art, and artwork. It includes theories about beauty and taste, the ontology of art, the meaning and value of art, the creation and appreciation of art and beauty, and the relation of art to other significant aspects of human life such as politics, economics, and moral values.

Logic

Philosophical theories in the Western tradition have employed logic to pursue their investigations. Logic is concerned with the procedures and rules of correct reasoning. For example, inferences are forms of reasoning that proceed from certain propositions, called premises, to reach a conclusion. An inference is good if the premises effectively support the conclusion. Logic offers tools to establish the validity of arguments, and to lay out the logical form of various types of arguments and fallacies (faulty arguments).

Plato's Academy

Plato, a student of Socrates, founded the Academy in 387 BCE in the outskirts of Athens. The Academy is considered to be the first university in the Western world. Aristotle was one of Plato's students at the Academy before he founded his own school, the Lyceum (334 BCE).

◄ Aristotle
Considered to be one of the greatest thinkers, Aristotle wrote and taught on a wide variety of philosophical issues.

Moral philosophy
How should we live our life? How can we know what is right or wrong? Moral philosophy is concerned with moral principles of human conduct and with moral values such as goodness, happiness, and justice. Competing ethical theories debate over these issues and are also applied to practical questions—for example, the issues of the rights of animals, euthanasia, and abortion.

Political philosophy
Central concerns in political philosophy in the Western tradition include the justification of the state, arguments for and against democracy, discussions of private property and the market, the nature of the law, liberty, justice, and human rights issues. Political theory exists at the intersection of philosophy, politics, history, sociology, and other related disciplines. It addresses interdisciplinary issues concerning, for example, power, race, identity, climate change, and religion.

Indian philosophy
The traditions of Indian thought include so-called "orthodox" (including Hinduism) and "unorthodox" (including Buddhism and Jainism) systems of thought.

Fundamental concepts of Indian philosophy are the self or soul (atman), actions or works (karma) understood in terms of their moral significance and efficacy, and liberation (moksha), the most important ideal of existence.

Buddhist philosophy
Buddhism evolved from the teachings of the Buddha (who lived in India between the mid-6th and mid-4th centuries BCE), and has developed into a number of schools and doctrines. At the core of Buddhism is a concern for an ideal of liberation from our limitations, delusions, and suffering, and an overcoming, through enlightenment, of the impermanence and ignorance, which are seen as characteristic of the human condition.

Chinese philosophy
An important characteristic of Chinese philosophy throughout the ages is its concern with human nature. Some fundamental concepts in relation to this, and more generally the question of the universe, are that of Dao (the Way or the Path) and its two opposing aspects, Yin and Yang—the elements of tranquillity and activity. In the human being, Dao gives rise to virtue (de). The most important virtues are ren (humanity, heartedness) and yi (righteousness).

In the Ancient period, Classical Chinese philosophy developed this philosophical framework in different schools of thought; two of the most important schools were founded by Confucius (551–479 BCE) and Laozi (6th century BCE).

Japanese philosophy
Philosophy in Japan developed throughout the ages through various interactions between local religious and spiritual views (in particular, the tradition of Shinto) and external influences exerted especially by Buddhism, Confucianism, and, in the modern age, by Western philosophy. In the course of its history, it has both focused on metaphysics and turned away from it toward social, moral, and political concerns. Different schools of thought have attempted to integrate various traditions in their systems of thought. Contemporary Japanese philosophy engages with Western philosophy and attempts to integrate it with Asian thought.

> "Learning without thinking is useless. Thinking without learning is dangerous."
>
> CONFUCIUS, *The Analects*, 5th century BCE

see also Philosophy through history pp.384–85 ▶ **383**

Philosophy through history

The history of philosophy as presented here reflects traditions with written records. Regions where philosophical thought was largely transmitted through oral traditions are therefore underrepresented; so too, are the many women philosophers, who were at times barred from academia and whose works have not been preserved. Western philosophy originates in ancient Greek teachings and thought. It is typically divided into four periods—ancient,

medieval, modern, and 20th century. Middle Eastern philosophy dates back to 3000 BCE. It includes Islamic, ancient Egyptian, and Jewish schools of thought, and has mostly developed out of a philosophy concerned with practical guidelines for life and speculative thoughts about the universe. The main traditions of Indian philosophy can be defined in terms of their position in relation to the Vedas— the oldest religious texts from ancient India.

c.624–546 BCE Thales of Miletus is one of the first ancient Greek thinkers to adopt a rational, scientific approach to explain nature. He proposes that everything is, or comes from, water.

EVERYTHING IS MADE FROM WATER

1265–73 Italian philosopher Thomas Aquinas writes *Summa Theologica*. He combines Aristotelian philosophy with Christian teachings to develop his doctrines that have become a central part of Roman Catholic theology.

1207–73 Persian mystic Rūmī proposes that all life exists in a continuum and expresses his beliefs through poetry.

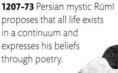

JALAL AD-DIN MUHAMMAD RUMI

1126–1198 Islamic polymath Averroes publishes commentaries on and summaries of Aristotle's works, introducing medieval scholars to the Greek philosopher.

426 CE Christian thinker Augustine of Hippo publishes *The City of God*, which outlines his vision of a state living according to Christian principles.

ENGRAVING OF AUGUSTINE'S *THE CITY OF GOD*

1509 Dutch humanist Desiderius Erasmus writes his famous satire *In Praise of Folly*, questioning the beliefs administered by the Roman Catholic Church, and endorsing a life based on strict moral principles.

ERASMUS WITH COLLEAGUE GILBERT COGNATUS

1620 Francis Bacon publishes *Novum Organum* in England. He advocates empiricism and the importance of experimental inquiry, laying the foundation for modern scientific methods.

Ships exploring seas beyond metaphorical pillars marking end of known world

TITLE PAGE OF *NOVUM ORGANUM*

Seven compartments filled with people exercising Christian virtues in order to prepare for heaven

1883–85 In his four-part treatise *Thus Spoke Zarathustra*, German philosopher Friedrich Nietzsche opposes what he sees as the meaninglessness of modern life with a life-affirming philosophy about the will to power—to strive to achieve one's fullest potential.

1908 EDITION OF *THUS SPOKE ZARATHUSTRA*

1848 German philosophers Karl Marx and Friedrich Engels publish *The Communist Manifesto*. This contributes to the emergence of Communist ideology leading to its implementation as a political system.

MARXIST POSTER

1739 Scottish enlightenment philosopher David Hume endorses empiricism in *A Treatise of Human Nature*. He, like Locke, believes that senses and experience, rather than reason, constitute the source of knowledge.

Symmetrical ornamental abstraction in burgundy and gold by Belgian painter Henry van de Velde

First page of elaborate double-page frontispiece

1910–13 English philosophers Alfred North Whitehead and Bertrand Russell collaborate to produce the three-part *Principia Mathematica*—a work that explores the logic-based foundations of mathematics.

1943 In *Being and Nothingness*, Frenchman Jean-Paul Sartre voices his existentialist view that "our existence precedes our essence." He denounces the concept of predestination and urges people to forge a purpose for themselves.

1949 French existentialist Simone de Beauvoir publishes her seminal feminist work *The Second Sex* on how women are defined in relation to men. She asks that prevailing notions of "femininity" be questioned as serving male interests.

JEAN-PAUL SARTRE AND SIMONE DE BEAUVOIR

PYTHAGORAS

c.569–495 BCE Greek philosopher and mathematician Pythagoras believes the order of the universe is governed by mathematical, moral, and divine principles. His followers include the philosophers Plato and Aristotle.

THE EIGHTFOLD PATH

Right mindfulness
Right understanding
Right action
Right speech
Right intention
Right concentration
Right livelihood
Right effort

c.563–483 BCE Born in modern-day Nepal, Siddhārtha Gautama uses meditation to gain fundamental insights into the nature of reality and human life. Later known as Buddha, he proposed the Eightfold Path that could lead one to enlightenment.

469–399 BCE Born in Greece, Socrates evolves a new, dialectical, way of thinking that involves examining life through a dialogue of opposing views. He is considered by many to be one of the founders of Western Philosophy.

SOCRATES

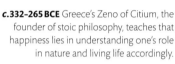

BALANCE IN NATURE

c.332–265 BCE Greece's Zeno of Citium, the founder of stoic philosophy, teaches that happiness lies in understanding one's role in nature and living life accordingly.

387 BCE Greek philosopher Plato establishes the Academy—the first western institution of higher learning. In 365 BCE, he meets his most famous student, Aristotle, whose thinking shapes the development of subsequent philosophical work.

MOSAIC DEPICTING PLATO'S ACADEMY

Central figure using a stick to point to globe is widely considered to be depicting Plato

Sacred olive tree associated with Athena, goddess of wisdom

Backdrop of the walls of Acropolis in Athens

Mosaic made of tiny, colorful stones called tesserae

1637 In his *Meditations*, French rationalist René Descartes applied his Method of Doubt (treat as if false any belief of which you cannot be certain). He was able to doubt all his beliefs about the external world, but was certain of the truth of "I think, therefore I am."

Is there a world outside?

Do I have a body?

Am I thinking?

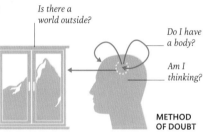

METHOD OF DOUBT

Theory

Experience

1689 In *An Essay Concerning Human Understanding*, Englishman John Locke suggests that at birth, the mind is a "tabula rasa" (blank slate), which then interacts with the world and forms ideas via theory and experience.

FORMING KNOWLEDGE

1961 In France, historian and philosopher Michel Foucault publishes his doctoral thesis *Madness and Civilization*, bringing into focus the subject of insanity and how it is perceived and treated in Europe.

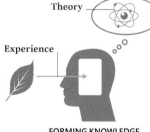

MICHEL FOUCAULT

1967 French postmodern thinker Jacques Derrida uses the term "deconstruction" in three titles—*Writing and Difference*, *Voice and Phenomenon*, and *Of Grammatology*—to refer to a methodology for engaging critically with the tradition of metaphysics.

OF GRAMMATOLOGY COVER

Feminist theorist Gayatri Spivak's English translation of this text made it even more widely accessible

1989 Slovene cultural theorist Slavoj Žižek's first book in English, *The Sublime Object of Ideology*, draws international attention. He uses and references popular culture to voice his political and philosophical beliefs.

POSTER FOR ZIZEK'S 2012 DOCUMENTARY FILM

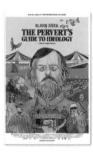

see also Great philosophers pp.386–87 ▶ Economics through history pp.400–401 ▶

Great philosophers

Throughout human history, people have tried to answer questions about the nature of the world and their place in it. Philosophy developed as extraordinary thinkers used their capacity for rational thinking to develop answers for these questions. It had wide-ranging implications, as the spread of new ideas inspired others to further develop arguments or to challenge these ideas. New understandings about knowledge, power, reality, and the function of belief in turn helped to shape developing societies. However, philosophers also reflect their time and place in history, drawing on the beliefs and culture that surround them. Listed here are just some of the many important and influential philosophers whose work help to shape our understanding of the world.

Painting based on descriptions of Confucius, as no contemporary portrait is known to exist

Traditional Chinese robe

CONFUCIUS

Thales of Miletus

Greece, c.624–c.546 BCE

Referred to as the first philosopher, his key concerns were metaphysics and cosmology (he believed everything came from water).

Siddhārtha Gautama (Buddha)

Nepal/India, c.6th–4th century BCE

A spiritual teacher whose enquiry into the nonself, suffering, karma, and nirvana forms the basis of Buddhist philosophy.

Confucius

China, 551–479 BCE

Venerated teacher whose interests included: the way of the sages; humanism; self-cultivation; ritual psychology; the state.

Zeno of Elea

Italy/Greece, 490–430 BCE

A pre-Socratic philosopher who is known primarily as the creator of a number of philosophical paradoxes.

Socrates

Greece, 469–399 BCE

One of the founders of Western philosophy. Areas of interest: the soul; ignorance; unity of virtues; induction; the Socratic method

Mozi

China, 470–391 BCE

Founder of Mohism, an influential social and philosophical movement. Theories/interests: ethical, spiritual, and political order

Plato

Greece, c.427–c.347 BCE

One of the most influential thinkers in Western philosophy. Theories/interests: the Forms; soul's immortality; philosopher kings

Aristotle

Greece, 384–322 BCE

Regarded as one the greatest philosophers. Theories/interests: essentialism; causation; happiness and virtue; formal logic

Colored copper engraving of Avicenna

Mengzi

China, 372–289 BCE

Confucian philosopher whose work examined human nature, the heart-mind, and the concepts of good and evil.

Zhuangzi

China, late 4th Century BCE

Influential philosopher who was concerned with Daoism, naturalism, ethical relativism, scepticism, and pragmatic utilitarianism.

Nagarjuna

India, 2nd Century BCE

Key figure in the development of Indian philosophy and the Buddhist "middle way," which is based on the idea of emptiness.

AVICENNA

Hypatia

Egypt, 355–415 CE

A Neoplatonist philosopher, she was famous as a mathematician, astronomer, and leader of the philosophy school in Alexandria.

Al-Kindi

Iraq, c.808–870

Sometimes called the father of Arab philosophy. Theories/interests: world's eternity; divine simplicity; the human soul

Avicenna (Ibn Sina)

Iran, 980–1037

Polymath who made vital contributions to philosophy and medicine. Theories/interests: Islam; Aristotelianism; the rational soul; God

Ramanuja

India, 1017–1137

Influential theologian and philosopher. Theories/interests: Hinduism; the qualified nonduality of matter and soul.

Abélard

France, 1074–1142

A brilliant philosopher whose key interests were nominalism, logic, wisdom and faith, and the issue of moral responsibility.

Averroes (Ibn Rushd)

Spain/Morocco, 1126–98

Religious philosopher who integrated Islamic philosophy and the Greek traditions of Platonism and Aristotelianism.

Jalāl ad-Dīn Muhammad Rūmī (Rumi)

Middle East, 1207–73

Scholar, mystic, and acclaimed poet who wrote about his beliefs in verse form. Key interest: Sufism (Islamic mysticism)

Saint Thomas Aquinas

Italy, 1225–74

Christian theologian and philosopher who wrote about God's existence and attributes; immortality and virtue; and natural law.

"The **unexamined life** is **not worth living.**"

SOCRATES, Attributed quote from Plato's *Apology, c.*399 BCE

Francis Bacon

England, 1561–1626

Important empiricist in the development of the scientific method. Theories/interests: natural philosophy; induction

René Descartes

France, 1596–1650

Influential rationalist philosopher. Theories/interests: rationalism, innatism, the Cogito, mind-body dualism, God

Elisabeth, Princess Palatine of Bohemia

England/Czech Republic, 1618–80

Known for her correspondence on philosophical matters with Descartes. Key interests: mind-body interaction; polity

Wang Fuzhi

China, 1619–92

Important Neo-Confucian thinker who was born toward the end of the Ming dynasty. Theories/interests: materialism; action; ethics

Margaret Lucas Cavendish

England, 1623–73

Prolific writer on a range of topics. Theories/interests: naturalism; materialism; vitalist theory of causation; free will

Gabrielle Suchon

France, 1632–1703

Prominent advocate of women's rights. Areas of interest: militant philosophy; women's education, autonomy, and liberty

John Locke

England, 1632–1704

Empiricist thinker and one of the most influential political philosophers. Theories/interests: social contract; personal identity

Mary Astell

England, 1666–1731

Proto-feminist known also for her critique of Locke. Theories/interests: women's education; dualist metaphysics

George Berkeley

Ireland, 1685–1753

One of the great empiricists of the 18th century. Theories/interests: empiricism; subjective idealism (immaterialism); religion

David Hume

Scotland, 1711–76

Influential thinker during the Enlightenment. Theories/interests: empiricism; scepticism; causation; induction; ethical noncognitivism

Immanuel Kant

Germany, 1724–1804

A key figure in the development of modern philosophy. Theories/interests: moral law and autonomy; transcendental idealism

Mary Wollstonecraft

UK, 1759–97

Moral and political philosopher who advocated for equality between sexes and asserted women's right to education.

John Stuart Mill

UK, 1806–73

One of the most influential English thinkers of the 19th century. Theories/interests: liberalism; utilitarianism; empiricism

Karl Marx

Germany/UK, 1818–83

Revolutionary thinker who has had a profound impact on the world. Areas of interest: historical materialism; Communism

Friedrich Nietzsche

Germany, 1844–1900

Philosopher and fierce cultural critic. Theories/interests: perspectivism; nihilism; will to power; the overhuman; death of God

Edmund Husserl

Germany, 1859–1938

His work on the structures of experience and consciousness influenced many other disciplines. Theory/interest: phenomenology

Kitarō Nishida

Japan, 1870–1945

Combined Western philosophy with the Oriental spiritual tradition. Theories/interests: consciousness; experience; nothingness

Bertrand Russell

UK, 1872–1970

A founder of modern analytic philosophy. Theories/interests: logicism; logical atomism; theory of language

Ludwig Wittgenstein

Austria/UK, 1889–1951

Thought to be one of the greatest philosophers of the 20th century. Theories/interests: language; meaning; certainty

Martin Heidegger

Germany, 1889–1976

Influential figure in contemporary European philosophy. Theories/interests: ontology; existentialism; hermeneutic phenomenology

Rudolf Carnap

Austria/US, 1891–1970

Prominent member of the Vienna Circle. Theories/interests: logical empiricism; inductive logic; verification and confirmation

Jean-Paul Sartre

France, 1905–80

Noted French intellectual. Theories/interests: existentialism; ontology; freedom; nothingness; bad faith; authenticity

Hannah Arendt

Germany/US, 1906–75

Prominent political theorist. Key interests: phenomenology of political existence, judgment, citizenship, and totalitarianism

Simone de Beauvoir

France, 1908–86

Significant intellectual and activist whose work was key in the development of existentialism and feminist theory.

Willard Van Orman Quine

US, 1908–2000

High-profile thinker in 20th-century Anglo-American philosophy. Key interests: naturalized epistemology; metaphysics

Michel Foucault

France, 1926–84

Controversial philosopher and historian. Theories/interests: post-structuralism; power and knowledge; sexuality; madness

Graciela Hierro

Mexico, 1928–2003

Notable feminist philosopher who specialized in ethics. Theory/interest: feminist ethics of pleasure

Jacques Derrida

France, 1930–2004

Best known for creating a form of analysis called deconstruction. Theories/interests: the Other; postmodernism; deconstructionism

Sandra Harding

US, b.1935

Distinguished standpoint theorist. Theories/interests: postcolonialism; feminist standpoint epistemology; strong objectivity

Chung-Ying Cheng

China/US, b.1935

Pioneer of Chinese philosophy in the US. Theories/interests: onto-hermeneutics; inner and outer; philosophy of management

María Lugones

Argentina/US, b.1948

Philosopher and activist who examines resistance to oppressions. Theories/interests: decolonial feminism, multiple selves

Iris Marion Young

US, 1949–2006

Political theorist who was interested in the phenomenology of the gendered body, and justice and politics of difference.

Horacio Cerutti Guldberg

Argentina, b.1950

Scholar who is part of the Latin American philosophical movement known as the philosophy of liberation.

bell hooks

US, b.1952

Writer and social activist whose work addresses issues of feminist identity and oppression, race, class, and gender.

BELL HOOKS

see also What is politics? pp.392–93 ▶   Political theory pp.396–97 ▶   Sociology pp.406–409 ▶

Mythology

Thought to have evolved in an attempt to understand concepts such as life and death, the natural world, the structure of the universe, and issues of morality like good and evil, myths are found in every culture on Earth. Originally passed from generation to generation orally, the invention of writing in Mesopotamia, West Asia, in 3300 BCE preserved many myths for posterity. As well as enhanced accounts of historic persons, myths include tales of magic, gods, goddesses, and otherworldly beings, as well as human heroes with supernatural powers.

Mesopotamian

Each of Mesopotamia's city-states (see p.304) had its own beliefs, but all worshipped similar supreme deities, including the supreme god, An (Anu); mother goddess, Ninhursaga; storm god, Enlil; and Enki, the divine craftsman. These controlled everything from crop fertility to underworld demons. Mesopotamia's most well-known mythic figure, however, is Gilgamesh. An actual human king of the Sumerian city of Uruk, in myths he became a warrior with superhuman powers. As well as battling lions, bulls, and monsters, Gilgamesh met and fought Enkidu, who subsequently became his best friend and brother. When Enkidu fell ill and died, Gilgamesh embarked on a journey of discovery, ending with him accepting his mortality.

ENKIDU AND GILGAMESH

"Who is there can rival his kingly standing?"

The Epic of Gilgamesh, c.2100–1400 BCE

Egyptian

From c.4000 BCE to 30 BCE, Egyptian ideas of life after death and mainly benevolent gods not only influenced every aspect of Egyptian society, but also the beliefs of other cultures, including those of Greece and Rome. Egyptian deities began as tribal gods in animal form, but by the time of the Old Kingdom they had taken on human shapes. Of the

hundreds of deities that remained, the earliest to be venerated were the firstborn children of Geb (Earth) and Nut (Sky): Isis, Set, Nephthys, Horus, and Osiris. Osiris was murdered by Set, but resurrected by Isis and became judge of souls and Lord of the Underworld— the next stage of existence for all ancient Egyptians.

Greek

As in Mesopotamia and Egypt, Greek myths chart the world's creation out of a void (Chaos), as well as the pantheon of deities on Olympus, Greece's highest mountain. Humanlike in form, they could change into animals at will and many had human flaws. There were 12 Olympians, including the king, Zeus, and Hera, queen

of the gods; Apollo, the sun god; Aphrodite, goddess of beauty and love; and others who specialized in everything from fire to wine. Humans, demigods, and creatures such as satyrs and centaurs abound in Greek myths, while legends such as the lost island of Atlantis, mentioned by Athenian philosopher Plato, served as cautionary tales.

THE LEGEND OF ATLANTIS

"In a **single day and night** ... the island of **Atlantis disappeared** into the depths ..."

PLATO,
*Timaeus and Critias, c.*360 BCE

Roman

Roman and Greek deities are so intertwined that some, such as Apollo, share the same name; Greek influence on the Italian peninsula had been present right from the foundation of Rome in the 8th century BCE. Yet Rome quickly put its stamp on its beliefs, starting with the city's creation story: Mars, god of war, fathered twin sons with a human king's daughter. The babies, Romulus and Remus, were thrown in a river to drown by a rival king. They were rescued and raised by a she-wolf, and grew up to found Rome; Romulus subsequently killed Remus to rule alone. Just as in Greece, Roman gods and goddesses were quick-tempered and often violent. However, they could be appeased by rituals that ensured a reward for the person involved.

Satyrs were woodland creatures *Roman satyrs had goat's horns and ears*

ROMAN SATYR MOSAIC, *c.***138–192 CE**

Celtic

Neither a single race nor nation, the ancient Celts (see p.307) developed hundreds of individual myths, which were passed down orally until some were recorded by monks in the Middle Ages. What survives today mainly reflects the mythology of Celtic Wales, Ireland, and Scotland, as well as of Brittany and Gaul. Each Celtic tribe had its own god and protector, but most recognized Lug, a god of light, healing, arts, and crafts, as well as Cernunnos, a horned god associated with animals and fertility. Female deities were especially important, particularly war goddesses such as the Morrígan; Brigid, goddess of learning and healing; and the horse goddess Epona. Magic, magicians, rebirth, and a supernatural "otherworld" humans could enter via *sidhe*—mounds or hills—loom large in Celtic mythology.

◀ The Riders of the Sidhe
The supernatural *aos sí* (Sidhe), the "fair folk" (fairies) of Irish and Scottish legend, depicted by John Duncan in 1911.

◀ see also Ancient Greece pp.312–13   ◀ Ancient Rome pp.314–15   **389**

>> Mythology continued

Suspension ring in shape of eagle's head

Interlaced bands on hammer's head typical of Norse art

10TH-CENTURY THOR'S HAMMER PENDANT

Norse

The Norsemen were North Germanic peoples who lived in what is present-day Scandinavia in the 8th–11th centuries. Those who went abroad to raid and trade were known as the Vikings. In the often brutal Norse myths of cold northern Europe, brother-gods Odin, Vili, and Ve created the universe from a giant's body, ordering it into various levels, or realms, connected by Yggdrasil, the great World Tree. Humans inhabited Midgard, or "Middle-earth," while the gods, the Aesir and Vanir, resided in the "heavenly level," often known simply as Asgard. The Aesir were gods of sky and war. Ruled by Odin, they were his wife, Frigg; their sons Thor, god of thunder, Baldr, and Tyr; and a trickster god, Loki. The Vanir were gods of love, fertility, and prosperity, and included Freyja (who cried tears of gold) and Freyr. The underworld, Niflheim, was ruled by Hel, Loki's daughter. The gods spent most of their time fighting each other or battling frost giants or other monsters, dwarves, or elves. Eventually, Ragnarök—the end of the world—ensued, destroying the universe in one version, but in another, a new world of gods and humans is allowed to rise from the destruction.

TYPES OF MYTHS

Most cultures have creation myths, dealing with how life and the universe began, as well as myths revolving around gods and goddesses. For example, the Aztec (see p.343) figures Oxomoco and Cipactonal (right) were believed to be the ancestors of all humans. Flood myths involving the destruction of a civilization are also common. Animals figure largely in the myths of Native American and Celtic cultures, while human heroes, such as the Greek Herakles (Hercules) loom large in others.

Maori

The Maori settled in New Zealand around the 13th century. According to Maori mythology, the sky god, Ranginui, and the Earth goddess, Papatuanuku, held each other in a tight embrace, with their many children living in the darkness between them. The world came into being when the children pushed them apart so that they could see light and have space to live. One of them, Tane, the forest god, tried to create living beings by using red ocher, but succeeded only in making trees, until he breathed on it and made Hina, the first woman. New Zealand was created when the trickster demigod, Maui, furious his brothers had left him behind when going fishing, stowed away on their canoe and used a magical hook to catch a monstrous fish that turned out to be North Island.

Indian traditional tales

Traditional Indian epics told stories rooted in the distant past. One such work, the *Mahabharata*, was composed between 400 BCE and 300 CE and relates the dynastic struggle between the Kauravas and Pandavas, two groups of cousins. The feud begins when Dhritarashtra, the forefather of the Kauravas, is passed over for the throne of Hastinapura because of his blindness, and his descendants try to wrest it back from the family of his brother Pandu. Rich in stories, such as an epic game of dice in which the Pandavas lose their kingdom back to the Kauravas, the *Mahabharata* ends in an epic battle said to mark the start of the current era of history.

▶ Mythical apparition

The 19th-century Japanese artist Utagawa Kunisada specialized in scenes from kabuki theater. Here he shows a female *yokai* ghost emerging from a lantern.

Oxomoco   Cipactonal

15TH-CENTURY AZTEC CODEX

Japanese

Japanese folklore populated the countryside with *yokai*—monsters, ghosts, and demons who preyed on unwary passersby. They came in many forms, most often animallike, but also as plants or inanimate objects. The *obake* were shapeshifters, able to transform themselves into foxes or badgers, while the monstrous Itsumade, with a human head, snake body, and razor-sharp claws appeared in the sky at times of plague, and the giant salamanderlike *kappa* were said to drown children who strayed into the river. The *Rokurokubi* were *yokai* who looked like humans, but their heads detached at night and roved around in search of victims. Propitiating the *yokai* was important, and offerings were made to them, such as cucumber thrown in rivers to appease the *kappa*.

Chinese

Chinese myth explained the creation of the world as the work of Pangu (or Pan Gu), a giant who grew within an egg that magically materialized out of primordial chaos. When Pangu broke out of the egg, the egg's lightest parts floated up to form the heavens, while its heavier parts sank down to form the Earth and sky. At the very corners of the Earth, four mythological creatures stood guard: the azure dragon of the east, the black tortoise of the north, the white tiger of the west, and the vermilion bird of the south. Much about society was attributed to legendary rulers such as Huangdi, the Yellow Emperor, under whom the Chinese calendar and writing were invented.

Maasai

The stories of the Maasai people of Kenya are strongly associated with the cattle whose herding dominated their way of life. Their chief deity, Enkai, had a dual aspect: as Enkai-Narok, the black god, he brought rain and prosperity, and as Enka-na-Nyokie, the red god, he inflicted famine on those who angered him. Enkai was said to have sent cattle to the Maasai at the time when the Earth and the sky split apart, by sending the cows down to Earth on a bark rope made from the oreti (wild fig) tree. All the cattle came to the Maasai, but Enkai also sent honey and wild beasts to the Torrobo, a hunting group, and seed to the Kikuyu people, who became farmers. Enkai is also said to have created these three groups by dividing a tree into parts that became human beings, and with what was left he gave a cane to the Maasai to herd cattle, a shovel to the Kikuyu to turn over the ground on their farms, and a bow and arrow to be used by the hunters.

> "I will **give you** something called cattle."
>
> ORAL LITERATURE OF THE MAASAI

Incan

The Inca people of Peru believed that the world came into being when Viracocha, the water god, emerged from Lake Titicaca. He then created the other gods, human beings, the sun, the moon, and the stars. His son, Inti, the sun god, was the brother and husband of the moon, Mama Quilla, and was the deity most revered by the Incas. An eclipse of the sun was said to be a sign of his anger, and he was seen as the ancestor of the Sapa Inca, the Inca emperors. Most of the gods lived in Hanan Pacha, the upper world, where those who had lived a good life hope to go after death. The wicked were punished by being sent to Uku Pacha, the land of Supay, god of the dead, who also demanded human sacrifices to populate his realm.

> "In the **beginning**, and before this world was created, there was a being called **Viracocha**."
>
> PEDRO SARMIENTO DE GAMBOA, *History of the Incas*, 1572

◀ see also World religions pp.378–81 **391**

What is politics?

Politics is the means by which societies and governments make decisions about governance, whether these concern war and peace, or local choices about garbage disposal. Finding solutions to these issues involves compromise and adjustment. Formal political processes typically follow constitutional or legal procedures, especially where enforceable rules are being considered. Therefore a decision on whether to increase or reduce taxes at local, state, or national levels will follow an agreed process.

Political moralism

Political moralism concerns the way that beliefs, ethics, and morality invariably shape how communities think, and thus play a major role in the political choices that are finally made. These beliefs can sometimes create systems that prejudice the interests of ethnic or religious minorities. Groups with similar beliefs will often form political parties to advance their agenda. Today, governing bodies generally preclude measures that favor a particular belief system, though bias still exists around the world and in politics.

Political realism

The idea that politics is about using power in pursuit of various objectives has been a dominant feature of national and international politics over the centuries, and is one reason why politics can sometimes be seen as a cynical and amoral process. Politics, in this context, is less about compromise and consensus than about exploiting advantages in economic or military imbalances in order to prevail in any given situation. Political realism often favors those groups with economic or social power over the weak and groups of marginalized people.

Wise counsel

In traditional societies and cultures, the idea that wisdom and good judgment come with age and experience often clashes with modern forms of democracy and equal rights. Most societies try to balance these considerations, but this is often difficult in societies that have traditionally favored the idea of filial duty (the duty of a child to its parents). Most countries now require a system of public consultation before decisions are taken. This process provides the time and space for experts or people with experience to provide counsel and advice.

◀ **EU Parliament**
The European Parliament, in Strasbourg, France, is the directly elected legislative body of the European Union (EU).

Representations of the industries of laborers

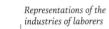

NORWEGIAN LABOR PARTY POSTER, 1930

Ideological thinking

While representative forms of government replaced traditional approaches to governance from the 18th century onward, new ideas of national identity that looked beyond religious or traditional beliefs still had to be found.

The growth of Communism and the rise of Fascism in the 20th century were two such secular ideologies, though in very different ways. While retaining some aspects of the modernizing agenda of industrial societies, they focused on social and economic organization, typically for a defined objective, within autocratic states.

SYSTEMS OF GOVERNMENT

Each form of government has its own characteristics. Governments whose power is concentrated in the hands of an individual are dictatorships or traditional monarchies. Democracies feature elected representatives who are held accountable. There are cases in which a few people control most policies (oligarchies), even if these are democracies, or in which religious beliefs determine policy (theocracies). Where there are no governing structures, the situation can be described as anarchic.

Socialism

Socialism is a political philosophy where workers control the generation of wealth. Socialist and Communist ideas have often been considered interchangeable, and were thought to be antidemocratic in essence. But a model of democratic socialism has emerged that blends socialist objectives with democratic processes. The traditional form of socialism (as in the former Soviet Union) establishes the Communist Party as the sole representative of the people. Party members are not elected, so such systems are characterized as single-party states.

Nationalism

Nationalism appears in different contexts. In a colonial context it is a means of pursuing independence or self-determination. India, Nigeria, Indonesia, and Egypt all had national movements for independence during the 1940s and 1950s. In other contexts, nationalism is a polarizing and dangerous force that expects individuals to subordinate their interests to defined national objectives. Fascism (a one-party dictatorship) and Nazism were extreme products of this form of nationalism, which violently persecuted minorities and marginalized groups.

Atatürk – founder and first president of the Republic of Turkey

KEMAL ATATURK, NATIONALIST LEADER

> "It is said that **democracy** is the **worst form of government**, except for all those **other forms**"
>
> WINSTON CHURCHILL, Speech to UK Parliament, 1947

Democracy

Democracy involves the periodic use of elections as the preferred form of selecting governments and is used in most parts of the world. An effective democracy, however, also requires checks on the executive power of the state, with powers and rights defined in a constitutional system. In practice, there is an extraordinary mix of democratic methods, ranging from plebiscites (votes from an entire electorate), directly elected officials, indirectly elected officials, and constituencies reserved for only certain types of electors.

Political institutions across the world

Every country develops its own system of government, with its own forms, and applies its own principles. This creates a wide mix of systems found across the world: federations, constitutional monarchies (as in the UK), religious states (as in Iran), dictatorships, and various forms of autocratic government. Most countries draw on democratic and liberal principles, while others draw on socialist principles. At the international level, ideas about the importance of constructive cooperation led to the creation of the United Nations in 1945.

SYSTEMS OF GOVERNMENT	RULE BY A SINGLE PERSON	RULE BY A SELECTED FEW	RULE BY THE MANY
	MONARCHY	THEOCRACY	DEMOCRACY
	DICTATORSHIP	OLIGARCHY	ANARCHY

see also Politics through history pp.394–95 ▶   Political theory pp.396–97 ▶   Sociology pp.406–409 ▶

Politics through history

From the dawn of time, every civilization and culture has developed ideas on how to govern people in order to ensure security and prosperity, as well as provide spiritual and ethical guidance. Wars, rivalries, and other forms of confrontation saw a distinctly European model of governance emerge as a dominant force, spreading across the world through imperial expansion and colonial subjugation. With roots firmly anchored in the Greek and Roman traditions—supplemented by largely Christian values and the evolution of political, civil, and human rights—this model of governance has significantly shaped various systems and practices around the world, often at variance with local traditions and beliefs.

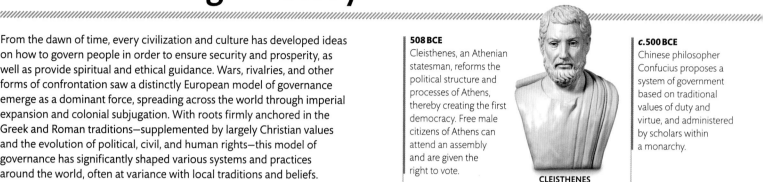

508 BCE
Cleisthenes, an Athenian statesman, reforms the political structure and processes of Athens, thereby creating the first democracy. Free male citizens of Athens can attend an assembly and are given the right to vote.

CLEISTHENES

c.500 BCE
Chinese philosopher Confucius proposes a system of government based on traditional values of duty and virtue, and administered by scholars within a monarchy.

1789 The French Revolution establishes a republic. The *Declaration of the Rights of Man and the Citizen*, drafted by revolutionaries, is a pioneering declaration of human rights.

Sharp blade makes guillotine, introduced 1792, a more humane mode of execution

REPLICA OF FRENCH GUILLOTINE

INDEPENDENT STATES

1783 In America, spurred by political differences, 13 British colonies defeat Britain, gain territory, and establish an independent United States. It is the first time major colonies break from European control.

KEY
■ Western territory ■ 13 states

1648 The Peace of Westphalia—a series of treaties—ends 30 years of conflict in Europe. It leads to the creation of the modern state system and establishes principles of sovereignty.

PEACE OF WESTPHALIA

1804 After a 14-year-long revolution, Haiti gains independence from France, becoming the first state in the Americas governed by black people, and the first country to abolish slavery.

Uniform of French National Convention member

HAITIAN REVOLUTIONARY JEAN-BAPTISTE BELLEY

1819 Venezualan statesman Simón Bolívar declares the independence of colonies of Gran Colombia (modern-day Panama, Colombia, Ecuador, and Venezuela).

SIMON BOLIVAR

Bolívar is depicted wearing his military uniform

1833 Slavery is abolished across the colonial British Empire. This is followed by France abolishing slavery in 1848, and the US in 1865.

1930 Mahatma Gandhi breaks British colonial law. This initiates a campaign of civil disobedience in India, whereby citizens refuse, in a nonviolent fashion, to obey the imperial British government.

JOSEPH STALIN

1922 In Russia, Joseph Stalin seizes control of the Communist Party, initiating radical policies of property confiscation, forced industrialization, and mass purges.

1918 The Armistice ends fighting in World War I. This is followed by the Treaty of Versailles, which imposes reparations and significant loss of territory on Austria and Germany.

1917 Military defeats by Germany and the subsequent civil unrest prompt Russia's Tsar Nicholas II to abdicate. Vladimir Lenin establishes a Communist state.

SOVIET PROPAGANDA POSTER

Flag bears the year of the revolution

FASCIST STATE

1939 With Adolf Hitler coming to power in Germany in 1933, fascist forces across Europe threaten the peace agreed upon at Versailles by forming alliances and invading Austria and Poland.

1945 The Allied leaders meet in Yalta in the Crimea to discuss the fate of Germany and Japan after the war. Later the same year, the United Nations is formed to preserve world peace.

1960 Sirimavo Bandaranaike is elected Prime Minister of Sri Lanka, becoming the first female elected head of government. Women's participation in politics sees a steady increase.

 ◄ see also The modern world pp.350–51 ◄ Self-determination and civil rights pp.366–67 ◄ What is politics? pp.392–93

Theodosius presents letter of appointment to official

c.380–360 BCE Ancient Greek philosopher Plato authors his best-known work, *The Republic*. In it, he advocates rule by philosopher kings who can use their knowledge of eternal realities to chart the course of good governance.

380 CE Emperor Theodosius I establishes Christianity as the official religion of the Roman Empire, beginning its institutional dominance in Europe. At this time in history, religion and politics are indistinguishable.

Palace guards

REPLICA OF MISSORIUM (CEREMONIAL DISH) OF THEODOSIUS

622 Prophet Muhammad's *Constitution of Medina* for Islamic and Jewish tribes advocates consultation and tolerance, and prohibits war to settle conflicts. It is an early example of religious tolerance put into practice.

8th–18th century European political tradition adopts the idea that monarchs derive the right to rule from a divine authority. Opposing this can be considered sacrilegious.

1513 Italian diplomat Niccolò Machiavelli composes *The Prince*, a treatise on governance that forms the foundation of modern political analysis. It analyzes men, rather than view politics as divine.

Christian knight

1095–1492 The Crusades bring Christians and Muslims into prolonged conflict over control of the Holy Land. The animosity between the two has centuries-long political ramifications in Europe and the Holy Land.

ILLUSTRATION OF THE CRUSADES

802–1463 Kingdoms of Southeast Asia adopt Buddhist precepts in their governing ethos, along with elements of Hinduism and Confucianism. They trade extensively with India and China.

ANGKOR WAT TEMPLE, ANGKOR

Dedication to Lorenzo de Medici, ruler of Florence

TITLE PAGE OF THE PRINCE

1871 Germany is unified as a single nation under the military governance of Kaiser Wilhelm I following the Franco-Prussian War, and the German annexation of the regions of Alsace and Lorraine.

Spike indicates this Prussian pickelhaube was worn by infantryman

PRUSSIAN HELMET

1893 New Zealand becomes the first self-governing country where most women acquire the right to vote in parliamentary elections, but they cannot become candidates until 1919.

WOMEN'S SUFFRAGE

1914 The assassination of Franz Ferdinand—heir to the Austrian-Hungarian throne—activates European alliances, marking a change in global politics and leading to World War I.

GUN USED TO KILL FRANZ FERDINAND

Semiautomatic pistol

Leather helmet

1912 After the last imperial dynasty in China is overthrown, ending an absolute monarchy, Chinese Nationalist Party leader, Sun Yat-Sen, establishes a republic, becoming president.

SUN YAT-SEN

1968 Martin Luther King, Jr. is assassinated. In the aftermath of this tragedy, the US Congress gives legal force to the agenda of the civil rights movement through the Civil Rights Act. It inspires many fights for equal rights across the globe.

1989 The Berlin Wall falls, initiating revolutions across Eastern Europe, the collapse of Communism and the reunification of Germany. The European Union adds 11 new member states.

US PRESIDENT AND LEADER OF THE SOVIET UNION

1990 In South Africa, anti-apartheid activist Nelson Mandela is released from prison. The first democratic elections occur in 1994, ending institutionalized racial segregation.

NELSON MANDELA

2016 Following the election of Donald Trump as President, US politics sees a shift towards unilateralism (in which foreign policy is made in the interest of a single nation).

see also Political theory pp.396–97 ▶ Sociology pp.406–409 ▶

Political theory

Political debate, political systems, and the way countries are governed, have all been influenced by many ideas from a variety of thinkers including philosophers and religious, military, and political leaders. Personal beliefs, wider social obligations and duties, and how political systems should operate dominate political debate. Presented here are just a few of the many theories that have been suggested throughout history.

Confucianism

Confucius's (551–479 BCE) moral standpoint was firmly rooted in traditional Chinese virtues of loyalty, duty, and respect, determined by social status. Reflected in the *junzi* (ideal man), whose proper conduct provides an example to others, Confucianism deepened an enduring tradition. Harmony in society would result from everyone behaving appropriately in their assigned role.

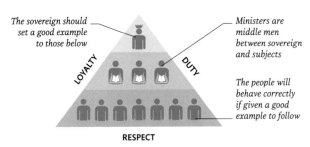

The sovereign should set a good example to those below

Ministers are middle men between sovereign and subjects

The people will behave correctly if given a good example to follow

LOYALTY · DUTY · RESPECT

CONFUCIUS'S TRIANGLE OF GOVERNMENT

FEMINIST SOCIAL THEORY

Though women have historically been deprived of property, legal, and political rights, feminist interpretations of political problems have been an important contribution to political theory. Early "first wave" feminism of the early 20th century focused largely on the fight for equal political rights. The liberation movements of the 1960s addressed reproductive rights and women's labour, constituting a "second wave". Contemporary "third wave" feminism centres on non-Western women, and the issues provoked by racism, homophobia, transphobia, and Eurocentrism.

Just wars

Current ideas of a just war can be traced back to Thomas Aquinas (1225–74). Although Christianity preached pacifism for its adherents, Aquinas believed it was sometimes necessary to fight in order to restore peace.

Restoring peace
Aquinas believed that the restoration of peace is the only just reason for war.

Authority of sovereign
Only with the authority of the ruler or sovereign can a just war be waged. All others are unjust.

Benefit of people
The war needs a just cause that will benefit the people, such as self-defense or to avoid invasion.

The social contract

Individuals in a social contract agree to surrender some liberties in exchange for security. Jean-Jacques Rousseau (1712–78) argued that this system could uphold inequalities, but attain freedom with the law. Thomas Hobbes (1588–1679) believed this assured peace, but not true freedom.

	WITHOUT SOCIETY	THE SOCIAL CONTRACT	FREEDOM
HOBBES	LIFE IS NASTY	GUARANTEES PEACE	EXISTS OUTSIDE LAW
ROUSSEAU	PEOPLE ARE CONTENT	PRESERVES INEQUALITIES	WON WITHIN LAW

Individual responsibility

While rights and liberties are guaranteed by law, it is expected that individuals take personal responsibility. Citizens have an obligation to obey the law.

Kant's categorical imperative

Kant's (1724–1804) categorical imperative (a rule that is true in all circumstances) states that a person should always act in such a way that he would be willing for it to become a general law for all people.

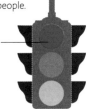

Driving through a red light is bad if everyone does it

Communism

While capitalism is an efficient economic system, in the 19th century philosopher Karl Marx (1818–83) suggested that it contains the seeds of its own destruction. He argued that profits from business benefit only the owners while workers are exploited, and that the only way to change this is eliminate private property and create a dictatorship of the working class.

Capitalism and alienation

The moment a worker hands over his finished products to his employer, he becomes disconnected from them. Marx argued that this disconnection causes a sense of alienation in a worker.

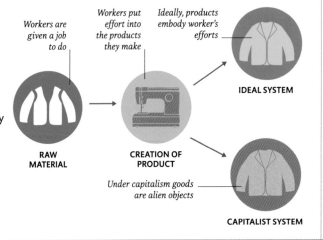

Workers are given a job to do

Workers put effort into the products they make

Ideally, products embody worker's efforts

IDEAL SYSTEM

RAW MATERIAL

CREATION OF PRODUCT

Under capitalism goods are alien objects

CAPITALIST SYSTEM

PHILOSOPHER KINGS

Plato argued that if people were to live well, they required rulers that would ensure this. In his opinion, only philosophers with knowledge of ethics and morality could do this, therefore political power should only be given to philosophers.

AN INTELLECTUAL RULER

> "If you **know both yourself** and **your enemy**,
> you can win a hundred battles without jeopardy."
>
> SUN TZU, *Art of War*, 6th century BCE

The art of war

Chinese general Sun Tzu (544–496 BCE) provided a framework for military strategy that can also be applied to political challenges. Principles include matters such as seasons, terrain, the moral influence of the ruler, the ability and qualities of the general, and the organization and discipline of the men.

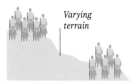

Varying terrain

Earth
A strategist must take into account the Earth, which comprises distances, danger and security, open or narrow terrain, and the chances of life and death.

Soldiers obey the general

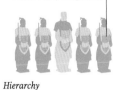

The Dao
Under the Dao (the Way), soldiers are in complete accord with the ruler, and will follow regardless.

Hierarchy creates order

Discipline
The army must be formed of proper subdivisions and organized by rank in order to instill discipline.

Opposites are in balance

Heaven
Heaven (Yin and Yang) signifies the cycle of the seasons, night and day, and the passage of time.

Command
A successful general must embody virtues such as wisdom, sincerity, courage, and benevolence.

Universal suffrage

Universal suffrage is the right that all adults have, subject to some minor exceptions, to vote, regardless of wealth, gender, race, ethnicity, property ownership, or any other restrictions.

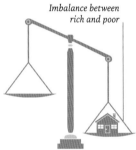

Imbalance between rich and poor

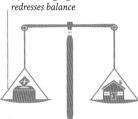

Equal voting rights redresses balance

VOTING RIGHTS BASED ON WEALTH

UNIVERSAL SUFFRAGE

Separation of powers

The division of power within a state between the executive (responsible for administration), the legislative (responsible for the passing laws), and the judicial (responsible for applying the laws), provides a check on the misuse of power by individuals or groups.

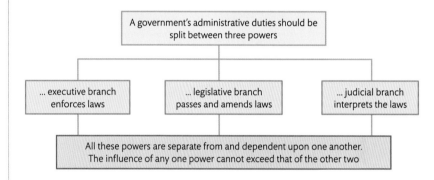

A government's administrative duties should be split between three powers

... executive branch enforces laws

... legislative branch passes and amends laws

... judicial branch interprets the laws

All these powers are separate from and dependent upon one another. The influence of any one power cannot exceed that of the other two

Social justice

The idea of social justice flows from a belief that everyone must benefit from their individual rights. While legal systems and institutions need to redress historic inequalities or exclusions in order to deliver social justice, the principles of democratic accountability should also sustain this process.

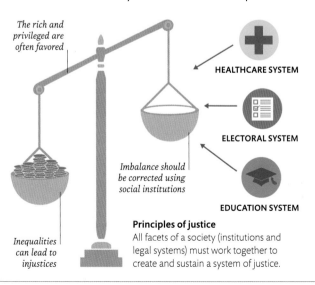

The rich and privileged are often favored

HEALTHCARE SYSTEM

Imbalance should be corrected using social institutions

ELECTORAL SYSTEM

EDUCATION SYSTEM

Inequalities can lead to injustices

Principles of justice
All facets of a society (institutions and legal systems) must work together to create and sustain a system of justice.

Individual liberty

Philosopher John Stuart Mill (1806–73) was interested in the balance between government interference and individual liberties. He argued for three basic liberties (below), and that the government may only interfere to prevent harm to others.

Freedom of opinion
People should be free to have opinions and express them in speech and writing.

Pursuing one's tastes
As long as it does not harm others, people may follow their own pursuits as they see fit.

Right to unite
People may gather and unite for any purpose that does not cause harm.

The rule of law

John Locke (1632–1704) argued for the liberal principles of government: that its chief purpose is to protect a people's life, liberty, and property, and to work for the public good. Therefore, in his view, lawmaking is the foremost role and responsibility of a government.

Good laws
Lawmaking is the chief purpose, and one of the most important functions, of a government.

Rights of the people
Laws should protect the rights of the people that the government represents.

Enforced laws
With the good of the public in mind, the government must enforce the laws it creates.

see also Economics through history pp.400–401 ▶   Sociology pp.406–409 ▶

What is economics?

Economics is the study of the ways in which people manage resources, and organize the production and distribution of goods and services. Building on other disciplines, such as law, psychology, and sociology, economics helps to explain how people make choices, as both consumers and as producers, and how they reconcile unlimited wants with the world's limited resources. There are many theories of how the economy works, and economists argue fiercely about the best explanation.

Making rational choice
Each time a consumer weighs the costs and benefits of the options available to them—trying to maximize the surplus of benefits over the costs—and comes to a decision based on their own preferences, they are making what microeconomists call a rational choice. Economists use this premise to predict how consumers will behave, assuming that they behave consistently to maximize their interests.

Ownership and property rights
The economic function of market exchange—the act of producing, selling, and buying—is based on the principle that resources are owned by someone, a construct referred to as property rights. These rights are intended to ensure peaceful, rather than violent, competition for resources. A private property right, for example, might be owning a house. As the owner of a house a person is entitled to delegate, rent, or sell the "rights" to any another party who is willing to meet mutually agreed terms, such as the price and timing of the exchange.

What is money?
Money is a unit of exchange and only has worth as long as people believe it represents a particular value—it is not the same as wealth. Historically, the earliest units of exhange were in the form of commodities—goods such as cocoa

◄ Floating market
The exchanging of goods for money takes place on many levels throughout society, from market traders selling their wares locally to intergovernmental trading.

beans, salt, or dried corn, considered valuable because they were in wide demand. Over the centuries this system gave way to paper notes and coins that were valued according to the price of gold, but in the 1970s, gold-backed currency was replaced by so called "fiat" money—inconvertible paper money that was made legal tender by governments.

The process of supply and demand
The amount of goods or services available in the marketplace is described as supply, and the quantity of goods or services wanted by consumers at any given time is known as demand. Together the two work to set the price of the goods or services. For example, according to the law of supply and demand, if there are 10 qualified accountants available for every accountancy job advertised then the salaries offered are unlikely to change. Conversely, if there is only one qualified accountant available for every 10 jobs advertised, then employers will raise offered salaries in order to attract scarce job applicants.

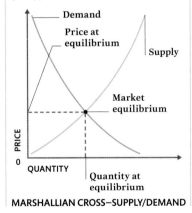

MARSHALLIAN CROSS—SUPPLY/DEMAND

MONOPOLY vs. PERFECT COMPETITION

Competition in the marketplace
A key driver of economic activity and a defining feature of capitalism, competition in this sense is rivalry between enterprises in the same line of business, each of which wants to increase its share of the market. To achieve this, producers or suppliers try to win over another business's customers or clients by varying price, innovating their product, introducing a promotion, or changing the location where the product is available. Competition can detemine market price: the greater the demand for a product, the higher the price a customer is willing pay. Monopoly occurs when a supplier has exclusive possession of a market, in which case it can set the price as it wishes. "Perfect competion" refers to multiple suppliers achieving a balanced price in a crowded marketplace.

Microeconomics
The study of microeconomics focuses on the behavior of both individual consumers and suppliers of goods and services. The starting point for this study is market mechanism, or the analysis of the key factors such as: the dynamics of supply and demand, illustrated with the Marshallian Cross diagram (see left); how

JOHN MAYNARD KEYNES
British economist John Maynard Keynes (1883–1946) revolutionized economic thinking in the 1930s by proposing that government spending was fundamental to maintaining full employment; this, in turn, stimulated economy by increasing demand.

resources are placed; the efficiency of production; how labor is allocated; and the effect of government regulation and tax on the entire process. It also looks at why individuals and producers respond to price in a particular way, and at what price level their behavior will change.

Macroeconomics
Macroeconomics deals with the behavior and performance of large-scale economic systems, assessing how they function at regional, national, or international levels. Macroeconomics focuses on changes in an economy's performance by examining indicators such as unemployment, growth rate, gross domestic product (GDP), and inflation. It connects elements, such as government, banking, and industry, which contribute to total, or aggregate, economic activity of a country, and anyalyzes the microeconomic factors that can influence them. Governments and corporations use macroeconomic models to help the formulation of economic policies.

> "A **national debt**, if it is not excessive, will be to us a **national blessing**."
>
> ALEXANDER HAMILTON, US Founding Father,
> In a letter to financier Robert Morris, April 30, 1781

TYPES OF ECONOMIES
Economic theory identifies four types of economies, each determined by the way resources are allocated. In a traditional, farming-based economy, supply just meets demand. In a planned economy (shown here), decisions are made by a central authority or government. A free market has no government intervention, and a mixed economy has some central intervention.

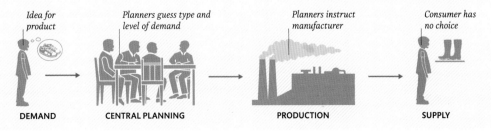

Idea for product — **DEMAND** *Planners guess type and level of demand* — *Planners instruct manufacturer* — **CENTRAL PLANNING** — **PRODUCTION** — *Consumer has no choice* — **SUPPLY**

◄ see also Modern globalization and economic growth pp.370–71   Economics through history pp.400–401 ►   Economic theory pp.402–405 ►   **399**

Economics through history

From bartering to cryptocurrency, economics has evolved from simple exchanges to complex financial algorithms and market mechanisms for global transactions. Economics—as a formal way of thinking about how goods and services are produced and consumed—developed in ancient Greece. However, it was not until the 18th century that theorists such as Adam Smith began to analyze how the buying and selling actions of individuals contributed to the way the economy of a nation worked. Other key thinkers including Karl Marx, John Keynes, and Milton Friedman further shaped the way economies worked in practice, influencing the actions of business leaders and governments.

Wheat crop grown by one party

Direct exchange of cow for bag of wheat

Cow owned by another party

BARTER SYSTEM

10,000–3,000 BCE The earliest economic transaction is a barter between individuals, directly swapping goods or services that each person agrees are of similar value. No money changes hands.

Wooden frame

Cotton fiber twisted into yarn

Thread spooled around bobbin

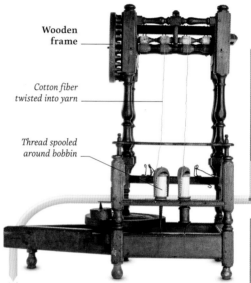

ARKWRIGHT'S WATER FRAME

1771 Inventor Richard Arkwright builds a water-powered spinning mill in Derbyshire, UK, marking the move from cottage industry to a centralized factory system.

Bronze statue depicts Hume wearing a philosopher's toga

1752 Scottish philosopher David Hume publishes his influential treatise *On the Balance of Trade*, arguing that governments should pay for public goods, such as street lighting and national defense, that benefit the masses.

DAVID HUME

1637 Demand for exotic tulips among the wealthy Dutch middle classes creates the first recorded bubble economy, as tulips are traded on stock exchanges for vast sums. Soon prices plummet, causing the "bubble" to burst.

SEMPER AUGUSTUS TULIP

1776 In *The Wealth of Nations*, Scottish economist Adam Smith describes the workings of an emerging industrialized capitalist society centered on the division of labor. He argues against monopolies and excessive government intervention.

1844 The full gold standard is adopted in the UK, establishing Bank of England notes as the official currency and tying the value of the British pound to a specific amount of gold.

GOLD STANDARD

Government holds reserves of gold and issues notes and coins

1867 German philosopher Karl Marx publishes *Das Kapital*, challenging the capitalist means of production and proposing a centralized system in which government plays a greater role to ensure the wellbeing of workers.

1960 The Organization of Petroleum Exporting Countries (OPEC) is founded by 14 major oil-producing countries to regulate supply and maintain fair prices.

OILFIELD PUMP

Pumping jack draws oil out of the ground

1958–60 The Great Leap Forward is implemented in China to increase the development of industrialization, but is thwarted by organizational issues and natural disasters.

1957 Six European nations sign the Treaty of Rome to establish the European Economic Community, which agrees to end tariff barriers and devise a common agricultural policy.

TREATY OF ROME

1971 President Richard Nixon abandons the gold standard to protect the US dollar, which is now overvalued due to foreign speculation, ending the system of fixed exchange rates.

Oil well drilled into rock

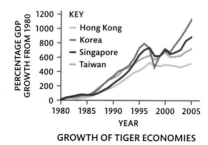

1989 American political economist Alice Amsden describes the rise of the east Asian tiger economies, attributing their success to state-promoted industrialization with strategies such as price controls and import reduction.

KEY
— Hong Kong
— Korea
— Singapore
— Taiwan

PERCENTAGE GDP GROWTH FROM 1980

0 200 400 600 800 1000 1200

YEAR: 1980 1985 1990 1995 2000 2005

GROWTH OF TIGER ECONOMIES

600 BCE–1100 CE The first true coins are used as a medium of exchange in Lydia, in modern-day Turkey. Trading entities decide the value of each coin based on its precious metal content.

Coin made of electrum—a mix of gold and silver

Hand-struck coin with image of lion head

LYDIAN COIN

Paper currency valid for three years

1120s The world's first government-issued paper money is introduced in China, notes being much lighter than coins to carry.

SONG DYNASTY NOTE

1397 The Medici family of Florence, Italy, founds a private bank specializing in investment opportunities. This establishment innovates with double-entry bookkeeping, letters of credit, and holding companies.

Medici Bank's 11 branches were managed by local junior partners rather than employees

MEDICI BANK

Poster reads "Communist youth, to tractors!," suggesting sufficient resources for all under collectivization

1492 Spanish voyager Christopher Columbus claims the Americas for Spain, flooding Europe with gold and silver from South American mines. This abundance lowers the value of of Spain's silver-based currency and causes prices to rise.

COLUMBUS IN WEST INDIES

c.1400s Bills of exchange become popular as cashless payment among merchants in Europe. Written by a notary, they are an obligation to pay, enabling secure trade.

1929 Under Joseph Stalin, the Soviet government implements the collectivization of farms, whereby wealthy farmers are compelled to give up their lands to join collective state-owned farms.

COLLECTIVIZATION CAMPAIGN

1929–40 The stock market crash of October 1929 and subsequent runs on the US dollar contribute to the Great Depression, the most severe and prolonged global economic downturn in history.

GREAT DEPRESSION PROTEST

WHY CAN'T YOU GIVE MY DAD A JOB?

1951 American mathematician John Nash's game theory—the study of how people behave in competitive situations such as while playing rock-paper-scissors—furthers economic modeling.

Scissors beats paper

Rock beats scissors

Paper beats rock

ROCK-PAPER-SCISSORS

1945 The International Monetary Fund is set up to promote global economic cooperation and a new system of exchange rates linked to the US dollar.

1999 Euro banknotes and coins are adopted by the 11 member states as the new legal tender of the European Monetary Union. Greece becomes the 12th member two years later.

European flag symbolizing European Union

EURO NOTES

Slow supply causes recessionary cycle

Money supply

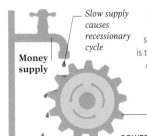

Wheel of economy

POWER OF MONEY

2008 The Great Recession, the worst financial crisis since the Great Depression, is triggered by the overselling of mortgages by US banks.

2009 An anonymous programmer or group known as Satoshi Nakamoto releases the first fully digital currency, or cryptocurrency, known as Bitcoin.

BITCOIN

see also Economic theory pp.402–405 ▶ **401**

Economic theory

Explanations of how economies work—or should work—have been devised for centuries by theorists such as Adam Smith and Karl Marx. Some theories have been adopted or adapted by governments and businesses, influencing their decisions on spending, taxation, borrowing, and other aspects of financial life.

The invisible hand

Conceived in 1759 by Adam Smith, the theory of the invisible hand is a metaphor for the unseen forces that are put in motion when one person acts in their own interests (by making a purchase, for example), resulting in economic benefit for society as a whole.

Changes in supply and demand

Smith used the invisible hand to support his view that the forces of supply and demand will naturally equalize in a free-market economy. Here, the umbrella factory will enjoy increased profits until other firms enter the market.

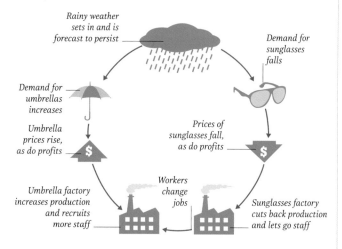

Rainy weather sets in and is forecast to persist

Demand for sunglasses falls

Demand for umbrellas increases

Umbrella prices rise, as do profits

Prices of sunglasses fall, as do profits

Workers change jobs

Umbrella factory increases production and recruits more staff

Sunglasses factory cuts back production and lets go staff

Friedman's monetarism

American economist Milton Friedman proposed that governments could manipulate interest rates to control the supply of money in the economy.

A fall in interest rates makes credit cheaper for consumers, encouraging them to spend more. Conversely, a decrease in interest rates makes credit more expensive for consumers.

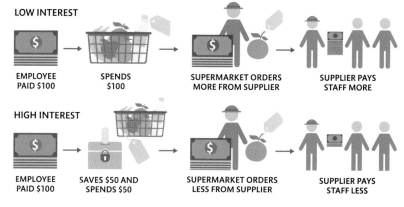

LOW INTEREST

EMPLOYEE PAID $100 → SPENDS $100 → SUPERMARKET ORDERS MORE FROM SUPPLIER → SUPPLIER PAYS STAFF MORE

HIGH INTEREST

EMPLOYEE PAID $100 → SAVES $50 AND SPENDS $50 → SUPERMARKET ORDERS LESS FROM SUPPLIER → SUPPLIER PAYS STAFF LESS

Effect of interest rates

When interest rates are low, the amount of money circulating in the economy increases. Consumers are willing to spend more, stimulating business and thereby job creation. The opposite applies when interest rates are high, as consumers spend less, fearing they may not be able to meet higher fees.

> "It is **not from the benevolence** of the butcher, the brewer or the baker that we expect our dinner, but from their regard to their self-interest."
>
> ADAM SMITH,
> *An Inquiry into the Nature and Causes of the Wealth of Nations*, 1776

The Keynesian multiplier

Developed by Keynes (see p.399) from British economist's Richard Kahn's work in 1931, the Keynesian multiplier is the number by which gross domestic product (GDP) will rise if money is injected into the economy, or fall if money is drained from the economy.

Keynes' general theory of money

Keynes argued that the effect of economic recession and depression can be counteracted by governments spending more and cutting taxes.

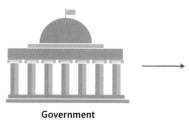

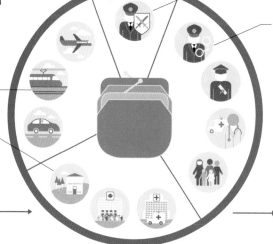

Defense

Policing, education, healthcare, and welfare

Transportation infrastructure

Buildings: houses, schools, and hospitals

Sales figures

Government
The economy can be stimulated toward full employment, if the government injects more money and cuts taxes.

Investment
Increased spending on public works and programs creates jobs in many sectors of society.

Stimulating demand
As more workers enter the workforce, they spend money they would not otherwise have.

Production increases
Because consumers spend more, sales of goods and services increase accordingly, triggering more production.

> "Economics brings into view that **conflict of choice** which is one of the **permanent characteristics of human existence.**"
>
> LIONEL ROBBINS, *An Essay on the Nature and Significance of Economic Science*, 1932

Entitlement theory

In 1976, Indian scholar Amartya Sen suggested that famine was not simply caused by a shortage of food. It would happen if workers were prevented from exchanging their "entitlement"—their economic power as laborers—for food.

Families **exchange their labor for money**, with which they buy food to survive

↓

If there is a **change in the price** of their labor or food ...

↓

... and wages **become too low** to buy the minimum amount of food a family needs ...

↓

... the family will **starve**, even if plenty of food is being produced

↓

Famine can happen in good harvests

Public goods

A public good is a product or service that is provided by a state or nation for the benefit of every member of the public, with no expectation of making a profit. Examples include defense forces, public parks, street lighting, health services, and even clean air.

STREET LAMP

BRIDGE

LIGHTHOUSE

LEGAL SYSTEM

EDUCATION

NATIONAL DEFENSE

Opportunity cost

An opportunity cost is a benefit missed out on when choosing one activity over another. A business, for example, must decide whether to put its resources into producing brakes or batteries. If it chooses brakes, the opportunity cost is the profit it might have made selling batteries.

Production possibility frontier

The PPF (production possibility frontier) compares how much of two different goods could be produced, given the same amount of fixed resources. It is usually plotted as a curve.

CONSPICUOUS CONSUMPTION

The American economist Thorstein Veblen coined the term "conspicuous consumption" in 1899 to describe how the emerging middle class spent money on a lavish scale—either on high-priced items or buying large quantities of items—in order to signal their wealth and status.

SHOPPERS IN TOKYO

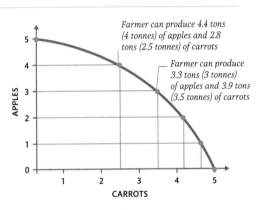

Farmer can produce 4.4 tons (4 tonnes) of apples and 2.8 tons (2.5 tonnes) of carrots

Farmer can produce 3.3 tons (3 tonnes) of apples and 3.9 tons (3.5 tonnes) of carrots

APPLES / CARROTS

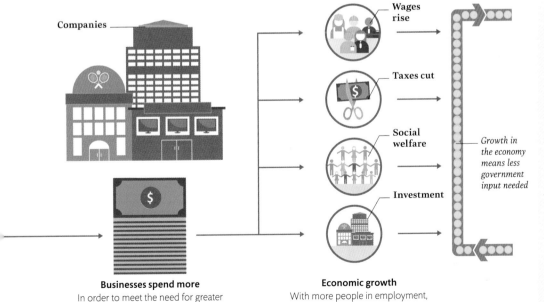

Companies

Wages rise

Taxes cut

Social welfare

Investment

Growth in the economy means less government input needed

Businesses spend more
In order to meet the need for greater production, businesses spend more on staff, buildings, and equipment.

Economic growth
With more people in employment, aggregate spending increases and economic growth is boosted.

MARXIST ECONOMICS

Karl Marx argued that capitalism divides humanity into the few who own the means of production, and the many who have only their labor to sell. Profit is taken by owners at the expense of workers.

1 PAIR OF SHOES = **2 HOURS' LABOR AT $10/HOUR** = **$20**

1 DRESS = **10 HOURS' LABOR AT $10/HOUR** = **$100**

Marx's labor theory of value

The value of a commodity can be objectively measured by averaging how many hours of labor were taken to produce it.

see also Sociology pp.406–409 ▶

Inflation

When the prices of household goods and services consistently rise over time, this upward movement is called inflation. The percentage rate at which prices rise is most commonly expressed as the Consumer Price Index (CPI), and is usually measured quarterly by a country's statistics bureau by monitoring the prices of a shopping basket of commonly purchased items.

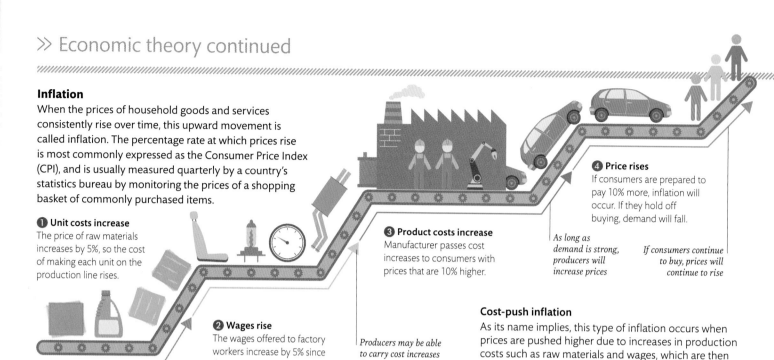

❶ Unit costs increase
The price of raw materials increases by 5%, so the cost of making each unit on the production line rises.

❷ Wages rise
The wages offered to factory workers increase by 5% since they are in short supply.

Producers may be able to carry cost increases for a limited time

❸ Product costs increase
Manufacturer passes cost increases to consumers with prices that are 10% higher.

As long as demand is strong, producers will increase prices

If consumers continue to buy, prices will continue to rise

❹ Price rises
If consumers are prepared to pay 10% more, inflation will occur. If they hold off buying, demand will fall.

Cost-push inflation

As its name implies, this type of inflation occurs when prices are pushed higher due to increases in production costs such as raw materials and wages, which are then passed on to consumers.

Financial crises

Triggers for a financial crisis include: investors rapidly selling overpriced assets; panic withdrawals from financial institutions; mass defaults on debt; or a sharp drop in the value of financial or real assets. This often leads to economic recession or depression.

ECONOMIC BUBBLES

When investors are attracted by a new asset and buy frenetically, the asset price surges dramatically. When no more investors are willing to buy, mass selling starts and the asset price plummets.

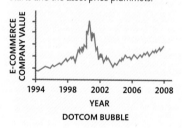

E-COMMERCE COMPANY VALUE

1994 1998 2002 2006 2008
YEAR
DOTCOM BUBBLE

The longer an economy remains stable, the greater **people's confidence** in the future

↓

The greater people's confidence in the future, the **more they borrow**

↓

Over time in a stable economy, **debt grows**, as risky lending increases and asset prices rise

↓

Eventually, asset prices peak and then fall, and borrowers start to default. **Lending collapses** and the economy goes into recession

↓

Stable economies contain the seeds of instability

Comparative advantage

When a person or business can produce goods or services at a lower cost than anyone else, this is known as comparative advantage. The seller with a comparative advantage is more profitable, as they enjoy higher margins.

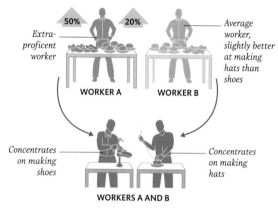

Extra-proficient worker

50%   20%

WORKER A   WORKER B

Average worker, slightly better at making hats than shoes

Concentrates on making shoes

Concentrates on making hats

WORKERS A AND B

Comparative advantage between factory workers
Since Worker A is 50 percent better at making shoes than Worker B but only 20 percent better at making hats, making shoes is the most profitable way to use his time.

Elasticity of demand

The degree to which a consumer's desire to purchase a good or service is influenced by price or other factors is called demand elasticity. It is typically calculated by dividing percentage change in quantity by percentage change in price. The more demand falls in line with price increases, the more elastic, or responsive, it is.

Types of demand

When prices increase, the resulting demand can be elastic, inelastic, perfectly inelastic, or perfectly elastic. Demand is said to be unitary when the price and demand change by the same ratio.

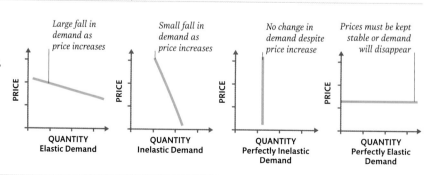

Large fall in demand as price increases

PRICE
QUANTITY
Elastic Demand

Small fall in demand as price increases

PRICE
QUANTITY
Inelastic Demand

No change in demand despite price increase

PRICE
QUANTITY
Perfectly Inelastic Demand

Prices must be kept stable or demand will disappear

PRICE
QUANTITY
Perfectly Elastic Demand

"Inflation is always and everywhere a monetary phenomenon."

MILTON FRIEDMAN, *The Counter-Revolution in Monetary Theory*, 1970

❶ Demand rises
Consumers have been holding off on purchasing new laptops, waiting for a new generation of computers featuring faster processing speeds.

❷ Manufacture at full capacity
New-generation laptop technology is put into production, which is reported in the media. Consumers who have held off now plan to purchase.

❸ Demand outstrips supply
Producers and marketers calculate the highest price consumers will be willing to pay, given the unique nature of the new laptops and pent-up demand for them.

❹ Prices rise
Until demand is satisfied, and there are more laptops for sale than there are consumers willing to buy them, the price will remain high.

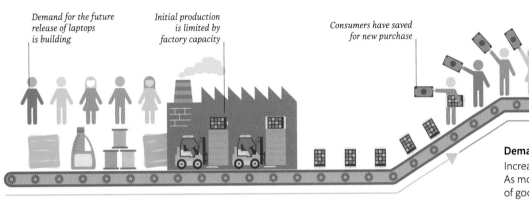

Demand for the future release of laptops is building

Initial production is limited by factory capacity

Consumers have saved for new purchase

Government and industry add to demand

Demand-pull inflation
Increased consumer demand can pull prices higher. As more people are competing for a limited number of goods and services, suppliers can charge more.

Division of labor

By carving up economic production into separate tasks, and allocating each task to the person or business best-equipped for it, labor is divided. At the simplest level, this means individuals who specialize in one task, such as surgery, can use their economic power to buy another person's specialization, such as dry cleaning.

Specialization increases productivity
By enabling each worker to specialize in a task, goods can be created more efficiently, such as on this production line.

"Every expansion of the personal division of labor brings advantages to all who take part in it."

LUDWIG VON MISES,
Socialism: An Economic and Sociological Analysis, 1922

Economies of scale

When producing a quantity of items, not all units will cost the same to make. The first units will be expensive to produce, because money has been invested in setting up production, but as each additional item is produced, the unit cost decreases, because the initial investment is spread over a larger number of units.

Graph of economies of scale
Plotted on a curve, economies of scale show that for each additional unit produced, the cost of production per unit changes.

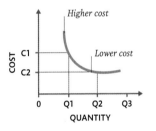

Higher cost

Lower cost

COST — C1, C2

0 Q1 Q2 Q3

QUANTITY

Game theory

Developed by John Nash in the 1950s, game theory mathematically models how any rational person is most likely to react in competitive scenarios. Applied to economics, game theory maps out an individual's or organization's beliefs, preferences, and potential actions, and determines how these are likely to change depending on what another individual or organization is offering. The "players" seek to maximize their own advantage.

Prisoner's dilemma

A theoretical setup to demonstrate how game theory can be applied, the "Prisoner's dilemma" involves two prisoners who are held separately for a crime. The best outcome for them collectively would be for them both to stay silent. However, both players are more likely to make the move that is better for them individually and so they will betray each other.

If both prisoners stay silent they will spend a shorter time in jail than if both confess

Betrayed prisoner suffers maximum penalty for staying silent

Confessing will only have a positive outcome for A if B stays silent

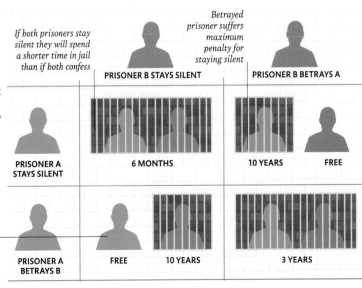

	PRISONER B STAYS SILENT	PRISONER B BETRAYS A
PRISONER A STAYS SILENT	6 MONTHS	10 YEARS / FREE
PRISONER A BETRAYS B	FREE / 10 YEARS	3 YEARS

Sociology

The discipline of sociology has its origins in the profound social and political changes of the 19th century. Sociology is the study of human society—more specifically, how the organization and structure of social groups, systems, and institutions shape the ways individuals think, act, and form social relationships. Sociology analyzes processes and structures such as social class, gender, sexuality, and ethnicity, as well as forms of collective identity.

The classical sociologists: envisaging society

Name	Karl Marx
Date	1818–1883

Philosopher, economist, and theorist Karl Marx's sociological writings center on the concept of alienation. Alienation refers to the processes by which individuals and groups are dominated by the consequences of their own actions. Modern capitalist society is highly alienating because the pursuit of wealth is the dominant activity, around which all social groups are organized. The result is that such societies are characterized by conflicts and inequalities between opposing social class groups competing for social and economic power.

Name	Emile Durkheim
Date	1858–1917

Emile Durkheim is regarded as the founding father of sociology. Durkheim defined sociology as the study of social facts. These comprise the aspects of society that shape all individuals, while not being reducible to any individual in particular. Religion, culture, and language are examples of social structures; suicide is also a social structure because it occurs in all societies. Durkheim's classic study, *Suicide: A Study in Sociology* (1897), demonstrates the terrible consequences that occur when social structures fail to integrate and regulate individuals.

Name	Max Weber
Date	1864–1920

The work of sociologist Max Weber represents the beginnings of historical sociology. Weber emphasized the role played by "ideal" as opposed to "material" factors in shaping social action. Weber's most celebrated study, *The Protestant Ethic and the Spirit of Capitalism* (1905), is an account of how the work ethic that arose from 16th-century Protestantism developed over time to become the work ethic motivating the capitalist drive for profit. Rooted in the concept of "unintended consequences," Weber's work stressed the largely unintended nature of the social and historical changes behind the rise of capitalism in the West.

Name	Georg Simmel
Date	1858–1918

Georg Simmel's analysis of society focuses on the distinction between "forms" of social interaction and their "contents." Human social life is expressed through a range of general forms of social interaction, such as conflict, cohesion, self, and more. All social interactions are structured by these forms, although their contents are expressed differently depending on the individuals, society, and historical period in question. In studies, Simmel analyzed how different forms of social interaction had developed and changed over time.

Structuralist and post-structuralist models

Name	Structuralism and post-structuralism
Date	1960s–present

Structuralism emphasizes the role social structures play in determining how individuals think and act. It is social structures, as opposed to individuals, that comprise the subject matter of sociology. Structuralists differ in their view of whether social structures enable people or constrain them: Marx regarded structures such as social class as constraining people's lives and identity, whereas Durkheim saw structures such as religion and culture as enabling because they integrate and regulate people. Post-structuralism evolved in the 1960s. The concept of discourse—the relationship between language and power—is central to post-structuralist thought.

Name	The Frankfurt School
Date	1918–present

The Frankfurt School was a group of German-Jewish sociologists and philosophers based at the University of Frankfurt. Having fled to America to escape Nazism in the 1940s, its members were critical of American capitalist culture and entertainment. The term "culture industry" describes the commercialization of American popular culture at the hands of large-scale capitalist organizations such as Hollywood. The culture industry supports the running of capitalism, and promotes the illusions of freedom, choice, and the capacity to define our identity as consumers. The Frankfurt School regards the culture industry as subjecting the members of capitalist societies to subtle forms of social and political manipulation.

Name	Michel Foucault
Date	1926–1984

Social theorist and historian Michel Foucault was highly influential in the development of structuralist and post-structuralist thinking in France. Foucault's historical study, *Discipline and Punish* (1975), identifies the increasing emphasis among Western governments on controlling and coercing the minds, as opposed to the bodies, of the citizenry. Foucault emphasized the different forms social power can take. Language is central to his analysis because language defines how we understand ourselves and other people. Through powerful forms of professional discourse, such as psychiatry

and criminology, Foucault explains how linguistic categories and structures are used to categorize people as, for example, sane or mad, normal, or criminal. The authority wielded by categories such as these forms the basis for Foucault's claims that power in late modern societies is increasingly governed through discursive categories defined and controlled by powerful institutions.

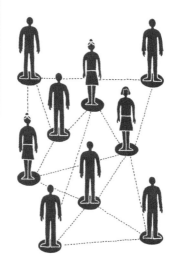

> ## "There is no sociology worthy of the name which does not possess a historical character."
>
> EMILE DURKHEIM,
> *Explanation in History and Sociology*, 1908

Individual-centred sociology

Name	Individual-centred sociology
Date	1920s–present

Individual-centred sociology analyses society from the perspective of the individual. It is associated with an analytical approach to human social life, known as methodological individualism. Society is made up of clusters of individuals working in small group settings and as part of wider collectives. The orderly and predictable feel of most social situations is not something that occurs naturally. Rather, individuals and groups achieve and maintain a state of social order by thinking and acting in patterned ways. First appearing in the work of Max Weber and Georg Simmel, individual-

Sociology emerged in Europe during the 19th century

WHAT DO SOCIOLOGISTS DO?

Sociologists in academia may find themselves lecturing, researching, or writing for publications. Outside of academia, sociologists may put their knowledge to use in public services, such as social work, policing, or politics. Understanding how people and society work can be useful in areas such as marketing and human resources.

 ◀ see also **Philosophy through history** pp.384–85   ◀ **Great philosophers** pp.386–87   ◀ **Political theory** pp.396–97

centered sociology was developed in a number of directions by American sociologists from the 1920s onward.

Name	Rational Actor Theory
Date	1950s–present

Rational Actor Theory (RAT) conceptualizes individuals as acting consciously and rationally in order to achieve goals. Rooted in the political philosophical ideas of thinkers such as Thomas Hobbes and J.S. Mill, RAT rose to dominance within American sociology during the 1950s. In studies such as *The Human Group* (1950) and *Bringing Men Back In* (1964), American social scientist George Homans and his colleagues at the Harvard University emphasized the view that all human relations comprise relations of exchange. Homans was critical of the overly socialized view of human behavior as determined by social structures. While RAT remains a presence within American sociology, it has been heavily criticized from a range of sociological perspectives for failing to explain the role that ideals and expectations play in regulating human social interaction.

Name	Symbolic interactionism
Date	20th century

Symbolic interactionism developed at the University of Chicago during the early 20th century. Thinkers such as George Mead, Charles Cooley, and Herbert Blumer stressed the importance of language for understanding the orderly basis of human social interaction. Language is key to forming an identity: it is only through using language to express to others how we think and feel that we arrive at a sense of our own identity. In this view, identity is not so much personal

▲ **American Legion parade, *c*.1950s**
Forms of sociation can be seen in most group activities, whether structured—as here—or informal.

as it is social. The work of Erving Goffman extended these ideas to include the non-linguistic, behavioral aspects of social interaction. Goffman's work compares social interaction to a form of ongoing, live drama. Like actors, people use the scripts embedded within social situations, which provide the cues that are used to interact with others.

◄ see also Economics through history pp.400–401   ◄ Economic theory pp.402–405   Sociology (continued) pp.408–409 ►   407

Critical-normativity

Name	Critical-normative perspectives
Date	19th century–present

Thinking critically about society is a key part of sociology. Rooted in Marx's highly critical analysis of modern capitalist society, critical-normative perspectives are concerned with issues of social injustice, social inequality, and the uneven distribution of power between groups. While Marx's work focuses on the economic inequalities between upper- and lower-class groups, sociologists have extended his critical ideas to explain how differences in power between individuals and groups are expressed through structures of gender, race, and more recently, sexuality. Critical-normative perspectives often regard sociology as a force for progressive social change.

Name	Feminism
Date	19th century–present

Feminism is a political movement that aims to challenge what it regards as the oppression of women by men. A society is described as patriarchal when the systematic oppression of women is characteristic of the majority of its social situations and institutions. The work of feminist sociologists such as Anne Oakley, Dorothy Smith, and various Marxist feminists have inspired political reforms that aim to address gender inequality. Oakley's *Sex, Gender and Society* (1972) was central in identifying the role played by parents in upholding patriarchal structures through forms of gendered play; Smith's concept of "line of fault" captures the estrangement women feel in a male-dominated culture.

Name	Neo-Marxism
Date	20th century–present

Neo-Marxism is a body of thought that adapts and develops the work of Marx, and Western Marxism more generally. A particularly influential strand of neo-Marxism is Immanuel Wallerstein's *The Modern World System* (1974). Wallerstein built on Marx's ideas to critically question global economic and political inequalities. Beginning with the colonial legacies of Western European nations, Wallerstein charts the dividing up of the world into "core," "semi-periphery," and "periphery." He states that Western Europe and North America comprise core nations, which depend on semi-peripheral nations such as Brazil and Portugal to mediate their exploitative relations with peripheral nations, including parts of Africa and South America.

Name	Critical-race theory
Date	1980s–present

According to critical-race theory, ethnicity refers to forms of collective identity organized around historical, religious, and cultural factors, whereas race is a socially constructed term with no biological foundation. Nevertheless, racial stereotypes and conflict remain major forms of division and inequality within modern society. Critical-race perspectives demonstrate how institutional and linguistic categorizations based on race are used by groups to dominate and exert power. Black feminist critical-race scholar Patricia Williams' book, *Seeing a Color-Blind Future* (1998), argues that even within multicultural and egalitarian societies, race is a central concept for understanding the lives and identities of marginalized groups.

▲ "Vessel" structure, New York
As in society, people can choose to move freely around this public installation, but only within a fixed framework.

Process sociology

Name	Process sociology
Date	19th century–present

Process sociology is critical of individual-centered and structuralist perspectives. Process sociologists see the separating out of individuals and society as meaningless. Rather, they view society as comprising multiple ongoing processes in which the patterned actions of individuals result in changes to society—and this social change transforms how individuals think, feel, and act. By emphasizing the fluid nature of human experience and social change, process sociology provides a detailed understanding of how long-term social processes shape, and are shaped by, the actions and interactions of individuals.

Name	Norbert Elias
Date	1897–1990

Norbert Elias's book, *The Civilizing Process* (1939), is a classic study in process sociology. Elias wanted to demonstrate how the "civilized" behavior, self-restraint, and courtesy that was characteristic of Western court society during the 15th century have filtered through and changed wider society over time. Elias shows how individuals felt pressure from one another, but also themselves, to behave and interact in ways considered respectful, restrained, and civilized. Elias' central claim is that changes to the personality structure, social relations, and cultural standards found in Western society are the largely unintended outcome of long-term civilizing processes.

Name	Pierre Bourdieu
Date	1930–2002

Pierre Bourdieu's most influential concept, "habitus," captures how the social class of individuals intimately shapes their sense of self identity in ways they are largely unaware of. Bourdieu's famous study, *Distinction* (1979), used statistical methods and interviews to demonstrate that people's personal tastes in a wide range of cultural forms such as music, food, hobbies, and more, are determined by the type of class-based group, or habitus, they are socialized into. It is social habitus, as opposed to personality traits or wider influences such as advertising, that determines people's personal tastes and preferences.

Sociology today: challenges and change

Name	Sociology today: social theory
Date	20th–21st century

Throughout the 21st century, sociology has expanded in a number of new directions. This has led to the flourishing of new questions, themes, and issues. A key index of these changes is captured by the turn away from sociological theory toward a more inclusive and interdisciplinary body of conceptual ideas known as social theory. Social theory combines theoretical concepts and methods from sociology with those taken from a range of humanities-based disciplines including literary theory, science and technology studies, and post-colonial studies. Sociologists draw on social theory to extend the range and scope of their interests to include the study of cultural symbols and meaning, the rising significance of technology in mediating social experience, and the role played by Western society in the making of global inequalities.

Name	Actor-network theory
Date	2000–present

Actor-network theory (ANT) has grown in prominence within sociology, particularly in the fields of science and technology. ANT conceives society as made up of multiple networks, or assemblages. Crucially, assemblages and networks consist not just of human actors, but include nonhuman actors too, such as animals as well as technological devices such as smartphones. ANT is critical of traditional sociological perspectives, which downplay or ignore the significance of nonhuman actors in shaping individuals' experiences and interactions.

Name	Cultural sociology
Date	20th century–present

Cultural sociology was founded by American sociologist Jeffrey Alexander. In studies such as *The Meanings of Social Life* (2003), Alexander emphasizes the patterned nature of meanings and values, and the role that cultural, as opposed to social structures, play in shaping how individuals respond to people, situations, and events. A central claim of cultural sociology is that social life is organized by emotionally and symbolically powerful narratives. Cultural sociologists understand conflict and cohesion between groups as arising out of differences in values as opposed to being rooted in class-based forms of antagonism.

RESEARCH METHODS
Sociologists draw on a wide range of methodological tools and data to conduct their research, including social surveys, statistics, historical studies, participant observation, and interviews with members of the groups they are studying. Sociological research is evaluated in professional journals and periodicals.

> Social media is the **defining** feature of modern culture

Name	Post-colonial theory
Date	19th century–present

Post-colonial theory is rooted in diverse strands of critical-normative thinking including critical-race theory and post-structuralism. Its primary concern is to explain how colonialism and imperialism have contributed to the dominance of North American and Western society on the global stage. While the colonial empires of the West had largely been dismantled by the 1960s, their oppressive legacies remain. Post-colonial theorists, such as US-based Julian Go, seek to develop critical concepts with which to construct a more egalitarian world.

> "**Different societies** appropriate the materials of **modernity differently.**"
>
> ARJUN APPADURAI, Anthropologist, *Modernity at Large*, 1996

see also Great writers pp.440–41 ▶

Arts and Leisure

Components of music

Music theory is the study of fundamentals—pitch, rhythm, harmony, and expressive qualities—considered individually and in combination. Musical literacy and performance can be broken down into a series of small component parts.

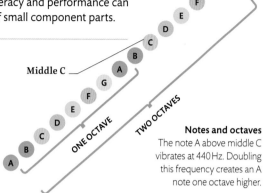

Pitch

Sound is created when air vibrates. When regular and consistent, the sensation is heard as pitch. A quicker, high-frequency sound wave creates a higher pitch; slower, low-frequency vibrations are lower pitched.

Middle C

ONE OCTAVE

TWO OCTAVES

Notes and octaves
The note A above middle C vibrates at 440 Hz. Doubling this frequency creates an A note one octave higher.

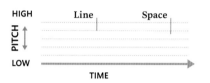

The staff
A note's placement on or between the five parallel lines of a staff indicates its name and pitch. Notes are played from left to right. Higher pitches are closer to the top.

Sharps and flats
A sharp sign directs musicians to play a note one half step higher in pitch (one key to the right on the piano.) A flat indicates one half step lower.

Clefs
A clef appears at the start of every staff, fixing the pitches of the lines and spaces. The treble clef indicates higher-pitched notes; bass clef denotes lower pitches will be used.

Curl of treble clef marks the position of the note G on the staff

TREBLE CLEF

Dots on either side of this line fix it as the position of note F

BASS CLEF

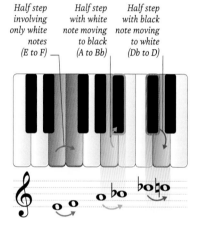

Half step involving only white notes (E to F) *Half step with white note moving to black (A to Bb)* *Half step with black note moving to white (Db to D)*

Half steps
A half step is the smallest interval possible between two pitches in Western music: two notes immediately next to each other on the piano keyboard.

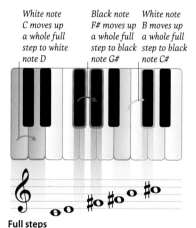

White note C moves up a whole full step to white note D *Black note F# moves up a whole full step to black note G#* *White note B moves up a whole full step to black note C#*

Full steps
A full step is the interval, or distance, created by going either up or down two half steps from a given pitch. An octave—also known as a perfect eighth—is divided into 12 half steps.

Rhythm

Rhythm is the placement of sound in time. A recognizable rhythm is created through a systematic arrangement of musical sound and silence, according to duration. Rhythm may have a regular or irregular pulse, or "beat."

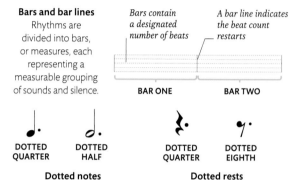

Bars and bar lines
Rhythms are divided into bars, or measures, each representing a measurable grouping of sounds and silence.

Bars contain a designated number of beats *A bar line indicates the beat count restarts*

BAR ONE   BAR TWO

DOTTED QUARTER   **DOTTED HALF**   **DOTTED QUARTER**   **DOTTED EIGHTH**

Dotted notes
A dot placed by the note head extends the duration of that sound by half again: a dotted half note lasts three counts.

Dotted rests
A dot placed by a rest denotes a lengthening, by one-half, of the silence. A dotted quarter rest lasts one and a half beats.

Scales

A scale is a set of notes in ascending or descending pitch order, usually between two notes that are one octave apart. The pattern of full steps and half steps in a scale gives it a unique sound and character. The difference between two successive notes in a scale is called a scale step.

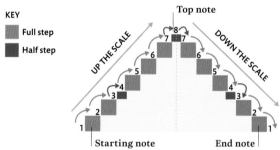

KEY
- Full step
- Half step

Top note

UP THE SCALE   DOWN THE SCALE

Starting note   End note

Major scales
All ascending major scales (sung do-re-mi-fa-sol-la-ti-do) consist of stepwise movement upward in the same pattern: full step, full step, half step, full step, full step, full step, and a last half step.

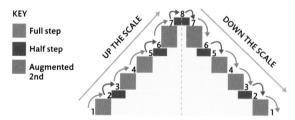

KEY
- Full step
- Half step
- Augmented 2nd

UP THE SCALE   DOWN THE SCALE

Harmonic minor scales
The three-half step interval between scale degrees six and seven creates the distinctive sound of the harmonic minor scale (so-called because its chords create minor music's foundational harmony).

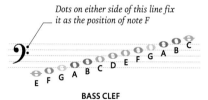

The earliest known form of **musical notation** comes from **Babylon,** *c.*1400 BCE

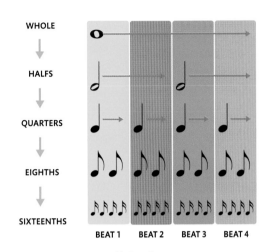

Two minims in each bar

2/2 TIME SIGNATURE

Four quarter notes in each bar

4/4 TIME SIGNATURE

Three eighth notes in each bar

3/8 TIME SIGNATURE

Time signatures
Time signatures indicate meter. The top number indicates the amount of beats in a measure, the bottom denotes the note value given to one beat.

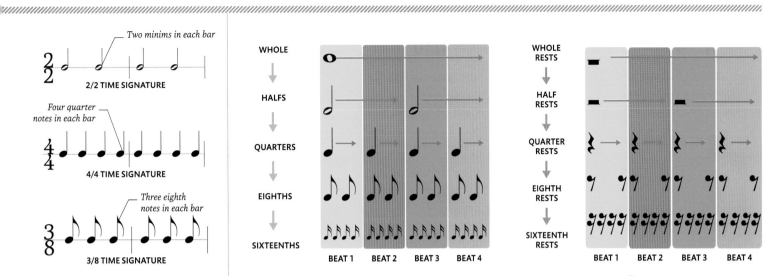

WHOLE → HALFS → QUARTERS → EIGHTHS → SIXTEENTHS

BEAT 1 BEAT 2 BEAT 3 BEAT 4

Note values
Note values are measured in relation to each other. Note durations are counted in beats: a whole note lasts four counts ("1-2-3-4") and a half note is half that ("1-2"). A quarter note is half of a half note; two eighth notes equal one quarter note.

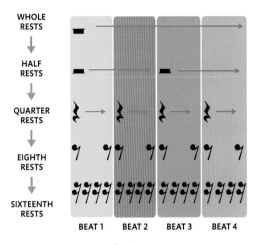

WHOLE RESTS → HALF RESTS → QUARTER RESTS → EIGHTH RESTS → SIXTEENTH RESTS

BEAT 1 BEAT 2 BEAT 3 BEAT 4

Rests
The duration of a rest, or period of silence, is measured and labeled like the sound of the correspondingly named note value. A whole rest is four counts of silence; a quarter rest is one silent beat.

Harmony
Two or more pitches sounding simultaneously, usually in a pleasing way, creates harmony. Harmony establishes a musical foundation for a piece of music.

C MAJOR   **C MINOR**

Major and minor chords
These chords are formed from the C Major and C Minor scales, by stacking scale degrees 1, 3, 5, and 8 on top of one another.

Key signatures
Music based on one scale (say, "the key of D,") use the same sharps or flats repeatedly: specified in a "key signature" at the beginning of each staff.

Sharps in a key signature are always written in this order

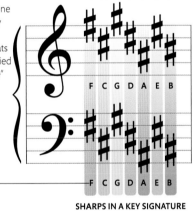

1 2 3 4 5 6 7

F C G D A E B

SHARPS IN A KEY SIGNATURE

Flats in a key signature are always written in this order

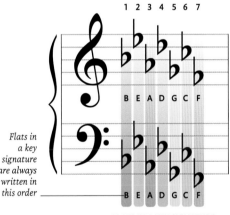

1 2 3 4 5 6 7

B E A D G C F

FLATS IN A KEY SIGNATURE

Performance directions
These notations convey to the musician important details beyond pitch and rhythm, such as volume, force, and whether notes should be connected smoothly or disjoined from each other.

Expression
Skilful musicians vary the energy of individual notes and phrases; they may employ various sustained, harsh, gentle, or waning sound production techniques to convey tone and character. Performers make these decisions guided by the composer's expressive markings.

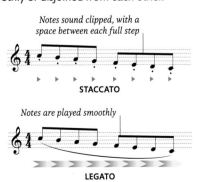

Notes sound clipped, with a space between each full step

STACCATO

Notes are played smoothly

LEGATO

Dynamics
This term refers to the volume and intensity of the music. Italian words such as *piano* and *forte* indicate to musicians the composer's intention about how the music should be played.

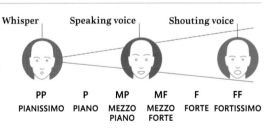

Whisper   Speaking voice   Shouting voice

PP — PIANISSIMO | P — PIANO | MP — MEZZO PIANO | MF — MEZZO FORTE | F — FORTE | FF — FORTISSIMO

Tempo
Tempo is the speed at which music is played. The composer's suggested tempo is indicated by numerical metronome markings in beats/minute, or with Italian words describing musical pacing.

	GETTING FASTER		FAST
ACCELERANDO		PRESTO	
PIU MOSSO		ALLEGRO	
STRINGENDO		MODERATO	
RITENUTO	GETTING SLOWER	ANDANTE	
RITARDANDO		ADAGIO	SLOW
RALLENTANDO		LENTO	

see also Music through history pp.414–15 ▶ The orchestra and musical instruments pp.416–17 ▶ **413**

Music through history

Music has probably existed since the dawn of humanity. Humans gained their full vocal range—and therefore the potential to sing—at least 530,000 years ago, and the oldest known musical instruments date to around 40,000 years ago. Shaped by social values,

traditions, and technology, music has been used in everything from religious ritual and folk storytelling, to entertainment. In the modern world, music remains a universal art form. It has become a popular entertainment industry, with varied musical styles evolving around the globe.

Gilded bull

c.2550 BCE The ancient Sumerian civilization produces woodwind and stringed instruments at Ur (in modern Iraq).

Wooden soundbox depicts donkey playing a lyre

SUMERIAN LYRE

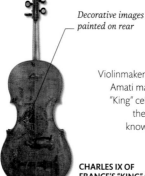

Decorative images painted on rear

1538 Violinmaker Andrea Amati makes the "King" cello (left), the earliest known cello.

CHARLES IX OF FRANCE'S "KING" CELLO (BACK VIEW)

c.9th–12th century Organum, a two-part harmonic religious chant, becomes the first known example of polyphony in Western music by combining different sounds simultaneously.

Colors used to depict personality traits

c.8th century The Pear Garden musical academy is founded in China, creating the first Chinese opera troupe, who perform drama set to music.

CHINESE OPERA MASK

OCARINA

Flute-like wind instrument has clay construction

c.8th century In South America, Pre-Columbian musicians play wind, string, and percussion instruments in social and cultural events.

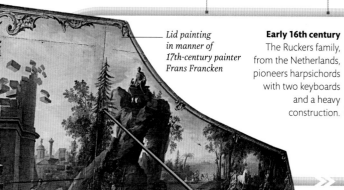

Lid painting in manner of 17th-century painter Frans Francken

Early 16th century The Ruckers family, from the Netherlands, pioneers harpsichords with two keyboards and a heavy construction.

1655 The invention of the piano allows players to produce notes with different dynamics.

Felt damper falls on string when key is released

Hammer strikes and vibrates string

Lever flicks hammer up

Pressing key pushes lever

PIANO MECHANISM

1763 At the age of 7, Austrian composer Wolfgang Amadeus Mozart begins his first concert tour, visiting Munich, Paris, and London.

WOLFGANG AMADEUS MOZART

Unlike a piano, harpsichord strings are plucked rather than struck when a key is pressed

Elaborate casing indicates status of owner

1913 *The Rite of Spring*—a ballet and orchestral concert work by Russian composer Igor Stravinsky—premieres, causing a riot with its avante-garde music, costume, and choreography.

Maiden sacrifices herself to Earth in this story of pagan Russia

THE RITE OF SPRING

Two keyboards known as manuals

Ornate carved legs

HARPSICHORD

Mouthpiece Valves

CORNET

1920–30 Jazz music evolves from ragtime and the blues into a new form of ensemble popular music, influenced by both European harmonic structure and African rhythms.

1950s The first electronic music studios pioneer the use of tape loops and synthesized sounds to create abstract musical works.

GERMAN ELECTRONIC COMPOSER KARLHEINZ STOCKHAUSEN

◄ see also Components of music pp.412–13

800 BCE onward Played on string instruments, *raga*—classical music from India, Bangladesh, and Pakistan—uses repeating notes on a scale to create a mood.

Strings are plucked

Gourd resonator at each end

VEENA

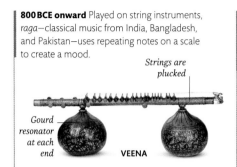

230 CE onward Gamelan, the traditional ensemble music of Java and Bali, Indonesia, features gongs and tuned metal instruments struck with mallets.

Sacred gong struck at the end of a section or piece of music

Supporting frame

GONG AGENG

c.8th century onward An Arabic string instrument out of North Africa, the wooden *oud* makes its way to Europe, where it influences the development of the lute.

Pear-shaped soundboard with inlaid decoration

OUD

618–c.906 Music played on the *pipa* (lute), the *sheng* (wind instrument), the *konghou* (harp), and the drums flourishes during the Tang dynasty in China.

Pipa   *Sheng*   *Konghou*

TANG DYNASTY FIGURINES

c.600 onward The Gregorian chant—a single melody sung by a choir of boys and men in unison—becomes a part of the Roman Catholic mass.

Stand used for sheet music

1730s–1820s The era of classical music popularizes the use of a clear melody over a subordinate chordal accompaniment.

SQUARE PIANO (1790)

1795–1827 Germany's Ludwig van Beethoven becomes the most influential composer of his era.

LUDWIG VAN BEETHOVEN

1820–1910 Composers such as Frédéric Chopin of Poland create patriotic music in response to a wave of nationalistic fervor sweeping across Europe.

Focus adjuster

ORNATE OPERA GLASSES

1895–1919 Piano players in the southern US pioneer ragtime music—a popular "ragged" or syncopated musical style and a forerunner to jazz.

"MAPLE LEAF RAG" SHEET MUSIC

Double-reed harmonica has reeds on both top and bottom

HARMONICA

1850s–1900s The blues is born as a form of folk music performed by African-American communities in the US.

c.1800 "Grand opera," a large-scale, elaborate version of Western opera, develops in Paris, France.

Excessive wear due to Elvis's aggressive strumming style

Tuners

ELVIS PRESLEY'S MARTIN GUITAR

1950s Rock 'n' roll music takes the US and Europe by storm, as musicians start making popular music influenced by the blues.

1960s Soul music enters the mainstream, as artists such as legendary singer Aretha Franklin have top 40 hits.

ARETHA FRANKLIN

1990s onward Electronic music, created using drum machines, synthesizers, and computer software, grows in popularity.

Controls allow different sounds to be balanced

ROLAND DRUM MACHINE

see also **The orchestra and musical instruments** pp.416–17 ▶   **Great composers** pp.418–19 ▶   **415**

The orchestra and musical instruments

An orchestra is a group of musicians playing together in various combinations of woodwind, brass, string, and percussion instruments. Musical instruments produce sound using pitched strings, membranes, resonators, or various percussive mechanisms.

Western classical orchestra
Musicians sit in a semicircle, facing the conductor. Louder instruments are placed in the back to balance the sound.

KEY

Conductor	Bassoons
First violins	Horns
Second violins	Trumpets
Violas	Trombones and tubas
Cellos	Harp
Double basses	Drums
Flutes	Other percussion
Oboes	Piano
Clarinets	

Woodwinds

Woodwind instruments amplify the sound created when air courses through tubes of wood, metal, or plastic. Some, such as the clarinet, have reeds – bamboo-like strips inside the mouthpiece that vibrate when blown on.

FLUTE

OBOE

CLARINET

ENGLISH HORN

CONTRABASSOON

Brass

Brass players use their mouths to control the flow of air through brass instruments of many different shapes. Some, such as trombones, have slides, while others use valves.

TROMBONE

Keys pressed to control valves and create different notes

TRUMPET

TUBA

Bell, or main opening

FRENCH HORN

Percussion

Percussion instruments are shaken (like the tambourine) or struck (like a drum). Some, like the xylophone, are pitched: carefully sized to be tuned to certain tones with preset frequencies. Others are unpitched, such as cymbals.

Metal shell

Tension rod

Copper body shell

SNARE DRUM

TIMPANI

Tone bars

Short bars have higher pitch

Resonators

XYLOPHONE

Strings

Stringed instruments create sound through tightly stretched, vibrating strings attached to and amplified by a wooden body. Strings of metal or gut (dried sheep intestines) are plucked or bowed: scraped by horsehair attached to a bow.

Neck, where fingers press strings to change notes

VIOLIN

Fingerboard is smooth

DOUBLE BASS

Thinnest string produces the highest notes

VIOLA

f-shaped sound hole typical of violin family

NOTE RANGE

The violin is the smallest, highest-pitched string instrument. The viola, cello (or violoncello), and double bass are the same shape but progressively increase in size, each with longer strings and a lower range of possible pitches.

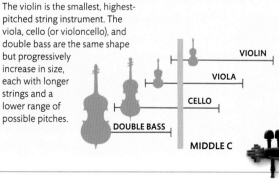

VIOLIN

VIOLA

CELLO

DOUBLE BASS

MIDDLE C

Traditional cello has spruce top

Chin rest

CELLO

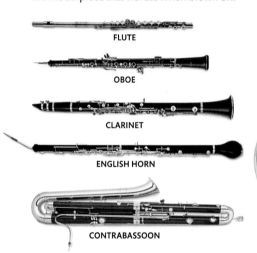
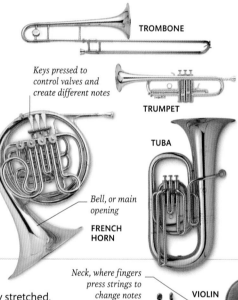
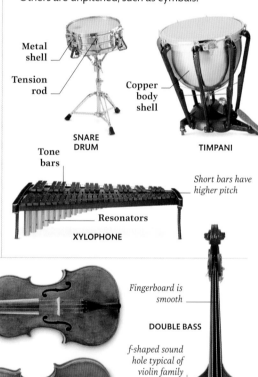

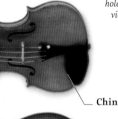

Piano

Played by pressing a row of keys with the fingers, piano keyboards produce sound when a corresponding hammer strikes a string in the instrument. Weighted keys help performers adjust volume.

Black keys are raised and set further back

Strings struck by hammer when keys pressed

Keys

PIANO KEYS

GRAND PIANO

The harp

Modern concert harps usually have 47 strings pitched in the same range as a piano. Harpists use the thumb and first three fingers of each hand to pluck or sweep across the strings; foot pedals control string pitch.

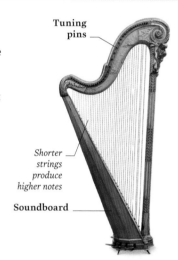

Tuning pins

Shorter strings produce higher notes

Soundboard

Harps have been used in **Africa, Asia, and Europe** from about **3000 BCE**

Global instruments

Folk and classical instruments from around the world produce a wide variety of sounds. Some use scales or note intervals that vary from those of Western music.

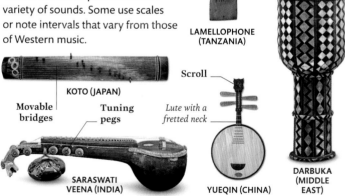

Metal plates

Stretched membrane

LAMELLOPHONE (TANZANIA)

KOTO (JAPAN)

Movable bridges

Tuning pegs

Scroll

Lute with a fretted neck

SARASWATI VEENA (INDIA)

YUEQIN (CHINA)

DARBUKA (MIDDLE EAST)

ELECTRONIC INSTRUMENTS

The mid-20th century saw the invention of purely electronic instruments such as synthesizers, magnetic tape machines, and even computers used to generate and adjust sound.

Keys

SYNTHESIZER

Guitar family

In an orchestra, or in flamenco music, a classical guitar can be used in a solo performance or as harmonic accompaniment. In folk music, acoustic guitars are strummed or fingerpicked. Electric guitars are played through amplifiers, which can distort their sound.

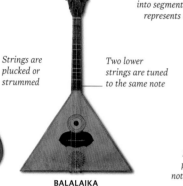

Neck

Strings are plucked or strummed

Two lower strings are tuned to the same note

UKULELE

BALALAIKA

Three nylon strings and three gut strings

CLASSICAL GUITAR

Electric guitar

The strings of electric guitars are made of metal, and their vibrations when played are converted into an electric signal by pickups. The signal is then converted into audible sound by a guitar amplifier.

Strings are typically made of chrome, nickel, or stainless steel

The fretboard is the laminated top layer of the guitar's neck

Frets divide the neck into segments; each one represents a semitone

Inlays help player find note positions

Strap button acts as anchor point for guitar strap

Pickup switch selects different pickups, changing the sound

Pickups act as transducers, converting vibrations into electric signal

Electric guitar body is typically made of solid wood

see also Great composers pp.418–19 ▶ Popular music pp.420–21 ▶

Great composers

In ancient times, music was largely passed on orally until the first musical notation systems in the 10th century CE heralded a new era in which a composer's work could be permanently recorded. The subsequent 1,000 years of musical history would come to be defined by composers who broke artistic ground across a variety of genres and cultures. Some composers enjoyed fame, fortune, and adulation. Others created music that achieved little recognition during their lifetime, but went on to receive acclaim on a global scale. In recent times, a number of composers have eschewed universal appeal in favor of experimentalism. Each historical period across the world has featured musical innovators. Below is just a selection of great composers throughout history.

> "**Whether I was** in my body or **out of my body** as I wrote it I know not. **God knows.**"
>
> GEORGE FRIDERIC HANDEL, On composing the "Hallelujah" chorus in his *Messiah, c.*1741

Ziryāb
Arabic: Iraq, Syria, Spain, 789–857 CE

A leading Arab musician at the Umayyad court of Córdoba, in modern-day Spain, he was said to know 10,000 songs by memory.

Adémar de Chabannes
France, 988–1034 CE

A Frankish monk, he devised the earliest known musical notation system to feature a vertical axis that indicated pitch.

Flames represent divine inspiration

HILDEGARD OF BINGEN

Hildegard of Bingen
Germany, 1098–1179

An abbess and composer, she claimed to be inspired by divine visions. Key work: *Symphonia armonie celestium revelationum*

Jiang Kui
China, 1155–1221

Composer of 17 *ci* (Chinese lyrical poems) known for their candidness and originality. Key works: *Anxiang*; *Shuying*

Josquin des Prez
France, 1450–1521

A master of vocal polyphony, he composed both secular and religious music. Key work: *Nymphes des bois*

Juan Navarro
Mexico, 1550–1610

Franciscan friar and composer of sacred music. Key work: *Liber in quo quatuor passiones Christ Domini continentur*

Yatsuhashi Kengyō
Japan, 1614–85

Innovative composer and player of the koto (Japanese stringed instrument). Key works: *Shiki no kyoku*; *Rokudan no Shirabe*

Barbara Strozzi
Italy, 1619–77

Soprano known for her ariettas, arias, and cantatas. Key works: *Madrigals, op. 1*; *Ariette a voce sola, op. 6*

Antonio Vivaldi
Italy, 1678–1741

Master of the Baroque era best known for his violin concertos. Key works: *Gloria*; *The Four Seasons*

Johann Sebastian Bach
Germany, 1685–1750

Celebrated composer who used French and Italian influences to enrich German styles. Key work: *Brandenburg Concertos*

George Frideric Handel
Germany, 1685–1759

Renowned composer of oratorios and more than 40 operas. Key works: *Xerxes*; *Messiah*

Keaulumoku
Hawaiian Islands, 1716–84

Known for musical chants and poems. Key works: *Haui Ka Lani, Auʻa ʻIa;" E Ninau Mai Ana Ka ʻOe*

Franz Joseph Haydn
Austria, 1732–1809

Pioneer of Classical string quartets and symphonies. Key works: *Symphony No. 45*; *String Quartet Op. 50 No. 1*

Belle van Zuylen
Netherlands, 1740–1805

Enlightenment composer during the French Revolution. Key works: *Oeuvres complètes*; *L'Olimpiade*

William Billings
US, 1746–1800

The first American-born choral composer, his music was infused with rhythmic vitality. Key work: *The Continental Harmony*

Wolfgang Amadeus Mozart
Austria, 1756–91

Prolific and highly influential Classical composer. Key works: *Le Nozze di Figaro*; *Symphony No. 41*; *Die Zauberflöte*

WOLFGANG AMADEUS MOZART

Ludwig van Beethoven
Germany, 1770–1827

Virtuoso pianist whose compositions bridged the Classical and Romantic eras. Key work: *Symphony No. 5*

Franz Schubert
Austria, 1797–1828

With a vast output, he composed intricate music known for its lyricism and beauty. Key work: *Die schöne Müllerin*

Fanny Hensel (née Mendelssohn)
Germany, 1805–47

Pianist who pioneered the genre of *Lieder ohne Worte* ("songs without words"). Key work: *String quartet in E-flat Major*

Juan Pedro Esnaola
Argentina, 1808–78

Nationalistic musician best known for his composition and arrangement of the Argentine National Anthem.

Giuseppe Verdi
Italy, 1813–1901

A master of Italian opera, he was also involved in the Risorgimento movement to unify Italy. Key work: *La Traviata*

Clara Wieck Schumann
Germany, 1819–96

One of the most distinguished pianists of the Romantic era. Key works: *Piano Concerto in A minor*; *Piano Trio in G minor*

Pyotr Ilyich Tchaikovsky
Russia, 1840–93

The most popular Russian composer in history. Key works: *Symphony No. 4*; *Piano Concerto No. 1*; *The Nutcracker*

Antonín Dvořák
Czech Republic, 1841–1904

Versatile composer known for channeling folk influences in his music. Key works: *Symphony No. 9*; *Rusalka*

IGOR STRAVINSKY

Gabriel-Urbain Fauré

France, 1845–1924

A highly influential pianist and director of the French Conservatoire. Key works: *Clair de lune*; *Pelléas et Mélisande*

Muhammad Uthman

Egypt, 1855–1900

Vocalist known for composing chamber music. Key works: *Ya Ma'nta Wahishni*; *Ishna w Shufna*

Ethel Smyth

UK, 1858–1944

Eclectic composer and dedicated suffragist. Key works: *The Wreckers*; *The March of the Women*; *The Boatswain's Mate*

Isaac Albéniz

Spain, 1860–1909

Post-Romantic pianist who used Spanish folk music idioms. Key works: *Chants d'Espagne*; *Asturias*; *Iberia*

Jean Sibelius

Finland, 1865–1957

Celebrated Finnish composer who produced nationalistic works based on folk tales. Key works: *Kullervo*; *Finlandia*

Scott Joplin

US, 1867–1944

Known as the "king of ragtime," he also composed operas. Key works: *Maple Leaf Rag*; *The Entertainer*; *Treemonisha*

Amy Marcy Beach

US, 1867–1917

The first successful female composer of large-scale classical music. Key work: *Symphony in E Minor*

Ralph Vaughan Williams

UK, 1872–1958

English symphonist and nationalistic composer. Key works: *A Sea Symphony*; *English Folk Song Suite*

Béla Bartók

Hungary, 1881–1945

Founder of the field of comparative musicology. Key works: *The Miraculous Mandarin*; *Concerto for Orchestra*

Igor Stravinsky

Russia, 1882–1971

Revolutionary modernist composer whose works garnered international acclaim. Key works: *Petrushka*; *The Rite of Spring*

Mana Zucca

US, 1885–1981

Opera composer and prolific songwriter. Key works: *Fugato Humoresque on the Theme of Dixie*; *I Love Life*

Kosaku Yamada

Japan, 1886–1965

Celebrated orchestral composer with more than 1,600 works. Key works: *Ochitaru tennyo*; *Ayame*; *Kurofune*

Heitor Villa-Lobos

Brazil, 1887–1959

A cellist and guitarist, he was an integral composer in the history of Latin American music. Key work: *Bachianas brasileiras no. 1*

Florence Price

US, 1887–1953

In 1933, she became the first African-American woman in history to have a symphony played by a major orchestra.

Aaron Copland

US, 1900–90

Expressive modern composer with an accessible style. Key works: *Piano Concerto*; *Billy the Kid*; *Appalachian Spring*

Fela Sowande

Nigeria, 1905–87

Music professor known for writing Nigerian art music in the classical European style. Key works: *Six Sketches*; *African Suite*

Ravi Shankar

India, 1920–2012

Known as the "sitar maestro," he founded the National Orchestra of India in 1949. Key works: *Saare Jahan Se Achchha*; *Arpan*

Peter Sculthorpe

Australia, 1929–2014

Composer heavily influenced by Australian Aboriginal music and instrumentation. Key works: *Kakadu*; *Requiem*

Toru Takemitsu

Japan, 1930–96

Known for mixing Western classical music with traditional Eastern instruments. Key works: *November Steps*; *Quatrain*

Krzysztof Penderecki

Poland, 1933–2020

A modern composer, he is known for his innovative and unusual orchestral work. Key work: *Threnody to the Victims of Hiroshima*

Arvo Pärt

Estonia, b.1935

Devout Orthodox Christian musician known for his medieval liturgical sound. Key works: *Fur Alina*; *Tabula Rasa*

Kaija Saariaho

Finland, b.1952

Composer known for combining traditional instruments with electronics. Key works: *L'Amour de Loin*; *La Passion de Simone*

Tan Dun

China, b.1957

A contemporary classical composer, he is most widely known for his film scores. Key work: *Crouching Tiger, Hidden Dragon*

TORU TAKEMITSU

Rachel Portman

UK, b.1960

An Academy Award winner, she has written more than 100 scores for film, television, and radio. Key works: *Emma*; *Chocolat*

Liza Lim

Australia, b.1966

Internationally acclaimed artist whose works range from orchestral scores to art installations. Key work: *Atlas of the Sky*

see also Popular music pp.420–21 ▶ Great dancers pp.426–27 ▶

Popular music

Popular music encompasses many genres, from rock 'n' roll, electronica, and heavy metal, to funk, hip-hop, and country. It is often confused with pop music, a genre of popular music based on catchy hooks that first sprang up in the 1950s. Popular music, because of its variety, can strike any tone: from earnest protest anthem to lighthearted love song. Usually produced by the multibillion-dollar music industry, popular music's wide appeal comes from its accessibility and the allure of its celebrity performers.

North America

Popular music in North America draws on diverse traditions rooted in its mix of cultures. Ragtime emerged from the South in the mid-1890s and gave rise to jazz shortly after, taking in African rhythms and European influences. In the 1920s, African-American blues were combined with Appalachian folk and cowboy tunes of the American West to form country music. The early 20th century sheet music from New York City's publishing hub Tin Pan Alley brought show tunes to the masses and solidified pop music forms such as the repetitive chorus and catchy "hook." In the 1980s, hip-hop rose in popularity, driven by looped beats and rhythmic vocals.

POP SINGER-SONGWRITER TAYLOR SWIFT

◀ **The sound of Motown, 1965**
The stars of Motown, a US soul and pop record label, are seen on a television special. Performers include Martha Reeves and the Vandellas, the Temptations, Dusty Springfield, Smokey Robinson and the Miracles, Stevie Wonder, and the Supremes.

Central and South America

Every Caribbean, Central, and South American country boasts its own unique musical tradition, from salsa and the Argentine tango, to the bossa-nova (meaning "new trend") of Brazil. Independently and in combination, the styles include a wide variety of rhythmic dance music, popularly referred to the world over as Latin music. Much of South America's music is rooted in folk instruments, such as panpipes from the Peruvian Andes and steel drums featured in the calypso tunes of Trinidad. These traditions have also led to hundreds of highly assimilated, blended, Latin American musical subgenres, including reggaeton, Latin ballads, and merengue.

THE BEATLES PICTURED IN LONDON, UK, IN 1967

Europe

Several popular music trends originated in late-20th-century Europe. The hugely successful Beatles, a rock band from Liverpool, UK, incorporated classical, Indian, and psychedelic influences into their music. This not only fueled the youth culture movement of the 1960s and 70s, but also led to the so-called "British Invasion" of US Top 40 music charts. The 1970s saw the rise of arena rock bands such as the UK's Queen, as well as the popularity of Swedish disco supergroup ABBA. The melodic Europop dance music of the 1980s grew along with the US club-influenced electronic sounds of techno, house, and other dance music sub-genres. The annual Eurovision Song Contest still celebrates pop music of all kinds from across Europe.

Africa

African popular music is a mix of indigenous and Western influences. In the 1940s, broadcasts of Cuban music—itself with African roots via the slave trade—popularized Afro-Cuban styles in the Congo. Musicians further reclaimed Latin pop styles when 1970s urban Senegalese musicians combined salsa with *mbalax*, Senegal's traditional dance music. *Mbube*, a powerful South African vocal genre sung in unaccompanied four-part harmony, has been popularized worldwide by groups such as Ladysmith Black Mambazo.

Russia

Pop and rock music grew in parallel to the West in the USSR from the 1960s. By the 1980s, up to 25 million people tuned in to hear BBC Worldwide DJ Seva Novgorodsev broadcast UK and US hits, despite the authorities' efforts to intercept the broadcast. After the fall of the USSR in 1991, Russian-language pop and rock continued to thrive, and in the early 2000s, Russian pop duo t.A.T.u scored hits in the US, Europe, Japan, and other countries.

East Asia

In Japan in the 1980s, J-pop, a blend of Japanese and Western styles, was dominated by electronica and grew to include hip-hop influences. Artists such as Cui Jian (known as the "father of Chinese rock") paved the way for an influx of touring international stars to China (including Beyoncé and the rappers Public Enemy) in the 2000s. South Korean K-pop relies mainly on "idol" groups of performing actor-models. K-Pop star Psy's "Gangnam Style" video was the first internet video to reach a billion views.

KOREA'S BTS (BANGTAN BOYS)

India

Known as Indi-pop, Indian popular music began in the 1970s as a fusion of Indian folk music, classical music, and Western rock. Today, it has a global sound that incorporates elements of world music such as hip-hop and reggae. Bollywood music, featured in Indian cinema, is popular for the starpower of the singer-actors as well as the showmanship of its emotional song-and-dance fantasies. Bollywood tunes typically feature the fiddlelike sounds of the short-necked *sarangi* and the tabla drum.

INDIAN SINGER-COMPOSER A.R. RAHMAN

Australia and New Zealand

Some of the world's biggest music acts, including the rock band AC/DC and the singer-songwriter "Princess of Pop," Kylie Minogue, are Australian exports. "Bush band" music, with its Celtic folk influences, has a country-folk sound and uniquely Australian subject matter. New Zealand's popular music industry is relatively young; the first hit produced there was 1949's "Blue Smoke," written by Ruru Karaitiana and sung by Pixie Williams. New Zealander Richard O'Brien wrote the 1970s musical *The Rocky Horror Show*, a tribute to cult sci-fi classic and B-movie horror films.

DOWNLOADING VS. STREAMING

Apple introduced a convenient music storage system, the iPod, which popularized downloading of music in the early 2000s. Listeners paid to retrieve and save tunes from an online library and stored them on their devices. Today's streaming services offer internet listeners on-demand access (often for a subscription) to millions of tracks—no saving or storage is required.

> "Music ... is an explosive **expression** of **humanity**. It's something we are all **touched by**."
>
> BILLY JOEL, US singer-songwriter

◀ see also Sound, light, and vision technology pp.270–71   ◀ Music through history pp.414–15   The history of dance pp.422–23 ▶

The history of dance

From its ancient origins as a form of ritual, dance has evolved over the centuries to serve many functions: as cultural expression in the ancient world, as a catalyst for aligning family and political partnerships in the Middle Ages, and a powerful social statement in the 20th century. Styles of dances were initially confined to the specific parts of the world where they arose, but as trade and communication crossed boundaries, dance fashions from the waltz to disco became popularized around the globe.

Prehistory

Evidence from cave paintings in India suggests that dance was a part of community life about 9,000 years ago. In Europe, Neolithic archaeological finds indicate annual harvest dances were enacted as a ritual to ensure the fertility of the land and people. Dance events were staged to celebrate young men and women coming of age, with choreography to emphasize male strength or female sexuality. At a time when most people were not literate, dance performance was also a popular way of communicating stories and events.

Indian classical dance

The oldest forms of Indian classical dance, Bharata Natyam from Tamil Nadu and Odissi from Odisha, originated as temple dances. Over time, other formal dances evolved in the different Indian states, including: Kathak from Uttar Pradesh; Kathakali from Kerala; Kuchipudi from Andhra Pradesh; Manipuri from Manipur; and Sattriya from Assam. Each form has its own style and costume but there are aspects common to all, such as distinct stances for men and women, feet stamping to keep rhythm, and *mudras*—symbolic hand gestures—that tell a story.

Small brass bells called *ghungroos* jingle in time with dancer's steps

String tie wraps around ankle

INDIAN MUSICAL ANKLETS

Folk dance

Folk dances have traditionally united local communities in performances involving learned sequences of steps and costumes, often with whole villages or towns participating regardless of experience. Passed down through the generations, folk dances reflect the cultural values and specific characteristics of the places from which they originated. Some of the best known are the Japanese odori, the Punjabi bhangra, the Czech polka, the Irish reel, the English morris dance, and the Anglo-American square dance.

PIETER BRUEGEL THE ELDER'S
***THE WEDDING DANCE*, 1566**

Dance and sub-Saharan Africa

The musical rhythms of the Bantu-speaking people underpin the dances of sub-Saharan Africa, with the body itself becoming a rhythmic instrument. Dances typically vary depending on whether the purpose is recreation or ritual, along with the gender, age, and social status of the dancer. The slave trade brought such dances to the Americas, where they generated new styles such as the cakewalk, which slaves developed to mock the way white people danced and became a craze in ballrooms in the US and UK around 1900.

Waltz and ballroom

Thought to have developed from Austrian and Bavarian folk dances, the waltz was a formal social dance of the Hapsburg court in Vienna. In the waltz—from the German word *walzen*, "to turn"—two people dance arm in arm, turning in three-quarter time. By the late 1700s, the waltz had become a craze across Europe, although it was considered risque because of the close physical contact. Its popularity spurred the opening of public ballrooms, and composers penned waltzes, of which "The Blue Danube" by Johann Strauss became the most famous.

Ballet

Derived from the Italian word *ballare*, "to dance," ballet originated in the aristocratic dances of 15th-century Renaissance Italy and became formalized as a dance technique in France when Catherine de Medici married the French king Henry II, bringing with her the dance styles of the Florentine court. France and then Russia developed ballet, introducing dancing in pointe shoes in the early 1800s, and the avant-garde costuming, choreography, and sets of the Ballet Russes in the early 1900s.

Latin forms

Named for the Latin American region they derived from, the Latin dance forms recognized today grew out of traditional indigenous dances, which fused with colonial European and African influences to produce new styles. Aside from social Latin dancing, there are five dances in international competitions: samba, cha-cha-cha, jive, paso doble, and rumba. Samba, with its origins in the music and dances of West African slaves in Brazil, was one of the first Latin genres to go global. Samba clubs had opened in Rio de Janeiro by the 1920s, and the dance made its international debut in 1939 at the New York World's Fair.

Swing

Most swing dances originated in African-American communities in the 1920s and 1930s, ignited by contemporary jazz music. Two of the earliest swing dances were the Collegiate Shag from the South, and the Lindy Hop, which evolved in New York's Harlem. Other forms include the Balboa, Lindy Charleston, Boogie Woogie, and East Coast Swing. Their common elements were a 6-count or 8-count rhythm and vigorous moves that involved swinging the body out and back. Band leader Cab Calloway popularized the use of the term "jitterbug" to refer to swing dances.

THE JITTERBUG

Disco

On the dance floors of US nightclubs, disco became the most influential cultural phenomenon of the 1970s. Unlike previous types of social dance, disco was freeform and did not require dancing as a couple, which had a profound effect on the gay scene in New York. Gay nightclubs fostered DJs who played music with no breaks between records and developed most of the DJ techniques used today.

Modern dance

Emerging in Europe and the US in the early 20th century, modern dance draws on contemporary culture to challenge audiences with experimental performances that emphasize the opposing bodily forces of tension and release. Pioneers include Isadora Duncan, Martha Graham (see p.427), and Merce Cunningham, and later, Twyla Tharp, and Alvin Ailey.

▶ Maasai warrior dance, Kenya

Maasai warriors perform a traditional competitive jumping dance to a percussive drum beat and singing.

STREET DANCE

Emerging in New York in the 1970s, people literally danced on the streets as a positive response to the music of pioneering DJs such as DJ Kool Herc, who created extended dance rhythms by mixing records played on two turntables. This style became known as hip-hop. Street dance was an escape from the deprivations of the inner city, and an important means of self-expression.

> "Dance is the **hidden language** of the **soul** of the body."
>
> MARTHA GRAHAM, *The New York Times*, 1985

Dance styles

Dance historically reflected local customs and religious beliefs. This led to a rich diversity, from the lion dance of China to the *haka* in New Zealand. However, as cultural influences traveled across the world, dance became internationalized. The medieval court dances of Italy spread through Europe, evolving into ballet, while from the mid-19th century on, African rhythms injected new energy into dance.

Fan used to accentuate movements of dancer

c.200 BCE In Hindu temples of southern India, dancers perform Bharata Natyam. Rhythmic footwork is combined with hand gestures called *mudras* that have symbolic meaning.

Red dye applied on soles of feet

INDIAN CLASSICAL DANCE

1700s Originating in Andalucia, in Southern Spain, flamenco dancing emerges from a mix of cultural influences. It is characterized by bright colors, hand clapping and percussive footwork.

Social dance, performed by couples, often involves vigorous steps

1700s Royal courts of Europe cultivate formal social dances, such as the minuet, while the country dances of England evolve into cotillions and quadrilles.

HAND-PAINTED FAN

FORMAL SOCIAL DANCE

1800 The waltz gains popularity in Austria and quickly becomes one of Europe's most popular pastimes. However, it is criticized by conservatives because couples dance so close to each other.

KEY
☐ Male   ☐ Female

THE WALTZ FOOTWORK

1832 Italian choreographer Filippo Taglioni's *La Sylphide*, with its ethereal ballerina and supernatural themes, represents a new taste for Romantic ballet. It is the first ballet to feature extensive pointe work (dancing on tiptoes).

ROMANTIC BALLET

Pleated gharana skirt eases dancer's movements

Ghungroos, or ankle bells, sound the rhythm

1933 American dancer Fred Astaire makes his screen debut in *Dancing Lady*, opposite Joan Crawford. Dance movies become one of Hollywood's most successful genres.

DANCE IN FILM

1923 The Charleston, an African-American dance originating in South Carolina, becomes all the rage after appearing in the musical theater show *Runnin' Wild*.

THE CHARLESTON

c.1920 Danced to a mix of Western jazz band instruments and West African drum rhythms, Highlife gains popularity in Ghana and Nigeria.

Wooden drum wrapped in coils that modulate pitch

AFRICAN HIGHLIFE

1960s With roots in Congolese dance, the twist takes off after American singer Chubby Checker demonstrates the moves to the rock 'n' roll song "The Twist" on television. The twist does not need to be danced in pairs and there are no formal steps to be learned.

Toe in, heel out, while twisting

THE TWIST

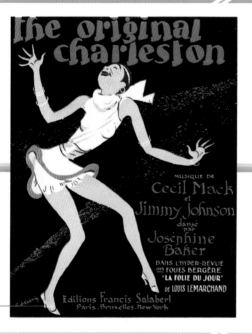

1970s Hispanic communities in New York propel salsa, a hybrid Latin dance style, to the heights of popularity at street parties and nightclubs. It involves a fast, rythmic dance between partners and moves to a four-step beat.

Dance characterized by swinging of hips

SALSA

Lion's head is operated by one person and tail, by another

CHINESE LION DANCE

c.200–700 CE Dances honoring the lion become popular in China. They are thought to chase away evil spirits and are usually performed at festivals.

c.1300 Maoris migrate from Polynesia to settle in New Zealand, developing a distinctive culture that includes the *haka*, or ceremonial dance. The skill with which tribes perform the dance reflects their power and prestige.

HAKA

1500s The galliard originates as a royal court dance in Italy. It involves energetic kicks, leaps, and hops, and is a popular way to show off athleticism.

THE GALLIARD

1661 King Louis XIV establishes the Académie Royale de Danse in Paris, France. The first dedicated ballet school, it marks the transition of ballet from court to stage.

COURT BALLET

Male dancers' costumes convey court rank

Elaborate costumes reflect styles of the day

1600s An all-female troupe launches kabuki, a style of Japanese dance-drama, which gains a reputation for being erotic. All female performers are later banned and it becomes an all-male dance.

KABUKI PERFORMER

c.1600 African slaves in Brazil, South America, develop capoeira, a blend of combat, dance, and music, which helps them disguise their fighting skills from slave masters.

CAPOEIRA

c.1840 The first tap dancing contests are held in the US, with competitors cutting in on one another to demonstrate their dexterity and rhythmic superiority.

Metal plates nailed or screwed to soles

TAP SHOES

c.1850 European writers traveling in Egypt document the Ghawazi belly dancers, who perform *baladi*—a local social dance. Belly dancing has its roots in the ancient Middle East.

Subtle hand movements

GHAWAZI BELLY DANCER

1890s–1900s Rejecting the rules of classical ballet, dancers such as Loïe Fuller experiment with improvisation, freedom of movement, and personal expression.

Loïe Fuller's performance poster

MODERN DANCE

1913 Russian ballet impresario Sergei Diaghilev's *The Rite of Spring* sparks controversy in Paris, France, for its primitive themes and confrontational choreography.

THE RITE OF SPRING

1913 English author H.G. Wells terms this the year of the tango, as the Argentine dance, with its rhythmic legwork, becomes a craze in cities across the US and Europe.

1895 In St. Petersburg, Russia, a new staging of *Swan Lake*, with music by Pyotr Ilyich Tchaikovsky and choreography by Marius Petipa and Lev Ivanov, captures the essence of Russian classical ballet.

CLASSICAL BALLET

c.1972 The fighting moves of New York gangs evolve into an improvised dance to the music of hip-hop DJs who mix record tracks with repeating drum "breaks".

Dancer performs signature headspin move

BREAKDANCE

Layered skirt derives from gypsy dress

2000 A new, high-energy style of Bollywood dancing emerges, melding Indian Classical dance with influences from Broadway, MTV video culture, and hip-hop.

BOLLYWOOD DANCE

see also **Great dancers** pp.426–27 ▶   **Cinema and film** pp.428–29 ▶   **World cinema** pp.430–31 ▶   **425**

Great dancers

Early history records the names of few individual dancers but by the 17th century, the cult of the dancer had begun to emerge. In 18th-century Europe, Jean-Georges Noverre and his contemporaries helped define dance as separate from opera, with narrative ballets in which movements revealed plot rather than serving as simply an aesthetic distraction. The rising popularity of dance performance helped individual dancers forge careers globally. By the early 1880s, a new athletic style pioneered by Auguste Vestris laid the foundations for modern dance, and training and technique became more significant than storyline. Below is just a selection of the great dancers that have graced royal courts, the stage, or the silver screen over the last two millennia.

Zhao Feiyan
China, 45 BCE–1 CE

A skillful dancer, she brought agility to the traditional court dances of the Han dynasty.

Pylades of Cilicia
Ancient Rome, c.22 BCE

Pioneered tragic pantomime dance based on Greek myths and was known for his grand style of performance.

Shizuka Gozen
Japan, 1165–1211

Shirabyoshi dancer, who performed formal court dances of the Heian period dressed as a man.

Domenica da Piacenza
Italy, c.1400–76

Formalized six requisite movements and techniques of the dancer, including coordination and floor space awareness.

Will Kemp
England, d.1603

Popularized Morris dancing, undertaking a much-publicized nine-day dance marathon over 100 miles from London to Norwich.

Louis XIV
France, 1638–1715

Danced in intricately choreographed ballets at his court, with cast and audience drawn from royalty and nobility.

Pierre Beauchamps
France, 1636–1705

Classical ballet dancer, choreographer, and composer, who clarified the five basic positions of feet in ballet.

John Weaver
England, 1673–1760

Known for pantomime ballet, experimental ballet, and narrative dance. Key work: *The Loves of Mars and Venus*

Louis Dupré
France, 1697–1744

Master of the noble style of ballet, with roots in earlier court ballets, admired for his elegant physique.

Ginger Rogers (1911–95) and Fred Astaire starred in 10 films together

POSTER FOR *TOP HAT* (1935)

Marie Sallé
France, 1707–56

Rejected the heavy wigs and costumes ballerinas were expected to wear at the time. Key work: *Pygmalion*

Marie Camargo
Belgium, 1710–70

Pioneered entrechats and complex footwork for female ballet dancers, as well as costume reform with shorter skirts.

Barberina Campanini
Italy, 1721–99

Ballet dancer famous for her athletic style, with precise movements, high jumps, and quick turns.

Jean-Georges Noverre
France, 1727–1810

Creator of ballet d'action, with an emphasis on expressive movement over costumes. Key work: *Psyché et l'Amour*

Gaétan Vestris
Italy/France, 1729–1808

Ballet dancer and choreographer who elevated the role of the principal male dancer.

Gasparo Angiolini
Italy, 1731–1803

Combined dance, music, and plot in dramatic ballet. Key work: *Don Juan, ou le festin de pierre*

Auguste Vestris
France, 1760–1842

Introduced a new athletic style of dance to ballet, based on rigorous training and barre work.

Marie Taglioni
Sweden, 1804–1884

Noted for her pointe work, she established the cult of the ballerina. Key works: *La Sylphide; Pas de Quatre*

Isadora Duncan
US/France, 1877–1927

Danced barefoot and noted for natural movement rather than strict ballet technique. Key work: *The Amazons*

Bill "Bojangles" Robinson
US, 1878–1949

Tap dancer and vaudeville performer who notably went solo and was famous for his "stair dance."

Anna Pavlova
Russia, 1881–1931

Russian ballet dancer who toured the world with her own company. Key work: *The Dying Swan*

Vaslav Nijinsky
Ukraine, 1889–1950

Early modern dancer famous for his leaps. Key works: *Afternoon of the Faun; Le Sacre du Printemps*

Michio Ito
Japan, 1892–1961

One of the pioneers of modern dance, inspired by Japanese Noh drama tradition. Key work: *Sylvia*

Martha Graham
US, 1894–1991

Modern dancer, who created a new system of movement. Key work: *Appalachian Spring*

Fred Astaire
US, 1899–1987

Combined tap, ballroom, and ballet in his routines. Key works: *Top Hat; Swing Time; Royal Wedding*

Rukmini Devi Arundale
India, 1904–86

Dancer and choreographer who revived and popularized the Indian classical dance form Bharata Natyam.

Carmen Miranda
Portugal/Brazil, 1909–55

Samba, samba-boogie, and Latin fusion dancer. Key works: *Down Argentine Way; The Gang's All Here*

RUDOLF NUREYEV

> "Sure [Fred Astaire] was great, but don't forget that **Ginger Rogers** did everything he did ... **backward and in high heels.**"

BOB THAVES, *Frank and Ernest*, c.1982

JIN XING WITH JIN XING DANCE THEATER OF SHANGHAI

Jin Xing
China, b.1967

Ballet and modern dancer with gender-fluid roles. Key work: *Cross Border–Crossing the Line (Cong dong dao xi)*

Vincent Mantsoe
South Africa, b.1971

Combines street dance, contemporary, African traditional, and Afro-fusion in his work. Key work: *NDAA*

Joaquín Cortés
Spain, b.1969

Classically trained ballet and flamenco dancer who fuses these with contemporary dance. Key work: *Pasión Gitana*

Akram Khan
UK, b.1974

Contemporary dancer who incorporates classical Bengali Kathak training in his work. Key work: *XENOS*

Gene Kelly
US, 1912–96

Athletic musical dancer who helped to change public perception of male dancers. Key work: *Singin' in the Rain*

Nicholas Brothers
US, Fayard 1914–2006; Harold 1921–2000

Theatrical dancers who merged tap, jazz, acrobatics, and ballet in their routines. Key work: *Jumpin' Jive*

Margot Fonteyn
UK, 1919–91

Renowned for her characterization and precise technique. Key works: *The Sleeping Beauty; Sylvia; Ondine*

Pearl Primus
Trinidad/US, 1919–94

Modern dancer whose work was infused with African influences. Key work: *The Negro Speaks of Rivers*

Merce Cunningham
US, 1919–2009

Modern dancer whose abstract style strove for "pure movement" without emotion. Key work: *El Penitente*

Bob Fosse
US, 1927–87

Musical theater dancer famous for his use of props and jazz-inspired moves. Key works: *Cabaret; Chicago*

Tatsumi Hijikata
Japan, 1928–86

Founder of Butoh, a postwar genre using stylized gestures and slow movements. Key work: *Forbidden Colors*

George Balanchine
US, 1929–83

Created abstract ballets with no story line, and fused classical ballet with musical theater. Key work: *The Nutcracker*

Mahmoud Reda
Egypt, b.1930

Modern dancer whose work draws on Arab traditions, jazz, ballet, and Hindu and Russian folk dance.

Alvin Ailey
US, 1931–89

Modern dancer who incorporated ballet and jazz styles in his choreography. Key work: *Revelations*

Rudolf Nureyev
Russia, 1938–89

Athletic classical ballet dancer renowned for explosive movements and high-speed turns. Key work: *Le Corsaire*

Pandit Birju Maharaj
India, b.1938

Classical Indian dancer and leading exponent of the Kalka-Bindadin Gharana style of Kathak.

Pina Bausch
Germany, 1940–2009

Modern dancer who created a surreal style now known as Tanztheater. Key work: *The Rite of Spring*

Twyla Tharp
US, b.1941

Contemporary dancer whose style combines classical, jazz, and pop. Key work: *The Catherine Wheel*

Mikhail Baryshnikov
Latvia, b.1948

Classical ballet dancer and proponent of modern dance. Key work: *Opus 19/The Dreamer*

Les Twins (Laurent and Larry Nicolas Bourgeois)
France, b.1988

New style hip hop and street dancers who introduced the concept of dancer as DJ.

Michaela DePrince
Sierra Leone/US, b.1995

Classical ballet dancer renowned for her technical expertise and spirited expression. Key work: *Mata Hari*

Arms held in fifth position, with elbows slightly bent and wrists relaxed

Foot en pointe

MICHAELA DePRINCE

Cinema and film

Science and creative ingenuity have driven the development of cinema, starting with the Lumière brothers' invention of the motion picture camera in France in 1895. Although filmmaking traditions developed around the world, Hollywood became the dominant force in movie production. Throughout cinematic history, films came to reflect social, cultural, and political trends, while also influencing them with powerful messages created by actors, directors, screenwriters, composers, and production teams.

Slits to view images through

Man bows and woman curtseys when disk spun

ZOETROPE DISK ENTITLED *POLITENESS*

19th century Various devices create the illusion of movement, including the French phénakistiscope of 1833 and the 1866 Milton Bradley zoetrope.

Hand-crank wound to photograph or project pictures

Film reel stored above camera projector

BIOKAM CAMERA-PROJECTOR

1895 In France, brothers Auguste and Louis Lumière demonstrate the *Cinématographe*—a movie camera and projector in one.

1933 The launch of King Kong causes a sensation, in part for its pioneering use of models, miniatures, and stop-motion effects, developed by US animator Wills O'Brien.

***KING KONG* POSTER**

1929 The first Academy Awards® ceremony, better known as the Oscars®, is held in Los Angeles, honoring the best films of 1927 and 1928. Among the winners are Emil Jannings for Best Actor, and Janet Gaynor for Best Actress.

1929 Entrepreneur George Eastman demonstrates the first Technicolor film made with a three-strip technicolor camera. The process is perfected in 1932, becoming the standard for color films in Hollywood.

EARLY TECHNICOLOR CAMERA

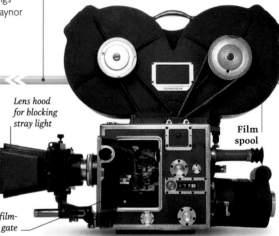

1934 The Motion Picture Production Code, or Hays Code—guidelines on what is unacceptable onscreen in the US—starts to be enforced. It is replaced in 1968 by the rating system.

1937 *Snow White and the Seven Dwarfs* is the first full-length animated feature. It uses a multiplane camera to create a three-dimensional appearance.

Lens hood for blocking stray light

Film spool

Film housing contains film-winding system and film gate

1995 US animator John Lasseter's directorial debut, *Toy Story* is the first animated feature to be made entirely with computer-generated imagery (CGI).

1988 Hindi-language film *Salaam Bombay!* depicts the struggle of children in Bombay's (present-day Mumbai) slums. Winning awards at the Cannes Film Festival, it propels director Mira Nair to fame.

STILL FROM *SALAAM BOMBAY!*

Film editor Marcia Lucas handles reel of film

Director of Star Wars, George Lucas, in the editing room

1997 Digital cinema becomes a reality as Texas Instruments' Digital Light Projector (DLP) is demonstrated in Hollywood; two years later, US director George Lucas uses DLP for *Star Wars: Episode I—The Phantom Menace*.

GEORGE LUCAS

1997 US director James Cameron's *Titanic* makes box-office history by grossing more than $1 billion, and holds the record for over a decade. It is nominated for 14 Oscars, of which it wins 11, matched by *Ben-Hur* (1959).

MAKING OF *TITANIC*

see also World cinema pp.430–31 ▶ Photography pp.492–95 ▶

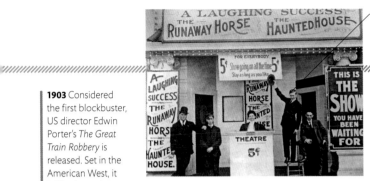

Ticket takers pose outside a nickelodeon theater

1903 Considered the first blockbuster, US director Edwin Porter's *The Great Train Robbery* is released. Set in the American West, it is 11 minutes long and is made on a purported budget of $150.

EARLY NICKELODEONS

1905 The first Nickelodeon, one of the earliest forms of amovie theater, opens in Pittsburgh, running back-to-back film screenings accompanied by piano.

1908 After starring in *The Red Girl*, Canadian-born Florence Lawrence emerges as the first Hollywood movie star. She appears in more than 300 films.

FLORENCE LAWRENCE

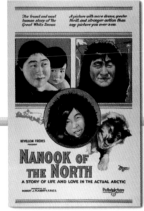

1928 *Steamboat Willie*, the first film featuring Walt Disney's Mickey Mouse with synchronized sound, debuts in the US, at New York's Colony Theater. Just eight minutes long, it marks the end of silent animation.

WALT DISNEY

NANOOK OF THE NORTH **POSTER**

1922 US filmmaker Robert J. Flaherty makes the first documentary, *Nanook of the North*, about a Canadian Inuit family.

1919 The Premier of the Soviet Union, Vladimir Lenin, nationalizes Soviet cinema. He declares that of all the arts, cinema is the most important.

1913 Based on a tale from the Indian epic *Mahabharata*, *Raja Harishchandra* is the first Indian feature film released in Bombay (present-day Mumbai), India.

1954 Japanese director Akira Kurosawa releases *The Seven Samurai*. It establishes the action film genre, with its storyline about a team of warriors assembled for a mission.

Poster informs public of film cast and crew

LA DOLCE VITA **POSTER**

1960 Director Federico Fellini's satire *La Dolce Vita* introduces Italian cinema to a global audience. Despite its depiction of excess, the film is a box-office hit in the US.

1964 Sidney Poitier becomes the first African-American to win the Best Actor award at the Oscars for his role in *Lilies of the Field* (1963).

SIDNEY POITIER

Magnetic tape stores video and sound

Takeup reel

1985 The launch of the Blockbuster home video chain transforms film viewing. It offers a supermarket-style checkout and a wider selection of films than existing video stores.

1981 German war film *Das Boot* captures global audiences with its documentarylike style. Director Wolfgang Petersen is admired for his use of close-ups to create a sense of claustrophobia.

STILL FROM *DAS BOOT*

1971 Sony introduces its U-matic cassette, the first successful videocassette format. Though originally aimed at the consumer market, it helps transform live location television.

DISASSEMBLED CASSETTE

Plastic case

2002 For her role in *Monster's Ball* (2001), Halle Berry becomes the first woman of African-American descent to win an Oscar for Best Actress.

HALLE BERRY WITH FELLOW OSCAR WINNER DENZEL WASHINGTON

2010 Kathryn Bigelow becomes the first woman to win the Best Director Oscar for her war drama *The Hurt Locker* (2008), which explores the psychological stress of combat in Iraq.

THE HURT LOCKER **POSTER**

2019 Written, produced, and directed by Bong Joon Ho, Korean comedy-thriller *Parasite* wins four Oscars, including Best Picture, awarded for the first time to a non-English language film. It also becomes the first Korean film to win the Palme d'Or, the highest prize awarded at the Cannes Film Festival.

World cinema

Despite early global domination by Hollywood, film industries in other parts of the world developed their own character, and often served an important social function in unifying individuals from different religious and ethnic backgrounds, notably in India and the Soviet Union. As films were exported globally, they inspired international audiences and filmmakers alike by offering insight into other cultures, while reaffirming the hopes and fears shared by people all over the world.

North America

Centered in sunny Los Angeles, the American film industry developed in Hollywood from 1910 onward, starting with the films of D.W. Griffith. By 1919, Griffith had joined forces with Charlie Chaplin, Mary Pickford, and Douglas Fairbanks to form United Artists, a production company set up in the interests of actors, rather than studios. As silent films gave way to sound, Hollywood's emerging studio system came to dominate film production, creating an aura of glamour through its careful curation of its stars and their public image.

POSTER FOR *E.T.*

Central and South America

As early as 1896, film screenings were held in Rio de Janeiro, Buenos Aires, and Mexico City, and over the next decade film industries developed across the continent. After filmmaking languished in the 1950s, the New Latin American Cinema movement grew out of a 1967 meeting in Chile of experimental, socially minded directors, reinvigorating film in Cuba, Colombia, and Brazil. From the 1990s onward, Mexico's *Like Water for Chocolate* (1992), Brazil's *City of God* (2002), and Argentina's *Roma* (2004) garnered international recognition.

Africa

South of the Sahara desert, indigenous filmmaking lagged until African nations gained independence. Senegal's Ousmane Sembène is considered the father of African cinema; his 1963 film *The Wagoner* is a landmark in the continent's film history. Burkina Faso became a prominent center of film production, focused on issues of culture and identity, and founded Africa's foremost film festival in 1969, now called FESPACO. In nearby Nigeria, director Ola Balogun helped to build a national industry in the 1970s and 1980s, adapting Yoruba plays for the cinema. Nigeria's film industry now rivals Bollywood as the world's second largest film industry by volume.

Western Europe

France was the pioneer of film and its early technology. When the Lumière brothers presented short films in Paris in 1895, they laid the foundations for 20th-century cinema. The Scandinavian film industry developed as an art form in the early 1900s. Germany pioneered expressionistic style in the 1920s, while Britain mastered documentary and comedy genres. Later 20th-century directors, such as Jean-Luc Godard and Federico Fellini, developed an international following for their emphasis on style and concept.

Eastern Europe

Polish filmmakers were active early in the 20th century, including Władysław Starewicz, who made a series of pioneering stop-motion films. By 1948, a film school had been founded in Łódź—among its graduates was Palme d'Or winner Andrzej Wajda. Members of the Czech new wave movement, Jiří Menzel and Miloš Forman, attracted plaudits until Soviet troops marched into Prague in 1968. During the Soviet era, indigenous cinema in Eastern Europe was stifled until the end of the Cold War in 1991 allowed national film endeavors to grow.

The Middle East

Egypt's film industry is one of the world's oldest; the first Egyptian cinema opened in 1906. Egyptian cinema flourished in the 1940s–1960s, drawing international attention for realist masterpieces such as Youssef Chahine's *Cairo Station* (1958). Syria produced its first feature film in 1928; Lebanon in 1929, and both countries continue to actively produce. Despite the restrictions facing Arab filmmakers through conflict and censorship, challenging features from Palestine, Yemen, Syria, Jordan, Algeria, Tunisia, and Lebanon have found critical success at home and internationally.

CHILDREN OF HEAVEN STILL, IRAN

Russia and Central Asia

A milestone of early Russian cinema was the pioneering use of two cameras in *Defense of Sevastopol* (1911). In 1925, Sergei Eisenstein's *Battleship Potemkin* introduced groundbreaking editing and camera techniques including montage and juxtaposition. Under Stalin, cinema became a tool for reinforcing state ideology, and Soviet-run Central Asian countries were set up as filmmaking hubs. After independence, some of these nations developed their own industries.

India

With over 1,500 films produced annually, in more than 20 languages, India supports the world's biggest film industry, including the Hindi cinema of Bollywood. Pivotal figures were Dadasaheb Phalke, who made the first silent feature film in 1913, and Ardeshir Irani, who made the first talkie in 1931. After independence from Britain in 1947, many films addressed national identity. A new wave of realist cinema appeared from the 1960s onward, but the box-office hits have been "masala" films, so-called because they blend romance, comedy, and action with song and dance.

China

Film came to China in 1896, when a short motion picture was screened as part of a variety bill in Shanghai. Inspired, Ren Qingtai began making films of Chinese opera performances; these were a hit and sparked the proliferation of film studios. Filmmaking flourished in Hong Kong and Taiwan in the 1950s and 1960s. In the 1970s, martial arts become the dominant genre before films such as *Yellow Earth* (1984) marked the return of mainland China to international cinema. Ang Lee's *Crouching Tiger, Hidden Dragon* (2000) brought together filmmakers from mainland China, Taiwan, and Hong Kong.

Walt Disney had **exclusive rights** to **Technicolor's 3-color process** between **1932 and 1935**

Artistic interpretations of scenes help to advertise the film

Japan

Immensely influential on filmmakers around the world, early Japanese films demonstrated the power of the long shot in establishing the emotional state of characters, and the interplay of light and shadow. The 1950s is considered the golden age of Japanese cinema, dominated by directors Akira Kurosawa, Yasujirō Ozu, and Kenji Mizoguchi. In the 1980s, Hayao Miyazaki cofounded Studio Ghibli, making some of Japan's biggest animated films, notably *Spirited Away* (2001), which became the first animated feature to win the top award at the Berlin Film Festival in 2002.

POSTER FOR *SPIRITED AWAY*

Australia and New Zealand

Following an early boom, including the world's first feature narrative film *The Story of the Kelly Gang* (1906), the Australian film industry slumped after World War I. It recovered in the 1970s thanks to government incentives, which spurred a new wave of films such as *Picnic at Hanging Rock* (1975), *Mad Max* (1979), and *Crocodile Dundee* (1986). Similarly in New Zealand, government initiatives in the 1970s encouraged filmmakers, who by the 1990s had gained an international reputation, notably Jane Campion with *The Piano* (1993) and Peter Jackson with *The Lord of the Rings* (2000).

Russian Ark (2002) was filmed in a **single** 99-minute take

▼ **Still from *House of Flying Daggers***
House of Flying Daggers (2004), directed by Zhang Yimou, is a Chinese martial arts film. The genre is known as *wuxia*, and in film it dates back to the 1920s.

see also Theater through history pp.432–33 ▶   Great writers pp.440–41 ▶   Photography pp.492–95 ▶

Theater through history

The history of theater has two distinct strands: productions for an elite audience, and those intended to appeal to popular tastes. In ancient China, for example, dramatic plays were performed for the aristocratic courts, while in medieval Japan, Noh's subtle metaphors were targeted to a knowing, educated audience. Parallel to this, theater also came to reflect the common concerns of all people through the popular commedia dell'arte (comic theater) of Renaissance Italy or the public theaters of Shakespearean London, where actors poked fun at the establishment and expressed the full range of human fears and other emotions within the controlled environment of the theater.

Isis, sister-wife of Osiris, stands behind throne

Osiris, god of the underworld and ruler of the dead

DECEASED WORSHIPS OSIRIS

c.2686 BCE–400 CE Ancient Egyptian writings and accounts by Greek historian Herodotus describe the annual Abydos passion play that tells the myth of Osiris.

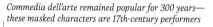

Commedia dell'arte remained popular for 300 years—these masked characters are 17th-century performers

1500s In Renaissance Italy, the commedia dell'arte attracts a mass audience with its comic action and by using vernacular Italian rather than Latin.

PULCINELLA

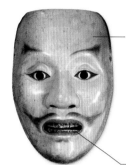

Carved cypress painted with natural pigments

14th century Japan's indigenous theater, Noh, evolves into a high art form that uses symbolism and metaphor to suggest a storyline rather than explain it.

Blackened teeth suggest high status

NOH MASK OF A SAMURAI

10th century In medieval Europe, folk dramas are merged into religious plays, but French playwright Adam de la Halle creates secular theater for an Italian court.

Le Halle writes satires and musical drama

ADAM DE LA HALLE

1500s In the kingdom of Benin, West Africa, ruler Oba Esigie founds the Ugie Oro festival, staging ceremonial enactments of military prowess.

1500s Four theaters open in London, England, including the Globe, and audiences flock to see popular entertainment such as plays by William Shakespeare.

GLOBE THEATER

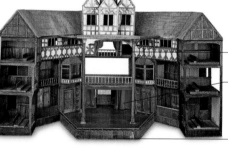

Central balcony for Romeo and Juliet's famous scene

Actors wait beneath stage

Outer stage projects into yard

1590–1680s Spain enjoys a golden age of theater, developing the three-act comedia verse drama, led by Lope de Vega and Pedro Calderón de la Barca.

Late 1800s French playwright Alfred Jarry's *Ubu Roi* is an extreme example of the Symbolists' use of language and objects to denote underlying meaning.

UBU ROI

Late 1800s Norwegian playwright Henrik Ibsen pioneers Realism with hard-hitting social dramas, such as *A Doll's House*.

HENRIK IBSEN

Late 1800s–1900s The growth of US cities and railroads sets the scene for the rise of modern musicals, leading to a century of shows on Broadway.

POSTER OF OKLAHOMA!

Late 1800s Russian producer Konstantin Stanislavski directs actors in *The Seagull* using his "method" training, which elicits a wider range of emotional expression.

SCENE FROM THE SEAGULL

"Mother Courage—Spices"

1930s In revolutionary plays such as *Mother Courage and Her Children*, Germany's Bertolt Brecht encourages the audience to question how plays are constructed and actors perform.

MOTHER COURAGE'S CANTEEN WAGON

Set on a farm in 1906, Oklahoma!'s characters include a cowboy just back from a trip to modern Kansas City

432 ◄ see also The Reformation pp.344–45 ◄ Mythology pp.388–91 ◄ Great dancers pp.426–27

Hair drawn up into double bun

Long sleeves emphasize movement of arms

TANG DYNASTY PERFORMER

Exaggerated expression so audience can tell characters apart

6th–1st century BCE The use of lightweight painted masks by actors in ancient Greece aids character recognition, and allows one actor to play multiple roles.

MODEL OF CHARACTER MASK

Tall stage front, several stories high

Seating capacity for 20,000 spectators

No roof, but theater could be covered with awnings

1st century BCE– 5th century CE Rome's first dedicated theater stages full-length scripted tragedies and comedies, with the audience segregated by social position. It is imitated across the empire.

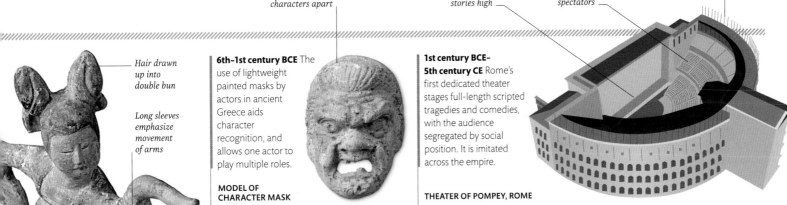

THEATER OF POMPEY, ROME

7th century During the Tang dynasty, the first classics of Chinese theater are performed, with military dramas, domestic farces, and political satires becoming established genres with recurring character types.

7th century In Persia (Iran), costumed performers use poems and songs to recount folk tales and epics in a form of dramatic storytelling called Naqqāli.

Barbad sings tales of Persia's ancient glory to the king

BARBAD ENTERTAINS KHOSROW II

1st–9th century CE Written in Sanskrit, poetic dramas with music and dance are staged throughout India. A common theme is the hero finding prosperity and love through righteous living.

1600s Izumo no Okuni and her female troupe create a new dance drama, kabuki. Considered too risqué, women are banned and kabuki becomes all male.

Male actor portrays female character

KABUKI ACTOR

Proscenium arch

Auditorium

Stage

ITALIAN THEATER

1600s–1700s Theaters in Italy introduce a frame separating stage and auditorium—the proscenium—through which the audience views the action.

Mid-1600s French playwright Jean Racine innovates drama with poetic language and an emphasis on characters motivated by love.

PHAEDRA AND HIPPOLYTE

Early 1800s After the French Revolution, melodramas telling tales of justice, such as *Le Chien de Montargis* (*La Forêt de Bondy*) become popular.

Illustration of set

LE CHIEN DE MONTARGIS

1775–1800s English playwright Richard Sheridan parodies the superficial behavior of polite society in *School for Scandal*, a comedy of manners.

LEAD CHARACTER, SIR PETER TEAZLE

1660–1710 Aphra Behn is England's first successful female playwright, creating satires and farces centered on the intricacies of Restoration society.

APHRA BEHN

1950–60s Absurdist dramatists abandon convention in favor of actors behaving irrationally, with little or no action or narrative, as a way of exploring human existence.

1960–70s As theater flourishes in newly independent African nations, Efua Sutherland combines Ghana's oral narrative tradition with Western dramatic devices.

THE MARRIAGE OF ANANSEWA

1960–2000s In the postmodern era, directors question the conventions of the theater, staging immersive dramatic experiences that involve members of the audience.

Water tank suspended above audience

FUERZA BRUTA (BRUTE FORCE)

see also The history of literature pp.434–35 ▶ The developing styles of poetry pp.438–39 ▶

◀ see also The Renaissance pp.338–39 ◀ The Enlightenment pp.346–47

The history of literature

Derived from the Latin word *literatura*, meaning "writing formed with letters," literature was once thought of as simply any written work, but its definition has changed over time. In the ancient world, literature was expected to have merit on the basis of its composition and expression. By the 18th century, literature was no longer considered to be simply any books or writing; it was writing that was imaginative, as distinct from purely historical or scientific.

Early literature

Two contenders vie for the title of oldest work of literature, both from Sumer, a region in the south of modern-day Iraq and Kuwait. Dating from *c.*2600–2500 BCE, the *Kesh Temple Hymn* is an ode to the temple at Kesh, and the *Instructions of Shuruppak* is a book of wise sayings and advice. A few centuries later, around 2100 BCE, the first fragments of the earliest fiction, the *Epic of Gilgamesh*, were inscribed into clay. In nearby Egypt, the rise of an intellectual elite led to a flowering of narrative works, inscribed on stone and on papyrus (a paper-like material).

The Classical period

During the Classical age, which roughly spanned the 8th century BCE to 6th century CE, ancient authors explored ideas about life, truth, and beauty. In Greece, Homer's *The Iliad* and *The Odyssey* were profound heroic epics, and in Rome, Virgil told the dramatic story of the city's origins in *The Aenid*. The Sanskrit literature of India encompassed sacred texts, plays, erotic stories, and folktales, while in China *fu* rhyming prose set the standard for creative writing, and the monumental *Shiji* became a milestone in historical literature.

EARLY MEDIEVAL WRITER ST. JEROME

Lectern

Early medieval Europe

For the first time, European writers used the vernacular rather than Latin. Ireland had the earliest European tradition of prose and poetry in the local language, with tales of saints and heroic figures; one of the main literary figures in the 6th century, Dallán Forgaill, became the national poet. In England, the epic poem *Beowulf* was written in Old English. In Europe, authors of folk tales used poetic meters to create a sense of drama.

Late medieval literature

Authors began to write under their own names, instead of anonymously as they did in earlier medieval times. The end of the 11th century marked a high point for Japanese literature with two stories of Imperial court life: Murasaki Shikibu's *Genji Monogatari* (The Tale of Genji) and Sei Shonagon's *Makura no Sōshi* (The Pillow Book). Other notable writers of the era include the Persian poet Rūdakī, 12th-century French poet Chrétien de Troyes, and England's Geoffrey Chaucer.

Stylus

Wax tablet

ANCIENT GREEK POET SAPPHO

◀ **In the library**
Poet and scholar al-Hariri (*c.*1054–1122) is depicted at the library in Basra (modern-day Iraq) reading from *The Maqamat* (The Meetings), a collection of stories.

The Renaissance

Bridging the transition from the medieval to a new age, Dante's *The Divine Comedy* helped to establish the cult of the author. From Italy, Renaissance literature spread across Europe, spearheaded by the rediscovery of writings from antiquity and the invention of the printing press in the 1450s. Key works of the age included Shakespeare's collected plays, *The Decameron* by Giovanni Boccaccio, the essays of Erasmus, and the poems of Edmund Spenser. Common themes were a rational approach to the world and to sensual pleasures.

The Enlightenment / Neoclassical

The "Age of Reason" in Europe (see pp.346–47) stimulated writers from the late 17th to early 19th centuries, spurred by the spirit of investigation and a desire for social and political change. Key works include Margaret Cavendish's science-based novel *Blazing World* (1668), *The Social Contract* (1762) by Jean-Jacques Rousseau, and *The Rights of Man* (1791) by Thomas Paine. African authors made an impact in Europe and America with slave narratives, such as Olaudah Equiano's *The Interesting Narrative of the Life of Olaudah Equiano* (1789).

The Romantics

Romanticism was the dominant literary theme in Europe in the first half of the 1800s. The importance of the individual's imagination, and the idea that creativity could help heal spiritual wounds, were the driving forces behind Romantic writers such as William Blake, William Wordsworth, Lord Byron, and John Keats. Mary Shelley's *Frankenstein* (1818) and Emily Brontë's *Wuthering Heights* (1847) were popular Gothic novels, focused on the supernatural and the balance between love and hate, and good and evil.

Realism

Depicting ordinary life was the aim of Realist writers, in a backlash against the literature of the mid-19th century. Some of the pioneers of Realism included Honoré de Balzac in France, Stendahl, Alexander Pushkin and Anton Chekov in Russia, and George Eliot in Britain. The movement also spread to America, where Henry James and Mark Twain, notably in

Huckleberry Finn, developed their own approaches. In Australia, Henry Lawson's raw descriptions of the harsh realities of life in the bush were groundbreaking.

Modernism

In response to rapid technological changes in the early 20th century, as well as momentous events such as the two world wars (see pp.362–63), writers experimented with new forms and themes, using the first person to describe the experience of the individual and the workings of the inner self. Capturing the zeitgeist were William Faulkner's *As I Lay Dying* and Virginia Woolf's *Mrs. Dalloway*. Other authors who became synonymous with modernism include Ernest Hemingway, F. Scott Fitzgerald, and Gertrude Stein.

MODERNIST AUTHOR VIRGINIA WOOLF

Postmodernism

From the 1950s onward, growing numbers of writers rebelled against the existing literary conventions and narrative forms in favor of interweaving different genres, creating illusions, blurring boundaries between fact and fiction, and challenging the reader to embrace disorder. Some of the most influential authors in this period include Jorge Luis Borges, Samuel Beckett, John Barth, Kurt Vonnegut, and Hunter S. Thompson. Key books include Joseph Heller's *Catch 22* (1961) and William S. Burroughs' *The Naked Lunch* (1959). More recently, Bret Easton Ellis's controversial *American Psycho* (1991) is also regarded as a postmodern classic.

"To **describe directly** the life of humanity ... appears **impossible.**"

LEO TOLSTOY, *War and Peace*, 1869

Books through the ages

Writing was initially used for trade, record-keeping, and disseminating the law of the land. The earliest examples of literature date back to c.2600–2500 BCE in Sumer, and much early literature is believed to have built on oral traditions. Since then literature has taken many different forms, including poetry, prose, theater, comedy, tragedy, and satire. It has been used in different ways at different times, but some works, such as *The Iliad* by Homer, have been valued more than others, and have had a huge influence on culture and society. Other works have marked significant technical advances in the printing or publishing process, which has either enabled a wider audience to enjoy them, or has allowed the production of works which are visual pieces of art in their own right.

c.750 BCE Greek poet Homer's epic *The Iliad* tells the story of the siege of Troy by the Greeks. It has roots in the Greek oral tradition and is regarded by many as the first masterpiece of European literature.

THE ILIAD

c.1590 Based on Buddhist scholar Xuanzang's journey to India in the 7th century, *Journey to the West* is one of the best-known novels from China. It includes the mischievous character Monkey, who has many adventures before finally reforming himself.

The birth of Monkey

ILLUSTRATION FROM JOURNEY TO THE WEST

1493 With more than 1,800 woodcut illustrations, the *Nuremberg Chronicle* is an impressive example of 15th-century printing. It presents an encyclopedic account of biblical and historical events, and has depictions of towns of the era.

Illustration shows God creating stars

ILLUSTRATION FROM THE NUREMBERG CHRONICLE

c.1600 Calligraphy flourishes in Persia (present-day Iran). Mir Emad Hassani perfects the Nasta'līq script, which is used for writing poetry.

1755 Containing more than 40,000 entries with 114,000 quotations, Samuel Johnson's *A Dictionary of the English Language* is the first comprehensive work of its kind in English.

Title page

JOHNSON'S DICTIONARY

1813 English author Jane Austen's *Pride and Prejudice* reacts against the sentimentality of previous novels with realistic, yet witty, portrayals of women and the world they lived in.

JANE AUSTEN

This page combines ink, watercolor, and gold leaf

ALBUM LEAF SIGNED EMAD HASSANI

1902 English author Beatrix Potter's *Tales of Peter Rabbit* is a gently humorous story of a mischievous young rabbit. Illustrated with watercolor images, it becomes one of the best-selling children's books of the 20th century.

BEATRIX POTTER

1901 *Buddenbrooks*, Thomas Mann's chronicle of the decline of a bourgeois German family, charms readers with its literary realism.

BUDDENBROOKS

1905–06 Japanese novelist Natsume Soseki's *I am a Cat* uses the comic device of an animal narrator to give an outsider's view of humans in modern society.

NATSUME SOSEKI

1935 Penguin becomes the first mainstream publisher to print cheap paperback books. With its unmistakable color-coded covers it creates a new mass market for literature.

Orange represents fiction

PENGUIN BOOKS

Leader of the Kaurava army

Conch signifies start of battle

ILLUSTRATION OF THE *MAHABHARATA*

c.400 BCE At 100,000 verses, the Indian epic *Mahabharata* is the longest poem ever written. It recounts the rivalry of the Pandava and Kaurava royal families and contains information about early Hindu philosophy.

c.150 BCE Written on vellum, papyrus, and copper—and discovered between 1946 and 1956 in the Judaean Desert in Israel—the Dead Sea scrolls contain scriptures that give a precious insight into the development of Judaism.

PAGE FROM THE GUTENBERG BIBLE

Illuminated with color

1455 Produced by the German printer Johannes Gutenberg, the Latin Bible is the first book printed in Europe using movable type. This process allows books to be produced economically and in greater numbers.

DIVINE COMEDY

1321 A philosophical allegory tracing the poet's fictional journey through the afterlife, Dante's *Divine Comedy* is the first major work in Italian and helps establish it as a literary language.

ILLUSTRATION FROM *BIRDS OF AMERICA*

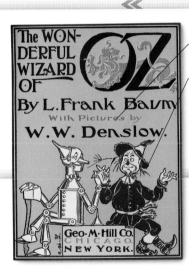

Both artist and author credited

Cover showing the characters Tin Woodman and the Scarecrow

COVER OF *THE WONDERFUL WIZARD OF OZ*

1827-38 Containing 435 life-size prints, naturalist John Audubon's *Birds of America* is published in four volumes. This 3 ft- (1 m-) tall book, with its hand-tinted illustrations, sets the standard for subsequent natural history publications. Each copper plate is engraved, printed, and colored by hand.

1900 American author L. Frank Baum's *A Wonderful Wizard of Oz* is the story of Dorothy, a girl whisked away to a magical land. It is later adapted for film and stage.

1869 Leo Tolstoy's *War and Peace* is a seminal work of Russian literature. It covers with unstinting realism the trials of the aristocratic society during the French invasion of Russia.

LEO TOLSTOY

1851 Herman Melville publishes *Moby Dick*, a key work of American literature. The novel charts the obsessive quest by Captain Ahab to hunt down and kill the whale Moby Dick.

MOBY DICK

1951 American author J.D. Salinger's novel *The Catcher in the Rye* captures the angst and alienation of a teenager faced with the superficiality of those around him.

COVER OF *THE CATCHER IN THE RYE*

First edition cover

1958 Chinua Achebe's *Things Fall Apart*, one of the first great African novels in English, chronicles precolonial Nigeria and the disintergration of its traditional society after the arrival of the Europeans.

THINGS FALL APART

1985 Canadian novelist Margaret Atwood publishes *The Handmaid's Tale*, a dystopian story of a society where women are subjugated by a new patriarchy, and the struggle of a brave few to resist.

Paperback cover

COVER OF *THE HANDMAID'S TALE*

The developing styles of poetry

Poetry is a literary form that exploits the sound and rhythm of a language for effect, normally breaking up the text into discrete lines. It lends itself to both powerful symbolism and allegory, and has been used by poets throughout history to push the boundaries of their languages, often making it very hard to translate. Many of the wide variety of poetic forms that have evolved over the centuries have ancient origins, while new types are still being created in modern times.

Verse fables

One of the oldest literary genres, verse fables commonly feature animals (and sometimes even inanimate objects) that are endowed with the ability to speak and reason. Their adventures encapsulate a simple moral, such as the virtue of hard work contained in the fable "The Ant and the Grasshopper" by the 6th-century BCE Greek fabulist Aesop. The grasshopper spends the summer singing, while the ant diligently stores up food; when winter comes, the grasshopper is forced to beg the ant for something to eat.

Dramatic poetry

Playwrights have often used poetic form to shape their plays, allowing for both a more creative use of language and the powerful distillation of emotions. It was pioneered by Greek dramatists such as Aeschylus in the 6th century BCE, and later reached the height of its developed form in English in the 16th century with the plays of William Shakespeare (see p.440), who used a poetic rhythm called iambic pentameter (also known as blank verse) to lend color to speeches and soliloquies.

Lyric poetry

Lyric poetry focuses on the expression of emotions and internalized states of mind more than the telling of a story. It derives its name from the lyre, the musical instrument that normally accompanied such poems in ancient Greece. Refined in Roman works such as the *Odes* of Horace in the 1st century CE, the lyric form appealed particularly to Romantic poets such as John Keats, whose 1819 "Ode on a Grecian Urn" is a fine example of the genre. In medieval

Europe, much of the lyric poetry set to music, often by traveling troubadors, was later collected in anthologies such as the 14th-century *Codex Manesse*.

Portrait of poet or subject   *Manuscript of lyric poetry*

ILLUSTRATION FROM THE *CODEX MANESSE*

Elegy

Elegy developed in ancient Greece, when the term was used to describe poems on serious or solemn subjects, especially poems of mourning or reflections on loss. Its subjects range from the sorrow expressed by a warrior for his exile from his lord's retinue encapsulated in the 10th-century Anglo-Saxon poem "The Wanderer," to "Le Lac," a lament by the 19th-century French poet Alphonse de Lamartine for the death of a female friend, expressed through a haunting description of the lake they once visited together.

Prose poetry

Prose poems infringe one of the most fundamental tenets of the poetic form by not being broken up into lines. However, they still use poetic devices such as rhyme,

sound patterns, repetition, and symbolic imagery to great effect. Although its origins were earlier, it was only in the 1860s that the style was popularized, most notably by the French poet Charles Baudelaire, in works such as "Be Drunk," and was subsequently taken up by later generations of poets such as Gertrude Stein and Pablo Neruda. After briefly falling out of favor, prose poetry had a resurgence in the mid-20th century, particularly among American "Beat" poets such as Allen Ginsberg and Jack Kerouac, and remains highly valued today.

THE BEAT GENERATION'S ALLEN GINSBERG

"Genuine poetry can **communicate** before it is **understood**."

T.S. ELIOT, American-English poet, 1929

Narrative

Poems that tell a story, narratives were often originally set to music in the form of ballads, such as those recounting the tale of Robin Hood and collected together in the late 15th century. Narrative poetry is also a very versatile form, and was used in the 18th century by Robert Burns, in "Tam o'Shanter," and in the 19th century by both Edgar Allan Poe, in "The Raven," and Alfred, Lord Tennyson, in "Enoch Arden."

SCENE FROM JOHN MILTON'S EPIC *PARADISE LOST*, ILLUSTRATED BY WILLIAM BLAKE

Epic

An epic is a longer version of a narrative poem, often telling the story of a hero or an adventure. Most ancient cultures had such forms, from the Sumerian *Epic of Gilgamesh*, composed around 2100 BCE in Mesopotamia, through the oldest European epic poems, such as *The Iliad*, in which the poet Homer relates the story of the Trojan War, to the Indian Sanskrit epic the *Mahabharata*, begun around 400 BCE.

Light verse

Addressing trivial or playful themes, light verse seeks to amuse the reader by the use of wordplay, puns, or nonsensical juxtapositions. Among its masters in the 19th century were poet and artist Edward Lear, who used limericks (a light verse form) in his *A Book of Nonsense*, and author Lewis Carroll, who incorporated nonsense poems such as "Jabberwocky" in his children's novel *Through the Looking-Glass, and What Alice Found There*.

Satire

Satirical poems poke fun at the follies and vices of the leading figures of the day, and are often thinly disguised as allegorical figures. Roman poets such as Horace and Juvenal popularized the genre in the ancient world, and, despite censorship and criticism from those it targets, satire today remains a popular tool of political commentary across many media forms.

Speculative

Speculative poets set their poems within imagined worlds or fantastic situations. Although the explosion in science fiction writing from the mid-20th century pushed speculative poetry to new prominence, it has its roots much earlier in 19th-century works such as the "The Hosting of the Sidhe," a fairy poem by the Irish poet William Butler Yeats.

▶ Visions of the afterlife

This scene from Dante's narrative poem *The Divine Comedy* was illustrated in 1857 by Gustave Doré.

HAIKU

Haiku is a Japanese poetic structure comprising three lines with a 5-7-5 syllable pattern, often juxtaposing two images to capture the essence of a moment. Developed in the 17th century by masters such as Matsuo Bashō, it has not only become Japan's most famous poetic style, but has also gained popularity as an English form.

POETRY WRITING, 17TH-CENTURY PRINT

Great writers

The last seven centuries have seen scores of literary traditions emerge, as writers chronicled both changes and continuities in their societies, as well as expounding more timeless themes of love, loss, and revenge. Literary cultures arose in all civilizations, many of them, such as those in China and India, having very ancient roots, but it is only more recently that we possess the names and works of writers across a wide range of cultures. The changing nature of communications has enabled many authors to find recognition far outside their homelands, a testament to the psychological insights, linguistic prowess, and powerful characterization of the truly great writers. Only a small selection of influential writers are featured here.

Dante Alighieri

Italy, 1265–1321

Poet whose allegorical masterpiece *The Divine Comedy* established Italian as a literary language.

Geoffrey Chaucer

England, *c*.1340–1400

Considered to be the greatest English poet of the Middle Ages and famous for *The Canterbury Tales*.

Christine de Pizan

France, 1364–1430

Poet, novelist, and biographer, she was a very early advocate for women's rights. Key work: *The Book of the City of Ladies*

Miguel de Cervantes

Spain, 1547–1616

Poet, playwright, and Spain's most renowned novelist, his *Don Quixote* is often considered the first modern novel.

William Shakespeare

UK, 1564–1616

Poet and England's greatest dramatist. His 37 plays include masterpieces such as *King Lear*, *Hamlet*, and *Romeo and Juliet*.

J.W. von Goethe

Germany, 1749–1832

Poet, playwright, novelist, philosopher, and pioneer of the German Romantic movement. Key work: *Faust*

Jane Austen

UK, 1775–1817

Used irony and realism to explore the social plight of women. Key works: *Pride and Prejudice*; *Emma*

Charles Dickens

UK, 1812–70

A consummate stylist with a concern for social issues, his 15 novels include *David Copperfield* and *Great Expectations*.

Victor Hugo

France, 1812–85

Poet, novelist, and dramatist. Lynchpin of the French Romantic movement, his masterpiece is *Les Misérables*.

Charlotte Brontë

UK, 1816–55

Novelist who explored the struggle of women to break free of stifling social confines in *Jane Eyre*.

Fyodor Dostoevsky

Russia, 1821–81

His psychologically powerful novels give penetrating insights into pathological minds. Key work: *Crime and Punishment*

Leo Tolstoy

Russia, 1828–1910

A master of realism, who rejected materialism, his masterwork is the epic *War and Peace*.

Emily Dickinson

US, 1830–86

Her highly personal, elliptical poems combine a metaphysical sensibility and sharp observation.

WILLIAM SHAKESPEARE

Henry James

US, 1843–1916

A virtuoso of literary realism with a deep understanding of conflicting psychological motives. Key work: *The Portrait of a Lady*

Oscar Wilde

UK, 1854–1900

Poet, novelist, playwright, and exponent of aestheticism, characterized by brilliant wit. Key work: *The Importance of Being Earnest*

Joseph Conrad

UK, 1857–1924

His complex plots deal with the plight of ethical men in morally compromised situations. Key work: *Heart of Darkness*

Selma Lagerlöf

Sweden, 1858–1940

Her lyrical style and idealism helped promote the Swedish Romantic movement. Key work: *Gösta Berling's Saga*

Rabindranath Tagore

India, 1861–1941

A polymath, but principally a poet, his blend of traditional and modern heralded a literary Renaissance in India.

Natsume Soseki

Japan, 1867–1916

Evokes a profound sense of alienation at a world where traditional values were no longer an anchor.

Lu Xun

China, 1881–1936

China's greatest 20th-century writer used the short-story form to pen biting critiques of Chinese society.

James Joyce

Ireland, 1882–1941

Irish novelist who used experimental stream of consciousness techniques in *Finnegan's Wake*.

Franz Kafka

Germany/Bohemia, 1883–1924

Avant-garde style juxtaposed the banal and fantastic to great effect. Key works: *The Trial*; *The Metamorphosis*

> ## "You can **never be wise** unless you **love reading**"
>
> SAMUEL JOHNSON, Letter to Francis Barber, 1770

Gabriela Mistral

Chile, 1889–1957

Her poetry rejected aestheticism to express the authentic experience of the marginalized. Key works: *Despair; Tenderness*

Anna Akhmatova

Russia, 1889–1966

Her poetry brought concrete expression and elegance in opposition to the prevailing Russian symbolism.

F. Scott Fitzgerald

US, 1896–1940

A master of modernist American fiction who chronicled the excesses of the jazz age. Key work: *The Great Gatsby*

Ernest Hemingway

US, 1899–1961

His spartan prose and adept understatement crafted masterpieces such as *For Whom the Bell Tolls* and *The Old Man and the Sea*.

Christina Stead

Australia, 1902–83

Employed satire and psychological insight in novels largely based in her native Australia. Key work: *The Man Who Loved Children*

George Orwell

UK, 1903–50

His lucid prose in works such as *Nineteen Eighty-Four* and *Animal Farm* attacked social injustice and totalitarianism.

Pablo Neruda

Chile, 1904–73

Latin America's most eminent poet moved from an early hermetic style to simple, direct expressiveness.

Naguib Mahfouz

Egypt, 1911–2006

His sweeping chronicles of modern Egyptian life are tinged both with national pride and social criticism.

Patrick White

Australia, 1912–90

Used allegory, shifting vantage points, and stream of consciousness to explore isolation and self-meaning in a growing country.

Aimé Césaire

Martinique, 1913–2008

Poet, playright, and a leading exponent of Négritude, the movement to restore a sense of cultural identity to Africans.

Iris Murdoch

UK, 1919–99

Novelist who used psychological insights to explore the inner lives of characters in *The Sea, The Sea*.

José Saramago

Portugal, 1922–2010

His allegorical approach subverts views of contemporary history, with a strong socialist perspective.

Italo Calvino

Italy, 1923–85

A master of fables in a neo-realistic and fantastic style, such as *The Baron in the Trees* and *If on a Winter's Night a Traveler*.

Latifa al-Zayyat

Egypt, 1923–96

Documents the pressures of young people to escape social conformism during the Egyptian nationalist struggle.

Wisława Szymborska

Poland, 1923–2012

Her deceptively simple poetry counterposes eternal problems of existence with the transitoriness of the present.

Nadine Gordimer

South Africa, 1923–2014

Produced powerful chronicles of exile and alienation against the backdrop of the anti-apartheid struggle.

NAGUIB MAHFOUZ

Gabriel García Márquez

Colombia, 1927–2014

A master of magical realism, mixing realistic settings with profoundly fantastical events. Key work: *One Hundred Years of Solitude*

Mariama Ba

Senegal, 1929–81

Her intimate prose illuminates the plight of African women struggling against the inequality of traditional values.

Chinua Achebe

Nigeria, 1930–2013

Chronicled the often-devastating impact of Western values on traditional African social structures. Key work: *Things Fall Apart*

V.S. Naipaul

Trinidad, 1932–2018

His elegant prose addresses questions of personal and collective alienation against the backdrop of colonialism.

Anita Desai

India, b.1937

Employs potent visual imagery and psychological insights into characters struggling with a society in transition.

Ngugi wa Thiong'o

Kenya, b.1938

Rejected English in favor of Gikuyu as a means of building an authentic African literature. Key work: *Wizard of the Crow*

Margaret Atwood

Canada, b.1939

Her dystopian fiction, notably *The Handmaid's Tale*, uses future disaster to reflect on present trends.

J.M. Coetzee

South Africa, b.1940

His novels examine the impact of colonization and the way in which language itself can enslave.

Halldór Laxness

Iceland, 1945–98

Poet and novelist who, with harsh yet lyrical realism in an epic style, chronicled the struggles of rural Icelandic life.

Keri Hulme

New Zealand, b.1947

Blends Maori and European culture, dream worlds, and reality into a complex narrative in *The Bone People*.

Lorna Goodison

Jamaica, b.1947

Her socially conscious poems celebrate the experience of the Jamaican struggle for self-determination.

Elias Khoury

Lebanon, b.1948

Uses multiple narrators and interior monologue to reflect on the catastrophic events of the postwar Middle East.

Haruki Murakami

Japan, b.1949

Uses magical realism to treat themes of alienation, loss, and trauma in the increasingly impersonalized modern world.

Orhan Pamuk

Turkey, b.1952

Explores identity and individuality to reflect on the clash between traditional and modern in society. Key work: *Snow*

ARUNDHATI ROY

Arundhati Roy

India, b.1961

Roy uses a carefully crafted nonsequential style to give insights into the social discrimination in post-independence India.

Shin Kyung-Sook

South Korea, b.1963

Examines loss and alienation in the decades of South Korea's rapid modernization. Key work: *Please Look After Mom*

see also The history of writing pp.462–63 ▶

The history of painting

Painting as an art form began with humans' discovery of pigments. Derived from the earth, and mixed with animal fat or other natural lubricants and fixatives, these pigments gave early artists their color palette. Over time, technological advancements made new paint colors and textures possible, along with more refined tools. These developments enabled different styles of painting to evolve, giving form to the ideas and social changes that inspired artists.

Prehistory

Our understanding of early human consciousness comes almost entirely from cave paintings dating back to around 44,000 BCE (see p.303), thousands of years before the advent of writing. These paintings, sheltered from the elements, and some rock engravings in open-air sites, are among the most enduring and evocative artifacts of prehistory. They demonstrate that humans consciously applied their creativity and imagination to producing artistic images, and did not simply paint in order to record events. Color palettes came from earth pigments—red ochre, yellow ochre, umber, and black from fired charcoal.

Stone surface

Images likely depict domesticated animals

BRONZE AGE ROCK ART

Portable art

At the same time as cave art was being made in the Stone Age, humans were also creating small, portable pieces of art, carved from bone or stone and painted. Found in Namibia, the oldest examples are stone plaques painted with rhinoceroses, zebras, and humans using red ochre, white clay, eggshell, hematite, and gypsum. In France, Spain, and Italy the Azilian culture of c.8000 BCE painted red geometric patterns on pebbles. In India, during the Bronze Age, portable art included religious paintings on plaques or small boxes. The painted pots of Mesopotamia (present-day Iraq) and decorated paddles of the Viking Age count as portable art too.

The ancients

Artistic painting matured in advanced ancient civilizations that developed writing systems, including China, India, Persia (present-day Iran), Egypt, Greece, and Rome. Many aesthetic and technical advances from this time proved influential on later art periods, including the Renaissance and Neoclassicism. The Imperial courts of China were devoted to landscape painting as well as calligraphy, which explored the nuances of black ink and brushwork to create expressive writing. Ancient Egyptians developed new paint colors for artworks on tomb and temple walls, and in ancient Greece artists created a new stylized form of painting on pottery.

Murals

Distinctive as an art form for being incorporated into architecture, murals were a natural evolution from cave painting. The ancient Egyptians pioneered synthetic green and blue pigments, which were mixed with agar gum as a fixative and applied over a smooth plastered surface. Murals decorate the palaces of the Bronze Age Minoan civilization, the Ajanta caves of India, and the Maya complex at San Bartolo in Guatemala. Tempera-style application was common, for which powdered pigments were mixed with raw egg and water. The ancient Greeks and Romans developed the encaustic method, grinding pigments into beeswax and applying them hot.

Frescos

A method of wall painting using pigment diluted with water and applied to wet, freshly applied lime plaster, the fresco (from the Italian for "fresh") is an integral part of the wall, rather than applied on top as a mural would be. The fresco designer makes an outline on an underlayer of lime plaster, and after the upper layer of wet

> ## "If you hear a **voice within you** say you **cannot paint**, then by all means **paint** and that voice will be **silenced**."

VINCENT VAN GOGH, *Van Gogh's Letters*, 1883

plaster is troweled on, the artists work quickly to paint over the just-visible outline, before the plaster is fully dried. The ancient Minoans developed an early technique for fresco, but the technique gradually became more refined during the early medieval period in India, from the 3rd to 7th century CE. It reached its peak in Renaissance Italy, where it can be found in churches, palaces, and government buildings.

◄ Kandinsky's *Composition 8*, 1923
Geometric forms reflect Modernist painter Wassily Kandinsky's spiritual interest in the properties of shapes.

Renaissance perspective
During the 15th and 16th centuries, European artists became interested in science and mathematics as the basis for a rational approach to art. One of their aims was to create paintings that resembled the way in which the human eye viewed the real world; with a sense of depth and perspective. Formal perspective models were based on the ideas of Italian architect Filippo Brunelleschi. The aim was to structure the composition around a vanishing point on the horizon line of the painting. This became known as linear perspective. To create this effect, objects become increasingly smaller the closer they are to the vanishing point. Artists noted for their linear perspective include Leonardo da Vinci and Raphael.

Baroque
The shifting political and religious life of Europe gave birth to Baroque art. The reform of the Catholic Church in response to Protestantism was the backdrop to a new art movement that emphasized bold, dynamic forms and an emotional connection to the viewer. Coinciding with these new artistic ideas, oil paints became the preferred medium thanks to improvements in oil refining technology. This trend had begun during the Renaissance but became entrenched during the Baroque period, and artists such as Peter Paul Rubens, Diego Velázquez, and Nicolas Poussin exploited the lustrous texture and deeply pigmented appearance of oils.

Neoclassicism
From the mid-18th century, artists looked back to the Classical age for inspiration. This was inspired by the discovery of the ruins at Pompeii in Italy, and also by general political unrest over the lack of equality in society. Neoclassical painters wanted to express the value of virtue over

MONET'S *IMPRESSION, SUNRISE*, 1872

superficiality, and as a result their subjects were often historical scenes. They believed that art had the power to transform and civilize society, and works often contained a lesson about morality. Leading painters of the age included Joshua Reynolds and Jacques-Louis David, who was influential in celebrating the cause of the French Revolution by portraying scenes from the Roman Republic.

Impressionism
The Impressionists rejected monochrome and championed vibrant color, aided by experimental synthetic paints. They were also influenced by Japanese paintings of town and country life. Sunflower yellow became a dominant hue, ideally suited to creating impressions of light and energy. J.W.M. Turner experimented with a new fluorescent yellow watercolor, called Indian Yellow, derived from the urine of mango-fed cows, and a poisonous lead-based synthetic Chrome Yellow. Claude Monet also made violet one of his signature colors. In 1841, painting was transformed by the invention of paint tubes, replacing the long tradition of storing paints in a pig's bladder. This made paints far more portable, spurring the landscape painting that dominated this particular art period.

Modernism
The industrial revolution was the impetus for a radical change in painting. As the pace of life became quicker, and trains, automobiles, and bicycles altered the human view, artists translated this new way of looking at things onto their canvases. Images were blurred, abstracted, and broken down into

parts. The Fauvists were among the first group of painters to experiment, using spontaneous brushstrokes and paint squeezed straight from the tube. Cubist painters such as Georges Braque presented objects from multiple points of view on the same canvas, pioneering abstract art. Other influential modernist painters were Kazimir Malevich, Salvador Dalí, Piet Mondrian, and Jackson Pollock.

Postmodernism
A reaction to the idea that avant-garde styles of modernism had become mainstream, postmodernism began in the 1960s with the Neo-Dada and Pop Art movements in the US, both of which questioned traditional views about the meaning and value of art. Andy Warhol, for example, painted mundane objects and pop culture icons, elevating the ordinary to the status of "special" by putting them on a large canvas. The emphasis of postmodern painting was on creating a visual spectacle that might shock or confront the viewer. Postmodernism also challenged the art hierarchy, dominated by European males, and paved the way for an appreciation of feminist and minority art.

> ## Paint made from **copper and arsenic** was proved to be **highly toxic** and was subsequently **banned**

Painting styles

The way in which a painting creates visual impact and elicits a response from the viewer has been a challenge for artists over many centuries. By exploring shape, line, color, shading, and texture, painters have created varying optical effects to change the way their work appears. Some endeavored to portray their subjects with realism—painters from the Han dynasty or the

Old Masters of the 17th century, for example; some invented a more stylized, romantic view of the world, evident in Japan's *c.*15th century *sumi-e*. Others have evolved new techniques to express pure emotion, especially since the mid-20th century. Experiments with the medium itself, and the method of application, have also shaped the stylistic progress of the art form.

44,000 BCE Figurative art on cave walls at Maros-Pangkep, Indonesia, is painted with black pigment. It depicts animals and human-animal hybrids.

EARLIEST-KNOWN CAVE PAINTING

Spare use of color to contain the action

TARTAR HUNT

Painted folding screen by Hasegawa Tōhaku

Mongol (Tartar) hunters are popular subjects

1338–1537 Japanese artists, such as Hasegawa Tōhaku, reinvent Chinese ink painting as *sumi-e* (ink wash painting), reflecting the essence of Zen Buddhism.

500–1400 CE In medieval Europe, much of the art produced is religious, reflecting how the Catholic Church dominates every aspect of life in Western Europe.

Bent body conveys pain

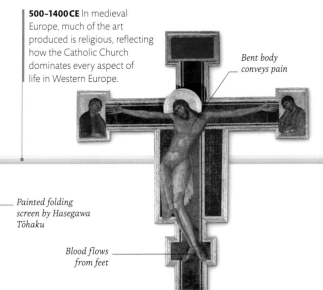

Blood flows from feet

THE CIMABUE CRUCIFIX, FLORENCE, ITALY

c.1800s Artists from the Native American Hopi tribe have long used natural pigments and yucca-leaf brushes to paint their pottery, but their art gains widespread recognition in the 19th century.

1787 Elisabeth Louise Vigée-Le Brun paints Marie Antoinette in the fashionable Baroque style; she will soon become portraitist to the French queen.

Use of gold leaf enhances brilliance of surface

GUSTAV KLIMT'S *THE KISS*

c.1615-1868 During Japan's Edo period, *ukiyo-e* woodblock prints celebrate everyday urban life, later influencing European Impressionists. They are produced en masse and sold cheaply.

CENTRAL PANEL OF WOODBLOCK TRIPTYCH

1874 Paul Cèzanne, Claude Monet, and Berthe Morisot are among 30 artists mounting the first exhibition of Impressionist art in Paris, France. Over 200 works of art are displayed.

MONET'S *ARGENTEUIL*

1897 Gustav Klimt founds the Vienna Secession, a group of Austrian painters, sculptors, graphic designers, and architects inspired by Art Nouveau.

1905 A new avant-garde movement, Fauvism, is helmed by French artists Henri Matisse and André Derain. They paint using strong, nonnaturalistic color.

HENRI MATISSE

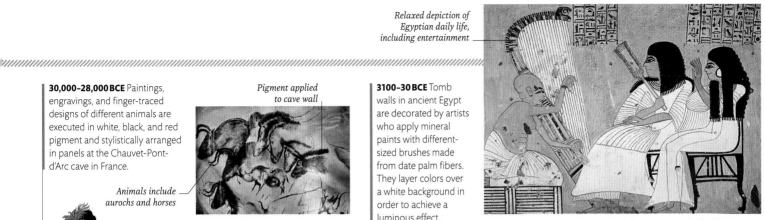

Relaxed depiction of Egyptian daily life, including entertainment

30,000–28,000 BCE Paintings, engravings, and finger-traced designs of different animals are executed in white, black, and red pigment and stylistically arranged in panels at the Chauvet-Pont-d'Arc cave in France.

Pigment applied to cave wall

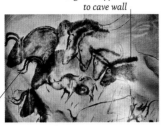

Animals include aurochs and horses

CHAUVET CAVE PAINTINGS, FRANCE

3100–30 BCE Tomb walls in ancient Egypt are decorated by artists who apply mineral paints with different-sized brushes made from date palm fibers. They layer colors over a white background in order to achieve a luminous effect.

WALL PAINTING FROM THE TOMB OF NEBAMUN AT THEBES

Drawn with fine lines

Accurate depiction of subject's fashion

GONGBI BRUSH TECHNIQUE

206 BCE–220 CE China's early calligraphic painting form, _gongbi_, develops during the Han dynasty, with emphasis on precise brushstrokes and nuanced coloring to recreate real life.

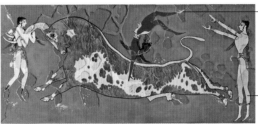

Depiction of bull-leaping ceremony

Women depicted with pale skin

REPLICA FRESCO FROM KNOSSOS, CRETE, GREECE

c.1550 BCE– c.467 CE In ancient Greece and Rome, frescoes adorn the walls of villas, tombs, and palaces exhibiting expert knowledge of mineral color pigments, including white and red lead, murex purple, and deep blue azurite.

1508–1512 In Italy, Raphael paints _The School of Athens_, demonstrating a mathematical approach to proportion, a principle Michelangelo applies to the ceiling of the Sistine Chapel.

1545 Italian painter Agnolo di Cosimo finishes _The Portrait of Eleanor of Toledo_, employing Mannerist tools such as flat lighting and a preoccupation with surface display to convey rich fabric detailing.

ELEANOR OF TOLEDO

16th–17th century In India's Mughal Empire, painting develops under the patronage of the courts with the focus on miniatures.

CEILING OF THE SISTINE CHAPEL, VATICAN CITY

17th century Dutch Masters such as Johannes Vermeer and Rembrandt van Rijn layer handmade oil paints to create subtle tonal shifts and convey the sparkling effects of natural light.

VERMEER'S _GIRL WITH A PEARL EARRING_

MUGHAL MINIATURE PAINTING

1937 Pablo Picasso paints _Guernica_, which blends Cubist and Surrealist elements. It is a powerful political statement that highlights the suffering often experienced by innocent civilians during wartime.

1952 American artist Jackson Pollock paints _Convergence_ using house paint flung and dripped. It is a milestone of Abstract Expressionism, channeling the physics and chemistry of paint in motion to express emotion.

JACKSON POLLOCK

Late 20th century American graffiti artists, including Keith Haring and Jean-Michel Basquiat, make graffiti and street art fashionable—in the process turning street art into high art and highlighting urban subcultures that had been previously overlooked.

Art applied with stencils

MODERN GRAFFITI

see also Elements of painting pp.446–47 ▶ Drawing and painting pp.496–97 ▶ **445**

Elements of painting

The appearance of an artist's finished work relies on the techniques applied throughout the creation process. Layering of colors, manipulating the characteristics of paint viscosity and opacity, varying brushstrokes, and size and positioning of objects are among the painter's most often used tools.

Subject and composition

The subject of a painting is the main idea, or theme, depicted. A subject may also determine a painting's composition, or arrangement of visual elements. Composition includes the devices the artist uses to direct the eye around the canvas, such as deploying proportional rules and radiating lines.

Light and shade

Contrast between light and shadow can focus the viewer's attention on a subject and, at the same time, heighten the emotional intensity of the painting, since the eye is drawn to the lightest area. This effect is called chiaroscuro, meaning light-dark, and can be employed to generate dramatic impact and impart three-dimensionality. Artists build up tonal graduations with layers of paint, working from dark to light, and using hatching, shading, and layering tones.

> Between 1912 and 1948, **art competitions,** including painting, were a part of the **Summer Olympics**

Direction of light
In *Girl with the Red Hat*, Jan Vermeer evoked a window beyond the visible scene by lighting one side of the face.

People
Jacques Louis-David contrasted Bonaparte's formal pose with rumpled hair and the intimate setting of his study.

Landscape
John Constable painted an open tree canopy and blue sky to frame *Salisbury Cathedral from the Bishop's Grounds*.

Quality of light
Caspar David Friedrich graduated tones of the same color and stippled with blue pigment to create *Winter Landscape*.

Still life
Paul Cézanne gave volume and three-dimensional form to fabrics and fruit to dynamically charge *Still Life with a Curtain*.

Abstract
In *Yellow-Red-Blue*, Wassily Kandinksy employed the power of movement along a diagonal axis.

Viewpoint and perspective

A painting's viewpoint—the position the artist wants the viewer to take—can be shaped by linear perspective, in which radiating vanishing lines intersect a central horizon line to generate the illusion of three-dimensional space.

Viewpoint
The viewer's eye is drawn in the direction of the river's flow in Ernst Ludwig Kirchner's *Rotes Elisabethufer*.

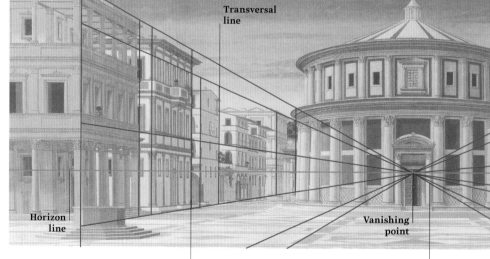

Transversal line

Horizon line

Vanishing point

The height or width between two orthogonal lines is established by transversal lines

The eyes are drawn to the vanishing point, where the "vanishing" lines meet the horizon

446 ◀ see also **The history of painting** pp.442–43 ◀ **Painting styles** pp.444–45

Media

The chemical and physical properties of pigments and paints can be manipulated by an artist to achieve a particular effect. Aspects to consider are the viscosity, or liquidity, of the paint on the canvas; its transparency or opacity; how quickly or slowly it dries; and the texture or sheen it has when dry.

Egg tempera
Duccio di Buoninsegna used the vivid matte tones and semitranslucency of egg tempera, the chief Renaissance medium.

Watercolor
Because watercolors form a thin layer, light reflects from the surface underneath, as evident in John Singer Sargent's work.

Oil painting
As J.M.W. Turner demonstrated, in the form of translucent glazes, oil paints can produce a luminous finish.

Acrylics
In emulsion form, acrylic paints lend clarity and spontaneity to paintings, such as in the work of Nand Katyal.

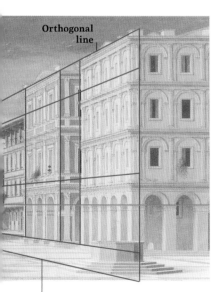

Orthogonal line

A series of imaginary, orthogonal (converging) lines follow objects in the painting until they vanish at the horizon line

Perspective
The Renaissance painting *The Ideal City* illustrates the linear perspective theories of architect Leon Battista Alberti.

RULE OF THIRDS
English portrait painter Joshua Reynolds is credited with the invention of the rule of thirds, a guideline that suggests that to achieve the ideal composition, a painting should be divided into thirds, horizontally and vertically.

Color

Theories of how color works have underpinned painting for centuries. The basis for such theories is the classification of color into hue, a pure color; tint, a hue with white added; tone, a hue with gray added; and shade, a hue with black added.

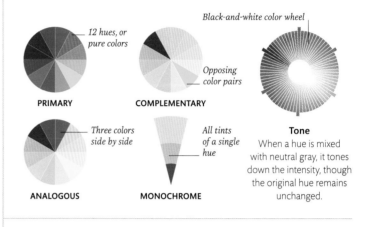

Black-and-white color wheel

12 hues, or pure colors

PRIMARY

Opposing color pairs

COMPLEMENTARY

Tone
When a hue is mixed with neutral gray, it tones down the intensity, though the original hue remains unchanged.

Three colors side by side

ANALOGOUS

All tints of a single hue

MONOCHROME

Brushstrokes and texture

The size and width of an artist's brush, the hair it is made from, the shape of the tip and the amount of paint on it, and the way it is held in the artist's grip, shapes the depth of paint applied and the resulting texture.

Invisible
Artists who wish to convey a sense of realism need to create a paint finish with virtually no trace of brushwork. To achieve this, they employ a very fine brush and make very small brushstrokes in order to create a unified surface with no conspicuous textures.

Jan Weenix's brush marks are imperceptible

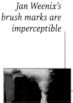

Visible
The thick swirls of paint in van Gogh's *Starry Night* reveal the artist's hand, a technique he often used very expressively. Heavy brushwork adds texture and signals the immediacy of the moment, creating an undulating surface that reflects light into the viewer's eyes.

Heavy brush strokes are obvious

Chinese brushstrokes
Painting with ink in the Chinese tradition requires a brush with a pointed tip. The artist controls stroke thickness with the pressure of the hand, and since the brush is working on porous paper or silk, the action must be fluid to create smooth, dynamic forms.

Dark colors from pressure applied to brush

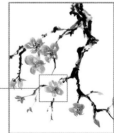

Great painters

Before the tradition of painting on canvas became established, artists created works on surfaces as diverse as pottery, plaster walls, wood panels, silk screens, vellum, and paper scrolls. As technology progressed, artists used new types of paints and developed techniques to express how they saw the world around them. Medieval Chinese artist Guo Xi strived to capture a scene from multiple perspectives rather than imitating how the eye views a scene, while Italian Renaissance figures Leonardo da Vinci and Michelangelo drew on science to realize their visions. Alongside technology, the life experiences of artists have helped to shape the course of painting as an art form, and only a small selection of great painters are included here.

Exekias

Greece, c.550 BCE

Considered one of the greatest practitioners of black-figure pottery painting. Key work: Vatican amphora (Ajax and Achilles)

Apollodorus

Greece, 5th century BCE

Noted for his development of *skiagraphos* (shadow painting) technique. Key works: *Odysseus; A Priest at Prayer*

Zeuxis

Greece, 5th century BCE

An innovative painter known for his art's realism. Key works: *Helen; Zeus Enthroned; The Infant Hercules Strangling the Serpents*

Gu Kaizhi

China, c.344–406 CE

Celebrated for his silk handscrolls. Key works: *Admonitions of the Instructress to the Court Ladies; Nymph of the Luo River*

Fan Kuan

China, c.950–c.1032

Song dynasty landscape painter. Key works: *Travelers among Mountains and Streams; Sitting Alone by the Stream*

Master of the Registrum Gregorii

Germany, c.972–1000

Gifted illuminator of religious codices. Key works: *Letters of Gregory the Great; Gospel Lectionary of Egbert of Trier*

Guo Xi

China, c.1020–90

A master of Northern Song dynasty landscapes. Key works: *Early Spring; The Coming of Autumn*

Aniko (Araniko)

Nepal, 1245–1306

Key figure in Nepalese and Chinese art during the Yuan dynasty. Key work: Lhakang Chenmo temple complex decorations

Guan Daosheng

China, c.1262–1319

Famous as a calligrapher and for her role in developing bamboo painting. Key work: *Bamboo Groves in Mist and Rain*

Theophanes the Greek

Turkey, 1330–c.1410

One of the greatest painters of the late Byzantine period. Key works: *Transfiguration of Jesus; Our Lady of the Don* (attributed)

Jan van Eyck

Belgium, c.1390–1441

Skilled at creating highly detailed and lifelike paintings. Key works: *The Adoration of the Mystic Lamb; The Arnolfini Portrait*

Black chalk lines on paper

PORTRAIT OF A YOUTH, RAPHAEL

Rogier van der Weyden

Belgium, 1399–1464

Known chiefly as a religious painter whose work displays great emotional intensity. Key work: *St. Luke Drawing the Virgin*

Leonardo da Vinci

Italy, 1452–1519

Polymath, painter, and a key figure in the Renaissance. Key works: *Lady with an Ermine; The Last Supper; The Mona Lisa*

Tang Yin (Tang Bohu)

China, 1470–1524

Exceptional painter during the Ming dynasty. Key works: *Tau Gu Presents a Poem; Court Ladies in the Shu Palace*

Michelangelo Buonarroti

Italy, 1475–1564

One of the most revered artists of his time, he excelled at sculpture and painting. Key works: *Doni Tondo*; the Sistine Chapel ceiling

Kanō Motonobu

Japan, 1476–1559

Created a technique that combined Japanese and Chinese painting. Key work: *Birds and Flowers of the Four Seasons*

Raphael (Raffaello Santi)

Italy, 1483–1520

Renaissance painter known for technical sophistication and realism. Key works: *The School of Athens; The Sistine Madonna*

Sultan Muhammad

Iran, early to mid-16th century

Persian master of miniaturist painting. Key work: *Shahnama* (Book of Kings) of Shah Tahmasp.

Kanō Eitoku

Japan, 1543–90

Grandson of Kanō Motonobu who further developed his grandfather's style. Key works: *Plum Tree; Chinese Lions*

Dong Qichang

China, 1555–1636

Primarily painted landscapes, combining elements from various schools of Chinese painting. Key work: *Mt. Qingbian*

Artemisia Gentileschi

Italy, 1593–c.1656

A successful professional artist at a time when it was seen as a vocation only for men. Key work: *Susanna and the Elders*

Manohar

India, late 16th century

Court painter for the Mughal emperors. Key works: *Emperor Jahangir Receiving his Two Sons; Bala Kanda*

Rembrandt van Rijn

Netherlands, 1606–69

Dutch master known for his use of light and shadow. Key works: *The Anatomy Lesson of Dr. Nicolaes Tulp; The Night Watch*

Francisco de Goya

Spain, 1746–1828

Portrait artist also known for his depictions of war. Key works: *The Third of May; The Execution of the Defenders of Madrid*

Katsushika Hokusai

Japan, 1760–1849

Famous Japanese creator of woodblock prints. Key works: *The Great Wave off Kanagawa; Fine Wind Clear Morning*

Joseph Mallord William Turner

UK, 1775–1851

One of the most important landscape artists of the 19th century. Key works: *The Fighting Temeraire; The Slave Ship*

Claude Monet

France, 1840–1926

One of the founders of the Impressionist movement. Key works: *Impression, Sunrise; Haystacks* series; *Water Lilies* series

Ilya Repin

Ukraine, 1844–1930

Influenced by European techniques, but depicted Russian themes. Key work: *Barge Haulers on the Volga*

Mary Cassatt

US, 1844–1926

A leading figure in the Impressionist movement. Key works: *Little Girl in Blue Armchair; The Child's Bath*

"I found that I could **say things with color and shapes** that I couldn't say in any other way—things that I had no words for."

GEORGIA O'KEEFFE, Show catalog, 1926

SELF-PORTRAIT, VINCENT VAN GOGH

Vincent van Gogh

Netherlands, 1853–90

An influential and prolific painter, though received little recognition in his lifetime. Key works: *The Starry Night; Irises;* self-portraits

Wassily Kandinsky

Russia, 1866–1944

Pioneering abstract painter whose work is characterized by vibrant colors. Key works: *Composition VII; On White II*

Piet Mondrian

Netherlands, 1872–1944

Known for his distinctive use of color blocks and black lines. Key works: *Tableau I; Composition II in Red, Blue, and Yellow*

Pablo Picasso

Spain, 1881–1973

Prolific artist, noted for his role in creating Cubism. Key works: *Les Demoiselles d'Avignon; Guernica; Weeping Woman*

Georgia O'Keeffe

US, 1887–1986

Modernist who combined abstract and figurative elements. Key works: *Black Iris III; Cow's Skull: Red, White, and Blue*

Tamara de Lempicka

Poland, 1898–1980

Painted stylish figures in an Art Deco style. Key works: *Autoportrait (Self-Portrait in a Green Bugatti); Young Lady with Gloves*

Mark Rothko

Latvia/US, 1903–70

Used color to evoke emotional response. Key works: *White Center (Yellow, Pink and Lavender on Rose); Orange, Red, Yellow*

Willem de Kooning

Netherlands/US, 1904–97

A leading figure in Abstract Expressionism. Key works: *Excavation; Easter Monday; The Cat's Meow*

Frida Kahlo

Mexico, 1907–54

Best known for her vibrant self-portraits. Key works: *The Two Fridas; Self-Portrait with Thorn Necklace and Hummingbird*

Francis Bacon

Ireland/UK, 1909–92

Celebrated master of figurative painting. Key works: *Study After Velasquez's Portrait of Pope Innocent X; Head VI*

Jackson Pollock

US, 1912–56

Abstract Expressionist artist best known for his action painting. Key works: *Autumn Rhythm (Number 30); Blue Poles; Convergence*

M.F. Husain (Maqbool Fida Husain)

India, 1915–2011

Modern artist who used contemporary European styles for traditional Indian subject matter. Key work: *Frolicking Ganesh*

Andy Warhol

US, 1928–87

Key figure in the Pop Art movement of the 1950s and '60s. Key works: *Campbell's Soup Cans; Shot Marilyns; Dollar Sign*

Ibrahim el-Salahi

Sudan, b.1930

Artist who combines elements from Arabic, African, and Western painting styles. Key works: *Self-Portrait of Suffering; The Tree*

Bridget Riley

UK, b.1931

Known for her use of subtle variations in shapes and colors to create movement. Key works: *Movement in Squares; Current*

Paula Rego

Portugal/UK, b.1935

Best known for her stylized figures depicting scenes from stories or folklore. Key works: *The Firemen of Alijo; The Dance; War*

David Hockney

UK, b.1937

Inventive artist known for his use of color and perspective. Key works: *A Bigger Splash; Mr. and Mrs. Clark and Percy*

Anselm Kiefer

Germany, b.1945

Creates intensely personal work, often drawing on German history. Key works: *Operation Sea Lion; Interiors; Osiris and Isis*

Marlene Dumas

South Africa, b.1953

Her unsettling, sometimes distressing portraits are acclaimed. Key works: *The First People; The Painter; The Visitor*

Jean-Michel Basquiat

US, 1960–88

Painter and graffiti artist whose vibrant works often explored personal and social issues. Key works: *Untitled* (1982); *Riding with Death*

FRIDA KAHLO

Takashi Murakami

Japan, b.1962

Known for blending popular culture and high art in his work. Key works: *The Castle of Tin Tin; Blue Flowers & Skulls*

John Currin

US, b.1962

Blends the traditional and contemporary, often with hyperrealistic detail. Key works: *Honeymoon Nude; The Teenagers*

Zeng Fanzhi

China, b.1964

One of Asia's most successful living artists. Key works: *Tiananmen; Mask Series 1996 No.6; Van Gogh III*

Julie Mehretu

Ethiopia/US, b.1970

Known primarily for her large, layered abstract landscapes. Key works: *Stadia II; Mogamma, A Painting in Four Parts*

see also Sculpture through history pp.450–51 ▶ **449**

Sculpture through history

The progress of sculpture through the ages can be seen as both a creative expression and an ongoing science experiment in which artists push technological boundaries to create works of wonder. Portable figurines from prehistory may have had totemic significance, but with larger-scale works becoming possible, monumental sculptures were commissioned to symbolize political and religious dominance. In contrast, sculptures on a more human scale signify both the strength and frailty of humanity. In recent decades, public art on city streets and in rural landscapes has made sculpture an influential and life-affirming art form.

Figure is 12 in (31 cm) tall

38,000 BCE Found in a cave in Germany and gradually pieced together, the *Lion-Man of the Hohlenstein-Stadel*—half man, half beast—is the oldest known figurative sculpture.

Made from mammoth ivory

LION-MAN OF THE HOHLENSTEIN-STADEL

Angel wields a gold spear aimed at Teresa's heart

Sense of movement as angel lifts Teresa's robe

THE ECSTASY OF SAINT TERESA

Marble drapery appears to cascade

1501 Two years in the making, the statue of David is created by 26-year-old Michelangelo from a block of Carrara marble abandoned by his contemporaries in Italy.

DAVID IN MARBLE BY MICHELANGELO

Eyes focus on different points

Relaxed leg gives posture dynamism

c.1455 CE Italian Renaissance sculptor Donatello carves the figure of Mary Magdalene from white poplar wood. Commissioned by the Baptistery of Florence, the *Penitent Magdalene* astonishes people with its realism.

150–100 BCE The fine white marble for the *Venus de Milo* is quarried on the Greek island of Paros. Parts of the body are sculpted separately and joined with vertical pegs.

Nudity contrasts with drapery

VENUS DE MILO

1647–53 In Italy, Lorenzo Bernini is commissioned to produce an altarpiece for a prominent church in Rome. This Baroque marble sculpture depicts the vision of Spanish nun and mystic Teresa of Avila as she has a spiritual encounter with an angel.

1875–76 Because of its naturalism and capture of pure emotion, *The Age of Bronze* by French sculptor Auguste Rodin is regarded as the first sculpture of the modern era.

Clasped hand conveys intense emotion

Life-sized figure about 6 ft (1.8 m) tall

THE AGE OF BRONZE

1961 Swiss sculptor Alberto Giacometti's *The Walking Man* is interpreted as an emblem of Existentialism. The figure's anonymous features and sense of frailty hint at the apparent meaningless of life in the postwar era of the 20th century.

1939 African-American artist Augusta Savage's monumental *The Harp* is reported to be one of the most viewed works at the 1939 New York World's Fair.

AUGUSTA SAVAGE

Hammer and sickle represent workers and peasants

1937 This monumental work of art by Latvian-born Vera Mukhina is installed as a political statement atop the Soviet pavilion at the Paris Exposition, in France.

INDUSTRIAL WORKER AND COLLECTIVE FARM WORKER

Sculpture is unpainted

1967 The large scale of Alexander Calder's public art in Montréal, Canada, is a collaborative effort with metal workers in a French foundry. This work is said to symbolize "human progress and power."

TROIS DISQUES (THREE DISKS)

1977 The Henry Moore Foundation is established by the renowned British sculptor, to care for and exhibit his work. Moore's large-scale figures and organic forms represent a belief in the integrity of humanity.

HENRY MOORE

Shaped from clay, fired, and polished

Remains of uraeus, Egyptian cobra, which is a symbol of royalty

38,000–10,000 BCE Small statuettes of female figures are carved from mammoth tusk, antlers, bone, and stone across Europe and Asia. They are thought to have been portable fertility symbols or aphrodisiacs.

VENUS OF LESPUGUE

5000 BCE Regarded as a masterpiece of Neolithic art, the *Thinker of Cernavoda* sits in a meditative position. It was excavated from a funerary site in Romania along with a female statuette.

Figure seated on small chair

THINKER OF CERNAVODA

1345 BCE The famous life-sized bust of the ancient Egyptian queen Nefertiti is crafted in the workshop of the court artist Thutmose. The right eye is inlaid with quartz, while the other eye is left blank.

Carved from limestone

Limestone covered with stucco, which is painted

BUST OF NEFERTITI

210 BCE Buried with the first emperor of China, Qin Shi Huang, the Terracotta Army numbers 8,000 statues. Some 2,000 have been excavated, each with unique hair styling and facial features.

TERRACOTTA ARMY OF XIAN, SHAANXI PROVINCE

1200–1000 BCE Metallurgists of China's Bronze Age refine existing alloys to make large sculptures, including the dozens of masks uncovered from the ancient civilization of Sanxingdui.

Angular facial features

SANXINGDUI BRONZE MASK

1881 French artist Edgar Degas' *Little Dancer Aged Fourteen* is revolutionary, and considered shocking, for its realism. The wax statue includes a silk tutu, linen slippers, ribbon, and real hair.

Bronze cast from original wax

LITTLE DANCER AGED FOURTEEN

1886 France presents the US with a sculpture, which is now known as the Statue of Liberty. Sculptor Frédéric Auguste Bartholdi oversees the work of assembling hammered copper sheets over a steel framework.

STATUE OF LIBERTY

c.1907–16 Romanian-French artist Constantin Brancusi pioneers abstraction and foreshadows Cubism with his sculpture *The Kiss*, which explores the separation of private and public lives.

Bronze cast of sculpture created posthumously

Marching figure appears deformed by wind and speed

Bronze with silver nitrate patina

Ribbed bronze legs

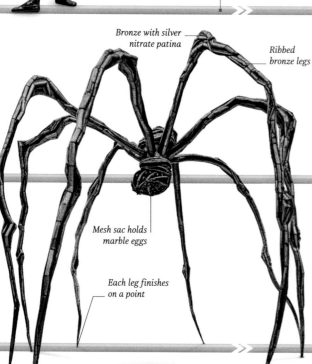

1917 An early example of conceptual art, American-French artist Marcel Duchamp's *The Fountain* challenges the idea of art objects as precious and unique by presenting an ordinary object, a urinal, as readymade art.

1913 Italian artist Umberto Boccioni's creation is a key work of the futurist movement, reflecting a new era of speed and industry, and expressing optimism about progress.

UNIQUE FORMS OF CONTINUITY IN SPACE

Curves to show constant motion

Mesh sac holds marble eggs

Each leg finishes on a point

1996 American-French artist Louise Bourgeois, the most celebrated female sculptor of the 20th century, creates the 30 ft- (9 m-) high spider sculpture *Maman* as a testimony to her mother's strength.

MAMAN

2006 Fusing architecture and art, British sculptor Anish Kapoor's *Cloud Gate* in Chicago is made from mirrored steel, reflecting the city and becoming an interactive public space.

ANISH KAPOOR

see also Sculpture techniques pp.452–53 ▶ **451**

Sculpture techniques

Although the processes of creating sculpture are varied, they have, in most cases, changed very little over time. Dating from the Stone Age, the earliest methods were carving and clay modeling. Casting metal has been in use since the Bronze Age, and only since the 20th century have new techniques such as constructing and assembling become accepted as fine art.

Young, bejeweled woman in confident pose

Mohenjo-daro bronze
Found at the ancient Indus Valley site of Mohenjo-daro in modern-day Pakistan, *Dancing Girl* (c.2500 BCE) is considered the oldest example of a bronze sculpture. It was cast using a lost-wax method.

Casting metal

Metal sculptures are formed by casting, a process in which the chosen metal—usually an alloy (see p.203) such as bronze—is melted at high heat and poured into a mold of the whole, or part of, the sculpture. The metal hardens as it cools and the mold is removed.

Bronze casting

Artisans in ancient civilizations from the Indus Valley River, China, and Egypt first mastered the technique of bronze casting, adjusting the mix of tin, copper, and lead to produce varying colors and degrees of hardness.

CASTING OTHER MATERIAL

Although bronze remains the most popular material for fine art casting, it is costly. Sculptors therefore have turned to less expensive alternatives, including plaster, resin, concrete, rubber, or fiberglass.

CRAFTSMEN POURING MOLTEN METAL

Sand casting

Models of the sculpture are set into compacted sand blocks, or shapes are carved directly into the moist sand, to create a mold. Then, molten bronze is poured in and left to cool before the sand is brushed away.

Lost-wax method

There are a few versions of this casting method. In one example, a plaster mold is lined with wax around a clay core. The wax is drained to leave a cavity; molten metal is poured into the cavity.

Plaster mold of original model

Mold cavity lined with wax and filled with clay

1 OUTER MOLD   **2** WAX ADDED

Mold baked and wax drained

Mold filled with molten metal

Bronze cast head

Feeders to be removed

3 IN THE OVEN   **4** METAL POURED   **5** SHELL REMOVED

Silicone mold into which plaster is poured

SILICONE MOLD

Fine detail replicated from silicone

Cavities from the mold are preserved

SCULPTURE

Modeling

An additive process, modeling requires the artist to build up malleable raw materials, using their hands and an array of small tools to add detail. The technique can be used to create finished sculptures, preliminary models, or molds for casting.

Stand connected to internal armature provides support

Colored wax gives skinlike finish

Clay
Polymer clay is often used for modeling because it is pliable until fired. Tools include needles, sponges, and loops.

Wax
Like clay, wax can be reworked during the modeling process, to fix mistakes or allow the artist to change direction.

Construction and assembling

Enabled by industrialization and a wider appreciation of what constitutes sculpture, artists in the modern age have turned to techniques such as welding, riveting, stitching, weaving, and gluing to fashion works in diverse materials from scrap metal to cardboard.

Welder uses both pressure and heat

Parts transported and assembled on site

Welding
Welding allows sculptors to work quickly and with an array of materials, including sheet metal and cast iron.

Weathering steel
British artist Antony Gormley employed 20 steelworkers to realize *The Angel of the North* using copper and weathered steel.

Studies suggest that **Classical Greek statues** were **brightly painted**

Carving

Unlike modeling, carving is a subtractive process, in which the artist begins with a solid mass of material and gradually reduces it to give shape to the emerging figure or object. A mason's axe is used to remove enough of the material to reveal a basic shape, followed by hammering and chiseling to impart detail. It may then be polished for a smooth finish.

The Kiss

Based on doomed lovers from Dante's *Inferno*, Auguste Rodin's statue became a symbol of romance.

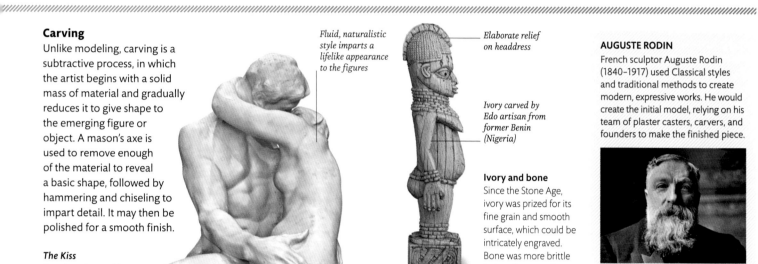

Fluid, naturalistic style imparts a lifelike appearance to the figures

Smooth bodies contrast with rough base

Elaborate relief on headdress

Ivory carved by Edo artisan from former Benin (Nigeria)

Ivory and bone

Since the Stone Age, ivory was prized for its fine grain and smooth surface, which could be intricately engraved. Bone was more brittle but easily sourced.

AUGUSTE RODIN

French sculptor Auguste Rodin (1840–1917) used Classical styles and traditional methods to create modern, expressive works. He would create the initial model, relying on his team of plaster casters, carvers, and founders to make the finished piece.

Chisel held at 45 degrees to stone

Stone carving

The modern stone sculptor's tools are virtually the same as they were in ancient times, with the majority of shaping done using a flat chisel.

Soft wood can be finely worked

Wood carving

After drawing an outline, the sculptor cuts the basic form with an axe before shaping with smaller tools to refine the details. The surface may then be sanded and treated.

Surface decoration

Historically, many finished sculpting surfaces were considered unrefined—rough sandstone, terracotta, or wood for example— so artists developed techniques for adding decoration. Demand for different aesthetic effects changed according to the tastes of the day.

Using mercury in gilding is illegal in many countries, because the process is highly toxic

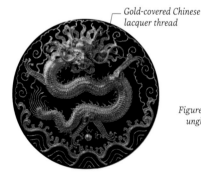

Relief work on base

Figures from Greek mythology

Gilding

Claude Galle's 1806 clock demonstrates lavish gilding (a thin layer of gold) applied to bronze using milled gold and mercury.

Gold-covered Chinese lacquer thread

Lacquers

Derived from tree sap, lacquer is applied thinly with as many as 30 or more coats. It can be inlaid, carved, or filled.

In Greek black-and-red figure technique, background is glazed

Figures are unglazed

Glazing

Used over terracotta or other ceramic forms, glazes can impart vibrant or subtle coloring in opaque or translucent finishes.

Shell inlaid into wood for the eyes in this Tlingit bear-shaped bowl

Inlay mimics teeth

Inlays

Sculptures of virtually any base material typically can be inlaid with glass, shell, quartz, precious metals, and wood.

see also Ceramics and glass pp.502–503 ▶

Elements of architecture

ARTS AND LEISURE

When architects design a new building, they have to make decisions about many different aspects of the project, from the materials that will be used to how the structure will fit into its surroundings. All elements of the project must combine to create a structure that works practically, is aesthetically suitable, and fits into the available time and budget.

The **Pantheon**, in Rome, has the **largest unreinforced concrete dome** in the world

Materials and techniques

The earliest builders used local materials such as wood, stone, and mud bricks. In ancient Rome, concrete was used to build complex structures such as vaults and domes, many of which still stand. Industrial materials such as steel, popularized in the early 20th century, made it possible to build huge bridges and skyscrapers.

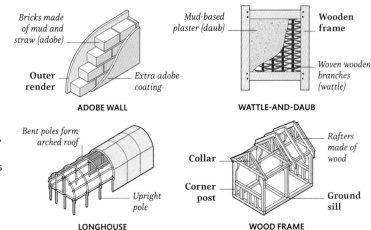

Bricks made of mud and straw (adobe)

Outer render

Extra adobe coating

ADOBE WALL

Mud-based plaster (daub)

Wooden frame

Woven wooden branches (wattle)

WATTLE-AND-DAUB

Bent poles form arched roof

Upright pole

LONGHOUSE

Collar

Corner post

Rafters made of wood

Ground sill

WOOD FRAME

Structure

Most buildings have either solid walls, which bear the weight of the structure, or less massive walls with a framework, like a skeleton, that bears the weight. With load-bearing walls, the taller the building, the thicker the walls have to be. With a framework, it is easier to build tall structures.

Steel, glass, and concrete

In many modern buildings, such as Seattle Central Library, the exterior is a skin made of steel and glass, and the weight is borne by a framework of steel posts and beams on a reinforced concrete base.

Seattle Central Library was **built using** more than **4,000 tons** (3,630 tonnes) of steel

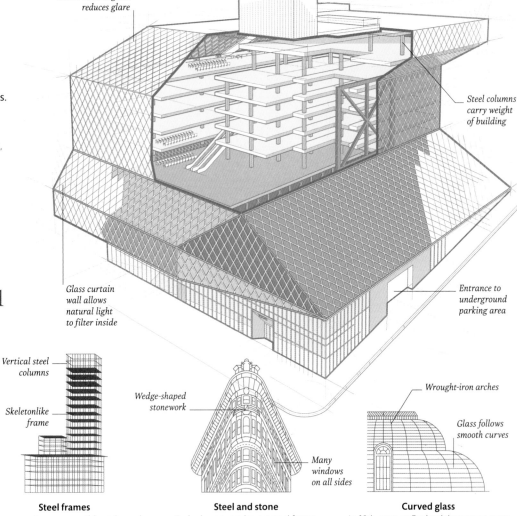

Metal mesh in glass reduces glare

Steel columns carry weight of building

Glass curtain wall allows natural light to filter inside

Entrance to underground parking area

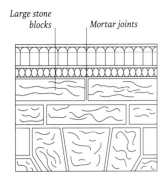

Large stone blocks

Mortar joints

Vertical steel columns

Skeletonlike frame

Wedge-shaped stonework

Many windows on all sides

Wrought-iron arches

Glass follows smooth curves

Stone walls
Many traditional buildings have stone walls. In order to bear the building's weight, these walls need to be substantial, so the size of the windows is limited.

Steel frames
Skyscrapers became possible at the end of the 19th century, when steel was good enough to make strong, rigid frameworks that could support many floors.

Steel and stone
Early skyscrapers have a steel frame, but are clad in stone, to give a decorative effect and to help the structure blend into its surroundings.

Curved glass
In 19th-century England there were great advances in glass making. This allowed for a new kind of structure where large panes of glass were inserted into iron frames.

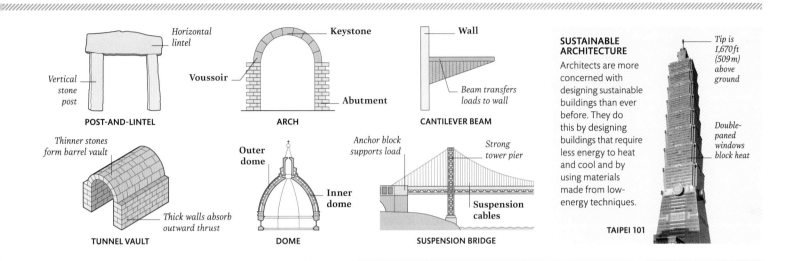

POST-AND-LINTEL
Horizontal lintel · *Vertical stone post*

ARCH
Keystone · *Voussoir* · Abutment

CANTILEVER BEAM
Wall · *Beam transfers loads to wall*

TUNNEL VAULT
Thinner stones form barrel vault · *Thick walls absorb outward thrust*

DOME
Outer dome · Inner dome

SUSPENSION BRIDGE
Anchor block supports load · *Strong tower pier* · **Suspension cables**

SUSTAINABLE ARCHITECTURE
Architects are more concerned with designing sustainable buildings than ever before. They do this by designing buildings that require less energy to heat and cool and by using materials made from low-energy techniques.

TAIPEI 101
Tip is 1,670 ft (509 m) above ground · *Double-paned windows block heat*

Plan
A building plan sets out what a building will look like and guides its construction. The way buildings are planned varies hugely, from rigidly symmetrical plans, such as a Palladian villa, to more informal layouts, where the position of each room is determined by its function or by the features of the building's site.

Symmetrical layout
In the Taj Mahal in Agra, India – which houses royal tombs of the Mughal Empire – order, balance, and solemnity are emphasized by a symmetrical building plan.

Asymmetrical layout
The Metropol Parasol in Seville, Spain, combines aerial walkways with a public plaza and market. Its asymmetrical design contrasts with the neat rows of old buildings that surround it.

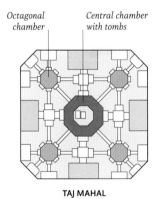

Octagonal chamber · *Central chamber with tombs*
TAJ MAHAL

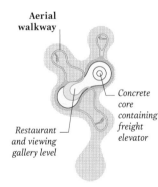

Aerial walkway · *Concrete core containing freight elevator* · *Restaurant and viewing gallery level*
METROPOL PARASOL

ORGANIC ARCHITECTURE
American architect Frank Lloyd Wright believed that architecture should be "organic." In 1935, he designed Fallingwater, a house that appears to be growing naturally out of its leafy surroundings. Inside, its rooms and spaces vary in size according to need.

FALLINGWATER

Use of interior space
An architect defines the character of a building's interior spaces by considering their use, their shape and size, their look, and how they are lit. Buildings designed to provoke awe or reverence, for example, such as churches, are often very tall.

Westminster Hall
Built for royal banquets and parliaments, this imposing medieval hall has a hammer-beam roof spanning a huge space without columns.

Amalienburg Pavilion
The main room of this Baroque hunting lodge is circular, richly decorated, and lined with mirrors to reflect the outside views.

Beauvais Cathedral
With the highest interior of any medieval cathedral, this interior reflects the aim of Gothic builders to make people look up to heaven.

Westminster Hall boasts the **largest** medieval wood roof in **northern Europe**

Structures in context
A building's context can range from a crowded city to custom-designed formal gardens, such as those at the palace of Versailles. Some buildings, such as skyscrapers, are designed to stand out, but still fit into a city block; others blend into their surroundings.

GARDENS OF VERSAILLES

Styles of architecture

In ancient times, local styles of architecture evolved in different parts of the world, whether it was Asia, Europe, Africa, or the Americas. When European countries began to colonize other parts of the world from the 16th century onward, they took the Classical, Baroque, and Gothic styles with them. From the 20th century on, as culture became increasingly globalized, architecture became even more international, with architects traveling worldwide and similar buildings appearing all over the globe.

c.2580 BCE In Egypt, the Great Pyramid of Giza is built to entomb Pharaoh Khufu. The 481 ft- (147 m-) tall pyramid is made of granite and limestone.

On the outside, 46 marble columns support horizontal friezes

Blocks, or acroteria, support roof ornaments above the triangular roof

438 BCE The Parthenon, built in Athens, Greece, in honor of the city's patron goddess, Athena, is completed. The temple exemplifies the Classical style, complete with fluted, baseless columns of the Doric order.

Two-tiered inner columns

Statue of Athena

CROSS SECTION OF THE PARTHENON

Outer terrace
Circular terraces with small, bell-shaped stupas
Large central stupa

c.842 The vast Buddhist stupa (shrine) of Borobudur, Java, Indonesia, is built as a series of nine stone terraces in the shape of a mandala— a sacred pattern, symbolic of the universe.

Tower leans due to unstable foundation

691 In Jerusalem, Israel, the Dome of the Rock, with its metal-clad wooden dome, is erected. The stone on which it stands is sacred to Muslims and Jews.

Five lower galleries with Buddhist sculptured reliefs

SITE PLAN OF BOROBUDUR

DOME OF THE ROCK

1010 With its pyramidal tower and tall gateways, the Brihadeshwara Temple in southern India exemplifies the Dravidian style of architecture. It is dedicated to the Hindu god Shiva.

Rounded dome tops the 13-story tower

Stone sculptures of Shiva adorn the temple's exterior

BRIHADESHWARA TEMPLE

1173 The Leaning Tower of Pisa, Italy, a round campanile (bell tower), is built in the round-arched Romanesque style, popular in Europe between the 10th and 12th centuries.

LEANING TOWER OF PISA

1182 With its stained-glass windows and carvings, the Notre-Dame Cathedral in Paris, France, is one of the best-known examples of the medieval Gothic style.

GROTESQUE CARVING

Extension added by way of 180 ft- (55 m-) high finial, or tip, to make it the tallest building in the city at the time

1930 The 1,047 ft- (319 m-) tall Chrysler Building in New York, designed by American architect William Van Alen in the Art Deco style, opens as the headquarters of the car manufacturer.

CHRYSLER BUILDING'S SPIRE

1929 Its open-plan layout and an innovative use of glass and concrete makes Villa Savoye in Paris, France, one of the best-known works of Swiss-French modernist architect Le Corbusier.

1894 London's Tower Bridge combines Gothic Revival architecture with modern engineering techniques to lift two sections of road to allow ships to travel along the Thames.

Gothic-style spires and turrets give a dramatic look

Lifting roadway powered by hydraulic mechanism

TOWER BRIDGE

Metal-clad spire designed with geometrical precision

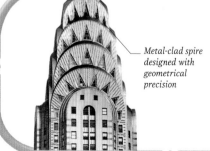

1973 Designed by Danish architect Jørn Utzon, the Sydney Opera House in Australia is world-famous for its distinctive concrete shell roofs.

SYDNEY OPERA HOUSE

1977 While designing the Centre Georges Pompidou in Paris, France, architects Richard Rogers and Renzo Piano place the utility pipes and escalators on the outside for an uncluttered interior.

1984 The modern AT&T Building in New York City is constructed with a Classical pediment on top—an example of humorous postmodern design by American architect Philip Johnson.

◀ see also The Renaissance pp.338–39   ◀ Elements of architecture pp.454–55   Details of architecture pp.458–59 ▶

c.30–15 BCE Roman engineer and architect Vitruvius writes *De architectura* (On architecture), a key work on the Classical style. It is the earliest surviving book on architecture.

c.128 CE In Rome, Italy, Emperor Hadrian rebuilds the Pantheon, a temple dedicated to all gods, which survives intact today.

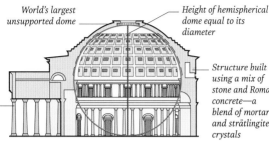

World's largest unsupported dome

Height of hemispherical dome equal to its diameter

Elaborate Corinthian columns line the entrance

Structure built using a mix of stone and Roman concrete—a blend of mortar and strätlingite crystals

CROSS SECTION OF THE PANTHEON

PYRAMID OF THE SUN

c.200 CE The five-tiered Pyramid of the Sun, one of the largest temples of the early Mesoamerican peoples, dominates the skyline of Teotihuacán in central Mexico.

607 The Horyu-ji temple complex is founded in Nara Prefecture, Japan. This wooden pagoda is supported on a large central post.

Pagoda is more than 105 ft (32 m) in height

Elegant, upward-curving roofs

FIVE-STORY PAGODA

537 CE The Hagia Sophia, a Byzantine church, is built in Constantinople, (present-day Istanbul, Turkey). Its interior is decorated with mosaics and marble.

Roofed with domes and semidomes

HAGIA SOPHIA

Statues and turrets adorn an ornate central facade

MAIN ENTRANCE OF CASA DE MATEUS

Three-tiered platform clad in marble

Throne hall

Upward-curved roof

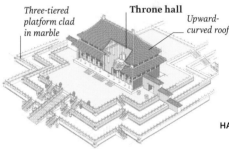

1420 In Beijing, China, the Forbidden City is built to house the imperial palace and other important religious and political buildings. Many of these buildings have wood frames.

HALL OF SUPREME HARMONY, FORBIDDEN CITY

COURTYARD OF PALAZZO RICCARDI

1444 Inspired by ancient Roman sources, Renaissance architects utilize round arches and Classical details, as at the Palazzo Riccardi in Florence, Italy.

1739 Italian architect Nicolau Nasoni designs Casa de Mateus, an elaborate Portuguese palace, in the Baroque style.

1889 The most famous landmark in Paris, the Eiffel Tower is constructed in wrought iron by French engineer Gustave Eiffel for the 1889 World Fair.

CONSTRUCTION OF THE EIFFEL TOWER

"Pompom" finials richly decorated with mosaics made with Venetian glass

1881 In Barcelona, Spain, the Sagrada Familia church is designed by Catalan architect Antoni Gaudí in his own adaptation of the Gothic style.

SAGRADA FAMILIA'S NATIVITY FACADE

1808 Lawyer and politician Thomas Jefferson introduces the Neoclassical style to the US, with the rebuilding of his house, Monticello, near Charlottesville, Virginia.

THOMAS JEFFERSON

1997 California-based architect Frank Gehry designs the Guggenheim Museum Bilbao, Spain, with curving and shimmering aluminum-clad walls outside and an innovative use of space within.

FRANK GEHRY

2009 At 2,716 ft (828 m) high, Dubai's Burj Khalifa in the United Arab Emirates becomes the world's tallest building. It is a mixed-use tower strengthened by a buttressed central core and Y-shaped plan.

2012 The Heydar Aliyev Centre in Baku, Azerbaijan, has a curvaceous and flowing design that is typical of the work of its Iraqi-British architect Zaha Hadid. It houses an auditorium, gallery, and museum.

HEYDAR ALIYEV CENTRE

Glass curtain wall

Roof covered in glass-fiber reinforced cladding

Details of architecture

Every building is made up of many different parts—from floors to walls to roofs. The way each part is designed affects not only how the building looks, but also how structurally sound it is and whether it is fit for its purpose. Architects have to consider all these details and put them together in a design that works as a whole.

The **stained glass** in the Cathedral of Brasília covers around **22,000 sq ft (2,000 sq m)**

Walls

By exploiting the texture of stonework or the different colors zof brickwork, architects can make walls attractive as well as simply strong. Another decorative technique is to use a cladding, such as brightly colored tiles, which are easy to keep clean as well as attractive to the eye.

Islamic colored tilework
Builders in the Islamic world often use colorful ceramic tiles, as on this building in Samarkand, Uzbekistan.

Renaissance rusticated stone
The masonry of Italian buildings like the Palazzo Medici-Riccardi, Florence, has exaggerated joints between the blocks.

Polychrome brick
Multicolored bricks (made using different clays or firing times) make patterns, as here on the Doge's Palace, Venice.

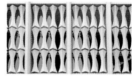
Brise soleil
This concrete structure on Vietnam's Reunification Palace is not load-bearing, but shades the interior from the sun.

Roofs, domes, and spires

A roof shelters the building from the weather, but can also have other functions—such as housing extra rooms, or creating a striking visual feature. Domes and spires make buildings such as mosques, churches, or town halls easy to find or even turn them into landmarks.

Roofs

Sloping roofs shed rain or snow readily and accommodate attic space for storage or an extra room. Flat roofs may provide space for a garden or a terrace.

Spires

Spires built of stone or wood began as a simple way of roofing square church towers. In the medieval period they developed into highly decorative, eight-sided structures that seemed to point toward heaven. Some spires almost double the height of the tower, producing a striking and graceful landmark.

Domes

Domes are often round and shaped like half a sphere, but may also be polyhedral, with a roof in several segments. Onion domes are common in Russia.

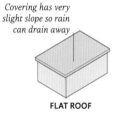
Covering has very slight slope so rain can drain away
FLAT ROOF

Pitch steeper in regions where it snows regularly
Vertical gable end
GABLE ROOF

Roof slopes on all four sides
HIPPED ROOF

Steeply sloping edges allow large attic rooms
MANSARD ROOF

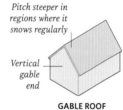
Double-curved onion shape
ONION DOME

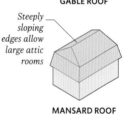
Dome stands on low cylinder called a "drum"
HEMISPHERICAL DOME

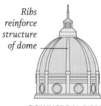
Ribs reinforce structure of dome
POLYHEDRAL DOME

Spire stands within low parapet
Parapet hides base of spire from view
NEEDLE SPIRE

Spire base comes up to top of tower wall
Broach helps support corner
BROACH SPIRE

Pinnacles adorn corners of tower
Pinnacles help direct thrust down toward ground
SPIRE WITH PINNACLES

Flying buttresses strengthen spire
BUTTRESSED SPIRE

Vaults

A vault is a way of building a ceiling using brick or stone. Between the 8th and 11th centuries, masons developed techniques for building vaults with elaborate networks of ribs, as a way of supporting the heavy stonework and counteracting the outward thrust that can otherwise make a vault weak.

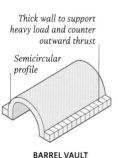
Thick wall to support heavy load and counter outward thrust
Semicircular profile
BARREL VAULT

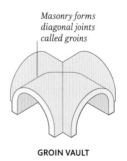
Masonry forms diagonal joints called groins
GROIN VAULT

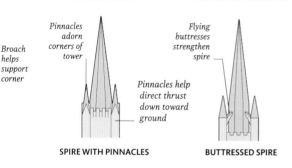
Longitudinal rib
Transverse rib
Pointed arch
Masonry ribs support joints between arches
RIB VAULT

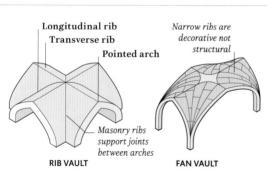
Narrow ribs are decorative not structural
FAN VAULT

"As an architect, you **design for the present**, with an **awareness of the past**, for a **future** which is **essentially unknown.**"

NORMAN FOSTER, *TED Talk*, 2007

Arches

An arch is a curve that directs the load around an opening in a wall. Arches are made up of wedge-shaped blocks called voussoirs that balance one another so that the structure can support weight.

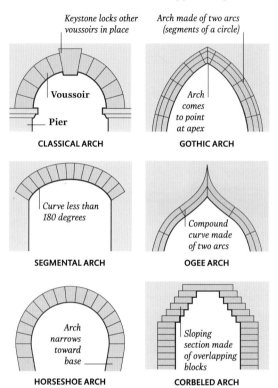

Keystone locks other voussoirs in place

Voussoir

Pier

CLASSICAL ARCH

Arch made of two arcs (segments of a circle)

Arch comes to point at apex

GOTHIC ARCH

Curve less than 180 degrees

SEGMENTAL ARCH

Compound curve made of two arcs

OGEE ARCH

Arch narrows toward base

HORSESHOE ARCH

Sloping section made of overlapping blocks

CORBELED ARCH

Columns

Many buildings are held up by columns, which can support arches or horizontal lintels. Although in some buildings the columns are hidden in the structure, they can be decorative and built of different materials, from stone to concrete.

Simple capital of Doric column

Classical
The ancient Greeks developed three styles (or orders) of columns, including Doric, each used to support a flat stone lintel.

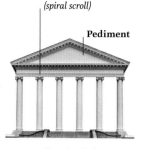

Semicircular arch

Decorative capital

Romanesque
Romanesque columns were sometimes highly decorative and topped with ornate carved capitals.

Capital of Ionic column has volute (spiral scroll)

Pediment

Neoclassical
In the 18th century, Classical columns became fashionable once more, as seen here in the Virginia State Capitol building.

Concrete columns join to form "crown"

Modernist
Columns in the 20th century ranged from plain cylinders to the highly sculptural supports of the Cathedral of Brasília.

CARYATIDS
The ancient Greeks created a kind of column called a caryatid, which took the form of a standing, draped female figure. These examples support part of the Erechtheion temple, which is part of the Acropolis in Athens. When Classical architecture was revived in the 18th and 19th centuries, some architects began to design buildings with caryatids once again.

ERECHTHEION TEMPLE

Windows

Window design has changed radically over time, as architects and builders have explored different materials, shapes, and structures. Gothic masons favored pointed windows, but rectangular windows are most common today.

Rose window
Medieval masons built intricate, circular rose windows, as in the Sainte-Chapelle, Paris.

Skyscraper window
Skyscrapers like Chicago's Reliance Building have a framework of uprights and horizontals.

Art Nouveau
Curvaceous forms are preferred by some architects, as shown on Gaudí's Casa Batlló, Barcelona.

Contemporary
Berlin's Jewish Museum has an outer "skin" of glass, which means its windows can be any shape.

TRACERY

The ornamental intersecting stonework in the upper part of a window is called tracery. The tracery of Gothic windows in Europe became more and more intricate between the plate tracery of the 13th century and curvilinear tracery of the 14th century.

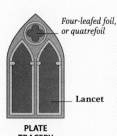

Four-leafed foil, or quatrefoil

Lancet

PLATE TRACERY

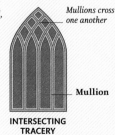

Mullions cross one another

Mullion

INTERSECTING TRACERY

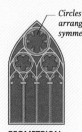

Circles arranged symmetrically

GEOMETRICAL TRACERY

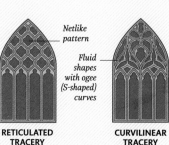

Netlike pattern

Fluid shapes with ogee (S-shaped) curves

RETICULATED TRACERY

CURVILINEAR TRACERY

◀ see also Styles of architecture pp.456–57

Fashion through history

Fashion and style have existed for as long as humanity itself. In ancient civilizations, clothing functioned primarily as a marker of rank and wealth, and styles took hundreds of years to develop. Later, changes in fashions were due to new technologies (spinning, or zips, for example) or shifts in political influence, such as the French Revolution, which made extravagant fashion outmoded, or the Roaring Twenties, when women gained more financial freedom, and with it, sartorial freedom. Many individuals have left an indelible mark on the history of fashion, from dandy Beau Brummell to punk pioneer Vivienne Westwood.

5000–3000 BCE China masters sericulture—the process of cultivating silk by farming mulberry worms. Raw silk thread is unwound from the cocoon of the worm, twisted to make yarn, and woven into cloth. The technique is a closely guarded secret, punishable by death.

Traditional hairpiece

1603–1868 Men and women of all classes adopt the kimono during Japan's Edo period. Kimonos bear motifs symbolizing the character of the wearer and reflecting changes in the seasons.

JAPANESE KIMONO

Landscape scene woven into fabric

Doublet front under scoop-neck jerkin

Collar and revers turned back

1500–1600 Catherine de Medici of Florence and Elizabeth I of England set a trend for extravagant court fashion. Styles, however, are strictly regimented by class.

RENAISSANCE SPLENDOR

1450–1624 During the Ottoman Empire, an Islamic political regime covering much of southeastern Europe, clothing is simple in cut but uses elaborate textiles.

Bright colors

OTTOMAN PERIOD WATERCOLOR

1625–1789 Ornate Baroque clothing gives way to the lightness and frivolity of Rococo, epitomized by Marie Antoinette at the court of Versailles.

ROCOCO FASHION

17th century Batik designs, originating in Java, an Indonesian island, come to West Africa through trade. They become an enduring fashion staple in the region.

CONTEMPORARY BATIK PRINT

1930s Retailers, exploiting the popularity of the film industry in Hollywood, sell copies of star-inspired costumes, hair, and makeup products.

FRED ASTAIRE AND GINGER ROGERS

Teeth

Slider

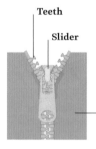

1930s Although invented in the late 1800s, the zipper becomes widely used in the 1930s. Sales assistants are trained to demonstrate the device to fashion shoppers.

Halves of fabric joined together

ZIPPER

1938 Nylon is invented, revolutionizing fashion with clothing that is easy to launder, does not crease, and is cheap enough to be replaced after one season.

NYLON STOCKING ADVERTISEMENT

Strips push together

Tiny loops

Hooks catch loops

TOUCH FASTENER

1955 Swiss engineer Georges de Mestral invents the first touch fastener, with two nylon strips that stick together. Later his invention becomes widely known as velcro.

c.1960s A traditional tunic from West Africa, the dashiki is adopted by racial equality supporters in the US to celebrate African-American heritage.

Bright cotton patterns

DASHIKI GARMENT

 ◀ see also Ancient Egypt pp.310–11 ◀ The Renaissance pp.338–39 ◀ Political revolutions pp.352–53

In Victorian England, women used **arsenic-based** beauty products to **lighten** their skin tone

2800 BCE The sari, a drape from the Indian subcontinent, begins to evolve. An early precursor is seen here on a figurine from Mohenjo-daro in present-day Pakistan.

Stonework depicts one-shoulder shawl
"PRIEST KING" STATUE

1330 BCE In ancient Egypt, cosmetic fashions are widespread, including antibacterial kohl (to prevent eye infection), eye shadow, lip balm, rouge, henna nail polish, and hair dye.

BUST OF NEFERTITI

750–30 BCE A rectangle of linen or wool cloth, the unisex chiton is draped around the body, belted, and pinned at the shoulders.

ANCIENT GREEK CHITON

600–476 BCE Imperial expansion brings design influences from all over Eurasia to the Byzantine capital, Constantinople, a global fashion center.

BYZANTINE EMPIRE CLOTHING

Yarn pulled by hand — **Drive wheel**

SPINNING WHEEL

13th century The spinning wheel, originally invented in the Middle East or China, is popularized in Italy, advancing cloth and carpet production in Europe.

600 CE–1449 Men in Europe wear a fitted jacket (doublet) with a pair of leggings (hose) attached to the hem of the doublet to keep them up.

206 BCE–220 CE During the Han dynasty, silk production becomes more refined, and wealthy women wear decorative silk robes wrapped and sashed at the waist.

Colored clay
CHINESE FIGURINE

509 BCE–476 CE The toga becomes a mark of citizenship in ancient Rome, and its color, fabric, and decoration are an indicator of the wearer's status, rank, and gender.

Toga
ROMAN STATUE

1770s–1830s During England's Regency period, self-styled dandy Beau Brummell sets new trends for the refined urban male in tailoring that emphasizes the male physique.

High-tied cravat
BEAU BRUMMELL

1790s–1820s In post-revolutionary France, fashion becomes simple and less extravagant, reflecting emerging ideals of democracy and equality.

Close-fitting stockings
REVOLUTION-ERA DUELIST

1870–90 As the emancipation movement grows, women adopt traditionally masculine garments that allow for more freedom to move while playing sports.

Riding habit
EMPRESS ELISABETH OF AUSTRIA

Tailored jacket

1920s As more women enter the workforce with the rise of equal rights campaigns, fashion rejects overtly feminine styles in favor of straight lines and boyish attire.

Crepe-de-chine trouser suit
ANDROGYNOUS CLOTHING

The Singer Automatic — LATEST AND BEST — THE SINGER MANUFACTURING CO.

1889 The first mass-produced electric sewing machine is launched by Singer. Within a year the company was selling 80 percent of the world's sewing machines.

Gold engraving
SEWING MACHINE ADVERTISEMENT

1873 Levi Strauss and Jacob Davis obtain a patent for the process of putting rivets into men's work trousers, creating blue jeans.

Low-heeled boots

1977 Rejecting the hippie aesthetic, Vivienne Westwood and her partner Malcolm McLaren draw on history, punk music, and youth counter-culture to create subversive fashion.

MALCOLM McLAREN AND VIVIENNE WESTWOOD

1980s–90s Women's clothing adapts the fashion language of businessmen in a new form of empowered attire known as "power dressing."

Cinch belt

Shoulder pads

White slacks

1980s FASHION

2000s Awareness of environmental problems compels some designers to use eco-friendly recycled fabrics and take an ethical approach, rejecting real fur and cheap labor.

Ethically sourced fabric

THE ETHICAL FASHION INITIATIVE

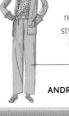

The history of writing

A writing system is a mark of human ingenuity. A recognizable, consistent script allows merchants to keep a tally of trade, historians to document events, and scholars to share knowledge widely. It enables people to exchange the complicated ideas of political and religious movements. Early writing systems seem to have emerged independently in various parts of Africa, Asia, and the Americas. The first systems tended to be based on visual representations of things, but over time, they began to represent language sounds too.

Pictograms and cuneiform

Date	c.3400 BCE–c.100 CE
Location	Mesopotamia

The earliest-known writing systems developed in Mesopotamia (present-day Iraq), and were based on pictograms, a system of stylized images that represented people or physical objects. Over time, these pictograms were simplified, and developed into abstract symbols and glyphs (simplified pictures), which could easily be written into wet clay tablets using a reed stylus. This new technique, known today as cuneiform, was initially used to record numerical information, such as sales or receipts, on clay tablets, and for the first few hundred years of its existence was used primarily for accounting. By 2800 BCE, cuneiform was incorporating symbols to represent the sound of specific syllables, which allowed scripts to express more complicated ideas. The earliest-known examples of literature (The Kesh Temple Hymn and a text giving advice on a virtuous life) date from about 200–300 years later.

This tablet discusses the distribution of grain

MESOPOTAMIAN PICTOGRAMS

Egyptian hieroglyphs

Date	c.3200 BCE–c.400 CE
Location	Egypt

In ancient Egypt, hieroglyphs ("sacred carvings") were used primarily on monuments and tombs, as well as in religious texts and formal documents. Hieroglyphic script consisted of a system of logograms (depicting words or ideas), symbols that represented individual syllables, and alphabetlike characters that represented consonants. The earliest examples date from about 3200 BCE, and at its height, hieroglyphic script comprised more than 1,000 characters. A simplified version of hieroglyphic script, known as hieratic, was adapted for writing with ink on papyrus. This simplified version may have provided some of the symbols that would be later used in the first alphabets.

> "The **princely** lord, the **princely** lord came forth from the **house**."
>
> THE OPENING LINES TO A SUMERIAN HYMN,
> *The Kesh Temple Hymn, c.2600–2500 BCE*

The first use of alphabets

Date	c.1800–c.1050 BCE
Location	Egypt

The first known alphabet, dating from about 1800 BCE, developed in Egypt. Known as Proto-Sinaitic because the best-known inscriptions were found in Sinai, it was derived from Egyptian hieroglyphics and may have been developed by workers who spoke a Semitic language. The Proto-Sinaitic alphabet was an "abjad," a writing system consisting of only consonants. Each consonant in the language was represented by a single character, so the number of characters used could be reduced to fewer than 30. The Proto-Sinaitic alphabet developed into the Phoenician alphabet—the ancestor of the Greek alphabet—and Aramaic, which developed into Old Hebrew and eventually the Arabic script.

Chinese characters

Date	c.1200 BCE – today
Location	China

According to a legend, Chinese characters were invented by Cangjie, a four-eyed historian who worked for the Yellow Emperor. The earliest historical evidence of writing in China dates to about 1200 BCE; archaeologists have identified more than 4,500 different symbols carved into animal bones that were probably used for ritual purposes. Modern Chinese characters have their roots in the system developed during the Han dynasty (206 BCE–220 CE). Chinese is a logographic script, in which each character represents a unit of language with a meaning, as well as a spoken sound. Elements of Chinese script were assimilated by Japan and Korea as the basis for their own written languages.

The Greek alphabet

Date	c.800 BCE – today
Location	Ancient Greece

The ancient Greeks took their alphabet from the Phoenicians, who traded alongside the Greeks throughout the Mediterranean region. In the Phoenician alphabet, each letter represented a single consonant, with no special characters to represent vowel sounds. The Greeks modified the alphabet, adapting some characters and adding new ones to represent vowels. Unlike the Phoenicians, the Greeks began to write from left to right. The resulting Greek alphabet had been standardized by 400 BCE, and a version of it remains in use in Greece and Cyprus today. It would form the basis of the Etruscan alphabet, which later developed into the Roman alphabet.

CANGJIE

The Latin alphabet

Date	c.700 BCE – today
Location	Italy

Between the 8th and 4th centuries BCE, the Etruscans, in central Italy, developed their own writing system by adapting the Greek alphabet. When the Romans conquered the Etruscans, they adopted the local alphabet for their own spoken language, Latin. As the Romans expanded, first through Italy and later into the rest of the Mediterranean world and much of Europe, the Roman, or Latin, alphabet went with them. After the fall of the Western Roman Empire in the 5th century, the Latin writing system continued to be used in much of Europe. Over time, it was adopted by non-Latin speakers, and new letters and sounds were added to the alphabet. Today, more than 2 billion people use a version of the Latin alphabet, making it the most popular in the world.

Writing innovation

The most significant changes in writing happened when there was a shift from systems that used images to represent words to systems that represented sounds. Many language systems spread with the expansion of empires.

4000 BCE

1450 BCE *Linear B, the first writing system based purely on syllable sounds, is used in Greece for the Mycenaean language*

1991 *Unicode is introduced for encoding the majority of the world's writing systems for computer use*

2000

*c.***2200 BCE** *Use of the Sumerian phonetic script spreads as the Akkadian Empire expands*

*c.***300 BCE** *The Mayan writing system develops in Central America, based on a system of symbols representing words or sounds*

*c.***400 CE** *The Arabic script is first used. Its use spreads with the expansion of Islam*

 ◀ **see also The first civilizations** pp.304–305   ◀ **The ancient world** pp.306–307   ◀ **Ancient China** pp.308–309

The winged sun is a symbol of divinity and power

The Ba bird symbolizes the dead person's soul

▲ Egyptian stele with hieroglyphs
This painted wooden stele (commemorative tablet) dates from the 3rd century BCE. It records the death of an Egyptian priest, and includes prayers asking for him to be granted a happy afterlife.

The hieroglyphic text includes the name and titles of the dead person, as well as funerary prayers

> "Reading maketh a **full** man, conference a **ready** man, and writing an **exact** man."
>
> FRANCIS BACON,
> "Of Studies" In *Essays*, 1625

Indian scripts

Date	268 BCE – today
Location	India

Most of the scripts of south and southeastern Asia are descended from the Brahmi script of ancient India. It was first recorded as being used in the Mauryan Empire in the 3rd century BCE, during the reign of the Emperor Ashoka, who used it to record his edicts. By the 2nd century BCE, Brahmi had evolved into several other scripts, notably Gupta, which developed into Nagari (used to write Sanskrit), which in turn evolved into Devanagari. Consisting of 48 characters, including 34 consonants and 14 vowels, Devanagari has remained largely unchanged since the 9th century. Today, this script is used to write more than 100 modern languages, including Hindi, Nepali, Rajasthani, Marathi, and Sindhi.

BRAILLE
Devised by Louis Braille (1809–52) as a code to enable the visually impaired to read by fingertip touch, braille is an arrangement of raised dots that can be used to write any language. It is based on the code invented in 1808 by French army officer Charles Barbier so that soldiers could communicate at night without lamps. Braille simplified Barbier's code, and released his own perfected system in 1829.

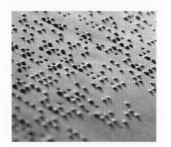

◀ see also Ancient Egypt pp.310–11   ◀ Ancient Greece pp.312–13   ◀ Ancient Rome pp.314–15   Writing Systems pp.464–67 ▶

Writing systems

The earliest writing systems emerged in ancient Egypt and Sumer around 3400–3100 BCE, and grew out of the need for documenting financial exchanges. As local and long-distance trade routes expanded, buyers and sellers realized the importance of noting what kinds of objects, and how many, were being transacted. Writing systems then evolved from crude numerical inscriptions to suit a variety of applications, from making laws to penning literary works.

PICTOGRAPHS

The earliest writing was made of pictographs developed by the Sumerians around 3400 BCE. Used to record commercial transactions, they were traced with a stylus on a clay tablet, with symbols denoting the types of goods, their number, and the names of buyers or sellers.

Inscribed with accounting entries

MESOPOTAMIAN ADMINISTRATIVE TABLET

Cuneiform

Pictographs evolved in Mesopotamia (present-day Iraq) into cuneiform. Instead of scratching shapes, scribes impressed a reed stylus with a triangular end into soft clay, making symbols of wedge-shaped marks. The cuneiform technique was used in many systems to write several languages over the next 3,000 years.

Impressed wedges

SUMERIAN TABLET

Symbol denotes quantity of beer sold

BABYLONIAN TABLET

Wedge-shaped markings

Etched in Sumerian and Akkadian

MESOPOTAMIAN TABLET

Symbols record exchange of goods

HITTITE TABLET

15th century BCE incisions in clay

HURRIAN TABLET

Kings listed by era

ASSYRIAN TABLET

Hieroglyphs

Hieroglyphs are ancient Egyptian symbols. Some, which represent sounds, are known as phonograms. Others, which symbolize concepts, are known as logograms (see below).

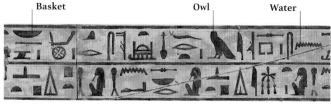
Basket   Owl   Water

EGYPTIAN COFFIN PANEL

HAND

SNAKE

OWL

BASKET

EYE OF HORUS

WICK

WATER

REED HUT

POT STAND

CROWN

Hieroglyphic script

Cartouche bears name of King Ptolemy

Greek scripts

Linear B, an early Greek script from c.1450 BCE, was derived from Linear A, an undeciphered script thought to be Minoan. These writing systems predate the arrival of the alphabet by centuries.

Unknown language

LINEAR A TABLET

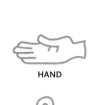

Mycenaean Greek letters

LINEAR B TABLET

Demotic script

Greek alphabetic script

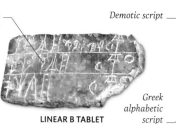

Rosetta stone

The Rosetta stone (196 BCE) is a royal decree bearing the same message in three different scripts—a feature that allowed French scholar Jean-François Champollion to first decode hieroglyphs in 1822.

Alphabets

Alphabets are sets of characters which represent the phonetics of spoken language. Originating in Semitic languages in the ancient Near East, most alphabets fall into two categories. An abjad—such as Phoenician and Arabic—is a type of alphabet that only features consonants, and where vowels are either implied by context or added as diacriticals. In the other type, known as a "true" alphabet, vowels have their own symbols.

EARLIEST ALPHABET

The oldest known alphabet emerged in Egypt around 1900–1700 BCE. It is sometimes called Proto-Sinaitic because it was first found in the Sinai Peninsula. Its 30 or so characters are thought to have been adapted from Egyptian phonetic symbols to match the sounds of a Semitic language.

Water symbol derived from hieroglyphs

FIRST ALPHABET

Phoenician

The Phoenician alphabet was made up of 22 consonants, written left to right. Its figurative forms echo Egyptian hieroglyphs, from which the letters are thought to have evolved.

| ALEPH | BETH | GIMEL | DALETH | HE | WAW |

Greek

The first alphabet to feature distinct letters for both vowels and consonants, Greek shares the same letter order as Phoenician, only expanded to include four new vowel sounds.

| ALPHA | BETA | GAMMA | DELTA | EPSILON | ZETA |

Etruscan

Trade spread the Greek alphabet westward to the Etruscans, who added some letters and changed others—"C" replaced "gamma," for example.

| A | B | C | D | E | F |

Roman

Further changes were made by the Romans: "Z" was dropped and later added back in at the end of the alphabet to avoid interrupting the established letter order.

| A | B | C | D | E | F |

Runic

Also called futhark (from the phonetics of its first six letters), runic was the alphabet of northern European Germanic tribes. Each rune is phonetic but also has a symbolic meaning.

| FEHU | URUZ | THURISAZ | ANSUZ | RAITHO | KAUNAZ |

Arabic

Written right to left and always in cursive, Arabic has 28 characters, 22 of which are descended from the Semitic alphabet. Apart from "alif," the letters are all consonants.

| ALIF | BA | TA | THA | GIM | HA |

Cyrillic

Based on Greek letters, this script grew in Slavic regions of the first Bulgarian empire in the 9th–10th century CE as a result of Christian missionary work. In its modern form it is used to write Russian and other slavic languages.

| AZŬ | BUKY | VĚDĚ | GLAGOLI | DOBRO | ESTŬ |

◄ see also The history of writing pp.462-63 **465**

›› Writing systems continued

Logographic and related scripts

Distinct from alphabetic script, in which each symbol represents a spoken sound, logographic scripts, such as Chinese, use each symbol to represent a morpheme—the smallest language component to have meaning, such as a word or an idea. This requires many more symbols than are needed in an alphabet. No writing system, however, is entirely logographic, as all scripts include a phonetic component.

ORACLE BONES

The earliest example of Chinese logograms are found carved into oracle bones, which date back to c.1200–1050 BCE. Around 5,000 characters have been identified. These pieces of animal bone or tortoise shell were used in ancient divination ceremonies.

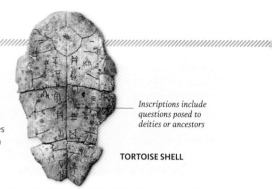

Inscriptions include questions posed to deities or ancestors

TORTOISE SHELL

Chinese characters

There are more than 8,000 individual Chinese logograms. They evolved from denoting simple units of language to indicate phonetics in some cases.

美	清	英	命	花
BEAUTY	**CLARITY**	**ELITE**	**DESTINY**	**FLOWER**

Japanese script

Adapting Chinese writing, Japan added 46 *hiragana* characters for Japanese sounds and 48 *katakana* characters for foreign-language sounds.

あ	か	さ	ア	カ
A Hiragana	**KA** Hiragana	**SA** Hiragana	**A** Katakana	**KA** Katakana

Korean script

Hangul has 24 characters written in blocks of two or three: 14 consonants and ten vowels. It replaced Chinese logograms in Korea in the 15th century.

P Hangul consonant

H Hangul consonant

YA Hangul vowel

Vertical line represents upright human

AW Hangul vowel

Horizontal line represents Earth (Yin)

YOO Hangul vowel

Olmec and Zapotec

These early Mesoamerican systems were similar in appearance to hieroglyphs. They were also written in vertical columns from top to bottom.

LORD/FLOWER Olmec

Coiled snake shape

SERPENT Olmec

ALLIGATOR Olmec

LORD/FLOWER Zapotec

Face visible in glyph

SERPENT Zapotec

Mayan writing

The Mayan script is the only Mesoamerican writing system to have been substantially deciphered. It consists of about 800 pictorial signs which use real life animals, people, or objects to signify ideas and sounds.

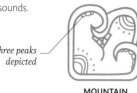

Fangs

SNAKE

WOMAN

Seeds scattered by hand

TO SCATTER

Three peaks depicted

MOUNTAIN

Flickering flames

FIRE

Flower petal

SUN

Surface inscribed with glyphs

Plaque made of jade

5TH CENTURY CE MAYAN PLAQUE

Flames depicted

In **Chinese writing**, a maximum of 64 strokes can be required to write a **single character**

Syllabic scripts

A syllabic script is a writing system in which each syllable is represented by a different symbol. For this reason, many syllabic scripts, such as native American Cherokee, require fewer characters than logographic scripts. In Indian scripts (see below), which are derived from Brahmi, the vowel symbol is secondary to the consonant symbol. This type of script is known as an abugida or an alphasyllabic script.

INDUS SCRIPT

The oldest writing on the Indian subcontinent is from the Bronze Age Indus Valley civilization (in modern-day Pakistan and India). Inscribed on clay seals and other objects, some 400 picture signs have been identified. The script they belong to, however, remains undeciphered.

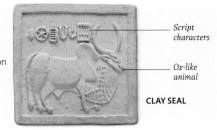

Script characters

Ox-like animal

CLAY SEAL

Brahmi

Written left to right, this script dates to the 8th century BCE. It is most likely a descendant of one or more Semitic writing systems.

A	Ā	BA	BHA	GA	GHA	DA

DHA	DA	DHA	HA	VA	U	Ū

Devanagari

In Devanagari, consonants are divided according to what part of the palate is used to pronounce them, and the action of the tongue for each.

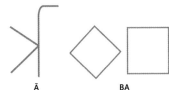

KA	KHA	GA	GHA

  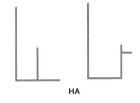  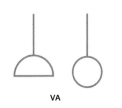 

NA	CA	CHA	JA	JHA

BHAGAVATA PURANA TEXT IN DEVANAGARI

Khmer

Also derived from Brahmi, Khmer has 33 consonants and a large inventory of vowels—24 diacritics (symbols that imply vowel sounds) and 14 independent vowels.

KA	KHA	KO	KHO

NGO	CA	CO	CHA	CHO

PREAH KO TEMPLE

Early examples of Khmer inscriptions can be found in Preah Ko ("The Sacred Bull"), a Khmer temple erected in 879 CE. It was built in Hariharalaya, then the capital of the Khmer Empire, in modern-day Cambodia.

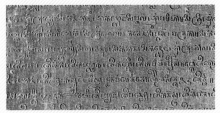

KHMER INSCRIPTIONS

◀ see also The history of writing pp.462-63   ◀ Writing systems pp.464-65   **467**

Team ball sports

Originating in Asia, Europe, and the Americas, team ball sports developed out of centuries-old games played with roughly spherical balls made of natural materials. They are watched by millions of people every week. The most popular is soccer, which is played on every continent in the world. Its biggest tournament, the World Cup, is one of the world's most eagerly anticipated sporting events.

HANDBALL
Circumference: 23½ in (59 cm)
Diameter: 7½ in (18.8 cm)

VOLLEYBALL
Circumference: 26 in (66 cm)
Diameter: 8¼ in (21 cm)

BEACH VOLLEYBALL
Circumference: 26½ in (67 cm)
Diameter: 8½ in (21.3 cm)

NETBALL
Circumference: 27¼ in (69 cm)
Diameter: 8¾ in (22 cm)

SOCCER BALL
Circumference: 27¼ in (69 cm)
Diameter: 8¾ in (22 cm)

BASKETBALL
Circumference: 29½ in (75 cm)
Diameter: 9½ in (24.2 cm)

Soccer

An 11-a-side soccer match is played over two 45-minute halves. Each team has a 24 ft (7.32 m) wide goal guarded by their goalkeeper (the only player allowed to touch the ball with hands). Players score goals by kicking or heading the ball across the other team's goal line. Then the conceding side restarts the game from the halfway line.

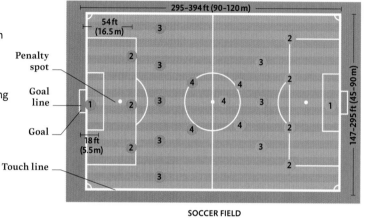

295–394 ft (90–120 m)
54 ft (16.5 m)
Penalty spot
Goal line
Goal
18 ft (5.5 m)
Touch line
147–295 ft (45–90 m)

SOCCER FIELD

KEY
1 Goalkeepers
2 Defenders
3 Midfielders
4 Forwards

3-5-2 formation
4-3-2-1 formation

FORMATIONS

Players line up in banks of defenders, midfielders, and attackers known collectively as formations. Some formations emphasize attack, and others, defense.

Attack

Teams attack by moving the ball into open space and toward their opponent's penalty area so they can score a goal via a shot or a header.

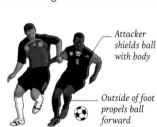

Attacker shields ball with body
Outside of foot propels ball forward

Dribbling

Quick feet and good balance allow players to maneuver the ball past opposing team members and through tight spaces.

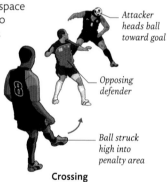

Attacker heads ball toward goal
Opposing defender
Ball struck high into penalty area

Crossing

Players kick the ball toward the center of the opposing team's penalty area so that attackers can score goals.

Head down as ball is struck powerfully
Shooting leg extended

Shooting

Shooting consists of a powerful kick at goal. Low corner shots are the most difficult for the goalkeeper to save.

REFEREE SIGNALS

The referee controls the match with the help of two assistant referees who patrol the touchlines. They use signals to convey decisions, and to penalize fouls by awarding free kicks and penalties.

Defense

A defending team tackles, blocks, and marks to avoid conceding a goal and to win back possession of the ball in order to launch their own attacks.

Defender slides to retrieve ball

Slide tackling

Slide tackling involves sliding under the opponent's feet to knock the ball away. Dangerous tackles constitute foul play.

Stretched leg stops opponent's pass

Interception

Players intercept the ball during an opposing player's pass by stopping it from reaching its intended target.

Defender shadows attacker, staying close
Attacker makes run into space

Marking

This technique involves one player staying very close to an opposing player to stop him or her from gaining control of the ball.

DIRECT FREE KICK

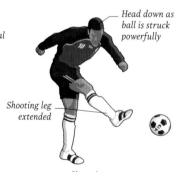
INDIRECT FREE KICK

YELLOW CARD (CAUTION)

RED CARD (SENT-OFF)

ADVANTAGE

In a **1962 NBA game Wilt Chamberlain** scored **100 points**, setting the single-game record

Hair held back by headband

Crossed arms propel ball

Lightweight cotton shirt frees up movement

Kneepads worn to prevent grazes

High-grip shoes create added stability

VOLLEYBALL PLAYER

Netball
This fast-moving sport pits two teams of seven players against each other. Each team passes the ball into the opposing team's goal circle and, from there, scores goals by throwing the ball into the netted hoop.

Goal ring stands 10 ft (3.05 m) high

Handball
Teams of seven bounce, pass, and shoot the ball at a rectangular goal during 60-minute games in which body contact is permitted.

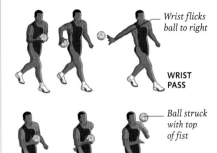

Wrist flicks ball to right

WRIST PASS

Ball struck with top of fist

FIST PASS

Volleyball
This sport consists of two six-a-side teams that must hit the ball into their opponents' half within a maximum of three touches. Common errors, which earn the opposing team points, include exceeding three touches and hitting the ball out of bounds.

Net
The net stands 8 ft (2.4 m) high for men and 7 ft 4 in (2.2 m) for women. A player touching the net at any time forfeits the point to the opposition.

Steel poles hold net in place

— 29 ft 6 in (9.5 m) —

Raised hand strikes ball with power

Hips twist as ball hit overarm

SERVE　**ATTACK**

Skills
Players defend by blocking opponents' shots and digging the ball—hitting it upward before it strikes the court floor for teammates to hit a powerful spike or a delicate tip.

Ball pushed gently over net

TIP

BEACH VOLLEYBALL
In this two-a-side variant of volleyball, played on sand, each team of two has to cover the entire 52 ft 6 in x 26 ft 2 in (16 x 8 m) court, and no substitutions are allowed. 21-point sets are played in a best-of-three format.

Basketball
Games feature five players on each side, and unlimited substitutions. Players control the ball by bouncing it, and pass and dribble with the ball on the hardwood court. They score with shots through the 10 ft (3.05 m) high hooped basket.

NBA OR FIBA?
FIBA (International Basketball Federation) games are played globally in four 10-minute quarters, while NBA (National Basketball Association) games are primarily played in North America in four 12-minute quarters.

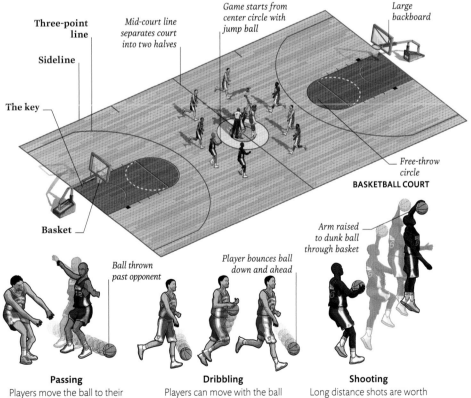

Three-point line

Sideline

Mid-court line separates court into two halves

Game starts from center circle with jump ball

Large backboard

The key

Basket

Free-throw circle

BASKETBALL COURT

Ball thrown past opponent

Passing
Players move the ball to their teammates with different types of passes such as overhead, bounce, flick, push, and chest.

Player bounces ball down and ahead

Dribbling
Players can move with the ball by bouncing it one-handed. When holding it two-handed, however, they cannot run.

Arm raised to dunk ball through basket

Shooting
Long distance shots are worth three points, while shots and dunks made within the three-point line are worth two points.

see also Snow and ice sports pp.480–81 ▶ Aquatic sports pp.482–83 ▶ Precision sports pp.484–85 ▶

» Team ball sports continued

Football

This sport is played over four 15-minute quarters and involves collisions, throwing, running, and strategy. The offensive team earns points during a set of downs (play periods) by entering the opposing team's end zone with the ball (a touchdown) or kicking the ball through the opposing team's goalposts (a field goal).

10 yd- (9.1 m-) deep end zone where touchdowns can be scored

The quarterback

The quarterback orchestrates a team's offense. Receiving the ball, he must choose which of his eligible receivers he will pass to or, if none are available, whether to advance with the ball himself.

Official signals first down

First down

If a team advances 10 yd (9.1 m) within 4 downs, the officials signal first down and they receive another set of downs. If they fail, their opponents receive the ball.

Numbers show yardage to goal line

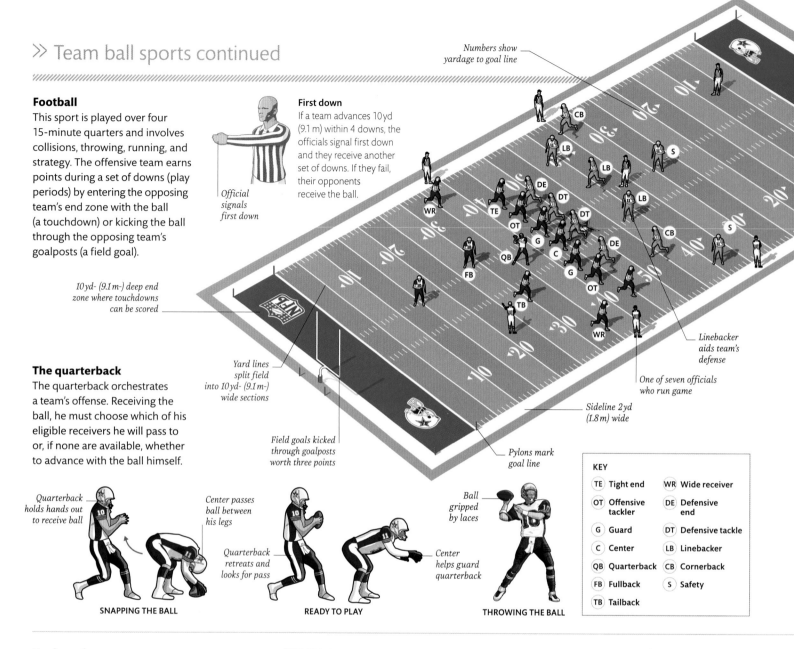

Linebacker aids team's defense

One of seven officials who run game

Yard lines split field into 10 yd- (9.1 m-) wide sections

Field goals kicked through goalposts worth three points

Sideline 2 yd (1.8 m) wide

Pylons mark goal line

Quarterback holds hands out to receive ball

Center passes ball between his legs

Quarterback retreats and looks for pass

Center helps guard quarterback

Ball gripped by laces

SNAPPING THE BALL **READY TO PLAY** **THROWING THE BALL**

KEY

TE Tight end	WR Wide receiver
OT Offensive tackler	DE Defensive end
G Guard	DT Defensive tackle
C Center	LB Linebacker
QB Quarterback	CB Cornerback
FB Fullback	S Safety
TB Tailback	

Rugby union

In this 15-a-side contact sport, teams score tries by grounding the ball in the opponent's goal area or score goals by kicking the ball through the opponent's goalposts. The ball can be kicked forward but, if passed by hand, can only be thrown backward.

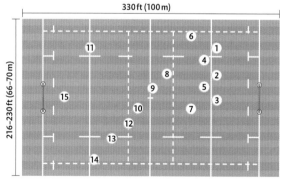

330 ft (100 m)

216–230 ft (66–70 m)

Scrum

All eight forwards in a team bind together with their opponents to form a central tunnel down which a scrum-half feeds the ball. Both packs of forwards compete for possession. The referee can call a foul if the ball is fed in incorrectly or if any player intentionally causes the scrum to collapse.

Line out

This restarts a game when the ball leaves the side of the pitch. One team's hooker throws the ball into play for rows of both team's forwards to catch.

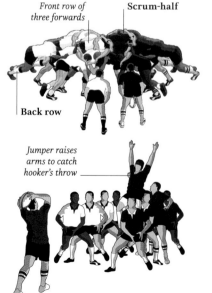

Front row of three forwards *Scrum-half*

Back row

Jumper raises arms to catch hooker's throw

KEY

1 Loosehead prop · 4 Left lock · 7 Openside flanker · 10 Fly-half · 13 Outside center
2 Hooker · 5 Right lock · 8 Number eight · 11 Left wing · 14 Right wing
3 Tighthead prop · 6 Blindside flanker · 9 Scrum-half · 12 Inside center · 15 Full-back

Goalposts 18.5 ft (5.6 m) apart

FIELD EQUIPMENT

Players are protected by broad shoulder and chest pads with a hard plastic outer layer and shock-absorbing foam inside. Quarterbacks' helmets can also be wired with a radio to allow them to receive instructions from their coach.

Helmet fitted with faceguard

Adjustable shoulder pads

Thigh pads

Knee pads

PROTECTIVE GEAR

Australian Rules

This 18-a-side sport sees players catch, tackle, hand pass, and kick the oval ball over four 20-minute quarters of near-continuous action. Points are scored for kicks through posts at each end of the enormous oval pitch.

443–607 ft (135–185 m)

360–508 ft (110–155 m)

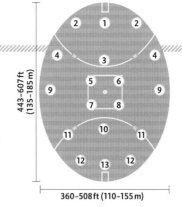

21 ft (6.4 m)   21 ft (6.4 m)

10 ft min (3m)   min 20 ft (6 m)

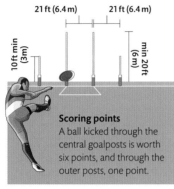

Scoring points
A ball kicked through the central goalposts is worth six points, and through the outer posts, one point.

Ball guided with hands

Ball moves end-over-end

Drop punt
This kick advances the ball medium to long distances upfield. The ball spins on impact, enabling accurate kicks.

KEY

1	Full forward	7	Rover
2	Forward pockets	8	Center
3	Center-half forward	9	Wingmen
4	Half-forward flanks	10	Center half-back
5	Ruckman	11	Half-back flanks
6	Ruck-over	12	Back pockets
		13	Full-back

Taking a mark
This catch, made from a kick 50 ft (15 m) or longer, leaves the catcher unobstructed and free to take the next kick.

Opponent tries to punch the ball away before mark taken

Gaelic football

This cross between football and rugby draws crowds of 80,000 to All-Ireland Senior Final matches. Two 15-player teams vie for control of the ball which earns three points if kicked or punched into the opponent's goal. An attempt that sails over the crossbar but between the posts is worth one point.

Defending player

Outstretched hands block the ball

Attacking kick thwarted

Gaining possession
A team needs possession of the ball in order to attempt to score goals. Players can tackle or block attempted kicks or passes by their opponents to gain possession of the ball.

Records of **Gaelic football matches** in Ireland date back to **1308 CE**

Rugby league

Originating in an 1895 breakaway by northern English rugby clubs, this sport shares many similarities to rugby union. However, it features 13-a-side teams scoring tries worth four points. There are also fewer set pieces, and more emphasis is placed on passing and running.

The **rules of rugby** were formalized after a **player was killed** during a practice match in **1871**

400 ft (122 m)

223 ft (68 m)

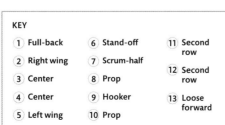

KEY

1	Full-back	6	Stand-off	11	Second row
2	Right wing	7	Scrum-half		
3	Center	8	Prop	12	Second row
4	Center	9	Hooker		
5	Left wing	10	Prop	13	Loose forward

Play-the-ball
After a tackle, the player with the ball rolls it back to a teammate. After six tackles, possession passes to the opposing team. Because of this, prior to the sixth tackle, the player with possession will often kick the ball far down the field to gain territory.

Skills and strategy
Successful rugby league sides are often defined by tough and accurate tackling in their defensive play. This is balanced with the slick handling and incisive running of their offensive players.

Sole of boot rolls ball back

ACTIVE PLAY

Attacker may offload ball before tackle is completed

TACKLING

see also The Olympics pp.488–91 ▶ **471**

Bat, stick, and club sports

Games based on hitting a ball or projectile with a bat, stick, or club have a long history. For example, ancient Egyptian artifacts depict a simple form of field hockey being played more than 4,000 years ago, while modern-day bat-and-ball sports have their origins in 18th- and 19th-century Europe.

There are **108 double stitches** on the seams of a **baseball**

Foul line—any ball that goes over this line is a dead ball

Foul pole   Centre field

BASEBALL FIELD

Right field

Baseball

A game features nine innings in which both teams attempt to make the most runs. To do that, the batter hits the ball, runs around the three bases, and returns to the home plate. An inning ends when three batters per side are out—when the ball is caught, when they miss three pitches, or when they are tagged out on a base.

Batting

A batter stands at the home plate and tries to hit a pitch, seeking to hit the ball as far as possible without it being caught.

Bat angled behind head

Arms and bat follow through

Bat swings as hips rotate

Batter's chest faces pitcher

STANCE   **SWING**   **FOLLOW-THROUGH**

Fastball

A pitcher places two fingers on the top of the ball to make it fly fast and straight. Major League Baseball (MLB) pitchers can throw at speeds of over 90 mph (145 kph).

Thumb provides support

Pitching

Pitchers strike out batters by pitching three balls past them into the strike zone—the area above home plate between knee and chest height.

Ball hidden behind glove

Hand swings hard overhead and forward

Gravel track warns player of wall ahead

Ball released as throwing arm extends

Front leg lifted

Body weight placed on front foot

WINDUP   **STRIDE**   **PITCH**

Cricket

Two teams of 11 each take turns to bat and score runs in pairs, or field. To score runs, the batter hits the ball and runs to the other end of the crease. The fielding team tries to get the batters "out" in a variety of ways, such as bowling the ball into the stumps, and catching the ball after it is struck.

Bowling

Bowlers bowl six consecutive balls, called an "over." They try to swing the ball or move it off the pitch to defeat the batsman.

Ball gripped in fingers

Front arm lifts up as bowling arm begins overhead swing

Ball released at top of bowling action

Weight transferred to leading leg

COIL   **DELIVERY STRIDE**   **DELIVERY**

Batsman protects stumps and tries to score runs

Wicketkeeper fields balls passing batsman

Closely mown crease measures 65 ft 7 in (20 m) between opposing stumps

Bowler throws ball overarm

Nonstriking batsman

Umpire judges whether batsman is out and if runs are scored

Batting

A batsman uses different shots (strokes) to propel the ball into gaps or over the boundary (the edge of the playing area) to score runs.

Bat made of willow wood

Front leg covered in protective pad

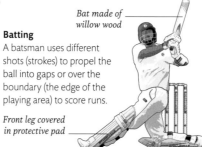

BATSMAN

Softball

This popular recreational sport shares many similarities with baseball, including nine-person teams that score runs by rounding four bases, and a diamond playing area—but with bases 60 ft (18.3 m) apart. Pitches are underarm, can be fast or slow depending on the competition, and are made with a ball larger than a baseball.

Flaps to protect ears and temples

Circumference of ball is typically 11.8 in (30 cm)

GLOVE AND BALL

HELMET

Bat has maximum length of 33.9 in (86 cm)

BAT

The **longest hole-in-one** in tournament golf traveled **1,551 ft (473 m)**

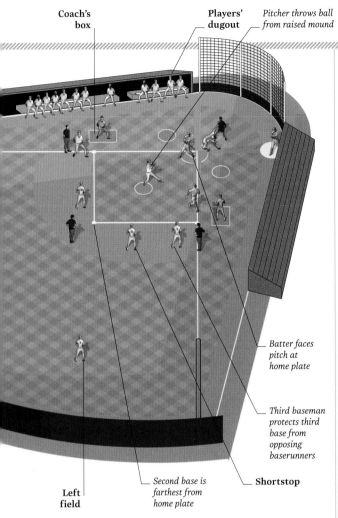

Coach's box

Players' dugout

Pitcher throws ball from raised mound

Batter faces pitch at home plate

Third baseman protects third base from opposing baserunners

Second base is farthest from home plate

Shortstop

Left field

Golf

Golfers aim to strike the ball into the hole—a cup embedded in a grass green—in as few shots as possible. There are usually 18 holes on a golf course, along with features such as trees, streams, and bunkers (pits of sand). These hazards act as obstacles the golfer must avoid or surpass in order to reach the green.

Golfer turns to face ball direction during follow-through

Club is raised and then swung downward

Good grip helps club face strike ball squarely

Swing extends up and around as player keeps head down

DOWNSWING POSITIONS

Clubs

Golfers carry up to 14 clubs, each of which can be used to propel the ball on different trajectories across varying distances.

Used for driving (taking first shot) on many long golf holes

Irons are numbered 1 to 9 depending on loft (angle) of club face

Heavily lofted face sends ball upward but with less distance forward than irons

Flat blade used to hit ball across green and into hole

DRIVER **LONG IRON** **WEDGE** **PUTTER**

Field hockey pitch

A competition hockey pitch measures 300 ft (91.4 m) long and 180 ft 5 in (55 m) wide. Each goal is surrounded by a D-shaped shooting circle. Goals can only be scored from this area.

Field hockey

Played in more than 100 nations, field hockey features teams of 11 players seeking possession of a small, hard ball which they pass, shoot, or dribble using only the flat side of their curved stick. A heavily padded goalkeeper tries to protect the goal.

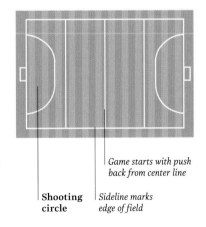

Game starts with push back from center line

Shooting circle

Sideline marks edge of field

Lacrosse

Deriving from native American games played as early as 1100 CE, lacrosse is played by teams of 10 men, or 12 women, each using a stick with a netted head to catch, carry, pass, and throw a sponge rubber ball at 5 ft 11 in (1.8 m) square goals.

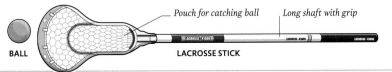

Pouch for catching ball

Long shaft with grip

BALL

LACROSSE STICK

Ice hockey

Played over three 20-minute periods, this fast-moving, physical sport sees teams of six ice skaters compete for a puck (rubber disc). Each 6 ft (180cm) wide goal is guarded by a goalkeeper, while the other players pass and shoot the puck using a 6 ft 6 in (2 m) long, flat-bladed stick. Unlimited player substitutions are permitted.

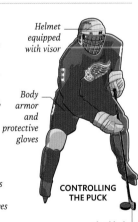

Helmet equipped with visor

Body armor and protective gloves

CONTROLLING THE PUCK

Flat blade connects with puck

Curved boards keep puck in play

Center line divides 200 ft (61 m) long rink into two halves

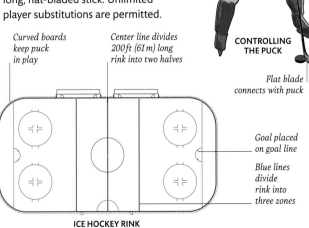

Goal placed on goal line

Blue lines divide rink into three zones

ICE HOCKEY RINK

see also The Olympics pp.488–91 ▶ **473**

Racquet sports

The first popular racquet sport was *Jeu de Paume* ("palm game") played in medieval Europe. Later, games played in Britain in the 19th century gradually developed into modern sports that employed a handheld racquet or paddle to strike a ball or shuttlecock around a court.

Badminton

In this indoor game, players hit a shuttlecock over a net and land it in the opposition half to score a point. Each game is first to 21 points, and matches are best of three.

Game area
The court is 44 ft (13.4 m) long and is divided in two by a net 20 ft (6.1 m) wide and 5 ft 11 in (1.55 m) tall.

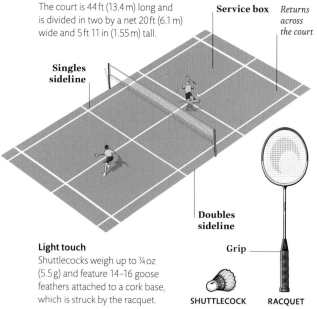

Singles sideline

Service box

Returns across the court

Doubles sideline

Grip

SHUTTLECOCK   RACQUET

Light touch
Shuttlecocks weigh up to ¼ oz (5.5 g) and feature 14–16 goose feathers attached to a cork base, which is struck by the racquet.

Serving and smashing
To serve the shuttlecock, the racquet must stay below shoulder height. Shots are played on the backhand and forehand, with the overhead smash the most powerful strike.

Shoulder is high

Arm is lowered

SERVE   HIT

Player times jump to hit shuttlecock at maximum height

Racquet head whipped through to impart power

Racquet follows through

SMASH

Squash

Players take turns to strike a small rubber ball against the front wall—and other walls—of an indoor court, creating difficult angles and positions for their opponent to return. First, the server must strike above the service line of the front wall, and a point is won if either the ball hits the ground more than once after hitting a wall or the opponent's ball hits the ground before the front wall. The winning score is 11 points or two clear points after 10–10.

Composite frame

Racquet and ball
A modern squash racquet can weigh up to 9 oz (225 g) and its synthetic strings can propel a hollow ball at speeds in excess of 161.5 mph (260 kph).

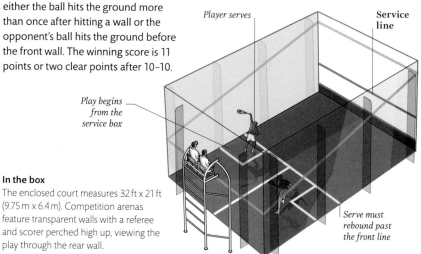

Player serves

Service line

Play begins from the service box

Serve must rebound past the front line

In the box
The enclosed court measures 32 ft x 21 ft (9.75 m x 6.4 m). Competition arenas feature transparent walls with a referee and scorer perched high up, viewing the play through the rear wall.

Table tennis

This sport sees players hit a lightweight ball over a net hanging 6 in (15.25 cm) above a table measuring 9 ft x 2 ft 6 in (2.75 m x 1.5 m). Games are played to 11 points or two points clear if the score reaches 10–10.

Net tautly strung

Dark, flat table surface

Quick to return

Speed and strength
Players need rapid reactions, footwork, and bat movement as they strive to strike the ball with spin, placement, and power and keep their opponent on the "back foot."

Wide, "ready" stance of feet

Bat covered with rubber

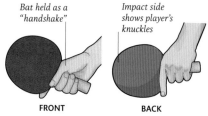

Bat held as a "handshake"

Impact side shows player's knuckles

FRONT   BACK

Orthodox grip
Nicknamed the "shake-hands grip," this hold with forefinger extended offers a good balance between defending and attacking play.

"Writing-pen" grip

Fingers shown

FRONT   BACK

Penholder grip
Developed in Japan in the 1950s, this grip offers a strong forehand attack but needs quick reactions to play backhand shots successfully.

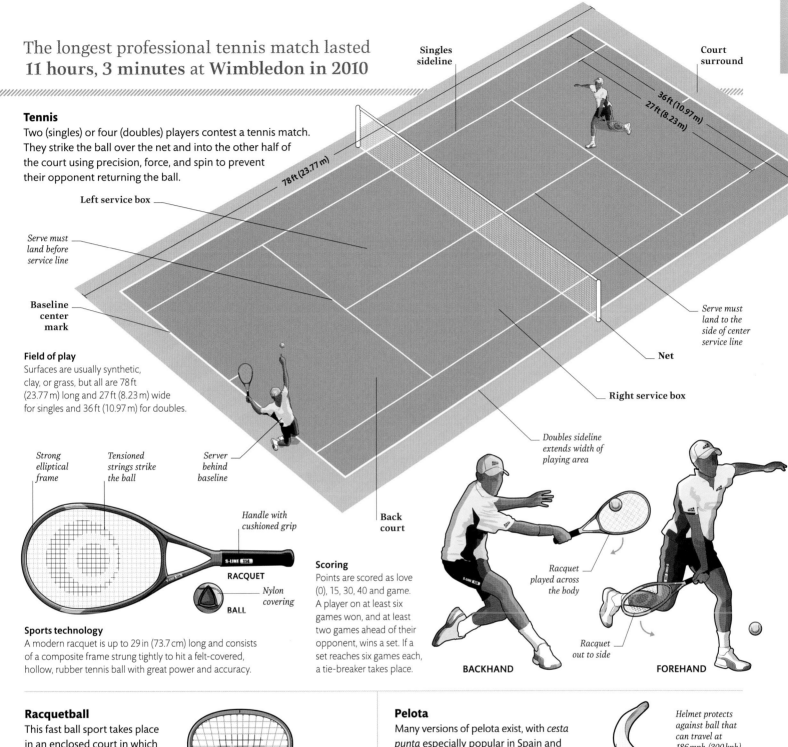

Singles sideline

Court surround

36 ft (10.97 m)

27 ft (8.23 m)

Tennis

Two (singles) or four (doubles) players contest a tennis match. They strike the ball over the net and into the other half of the court using precision, force, and spin to prevent their opponent returning the ball.

78 ft (23.77 m)

Left service box

Serve must land before service line

Baseline center mark

Serve must land to the side of center service line

Net

Right service box

Field of play

Surfaces are usually synthetic, clay, or grass, but all are 78 ft (23.77 m) long and 27 ft (8.23 m) wide for singles and 36 ft (10.97 m) for doubles.

Doubles sideline extends width of playing area

Strong elliptical frame

Tensioned strings strike the ball

Server behind baseline

Handle with cushioned grip

RACQUET

Nylon covering

BALL

Back court

Sports technology

A modern racquet is up to 29 in (73.7 cm) long and consists of a composite frame strung tightly to hit a felt-covered, hollow, rubber tennis ball with great power and accuracy.

Scoring

Points are scored as love (0), 15, 30, 40 and game. A player on at least six games won, and at least two games ahead of their opponent, wins a set. If a set reaches six games each, a tie-breaker takes place.

Racquet played across the body

Racquet out to side

BACKHAND

FOREHAND

Racquetball

This fast ball sport takes place in an enclosed court in which all four walls, ceiling, and floor can be played, providing each player's serve strikes the front wall first and does so without hitting the floor on the way. A point is won when the ball bounces twice or a player cannot play a shot.

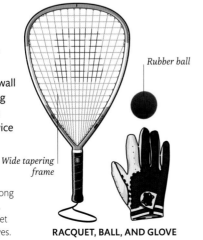

Rubber ball

Wide tapering frame

RACQUET, BALL, AND GLOVE

Varied equipment

Racquets are up to 22 in (55.9 cm) long with a short handle and wrist strap. Players wear a glove on their racquet hand and goggles to protect the eyes.

Pelota

Many versions of pelota exist, with *cesta punta* especially popular in Spain and other Spanish-speaking nations. Two players use a *cesta*—a basket attached to a glove—to hurl a rubber-cored, leather-clad ball at a wall in a fast, flowing movement. Anything between 25 and 50 points wins the match.

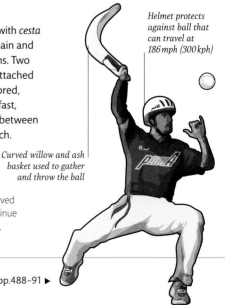

Helmet protects against ball that can travel at 186 mph (300 kph)

Curved willow and ash basket used to gather and throw the ball

Rally play

Each point begins with the ball served against the single wall. Rallies continue until the ball goes out of the court, bounces twice, or is not returned.

see also **Riding and racing sports** pp.486–87 ▶   **The Olympics** pp.488–91 ▶

Track and field

Running, jumping, and throwing competitions are amongst the oldest sports. Running was featured at the Olympics in ancient Greece from 776 BCE and, together with racewalking, includes a range of races covering different distances held on a track. Throwing, jumping, and vaulting competitions are field events. The seven-discipline heptathlon and the 10-discipline decathlon include both track and field events.

Middle- and long-distance running

These are multilap track events that require speed, stamina, a tactical brain, and a sprint finish. They comprise a range of events from 800 m to 10,000 m, and the 26¼ mile (42.2 km) marathon. The latter is often run on roads, but at major events such as the Olympics it ends with runners making a lap of the track.

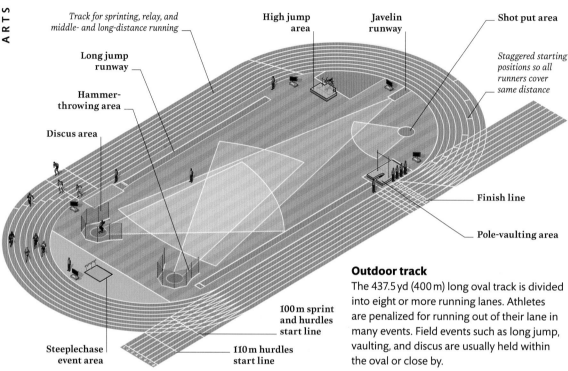

Track for sprinting, relay, and middle- and long-distance running

High jump area

Javelin runway

Shot put area

Staggered starting positions so all runners cover same distance

Long jump runway

Hammer-throwing area

Discus area

Finish line

Pole-vaulting area

100 m sprint and hurdles start line

110 m hurdles start line

Steeplechase event area

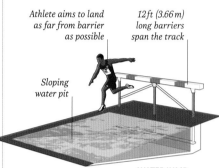

Athlete aims to land as far from barrier as possible

12 ft (3.66 m) long barriers span the track

Sloping water pit

WATER JUMP

Steeplechase

This is a gruelling long-distance race that is typically held over 3,280 yd (3,000 m). During the event athletes must cross a water jump seven times and jump the four barriers that span the track a total of 28 times.

Outdoor track

The 437.5 yd (400 m) long oval track is divided into eight or more running lanes. Athletes are penalized for running out of their lane in many events. Field events such as long jump, vaulting, and discus are usually held within the oval or close by.

Sprinting

Held indoors over 60 m and outdoors over distances of 100 m and 200 m, the sprints call for explosive power out of the starting blocks as athletes drive into an upward stance and then race to cross the finish line ahead of rival competitors.

Crouched on one knee, feet pressing into blocks

Shoulders positioned forward of hands

Rear leg drives athlete forward

"ON YOUR MARKS" **"SET"** **"GO"**

Hurdles

The 110 m (men) and 100 m (women) sprint hurdles, and the 400 m event for both sexes, all feature 10 gatelike barriers (hurdles) that athletes must jump as efficiently as possible while maintaining sprint speed.

Crossbar

Feet toward runner

HIGH HURDLE **INTERMEDIATE HURDLE**

Knee raised on approach

Body angled as front foot clears hurdle

Leading leg descends to land

Rear foot pushes off

CLEARING A HURDLE

Starting blocks

Set on the running track for sprint events, starting blocks have adjustable, angled footrests that provide a platform for a sprinter's feet to push hard against as the starter's pistol fires and a race begins.

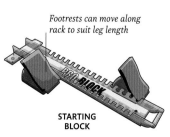

Footrests can move along rack to suit leg length

STARTING BLOCK

In the 1932 Olympics **men's steeplechase** final, athletes **ran an extra lap** as track officials lost count

RELAYS

Four athletes per team each run 100 m or 400 m before passing a baton to their teammate. Dropping the baton or failing to complete the changeover results in disqualification.

DOWNSWEEP CHANGEOVER

High jump

Athletes jump off one foot and attempt to clear a bar resting on two supports. Each competitor is allowed three attempts to clear a set height, but is eliminated if they fail. The bar is raised in increments and the athlete who can jump the highest is the winner.

Launching leg pushes off ground

Outside leg drives upward during takeoff

Hips rotate as inside arm and shoulder clear the bar first

Feet lifted together over the bar

Back arches and legs are brought together

Athlete lands on shoulders

The "Fosbury Flop"
Popularized by US athlete Dick Fosbury in the 1960s, this shoulders-first jump technique is now adopted by all elite jumpers.

The **women's high jump** debuted at the **Olympics** in **1928**

Long jump

Athletes sprint, then leap into a sand pit from a takeoff board; if they overstep it, the jump does not count. Distance is measured from the front edge of the board to the first mark the athlete makes in the sand.

Foot must not cross front of board

TAKEOFF BOARD

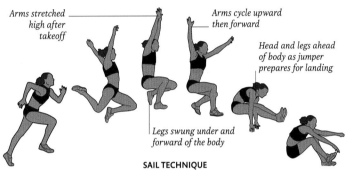

Arms stretched high after takeoff

Arms cycle upward then forward

Head and legs ahead of body as jumper prepares for landing

Legs swung under and forward of the body

SAIL TECHNIQUE

Pole vault

Vaulters use a long, flexible pole, one end of which is planted in a vaulting box. The pole initially bends under the vaulter's weight, then straightens, propelling the vaulter, in an upside-down position, up and over a bar. Like high jumpers, vaulters have three attempts.

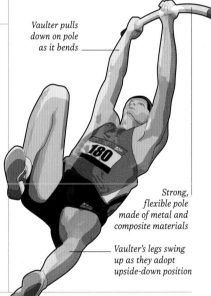

Vaulter pulls down on pole as it bends

Strong, flexible pole made of metal and composite materials

Vaulter's legs swing up as they adopt upside-down position

Javelin

Athletes run and throw a 7 ft 3 in–8 ft 10½ in (2.2–2.7 m) projectile, or javelin, toward a landing area. They must ensure a perfect angle as they release the javelin as its tip must touch the ground first for the throw to be valid.

Landing sector

Approx 328 ft (100 m)

Runway

TARGET AREA

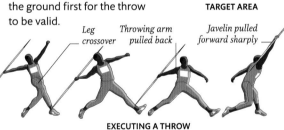

Leg crossover

Throwing arm pulled back

Javelin pulled forward sharply

EXECUTING A THROW

Hammer throw

Competitors use a steel ball (weighing 16 lb/7.26 kg for men or 8 lb 12 oz/4 kg for women) attached by a steel wire to a handle. An athlete spins to build momentum before releasing the ball.

Throwing area

CAGED CIRCLE

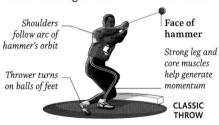

Shoulders follow arc of hammer's orbit

Thrower turns on balls of feet

Face of hammer

Strong leg and core muscles help generate momentum

CLASSIC THROW

Shot put

Athletes get several attempts at putting (pushing) a heavy metal ball (shot) as far as possible. Elite athletes can "put the shot" more than 66 ft (20 m).

8 lb 12 oz (4 kg)

16 lb (7.26 kg)

WOMEN'S SHOT

MEN'S SHOT

Athlete faces away from the direction of throw

Body twists as weight shifts sides

Non-throwing arm points to target

Left side stays braced as shot released

Shot departs at 40°

PUSH OFF

SPIN

THRUST

Discus

After making a number of turns across a 8 ft 2½ in (2.5 m) throwing circle, a thrower releases their discus from a sidearm position. The fingertips press down on the discus's edge to help control angle and flight.

2 lb 3 oz (1 kg)

4 lb 7 oz (2 kg)

WOMEN'S DISC

MEN'S DISC

Athlete grips top of discus, wrapping fingertips around rim

THROWER IN CIRCLE

see also The Olympics pp.488–91 ▶

Combat sports

Wrestling, boxing, and other tests of fighting prowess began thousands of years ago, and were popularized by armies and other fighting forces. Some combat sports feature demonstration routines showing stances and skills, but most pit two opponents in timed contests overseen by referees or judges.

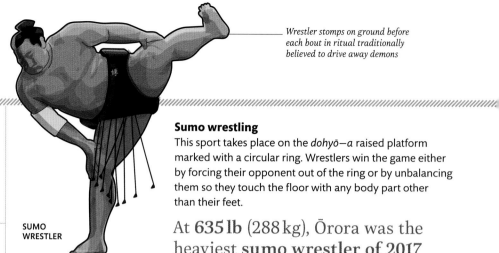

Wrestler stomps on ground before each bout in ritual traditionally believed to drive away demons

SUMO WRESTLER

Sumo wrestling

This sport takes place on the *dohyō—a* raised platform marked with a circular ring. Wrestlers win the game either by forcing their opponent out of the ring or by unbalancing them so they touch the floor with any body part other than their feet.

At **635 lb** (288 kg), Ōrora was the heaviest **sumo wrestler of 2017**

Opponent driven back and down

Charging wrestler toppled by push

Wrestler forces opponent out of ring

YORITAOSHI　　　HATAKIKOMI　　　YOKIKI

Judo

In Judo, *judoka* (judo fighters) aim to throw, hold, or pin their opponent to the mat. Players win by gaining an *ippon* (a full point), either with a controlled 25-second hold or a perfect throw, landing the opponent on their back.

Opponent thrown over shoulder

Belt, or obi, color indicates rank

FULL SHOULDER THROW

Boxing

Fighting in a roped square ring, boxers score by landing clean punches on their opponent's body. Judges pick a winner after a maximum of 12 three-minute rounds, unless either boxer is knocked out before.

Arm extends fully on impact

Opponent takes punch in body

Boxer swivels on ball of foot

JAB　　　HOOK

KICKBOXING

This mix of boxing and attacking martial arts takes place in boxing rings. Opponents punch and strike with high and low kicks, scoring points for blows made with good contact. Bouts can also be won by knocking out an opponent.

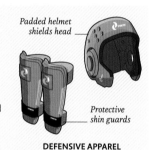

Padded helmet shields head

Protective shin guards

DEFENSIVE APPAREL

Kendo

This ritualized version of traditional Japanese sword-fighting swaps metal swords, or *katana*, for a bamboo *shinai*. Players score points by striking one of seven permitted areas on an opponent's head, body, or wrists.

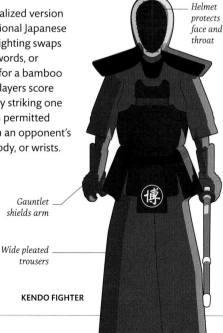

Helmet protects face and throat

Gauntlet shields arm

Wide pleated trousers

KENDO FIGHTER

Taolu

In Taolu—a major form of kung fu—choreographed routines of stances, leaps, and balances demonstrate skill, precision, and dexterity. Routines with or without weapons are performed on a padded rectangular mat and marked by a 10 person judging panel.

GUN

QIANG

TAIJIJIAN

JIAN

DAO

NANDAO

Weapons

Traditional weapons range from the 7 ft (2.1 m) gun staff to the 3¼ ft (97 cm) *nandao* broadsword.

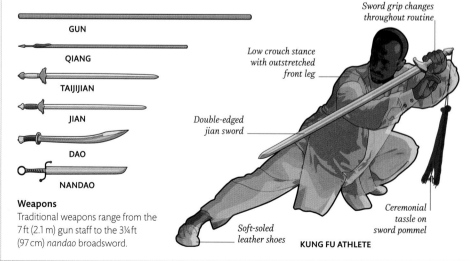

Sword grip changes throughout routine

Low crouch stance with outstretched front leg

Double-edged jian sword

Soft-soled leather shoes

Ceremonial tassle on sword pommel

KUNG FU ATHLETE

Jiu-jitsu

Two main events exist. In one, points are scored for punches, kicks, or throws. In the other, fighters are judged on how they defend against attacks called by the referee (as below).

Attacker places arms around neck

Attacker thrown over shoulder

SHOULDER THROW

Wrestling

This sport is usually played either freestyle or in the Greco-Roman style, the latter only involving the upper body. Both styles involve holds, throws, and attempts to pin the opponent on the mat.

Opponent held by chest

Back bends during lift

LIFT-OFF

Opponent pulled over

START

PITCH

SAMBO

This Russian sport developed in the 1920s out of different wrestling styles influenced by minor elements of karate and judo. Each round takes place on a circular action area with the contest judged by a mat referee. Points are awarded for throws, holds, and leg locks, and the first player to gain a 12-point lead is the winner.

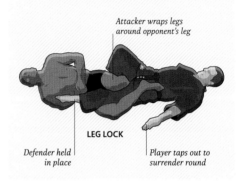

Attacker wraps legs around opponent's leg

LEG LOCK

Defender held in place

Player taps out to surrender round

Karate

More than 70 styles of this Japanese unarmed martial art exist with varied competitive elements, including *kumite*—sparring between pairs of opponents—and *kata*—choreographed displays of combat moves. Both call for high concentration, balance, and precise control of all parts of the body.

Ball of foot leads with toes pulled back

Fists together with thumbs on top

Palm open with wide stance

Right fist at chest height

Right fist punches

Left arm rapidly straightens out

Knuckles of both fists face backward

FRONT KICK   **DOUBLE PUNCH**   **KNIFE HAND BLOCK**   **BACK FIST BLOCK**   **REVERSE PUNCH**   **ARM STRIKE**   **DOUBLE-HANDED BLOCK**

Fencing

Bouts are fought using one of three types of blunt-tipped sword: foil, saber, or épée. Fencers time feints, lunges, and defensive skills as they duel on a 46 ft- (14 m-) long piste platform. Both combatants are rigged up to electronic sensors which register scoring hits on their torso.

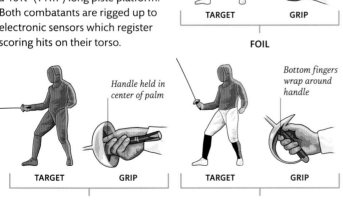

Thumb and forefinger inside hand guard

TARGET   **GRIP**

FOIL

Handle held in center of palm

TARGET   **GRIP**

EPEE

Bottom fingers wrap around handle

TARGET   **GRIP**

SABRE

Tae kwon do

Originating in Korea and making its Olympic debut in 2000, this sport of kicks and blows takes place on a 35 ft 9 in (11 m) square mat. Fighters are assessed by four judges and a referee.

Protective clothing
Extensive padded clothing is worn by competitors over their white *dobok* (competition uniform).

Fighter balances on left leg

Right leg thrust outward to strike opponent

Torso parallel with kicking leg

WIND UP   **SIDE KICK**

Helmet protects jaw and ears

Torso guard

Forearm guard

Groin guard

◄ see also Bat, stick, and club sports pp.472–73   Precision sports pp.484–85 ►   The Olympics pp.488–91 ►

Snow and ice sports

Skiing, skating, and sledding sports developed from the use of these devices as transportation in Arctic and alpine environments. There are a number of major international competitions where participants demonstrate both speed and athletic skill, including world championships, world cups, the X Games, and the Winter Olympics, which is held once every four years.

Alpine skiers can experience **3.5 times the force of gravity** during fast turns

Alpine skiing

Mimicking the skiing that millions of winter sports enthusiasts enjoy, this group of events features timed runs down mountain slope courses. Skiers require great skill and body strength to maintain their streamlining and form to complete the course in the quickest time.

Padded insert

Hard outer shell

Tinted eyepieces reduce glare

HELMET

SKI BOOTS

GOGGLES

POLES

Basket stops pole from sinking in snow

Deep side cut for faster turns

Strap held between palm and handle

SLALOM SKI

Pole out for balance

Low crouch allows a faster turn

Gates mark out course

Skis moved parallel to regain speed

Downhill racing

This is the fastest alpine event. Skiers reach up to 93 mph (150 kph) and make long airborne jumps along a 1½–3 mile (2.5–5 km) course marked by gates.

Tighter turns make for shorter, faster runs

Skis pass in front of gate pole

Skier pushes flexible gate poles aside

Skier shifts weight for next turn

Slalom and Giant Slalom

In these technically challenging events, skiers aim to complete a course with numerous twists and turns—and up to 75 gates—in the shortest possible time.

Safety helmet and goggles

Body-hugging suit

Starting gate

Inrun allows jumper to accelerate

Ski angle held throughout jump

Jumper flies off take-off ramp

Outrun (stopping area)

Form maintained through the air

Ski length set at 145 percent of jumper's height

Landing made on both skis

JUMPING HILL

Ski jumping

Jumpers accelerate down a sloping ramp before leaping long distances—in 2017, Austria's Stefan Kraft set a world record of 832 ft (253.5 m). Jumpers must land with one ski ahead of the other. Points are awarded for distance and "style"—a good body position during take off, flight, and landing is crucial.

CROSS-COUNTRY SKIING

Popular in Scandinavia and Eastern Europe, athletes use light, narrow skis to cover long distances, including 31 mile (50 km) marathons. Competitions include relays for teams of four.

Skier leans on left pole and slides foot forward

Right arm moves forward

Rear leg lifts for next stride

Gliding motion

DIAGONAL STRIDE

Figure skating

Individual skaters, or pairs, perform routines that combine movements demonstrating power and grace, often in time to a piece of music. Contact with the ice is made only with the ⅛ in (4 mm) wide blade, with marks deducted for errors and falls.

Jumps

Skaters leave the ice and may rotate up to three or four times. In axel jumps, the arms are clasped around the body.

Take off from left foot

Backward landing on right foot

Spins

Techniques such as the Biellmann spin display speed and control; the speed of the spin dictates the number of possible rotations.

Skater takes hold of blade

Right leg raised and held

Left leg rotates on ice

Teardrop shape

SPEED SKATING

Demanding immense power and agility, speed skating races cover a range of distances from 500 m (547 yd) sprints to 10 km (6.2 mile) endurance events. "Long track" events are held on a 400 m (437 yd) oval rink. "Short track" racing takes place on a 111.12 m (122 yd) circuit that sees frequent crashes as skaters jostle for position and sweep low around corners.

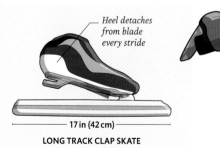

Heel detaches from blade every stride

17 in (42 cm)

LONG TRACK CLAP SKATE

Freestyle skiing

Judges mark for technical merit, accuracy, and style as a competitor travels down a slope performing jumps and tricks. Different types of slopes exist: aerial slopes feature high ramps for mid-air twists and spins, while on mogul courses covered in small mounds, skiers jump off kicker ramps to perform twists and somersaults.

Skier jumps and starts to turn

Skier builds up speed on slope before jump

Skier completes a 360-degree turn while still airborne

Skier continues to turn another 180 degrees

Skis held together throughout twisting move

Knees bent to absorb landing impact

540-DEGREE AERIAL TURN

82 ft (25 m)

Starting gate

Mogul mounds set about 11 ft 6 in (3.5 m) apart

Control gate

Kicker ramps

Finish area with stand for judges

218–295 yd (200–270 m)

Finish line

MOGUL SLOPE

"**Mogul**" comes from the **Austrian word** "**Mugel**," meaning **small hill** or **mound**

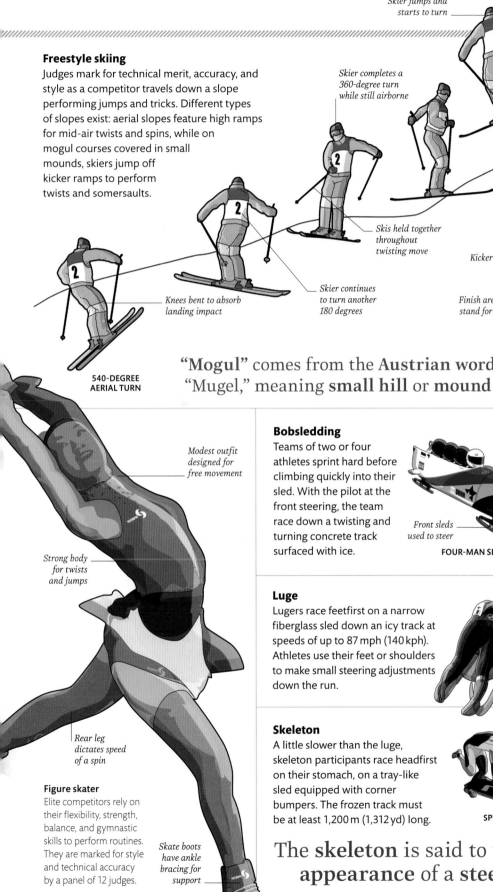

Modest outfit designed for free movement

Strong body for twists and jumps

Rear leg dictates speed of a spin

Figure skater

Elite competitors rely on their flexibility, strength, balance, and gymnastic skills to perform routines. They are marked for style and technical accuracy by a panel of 12 judges.

Skate boots have ankle bracing for support

Bobsledding

Teams of two or four athletes sprint hard before climbing quickly into their sled. With the pilot at the front steering, the team race down a twisting and turning concrete track surfaced with ice.

Front sleds used to steer

FOUR-MAN SLED

Luge

Lugers race feetfirst on a narrow fiberglass sled down an icy track at speeds of up to 87 mph (140 kph). Athletes use their feet or shoulders to make small steering adjustments down the run.

LUGE RACER

Skeleton

A little slower than the luge, skeleton participants race headfirst on their stomach, on a tray-like sled equipped with corner bumpers. The frozen track must be at least 1,200 m (1,312 yd) long.

Wrist guards reduce injuries

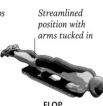

Water resistant trousers

SNOWBOARDER

Snowboarding

Riding a sculpted board fitted with boots and bindings, snowboarders compete in fast snowboard cross races, timed slaloms, or perform a routine of tricks and moves off ramps or tubular arenas known as half-pipes.

Crouched running start

Athlete leaps on to sled

Streamlined position with arms tucked in

SPRINT **JUMP** **FLOP**

The **skeleton** is said to take its name from the **bony appearance** of a **steel sled** introduced in **1892**

see also Aquatic sports pp.482–83 ▶ The Olympics pp.488–91 ▶ **481**

Aquatic sports

Swimming and the racing of simple rafts and canoes are among the oldest of all sports, dating back thousands of years. Watersports have been part of the Olympic Games since it first began in 1896. A number of watersports take place in indoor aquatic arenas while other events, from open-water swimming to boat races, are held outdoors.

Swimming

Swimmers take part in single-stroke events, where only one type of stroke is permitted, or medleys, where they must swim a quarter of the race distance using each of the four main strokes (see below) at different stages. Races in the pool vary from 50 m (164 ft) sprints to gruelling 1,500 m (1,640 yd) events.

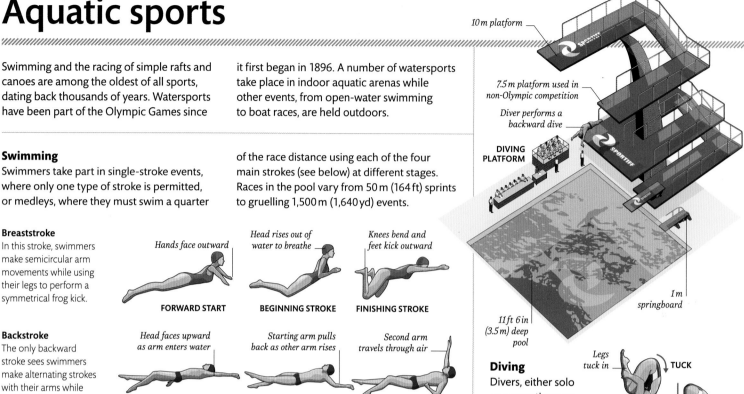

10 m platform

7.5 m platform used in non-Olympic competition

Diver performs a backward dive

DIVING PLATFORM

11 ft 6 in (3.5 m) deep pool

1 m springboard

Breaststroke
In this stroke, swimmers make semicircular arm movements while using their legs to perform a symmetrical frog kick.

Hands face outward

Head rises out of water to breathe

Knees bend and feet kick outward

FORWARD START **BEGINNING STROKE** **FINISHING STROKE**

Backstroke
The only backward stroke sees swimmers make alternating strokes with their arms while gently kicking their feet.

Head faces upward as arm enters water

Starting arm pulls back as other arm rises

Second arm travels through air

BACKWARD START **BEGINNING STROKE** **FINISHING STROKE**

Front crawl
In the fastest stroke, swimmers' bodies roll from side to side as their legs perform flutter kicks just under the water.

Arm stretched out fully to enter water

Second arm bends at elbow

Second arm extends out as first pulls back

FORWARD START **BEGINNING STROKE** **FINISHING STROKE**

Butterfly
The butterfly stroke, in which the arms and legs move in unison, requires great strength, stamina, and timing.

Legs whip through water in dolphin kick

Hands pull back through water

Swimmer lifts head for air

FORWARD START **BEGINNING STROKE** **FINISHING STROKE**

Diving

Divers, either solo or competing as a synchronized pair, perform a series of dives marked by judges on various criteria, including the execution of moves in the air and cleanness of entry into the water. Dives are made from raised platforms of several heights or from a smaller springboard by the pool's edge.

Legs tuck in **TUCK**

PIKE

Feet point down

STRAIGHT

HUMAN TORPEDO

Diving manoeuvres
There are six categories of dives: forward, backward, reverse, inward, twist, and handspring (or armstand).

Water polo

This seven-a-side sport is played over four eight-minute periods. Teams move a small ball around the pool by passes or by swimming with it in front of them, and opponents try to intercept to gain possession of the ball. Each successful shot at goal earns one point.

32–66 ft (10–20 m)

66–230 ft (20–30 m)

KEY

- **FW** First winger
- **SW** Second winger
- **FD** First driver
- **SD** Second driver
- **PM** Point man
- **CF** Center forward
- **GK** Goalkeeper

9 ft 9 in (3 m) wide goal rests 3 ft (90 cm) above water

First driver moves into attacking position

Point man prepares to pass

WATER POLO MATCH

Canoeing

Competitors propel their canoes using a single-bladed paddle. Flatwater races are held from 200 m (217 yd) to 5,000 m (5,468 yd) on still water while slalom events are timed events held on a whitewater course.

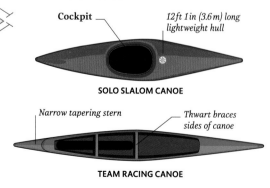

Cockpit

12 ft 1 in (3.6 m) long lightweight hull

SOLO SLALOM CANOE

Narrow tapering stern

Thwart braces sides of canoe

TEAM RACING CANOE

In 2017, **Brazilian surfer Rodrigo Koxa** rode
a **80 ft-** (24.4 m-) high wave off the coast of Portugal

Windsurfing

Windsurfers race around courses marked with buoys or perform spectacular freestyle routines with jumps and turns. Their boards feature a mast and sail attached to a movable wishbone boom which angles the sail in and out of the wind. Windsurfers can reach speeds of more than 50 mph (80 kph).

Sail reinforced with horizontal battens

Light polyester material

WINDSURFER

Surfing

Standing on a narrow surfboard, surfers use balance and timing to ride breaking waves. In competition surfing, the tricks performed and the length of the ride earn marks from judges.

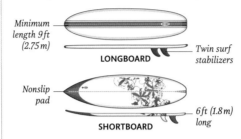

Minimum length 9 ft (2.75 m)

LONGBOARD

Twin surf stabilizers

Nonslip pad

SHORTBOARD

6 ft (1.8 m) long

Dragon boat racing

Often cramming 18 paddlers into their slim hulls, dragon boats race against up to six other crews. Events vary from 200 m (217 yd) sprints to 50 km (31 mile) marathons.

Drummer beats out stroke rhythm

Helmsman steers

Modern fiberglass hull

DRAGON BOAT

Waterskiing

Waterskiers grip the handle of a towline attached to a powerboat and compete in a variety of events, including slaloming in and out of buoys on just one ski and ski jumping for distance using angled ramps set in the water.

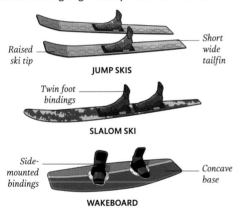

Raised ski tip

JUMP SKIS

Short wide tailfin

Twin foot bindings

SLALOM SKI

Side-mounted bindings

WAKEBOARD

Concave base

Kayaking

From a seated position, competitors power their kayak with a two-bladed paddle. They compete in straight line races in single (K1), pairs (K2), or four-man (K4) crews, or take part in timed slalom events where they must pass through numbered gates set on a challenging whitewater course.

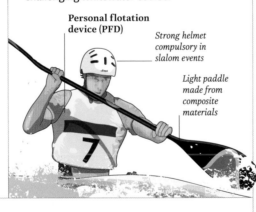

Personal flotation device (PFD)

Strong helmet compulsory in slalom events

Light paddle made from composite materials

Sailing

Sailing boats vary from solo laser dinghies to giant ocean-racing catamarans. In races, the crew steers the boat and controls its speed by adjusting its sails and riggings.

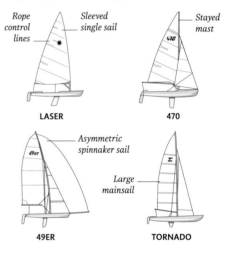

Rope control lines

Sleeved single sail

LASER

Stayed mast

470

Asymmetric spinnaker sail

49ER

Large mainsail

TORNADO

Rowing

Rowers race on slim boats on straight-line courses typically 2,000 m (2,187 yd) long. Facing backward, each rower propels one oar, or in sculling, two oars, to power their boat through the water.

Equipment

Lightweight rowing shells with sliding seats and stiff oars are usually constructed from carbon fiber and other composites.

Loom shaft

Plastic sleeve

ROWING OAR

SCULLING OAR

BOAT

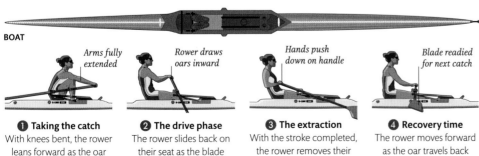

Arms fully extended

Rower draws oars inward

Hands push down on handle

Blade readied for next catch

❶ Taking the catch
With knees bent, the rower leans forward as the oar blade enters the water.

❷ The drive phase
The rower slides back on their seat as the blade pushes through the water.

❸ The extraction
With the stroke completed, the rower removes their blade from the water.

❹ Recovery time
The rower moves forward as the oar travels back to its starting position.

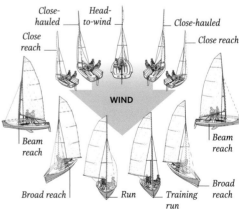

Close-hauled *Head-to-wind* *Close-hauled*

Close reach *Close reach*

WIND

Beam reach *Beam reach*

Broad reach *Run* *Training run* *Broad reach*

Points of sail

Every time a boat changes its angle relative to the wind, it changes its point of sail and must adjust its sails accordingly. Each point of sail has a name.

Precision sports

In precision sports, accuracy is prized above all else. These sports often involve aiming a ball or shooting a projectile at a target with perfect precision over and over again. Alternatively, in other disciplines in gymnastics and trampolining sports, athletes use precision in the exact body movements required to complete demanding performances. The efforts of the competitors in these routines are usually then marked by a panel of judges.

Artistic gymnastics

Acrobatics are performed on a variety of apparatus in artistic gymnastics. Routines are for men, women, or both, and include the vault, floor exercise, parallel bars, balance beam, and pommel horse.

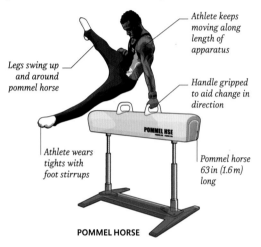

Athlete keeps moving along length of apparatus

Legs swing up and around pommel horse

Handle gripped to aid change in direction

Athlete wears tights with foot stirrups

Pommel horse 63 in (1.6 m) long

POMMEL HORSE

Rhythmic gymnastics

Routines are balletic and choreographed to music, and are performed individually or in teams in a matted performance area. Objects must be kept in constant motion throughout.

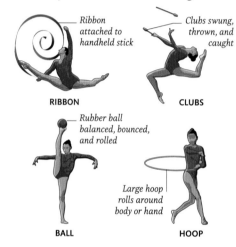

Ribbon attached to handheld stick

Clubs swung, thrown, and caught

RIBBON

CLUBS

Rubber ball balanced, bounced, and rolled

Large hoop rolls around body or hand

BALL

HOOP

Trampolining

The trampoline was invented by US gymnast George Nissen in the 1930s. In competitive trampolining, athletes build height with bounces, then perform a short routine of somersaults and other acrobatic moves in midair.

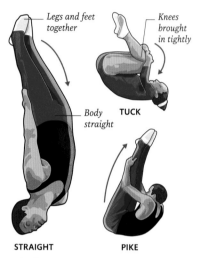

Legs and feet together

Knees brought in tightly

Body straight

TUCK

STRAIGHT

PIKE

Body shapes

All moves in trampolining begin with a basic jump. More elaborate acrobatic positions can then be linked together with twists.

Snooker

In a frame of snooker, players earn points by potting balls into the table's pockets in sequence. Within each break (individual turn at the table) a referee calls the number of points scored as each ball is potted. Once all 15 red balls have been potted, the six colored balls are then potted in ascending points order.

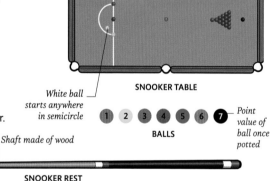

White ball starts anywhere in semicircle

SNOOKER TABLE

① ② ③ ④ ⑤ ⑥ ❼

Point value of ball once potted

BALLS

Rest helps player take tricky shots

Shaft made of wood

SNOOKER REST

Cueing

A good cueing position uses the hand as a stable guide for the movement of the cue as the player directs it forward to strike the ball.

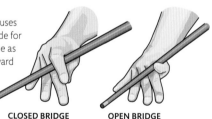

Cue tip makes contact with ball

CLOSED BRIDGE

OPEN BRIDGE

Ronnie O'Sullivan scored the **fastest snooker maximum break** (147 points) of all time at **5 minutes, 8 seconds**

Pool

Many versions of this cue sport exist, with different scoring systems. Most feature a table with six pockets into which players try to pot balls. The cue ball is hit in different ways to manipulate it into an ideal position for the next shot.

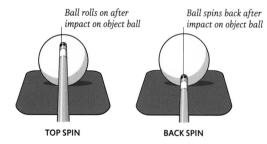

Ball rolls on after impact on object ball

Ball spins back after impact on object ball

TOP SPIN

BACK SPIN

BILLIARDS

In most versions of billiards, players play a cue ball so that it hits the red object ball and their opponent's cue ball in order to earn points. Pocket billiards (top row) features two cue balls and a red. In carom billiards (bottom row), one cue ball is yellow.

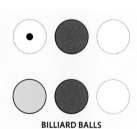

BILLIARD BALLS

Archery

The first **organized archery tournament** was held in England in 1583 and attracted **3,000 participants**

For each arrow that hits the target of 2 ft 7 in (80 cm) or 3 ft 11 in (120 cm) in diameter, archers score between one point, for hitting the outer white ring, and ten points, for hitting the central gold circle. Olympic archers shoot from a distance of 229.7 ft (70 m).

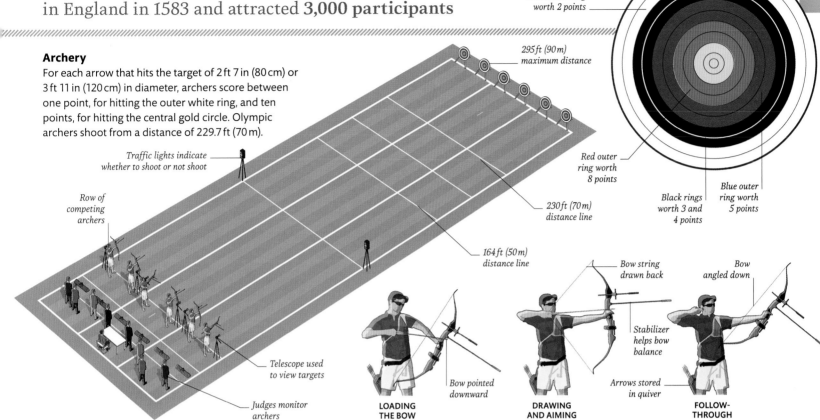

White inner ring worth 2 points

295 ft (90 m) maximum distance

Red outer ring worth 8 points

Blue outer ring worth 5 points

Black rings worth 3 and 4 points

Traffic lights indicate whether to shoot or not shoot

Row of competing archers

230 ft (70 m) distance line

164 ft (50 m) distance line

Telescope used to view targets

Judges monitor archers

Bow string drawn back

Bow angled down

Stabilizer helps bow balance

Bow pointed downward

Arrows stored in quiver

LOADING THE BOW

DRAWING AND AIMING

FOLLOW-THROUGH

Shooting (rifle)

Shooters aim from a standing, kneeling, or prone position at a small target made up of concentric rings a set distance away, often 164 ft (50 m) or 328 ft (100 m). In 50 m events, the innermost ring, worth 10 points if hit, measures just 1/4 in (0.5 cm) across.

Foresight aids aim

Rifle butt rests on shoulder

Knee patch

STANDING

Darts

Two players take turns throwing three darts at a dartboard 7 ft 9¼ in (2.37 m) away. Starting at 301 or 501 points, players aim to reach zero by hitting different parts of the board. The bullseye is worth 50 points, and its green ring, 25 points.

Sharp steel point

Hitting outer ring earns double points

Dart steadied by middle and third fingers

Dart gripped by thumb and forefinger

STANDARD GRIP

PENCIL GRIP

DART

DARTBOARD

Croquet

Players use long-handled mallets to strike balls through six hoops fixed in the playing area. Players take turns until one has negotiated all the hoops and strikes the ball into the central pole, known as the last post.

BALL

LAST POST

Hoop 0.1 in (0.3 cm) wider than ball

18 in (46 cm) tall

WIRE HOOPS

CROQUET MALLET

Ten-pin bowling

Bowlers hurl a heavy ball down a lane aiming to knock over ten pins arranged in a triangle. Knocking all ten pins down in one attempt is called a strike and earns bonus points. Games score a maximum of 300 points.

Bowler must not cross foul line

Polished wood lane

Rounded point

Thumb hole

Polished wood lane

BOWLING LANE

BALL

PIN

LAWN BOWLS

On a grass green or indoor carpet, players typically bowl two or four woods, aiming to get as close to the "jack" (target ball) as possible, which earns points. The first player to 21 or 25 points wins the game.

Polished exterior

Central disk

WOOD

see also The Olympics pp.488–91 ▶

Riding and racing sports

Races and contests of skill on horseback have occurred for thousands of years, but wheeled sports are mainly more recent arrivals. The invention of the bicycle and motorized vehicles such as the motorcycle, automobile, and airplane—all in the 19th century—led to a broad range of sports, with skateboarding and mountain biking arriving in the 20th century.

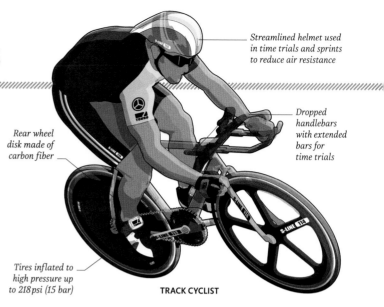

Streamlined helmet used in time trials and sprints to reduce air resistance

Dropped handlebars with extended bars for time trials

Rear wheel disk made of carbon fiber

Tires inflated to high pressure up to 218 psi (15 bar)

TRACK CYCLIST

Cycling–road racing

These grueling tests of riders' speed and stamina involve steep hill climbs, sprints, and long-distance stages held on roads for teams of cyclists. The pinnacle of the sport is the annual Tour de France, which features 21 daily stages.

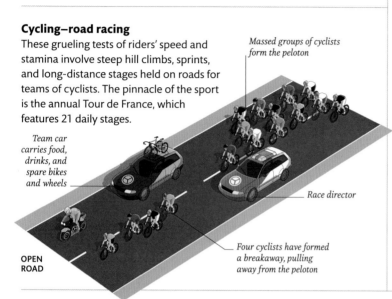

Massed groups of cyclists form the peloton

Team car carries food, drinks, and spare bikes and wheels

Race director

Four cyclists have formed a breakaway, pulling away from the peloton

OPEN ROAD

Track cycling

A track bike has a single fixed gear and no brakes. Cyclists ride these lightweight bikes around a banked oval track, which measures 273 yd (250 m) in Olympic competitions. Races vary from two-rider sprint events to team pursuit and the multi-event omnium.

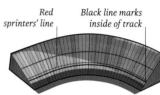

Red sprinters' line

Black line marks inside of track

Banking angles

The heavily angled bends of the track enable cyclists to keep their speed through the corners or to launch an attack.

Mountain biking

As soon as these rugged, multi-geared bikes were introduced in the late 1970s, they were raced on cross-country courses and later downhill, either in time trials or four-rider events.

Rear suspension

Front suspension

Rigid frame (hardtail) at rear

Disk brake

FULL SUSPENSION MOUNTAIN BIKE

"HARDTAIL" MOUNTAIN BIKE

The **highest mountain bike race** reaches altitudes of **17,000 ft** (5,200 m) above sea level

Formula One

One of the most well-known motorsports is the annual Formula One (F1) series. F1 sees races held on circuits around the world. Drivers compete against one another to be first to finish the number of laps needed to reach 190 miles (305 km).

DRY TYRES

MEDIUM WET TYRES

EXTREME WET TYRES

Points of contact

Tires are designed to maximize the contact with the track surface, with different patterns for wet or dry weather.

Air motorsports

In this sport, pilots individually navigate a challenging slalom race course in the quickest possible time. The pilot with the fastest lap time wins the race.

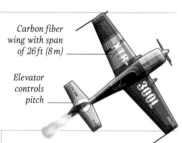

Carbon fiber wing with span of 26 ft (8 m)

Elevator controls pitch

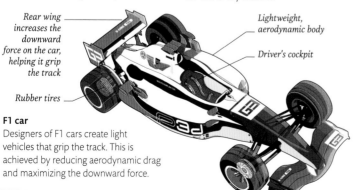

Rear wing increases the downward force on the car, helping it grip the track

Lightweight, aerodynamic body

Driver's cockpit

Rubber tires

F1 car

Designers of F1 cars create light vehicles that grip the track. This is achieved by reducing aerodynamic drag and maximizing the downward force.

Powerboating

This is the fastest of all water sports, with powerboats capable of reaching speeds up to 140 mph (225 kph) as they race around a defined course.

Rear wing gives greater stability at high speeds

Strong, lightweight frame

UNLIMITED HYDRO CLASS

Motorcycle racing

Road races usually take place on specially built racing tracks. Races are between 60–80 miles (95–130 km) long, depending on the length of the track.

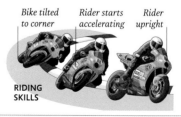

Bike tilted to corner

Rider starts accelerating

Rider upright

RIDING SKILLS

Skateboarding

Riding skateboards has two main competitive elements: street, where skateboarders perform tricks on level surfaces or street furniture such as rails; and vert (short for vertical), where moves are made inside and above a half-pipe—a large U-shaped structure with steeply sloping walls.

The ollie

The boarder snaps the board's tail downward while jumping, which propels the board into the air.

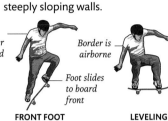

Boarder rises upward

Front leg bends at knee

POPPING THE TAIL

Border is airborne

Foot slides to board front

FRONT FOOT FORWARD

LEVELING OUT

Roller skating

This sport includes many different forms from speed skating on oval tracks to street skating using curbs and rails to perform tricks and moves. Artistic roller skating is performed in routines similar to ice figure skating.

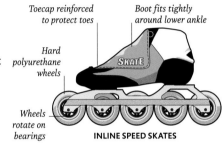

Toecap reinforced to protect toes

Boot fits tightly around lower ankle

Hard polyurethane wheels

Wheels rotate on bearings

INLINE SPEED SKATES

Roller hockey

This fast-moving sport is based on ice hockey but with players wearing either roller skates or inline wheeled skates competing on a hard, flat rink surrounded by boards. Teams of five players (with rolling substitutions) pass and shoot the puck or ball, aiming at their opponent's goal.

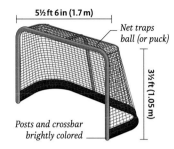

5½ ft 6 in (1.7 m)

Net traps ball (or puck)

3½ ft (1.05 m)

Posts and crossbar brightly colored

Rink goal

The goal is guarded by a goalkeeper who stands in a semicircular area 10 ft (3 m) in diameter.

Puck and stick

Roller hockey is played using either a ball or solid puck (rubber disk). Sticks are made of wood, aluminum, carbon composite, or graphite.

Inline stick blade up to 3 in (7.6 cm) deep

3 in (7.6 cm) across

PUCK

Inline hockey sticks are 65 in (163 cm) in length

HOCKEY STICK

Equestrianism

A group of horse-riding disciplines have appeared at every Olympics since 1912. They involve the rider showcasing their skill and teamwork with their horse in timed or judged events. Cross-country and show jumping involve horse and rider clearing jumps without incurring faults for knocking down barriers.

Formal riding clothing

Front and rear leg raised to same height

Dressage
Horse and rider perform a precise, choreographed routine of movements in an arena.

Rider pulls hard on reins as horse lands

Protection for legs knocking obstacles

Eventing
This features dressage, show jumping, and cross-country where horses are timed around a long course.

Rider wears protective helmet

Show jumping
Competitors negotiate an arena course as quickly as possible while clearing water jumps and barriers.

Horse racing

This sport is divided into flat racing on smooth grass or dirt tracks and jump racing (steeplechase), in which the horses, ridden by small but strong jockeys, have to clear a number of large barriers or jumps.

Jockey wears colors of horse owner

STEEPLECHASE JUMP

Polo

Originating in Persia around 600 BCE for training cavalry, polo is mostly contested on 300 yd (274.3 m) outdoor fields. Games are divided into time periods called chukkas during which teams on horseback attempt to strike a ball through their opponent's goal using a long-handled mallet.

Mane is clipped to stop from getting tangled

Attacker aims shot at an 8 yd (7.3 m) wide goal

OUTDOOR POLO

Different forms of polo are played using **yaks, camels, and elephants** instead of horses

RODEO

Popular in the United States and Mexico, competitors take part in various riding and roping events, including bucking bronco and bull riding where the object is to stay on your ride for as long as possible.

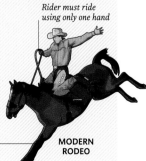

Rider must ride using only one hand

Horse attempts to throw rider

MODERN RODEO

The Olympics

The modern Olympics is the biggest international multisports event in the world. The 2016 Summer Games held in Rio de Janeiro, Brazil, featured 11,238 athletes competing in 306 medal events. The very first Olympic Games, held in ancient Greece 2,800 years ago, featured just one competition—a foot race the length of the stadium at Olympia—approximately 630 ft (192 m). The ancient Olympics died out in the 4th century CE, but the idea was revived toward the end of the 19th century. The Modern Games of the Olympiad have been staged in summer every four years since 1896 with only three interruptions—for two world wars, and the 2020 coronavirus pandemic. A quadrennial Winter Games is also held, attracting winter sports athletes dreaming of gold and glory.

Early discuses were initially made of stone, then bronze, lead, or iron

776 BCE The first ancient Olympics are held in honor of Greek god, Zeus. In 708 BCE, the pentathlon—including discus, javelin, wrestling, running, and jumping—is introduced to the games.

DISCOBOLUS LANCELLOTTI

French newspaper celebrates the arrival of the Winter Olympics

NEWSPAPER COVER, FEBRUARY 1924

Racing helmet made of leather

January 25–February 5, 1924 The first Winter Olympic Games are held in Chamonix, France, with 258 athletes competing in 16 medal events, including ski jumping and curling.

April 20–September 12, 1920 The five-ringed Olympic flag is raised for the first time at the VI Summer Games in Antwerp, Belgium. Italy wins the Team Pursuit cycling event.

ITALIAN CYCLIST FRANCO GIORGETTI

Skilled riflework earns Oscar Swahn a gold medal in the team running target, single shots event

May 5–July 27, 1912 The V Summer Games in Stockholm, Sweden, introduce automatic timing and photo finishes to athletics events. Modern pentathlon and dressage debut.

SWEDISH SHOOTER OSCAR SWAHN

May 4– July 27, 1924 The VIII Summer Games are held in Paris, France. Runner Paavo Nurmi—also known as "the flying Finn"—wins five gold medals, with two wins coming within hours of each other.

Competition number helps officials and spectators identify runner

FINNISH RUNNER PAAVO NURMI

February 11–19, 1928 The II Winter Games are held in St. Moritz, Switzerland. Norway's Sonja Henie wins the first of three figure skating gold medals at consecutive Olympics.

FIGURE SKATER SONJA HENIE

Henie's trademark white ice skating boots

July 19–August 3, 1952 The XV Summer Games are held in Helsinki, Finland, the host of the canceled 1940 games. Indonesia, Israel, and the People's Republic of China make their Olympics debuts.

GOLD MEDAL, 1952

Nike, the ancient Greek goddess of victory

February 14–25, 1952 The VI Winter Games are held in Oslo, Norway. Hjalmar Andersen delights home crowds by winning three out of the four men's speed skating events.

July 29–August 14, 1948 After an explosives injury to his right hand, Hungary's Károly Takács shoots with his left to win the rapid-fire pistol shooting event at the XIV Summer Games in London.

SHOOTING TARGET

January 30–February 8, 1948 The V Winter Games are held at St. Moritz, Switzerland. In the wake of WWII, Japan and Germany are excluded; 28 nations compete across 22 events.

SWISS ALPINE SKIER KARL MOLITOR

January 26–February 5, 1956 The VII Winter Games are held in Cortina d'Ampezzo, Italy. The Soviet Union debuts and tops the medal table, winning 7 of the 24 events. Italy wins bobsled events.

BOBSLEDDERS EUGENIO MONTI AND RENZO ALVERÀ

Brakeman tucks in behind driver

Smooth, aerodynamic hull cuts down drag

November 22– December 8, 1956 The XVI Summer Games in Melbourne, Australia, are the first Games held in the southern hemisphere. Australia wins 8 of the 13 swimming gold medals.

AUSTRALIAN SWIMMER DAWN FRASER

April 6-15, 1896 Proposed by International Olympic Committee (IOC) founder Pierre de Coubertin, the first modern Olympiad begins with the Games held in Athens, Greece, with 241 athletes from 14 countries attending.

FRENCH EDUCATOR PIERRE DE COUBERTIN

May 14-October 28, 1900 The Games of the II Olympiad are held in Paris, France, as part of the World's Fair. With events spread over 5 months, the Olympics could not maintain people's interest. Women compete at the games for the first time—in sailing, tennis, and golf.

Fencing was a major attraction, with épée drawing up to 155 participants

OFFICIAL POSTER OF THE 1900 SUMMER OLYMPICS

Three types of fencing sword: foil, sabre, and épée

April 21-October 28, 1908 A dedicated stadium is built for athletic events, such as the marathon, at the IV Summer Games held in London. The organizing committee sets the length of the marathon at 26 miles, 385 yd (42.195 km).

ITALIAN MARATHON RUNNER DORANDO PIETRI

July 1-November 23, 1904 The III Summer Games are held in St. Louis, MO. Medals are awarded for the first time. US gymnast George Eyser wins six medals, despite having an artificial leg.

GEORGE EYSER

Fencing medalists received cash prizes in the 1900 Olympics

May 17-August 12, 1928 The Netherlands hosts the IX Summer Games in Amsterdam. Women's athletics debuts and India begins a run of six straight golds in men's hockey.

POSTER FOR IX OLYMPIAD

February 4-15, 1932 At the III Winter Games in Lake Placid, NY, America's Eddie Eagan becomes the first Olympian to win a gold medal at both a Summer and Winter Games in different sports—boxing (1920) and bobsled (1932).

July 30-August 14, 1932 The X Summer Games held in Los Angeles, CA, last 16 days. They include a dedicated Olympic village for male athletes and podiums for medal presentations.

US FENCER GEORGE CALNAN TAKES OLYMPIC OATH, 1932

August 1-16, 1936 The XI Summer Games in Berlin, Germany, are the first to feature a torch relay from Greece to the host city. US athlete Jesse Owens wins four gold medals, undermining German Führer Adolf Hitler's discourse of a superior Aryan race.

Specially made shoes with lighter spikes and laces

US ATHLETE JESSE OWENS

February 6-16, 1936 At the IV Winter Games in Garmisch-Partenkirchen, Germany, alpine skiing debuts with a combined slalom and downhill event. Norway's Ivar Ballangrud wins three speed-skating golds.

SPEED SKATER IVAN BALLANGRUD

February 18-28, 1960 Squaw Valley, CA, hosts the VIII Winter Games. Biathlon and women's speed skating are added, but bobsled is omitted—the only time in Olympic history.

August 25-September 11, 1960 The XVII Summer Games are hosted by Rome, Italy. Hungarian fencer Aladár Gerevich wins his seventh gold. Paralympic events are competed by 400 disabled athletes.

Fencer avoids opponent's lunge

OLYMPIC FENCING

January 29-February 9, 1964 At the IX Winter Games in Innsbruck, Austria, the French Goitschel sisters finish first and second in the slalom and giant slalom events.

October 10-24, 1964 The XVII Summer Games are held in Tokyo. Judo, volleyball, and women's pentathlon debut. Soviet gymnast Larisa Latynina wins six medals. Her career total of 18 medals holds the record for 48 years.

Stamp depicts game of volleyball

POSTAGE STAMP

◀ see also Snow and ice sports pp.480–81   ◀ Riding and racing sports pp.486–87   **489**

>> The Olympics continued

February 6–18, 1968 The games are broadcast in color for the first time, with the X Winter Games, held in Grenoble, France. Norway tops the medal table with six gold medals.

DICK FOSBURY'S HIGH JUMP

Feet hitched up and lifted over bar

October 12–27, 1968 The XIX Summer Games in Mexico City are the first to be held in Latin America. US high jumper Dick Fosbury wins gold with his unique technique.

Thin, synthetic fabric helps reduce wind resistance

Chest held parallel to ground

JAPANESE SKI JUMPER YUKIO KASAYA

Boots in bindings allow movement at ankle

Long skis angled upward for lift

February 3–13, 1972 Hosted in Sapporo, Japan, the XI Winter Games are the first to be held outside of Europe or the Americas. A total of 35 nations participate.

September 17–October 2, 1988 At the XXIV Summer Games in Seoul, South Korea, athlete Christa Luding-Rothenburger becomes the only person to win medals in the Winter and Summer games in the same year.

Circular scoring area called house

Eight rocks per team

CURLING INTRODUCED

February 13–28, 1988 The XV Winter Games are hosted in Calgary, Canada, for the first time. Despite not winning medals, the Jamaican bobsled team earn fame and goodwill for participating against all odds. Curling is introduced as a demonstration sport.

July 28–August 12, 1984 Synchronized swimming and women's marathon events make their debut at the XXIII Summer Games in Los Angeles, CA. American athlete Carl Lewis wins four golds.

SYNCHRONIZED SWIMMING

Protective helmet

February 8–23, 1992 Moguls skiing, short-track speed skating, and the women's biathlon make their Olympic debut at the XVI Winter Games in Albertville, France.

OLYMPIC DEBUT OF MOGULS FREESTYLE SKIING

Boots are attached to skis using standard ski bindings

July 25–August 9, 1992 The XXV Summer Games are hosted in Barcelona, Spain. Baseball and women's judo become medal events. Slalom canoeing returns to the Olympics.

Indonesia's Susi Susanti wins gold in Barcelona

BADMINTON INTRODUCED

February 12–27, 1994 Lillehammer, Norway hosts the XVII Winter Games, the first games to be held in a different year from the Summer Olympics. Speed skating moves indoors.

Usain Bolt strikes his trademark "lightning bolt" pose

August 8–24, 2008 US swimmer Michael Phelps wins eight gold medals at the XXIX Summer Games in Beijing, China. Usain Bolt breaks the 100 m and 200 m world records.

February 10–26, 2006 At the XX Winter Games in Turin, Italy, Germany tops the medal table with 29 medals. Enrico Fabris becomes the first Italian to win a gold medal in speed skating.

One arm behind back to reduce drag

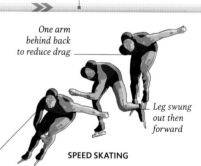

Leg swung out then forward

Skater stays low to maintain speed

SPEED SKATING

February 12–28, 2010 Held in Vancouver, Canada, the XXI Winter Games mark the debut of ski cross. Canada tops the medal table with 14 gold medals.

Jamaican national colors

JAMAICAN SPRINTER USAIN BOLT

July 27–August 12, 2012 At the XXX Summer Games in London, 38 world records are set and women's boxing is introduced in three weight classes: 51 kg, 60 kg, and 75 kg.

WOMEN'S BOXING

February 7–23, 2014 Held in Sochi, Russia, the XXII Winter Games feature 12 new events including luge relay, team figure skating, and ski half-pipe.

August 26– September 11, 1972
A Palestinian terrorist attack at the XX Summer Games in Munich, Germany, results in the deaths of 11 Israeli athletes and officials. The games continue in defiance of this attack.

ARCHERY RETURNS TO THE OLYMPICS

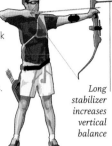

Recurve bow fires arrows at more than 124 mph (200 kph)

Long stabilizer increases vertical balance

February 4–15, 1976
The XII Winter Games are held in Innsbruck, Austria, for the second time in 12 years. Ice dance makes its debut. Luge and bobsled events are held on the same track for the first time.

AUSTRIAN SKIER FRANZ KLAMMER

Klammer wore his own yellow ski suit because he found the Austrian team's ski suit too tight

July 17–August 1, 1976
The Soviet Union wins 125 medals at the XXI Summer Games held in Montreal, Canada. Nadia Comǎneci becomes the first gymnast to earn a perfect 10 score.

ROMANIA'S NADIA COMǍNECI

February 8–19, 1984 Sarajevo, in former Yugoslavia, hosts the XIV Winter Games. Great Britain's Jayne Torvill and Christopher Dean win gold in ice dancing, scoring 12 perfect sixes for artistic interpretation.

Balletic moves choreographed to French composer Maurice Ravel's Bolero

JAYNE TORVILL AND CHRISTOPHER DEAN

Shorter blades allow for faster footwork

July 19–August 3, 1980
At the XXII Summer Games, held in Moscow, Soviet Union, home gymnast Aleksandr Dityatin wins eight medals. He is the first male gymnast to earn a perfect 10 score.

February 13–24. 1980
The XIII Winter Games are held in Lake Placid, NY. The US ice hockey team defeats four-time Olympic champions, the Soviet Union, in a win touted as "the miracle on ice."

US DEFEAT SOVIETS 4–3

July 19–August 4, 1996
At the XXVI Summer Games in Atlanta, GA, Marie-José Pérec of France becomes the first woman to win the 400 m at two consecutive Olympics. She also wins the 200 m.

OLYMPIC GOLD MEDALLIST MARIE-JOSE PEREC

Pérec's speed and slender physique earns her nickname "La Gazelle"

February 7–22, 1998
The XVIII Winter Games in Nagano, Japan, feature the return of curling as an Olympic medal sport, for both men and women. Snowboarding and women's ice hockey appear for the first time in the Olympics.

August 13–29, 2004 With the XXVIII Summer Games, the Olympics return to Athens, Greece. Shot putters compete at the ancient Olympia stadium. Women's wrestling and saber fencing debut.

OPENING CEREMONY

February 8–24, 2002
The XIX Winter Games are held in Salt Lake City, UT, with 78 nations taking part. Speed skater Yang Yang wins China's first ever gold medal in the Winter Games.

September 15– October 1, 2000 The XXVII Summer Games are held in Sydney, Australia. Cathy Freeman becomes the first athlete to light the Olympic flame and win gold in the same Olympics.

AUSTRALIAN ATHLETE CATHY FREEMAN

August 5–21, 2016
At the XXXI Summer Games in Rio de Janeiro, Brazil, Michael Phelps takes his career medal tally to 23 gold, 3 silver, and 2 bronze medals before announcing his retirement.

Phelps is often called "the flying fish"

US SWIMMER MICHAEL PHELPS

February 9–25, 2018
Six nations make their Winter Games debut in Pyeongchang, South Korea, taking the total number of participating teams to 98. Big air snowboarding is among the new events introduced.

Athlete grabs front of board

Body turns to board front

Board is released

Board angled to land flat on slope

SNOWBOARDING ALLEY-OOP TRICK

2020 Games of the XXXII Olympiad in Tokyo, Japan, are delayed, until 2021 or later, due to the Coronavirus pandemic. Freestyle BMX is slated to make its Olympic debut.

◀ see also Track and field pp.476–77   ◀ Snow and ice sports pp.480–81   **491**

Photography

Photography began in the 19th century as a process in which light prompted chemical reactions on film coated with an emulsion. Digital cameras were invented in 1975 and replaced film with light-sensitive sensors. The sensors' electric output signals are processed by the camera to produce a digital image file stored in memory, and is downloadable and editable using computers.

Camera types

Digital cameras range from slim compacts to bulky yet powerful DSLRs (see p.271). Image quality is often dependent on the lens and the sensor quality. Many enjoy taking images with the increasingly powerful camera options of smartphones.

Enthusiast compact
Compact cameras have excellent build and image quality but are expensive and sometimes have only a narrow zoom range.

Bridge/Prosumer
Bridge cameras feature a wide zoom range and smaller bulk than a DSLR, but, like compacts, no ability to change the lenses.

Mirrorless
Smaller, lighter, and quieter than DSLRs, mirrorless cameras provide users with some choice of interchangeable lenses.

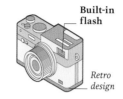
Built-in flash
Retro design

DSLR
DSLRs offer users control, high-quality images, and the ability to accept a wide range of interchangeable, high-quality lenses.

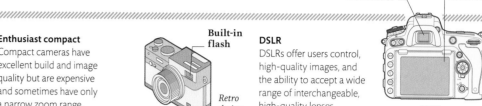
Viewfinder
Large LCD viewscreen
BACK

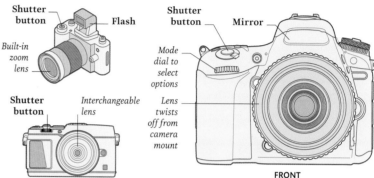
Shutter button
Flash
Built-in zoom lens

Shutter button
Mirror
Mode dial to select options
Lens twists off from camera mount

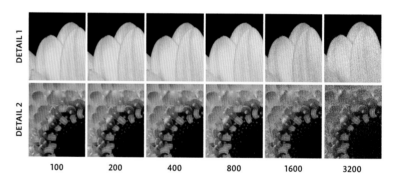
Shutter button
Interchangeable lens

Shutter button
Lens twists off from camera mount
FRONT

ISO

A legacy from film cameras, ISO determines the amount of light needed during an exposure. Cameras have a typical ISO range of 50 to 3200. A higher ISO boosts the signals sent from the camera's sensor, enabling the capture of low-light images, but at the expense of graininess, called "noise", in the resulting image. Noise is a kind of interference that can also appear in an image as colored dots.

Increasing ISO
In close up, it is clear how fine details change at different ISO sensitivities.

DETAIL 1

DETAIL 2

| 100 | 200 | 400 | 800 | 1600 | 3200 |

Aperture

A series of blades in the lens open to form an aperture to let light in. The aperture's size can be adjusted in a series of steps known as f-stops (typically f/1.4 to f/22). The smaller the f number, the larger the aperture and the more light admitted.

Changing aperture
A smaller aperture, such as f/16, increases depth of field—the amount of the scene in focus (see p.494). A wider aperture, such as f/4, results in a blurred background.

Aperture blades

Blades close to produce small aperture

MORE LIGHT
f/2
f/4
f/5.6
f/8
f/11
f/16
LESS LIGHT

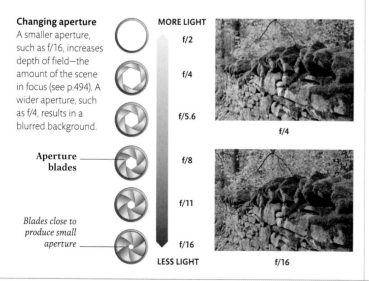
f/4

f/16

Shutter speed

Shutter speed determines exposure time—the length of time light is permitted to reach the camera's sensor. It is usually measured in fractions of a second. High shutter speeds freeze rapid action into a sharp image, but often require higher ISO or a larger aperture to obtain enough light.

Shutter speed dial
Shutter speed can be manually controlled. The fastest shutter speed setting will freeze movement and is best-suited for shooting in very bright light.

Fast shutter speed

Mid-range speed

Slow shutter speed

1/500 SEC

1/125 SEC

1/15 SEC

Exposure and movement
The slower the shutter speed, the greater the blur exhibited by moving elements in an image and the more light is let in by the shutter.

1/500 SEC

1/125 SEC

1/15 SEC

Focal length

This is the distance, usually measured in millimeters, between the lens and the camera's image sensor when the subject is in focus. Prime lenses have one focal length, while zoom lenses vary. Focal length determines the angle of view—how much of a scene is captured.

Focal length and view

The longer the focal length of a lens, the narrower the angle of view, the smaller the area captured, and the larger the subject appears to be.

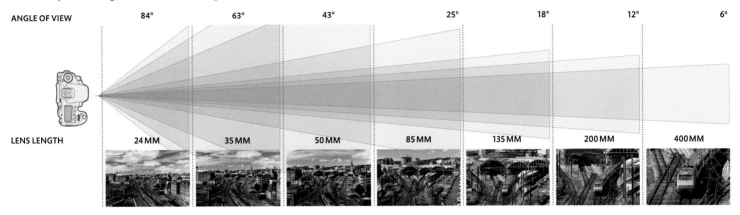

ANGLE OF VIEW	84°	63°	43°	25°	18°	12°	6°
LENS LENGTH	24 MM	35 MM	50 MM	85 MM	135 MM	200 MM	400 MM

Lenses

Lenses may be prime (with one fixed focal length) or zoom (variable focal lengths). Prime lenses tend to have a faster maximum aperture, so they can let in more light at higher shutter speeds.

Wide angle
Focal lengths below 35 mm give a wider field of view used in landscape, travel, and abstract shots.

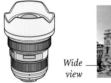

Wide view

Standard
Lenses of 35–50 mm produce images with a perspective comparable to the naked eye.

Natural perspective

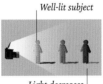

Telephoto
Focal lengths of 75 mm and above bring distant subjects closer. Long telephoto is used for wildlife photography.

Distant subject large in frame

Macro
These allow focusing at much closer distances than other lenses, enabling small subjects to fill the frame.

Extreme close up

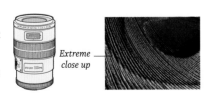

A **Leica f5.6/1600 mm** telephoto lens sold for **$2,064,500** in 2006

Flash

Flash is built-in to many digital cameras or can be provided by an external flashgun that can be deployed off camera or fitted to the camera via a hot shoe (mount). Flashes provide a short but intense burst of light to illuminate a scene. The output is measured in guide numbers (GN): the higher the number, the more powerful the flash.

Light decreases with distance
A flash guide number suitable for close-up subjects may not work at greater distances.

Well-lit subject

Light decreases with distance

Subject at long range, low GN
Flash is unable to light the subject fully. The image is underexposed as a result.

Subject poorly lit

Subject at short range, low GN
A lower power flash can brighten a close subject poorly lit or in partial shadow.

Subject brightened

Subject at long range, high GN
Increasing ISO sensitivity increases the flash's GN, providing enough light for exposure.

Light reaches subject

Filters

Filters are mounted in front of a lens to perform a variety of tasks. Polarizing filters reduce reflections and help create images with saturated colors; others diffuse light, producing a soft image.

Filter holder attached to lens via adapter

Filter ring attaches directly to lens

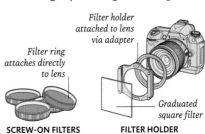

Graduated square filter

SCREW-ON FILTERS

FILTER HOLDER

TRIPODS

Tripods provide a stable support for a camera so that it does not move during exposure. The height can be adjusted by raising or lowering the legs.

Axes can be adjusted

THREE-WAY HEAD

Ball and socket joint

BALL HEAD

Tripod head

TRIPOD

≫ Photography continued

Composing pictures

Composition comprises a series of decisions by the photographer on the arrangement, placing, and importance of the different elements within their image. It can involve experimenting with different viewpoints, framing techniques, shutter speed, and depths of field. A large aperture, for instance, can blur many elements, thus increasing the importance of those elements that remain sharp.

> "For me, the camera is a **sketch book**, an instrument of **intuition** and **spontaneity**."
>
> HENRI CARTIER-BRESSON,
> *The Mind's Eye*, 1999

Manipulating depth of field

Depth of field is the area of relative sharpness within an image either side of the subject being focused on. Changing the lens aperture can alter the depth of field in order to bring greater or fewer elements into clear view.

The figure is the only part of the image that is in focus

Background of image is blurred

f/8 aperture produces deeper depth of field

Large f/2.8 aperture results in shallow depth of field

Aperture set at f/2.8

All of the image (foreground and background) is sharp

Small f/22 aperture produces very deep depth of field

Subject focused on by camera is 30 ft (10 m) away

Aperture set at f/8

Aperture set at f/22

Composition frameworks

Arranging and placing elements within a photograph can be a tricky skill for inexperienced photographers to master. Simple compositional frameworks, such as following the rule of thirds or seeking out diagonals in the scene to work with, can assist new photographers when trying to select their precise viewpoint and composition.

Subject's body centered between the two horizontal lines

Diagonal formed by bird and leaf lead viewer's eye into scene

Rule of thirds

The rule of thirds involves dividing up a scene into a grid using two evenly spaced vertical lines and two evenly spaced horizontal lines. Placing elements of interest along these lines and where they intersect helps balance shots.

Diagonals

Diagonal lines in a scene can add dynamism, leading the viewer's gaze to a point in the image and creating further points of interest where they intersect other lines. Diagonal lines can be more engaging than horizontals and verticals.

Light and contrast

Contrast is the difference in tone and color between different parts of a scene. Hard light produces strong contrast, accentuating shapes and shadows. Soft, more diffuse light, such as sunshine through clouds or filtered through blinds, produces less contrast and softens subjects. Different subject types require different qualities of light.

Source of light

Diffused light source

Bright, focused highlights

Soft, subdued highlights

Strong, hard-edged shadows

Pale, soft-edged shadows

HARD LIGHT

SOFT LIGHT

THE GOLDEN RATIO

The irrational number 1.618034 is known as the golden ratio (1:1.62) or phi. Widely found in nature, the ancient Greeks discovered the attractiveness of rectangles with short and long sides in these proportions. The golden ratio and its close relation, the golden spiral, are adopted in photography to compose images that are naturally pleasing to the eye.

Center of spiral forms focal point of image

GOLDEN SPIRAL

Rhein II, a photo taken by Andreas Gursky, sold at a 2011 auction for $4,338,500

Subject types

There is a great variety of photographic subject types, from astrophotography (imaging the night sky) to architectural. Each type may make different demands on a photographer's eye for composition, their technical understanding, and the equipment used. Some choose to specialize in one area, developing their specific skills and sometimes purchasing dedicated equipment.

POST-PROCESSING

Photographs can be transferred from a camera's memory card to a computer, where software packages can edit the data stored in the digital image file to process and enhance the images. Particular parts of images can have their exposure or color saturation altered, effects and filters applied, or small, unwanted objects removed from the image entirely.

IMAGE PROCESSING SOFTWARE

Color sampling pull-down menu

Document window features image undergoing editing

Landscape
The perfect capturing of a natural scene requires sound composition and management of contrast, saturation, and depth of field. Color filters are sometimes used to bring out the landscape's natural colors.

Street
Street photography is the documenting of public space as the photographer sees it. Their focus may be on saturated, vibrant colors, architectural angles using wide-angle lenses, or candid photography of street life.

Action
Freezing fast movement for sharp images in sports requires a high shutter speed. Long lenses can bring the action closer. Some cameras' burst modes take multiple images per second.

Abstract
Abstract photography involves seeking out textures and unusual perspectives in nature or everyday things. It can involve macro photography or long exposures to create blur or streaks of moving light.

Macro
This extreme close-up photography, with 1:1 or higher reproduction, often requires dedicated lenses or extension tubes to magnify objects and reveal textures and details previously unnoticed by the naked eye.

Portrait
Capturing peoples' personalities and expressions is an art that requires careful management of light, contrast, and background. Some portraiture is candid, while indoor portrait work may utilize special studio equipment.

Travel
A bridge camera or DSLR with zoom provides the versatility to capture images in a wide range of conditions. An eye for the unusual and noteworthy, and understanding of light, can be invaluable.

Wildlife
Great patience and intense concentration can capture extraordinary images in the wild. Long lenses may be required for imaging animals at a distance, blurring backgrounds to put the subject center stage.

Documentary
Seeking out scenes that tell a story, some documentary photography is taken in black and white for added impact. Photographers may have to sum up a situation and shoot in a moment.

Drawing and painting

Among the oldest of all art forms, painting and drawing were first performed by humans during the Old Stone Age. They have been used ever since to express ideas and emotions, tell a story, and capture scenes and likenesses of people, animals, and objects. These art forms utilize a wide variety of media and many different strokes and techniques. Before the invention of photography in the 19th century, paintings and drawings provided much of the visual documentary evidence we have of the historic world.

Drawing

Drawing is the construction of art consisting of lines and shading made using various tools. It emphasizes form and shape over mass blocks of color and is very versatile. Sketches and preparatory drawings are often made by painters to aid composition.

Tools

Artists can pick from a variety of black graphite pencils, pens, charcoal, and richly colored pastel crayons with which to draw.

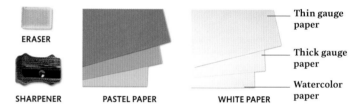

PENCIL   OIL PASTEL

COLOR PENCIL   CHALK PASTEL

CHARCOAL PENCIL   COMPRESSED CHARCOAL   TECHNICAL PEN

PENCIL GRADES

Pencils can be graded on a scale from ultra-soft and dark (9B) to ultra-hard and light (9H). These are determined by the amounts of clay and graphite the pencil contains.

| 9B | 8B | 7B | 6B | 5B | 4B | 3B | 2B | B | HB | F | H | 2H | 3H | 4H | 5H | 6H | 7H | 8H | 9H |

SOFT ←→ HARD

ERASER

SHARPENER   PASTEL PAPER   WHITE PAPER

Thin gauge paper
Thick gauge paper
Watercolor paper

Building a drawing

Many drawings can be built from a series of rough lines and geometric shapes all in proportion to the object or person portrayed. These form a guide that shows how the differing parts relate to one another.

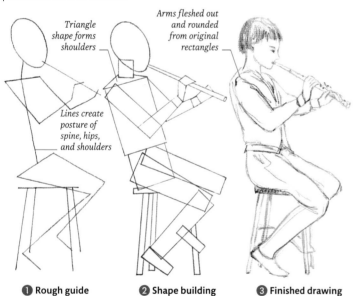

Triangle shape forms shoulders

Arms fleshed out and rounded from original rectangles

Lines create posture of spine, hips, and shoulders

❶ Rough guide
The proportions, orientation, and angles of the different parts of the figure are sketched out.

❷ Shape building
Geometric shapes are added—from rectangular limbs and torso to a cylinder for the oboe.

❸ Finished drawing
The complete figure is drawn by altering the geometric shapes to create more detail.

A 73,000 year old drawing was found in South Africa's Blombos Cave

Gripping

A lighter, more relaxed grip than when writing allows control of pencils and charcoal. Pastels are applied via their ends or side.

Pressing harder produces denser color

PENCIL   CHARCOAL   PASTEL

Hatching and crosshatching

These line-drawing techniques can add weight or texture to a drawing or create light and shadow.

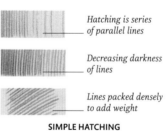

Hatching is series of parallel lines

Decreasing darkness of lines

Lines packed densely to add weight

SIMPLE HATCHING

A series of parallel lines intersect at right angles

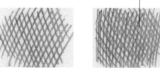

CROSS-HATCHING

Adding tone

Variations in tone (light and dark) can convey how light falls on an object from different directions.

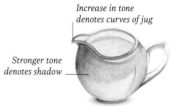

Increase in tone denotes curves of jug

Stronger tone denotes shadow

BACKLIGHTING

Light strikes object from front-right

Darker shading conveys shadow

THREE-QUARTER LIGHTING

Painting

A painting is an image created using dry pigments (colors) mixed with a medium (a liquid such as water or oil). This is then applied to a surface such as paper, wood, or canvas. This is most commonly achieved using brushes, but custom knives, scrapers, and shaped sponges can produce a range of different effects.

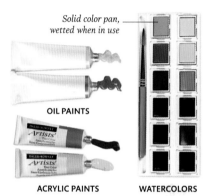

Solid color pan, wetted when in use

OIL PAINTS

ACRYLIC PAINTS   WATERCOLORS

Paints

Slow-drying oils allow layering and vibrant color buildup. Acrylic paints dry quickly but may darken, while watercolors dry matte.

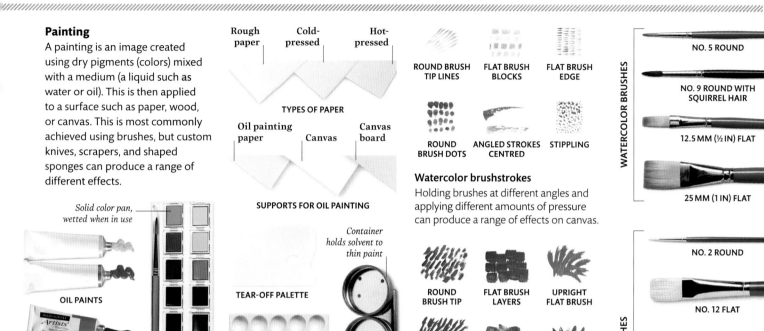

Rough paper   Cold-pressed   Hot-pressed

TYPES OF PAPER

Oil painting paper   Canvas   Canvas board

SUPPORTS FOR OIL PAINTING

Container holds solvent to thin paint

TEAR-OFF PALETTE

WELL PALETTE   DIPPERS

Tools

Brushes for different paints come in different sizes and shapes. Palettes enable the mixing of paint before application onto paper or canvas.

ROUND BRUSH TIP LINES   FLAT BRUSH BLOCKS   FLAT BRUSH EDGE

ROUND BRUSH DOTS   ANGLED STROKES CENTRED   STIPPLING

Watercolor brushstrokes

Holding brushes at different angles and applying different amounts of pressure can produce a range of effects on canvas.

ROUND BRUSH TIP   FLAT BRUSH LAYERS   UPRIGHT FLAT BRUSH

FILBERT BRUSH   KNIFE COLORING   KNIFE DAB

Oil paint brushstrokes

Oil brushes come in fan, filbert, flat, and round designs. Each can be applied to the canvas in a variety of different ways.

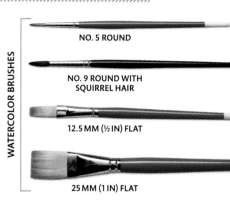

WATERCOLOR BRUSHES

NO. 5 ROUND

NO. 9 ROUND WITH SQUIRREL HAIR

12.5 MM (½ IN) FLAT

25 MM (1 IN) FLAT

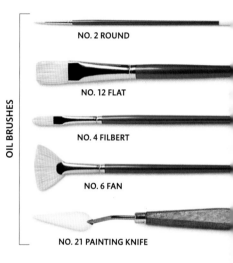

OIL BRUSHES

NO. 2 ROUND

NO. 12 FLAT

NO. 4 FILBERT

NO. 6 FAN

NO. 21 PAINTING KNIFE

Building a painting

Preparatory sketches determine composition and the focal point—where the viewers' eyes are first drawn. These first sketches can be erased and reworked if necessary. Lightly sketched outlines on the canvas are first filled in with base layers of paint from the edge of the canvas or paper inward. Fine detail is gradually added and layered on top with different tools, such as knives or brushes.

❶ Outline and background
With the painting's outline sketched out, the background is filled in, working from the edge inward.

❷ Background complete
The background between flowers is filled in using a painting knife. The lower jug is rag-rubbed to achieve a lighter color.

COLORS

The relationships between colors can be shown on a color wheel. There are three primary colors (red, blue, and yellow), which can be mixed to form three secondary colors (green, orange, and violet). Six further intermediate colors can be created by adding more of one primary color to a secondary color to form a color wheel of 12 colors. Opposite pairs are called complementary colors.

❸ Starting the flowers
A bright mixture of magenta and white paint is applied as a base color for the anemones, using a knife.

❹ Blues added
Blues are applied by brush to the flowers and the jug, and to create the subtle folds in the tablecloth below.

❺ Completed painting
A striking arrangement of strong, bright flowers and vase is presented against the simple background.

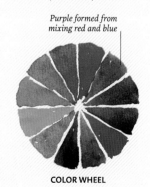

Purple formed from mixing red and blue

COLOR WHEEL

◄ see also Great painters pp.448–49   Ceramics and glass pp.502–503 ►

Sewing, knitting, and crochet

The need to create fabric and stitch it together emerged in human prehistory, with animal furs and skins stitched together using animal sinews or plant fibers as sewing thread. Knitting with needles and wool is thought to have originated in the Middle East around 1,500–2,000 years ago. Crochet, using hooks and yarn, is a more recent, 19th century, invention.

MEASURING TAPE **CUTTING SHEARS** **THIMBLE**

Sewing

Sewing uses stitches made of thread to join fabrics together or affix objects to fabrics. It is used to create clothes, soft toys, and household furnishings from scratch, and to resize clothing, or perform repairs. Sewing is also the basis of other crafts including embroidery, quilting, tapestry, and appliqué.

Threads

Threads vary in color, thickness, material, finish, and elasticity. Standard cotton threads stretch less than polyester threads, for instance.

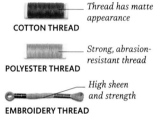

COTTON THREAD — *Thread has matte appearance*

POLYESTER THREAD — *Strong, abrasion-resistant thread*

EMBROIDERY THREAD — *High sheen and strength*

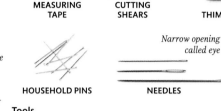

Narrow opening called eye

HOUSEHOLD PINS **NEEDLES**

Tools

A typical sewing box contains needles of different sizes, fabric-cutting shears, and pins to hold fabrics in place prior to stitching. A metal or plastic thimble protects the middle or index fingertip from sharp points.

Common stitches

A variety of stitches can be employed for different hand-sewing tasks, from the simple but weak running stitch to cross stitches used to finish a hem (folded edge of fabric). Some stitches are purely functional, while others can be employed for decorative purposes on clothing and fabric.

Strong stitch, usually used to sew seams
BACK STITCH

Small, even stitches used for decoration or seams
RUNNING STITCH

Stitch wraps round edge of fabric to prevent fraying
WHIP STITCH

Thread forms knots along edge of fabric
BUTTONHOLE STITCH

Short stitches cross each other
HERRINGBONE STITCH

Straight stitch holds two layers together
FLAT FELL STITCH

Short, horizontal stitch
SLIP HEM STITCH

A slip hem stitch hidden under fabric edge
BLIND HEM STITCH

Stitch wraps up and over fabric edge
BLANKET STITCH

Rows of diagonal stitches crossing in center
CROSS STITCH

Knitting

Knitting uses long needles to knot or interlink a series of loops to construct fabric from a continuous thread of wool or yarn. Knitted fabric generally stretches more than woven cloth.

BAMBOO NEEDLES

PLASTIC NEEDLES

METAL NEEDLES

BAMBOO DOUBLE-POINTED NEEDLES

STITCH HOLDER

Tools

Needles can be straight, flat, or circular, and made from different materials. Plastic and bamboo needles are lightweight, while metal needles allow yarn loops to slip off smoothly.

KNITTING NEEDLE CONVERSION CHART

Needles vary in size from tiny, for intricate lace projects, up to to 1 in (2.5 cm) wide for thick yarns.

EU METRIC	OLD UK	US
1.5 mm	n/a	000
		00
2 mm	14	0
2.25 mm	13	1
2.5 mm		
2.75 mm	12	2
3 mm	11	n/a
3.25 mm	10	3
3.5 mm	n/a	4
3.75 mm	9	5
4 mm	8	6
4.5 mm	7	7
5 mm	6	8
5.5 mm	5	9
6 mm	4	10
6.5 mm	3	10.5
7 mm	2	n/a
7.5 mm	1	n/a
8 mm	0	11
9 mm	00	13
10 mm	000	15
12 mm	n/a	17
15 mm	n/a	19
20 mm	n/a	35
25 mm	n/a	50

Yarns

Yarns vary in weight (thickness) and are made from natural (wool, fleece, cotton, and silk) or artificial (nylon, acrylic, polyester) materials, or even a hybrid of both.

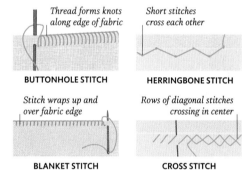

Warm and durable
WOOL

Extremely soft (from Merino sheep)
MERINO WOOL

Smooth, machine-washable yarn
ACRYLIC

Making a slip knot

The starting point of many knitting projects, the slip knot securely anchors one end of a ball of wool or yarn to a needle and is the first loop on a needle. It is a key technique and forms the first stitch in the casting on row. It is used for the same purpose in crochet.

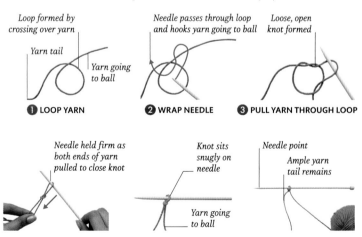

Loop formed by crossing over yarn
Yarn tail
Yarn going to ball
❶ LOOP YARN

Needle passes through loop and hooks yarn going to ball
❷ WRAP NEEDLE

Loose, open knot formed
❸ PULL YARN THROUGH LOOP

Needle held firm as both ends of yarn pulled to close knot
❹ FORM AROUND THE NEEDLE

Knot sits snugly on needle
Yarn going to ball
❺ TIGHTEN KNOT

Needle point
Ample yarn tail remains
❻ READY TO KNIT

The world's **fastest knitte**r, Miriam Tegels, can knit **118 stitches in 1 minute**, an average knitter can manage 20–30

Crochet

Deriving from the French word for "small hook," crochet creates textured fabric from looped and linked chains of thread using a single hook to hold and pull the thread through. Crocheted objects, apart from clothing, include hats, toys, lacework, and bags.

AMIGURUMI

These crocheted stuffed dolls and plush toys originate from Japan. They are usually constructed by crocheting a spiral with a small-gauge hook. Prior to stuffing, many amigurumi are weighted with stones in the feet so they can stand up.

Felt lining attached with stitches

CROCHETED SOFT TOY

Tools

One of crochet's most appealing aspects is just how little equipment the craft requires—just crochet hooks of different gauges and a blunt-ended yarn needle, to securely sew in and hide loose ends of yarn.

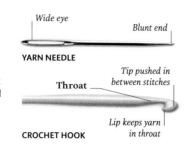

Wide eye · *Blunt end*

YARN NEEDLE

Throat · *Tip pushed in between stitches*

Lip keeps yarn in throat

CROCHET HOOK

Holding hook and yarn

The hook can be held like one would a knife, or a pencil (pictured, right). The flow of yarn is controlled by lacing it around the little finger and then under the two middle fingers.

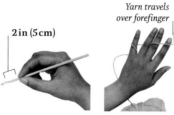

2 in (5 cm)

Yarn travels over forefinger

HOLDING THE HOOK · **HOLDING THE YARN**

Fastening off a row of stitches

The loop is removed from the crochet hook, enlarged, and the end passed through and pulled to tighten the loop and fasten off.

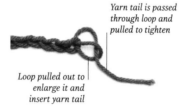

Yarn tail is passed through loop and pulled to tighten

Loop pulled out to enlarge it and insert yarn tail

Making a foundation chain

A foundation chain is the starting row of most crochet projects. Simple chain stitches create spaces for other crochet stitches to link to.

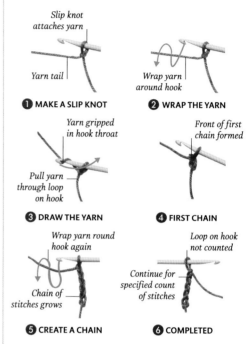

Slip knot attaches yarn

Yarn tail

① MAKE A SLIP KNOT

Wrap yarn around hook

② WRAP THE YARN

Yarn gripped in hook throat

Pull yarn through loop on hook

③ DRAW THE YARN

Front of first chain formed

④ FIRST CHAIN

Wrap yarn round hook again

Chain of stitches grows

⑤ CREATE A CHAIN

Loop on hook not counted

Continue for specified count of stitches

⑥ COMPLETED

Single cast-on

Also known as the thumb cast-on, the single cast-on is the easiest cast-on technique to learn. It uses a single strand of yarn that is looped around the left thumb. The needle tip is brought under and up through the loop to cast on. The technique can be repeated as often as needed to get the required amount of loops on the needle.

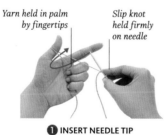

Yarn held in palm by fingertips

Slip knot held firmly on needle

① INSERT NEEDLE TIP

Release loop from thumb

New loop on needle tightened by pulling yarn

② NEW LOOP

Cast-on loops pushed together

Yarn going to ball

③ REPEAT FOR REQUIRED STITCHES

Working a knit stitch

With the right needle inserted into the back of the left's first loop, the yarn is wrapped under and around the right needle. The yarn is then drawn through the loop on the left needle to form a new stitch. The yarn is held firmly (but not tightly) to achieve an even level of tension. Any stitches that come off the needle can be sewn in later.

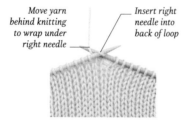

Move yarn behind knitting to wrap under right needle

Insert right needle into back of loop

① INSERT AND WRAP

Draw yarn through loop

Yarn held at back of knitting

② DRAW YARN THROUGH

Old loop drops off left needle

Completed new stitch

③ COMPLETED STITCH

Casting off knitwise

Casting off is the technique used to end a column of stitches and close off loops. When completed, casting off removes the yarn from the needles and avoids stitches unraveling. The following technique sees the needle tip lift one stitch over the next to form a secure edge. The yarn tail should be cut long enough so that it can be darned into the knitting later.

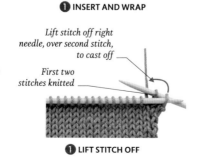

Lift stitch off right needle, over second stitch, to cast off

First two stitches knitted

① LIFT STITCH OFF

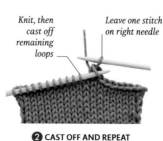

Knit, then cast off remaining loops

Leave one stitch on right needle

② CAST OFF AND REPEAT

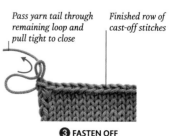

Pass yarn tail through remaining loop and pull tight to close

Finished row of cast-off stitches

③ FASTEN OFF

see also Knots pp.504–505 ▶ **499**

Woodworking

Wood is one of humankind's oldest building materials. It is phenomenally versatile—capable of being bent, cut, drilled, shaped, and joined in a great variety of ways. Equally numerous are the many tasks and projects for which you can use wood. Millions of people enjoy the craft of woodworking and employ it to produce useful or decorative items, from benches, cabinets, tables, and chairs, to toys and jewelry.

Types of wood

Woods and artificial boards, such as plywood, all exhibit different attributes. Softwoods include pine and cedar. Slower-growing deciduous trees yield hardwoods such as teak, walnut, and beech.

Walnut is fine-grained and durable

HARDWOOD

Pine is light and resinous

SOFTWOOD

Formed of a sandwich of layers

PLYWOOD

Hand tools

Most woodworking tools are operated and controlled by hand. Saws and chisels allow wood to be cut, and slots and joints created, while striking tools such as hammers drive chisels or nails. Clamps and vises hold work in place.

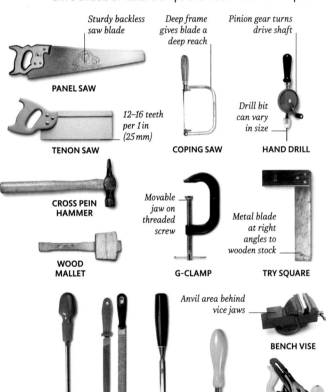

Sturdy backless saw blade

PANEL SAW

Deep frame gives blade a deep reach

Pinion gear turns drive shaft

12–16 teeth per 1 in (25 mm)

TENON SAW

COPING SAW

Drill bit can vary in size

HAND DRILL

CROSS PEIN HAMMER

Movable jaw on threaded screw

Metal blade at right angles to wooden stock

WOOD MALLET

G-CLAMP

TRY SQUARE

Anvil area behind vice jaws

BENCH VISE

SCREW-DRIVER

RASP AND FILE

CHISEL

BRADAWL

BENCH PLANE

POWER TOOLS

Electric power tools ease the effort required by some hand tools. Some electric devices, such as jigsaws and drills, enable tasks that are difficult for many to achieve using hand tools.

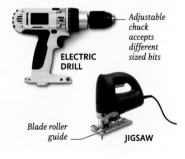

Adjustable chuck accepts different sized bits

ELECTRIC DRILL

Blade roller guide

JIGSAW

Sawing

A saw's outward-set teeth create a small channel in wood called a saw kerf. Wood behaves differently when sawed with the grain or against it, so it usually requires different saws. In both cases, cut lines are measured and marked out before the saw is drawn back to make its initial cut. Panel saws work well for both ripping and cross-cutting wood.

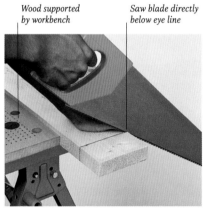

Wood supported by workbench

Saw blade directly below eye line

Cross-cutting

Cutting across the grain requires a saw with more teeth, which sever the wood fibers cleanly. The wood can be clamped or steadied with the supporting hand as the saw cuts.

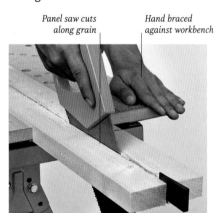

Panel saw cuts along grain

Hand braced against workbench

Ripping

Cutting along the grain requires a steady rhythm. When using a large-toothed panel saw, the wood should be cut on the waste side of the cutting line so that any excess can be planed down.

Planing

A plane's steel blade enables woodworkers to shave off thin layers of wood in the process of flattening, smoothing, or reducing the thickness of wood. The blade's depth can be adjusted to suit the task. Planing is conducted via repeated strokes made by the woodworker in line with the wood, and should move with the grain of the wood.

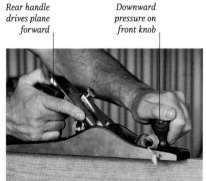

Rear handle drives plane forward

Downward pressure on front knob

USING A BENCH PLANE

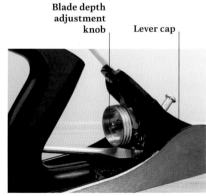

Blade depth adjustment knob

Lever cap

ADJUSTING THE BLADE DEPTH

Early examples of the **dovetail joint** can be found in **ancient Egyptian** cabinetwork from the First Dynasty

Clamping

Clamps are applied to hold work securely when sawing or chiseling, or to apply consistent pressure when a joint or frame is glued and left to set. A range of clamps can be employed for different tasks. A band clamp is ideal for clamping a frame made of four right-angled miter joints.

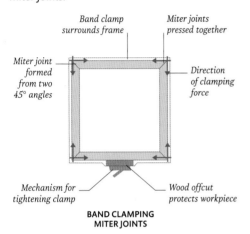

Band clamp surrounds frame
Miter joints pressed together
Miter joint formed from two 45° angles
Direction of clamping force
Mechanism for tightening clamp
Wood offcut protects workpiece

BAND CLAMPING MITER JOINTS

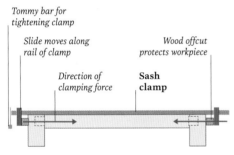

Tommy bar for tightening clamp
Slide moves along rail of clamp
Wood offcut protects workpiece
Direction of clamping force
Sash clamp

SASH CLAMPING MORTISE AND TENON JOINTS

> "It is the most **humanly intimate** of all materials ... Wood is **universally beautiful** to Man."
>
> FRANK LLOYD WRIGHT,
> *In the Cause of Architecture*, 1928

WORKING SAFELY

Working in a neat, well-lit, and well-ventilated workshop helps prevent accidents. Tying back loose hair and keeping power cords and sharp tools stored safely is very important. Wearing loose-fitting clothing or jewelry should be avoided, as they can catch in machinery. Eye goggles or safety glasses can protect from flying splinters, and dust masks provide a barrier against small particles. Feet should be protected by steel toe-capped boots in case heavy loads are dropped.

Joints

The joining of two pieces of wood can be as simple as two edges butting up to each other, to intricately cut and chiseled dovetail joints. Strength, visibility, and ease of construction can determine joint choice. Some hold together mechanically, but many require assistance via glue, screws, or nails.

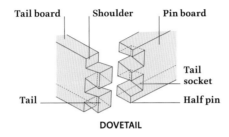

Tail board
Shoulder
Pin board
Tail socket
Half pin
Tail

DOVETAIL

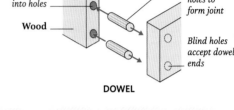

Mortise piece
Edge
Cosmetic shoulder
End wall
Tenon piece
Bottom
Structural shoulder
Face

MORTISE AND TENON

Dowel pin pushed into holes
Wood
Dowel pins align with holes to form joint
Blind holes accept dowel ends

DOWEL

TYPES OF SCREW HEADS

Screws utilize different drive systems to affix them. These include slotted, the cross-shaped Phillips system, and hexagonal heads that can be driven using an allen key or hex screwdriver.

SLOTTED

PHILLIPS

HEXAGONAL-HEADED

DUAL-PURPOSE

Gluing

Many joints and parts of woodworking projects require glue to hold them in place. Surfaces to be bonded need to be free of dust, paint, or varnish, and an even coating of glue is best. Some glues are fast acting, while polyvinyl acetate (PVA) glues can take up to 12 hours to cure completely.

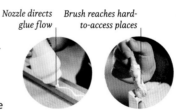
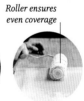

Nozzle directs glue flow
Brush reaches hard-to-access places
Roller ensures even coverage

USING BOTTLE   **USING BRUSH**   **USING ROLLER**

Sanding

The abrading (wearing away) of wood to create a smooth finish most commonly involves sandpaper. This comes in a range of grit sizes from below 100 (coarse) to over 240 (very fine). Although power sanders work rapidly, many prefer hand sanding—stretching sandpaper over a sanding block.

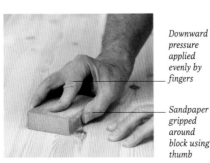

Downward pressure applied evenly by fingers
Sandpaper gripped around block using thumb

SANDING A FLAT SURFACE

Varnishing

Wood can be finished in a range of ways including varnishing, staining, and painting. Varnishing is the application of one or more coats of hard, clear, or translucent liquid, typically available in matte, gloss, and satin (semigloss) finishes. It dries to form a tough, water-resistant surface.

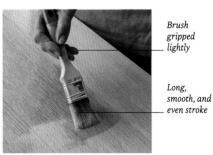

Brush gripped lightly
Long, smooth, and even stroke

VARNISHING SURFACES

Ceramics and glass

As a craft, ceramics involves the shaping, hardening, and decorating of clay products. Ceramics comes from the ancient Greek word, *keramos*, meaning potter or pottery. Potter's wheels originated in Mesopotamia about 5,500 years ago. Glass can only be produced by specialist craftsmen, but premade glass objects, such as vases, can be decorated at home.

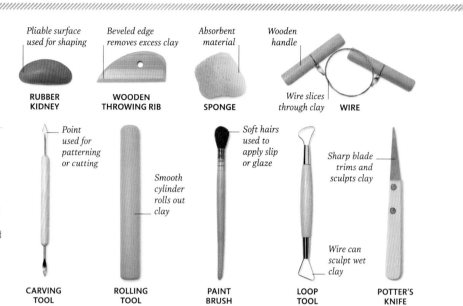

Pliable surface used for shaping
RUBBER KIDNEY

Beveled edge removes excess clay
WOODEN THROWING RIB

Absorbent material
SPONGE

Wooden handle
Wire slices through clay **WIRE**

Point used for patterning or cutting
CARVING TOOL

Smooth cylinder rolls out clay
ROLLING TOOL

Soft hairs used to apply slip or glaze
PAINT BRUSH

Sharp blade trims and sculpts clay
Wire can sculpt wet clay
LOOP TOOL

POTTER'S KNIFE

Pottery

Pottery is damp, worked clay that has been formed and shaped, dried, and then fired—heated to very high temperatures in a special oven called a kiln. The resulting substance, known as bisque, is solid, but porous. The application of glazes (powdered glass that forms a smooth, durable coating) and further firing in a kiln can make it impervious to water.

Tools

Pottery requires simple tools to cut, roll, shape, and pattern clay. Some tools have more than one purpose. Loop tools, for example, can also be used to carve soft clay and to produce clay coils with which to build pots using the hand-thrown coiling method (below).

Hand-thrown clay

Pottery formed by hand uses a variety of techniques, from pinching and manipulating soft lumps of clay into pots and bowls and building pots with coils of clay, to producing flat slabs to create tiles, containers, or rolled tubes that can function as pipes.

Clay supported in one hand
Fingers squeeze clay to build wall height
PINCHING

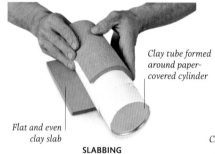

Clay tube formed around paper-covered cylinder
Flat and even clay slab
SLABBING

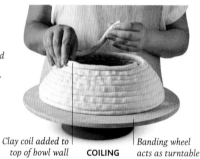

Clay coil added to top of bowl wall **COILING** *Banding wheel acts as turntable*

The potter's wheel

An electric or mechanically powered horizontal disk (the wheel) rotates, allowing wet clay to be worked into a wide range of circular objects by hand or with handheld pottery tools.

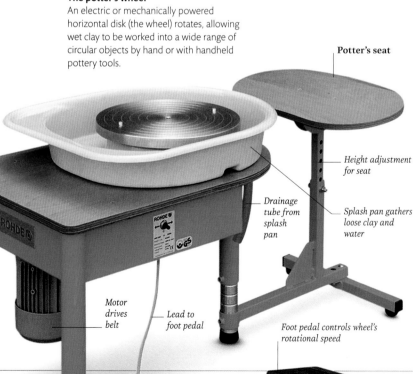

Potter's seat

Height adjustment for seat

Drainage tube from splash pan

Splash pan gathers loose clay and water

Motor drives belt

Lead to foot pedal

Foot pedal controls wheel's rotational speed

Wheel-thrown clay

Wet clay is first centered on the spinning wheel. It is then worked using downward and outward pressure to open the clay, form, raise, and thin its walls and provide the piece's overall shape.

Thumb presses and steadies clay as inside pressure raises wall

Work is placed on wooden bat on top of wheel

Overglaze (glaze on top of another glaze) applied by brush

Glazing

Glazes seal clay and typically add great decorative value. Pieces can be dipped in glaze or it can be applied as designs by spray or brush.

Mosaics

The decoration of a surface with small, colored pieces of ceramics, known as tesserae (tiles), as well as items like sea shells, has a long history. Tesserae are arranged and cemented onto the surface of a base to form eye-catching patterns or tile paintings.

Tools and materials

Tools are required to cut tiles—made of glass, stone, or pottery—to size and to apply cement and grouting. Grout can irritate bare skin and should not be applied by hand.

GLAZED CERAMIC

Tungsten-tipped cutting blades

Point scrapes out excess adhesive

Trowel end

TILE NIPPERS **PLASTERER'S SMALL TOOL**

Uniform tiles, 0.75 in (2 cm) square

VITREOUS GLASS

GOLD, SILVER, AND MIRROR

Tiles sizes may vary

UNGLAZED CERAMIC

CEMENT-BASED GROUT

Edges of tile may be uneven

MARBLE

CEMENT-BASED ADHESIVE

HISTORICAL MOSAICS

Mosaics originated in Mesopotamia over 4,000 years ago and were popular among the Ancient Greeks and Romans. One mosaic in the remains of the Roman city of Pompeii, depicting Alexander the Great, is made of 1.5 million tiles.

Gold tiles form backdrop

CHRISTIAN MOSAIC, 1907, RUSSIA

Design mapped out on base

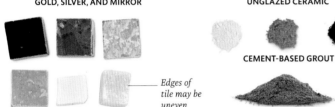
Cement applied by palette knife

Applying mosaic tiles

The mosaic's base is covered with an adhesive bed of cement into which individual tesserae are pressed.

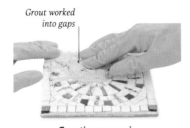
Grout worked into gaps

Grouting a mosaic

A mosaic is completed by filling and sealing the gaps between tesserae using grout applied by hand or a spatula.

Glass decorating

There are many ways to decorate glass, including the application of tinted film and lead strips to create faux stained glass. More commonly, glass is painted using special enamel or acrylic glass paints. For an opaque design, an undercoat may be applied first.

Tools and materials

Other than paints, brushes, outliners, and cutters, crafters also make use of solvents to degrease glass and tracing paper for design templates.

Fine, pointed brush for intricate decorating

ARTIST'S PAINTBRUSHES

Sharp cutting wheel

Handle squeezed to apply pressure

Airtight lid

Narrow applicator nozzle

DOUBLE-WHEEL CUTTER   **GLASS PAINTS**   **GLASS OUTLINER**

Glass paint applied within outline

Painting glass

After applying thick outliner around the boundaries of a design and letting it dry, glass paint is applied with a fine brush.

Stained glass

Commonly seen in places of worship, colored glass is typically placed within a soldered lead framework to form a mosaic-like pattern or scene. Color is achieved by adding chemicals to the mix.

Leading marks edge of glass fragment

GLASS BLOWING

The skill of glass blowing, in which molten glass is shaped using a long iron or steel blowpipe and a range of tools to produce hollow glassware, dates back more than 2,000 years. The tools required include wooden bats called blocks, and paddles and gathering irons that can add extra molten glass during the process. Impurities and threads may also be added to create different patterns and colors within the glass.

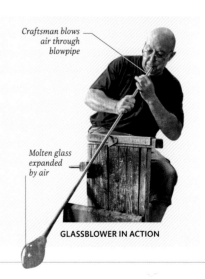
Craftsman blows air through blowpipe

Molten glass expanded by air

GLASSBLOWER IN ACTION

◀ see also Materials pp.264–65   ◀ Sculpture through history pp.450–51   ◀ Sculpture techniques pp.452–53

Knots

Knots are a relatively simple skill with many applications. These twists, bends, and turns in a length of rope or line enable objects to be bound or joined together without slipping. In the case of climbing ropes, rescue harnesses, and sutures used to fix or tie parts of the body during surgery, knots can be lifesaving. Modern knots evolved particularly through historic areas of human endeavor, such as construction and hauling heavy objects, sailing, and textiles work. This gallery is a selection of typical knots.

HISTORY OF KNOTS

Historians believe knots have been tied for at least 15,000 years. Early peoples used twisted plant fibers, animal sinews, and hair to form cords or ropes. The quipu, an Inca invention, used knotted strings of various lengths, thicknesses, and colours to convey information, and was used to keep records.

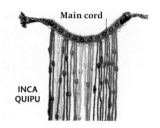

Main cord

INCA QUIPU

Stopper knots

Used in climbing and elsewhere on the ends of rope, these knots create a thicker area to act as a stopper. This prevents the rope or line from passing or slipping through an opening or another knot down the line.

Four wraps

Standing end pulled to tighten

MONKEY'S FIST

End passed through loop twice

Knot forms large core

DOUBLE OVERHAND KNOT

Working end

Crossed loops form "8" shape

FIGURE 8

End pulled to adjust knot

Rope passes through loop

Standing end

OVERHAND KNOT (SEE OPPOSITE)

Binding knots

Binding knots are used to secure or wrap loose objects such as both ends of the same rope or cord, or even shoelaces. Some binding knots, such as the sailor's cross (see right), are purely decorative in function.

Rope wrapped around and under

End pulled to adjust

CLOVE HITCH

Rope passes through linked overhand knot

Second overhand forms matching decorative knot

TRUE LOVE'S KNOT

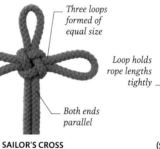

Three loops formed of equal size

Loop holds rope lengths tightly

Both ends parallel

SAILOR'S CROSS

Ends of same rope run parallel

REEF KNOT (SEE OPPOSITE)

Bends

A bend is a knot that ties the ends of two ropes together. Some, such as the sheet bend, are good for ropes of different thickness. Others, such as the blood knot, tie fishing lines together.

Other rope turns in opposite direction

Five turns of rope around other rope

BLOOD KNOT

Standing end pulled to tighten

Rope turn locks knot together

HUNTER'S BEND

Overhand knot tied

Two knots seated together

FISHERMAN'S KNOT

Both short ends on same side of knot

Initial loop

SHEET BEND (SEE OPPOSITE)

Hitches

A hitch attaches a single rope to a fixed object, such as a tree, mooring ring, or, when climbing, a carabiner. Lashings are hitches used to secure two or more objects together. Hooks are often fastened to fishing lines with hitches.

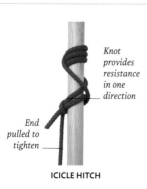

Knot provides resistance in one direction

End pulled to tighten

ICICLE HITCH

Three bights grip each other

Single tug of working end releases knot

HIGHWAYMAN'S HITCH

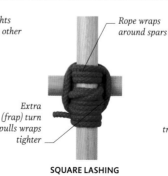

Rope wraps around spars

Extra (frap) turn pulls wraps tighter

SQUARE LASHING

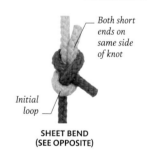

Two wraps of rope around object

Half hitches travel in same direction

ROUND TURN AND TWO HALF HITCHES (SEE OPPOSITE)

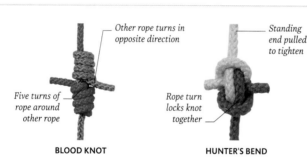
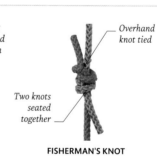
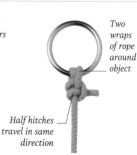

The **reef knot (or square knot)** is thought to date back **more than 10,000 years**

TERMS TO REMEMBER
- **Ends of the rope** The active end moved to tie a knot is called the working end and the other, the standing end.
- **Shaping the rope** A rope can be fashioned into loops, circles, and bights—a rope section that does not cross itself.
- **Turns around an object** Passing a rope around another rope or object is known as making a turn.

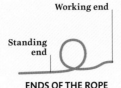
Working end
Standing end
ENDS OF THE ROPE

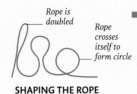
Rope is doubled
Rope crosses itself to form circle
SHAPING THE ROPE

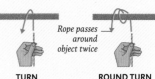
Rope passes around object twice
TURN **ROUND TURN**
TURNS AROUND AN OBJECT

Overhand knot

The easiest knot to tie and often the first children experiment with, this knot (also known as the thumb knot), involves a simple loop and is hard to untie after tightening. It forms part of a number of other knots.

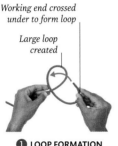
Working end crossed under to form loop
Large loop created
1 LOOP FORMATION

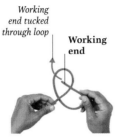
Working end tucked through loop
Working end
2 THREADING

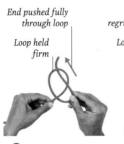
End pushed fully through loop
Loop held firm
3 PUSHING THROUGH

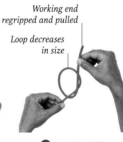
Working end regripped and pulled
Loop decreases in size
4 TIGHTENING

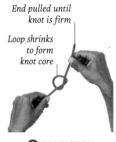
End pulled until knot is firm
Loop shrinks to form knot core
5 COMPLETION

Reef knot

This common, quick, and simple binding knot is also known as the square or Herakles knot. It can be used to join two ropes or to secure a line around an object. Historically it was used to tie up reefs (sails).

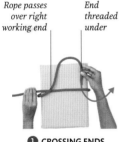

Rope passes over right working end
End threaded under
1 CROSSING ENDS

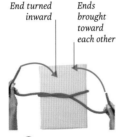
End turned inward
Ends brought toward each other
2 ENDS TOGETHER

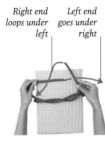
Right end loops under left
Left end goes under right
3 CROSSOVER

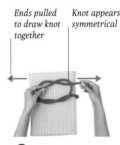
Ends pulled to draw knot together
Knot appears symmetrical
4 DRAWN TOGETHER

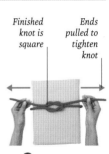
Finished knot is square
Ends pulled to tighten knot
5 TIGHTENING

Sheet bend

Also known as the weaver's knot or becket's bend, this knot is used to join ropes of different diameters or materials together. The thicker rope is used to form the initial loop.

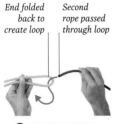
End folded back to create loop
Second rope passed through loop
1 LOOP FORMATION

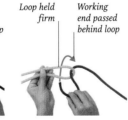
Loop held firm
Working end passed behind loop
2 PASSING AROUND

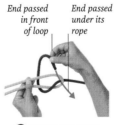
End passed in front of loop
End passed under its rope
3 UNDER AND OVER

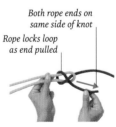
Both rope ends on same side of knot
Rope locks loop as end pulled
4 LOCKING THE KNOT

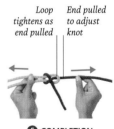
Loop tightens as end pulled
End pulled to adjust knot
5 COMPLETION

Round turn and two half hitches

This common marine knot is principally used to attach a rope to a ring, pole, or other fixed support when mooring a boat. It is relatively strong and can be untied even when the rope is under heavy load.

End threaded through ring from behind
1 STARTING THE TURN

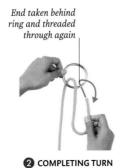
End taken behind ring and threaded through again
2 COMPLETING TURN

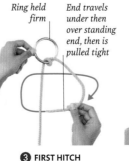
Ring held firm
End travels under then over standing end, then is pulled tight
3 FIRST HITCH

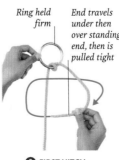
Standing end gripped
Working end passed under then over standing end
4 SECOND HITCH

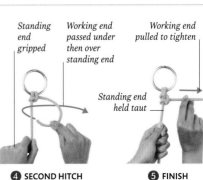
Working end pulled to tighten
Standing end held taut
5 FINISH

Glossary

This glossary is intended to provide additional clarification for selected terms. Italics denote words that appear elsewhere in the glossary.

Abstract Expressionism Movement of painting evoking strong expressive content using varying degrees of abstraction that emerged in New York City in the 1940s.

albinism Inherited condition in which the pigment that gives skin, hair, eyes, and feathers color is absent.

algae Simple, flowerless, mainly aquatic organisms that contain the green pigment *chlorophyll*, helping them make food using energy from sunlight.

algorithm A systematic procedure used in mathematics and computer science to find a solution to a problem.

amino acid A simple molecule used by the body to build proteins. The body's digestive system also breaks down proteins in food into amino acids.

analog Relating to or using signals or information represented by a continuously varying value, such as a wave.

anarchy A state of disorder arising from absence or nonrecognition of authority or other controlling systems.

Animism The belief that all plants, inanimate objects, and natural phenomena have a soul.

anion An atom (or group of atoms) that carries a negative charge, formed when an atom gains one or more electrons in its outer shell.

apartheid Government policy in South Africa during the 20th century that sanctioned segregation and discrimination between the country's white minority and the majority non-white population.

apogee The point in the orbit of the moon, or an object such as a satellite, when it is farthest away from the Earth.

arboreal Resembling a tree, or an organism (plant or animal) that lives fully or partly (semiarboreal) in trees.

Archean The earliest part of the Precambrian division, beginning about 4 million years ago and ending 2.5 million years ago. Life first formed on Earth during this period.

aria A piece of music for a solo voice in an opera or oratorio.

Art Deco (architecture) A decorative arts movement characterized by geometric and stylized forms. It originated in Europe in the 1920s and flourished in the 1930s.

atheism The total denial or disbelief in the existence of God or spiritual beings.

autocracy Also known as absolutism, a community or state in which unlimited authority is exercised by a single individual.

axiomatic A mathematical statement or proposition on which an abstractly defined structure is based.

barbarian Term first used by the ancient Greeks to describe all foreigners, later adopted by the Romans to mean all tribes outside the Greco-Roman Empire.

Baroque (architecture and art) An art movement that flourished in 17th-century Europe, often characterized by dynamic movement, emotional intensity, and theatrical effects. The architecture is characterized by complex shapes.

Baroque (music) Style of European music composed between 1600 and 1750, characterized by the introduction of many new complex musical forms.

base (baseball and softball) One of four points around the infield that a player must make contact with to score a run.

black body radiation The continuous spectrum of radiation reemitted by an object known as a black body after that radiation has fallen on its surface.

Bollywood Slang term for the Hindi-language, Mumbai-based film industry that began in the 1930s.

botryoidal Mineral or plant with a globular form resembling a bunch of grapes.

bract A leaf that has modified into an attractive or protective structure—usually to protect buds—around the base of a flower or flower cluster.

calculus The branch of math concerned with the calculation of instantaneous rates of change from one moment to the next (differential calculus), or the joining of infinitely small factors to determine a whole (integral calculus).

caliph Leader of an Islamic political and religious state or empire (caliphate), regarded as a successor of Muhammad.

cantata A piece of music for one or more voices and orchestra designed to tell a story; it can be secular or religious.

cantilever A beam that is supported at only one end and carries the weight on the other, unsupported, end.

capillary The tiny blood vessels that carry blood between the arteries and veins and in which oxygen, nutrients, and waste are exchanged between blood and tissues.

caravel Lightweight, fast sailing ship often employed by Spanish and Portuguese fleets in the 15th to 17th centuries.

carbonates Any of two classes of chemical compound derived from carbonic acid or carbon dioxide.

Carboniferous Geological period of the Paleozoic Era between the Devonian and the Permian periods that spanned approximately 60 million years.

carnivore Any animal that eats meat. It can also be used to describe mammals of the order Carnivora.

carpel Also known as a *pistil*, this is the female reproductive part of a flower, which consists of an ovary, style, and stigma.

carrack Deep, broad, usually three-masted sailing ships of the 14th- to 17th-century European merchant fleets.

catalyst A substance that enables a chemical reaction to occur more rapidly, but is not changed by the reaction.

cation An atom (or groups of atoms) that carries a positive charge.

causation (philosophy) The relationship between two successive events when one (the cause) brings about the second (seen as the effect).

chlorophyll Green pigment inside plant cells that enables them to absorb light and carry out photosynthesis.

chloroplast The chlorophyll-containing particles inside plant cells, where *starch* is formed during photosynthesis.

chromists Mostly photosynthetic single and multicellular microorganisms of the Kingdom Chromista, including ciliates, diatoms, and some *algae*.

clade A group of organisms that includes all the evolutionary descendants (living and extinct) of a common ancestor (organism, population, or species).

Classical (art and architecture) Art and architecture of the ancient Greek and Roman civilizations. It is also used to describe architecture of later periods that employs Greek or Roman forms.

Classical (music) Style of European music written around 1750–1820. Using a simpler style than *Baroque*, it was a period when the symphony, concerto, and sonata forms were standardized. It is also a term used to distinguish Western music intended for a formal context from more informal styles.

Cogito, the Philosopher René Descartes' argument—"Cogito, ergo sum", or "I think, therefore I am"—that knowledge is attained through reason, not experience.

colonization The action of a plant or animal establishing itself in a certain area. Or the act of sending settlers to establish a colony in another country.

Communism The political and economic belief in a society in which ownership of both property and wealth is shared among the people.

conquistador A leader (conqueror) of the Spanish conquest of the Americas in the 16th century.

core The dense central region of a planet—for example, the innermost and hottest part of Earth, which consists of a liquid outer layer around a solid center, both thought to be made of iron and nickel. It also refers to the central region of a star within which energy is generated by means of nuclear *fusion* reactions. Can also refer to a dense concentration of material within a gas cloud.

corona The outermost part of the sun or a star's atmosphere, only visible during a solar eclipse when it appears as a white "halo."

cosmology The bringing together of different natural sciences, in particular astronomy and physics, to study the universe as a whole.

coulomb The unit of electrical charge transported in one second by a current of one ampere when objects are attracted or repelled because of their electric charge.

Council of Trent Ecumenical council of the Roman Catholic Church held in Trento, northern Italy, between 1545 and 1563 as a response to the Protestant Reformation.

crease (cricket) The area around the wicket indicated by white lines that defines where the bowler and the batsman must be during play.

Cubism A revolutionary style of art begun by French artist Georges Braque and Spanish artist Pablo Picasso in 1907. They combined multiple views of an object in one painting, thereby producing a fragmented and abstracted image.

crust The thin, rocky, outermost layer of a planet such as Earth or a major planetary satellite that has separated into layers.

declination The angular distance of a celestial body that is north or south of the celestial equator. Declination is positive (+) if the object is north of the celestial equator, and negative (-) if the object is south of the celestial equator.

decolonization The process of giving back political control to a former colony, resulting in its independence.

deconstructionism A philosophical movement and theory of literary analysis originating in the 1960s that questions assumptions about certainty, identity, and truth.

democracy A political system in which the people of a country or state have the power to control their government, usually by electing politicians to represent them.

dialectic The use of intellectual investigation to seek the truth through discussion and reasoning.

digital Signals, data, and sound that are expressed in binary code—using only the digits 0 and 1.

dinoflagellate Microscopic plantlike organisms with complex outer shells and whiplike tails (flagella) that help them move through fresh or salty water.

discourse Defined by 20th-century French philosopher Michel Foucault as ways of talking, thinking, or representing a subject to produce useful knowledge that can influence social practice and have consequences.

DNA Short for deoxyribonucleic acid, DNA is the chemical substance found in the cells of all living organisms that determines their inherited characteristics and is individual to each organism.

Doric One of the orders of Classical architecture developed in the second half of the 7th century BCE, characterized by simple fluted columns with a plain top.

doublet A close-fitting, waisted, padded jacket worn over a shirt by men from the 15th to 17th centuries in Western Europe.

Dravidian Style of architecture employed for building Hindu temples in southern India from the 7th to 18th centuries, characterized by a square sanctuary topped by a pyramidal tower.

dribble (sports) A method by which a player maneuvers a ball or puck while moving in a set direction.

dynasty A family that has ruled a country for successive generations.

echolocation A way of sensing objects by transmitting pulses of high-frequency sound that bounce back from obstacles.

ecliptic The track along which the sun appears to travel around the celestial sphere, relative to the background stars, in the course of a year.

economy The state of a region or country in terms of production, distribution, and consumption of goods in relation to the supply of money.

electron A subatomic particle with a negative electric charge that orbits the *nucleus* of an atom in a "cloud." An electric current consists of a "flow" of electrons.

electroreceptor Organ found in some animals that has the ability to detect weak, naturally occurring electrostatic fields.

empiricism The view that knowledge of any concept, belief, or proposition can only be derived from experience.

enlightenment The state of mind (also known as nirvana) achieved by Siddhartha Gautama, or Buddha, through meditation.

epistemology The dominant branch of philosophy concerned with what humans can know, how they know it, and exactly what knowledge is.

equator An imaginary line around the center of any planet, halfway between its north and south poles.

essentialism The view in philosophy that the essence, or properties, of an object are more important than its existence.

exoskeleton The tough external skeleton of an animal, such as an insect, that supports and protects its body.

factor In mathematics, one of two or more numbers or quantities that when multiplied with another produces a given number or quantity; likewise a number or fraction that can divide another evenly, with no remainder.

fascine Long bundles of wooden sticks bound together and used to support river banks, fill ditches, or construct roads, embankments, and fortifications.

Fascism A political ideology and movement that supports *nationalism* and values the importance and strength of the state over the welfare of individual citizens.

feudalism A social system developed in medieval Europe and Japan, in which the serving classes (peasants) pledged support to their landowner in return for protection.

flamenco A type of song, instrumental (guitar and percussion) music, and dance from southern Spain, commonly associated with the Andalusian Romani people.

fusion Joining together; nuclear fusion is the joining of two atomic nuclei to generate energy.

galleon Three- or four-masted sailing ship with a characteristic beaked prow, developed in the 15th and 16th centuries and primarily used for fighting.

gas giants The larger outer planets Saturn and Jupiter, which are composed mainly of the gases helium and hydrogen, and have small cores of rock and ice.

germination The physical and chemical changes that take place within a seed, causing it to start to grow.

glucose A simple carbohydrate, or sugar, that circulates in the bloodstream and is the main energy source for the body's cells.

Gothic The style of art and architecture prevalent in Europe in the late Middle Ages. The architecture is characterized by pointed arches and soaring, light interiors; paintings and sculptures by graceful swaying figures.

halide A chemical compound that contains halogen and one other element.

herbivore An animal that feeds only on plants or plantlike *plankton*.

hibernation A period of dormancy that some animals undergo during winter, when their body processes slow to a low level.

hoplite Heavily armed ancient Greek foot soldier introduced in the 8th century BCE.

hormones Chemical messengers produced by glands that change the way another part of the body works. They are carried around the body by the blood.

ice dwarf Also known as plutoids, these are small planets with an orbit outside Neptune that have cold surface temperatures—the largest of these are Pluto, Eris, Haumea, and Makemake.

ice giants The outer planets Uranus and Neptune, which although formed largely of helium and hydrogen, have rocky-icy cores that are proportionately greater than the gas they contain.

igneous rock Rock formed from the hot, liquid material inside Earth (known as *magma*) that has come to the surface, cooled and hardened.

immolation To sacrifice, or destroy something as an offering, often by burning.

imperialism The policy of extending the dominion of a nation through direct intervention in the affairs of another country, and the seizure of territory and subjugation of its peoples that happens in the process of building an empire.

indehiscent A fruit that does not split open to release its seeds when ripe—for example, a hazelnut.

inductive logic In philosophy, reasoning from the particular to the general. For example, stating that Socrates died, Plato died, Aristotle died, and every individual man who was born more than 130 years ago has died, so therefore all men are mortal and will eventually die.

infrasound Sound waves at such low frequencies they are inaudible to humans.

ingest To take food or drink into the body through the mouth.

inning(s) The division in a game of baseball or cricket, for example, when one team has their turn at batting.

interference The disturbance of signals that occurs when two or more waves meet.

isometric (crystal) Also known as cubic, this is a crystal that has three axes of equal length that are perpendicular to each other.

Jacobson's organ An organ in the roof of the mouth of some animals that is sensitive to airborne scents. Snakes often use theirs to detect their prey, while some male mammals use it to find females that are ready to mate.

kabuki A traditional Japanese dramatic art form dating back to the 17th century. It combines music, vocals, dance, and mime with spectacular costume and scenery.

karma Meaning "action" in Sanskrit, this is the force generated by a person's actions (good and bad) which, according to Hinduism and Buddhism, will determine their fate in future existences.

khanate A central Asian political region or entity ruled over by a khan. After the death of Genghis Khan in 1227, the Mongol Empire was divided into four khanates.

kimono Traditional ankle-length gown with long, wide sleeves worn by Japanese men and women from the Hakuhō period (c.645–c.710 CE) to the present day.

larva An immature but independent animal that looks completely different from its adult form and develops the adult shape by metamorphosis. In many insects, the change occurs in a resting stage (pupa).

leucism A genetic mutation that prevents melanin and pigments being deposited in feathers, hair, and skin of affected animals. Results in pale coloring overall or light patches.

liberalism A political philosophy that emphasizes the freedom of the individual above all else, believing that a government is needed to protect the individual, but that it can also pose a threat to a person's liberty.

light year A measurement used by astronomers, based on the distance that light travels in one year.

Low Countries The historical term used to describe a coastal lowland kingdom of northern Europe that included what is now the Netherlands, Belgium, Luxembourg, and northeast France.

luminosity The amount of light given off by an object such as a star.

magma Liquid, molten, or partially molten material between the Earth's *core* and *crust*, or *mantle*, that cools to form *igneous rock*.

magnetoreception The innate ability of certain animals, such as birds, fish, and cetaceans, and other organisms to detect and respond to Earth's magnetic fields during *migration*.

magnetosphere The region in space within which the motion of charged particles is controlled by the planetary magnetic field.

magnitude The measurement of brightness of a celestial object, such as a star. The brighter the object, the lower the number it is assigned.

mantle The layer of hot rock that lies between the *core* and the *crust* of a rocky planet or large moon.

materialism In philosophy, the belief that all facts are causally dependent on something material.

matter A physical substance that has a mass and occupies a space.

mechanics The science concerned with energy and forces and their effect on moving and stationary bodies.

mechanoreceptor Sense organ that responds to mechanical stimuli such as vibration, touch, and smell.

melanism Excessive production of the melanin granules in the skin, which causes abnormal darkening or blackening of skin, feathers, and hair in animals.

mesophyll The soft, inner tissue of a leaf, between the upper and lower layers of the epidermis that contains *chloroplasts* for photosynthesis.

metamorphic rock Preexisting rock that has been changed by heat, pressure, and environmental stress to form new rock consisting of new materials; preexisting rock can be *igneous*, *sedimentary*, or other metamorphic rock.

metaphysics The branch of philosophy concerned with the ultimate nature of what exists. It questions the natural world "from outside," and its questions cannot be answered by science.

meteor Also described as a shooting star, this is a tiny piece of dust or rock from outer space that burns up as it enters Earth's atmosphere, creating a visible streak of light.

meteorite A piece of rock or metal in space that enters Earth's atmosphere and reaches the ground without burning up. It is classified according to its composition as stony, iron, or stony-iron.

migration A journey taken by animals to a different region, following a well-defined route, generally to take advantage of good breeding conditions in one place and wintering ones in another.

mitochondrion (plural mitochondria) Tiny organs inside a body cell that create energy to keep the cell alive.

mitosis The process of cell duplication when one cell divides into two new, identical cells.

Mohs scale Quantitative scale denoting the hardness of a mineral. Any substance with a higher number can scratch substances with a lower number.

monasticism Institutionalized religious practice used by many religions from Christianity to Buddhism, Hinduism, and Jainism. Members separate themselves from society, living by specific rules on their own or in communities.

monophyletic An organism, or group of organisms, that are descended from one evolutionary group or ancestor, not shared by another group.

monotheism The belief in the existence of one god.

multituberculate A member of a group of small rodentlike fossil mammals with three rows of molars, which existed from the middle of the Jurassic period to the early Eocene epoch.

mutation The altering of the genetic material of a cell in a living organism (or virus) in a way that it can be transmitted to the cell's descendants.

mystery cult Highly secretive religious cults of the ancient Greeks and Romans.

nanotechnology Minute technology on an atomic or molecular scale.

nationalism Ideology that promotes an individual to identify and support their own nation or nationality to the exclusion of the interests of any other nation.

native element Chemical elements that can occur naturally not combined with others—for example arsenic, iron, and diamonds; atmospheric gases are not native elements.

Neoclassical (architecture) Art form that dominated in late 18th-century Europe, which revived the architectural forms of classical antiquity.

Neolithic The period from about 10,000–3000 BCE, characterized by the use of stone hand tools that are shaped by grinding and polishing, and by permanent settlements and the domestication of plants and animals.

neutron Particle in the *nucleus* of an atom that has no electrical charge.

nihilism The philosophical belief that nothing in the world has a real existence, and therefore rejects the possibility of knowledge or communication.

nominalism A doctrine that flourished in Medieval times based on the belief that general ideas and universals did not imply existence or correspond to reality.

nucleus The central part of an atom, made up of *protons* and *neutrons*. Or the structure in most plant and animal cells that contains genetic material.

omnivore An animal that eats both plant matter and meat.

ontology The branch of philosophy that asks what actually exists, as distinct from the nature of our knowledge of it, which is covered by the branch of *epistemology*.

ophthalmoscope A handheld instrument used to examine the inside of an eye.

oracle Person who communicated advice from the gods of Classical antiquity to those who sought it, or the place where a message was delivered.

orbit The path taken by an object, for example a planet or satellite, as it circles around another body, such as a planet.

oscillation A regular back-and-forth movement. In physics, a regular variation in position around a central point, especially of an electric current.

ossicle A very small bone, especially any of three bones in the middle ear that carry sound from the eardrum to the inner ear.

ostracon A piece of pottery or limestone flake on which the ancient Egyptians, Greeks, and Hebrews wrote and depicted scenes of nature and everyday life.

otoscope Instrument, also known as an auroscope, used to examine the outer ear and eardrum.

overhuman, the A concept proposed by German philosopher Friedrich Nietzsche, that human life is given meaning through the advancement of a new generation of humans—known as the Übermensch.

oxide Any compound formed between oxygen and another element.

pathogen An agent, particularly a microorganism, that causes disease.

perigee The point in the orbit of the moon, or an object such as a satellite, when it is nearest to the Earth.

perihelion The point on its orbit where a planet, or other body in the solar system, is closest to the sun.

perimeter The line that forms the outer edge of a geometrical figure, or the outer limits of something.

perspectivism The philosophical concept that knowledge, perception, and experience are always seen from the viewer's vantage point.

phenomenology A philosophical approach that investigates objects of experience (phenomena), but only to the extent that they manifest themselves in a person's consciousness.

phonetics The study of the acoustic and physiological quality of speech sounds and how they can be combined to make syllables, words, and sentences.

phosphate A chemical compound that contains the element phosphorus (P).

photon A "package," or quantum, of electromagnetic energy, which may be seen as a "particle" of light. The shorter the wavelength of the radiation and higher the frequency, the greater the photon's energy.

photosphere Thin, gaseous layer at the base of the solar atmosphere, from which the sun's visible light is emitted, that corresponds to its visible surface.

physiology The study of the normal functions of all parts of living organisms.

pistil Also known as a *carpel*, this is the female reproductive part of a flower and consists of an ovary, style, and stigma.

plankton Floating organisms—many of them microscopic—that drift in open water, particularly near the surface of the ocean.

plasma The fluid part of the blood that remains if all cellular components are removed; or a gaslike cloud of electrically charged matter.

polity The condition of being constituted as a state or organized community proposed by ancient Greek philosopher Aristotle. He called it a form of popular government in the common interest.

polytheism The belief in the existence of many gods.

precipitation Any water particle (liquid or solid) that falls from the clouds and reaches the ground.

primary growth The increase in the length of roots and shoots at the tips of stems as a result of cell division.

principality A country or small state ruled by a prince or princess, from which they draw their title.

protein A complex substance found in all living organisms and needed by the body for growth and repair.

proton A particle in the *nucleus* of an atom that has a positive electric charge.

protozoa Typically microscopic, single-celled organisms with a clearly defined *nucleus* encased within a membrane.

rationalism The view that people can gain knowledge of the world through the use of reason, without relying on perception via their senses. The opposite is known as *empiricism*.

reactant The substance that is changed when a chemical *reaction* takes place.

reaction Any process that alters the properties of a chemical substance or forms a new one; or a force that is the same in magnitude but opposite in direction to another force.

republic A state or country with no monarch, in which power resides usually with a president who may or may not have been freely elected by the people.

Restoration, the Period in British history from 1660 when the monarchy (King Charles II) returned to power after Oliver Cromwell's Republican Commonwealth, marked by period of colonial expansion and revival of art and literature.

RNA Short for ribonucleic acid, RNA is a molecule that forms simple, single long strands of nucleotide bases and carries "messages" between *DNA* and the rest of a cell.

Rococo Initially a style of early 18th-century French decoration combining relief scrollwork with shell motifs. The term was later expanded to describe all the art of that period.

ROM (read-only memory) The permanent part of a computer's memory where information is stored and "read," but cannot be changed.

Romanesque A style of architecture prevalent in Europe from the mid-11th century until the *Gothic* period, characterized by large churches with vaulted ceilings, large naves, semicircular arches, and few windows.

Romantic (music) The style of music that dominated Europe in the 19th century, characterized by the abandonment of traditional musical forms, and the introduction of large-scale compositions.

secondary growth The increase in stem and root thickness that develops in *vascular plants* after *primary growth*.

sedimentary rock Rock formed by rock fragments, organic remains, or other materials that settle on the floor of a sea or lake and cement together over time.

seismic wave The shock waves that travel through the ground and can be felt after an earthquake or explosion.

sepal Usually green, this is the part of the flower that surrounds and protects the bud.

shogunate Government of the Japanese shogun, the hereditary dictators in charge of the military from 1192–1867.

sociation In sociology, a process of associative or dissociative interaction.

Society of Jesus Also known as the Jesuits, this is a Roman Catholic religious order founded by Ignatius of Loyola, and approved by Pope Paul III in 1540.

Socratic method A method used by Socrates to expose contradictions in the thoughts and ideas of his opponents and students through engaging in argument.

sphygmomanometer An instrument used to measure a person's blood pressure.

spore The minute, reproductive structure of flowerless plants, such as ferns and mosses, and fungi.

stamen The male reproductive part of a flower—the pollen-producing anther and its supporting filament or stalk.

starch An odorless, white substance produced by all green plants, in which their energy is stored. Starch obtained from potatoes, rice, and wheat forms a key part of the human diet.

stela A stone or wooden slab erected as a monument by ancient cultures, often featuring text or decorative elements.

stoicism A belief that perception is the basis of true knowledge and that those who are virtuous are indifferent to fortune, pleasure, or pain.

stupa A hemispherical Buddhist monument, or shrine, housing sacred relics.

sulfate A naturally occurring salt of sulfuric acid.

sulfide A compound of sulfur and another element, or group of elements.

sultan Originally used to describe an Islamic spiritual leader, but later denoted political power. From the 11th century onward, the title given to the sovereign of an Islamic state.

suture A type of joint found only between the bones, or plates, of a skull.

theocracy A government whose leaders are members of the clergy, with a legal system that is based on religious laws.

thorax The middle body division, between the head and the abdomen, of insects and some other arthropods; also, the chest region of mammals and other land vertebrates, containing the heart and lungs.

topology The branch of mathematics concerned with continuity in geometric figures whose properties remain unchanged when stretched or shrunk.

totalitarianism A centralized, dictatorial form of government that permits no personal freedom.

transpiration A plant's loss of water by evaporation from leaves and stems.

USB (universal serial bus) A hardware interface, or port, used to connect a computer to external devices.

utilitarianism A theory of ethics and politics that judges the morality of actions by their consequences—therefore an action is right if it promotes happiness.

vanadate Rare, naturally occurring mineral that is a compound of vanadium, oxygen, and other metals.

vascular plant A plant that has both food-conducting tissues (phloem) and water-conducting tissues (xylem).

vitreous A substance that is glasslike in appearance or quality.

votive offering Objects or money left at sacred places as gifts to the gods, or to gain favour with supernatural forces.

Index

Acknowledgments

Dorling Kindersley (DK) would like to thank Garima Agarwal, Sanjay Chauhan, Ankita Das, Meenal Goel, Arshti Narang, Pooja Pipil, Ira Sharma, Steve Woosnam-Savage, and Francis Wong for design assistance; Tom Booth, Sam Borthwick, Jemima Dunne, Peter Preston, Laura Sandford, Tia Sarkar, and Marcus Weeks for editorial assistance; Nand Kishore Acharya, Sonia Charbonnier, Jaypal Chauhan, Satish Gaur, Ashok Kumar, Mrinmoy Mazumdar, Tom Morse, Rajdeep Singh, Bimlesh Tiwary, and Tanveer Zaidi for technical assistance; Suhita Dharamjit, Rakesh Kumar, Priyanka Sharma, and Saloni Singh for the jacket; Vagish Pushp for picture research assistance; Suresh Kumar for cartographic assistance; Joy Evatt for proofreading; and Helen Peters for indexing.

The publisher would like to thank the following for their kind permission to reproduce their photographs:

(Key: a—above; b—below/bottom; c—center; f—far; l—left; r-right; t—top)

1 Alamy Stock Photo: agefotostock / J.D. Dallet (crb). **Dreamstime.com:** Lateci (cra). **Fotolia:** valdis torms (clb). **2 Alamy Stock Photo:** imageBROKER / Oleksiy Maksymenko (cra). **DK:** Gary Ombler / Durham University Oriental Museum (cla); Gary Ombler / University of Pennsylvania Museum of Archaeology and Anthropology (clb). **Science Photo Library:** KTSDESIGN (crb). **4–5 Getty Images:** Sabine Lubenow / LOOK-foto (cb). **6 SpaceX:** (tl). **7 DK:** Gary Ombler / National Railway Museum, York / Science Museum Group (tr). **Science Photo Library:** Alfred Pasieka (tl). **8 DK:** Angela Coppola / University of Pennsylvania Museum of Archaeology and Anthropology (tc). **Dreamstime.com:** Jaroslav Moravcik (tl). **iStockphoto.com:** DigitalVision Vectors / ZU_09 (tr). **9 DK:** Dave King / Science Museum, London (tl); Gary Ombler / National Music Museum (tc). **Getty Images:** De Agostini / DEA / G. CIGOLINI (tr). **12 123RF.com:** solarseven (cra). **NASA:** NASA / ESA and The Hubble Heritage Team STScI / AURA (cla). **12–13 M. Meyer, Linter, Germany:** http://www.comethunter.de/academie.html (t). **13 Alamy Stock Photo:** Panther Media GmbH / Shing Lok Che (cla/Asterism). **Dreamstime.com:** Neutronman (ca). **EHT Collaboration:** (cra/Black holes). **NASA:** CXC / M.Weiss (crb); ESA / Hubble & NASA (cla); JPL-Caltech (cra, fcra). **16 DK:** Peter Bull / NASA (tr). **16–17 Dreamstime.com:** Vjanez (Used multiple times on the spread). **17 DK:** Peter Bull / NASA (cr). **18 NASA:** JPL (cb, crb); NEAR Project, NLR, JHUAPL, Goddard SVS (crb/Stony Asteroid). **19 Dreamstime.com:** Suyerry (crb). **ESO:** H.H.Heyer https://creativecommons.org/licenses/by/4.0 (br). **Getty Images:** AFP / George Shelton (crb/COMET HYAKUTAKE). **NASA:** (ca/Eris, ca/Makemake, ca/Haumea, cra); JPL-Caltech / UCLA / MPS / DLR / IDA (cla); JPL / Johns Hopkins University Applied Physics Laboratory / Southwest Research Institute (cla/PLUTO). **20 NASA:** SDO (cra). **SOHO:** Courtesy of SOHO / LASCO consortium. SOHO is a project of international cooperation between ESA and NASA (cb). **21 Getty Images:** Steffen Schnur (cra). **23 NASA:** ESA, M. Livio and the Hubble 20th Anniversary Team (STScI) (bc). **Schlesinger Library, Radcliffe Institute, Harvard University:** (tr). **24 ESO:** ALMA (ESO/NAOJ/NRAO)/H. Kim et al., ESA/NASA & R. Sahai, https://creativecommons.org/licenses/by/4.0 (tr). **NASA:** J.P. Harrington and K.J. Borkowski (University of Maryland), and NASA / ESA (ftr); NASA, ESA, N. Smith (University of Arizona) and J. Morse (BoldlyGo Institute) (br). **25 NASA:** ESA, H. Bond (STScI) and M. Barstow (University of Leicester) (tl); NASA, ESA, G. Dubner (IAFE, CONICET-University of Buenos Aires) et al.; (tr). **26 Dreamstime.com:** Zhasmina Ivanova / Zhasminaivanova (tc). **26–27 NASA:** JPL-Caltech (c). **28 ESO:** https://creativecommons.org/licenses/by/4.0 (cra, c/Fornax). **Getty Images:** The Image Bank / Derek Berwin (cla). **NASA:** Carnegie-Irvine Galaxy Survey / JPL-Caltech (ca/Horologium); The Hubble Heritage Team (AURA / STScI) / S. Smartt (Institute of Astronomy) and D. Richstone (U. Michigan) (ca); ESA / Hubble & NASA, A. Riess (STScI / JHU) (cl); ESA / Hubble & NASA / Judy Schmidt (cra/Pavo, cb); ESA, and The Hubble Heritage Team (STScI / AURA) (c, bl); ESA / Hubble & NASA (cr); NASA's Goddard Space Flight Center / ESO / JPL-Caltech / DSS (cr/Pavo); ESA, P. Goudfrooij (STScI) (clb); ESA, and The Hubble Heritage Team (STScI / AURA) / W. Keel (University of Alabama, Tuscaloosa) (cb/Draco); ESA and The Hubble Heritage Team (crb); ESA / Hubble & NASA / J. Barrington (crb/Telescopium); ESA / Hubble & NASA, J. Blakeslee, P Cote et al. (bc); ESA, and Z. Levay (STScI) (bc/M87 VIRGO); CXC / Penn State / G. Garmire (br). **Sloan Digital Sky Survey (SDSS):** (br/NGC 4623). **29 ESO:** ESO / WFI (Optical); MPIfR / ESO / APEX / A.Weiss et al. (Submillimetre); NASA / CXC / CfA / R.Kraft et al. (X-ray) https://creativecommons.org/licenses/by/4.0 (cr); VISTA VMC https://creativecommons.org/licenses/by/4.0 (tr); IDA / Danish 1.5 m / R. Gendler and J.-E. Ovaldsen https://creativecommons.org/licenses/by/4.0 (br). **NASA:** ESA / Hubble & NASA / Judy Schmidt (tl); ESA, and A. Aloisi (European Space Agency and Space Telescope Science Institute) (tc/I ZWICKY 18); ESA and the Hubble Heritage Team (STScI / AURA) / J. Gallagher (University of Wisconsin), M. Mountain (STScI) and P. Puxley (NSF). (tc); ESA, and D. Elmegreen (Vassar College), B. Elmegreen (IBM's Thomas J. Watson Research Center), J. Almeida, C. Munoz-Tunon, and M. Filho (Instituto de Astrofisica de Canarias), J. Mendez-Abreu (University of St. Andrews), J. Gallagher (University of Wisconsin-Madison), M. Rafelski (NASA Goddard Space Flight Center), and D. Ceverino (Center for Astronomy at Heidelberg University) (cla); ESA / Hubble & NASA, L. Ferrarese et al. (ca/M110); ESA / Hubble & NASA / Alessandra Aloisi (STScI) and Nick Rose (ca); ESA, and The Hubble Heritage Team (STScI / AURA) (ftr, cra, crb); ESA / Hubble and NASA / Judy Schmidt (fcra); ESA / Hubble & NASA (cl, bc); JPL-Caltech / Roma Tre Univ. (c); ESA / Hubble Heritage (STScI / AURA)-ESA / Hubble Collaboration (c/Perseus); ESA / Hubble & NASA / Judy Schmidt (Geckzilla) (fcr); ESA, the Hubble Heritage Team (STScI / AURA)-ESA / Hubble Collaboration, and W. Keel (University of Alabama, Tuscaloosa) (fcrb, fbr). **30 2dF Galaxy Redshift Survey Team (www2.aao.gov.au/2dFGRS):** www.2dfgrs.net (bl). **32 Getty Images:** The LIFE Images Collection / Fred Rick (crb). **NASA:** CXC / M.Markevitch et al. / STScI; Magellan / U.Arizona / D.Clowe et al. / STScI; ESO WFI; Magellan / U.Arizona / D.Clowe et al. (bc); ESA / Hubble (br). **34 ESO:** https://creativecommons.org/licenses/by/4.0 (cr). **36 Alamy Stock Photo:** Zvonimir Atletić (cl); World History Archive (cla). **DK:** Jason Harding / TerraBuilder / squir (Turbosquid) (ca). **NASA:** (r). **37 Alamy Stock Photo:** DBI Studio (cla); Heritage Image Partnership Ltd / © Fine Art Images (tc); Everett Collection Historical (c); World History Archive (bl). **DK:** Bob Gathany / Space and Rocket Center, Alabama (tr). **NASA:** (cb); Jim Ross (cl). **38 NASA. 39 ESA:** ATG Medialab (br). **NASA:** (clb); JPL-Caltech / MSSS (c). **46–47 DK:** Peter Bull. **49 Alamy Stock Photo:** Tom Bean (cb); Science History Images / Photo Researchers (br). **50 DK:** James Kuether (bl). **Dreamstime.com:** Dmitry Pichugin / Dmitryp (crb). **Science Photo Library:** Mikkel Juul Jensen (c). **51 Dreamstime.com:** Matauw (br). **iStockphoto.com:** Aunt_Spray (bc). **56 Alamy Stock Photo:** Stocktrek Images, Inc. / Stocktrek Images (cr). **Dreamstime.com:** Tusharkoley (crb). **Science Photo Library:** NASA (br). **57 Alamy Stock Photo:** Nature Picture Library / Alex Mustard / naturepl.com (cb). **DK:** Peter Bull / NASA: Earth Observatory / NOAA (br). **59 DK:** Peter Bull / U.S. Geological Survey / Elevation data USGS NED (c). **60 DK:** Colin Keates / Natural History Museum, London (cr); Gary Ombler / Oxford University Museum of Natural History (crb). **61 DK:** Harry Taylor / The Natural History Museum, London (bc). **Dreamstime.com:** Vlad3563 (br).**62 DK:** Colin Keates / The Natural History Museum, London (fcrb, fbr). **Dreamstime.com:** Sdbower (crb). **63 123RF.com:** welcomia / welcomia (tr). **DK:** Ruth Jenkinson / Holts Gems (bc). **65 © Caladan Oceanic:** (bc). **NOAA:** © Submarine Ring of Fire 2014 - Ironman, NOAA / PMEL, NSF (cr). **66 Alamy Stock Photo:** RKive (tr). **67 Dreamstime.com:** Puntasit Choksawatdikorn (tc/Copepod); Christopher Wood / Chriswood44 (crb). **naturepl.com:** Visuals Unlimited (tc). **PunchStock:** Digital Vision / Tim Hibo (cb). **70 NASA:** (bc). **71 NASA:** NASA Ozone Watch (fcla, fclb, clb, clb/2019); NASA's Goddard Space Flight Center (cla). **72 Alamy Stock Photo:** The Picture Art Collection (br). **PunchStock:** Digital Vision / Peter Adams (clb). **75 Ed Merritt / DK:** Merritt Cartographic: Ed Merritt (bc). **77 Dreamstime.com:** Fourleaflover (cla). **83 NASA:** NASA's Scientific Visualization Studio (tr). **86 Alamy Stock Photo:** Archive PL (br); Sabena Jane Blackbird (cra). **DK:** Peter Minister and Andrew Kerr / Dreamstime.com: Xunbin Pan (clb). **87 123RF.com:** Corey A Ford (fcrb). **DK:** James Kuether (cb). **Dreamstime.com:** Anthony Aneese Totah Jr (clb). **Pavel Škaloud:** (cla). **Roman Uchytel:** (br). **88 123RF.com:** Corey A Ford (bl). **89 DK:** Colin Keates / The Natural History Museum, London (tc); Colin Keates / Natural History Museum, London (clb). **90 123RF.com:** Mark Turner (bl/Plesiosaurs). **DK:** James Kuether (clb, cb). **Science Photo Library:** James Kuether (bl). **91 DK:** James Kuether (bl/Velociraptor, bl). **92 DK:** Jon Hughes (cb); Colin Keates / Natural History Museum, London (tc/Dog teeth). **Science Photo Library:** Jose Antonio Penas (bl). **93 DK:** Jon Hughes (cb, crb/Early horse); James Kuether (crb). **94 DK:** Kennis & Kennis / Alfons and Adrie Kennis (fcla, cla, ca, cra, fcra); Dave King / Natural History Museum, London (crb); Royal Pavilion & Museums, Brighton & Hove (br). **95 DK:** Kennis & Kennis / Alfons and Adrie Kennis (fcla, cla, ca, cra, fcra). **96 Alamy Stock Photo:** Don Johnston_PL (ca/Southern Ground Cedar). **DK:** Gary Ombler / Centre for Wildlife Gardening / London Wildlife Trust (fcra). **FLPA:** Arjan Troost, Buiten-beeld / Minden Pictures (cra). **Getty Images:** age fotostock / Daniel Vega (cla/Hornwort); J&L Images (cla/Haircap Moss). **iStockphoto.com:** Alkalyne (ca). **Science Photo Library:** Bjorn Svensson (fcla). **97 DK:** Alan Buckingham (br). **Dreamstime.com:** Cloki (cr). **98 Bikash Kumar Bhadra:** (c). **Sandy Cleland:** (bc). **DK:** Colin Keates / The Natural History Museum, London (c/Clubmoss). **naturepl.com:** Adrian Davies (ca). **99 123RF.com:** Alfio Scisetti (cra). **DK:** Neil Fletcher (cra/Adder's-tongue Fern). **100 Dreamstime.com:** Chernetskaya (bl). **101 Fotolia:** Yong Hian Lim (r). **iStockphoto.com:** E+ / pixhook (ca). **102 DK:** Gary Ombler / Green and Gorgeous Flowers (bl); Gary Ombler: Centre for Wildlife Gardening / London Wildlife Trust (fbr). **Dreamstime.com:** Paop (ftr). **iStockphoto.com:** Sieboldianus (cl). **103 Alamy Stock Photo:** Nigel Cattlin (ftl); EyeEm / Birte Möller (crb). **DK:** Gary Ombler / Green and Gorgeous Flowers (fclb). **Dreamstime.com:** Daniil Kirillov (fcrb); Voltan1 (ftr); Yurakp (cr); Jan Martin Will (fcr). **Getty Images:** Getty RF / F. Lukasseck (tc). **104 Dreamstime.com:** Martin Green / Mrgreen (cla); Rasmapuspure (fcla). **106 DK:** William Bourland (fclb); David J Patterson (cb, cb/Arcella Bathystoma, crb/Green Euglena); Guy Brugerolle (crb); David Patterson / Linda Amaral Zettler / Mike Peglar / Tom Nerad (fcrb); Hwan Su Yoon (fcrb/Scaly Cercozoan). **Science Photo Library:** Alexander Semenov (c). **107 DK:** Linda Pitkin (c, fclb, br). **Getty Images:** Universal Images Group / Auscape (fcl). **NOAA:** Image courtesy of the NOAA Office of Ocean Exploration and Research, Deep-Sea Symphony: Exploring the Musicians Seamounts (cl). **SuperStock:** Universal Images (clb). **108 DK:** Linda Pitkin (ca, ca/Gorgonia Ventalina, cra, fcr). **109 DK:** Linda Pitkin (tc, ca/Cassiopea Andromeda, br). **Dreamstime.com:** Eugene Sim Junying (fclb); Kristina Kostova (ca); Jolanta Wojcicka (cra); R. Gino Santa Maria / Shutterfree,LLC / Ginosphotos / Shutterfree,Llc (c); Lukas Blazek / Lukyslukys (clb). **110 DK:** Frank Greenaway / The Natural History Museum, London (bl); Linda Pitkin (cb, br). **111 DK:** Linda Pitkin (tl, fclb). **Dreamstime.com:** Stevenrussellsmithphotos (cb). **NOAA:** OAR / OER, 2016 Deepwater Wonders of Wake (bl). **112 123RF.com:** Eric Isselee / isselee (crb). **DK:** Forrest L. Mitchell / James Laswel (fclb); The Natural History Museum, London (c, cr). **Dreamstime.com:** Henrikhl (fbr); Dmitrii Pridannikov (fbl). **113 123RF.com:** Andrey Pavlov (bl). **DK:** Frank Greenaway / The Natural History Museum, London (fcra, fcr, fclb, clb); Koen van Klijken (cr); Jerry Young (cb); Colin Keates / The Natural History Museum, London (ftl, ftr, crb). **Dreamstime.com:** Aetmeister (tl); Fotofred (fbl). **114 DK:** Linda Pitkin (cra, cb). **Getty Images:** NNehring (bc). **115 DK:** Shane Farrell (bl); Jens Schou (fcra); Jerry Young (ca); Paolo Mazzei (cra, cr). **Dreamstime.com:** Kerry Hill / Kezza53 (fcra/Australian Redback Spider). **116 Dreamstime.com:** Sneekerp (tc). **118 DK:** Dr. Peter M Forster (bl). **Dreamstime.com:** Greg Amptman / Thediver123 (br). **119 123RF.com:** Corey A Ford (bc). **DK:** Colin Keates / The Natural History Museum, London (cla). **120 DK:** Jason Hamm (crb); Jerry Young (tr, ca, fclb, clb); Professor Michael M. Mincarone (bl); Linda Pitkin (fcrb). **121 123RF.com:** Micha Klootwijk / michaklootwijk (bl). **DK:** Frank Greenaway / Weymouth Sea Life Centre (cb/Weedy Seadragon); Joseph McKenna (cla); Jerry Young (clb, cb); David Harasti (crb); Linda Pitkin (fcrb, clb/Short dragonfish, fbl, bc, br). **122 DK:** Twan Leenders (crb); Harry Taylor / The Natural History Museum, London (cra). **FLPA:** Photo Researchers (cr). **naturepl.com:** Daniel Heuclin (br). **123 DK:** Geoff Brightling / Booth Museum of Natural History (t); Twan Leenders (cb, clb, cb/Striated Salamander); Bill Peterman (bc). **124 DK:** Twan Leenders (tl). **125 DK:** Twan Leenders (fcla, fcra, br). **Dreamstime.com:** Isselee (fcrb); Janpietruszka (cl); Ondřej Prosický (c). **126 DK:** Colin Keates / The Natural History Museum, London (crb). **iStockphoto.com:** Somedaygood (clb). **127 DK:** Frank Greenaway / The Natural History Museum, London (c); Twan Leenders (fcla, ca); Jerry Young (cl); Colin Keates / The Natural History Museum, London (bl). **Dreamstime.com:** Peter Leahy / Pipehorse (tr); Stephanie Rousseau / Stephanierousseau (cra). **128 DK:** Colin Keates / The Natural History Museum, London (c). **129 Dreamstime.com:** Outdoorsman (tc). **130 DK:** Twan Leenders (cl); Gary Ombler / Cotswold Wildlife Park (cr). **131 Dreamstime.com:** Industryandtravel (bc). **Fotolia:** Steve Lovegrove (cb). **132–133 DK:** Jerry Young (t, b). **132 naturepl.com:** Anup Shah (cr). **133 Dreamstime.com:** Mikhail Blajenov / Starper (clb). **Getty Images:** Shubham Kumar Tiwari / EyeEm (br); Chris Mattison (ca). **134 DK:** Andy Crawford / Senckenberg Nature Museum (cl). **iStockphoto.com:** igorkov (c); KenCanning (r). **135 DK:** Peter Chadwick / The Natural History Museum, London (cra/Tawny Owl Feather, fcr/Owl Feather). **136 DK:** Chris Gomersall Photography (cr); Roger Tidman (c). **Dreamstime.com:** Bouke Atema (bl); Steve Byland (fclb); Oleksandr Panchenko (clb); Teh Soon Huat / Shunfa (cb); Christopher Elwell / Celwell (fbl). **FLPA:** Jurgen & Christine Sohns (fbr). **137 DK:** E. J. Peiker (fcl). **138 123RF.com:** BenFoto (cl); Keith Levit / keithlevit (fbl); Eric Isselee / isselee (fbr). **DK:** Jan-Michael Breider (bc); Jerry Young (ca); Mark Hamblin (c); Mike Lane (fclb); Gary Ombler / Cotswold Wildlife Park (clb); George Lin (cb); Roger Tidman (crb); Liberty's Owl, Raptor and Reptile Centre, Hampshire, UK (bl). **Dreamstime.com:** Natalya Aksenova / Natalyaa (fcl). **Getty Images:** Sjoerd Bosch (fcr); David Tipling / Digital Vision (tr). **naturepl.com:** Pete Oxford (br). **139 DK:** Chris Gomersall Photography (tl, tr); Hanne Eriksen / Jens Eriksen (tc, cb); Andy and Gill Swash (fcla); Mark Hamblin (cra, bc); E. J. Peiker (cr). **iStockphoto.com:** GlobalP (r); twildlife (ca). **naturepl.com:** Edwin Giesbers (fclb). **140 DK:** Dave King / Booth Museum of Natural History, Brighton (crb); Jerry Young (cb). **141 123RF.com:** Eric Isselee / isselee (br); Sommai Larkjit / sommai (bc). **DK:** Ramon Campos (fcr); Anahi Fornoso (cra); Tom Swinfield (cr). **Dreamstime.com:** Julian W / julianwphoto (ca); Marco Tomasini / Marco3t (cb). **Fotolia:** Mark Higgins (tl). **Getty Images:** Heath Holden (tr). **142 Alamy Stock Photo:** Helen Davies (tr). **DK:** Blackpool Zoo (crb); Malcolm Ryen (cb); Harry Taylor / The Natural History Museum, London (bc); Harry Taylor (br). **Dreamstime.com:** Isselee (clb); Matthijs Kuijpers (fclb). **naturepl.com:** Michael & Patricia Fogden (bl). **143 123RF.com:** wrangel (br). **Alamy Stock Photo:** Life on white (t). **DK:** Greg Dean / Yvonne Dean (crb). **144 123RF.com:** Robert Eastman (cl). **DK:** Jerry Young (ca). **Dreamstime.com:** Broker (clb); Seadam (crb); Isselee (fcrb); Derrick Neill / Neilld (bl); Scattoselvaggio (bc); Kajornyot (br). **Getty Images:** Encyclopaedia Britannica / UIG (fcrb/Colugo). **145 123RF.com:** Eric Isselee / isselee (bl); wrangel (fclb). **Alamy Stock Photo:** Rick & Nora Bowers (bc). **DK:** Blackpool Zoo, Lancashire, UK (cb/Hydrochoerus Hydrochaeris); Frank Greenaway / Marwell Zoological Park, Winchester (c); Jerry Young (clb). **Dreamstime.com:** Musat Christian (br); Isselee (fcl). **Fotolia:** Matthijs Kuijpers / Mgkuijpers (cb). **146 Alamy Stock Photo:** GFC Collection (bc); Nature Picture Library / Andy Rouse (fbl). **DK:** Blackpool Zoo, Lancashire, UK (c). **Dreamstime.com:** Lukas Blazek (crb); Dennis Van De Water (cb); Lukas Blazek / Lukyslukys (bl); Outcast85 (br). **iStockphoto.com:** apple2499 (tc). **147 DK:** Cotswold Wildlife Park & Gardens, Oxfordshire, UK (cr); Andy and Gill Swash (bl, bc). **Dreamstime.com:** Lawrence Weslowski Jr / Walleyelj (cb). **148 123RF.com:** Maurizio Giovanni Bersanelli, / ajlber (fclb); Uriadnikov Sergei (cb/Bonobo). **Alamy Stock Photo:** imageBROKER / jspix (fcra); Juniors Bildarchiv GmbH / Juniors Bildarchiv / F279 (cra). **DK:** Blackpool Zoo, Lancashire, UK (clb). **Dreamstime.com:** Isselee (cb); Norbert Orisek / Noron (fcrb). **iStockphoto.com:** ePhotocorp (crb). **149 Ardea:** Steve Downer (crb). **DK:** Frank

Greenaway / The Natural History Museum, London (cr, bc); Jerry Young (cb, br). **150–151 Dreamstime.com:** Nialldunne24 (t). **150 Alamy Stock Photo:** National Geographic Image Collection / Joel Sartore (bc); Newscom / BJ Warnick (bl). **Avalon:** © NHPA / Photo Researchers (tr, crb). **Dreamstime.com:** Isselee (br); Martin Sevcik / Martinsevcik (tc); Rudmer Zwerver (cb). **iStockphoto.com:** 2630ben (clb). **152 123RF.com:** Steve Byland / steve_byland (bl); Michael Lane (cb/Arctic Fox); Achim Prill (fcrb). **DK:** Blackpool Zoo, Lancashire, UK (fcl); Alan Burger (cl); Jerry Young (bc/Maned Wolf, br, crb). **Dreamstime.com:** Pablo Caridad / Elnavegante (cr); Vladimir Melnik / Zanskar (fcr); Maria Itina (cb); Isselee (bc). **iStockphoto.com:** SKapl (tl). **153 DK:** Dave King / Whipsnade Zoo, Bedfordshire (tc); Tracy Morgan (cb). **iStockphoto.com:** GlobalP (tr); Cody Linde (cr). **154 DK:** Wildlife Heritage Foundation, Kent, UK (ca). **Dreamstime.com:** Anan Kaewkhammul / anankkml (cla); Volodymyrkrasyuk (fclb); Outdoorsman (cb). **Getty Images:** Martin Harvey (c); Westend61 (br). **155 123RF.com:** Eric Isselee / isselee (bc). **DK:** British Wildlife Centre, Surrey, UK (fclb); Jerry Young (fcra); Greg and Yvonne Dean (c); Cotswold Wildlife Park & Gardens, Oxfordshire, UK (cb). **Dreamstime.com:** Cathywithers (cra); Isselee (clb). **156 DK:** Jerry Young (cl, c). **Dreamstime.com:** S100apm (cra). **157 123RF.com:** Jatesada Natayo / mazikab (tc). **DK:** British Wildlife Centre, Surrey, UK (cb); Geoff Dann / Cotswold Farm Park, Gloucestershire (crb/Bagot Goat); Colchester Zoo / (bc/Greater Kudu). **Dreamstime.com:** Isselee (cla, cr); Iakov Filimonov / Jackf (c); Shailesh Nanal / Shaileshnanal (cb/Indian Bison); Lukas Blazek / Lukyslukys (bc). **Fotolia:** Eric Isselee (crb). **Getty Images:** Life On White (r). **167 Alamy Stock Photo:** FLHC 52 (br). **iStockphoto.com:** matejmo (crb). **168 Alamy Stock Photo:** Granger Historical Picture Archive / NYC (cr). **170 Getty Images:** Universal Images Group / SVF2 / Sovfoto (tr). **171 Alamy Stock Photo:** Garry Gay (bc). **175 iStockphoto.com:** DigitalVision Vectors / ZU_09 (br). **178 123RF.com:** zentilia (cr). **Getty Images:** Michael Ochs Archives / Donaldson Collection / NASA / Bob Nye (bc). **183 123RF.com:** Georgios Kollidas (fbl). **185 Alamy Stock Photo:** Science History Images / Photo Researchers (bl). **197 Alamy Stock Photo:** Shawshots (cr). **198 DK:** Clive Streeter / The Science Museum, London (bl). **201 SuperStock:** Fine Art Images / A. Burkatovski (tr). **204 123RF.com:** Nataliia Kravchuk (cb); lightvisionftb (cra). **Alamy Stock Photo:** studiomode (fcla, ca/IRON FILINGS). **Getty Images:** Hulton Archive / Keystone (tr). **iStockphoto.com:** Turnervisual (cla, ca/Sulfur). **Science Photo Library:** Martyn F. Chillmaid (ca). **210 Alamy Stock Photo:** kpzfoto (cr). **Dreamstime.com:** Georgios Kollidas (bl). **212 Dreamstime.com:** Rechitan Sorin / Rechitansorin (tr). **214 DK:** David J Patterson (cb). **215 naturepl.com:** Aflo (br). **218 DK:** Rajeev Doshi (Medi-mation) (c). **219 Alamy Stock Photo:** Photo12 / Ann Ronan Picture Library (br). **222 Alamy Stock Photo:** Keystone Press / KEYSTONE Pictures USA (tr). **223 Science Photo Library:** Biophoto Associates (tc). **224 Alamy Stock Photo:** Science History Images / Photo Researchers (bc). **227 Alamy Stock Photo:** Biosphoto / Adam Fletcher (cl/DANCING); David Osborn (c); Historic Images (br). **Dreamstime.com:** Elena Duvernay / Elenaphoto21 (c/BONDING); Mikelane45 (fcl). **228 iStockphoto.com:** Grafissimo (bc). **229 Alamy Stock Photo:** All Canada Photos / Roberta Olenick (br). **DK:** Jon Hughes (bc). **Dreamstime.com:** Carol Buchanan (bc/SHARK); Kotomiti_okuma (ca). **233 DK:** Arran Lewis(science3) / Rajeev Doshi (medi-mation) / Zygote (bc). **240 DK:** Arran Lewis(science3) / Rajeev Doshi (medi-mation) / Zygote (cla). **250 Alamy Stock Photo:** dpa picture alliance / dpa (bl). **DK:** Dave King / Science Museum, London (cl). **Getty Images:** Hulton Archive / Culture Club (c); Universal Images Group / Universal History Archive (cla); Hulton Archive / Central Press (clb). **Wellcome Collection:** Attribution 4.0 International (CC BY 4.0) (ca); Science Museum, London, Attribution 4.0 International (CC BY 4.0) (tr, cr). **251 Alamy Stock Photo:** BSIP SA / IMAGE POINT FR - LPN (br); dpa picture alliance / Soeren Stache (cl); Emilio Ereza (c). **Los Angeles County Museum of Art:** Gift of Emeritus Professor and Mrs. Thomas O. Ballinger (M.87.271a-g) (tl). **University of Virginia:** Courtesy of Historical Collections & Services, Claude Moore Health Sciences Library, University of Virginia (cla/Scalpels). **Wellcome Collection:** Attribution 4.0 International (CC BY 4.0) (tr, cla); Science Museum, London, Attribution 4.0 International (CC BY 4.0) (tc, cla/Surgical knife, cla/shears). **252 123RF.com:** Nicola Simpson (b/X 4, crb). **Dreamstime.com:** Arkadi Bojaršinov (cb/Cardiology); Keng62fa (cb); Anatolii Riabokon (crb/Oncology). **253 123RF.com:** kotoffei (clb/Pharmaceutical medicine); Nicola Simpson (bc/X 3, clb). **Dreamstime.com:** Miceking (bl); Oleksandr Yershov (clb/Pathology). **254 Wellcome Collection:** Attribution 4.0 International (CC BY 4.0) (bl). **255 iStockphoto.com:** pixelfit (br). **256 Dreamstime.com:** Katarzyna Bialasiewicz / Bialasiewicz (ca/Ear check); Peter Sobolev (crb). **Getty Images:** Jacobs Stock Photography (ca). **257 123RF.com:** jovannig (c). **Dreamstime.com:** Sopone Nawoot (bc); Rattanachot2525 (cla); Robert Semnic / Semnic (ca). **Science Photo Library:** ZEPHYR (bl). **Wellcome Collection:** Dr Jim Myers, Imperial College London, Attribution 4.0 International (CC BY 4.0) (cl). **258 Alamy Stock Photo:** Peter Horree (br). **259 Dreamstime.com:** Ironjohn (br); Piyapong Thongdumhyu (cr). **Wellcome Collection:** William R. Geddie, CC0 1.0 Universal (cra). **260 Getty Images:** Amir Levy (tr). **Science Photo Library:** Alfred Pasieka (bl). **278 DK:** Gerard Brown / Llandrindod Wells National Cycle (ca). **Getty Images:** Bettmann (cb). **279 DK:** Gary Ombler / Dave Shayler / Astro Info Service Ltd (crb). **Getty Images:** Corbis Historical / David Pollack (l). **280 Alamy Stock Photo:** Heritage Image Partnership Ltd / © Fine Art (cb); Danita Delimont (tc); Chris Hellier (ca). **DK:** James Stevenson / The Science Museum, London (br); Clive Streeter / The Science Museum, London (crb). **281 123RF.com:** Nickolay Stanev (r). **DK:** Gary Ombler / Whipple Museum of History of Science, Cambridge (tc); Clive Streeter / The Science Museum, London (ca). **Dreamstime.com:** García Juan (cr); Mr1805 (tr); Ml12nan (bl). **Getty Images:** Bettmann (cb). **283 Getty Images:** De Agostini / DEA / A. DAGLI ORTI (crb). **284 DK:** Gary Ombler / National Railway Museum, York / Science Museum Group (tr); Gary Ombler / Railroad Museum of Pennsylvania (cb); Gary Ombler / Christian Goldschagg (bl). **Dreamstime.com:** Michelle Bridges (cla); Alexander Mitr (cra); Sean Pavone / Sepavo (br). **284–285 Getty Images:** Science & Society Picture Library (c). **285 Alamy Stock Photo:** Chronicle (crb/Fliegende Hamburger). **DK:** B&O Railroad Museum, Baltimore, Maryland, USA (tr); Gary Ombler / Didcot Railway Centre (cb); Gary Ombler / Railroad Museum of Pennsylvania (crb); Mike Dunning / National Railway Museum, York (clb); Deepak Aggarwal / Safdarjung Railway Station (bc). **Library of Congress, Washington, D.C.:** LC-USZ62-92130 (tl). **286 Getty Images:** fStop Images - Caspar Benson (cra). **287 DK:** James Mann / Rodger Dudding (cr); Gary Ombler / R. Florio (fcra); James Mann / Colin Spong (fcra/Lincoln Zephyr); Matthew Ward / Garry Darby (crb); Matthew Ward (fcrb); James Mann / Peter Harris (crb/Lamborghini Countach). **288 Alamy Stock Photo:** Pictorial Press Ltd (c); World History Archive (cr). **DK:** Gary Ombler / Flugausstellung (cl, crb); Gary Ombler / Royal International Air Tattoo 2011 (clb). **Dreamstime.com:** Viktor Gladkov (tr); Lefteris Papaulakis (br). **Getty Images:** Popperfoto (cla). **Library of Congress, Washington, D.C.:** LC-DIG-ds-08348 (digital file from original) LC-USZ62-15740 (b&w film copy neg.) (fcla). **U.S. Air Force:** Staff Sgt. Aaron D. Allmon II (bl). **289 Dreamstime.com:** Steve Mann (bc); Susan Sheldon (clb). **Library of Congress, Washington, D.C.:** photograph by Harris & Ewing LC-DIG-hec-04727 (cra). **© Solar Impulse:** (br). **290 Alamy Stock Photo:** Greatstock / Horst Klemm (clb). **iStockphoto.com:** anouchka (crb). **SpaceX:** (c). **291 iStockphoto.com:** Nikada. **294 Science Photo Library:** Babak Tafreshi. **295 ESA:** Planck Collaboration (cb). **Science Photo Library:** Emilio Segre Visual Archives / American Institute Of Physics (br). **296 NASA:** The Hubble Heritage / STScI / AURA (tr). **297 ESO:** L. Calçada/M. Kornmesser https://creativecommons.org/licenses/by/4.0 (ca). **298 Alamy Stock Photo:** Science Photo Library / Mark Garlick (bl). **300 Alamy Stock Photo:** The Natural History Museum, London (clb). **Science Photo Library:** Mikkel Juul Jensen (tc). **301 Alamy Stock Photo:** The Natural History Museum, London (br). **DK:** NASA (tr). **302 Alamy Stock Photo:** Peter Barritt (br); Eddie Gerald (ca); Peter Horree (clb). **DK:** Gary Ombler / The Walled Garden, Summers Place Auction House (cl). **303 Alamy Stock Photo:** Images & Stories (bc). **Adam Brumm:** Adam Brumm,Ratno Sardi, Adhi Agus Oktaviana (tr). **DK:** Dave King / The Natural History Museum, London (bl); Harry Taylor / The Natural History Museum, London (cra); Gary Ombler / University of Pennsylvania Museum of Archaeology and Anthropology (crb). **Dreamstime.com:** Briancweed (c). **304 Alamy Stock Photo:** agefotostock / Historical Views (bl). **DK:** Gary Ombler / University of Pennsylvania Museum of Archaeology and Anthropology (cl). **304–305 DK:** Gary Ombler / University of Pennsylvania Museum of Archaeology and Anthropology (c). **305 Alamy Stock Photo:** The History Collection (tr); INTERFOTO / Fine Arts (br). **Getty Images:** George Steinmetz (bl). **306–307 DK:** Gary Ombler / University of Pennsylvania Museum of Archaeology and Anthropology (c). **306 Alamy Stock Photo:** Robert Kawka (br); Werner Forman Archive / N.J Saunders / Heritage Images (ca); Ariadne Van Zandbergen (bc). **DK:** Angela Coppola / University of Pennsylvania Museum of Archaeology and Anthropology (cb); Gary Ombler / Durham University Oriental Museum (bl). **Rex by Shutterstock:** Gianni Dagli Orti (cl). **307 Alamy Stock Photo:** © Fine Art Images / Heritage Images (cb); Dmitriy Moroz (c); Peter Horree (bl); INTERFOTO / Personalities (br). **DK:** Angela Coppola / University of Pennsylvania Museum of Archaeology and Anthropology (cla); Aditya Patankar / National Museum, New Delhi (tl). **Dreamstime.com:** Angellodeco (cr); Anna Pakutina (r); Spiroview Inc. (clb). **308 DK:** Dave King / University Museum of Archaeology and Anthropology, Cambridge (ca); Gary Ombler / Durham University Oriental Museum (clb). **308–309 Bridgeman Images:** © Archives Charmet (c). **309 Getty Images:** © Asian Art & Archaeology, Inc. / Corbis / Martha Avery (crb). **310 DK:** Gary Ombler / Newcastle Great Northern Museum, Hancock (bl). **Dreamstime.com:** Jaroslav Moravcik (cb). **310–311 Getty Images:** De Agostini / DEA / S. Vannini (c). **311 Getty Images:** De Agostini / De Agostini Picture Library (cra). **312 Alamy Stock Photo:** adam eastland (br). **DK:** Gary Ombler / Newcastle Great Northern Museum, Hancock (ca). **Dreamstime.com:** Sergio Bertino (bl). **313 Alamy Stock Photo:** Azoor Photo. **314 DK:** Gary Ombler / Ermine Street Guard (cr). **314–315 Alamy Stock Photo:** Granger Historical Picture Archive (b). **315 Alamy Stock Photo:** Granger Historical Picture Archive (cr). **316 DK:** Dave Rudkin / Birmingham Museum and Art Galleries (cra). **Getty Images:** De Agostini / DEA / G. DAGLI ORTI (clb). **316–317 Getty Images:** De Agostini / DEA / G. DAGLI ORTI (c). **317 DK:** Gary Ombler / University of Pennsylvania Museum of Archaeology and Anthropology (cr). **318 Alamy Stock Photo:** Granger Historical Picture Archive (c). **DK:** Dave King / Museum of London (clb); Gary Ombler / University of Pennsylvania Museum of Archaeology and Anthropology (fcla). **319 Bridgeman Images:** Photo © Boltin Picture Library. **320 Alamy Stock Photo:** Everett Collection Inc (cla). **Bridgeman Images:** Pictures from History (tr). **DK:** Constantin Sava / Savcoco (clb); Michel Zabe (cra). **Getty Images:** Archive Photos / GraphicaArtis (bc). **320–321 DK:** Gary Ombler / University of Pennsylvania Museum of Archaeology and Anthropology (bc). **321 akg-images:** Roland and Sabrina Michaud (bc). **Alamy Stock Photo:** agefotostock / Historical Views (cla); Andrew Paul Travel (cl); Prisma Archivo (cb); GL Archive (br). **Dreamstime.com:** Yuriy Chaban (c). **Getty Images:** ullstein bild (tr). **iStockphoto.com:** DigitalVision Vectors / whitemay (clb); Azhar Khan (ca). **322 Alamy Stock Photo:** Pictorial Press Ltd (ca). **DK:** Gary Ombler / Durham University Oriental Museum (clb, crb). **323 Alamy Stock Photo:** Granger Historical Picture Archive / NYC. **324 Alamy Stock Photo:** World History Archive. **325 DK:** Gary Ombler / Durham University Oriental Museum (cl); Gary Ombler / Board of Trustees of the Royal Armouries (bc). **326 Alamy Stock Photo:** Granger Historical Picture Archive (bc). **DK:** Gary Ombler / Durham University Oriental Museum (crb). **326–327 Alamy Stock Photo:** Artokoloro (c). **327 DK:** Dave King / Pitt Rivers Museum, University of Oxford (fcra); Gary Ombler / Board of Trustees of the Royal Armouries (cra). **328–329 Alamy Stock Photo:** funkyfood London - Paul Williams (t). **328 DK:** Gary Ombler / Canterbury City Council, Museums and Galleries (cr). **329 Alamy Stock Photo:** Science History Images / Photo Researchers (br). **DK:** Gary Ombler / Newcastle Great Northern Museum, Hancock (bl). **330 DK:** Geoff Dann / Wallace Collection, London (cra). **Dreamstime.com:** Steven Langford (bl). **330–331 SuperStock:** DeAgostini (c). **331 DK:** Richard Leeney / Faversham Town Council (cr). **332 Alamy Stock Photo:** Photo 12 (br). **DK:** Gary Ombler / Whipple Museum of History of Science, Cambridge (ca). **The Metropolitan Museum of Art, New York:** Theodore M. Davis Collection, Bequest of Theodore M. Davis, 1915 (crb). **333 Alamy Stock Photo:** Prisma Archivo. **334 DK:** Geoff Brightling / 95th Rifles and Re-enactment Living History Unit (cra); Dave King / Durham University Oriental Museum (tr); Gary Ombler / English CIvil War Society (ca); Dave King / Robin Wigington, Arbour Antiques, Ltd., Stratford-upon-Avon (cl); Gary Ombler / Board of Trustees of the Royal Armouries (cr, br). **Dreamstime.com:** Adam88x (tc). **Getty Images:** Roger Viollet / Boyer (clb). **Library of Congress, Washington, D.C.:** LC-DIG-pga-03240 (cb). **335 Alamy Stock Photo:** Science History Images / Photo Researchers (cb). **DK:** Gary Ombler / Combined Military Services Museum (CMSM) (cl, tr); Gary Ombler / Southern Skirmish Association (cr); Gary Ombler / Board of Trustees of the Royal Armouries (crb, bc). **Getty Images:** ullstein bild (tc). **336 Alamy Stock Photo:** Heritage Image Partnership Ltd / © Fine Art (cr). **336–337 Alamy Stock Photo:** Heritage Image Partnership Ltd / © Fine Art (b). **337 Getty Images:** Hulton Archive / Heritage Images (c, cra). **338–339 Dreamstime.com:** Ungureanu Vadim (bc). **339 Alamy Stock Photo:** IanDagnall Computing (br). **Getty Images:** Universal Images Group (cla). **340 Alamy Stock Photo:** Art Heritage. **341 DK:** Ranald MacKechnie / Pitt Rivers Museum, University of Oxford (tl). **Dreamstime.com:** Pancaketom (cr). **SuperStock:** Universal Images (br). **342 Alamy Stock Photo:** Prisma Archivo. **343 DK:** Angela Coppola / University of Pennsylvania Museum of Archaeology and Anthropology (cb); Gary Ombler / University of Pennsylvania Museum of Archaeology and Anthropology (clb, bc). **344 Alamy Stock Photo:** Prisma Archivo (c). **344–345 Alamy Stock Photo:** © Fine Art Images / Heritage Images (b). **345 DK:** Geoff Dann / Wallace Collection, London (crb). **346 Alamy Stock Photo:** The Granger Collection (bc); Science History Images (tr). **DK:** Dave King / Science Museum, London (c). **346–347 Alamy Stock Photo:** Photo12 / Ann Ronan Picture Library (b). **348 akg-images:** Pictures From History (clb). **348–349 Alamy Stock Photo:** Peter Horree (c). **349 Alamy Stock Photo:** agefotostock / Historical Views (tr); incamerastock / ICP (br). **350 akg-images:** (tr). **Alamy Stock Photo:** American Photo Archive (c); Shawshots (cr); Panzermeister (clb); World History Archive (bl). **Getty Images:** Stefano Bianchetti / Corbis Historical (ca); Time Magazine / The LIFE Picture Collection / Larry Burrows (crb). **Rex by Shutterstock:** Peter Horvath (bc). **351 akg-images:** Fototeca Gilardi (fcrb). **Alamy Stock Photo:** Granger Historical Picture Archive (tr); iWebbstock (bl). **DK:** Gary Ombler / Wardrobe Museum, Salisbury (cl). **Dreamstime.com:** Gary Blakeley / Blakeley (clb). **Getty Images:** DEA Picture Library / De Agostini (tl); Archive Photos / Stringer (cla); ullstein bild / ullstein bild Dtl. (cr); Patrick Robert - Corbis / Corbis Historical (crb). **Library of Congress, Washington, D.C.:** LC-DIG-ggbain-07650 (digital file from original neg.) (fcla). **Rex by Shutterstock:** The Art Archive (cra). **352 Alamy Stock Photo:** World History Archive. **353 Alamy Stock Photo:** Photo12 / Archives Snark (br). **DK:** Andy Crawford / Imperial War Museum, London (tr). **354 Alamy Stock Photo:** SOTK2011 (cra). **DK:** Dave King / The Science Museum (cla). **354–355 Alamy Stock Photo:** North Wind Picture Archives (b). **355 Alamy Stock Photo:** Niday Picture Library (crb). **356 akg-images:** (bc). **Alamy Stock Photo:** incamerastock / ICP (ca). **356–357 Alamy Stock Photo:** Artokoloro (c). **357 Getty Images:** Pete Holdgate / Crown Copyright. Imperial War Museums (crb); Universal Images Group / Leemage (ca). **358 Alamy Stock Photo:** © Fine Art Images / Heritage Images (ca). **358–359 Getty Images:** Archive Photos / Buyenlarge / Matthew Brady (b). **359 Alamy Stock Photo:** Trinity Mirror / Mirrorpix (tr). **Getty Images:** Hulton Archive / Robert Nickelsberg / Liaison (br). **360 Alamy Stock Photo:** Granger Historical Picture Archive. **361 Alamy Stock Photo:** Chronicle (tr); Science History Images / Photo Researchers (crb). **362 DK:** Gary Ombler / The Tank Museum, Bovington (crb). **Dreamstime.com:** Nigel Spooner (ca). **Getty Images:** ullstein bild (tr). **363 Alamy Stock Photo:** US Air Force Photo. **364 Alamy Stock Photo:** Heritage Image Partnership Ltd / © Fine Art Images. **365 Alamy Stock Photo:** incamerastock / ICP (bc); Science History Images / Photo Researchers (cb). **SuperStock:** Marka / Fototeca Gilardi (crb). **Wellcome Collection:** Science Museum, London, Attribution 4.0 International (CC BY 4.0) (ca). **366–367 Alamy Stock Photo:** World History Archive (b). **367 Alamy Stock Photo:** Art Collection 3 (tl). **Getty Images:** AFP (cra). **368 Getty Images:** Sygma / Daniele Darolle. **369 Alamy Stock Photo:** Pictorial Press Ltd (bc); Bjorn Svensson (ca); World History Archive (br). **370–371 Getty Images:** Carlina Teteris (b). **370 Alamy Stock Photo:** Classicstock / H. Armstrong Roberts (clb). **371 Alamy Stock Photo:** Westend61 GmbH (cla). **372 Getty Images:** Mirrorpix. **373 Alamy Stock Photo:** Science Photo Library / Steve Gschmeissner (cr); Science History Images / Photo Researchers (clb).